Handbook of Modern Personnel Administration

JOSEPH J. FAMULARO *Editor-in-Chief*

Vice President, Personnel Relations
McGraw-Hill, Inc.

McGRAW-HILL BOOK COMPANY
New York   St. Louis   San Francisco   Düsseldorf   Johannesburg
Kuala Lumpur   London   Mexico   Montreal   New Delhi
Panama   Rio de Janeiro   Singapore   Sydney   Toronto

For Mary, Bea, and Louise

The editors for this book were M. Joseph Dooher, Karen Kesti and
Lydia Maiorca, the designer was Naomi Auerbach, and its produc-
tion was supervised by George E. Oechsner and Teresa F. Leaden.
It was set in Caledonia by University Graphics, Inc.

It was printed and bound by Kingsport Press, Inc.

Total number of pages: 1268.

Contents

Part 14. SPECIAL PERSONNEL PROBLEMS

Part 15. SPECIAL EMPLOYEE GROUPS

Part 16. COMMUNICATING TO EMPLOYEES

Part 17. RECORDS, REPORTS, AND STATISTICS

Part 18. PERSONNEL RESEARCH

INDEX FOLLOWS PART 18

Contributors

JOHN C. AGATHON *Director of Management Development, Celanese Corporation, New York, New York (Chap. 22)*

JOSEPH C. AUGUSTINE *Personnel Administrator, Medical Center Personnel Office, The University of Michigan, Ann Arbor, Michigan (Chap. 62)*

JAMES J. BAMBRICK *Labor Relations Representative, The Standard Oil Company (Ohio), Cleveland, Ohio (Chap. 54)*

BURTON E. BAUDER *Vice President, Sibson & Company, Inc., New York, New York (Chap. 29)*

ROBERT L. BAUER *Activity Advisor, Armco Association, Armco Steel Corporation, Middletown, Ohio (Chap. 46)*

RICHARD J. BENOIT *Manager, Recruiting and Training, Interstate United, Chicago, Illinois (Chap. 67)*

JOHN S. BERCEN *Director, Industrial Relations, Coro Inc., Providence, Rhode Island (Chap. 77)*

ROGER D. BORGENSON *Vice President and Personnel Director, Abraham & Straus, Brooklyn, New York (Chap. 6)*

WILLIAM H. BROWN III *Chairman, Equal Employment Opportunity Commission, Washington, D.C. (Chap. 53)*

BERNERD H. BURBANK *Medical Director, McGraw-Hill, Inc., New York, New York (Chap. 49)*

EDGAR M. BUTTENHEIM *President, Buttenheim Publishing Corporation, Pittsfield, Massachusetts (Chap. 74)*

WESLEY S. CALDWELL *Program Director, Porter Henry & Co., Inc., New York, New York (Chap. 43)*

DAVID N. CAMPBELL *Personnel Director, Sealtest Foods, Division of Kraftco Corporation, New York, New York (Chap. 4)*

DANIEL D. CANTOR *Deputy Director, Peace Corps, India, Formerly: Vice President Employee Relations, Itek Corporation, Lexington, Massachusetts (Chap. 76)*

RICHARD CROOK *President, Selling Systems, Inc., Lake Forest, Illinois (Chap. 44)*

THEODORE P. CURTIS *Manager-Employee Services, McGraw-Hill, Inc., New York, New York (Chap. 23)*

ANN M. DAVIS *Employee Benefits and Workmen's Compensation Administrator, The J. L. Hudson Company, Detroit, Michigan (Chap. 51)*

PETER A. DAVIS   *Partner, Hooper, Hathaway, Fichera, Price & Davis, Attorneys at Law, Ann Arbor, Michigan (Chap. 50)*

ROBERT I. DAWSON   *Director, Research and Consulting, Personnel Department, The Equitable Life Assurance Society of the United States, New York, New York (Chap. 80)*

CARLTON W. DUKES   *Industry Manager, Information Science Incorporated, New City, New York (Chap. 17)*

PHILIP H. DUTTER   *Director, McKinsey & Company, Inc., New York, New York (Chap. 32)*

ROBERT S. DVORIN   *Consultant, Westport, Connecticut (Chap. 26)*

LOUIS M. ELLISON   *Director of Employee Relations, United Utilities, Inc., Kansas City, Kansas (Chap. 58)*

ALFRED J. FIGLIOLA   *Assistant Vice President, International Banking Group Personnel, Salary Systems Development and Research, First National City Bank, New York, New York (Chap. 57)*

GLENN T. FISCHBACH   *Director of Engineering Services, American Association of Industrial Management, Melrose Park, Pennsylvania (Chap. 41)*

FRANK E. FISCHER   *Vice President and Director of Personnel Services, Cresap, McCormick and Paget Inc., New York, New York (Chap. 9)*

CHARLES H. FROST   *Vice President–Employee Relations, USLIFE Corporation, New York, New York (Chap. 59)*

JAMES E. GARDNER   *Training Manager, Fieldcrest Mills, Inc., Eden, North Carolina (Chap. 48)*

WALLACE W. GARDNER   *Professor of Management, The University of Utah, Salt Lake City, Utah (Chap. 78)*

LEE S. GASSLER   *Director of Industrial Relations, Kodak Park Division, Eastman Kodak Company, Rochester, New York (Chap. 69)*

SAUL W. GELLERMAN   *President, Gellerman Kay Corporation, Harrington Park, New Jersey (Chap. 2)*

HARRISON GIVENS, JR.   *Second Vice President, The Equitable Life Assurance Society of the United States, New York, New York (Chap. 35)*

LOUIS S. GOODMAN   *President, Louis S. Goodman & Associates, New Rochelle, New York (Chap. 18)*

WILLIAM A. GROENEKAMP   *Management Consultant, Los Angeles, California (Chap. 27)*

ROGER H. HAWK   *Manager Individual Resources Development and Education Operation, General Electric Company, Management Development Institute, Ossining, New York (Chap. 11)*

DAVID A. HEENAN   *Instructor of International Business, Wharton School of Finance and Commerce, University of Pennsylvania, Philadelphia, Pennsylvania (Chap. 56)*

KENNETH F. HERROLD   *Professor, Department of Psychology, Teachers College, Columbia University, New York, New York (Chap. 40)*

JOAN E. HOLLAND   *Assistant Personnel Director, Lenox Hill Hospital, New York, New York (Chap. 23)*

CHARLES L. HUGHES   *Director, Corporate Industrial Relations, Texas Instruments Incorporated, Dallas, Texas (Chap. 45)*

JOHN PAUL JONES   *Senior Vice President, Federated Department Stores, Inc., Cincinnati, Ohio (Chap. 1)*

JAMES M. KELLY   *Dean, College of Business, Idaho State University, Pocatello, Idaho (Chap. 70)*

ROBERT J. KELLY   *Personnel Administrator, McGraw-Hill, Inc., New York, New York (Chap. 28)*

DOUGLAS J. KENNEDY   *Director of Employee Benefits Administration, The Greyhound Corporation, Phoenix, Arizona (Chap. 37)*

THOMAS A. KINDRE   *Senior Vice President, Hill and Knowlton, Inc., New York, New York (Chap. 72)*

W. EUGENE KOGER *(deceased)   Formerly: Vice President, Personnel and Industrial Relations, Ingersoll-Rand Company, New York, New York (Chap. 68)*

MARKUS M. LOFTIN III *Second Vice President, Human Resources Department, The Chase Manhattan Bank, New York, New York (Chap. 19)*

FELIX M. LOPEZ *Felix M. Lopez & Associates, Roslyn, New York (Chap. 13)*

ROBERT L. LoPRESTO *Manager, Corporate Staffing, Fairchild Camera and Instrument Corporation, Mountain View, California (Chap. 12)*

RICHARD M. MACHOL *Electrical World, McGraw-Hill, Inc., New York, New York (Chap. 74)*

HOWARD T. MAIER *Director of Personnel Administration, McGraw-Hill, Inc., New York, New York (Chap. 75)*

PAUL MALI *Certified Management Consultant and Professor of Management, Graduate School of Business, Hartford University, Hartford, Connecticut (Chap. 14)*

BERNARD MANDEL, ESQ. *Terrell, Williams and Salim, Cleveland, Ohio (Chap. 39)*

IAN E. McLAUGHLIN *Director of Sales Training, Del Monte Corporation, San Francisco, California (Chap. 31)*

MURIEL E. MERKEL *Staff Communications, Personnel Department, The Port of New York Authority, New York, New York (Chap. 47)*

MICHAEL L. MOORE *Assistant Professor, School of Labor and Industrial Relations, Michigan State University, East Lansing, Michigan (Chap. 5)*

DOROTHY MOULTON *Training Director, Anchor Savings Bank, Brooklyn, New York (Chap. 24)*

JOHN K. MOYNAHAN *Consultant, Towers, Perrin, Forster & Crosby, Inc., New York, New York (Chap. 34)*

CHESTER T. O'CONNELL *Vice President, Industrial Relations KLEINSCHMIDT, Division of SCM Corporation, Deerfield, Illinois (Chap. 71)*

GEORGE S. ODIORNE *Dean, College of Business, The University of Utah, Salt Lake City, Utah (Chap. 8)*

AURORA PARISI *Personnel Administrator, McGraw-Hill, Inc., New York, New York (Chap. 65)*

ROBERT J. PAUL *Associate Professor of Management, University of Missouri, Columbia, Missouri (Chap. 81)*

N. T. PHILLIPS *Corporate Compensation Manager, Midland-Ross Corporation, Cleveland, Ohio (Chap. 52)*

ROBERT B. PURSELL *Director, Coloney, Cannon, Main & Pursell, Inc., New York, New York (Chaps. 30 & 42)*

W. F. RABE *Professor of Management, San Fernando Valley State College, Northridge, California (Chap. 7)*

ROBERT R. REICHENBACH *Vice President, Organization Resources Counselors, Inc., New York, New York (Chap. 21)*

JULIUS REZLER *Professor of Economics, Loyola University of Chicago, Chicago, Illinois (Chap. 63)*

FRANKLIN R. ROOT *Associate Professor of International Business, Wharton School of Finance and Commerce, University of Pennsylvania, Philadelphia, Pennsylvania (Chap. 56)*

BENJAMIN ROTER *Assistant Treasurer, Human Resources Department, The Chase Manhattan Bank, New York, New York (Chap. 19)*

GEARY A. RUMMLER *President, Praxis Corporation, New York, New York (Chap. 25)*

NELSON L. RUNGER, JR. *Editorial Director, New Jersey Bell Telephone Company, Newark, New Jersey (Chap. 73)*

ROBERT H. SAND *Labor Counsel, Allied Chemical Corporation, New York, New York (Chap. 66)*

JOHN E. SHEA *Division Vice President, Industrial Relations, Union Tank Car Company, Chicago, Illinois (Chap. 36)*

JAMES F. SHERIDAN *Director of Compensation & Benefits, Bristol-Myers Products, New York, New York (Chap. 33)*

EVERETT G. SHERMAN *Manager Employee Benefits, Honeywell Inc., Minneapolis, Minnesota (Chap. 38)*

J. C. SMITH *Plant Manager, The Pantasote Company, Point Pleasant, West Virginia (Chap. 20)*

JOHN SMITH *Associate Employment Consultant, Division of Employment, New York State Department of Labor, Albany, New York (Chap. 15)*

LAWRENCE L. STEINMETZ *Professor and Head, Management and Organization Division, Graduate School of Business Administration, University of Colorado, Boulder, Colorado (Chap. 64)*

C. J. STERNHAGEN *Medical Director, Kerr-McGee Corporation, Oklahoma City, Oklahoma (Chap. 61)*

HAROLD STIEGLITZ *Vice President, The Conference Board, New York, New York (Chap. 3)*

JOICS B. STONE *Consulting Psychologist, Hacienda Heights, California (Chap. 16)*

RICHARD A. WAMBOLD *Director of Benefits and Personnel Services, Tenneco Inc., Houston, Texas (Chap. 60)*

DAVID R. WEBB *Management Information Systems Manager, Ritter Company, Rochester, New York (Chap. 79)*

FRANK JAY WOLLING *Manager, Reference and Library Service, The Rockefeller Foundation, New York, New York (Chap. 77)*

JAMES C. WORTHY *Vice President, Cresap, McCormick and Paget Inc., Chicago, Illinois (Chap. 10)*

JOSEPH P. YANEY *Associate Professor of Management, The Ohio State University, College of Administrative Science, Columbus, Ohio (Chap. 55)*

Editorial Planning Committee

FREDERICK G. ATKINSON
Senior Vice President
R. H. Macy & Co.
New York, N.Y.

LYLE H. FISHER
Vice President
Personnel and Industrial Relations
Minnesota Mining & Manufacturing Co.
Saint Paul, Minnesota

ROBERT L. GARDINER
Retired–Vice President Personnel
Warner-Lambert Pharmaceutical Co.
Morris Plains, N.J.

S. AVERY RAUBE
Vice President
The National Industrial Conference Board
New York, N.Y.

EDWARD A. ROBIE
Vice President and Personnel Director
The Equitable Life Assurance Society
New York, N.Y.

PAUL F. SHAW
Vice President
The Chase Manhattan Bank
New York, N.Y.

WILLIAM R. SPRIEGEL
Professor of Management
The University of Texas
Austin, Texas

JOSEPH W. TOWLE
Professor of Management
Washington University
St. Louis, Missouri

Preface

The goal of this Handbook is to provide comprehensive, authoritative, and understandable information on all aspects of modern personnel administration. When the user of this Handbook finds himself confronted with a personnel problem, he can reach for the Handbook and find an answer or at least guidance toward an answer in its pages. This Handbook is replete with practical how-to-do-it information as any handbook should be. In addition to a "nuts and bolts" approach, the authors have included their observations, the philosophy and background of their subjects, and their feelings on the practical application of what they are writing about in the real world of business and industry.

This Handbook was planned to serve the needs of three groups of people:

1. Personnel administrators: This group includes vice presidents of personnel and industrial relations, personnel directors, personnel managers, wage and salary administrators, recruitment specialists, employee benefits administrators, labor relations specialists, training directors, employee services managers—in other words, *all* those in the field of personnel in private and public organizations. This also includes management consultants and teachers of personnel administration and related courses.

2. Top management to supervisors inclusive: This group includes all those individuals who have responsibility for leading and managing people including top executives, middle management people, and first line foremen and supervisors.

3. Students of personnel administration: This group includes any individual who seeks greater responsibility and all students taking personnel administration and related courses.

Almost a year was spent just in the planning of this book. But at the end of that year, those who had worked on it felt that a sound practical framework for a discussion of the many facets of personnel administration had been developed.

This Handbook is the result of endless hours of serious work on the part of many sincere people with years of experience in the field of manpower management. These individuals have expressed their convictions honestly and forcefully. Of course, there were some compromises along the way.

However, when the Handbook was finally put to bed, there was not a question in any of our minds that it had our full endorsement.

There are probably differences of opinion on the methods by which the job of managing people may best be carried out. After all, managing people is a very complex function. The reader will surely feel this as he reads through the Handbook, and he will also be impressed with the number and variety of people problems which must be dealt with by supervisors, foremen, managers, directors, department heads, and executives. People problems are evident in every chapter; but for every problem, a suggested and workable solution is offered. Although no one would claim that the methods and techniques in personnel administration are perfect and that no further improvement is possible, the reader will nevertheless find reasonable solutions to most of his problems as set forth here in these pages. The reader will realize that there are no simple answers. Each chapter will give him added insight which will help him manage people more effectively than ever before. This is what the planners of the Handbook had in mind from the start.

The person who is seriously interested in knowing more about the art and science of personnel administration will find it helpful to study the entire Handbook. He can read a chapter a day. In approximately three months, he will have read the entire book and at that time he will surely have a breadth of understanding of personnel administration far greater than he might acquire in any other way. The Handbook, in this way, offers an excellent way for self-development.

The need for the Handbook was first recognized by the McGraw-Hill Book Company. Nowhere within the covers of one volume, which could be referred to for guidance in time of need, could they find an up-to-date and authoritative discussion of the many problems faced by literally thousands of managers.

The Handbook is, of course, the work of many, many people. The authors were selected because of the knowledge of their subjects they are known to possess. As a group, they form an excellent cross section of personnel practitioners, including as they do, practicing general personnel executives, management consultants, teachers of personnel administration, and experts from the many professional and specialized fields in personnel management.

The Editor-in-Chief wishes to express his sincere appreciation to the members of the Editorial Planning Committee, to all the authors, and to the many others who have made this Handbook possible. Special credit must go to Joan Muessen whose efforts were tireless in handling many administrative and other responsibilities that a Handbook of this magnitude necessarily involves. Without her "beyond the call of duty" devotion, this book would not be in your hands today.

Joseph J. Famularo

Part 1

Management and Personnel Administration

chapter 1

Today's Role and Scope
of Personnel Administration
in Management

JOHN PAUL JONES *Senior Vice President, Federated Department Stores, Inc., Cincinnati, Ohio*

In the years since the end of the Great Depression and the beginning of World War II, the personnel function has grown and matured until it now plays an indispensable role in the management of most American corporations. From an early concentration on blue-collar employment and welfare programs, personnel has developed into a major function and a constellation of special skills and talents covering a broad spectrum of activities concerned with the recruitment, training, assessment, selection, placement, development, appraisal, compensation, organization, and conservation of business and industry's most critical resource: the people who make the enterprise productive. Indeed, the personnel function may be said to be principally responsible for the human values of the organization, and this responsibility is discharged not only internally but also when dealing with unions where they represent any portion of the company's human resources.

Objectives

It is a truism to say that the objectives of a personnel function must be consistent with those of the enterprise it serves. Peter Drucker[1] has suggested that the principal objective of any organization is survival, and that from this all other objectives flow. Thus, if profit is needed for survival, profit is an objective. If survival de-

---

[1] Peter Ferdinand Drucker, *The Practice of Management,* Harper & Brothers, New York, 1954.

pends upon growth, then growth—usually profitable growth—becomes an objective, and so on.

Most American corporations at this stage of history are also considering and acknowledging social and public objectives which often may seem to be in direct conflict with their fiscal and operating goals. These new objectives cover a wide range of problems, many of which have been recognized only recently as areas in which business organizations must develop goals and strategies. Urban renewal, employment of the disadvantaged, ghetto redevelopment, and air and water pollution are among these problems. Also, there are "conscience" questions involving such issues as the manufacture of war material, food additives, insecticides and the whole issue of consumer protection.

Therefore, although it is self-evident that the objective of a good personnel function should be completely supportive of the profitable growth of the enterprise of which it is a part, the problem of what contributes to or detracts from profitable growth is becoming more complex each year in terms of the total sociopolitical-economic milieu of our times. Furthermore, of all the functions of the business enterprise (manufacturing and selling, buying and selling) personnel is one of the few whose responsibilities and commitments encompass all the objectives of the business: economic, social, and political. Thus, objective setting within the personnel function must be done utilizing all corporate objectives and with considerable guidance and input from the top management of the enterprise.

THE SCOPE OF PERSONNEL ADMINISTRATION

The personnel function occupies a paradoxical position in the business enterprise unlike any other business function. On the one hand, as noted earlier, the well-performed personnel function probably touches on or is involved in a wider range of activities than any other business function. On the other hand (as many personnel executives have ruefully observed), everyone in the enterprise is a personnel man. The hopes, aspirations, fears, problems and apathies, actions, balance, creativity and innovativeness of people determine the ultimate success or failure of the business. Every manager in the enterprise takes actions every day which affect the people he manages. Thus, he may create or avoid problems, support or suppress creativity, or inspire or frustrate his portion of the larger human organization. The professional personnel executive accepts the paradox and the fact and builds his own skills and genuine reputation by being both a skillful guide and a trusted challenger to the line manager at all levels.

THE DEVELOPMENT OF RESPONSIBILITIES, FUNCTIONS, AND SERVICE

The Beginnings

One way to see the total personnel function is to look at the history of the development of specialties within the function—specialties which were created and developed to meet specific needs of the business as these needs occurred and developed over the years.

As noted before, in the years prior to 1930, the personnel man (where he existed) was primarily an employer of blue-collar people and a welfare administrator within the more paternalistic modes of the organization of that day. In the same vein, he might also have directed the recreation and social programs of the company, recruited athletic teams, and arranged the annual picnic and dinner dance. Very often, he also was the "hatchet man" of the organization, wielding the termination ax when economic conditions suggested a cut in the work force.

The Depression and World War II

With the rise of big unionism in the thirties, labor relations skills began to be in high demand. Because during these years both labor and management were feeling their way into the collective-bargaining relationship, many personnel men learned along with their union counterparts how to handle arbitrations and how to negotiate collective-bargaining agreements.

During World War II, while labor relations continued to occupy its preeminent position in the personnel function, psychological testing and selection and training activities began to become important because of the shortage of skilled workers during wartime. Wage and hour competence also became a needed skill as government wage and price controls were imposed, and from the same base of interest, many personnel departments also developed a continuing interest in and audit of social legislation of all kinds.

Many companies had benefit programs long before World War II, but quite generally these were administered by the financial function. As the programs became more and more a subject of collective bargaining, it was a natural evolution in the personnel area for skills and benefit plan development administration and costing to be added to the personnel function. Thus, generally, we ended World War II with the better personnel functions having represented in their constellation: labor relations, employment, wage administration, employee recreation, and benefit plan development and administration. Safety had also become a predominant need in the World War II plants, and very often safety became a part of the personnel function as did employee feeding (primarily spurred by experiences in the huge isolated manufacturing facilities so common during the war).

The Immediate Postwar Years

Two things happened in the late forties and early fifties to increase the scope of personnel administration. The burst of technology engendered by World War II geometrically increased the need for college-trained people in business and industry — particularly engineers and technically trained people. Thus, college recruitment and college relations bloomed during that era. At the same time, the inflation experienced after World War II made it necessary to pay a considerable amount of attention to both the rise in hiring rates on the campus and the impact of these rates and general inflation on the salaries of managerial, executive, professional, technical, and administrative people. Thus, many companies in the late forties and early fifties began to move toward incorporating into the personnel function the motivational and competitive aspects of exempt salary administration.

As a direct consequence, most personnel functions began to concern themselves with appraisal techniques, moving from the well-established processes of the merit rating of the hourly employees to the more speculative and experimental processes of judging managerial performance. By the same token, the need for more systematic knowledge in many of these areas encouraged the formation of personnel research functions.

The Recent Years

During the early fifties, employee communication seemed to be one of the major areas of concern. Company publications proliferated, and attitude and morale surveys began to flourish. Management development and manager training activities also began to become more important and more complex in our larger corporations. During the late fifties and early sixties, the impact of behavioral science research began to make itself felt with consequent changes in approaches to management development, including the advent of concepts such as continuing education and manager renewal opportunities.   About the same time, staff activity concerning the organization of work moved quietly from the industrial engineering area, where the focus was on the relationship of man to machine, to the personnel area, where the concern was the relationship of man to man, group to group, and both groups and men to objectives.

Finally, during the middle sixties, after some disastrous experiences had convinced many managements of the advisability of personnel involvement, personnel functions began to be deeply involved in acquisitions and mergers, particularly in the assessment of problems connected with the merging of benefit plans and the difficulties often accompanying the acquisition of added labor problems along with the assets of the business.   Additionally, the trend of this activity is toward more participation of the personnel function in the problem of merging organizational components and concepts as the pace of mergers and acquisitions increases.

THE NEWER SPECIALTIES

As this book goes to press, at least three other special areas are beginning to emerge within the personnel function.

As noted earlier, urban affairs and minority-group employment and upgrading have begun to take a major role in American corporations and, therefore, on the personnel function.   The impact of civil-rights legislation over the last five or ten years has brought the plight of the minority person and the disadvantaged person strongly into focus before business and industry, and personnel people are becoming deeply involved in minority-group affairs.

Secondly, as the generation of youngsters leaving school and entering business makes its impact on the scene, the role of "ombudsman" is becoming more and more important within the personnel functions of advanced organizations.   Striking changes have taken place in the values, aspirations, hopes, and expectations of young people over the past ten years.   Alert personnel groups are making certain that people now have a spokesman within the enterprise who will stand up fearlessly and represent their point of view.

Finally, the whole area generally known as organization development is beginning to play a major role in large corporations.   This function picks up the old principles of attitude surveys and converts them into more sophisticated methods of securing feedback from the organization in terms of roadblocks, communication blocks, and frustrations, and spends a major amount of effort applying the findings of behavioral science research in such areas as interpersonal and intergroup conflict and dynamics. Basically, organization development focuses on the whole process of freeing the climate of organizations to enhance the productivity and creativity of the people who work within it.

Thus, the role and scope of personnel administration have come a long, long way in the past fifty years.   It seems likely that the challenges of the years ahead may produce even more dramatic changes in the fifty years to come.

chapter 2

Motivation and Performance

SAUL W. GELLERMAN *President, Gellerman Kay Corporation, Harrington Park, New Jersey*

The behavioral science movement has gone through three distinct historical stages, and its impact on management has been rather different at each stage. The first period ran from the end of the World War I through the mid-thirties, and might be called the period of emphasis upon *selection*. This was due largely to the success of the armed forces in classifying large numbers of soldiers into occupational groups on the basis of paper-and-pencil tests. During this period, the problem of motivation was approached largely through the attempt to identify potential shirkers prior to hiring by means of various tests.

While this approach is still being used, it began to be supplanted during the thirties by a new emphasis on *paternalism*. At this time, management became concerned with the importance of maintaining employee loyalty and morale through the elimination of irritants from their environment. Initially the emphasis was on physical irritants such as temperature and noise, but later this was broadened to include a much wider spectrum of disturbing influences, such as feelings of insecurity with regard to employment, feelings of unfairness on the part of supervision, and feelings of not being accepted by one's fellow workers. During this period, management put great emphasis on providing recreational facilities for employees and training supervisors in methods of dealing with their subordinates in a friendly and, above all, a fair manner.

During the latter part of the 1960s, managers began to take a renewed interest in motivation. There were two reasons for this: (1) the constantly increasing economic pressure for increased labor productivity, coupled with the recognition that productivity was very often influenced by the extent to which workers were willing to devote their best efforts to their jobs; (2) the popularization of concepts and techniques which emerged from recent research in the behavioral sciences.

The earlier (post–World War I) research had centered upon that aspect of motivation which is *inherent* in individuals, and which tends to characterize their behavior over long periods of time.   This corresponds roughly to what the layman means when he speaks of "personality" traits.   Because of this historical background, it is not surprising that for many people the term "motivation" still has strong connotations of traits which are "built in" to certain individuals, especially desirable ones such as zeal, enthusiasm, determination, and intense commitment to the accomplishment of goals.   But as more behavioral science research data became available to managers, it became increasingly apparent that the actual behavior of workers could often be best understood as a *reaction* to the situation in which they found themselves, rather than an expression of any inherent traits.   In other words, most people are capable of a wide variety of behavior, and their actual conduct in any given situation will depend on the way in which the environment draws upon their available "inventory" of possible responses.   Further, the "environment" had to be understood more broadly: it included not only working conditions, compensation, and supervision (the main concerns of the "paternalistic" phase), but also the experiences generated by doing the job and the web of communications in which the job was embedded.

With the recognition that behavior was in fact adaptable and largely molded to circumstances, rather than preordained by any immutable traits, management was enabled to move forward into the current phase of behavioral science application.

This by no means indicates that the attempts to classify people according to their behavior potentialities, or to maintain morale, have been abandoned.   Rather they have been placed in a more realistic perspective as parts of the larger complex of factors that affect employee behavior on the job.   The current phase, which might be called the *experimental* phase, has been characterized by the development of new approaches to managerial problems, largely under the influence of behavioral research results which have been successfully popularized and interpreted to management.

In particular, this phase has been influenced by the work of the late Douglas McGregor (1906–1964) who was Professor of Industrial Administration at the Massachusetts Institute of Technology.   McGregor is best known for his emphasis on the importance of the assumptions which managers make about the process of human influence, the nature of work, and the nature of human nature itself.   He noted that for many managers, these assumptions were rather cynical, and included the notions that most people were not naturally attracted to work and would not engage in productive work unless either coerced or coaxed into doing so.   McGregor also noted that these assumptions tended to become a "self-fulfilling prophecy" in the sense that the assumptions would color the manager's own behavior in subtle ways which would tend to motivate his subordinates to act in ways which were consistent with his assumptions.   In other words, the manager's behavior acted selectively upon the repertoire of various behavior styles available to subordinates, and elicited from them chiefly actions which tended to confirm the beliefs of the manager.

McGregor's ability to popularize this notion led to a great deal of emphasis by managers on examining their own behavior, and the assumptions underlying it, in an attempt to develop managerial styles which had a more constructive influence on employee behavior.   This has been manifested in many ways, the best known of which are sensitivity training and that group of procedures which are known collectively as organization development.   The research data presently available concerning the efficacy of these procedures are not very large, and for that reason they must, despite their popularity, be considered largely experimental.

The influence of McGregor can be seen in the concern modern managers have shown in the effects of their own behavior on the behavior of their co-workers and subordinates.   Recognizing that behavior is usually a response, rather than an inevitable acting out of some inner drive, managers have become increasingly concerned with the extent to which they can deliberately shape the environment in which the response is made. In other words, they have become more interested in that aspect of motivation which they are in a position to influence (the environment in which workers cope with their assignments) and correspondingly less interested in that aspect over which they can exert relatively little control (the individual's traits and predispositions). Thus, to the behaviorally sophisticated manager, the term "motivation" is more likely to connote an action or event which produces a change in behavior than a desire by an individual to behave in a particular way.

This is a more pragmatic view of motivation. It is more compatible than the older, trait-oriented view with the desire of managers to get down to specifics and cope with tangible problems, and also with the implications of increasingly sophisticated studies in the behavioral sciences. As a result, attention is increasingly focused on the specific kinds of on-the-job behavior, which can be influenced by managerial action and which have a direct relationship to productivity.

It has been recognized that some forms of on-the-job behavior can be influenced by managerial action in more or less direct, readily understood ways; while others can be influenced only subtly and indirectly. It is also clear that both desirable and undesirable forms of behavior can be motivated by managerial actions, and that in this sense motivation is neither positive nor negative, but simply refers to actions which cause behavior to change.

The most tangible and fundamental aspect of behavior which is subject to motivational influence is membership, that is, those actions involved in joining an organization, remaining in it, or leaving it. It is now understood that the process of recruitment is not a one-sided affair at all. It also involves "selection" of the company by individuals in the pool of available candidates who elect to apply to the company for and to accept offers of employment. This is especially true in tight labor markets when candidates tend to be quite selective about which employers they will even consider; but it is increasingly true of very loose labor markets as well. For example, workers whose jobs are eliminated by automation will frequently refuse job opportunities that involve relocating. Unemployed workers have been known to refuse job opportunities which paid reasonably good wages, but which they considered menial or beneath their dignity.

In other words, there is a trend toward increasing selectivity on the part of prospective employees. They are responding to the "image" or reputation of a company, an industry, or an occupation as much as to the income opportunities which are offered to them. This in turn reflects a major reorientation of attitudes since the depression and immediate postwar years: instead of being chiefly concerned with income and security of employment, workers are increasingly concerned with whether they would enjoy the work and derive enough dignity and status from it to satisfy their needs. This is not to suggest that workers have become indifferent to either income or security, but rather that the relative ease with which both can be achieved in an affluent economy has made people less sensitive to them than before, and more willing to indulge themselves in interests which previously were of secondary importance.

The importance of effectively motivating membership cannot be overstated. Basically what is at stake is the company's access to a sufficient number of properly qualified people to accomplish its work. Unless the requisite talent can be attracted and retained, a company's ability to effectively utilize its physical and financial assets can be seriously jeopardized. Recognizing this, many managements have moved forcefully to make their companies as attractive as possible to the kinds of people needed to accomplish their work. Among other things, this involves assuring that salary and other aspects of financial compensation are competitive, that physical working conditions are pleasant, that jobs are as stimulating as possible, and that as many petty irritants as possible are eliminated. In some cases, these efforts to make the company more attractive to employees has required a reexamination of some time-honored practices, and modifying or even abandoning them.

Attention also began to be focused on the problem of absenteeism; in many cases it was recognized that the chronic absentee was really coping in a somewhat less drastic manner with the same kind of job frustrations that motivated other more "marketable" people to resign from their jobs. In fact, absenteeism can frequently be best understood as a temporary escape from an undesirable job. It is a tactic favored by people whose skills are relatively less in demand than others, or who have a strong vested interest in remaining on the payroll of their present employer. It is, in other words, more characteristic of the hourly employee. On the other hand, voluntary turnover is more likely to occur among the more mobile employees found at the professional and managerial levels whose skills are highly marketable. Although the behavior in these two cases is different, the motivation tends to be similar (escape from an undesirable job). The effect on productivity is also similar (increased cost of operations).

While membership is of fundamental importance, it is only a part of the larger problem of labor productivity. In addition to attracting and retaining qualified personnel, the company also needs to find ways to encourage ingenuity, attention to quality, communication, cooperation, and other forms of on-the-job behavior which in total contribute to productivity. It also needs to find ways to minimize negligence, uncooperativeness, deliberate restriction of output, and other actions which detract from productivity. Initially, these problems were approached through a combination of rewards and punishments, such as wage increases or threats of dismissal. While these are still used, it is increasingly recognized that the greatest managerial leverage upon these forms of behavior is obtained through programs designed to foster the *development of individual talent.*

There have been four major approaches to the development of talent. While each tends to have its advocates and detractors, they are not really incompatible with each other, and many companies blend them into an effective overall program. The two older techniques are training programs (including classroom, vestibule, and on-the-job training) and instructing supervisors in more effective methods of dealing with subordinates (usually emphasizing fairness, accessibility, and individual attention and discouraging the ever-present temptation to resort to a coercive approach). The two newer approaches are job enrichment (which attempts to restructure the duties of a job so as to make the work itself more interesting and stimulating) and team building (in which an attempt is made to build greater candor and clarity into the communication that occurs within and between work groups).

Part of the reason for the rising concern with developing talent is a recognition that the alternative to development is stagnation, and that this not only is costly in itself but also helps to breed more severe problems such as work restriction (and in the case of companies with union contracts support for strikes, boycotts, and other militant tactics).

It would obviously be an oversimplification to ascribe such complex acts as these to any single cause; but it seems clear that when people feel unable to influence their future and/or to tolerate the present, they become increasingly predisposed to actions which are basically retaliatory and revengeful. Therefore, the emphasis on personal development is motivated not only by the desire to increase productivity but also by the need to "defuse" tendencies toward costly, destructive behavior in people who have come to feel trapped and unable to progress.

Just as absenteeism is essentially a milder form of escape from an undesirable job than is turnover, so can restrictive practices and flouting of work rules be understood as essentially milder forms of the same impulse (retaliation) that gets its most dramatic expression in strikes or acts of sabotage. The modern behavioral approach emphasizes trying to identify and eliminate their root causes, while the traditional approach emphasizes means of suppressing them (usually through tighter supervision and discipline). Identifying the causes usually involves an attempt to understand the way in which the employees see their own situation, through such methods as interviews and opinion surveys. Some of the causes revealed by these methods are beyond management's ability to control, and others involve changes which management may be reluctant to make for technical, financial, or other reasons. But in many cases the undesirable behavior is being stimulated by factors which management can control, and by addressing effective action to these sources significant reductions in undesirable behavior can be obtained.

In this connection, it is important to note that employee dissatisfaction is not always based on financial factors, and that the resolution of these problems does not always require substantial expenditures of money. In fact, the major obstacle to the solution of many motivation problems is not the company's budget, but the willingness of management to modify some of its favorite practices, especially with regard to control procedures such as routine reports, time clocks, approvals.

Since McGregor, the most substantial contribution to applied behavioral science has been made by Frederick Herzberg, Professor of Industrial Psychology at Case Western Reserve University. In a well-known series of experiments beginning in the late 1950s, Herzberg and his associates drew a distinction between two kinds of motivational influences which seemed to have markedly different effects on behavior and performance. The first they called *hygiene* factors, since they were essentially aspects of the working environment which, when ineffectively administered, resulted in resentful attitudes and diminished effort or even hostile acts against the organization, but which when effectively administered resulted in a more or less neutral situation, without any marked or lasting enthusiasm for the work or increase in productivity. The term "hygiene" was used because the effect is essentially the same as that achieved by public health measures such as water purification: in itself it does not make people healthier, but failure to give proper attention to it would endanger the health of many people. Herzberg included among hygiene factors most of the factors traditionally emphasized by personnel departments: pay, fringe benefits, supervisory styles and policies, working conditions, etc.

The other set of influences were called *motivators,* since they seemed to produce lasting satisfaction and commitment of the individual's energies to the job. These were experiences generated by work which were sufficiently challenging to engage the bulk of the individual's abilities and included the sense of accomplishment, the sense of increasing mastery or competence, recognition through increased responsibility, etc. In one sense, the term "motivators" is a bit unfortunate since Herzberg uses it in a more restricted sense than do most behavioral scientists. This has led to some avoidable but vigorous controversies, such as the question, "Is money a motivator?" (If we accept Herzberg's definition, money is usually a hygiene factor and not a motivator, but if by motivator we mean something that influences behavior, then money clearly is a motivator, especially of membership. Its influence on productivity is not marked except as a negative influence in the case of inequitable payment.) However, more than semantics is involved in the controversy over Herzberg's work.

The two basic reasons why Herzberg's work has attracted so much attention are that it calls into question the efficacy of most of the traditional practices of personnel departments with respect to motivation, and his conclusion that satisfaction and dissatisfaction are not opposites but instead are entirely distinct and independent feelings. With regard to the former, Herzberg holds that hygiene factors cannot be dispensed with, and indeed require constant skilled administrative attention, but that it would be unrealistic to expect them to generate commitment or enthusiasm. The best that can be expected is a lack of negative attitudes. Positive attitudes toward work, if they are to occur at all, are more likely to be the result of building "motivators" (in Herzberg's sense) into the job. With regard to the relationship of satisfaction and dissatisfaction, this is a theoretical point of greater interest to academicians than to practitioners or managers. The methods by which Herzberg's experiments were designed and by which the statistical results were interpreted have been questioned by some academicians, resulting in a lengthy series of articles in professional journals that have little or no relevance to management problems but have generated considerable heat, some of which has come to the attention of managers.

The best known application of Herzberg's work has been the job-enrichment experiments carried out in certain units of the Bell System and of Imperial Chemical Industries. These involved the redesign of jobs in such a way as to eliminate or at least reduce the amount of time spent in essentially dull, unstimulating tasks; the incorporation of related tasks previously separated into several jobs into one job, so as to provide clear responsibility by each individual for a definable unit or sub-unit of work; and the addition of more challenging responsibilities related to the work, such as scheduling, setting priorities, and on-the-spot decisions related to the product or process with which the work was involved. These experiments indicate a promising opportunity for applying the job-enrichment technique to the reduction of turnover and absenteeism and to the improvement of quality and efficiency.

Experiments in team building represent the current extension of the earlier work by McGregor and his associates. Perhaps the best known experiments have been carried out by Sheldon Davis of TRW Systems Division in Redondo Beach, California. The intent of these exercises is to enable people whose jobs require them to collaborate with each other to maximize their ability to facilitate each other's work and to minimize the interference of normal, but impeding, trends such as lack of candor or uncertainty about implications. The focus, in other words, is on the extent to which behavior by one team member facilitates or impedes the effectiveness of other team members, and on teaching them to confront any difficulties between themselves openly and constructively. The approach is similar in some respects to sensitivity training, but it is more definitely programmed and more sharply focused on specific objectives.

Looking to the future, behavioral scientists have become concerned with the possible impact of their own work on management, and also with the inevitable impact which the changing values of younger workers will eventually have upon the labor force as a whole. It is clear that the successful introduction of techniques such as job enrichment and team building will bring substantial improvements in efficiency, but will also present new challenges. Managing a highly motivated team of collaborative employees will in some respects be more difficult than managing a less effective team, and steps may be necessary to help managers develop wholly new procedures for operating in such an environment. The gradual change in employee's values will probably move to less emphasis on job security and to more emphasis on relatively rapid satisfaction of desires for meaningful, challenging assignments. The result, unless effective means are found through job enrichment and other procedures for coping with these needs, is likely to be substantially higher rates of turnover, absenteeism, and "opting out" of the labor force altogether than have previously been experienced.

Thus the role of the behavioral sciences in contributing to the management of performance is continuing to evolve, and appears likely to play an even more critical role in the foreseeable future than it has in the past.

BIBLIOGRAPHY

Ford, R.: *Motivation Through the Work Itself,* American Management Association, New York, 1969.

Gellerman, S. W.: *Management by Motivation,* American Management Association, New York, 1968.

Herzberg, F.: *Work and the Nature of Man,* World Publishing Company, Cleveland, 1966.

McGregor, D.: *The Human Side of Enterprise,* McGraw-Hill Book Company, New York, 1960.

—— : *The Professional Manager,* McGraw-Hill Book Company, New York, 1967.

chapter 3

Organization Planning[1]

HAROLD STIEGLITZ *Vice President, The Conference Board, 845 Third Avenue, New York, N.Y. 10022*

In a free competitive economy, a company's only long-term advantage lies in its human resources. Other advantages that arise from technological improvements, the opening of new markets, and lower material or labor costs all prove to be relatively short run. So basically it is the initiative, the will and the motivation people bring to their work, that companies are learning to rely upon for survival and growth.

To nurture this motivation, more and more companies are seeking fundamental elements to provide just the right climate for its growth. Part of this search stems from the growing realization that, even with the present affluent society, there is just not enough money printed to buy motivation. Possibly more important is the recognition that even the most broadly conceived compensation structure can provide satisfaction only off the job.

So far the search has unearthed no startling panacea. However, it has produced growing appreciation of several very basic—but still rather elusive—elements, and ever-increasing emphasis on the vital impact they can have on people:

Policy—that sets out the company's code of ethical values which governs all employee, customer, public, and governmental relationships.

Communication—down, up, across and in between that makes for maximum participation of people in decisions affecting them.

Organization—that integrates and coordinates the efforts of different individuals and gives purpose to their efforts in terms of objectives to be accomplished.

ORGANIZATION PLANNING: A DEFINITION

Essentially, a business organization is a combination of men, money, and machines so coordinated that they can fulfill an economic objective.

[1] Reprinted with permission of The Conference Board from their report "Organization Planning: Basic Concepts: Emerging Trends, 1970."

Organization planning is simply figuring out how this coordination is to be achieved. Of course if the result of organization planning is to be sound organization rather than disorganization, the planning required may not be so simple. For involved in "coordination" are such major considerations as objectives, activities, authority, and relationships. One of the accepted definitions of organization planning brings these four elements together as follows: "Organization planning is the process of grouping activities, assigning authority and establishing relationships so as to accomplish the objective of the enterprise."

However, this is a somewhat traditional definition. To give fuller emphasis to the importance of human resources and to underscore the need for personal motivation, another definition might be more appropriate: "Organization planning is the process of logically grouping activities, delineating authority and responsibility, and establishing working relationships that will enable both the company and the employee to realize their mutual objectives."

This definition gives organization planning a broader scope. It emphasizes that corporate objectives are accomplished through people. And it squares with companies' increasing realization that people identify themselves with company objectives only to the extent that their own objectives are also achieved.

It also recognizes, as most organization planners know, that short-term organizing is a very pragmatic process. There is a huge difference between the abstract, impersonal structuring of an "ideal" long-range organization plan and the accommodation of that "ideal" to current realities in the form of existing personnel.

Objectives

Yet, in emphasizing people and their objectives, the definition does not undercut the prime importance of corporate objectives. For in terms of planning, corporate objectives are the starting point.

Conceived of in the largest terms, survival and perpetuation are the basic objectives of a company. The company's ability to achieve these objectives is measured in terms of profit and growth. More recently, some business executives have begun to cite a third objective, which, for lack of more precise terminology, is usually phrased as "maintenance of a corporate image." This objective concerns the character and reputation of the company. Spelled out, the "corporate image" viewpoint stresses that the company, like other citizens, has certain civic and social responsibilities that it must fulfill and certain social and ethical values that it must sustain. There are business executives who insist that the intelligent corporation pursues a favorable corporate image as a means of furthering its basic objectives of survival and perpetuation. But others regard the corporate image as an end in itself that merits the same emphasis as the other two objectives.

Although these are the basic objectives of most companies, organization planning is based on the more specific objectives of the particular company: What goods or services does the company produce or plan to produce? Will it be a single-product company or will it diversify and produce several products? If diversified, what form will the diversification take:

Integration, whereby the company will produce major components that it might otherwise have to buy from other suppliers?

Production of products that are related, either because of the similarity of the manufacturing process (typewriters and guns) or because they serve a common purpose (all types of containers, rather than just cans)?

Production of totally unrelated products with similar marketing channels (hosiery and perfumes) or completely dissimilar distribution channels (recreation equipment and electronic devices)?

Obviously, answers to these questions in the producing side of the business materially affect the structure of the organization. On the selling side, answers to the following questions also affect the structure:

What market does the company serve or plan to serve in terms of geography and customers?

Is the market local, national, or international?

Do all the products have similar geographic markets?

How about the customers? Is the company catering to the consuming public, industry, or government?

Is the market stable or is it shifting?

The objectives of the company—plus a host of other environmental factors like the degree of competition in the industry, the relative degree of change in the technology involved, the legal environment—affect the type of work or activities the company must engage in, the structure of authority that can be allowed, and the relationship that will obtain between the various units of the organization. For, once objectives are established, the work of organization planning is largely concerned with these three elements: work or activities, authority, and relationships.

TOOLS OF THE TRADE

To carry out the job of organizing or organization planning, certain tools have been developed. Some tools are terms used in organization planning and communicating about it; others are principles of organization which act as guides in planning the structure.

Common Terms Defined

Without certain terms, the organization planner would be lost. Strip his vocabulary of such words as *manager, delegation, responsibility, accountability, authority, line,* and *staff,* and it becomes exceedingly difficult for him to discuss organization structure. Even with these terms, however, all is not smooth, for not all of them have a precise, universal meaning. Because the above-mentioned words are those most often used in discussing organization, the following estimate of their meaning in current usage is offered:

Manager: a person whose work calls for him to plan, organize, motivate, and control the work of others. The verbs used to characterize the work of a manager can be increased to eleven or twelve by including such other verbs as forecasting, programing, staffing, integrating, directing, measuring, correcting; or all these can be reduced to just one word—coordinating. But the four above seem adequate to encompass the basic characteristics of a manager. He is a person who accomplishes his work through other people. The scope of planning, organizing, motivating, and controlling done by the manager may be large or small. A manager may carry the title "foreman" to show that the scope of his managing is relatively small; he may carry a more lofty title, "president" or "chief executive," to indicate that his scope in terms of the company is all-encompassing. Regardless of the title, he is a manager by virtue of the fact that he coordinates the work of others.

Delegation: the act of entrusting to someone else (a subordinate) part of the job the person (superior) is expected to carry out. This entrustment is usually subject to recall by the superior. Sometimes the recall occurs without the subordinate's even knowing it; for example, when the superior intervenes in a situation or makes a decision that the subordinate thinks was delegated to him.

Delegation takes place between the individual and his subordinate. (When carried out on a company-wide scale, when the company encourages maximum delegation throughout the organization, it is termed "decentralization.") What is delegated is responsibility and authority: responsibility in terms of a job to be performed, authority in terms of the power to act.

For delegation or decentralization to be effective, there must be clearly defined controls in the form of objectives and policy, and means of measuring action against the controls or limits that have been established.

Responsibility: the work, function, or activities assigned a particular organizational component or person. Responsibility may be delegated and redelegated. A total responsibility, or a total function, may be split into several parts and the subparts be delegated and redelegated to lower levels in the organization. The manufacturing responsibility, for example, may be split into production and engineering, and the head of manufacturing may delegate these responsibilities to subordinates. The head of engineering, in turn, may split his responsibility into several parts, e.g., production engineering and plant maintenance, and redelegate these parts to his subordinates. In each case, however, certain parts of the overall responsibility cannot be delegated. These "reserved responsibilities" pertain to the management and coordination of the several parts that have been delegated.

Responsibility, in the sense used here, should be distinguished from accountability.

Accountability: an obligation to answer to a superior for carrying out delegated responsibilities; obligation to produce and account for results, in terms of objectives or work which have been delegated. Whereas responsibility may be delegated and redelegated, accountability may never be delegated. It emerges each time responsibility is delegated. The subordinate, in accepting the responsibility, also accepts the obligation to account. However, the superior, having delegated responsibility to subordinates, retains accountability for results of delegated work. This proposition is basic to organization planning and is enunciated most forcefully in the principle of organization that states: "The accountability of higher authority for the acts of its subordinates is absolute."

Authority: the right, power, and freedom to take action necessary to carry out work or obtain results for which the person is accountable. The essence of a manager's authority to act is his right, power, and freedom to make decisions.

Authority is delegated, as is responsibility. However, within a company, no manager has complete authority or complete freedom to act. His authority is subject to restraint in the form of such overall corporate controls as objectives, policies, and budgets. Delegated authority thus emerges as freedom to act or make decisions within, and in conformity with, overall corporate objectives and policies.

The relationship between responsibility and accountability and authority thus becomes self-evident. The acceptance of responsibility brings about accountability which, in turn, gives rise to authority required to carry out that which a person is accountable for.

Again, there is an often-quoted principle of organization that enunciates this relationship: "Responsibility should always be coupled with corresponding authority," or more explicitly, "Authority and responsibility must be equal." With the major emphasis today on accountability, a more reasonable statement of the principle is: "Accountability should always be coupled with corresponding authority."

Line and Staff: organization terms used to define the relationship between the work and authority of organization components.

"Line" and "staff" are two of the most perplexing, ambiguous, overworked, and overdefined terms in the lexicon of the organization planner. It might also be said that they are two of the most misunderstood terms, but this would imply that someone, somewhere, has arrived at a "true meaning" of the terms.

Attempts have been made by some companies to dispense with these terms. "Operating" is quite often substituted for "line"; "auxiliary" and "service" are the most common substitutes for "staff." But substitution of terms is of doubtful value in clarifying the organization relationships involved. An explanation that is offered in the organization manual of a large manufacturing company illustrates this point: "The nature of our organization requires a thorough understanding of the relationship between *operating men* and *administrative specialists.* There is no innovation here. It is the same relationship that has always existed between *line and staff when these words are properly used."* (Italics added).

Since these terms are encrusted with military overtones and the nuances given them by organization planners and writers, it is only possible to point out what most people most of the time connote (as opposed to mean) when they use these two terms.

In general usage, the terms are used in two quite different settings: (1) to distinguish or characterize types of work; and (2) to distinguish and characterize types of authority.

As a matter of fact, a good part of the confusion arises from the general conclusion that "staff work" necessarily implies "staff authority."

In terms of work, "line" connotes the work, functions, or organization components that are accountable for fulfilling the economic objectives of the organization. They are the income-producing components of the organization. This is not to imply that any unit of the company does not contribute to the company's income. But most explicitly, line units are those directly concerned with producing the values in the form of goods and services that the customer will pay for. In terms of basic economics, line units are those that produce "time, place, and form" utility. In a manufacturing company, these are generally identified as manufacturing and sales and sometimes engineering when it is an integral part of manufacturing.

In terms of work, "staff" connotes work, functions, or organization components that are required to supply information and services to the line components.

The nature of the work performed is of three types:

1. *Advice and Counsel.* Staff gathers and disseminates information, often of a specialized nature, to other elements of the organization that require information. Relative to its superior, the staff unit advises and counsels on procedures, methods, and systems that will most effectively accomplish the objectives of the organizational unit. When the organizational unit is the company as a whole, staff units advise and counsel the president in his planning on overall corporate objectives and policies. Relative to other units in the organization, staff acts not only as an adviser but as a counselor and interpreter, especially in the case of corporate objectives and policies.

2. *Service.* Staff supplies to other units services that can be provided more economically by centralizing them. A unit may be created, for example, to recruit and screen new employees, rather than have the several components doing their own recruitment and screening. Or a purchasing department may be created to handle the purchasing of several departments. In such situations, staff may be viewed as relieving the line unit of chores. In other situations, however, the services required are of a more specialized nature that cannot be adequately performed by line units. The special skills and knowledge required to negotiate a legal contract, for example, or to provide medical attention, give rise to staff units providing these specialized services.

3. *Functional Control.* Staff acts in behalf of its superior to see that certain controls, in the form of objectives and policies, budgets, plans, and procedures, are being adhered to by other units. In behalf of its superior, it inspects, measures, and evaluates performance within its sphere of functional competence, relative to the standards and controls that have been established. In this respect, staff is working within the area of its superior's reserved responsibility to plan and to control.

Very often, in speaking of staff, consideration is restricted to its work as an advisory and counseling unit only. This leads to the contention that staff is actually line when it performs certain services or exercises functional control. Very often, too, statements are made to the effect that "the traditional role of staff" is that of merely providing advice and counsel. This, too, neglects the historical fact that the need for special services—as opposed to just advice and consent—gave rise to some of the earliest types of staff units; for example, finance, purchasing, legal, and medical departments. And functional control is also a traditional role—so traditional that when "control" is mentioned, one automatically thinks of a controller.

In many companies, there are staff units whose work is primarily to advise and counsel—a long-range planning unit, for example; there are other units that are primarily service units—purchasing or press relations, for example; and there are units that are solely functional control units, like the auditor or controller. But more and more it is recognized that staff units perform all three types of work. Personnel administration, for example, advises and counsels top management and other units on effective personnel programs and procedures; provides services in the form of recruitment, selection, and testing; and exercises functional control in behalf of its superior in overseeing adherence to corporate personnel policies.

As was previously indicated, this distinction between "line" and "staff," when used to characterize different types of work, may confuse the relationship between the two units when they are characterized in terms of authority. It is generally assumed, for example, that units doing line work automatically have line authority, and that units doing staff work have no authority over the line and thus no line authority. Or (more to the point) line work is often believed to be synonymous with line authority, staff work synonymous with staff authority.

Possibly the simplest way to clarify the authority relationship between staff and line is to express it in terms of accountability for results.

In any organizational relationship, the unit or person held accountable for the specified result has authority to make the necessary decision. *"Line," in this authority context, connotes authority to take action, authority to make decisions.*

Staff, on the other hand, connotes the unit (or units) that supplies facts and information that will enable the accountable manager to make the best decision. *Staff supplies services designed to help the line manager achieve the best results.* But it cannot impose its judgment or its services on the manager with line authority.

These distinctions—between line work and line authority and staff work and staff authority—become more evident in a given situation. The head of a department doing staff work—finance, for example—is accountable for the effective performance of his unit. To further his effectiveness, he may call on the organization planning department to analyze his organizational setup (he has requested a service) and recommend a better structure (he has asked for advice). In accepting or rejecting the recommendation of the organization planning department, the head of finance is exercising line authority.

To further improve his department's effectiveness, he may seek the advice of the manufacturing division on measures that will simplify accounting problems. Again he may accept or reject the suggestions that the manufacturing unit makes. In this case the manufacturing unit, though labeled "line" in terms of work is operating in a staff capacity to a unit conventionally labeled "staff" (in terms of work) that is now exercising line authority.

Thus, when the question of authority is at issue, it is accountability for results that determines where the line authority resides. The most obvious example of a situation under which a department doing staff work apparently assumes line authority occurs when it exercises functional control relative to overall corporate objectives or policies. As one company states:

When standards have been developed for [company-wide] application and have been incorporated in an official statement of policy or where [the chief executive] has made it clear through other media or methods that certain standards are to be observed, the role of the staff department is no longer advisory but becomes one of inspection and reporting.

Another company states:

The head of a functional [staff] unit, industrial relations, for example, may see a need for a corporate-wide policy relating to his particular function. The policy may impose requirements upon the operating organization. Conformance to the policy is still a matter of line relationships. However, the head of the functional unit would have responsibility to audit performance relating to the policy and to advise and counsel in its application.

In each of these cases, the accountable line manager may be advised that he is violating company policy; he may be advised that "you can't do that." In turn he may cry that staff has usurped line authority. But the usurpation of authority in such a situation is more apparent than real, for when corporate policy has been enunciated, the scope of authority of all managers is immediately limited. Authority or freedom to act, as previously stated, means freedom to act within the confines of corporate policy. Authority that has not been delegated cannot be usurped.

Principles of Organization

It is rather evident from the discussion above that more is involved here than mere definition of terms: the definitions involve concepts of organization, and it is the concepts that are the organization planner's tools.

The concepts also take the form of "principles of organization," that are to be followed in structuring organization. To a large extent, these principles have been derived from analysis of how work and people have been best coordinated in achieving an objective. To a lesser extent, some "principles" have been derived through abstract reasoning on the nature of coordinated effort. In either case organization planners who have developed (but more importantly, applied) principles emphasize that they are not immutable laws. Rather, these principles are guides or cautions that in no way relieve the manager from using his discretion and judgment in their application. In some cases, to attempt to invoke these principles blindly would lead to an organizational impasse. A prime example of such an impasse might grow out of the application of two often-repeated principles: one calling for a minimum number of levels in an organization, another for a limited span of control. Obviously, the two are not mutually exclusive; none of the principles are. Given a number of people to do a given body of work, a more limited span of control calls for more levels, and vice versa.

The emphasis on principles as guides rather than dogma also stems from the fact that very few of them are stated in terms of absolutes. The principle that "everyone should report to only one boss" is one of the examples of an unequivocal directive. However, the key words in most of the other statements of principle call for judgmental interpretation. To refer again to the principle of minimum levels, for example, what is "minimum" is a matter of judgment in a particular situation.

The body of principles that have been enunciated by both companies and analysts is very large. Some analysts have enunciated as many as eighty or ninety "principles" of organization; some companies are satisfied to emphasize only four or five principles. There is, of course, considerable duplication and overlap. From this large body of principles, The Conference Board has selected eleven that might be labeled a consensus: they include those most frequently mentioned or emphasized by both analysts and companies. These eleven principles can be classified in terms of the elements of organization to which they have most pointed application.

Principles of Organization

Objectives

1. The objectives of the enterprise and its component elements should be clearly defined and stated in writing. The organization should be kept simple and flexible.

Activities and Grouping of Activities

2. The responsibilities assigned to a position should be confined as far as possible to the performance of a single leading function.
3. Functions should be assigned to organizational units on the basis of homogeneity of objective to achieve most efficient and economic operation.

Authority

4. There should be clear lines of authority running from the top to the bottom of the organization, and accountability from bottom to top.
5. The responsibility and authority of each position should be clearly defined in writing.
6. Accountability should always be coupled with corresponding authority.
7. Authority to take or initiate action should be delegated as close to the scene of action as possible.
8. The number of levels of authority should be kept to a minimum.

Relationships

9. There is a limit to the number of positions that can be effectively supervised by a single individual.
10. Everyone in the organization should report to only one supervisor.
11. The accountability of higher authority for the acts of its subordinates is absolute.

As indicated in the previous definition of organization planning, there are four basic elements involved: objectives, activities, authority, and relationship. The box on this page groups the eleven principles in terms of these four elements.

Most of the principles relating to activities, authority, and relationship flow from the first principle: *"The objectives of the enterprise and its component elements should be clearly defined and stated in writing. The organization should be kept simple and flexible."*

And most of the principles need no further elaboration. The advantages of following them are implicit in the principles themselves and the previous definitions of terms. However, in light of company experience and recent developments in organization planning, several of the principles merit greater consideration.

Span of control. The span-of-control principle generally used today is: *"There is a limit to the number of positions that can be effectively supervised by a single individual."* This is quite different from the somewhat arbitrary statement still used by relatively few: "The number of people supervised should be no more than five."[2] The modification has been due to company experience. There is recognition that a number of very practical factors affect span of control, and none of these factors operates independently of the others:

1. The competence of both the superior and the subordinates
2. The degree of interaction between the units or personnel being supervised
3. The extent to which the supervisor must carry out nonmanagerial responsibilities and the demands on his time from other people and units

[2] See also, "Span of Control," *Management Record,* July–August, 1960.

4. The similarity or dissimilarity of the activities being supervised
5. The incidence of new problems in his unit
6. The extent of standarized procedure
7. The degree of physical dispersion

This brief list by no means exhausts the factors that affect a supervisor's span of control. But, consideration of them has led companies away from attempts to set arbitrary limits on the number of people that can be supervised at any level. A large textile company, for example, states its span-of-control principle in these terms: "The employees reporting to one executive should not exceed the number which can be effectively directed and coordinated. The number will depend largely on the scope and complexity of the responsibilities of the subordinates."

A large transportation company summarizes the points of view of many organization analysts in the following statement of principle: "There are no fixed rules for determining span of control; the number of subordinates reporting to one executive should be determined by the capacities of the individuals involved and the nature of their responsibilities."

Homogeneous grouping of activities. In regard to activities and their grouping, one basic principle calls for specialization; that is, breaking down the work into small specialized functions. But then, having achieved specialization, the organization planner is concerned with the coordination of these specialties by grouping them into larger units. The principle that has application to grouping is: *"Functions should be assigned to organizational units on the basis of homogeneity of objectives to achieve most efficient and economical operations."*

This statement is a composite of different principles used by companies in grouping activities. As examples, consider the progression in thinking evident in the following statements of principle selected from five different companies:

> Related activities and functions should be combined when practical. (A petroleum company)
> Similar activities should be grouped together to obtain the most effective use of people and facilities. (An electric utility company)
> Activities should be grouped in the best way to meet objectives. (An insurance company)
> Activities should be grouped to produce the most efficient and economical operation. (A diversified manufacturing company)
> Responsibilities should be grouped where possible so that overall control of a function, activity, or product can be established and preferably so the manager can be held accountable for profit. (A large diversified manufacturing company)

From these different statements, it becomes evident that there is no one best method of achieving optimum grouping of activities. The terms "similar activities" or "related activities" evidently have meaning only when viewed in terms of a common objective. Thus, in a company producing and selling one product, manufacturing and sales may be considered unrelated. In a diversified company, however, production of product A may be more closely related to sales of product A than it is to production of product B. The common objective provided by product A (or product B) makes for the close relationship between the two and leads to grouping on the basis of product.

Companies have applied the same reasoning and arrived at groupings on a regional basis.

Thus, in business and in industrial organization today three major methods of grouping are evident:

Functional, where activities are grouped on the basis of similarity of function alone. All production is grouped under one head, all sales under one head, all financial activities under one head.

Regional, where dissimilar functions that occur in different regions are grouped under one head. Production, sales, and financial activities, as they apply to the western region of a company's organization, for example, are grouped under one head.

Product, where all production, sales, financial, or other activities incident to a given product are grouped under one head.

Companies tend to identify their type of organization as product, regional, or functional on the basis of the delegations the chief executive has made to line managers reporting to him. Not all companies can be identified as only one of the three types. Some are mixed: production activities may be grouped on a product basis, while all sales activities are grouped under one functional head. Then too, regardless of the major grouping, the modular units from which it is built are functional. Thus, within a product or regional division of a company, a functional type of organization characteristic of the single-product company makes its appearance.

As already indicated, the basic question involved in grouping by product, region, or function is economic: What will most economically achieve the objective? The nature of the production processes, the nature of the markets being served, the sources of supply for material and labor, transportation costs, and size are a few of the more important factors that come to bear on this decision.

Essentially, however, a diversified company finds that there are three key factors most conducive to a product type of organization:

1. Differing production processes; i.e., the technology involved in the products differs.

2. Differing markets; i.e., the customers for each of the products are different.

3. Sufficient demand for the product to sustain a full-time operation.

When a company organizes regionally, the dominant economic considerations seem to be whether the sources of supply are available within the region, whether supplies are sufficient to meet the demand, and whether the manufacturing facility can be economically reproduced within the region.

For the most part, it is companies in service-type industries, as opposed to manufacturing, that are more often organized on a regional basis. Manufacturing companies, when diversified, more often move to product-type organization. Companies in the refining and extracting industries and smaller manufacturing companies are most typically functionally organized.

Decentralization. The grouping of activities on the basis of product or region has been loosely termed "decentralization." Upon reflection, however, company organization analysts are finding it necessary to distinguish sharply between "decentralization" and "divisionalization," the term more often now used to denote a product or regional type of organization.

Although decentralization most often follows divisionalization, companies with a functional type organization may also be highly decentralized. On the other hand, as some companies have discovered, it is also possible to have little decentralization in a divisionalized company. For decentralization relates to authority rather than to the grouping of activities. And the principle of decentralization, as most widely stated, says: *"Authority to take or initiate action should be delegated as close to the scene of action as possible."*

The advantages of decentralization—in terms of quicker and better decisions, manager development, reducing levels of organization, freeing supervisors to concentrate on broader responsibilities—have been extolled for many years. So whether to decentralize has become an academic issue. Rather, the perplexity arises over two questions relating to the degree of decentralization: (1) How far down in the organization can authority be delegated? and (2) What limitations, if any, should be placed on decentralized authority?

To the question, "How far down can authority be delegated?" the flip answer comes back: "It all depends." Three criteria can be isolated upon which the delegation of decision-making authority is dependent:

1. *Competence* to make decisions on the part of the person to whom authority is delegated; confidence in that competence on the part of the superior is also an essential element.

2. *Information.* The person making the decision requires adequate and reliable information, pertinent to the decision. Decision-making authority thus cannot be pushed below the point at which all information bearing on the decision is available.

Both of these points are covered in a manufacturer's statement of principle: "Responsibilities and authority should be delegated to the lowest level of organization at which the required knowledge and judgment are available to reasonably assure correct decision."

3. *Scope of impact of the decision.* Decisions made by one unit head may affect only the men, money, or material within his own sphere of accountability. However, they may also affect other units. If a decision affects more than one unit, the authority to make the decision rests with the manager accountable for the several units. Thus, authority can be decentralized to the level where the impact of the decision is local. Certain decisions having company-wide effect, e.g., corporate objectives, policies, budgets, are usually not decentralized at all.

To a large extent, this point concerning scope of decisions also answers the second perplexing question: "What limitations, if any, on decentralization?" For in a real sense, the decisions made at the top of the organization that take the form of objectives and policies are the limits on decentralized authority. And as previously stated by way of definition, authority means freedom to act or make decisions within, or in conformity with, overall corporate objectives and policies. This latter point is included in one company's statement of principle on decentralization as follows: "Authority and responsibility for action should be decentralized to organizational units and individuals responsible for actual performance to the greatest extent possible without relaxing necessary control over the policy or the standardization of procedure."

Still another way to view the limits on decentralization is to examine the term itself: de-centralization. Viewed in this way, there is something (an organization) that must be centralized before it can be decentralized. And to keep decentralization from resulting in complete fragmentation, some part of the central core must remain as the unifying element.

Thus, decentralization in practice becomes a matter of degree—with the degree being determined by how far down authority has been delegated and how stringent the limits are that have been placed on authority. It is this fact that leads organizational analysts to declare that no company is completely decentralized. Companies are only more or less decentralized.

THE ORGANIZATION PLANNING PROCESS

Terms, principles, and the organization concepts involved in both are the major tools of the organization planner contemplating the organization or reorganization of a unit of a company or the whole company. Few organization planners, if any, have had the opportunity to organize a company from scratch. Most often, an existing organization reorganizes. The move may be instigated by any of a number of external factors that contribute to changing markets or increasing competition, or by internal factors having to do with personnel and their work. The move to reorganize may be an attempt to correct a poor situation or improve an already satisfactory situation. The reorganization may be large, affecting many units of the company, or small, confined to just one unit.

There are certain identifiable steps, certain priorities, that organization planners attempt to follow when approaching a reorganization. Briefly, they are as follows:

1. *Determination of Objectives.* The top-priority step is clear determination of the objectives of the company. For some companies, this amounts to a redefinition of the nature of the business the company is in. For some, it requires a reevaluation of the company's markets; for some, it is a reevaluation of the company's products or services. However, without the determination of objectives, the organization planner lacks direction for organizing. As part of the determination of objectives, the company enunciates the policies it will adhere to in pursuit of its objectives and the organization principles it plans to follow in organizing to meet these objectives.

2. *Analysis of the Existing Organization.* Essentially, this step amounts to an inventory of existing personnel, functions, and relationships. The organization planner is here concerned with who does what. What are the current assignments of responsibility and authority? What reporting and work relationships now exist? Is there overlap or duplication?

As part of this process, which is most often carried out through questionnaires accompanied by extensive interviews, the organization planner usually prepares a chart or charts of the existing organization and its components. He may also prepare an organization manual which usually includes the charts and position guides of existing positions. The manual may, in addition, contain statements of the company's objectives, principles of organization, and standard nomenclature.[3] This analysis not only provides a snapshot of the existing organization but also provides information that can be used to improve the organizational situation and may generate ideas useful in the next step of the organization planning process.

3. *Preparation of the Long-term "Ideal" Structure.* This is a wholly impersonal plan drawn up to approximate the structure best suited to meet the company's redefined objectives. It is "ideal" only in the sense that it is the structural goal the company will work toward. Organization planners hesitate to equate the "ideal" with the "perfect" plan.

The ideal plan is impersonal in that existing personalities, existing assignments of responsibility and authority, and existing reporting relationships are disregarded in constructing it.

Thus, the only elements that bear on the construction of the ideal long-range plan are the objectives of the company, the principles of organization, ideas for improvement generated by the analysis of the existing organization, and the judgment of those responsible for recommending the ideal structure.

The ideal plan usually takes the form of a chart. But more important than the chart itself are the definitions of the objectives of each major component called for by the ideal, the assignments of responsibility and authority in accord with the objectives that each component manager will be held accountable for achieving, and the clarifying of relationships.

In a true sense, construction of the ideal plan is the only place in the reorganization process where the organization planner divorces himself from the realities of the existing situation. He can, in effect, start from scratch and construct and chart the organization structure judged most desirable to meet the company's objectives. The ideal plan may or may not have a set target date. It is set up as a plan to be

---

[3] For detailed analysis of the organization manual, see "Preparing the Company Organization Manual," *Studies in Personnel Policy,* No. 157.

accomplished in the foreseeable future—which may be two or three months from now or four or five years from now.

4. *Determination of the Method of Change.*   Having set up the ideal, the next problem is how to get from the existing organization to the ideal.   Here the organization planner is confronted with reality in terms of existing personalities and facilities.   For whether the reorganization can be accomplished over a short or long period of time depends not only upon the scope of the reorganization called for by the redefined objectives, but also upon the adequacy of present personnel and facilities.

Two methods are generally referred to in speaking of methods of change: (1) the "earthquake" approach, and (2) gradual change through phase plans.

The earthquake approach contemplates a drastic change in the organization within a relatively short period of time.   It is difficult to ascertain whether the term "earthquake" is used to connote the major regrouping of activities and reshuffling of responsibilities that occur, or whether it connotes the quaking and shock experienced by the individuals subject to the change.   The earthquake may hit the whole organization, or it may be confined to one or two organization components.

Organization analysts and planners generally warn against the earthquake approach.   Even though the organization may require major changes, experience indicates that the lingering after effects of drastic remedies administered in a drastic manner often cancel out many of the sought-for benefits of the reorganization.

The more desirable alternative, it is emphasized, is gradual change through phase plans to bring the existing organization into conformity with the ideal.   The time period involved depends upon the degree of difference that exists between what the company has (in terms of personnel and facilities) and what it needs.

5. *Preparation of Phase Plans.*   Phase plans are short-term, intermediate structural changes viewed as feasible steps toward the ideal.   They provide for changes in facilities, changes or regroupings of activities, changes in personnel, changes in responsibility and authority, and changes in relationships in an orderly way.   They are designed to correct existing deficiencies, provide for additional units and personnel, and allow for accommodations to new and possibly expanded responsibility and authority called for by newly created positions.

The organization planner may design one, two, or more phase plans as realistic steps toward the ideal.   But in sharp contrast to the construction of the wholly impersonal ideal plan, in the construction of phase plans and especially in the movement from one phase to another, the planner and the company are greatly concerned with existing personnel and personalities.   One phase plan, for example, may be predicated upon the retirement of one or more individuals; another may be predicated upon the development of sufficient managers to manage.

Not only personnel, but facilities, sources of supplies, finances and markets bear on the development of phase plans and the transition from one phase to another. For the changes called for by a phase plan may be predicated on any or all of these factors.

6. *Implementation.*   Putting the plan into effect, or moving from the planning stage of reorganization to the organizing stage, requires first the approval of the plan by the accountable manager.   If the reorganization encompasses the total organization, the chief executive, of course, must approve the plan and set the stage for its implementation.

Presumably, the stage setting required for effective implementation of a reorganization plan will have been taking place throughout all the steps of the planning process.   For organization planning does not occur in a vacuum.   Analysis of the existing organization, setting up of an ideal plan, and preparation of phase plans call for joint efforts and constant checking and communication with the personnel and the managers affected.

The degree of communication and involvement often varies at different steps. The "ideal" plan, for example, may be kept highly confidential and often is. But organization planners with long experience in planning and implementing organization changes stress that communication during the planning stage helps accommodate people to the fact of the change when implementation occurs.

Implementation, of course, involves the actual personnel changes, regrouping of activities, changes in responsibility and authority called for by the phase plan. This part of the process is in the hands of the line managers rather than the staff organization planning unit. The staff unit assists the accountable line managers in making the changes. In many companies, the organization planner at this implementation stage becomes both a teacher and a maintenance man: a teacher in familiarizing personnel with the concepts involved in organization planning in general, and those involved in the particular plan adopted; a maintenance man in keeping the company's organization manual current in terms of changes in the organization charts and changes in position guides. But his key role during the implementation stage is in reviewing all organization changes to see that they are in conformity with the long-range plans—or will not impede the realization of the "ideal."

Implementation—short-term organizing—tends to be very pragmatic. For here the company is confronted with adapting reality to the plans and plans to reality. Organization planners find implementation, rather than being the last step in the organization planning process, becomes just another step in a continuous cycle. The "ideal" is seldom attained. For through constant revaluation and adaptation, the company may find that as it approaches the ideal, it too has become another phase plan on the road to a new ideal plan.

BIBLIOGRAPHY

Holden, Fish, and Smith: *Top Management Organization and Control,* McGraw-Hill Book Company, New York, 1951.

Koontz: "The Management Theory Jungle," *Journal of The Academy of Management,* vol. 4, no. 3.

Sherman, Harvey: *It All Depends, A Pragmatic Approach to Organization,* University of Alabama Press, Alabama, 1966.

Stieglitz and Janger: "Top Management Organization in Divisionalized Companies," *Studies in Personnel Policy,* no. 195, The Conference Board, New York, 1965.

Part 2

Organization and Operation of the Personnel Administration Department

chapter 4

The Personnel Director, His Staff, and Structure of the Department

DAVID N. CAMPBELL *Personnel Director, Sealtest Foods, Division of Kraftco Corporation, New York, New York*

Few modern corporate managements would quarrel much with the following mission for a personnel department: to provide for a steady supply of competent, well-trained people at all levels and, further, to help operating management provide the climate wherein these people can work together toward their own fulfillment through the accomplishment of the goals of the corporation.

From that point on, however, as they got into such subjects as precisely what the chief personnel executive should do, what kind of a man he should be in terms of experience and personality, how he should staff his department to do the job, and what the organization chart of his department should look like, the quarreling would get strident, extended, and go, predictably, unresolved.

The reasons should be obvious: corporations differ greatly in their products, degree of labor intensiveness, type of labor required, complexity of organization, style of management, and the personality of their chief executive officers. Regardless of these vagaries, at some point each corporation must arrive at its own decision as to who the chief personnel officer should be, what he should do, how he should staff his department, and how the personnel organization should be organized and structured in relation to other departments.

By honestly answering the following types of questions, the person making these decisions should make a good start toward assessing corporate needs in the personnel area:

1. Are we a company which is growing or shrinking in employee population? Is this trend likely to continue?

2. If we are not organized by unions now, are we likely to be? Why? Are we accomplishing our labor relations objectives?

3. What type of employees will we need the most of? How many? How soon?

4. Will we have to train large groups of people? What levels? How fast?

5. Are we in poor shape in the areas of minority hiring and upgrading?

6. What do our employees think of our personnel program now? Do we need to change those attitudes?

7. Do we give appropriate personnel service to all levels of our business?

8. What level of personnel service can we afford over the next few years?

This type of assessment should help in determining such requirements as the professional qualifications needed by the personnel chief, his management style, and even his attitudes toward youth and minorities, so important in the climate of today and of even greater importance for our business future. Further, it should help determine whether the department should be staffed by generalists or specialists, how centralized or decentralized it should be, and how department talents should be skewed in relation to needs. Finally, a determination should be made as to whether the function can weather some minor dips in the profitability chart over the next few years since an "on again–off again" personnel program is downright dangerous to the general management climate of a corporation.

The following sections of this chapter will present no absolutes. The approach is aimed at offering help to an executive selecting a new personnel chief or to a personnel professional reorganizing his department.

THE PERSONNEL DIRECTOR

In this chapter we shall use the following definition for the personnel director: the chief personnel officer of an organization or of an organizational subdivision who reports directly to the top-line executive of the unit and who bears the responsibility for the complete mission of the personnel function.

This definition dictates that the individual who fills the position should be a generalist. Only a generally experienced personnel executive can adequately carry out the responsibilities of a position of this scope. He must have the confidence required to report to the top-line official and interface daily with other highly skilled department heads as they solve serious management problems. The specialist or individual contributor, no matter how talented, cannot cope with this job.

When considering what the personnel director does, we should be on safe ground by using the following position description from the *1969 American Management Association Top Management Report.*

TOP INDUSTRIAL RELATIONS EXECUTIVE

BASIC FUNCTION

Develops, implements, and coordinates policies and programs covering the following: employment, labor relations, wage and salary administration, indoctrination and training, placement, safety and health, benefits and employee services. Originates policies and activities which will provide a balanced program throughout all locations of the company.

RESPONSIBILITIES

Directs the interpretation and application of established industrial relations policies throughout the company.

Formulates and recommends industrial relations policies and objectives of the company.

Responsible for administration of wage and salary policies and structures, and for personnel rating programs. Provides adequate personnel through employment office. Protects interests of employees in accordance with company's personnel policies.

Maintains overall supervision of the company's recruitment, placement, and training programs.

Directs the preparation for and represents the company in collective bargaining, contract negotiations, contract administration, and grievances.

Exercises general supervision over all company benefit programs and services.

Responsible for company health and safety programs.

Conducts a continuing study of all industrial relations policies, programs, and practices to keep the company abreast with current practice and informed of new developments.

Directs the preparation and maintenance of such reports as are necessary to carry out functions of the department.   Prepares periodic reports to the top general management executive, as necessary or requested.

Directs and maintains various activities designed to promote and maintain a high level of employee morale.

Now we have both a definition and a working position description.   We are close to being able to ascertain what it is we want the personnel director to do in the organization.   Before we get beyond this point, let us explore some of the varying roles of the personnel director in a modern corporation.

THE PERSONNEL DIRECTOR AS A CRAFTSMAN

If the personnel director is not the best personnel craftsman in the organization, he should be close to it.   He should take professional pride in his own individual contributions.   When *he* undertakes to write a policy statement himself, the draftsmanship should be excellent, the research behind it should be definitive, and the need well established through testing of internal attitudes.   If the personnel director conducts a high-level management search himself, his methodology should be current, his interviewing skills up to date and crisp, and he should use the same controls on his own judgment as he would expect his subordinates to use.   In other words, he must establish a fine example of craftsmanship in his department by being a fine craftsman himself.

The personnel director must know more than how to do the job well; he must know how to do it at the lowest possible cost.   The personnel director who contracts out all job openings over a set salary to management search firms, without assessing other methods from a cost-effectiveness standpoint, is not being a good craftsman.   Consulting outside labor counsel on routine legal matters which could be answered just as well by consulting a labor law loose-leaf service is not being a good craftsman.

Many personnel directors are tempted to make the dangerous mistake of assuming that as soon as they get to this level, they no longer need to be craftsmen.   If they fall into this trap, this may lead to their own professional deterioration, as well as make it more difficult for them to direct the activities of their department.   Also, since most personnel directors got where they are by being skilled craftsmen, to stop being one is playing dangerously with their own self-esteem and assurance.

A third factor in craftsmanship is availability.   If your bathtub is leaking and you call a plumber, you do not want him to come next week.   You want him now when you have the problem.   Similarly, the personnel director who is unavailable because of constant meetings, or because he lets his associates know that "the work of *our* department comes first" is not being a good craftsman.   Others in the company must feel that the personnel shop is always open when they need service, and in many companies that means twenty-four hours a day, seven days a week.

The last aspect of craftsmanship is promptness in completing assignments. Just as you do not want the plumber to take a week to come to fix your leaking pipes, you also do not want him to take a week to fix them once he gets there.

The same is true of the personnel craftsman. He must habitually set and meet deadlines. He must establish proper priorities based on urgency, and he must not mislead his associates into thinking that the job will take a shorter time than he knows it will, since to do this may upset their plans needlessly. Conversely, he should not dillydally over minor requests and make mountains out of molehills.

In case the reader feels that superior personnel craftsmanship—workmanship, cost effectiveness, ready availability, and promptness of response—is commonplace, just ask a few friends about the craftsmanship in the personnel departments in their organizations and see what kind of answers you get.

THE PERSONNEL DIRECTOR AS AN EDUCATOR

Since the personnel director cannot possibly know everything that happens in other departments with "people" implications, he must expand the number of eyes and ears aware of how personnel policies and programs, labor laws, and bargaining agreements can and should affect decisions.

In his role of an educator, he must devise ways and means of effectively keeping management in other departments informed. This educational program starts with the personnel director being readily accessible, as discussed earlier. By being accessible, he is generally aware of what is bothering his associates in other departments and can head off problems early when misconceptions about personnel matters occur.

Other things which he in his role of educator can do are:

1. Participate in other departments' staff meetings
2. Circulate clippings and articles on pertinent subjects
3. "Copy" appropriate department heads with internal department reports
4. Involve line executives on task forces, policy committees, and project groups which are planning or developing programs
5. Invite other executives to his staff meetings
6. Maintain a library of films, periodicals, and books on industrial relations subjects and encourage its use by executives in other departments.

So far in our discussion of the personnel director in the role of educator, we have covered the subject only in relation to the improvement of internal working relationships and the decision-making machinery of other departments. Another aspect of the "educator" role is in the area of improving managerial skills. Certainly the personnel director must play a key role in integrating the new applications of behavioral sciences into business applications. In order to do this effectively, he must stay abreast of new developments himself and then spread the concepts best fitting the total organization among his associates, including his boss.

We must add here that there is as much danger in "too much" as "too little." Executives could recite hours of horror stories about fadism in this area. For example, many executives can recall the "human-relations" era of management with the only pleasure coming from the fact that we all survived it. If the personnel director really educates well, however, he will be able to stop headlong plunges into the arms of quick-buck consultants who will not stay around long enough after the last fee is collected to survey the damage they have done.

As the personnel director plays his role of educator, he should not be afraid to experiment. In order to avoid the "do as I say, not as I do" posture, he might well experiment with new concepts within his own department. If he uses the task force effectively to plan a training program, has management performance standards for his department staff, and truly manages by objective, he is much better armed to advise others on the application of these principles to their areas of work.

Finally in his role of educator, he may find himself with a new job as the 1970s progress. At no time in recent history has the gulf between the universities and business been wider. Yet the personnel director needs good relations with the universities in order to do his job—from recruiting, to management advanced education, to personnel research. The 1970s may find the personnel director reintroducing educators and businessmen to the fact that they need each other.

THE PERSONNEL DIRECTOR AS AN ADMINISTRATOR

While the personnel director is advising his superior on vital personnel matters having far-reaching effects, the day-to-day work of the department must go on. Telephones must be answered, letters written, bills paid, budgets prepared, and reports completed. It seems that at certain times of the year the entire department is embroiled in "doing its own work"—that is, the work that exists just because the department exists. It is this very condition which requires the modern personnel director be an outstanding administrator. Obviously the less time and effort the personnel department spends on these activities, the more it has to spend on carrying out its mission. It is highly important, therefore, that the personnel director organize and train his department to make the administrative activities flow smoothly.

Following is a list of the types of questions which personnel directors can use to check their own performance as administrators—or which a president can use to check his personnel director:

1. Is the quality of your clerical and secretarial staff up to the standard set by other departments?

2. Have you set aside training time for your staff in administrative skills? How about the clerks and secretaries?

3. Do you use administrative assistants to relieve professionals of as much administrative detail as possible?

4. Are you proud of the housekeeping in the department?

5. When you call your office are you pleased by the way you are handled on the telephone?

6. Do you purge your files regularly?

7. Have you examined the need for all reports required by your department within the last twelve months?

8. Do you check your policy and administrative manuals at least annually?

9. Have you established controls so that approvals may be given as low as possible in the organization without worrying that someone will "give the store away"?

10. Do you use your company's computer effectively to improve and simplify the administrative work of the personnel department?

Often professionals downgrade the administrative details of their jobs. However, this cannot—must not—be allowed in the modern personnel department. Tight administrative control is necessary for good departmental discipline. Also, for many people, such as job applicants, employment agencies, and insurance claimants, the personnel department is "the company," and the way they are handled administratively reflects on the whole organization. Finally, for the personnel director in the field who is angling for a chance at the big job, we would admonish him that, for many in the home office, he is known more by the quality of his internal administrative activities than for his professional skills.

THE PERSONNEL DIRECTOR AS A PROPHET

At least a generation of personnel directors have been wagging their fingers under the noses of errant line managers, making dire predictions that "the plant will get organized if you do not change your ways." By using the same approach, elementary predictive analysis, they have also predicted impending turnover crises, strikes, and dramatic increases in accident frequency and severity.

The same professionals who had read the signs of deteriorating relations and economic and political pressures building up within their organizations failed to translate this skill beyond their own four corporate walls in the late 1960s. Even though personnel directors in the United States read of growing unrest in the South and burgeoning civil discord in large Northern cities, they did not predict the impact of the Negro revolution on their corporations. The Civil Rights Act of 1964 was passed, and still no concerted professional warning signs went up. In the late 1960s the Office of Federal Contract Compliance got the power to cancel the contracts of companies which did not carry out affirmative action programs to hire and upgrade minority workers. This failure to read the social, economic, and political signs of the times left many companies wide open to attack in the marketplace by minority pressure groups seeking to accomplish gains in job opportunities.

Even if we are charitable and forgive the personnel professionals for allowing organizations to miscalculate so badly, we must still call their insensitivity what it was—a collective professional disaster—and mark it as a failure of the profession at a crisis point.

The personnel directors of the 1970s have an opportunity to recoup. They still have an opportunity to respond to the needs and demands of blacks and other minorities seeking employment and increased job opportunity, for giving some attention to a changing role for women, and they still have time to prepare management for the differing attitudes of a growing legion of young professionals now swelling the ranks of corporations and institutions. If the modern, aware personnel director does not keep his eye turned to the swirling winds of political and social change and keep his organization from making dangerous errors, he may come very close to losing his "oracle's license" even on internal matters.

THE PERSON FOR THE JOB

Although the personnel director is becoming more professional all the time, there is no standard educational background necessary to hold the position, nor is there an examination given to qualify for the job.

If we were to take a survey of all the educational backgrounds of personnel directors in North America, we would find lawyers, engineers, psychologists, teachers, and accountants. Both sexes would be represented and so would all ages. With so few guidelines, how then do you select the person who will guide the personnel function in your organization? Let us first look at some general qualifications:

1. Although the personnel director is not a general manager, he is a generalist. He must have the capability of taking a myriad of ofttimes conflicting factors into account when creating a consistent, balanced, ongoing program. Therefore, before your personnel director is given the job, he should have had experience in most of the specialties under his supervision as well as prior supervisory experience.

2. The personnel director should be intellectually curious. He must have an overwhelming desire to know what is going on in the organization. If he does not demand to be involved in all facets of the business, he will be left out—just because it is easy for others to leave him out.

3. The personnel director must be knowledgeable, not only about his own field but about the business in general and the social and political climate in which he lives and works. Only by being aware can he make the multitude of crucial judgments varying from management selection to whether a strike should be taken.

If we assume that there is agreement upon a generally experienced, intellectually curious, and knowledgeable personnel director, what else is required? The following types of questions may help you in selecting the right person to fill the position in your organization:

1. What is the intellectual and academic climate of your organization? (It would be tough to fit a non-degree man into a research and development firm where 50 percent of the employees have Ph.D.s.)

2. Is previous success in your industry or a related one an important value to the people of your organization? (Do not give your new personnel director the stigma of being called "the chain-store genius" if you happen to be in the steel-fabrication business.)

3. What specific factors of performance are most important over the short run? (Being an expert at wage and salary administration will not help him if you have continuous "make-or-break" strike situations.)

4. Must he build an organization from scratch? (The person from an organization with three people standing in line for every job might have trouble with this one.)

5. Is your organization youthful now, or will you need many new young people over the next few years? (If your personnel director is not open-minded about longer hair, a little rebelliousness, and loud music, he may have a tough time in this assignment.)

6. Do you expect your personnel director to move through that slot into other management jobs?

These are just a few of the questions one should ask before selecting a new personnel director. They are also the kind of questions to be used when assessing why the incumbent is not performing well. It may just be that the job has changed, or that the company's objectives have changed, or that the management climate has changed sufficiently so that there is no way he can be successful.

THE PERSONNEL DIRECTOR'S STAFF

Basically, the personnel director has several factors to consider when he structures and staffs his department. Among these are:

1. How much staff can the organization afford?
2. What are the key priority items which must be accomplished in short order?
3. What are the personnel director's areas of weakness?
4. Who is available in the department to fill the staff positions?
5. How are other departments structured?

Obviously there are countless variations in staffing the department. In this chapter we will explore two methods which seem most opposite in concept and list the advantages of each method.

The "Assistant Personnel Director" Method

This method of staffing would present an organization chart such as that shown in Figure 1. This approach is most often found in divisionalized organizations. It offers the following advantages:

1. Although all staffers should be generalists, it allows the staffer with either the most experience or the lightest work load to take on new assignments.

2. Staff assignments can be moved about periodically to give experience or for job-enrichment purposes.

3. It is an excellent method by which to broaden the experience of specialists in order to train them for the top personnel position.

4. It allows for maximum flexibility when expanding or contracting the department.

5. It allows the personnel director to delegate supervision of a small division or subsidiary without appearing to put it "under a specialist." It is more palatable

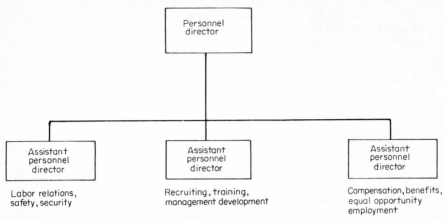

Figure 1. The "assistant personnel director" method of staffing.

to the personnel manager of a new division to report functionally to an assistant personnel director than to the training director, for example.

The "Staff Specialist" Method

This type of organization is charted in Figure 2 and represents the most common type of staffing in large corporate personnel departments. The advantages of this organization are numerous:

1. Staff positions can be filled by people who are most expert in their fields.

2. The personnel director can achieve constant emphasis and a continuing program in each functional area.

3. It is possible to recruit from outside directly into these positions since there are usually excellent carry-over skills from one company to another.

4. Trainees may rotate for periods in each staff specialty in order to get a well-rounded, yet thorough early training.

5. The personnel director can make up for a weakness in his own background by "overhiring" in certain skill areas.

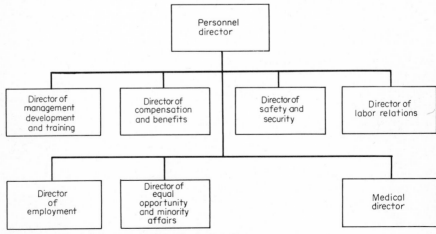

Figure 2. The "staff specialist" method of staffing.

6. This organization will serve either a centralized, highly functional organization or a large divisionalized organization at headquarters or division level.

Regardless of the organizational form the personnel director uses, the department wheels turn smoothly only when the positions are filled with strong people. Although the personnel director may place many executives in his career, none will affect his ultimate success more than those he places on his own staff.

The personnel department must provide a method of checking its own selections for the same reason that it acts as a check and balance on other departments' selections. Outside consultants may provide this service, group interviews may be used, or even executives in other departments may be asked their opinions. The need to select well is obvious because if the department which selects people for other departments cannot choose well for itself, it will certainly find other departments losing confidence in its performance of this function. Because high-placed personnel staffers have such a strong organizational impact, irreparable harm may be done by a poorly selected or improperly trained personnel man before it is found out.

THE STRUCTURE OF THE PERSONNEL DEPARTMENT

We have already discussed two approaches to staffing the personnel department directly under the personnel director. This section will deal with the structure of the personnel department in a multilevel company. For purposes of discussion, we will explore a tri-level organization—headquarters, division, and local plant or market.

To avoid duplication of effort and to provide for an appropriate and efficient division of labor, the first thing that must be decided is *which* level does *what* work. This step must be taken regardless of whether the department is structured divisionally or functionally. (The differences in these two structural forms will be discussed later.)

Although these responsibilities may differ slightly from organization to organization, the following assignments are typical in large organizations.

Level	Duties
Headquarters	Industrial relations broad strategy Top policy development and enforcement Program development High-level consulting Communications Broad supervision of department activities
Division	Industrial relations division strategy and tactics Policy enforcement Program implementation Consulting Communications Personnel service
Local plant or market	Day-to-day industrial relations activities Policy enforcement Program execution Communications Personnel service

In Figure 3 are shown two organization charts which graphically illustrate the main difference between divisionalized and functional organizations. In the divisionalized form, the division personnel director reports directly to the division chief executive and reports to the top personnel executive only through a staff relationship. In the functional organization, the personnel department reports in a straight line all the way from the bottom to the top.

Although the mission of the personnel department in both types of organization may be the same, the professional methods may differ considerably in order to accomplish that mission. An important caveat to the executive who is establishing a new personnel department or reorganizing his present one is that the struc-

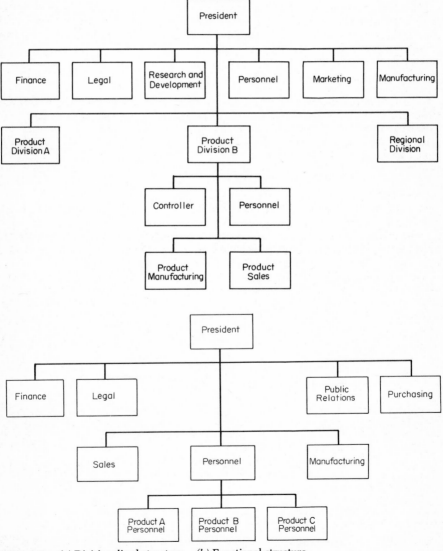

Figure 3. *(a)* Divisionalized structure. *(b)* Functional structure.

ture of the department should conform to the style of organization in other departments. If it does not, the personnel director is likely to find that his people are being cut out of decisions because they lack counterparts in other departments with whom they can comfortably and appropriately interface. Status is as necessary as specialized knowledge to communicate effectively. Only organizational comparability can make this status clear.

THE TASK FORCE AS A STAFF METHOD

Personnel directors should not overlook the task force as a staff method as it offers many advantages to all sizes of organizations, when it is used properly as an ad hoc, high-powered, well-staffed group commissioned to accomplish specifically defined objectives over a short time cycle.

The task-force method allows the personnel director to call on talent from headquarters, divisions, and local markets, as well as both departmental and nondepartmental people. If the need for a program is crucial enough to form a task force to accomplish it, it means that top people should be assigned to it. Also because assignments are temporary and everyone still has a job to do, the work is usually completed quickly.

The task force has advantages for its members—job enrichment, new experience, recognition by top management, as well as the opportunity to interface with and learn from others. For the personnel director who must have a sound program quickly and does not have, or does not want, excess staff, the task force may be the best answer yet invented.

Personnel Department Staff in the International Division:

There are two basic functions to be performed by the personnel department in the international division of a corporation. One is solving the personnel problems related to United States citizens and third-country nationals working outside their country of citizenship, e.g., a German working in Sweden. The other is the day-to-day personnel services to be provided to citizens working within their own countries.

Generally speaking, United States citizens and third-country nationals are looked after by the corporate headquarters, either by specialists within the personnel department or by a personnel director reporting to the head of the international division. Such matters as compensation, living allowances, home leave, and benefits usually come under close supervision by the corporate personnel people since it is in these areas that matters of internal equity are concerned, not only among employees of the international division, but also between them and the United States personnel.

The internal running of the personnel department within a foreign subsidiary is usually left to the managing director of the subsidiary working through his own personnel department. Most corporations give only very general supervision to these activities. That supervision may come either directly from the corporate personnel department or from an international division personnel director.

Canadian divisions of United States corporations are usually not considered in the same light as subsidiaries in other countries, however. Since similarities between these two countries are far greater than the differences in terms of law, language, and custom, the Canadian division is usually considered more like a United States division in terms of staffing, structure, and supervision.

CONCLUSION

The field of personnel has come a long way from the days when a close relative of a top executive occupied a prominent position in the department because it was a safe receptacle for his incompetence. There are still today, however, no standard selection criteria for the personnel director.

It is for this precise reason that so much space was taken in this chapter on the subject of the position of the personnel director. Unless the function of the personnel director in the organization is well understood and the position filled with a mature, able, and knowledgeable executive, the material in the remainder of the chapter is academic.

A well-trained personnel chief is most likely to choose superior subordinates, staff the department well, and properly integrate his function into the decision-making and executing-machinery of the organization—whether a corporation, institution, or governmental department.

Perhaps someday the field will have a code of ethics, professional prerogatives, accreditation, or even licensing so that selection may be made easier.

Until then, you are on your own.

BIBLIOGRAPHY

Blood, Jerome W. (ed.): *The Personnel Job in a Changing World,* American Management Association, New York, 1964.

"The Evolving Role of Personnel Administration," *The Conference Board Record,* New York, July–August, 1962.

McFarland, Dalton E.: *Cooperation and Conflict in Personnel Administration,* American Foundation for Management Research, Study, New York, 1962.

—— : *Company Officers Assess the Personnel Function,* American Management Association, Research Study 79, New York, 1967.

Myers, Charles A.: "New Frontiers for Personnel Management," Department of Economics and Social Science Publications, *Social Science,* ser. 2, no. 86, reprinted from *Personnel,* May–June, 1964.

"The Personnel Man—in Transition?," *The Conference Board Record,* New York, December, 1963.

Rico, Leonard: "Managerial Schizophrenia: The Personnel Function in a Firm," reprinted from *Management of Personnel Quarterly,* Bureau of Industrial Relations, Ann Arbor, Mich.

Ritzer, George, and Harrison M. Trice: *An Occupation in Conflict: A Study of the Personnel Manager,* New York State School of Industrial and Labor Relations, Cornell University, Ithaca, N.Y., 1969.

"Structuring the Corporate Personnel Staff," *The Conference Board Record,* New York, May, 1965.

Top Management Organization in Divisionalized Companies, Studies in Personnel Policy, no. 195, a Research Report from the Conference Board, New York.

chapter 5

The Personnel Staff:
Recruiting, Training,
and Determining Standards
of Performance

MICHAEL L. MOORE *Assistant Professor, School of Labor and Industrial Relations, Michigan State University, East Lansing, Michigan*

The type and quality of data available for management decisions at a given time determine the validity and reliability of any choice process. In discussing the acquisition and training of personnel staff members, the initial approach will illustrate the development of a decision-making data base, including determination of performance contribution areas, standards, updating processes, and relative quality of job-analysis information as well as illustrations of the specific relevance of organizational culture items including norms, values, and informal relations. This data base will be used in the subsequent formulation of selection, recruitment, and training issues for personnel relations staff positions.

PERSONNEL RELATIONS AND THE MARKETPLACE

The economic marketplace for the services of specialized personnel has sometimes been viewed as a somewhat capricious evaluator of values. In surveying the previous forty years, one can only reach the conclusion that the system works rather well, except, perhaps, from the viewpoint of personnel staff members. Demand for services and top management support for the personnel relations function as represented by staff growth and salary arrangements have rarely tended to approach the commitment wished for by personnel staff members.[1]

Crucial Job Functions 1930–1970

In the 1930s, sales and especially marketing became prominent as organizations tried to revive failing markets during depression years.   During World War II, the 1940s saw a reemphasis and strengthening of production, research, and engineering as the market problems of the thirties were replaced with strong military and consumer demands but often in new product lines.   Following World War II and at present, marketing has remained prominent although the Sputnik scare of the 1950s and the United States Apollo moon-exploration program strengthened work in basic and applied science.   New levels of financial knowledge were necessary to cope with new organizational forms such as conglomerates to finance the increasing rate of technological and social change facing organizations in the 1960s.   The common factor running through the probable reasons for the prominence of any specific function was that the executives considered that function to have the relevant areas of expertise for dealing with the most valuable variables needed at that time. Despite the glowing statements expressed in annual reports about "people being our most important resource," executives have rarely been willing to acquire and utilize the personnel relations staff as a crucial factor in the organizational decision-making processes, except for the use of a labor relations staff to meet the needs of collective bargaining in the 1940s.

The time of personnel relations may be arriving sooner than anticipated.   While other functions such as information processing and systems science are also predicted to grow in stature, the functional areas such as personnel relations or the manpower subsystem area may well be seen as having the expertise to deal with increasingly unpredictable and valuable variables, the organization's human resources, its human capital, to use Shultz's term.   The 1960s have seen a tremendous resurgence of programs representing public and joint public-private attempts to deal more effectively with human resources.   The Manpower Development and Training Act, 1962, Office of Economic Opportunity, Job Corps, Upward Bound, JOBS, Project Headstart, and hiring and training programs with groups such as the National Alliance of Businessmen have served to focus public attention on the manpower function, as defined narrowly here, to represent the various categories of disadvantaged job seekers and a tendency to view the economic equation from the supply side only.   In addition, societal pressure for increased leisure, more satisfying work, and the "youth culture" all pose challenging issues for the future operations of organizations.

Crucial Functions in the 1970s and 1980s

The 1970s and 1980s are likely to illustrate the increasingly crucial nature of developing, diffusing, and utilizing knowledge concerning high-talent manpower. Drucker (1969) defines high-talent people and specifically executives as "knowledge workers."   They are viewed as being effectiveness oriented and as making contributions to organizations based on the application of knowledge, as opposed to apprenticeship-type expertise.   The personnel relations staff already is moving toward the evolution of manpower specialists (Patten, 1970), change agents (Bennis, 1969), and organizational development specialists as mentioned by many authors.   The personnel relations staff can be expected to play a larger role in organizational effec-

[1] Dalton McFarland, *Company Officers Assess the Personnel Function,* American Management Association, Research Study 79, New York, 1967, p. 59.

tiveness, survival, and growth in economic terms and in efficiency, development of communication, and authority systems to facilitate adaptability for external adaptation and innovation.

THE TASK-SPECIALIZATION PROCESS

In order to recruit, select, train, and effectively evaluate the personnel staff, it is perhaps most useful to begin with the task-specialization process (French, 1970). In brief, the process involves the following factors: (1) determining organizational objectives; (2) relevant planning in terms of meeting these objectives, which might involve organization, design, and job-design concepts based on the technology needed to meet objectives; (3) development of information such as job descriptions of the work to be performed; (4) development of the human resource qualifications required, such as job specifications; (5) development of standards of performance; and (6) establishment of specific work rules and other aspects of task facilitation. This process is the infrastructure underlying all job creation and must be considered in employment decisions. It implies that organizational needs and objectives are intimately related to job creation and should receive primary consideration in the process of employing a personnel staff.

This chapter will discuss all the steps of the process and focus on the work of personnel and how to determine recruiting and selection procedures from work descriptions. Before any search of the organization's internal or external labor markets is made, certain data concerning organizational objectives, the work to be performed, and how the work is to be evaluated in the organization must be assembled.

SOURCES OF JOB INFORMATION

Position information for job analysis is typically assembled from many sources, including the following: (1) the position incumbent, (2) his organizational superior(s), (3) his work group and peers, (4) his subordinates. Methods of collecting information include interviews conducted with all the above sources singly or in various combinations. Typically, questionnaires are utilized early in the process to aid in data collection, comparison, and facilitation of focused interview formats. Other methods include tests of position incumbents. Often, for uniquely skilled work, direct observation of the performer may be used to supplement information collected by the other methods. Further, most organizations try to utilize their own records to put some of the work dimensions into historical or other comparative framework. The *Dictionary of Occupational Titles* and other publications of the United States Employment Service may also be found valuable at this stage. Job data sources and methods will receive more detailed treatment in other chapters of this handbook, but their relevance to this chapter demands their mention at this point.

Job Data Changes

Positions in organizations are rarely static in nature but more likely will be seen as reflecting many changing trends. For example, a personnel job typically is unstructured enough even after job analysis for the position incumbent to facilitate personal redirections in position role. In other cases, the changes may be forced from external sources such as economic conditions or recessions, or by changing aspects of the labor market supply, such as more women, youths, or minority group members in the labor force. Jobs may also be changed through technological change, the actions of the informal organization (work groups) in altering assignments and instilling norms for work, as well as by historical differences of orientation among organizations reflecting geography, social philosophy, recruiting practices, and other values, social customs, and practices consistently implemented over time.

Types of Position Information

By surveying the previously mentioned sources and utilizing the various methods mentioned, it is possible to develop the levels of information shown in Figure 1 as bases for later personnel decisions to recruit, select, hire, appraise, develop, and compensate personnel relations staff manpower.

From this framework the most useful position information to bring to the personnel decision is that which discusses multiple criteria of job success, how these criteria are related in priority, measures and especially performance ranges where appropriate, and lastly focuses on the time constraints in which these performances must typically be produced, i.e., daily, quarterly, at project deadlines. It is further suggested that a historical perspective of how job criteria for a given function have been altered over time due to other factors may be valuable information for selection. The development of complete job data for personnel staff positions is treated in a systematic manner in subsequent sections.

Figure 1.   Types of position information.

Usefulness of information	Position information
Useful	Job title
	Job description
	Job activities—instrument based
	Job behaviors—observer based
	Time analysis—multiple sources
	Total behavior inventory— multiple sources combined
	Total behavior inventory
	Unitary criterion—effectiveness measure
	Unitary criterion—effectiveness ranges
	Multiple criteria—single measures
	Multiple criteria—ranges and trade offs
	Multiple criteria—trade offs— ranges of job success
More useful	Time evaluations and longitudinal measures

ANALYZING THE PERSONNEL FUNCTIONAL JOBS

In order to discover job criteria for personnel staff positions, it is useful to consider a simple systems formulation as a basis. Thus, every personnel job may be analyzed according to the schematic shown in Figure 2.

Key Results Areas for Personnel Relations

Most of the management by objectives literature or its semantic counterpart work planning and review groups all work outputs into one category. A more detailed

Figure 2. Positions as simple systems.

Inputs	Transformation process (Job activities)	Position outputs

Staff
Dollars
Facilities
Information
	General Activities
	  Plan, organize, direct, control, motivate, communicate, write, check work, travel, conferences
	
	Specific Activities of Personnel
	  Manpower planning, recruiting, selecting, inducting, training, compensating, appraising
		Personnel Department: Internal Evaluation
		  Budgets
		  Quotas
		  Reports
		  Projects
		Organization and Community: External Evaluation
		  Job competence
		  Job satisfaction and morale
		  Public and community relations
		  Competence of employees hired, developed, compensated

and descriptive system is formulated for general management personnel decisions (Odiorne, 1965) and selection (Odiorne and Miller, 1966). This approach involves identification of key result areas in four different job categories, as illustrated in Figure 3.

Since the regular objectives are viewed as forming the basis for the development of all higher order objectives of the position, typical regular objectives and subobjectives for personnel relations work will be considered at this time. Once these are established, criteria will be established and the relevance of the information to the next step of selection will be discussed.

Figure 3. Four types of key result areas.

Type	Definition
Personal development objectives.	Contribution made to increase general and specific personal skills relative to work roles
Innovative objectives	Contributions made to improve performance in areas where performance is still acceptable but possibly improvable
Problem-solving objectives	Contributions undertaken to restore regular objectives to acceptable levels once they have been disrupted and appear to be stabilizing at intolerable levels
Regular system objectives	Basic contributions required by the organizational role. Recurring products of services from the job

In subsequent pages, a portrayal of key result areas for a wide number of personnel staff functions will be provided. In any given organization, certain functions may not be required or may not be grouped in the manner presented in this chapter and thus require specific regroupings to meet the needs of the relevant situation. The following key result areas are presented as general guidelines for preparing for selection and performance decisions.

The first areas to be listed will be the specific personnel functional areas with typical but not necessarily exhaustive subdivisions noted. Then, general areas of contribution for all or most personnel functions will be presented.

PERSONNEL FUNCTIONS—SPECIFIC

Key Result Areas

Manpower planning: Demand analysis, organizational planning, supply analysis of labor market, projections

Recruiting: Executive, college, other

Selection: Continuing validation programs for predictors utilized, executive, exempt-nonexempt

Identification of high-potential manpower: Programs for specific talent groups

Induction, orientation, and assimilation: Hard-core programs, college programs, other programs

Training: Executive, middle management, general management, foreman training, skill training, apprenticeship programs, cooperative programs, on-the-job-training, Manpower Development and Training Act and/or JOBS programs, job-design programs.

Development: Succession plans, development plans, team development, organization development

Compensation—direct: Salary programs, (Nonmanagement, management), surveys, job analyses and ranking proposals, bonus programs, incentive programs, executive compensation, appraisal

Compensation—indirect: benefits: Insurance, pensions, profit sharing, savings or stock plans, vacations and holiday, leaves, other

Labor Relations: Contract administration, grievances, discipline, negotiation preparation projects

Employee services: Health, medical, counseling, financial, moving, recreation programs, parking, cafeteria, records

Communications: Employee publications, management publications, suggestion programs

Public and Community Relations: Educational and scholarship programs, public service, legal obligations

Safety   programs

Personnel research: Projects

PERSONNEL STAFF POSITIONS

Each of the previously listed key result areas may be performed by personnel specialists with unique skills in that area. In addition to making specialized contributions to the organization, members of the personnel staff typically are responsible for general administrative contributions as well. These key result areas represent responsibilities of members of the personnel management function in an organizational setting and may be considered as additional to the previously mentioned fifteen result areas.

PERSONNEL FUNCTIONS—GENERAL (PERSONNEL STAFF ONLY)

Reports: Regular reports on the fifteen specific areas and subareas, special reports

Budgets: Direct costs, indirect costs

Employee relations: Absenteeism, turnover, grievances, or complaints

Staff development

Quality of personnel work: Complaints from users

Projects: Management projects, internal personnel projects

Policy development: Policy area, company-wide, personnel staff

Problem-solving, Innovative, and Personal Development Objectives

The twenty-two key result areas listed represent as a whole and in various combinations the typical regular objectives of personnel relations staff members. At any point, priorities and performance in these results areas may differ. Thus, staff members would probably have a limited number of problem-solving and innovative objectives as part of their commitment during any specific work cycle, such as a quarter.

Thus, every personnel relations staff member could possibly have some regular, problem-solving, innovative, or personal development objectives in each of the twenty-two key result areas mentioned. The possible ways for the personnel rela-

---

PROBLEM-SOLVING OBJECTIVES
(REACTING TO SITUATIONS WHERE CURRENT
PERFORMANCE IS UNACCEPTABLE)

Position	Objective
Labor relations analyst and representative	Reduce foreman working grievances by half for the foundry core room. Project time, 2 months.
Employee representative	Improve ratio of hires to college graduate interviews at our location from 1 in 4 to 1 in 2.5. Project time, 6 months.

INNOVATIVE OBJECTIVES (THE CURRENT CONTRIBUTION IS
ACCEPTABLE BUT COULD BE IMPROVED THROUGH INNOVATION)

Position	Objective
Compensation analyst	Cost-benefit analysis of benefit programs in report form. Project time, 1 month.
Employment specialist	Develop and implement an affirmative action program. Project time, first stage of report in 3 months.

PERSONAL-DEVELOPMENT OBJECTIVES

Position	Objective
Personnel research analyst	Take a university extension course in test design and construction to facilitate selection research background. Next term offered.

---

tions function to contribute to organizational effectiveness in its markets and internal well-being are recognized as being extremely diverse when viewed this way. Needless to say, a knowledge of key results areas alone is insufficient to appreciate these positions. This knowledge must be coupled with information about how these contribution areas are evaluated in order to form a more accurate picture of the job attributes for any specific personnel position.

MEASURING PERSONNEL POSITIONS

Key results contributions are evaluated against commitments made mutually by individuals and their superiors. In many cases, performers in complementary work areas find it advisable and informative to utilize group objective setting to determine areas of contributions and appropriate measurements for the period under consideration.

Typically, personnel staff members may be measured against the indicators shown in Figure 4.

Figure 4.   Typical measurement indicators for personnel staff positions.

Classification	Type	Examples
Objective measures	Raw data	Number of college graduates hired Average starting salary of college recruits
	Percentages	Turnover per 100 employees Entire firm Job categories Job classifications By length of service By reason of separation
Subjective measures	Scale (requires that a valid average rating be determined)	Training program ratings by participants
	Discussions (requires knowledge of the subject being discussed by all parties concerned)	User complaints about personnel services (quality measure) Management development Deficiencies noted? How corrected? How promotable? When?

Since an entire chapter has been devoted to evaluating the personnel function, this chapter will emphasize the importance of determining performance measures as an *input* to decisions related to recruiting, selecting, and training personnel relations staff members. Although quantitative measures of performance are often preferable and available (Rabe, 1967; Hawk, 1967), the previous section also stressed that subjective discussions and assessments may also be acceptable when conducted by informed personnel and prepared for on a consistent and regular basis as part of a formal individual or group goal-setting process involving dialogue and commitment from all parties involved.

Determining Standards of Performance

Formal goal-setting discussions provide systematic feedback as to the relevance of each contribution area to specific organizational needs. Measurement indicators based on work cycles provide for individualized and continuous feedback to job performers and help identify changes in the organization or the work. Thus, the system depends on mutual and occasionally group involvement in standard setting where teamwork is the appropriate unit under consideration. Standards are discussed in a process which involves an assimilation by both parties of general information and objectives from the higher levels of the organization with recommendations and detailed information from position incumbents as to how goals may be reached. Often the outcome of this process may be ranges of performance possible under varying conditions for a given key result area indicator. Only after a standard, its measures, ranges, and repeating feedback loops are established and agreed upon do the superior and subordinates make mutual commitments concerning results achievement. It is through the time-control facet of each indicator that the unit of achievement measured either as a single goal or as a goal range is available to position performers and their related role members as performance feedback. Thus, any position is part of an open, adaptive system. The system is open because of the diverse contacts made with other parts of the organization and community previously mentioned in the key result areas and adaptive because indicators representing units of achievement in time perspectives have been identified and are viewed on a continuous basis for change and updating. These are the realistic and current standards which are discussed here as the data bases for manpower planning, recruiting, selection, training, and other employment decisions.

SELECTING THE PERSONNEL STAFF

It has been suggested that in the selection and utilization of personnel staff considerable attention be paid to organizational needs and specifically to the job analyses of the position(s) to be filled. To summarize, it was emphasized that before any selection or manpower search takes place, the organization should typically perform certain functions to assure itself of the types of information needed for later personnel decisions. These functions were identified:

  1. Analysis of the task specialization process to determine the organization's needs to be filled
  2. Analysis of the needs to identify which of the twenty-two or more general contribution areas are crucial to the organization
  3. Identification of the specific behavioral requirements within each of the contribution areas
  4. Determination of how each type of contribution will be measured by the organization
  5. Determination of specific measures of success including recognition of ranges of performance representing unacceptable to excellent whenever possible
  6. Setting priorities for contribution areas and identifying typical trade offs applicable to job performance
  7. Locating problem-solving and innovative objectives relevant to *each* contribution area.

Utilizing a Personnel Staff

All the previous criteria focus directly on the degree of involvement of the organization in utilizing its human resources. To the degree that criteria of job performance success can be identified by members of the organization, including the personnel staff and users of personnel services when appropriate, the induction and assimilation process whereby the person is socialized into the organization's work and culture is facilitated accordingly. Thus, factors in the organization's culture including information relations are appropriate inclusions in the decision process.

SELECTION STRATEGIES

Before the recruitment process begins, certain selection objectives are considered. As an institutional decision-making process, several objectives are possible:

Rejecting unqualified candidates

Ordering qualified candidates

Classifying a fixed number of candidates to jobs having unlike requirements

Having obtained, through job analysis, a statement of job criteria (contribution areas and subareas) and information on measurement (ranges and trade offs plus a measurement format identified for each contribution area), the selection process represents a screening of information obtained from and about potential job candidates from different sources. This screening attempts to evaluate how well the information about the person fits the information about the job and focuses on whether the probable future job result areas can be achieved by a candidate having a record of past accomplishments and probable future skills.

Predictors

In developing the job criteria, the focus was on contributions and accomplishments related to organizational goals and subgoals. To determine these factors, it was recognized that candidate performances of necessity would take place in diverse job situations. It is further accepted that different candidates might behave differently within the context of these different situations. In accordance with the previously mentioned systems framework, the orientation utilized here will focus on results and accomplishments against organizational criteria and commitments, although others might choose to stress individual behavior as a focus for selection. It is appropriate to recognize that if situations for performance become sufficiently standardized as in many hourly jobs, patterns of behavior may be of more value as indicators of success.

The requirement for the selection process becomes one of developing predictors which abstract relevant information about job candidates and allow for this to be matched with job criteria.

Job performance is a multidimensional concept. Typically, it includes not only the productivity, quality, timeliness, and cost factors of the key result areas, but factors such as tenure and turnover with the organization as well. Other items considered in predicting results may include candidates' trainability and ultimate managerial potential. In many situations, relative performance against results is also a factor in making peer comparisons for selection or promotion decisions.

Types of Predictors

Broadly speaking, any objective or subjective information utilized in determining whether candidates will be hired can be considered as a predictor. Typical predictors utilized in selecting the personnel staff may include the following:

Interviews......	Directive Nondirective Stress Group or panel	Biographical data.......	Application blanks Biographical inventories Reference checks Weighted application blanks
Tests	Personality General aptitude Specific aptitude Skill and ability Work samples Performance tests	Clinical data	Appearance Personal mannerisms Physical examination

Selection strategies utilizing these predictors may involve the candidate's making his way over successive hurdles or possibly through some type of multiple cutoff. Ideally, a selection strategy puts its most valid predictors at the beginning of the process so that the expense of dealing with unsatisfactory candidates is minimized. Also, though, an attempt is made to include the less costly of the predictors at the beginning of the strategy for the same reasons. Thus, the typical strategy involves trade offs in validity and costs of selection and becomes a hybrid process individualized to the needs of the organization.

Although single criteria are sometimes used, the selection strategies applicable to selecting a personnel staff member would probably be multiple predictor and multiple stage. This means that a decision would not be made until considerable evidence was collected from several sources and due consideration would be given to the candidate's personal time involvement in the process.

Degrees of Candidate Information

Having determined various levels of job information ranging from position title through position key result areas, priorities, trade offs, ranges of measurement, and time criteria for performance, it is necessary to construct a similar framework for evaluating information collected about people applying for personnel positions. This is shown in Figure 5.

The validity of the selection process is the relationship between the predictor information and the job-success criteria as determined from organization and job analysis. For any particular predictor, its validity is determined by the relation-

Figure 5.   Levels of candidate information.

Usefulness of Information in decision	Personal information
Useful	Name
	Personality measures
	Self reports
	Uninformed clinical
	Clinical projective
	Professional clinical
	General aptitude (IQ)
	Specific aptitude
	General demographic data
	Specific biographical data
	Weighted biographical data
	General skill measures
	Specific skill measures
	Behavior simulations (assessment centers)
	Work samples
	Single goal achievements against commitments
	Multiple achievements, including trade offs against commitments
	Multiple achievements: Performance ranges
Most useful	Priorities
(in a general sense, although the order might change based on situational validities)	Trade off achievements
	Time control
	Longitudinal achievements

ship between its informational contribution and job success criteria. In addition to predicting accurately (validity), the consistency of prediction in subsequent reuses in identical or similar situations (reliability) is also crucial. Thus, both predictors and job success criteria typically require constant reevaluation to assure relevance and reliability. Selection decisions involving jobs other than the work at hand, such as promotion potential, require even more information analyses of positions and candidates before the hiring decision.

Approaches to Selection—Summary

A selection decision may involve any combination of predictors. A typical strategy might be similar to the sequence shown in Fig. 6.

Figure 6.   Typical selection strategy sequence.

Sample application blank → Screening interview → Biographical inventory → Tests → Interviews → Physical exam

In relating job requirements to candidate information, Odiorne and Miller (1966) identify four typical approaches to hiring decisions.

Personal preference: This is essentially a matching of personal biases relating candidate personality factors to real or perceived performance criteria through subjective processes of those doing the choosing. It focuses on clinical types of data as the major sources of prediction.

Occupational characteristics: This approach focuses on aptitude measures as predictors, typically applies only to broad categories of positions, and is generally seen as being of limited value for managerial jobs.

Behavior: This focuses on skill measures and simulations of the work itself whenever possible. It can be quite specifically linked to job performance in some cases, such as a typing skills test for typists.

Background: This involves the evaluation of demographic and specific background factors, including type and degree of formal education as inputs to the selection decision. It attempts to determine demographic items from the background of successful performers and to locate job candidates with similar qualifications.

A typical decision regarding the hiring of a manpower specialist, recruiting specialist, compensation trainee, training and development man, or labor relations representative might include all four approaches to some extent. Odiorne and Miller discuss a fifth approach, *selection by objectives,* as a method of increasing validity. This approach was the basis for the previous information presented in this chapter and represents a selection focus based on matching the strongest possible job success criteria and measures these with the equivalent measure of the candidate, i.e., his goal achievements on comparable criteria of key results, against comparable measures, over some organizationally relevant period.

This fifth approach has sometimes been neglected because of the demands it makes in terms of requiring organizations to understand the position being filled and because of the problems of ascertaining the relevance of data put forward by the candidate.

IMPLEMENTING SELECTION BY OBJECTIVES

Selection by objectives makes deterministic assumptions about human performance, i.e., it assumes that past behavior and accomplishments are the best predictors of short-run behavior in the future. Thus, the less adequate the data sources on past performance, the lower are the chances for prediction success. Or, conversely, the farther into the future the prediction, such as success initially plus the four next higher job levels, the less are the chances of prediction success as individual changes in learning, socialization, and maturation and changes in position requirements and success criteria work to alter an originally valid linkage between candidate and initial job requirements.

For each key result area of the job and for each of the subareas under that criterion, the following information may be appropriately gathered to facilitate the hiring choice:

Has he (the candidate) ever achieved anything in this area before?
Were his achievements shared with others? If so, what did he accomplish?
How were his accomplishments measured?
Was he effective against these measures?
How similar was this prior work to the position under consideration?
What changes did he make?
Were these changes successful?

Similar information should also be gathered for the problem-solving and innovative objectives of the position under consideration.

INFORMATION SOURCES AND PROBLEMS

Sources of this information should rest heavily on interview strategies, patterned to highlight areas not explained fully by other predictors, and considerable use of reference checking and biographical inventories. Information presented by the candidate should be viewed with "cautious skepticism" until verified through interview or reference checking to the degree discussed previously. Gaps and discrepancies should provide points for further discussion with the candidates. Problems involving acquisition of this information include the time and expense in checking, the positive biases of the candidate's chosen references, and uncertainties as to how comparable the work situations really were.

This discussion has viewed personnel staff members as technical specialists in personnel decision-making processes which assist in determining issues related to the contributions made by the organization's human resources in an often rapidly changing organizational environment. This chapter has tended to downplay the concept of a "personnel personality" as a selection criterion. Instead, the focus has been primarily on the contributions made on the position with discussions of skills, background factors, and personality traits and syndromes noted as being of possible relevance but only within the framework of performance achievement against commitments. In terms of the data quality, especially its reliability, a data search for additional information to aid in evaluating a candidate might follow the following stages:

In the absence of goal-achievement measures in relevant key result areas by the candidate, the next place for analytical consideration would be whether the candidate's demonstrated skills or behaviors are relevant to work situations. If determination of this information is still doubtful, a check into his formal education and accomplishments in specific course-work areas is a possible source of insight into probable work contribution. The applicant's personality structure too may come into consideration if evidence of work problems due to personal matters is apparent. Despite this extended discussion of the relevancy of various types of candidate information, interviewers and some executives may still prefer extrasensory perception or "vibrations" to choose the man for the job and may never assemble any of the other information viewed in this chapter as vital to the process. Hopefully, statistical and human prediction can be combined in a valid selection decision.

THE PERSONNEL STAFF RECRUITMENT PROCESS

The purpose of the recruitment process is to provide a flow of suitable candidates to the selection process and thus assure the organization of a nonunitary selection ratio. A nonunitary ratio simply means that for each of the personnel staff positions under consideration, more than one candidate can be found who is interested in working for the organization. Stated simply, the recruitment process is designed to provide the selection process with a choice so that the decision-making strategies previously discussed can be utilized.

Given the job requirements data derived from the task specialization process and conceptualized as previously discussed for the selection process, the task of deciding how to best approach the manpower market for personnel staff specialists becomes relevant. The organization may decide to make its own direct contact with the market, utilizing its own recruiter. It might attempt an indirect approach involving advertisements and communications in various journals, magazines, and other media. Or, it could conceivably contact an outside specialist such as an executive or personnel search firm or, indeed, develop a hybrid strategy using any combination of these approaches. The difference between method and source is not always easily determined as may be noted from a study of typical manpower sources.

Source Identification

Typical manpower sources are identified by Hawk (1967). These are conceptually grouped into two categories: (1) sources external to the organization and (2) internal sources.

External sources	*Internal sources*
Advertising—journals, radio, television, newspapers handbills	Staff referrals Promotions Unions Manpower inventories
Agencies—public, government, search firms, private fee charging	
Field trips	
"Rented" personnel	
Professional conventions and meetings	
Retired military	
Schools and colleges	
Walk-ins	
Write-ins	

Any combination of these sources may be utilized, depending on source selection criteria. The list stresses the internal labor market of currently employed personnel as well as external sources as legitimate places to search for required personnel.

Source Selection Factors

In choosing any recruiting source, certain factors might be considered, including: (1) characteristics of the employee desired; (2) characteristics of the source, specificity, cost, etc.; (3) geographic considerations; and (4) characteristics of the labor market. For example, in a loose market with plenty of job seekers available, recruitment efforts might be focused more heavily on the local area and its public and private agencies.

The major sources for locating prospective personnel staff members would be executive search firms for top-level staff and private fee-charging agencies for reaching experienced staff personnel. Both of these sources offer some degree of specificity in providing personal and individualized treatment for the contacted prospective employee.   Their major disadvantages involve their possible delay in locating suitable candidates and their costs, which may be as high as 25 percent of the candidate's first year salary for applicants referred through executive search firms, although in a loose market, the candidate may pay the fee.

Most personnel staff trainee or introductory level positions are filled by recruiting candidates directly from colleges and universities.   Applicants with relevant course work typically graduate from schools of industrial relations, colleges of business administration, or departments of industrial or personnel psychology.   Labor relations specialists may also be obtained from law schools.   In addition, some firms prefer to recruit liberal arts graduates as inputs into structured training programs which the organization may feel to be the equivalent of further specialized education.

Figure 7 illustrates a typical summary of educational and work interests of master's degree graduates in Michigan State University's School of Labor and Industrial Relations.   Note that degree programs are oriented toward both private and public sector employment and that all students receive course work in research methods and economics as part of the degree preparation.

Figure 7.   1971–1972 graduates, Master of Labor and Industrial Relations, Michigan State University.

WORK INTERESTS

Students who graduate with a Master of Labor and Industrial Relations (MLIR) degree seek employment primarily in private business but also in trade unions and in federal, state, and local governments.

In business they seek employment as generalists or specialists in personnel positions, including recruitment, selection, induction, placement, training, appraisal, compensation, and planning, or in organizational development work.   Alternatively, they may seek labor relations positions, including contract and grievance administration, contract negotiation, and union-management relations generally.

In unions they may seek work in education and research positions.   In government they may seek work with the National Labor Relations Board and similar agencies at the state level, with personnel and labor relations departments of state and municipal governments, and with various public manpower agencies, including retraining and rehabilitation programs, state manpower planning departments, state employment services, and government statistical and research agencies.

COURSEWORK IN THE MASTER OF LABOR AND INDUSTRIAL RELATIONS PROGRAM

All students in the program take three courses in labor-management relations, manpower economics, and data sources and research methods.   Those who enroll in the collective bargaining and employment relations option take four courses in American trade unionism, grievance administration and arbitration, employment relations, and organizational behavior.   Students in the manpower policies and programs option take four courses in manpower programs and institutions, income maintenance programs, labor force behavior, and methods of program evaluation.   A master's thesis is optional. Those not writing a thesis take at least four elective courses.   Electives are usually taken in labor and industrial relations, management, psychology, or sociology.

WORK EXPERIENCE

Students often have one or several years of full-time work experience in labor and industrial relations before starting in the master's program.   Those who hold assistantships in the school acquire further work experience either in research and analysis or in the adult education programs of the school: the personnel management program, the labor program, and the manpower program.

OTHER ACADEMIC PREPARATION

All students take undergraduate principles of economics and undergraduate statistics, usually before entering the Master of Labor and Industrial Relations program.   They usually major in one of the social sciences or in business administration, but majors in natural science, engineering, and other fields may also be acceptable if they have course work in the social sciences.   A grade average of B in junior and senior years is normally required for admission into the program.

Business school graduates may have slightly less concentration in personnel subjects but more information about other functions in a firm, such as accounting, marketing, finance, production management, quantitative methods, and similar areas. Through elective course work, any student may well have combined some business, law, or psychology courses with his personnel and industrial relations core courses. In each case, since no one definite definition of success in personnel management is available, no single route may be prescriptively described as the "best" background or source.

Students acquired directly from academic programs typically possess useful general functional knowledge in their chosen field. Their job performance in the organization, however, may depend more on the specific attention devoted to their utilization and training in the specific knowledge of the firm than their college preparation in short-term measures of success and tenure.

Other sources of experienced applicants include alumni placement services of colleges and universities. These services will list job openings and survey interested alumni periodically, generally on a quarterly basis. Additional sources of personnel staff members include "pirating" from other firms. Consulting firms may be especially vulnerable to losing staff to clients who have utilized the time spent on consulting services to evaluate consultants for possible positions with the organization. Experienced personnel may also be found at professional meetings of the American Society of Personnel Administrators, the American Society for Training and Development, Public Personnel Administrators, and the Society for Personnel Administration. Advertisements in trade journals such as *The Personnel Journal* or "The Mart" of the *Wall Street Journal* may attract candidates, although initial selectivity is diminished from the more individual approaches previously mentioned, such as agencies.

Factors in Job Choice

This chapter has stressed the importance of assembling job information, including key result areas, trade offs, and probable measures of effectiveness in ranges and with time constraints considered as well as valid data from the organization's point of view. The candidate, on the other hand, assesses the job from his viewpoint. Behling (1968) discusses a three-factor theory related to job choice by college graduates which is of value and may be extended to experienced job seekers as well. His three decision approaches imply a Maslow-like hierarchy and assume a prepotency of needs concept. Certain factors are viewed as basic and are believed to result in job rejection if they are not present. Higher levels of needs have a crucial effect in the decision process as jobs are viewed as essentially comparable on lower level factors. The description of each theory is stated as follows:

Objective factor theory: The selection of a position by a college graduate is basically a process of objectively weighing and evaluating a limited number of measurable characteristics of employment offers, such as pay, benefits, location, opportunity for advancement, nature of work to be performed, and educational opportunities. Although the importance of these factors may vary from individual to individual, there is a fairly consistent weighting pattern which, if detected and used as a basis for structuring the firm's offer of employment, will significantly increase the hiring effectiveness of the firm.[2]

Subjective factor theory: The selection of a position by the college graduate is the result of a perceived high degree of congruence between deeply seated and

[2] Orlando Behling, "College Recruiting: A Theoretical Base," *Personnel Journal,* 50, (7):15, January, 1968.

poorly understood emotional needs and the ability of the firm, or, more accurately, its image, to satisfy those needs of the individual candidate. The decision is not based upon weighting of objective factors in a pattern which is fairly consistent from individual to individual, but, rather, is made on a highly personal and emotional basis.[3]

Critical contact theory: The typical candidate is unable to make meaningful differentiations among firms or offers in terms of either objective factors or subjective image because the length of contact is short, offers tend to be constant, and the student lacks the necessary experience to readily evaluate them. The candidate still, however, must make a decision and is forced to rely on differences in treatment which he can perceive. The selection of a position by a college graduate is generally the result of the student's evaluation of the recruiter and his treatment during the plant visit.[4]

Thus the job seeker is viewed as attempting to weigh measurable job factors and decide objectively in the first case among various firms and their offers. Lacking clear objective grounds, the candidate is viewed as using his emotional reactions to industry image or perceived friendliness during interviews as the basis for deciding. These reactions are individual and highly subjective in orientation. The final level of decision is viewed as occurring when no clear objective factor or subjective reaction differentiates between position choices, and thus this situation would be less likely to occur among experienced job seekers. When no clear decision basis is found, it is assumed that the candidate proceeds by hunch or extrapolation from minor items such as quickness of response to correspondence or some other form of critical contact.

To some extent each of these factors may be viewed as having a role in hiring personnel staff members. By being prepared for the decision in terms of job analysis and contributions, the organization increases the likelihood of introducing objective criteria into the mutual choice process of applicant and organization. Subjective factors may also be more easily communicated once position roles and contributions are available for consideration in the manner indicated.

TRAINING THE PERSONNEL SPECIALIST

Training is viewed as the specific skills learning planned by the organization to further organization goal accomplishment by the trainee after he has joined the organization. Development is viewed similarly but with more stress on communicating organizational norms and values for given roles and thus becomes, in part, a socialization process.

Although training can focus on changing attitudes and values, most organizations try to focus directly on changing skills and performance. Before providing any training, the following analysis is appropriate to consider:

1. Analysis of performance desired: Do we know what a master performer achieves in this specific work area?

2. Analysis of system in which performance is to occur: What happens to someone who performs exactly as desired? What are the advantages? What are the disadvantages?

3. Design support system for the desired performance.

4. Design and implement an instructional system to acquire the desired performance.

[3] *Ibid.,* p. 17.
[4] *Ibid.,* p. 18.

Note that the analyses stressed the environmental support (organizational, in most cases) for the performance change desired *before* any consideration for delivering and designing any type of training was considered.

Training Methods

Training methods are summarized by many authors (Bass and Vaughan, 1966; Campbell et al., 1970) and include information presentation techniques, lectures, T-groups and variations, programmed instruction, films, readings, systematic observation of master performers, and the conference method. Simulations include cases, the incident process, role playing, business games, in baskets, and task simulations. A member of the personnel staff may be exposed to all these at various points in his career in connection with acquiring self- and subject-matter knowledge. Most likely, his major learning will come from on-the-job training. A member of the personnel staff may expect to engage in continuing job rotations through different aspects of the personnel function, or his position on general management committees may be used to extend his learning experiences. On-the-job coaching from co-workers and superiors is typical as is the use of performance appraisal to aid in identification of learning needs and for evaluating progress.

As previously mentioned, training content may focus on self-knowledge, attitudes, and skills, as well as on specific factual content and approaches to using information in problem solving and decision making.

University program services and bureaus as well as the American Management Association have expanded their efforts over the last decade in offering short-term courses (two days to one week) on technical subjects in personnel management. A partial listing of some of the course offered recently in the Midwest included:

Managing employment relations by objectives
Fringe benefits
Basic and advanced wage and salary administration
Recruiting high-talent personnel
Manpower planning for high-talent personnel
Affirmative action programs
Job enlargement and enrichment
Personnel testing
Training systems workshop
Orientation programs for disadvantaged workers
Employment interviewing (basic and advanced)
Technical graduate recruiting

Personnel staff members might attend seminars such as these, in coordination with job-rotation programs as part of a many-faceted and individualized career learning and building process.

This chapter has emphasized the diversity of contributions possible from the personnel staff. From their assistance to organizational goal determination and planning, they formulate the formal structure of the organization on a continuing basis. From the knowledge of job interfaces in the personnel decision functions, they have the potential to greatly influence human contribution and development in the organizational setting. The crucial interface of whether an organization is *deterministic*, i.e., the formal structure of legitimate control and communication determines the scope of human behavior, or *resultant*, i.e., human behavior determines the organizational structure and functioning, is the increasingly important area of expertise relevant to the personnel function and its staff. Specialists in personnel decisions, organizational behavior, and organizational development will be increasingly viewed as having the relevant expertise to enable organizations to continue to function in their environment and to become places of greater psychological health for their members.

BIBLIOGRAPHY

Bass, Bernard M., and James A. Vaughan: *Training in Industry: The Management of Learning,* Wadsworth Publishing Company, Inc., Belmont, Calif., 1966.
Behling, Orlando: "College Recruiting: A Theoretical Base," *Personnel Journal,* vol. 50, no. 7, January, 1968.
Bennis, W. G.: *Organizational Development: Its Nature, Origins, and Prospects,* Addison-Wesley Publishing Company, Inc., Reading, Mass., 1969.
Campbell, John P., Marvin Dunnette, Edward E. Lawler, III, and Karl E. Weick, Jr.: *Managerial Behavior, Performance, and Effectiveness,* McGraw-Hill Book Company, New York, 1970.
Drucker, Peter F.: *The Age of Discontinuity,* Harper & Row Publishers, Incorporated, New York, 1969.
Dunnette, Marvin: *Personnel Selection and Placement,* Wadsworth Publishing Company, Inc., Belmont, Calif., 1966.
French, Wendell: *The Personnel Management Process,* Houghton-Mifflin Company, Boston, 1970.
Hawk, Roger H.: *The Recruitment Function,* American Management Association, Princeton University Press, Princeton, N.J., 1967.
McFarland, Dalton: *Company Officers Assess the Personnel Function,* American Management Association, Research Study 79, New York, 1967.
Odiorne, G. S.: *Management by Objectives,* Pitman Publishing Corporation, New York, 1965.
―――― and Edwin L. Miller: "Selection by Objectives," *Management of Personnel Quarterly,* vol. 5, no. 3, Fall, 1966.
Patten, T. H., Jr.: "The Education of Manpower Specialists for Large Scale Organizations," unpublished paper presented at "Manpower for the Manpower Field," a conference sponsored by the New York State School of Industrial and Labor Relations, Cornell University, Ithaca, N.Y., 1970.
Rabe, W. F.: "Yardsticks for Measuring Personnel Department Effectiveness," *Personnel,* January–February, 1967.

chapter 6

Planning the Personnel Function Program and Budget

ROGER D. BORGESON *Vice President and Personnel Director, Abraham & Straus, Brooklyn, New York*

Among the many factors which separate the routine, unresponsive style of personnel administration from the well-run, sophisticated management of human resources found in an increasing number of companies, one of the most important is the skill and foresight with which personnel department programs are established and controlled to meet the demonstrated needs of the enterprise. Effective planning and budgeting are the keys to achieving this result.

This chapter examines the management planning and control process as it applies to the personnel function. The process is considered in terms of (1) the setting for personnel function planning and budgeting, (2) how the program planning process can function as an effective management tool, and (3) how to establish a personnel function budget and cost reporting system which permits meaningful control of the department's operations. At the outset, however, it is necessary to define our terms. What is personnel function planning? What do we mean by effective personnel function budgeting? What are the essential elements in the process?

THE PLANNING AND BUDGETING CONCEPT

Planning the personnel department program is not significantly different from planning the work of other staff departments. It involves developing a series of specific objectives which advance the defined, particular mission of the function, as well as the means of reaching these objectives, and a timetable. Budgeting involves deciding how much of the company's financial resources will be devoted to each aspect of the work of the department, and thus is an inexorable part of the planning process. Moreover, budget preparation, together with cost reporting, provides part of the information needed to control and measure the effectiveness of the department's operations.

The personnel administration function, more than most staff activities, is susceptible to directionless growth and the absence of a continuing close relationship between process and purpose. Good program planning and budgeting help ensure that the department has focus, that its activities are directly related to meeting the bona fide personnel administration needs of the organization. Without good planning of goals, and budgets to achieve them, objective judgment of the department's effectiveness gives way to visceral "feel" and subjective opinions. This is unacceptable as a management practice and can be hazardous to a function, such as personnel administration, which is difficult to evaluate with accuracy and neutrality.

ESSENTIAL ELEMENTS IN THE PLANNING AND BUDGETING PROCESS

The program planning and budgeting process for the personnel function contains the following basic elements:

A detailed understanding of the framework within which personnel department goals must be set, including the mission and philosophy of the department, the organizational environment, and the capabilities of the staff.

An understanding by the personnel department staff of the purpose and characteristics of the department's goals.

A procedure for determining specific goals in a manner that maximizes the probability of meeting the needs of the organization on a first-things-first basis. The procedure should spell out who participates in goal setting, in what sequence, in what role, and with what information and assumptions. It should also provide a means of evaluating proposals and identifying costs.

An awareness of common pitfalls and problem areas in setting goals for the personnel function.

An established budgeting and cost reporting procedure which facilitates managing and evaluating the work of the department in accordance with agreed-upon goals.

An operating budget for the department which corresponds to the goals of the department.

The remainder of this chapter considers each of these basic elements of the goal setting process and the budgeting process, respectively.

SETTING GOALS FOR THE PERSONNEL FUNCTION

The Framework for Planning Goals

Three conditions are imperative if the personnel department is to plan its programs effectively and control them successfully: (1) a clear understanding in depth of the department's mission, philosophy, organization, and scope; (2) an appreciation of the environment within which the department operates; and (3) the existence of a dedicated professional staff which is capable of moving effectively toward the mission within the existing environment.

Part I, particularly Chapters 1 and 2, discusses the overall philosophy, role, and scope of the modern personnel administration function and describes the setting within which specific activities and programs can be established for the department, each of its units, and individual members of the staff. A detailed statement of the mission and organization of the department helps to establish specific goals within a coherent plan of organization.

The normal and most useful formal expressions of the role, organization, responsibilities, and scope of the department are clear, detailed organization unit charters, position descriptions, organization charts, and operating guides. Together, these instruments should spell out the continuing formal responsibilities, specific duties, and relationships of each person and unit in the department. While scope and approach will vary from one company to another, the mission of the personnel function should include at least the following responsibilities:

1. Undertake manpower planning and related personnel recruitment, placement, and development activities to meet the needs of the organization for human resources now and in the future

2. Establish plans and programs which motivate individual and group performance, including compensation, benefits, training and promotion opportunities, position enrichment, attitude development, and employee communications

3. Develop, apply, and monitor personnel policies and practices which are conducive to constructive relationships between the individual employee and the organization

4. Establish and maintain productive relationships with recognized employee groups where necessary.

5. Provide various personnel services, such as recruitment, selection, placement, counseling, training, compensation and benefits administration, and safety.

The second requirement for successful goal setting in personnel administration is to understand the dynamics of the environment within which the personnel department operates. Environmental factors which influence personnel goal setting exist both within and outside the organization.

Within the organization, it is essential to understand the existing and continuously changing relationships and restraints. It is particularly important to understand what top management and others expect of the personnel function, and what unavoidable demands are imposed on it. For example, if the chief executive officer forces the personnel director into the role of a personal administrative assistant, he may not be able to lead a major staff effort effectively. It is important to appreciate that there are unpredictable factors about the environment which influence the work load of the department. More often than not, unforeseen (if not always unforeseeable) circumstances will deflect the department's efforts away from agreed-upon goals, or will require modifying these goals, or will cause delays in achieving them. Finally, it is important to understand the economic condition of the company, and any future business plans which affect personnel program planning.

Outside the organization, there are additional environment factors which should be understood and taken into account. These include competitive factors in the labor market, such as the levels of compensation, benefit programs, and personnel policies of other employers. They also include legal requirements, such as laws and regulations governing employment practices, and labor relations.

The third imperative for successful personnel program planning is the availability of staff members who are both qualified and motivated to achieve the particular objectives which must be met to advance the department's mission within the existing environment.

A personnel director can do an outstanding job of identifying personnel administration needs and priorities for his company, and may plan an intelligent array of programs for his department to meet these needs. However, if he does not have the professional talent required to implement these plans, he has wasted his time, and may even have raised a question regarding his judgment. Furthermore, even if he has a qualified staff, he may be in trouble if he fails to take their interests and goals into account when planning the activities of the department.

Characteristics of Personnel Goals

In addition to understanding in depth the mission of the department, the environment in which it functions, and the capabilities of the staff, it is essential for the personnel director and his staff to understand what a personnel function goal is, and what it is not. Experience shows that it is helpful to consider personnel function goals as falling into three general categories: program goals, procedural goals, and professional goals.

1. *Program goals achieve specific new results in response to demonstrated needs for better management of human resources.* Goals of this type can cover the full spectrum of personnel administration. They require undertaking a specific new activity which is likely to produce a specific, tangible result. The activity may be a continuing one, or it may be a single project with an identifiable beginning and end, such as undertaking a particular study or reconsidering a particular personnel policy.

Program goals should be as specific as possible, and should not be confused with generalized statements of the mission or policy of the department. For example, a recruitment section may have a "mission" of finding the best qualified candidates for each vacancy, without regard to race, religion, national origin, sex, or age; as a "goal," it might set the reexamination of its recruiting sources and selection tests to determine whether they conform to the mission. A wage and salary section might have the mission of developing compensation plans designed to attract and retain high-talent management personnel, and might set as a goal the development and implementation of a particular stock option plan or incentive compensation plan. A training and development section could have the mission of identifying employee education and development needs in the organization, and might set as a goal the development or modification of an appraisal plan to assist in identifying those needs.

2. *Procedural goals improve the efficiency and economy of the personnel department in meeting agreed-upon program goals and in fulfilling its mission.* Procedural goals are intended to improve the quality, timeliness, and cost effectiveness of the activities of the department, by identifying and overcoming inadequacies in existing processes. In some companies which follow the practice of "management by objectives," possibilities for procedural improvements are not given adequate attention in the goal-setting process. The result can be a proliferation of personnel department programs, accompanied by a diminution in the quality of program execution.

The possibilities for procedural goals are almost limitless. For example, a recruitment section could establish the goal of reducing the average time of "open" personnel requisitions, or of eliminating some of the paper work involved in placing new employees on the payroll. A wage and salary section might set a goal of simplifying the process for reviewing merit increases, or of exploring ways of streamlining the process for administering certain fringe benefits. The training and development section might decide to review the process for gaining approvals under a tuition assistance plan, or to change its handling of expenses in connection with certain in-house training activities.

3. *Professional goals improve the professional capability of the personnel department staff, and thereby the quality of the program goals and the means of achieving them.* Some personnel directors and training managers are fond of pronouncing as axioms certain opinions of their profession. One of these is that the main growth process for an employee occurs on the job, that "employee development is primarily a line department responsibility." Ironically, personnel department professional staff are frequently among those with stunted growth whose development needs are being neglected. While the development of personnel department staff may logically be considered a procedural goal, experience shows that establishing a separate category of professional goals helps ensure that this important task is not ignored.

Goal-Setting Procedure for the Personnel Function

The procedure which should be followed in establishing management objectives for the personnel department depends in part on the factors which define the framework for planning goals (as described earlier), particularly the organization principles and management climate of the organization. There is a growing body of experience, however, which suggests that goals for the personnel function are most likely to be met when there has been broad-based participation in their formulation. The personnel department is a cost center serving the entire enterprise; as such, it must earn the acceptance and support of the enterprise if it is to be successful. This can frequently be facilitated by obtaining the specific involvement of both headquarters and key field-level managers in departments being served by the personnel function. The goal-setting process should include soliciting their suggestions as an early step.

In addition, of course, the process must involve professional staff throughout the personnel department. Professional personnel staff should be an excellent source of ideas. Furthermore, if the department's goals are set unilaterally by the personnel director, they are not likely to be fully supported by the staff. Where the personnel function has staff situated in the field, experience indicates it is usually best to involve them in goal setting *before* headquarters personnel; and they should have a definite role, regardless of whether they report to the headquarters personnel function on a direct or functional basis.

The accumulation of ideas for new goals and improved ways of achieving established goals should be considered a year-round duty of everyone in the personnel department. For the astute manager, however, there are many additional sources of ideas for personnel goals, as illustrated by Figure 1.

Figure 1.   Illustrative sources of ideas for personnel department objectives.

Day-to-day observations of personnel department management
Complaints and comments by management of other departments
Reactions of top management to periodic activity reports
Periodic staff meetings within the personnel department
Analysis of grievances
Employee attitude surveys
Personnel research; comparison with the practices and programs of others
Contacts with outside sources such as competitor companies, professional associations, consultants, and educational and development programs

---

While details of the goal-setting process will vary from company to company, it should normally include the following seven general steps:

Step 1:   Evaluate past achievements and the present situation.
What were the past agreed-upon objectives?
Have they been achieved successfully?
If not, why not?
If not, are they still appropriate objectives?

Step 2:   Develop inputs concerning the environment which are needed to evaluate proposed objectives, including:
Limiting factors in the organizational climate
The expectations of top management regarding the role of the personnel function
Future business plans of the enterprise
The policies, programs, compensation, benefits, and personnel-related activities of competitors in the labor market

Assumptions about changes in personnel costs, such as increases in compensation.

Step 3:   Solicit suggested objectives from field and headquarters management outside the personnel department.

Step 4:   Solicit suggested objectives from personnel department staff, including, for each recommended objective:

A description of the objective

Reasons for recommending it

The approximate staff time required to achieve it

The relative priority it should be given

An estimate of the timetable for implementation

A rough approximation of costs.

Step 5:   Discuss and evaluate suggested goals in collaboration with key personnel department staff and possibly others in management.

Step 6:   Develop a definitive set of departmental objectives, including staffing estimates, cost estimates, and an implementation timetable.

Step 7:   Present recommended objectives to higher management for discussion and approval.

The specific techniques used in each of these steps depend on the special and frequently unique combination of relevant factors present in each company.

The key person in the goal-setting process is the top personnel executive of the organization. While he may delegate much of the preliminary planning work to the heads of subordinate units, and while he should establish goals in collaboration with his staff, he cannot delegate final responsibility for establishing and achieving the department's goals. He alone must decide on the specific techniques which will be employed in completing each of the seven basic steps in the goal-setting process. Inputs from executives of other departments should normally come through him.

It is also his job to work out disagreements among units in his organization. He must evaluate and harmonize various suggestions, "sell" his own ideas to the staff, coordinate the overall effort, make the final decisions, and develop staff support for these decisions. He personally must convince his superiors that the program, procedural and professional goals ultimately recommended express what his superiors should expect from the personnel function during the coming year or longer.

Avoiding Some Common Pitfalls

Goal setting for the personnel function frequently leads to certain pitfalls which are familiar to the experienced personnel executive. Some of these are described below. Those who plan for personnel administration should be mindful of each of these pitfalls and their implications for goal-setting strategy.

Top management sometimes has unrealistic, unenlightened or even naïve expectations regarding the personnel function, its role, and what it can and should be doing for the company. This condition can have serious repercussions in planning and executing the work of the department. A common example is the senior line executive who diagnoses an organization problem as a "training problem which personnel should do something about." Another is the chief executive who gives lip service to the manpower planning function but excludes the personnel director from the business planning councils of the enterprise. Still another is the executive who considers the personnel department as his personal service bureau. One task of every personnel executive is to educate top management regarding what it can and should realistically expect from the personnel function.

Another potential problem area involves the interactions among personnel department staff competency, authority, esteem, and goals. Certain goals, however desirable, may be unachievable at a given point in time for any one of several reasons having to do with the strength of the personnel department. If the department does not have high acceptance in the organization, sufficient staff resources, or adequate formal and informal authority, certain goals may be out of reach for the present.

A closely related potential pitfall is the question of priorities and timing. Eager but inexperienced personnel directors can fall into the trap of sponsoring an advanced, sophisticated personnel activity (perhaps for prestige purposes) before the time for it is ripe. As with most staff organizations, the personnel department typically faces a world of unlimited needs (the human resources aspects of the organization) with limited resources (the levels of staffing and expertise within the department). In this circumstance, it is important to set priorities—to meet first the most pressing needs which can be met. A good technique is to divide all the possible activities into three groups: (1) those which are absolutely essential to ensure effective performance of the function; (2) those which are clearly desirable, but not essential; and (3) those which are desirable but could be postponed. In short, the successful personnel director will promise only what he can and should deliver.

A final common pitfall in personnel administration planning can be called the triumph of process over purpose. This phenomenon is most noticeable in very large organizations with large personnel departments, where there sometimes seems to be a greater tolerance for (or concealment of) inefficiency. A major performance measurement of any personnel department will always be the results achieved, that is, to what extent the rest of the organization is satisfied with the personnel department's ability to meet reasonable demands for service. This suggests that personnel department planning should avoid elaborate, time-consuming, and excessively expensive programs. A good question to ask about every personnel department activity or objective is this: Does the value of the result warrant the cost of the process?

PREPARING A BUDGET FOR THE PERSONNEL FUNCTION

Most personnel executives and administrators have not distinguished themselves in developing effective budgeting techniques as a means of managing the activities of their department, measuring costs, and assessing program effectiveness. In consequence, many companies find the traditional personnel administration activities being continued, year after year, without adequate determination of how much the company is paying for each activity or whether it is getting its money's worth. In addition, new programs are born and thrive or die without reference, except in general terms, to what they cost the company. The typical personnel department budget is confined to forecasting salaries and miscellaneous expenses by organization unit within the department, and distributing estimated overhead items. Often it is prepared in a mechanical way, with little attention to the department's objectives, and then placed in a drawer and ignored until the following year.

One result can be burgeoning costs of personnel administration. Another is the absence of a suitable cost information base to be used in determining which plans and programs would meet economically the particular, demonstrated personnel needs of the enterprise. As a consequence, personnel directors are left unnecessarily vulnerable to charges of expending corporate assets without apparent concern for the impact on net profits, of concocting activities which have no "provable" impact on the success of the company. No professional manager—and particularly not the manager of a major cost center such as personnel administration—can accept this situation.

Obstacles to Better Budgeting

Why, then, has so little progress been made in developing satisfactory budgeting techniques for the personnel function? Several factors have had their effect:

It is difficult and time consuming to identify, forecast, and measure the costs of many personnel administration activities.

There are special and sometimes insuperable difficulties in measuring the effectiveness of most personnel activities in terms of dollar value received; indeed, most can be "justified" only on the basis of necessity, logic, and experience (or even faith), rather than in terms of how they made or saved money for the company.

It is erroneously, but commonly, believed that little or nothing can be done about controlling most personnel function costs—that most costs are unavoidably incurred as the personnel department responds to the demands of the organization.

Budgeting and expense reporting procedures are sometimes developed unilaterally by finance administration personnel, and thus may be unnecessarily complex, burdensome, and poorly understood by those in the staff departments (such as personnel) who have to understand, use, and support the procedures.

Since many key personnel activities necessitate working on more than one program or activity at a time and also call for interunit collaboration, it is difficult to allocate staff costs among programs.

Personnel managers sometimes experience a problem common to many managers of staff services—an underdeveloped awareness of costs, coupled with a fully developed desire for growth, recognition, professional achievement, and advancement for themselves and their departments.

The Traditional Approach to Personnel Budgeting

Because of these obstacles to better financial planning and control, the characteristic approach to budgeting (and expense reporting) for the personnel function in a majority of companies is confined to the classification of expenses by type of expense and by organizational unit within the department. For example, the employment section will receive an approved budget (which it may or may not have helped develop) which authorizes paying (up to a specified amount) total salaries to a specified number of professional and clerical staff, and incurring (up to specified levels) additional expenses which typically must be classified and coded according to type of expense. In addition, the employment section will be charged with a proportion of the personnel department's overhead costs (rent, utilities, etc.), normally on the basis of number of employees within the unit or amount of space occupied.

As a rule, unit heads within the department will be asked to estimate their budget needs, but the level of bona fide involvement will be minimal, and predictably, their level of commitment will be correspondingly low. Unit heads may or may not be asked to explain variations in actual expenses from the budget as the year progresses; however, since expenses are not identified in accordance with the specific objectives of the unit, it is frequently difficult to pin down the real cause of the variance.

The traditional approach to budgeting by classification of expense within each unit provides only a modicum of assistance in planning and controlling the overall work of the unit. It provides little help in managing the work of the unit and the department in terms of detailed, approved activities and goals.

Role of Effective Personnel Budgeting

During the 1960s, progress was made in an increasing number of large companies in developing more meaningful budgeting techniques for the personnel department. In general, this has occurred among the more sophisticated organizations, where the budgeting process is seen as a useful management tool rather than an annual, time-consuming, semiclerical ritual.

With effective budgeting, the activities and programs of the personnel department can be planned and established in full awareness of their probable cost. Thus, cost consciousness in the best sense, that is, an awareness of the importance of maintaining a suitable relationship between expenses and results, will be fostered within the personnel department. In turn, the company's top management will have a better basis for judging the effectiveness of personnel programs, and the expenditure of company funds can be measured and controlled in terms of achieving specific, approved objectives.

These benefits will be realized if certain underlying principles and conditions are present in establishing budgeting procedures: (1) the corporate climate, from the top down, must be conducive to good financial planning and control practices; that is, managers must believe they are measured in part by their budgeting and expense control practices; (2) there must be effective collaboration between the top personnel executive and the financial planning and control executive of the organization; (3) budgeting, coding, and related procedures must be kept as clear and simple as possible, consistent with generating the information needed in sufficient detail; (4) a plan must be developed for ensuring understanding and acceptance of the procedures and their purposes by organizational unit heads within the personnel function.

Where these elements are present, the personnel function can be managed with the advantage of adequate financial control intelligence. The most successful financial planning and control technique for the personnel function is program-oriented budgeting within each organization unit of the department.

Program-Oriented Budgeting

In a program-oriented financial planning system, the main thrust of personnel department budgeting and reporting is to identify, forecast, and report costs in terms of each of the basic purposes, ongoing tasks, and special projects of each unit in the department as and where they occur.

A company adopting this procedure should construct and use three basic sources of information in establishing the personnel function budget, in reporting expenses, and in measuring results: (1) a system for budgeting and coding nonstaff expenses as they occur, by program and by type of expenditure; (2) monthly estimates of staff time devoted to each program; and (3) annual assumptions regarding the allocation of overhead expenses by program. Separate budget and reporting data should be maintained for each organization unit within the department.

The first of these sources of information involves costs which can be isolated by program; the second and third sources have to do with costs which are most conveniently allocated periodically among programs, according to estimates or formulas. The result is a workable system for gathering, in useful but not burdensome detail, reasonably accurate cost data for each major, continuing task and subtask, as well as for each major special project, of the personnel function.

Coding nonstaff expenses. For the purpose of coding expenses, Figure 2 contains a list of the programs which are characteristic of the personnel function in a medium-to-large organization.

Programs are added or deleted during the course of each year to reflect the actual work of the department. Each program is carefully defined, and the list of coded, defined programs is an important document for each person within the department who has authority to approve invoices and expense accounts. When expenditures are not readily identified with one program exclusively, they are coded according to the primary program served or, if none, to one of the "administration" codes.

In addition to the coding of each expense according to the program objective being served, each is identified according to classification or type of expenditure involved. Figure 3 lists characteristic expense classifications, each of which should be clearly defined.

Figure 2.   Characteristic personnel function "program" accounts.

Recruiting and Selection

01 College recruiting
02 Executive recruiting
03 Recruiting other "exempt" personnel
04 Clerical recruiting
05 Hourly recruiting
06 Orientation and induction
07 Promotions, transfers, and reassignments
08 Manpower planning activity
09 Temporary manpower

Training and Development

10 Outside short-term courses
11 Outside executive development programs
12 Supervisory training
13 Tuition assistance
14 In-house knowledge or skill training
    (identify by program)
15 Special development activities (identify
    by program)
16 Personnel appraisal and employee
    counseling

Compensation

17 Salary and wage planning and admin-
    istration
18 Surveys
19 Job evaluation and classification
20 Executive compensation planning and
    administration
21 Benefit planning
22 Benefit administration

Communications

23 Periodic employee publications
24 Special publications
25 Attitude surveys
26 Suggestion plan administration

Personnel Services and Research

27 Periodic medical examinations
28 Diagnostic medical services
29 Preventive health programs
30 Employee recreational and social
    activities
31 Employee safety
32 Personnel information storage and
    retrieval systems
33 Minority group improvement activity
34 Employee relocation subsidy
35 Personnel policy development
36 Personnel policy interpretation
37 Personnel research

Labor Relations

38 Bargaining and related activity
39 Grievance handling and arbitration
40 Employee relations counseling of other
    departments

Administration

41 Planning and reporting activities
42 Professional development of staff
43 Initiating or reviewing personnel
    transactions
44 Special projects (identify)
45 General administration

Inspection of this list shows that expense classifications include those kinds of expenses which are frequently generic to more than one organizational unit within the personnel function but are readily capable of being "charged" directly to the unit which incurs and benefits from the expenditure. Again, as with program codes, expense classification codes should be modified whenever necessary to reflect the actual expenses of the department.

Expenses subject to coding to specific programs as they occur do not include two major categories of personnel function costs—staff salaries and fringe benefits, and overhead costs which can be conveniently distributed among units of the department on some ratio basis. The methods employed for budgeting and reporting these costs constitute the remaining two sources for personnel function program-oriented budgeting.

Staff time allocations. By far the largest expense in performing the personnel administration function in any organization is the cost of salaries and benefits to the department's staff. The main problem with program-oriented budgeting is that many staff members in the personnel department, particularly those holding professional and supervisory positions, spend time on more than one program concurrently. In addition, many of the most critical activities of the department require interunit collaboration within the department. Consequently, in order to budget and report costs on a program basis, it is necessary to allocate staff time among programs. The problem is to accomplish this in a way which is reasonably accurate without imposing time-consuming burdens on the staff and thereby taking time away from the substantive work of the department.

One solution is to establish a program-related time-reporting system for staff within the personnel function. In such a system, all employees provide monthly estimates of the working time spent on each identified and coded program of the department during the preceding month. Precise, hour-by-hour reporting frequently takes more time than it is worth, and may be resented. A good approach is to require estimates of time spent each month (or each week) on identified programs, broken down in either half-day or percentage units.

Under such a plan, organizational unit heads in the personnel function are charged with accumulating the estimates of individual staff members within their units and including this information in monthly activity reports to higher management and separately to the accounting department. The primary purpose of estimating staff time by program is to permit the accumulation of actual program costs, but an important secondary purpose is to focus the attention of staff members on the objectives of the department and the costs of achieving them.

While it is desirable to get time-reporting data from all staff in the department, this may be unduly burdensome under some circumstances. In some companies, sufficient accuracy is achieved by prorating clerical salaries by program within each organizational unit comprising the personnel function, in the same manner as other general overhead costs. This approach has the advantage of avoiding the necessity of training clerical staff in time-reporting procedures, and reduces the quantity of paper work required in the financial control process.

Prorating overhead costs. Overhead costs should be prorated among organizational units within the personnel function, either on the basis of employee head count or amount of space occupied. These costs typically include rent, utilities, communications equipment charges, postage, and general supplies. If project-related time reporting is not required of clerical staff, their salaries and benefits should be charged to each employing organizational unit as an overhead item. Clerical overhead costs should be allocated to programs within each organizational unit in the same ratio as professional salaries. After some experience, it is possible to make reasonably accurate annual assumptions concerning the percentage allocation of overhead costs by program within each organizational unit.

The three classes of data described above are forwarded to the appropriate unit of the accounting department, and provide the basis for periodic (typically, once every three months) budget performance reports to the personnel director and

Figure 3. Characteristic personnel function expense classifications.

01 Travel and subsistence—employees	12 Educational supplies
02 Travel and subsistence—applicants	13 Meal allowances
03 Employment agency fees	14 Meeting expenses
04 Executive search fees	15 Tuition payments
05 Testing materials and services	16 Equipment purchase and rental
06 Preemployment medical examinations	17 Office remodeling
07 Interviews and reference checks	18 Furniture and furnishings
08 Outside service fees	19 Computer time
09 Professional fees and retainers	20 Special purposes
10 Advertising	21 Professional and club memberships
11 Books, periodicals, and trade publications	22 Sundries

Figure 4.   Summary of program-oriented personnel expense reporting.

Organizational unit	Type of expense		
	Chargeable nonstaff expenses	Staff time	Overhead distribution
Each personnel department unit	Within limits of authority, approve and code expenses as they are incurred 1. By program and 2. By expense classification	Code hours by program each month	Identify employee head count or size of space annually
Office of personnel director	Approve and code expenses for which authority is not delegated	Review	Review
Accounting department . . .	1. Accumulate and distribute expenses by program and unit	1. Convert to salary and benefit costs; distribute by program and unit	1. Calculate overhead costs, and distribute by program and unit in accordance with agreed-upon formula
Accounting department . . .	2. Consolidate all data into quarterly report to personnel director, showing operating results by unit, classification of expense, and program		

other appropriate persons.   These data enable the accounting department reports to show personnel department costs according to any combination of the following variables: organization unit, classification of expenditure, and departmental program.   More complex reporting systems enable additional cost accumulations, according to organization units being served (such as divisions or profit centers) and according to geographic area.

The process of reporting, accumulating, and feeding back personnel department operating expenses under the program-oriented budgeting procedure can be summarized by Figure 4.

Charging Personnel Department Costs to Users

One important question of policy related to personnel function budgeting remains for consideration: Should all the expenses of the personnel department be distributed as overhead to the rest of the organization in accordance with a general formula, or should expenses be charged back to using departments, whenever possible, in accordance with the actual amount of use or benefit received?   This question frequently arises in connection with temporary manpower costs, employment agency and executive search fees, travel costs of job applicants, employee relocation costs, tuition assistance, the cost of outside training programs, and the cost of inside training course development and administration, among others.

Unfortunately, there is no hard-and-fast answer to the question.   The best practice for a particular company depends on such factors as its management and budgeting philosophy, degree of acceptance of the personnel department, whether the service can be isolated to a particular using department, and so forth.   In considering how to resolve this question in a particular situation, it helps to keep in mind the advantages of each approach:

Advantages of overhead distribution (unrelated to actual use):

Encourages fuller utilization of personnel department services, since cost is not directly related to use

Recognizes that personnel services often have a beneficial impact on more than one unit, and therefore cannot fairly be charged to one unit

Facilitates desirable independence of action and enhances the stature of the personnel department in its policy-making and control roles, since it makes the personnel function less dependent on support from user departments

Ensures less interference with the management of the personnel function by using departments

Is simpler to administer than a charge-back system.

Advantages of a charge-back system (related to actual use):

Is a more equitable system, since using departments pay only for services rendered, thereby reducing overhead distributions and enhancing profit-center and cost-center accountability

Improves the probability that personnel services will be more directly related to the actual, immediate needs of the enterprise

Ensures greater participation and involvement by user departments in the activities of the personnel function

Tends to restrain the personnel department from unduly expensive activities

SUMMARY

Effective program planning and budgeting can spell the difference between haphazard personnel administration and a well-organized effort which is efficiently responsive to the organization's needs. For the goal-setting and planning process to work well in the personnel department, it is necessary to have a detailed understanding of the mission of the department in the particular enterprise, the environment within which it must function, and the capabilities of the personnel staff.

Personnel department goals can be grouped conveniently into three categories: those which initiate activities intended to produce tangible new results that advance the mission of the department; those which improve the procedures of the department; and those which enhance the capacity of the department by upgrading the capabilities of personnel staff.

Details of goal-setting procedures vary among company personnel departments according to many environmental and other factors, but normally should include seven basic steps: evaluating past accomplishments, developing environmental inputs, getting suggestions from the rest of the company, getting suggestions from the personnel function staff, evaluating recommendations, developing recommended objectives, and obtaining approval and support from higher management.

In developing personnel department objectives, it is important to adopt measures which will overcome a number of common problem areas. Strategies include: working with top management so that it acquires realistic and appropriate expectations about the function; assessing accurately the relationship of the stature, influence, and capacity of the department to possible goals; setting appropriate priorities; and avoiding complex procedures which hamper the achievement of results.

By and large, effective budgeting and cost reporting as a means of planning and controlling personnel department activities is a rarity. Typically, personnel budgeting has been limited to forecasting and reporting costs for each organizational unit in terms of broad classifications such as salary and benefits, miscellaneous expenses, and overhead distributions. More effective budgeting procedures can be established where there is a suitable corporate climate, and where there is cooperation between financial planning and personnel executives.

Program-oriented budgeting has emerged as a successful planning and control tool in an increasing number of companies. In a program budget system, personnel function costs are projected and reported by specific activity or program, as well as by organizational unit and classification of expense. This approach requires coding all expenses (including estimates of staff time) by program served, and distributing overhead by program. The result permits planning and measurement of the department's activities in terms of the specific goals it is undertaking to achieve.

BIBLIOGRAPHY

A Look at Personnel through the President's Eye, American Management Association, Management Bulletin 66, New York, 1965.

Chruden, Herbert J.: *Personnel Management,* 3d ed., South-Western Publishing Company, Incorporated, Cincinnati, 1968.

Finlay, Robert E.: *The Personnel Man and His Job,* American Management Association, New York, 1962.

Flippo, Edwin B.: *Principles of Personnel Management,* 2d ed., McGraw-Hill Book Company, New York, 1966.

McFarland, Dalton E.: *Company Officers Assess the Personnel Function,* American Management Association, Research Study 79, New York, 1967.

Pigors, Paul, and Charles A. Myers: *Personnel Administration,* 6th ed., McGraw-Hill Book Company, New York, 1969.

Scott, Walter D., Robert C. Clothier, and William R. Spriegel: *Personnel Management,* 6th ed., McGraw-Hill Book Company, New York, 1961.

The Personnel Job in the 1960's, American Management Report 63, New York, 1961.

chapter 7

The Role of the Personnel Administration Department in Creating and Controlling Personnel Policy

W. F. RABE *Professor of Management, San Fernando Valley State College, Northridge, California*

THE NEED FOR STATEMENTS OF PERSONNEL POLICY

In any large business organization many individuals make decisions regarding how employees will be handled. Employees are hired, transferred, promoted, granted vacations, sick leaves, increases in pay, and terminated for many reasons. The question exists as to whether all these different decisions are consistent with the best interests of both the company and the employee. Without guidance such decisions can defeat the purposes of the company, can encourage employee dissatisfaction, and can ultimately win the firm the reputation of being an unsatisfactory employer. Such decisions must be made with certain guidelines, and statements of personnel policy serve as these guidelines. The greater the number of decision makers in the organization with regard to personnel, the greater the need for guides for their decisions, and thus the greater the need for statements of policy.

However, even the small firm has a need for personnel policies. A single manager operating a small enterprise has to make decisions regarding his personnel. Even though he may be the only person for the moment making such decisions, he may run into difficulties in maintaining consistency over a period. A decision made at one time may be forgotten when a similar situation arises later. Thus a highly erratic pattern of on-the-spot decisions grows. In addition, the small organization will grow and thus inherit a pattern of personnel practices that, while workable for the small firm, may be impossible for a large firm.   Thus even the small enterprise needs guides for its personnel decisions.

In the final analysis there is an even more basic reason for personnel policy.   A business firm exists for certain specific purposes.   All resources must be directed toward the achievement of those purposes.   All actions and decisions taken by any member of the organization must be guided toward the achievement of those objectives.   Personnel decisions must be directed toward the firm's purposes as would any financial, production, marketing, or research decision.   Personnel policy statements serve as guides toward the firm's purposes, and their existence can assist in preventing decisions counter to the firm's objectives.

Needless to say, a prime purpose of the firm is profit, and that cannot be achieved without control of costs.   Every decision or action concerning employees costs money.   Spending the firm's income through erratic, inconsistent, and contradictory personnel decisions is to be avoided.   Personnel policies define the limits, and thus the cost, to which a firm is willing to go with regard to its employees.   Compensation policies, vacation practices, and many other factors constitute defined cost limits, and thus meet a crucial need.

While many other reasons for policy statements may exist for specific firms, the basic reasons common to all are threefold: (1) The achievement of common purposes at the lowest cost by many members of an organization requires common guidelines for decisions and actions.   (2) Comparable action among many personnel decision makers requires comparable guidelines for the various members of the organization. (3) Consistency over a period of time furthermore requires statements which remain though managers and personnel may change.

THE NATURE OF EFFECTIVE PERSONNEL POLICY

The needs for a personnel policy determine its nature.   Defined, a personnel policy is a statement of what the firm wishes done with regard to its employees in order to meet the firm's objectives.   All members of the organization who must decide and act on matters affecting employee relations must follow the guides and cost limits set in the policy statements.   All employees can then enjoy a degree of certainty as to how they will be treated under varying circumstances.   The firm can thus build sound and productive relations with its work force.

In its most useful form, the policy statement includes several parts.   First the purpose of the policy is stated.   This in some measure establishes why the policy is to be observed.   For example, a firm may examine the reasons for a vacation policy. It may determine that a vacation is earned by the employee and accrues to him as a form of deferred compensation.   On the other hand, the firm might determine that the vacation is to improve productivity and to give the employees needed rest and relaxation from the job.   If the former is decided upon as the purpose, the firm may adopt a policy which allows a vacation to accrue indefinitely or may give the employee two extra weeks of pay during the year if he does not take the vacation. If the latter is the case, the employee might be required to take a vacation each year or lose it, since the purpose is defeated if he does not take it annually.   Similar reasoning should apply to each personnel policy; first the purpose followed by the implementation, or first the why and then what may be permitted.   These two parts constitute the first portions of any policy statement.

These parts must be followed by a third which clearly establishes who has the authority to implement policy.   Is the policy a matter of supervisory discretion? Must the matter be submitted to higher managerial authority for decision?   Or is the personnel department the only approving authority?   Authority for decision and action on a policy must be defined as part of the policy.

The fourth portion of a policy includes the procedure that must be observed in carrying out the policy. This establishes the flow of any paper work connected with the action. In almost all cases something of this nature will be involved. Records must be maintained, and visibility on what is being done offers advantages. Therefore a procedure that all personnel decision makers can follow is wise.

Effective written personnel policies thus consist of several parts. The heart of the policy is a statement of what the firm wishes done on the matter. This is preceded by a statement of the purpose to be achieved. Authority for action is defined in the third section, and the whole document is supported by a statement of procedure.

THE PERSONNEL DEPARTMENT'S ROLE IN POLICY DEVELOPMENT

The development and maintenance of any policy gain if specialized experts can be used. This is particularly true of personnel policy. The small firm with limited ability to hire experts in all its functional areas requiring policy statements may resort to outside services. Instead of a personnel staff, consulting services may be useful, local or industry personnel associations may be helpful, or bureaus of research attached to schools of business or universities may function as temporary personnel departments to develop policy.

Whether the service is supplied from outside or by an established department, the same basic steps in developing policy will be necessary. Identification of the purposes and objectives the firm wishes to attain with regard to its work force is the first activity. Consultation with upper levels of management by the personnel staff can lead to a clarification of these points. The second step will require analysis of all the factors under which the firm's personnel policy will be operating. In some instances there may be limitations outside the firm as well as inside. These are dealt with in detail in the next section of this chapter.

The third step will require that the personnel department examine the possible alternatives in each area in which a personnel policy statement is necessary. What are the various transfer and promotion policies which the firm could adopt? What retirement policies may serve the firm's purposes? What kind of training and education programs are open to the firm? Extensive research is essential, and continuing familiarity with industry practice is mandatory. A forward-looking personnel staff may want to project trends into the future to determine innovations implied in contemporary developments. Even study of practices of foreign firms will suggest interesting alternatives that may offer significant cost savings. Mere adoption of local industry practice, for instance, without consideration of alternatives may not be of greatest advantage. What other firms do or do not do grows out of their unique problems and experience and is not necessarily "exportable" to other firms with their own problems and their own work force. Thorough and practical research is one of the distinct contributions to policy development that the personnel staff may make.

Choice of the alternative is determined by the purpose to be achieved and by the cost burden the alternative will place upon the firm. In this fourth step of policy development, the personnel department must reduce the policy to as tangible a level as possible. The cost per hour of the policy requires careful consideration. Surprisingly enough, the cost of not adopting a particular policy may become a determining point. For example, the cost of not having a fixed retirement age for all employees may become evident in a burdensome group of unproductive workers and a high turnover of young people who see little or no opportunity to get ahead. The cost of uncontrolled coffee breaks may well exceed the defined break in a policy which offers some opportunity for control.

The fifth step in development is to provide for implementation of the policy through the development of a procedure to support the policy and the definition of authority for implementation. Many personnel departments may turn to the firm's systems and procedures group for major assistance. An attempt to develop procedures independent of the firm's other systems and paper-work flow may be a duplication of effort and result in conflicting procedures. With the large-scale use of electronic information systems, the personnel department needs to integrate as many as possible of its personnel procedures with the total system in order to enjoy the lowest cost and greatest speed in the movement of information throughout the firm. The personnel department may thus desire to delegate the development of procedures to the specialists on electronic data systems.

The sixth step in policy development consists of a broad program of communication of the policy and procedures adapted to the entire organization. This step is of such importance that it is dealt with in a special section of this chapter as is the seventh step regarding audit of policy.

The eighth step in development is the continuing reevaluation and revision of policy as audit reveals the necessity for change. Effective personnel policy means that it meets current needs. A personnel department will find it essential to review each policy annually. In the light of facts and experience, which the personnel department must be constantly gathering, revisions and modification must be proposed for management approval. Certain policies may not prove worth maintaining and must be scrapped. Others may have to be adopted in their place. New needs may make themselves apparent, and new approaches may have to be created.

The responsibilities of the personnel department in policy development offer a unique opportunity for it to prove its worth. How well it does its job will determine in part the firm's labor costs and how productive that work force can become. The department must manage the entire process of policy development through careful organization of each step. (1) Purposes must be established. (2) All factors affecting each policy require identification. (3) Alternatives need research. (4) Evaluation of alternatives against purposes and costs is essential. (5) Provision for implementation through procedures requires special assistance. (6) Communication through the organization demands special attention. (7) Audit of performance leads to the final step of revision and updating.

Policy development is managerial decision making at its more complex levels. Its consequences must be lived with for a long time, and a great number of people will be affected. The personnel department's mastery of the process therefore is crucial.

FACTORS INFLUENCING POLICY

Personnel policy functions within the framework of many influencing factors. Policy developed in contradiction to these factors or which ignores them will serve the firm badly. In the process of policy development, the personnel department must test each statement against such factors and adapt it accordingly. Some of the more constraining factors to be considered are as follows:

The Social Values of American Democratic Society. The preeminent place granted human rights and liberty by our society makes it mandatory that personnel policy do the same. American democracy places the human being at the center of its consideration and surrounds him with protective legal processes and defenses. So also must personnel policy statements. It is the responsibility of the personnel staff to see that statements of policy constitute an extension into the employment life of the citizen of the democratic rights basic to his society. Furthermore, the firm must develop a policy which supports the political system which permits it to exist and function. It is unthinkable that a firm's policies would operate in a fashion subversive to the interests of society.

Legislation.   The entire work life of the employee is protected with a myriad of legislative restrictions. Federal, state, and local regulations, codes, and statutes place constrictions on both the employee and employer. All must be taken into consideration in the development of personnel policy, and it is the responsibility of the personnel staff to possess expertise on such legislation.

Industry Patterns.   Policy patterns exist within each industry. Certain practices are traditional and are reinforced by the tests of time. Any firm that wishes to compete for the labor supply must at least match the pattern of the industry if not take steps beyond it. A personnel staff that is not cognizant of industry patterns will ill serve the interests of its firm. Policy reflecting the best industry practice places the firm in the most favorable position in the labor market.

Professional Trends.   Research in the behavioral sciences is increasing our knowledge of relationships among individuals and groups, employees and employers, as well as workers and their supervisors. Ideas on motivation, productivity, morale, and discipline have gone beyond mere assumption and possess factual and experimental support. These concepts need to be incorporated into statements of personnel policy in order for the firm to use the best means of achieving its objectives. With roots in the behavioral sciences, personnel administration has become a more professional field of endeavor. It too is developing and revising its standards on the best practices. Contemporary rethinking of personnel administration needs to be incorporated in policy statements.

Community Mores.   American society displays many diversified and provincial attitudes toward industrial relations. What is acceptable personnel practice in one area of the country, may not be so in another. Such local differences must be taken into account. If the firm is an international one, the differences become even greater. An American firm with overseas operations may find itself confronted with the need for varied personnel policies, depending on the cultural climate in which it is operating. Comparative study of personnel policy and practice from one community to another or from one nation to another is a responsibility of the personnel staff.

Union Objectives and Practices.   If the firm's employees are represented by a bargaining unit, its objectives, strength, and pressure techniques will constitute a major factor in personnel policy. This must be taken into account when the staff develops or revises policy.

Management Philosophy and Values.   A top management team does not work together for any length of time without forming a broad philosophy and a general set of values which influence their actions on matters concerning the work force. Any attempt by a personnel staff to submit personnel policy statements that diverge significantly from this general philosophy may meet with outright rejection. Adoption of such policy may result in a policy more honored in the breach than in implementation, and the firm will be viewed as hypocritical and insincere by the work force. Either the personnel department recommends policy within the philosophical limits of top management's view, or it undertakes a process of prolonged reeducation and redirection of thinking directed toward the upper levels.

Stage in the Firm's Development.   No firm exists without proceeding through various changes. The size of operations will expand or decrease, change in scale; technological innovations will intrude; the composition of the work force fluctuates; a decentralization of authority may be required; and financial structures may also change drastically. All these changes, with others, will necessitate adaptation of personnel policy. Increasing professionalization of the work force may call for new policy approaches; decentralization may call for a policy that permits some new differentiation at lower levels.   The reverse may also be desirable.   A strong policy audit may be demanded.   The personnel staff, therefore, must be sensitive to such changes and be alert to adapt policy to the dynamics of the situation.

The Firm's Objectives.   Enough has already been said with regard to the contribution personnel policy must make toward the achievement of the firm's objectives. To this contribution the personnel department must always direct the development of policy.

Financial Position of the Firm.   As has already been stated, personnel policies cost money.   The ability of the firm to absorb such costs into its prices sets the absolute limit to the firm's policies.   No other factor in policy development is so final or so tangible.

Type of Work Force.   Each work force has its unique nature.   The percentage of women workers, the educational level, the average age, the ratio of supervision to workers, the stability of the industry, and thus the sense of security of the workers are but a few of the many dimensions of these phenomena.   Any group develops certain attitudes and perceptions based on its unique characteristics.   These constitute a limiting factor on what they will accept as meaningful personnel policy. Assessment of the characteristics of the labor force and what is acceptable to them is the responsibility of an effective personnel staff.   A policy that is inappropriate to the situation is hardly worth the implementation.

The peculiar nature of each factor as it relates to a particular firm needs intensive study by the staff.   Translation of that nature into as tangible terms as are possible so that its influence on the firm can be recognized is essential.   The strength of its influence needs measurement.   Factor analysis is a major aspect of policy development.

METHODS OF POLICY DEVELOPMENT

For varying practical reasons, firms adopt diverse methods of translating research into written statements.   In some instances, the personnel department may be solely responsible for the entire process.   In other cases, the department will germinate the ideas which a policy and procedures group will reduce to the formal statement. A variation of this method is consultation with all levels of supervision.   Groups of supervisors representing the various departments assemble to meet with the personnel staff.   Open discussion of a proposed policy will yield points which are worthy of consideration.   In addition, a policy in which all levels of management have participated in its development will have better chances of being accepted and implemented with wholehearted cooperation by those participating.

Another variation involves employee participation.   Representatives from all levels and all departments are brought into groups with personnel department staff to consider the policy to be adopted.   Involvement of employees in the formulation of policy that will affect them contributes much toward the construction of morale and respect for management.   While this may seem strange, firms might well consider that a form of this approach is widely in use through collective bargaining.

Another approach is to consult with representatives of other firms in the same industry.   Trade associations or industry meetings of personnel staff offer opportunities for exchange.   While this approach may not afford detailed discussion, general principles can be evaluated and the experience of other firms may prove helpful.

Combinations of the above are used by personnel staff to advantage.   Participational approaches reveal problems before adoption, offer a chance to explain management problems, and can win acceptance of an unpopular policy.   Rejection of these approaches should not be without good reason.

COMMUNICATION OF POLICY

The role of the personnel staff in the issuance of formal personnel policy statements is usually limited. The manual on policy, incorporating all policy, is maintained by a department on policy and procedure. Since the distribution is limited in many organizations, the personnel staff will find it necessary to take further steps to obtain wide understanding of both the letter and the intent throughout the organization.

Many personnel departments find a handbook on policy and practice a highly useful device. This takes the form of a compact publication that can be used easily on the job by supervisors. It may be bound in loose-leaf fashion so that revision is simplified. The language is informal, and it may include illustrative material.

To encourage full understanding, training sessions for supervisors on policy and practice are conducted. Special sessions for new supervisors are mandatory. Review sessions for supervisors on the job will update their understanding and facilitate compliance.

Booklets on personnel policy which summarize points of interest to employees are often issued. Special booklets on the various benefit programs are useful, particularly if different plans are in effect for different groups of employees. Periodic restatement and publicity may be practical. Some departments adopt the practice of developing an annual restatement of personnel policy in the firm's house organ. In the spring of each year a general review of vacation policy is the subject of a major article. Toward the end of the year a review of holiday policy and an announcement of holidays for the coming year may receive publicity. Other aspects of policy will be subjects of special treatment throughout the year.

Little of this can substitute for the continuing close relationship that the personnel staff maintains with all members of supervision to encourage consultation on policy interpretation. Special cases will always arise; the staff must be viewed as capable of giving authoritative and useful interpretations on all matters.

PERFORMANCE AUDIT

Effective maintenance of policy requires acquisition of information on how policy is being implemented in time to take any corrective action necessary. This is a major function of the personnel department, and establishment of channels through which information is accessible constitutes a major activity.

While it is possible to determine the extent to which policy is being followed, most personnel departments experience difficulty in determining whether its purpose is being achieved. Measurable causal relationships between policies and increased productivity, job satisfaction, or morale are yet to be established. Thus personnel finds it is auditing what is being done, and not whether the objectives of policy are being achieved.

How does a personnel department obtain information on what is being done? Two broad types of approach are possible. The first is the continuing review of operations. This is accomplished by routing all paper work concerning employees through the personnel department for review and approval. Current developments in electronic information systems make it possible for personnel departments to eliminate the review of each document. Instead, daily or weekly print outs are audited by the department, deviations are noted, and corrective action is initiated. This method may be difficult to implement since corrective action is delayed until after the fact, and personnel problems result.

The periodic audit is the second general type of approach and takes several forms. Some personnel departments delegate this to internal audit, specifying what information is desired and what organization unit is to be audited. All aspects of how that unit is implementing personnel policy are reviewed as defined by the personnel staff, and summary reports are submitted by internal audit.

Another method is to have the personnel staff do the entire job instead of internal audit. Still another approach is to develop a committee to conduct the audit. This can take the form of a three-man team that functions once a year. The composition of the committee will vary for each organization unit being audited. It should include a representative of the personnel staff, another from the controller's staff, and a third from the unit being audited. This team evaluates policy performance and reports to both the personnel director and the head of the unit being audited. Another approach is to have the organization unit audit itself according to procedures established by the personnel staff and submit the findings to both the personnel director and the firm's chief executive.

The participation by the organization unit in the audit or even the idea of self-audit may appear questionable. However, a firm may wish to place the full burden for effective policy implementation on managers throughout the organization. The firm does not wish the personnel staff to assume the role of policeman or assume any semblance of responsibility for policy implementation. The firm desires that the head of each unit and his subordinates become "personnel managers" in the fullest sense of the word. The assumption is that the personnel staff does not manage personnel; managers do that and must assume full responsibility.

In addition, specialized audit activities are found useful by many personnel departments. Each is designed to fulfill a specific purpose and takes a unique form. Some departments require employment interviewers to follow up on each employee they hire several times during the initial months on the job. Interviews are held with the employee as well as his supervisor to determine how effectively he has been working. Another type are the audits undertaken among terminated employees. Pretermination interviews, follow-up interviews, follow-up questionnaires are devices to study policy on terminations. Special analysis of managerial promotion and replacement potentials may reveal the effect of an education policy. Study of trends in type and cost of grievances is still another example.

STANDARDS FOR AUDITS

Extensive quantitative standards have evolved in the areas of finance, sales, accounting, and production. Such standards have universal acceptance in business. The personnel function has been slow in developing many such statistical standards, and universal acceptance is limited. Seemingly, standards of such a nature can be developed with experimentation, but their meaning is relative to the industry, the firm, and even the region in which the firm is located. What constitutes a good turnover ratio for a firm will vary over a period of time and under changing conditions. An analysis of claims experience for health benefits may yield all sorts of statistical information, but whether such information is indicative of a policy failure is relative to the firm and the attitudes of those using the information.

Probably the most important function of a personnel staff is to maintain information on all aspects of policy over a long enough period so that useful statistical data can be revealed. More often than not personnel fails to retain historical records on enough aspects of policy to discover just what is useful and what constitutes acceptable standards. Comparisons of data over a period can lead to the development of significant standards. Such internally developed standards are often of greater use than externally applied ratios and data. Industry or regional standards have their uses but hardly tell the whole story. Ingenuity and historical fact constitute the basis for effective standards of performance for any personnel policy evaluation.

REPORTS TO MANAGEMENT

Many aspects of personnel administration deserve the attention of top management and should be the subject of reports for their review. The concern here is reports that focus thinking on how personnel policy is implemented to serve the purposes of the firm. The reporting efforts of the personnel staff must be directed to closing the gap in understanding between management's thinking and policy in action. In fact the personnel staff becomes a central intelligence unit for management on personnel policy. It functions much as a consultant to a client, providing needed information gathered and interpreted in the most concise and useful format possible.

Reporting to management begins with an analysis of information needs. It is a question of who needs what. The executive or top group needs certain overall information. Other subdivisions of the firm need information on their specific areas of responsibility. Different reports will therefore have to be developed and submitted. What is needed must be specified by the client or at least with the client's participation. Nine broad areas in which information is needed seem somewhat standard among large firms. They are manpower utilization, employment analysis, separations, wages and salaries, benefit programs, education and training, safety, labor relations, and employee morale and participation.

The second phase consists of developing indices of what is occurring as a result of a particular policy or group of policies. These are ratios, statistics, or cost figures which are indicative of deviation or change in the way policy is implemented. They serve diagnostic purposes in that they will alert management to needed corrective action or to problem areas requiring attention. In preparing the report the personnel staff may define the problems suggested by the indices and recommend necessary action. A survey of the more standard ratios and indices in use is available in reference 4.

The question of timing the reports offers some coordination difficulties. Certain items of information are useful and meaningful on a weekly basis. Others may be deferred to monthly, quarterly, or semiannual reports. Still others need only annual review by management.

Format is open to many alternatives. Many top management groups respond most readily to the brief factual presentation with a minimum of text. Concise interpretative comment is helpful, accompanied by the action being taken. Even graphic presentations have considerable merit. These often say more than words or dry statistics. A possible format for one of the nine areas listed above is shown to illustrate what might be done. In the final analysis, the report must be adapted to the needs of the "client" who is most sensitive to costs both hidden and obvious.

THE FINAL RESPONSIBILITY

Any study of trends in personnel practice abroad will reveal a decided movement toward the nationalization of personnel policy. More and more personnel policy which private firms must follow is being established by government through legislation and through state agencies. At the same time, foreign firms do not seem to have made use of personnel departments in a manner similar to the American

SEPARATION ANALYSIS: QUARTER ENDING MARCH 27, 1970

Turnover per 100 employees	This period	Last period	Year ago	Recommended action
Company total	5	4	6	
Plant A	6	5	5	None: Plant B has
Plant B	7	8	4	been laying off
Plant C	5	5	6	staff during the
Corporate office	3	2	4	past 6 months.
Salary exempt	4	5	2	
Salary nonexempt	7	8	3	None: see above
Hourly	8	10	3	
Labor grade 1	1	1	2	
2	1	1	1	Labor grade 14 is
3	1	1	2	experiencing high
4	4	5	3	turnover and as
5	5	0	0	indicated below
6	0	1	6	the reasons for
7	2	8	7	separation are
8	0	3	5	better pay and
9	4	0	0	work elsewhere.
10	1	2	0	Wage and salary
11	0	0	0	is making a com-
12	0	1	0	parative analysis
13	0	0	0	and will submit
14	12	10	2	recommendations
15	1	0	1	within the month.

Reasons for Separation:				
Total number	185	200	82	
Probationary	20	25	18	
Involuntary	100	100	8	
Voluntary	65	75	66	
More pay	9	15	3	
Better job	10	12	2	
Move from area	2	4	0	
Illness	13	10	12	
Death	11	15	18	
Retirement	12	14	17	
Education	5	0	98	
Other	3	5	6	(All figures are fictitious)

firm. Such departments abroad do not appear aggressive in their leadership; seemingly, nationalization of policy fills a void. The implications for American industry are important. Personnel departments need to exert leadership in developing and maintaining personnel policy. Failure to do so leaves a void that invites several alternatives. Imposition of policy on the firm from external agencies may be one of these and will prevent the firm from establishing policies that serve its needs and purposes. Personnel departments must, by their efficient development and maintenance of personnel policy, protect the firm and permit it to serve social and economic needs with as much freedom and responsiveness to change as has been characteristic of the continued growth of the American business system.

REFERENCES

Appley, Lawrence A.: "Essentials of a Management Personnel Policy," *Personnel,* May, 1947, pp. 430–435.

French, Wendell: *The Personnel Management Process,* Houghton Mifflin Company, Boston, 1964.

Odiorne, George S.: *Personnel Policy: Issues and Practices,* Charles E. Merrill Books, Inc., Columbus, Ohio, 1963.

Rabe, W. F.: "Yardsticks for Measuring Personnel Department Effectiveness," *Personnel,* January–February, 1967.

Rogers, Robert C.: "Written Policies and Standard Practice Instructions in Personnel Administration." *Personnel Journal,* April, 1959, pp. 32–37.

Turner, J. Howell: "Essentials in the Development of Personnel Policy," *Addresses on Industrial Relations, 1957 Series,* Bureau of Industrial Relations, Bulletin 25, University of Michigan, Ann Arbor, Mich.

Publications of the National Industrial Conference Board and the American Management Association are highly recommended. Inquiries should be directed to either organization to determine what is currently in print and available.

chapter 8

Evaluating the Personnel Program

GEORGE S. ODIORNE *Dean, College of Business, The University of Utah, Salt Lake City, Utah*

How can you evaluate whether or not your personnel administration staff is adequate, its activities are germane, its effectiveness is high?

At present we find five major yardsticks which are being used to audit and evaluate personnel departments.   They include the following:

1. You might audit yourself by comparing your personnel programs with those of other companies, especially the successful ones.

2. You might base your audit on some source of authority, such as consultant norms, behavioral science findings, or simply use a personnel textbook as a guide.

3. You might rely upon some ratios or averages, such as ratios of personnel staff to total employees.

4. You might use a compliance audit, to measure whether the activities of managers and staff in personnel management comply with policies, procedures, and rules, using what I would call the internal-audit approach.

5. Finally, and my own personal recommendation, you might manage the personnel department by objectives and use a systems type of audit.

My general plan is to discuss each method.   Since you already know my bias in favor of the last method, you will note that I will employ an abstraction ladder technique to destroy the first four approaches.   This will leave the final systems approach as the recommended method for auditing your own personnel activities.

The recommendations are not simply based on speculative or pipe-smoke cogitation, but rather on actual field attempts at experimental installations of such a system, with some tangible evidence in such substantial companies as Ford, Honeywell, General Mills, Aetna, and other similar firms to confirm its value in practice.

I would not be candid if I did not admit that not every facet of this approach is without some controversial aspects.   But I freely predict that it is the method which will be increasingly accepted.   In our seminars at the Bureau of Industrial Relations we have adopted a unifying theme which runs through the hundreds of seminars which are attended by 10,000 managers each year. Much of my confidence lies in the favorable response which we at the Bureau have received to our approach to the personnel and industrial relations job.

After discussing the shortcomings of other approaches, I should like to outline the major facets of what we rather immodestly refer to as the Utah approach.

Let us look at each audit system in turn:

COPYING OTHER COMPANIES

It is fairly natural and not without some merit that we should try to imitate the successful. If we learn that GE, IBM, RCA, Dupont, or General Foods is practicing a certain kind of personnel technique, it is not surprising that we tend to imitate them. They are successful in the overall results which their companies achieve. We presume that copying individual programs is to increase the likelihood of achieving similar overall results from their experience for our own.

Yet, the model which calls for imitating the best is not without dangers. We may imitate the wrong things. We might copy some irrelevancies rather than the fundamental germ of the idea. We may copy something which was designed to meet a specific local problem within the model firm, but which does not suit the needs of our own firm and its problems. Even worse, we may imitate those things which a few isolated individuals, whose low work pressure permits them to appear most frequently at conventions as speakers, declare to be their company practice, but which the great bulk of their managers have never practiced nor do they ever intend to try.

Many personnel and training men fall into the self-deluding habit of describing their own desires and plans to outsiders in terms that would create the impression that their firms are smoothly operating monolithic machines which have none of the real-life problems and obstreperous people which you and I always seem to encounter in our own shops.

Learning from another's experience is valuable if you can learn all the details of that experience. Short of that, constructing new programs based on copycat thinking might mean borrowing the other fellow's troubles along with his gains.

BASING YOUR AUDIT ON SOME OUTSIDE AUTHORITY

A second method of devising yardsticks for evaluating your personnel department is to find an expert authority and adopt his criteria.

The search for experts who will do our thinking and decision making for us often starts with a checklist. A list of all the personnel functions and a rating scale of how well each is done usually comprise the basic audit instrument. This list can come from a textbook, from a manual, or from some commonly applied audit. The University of Minnesota's Triple Audit would be one such example; the Industrial Relations Counselors Procedure is another. There are a number of such lists, many of which are constructed by copying from the others.

A consultant's observations comprise another type of expert or authoritative rating. The consultant has visited and worked for numerous firms. He has a well-stocked memory drum of personnel practices he has seen elsewhere. He will tell you how your personnel program stacks up against the others he has seen. He may also tell you how to correct any shortcomings.

The findings of behavior science research are one of the most amazing sources of expert knowledge in recent years against which present practices are rated. Such norms as theory X or theory Y, managerial grid, and autocratic-democratic scales would be examples of norms and values which are proposed by academic researchers as tests of personnel administration effectiveness.   The X guys are bad, the Y types are the good guys, and so on.

The common ingredient of all such standards for personnel departments is that they are general in scope and are applied to specific departments, located in specific companies, at a specific time.   Not without some uses in obtaining estimates of how you compare with others, such authoritative guides are a poor beginning point for measuring personnel effectiveness.   As ultimate criteria they have many shortcomings.

MEASURING YOUR DEPARTMENT AGAINST AN AVERAGE

Closely related to the other methods is the practice of determining certain data and rating the findings against some averages.   The ratio of personnel people to other employees, the ratio of professional staff to clerical staff, the ratio of managers to workers, or the ratio of offers to acceptances in college recruiting are common terms in personnel department evaluation efforts.   The answers can be calculated in dollars to results ratios, percentages of total work-force ratios.   Negroes, females, impending retirements, turnover, absenteeism are examples of averages we use. In the use of personnel statistics, the use of averages of one kind or another is commonplace.   Frequently, it is enlightening and useful.

Some limitations do exist here.   Such statistics have meaning only as internal control devices, not as evidences of success or failure.   When the statistics for your firm are matched against the averages for all firms, or even for leading firms, you may be commiting an error in logic.   By some, the use of averages or statistics is mistaken for managing by objectives.   While we may use such data in setting and evaluating performance against targets, there is more to managing by objectives.

MEASURING COMPLIANCE AGAINST POLICY, PROCEDURE, RULES

The fourth approach to evaluating the performance of personnel departments is that of auditing compliance with policies, procedures, and regulations out in the work force and sales office.   With increasing frequency, the trend seems to be toward turning the dirty job of conducting such inspections over to the internal auditing department.   The steps in preparing such audits are about as follows:

1. The personnel department in cooperation with the internal auditor takes out the policy and procedure manuals on employment, selection, testing, grievance handling, time off with pay, leaves of absence, and all the other areas of concern and converts them into a checklist.

2. From some available checklists they add other such areas and compile them all into an internal auditor's guide to policing the line organization on behalf of the personnel department.

3. The internal auditor, along with the regular duties of checking revenue and expense procedures, also probes into personnel practices and issues a compliance or noncompliance report.   The personnel department is thus removed from the unpleasant task of being policeman.   When the report is unfavorable, it is then properly sympathetic and helpful in correcting the deficiencies.

As a kind of manipulative system, it helps protect the good-guy image of the personnel department.   As one personnel manager put it to me: "It's really a wonderful plan—the auditors are all viewed as snoopers and busybodies, anyhow."

The main advantage of the system is that it takes the personnel department out of the role of controller and turns it into a service and advice department, which is a softer and more pleasant image.   The disadvantage is that it turns over to the controller some personnel functions which may not be as cleverly concealed as we suppose. The general manager who gets a favorable financial audit, but is criticized because he has varied from a personnel policy for good reason, will hardly welcome innovative suggestions from the personnel people. This system also implies that exact and slavish conformity to every personnel regulation and rule is to be placed in the same category as a violation of the rules for handling cash receivables, inventories, billings, and purchase orders. There is a difference between personnel practices respecting people and accounting practices regarding control of cash. Each in its way has some useful purpose. Auditing people for their management of cash is nothing more than removing temptation—a biblical kind of work. Intervening between manager and subordinate by strict definition of every detail of that relationship is hardly biblical, or even human.

USING OBJECTIVES APPROACH TO AUDIT PERSONNEL DEPARTMENTS

My own preference, based on close observation of each method, is the fifth approach to auditing the personnel department. To wit: Did it set sound objectives? How well did it achieve the objectives which it set for itself? Measuring results against objectives for personnel departments offers the best chance for integrating the personnel department into the parent organization which created and sustains it.

Yet, an anomalous situation exists in many firms. The personnel, management development, and the training departments have been leaders in espousing management by objectives for other managers but have been amazingly reluctant to install the same system in their own shop. The reasons they give often include such evasions as, "Our work is too intangible and can't be measured." This invites two immediate questions:

1. How can you be so insistent that everyone else do something which you yourself evade?

2. If your output is so vague that it cannot be described or measured, what would the company be missing if it were eliminated?

The plain facts are: Many personnel departments are being managed by objectives. They do it and find it exciting and helpful. They are more successful than those which are not managed by objectives.

What is success for a personnel department? Personnel departments do not produce tangible products. They produce intangible soft wares. These intangible soft wares are made and sold for a captive market consisting of line departments and other staff departments, plus top management. By applying management by objectives to your personnel department, you are able to use a marketing approach to personnel department administration.

A marketing approach to personnel administration? The beginning point for managing the personnel function by objectives is to determine that we are in the business of making and selling certain kinds of products for a captive market. What is this captive market? It consists of those departments which produce and sell the hardware or are themselves staff departments to these same producers and sellers.

The purposes of the firm are to make and sell such items as automobiles, chemicals, soap, or cereals or to produce and sell some kind of consumer services which will be sold such as insurance protection, investment advice, or education. The purposes of its own captive departments such as personnel, public relations, traffic, and legal are to help the hardware departments succeed or to help the top management of the firm manage the organization. It is the loss of insight into its own purposes which gets a personnel department into low repute inside its own firm, or leads to its being crippled in size, budget, and effectiveness.

It is precisely in this regard that the four criteria for auditing personnel departments can contribute to lowering rather than raising its effectiveness.   Outside authorities, behavioral sciences, practices of other firms, ratios, compliance with policy, and consultants have value only to the extent that they impel the personnel department in your organization toward the objectives of your customers.   The demand for personnel services is a derived demand.   Personnel functions are like an organ which depends upon the entire organism for its sustenance.   At the same time, it comprises a part of the organism and strengthens it by performing a vital function.

What are the stages in setting sound objectives for the personnel department? Since the personnel department is primarily a producer of soft wares, it must research its markets and find out what its customers, the primary producing departments, need, want, or will buy.   This requires that line objectives be reasonably clear.   In too many cases the line departments are unclear on where they are going, and the personnel department is trying to help them get there.

If operating departments are not clear on objectives, the personnel department has a challenge—to train them in setting objectives, and in selecting people by objectives, appraising performance against objectives, and administering salaries by objectives.

With these primary department objectives, the personnel department has the basis for establishing its own targets.   As an intangible soft-wares department, it works at an organization-wide level.   And it should be working on five-year plans, with one-year objectives and commitment to them.

At the beginning of each year, every staff member in the personnel department should be required to make a commitment to his immediate superior, with respect to three kinds of responsibilities.   They should reflect what each staff member intends to contribute on his job during that period, with perhaps some quarterly indicators and measuring points noted in advance.   These three objectives should include, in ascending order of importance, the following goals:

Regular Routine Chores

In this category he states those regular, ordinary recurring responsibilities for which he accepts responsibilities.   The outcome here should be stated in terms of average expected outcome but should always include a range of high and low expectations as well.   The importance of this kind of range cannot be overestimated.

No personnel man worth his salt would reasonably expect that he can predict exactly how many college graduates or computer programmers he will hire during the coming year.   He could state the range of expected successes and failures.   This is more than a wild guess because it is based on present levels in stating the average expected.   The lower level of expectation is the figure below which he must inform the boss in time to take action, if he fails.   The highest expected outcome states the most optimistic possibility and would indicate superior performance.

It is always a mistake to set targets for a single outcome in regular duties.   Even more foolish is the practice of those managers who simply take last year's outcome and add 2 percent.

The first major mistake in setting personnel objectives is to set a single target rather than a range of possible outcomes.   The second is to give a man a single responsibility area upon which his entire performance will be measured.   Such areas of routine responsibility should be stated to permit trade offs of one outcome for another.

You could get all the college recruits you need if you could have an unlimited budget for recruiting.   Budget compliance must be a trade-off responsibility with head count of campus hires.   You could operate with no grievances for a whole year, but labor costs would go through the roof.   You must trade off certain numbers of grievances in order to keep labor costs down. Grievance levels often are trade offs for labor cost levels. The number of regular responsibilities must include the trade offs of cost, quantity, quality, service, and time pressures.

Problem-solving Objectives

The second major category of objectives for personnel departments begins where the regular routine responsibilities leave off. These objectives consist of immediate and on-the-spot problems which exist in the organization and that the personnel department must solve. Usually they are found in the indicators for the routine responsibility. An indicator running below minimum acceptable levels is a problem. A problem very specifically stated is the best kind of objective possible. Every staffer in your personnel department should be identified as responsible for some problem or problems upon which he will work. This does not mean he will solve two problems per year. He may solve only part of one, or he may solve a dozen. The key point here is that he has two or more in front of him at all times. They are before him with a known order of priority and an agreement with his boss that they are important. Also, he knows what priorities exist for their solution.

Innovative Goals

The hardest of all to measure but probably the area of greatest contribution for personnel departments is that of innovating, introducing changes or raising the quality of employee relations to higher levels than before. This may mean introducing new ideas from the outside which will enhance the performance of the customer departments. It means keeping abreast of new developments which might contribute to such growth. It means making orderly feasibility studies of their application to your business. It means intelligent and aggressive action in installing new programs and making them work.

This trio of categories, routine, problem solving, and innovative, comprises an ascending scale of excellence in personnel work. It also comprises an ascending scale of need fulfillment for the people involved, whether you prefer Maslow's hierarchy of needs or Herzberg's motivation and maintenance factors.

More important, it attunes the personnel program, budget, and staff toward the needs of the parent organization, not to some theoretical, unrelated checklist of audit items. The personnel departments make available only those items of advice, service, or control which its market research among its customers shows are needed, have been asked for, or can be sold.

Should personnel departments sell their wares to other departments? The personnel man can take the position that selling is not part of his job description; otherwise he would have joined the sales department or marketing staff. Such beliefs lead to these standards errors of the frustrated personnel staff man:

He sees the line manager as an enemy who seeks to frustrate him—an obstacle on the path to professional success—rather than as a customer whose needs must be met and around whom his wares must be shaped.

He relies too heavily on faith in top management backing to knock down the barriers to his programs.

When line managers will not buy his wares, he cites this as proof of their autocratic nature, incompetence, or uncooperative nature. He creates a special island empire and either abandons the project or goes along with it without line help. Often the personnel department has attached ogre images to some of the most influential managers.

To survive, he measures his success more and more in intradepartmental terms: the number of programs installed, trainees covered, forms approved or processed, man hours devoted to each project, and similar symptomatic measures.

Ultimately, he is a likely candidate to start searching for more felicitous grounds, a more enlightened management climate, or a more progressive company where all obstacles to his plans will be removed.

BIBLIOGRAPHY

American Management Association, Personnel Division: *A Look at Personnel through the President's Eye,* American Management Association, New York, 1965.

Blood, Jerome W. (ed.): *The Personnel Job in a Changing World,* American Management Association, New York, 1964.

Hersey, Paul, and R. K. Blanchard: *Management of Organizational Behavior,* Prentice-Hall, Inc., Englewood Cliffs, N.J., 1969.

Jucius, Michael J.: *Personnel Management,* Richard D. Irwin, Inc., Homewood, Ill., 1967.

Kindall, Alva F.: *Personnel Administration,* 3d ed., Richard D. Irwin, Inc., Homewood, Ill., 1969.

Odiorne, George J.: *Personnel Policy: Issues and Practices,* Charles E. Merrill Books, Inc., Columbus, Ohio, 1963.

Pigors, Paul, and Charles A. Myers: *Personnel Administration,* 6th ed., McGraw-Hill Book Company, New York, 1969.

Ritzer, George, and Harrison M. Trice: *An Occupation in Conflict,* New York State School of Industrial and Labor Relations, Cornell University, Ithaca, N.Y., 1969.

Yoder, Dale: *Personnel Management and Industrial Relations,* Prentice-Hall, Inc., Englewood Cliffs, N.J., 1970.

Part 3

Development of
Personnel Resources

chapter 9

Manpower Management

FRANK E. FISCHER *Vice President and Director of Personnel Services, Cresap, McCormick and Paget Inc., New York, New York*

Manpower management, like financial management or materials management, is concerned with the utilization of resources to help attain an organization's objectives. It does so by ensuring that the required manpower is available when needed and that it is used efficiently. The task of manpower management is to forecast job requirements and the number and types of people needed to fill those requirements, and to prepare plans for seeing that this is done within the projected time span.

Manpower management literally includes all those activities of an enterprise involved with the management of its human resources and therefore, in a sense, encompasses the whole of this handbook. Although other facets of manpower management will be discussed, this chapter concentrates on the methods used by business organizations to forecast their manpower requirements and plan for effective utilization of manpower. After a general discussion of the management of human resources, major attention is given to the definition of manpower planning, the description of the manpower planning process, and methods for establishing the manpower plan, followed by an evaluation of the present status of manpower planning and conjectures regarding its future development.

THE MANAGEMENT OF HUMAN RESOURCES

Manpower management, of course, is not new; businesses have always "managed" their manpower. What is new is the serious and systematic attention given by a growing number of companies to the planning and deployment of their human resources. As late as ten years ago, Prof. Frederick Harbison noted that "of all economic resources, high-talent manpower takes the longest to develop . . . [yet] most companies are doing little or nothing about this." A number of recent developments, however, have made companies aware of some serious manpower problems they soon will be facing:

There is a great and growing shortage of high-talent manpower. By 1980, although the population will grow by 22 million, there will be a net decrease of one million in the pool of management represented by the thirty-five to forty-four age group.

There will be an increasing need for managers. It has been estimated that one-third more managers will be needed by 1975—this in the face of the expected decrease in the supply of management talent mentioned above.

The manager's job will become more demanding. Business organizations will get bigger, and so will their manpower problems. In addition, management processes are likely to become more rather than less complex.

There will be increasing competition for managers. Our government and educational institutions, for example, are successfully competing with industry for management talent.

Companies have responded to manpower problems in various ways. Some have sharpened their recruiting practices or inflated salaries in order to pirate key employees; others, particularly in defense industries, have protected themselves by overrecruiting. Still other companies have been forced to alter their business plans and cut back on their staffing requirements.

All these are reactive, short-term solutions—the "bits-and-pieces approach" to manpower management, as Prof. Mason Haire has called it. A few companies, beginning with the 3-M Company back in 1952, began to attack the problem systematically and to develop techniques for forecasting their manpower requirements. Still later, other companies began to examine the total manpower planning system in an effort to delineate the process for projecting future manpower requirements and developing action plans for meeting them.

Professor Haire sees the problems of manpower management in still broader terms, and urges that we move "toward an explicit management of human resources." In his McGregor Memorial Lecture in March 1967, he said:

> We have a tradition of planning expansion in terms of market growth, product diversification, and capital availability, and trusting that the flexibility of people and a loose labor market will protect us from the results of not planning in the human area. . . . We have not, in general, taken responsibility for what is, from the side of the organization, manpower planning, or what is, from the side of the individual, career development. . . . Pay, promotion, training, job rotation or cross-functional assignment, performance evaluation, supervision—all of these are immensely strong levers to modify behavior. They can usefully be thought of, in organizational terms, as variable inputs which can be applied at the discretion of management to shape the manpower pool for present productivity and future promotability. Or, on the other hand, they can be viewed as optional interventions in the career development process. In either case, they are the company's repertoire of things that it can do or not do in treating the problem of human resources.

An overall approach, linking key manpower plans and actions to the basic management process, is shown in Figure 1. This model, the Management of Managerial Resources, is an attempt to provide managers with a conceptual framework for analyzing the factors affecting their human resources so that they may better understand how to manage them.

Whether fragmented or seen as a total human resource system, manpower management includes all those activities concerned with the planning, staffing, development, motivation, and utilization of people. This chapter will discuss me of these activities in terms of methods used by companies in planning their power requirements and for achieving their manpower objectives.

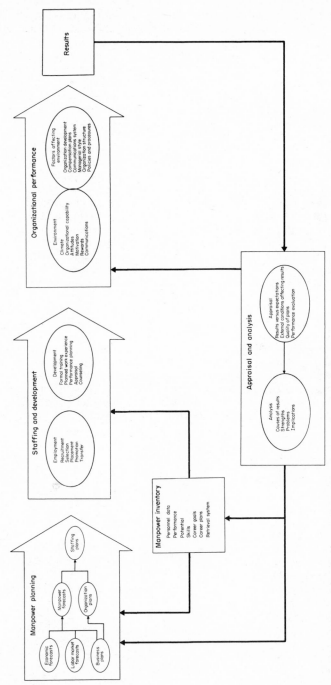

Figure 1. Management of managerial resources. Planning and performance cycle — the organization. (*Cresap, McCormick and Paget, Inc., Management Consultants.*)

MANPOWER PLANNING: DEFINITION AND SCOPE

Professor Eric Vetter has defined manpower planning as the process by which a firm ensures that it has the right numbers and kinds of people, in the right places at the right time, doing the things for which they are economically most useful. Essentially, it is a method for determining future manpower requirements and developing action plans for meeting them. Manpower planning is part of a firm's total resource planning. It influences and is influenced by the firm's business plans, interacts with organization plans, and contributes to business decisions concerning, for example, the development of new products, markets, facilities, or production processes and mergers and acquisitions.

Manpower planning helps evaluate and implement management's plans and decisions by assessing their manpower implications. For example, the plans of a defense contractor for shifting his business from the military to the commercial market would depend greatly on his ability to convert or supplement the skills of his existing manpower resources. An example of how some business plans can affect long-range manpower planning is offered by a company which recently decided to diversify within three years into two fields in which it had little or no experience, namely, motels and plastics. Its ability to do so will depend largely upon the phased recruitment of staffs for these two unrelated projects. The company's present plans call for recruiting managers as the new motel building sites are selected. Recruiting for the new plastics operations is being approached two ways. By using manpower inventories, certain chemists are being selected from the company's existing chemical operations for training in plastics; the remainder it plans to hire from existing plastics producers at premium salaries. Obviously, this company is well aware of the manpower problems it is facing, and is planning well ahead in order to meet them.

As with business planning, manpower planning frequently interacts with organization planning and development. For example, it may measure the impact of planned organizational changes such as the consolidation of staff functions, decentralization or recentralization, changes in function or structure, and changes in operating systems such as the shift from functional to project management. All these changes affect and are affected by a company's manpower plans and resources.

THE MANPOWER PLANNING PROCESS

The manpower planning process, as we have seen, involves a determination of future manpower requirements and action plans for meeting those requirements. The process includes three key elements:

Manpower inventory: data which describe the present work force in quantitative and qualitative terms

Manpower forecast: the manpower required at specified times in the future, described either in gross numbers or in specific categories such as skill, educational level, and experience

Manpower plans: specific action plans or blueprints for bridging the gap between the forecast and the inventory.

A schematic diagram of the manpower planning process is presented as Figure 2. Here is shown the work force required to carry on the existing business and, with the passage of time, changes in the composition of this work force as a result of transfers, promotions, and separations. Projected new business, translated into work load, determines future manpower requirements. To the extent that these are not expected to be met as a result of changes in the existing work force,

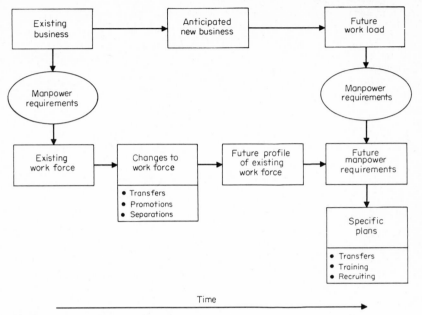

Figure 2. **The manpower planning process.**

specific plans will have to be developed for the recruitment, training, and transfer of the necessary personnel.

Manpower Inventory: Assessment of Available Resources

Essential to systematic manpower planning is an up-to-date system for classifying and locating personnel within an organization. Most companies have such an inventory, although its content may vary widely. Most inventories will include information on age, experience, and education. Less commonly, the inventory will include information on the quality of the person's performance, his potential for promotion, and perhaps his career goals. These data permit management to assess the depth of their manpower resources in terms of ability, capacity, and potential for growth. The personnel inventory may be recorded manually or kept on punched cards or on the computer. The 3-M inventory file has data on about four thousand persons, including their past history, performance appraisals, and estimates of potential. The company finds that this inventory can be updated easily and accurately, and prefers not to computerize it because the computer cannot recognize the person who almost fits. However, when companies use summaries of the manpower inventory for statistical studies as an input for manpower planning, they usually keep the inventory on computers.

Typically, the manpower inventory is initiated by asking each employee to fill out a questionnaire which provides the initial data inputs. The inventory is usually updated by entering changes, for example, in position title, salary, and appraisals; this is accomplished automatically through changes in the personnel status file. Frequently, a printout of at least some of the information is given annually to each employee who is asked to supply corrections or new information. This is the practice, for example, in a product division of IBM with 15,000 employees. The data in this system include the employee's profile, his employment history, a record of previous employment and significant achievements, and his education and skills. In addition to using the data system for quickly retrieving information for placement purposes, simulation is used to help management review and evaluate alternative manpower plans—including hiring, transferring, and retraining —for coping with changing workloads or technological advances.

Since a company's work force is subject to changes over time, the manpower inventory may include a projection of the future composition of the work force now on board. Turnover in the form of voluntary and involuntary terminations, deaths, and retirements can be projected or estimated, as can transfers and promotions. Formal appraisal plans assist in determining the performance level of personnel. Potential or promotability is harder to determine, but a number of companies have established assessment centers for this purpose.

In many companies, managers rely on replacement charts or tables as a means of quickly ascertaining the management depth of their organizations and as a basis for developing manpower plans. The form used by one company to chart its managerial replacements is illustrated by Figure 3.

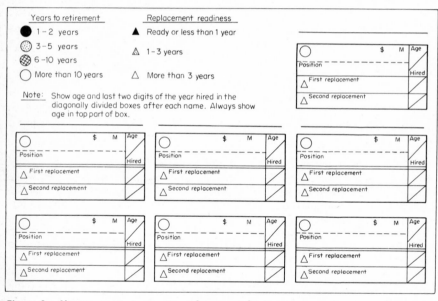

Figure 3.   Management manpower replacement chart.

Manpower Forecast: Determination of Future Requirements

Surveys of company practices reveal widely varying approaches to manpower forecasting. One survey of 115 large companies, conducted jointly by the American Management Association and Cresap, McCormick and Paget Inc., indicated that some companies, particularly in stable businesses like utilities or insurance, simply projected requirements on the basis of past manpower growth. A substantial number related their manpower forecasts to some element of their economic or business forecast; the most common link was with sales forecasts. Relationships were also established, in declining order, with projected organization changes, planned new products or services, productivity changes, and technological developments; and a few tied their manpower forecasts to research and development expenditures, capital investment forecasts, and projections of GNP. The forecasts differed in several ways, from gross long-term estimates to specific near-term forecasts of manpower by numbers, organizational units and levels, and occupational categories.

In addition to the simpler techniques described above, some companies establish their forecasts by analyzing a number of factors, including general economic conditions, the company's business plans (for example, sales volume, new products, and acquisition plans), expected changes in organization structure, manpower mix and productivity, past employment trends, and anticipated changes in personnel policies and programs.

In most companies, however, factors like economic forecasts, corporate policies, and business objectives are probably still reflected in the manpower forecast in an informal rather than scientific or rigorous manner. In a divisionalized company, manpower requirements are typically projected for the next year or two ahead by the various divisions, which are expected to take into account their business plans (production, sales, etc.) as well as statements of company policy and overall corporate objectives. Usually, this is done somewhat subjectively, and both the process used and the implicit assumptions tend to vary significantly among the divisions. Guidelines for preparing the forecast are sometimes disseminated by the corporate planning group, but they are not always followed or rigorously controlled.

Nonetheless, a few companies seem to have adopted a systematic and successful approach to manpower forecasting. In the Cleveland Electric Illuminating Company, for example, manpower forecasting is essentially a line responsibility and is done on a departmental basis. The central personnel department distributes annually a statement of "corporate assumptions for planning" which summarizes the general economic outlook, the specific sales and production plans for the next five years, a statement of overall objectives for the next year, and statements of company policies which affect manpower planning. These projections or assumptions are used by the various departments in making their manpower forecasts, and the corporate personnel department controls the process by auditing the departmental forecasts and questioning any deviations from the corporate projections and assumptions.

Although the methods they use in manpower forecasting are not as sophisticated as in the Cleveland Electric Illuminating Company, most companies aggregate departmental, plant, or divisional manpower estimates in order to arrive at an overall manpower plan. Others attempt to forecast manpower at the corporate rather than the division level (for example, Standard Oil of Ohio and the Bendix Corporation), and a few are attempting to forecast their manpower requirements by means of formal models constructed and applied at the corporate headquarters. One electronics equipment company has developed a manpower balancing equation incorporating a number of overall corporate variables affecting employment levels.[1] In utilizing the equation, the company makes various assumptions about the future course of productivity, output, intermediate purchases, and other critical variables. The likelihood of various combinations of these assumptions is appraised, employment levels corresponding to the most probable combinations are derived, and their implications are studied. Several other companies have developed statistical inference models to estimate relationships among such variables as production, sales, assets, and manpower. A regional telephone company, for example, uses relationships among managerial and nonmanagerial employment, the number of telephones, the number of customer accounts, and forecasts of

[1] Described in *The Conference Board Record,* August, 1968, pp. 39–40.

business growth to predict employment levels for the total nonmanagerial work force and for the six company divisions by managerial level.

The manpower forecast, of course, has to take account of many factors other than business projections and economic forecasts, for example:

It should estimate changes in the existing work force resulting from promotions, separations, and transfers.

It should predict the probable effect of changes in personnel policies and programs. As an illustration, changing the pension plan to liberalize the early retirement formula might accelerate the rate of retirements in the next few years.

It should take account of technological developments which may change the mix and levels of skills and the relative size of occupational groups.

It should consider changes in the amount of time needed to train or recruit personnel to fill the increasing number of technical and professional openings.

It should incorporate changes in labor productivity, a key element in forecasting manpower, particularly hourly employees. As Professor Vetter has pointed out, forecasting labor productivity on the basis of analyzing past experiences to determine changes in labor efficiency is beset with difficulties. These include the availability and reliability of the data used to measure output and input. Moreover, there is no assurance that current manpower staffing necessarily reflects good manpower utilization.

Finally, the manpower forecast has to take into account expected changes in a company's organization plan. Shifts toward greater decentralization, the consolidation of functions, or the transfer of international operations to the product divisions, for example, will obviously affect the staffing of an organization and the size and composition of the future work force.

Manpower Plans: Action Steps to Meet Manpower Needs

The third key element in the manpower planning process is the design of implementation plans and action programs to help achieve manpower objectives. Here many options are open. Typically, the company first looks within itself to see what candidates are now available or can be trained in time to fill anticipated openings, or it makes plans to recruit the necessary personnel from outside. A third approach to meeting future manpower needs is to improve the utilization of the existing work force. Many ways of accomplishing this are available to an organization, some of which are described later in this section.

The matching of staffing requirements with staff capabilities is facilitated in many companies through the development and analysis of manpower inventories and replacement tables. This is a mechanically complex task which even medium-size companies today may find economical to computerize. The computer programs may range from a simple series of "go or no go" types of decisions to extremely complex, fully integrated programs. Regardless of their complexity, all such programs require the development of initial replacement recommendations at the lowest possible organizational level. The computer is useful to ensure that:

1. All qualified candidates are considered for anticipated openings.

2. Plans are not developed for an executive to fill more than one anticipated opening at one time.

3. Development efforts can be undertaken in time to train replacements for expected openings or, if this is not possible, steps can be taken to recruit candidates.

4. All key positions without potential replacements are identified.

5. High-potential and immediately promotable executives for whom no promotions are forecast can be identified, and plans developed for their utilization.

At the 3-M Company, the process for matching the manpower forecast with the inventory has been developed to the point that corporate personnel can quite accurately inform the divisions how many people they will need over a given period for growth and replacements. This enables the divisions to determine the extent to which they can take care of their own needs on the basis of how many are ready and available in the inventory, and how many will have to be developed by the time they are needed. They will also know how many high-talent personnel can be pried from other divisions, and how many will have to be hired from outside.

To be effective, a plan for closing the gap between manpower requirements and capability must be supported by sound personnel objectives and programs, and priorities for implementation must be established. Employment policies and goals governing turnover and retirement as well as outside recruitment have to be clearly spelled out, as do the policies and goals for training and upgrading personnel.

The primary output of manpower planning in most companies is the determination of hiring goals to meet future manpower needs. Unfortunately, some companies do not fully appreciate the extent to which their needs can be met through better manpower utilization. As Professor Haire has observed, an organization can initiate a number of actions to effect structural and behavioral changes, for example:

1. Rigorous analysis of organizational arrangements will often disclose examples of excessive layering, unnecessary overlapping or fragmented functions, and numerous assistant and assistant-to positions which, if identified, could result in the elimination of certain positions.

2. Similar opportunities for personnel reductions may result from the examination of staffing levels. Symptoms of overstaffing may be revealed by comparing the staffing levels of similar organizational units, comparing the ratio of employees in an organizational unit with total employment over a period of time, or comparing changes in a unit's staffing level with changes in sales or other output data. Some companies in industries that experience swift and sometimes drastic changes in volume have a rule of thumb for determining and controlling staffing levels. A West Coast electronics firm that works almost entirely on defense contracts has set its staffing level at $22,000 of sales per employee in order to meet its profit goal.

3. In recent years, a number of companies have improved manpower utilization through changes in job design. These have ranged from the creation of job families to programs for job enlargement or enrichment which, in Texas Instruments and other companies, have significantly increased employee productivity or reduced the size of the work force.

4. Training and development programs, using team building and other behavioral approaches, are found in an increasing number of companies interested in improving employee motivation and manpower utilization. In addition, innumerable training opportunities are provided through selected job experiences as well as formal training courses. Farsighted companies will initiate retraining programs in anticipation of technological innovations, as one company did, for example, when it foresaw the displacement of the vacuum tube by the transistor and acted in time to salvage its skilled tube-circuit designers.

5. Innovations in staffing and personnel placement seem to be helping to meet the manpower needs of a number of companies. Many have learned in recent years that they must give their high-talent manpower challenging tasks and meaningful responsibilities if they wish to retain these men. Various forms of temporary organizations, including task forces, project teams, and venture management

teams, are being tested by a number of companies trying to escape the wasteful rigidities of conventional organizational patterns. The design of career paths and the assignment of personnel to such temporary organizations are helping to create a mobile work force responsive to rapidly changing technology.

6. Still another means of improving manpower utilization involves the commitment of employees to the attainment of personal and organizational goals as part of an overall performance planning and review process. Appraisals that measure achievements against expectations are found to be far better than conventional merit reviews as evidence of a man's abilities, and an earlier indicator of his talents.

7. The design of a company's reward system can also be a powerful tool for improved manpower motivation and utilization. Well-designed incentive plans and selective compensation approaches are considered important motivators by a number of companies. Another imaginative use of the reward system to retain and motivate high-talent personnel is the recent practice of rewarding venture team managers with stock participation when a company is created out of a successful venture.

In the future, particularly when manpower is scarce, it is believed that companies will increasingly seek to meet their needs through improving the utilization of their existing manpower resources instead of simply replenishing or supplementing them from inventory or outside sources.

Implementing and Controlling the Manpower Plan

As the staff department chiefly responsible for the deployment and development of the firm's human resources, the personnel department has the major role in designing and implementing the manpower plan. The success of the manpower plan, therefore, rests largely on the department's ability to establish viable policies and practices in all aspects of manpower management, including recruitment and selection, staffing, career planning, performance planning and review, pay plans, training and development activities, and organization planning.

An important—and in larger companies perhaps an essential—aid in implementing and controlling the manpower plan is an inventory and retrieval system. Properly designed, such a system provides information on the status of a firm's current manpower resources and enables management to identify personnel qualified to fill vacancies. It also generates manpower planning reports based on appraisals of potential. In addition, it may include manning tables which provide data for management succession purposes and information for replacement charts showing positions which can be filled in the near term and those which cannot.

In most companies, top management reviews manpower plans at least annually. The report on these plans typically presents a manpower forecast for the coming year and perhaps for the longer term, including figures on anticipated turnover, the number of additions required for replacement or growth, and the numbers to be recruited for the coming year. The report may also include a review of management succession and development plans covering key positions in the organization.

Manpower planning is not sufficiently advanced to have developed effective controls or reliable criteria for measuring its effectiveness. However, there are several indicators or questions that might be asked to test the soundness of the manpower planning process, for example:

Are managers keeping to their staffing forecasts and salary budgets?

Have policies and controls been established, and are procedures being followed for new hires, for example, to ensure that requisitions have been submitted for legitimate replacements?

Are jobs properly analyzed and described, and are job specifications accurate?

Are they updated to reflect changes in job content and skill requirements, so that they provide valid inputs to the determination of manpower requirements?

Is turnover of managers or high-talent personnel increasing and, if so, for what reasons?

Are manpower levels related to levels of operations to yield manpower ratios?

Are college recruitment quotas being met?

Are there backups for all key positions?

What percentage of persons promoted into open jobs were identified for those jobs in the company's succession plans?

In addition to the criteria suggested by these questions, inferences regarding the effectiveness of manpower plans might be drawn from whether the organization is achieving its objectives, whether its structure is lean and flexible, and whether it is properly motivating and rewarding its high-potential personnel.

ESTABLISHING THE MANPOWER PLAN

This section discusses provisions for the management and planning of manpower, and methods of establishing a manpower planning activity.

The Management of Manpower Management

The management of manpower is, of course, the responsibility of all managers. Every manager, in his day-to-day role, influences the human resources assigned to him, and his effectiveness ultimately depends on how well he trains and utilizes them. His effectiveness depends also on the counsel and help he gets from staff in recruiting, selecting, training, and assigning his people. In the past, staff support in these areas was generally provided on an ad hoc basis. It was rarely planned or coordinated, and no one individual or unit had responsibility for the company's overall manpower planning function. Today, however, an increasing number of companies have made provision for this activity at the corporate staff level. In about two-thirds of some fifty companies surveyed for the American Management Association in 1966, the manpower planning and control function was found to be centralized and, in most of them, to report to the principal personnel officer. This is understandable, since the activities involved in implementing the manpower plan are generally assigned to the personnel department. However, where manpower planning is principally an input to an overall business forecast and plan, this function may be carried out by a corporate planning unit.

Wherever the responsibility resides, it is mandatory that the manpower plan be coordinated with the corporate business plan. In addition to tying manpower plans to business plans, it is essential, as Frank Cassell has written, that the personnel department view the functions of employment, training, compensation, and job structure as interacting cost variables that can be adjusted so as to increase the effective supply of labor.

Finally, it is important that the roles of top management, division heads, and personnel units be clearly delineated. In one large company, for example, responsibilities for the manpower planning system are assigned as follows:

1. The manpower resources committee, with the president as chairman, formulates policy relating to the acquisition, development, deployment, and utilization of the company's manpower resources, and periodically reviews reports on the status of overall manpower resources.

2. Division heads are responsible for implementing company-wide manpower resources policy and manpower planning procedures within their divisions.

3. The corporate manpower planning unit is responsible for proposing manpower resources policy and plans, establishing procedures for implementing the plans,

monitoring and reporting on the execution of corporate and division manpower plans, developing improved manpower planning techniques, and counseling and assisting the divisions on manpower plans and problems.

4. Division personnel units provide division management with staff services relating to manpower planning.

Surveys of the manpower planning activity indicate that the number of staff people involved varies greatly, depending upon the scope of the activity, the degree to which it is centralized, the size of the company, the extent to which operating people and top management are involved, and the organization's experience with and acceptance of the manpower planning function. In the 3-M Company, for example, which has been doing manpower planning for almost twenty years, manpower planning is only a part-time activity of two staff people. In the Ford Motor Company, on the other hand, as many as fifty to seventy-five people are involved in one or more aspects of personnel planning. Separate groups are engaged in planning for hourly, salaried, and management personnel. In addition, each functional staff department has one or more "manpower brokers" who maintain the inventories and counsel on career planning.

Introducing Manpower Planning

There are several ways for a company to get started in manpower planning. The person responsible can:

1. Design and install a total corporate manpower planning system, intended to produce annual and long-term corporate manpower plans.

2. Formalize certain existing manpower activities, with the expectation that these may later become building blocks for an integrated manpower planning system.

3. Analyze and solve specific manpower problems, and furnish manpower planning assistance on a project basis.

The first approach, while theoretically seductive, has been found difficult to accomplish. Companies in which manpower planning has not succeeded are likely to be those which adopted a highly theoretical, mathematical, and involved approach to manpower planning. Often it took so long to design the system, and the benefits were so uncertain, that manpower planning came to be regarded as a personnel program rather than a tool for management's use.

The second approach—to begin with one or two parts of the manpower system, especially if not too complex and there is promise of early returns—is often a better way to enlist management interest and support. Professor Vetter suggests that a good starting point is to inventory existing management manpower, since top management's attention is thus almost assured, especially if the analysis indicates lack of depth in critical areas of the organization.

The third way to get started, particularly if faced with a skeptical management, is to help solve some actual and pressing manpower problems. If successful, the manpower planner may have a better chance of later winning support when introducing the overall planning process. One newly appointed head of manpower planning for an oil company began by conducting a survey among division executives of needs and problems in the manpower area. Specific projects he was asked to address himself to included more formalized approaches to management replacement planning, improved mobility of professional and management employees, and the need for simpler, improved employee performance appraisal systems.

Of course, no single approach can fit every company situation. It is suggested, nevertheless, that a strategy for introducing manpower planning should include most of the following steps:

1. First, assess the organization's receptivity to changes, particularly those in the

area of human resources, and identify the executives and organizational units most and least likely to support a manpower planning program.

2. Identify the actual and perceived manpower planning needs and problems of the organization. Is the company in an abnormally tight labor market? Is its technology changing rapidly? Do many positions require a long lead time for training or developing replacements? Is management succession a concern of management?

3. Establish the objectives and scope of the manpower planning process. Should it be to seek lower recruitment costs or a more stable work force? Should it cover all occupational levels or only the management group?

4. Determine the time horizon of the manpower plan. Should it be tied to the annual operating budget or to the long-range corporate business plan, or both?

5. Delineate the respective roles of corporate staff and the divisions in administering the plan.

6. Consider how to enlist the support and involvement of top management in manpower planning.

7. Identify the key interfaces in the company. These would probably include persons responsible for long-range planning, business research, and organization planning, as well as personnel managers and EDP executives.

8. Outline in principle the design of the manpower planning process, for top management approval.

9. Prepare a formal, detailed implementation plan, including provision for progress reporting.

10. Develop methods of monitoring the plan, in order to evaluate the accuracy and practicality of the forecasting and planning process, and to learn whether recommendations are acted upon.

11. Plan for later revision and improvement of the plan. Experience with even the most carefully designed plans will often uncover mistaken assumptions and expectations.

12. Institutionalize the planning process, to make its place secure within the management system.

MANPOWER MANAGEMENT: A STATUS REPORT

This section briefly reviews the state of the art and the uses and benefits of manpower planning systems and utilization techniques. It also cites some of the limitations and problems, and some expected future developments in manpower planning and management.

State of the Art

As with most emerging management concepts, little systematic effort has been made to date to assess the contribution of manpower planning and other manpower management techniques to improving company performance. We know more about the amount of *activity* in this area than we know about the *results* of this activity. Joint studies by members of the Department of Economics at Harvard University and The Conference Board identified several advances in manpower planning in fourteen major companies surveyed in 1965 and 1967. Specifically, they reported a broadening of occupational coverage (Figure 4). Advances were also noted in the techniques of corporate manpower forecasting, as well as greater variety in methods of translating these forecasts into short- and long-term operating plans. The companies surveyed, however, were relatively sophisticated in manpower planning. A larger sampling of 115 companies by the American Management Association and Cresap, McCormick and Paget Inc., in 1966, supplemented by a detailed study of manpower planning in twelve of these companies, indicated that not a great deal

Figure 4.   Occupational categories projected by fourteen companies.

Company and general industry description	Managers	Scientific and technical	Clerical	Total non-exempt	Non-exempt salaried	Non-exempt hourly	Total blue-collar	Skilled	Unskilled
A. Non-ferrous metals......	x	x							
B. Telephone utility......	x	x	x	x					
C. Petroleum....	x	x	. . .	x					
D. Domestic airline......	x	x	x	. . .	. . .	. . .	x	x	x
E. Electrical equipment....	x	x	. . .	x	x	x			
F. Diversified....	x	x							
G. Diversified....	x	x	x	. . .	. . .	. . .	x	x	x
H. Automobiles...	x	x	x	. . .	. . .	. . .	x		
I. Engines......	x	. . .	. . .	. . .	. . .	. . .	x		
J. Electrical equipment	x	. . .	. . .	x					
K. Office machines.....	x	. . .	. . .	x	. . .	. . .	x	x	x
L. Aerospace....	x	x	x	. . .	. . .	. . .	x	x	x
M. Aerospace....	x	x	. . .	. . .	. . .	. . .	x		
N. Diversified....	x	. . .	x	. . .					
Total........	14	10	6	5	1	1	7	4	4

SOURCE: *The Conference Board Record*, August, 1968, p. 39.

of manpower planning was actually being done at that time.   In some companies, programs were only getting under way, and in others a well-conceived program existed but had not been put to practical use.   Interviews in these and other companies three years later, however, indicated that more advanced approaches were being introduced, including quantitative techniques, the factoring in of the external environment, and the use of EDP in manpower inventories.   In addition, manpower planning was often tied to corporate business planning and made part of a total manpower management support system.   Whereas in 1966 it was rare to find companies in which manpower planning involved more than one full-time member of the corporate staff, three years later a number of companies had established manpower planning units.

As is to be expected, the most practical advances in manpower planning and utilization have been in labor-intensive and defense-oriented industries, while more theoretical, longer term manpower forecasting techniques have been developed in larger, more stable companies, especially those with longer planning cycles and more predictable growth rates.

Uses and Benefits

Companies in which manpower planning is a key element in manpower management cite a number of uses or benefits they derive from this activity.   In summary, these include:

The determination of long-term manpower requirements for anticipated operations, and forecasts of compensation costs

Improved manpower utilization, with corresponding reduction in manpower costs

More stable employment (especially in volatile defense businesses)

Development of plans for management succession

Decisions regarding placements, transfers, and promotions (especially mentioned by companies with assessment centers)

Assistance in career planning
Determination of training and development needs
Establishment of college recruitment levels
Input to and assessment of acquisition and expansion plans
Assistance in long-term organization and facilities planning

One manpower planner summed up the benefit of manpower planning to his company by saying that it helped the operating divisions to be aware of their problems, instead of solving the problems for them. Another manpower planner observed succinctly that the real test of the manpower plan was that its benefits outweighed the costs of developing it.

Limitations and Problems

There appear to be some inherent limitations in forecasting and planning manpower requirements. Although many companies are advancing the state of the art on several fronts, it is doubtful whether any has or ever will have a viable blueprint for the planning and utilization of future manpower. A major oil company, for example, has developed manpower forecasts, succession plans, and a skills inventory; it also has career counseling, and operates an assessment center as well as an active management development program. In a very real sense, then, it is continually engaged in manpower planning; yet it does not have a formal manpower planning document.

Among the limitations to manpower planning identified by a number of companies are the following:

1. Long-range forecasts are difficult, and the plans are likely to be inaccurate. They are vulnerable to changes in economic conditions and market conditions, as well as changes in technology and management methods. Because of these and other limitations, no company seems to have forged an effective link between long-term manpower forecasts and near-term manpower plans.

2. Although it is possible to predict the approximate number of vacancies that will occur in an organization as a result of deaths, early retirements, and resignations, there is no way of knowing *which* managers will have to be replaced or *when* this will occur.

3. Forecasts can yield gross estimates of personnel requirements in the future, but management, as one manpower planner commented, "takes action on specifics, not on totals."

4. As Frank Cassell has pointed out, few if any companies have successfully incorporated in their manpower plans the impact of both internal and external labor markets and their interaction.

In addition to limitations in the state of the art, some problems experienced by companies in performing manpower planning are of their own making, for example:

1. Frustrated manpower planners frequently complain of the lack of top management support for their activity and, partially as a result, a lack of confidence among managers in their manpower plans and forecasts.

2. The gap between manpower forecasts and the use of such data by management is sometimes attributable to the overzealousness of staff in designing and introducing elaborate manpower planning techniques. This occurred in an automobile company which for some years had a fairly simple and practical method of forecasting manpower needs. It ran into difficulties when the planners decided to establish a better forecasting system, based on more accurate data, which provided outputs on all manpower transactions by salary grade, location, and other criteria. Additional data were cranked into the system in the belief that they would yield better forecasts, and detailed projections were prepared for each organizational unit. The divisions were then asked to add still more data on such things as plant openings and changes in technology, to quantify this data, and on the basis of formulas they were given, to modify the extrapolation provided by the manpower planners. Losing confidence

in this input, division management not surprisingly lost confidence in the output also. As one manpower planner put it, "The damned thing was so elaborate nobody wanted to do it." The company then went back to the old system, which leaned heavily on past experience and discussions with the managers who made the decisions for their operating units.

3. As might be expected, the impact of manpower planning on an organization is often governed by the level at which the activity reports. In one petroleum company, for example, responsibility for manpower planning is divided among several units reporting four levels below the president. As a result, the planners complain, management makes no use of their manpower forecasts.

4. One of the more frequent miscalculations in manpower planning occurs when the corporate staff simply aggregates forecasts submitted by the operating divisions without subjecting them to critical scrutiny. A somewhat related mistake was made by a manpower planner who assumed that a forecasting system that was useful in one division was applicable to all, and ended up with a totally unrealistic corporate manpower plan.

5. Perhaps one of the most common problems in manpower planning arises when it is regarded simply as a technical problem, rather than also a problem in effecting organizational change.

Future Developments

The future importance of manpower planning is almost assured. The need on the part of management to control costs in a time of full employment and swift technological changes can be expected to lead to increased emphasis on better manpower management. Manpower planning is likely to receive the same attention in the future as financial planning, marketing planning, and product planning do today. Other developments, many of them already nascent, will probably include the following:

1. Sophisticated control systems to monitor manpower performance

2. More reliable manpower plans resulting from improvements in input data (for example, in the identification of potential, performance appraisals, and forecasting techniques)

3. Better productivity measures and other tools to help reduce labor costs

4. New organizational concepts such as matrix management, project teams and other forms of temporary organizations, resulting in improved mobility and manpower utilization; also, more imaginative job designs, and ways of enriching job content at all levels

5. Better planning and tracking of manpower movements in an organization

6. Possible management-union collaboration in eliminating work rules restricting manpower movements and utilization; also, better techniques for stabilizing employment to counter the effect of Subsidiary Unemployment Benefits provisions, and accelerated automation to counter escalating wage costs

7. Linkage of near-term planning to long-term forecasts through the use of simulation techniques and personnel data systems

8. Closer collaboration between manpower and corporate planning staffs, resulting in better integration of manpower planning and business planning

9. Improved ability to anticipate future organizational structures and to determine the qualifications of the persons needed to fill them

10. Manpower plans for specific types and levels of employees, such as professional, technical, and other "knowledge" workers, and techniques for utilizing them more effectively.

SUMMARY

Effective management of an enterprise ultimately depends on how well its human resources are managed. They represent, as has been said, an asset that can appreciate if properly nurtured and utilized. This is especially true of managerial resources, since the future of an organization is shaped by the care with which it plans for, deploys, and motivates its high-talent manpower.

The scarcity of talent, the difficulty of discovering it, and the time required to develop it fully have forced companies to think about their manpower in a systematic way. Many now inventory their manpower resources, develop and appraise their executives, draw up management succession plans, and calculate the replacements that will be needed for retirements and other causes. A few companies adopt a broader approach to the manpower planning process, beginning with their business plans and manpower projections based on economic and labor market forecasts. The manpower forecast is then combined with an analysis of future organization plans, and translated into staffing plans which define the skills and qualifications of those needed to man the future organization. The process includes action plans for the recruitment or training of the required personnel. In addition, progressive companies also try to meet their manpower requirements by improving manpower utilization, using many of the strategies available to them for motivating people and changing their behavior, such as job enrichment, training, incentive pay plans, career counseling, promotions, and performance planning and review systems.

Although manpower management can never be a science, behavioral research and systematic approaches to manpower forecasting and planning are contributing substantially to the better utilization and control of our human resources.

BIBLIOGRAPHY

Bennis, Warren: *Organization Development: Its Nature, Origins and Prospects,* Addison-Wesley Publishing Company, Inc., Reading, Mass., 1969.

Burton, Wendel W.: *Forecasting Manpower Needs: A Tested Formula,* American Management Association, Personnel Series 172, New York, 1957.

Cassell, Frank H.: *Corporate Manpower Planning,* Industrial Relations Center, University of Minnesota, Minneapolis, February, 1968.

Doeringer, P. B., M. J. Piore and J. G. Scoville: "Corporate Manpower Forecasting and Planning," *The Conference Board Record,* New York, August, 1968.

Foulkes, Fred K.: *Creating More Meaningful Work,* American Management Association, New York, 1969.

Geisler, Edwin B.: *Manpower Planning: An Emerging Staff Function,* American Management Association, Management Bulletin 101, New York, 1967.

Haire, Mason: *Coming of Age in the Social Sciences,* Massachusetts Institute of Technology, Cambridge, Mass., 1967.

———— : "The Management of Human Resources: A Symposium," *Industrial Management Review,* Cambridge, Mass., Winter, 1970.

Sinha, N. P.: *Manpower Planning: A Research Bibliography* (rev. ed.), Bulletin 52, Industrial Relations Center, University of Minnesota, Minneapolis, January, 1970.

Tulk, Allan V.: *Information Systems for Better Management of Manpower Resources,* American Management Association, Management Bulletin 79, New York, 1966.

Vetter, Eric W.: *Manpower Planning for High Talent Personnel,* Bureau of Industrial Relations, Graduate School of Business Administration, The University of Michigan, Ann Arbor, 1967.

chapter 10

Management Succession

JAMES C. WORTHY *Vice President, Cresap, McCormick and Paget Inc.,*
Chicago, Illinois

Organizational survival, continuity, and viability are among the primary responsibilities of top management of all corporations and of most other organizations and institutions. These responsibilities to the organization's employees, stockholders, or sponsors and customers, clients, or beneficiaries cannot be fulfilled effectively unless adequate provision is made for management succession. Responsible managers cannot leave the development of the future management of their organizations to chance. Future management needs can be forecast and budgeted as well as capital needs, and managerial resources can be managed to ensure that the organization has the right number and the right kind of management employees at the right time and in the right positions to provide for continued organizational strength.

In recent years, as the necessity of providing for effective management succession has become more acute, organizations have become increasingly aware of their needs in this area. Members of the academic community in various disciplines as well as professional managers and practitioners have addressed the problem, and new approaches and techniques have been developed and applied. It has been recognized that managerial resources, unlike other organizational assets, have the potential to increase in value through use; the more intensively the capabilities and capacities of management resources are used, the more valuable they become.

In this chapter, we will discuss the need for developing and implementing effective management succession programs, describe several approaches and their strengths and weaknesses, and review certain significant new developments.

NEED FOR MANAGEMENT SUCCESSION PLANNING

In the past, many organizations relied on intuition and a haphazard approach to management development and succession. They have had a tradition of planning for organizational success and expansion in terms of market growth, diversification, and the availability of capital, without consideration of their potential management needs; they have tended to rely on the flexibility of their management group and on a relatively loose labor market to protect them from the results of failing to plan for their managerial needs. They have not assumed responsibility for management planning for the benefit of the organization, nor for planned career development in the interests of their employees. Organizations such as these now often find they are losing out to competitors who are using more progressive and more systematic methods. The problems associated with inadequate management succession planning are accelerating for several reasons.

The quantity of available management manpower is declining because of the low birth rate in the United States during the 1930s. In the 1970s there will be a million less men age thirty-five to forty-five than there were in the mid-1960s. This age group is particularly significant, as it is from this pool that most of the top managers in the 1970s will be selected. At the same time, the number of managers required in business, government, education, and other types of organizations is increasing at a relatively rapid rate.

The age-distribution factor is a problem in some firms. Fifteen years of restricted hiring of young managerial talent during the depression of World War II has resulted in an additional shortage of experienced executives in their fifties. This has become particularly acute as managers who started their careers in the 1920s have reached retirement age.

The accelerating rate of change, both within organizations and in the environment within which they function, has created an ever-increasing need for management succession programs that are fully integrated and systematic, but flexible and effectively implemented. Technological changes, creating new products, markets, and techniques, are changing demands on management groups, particularly in expanding organizations. Advances in information technology, providing new internal tools for management's use, are changing management concepts and requirements. Changes in the social, economic, and political environment will require professional managers whose career experiences, as well as personal skills, have equipped them to cope successfully with environmental changes. Finally, the expectations, as well as managerial and personal philosophies, of today's younger managerial employees have changed. They are no longer content to be placed in a starting position in an organization, with an indication that, if they do well, they have unlimited opportunity to rise to the top—then are left on their own to do so. They expect to be able to mature and progress in a professional management atmosphere, receiving guidance, education and training, and career planning activities that will permit them to realize their full potential. If, after some exposure in an organization, they feel their expectations will be left to chance, they may decide that opportunities may be better elsewhere.

Each organization must have a well-designed and understood system of management succession, which carefully spells out principles and guidelines. All levels of management must know each of the processes and understand how they fit into the total system. A hard-hitting total effort, which is more powerful than the total of the independent parts, will result.

APPROACHES TO MANAGEMENT SUCCESSION

In this section we will discuss tools and techniques used by various organizations in management succession programs and discuss methods of integrating these approaches into a total management of managerial resources system. In discussing each activity, technique, or tool in the management succession process we must consider it from the standpoint of three time frames:

Immediate: within one year
Intermediate: one year to five years
Long range: beyond five years

It has been our experience that many organizations gear most, though not necessarily all, of their management succession activities to the immediate future. This is not difficult to understand because management manpower projections and plans which are integrated closely with the annual planning and budgeting cycle of the total organization can be relatively precise and accurate. However, any realistic succession program has intermediate and long-range effects and must be planned accordingly.

In reviewing the approach to a total management succession program, we will consider the following elements:

Management manpower planning
Staffing and development
Organizational performance
Appraisal and analysis
Manpower inventory

All organizations engage in many or all of these aspects of personnel management, either on a formal or on an informal basis. Few of these firms, however, tend to think of their activities in these areas as parts of an overall approach to the management of managerial resources which will provide for an integrated and effective management succession program. Typically, each is considered a separate activity without regard for its interaction with other elements. In this discussion of the major elements of an overall management succession program, it will be important to keep in mind the continuing interaction and effect of one element on another, as indicated in Figure 1.

Management Manpower Planning

Management manpower planning must be the foundation upon which the total management succession program is built. The objective of this process should be fully developed management staffing plans. These plans should be prepared on an individual basis for all anticipated needs in the immediate year ahead and for key positions in the intermediate and long-range future. They should also be prepared

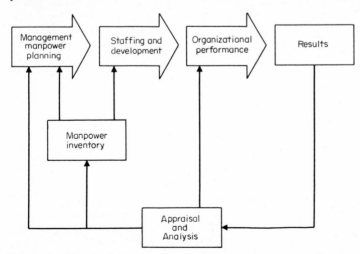

Figure 1. Management succession system.

on a numerical basis for all other management positions for the intermediate and long-range future.

As a first step in management manpower planning, the potential effects of external factors, such as *economic forecasts* and overall *labor market forecasts* should be reviewed and considered.   At the same time, the business plans should be reviewed to determine their effect on managerial needs.   As business plans for both the near and the long term are developed, the *organization plans* and *manpower forecasts* should be determined.   All this preliminary analysis and planning should permit the development of appropriate *staffing plans.*   Figure 2 illustrates the sequence of events in management manpower planning.

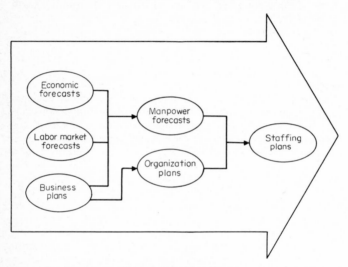

Figure 2.   Management manpower planning.

Although we look upon management manpower planning as an integral part of the total management of managerial resources program, its practice varies in different organizations.   In many organizations this activity is confined to forecasting management needs for the year ahead based upon known openings.   Such forecasts, which are normally integrated with annual organizational plans and budgets, can be quite accurate in setting up staffing and development plans for the year ahead. However, because of the long-term requirements of many development activities, intermediate and long-range forecasts must be made.   As the forecasting time span increases, the forecasts become more judgmental and subject to inaccuracies.

Much of the work that has been done in intermediate and long-range forecasting has been concentrated in the numeric area, with emphasis on the numbers of people who will be needed at various organizational levels.   Such forecasts can be reasonably accurate for the intermediate future if the forecasters have access to business and organization plans as well as turnover data and other statistics.   Most organizations project their plans for product demand, expansion, new facilities, products, and markets, etc., up to five years in advance.   It is relatively easy, then, to determine additional management needs; the accuracy of the forecast will vary with the accuracy of the information provided.   To this, however, must be added less accurate inputs, based upon historic statistics: turnover, internal movement, and anticipated development of present and potential managers.

Annual management staffing plans, therefore, can be numerically general, particularly at lower levels and for long-range needs, and fairly specific for immediate needs.

Several large firms have been relatively successful at forecasting numerically general needs for annual college recruiting programs, based at lower and middle management levels. Gross number forecasts of potential openings are refined by application of historical information as to turnover and normal progression of incumbents and new college recruits. It is assumed that the movement of each year's crop of management recruits through the organization will be adequate to meet future needs as they develop. The success of this approach to management succession, of course, is dependent upon implementation of an effective, fully integrated management of managerial resources program as well as upon the adequacy of the forecasts. It also requires continuity of staffing effort from year to year. Normally, however, starting a college recruiting program is not sufficient to provide for all the management needs of an organization; staffing plans for specific, immediate, and anticipated openings at the middle and senior management levels, based upon additional manpower planning inputs, must also be made.

Fairly reliable numeric forecasts of management requirements can be consolidated after thoughtful analysis of all these inputs. Gross historical information should be used cautiously, however, as trends of the past can be deceptive when applied to the future. They do not take individual changes into account. Such changes, related to individual performance and expectations, should be an objective of the management succession program. Inputs from organization plans and the manpower inventory must be added before staffing plans can be completed. Organizational restructuring, based upon anticipated technological change or management emphasis, should be considered. Potential movement of key positions, which will create vacancies, beginning with the chief executive officer, and movement of incumbents of lower level positions up to these vacancies should be determined. These inputs will provide additional information to be considered in the preparation of staffing plans.

The process described briefly above must, of necessity, vary between organizations, and is more difficult as organizational size and complexity increase. Segmentation can simplify the problem in large organizations if each segment has the necessary information and time. However, centralized coordination is normally required to provide balance, guidance, specific inputs in some cases, and forecasting and staffing plans for higher organizational levels.

Staffing and Development

An effective staffing and development activity should provide sufficient numbers of qualified candidates to fill current and anticipated vacancies promptly, and provide for evaluating them to ensure selection of the best candidate in each case. It results in the establishment of a comprehensive program to provide necessary basic training, both for managerial personnel currently employed and for new personnel hired as immediate replacements or as trainees, as well as opportunities for furthering the individual development of all managerial employees. The end result should be to provide for utilization of managerial personnel most effectively, to ensure promotion for those best qualified, and to provide job progression opportunities for all.

Staffing and development is obviously a twofold process. The first phase includes the actions involved in the initial and continued *employment* of managerial personnel, that is, the *recruitment, selection,* and *placement* of candidates from the outside, as well as selection and movement of present personnel through *promotion* and *transfer.* The employment function must guide managerial personnel to the job progression opportunities which will enable them to achieve their own objectives while helping the organization to reach its goals. It is the point in the process of managing managerial resources at which the data collected and the subsequent planning must be translated into action.

The second phase of this function involves the *development* of managerial personnel, through approaches such as: *formal training,* both within the organization and outside; *planned work experience,* or on-the-job learning; *performance planning,* or the setting of objectives, followed by *appraisal* of performance; and last—but quite important, least expensive, and probably least utilized—*counseling* and coaching. The thrust in this area should be to establish opportunities for individuals to develop themselves, and to correlate the potential rewards with the effort involved. Thus, a capable development function determines managerial development needs, collects information on available techniques and programs, and analyzes the effectiveness of the various programs in meeting the needs. Such a function also develops and provides appropriate programs and advises individual executives or groups of managers regarding the availability of additional appropriate development activities.

It is generally recognized that the selection of junior management trainees should be based upon, hopefully, realistic appraisals of potential for advancement in management at least two levels above trainee status. There must be an assumption of possible further progression in time. However, advancement potential requirements for middle and senior management and executive candidates must be determined for each situation independently. Consideration should also be given to a realistic assessment of advancement opportunities which may, or may not, relate to the candidate's expectations.

The need for top management support of, and participation in, the development function is recognized as essential to its success. One result of this support is the provision of consistently adequate budgets which must be justified in terms of results. In some organizations that provide apparently adequate budgets for the development functions, however, resistance of line management to some development activities is created by salary control requirements. Management trainees at various levels and individuals placed in positions in anticipation of movement to higher levels are often either added to an organization or paid higher salaries than their positions would normally justify. The increased payroll cost, particularly in a profit center, should be recognized. Pressure on the line manager for payroll con-

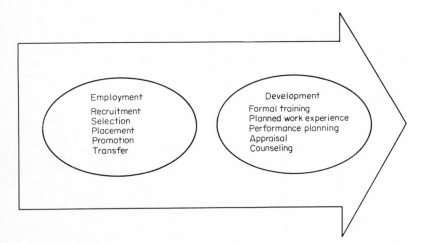

Figure 3. Staffing and development.

trol can be relieved through accounting procedures which identify the required excess payroll or through centralized subsidy of the excess payroll.

Organizational Performance

The establishment of a hospitable environment for the individual, with careful and continuing attention to the factors affecting that environment, should provide for retention of the most desirable employees and outstanding performance from the management group.

An *environment* which results in effective organizational performance consists of many elements, both tangible and intangible. It is probably true that they do not exist in perfect form in any one organization at any one time, but each organization should be aware of the environment it provides. The *climate* must afford opportunities for meaningful achievement and treatment of each manager as an individual. The level of *organizational capability* should provide a challenge to each manager to keep up rather than permitting him to function with passivity at less than his true potential. The *attitudes* of managers should reflect a greater interest in where the company is going than in what it has been. *Motivation,* in the form of challenging jobs, should foster a feeling of achievement, responsibility, growth, and earned recognition. Managers must see the relationship of *rewards* to performance results. Effective *communications* should permit uncomfortable questions to be asked and honest answers to be given.

Obviously, the *factors affecting environment,* which are under the control of the organization, must be geared to achievement of the environment indicated above. *Organization development* must keep pace with the actual growth and complexity of the business rather than be structured in an inflexible fashion to solve problems that no longer exist. The rewards offered by *compensation plans* must be related to performance and must provide incentive for improved performance and assumption of greater responsibility. The *communications system* must permit rapid and accurate transmission of pertinent information upward and across organizational lines as well as downward. The *managerial style* of key executives should stimulate enthusiasm, indicate a willingness to listen to new ideas, and acknowledge that risk taking may result in error. The *organization structure* should be flexible, permitting it to move quickly to solve problems. *Policies and procedures* should provide an

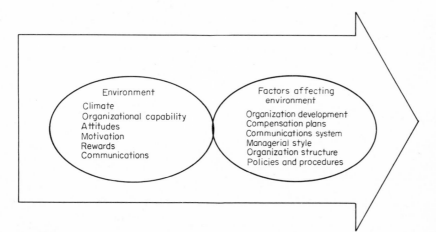

Figure 4. Organizational performance.

effective framework within which managers can operate easily, rather than bonds which restrict movement and action.

Considerable attention must be paid to these factors to ensure that management employees perform and develop effectively, both as individuals and as the group responsible for present and future performance. The establishment and maintenance of a satisfactory environment, while difficult and time consuming, is necessary for the successful implementation of a management succession program.

Appraisal and Analysis

Appraisal and analysis of results achieved should provide an organization with essential feedback on the performance and potential of management personnel, on the need for changes in plans, and on the need to modify any of the factors which affect organizational performance. At the same time, effective appraisal and analysis of individual performance results should be reviewed with each manager to provide him with a clear understanding of the level of his performance and any areas requiring improvement, and should provide for recognition and reward if any has been earned. It should also form the basis for mutually determined development needs and objectives for the period ahead.

Appraisal and analysis is a process that is constantly taking place, formally or informally. It works best, however, when it measures achieved results against clearly defined standards, plans, and objectives. Performance planning, or the setting of specific goals and objectives, is a key requirement for the effective appraisal and analysis of results. Moreover, performance planning is essential not only as a step in this process of feeding back information for future development and improvement, but also as a tool for the control and direction of current operations.

Appraisal usually begins with an evaluation of *results versus expectations*. Obviously, two other major factors must also be considered if the appraisal is to be meaningful. First, *external conditions affecting results* should be determined and considered. Second, the *quality of plans* which were originally established should have been at an acceptable level. As the final but most important aspect of appraisal, overall *performance evaluation* must be undertaken to establish how well the manager has performed in achieving previously agreed-upon objectives for which he was assigned and had accepted responsibility.

Analysis of the results achieved should follow appraisal. Many companies unfortunately stop with the appraisal, and fail to ask the crucial questions: What are the *causes of results?* What *strengths* are indicated? What *problems* still exist? What are the *implications* for the future? Unless analysis follows appraisal, the necessary feedback for improvement or change is not likely to be gained.

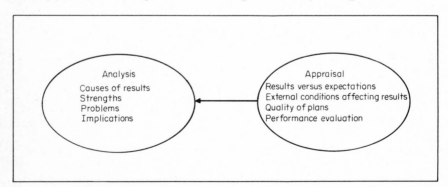

Figure 5.   Appraisal and analysis.

Realistic analysis, as well as appraisal, of a manager's performance is an essential part of the assessment of his potential for advancement. In addition to obviously inadequate recommendations based upon superficial qualities or long and satisfactory service, recommendations of advancement potential which are based strictly upon outstanding performance on a job can result in placing managers beyond their capacity. An analysis of strengths and weaknesses and their implications must be made and related to the requirements of the position or level to which the man is considered promotable. Additional skills or experiences required and the time needed to achieve them must be determined. Specific development plans must be established and followed.

```
Personnel data
Performance
Potential
Skills
Career goals
Career plans
Retrieval system
```

Figure 6. Manpower inventory.

Management Manpower Inventory

A management manpower inventory, properly prepared and maintained, should help identify the best qualified employees for filling present and potential management vacancies. It should also indicate what training and development activities are necessary to prepare current employees for prospective vacancies. Finally, it should offer early warning that certain vacancies cannot be filled from within, eliminating loss of time before beginning an outside search.

Of primary importance in establishing a management manpower inventory is careful determination of the information needed to reach decisions on promotion or transfer of managers, on the need for training and development programs, on the extent of external recruiting, etc. Obviously, basic *personnel data* are needed, ranging from personal information such as age, education, and family status to work experience and demonstrated job skills. As a separate element, a history of each manager's level of *performance* should be developed. If possible, performance should be noted in quantitative terms, but information pertaining to the analysis of performance should be added. Indicated *skills and potential* for advancement should be determined and included in the inventory. Each manager's *career goals* and objectives should be recorded, and *career plans* should be established. As a final step, a *retrieval system* should be developed to provide easy access to pertinent information.

Management manpower inventories can range from complex computer programmed systems to simple typed sheets that can be reviewed in several minutes; organizational size and complexity are determining factors. Regardless of the type of system used, however, appropriate, accurate, and up-to-date information is necessary for practical use of an inventory, which should be considered the focal point in an integrated management succession program. The information in a manpower inventory must be put to effective use; it must be available to the decision makers in the manpower planning, staffing, and development functions.

In relatively large organizations, the information available in a manpower inventory can be summarized in several reports.

An *analysis table* provides basic data that show advancement data for each manager in the organization. It lists each individual and provides pertinent personal and personnel information. In addition, it indicates potential for advancement, including future possible positions or levels and when the person should be ready for promotion. The analysis table can be used as input for determining training and development needs and activities, as well as the source of information for manning tables and replacement charts.

A *manning table* identifies all incumbent managers included in the system and indicates anticipated tenure in their present positions. It identifies candidates for emergency replacements and for future replacements, if the incumbents should leave, and indicates the time when they should be ready for promotion. Although it does not identify the precise man who will fill the vacancy, it serves as a tool for determining the best qualified candidates for consideration when needed. The manning table can permit formulation of shortage reports or replacement charts from which hiring and training programs can be developed.

Replacement charts are a useful tool showing positions for which short-term needs (up to two years) can be met, and those for which they cannot. They specify whether there is a promotable replacement for each position ready immediately or within two years and identify cases where there is only a temporary replacement ready or none.

The need for these management inventory reports and their complexity, of course, will vary, depending upon the size and complexity of an organization. They can be segmented by functional unit or by other appropriate organizational segments. In many large organizations, however, even though management inventories may be maintained by organizational segments, it is advisable to maintain centralized inventories to provide for interorganizational movement of qualified managers; this is particularly necessary above the junior management level.

Although all the information indicated above is essential to an effective manpower inventory, the necessity of realistic appraisal of advancement potential cannot be overemphasized. Many different systems or approaches are available for assessing promotability. Because no single method is perfect, they are generally most effective when used in combinations and, regardless of what combination is used, one of the elements should be the appraisal and analysis of performance results.

The management of managerial resources concept, described in this section, provides a fully integrated management succession program. It commits the top management of an organization to a realistic approach to managing the organization's human resources as thoughtfully and effectively as they have managed other resources in the past.

TOP MANAGEMENT SUCCESSION

Selection and development of a potential successor, or successors, to the chief executive officer is a unique and difficult problem which must be resolved by every organization regardless of size. The importance of this process to the long-range success of any organization is obvious. Yet, all too frequently it is delayed until after the time remaining is too short for orderly action. Top management succession, therefore, is a topic that warrants separate consideration, even though the basic principles outlined in the preceding section are necessary ingredients.

Planning for succession to the top position should begin almost immediately after the incumbent is appointed. Even though it may be anticipated that he will function effectively in that position for an extended period of time, contingency plans should be made to deal with possible untoward developments. The plans should be revised periodically as the needs of the organization and the strengths and characteristics of potential successors change. It is wise for an organization to have options, but to keep its options open, to make no commitments on succession until it has to, to push the development of several possible successors, and to select, when the time comes, that individual whose particular strengths and characteristics best meet the needs of the organization as they at that time appear to be.

Of primary importance in planning for succession to the position of chief executive officer is a realistic audit of the abilities and potential of the key management group to identify individuals who appear to have potential which, with refinement and development, could qualify them for the position. Identification of these individuals does not necessarily mean that they will qualify for advancement to chief executive officer, but it provides a pool of potential resources from which future higher levels of leadership may possibly be drawn. If no near-term emergency occurs, there should be sufficient time to round out the preparation of several members of this group with good likelihood that they will be adequately qualified to take over in due course.

Specifications for Chief Executive Officer

Without attempting to catalog the various attributes and virtues desirable in the top executive of an organization, the following paragraphs consider some general requirements, under three headings: experience, age, and personal qualities.

It is generally recognized that, for fairly obvious reasons, the experience required to run one organization is quite likely to be different from that required to run another. What is less generally recognized, however, is the fact that the experience required to run the same organization at different stages of its development may also be quite different. Each organization must be able to determine if technical, financial, sales, production, or general business know-how, or a combination, is most important. In addition, it must be emphasized that experience at managing activities on a relatively autonomous basis, with freedom to function with a fairly wide range of independence and responsibility for results, is of paramount importance.

Age is another important element in the selection of a successor for the top position. It is most advantageous if the successor can look forward to a fairly substantial period of time in office before reaching the normal age of retirement. This is not meant as a rigid requirement, but to make the point that a really good man should have enough time to make a significant contribution to the development of the organization. Any such major contributions inevitably take time, and if a chief executive's time is too short his potential contribution is limited accordingly. An expected service of fifteen to twenty years is suggested as a guide; on this basis, the successor should ideally be forty-five or fifty at the time he moves into the top position.

As for experience, a different constellation of characteristics may be required by different organizations and by the same organization at different times. It is almost impossible to duplicate personal characteristics in successive leaders, and if it were possible, it would be a mistake to try to do so. Two characteristics, however, are essential to any successor: the ability to delegate responsibility and authority and personal concern for the development of people.

NEW DEVELOPMENTS IN MANAGEMENT SUCCESSION

As with any area of human endeavor, the processes of management succession, as well as the practices of management, are in a state of constant evolution. Although this chapter does not provide space for amplification, the growing contributions of the behavioral sciences must be noted, particularly in the areas of selection, assessment of performance and potential, individual motivation and development, group dynamics, and the emerging field covered by the general title of organization development. Continued interaction and mutual support between behavioral scientists and practicing managers should provide further accelerating developments in these areas. The application of modeling techniques for managing human resources, as well as for forecasting management needs, is a relatively new field, but should aid top management in treating the organization as a system, in determining alternative strategies and their benefits, and in the development of effective management manpower policies. Models have been developed with analytic as well as accounting functions.   The accounting models show the results of a given set of personnel policies over a period of time.   The analytic models describe results under feedback conditions or under constraint conditions.   Both of them can indicate potentially workable manpower policies and diagnoses.

GENERAL OBSERVATIONS

Management succession is essentially a top management function, a direct responsibility of the chief executive officer and the top management group.   In carrying out this responsibility, the top management group must guard against a normal bias, i.e., the tendency to give preference to the people who are similar to themselves in background and thinking.   This is a human tendency, but it can present a serious organizational problem: conformity that can seriously inhibit adaptability, innovation, and growth potential.   A premium must be placed on diversity — diversity in experience, education, interests, and temperament.   Innovation must not be discouraged.   Maintaining the vitality and creativity, and thereby the longevity, of the organization is at stake.

A policy of promotion from within is generally considered to be in an organization's best interest.   It is a useful policy and an effective administrative procedure helping to ensure that people in key positions will have an applicable background of experience in, and knowledge of, the organization.   It provides an opportunity for people to rise in the organization and ensures that qualified employees will be considered when opportunities arise and promoted if they are qualified. However, a policy of automatic promotion in lockstep fashion, regardless of qualifications, can have serious repercussions.   If, after realistic appraisal of all candidates from within, it is found that there is no one who is qualified, candidates from outside the organization should be recruited and a qualified individual should be selected.

A policy of promotion from within can present another serious problem: a tendency to give undue weight to length of service.   People who have ability must be recognized early and must have opportunities for continuous growth; the organization cannot afford to have that growth stifled by a system in which seniority plays a determining role in advancement.   This is particularly true of the top positions in an organization.   High leadership capacity matures early.   If an individual demonstrates outstanding leadership capacity, the system must be open enough to permit him to move ahead rapidly, vaulting over many who may be his senior in age and service.   If this does not happen, he is not likely to stay with the organization long; he is likely to do his "vaulting" by moving to another organization.   A potentially topflight man may be lost.

The chief executive officer plays the key role in the management succession process.   He has the ultimate responsibility for seeing that this important need of the enterprise is met.   He is responsible for seeing that the system functions not only with efficiency but with integrity as well.   In no phase of business life is integrity as important as in making promotion decisions.   Nothing destroys confidence in management more quickly than evidence—even suspicion—of favoritism.   The people in the organization must have confidence that those promoted actually merit promotion, that selections are made carefully, thoughtfully, and fairly, that what is important is not whom you know but what you are.   It is the business of the chief executive to make sure that the system operates in this way; if he does not do it, no one else can.

BIBLIOGRAPHY

Argyris, Chris: *Integrating the Individual and Organization,* John Wiley & Sons, Inc., New York, 1964.

Crooks, Lois: *Issues and Problems in Managerial Manpower Planning,* Educational Testing Service, Princeton, N.J. 1967.

Drucker, Peter F.: *The Practice of Management,* Harper & Brothers, New York, 1954.

Ewing, David W. (ed.): *Long-range Planning for Management,* Harper & Brothers, New York, 1958.

Haire, Mason, (ed.): *Modern Organizational Theory,* John Wiley & Sons, Inc., New York, 1959.

Likert, Rensis: *New Patterns of Management,* McGraw-Hill Book Company, New York, 1961.

——— : *Manpower Planning and Forecasting in the Firm: An Exploratory Probe,* Industrial Relations Center, University of Minnesota, Minneapolis, 1968.

——— : *Manpower Planning: An Emerging Staff Function,* American Management Association, New York, 1967.

McGregor, Douglas M.: *The Human Side of Enterprise,* McGraw-Hill Book Company, New York, 1960.

——— : *Organization and Manpower Planning,* Business Publications Limited, London, 1966.

Payne, Bruce: *Planning for Company Growth,* McGraw-Hill Book Company, New York, 1963.

Part 4

Recruitment, Selection, and Placement

chapter 11

Development of an Employment Policy

ROGER H. HAWK *Manager, Individual Resources Development and Education Operation, General Electric Company, Management Development Institute, Ossining, New York*

Cultural anthropologists in their studies of societies, both primitive and contemporary, have reported the universality of a division of labor within societal groups. The considerable variety in the assignment of work in different cultures is an interesting study in itself, but this organizational phenomenon is so pervasive that it should not surprise us when we discover that the roots of employment policy lie within the culture itself.

Contemporary man is man in organization; so employment, by definition, becomes a social concept. Personnel administrators might be more comfortable if they could believe that the policies they propose and subscribe to were invented in a pragmatic way to meet the needs of the enterprise. Even casual observation of rapidly changing practices tends to deny them this comfort. But employment policies are formulated and, for the most part, seem to meet the needs of the organization and the people to whom they apply.

Employment policy, as a subfunction of general personnel policy, has received little attention in the literature on personnel administration as a subject for further development. This neglect probably is due to the close relationship of policy and practice to the beliefs of a particular culture about the organization of work. Practices that are accepted in the United States, for example, would be totally unacceptable in Europe to management and employees alike. The major challenge to date, therefore, has been to make relevant to the employment situation explicit attitudes and behavior that are already widely accepted in the culture.

As recently as 1950, a popular work on business management treated employment policy as follows:

> *Employment policies:* Before an employment manager can start hiring for the openings in a company, he must know both the written and unwritten employment policies

of that company and its various divisions.   Does the company attempt to maintain a balance of the minority groups in the community in its company population?   Does the company employ all religious groups?   Is the particular opening suitable for members of all races?   Are the sexes considered equal?   Are there promotional policies that make physically or mentally handicapped individuals unemployable?   Are left-handed or glasses-wearing employees subjected to unusual safety risks?   Must the oil-allergic or chemical-sensitive be limited to specific departments?   What about the color-blind?   The illiterate?   The foreign-speaking only?   The answers to these and similar questions constitute a company's employment policy.[1]

The most inexperienced personnel administrator in today's environment would find little help or satisfaction from the above.   And while the questions posed here are still relevant, a quarter century of evolution makes this summary appear superficial and inadequate.

Modern management is increasingly sensitive to our changing environment, and the personnel administrator must be astute and responsive to a leadership role in anticipating changes that will have an impact on employment philosophy and practice.

For many, a new, and hopefully rewarding, requirement will be that they understand more fully the system of personal and social relations that influences and controls the behavior of group members.   If personnel administrators rise to this challenge, policies and practices in the employment arena are certain to be improved.

DISTINGUISHING AMONG POLICIES, PROCEDURES, AND PRACTICES

In its excellent summary report on personnel policy, the National Industrial Conference Board has introduced seven criteria to determine the use of the word "policy."   They are:

1. A policy is a statement of a company's intent or goal as a guide to individual action.
2. Policies are in writing.
3. Policies are stated in broad terms.
4. Policies are inviolate, insofar as this is within the power of management.
5. Policy formulation requires an unusually high level of thinking and contemplation.
6. Policies are approved by the highest authority in the organization.
7. Policies are long range, long term.[2]

To this list we would add: the content of policies is to be communicated to all members of the enterprise who are or may be affected.   Perhaps it is obvious that in achieving the objectives of management, the mere formulation of a policy statement is inadequate.   But it seems important to acknowledge that the statement must be fully communicated so that all can address themselves to the stated objectives.   The requirement for full communication cannot be overstated.

Personnel administrators are generally conversant with the distinctions between policies and procedures and between them and practices.   Specific, uniform, and obligatory courses of action required to achieve common objectives are defined by policy statements and supported by procedures.   A policy tells why a certain course of action must be taken, and the procedure details how this is accomplished.   A practice, of course, describes what is actually done; it may or may not be related to a policy or procedure.

[1] L. L. Bethel, G. H. E. Smith, F. S. Atwater, and H. A. Stackman, *Industrial Organization and Management*, McGraw-Hill Book Company, 1950, p. 489.

[2] "Statements of Personnel Policy," *Studies in Personnel Policy*, No. 169, National Industrial Conference Board, 1959.

The personnel administrator must discipline himself to keep these distinctions in mind in the conduct of his work. Otherwise, certain practices may evolve within the organization that are counter to the intent of management. Frequent monitoring of procedures and practices is necessary to assure that employment policies are being observed.

ESTABLISHING EMPLOYMENT POLICY

The impact of culture makes it virtually impossible to conceive of an organization being initiated in the absence of preconceived objectives in the employment arena.

In contemporary, complex societies, the role of social control is increasingly exercised in law, contract, and regulations. Governmental components at all levels have produced constraining legislation that tends to define the limits of freedom of choice in employment policy. Legal restraints arise when organizations are no longer responsive to the needs of the individuals who make up and support the organization. Abuses of acceptable social behavior, whether accidental or intentional, inevitably lead to restrictive legislation.

One need only consider the evolution of child labor laws to recognize the degree of responsiveness to the perceived needs of society. In frontier days in the United States, children were important citizens in the performance of necessary work. They were assigned a myriad of chores, such as bringing in wood and water, making fires, pounding corn, and tending stock. As the society became more urbanized and mechanized, there was a diminishing need to use children in this way, and many young people were diverted to industrial employment. At the same time, sentiment for primary and secondary education for all youth was growing to the point where compulsory school attendance and minimum-age work laws were established. If employers had adequately anticipated these changes in attitude, the legislation might not have been necessary.

AVOIDANCE STRATEGY

It is easy to visualize the development of an employment philosophy based solely on avoidance of conflict with existing laws, that is, to develop policies that will help assure that responsible hiring managers avoid all actions that might be suspect if subjected to ethical and legal tests. Such policies would, in 1970, constrain the manager from discrimination in hiring based on race, creed, color, national origin, age (within certain ranges), union affiliation, prior employment with a competitor, and the like. Also, the most recent executive order requires that certain steps be taken to ensure that certain minorities receive special employment efforts.[3]

It is only prudent, of course, to assure that employment policy does not run afoul of federal, state, and local laws on the subject. Statutory requirements will of necessity, then, form the basis for development of an employment philosophy.

PARTICIPATIVE STRATEGY

The modern personnel administrator is encouraged to take a more expansive and developmental view of policy. As the role of the personnel administrator in the conduct of business expands, so also does the requirement that policy reflect the needs of people, both within and outside the organization.

It is assumed here that the administrator is strongly motivated to continually upgrade his knowledge about changes in people needs. He perceives the need to be-

[3] For a detailed discussion of government controls, see Part 10.

come increasingly sensitive to change so that he is better equipped to anticipate and plan for these changes.

Implicit, also, is the requirement that the administrator be current in the state of the art in the behavioral sciences as well as related new developments and trends within government circles.

Increased involvement in the enterprise at the policy level demands high levels of recognition and response to social change. Those who anticipate change and encourage appropriate action may be rewarded in the long run by the relative absence of restrictive legislation.

While policy determination remains with top-line executives, it is the responsibility of the administrative staff to assume leadership in the recommendation of a policy that is responsive to the changing environment. Thus, those administrators who adopt an activist and participative strategy with respect to employment policy will be enhancing their value to the enterprise.

WHAT SHOULD POLICY COVER?

It is axiomatic that employment policy should guide and assist the enterprise in meeting its manpower objectives. No single policy statement seems to cover adequately the concerns of both management and the participating individuals. While policy statements should be broadly conceived and stated, the sheer range of employment activity defies single-sentence or even one-paragraph summaries.

The checklist in Figure 1 is devised to assist the administrator in evaluating the length and breadth of his operational responsibilities and to test the comprehensiveness of applicable policy statements. The checklist will also be useful in identifying the need for supportive procedures to assure that stated policy can and will be observed.

Figure 1. Policy and procedure checklist.

Manpower planning	Policy	Procedure
Forecast of requirements for personnel		
Internal promotion and transfer		
Seniority and skill experience considerations		
Man specifications—selection criteria:		
Age—Minimum age: employment of minors		
Maximum age: mandatory retirement		
Educational requirements		
Experience requirements		
Health requirements—degree of physical fitness required		
Handicapped		
Citizenship		
Military service and/or draft status		
Marital status		
Personal characteristics, attitude, character, appearance		
Travel—travel required in position		
Willingness to relocate		
Union membership, participation		
Fidelity bonding, security clearance		
Nondiscrimination—race, creed, color, national origin, etc.		
Job posting		
Preferential treatment:		
Former employee preference		
Relatives of employees		
Employees on strike from another company		

Figure 1. Policy and procedure checklist. (continued)

Recruitment	Policy	Procedure
Application forms		
Recruiting relationships with		
Colleges and universities, public schools, etc.		
Employment agencies		
Private		
Federal, state, local government		
Professional societies		
Recruitment advertising		
Field recruiting visits to other locations—offshore		
(foreign) recruiting		
Minority and hard-core sources		
Proselyting and/or pirating		
Résumé review and acknowledgement, follow-up		
Handling of submitted ideas		
Interviewing:		
Preliminary		
Placement		
Arrangements:		
Travel reimbursement		
Salary discussions—negotiations		
Testing:		
Skills		
Interest		
Psychological		
Reference checks:		
Credit		
Security		
Character		
Work performance prior employment		
Academic records		
Employment offer:		
Contract document		
Duration of open offer—period of consideration		
Salary negotiations		
Probationary period		
Preemployment physical		

Employment processing—induction and orientation	Policy	Procedure
Relocation assistance		
Reporting-in expenses		
Housing search		
Expense accounting		
Physical examination		
Work rules: hours of work, location, dress, safety		
requirements, garnishees, discipline		
Salary: tax and other withholding requirements,		
pension plan, health and accident plans		
Benefits, vacations, holidays. Savings plan.		
Training opportunities		
Fingerprints, photographs		
Fidelity bond application		
Patent agreement		
Performance reports (see probationary period)		
Outside employment		

No doubt there are other items that could be added to the checklist, particularly if the organization is large and complex.   The intent here is to highlight basic areas where attention should be directed if the policy statements are intended to be inclusive.

Additionally, the checklist will focus for personnel administrators and top management alike some of the factors that are likely to be dynamic and responsive to positive change.   The days when policy can be established for the millenium, reduced to writing, and assigned to a clerk to administer are gone.   The modern personnel administrator must have the capacity and the willingness to assume vastly increased responsibilities to cope intelligently with inevitable change.

Consider briefly policies related to the management of manpower resources.   A prerequisite is obviously some sort of manpower planning or forecasting.   All too frequently, this activity, if accomplished at all, has been the exclusive province of various functional line managers, and any attempt at coordination or overview has been considered suspect and an invasion of long-established prerogatives.   Future enterprises will discover that effective policy for manpower management will require a more critical overview of the entire establishment's human resources.

Recruitment itself can no longer be "catch as catch can."   The ensnarement of new employees, once merely a fascinating game of chance, now becomes the demanding activity of ensuring responsible behavior across the spectrum of employable people.   A reexamination of once sound but now outmoded employment philosophies and practices will undoubtedly result in a healthy respect for the insights and abilities of the modern personnel administrator.

Finally, it is apparent that the employment process goes beyond adding a pair of hands to the payroll.   The employment manager's responsibility continues through the initial orientation and adjustment phase to assure that the entire process is viable for all.

Reducing all the above to policy statements is left to the reader who can and must tailor his employment policies to the realities of his particular organization and environments.   It is clear that there are no foolproof formulas, no universal panacea, no easy way.   Yet, many companies have well-defined policies; two examples of these are shown in Figures 2 and 3.

Applying a participative strategy, using the knowledge of a full spectrum of involved persons, and coupling these with a thorough understanding of the total process will result in policy with integrity.   And policy with integrity is the only basis for consistent and sound decisions in a changing environment.

Figure 2. Policy statement on equal employment. *General Electric Company.   Reprinted by permission.*

EQUAL EMPLOYMENT OPPORTUNITY AND AFFIRMATIVE ACTION*
NEED FOR A POLICY
General Electric is committed to equality of opportunity, a basic goal of a free society. Profitable, responsible growth, and the business success of the General Electric Company, as well as the personal growth of individuals, result from enhancing and utilizing the abilities of individuals to the fullest extent practical within the framework of the business environment.   By hiring, compensating, training, promoting and in all ways providing fair treatment to employees on the basis of merit, the effectiveness of the Company's operations can be maintained while enhancing both the nation's economic progress and that of individuals.

To further this goal, there is need for a Company Policy concerning Equal Employment Opportunity and Affirmative Action.

*From General Electric Organization and Policy Guide, 1969.

Figure 2.   Policy statement on equal employment. *General Electric Company.   Reprinted by permission.*   (**continued**)

Beyond just equality of opportunity, however, there currently is a national problem of relative deprivation for some citizens, concurrent with prosperity for the great majority.   Industry, as an important segment of the nation's economy, often can make many vital business contributions to the solution of these problems.   Within the Company there is a determination to take voluntary, positive, business-oriented action which will contribute to the reduction of this national problem, as well as to further Company progress.   A related determination is to assure that managers and employees at all locations, as a basic minimum, comply with both the spirit and intent of federal, state and local legislation, government regulation and executive orders in providing equal opportunity without regard to race, color, religion, national origin, sex or age.

Thus, there is a continuing and urgent need for managers to take affirmative action in providing Equal Employment Opportunities.   Managers must assure, through action and teaching, that positive steps are being taken to comply with this Policy, to meet the requirements of law, and the stated objectives of the Company for continued profitable, responsible growth and success.

STATEMENT OF POLICY

It is the policy of the General Electric Company to provide employment, training, compensation, promotion and other conditions of employment without regard to race, color, religion, national origin, sex or age, except where age or sex are essential, bona fide occupational requirements.

In addition, while it is the policy to apply appropriate job related standards to the conditions of employment and to maintain such standards at a level consistent with the healthy growth of the Company's business in a highly competitive economy, it is also the policy to take affirmative action to seek out individuals whose potential has not been developed, with the objective of assisting them to meet these standards.   Affirmative action will include finding additional sources of applicants who can become qualified, utilizing appropriate training which will assist these individuals towards full qualification, and developing programs to assure upward mobility for qualified individuals.

A major goal of the Company is also to become a civic leader in programs and activities which enhance equal employment opportunities within the various communities in which the Company operates and throughout the Nation.

APPLICATION OF POLICY

Each manager is responsible for the application of this Policy within his component. This includes initiating or supporting programs and practices designed to develop understanding, acceptance, commitment and compliance within the framework of this Policy. All employees and specifically each manager will be responsible for complying with all the requirements and laws of the government, and in applying this Policy to achieve Company objectives.

Specifically, each Manager will be responsible for:

▪ Making certain that individuals in his components who make or recommend employment and other personnel decisions are fully aware and comply with this Company Policy

▪ Notifying both applicants and sources of applicants that the Company is an "Equal Opportunity Employer"

▪ Taking affirmative steps to encourage the application and qualification of individuals for available job openings

▪ Assuring that promotion and development opportunities at all levels within his component are made without regard to race, religion, color, national origin, sex or age, except where sex or age are essential bona fide occupational requirements

▪ Cooperating with compliance reviews by appropriate government agencies

▪ Demonstrating leadership among other responsible business and civic leaders in observing the spirit and intent of federal, state and local laws concerning nondiscrimination.

Each Division General Manager, Department General Manager and Corporate Staff Officer will assure that this Policy on Equal Employment Opportunity and Affirmative Action is appropriately communicated and uniformly applied by all levels of management.

At least once each year progress and performance in the area of Equal Opportunity

Figure 2.   Policy statement on equal employment. *General Electric Company. Reprinted by permission.* **(continued)**

and Affirmative Action will be measured for each Department, Division, Group, Corporate Staff, as well as the Company as a whole.

RESERVATIONS OF AUTHORITY

Presidential Executive Order requires affirmative action plans within the Company. These must be updated yearly. Copies of these plans should be sent to Corporate Industrial Relations Staff — Equal Opportunity/Minority Relations (EOMR). Corporate EOMR working with Corporate Employee Relations and Management Manpower Development has responsibility for auditing performance under this Policy. Proposed EOMR actions or programs which could have significant effects on the Company's public posture, as well as any proposed settlement or agreement resulting from a compliance review shall be reviewed with Corporate EOMR and appropriate Corporate Staff.

RESPONSIBILITY OF OPERATIONS

Division General Managers, Department General Managers and Corporate Staff Officers are responsible for measuring progress and assuring that effective equal employment opportunity practices and programs are developed in accordance with this Policy and implemented for their component. Advice and counsel should be obtained from Corporate Industrial Relations, Employee Relations, Management Manpower Development and other functional components as appropriate during various phases of designing, revising, documenting and implementing the component's Equal Employment Opportunity/Affirmative Action plans and programs. Compliance reviews and complaint cases initiated by governmental agencies at the operating level should be communicated to Corporate EOMR for appropriate advice and counsel.

RESPONSIBILITY OF CORPORATE FUNCTIONAL COMPONENTS

Corporate Industrial Relations Staff (EOMR), working with Corporate Employee Relations and Management Manpower Development has responsibility for the following:

▪ Providing advice and counsel on the interpretation and implementation of this Policy

▪ Reviewing proposed plans and programs and preparing written recommendations to operating components and/or the Corporate Executive Office

▪ Recommending policy to the Corporate Executive Office

▪ Searching out and evaluating new concepts and approaches in the field of equal employment opportunity/minority relations

▪ Working with Company components in appraising the effectiveness of equal employment opportunity/minority relations programs and practices, as well as recommending changes through appropriate management channels

▪ Auditing effectiveness and recommending needed changes in affirmative action programs of operating and staff components

▪ Developing guides, criteria, measurements and needed communications to staff and field.

Other Corporate staff components are responsible, as appropriate, for developing, recommending and supporting effective plans and programs in their specific areas of responsibility which will further the Company's Equal Opportunity/Affirmative Action programs.

Figure 3.   A portion of United Air Lines' extremely comprehensive employment guide. *Reprinted by permission.*

PLACEMENT INTERVIEW*

1. GENERAL. At the placement interview, information about the applicant gathered from the review of the Personal History, test results, screening comments and general observations made during the actual processing can be brought together for total analysis.

The interview is the most frequently used selection method. The interviewer can get much information during this portion of employment processing if he learns to probe deeply, tie applicant comments together and encourage the applicant to express his normal personality and attitudes.

*From United Airlines Employment Guide, 1970.

Figure 3.   A portion of United Air Lines' extremely comprehensive employment guide. *Reprinted by permission.* **(continued)**

Normally 30 minutes is considered a practical time to spend in a placement interview. While it is not enough time to observe a person completely, it does afford ample time to make a sound, professional placement decision.

2. PREPARATION. Planning is essential before the interview; review information already available carefully, looking for points that need coverage.

The Employment Representative must know the position or positions for which the applicant is being considered. "Placement interview" is the key here. *We are not looking for excuses for not employing an individual. Instead, we are interested in his strong points. What are they? Where can they be of greatest value to U A? If his weaknesses predominate, or if his strong points do not relate to any vacancy, then the applicant cannot be placed.* This means the Employment Representative must know, and know well, the physical, mental and personality requirements, working conditions and lines of promotion.

Before the actual interview, much information is already available about the applicant.   The screening interviewer has recorded his comments, the tests have provided certain insights, and the Personal History can be evaluated (see appropriate section). With this information in mind, begin to get an idea of the applicant's strong and weak points as they relate to the job in question. *Decide, before sitting down with applicant, what areas must be covered and plan how to cover them.*

3. RAPPORT.   The interviewer's manner determines rapport.   Friendly, courteous interest in the applicant as an individual usually is all that is necessary. Light genial conversation of interest to both at the outset accustoms the applicant to talking, but prevent what should be an interview from becoming a "coffee klatch."   Once the applicant starts talking, turn the conversation towards himself.   There are no gimmicks with which to do this.   It takes practice.   If you make notes during the interview, avoid becoming so engrossed in the note taking that you lose touch with the applicant.   Also, too much preoccupation with note taking puts the applicant on guard.   For this reason some interviewers prefer to wait until after the interview to make notes.   Avoid glancing at a clock or watch. Such action destroys rapport and gives the applicant an impression that the interviewer has other things on his mind.   As long as the applicant feels that at the moment the interviewer is concerned only with the subject at hand, information is much more readily accessible.   Privacy is a must.   Eliminate distractions from adjoining rooms, whether visual or audible.

4. TECHNIQUES FOR OBTAINING INFORMATION.   There are no sure-fire techniques for interviewing.   However, there are several aids.   All-encompassing questions such as "Tell me about your education: what subjects did you like best?" involve a wide area and the applicant cannot answer "yes" or "no."   The answer may not contain a great deal of useful information, but it accustoms the applicant to talking.   From the general, the questions can be guided to the specific.   As a rule, "yes" or "no" answers do not solicit a great deal of information; avoid them except when a specific fact must be determined. "Have you ever been arrested?"

Obviously you must be clearly understood.   Slang or technical terms relating to the airline industry are usually best avoided.   How questions are phrased, in part, determines the success of the interview.   Asking too many at one time may confuse.   Leading questions—ones that seem to imply the desired answer—may lead to inaccurate replies.   Let the applicant do most of the talking while you listen, making mental notes that will tie your evaluation together at the close.

There are bound to be uncommunicative applicants.   Somehow, they manage to answer every question in one or two words.   Usually, gentle pressure solves the problem.   Rather than probing for more information with additional questions, pause at the end of an answer, as if anticipating more.   Use this technique early in the interview, before the applicant can establish a rhythm of short answers.   Otherwise, the result may be an embarrassing waiting game.

Do not moralize during an interview.   If the applicant says he is an Anarchist, it is not your place to agree or disagree.   Avoid trapping the applicant.   Remember, he has applied for employment; he isn't on trial.   If obvious fallacies or discrepancies appear, approach them gently; they could be the result of honest confusion.   Employment practice laws prohibit asking certain discriminatory questions.

Figure 3.   A portion of United Air Lines' extremely comprehensive employment guide. *Reprinted by permission.* **(continued)**

5. EVALUATING AND INTERPRETING INFORMATION.   Be realistic and objective. Know exactly what information you have obtained from an applicant.   It is easy to come to believe in one's "intuitive knack for sizing up people."   United has neither the time nor the money to psychoanalyze its applicants.   We are interested in such things as maturity, motivation, stability, compatibility.   In attempting to place an individual into an industrial situation, a careful evaluation of past experience is the most productive source of useful information.   There is some leeway here for conjecture about such things as attitudes and how they were formed.   Past behavior usually predicts future behavior. If an individual shows evidence of job hopping, we can only assume he will continue it. If he has always given up when faced with obstacles, we can assume he will continue to do so.   If he speaks poorly of all his previous supervisors, he probably experiences difficulty coping with authority.

However, carefully analyze all facts.   Perhaps there are legitimate reasons for apparent job instability.   Thoroughly investigate indicators of problem areas.   Get as many facts as possible.   Without complete information, there is danger of doing the applicant an injustice.

Throughout the interview, maintain objectivity.   Everyone has personal prejudices and biases.   An interviewer owes it to himself and to the applicant to examine these carefully, and make sure they assume no importance in the evaluation.   Such things as a dislike for bow ties, a particular color sock, or a manner of dress have no correlation with job success.

6. TERMINATING THE INTERVIEW.   This is the best time for giving information about the company and the job, because it:

a. *Decreases the Possibility* of having the applicant consciously slant his qualifications to "meet the bill" and

b. *Decreases the Time* the interviewer would have to devote to these topics with unqualified applicants.

Communicating the unfavorable decision can best be left to the various region's local procedures.   Regardless of which system of notification is used, handle it with the utmost tact and finesse.

When the applicant is to be considered further, discuss in detail job and company specifics, as well as fringe benefits.   Walk a fine line between selling the position and the company, but not overselling them either.

When a decision is made to refer the applicant, advise him of this and how he will be notified of the eventual outcome.   At this time you should know the applicant's assets and liabilities.   Without this information, you have conducted a poor interview.

Make appropriate notations on the Personal History (UPE 128).   These should resolve apparent inconsistencies, clarify information given by the applicant and in general add to the total information available.

These notations also reflect a thorough interview job and indicate emphasis on important areas.   Make your comments on the Personal History in red pencil to distinguish your remarks from the applicant's.

7. CONCLUSION.   This chapter is not intended to make someone into a qualified interviewer, but to provide some general guidelines.   There is a wealth of written material available on interviewing technique.   Seek out this information on your own initiative. Role playing has considerable merit.   Having inexperienced interviewers observe a more experienced person conduct an interview offers great potential for critical analysis.   The best teacher is still experience.   The important thing is to analyze the experience.

SUMMARY

Solving the problems of employment in today's complex society is going to require a complete reorientation in the personnel administrator's attitude toward the development of employment policy.

New statutory requirements have now imposed on the personnel administrator the need for new strategies and techniques in the application of personnel policy. In this regard, the modern personnel administrator can no longer maintain a passive philosophy about the social, political, and economic forces at work in the society that challenges the foundations on which the original policy was based.

Further, the new statutory requirements make it necessary for personnel administrators to adopt an activist and participative role in formulating policies that are broadly conceived, that enhance their value to the system, and that reflect the needs of the people both within and outside the organization.

Developing policy is not an easy task, and once a policy is formulated and accepted by top-line management, it must continuously undergo revisions. A broadly conceived employment policy might be constructed using an analysis checklist which focuses on policy and procedure requirements regarding manpower planning, recruitment, and employment processing-induction and orientation. This technique will provide assistance and guidance in meeting manpower objectives of the enterprise.

Knowledge and participation from the full spectrum of interested persons should be brought to bear in the development process. This involvement should result in a well-defined, meaningful employment policy that is broadly conceived and sufficiently flexible so that it can be implemented with integrity.

BIBLIOGRAPHY

Aspley, John C. (ed.): *Handbook of Employee Relations,* 1st ed., The Dartnell Corporation, Chicago, 1955.
  Employee relations in a free economy. GE's statement of company policy.
Blood, Jerome W. (ed.): *The Personnel Job in a Changing World,* American Management Association, New York, 1964.
  Forty-one top executives review problems of personnel management and discuss steps they have taken to alleviate these various problems. (Alcoa, American Can, U.S. Steel, etc.)
Hawk, Roger H.: *The Recruitment Function,* American Management Association, New York, 1967.
"Horse-and-Buggy Techniques Lose in Jet Age Recruiting Race," *Employee Relations Bulletin,* July 5, 1967, pp. 10–11.
  Recruiting program about Sun Chemical Corp. Checklist.
"How 141 Companies Recruit Employees," *Dartnell Industrial Relations Report, part 2,* June, 1952.
  Programs of particular companies. Charts showing practices by type of company.
Lester, Richard A.: *Adjustments to Labor Shortages,* Princeton University, Industrial Relations Section, 1955.
  Recruitment and employment policies of expanding firms in Trenton area and impact of their expansion on industrial policies of 78 other firms.
Mandell, Milton M.: *Selection Process: Choosing the Right Man for the Job,* American Management Association, New York, 1964.
  Explains methods, practices, procedures of selection and demonstrates how to use techniques. Corporate examples include GE, GM, Lever Bros., Inland Steel, 3-M, Colgate.

"Recruiting and Selecting Employees" *NICB Studies in Personnel Policy, no. 144,* September, 1954.

Sixty companies study current trends in employment practice, policies.

"Recruiting Practices," *Personnel Policies Forum Survey no. 86,* The Bureau of National Affairs, Inc., Washington, D.C., March, 1969.

Survey of corporate practices among large and small firms, policies.

Schein, Edgar H.: *Organizational Psychology,* Foundations of Modern Psychology Series, Richard S. Lazarus, ed., Prentice-Hall, Inc., Englewood Cliffs, N.J., 1965.

Spriegal, William R., and Virgil A. James: "Trends in Recruitment and Selection Practices," *Personnel,* November-December, 1958, pp. 42–48.

Five surveys of personnel management by authors.   Procedures.

Stone, C. Harold, and William E. Kendall: *Effective Personnel Selection Procedures,* Prentice-Hall, Inc., Englewood Cliffs, N.J., 1956.

Employment policies.   Organization for the task.

Strong, Lydia: "Executives Wanted: The Managerial Manhunt," *Management Review,* February, 1957, pp. 53–68.

Results of American Management Association's study of 469 companies to find out about current company practices in executive recruiting.

Yoder, Dale, H. G. Heneman, Jr., John Turnbull, and C. Harold Stone: *Handbook of Personnel Management and Labor Relations,* McGraw-Hill Company, New York, 1958.

Factors influencing recruitment.   Policy.   Techniques.

chapter 12

Recruitment Sources and Techniques

ROBERT L. LOPRESTO *Manager, Corporate Staffing, Fairchild Camera and Instrument Corporation, Mountain View, California*

The acquisition of new employees is a most important and complex task. To find and employ the best individuals available is every personnel manager's goal. Far too many organizations have underestimated and neglected the importance of the human equation in the profit and loss formula. A company cannot prosper, grow, or even survive without adequate human resources. Shortages of trained manpower in recent years have created a pressure on organizations to establish an efficient recruitment function. Personnel managers and line managers must, therefore, be dynamic and creative in finding, screening, and selecting the quality and quantity of personnel needed for both short- and long-range manpower requirements. The emphasis should be on the quality of applicants, since it is time consuming and costly to process unqualified candidates. Due to the individual differences of organizations, such as geographical location, size and makeup of work force, and type of industry, there is no standard recruitment package that will work for everyone. The purpose of this chapter, therefore, is to examine the many recruitment sources and techniques available to the modern-day personnel or administrative manager so that a recruitment program can be organized in relation to specific situational needs.

THE LABOR MARKET

The variations between the supply and the demand for manpower is commonly referred to as the "labor market." Complex variables, which create a constantly shifting availability of qualified personnel, include: (1) government spending, affected by new administrations, defense and space budgets, limited hot and cold wars, national and local economic climates; (2) demographic changes in population; (3) a highly mobile work force; and (4) emerging technology. The low birth rates of the depression years have created a shortage of prime management talent in the ages of thirty to forty-five, which will not subside until the late 1970s. The post-war baby boom in turn has created a great number of young people entering the work force without previous work experience. The work force has become highly mobile and elastic through increased levels of educational attainment, affluence, planned parenthood, the availability of occupational information communicated by mass media, and the ease of geographic mobility with jet transportation and short-term lease apartment living, all contributing to an erosion of company loyalty and higher turnover rates. Unemployment, underemployment, and other serious manpower problems have been bred by the immigration of unskilled agricultural workers to the cities at a time when occupational requirements are changing in favor of jobs requiring greater education and training. Unskilled farm and blue-collar positions have decreased in favor of a rapidly expanding growth of white-collar technical and professional occupations. Jobs in teaching and government also have expanded in direct proportion to population growth.

The Government Printing Office publishes an abundance of information in this regard. An annotated bibliography of manpower information is available from the U.S. Department of Labor, Bureau of Labor Statistics, Washington, D.C. 20402. The Bureau also publishes monthly reports on levels of employment and unemploy-ment on a national and regional basis which are the best indicators available for labor supply and demand. Several states, such as New York, also publish similar monthly reports. Other indices of the labor market include: *The Help-Wanted Advertising Index,* published by the National Industrial Conference Board, Divi-sion of Economic Research, New York, N.Y. 10022, and the *Engineer/Scientist Demand Index,* published monthly by Deutsch, Shea & Evans, Inc., New York, N.Y. 10022. Three annual reports from the College Placement Council, Inc., Bethlehem, Pa. 18001, summarize the supply, demand, and starting salaries of-fered recent bachelors', masters', and doctoral candidates during each college re-cruitment season. The Engineering Manpower Commission of the Engineers Joint Council, New York, N.Y. 10017, publishes significant data on the supply and de-mand of technical manpower. For example, the commission published a survey titled *Demand for Engineers and Technicians, 1968.*

Recruitment activity begins when an approved personnel requisition is received by the individual responsible for recruiting. Ideally, the requisition (Figure 1) should be based on an accurate job description written by the hiring manager with the assistance of a job analyst. The requisition should clearly indicate the duties of the job and realistic qualifications required. The requisition is, therefore, man-agement authorization to spend recruitment expenses and add an individual to the payroll, and serves as a communications device between management and the per-sonnel department.

INTERNAL SOURCES OF LABOR SUPPLY

Internal sources include: (1) transfer and promotion of present employees, (2) employee referral programs, (3) mobilization of the management staff, and (4) reemployment of former employees.

Present Employees

When a specific opening occurs, the first place to look for candidates is in your present work force. Through transfer and promotion, you should be able to fill many vacancies for experienced personnel. This will have the effect of creating more entry level positions, which should be easier to fill and less costly when recruiting outside the company.

The basic ingredients for maximizing internal promotions and transfers are:

PERSONNEL REQUISITION

Job Title_____ Grade Level_____ Date Needed_____

Div/Co_____ Pub/Dept._____

Section_____ Work Location_____

Pay Agency Fee: ☐ Yes ☐ No   Pay New Employee Relocation Expenses, If Necessary: ☐ Yes ☐ No

Refer Questions and Applicants To:_____ Location_____ Fl._____ Ext._____
In His Absence To:_____ Location_____ Fl._____ Ext._____

JOB REQUIREMENTS

I. Brief Description of Duties _____

II. Special Experience or Qualifications Required_____

III. Education Required_____

SALARY AND WORK STATUS

I. Hiring Range: From $_____ To $_____ Per Year_____ Month_____ Week_____ Hour_____
II. Charge Salary   G/L_____S/L_____Dept._____%_____   G/L_____S/L_____Dept._____%_____
   Expense To: G/L_____S/L_____Dept._____%_____   G/L_____S/L_____Dept._____%_____
III. ☐ Permanent ☐ Temporary If Temporary, For How Long _____
    ☐ Full Time ☐ Part Time If Part Time, What Hours & Days _____
    ☐ Day Shift ☐ Night Shift If Night Shift, What Hours _____ What Rate Differential _____

JUSTIFICATION AND HISTORY

I. Is This an Increase to Staff? ☐ Yes - Give Reasons In "Comments"
                                 ☐ No - Replacement For: Name_____
Salary_____ Per_____ Date Off Job_____ Reason (Check One Below)
☐ Promoted ☐ Transferred ☐ Terminated ☐ Military Service ☐ Other (Explain)_____

II. Is This Position Budgeted? ☐ Yes ☐ No   If No, Explain in "Comments"

COMMENTS

_____
_____
_____
_____
_____

APPROVALS

		PERSONNEL DEPT. ONLY
First_____	Date_____	Job Class Code_____
Second_____	Date_____	Grade Level_____
Third_____	Date_____	FLSA_____
Agency Fee_____	Date_____	Signature_____ Date_____
Relocation Expenses_____	Date_____	Signature_____ Date_____

Figure 1. Personnel requisition.

(1) a good communications system, (2) the cooperation and backing of management, and (3) an employee information system or skills inventory.

Communications. Whether a company uses job posting on bulletin boards, special printed announcements of opportunities to each employee, or coverage in an employee newspaper, a good communication system is essential for motivating interested employees to come forward. The openness of sharing this information with employees can boost morale, retain good employees, and increase productivity. A very important factor in a good communication system is to notify all successful and unsuccessful employees of decisions as soon as possible. Unsuccessful employees should be diplomatically told why they were not selected and counseled on how they can develop into being more promotable.

Management backing. The cooperation and backing of management is very important to the success of an internal transfer and promotion program. Top management obviously must weigh the advantages and disadvantages of internal movement and spell out company policy on this matter. There is a natural reaction for managers to jealously guard their best employees and, therefore, to resist internal movement. If top management makes it clear that all managers will be held responsible and recognized for the development and promotion of personnel for the organization, internal promotions will flourish. Most organizations adopt a policy of first priority for promotions from within and outside recruiting only after it has been determined that there are no qualified employees available.

Skills inventory. Since Chapter 17 will be devoted to skills and interest inventories and promotion systems, the following shall be only a brief orientation to this subject as it applies to internal sources of labor supply.

A computerized employee information system or skills inventory can be installed as a satellite to an existing payroll or personnel data system, thereby minimizing the cost. Matching qualifications of employees with openings can be efficiently handled in a minimal amount of time by the recruiting staff prior to expensive outside recruiting. Input to the system normally consists of a periodically completed employee questionnaire. The output, a computer-produced directory of skills, education, and interests, becomes the tool for matchmaking with open requisitions.

Employee Referral Programs

Many organizations have found that employee referrals are a valuable source of good-quality workers. Since an employee is inclined to do some prescreening rather than embarrass himself, a friend, or his company, the quality of the referral tends to be higher than from most outside recruitment sources. Minimal cost is another major reason for considering this method.

A variety of techniques can be aimed at encouraging employee referrals. Internal communication of job openings, as mentioned earlier, can remind employees to refer their friends, neighbors, and former business associates. Bulletin boards, special circulars, employee newspapers, employee handbooks, new employee orientation sessions, paycheck inserts, and lobby, lunchroom, and elevator displays can be used to promote referrals. Special incentives can be offered in the form of cash awards, savings bonds, company merchandise, trading stamps, or sweepstakes for trips and prizes. Some firms program the full amount of the award in stages based on the length of time an employee stays with the company. Recruitment awards are considered wages, subject to income and social security taxes; therefore, make sure employees know this, or increase the amount of the gross award to absorb the deductions. Some companies report that retirees are a good source for referrals and should, therefore, remain eligible for awards after retirement.

It is suggested that each organization develop its own program to meet the specific needs and individual differences of the company and that a trial program be used for a specific period of time to test its effectiveness. Some companies, especially in small communities, find that employee referral programs may result in cliques or nepotism. These possibilities can be minimized if employee referrals are only one of several recruitment sources and if all applicants are processed the same way without favoritism, regardless of source. Another word of caution is that government agencies look down upon employee referrals for companies with a low percentage of minority group workers. Their logic is that a company only perpetuates its nonminority group work force with employee referral programs; therefore, it will not meet the conditions and goals set forth in equal opportunity employment policies and civil rights legislation.

Mobilization of Management

In most cases, no one is more aware and interested in recruitment than your own management staff. They are personally affected by manpower shortages and turnover problems, and are held responsible for meeting production schedules, research and development goals, and sales quotas. Supervisors and managers are, therefore, primed to help recruit and, in turn, help themselves. Ask for their cooperation and ideas by encouraging them to become recruitment specialists for your company. By doing so, you instantly multiply the size and scope of the recruitment staff. You may be surprised to find that many of your managers are already doing their own recruiting; so they might as well be part of an organized effort. Since most managers are traveling on business, are teaching at night, or are active in community affairs, they come in contact with many potential applicants. Every supervisor and manager can be a goodwill ambassador and part-time recruiter when he attends conventions, meetings, or talks with clients, customers, suppliers, or salesmen.

A first step could be to hold a special meeting, for example, a breakfast, lunch, or dinner discussion. Since manpower is a top-priority subject, executives should be there to lend the air of importance which fosters results. Department heads are the best persons to get involved, as they will in turn mobilize their subordinate supervisors. It is best to explain why recruitment is difficult and to make the managers, who are present, understand their importance by pointing out how they are in a position to help. Give a detailed listing of job openings and specifications, which includes hiring salaries, to these managers so that they are armed with the information needed to do a good job. A short course in interviewing techniques with role playing might be appropriate. If your company has an award for employee referrals, ask your managers to speak to all their employees and to remind them of the award. Suggest that employees also enlist the help of the members of their families in recruiting their acquaintances. Stress the importance of each manager looking at his present employees as possible candidates for upgrading into promotional opportunities, and make sure that top management learns of those managers who make recommendations. Encourage managers to pass on to the recruitment staff those applicants which they cannot use, and have them provide suggestions on where else these candidates for employment might fit into the company.

It will be important for you to keep records on all applicants and hires which result from this campaign, so it can be evaluated and improved for the future. Also, you will want to compare turnover before and after the program. You will probably find that managers are doing a better job to keep their best employees once they find out how difficult it is to recruit and attract good people. A little empathy can go a long way in securing management cooperation. At the meeting, also ask your managers to think about the best employees who have previously left the company. This leads us into our next subject.

Reemployment of Former Employees

As mentioned earlier, the shortage of trained manpower and the increased mobility of the work force have created an erosion of company loyalty and higher turnover. Therefore, resignations do not carry the stigma of disloyalty that they did some years ago. These changes have caused companies to reexamine their policies on reemployment. The return to a former employer, particularly at the level of professionals and executives, is a growing trend. Many companies have either relaxed or abandoned long-standing policies against rehiring former employees. Many firms are keeping better records of desirable departing employees as a potential recruiting source. Most companies also will admit that a former employee's experience gained while with a competitor can be an asset upon returning. Also, the former employee's competence is a known quantity in comparison to a new recruit. Perhaps the best example of reemployment activity involves scientists and engineers who move between the aerospace and electronics companies individually or in teams as major government contracts shift between these firms. In attracting office personnel, a company in New York City wrote a letter to all secretaries who had left their employment in good standing during the past five years asking them to come back or refer a friend. It is usually flattering to an ex-employee to know that a company for whom he may still hold positive feelings wants him back. It also overcomes any reluctance based on pride that former employees may hesitate to admit they made a mistake in leaving. It is important to tap the grapevine of employees who may hear that a former employee is not completely happy with his new job and might be receptive to coming back.

The biggest danger in the reemployment of former employees is the creation of salary relationship inequities, which lower morale and increase turnover. Former employees should not be rewarded for leaving, nor should employees be penalized for staying. As a general rule, a former employee who is reemployed at his prior level should receive a salary increase which does not exceed the merit increases he would have received if he had stayed. Where it can be demonstrated to the present staff that a former employee is returning in a higher level position with more responsibilities, then a corresponding salary increase may be justified.

EXTERNAL SOURCES OF LABOR SUPPLY

Schools

Educational institutions are an excellent source for filling entry-level or training-program type positions. High schools, trade and vocational schools and institutes are usually anxious to place their graduates in industry and government. For example, graduates of business courses in high schools and private business schools are an excellent source for clerk typists and secretaries. The key to successful recruiting at school is the development of good contacts among teachers and guidance or placement directors. Plant tours, cooperative work-study programs, after-school and summer jobs, guest speakers, and recruitment literature are all techniques for promoting an effective school recruitment program. High school career conferences have recently become popular, especially in large cities; however, early indications from participating companies are that most are conducted in a circus-type atmosphere with students primarily looking for company giveaways.

Colleges

Since the 1950s, when shortages of college-trained engineers and scientists became critical, the recruitment of college graduates has become an extensive and extremely competitive operation. Most large companies have set up training programs for recent college graduates; these programs serve as pipelines to fill the increasing demand for professional and management personnel.

Before organizing a college recruitment program, it is best to determine the annual needs of your organization for college graduates. College recruitment is normally done at these levels: (1) junior or community colleges for the associate degree graduate, (2) colleges and universities for the four-year bachelor's degree holder, and (3) graduate schools for master's and doctoral candidates.

College relations must involve a continuous program with long-term contracts and relationships between recruiters, alumni, faculty, and placement directors. The regional placement associations of the College Placement Council hold annual meetings, which offer an excellent opportunity to establish, maintain, and build close working relationships between recruiters and placement officers. The image that students and faculty have of your company is an important factor in the success of a college relations program.

Large, better-known consumer product firms hold an advantage over smaller companies in this respect. They usually are also well staffed and organized for effective college recruiting. College recruiting is normally centralized at their corporate headquarters, with divisional and regional personnel pitching in to fulfill a large nationwide recruitment schedule.

Most companies develop college recruitment quotas for an academic year. This is usually done by contacting various department heads and training directors to determine: (1) how many graduates are needed; (2) the kinds of graduates required, for example, electrical engineers or accounting majors; and (3) the number of colleges and universities that must be visited to fulfill the demand. The decision as to which colleges you will visit depends on the type of graduates needed and which schools have the best reputation for specific majors. Individual' college directories or the College Placement Council can give you information on the degrees awarded at specific colleges. For example, the council publishes an *Annual Directory of College Placement Offices.* Recruiting at local colleges as much as possible will keep expenses down and increase results since area residents are probably your best prospects for local employment.

Records of your annual college recruitment efforts and results should be evaluated to determine which schools to revisit, although it may take a few years to establish yourself at some schools. Interview-to-offer and offer-to-acceptance ratios will aid your evaluation, and in time, the performance ratings and promotions of graduates will point out those colleges which provide the best material for your organization. As the smaller colleges have been somewhat overlooked by many in favor of "big-name" schools, a well-balanced schedule is recommended. The black colleges have been previously untapped as a source for talent, although this is changing due to the shortage of qualified manpower and equal opportunity employment legislation.

While most campus recruiting is done through the college placement office, supplementary contacts with professors can help if channeled through the placement director. *Principles and Practices of College Recruiting,* available from the College Placement Council, is an excellent guide. A schedule of recruitment visits should be set up early in the school year, and some colleges will schedule your recruitment date a year in advance. It is important to provide the placement office with detailed information on the starting assignments or training programs, salaries, employee benefits, and advancement prospects which you offer. Most colleges send an information form to companies for completion in advance of the recruitment visit (see Figure 2). Companies can supplement this with recruitment literature, annual reports, etc. Most universities have placement libraries containing handout literature and a permanent binder of company material which can be updated annually. It is vital to keep students and placement officers informed of the results of campus interviews. Placement directors should be sent copies of correspondence turning down or inviting students to visit the company and offer letters. If a candidate must travel a considerable distance to visit a company, or if relocation is necessary, his expenses are usually paid by the company.

Some firms enhance their college relations program through cooperative work-study plans, summer intern programs, scholarships, and fellowships. Company visits and summer work assignments for professors and placement officers also strengthen ties with colleges. Some companies donate scientific and engineering equipment to schools to enhance their relationships with the students and faculty. There is no question that graduates of colleges and universities represent the major

2c	⟨CP⟩ **CAMPUS RECRUITING INFORMATION FORM** (For submission by colleges to employers for data pertinent to setting up campus interviews.) (USE SEPARATE FORM FOR EACH RECRUITING VISIT. Retain one copy for your file and return this form at least 4 weeks prior to interview date.)	(COLLEGE NAME) Address

EMPLOYER	ADDRESS	PHONE (Include Area Code)
NAME OF PERSON RESPONSIBLE FOR ARRANGEMENTS		TITLE

Types of Job Openings or Groups to be Interviewed*

POSITIONS AVAILABLE   ACADEMIC BACKGROUNDS AND DEGREES DESIRED

DATE(S) OF INTERVIEWS	INTERVIEWS START AT	INTERVIEWS END AT: (Be sure of departure time before completing)

INTERVIEWING FOR THE FOLLOWING LOCATIONS

SCHEDULING INFORMATION*

Interview Information	NUMBER OF SEPARATE SCHEDULES WHICH SHOULD BE SET UP EACH DAY	LENGTH OF INTERVIEW (Indicate Choice) ☐ 20 Minutes	☐ 30 Minutes	☐ Other
Areas Of Employment And Training	☐ Design ☐ Research and Development	☐ Sales	☐ Sales Engineering	☐ Training Program
	☐ Accounting ☐ Finance	☐ Biochemistry	☐ Mechanical Engineering	☐ Other
Will Interview	☐ October Graduates ☐ January Graduates	☐ June Graduates	☐ Summer Graduates	☐ Other
Will Interview for Summer Work	☐ Freshmen ☐ Sophomores	☐ Juniors	☐ Seniors	☐ Graduate Students
Check (X) As Applicable	☐ Only recruiting visit to this office this school year	☐ Citizenship required	☐ Employer literature will be mailed 4 weeks prior to interview visit.	

NAMES AND TITLES OF INTERVIEWERS

NOTE TO EMPLOYERS: For campus interviews, students use the College Interview Form CPC #1 as their resume.	DATE COMPLETED

CPC #2 — FORM ADOPTED BY THE COLLEGE PLACEMENT COUNCIL   *THESE ITEMS CAN BE ADJUSTED TO LOCAL SITUATIONS.

Figure 2. Campus recruiting information form.

source for future key positions in American business, government, and education. Most major firms now visit more than 100 colleges per year to employ 300 to 500 graduates annually.

Private Employment Agencies

Employment agencies can supplement the recruitment staff in finding and screening qualified applicants for several companies at one time.   They can save time for the company and the job seeker by serving as a clearinghouse of job information.   Details of jobs can be discussed with applicants without revealing the name of the company, and likewise, the agency can submit résumés without identifying the applicant.   Upon receipt of new requisitions, a telephone call to an agency can provide qualified candidates in a few hours.   Several employment agencies are now using data-processing techniques to quickly match jobs with applicants on file. The most significant advantage of using agencies is that no costs are incurred by the company, until the position is filled. This is true only on company fee paid positions, which are most likely for higher level positions and for occupations in short supply, e.g., engineers and secretaries. In extremely tight labor markets, almost all fees are company paid. For lower-level positions, normally the applicant pays the fee.

It is important to select a few good employment agencies that are reliable, ethical, and produce consistent results. Establish and maintain a good relationship with a few selected agencies by keeping them informed of job requirements and hiring decisions. Normally, companies send a printed list of job openings, salary ranges, and contact information to agencies on a regular basis. The telephone is even quicker and can serve as a "hot line" for an agency when an outstanding candidate comes in. Carbon copies of reject and offer letters to applicants can keep the agency informed. In many cases, a good account executive who knows your company can persuade the applicant to join your firm. Plant and office visits by agency personnel are valuable, and the agency should have a supply of company recruitment literature on hand. An agency that derives continuing revenue from a company has an incentive to maintain a good-quality referral record. Most companies will put new agencies on a trial period and continually revise its list of agencies on the basis of results.

One good indicator of selecting an agency is its membership in a state or national association that subscribes to certain professional or ethical standards. A nationwide directory of private employment agencies is published by the National Employment Association, Washington, D.C. 20006. The classified want-ad sections of newspapers are a good source of information, for an agency who can afford extensive and regular advertising must be placing applicants to pay for its advertising. Another good approach in evaluating an agency is to visit the office to see what facilities and procedures are used in screening applicants.

Some organizations will ask an agency to sign a contract or set of ground rules covering the fee schedule, reimbursement of fees in case of short-term employment, and placement credit for duplicate referrals from two or more agencies on the same applicant. Normally, fees will vary in different parts of the country, based on labor markets. The most prevalent fee schedule is based on a percentage of the annual salary, e.g., 1 percent per thousand dollars of annual salary or a fee of 15 percent on $15,000 per year.

Today, private employment agencies constitute a big business, consisting of over 10,000 agencies doing a volume of more than 300 million dollars in fees. The large agencies are branching out into the suburbs and sharing jobs and applicants through computer-type matching on a regional and nationwide basis. The quality of personnel in the agency field has improved as several personnel recruitment specialists have left industry to set up their own business. These men and women are in a good position to understand the needs and procedures of client companies, having formerly been on the other side of the fence.

Public Employment Agencies

The United States Employment Service and affiliated state employment services are made up of 2,000 public employment offices across the nation. The state offices were set up originally to handle unemployment compensation claims and to find jobs for the unemployed. Over the years, they have expanded services into professional level placement and special manpower programs for placing older workers, the handicapped, returning servicemen, and minority groups.

A new computerized job bank system should increase the effectiveness of the United States Employment Service in statewide and national job matching and placement. The major advantage of utilizing the public employment agencies is that no fee is charged. State and government employment services are funded by the government through general taxation. More information is available from the United States Employment Service by writing the Bureau of Employment Security, U.S. Department of Labor, Washington, D.C. 20210.

Executive Search

When filling top-level positions, many companies use management consulting firms that specialize in the recruitment of executive personnel. They find and screen candidates, check references, and present the most qualified candidates. The usual agreement is to pay the consultant on a retainer basis, whether they provide a successful candidate or not, plus expenses and a flat fee or percentage of the first year salary of the executive placed. The fee is normally 25 percent and up, of the annual salary.

The choice of an executive recruitment firm is crucial. An assignment will be successful only if there is a mutual understanding of the requirements of the job to be filled. If the specifications are not made clear or shift a lot, a search can be prolonged and costly. A search firm and the client company's management should be compatible, and the assignment should be reduced to writing, so that there are no false starts and blind alleys. When selecting a search firm, investigate the reputation of several and obtain the names of satisfied clients. Consider the firm's experience in your industry and in the specific field of the opening. Determine exactly who will handle the assignment and if there is a good relationship between the individual consultant and the executive making the hiring decision.

The advantages of using search firms are several. Consultants can operate tactfully and with discretion and avoid embarrassment to the client, company, and candidates and without upsetting customer or competitive relationships. They can go after successfully employed executives in other companies who may not even be looking for another position, and your company can remain anonymous until real interest is generated.

Executive search is costly but well worth the investment when dealing with the selection of top management staff. If the search firm is chosen wisely, company time and money will actually be saved. Some large firms which have continuous needs for top-level personnel employ an executive recruiter on their own staff to keep the costs down.

Advertising

Help-wanted advertising in newspapers, magazines, radio, and TV is one of the major recruiting techniques available. In advertising, the selection of the medium is just as important as the message. A good recruitment advertising agency or company advertising department can be of great assistance in recommending media and creating ads. A log of ad responses will prove which media are most productive for continued use. Institutional advertising creating a good image for a company can indirectly assist in recruiting, but specific classified and display ads are much more effective. Where and when to place ads will depend on your recruiting needs.

When recruiting salespeople, executives, or technical and professional people, consider running a display ad in one or more industry, trade, or professional journals. You may also find likely candidates in the journal's "positions wanted" section. You will receive fewer candidates from trade magazine ads than you will from newspapers; but the ones you get will normally be better qualified, interested, and experienced in your type of industry.

In most areas, there is usually one newspaper carrying the largest help-wanted advertising section. Sunday editions of newspapers are usually best, and there is normally one other day during the week that carries a volume of recruiting advertising. Advertising during a holiday weekend is usually not productive.

Classified ads are the most frequently used for recruiting. They can be prepared and placed promptly and are less expensive than display ads. Display ads are usually larger and appear in other sections of papers such as the sports page for engineers and salesmen, the business section for management positions, and the women's page for secretaries. Blind ads, without company identification, ask applicants to mail résumés to a box number. This kind of advertising is good for screening applicants for confidential higher-level positions or when you expect a large number of responses which you do not wish to acknowledge. Open ads are placed to capitalize on the company's reputation and are more often used in tight labor markets, for critical skills, and for lower-level positions.

When writing recruitment ads, keep the following guidelines in mind: Classified ads are normally listed alphabetically by titles; so the first word or phrase following the title should attract the reader and motivate him to read on. Be specific about requirements of skills, education, and experience, and list salary ranges, hours, and job location. Highlight benefits such as vacation, cafeteria. Close with specific information on when, where, and how to apply, e.g., by mail, telephone, or in person.

Check your advertising copy to be sure it does not violate legislation against discrimination. Federal and state laws prohibit references to race, color, religion, sex, age, or national origin, unless they are a bona fide occupational qualification. Government regulations on affirmative action also require advertising in media read by minority groups such as ethnic newspapers and magazines.

Recruitment messages on radio and TV reach large numbers of people. The major disadvantages are higher costs than newspaper or magazine advertising and the possibility of being overwhelmed with many unqualified responses. TV recruitment programs often conducted with state employment offices have been successful. A TV commentator normally interviews a company representative who describes specific job openings, and interested viewers are requested to follow up by telephone. Special operators at the State Employment Service take the calls and arrange screening interviews with candidates and then refer only qualified applicants to the company. This program has worked well in large cities and for disadvantaged groups. Display ads on bus and subway car cards and diaroma displays in bus terminals and train stations have proved effective in some cases. However, the ad must be eye catching and the message short, due to limited reading time.

Recruitment Literature

Most companies prepare special recruitment literature aimed directly at high school and college graduates. Literature should be attractive, descriptive, and motivate the reader to want to work for the company. It should highlight advancement and educational opportunities, working conditions, and company growth. The heavy use of action photographs of employees in the work setting is recommended, and there could also be photographs of residential, educational, cultural, and recreational areas. The most important guideline is to aim the graphics and the copy to the specific audience you wish to reach. The paper and colors used should be rich looking and feeling but not slick. The front cover must motivate someone to pick it up and read on. A pocket in the back cover can accommodate inserts such as the annual report. All recruitment literature should clearly outline job qualifications and how to apply.

Walk-Ins

An individual without an interview appointment is considered a walk-in. Large well-known companies receive thousands of walk-ins each year, depending on the labor market. If possible, it is good public relations to interview each walk-in even if it is only a short interview. Although the quality of walk-ins is normally lower than from other recruitment sources, a walk-in can influence his friend, neighbors, and relatives. Therefore, courteous treatment can turn a walk-in into a walking goodwill ambassador.

Write-Ins

Writing to companies for employment is a popular job-finding method. It is important to answer every personal letter as soon as possible. Courteous well-written form letters can be sufficient, and if there is some initial interest, more information can be requested such as a completed application or résumé. An interesting write-in can be called in for an interview or, if there is no suitable opening, kept on active file for future contact.

Applicant Files

By setting up an organized filing system, many companies cash in on former qualified applicants when new openings occur. A filing system of critical occupational categories with a cross-indexed alphabetical card locator can be an inexpensive setup. A computerized applicant filing system may be feasible for large companies, or for technical firms who employ professionals which are in short supply such as engineers. The disadvantage of course is unavailability due to aging of applicants. However, old files can be reviewed on a periodic basis and tossed out if a candidate indicates no further interest or does not respond. Normally, applicant files are kept six months to a year and critical skills indefinitely. Prime candidates in the file should be identified such as candidates who previously rejected an offer of employment in order to go with another company and may have made a mistake.

Field Recruiting Trips

Some companies find out-of-town recruiting productive for experienced managerial, technical, and professional personnel. It is particularly effective when visiting a competitor's location or when the competitor is reducing staff, relocating, or closing down. It is advisable to advertise a week or two in advance and to contact a few employment agencies prior to a trip to ensure a full schedule of interviews. A good college recruiter can combine his school visits with field recruitment trips for experienced people.

Professional Associations

Most professional and technical societies maintain regular placement services for their members. The existence of professional standards by these organizations helps to certify the qualifications of their membership. It is also possible to place recruitment ads in association journals and newsletters.

Computer-assisted Recruitment

Several nationwide job-matching organizations are using computers to match applicants' interests and qualifications with employer needs. The college placement council sponsors an alumni placement service called GRAD. Employers submit searches for candidates to the GRAD computer, and proper matches provide résumés of prospects for a nominal cost to the company. As mentioned earlier, several private and public employment agencies are using computer matching retrievals. A private computerized retrieval firm called Re-Con is working with college seniors and graduate students. Several college placement offices are also experimenting with computerized placement. Video tape recorders have also been used for interviewing on a trial basis, especially for out-of-town recruiting. It is costly, however, and is recommended for companies who have other uses for the equipment.

Older Workers

Due to shortages of trained manpower and the Age Discrimination in Employment Act of 1967, many companies are now hiring older workers age forty and up. Even with a compulsory age sixty-five requirement policy, some companies are employing retired workers on a part-time basis. Studies by the U.S. Department of Labor's Bureau of Labor Statistics show that the productivity of older workers compares favorably with that of the lower age group. The Forty Plus Club located in most major cities is a free source for older managerial and professional personnel.

Women

For the most part, womanpower has been properly used only in times of critical shortages such as during World War II. Women are the largest minority in the work force, comprising 40 percent of the labor pool. Family planning and reduced tasks of homemaking due to technological advances have freed many women for a second career. The Civil Rights Act of 1964 bans discrimination based on sex in employment except where sex is a bona fide occupational qualification. Studies by the U.S. Department of Labor indicate that previous stereotype notions regarding women workers are invalid. Reports state that women workers have favorable records of attendance and turnover when compared with men employed at similar job levels and under similar circumstances. Detailed analysis indicates that the skills level of the job, the marital status and age of the worker, the length of service and record of job stability provide better clues of differences in work performance than whether a worker is a man or a woman.

Minority Groups

The shortage of qualified manpower, riots in the cities, and the Civil Rights Act of 1964 have recently brought more minority group individuals into the mainstream of employment opportunities. Blacks, Puerto Ricans, Mexican Americans, Orientals, and American Indians are overcoming environmental and educational handicaps due to the willingness and needs of American industry to train qualified workers. The Urban Coalition, National Alliance of Businessmen, and the U.S. Department of Labor have joined together to set up "Jobs" training programs. Industry provides the jobs and training, and the government reimburses companies for training costs. Through the College Placement Services, Inc., the National Urban League, and the college cluster program of the National Alliance, industry is working with colleges to provide a better education and more opportunities for minority groups to attain a college degree to qualify for the better jobs in business. The Urban League, numerous community agencies, state employment services, and church groups are all sources for minority-group personnel.

Handicapped

Placed in suitable jobs, physically or mentally handicapped workers compare favorably in achievement, attendance, punctuality, safety, attitudes, dependability, company loyalty, and turnover. The blind and deaf can perform many jobs better because of their handicaps. Success in using handicapped employees depends on proper placement, job modifications, where necessary, and a practical program for integrating them into your work force.

Veterans

Men about to be released from military service are a good recruiting source. In some cases, they have been trained in highly technical fields. Others have undergone special training during the last six months of their tour of duty under the Project Transition Program of the United States Manpower Administration and United States Employment Service. Junior officers about to leave the service are recruited for engineering, professional, and management jobs. A number of firms are now specializing in military recruitment centers held in cities near major military installations. Other techniques used are: advertising in military publications, sending recruitment literature, and interviewing at separation centers. Retired officers are another source for employing military personnel. Many officers retire with twenty years of service while they still have many productive years ahead of them. Military leadership training and responsibility can be transferred as experience to management positions in industry. The Retired Officers Association in Washington, D.C., serves as a clearinghouse for employment, and there is no fee.

SCREENING AND SELECTION

Assuming we have recruited a sufficient number of qualified applicants from the previously mentioned sources and techniques, we will now discuss the various methods of screening and selecting candidates. Since employment interviewing will be covered in depth in Chapter 13 and testing in Chapters 14, 15, and 16, we shall limit our discussion to résumés, regular and weighted application blanks, reference checking, preemployment physical examinations, and the selection decision. It is recommended that all available screening techniques be used to obtain a total profile of an applicant. All selection methods should be validated in follow-up studies to see if they truly predict success on the job.

Résumés

Unfortunately, résumés are used too often as the only factor in initially deciding to interview an advertising response, an employment agency referral, or a write-in candidate. A résumé is normally a subjective narrative description of an individual's education, experience, and personal data, slanted the way he wants to present it. The individual may stress unimportant material and minimize essential information. A trained recruitment specialist must, therefore, read between the lines and not reject a résumé too quickly without checking it out further. An application form on the other hand requires the candidate to present his qualifications in a structured, factual manner which is important to the company.

Application Blanks

When there is a large volume of walk-in candidates to be screened, two application forms may be used: one short form for preliminary screening (Figure 3) and a more detailed blank for those passing the initial screening. Many companies have different forms for contrasting job levels. Normally, there is one for clerical and blue-collar positions and another for managerial, professional, and technical positions where job requirements are more complex. If possible, it is desirable not to require candidates to complete more than one application form. The forms should be designed in relation to the nature of the company's business and job requirements. They should be durable, easy to read, clear, concise, and sufficiently spaced. Since most companies keep applications of those employed as a permanent record in the personnel file, they should be properly sized for filing and the last name should appear first, so as to be easily identifiable.

Preemployment inquiries are closely regulated by federal, state, and city fair employment legislation; therefore, questions should not violate the law. The principal information requested should include name, address, telephone number, social security number, health and physical handicaps, education, job history, and military service. Similar questions should be grouped together and enough space allowed

MCGRAW-HILL POLICY AND FEDERAL LAW FORBID DISCRIMINATION BECAUSE OF RACE, COLOR, RELIGION, AGE, SEX OR NATIONAL ORIGIN.

PERSONNEL RELATIONS

McGRAW-HILL, INC.

PRELIMINARY
EMPLOYMENT APPLICATION

Date_____

Personal Data

Applying For Position As _____ Salary Desired _____ Date Available _____

Name:_____
(Last)   (First)   (Middle)

Address_____
(Street)   (City)   (State)   (Zip Code)

Telephone No._____ Social Security No._____ Are you a U. S. Citizen or an
(Area Code)   Alien Immigrant? ☐ Yes ☐ No

Are you (check appropriate box) over 16 ☐, over ☐ 18, and/or under ☐ 65?

How were you referred to McGraw-Hill, Inc.?   ☐ Agency ☐ School ☐ Advertisement ☐ Direct Contact ☐ McGraw-Hill Employee ☐ Other

Name of referral source above:_____

Educational Data

SCHOOLS	NAME OF INSTITUTION	ADDRESS	MAJOR	COURSES TAKEN	No. Yrs. Attended	Yr. Grad.	Degree
GRADE			✕✕✕✕✕	✕✕✕✕✕			✕✕
PREPARATORY OR HIGH			✕✕✕✕✕				✕✕
COLLEGE							
OTHERS							
PRESENT							✕✕

Employment Data Begin with more recent employer.

FORMER EMPLOYERS and ADDRESS	YOUR POSITION and DUTIES	DATES	SALARY RECEIVED	SUPERVISOR'S NAME	REASON FOR LEAVING
		From	Start $		
NATURE OF BUSINESS		To	Finish $	TITLE	
		From	Start $		
NATURE OF BUSINESS		To	Finish $	TITLE	

Skills

Typing Speed_____words per minute ☐ Electric ☐ Manual   Steno Speed_____words per minute Method_____

Business Machines _____

Figure 3. Preliminary short-form employment application.
(McGraw-Hill.)

for write-in answers. Application forms normally conclude with a signed statement that the information given is correct, and that the individual understands he is subject to discharge for falsification. In some cases, the final statement also includes company rules or an agreement to undergo a security clearance check for government contractors. Application blanks tend to grow over a period of time and should be periodically revised to eliminate irrelevant questions or items ruled discriminatory by new fair employment legislation.

Weighted Application Forms

It is possible to score application blanks numerically, based on statistical research on item selection and weighting. The research techniques must be systematic, with results yielding significant correlation between an employee's future job behavior and the weighting factors. It is recommended that instead of a cutoff score, an acceptable range of scores be used to narrow the field of applicants for total profile analysis, using other selection criteria (interviews, tests, reference checks, and physical examinations).

Reference Checking

The verification of information obtained on application forms and during interviews is essential in the screening process. There is nothing more tangible for predicting an applicant's future performance than past success in employment. Therefore, discussions with former supervisors regarding the strengths and weaknesses of an applicant can be the deciding factor in the selection procedure. Too often, in many companies, reference checking is treated very casually or omitted entirely. Unfortunately, many applicants know this and, therefore, stretch the truth on application blanks. A good reference check involving someone who really knows the applicant gives the recruiter an opportunity to verify or nullify facts or impressions. If the applicant is employed, the information obtained can assist his new supervisor in doing a better job of developing and motivating him.

To perform reference checking properly requires good interviewing skills and the art of persuasive diplomacy. It is too important to be delegated to a secretary or clerk. The higher the level of the person conducting the checking, the more it conveys an implication of importance to the company being contacted. The names of former supervisors should be obtained on an application form or during an interview. Personal references are almost worthless, for a friend will most likely only say nice things about the applicant. The candidate's former supervisor is in the best position to give an objective evaluation of work performance, and the personnel department can usually verify factual information, such as dates of employment, salary history, attendance. Normally a five- to ten-year period of past employment is checked, and the highest degree or diploma is verified.

The most important reference probably is the applicant's present employer; however, care must be taken not to check without permission from the applicant. The applicant can be asked if there is anyone in his present company who can be contacted without jeopardizing his position, or if one of his former supervisors has left the company. If it is impossible to check the present employer, condition an offer of employment on receiving a satisfactory reference check after the applicant has given notice of resignation.

Most companies use both the telephone and the mail for checking references. A personal visit with a former supervisor would be ideal; however, time and cost factors typically prohibit this practice. Telephone reference checks are preferable because they save time and produce information the former supervisor may not want to put in writing. Many firms use a telephone reference check form to make sure specific points are covered (see Figure 4).

School and college records are the most valuable source for reference information on applicants with little or no pertinent job experience. Educational information is extremely difficult to obtain by telephone, and, therefore, a written request for verification of a degree or diploma is suggested. Many colleges require a signed request by the former student before they will release information. A self-addressed, stamped envelope will facilitate returns. Requests for reference data normally carry two stipulations: that any information given will be held in confidence, and that reciprocal courtesy will be provided in the future. In addition to employment and educational references, the requirements for some jobs also make it advisable to check police records, military service, or credit standing. Investigation agencies can inexpensively check these items through established contacts.

PERSONNEL RECRUITMENT AND SELECTION

TELEPHONE REFERENCE CHECK

Applicant's Name _____

Firm Contacted _____

Person Contacted _____ Position _____

Confirm Dates of Employment: Started _____ Left _____

Job Title and Brief Description of Duties: _____

_____

_____

Overall Job Performance: ☐ Outstanding ☐ Average ☐ Poor

Did the Applicant Work Well with Others? ☐ Yes ☐ No

Strong Points: _____

_____

Weak Points: _____

_____

Reason for Leaving: _____

Rate of Pay: _____ Absenteeism: _____

Would You Recommend for Our Position? ☐ Yes ☐ No

Would You Rehire? ☐ Yes ☐ No   If Not, Why? _____

_____

Additional Specific Questions: _____

_____

_____

_____

Reference Done By: _____ Date: _____

STRICTLY CONFIDENTIAL
Upon Completion Forward To Personnel Relations Department

Figure 4.   Telephone reference check.

Dun and Bradstreet, Retail Credit, and Fidelifacts are agencies which have representatives in most areas of the country.

If one or two unfavorable comments are uncovered in reference checking, do not automatically eliminate the applicant. Consider whether the respondent might be biased, and check with other sources for verification.

Preemployment Physical Exams

Medical examinations are usually the last step in the employment process, but in some cases they are not given until after the new employee starts work. If possible, it is desirable to have an applicant pass a preemployment physical before resigning his present position. Exceptions to this should be granted only with the applicant's clear understanding that his final employment is subject to passing the examination. The main reasons for preemployment medical examinations are: (1) to determine if the applicant qualifies for the physical requirements of the position, (2) to discover any medical limitations that should be taken into account in the placement of the applicant, (3) to establish a record of the applicant's health at the time of employment in case of future insurance or compensation claims, (4) to detect diseases unknown to the applicant which may be contagious, treated, and cured, (5) to prevent absenteeism and reduce accidents.

Large companies normally use their own medical department for preemployment physicals. Smaller firms usually retain a doctor on a consulting basis and have the applicant go to his office for the examination. In many states the employer is required to pay the costs of preemployment physicals; however, most companies normally assume this expense.

The Selection Decision

Normally the personnel department screens all candidates and only refers the most qualified to line management for consideration. Once a candidate has completed an application form, multiple interviews, preemployment tests, reference checks, and a medical examination, it is time for a selection decision. It is recommended that more than one person interview and evaluate candidates; however, the manager responsible for the performance of the new employee should make the selection decision based on the total profile of the applicant.

The critical element in the selection process is timing. Steps in the process should be streamlined so that applicants are not left hanging for long periods of time. The personnel department should keep in constant touch with requisitioners and keep applicants posted on their status by telephone. Too many companies take up to a month or more to process an applicant to the final step only to lose him to a faster competitor. All applicants deserve to know of their final status in the selection process within a reasonable period of time. Most firms send a diplomatic turndown letter to all candidates once a selection decision is made. It is normally best not to tell applicants the reasons for rejection if they are of a personal or subjective nature. The most common reason given is that the most qualified person has been selected from a few well-qualified final candidates. If a rejected candidate is well qualified, tell him he may be recontacted as new positions develop. It is important to document reasons for employment decisions in case of any future charges of discrimination. Many organizations use an interview evaluation check-off form for each interview conducted.

SUMMARY

Effective recruitment screening and selection procedures contribute to your company's success and profit-making potential by attracting the best employee for each job. It is important to record all recruitment costs by source and continually determine by which methods you are obtaining your best employees. This can be done by periodically analyzing cost per hire, turnover reports, performance evaluations, promotions, and company profits.

BIBLIOGRAPHY

A.M.A. Book of Employment Forms: American Management Association, New York, 1967.
Bibliography: College Trained Manpower, College Placement Council, Bethlehem, Pa., 1967.
Calvert, Robert J.: *Employing the Minority Group College Graduate,* The Garrett Park Press, Garrett Park, Md., 1968.
Coss, Frank: *Recruitment Advertising,* American Management Association, New York, 1968.

Endicott, Frank S.: *Trends in Employment of College and University Graduates in Business and Industry,* Northwestern University Press, Evanston, Ill., 1970.

Hawk, Roger S.: *The Recruitment Function,* American Management Association, New York, 1967.

Kellog, Frazer: *Computer Based Aids to the Placement Process,* M.I.T. Sloan School of Management, Industrial Relations Section, Cambridge, Mass., 1969.

Pell, Arthur R.: *Recruiting and Selecting Personnel,* Simon & Schuster, Inc., New York, 1969.

Preparing the Recruitment Brochure, College Placement Council Inc., Bethlehem, Pa., 1964.

"Recruiting Practices," *Personnel Policies Forum Survey no. 86,* The Bureau of National Affairs, Inc., Washington, D.C., March, 1969.

Supplement to the Bibliography: *College Trained Manpower,* College Placement Council Inc., Bethlehem, Pa., 1969.

Teal, Everett: *A Manual for Campus Recruiters,* The College Placement Council Inc., Bethlehem, Pa., 1962.

Technical Manpower Recruitment Practices: Deutsch, Shea and Evans Inc., New York, October, 1969.

The Fine Art of Designing Your Company's Recruiting Brochure: Champion Papers Inc., Hamilton, Ohio, 1964.

Uris, Auren: *The Executive Job Market,* McGraw-Hill Book Company, New York, 1966.

Trade Journals and other reference works

Journal of College Placement, College Placement Council Inc., Bethlehem, Pa.

Personnel, American Management Association, New York.

Personnel Administration, Society for Personnel Administration, Washington, D.C.

Personnel Journal, The Personnel Journal Inc., Swarthmore, Pa.

Personnel Management, The Bureau of National Affairs Inc., Washington, D.C.

Personnel Management, Prentice-Hall, Inc., Englewood Cliffs, N.J.

Recruiting Trends, Enterprise Publications, Chicago, Ill.

chapter 13

The Employment Interview

FELIX M. LOPEZ *Felix M. Lopez & Associates, Roslyn, New York*

The interview is the heart of the employment process. One of man's oldest and most universal methods of assessment, it is also the most misunderstood. Although it simulates a conversation between an applicant and a prospective employer, it is really a highly complicated tool.

It is the principal means by which an employer secures the information necessary to describe an applicant accurately, in reference to the requirements of a position, to enable him to make an accurate statement about the applicant's probable performance in a position. It is also an employer's principal means of persuading the applicant of the advantages of employment with his organization.

The interview is, therefore, a most indispensable tool, not only because of its information potential, which is considerable, but also because of its distinctly human aspects. No applicant wants to be judged for a position without an opportunity to discuss it face to face in a meeting with a company representative. The interview gives the applicant the feeling that he matters, that he is being considered by a human being rather than by a computer. The interview also gives him a chance to ask questions about the job, the company, or its benefits. It gives the interviewer an opportunity to do some selling, if that is necessary, as it so often is and, finally, because it gives an applicant a chance to feel that he is the one doing the deciding, it enables him to maintain his dignity in what can become a very impersonal process.

THE INTERVIEW AS A SELECTION TOOL

Skill in employment interviewing is not easily acquired. As a selection tool, the interview has been the subject of repeated criticisms that have centered principally on the interviewer rather than on the technique, but when the interviewer is well prepared and uses proper techniques and procedures, the interview becomes a most powerful tool in the selection process.

Interview Issues

Research by various investigators in the past twenty-five years has produced little evidence to testify to the validity of the employment interview. It has, on the other hand, raised a number of issues that can be summarized as follows:

Untrained interviewers. The average interviewer has never been exposed to formal interview training. He is simply unprepared to conduct a proper employment interview. Without realizing it, he is likely to obtain so little relevant information that, at the end of the interview, he has to fill in his sketchy impressions with information from his own biases.

Content variability. The interview content is covered haphazardly and indiscriminately. Each interviewer tends to question the applicant on areas that are of interest to him or which he deems to be most relevant. There is no uniformity of information covered among interviewers nor even by interviewers in speaking to several applicants for the same job in the same company.

Question variability. Interviewers vary considerably in the way they ask questions, not realizing that the form of the question affects its answer. An interviewee usually tries to determine the answer the interviewer wants, rather than the answer he prefers to give.

Uneven interpretation. Even when interviewers obtain the same information about an applicant, they are likely to interpret or weight it differently. One investigator found that interviewers differ widely on how much certain items of information impressed them. The same items created quite unfavorable impressions on some interviewers and quite favorable impressions on others.

Premature decisions. Most interviewers tend to make their decisions early in the interview and thereafter merely look for information to support that decision. Their initial appraisals of information derived from an application blank, or the applicant's personal appearance, are usually decisive. The often-stated observation, "I sized him up the minute he walked into the office" is one example of this failing.

Negative approach. The attitudes of untrained interviewers affect the information obtained. The fact that such interviewers are more likely to be influenced by unfavorable rather than by favorable information, or to change their original favorable impressions to unfavorable impressions, suggests that their purpose is to search for negative information about an applicant.

Unreliable decisions. The decisions made as a result of an interview are often unreliable and inconsistent. As usually conducted, the interview has been shown to be so inconsistent that the results depend more on the interviewer than on the interviewee. An applicant who is interviewed by different persons for the same job can be assessed as to his employability in absolutely contrary ways by them.

Selection and Preparation of Interviewers

The employment interview becomes effective when it is conducted uniformly, relevant information is obtained and interpreted consistently, and it contributes to the selection of successful employees. These requirements can be met by selecting and training competent interviewers and by using appropriate employment interviewing techniques.

The selection and preparation of interviewers are important because not everyone is emotionally disposed, nor adequately prepared, to engage in this rather delicate and sensitive task. Two errors are commonly made in this regard. The first consists of assigning a relatively immature and inexperienced person as an employment interviewer in the personnel department. This error is based on the mistaken assumption that employment interviewing is largely a clerical function. The second error consists of permitting a line supervisor to interview candidates for positions in his unit. Even though he has the ability to judge technical competence, he usually has little skill or inclination to interview adequately.

Interviewing is a complex skill, and for an employer, there is a lot at stake. Interviewing errors are costly. No one should be assigned to this task unless he is carefully selected and trained for it.

Interviewer selection.   A prospective interviewer must have a reasonably attractive appearance and diction to enable him to establish rapport and to communicate easily with applicants. He must be mature, free from overt emotional problems, from obvious biases, and from neurotic tendencies. Above all, he must have a positive conviction about the basic dignity of a human being—a dignity that entitles him to respect and consideration regardless of his background. This means that he must not merely "like people" but must possess the flexibility and the tolerance to approach others with respect and to establish helpful relationships with them.

Besides these personal qualities, an interviewer must know thoroughly the requirements and the circumstances surrounding the positions for which he interviews. He must be familiar with the details of the company's products, customers, organization structure, personnel policies, salary rates, position's duties, and even the personal characteristics of individual supervisors. But, most importantly, he must have a clear idea of the critical factors that mark the difference between successful and unsuccessful job performance. It is inappropriate for an interviewer merely to guess at these; he must find out for sure by adequate investigation.

Interviewer training.   Interviewer training must cover (1) the basic principles of individual differences, human motivation, and personal adjustment; (2) the functions of modern personnel administration; (3) the basic products, policies, and practices of his organization; and (4) the principles and the components of the interview as a communications process.

The format of an effective training program for interviewers consists of at least forty hours of formal instruction. Ample opportunity must be provided for role playing, personal coaching, and feedback sessions via audio and video tape recordings of practice interviews. Without this intensive training a person simply cannot acquire significant skill in the interview process on his own.

It is apparent that these requirements preclude the assignment of line supervisors and managers to an extensive role in the employment program. They should confine themselves to an evaluation only of an applicant's technical competence for the position under consideration if it cannot be judged in a more objective fashion.

Interview Procedures

Besides a well-prepared, competent interviewer, the effectiveness of the interview as a selection tool is a function of the procedures used. This depends upon the type of interview conducted and the information required of the applicant.

Types of employment interview.   Basically, there are two types of employment interview: the initial and the evaluation interview. Each differs according to its immediate purpose and its place in the employment sequence.

The initial interview which is designed to eliminate obviously unqualified applicants and to interest qualified applicants in employment is conducted at the beginning of the selection sequence and results only in a tentative decision. Initial interviews last between fifteen and thirty minutes.

There are many ways to conduct this interview, but the most effective is a screening approach. After indicating that the interview will be brief, the interviewer asks the applicant "make-or-break" questions that tell him whether the applicant meets the bedrock qualifications of the job. To do this, the interviewer must have ready a list of questions for which there is incontrovertible evidence that certain answers will disqualify the applicant immediately.

A few examples of such questions are:
"What are your salary requirements?"
"Can you work overtime?"
"Do you have a driver's license?" (for a chauffeur's position)
"Do you type?" (for a typing position)
If the applicant qualifies on these critical questions, the interviewer then explores briefly his education and full-time experience. Once the interviewer obtains a rough outline of the applicant's background, he may then explore briefly his attitudes toward the occupation, the industry, or the company. Broad open-ended questions such as these are effective:
"What is there about selling that appeals to you?"
"What makes you feel that you would do well in clerical work?"
If, at this point, the applicant looks like a good prospect, an appointment for testing or an evaluation interview can be arranged. In some cases, that is, for part-time or temporary help, this brief initial interview may be all that is necessary.

The evaluation interview, which is designed to provide a thorough review of the applicant's qualifications to enable the interviewer to make a final decision, is usually conducted last in the selection sequence. Evaluation interviews last usually between thirty and sixty minutes and will be discussed throughout the balance of this chapter.

Interview styles. There are two major interviewing styles: the patterned and the nondirective. The patterned style is always used in the initial interview, while both styles are used in the evaluation interview.

The patterned interview style follows a predetermined outline of questions carefully designed to reduce the variability in the form of information obtained from the interview. The information supplied by the interviewee is usually recorded on a preprinted form during the interview. Later, the data are classified, tabulated, and used to build standards with which the responses of many applicants can be compared. The drawback of this style is that its standardization results in less interviewer flexibility and a restriction in the amount of information exchanged. It is usually possible, therefore, to obtain only the information planned before the interview.

Most professional interviewers adopt a more open-ended style, which is referred to as "nondirective." In this style, the interviewer uses comprehensive questions and encourages the interviewee to take the lead in covering the information relevant to the job. Thus, it is more likely that unexpectedly significant information can be obtained.

In most employment situations, the nondirective style is more effective, but it requires considerable training and experience to employ skillfully, and it is also much more time consuming. The interviewer must weigh the value of the additional information obtained against the time required to obtain it. The style of most interviewers lies somewhere between the patterned and the nondirective. In the more sensitive managerial positions, the interviewing style will tend to be more nondirective, while in the clerical, production, and sales positions, the most efficient style will be patterned.

Interview content. Knowing what to discuss with an applicant is central to effective interviewing. The applicant's previous life history, education, work experience, and personal qualifications form the basic content of the interview.

1. *Personal Qualities.* This area includes the personal qualifications required in the position: physical appearance, health, dress and grooming, voice quality, diction, vocabulary, poise, alertness, and aggressiveness. Most of these qualities are assessed by the interviewer's observations rather than by the applicant's answers to his questions.

2. *Academic Achievement.* This area covers the type of schooling, quality of grades, class standing, social activities, relationship with teachers, honors and awards, and athletic accomplishments. Questions in this area can provide a good indication of an applicant's initiative, independence, reliability, intellectual competence, and emotional stability. Fruitful avenues to explore are the reasons why the applicant chose the schools he attended, the amount of advice he received while in school, the degree to which he financed his own education, and his personal appraisal of his scholastic achievements.

3. *Occupational Experience.* This area emphasizes not merely an applicant's technical competence but also the level of responsibility and skill he has attained in previous jobs, the position level and salary progression he has achieved, and his reasons for leaving former jobs. Questions in this area should be directed at obtaining evidence of good judgment, initiative, drive and energy, and ability to assume responsibility.

4. *Interpersonal Competence.* This area includes the applicant's ability to get along with others. It is not enough to evaluate this area on the basis of the applicant's behavior during the interview. Specific questions must be asked about his family history, leisure-time activities, hobbies, and community interests to ascertain his degree of social adjustment.

5. *Career Orientation.* This area covers the applicant's career aspirations, his immediate and long-range goals, and his potential for advancement. Answers to questions in this area form the heart of a managerial applicant's qualifications. The internal consistency and realism of his career progress are important road signs pointing to eventual success.

The interview record. Each employment interview must be carefully recorded on a preprinted form. Many forms are available, ranging from precisely structured checklists to forms that allow for extensive expression of an interviewer's reactions. The more structured the form, the easier it is to make comparisons between different applicants and different interviewers.

In initial interviews, it is more desirable to use the checklist. In evaluation interviews, the open-ended form is more desirable. It is best to strike a balance between a form that narrowly confines an interviewer and one that gives him no guidelines at all.

It is also most desirable to record interview judgments and observations while the interview is in progress. If the interviewer waits until afterward, he is apt to forget many important details. There is little danger that, by writing during the interview, he will distract the interviewee. If an interviewer waits until the interview is over to make notes, interruptions may prevent the completion of this task for an hour or even a day. Even though he has an excellent memory, the later the task is postponed, the less reliable will be the final evaluation.

Therefore immediately after the interview, the interviewer must complete his notes and make a final summary of his impressions indicating his evaluation of the applicant. This summary, written while the interview is still fresh in his memory, is invaluable later if there is an occasion (such as in a civil rights complaint) to review this final evaluation and the reasons for it.

CONDUCTING THE INTERVIEW

Like the football coach who always has his "game plan," the interviewer conducts an effective interview when he follows a careful plan. A haphazard interview is not only disconcerting to the applicant, it inhibits the coverage of the applicant's qualifications and distorts his final evaluation.

An interview plan includes not only those areas previously described under

Interview Content but such preliminaries as interview location, time allocation, and interview sequence.

Interview Preliminaries

If possible, the interviewer reviews the application before the interview, looking for unusual items, inconsistencies, gaps, or other information that he will want to discuss with the applicant. It is good practice to require the applicant to complete the company's application form rather than to submit a résumé, and it is quite undesirable to interview with no written biographical information available.

Interview location.   The location in which the interview is conducted must be arranged meticulously. It is a poor practice to conduct an employment interview in an open area or even in semiprivacy. Without exception, an interview must be conducted in private, which means a closed office where no telephone calls can be received and where the interview conversation cannot be heard by others. It is discourteous and distracting to permit interruptions in the form of telephone calls or personal visits during an interview. Privacy and courtesy mean also that the interview area is neat and tidy, the interviewer's desk clear of papers and books, and the interviewer dressed appropriately. An untidy desk or a disheveled interviewer creates the impression that the applicant is either intruding or being treated indifferently.

The time allocated to an interview is divided into three broad phases: the warm-up, the main sequence, and the wrap-up.

The warm-up.   The warm-up phase, which should consume about 15 percent of interview time, is designed to establish a communications bridge between interviewer and interviewee over which information can flow freely. The interviewer must convey the impression of being sincerely interested in the applicant. As the applicant enters the office, the interviewer welcomes him warmly, greets him with a handshake, and introduces himself. He then seats the applicant in a comfortable chair in full view so that he can observe his physical appearance from shoes to headdress, his style and taste in clothing, neatness, decorum, and personal cleanliness.

The interviewer then opens by discussing some item on the application blank —the applicant's hobbies, cultural interests, or social affiliations—something that is comfortable for him to discuss. Hopefully, the area selected is of mutual interest so that the interviewer can establish a subtle bond with the applicant. During this phase, the interviewee should be given frequent pats on the back, and the interviewer should show enthusiasm and approval of the interviewee's remarks and accomplishments. But, gradually, and almost imperceptibly, the interview moves into the main sequence.

The Main Interview Sequence

The main interview sequence requires about 70 percent of the interview time budget. There is no set way of entering this phase. Ideally, the interviewer moves into it without realizing it by building his questions on the applicant's remarks during the warm-up phase. If the introductory conversation goes well, the applicant will be talking freely. It is best to have him talk about himself first. Then, after he has completed his presentation of his qualifications, the interviewer can talk about the job. But the main idea is to get the applicant to do most of the talking so that the interviewer can listen carefully, making sure the appropriate areas are covered and interpreting what he hears accurately.

Obtaining information.   Without resorting to the subtle probes of professional psychologists, the interviewer can look for signs of stability, truthfulness, or other physical and mental characteristics that are employment assests. This review is greatly facilitated by sketching mentally a chronological outline of the applicant's life history. By following such a procedure, the interviewer is apt to uncover gaps in the applicant's history, clear up confusion in dates, and rectify other errors in the record.

Details are important even though the interview must move along fairly rapidly. Little things—casual remarks, confusion on dates, faulty memory, minor periods of unemployment—are often significant. When picked up, they are followed up carefully but unassumingly or noted for future checking.

The interviewer must not hesitate to discuss sensitive topics if they arise. But he must avoid showing any outward sign of disapproval or distress if unfavorable information is brought up. If the interviewer projects an understanding and accepting attitude, he is likely to obtain more information than by displaying displeasure or disbelief. However, he must avoid probing in areas that are irrelevant to employment no matter how interesting.

Giving the applicant information. Another important task of the interviewer is to sell the interviewee on the job and the company. He succeeds, or fails, to do this mainly by the way in which he conducts the interview. Success also depends on the adequacy of the information given to the applicant about the job and the company. This task should require about 15 of the 70 percent allocated to the main sequence of interview time.

The interviewer first describes the company and its policies, then the duties, responsibilities, and opportunities in the job under consideration and, finally, the way employment is secured, emphasizing that a thorough check will be made of the applicant's background. In describing the job, it is important to keep in mind that there are good and bad features to every position. The bad features should not be overemphasized. As a matter of fact, the favorable aspects should be stressed after the presentation of a position's undesirable features.

It is well to keep in mind that the employment interview is not the time to describe the intricacies of the pension or incentive compensation plans. The interviewer merely mentions the employee benefit programs and gives the applicant a brochure that describes them in detail. And, last, he should mention the salary if it is fixed or the salary range if it is subject to negotiation, noting in the latter instance that a precise figure will be discussed after the final employment decision has been made.

The Interview Wrap-Up

When the interview reaches the 85 percent mark with respect to time passage, the interviewer begins to bring it to a close. By now, he has a clear idea of the applicant's basic strengths and limitations for the job under consideration, and the applicant understands the job opportunity and important company personnel policies. To double check this understanding, the interviewer gives the applicant, at this point, a chance to ask questions. He then terminates the interview with a brief summary of what has been discussed and what the next step in the employment process is to be.

As a rule, it is undesirable to terminate an interview by announcing an unfavorable decision unless it is absolutely unavoidable. When an applicant is rejected out of hand, it can prolong the interview unnecessarily. If it appears that the decision is likely to be unfavorable, it is more convenient and usually more graceful to tell the applicant that the interviewer will let him know in a day or two what the decision is to be. Of course, this commitment must be kept. If it appears that the applicant is qualified, the interviewer makes an appointment for medical examination or other employment procedure. Immediately after the applicant leaves the interviewer, he reviews his notes and writes a careful summary of his evaluation.

THE INTERVIEW INFORMATION PROCESS

A sound interview decision is made only if the right information is obtained and interpreted correctly. The object of the interview information process, therefore, consists in getting the interviewee to talk, listening carefully to what he says, and interpreting what he says correctly.

Getting the Interviewee to Talk

The interviewer gets the interviewee to talk freely by asking questions properly, by maintaining silence at appropriate times, and by reflecting or restating what the applicant says to him.

Asking questions properly. Since it is up to the interviewer to take the lead in the interview, he must ask questions to suggest what he wants to know. The art of interviewing lies in the number of questions and the way they are asked. If the interviewer asks too many and too direct questions, the interview will become just an interrogation; if he asks too few and too broad questions, it will assume the rambling quality of a mere conversation. Here are a few general rules for asking questions:

1. It is best to try to phrase questions in a declarative form. The suggestion "Tell me about your present job" is preferable to the question "What kind of work do you do?"

2. Open-ended questions, that is, questions that cannot be answered with one or two words, are much more effective than closed questions.

3. Comprehensive introductory questions such as "Tell me about yourself" are excellent stimulants for the applicant because they suggest subtly to him that he is expected to do most of the talking.

4. Questions that are based on what the applicant has just said show that the interviewer is listening carefully and encourages the applicant to continue to talk.

The immediate purpose of the interview determines largely the type of questions to be asked. In the initial interview, for example, the emphasis is upon the "what," the "where," and the "when." Such questions would include the following:

"What schools did you attend?"
"When and where did you work?"
"What kind of work did you do?"

In the evaluation interview, the purpose is to describe the underlying life style and motivational patterns of the interviewee. Questions, therefore, focus on the "why," the "who," and the "how."

"Why did you choose your college?"
"How did you like your last supervisor?"
"Who influenced you most in your early life?"

Using silence effectively. Often the most significant information is offered by an applicant after a period of silence. Using silence effectively, therefore, is one of the most powerful tools the interviewer has. Few know how to employ this technique because, for the uninitiated, there is a natural tendency to become somewhat anxious when silence occurs in the interview. A few seconds seems like ten minutes. The untrained interviewer will interrupt this meaningful period by introducing another thought or another question.

To avoid this pitfall, the interviewer must keep in mind that during a period of silence, an applicant is usually trying to formulate an answer, that the pressure to speak is building up in him too, and that the silence is another subtle suggestion to the applicant that he must do the talking.

There are two ways to make silence work. (1) After asking a question, the interviewer should wait until the applicant answers in some way, no matter how many seconds of silence pass. (2) After the applicant answers a question, it is desirable to avoid jumping in with another question immediately. The interviewer can nod his head and say, "I see" or "I understand." Often, the applicant will continue to elaborate on what he has just said in a very meaningful way.

Reflecting and restating. The essence of nondirective interviewing consists of using silence effectively and of reflecting and restating the ideas of the interviewee. Silence is the interviewer's most powerful tool, but reflection and restatement are his sharpest and most incisive. They are also the most difficult to master.

Reflecting an applicant's ideas is the best way of showing him that the interviewer accepts them and is trying to understand him. For example, an applicant might say, "My supervisor on my last job gave me a raw deal." The interviewer then says, "You feel he didn't treat you fairly." This restatement accepts what the applicant said, avoids an indication of disapproval or concern, and merely continues the conversation.

Restating also gives the applicant an opportunity to hear what he has just said, to correct or modify it if the interviewer did not hear him accurately, or to elaborate on it. For example, an applicant might say, "I want a sales position because I like to be on the go and to work with people. I think it gives you an opportunity to really prove how effective you are." The interviewer restates this by saying, "You feel that sales work will give you a chance to show how effective you are with people." This restatement gives the applicant a chance to confirm, elaborate, or modify the notion. The result is a much deeper level of communication between the interviewer and the applicant.

Restatement, however, is quite difficult because it requires the interviewer to listen carefully and intently, an art with which few adults have more than a nodding acquaintance.

The Art of Listening

Listening is what one hears, understands, and remembers. Most adults are quite surprised to learn how poorly they listen to others' conversations. The average adult listens with only about 25 percent efficiency but deceives himself into believing that he listens intently when actually he does not.

Listening is crucial to an interviewer. He must hear, understand, and remember what happens and what is said during the interview. Although his eyes are used, he relies most heavily upon his ears. Many interviewers fall down in this regard not because they do not cover all the areas of the interview, nor because they do not ask the proper questions, but simply because they are not accustomed to obtaining information through their auditory senses.

Listening pitfalls. Some of the listening pitfalls that interviewers fall into are:

1. *Anticipation.* When an applicant begins a sentence, interviewers have a tendency to anticipate the remainder of the sentence. They then stop listening and begin to think of what they will ask next.

2. *Intolerance.* Interviewers are often so intolerant, that is, mentally critical of the physical speech, appearance, or mannerisms of an applicant, that they will either pay little attention to what he is saying or interpret it inaccurately.

3. *Impulsivity.* Interrupting an applicant before he can complete an answer and asking him another question before he has had time to answer the previous one are examples of interviewer impulsivity. Every interviewer should stamp on his consciousness the word "wait."

4. *Indolence.* Listening takes such hard mental effort that many interviewers become lazy and let their attention wander.

5. *Suggestibility.* Interviewers are often influenced by emotionally loaded

terms. If an applicant says his former supervisor was "unbearable," the interviewer should ask him what he means by that word.

Aids to good listening. Besides interviewing in a distraction-free area and taking notes, there are a number of ways in which an interviewer can improve his listening.

1. *Interest.* Interviewers tend to listen more intently when they are interested in the applicant. The interviewer must, therefore, consider the interview to be quite important and strive consciously to do the best job he knows how to do.

2. *Patience.* The interviewer must be patient and take his time. Rapid-fire interviews are rarely effective. After he asks questions, he must give the interviewee time to think.

3. *Linking.* The interviewer must try to form his questions on the basis of what the applicant says. He can begin with a broad introductory question and then build his subsequent questions on these replies. This frees him from the distraction of thinking of his next question—a distraction that is the main root of poor listening.

4. *Alertness.* The interviewer must listen for key words and phrases the applicant uses. He must ask him to explain them further, when necessary, to be absolutely certain that he understands these words and phrases in the same way in which the applicant uses them.

5. *Concentration.* The interviewer must listen for main ideas rather than for mere facts. It is best to concentrate on what the applicant is trying to convey, to listen for the inner meaning, for ideas, patterns, or trends. The interviewer must ask himself constantly, "What is the applicant telling me?"

6. *Deliberation.* The interviewer must withhold evaluation until comprehension is complete. He must hear the man out before he judges him and then frequently summarize what has been said to be certain that comprehension is really total.

Interpreting Interview Information

The validity of a selection procedure lies not in obtaining relevant information about an applicant but primarily in interpreting it correctly. Interviewers often fail because they make one or all of these three fundamental interpretation errors:

1. They do not obtain information from the applicant that is relevant to effective job performance.

2. They draw invalid conclusions from the information they do obtain.

3. They fail to recognize that there are several plausible conclusions to be drawn from the same set of facts.

Interviewers tend to draw conclusions from different bits of information, then accept them as positive truths rather than as mere hypotheses that must be confirmed by additional information. In a sense, therefore, interpretation of interview data consists of the ability to resist leaping to erroneous conclusions.

Interpretation is essentially a logical rather than an intuitive process. The interviewer must elicit information about a person, put it together to posit a hypothesis that explains the information, seek confirmation in other information about the person, and apply the whole to determine the probability of success in performing the job. Basically, therefore, interpretation is a process of continuous generation of hypotheses from the applicant's life history as he describes it and his behavior during the interview as it occurs and their confirmation or rejection on the basis of other evidence obtained in the same interview.

Therefore, during the interview, the interviewer must obtain material with which to generate hypotheses. Obviously the broader and the richer the material, the more fertile it will be for hypotheses generation. The applicant's past history, of course, provides the best source for these hypotheses. However, the same sources must also be used to confirm or reject them. One approach is to use early life history and schooling as places from which to generate ideas and thoughts about the individual and then to confirm them by questions from his current life history. For example, if an applicant indicates that he had difficulty with some of his teachers in school, the hypothesis that he had a negative attitude toward authority could be formulated and then confirmed or rejected by careful questions about his relationships with past and present supervisors.

Another approach is to ask questions that require the applicant to make self-evaluations. For example, the question, "What do you consider to be your chief asset?" is a straightforward self-evaluative query. But, there are many other ways to ask the same question. Suppose an applicant says, "I believe that I can become a manager in five years." An evaluative question might then be, "What would you say you have going for you that will make that level of attainment possible?"

Answers to self-evaluative questions can confirm the hypotheses about his strengths and weaknesses that the interviewer has already formulated. The most interpretable information comes from these self-evaluation questions.

Facts in and of themselves mean very little. The fact that an applicant obtained high grades in school does not really tell anything about how he is functioning as an adult. What the interviewer wants to know is whether the applicant's school grades are consistent with his present achievement.

The hypothesis-testing approach is reinforced or deterred by the interviewer's basic attitude toward his task. Most interviewers follow the traditionally cautious approach of seeking an applicant's weaknesses because they wish to avoid, at all costs, the error of recommending an unqualified applicant for employment. But the opposite error of rejecting a qualified applicant can be, and often is, much more damaging to an organization because it is irreversible.

Interviewers must remember that each person has strengths and limitations and for every limitation there is usually a counterbalancing strength. The most satisfactory interview approach, therefore, concentrates upon an applicant's strengths and compares them with his limitations to determine how compensatory they are. This is the essence of the applicant-centered approach, by far the most effective interviewing technique. Basically, it consists of obtaining the facts, asking self-evaluative questions about the facts, formulating hypotheses, and then confirming or rejecting them by additional questioning.

In summary, there are three important guidelines to effective employment interviewing:

1. In obtaining and interpreting information about an applicant, the interviewer must always keep the job requirements in mind. No matter how socially desirable or undesirable a personal characteristic may be, it is of no significance unless it affects job performance.

2. The interviewer must wait until the interview has been completed before making a final decision. The biggest pitfall in interviewing lies in making an evaluation on the basis of facts or impressions formed early in the interview.

3. The interviewer must evaluate the *whole man* in relation to *total job performance*. People have a way of compensating for their weaknesses by strengths in other areas.

The interviewer who follows these guidelines will find that his job is much more difficult and challenging than he first thought, but his overall judgments will be right far more often than they would be wrong.

BIBLIOGRAPHY

Bassett, Glenn A.: *Practical Interviewing,* American Management Association, New York, 1965.

Drake, John: *Interviewing for Managers,* American Management Association, New York, 1971.

Fear, Richard A.: *The Evaluation Interview,* McGraw-Hill Book Company, New York, 1958.

Hariton, Theodore: *Interview! The Executive Guide to Selecting the Right Person,* Hastings House, Publishers, Inc., New York, 1970.

Kahn, Robert L., and Charles F. Cannell: *The Dynamics of Interviewing,* John Wiley & Sons, Inc., New York, 1958.

Lopez, Felix M.: *Personnel Interviewing: Theory and Practice,* McGraw-Hill Book Company, New York, 1965.

Webster, Edward C.: *Decision-Making in the Employment Interview,* Industrial Relations Center, McGill University Press, Montreal, 1964.

chapter 14

Testing and the Employment Procedure

PAUL MALI, Ph.D. *Certified Management Consultant and Professor of Management, Graduate School of Business, Hartford University, Hartford, Connecticut*

Choosing the right person for the right job is probably the most challenging decision faced by management today. In many cases, the results of such a decision must be tolerated and accepted for twenty to thirty years. This type of decision is not getting any easier. Changing job contents, changing job procedures, product obsolescence, personnel mobility, and labor scarcity are but a few variables causing us to take a hard and careful look at how we get accurate information about people. How reliable is this information? How do we use this information in making long-term decisions? How do we mix information collected from several sources to predict the performance of an applicant before he is placed on the job or before we promote him to a higher job?

PERSONNEL TESTING AS A FUNCTION

Personnel testing in recent years has developed some strong opponents as well as some strong adherents. The mention of personnel testing as a part of the personnel processes within a company always elicits a response or a challenge. There are those who will cite experiences which show it to be ineffective, and there are those who can make claims of great decisions based on its output. Regardless of the position that one might take in the use of personnel testing in industry, the following might be found in agreement with both points of view:

Personnel Testing Is Here to Stay

More than 28 million applicants each year are screened and tested in industries, business, government, and educational institutions. Is there a suitable alternative to handle this gigantic task of recruiting, admitting, transferring, and placing each year with reasonable cost, high objectivity, and efficiency? The trend in the use of tests is up. More than 2,600 tests are available, and more are in preparation. We are now beginning our third generation of tests with performance and simulation devices.

Personnel Testing as a Function Is Misused

Personnel testing like any professional activity should be directed, supervised, and carried out by qualified and trained individuals. When it is, meaningful results can be expected. Individuals chosen to carry out this function should collect as much know-how and experience as they can. The alert tester learns the value and limitations of tests. He does not expect miracles. He knows of testing intangibles. He is suspicious when a test claims to do all. He has learned the hazards and pitfalls in testing. He has come to realize the chief value of these devices, as information collecting instruments.

Personnel Tests Vary in Worth

Tests like other managerial tools vary in their worth and value. Are interviews without fault? Are application blanks good sampling devices? Are high school transcripts accurate? Some tests are better than others. Some tests are next to worthless. Some have proved their value, some have not. How a test is used and validated determine in a significant way the quality of the results.

USES OF PERSONNEL TESTS

A test is a systematic procedure for comparing the behavior or performance of two or more persons as it relates to job criteria. It is a simple measure to imply the totality of an applicant's ability. The test score is a numerical approximation of the amount of this ability in the applicant. At best, it is an indicator of the degree of the ability held by the testee. Obviously, it becomes an important piece of information in the decision process and should be handled as such. When used properly, along with other selection devices, it is effective in discovering abilities and predicting success or failure on the job. Personnel tests when they are properly designed and administered help employ, develop, and control personnel.

For existing employees, tests:
1. Determine fitness for the job held; improve matching
2. Indicate potentialities for greater efficiency
3. Discover promotables on a fair, impartial, and equitable basis
4. Indicate which positions pay off for employee training
5. Improve supervisor-subordinate understanding of job requirement
6. Help plan inventory for replacement planning
7. Reduce the costs of training and performance errors
8. Reduce turnover in giving "in-house" opportunity for new openings
9. Validate training programs with pretest and posttest measures
10. Reduce favoritism and nepotism through greater objectivity
11. Improve employee confidence through a feeling of "I can do it"
12. Help formulate standards of performance and cutoff norms.

For prospective employees, tests:
1. Predict acceptable or unacceptable performance on the job
2. Discourage hit-or-miss selection of new employees
3. Reduce hiring failures by discovering unfit applicants
4. Help identify responsible people for distant and unsupervised jobs
5. Reduce the costs of recruiting, selecting, and hiring
6. Identify "future" job factors of placement in the organization
7. Safeguard against the misleading and shrewd applicant

8. Identify workers who are slow or fast to catch on

9. Reduce the costs of close supervision for indoctrination of new workers.

The uses of personnel tests in any organization will vary in degree and application according to the type of jobs under consideration. All companies have some jobs that are regarded as "problem types." For such jobs, tests are available with considerable worthwhile research experience behind them. Standardized tests developed and evaluated on similar jobs in other companies hold promise for tryout and are less costly than unproved tests. Tests can be used most effectively in certain types of jobs where:

1. The performance of employees can be easily differentiated into acceptable or unacceptable levels.

2. Jobs can be clustered for having similar performance abilities.

3. The climate is permissive and testees are willing to take tests without management pressures and union resistance.

4. The selection ratio is high, that is, many applicants are available for a single opening.

5. Performance abilities to meet job requirements are easily identified.

6. Job criteria are not vague and constantly changing.

7. The cost of hiring, placement, and retention of employees is high.

8. A formal selection procedure exists to allow tests to "fit in" with their contribution.

Benefits accrued from test usage will vary in degree. This is simply due to the varying accuracy the state of the art allows in measuring human qualities and characteristics. Therefore, accuracy of test measurements will vary with the type of job ability to be predicted. Figure 1 shows the relative accuracy in tests used for various jobs.

TEST USAGE IN THE EMPLOYMENT PROCEDURE

The chief value of a test is that it can collect unbiased information about people not easily available by other methods before. Tests give information for predicting job performance. They do not solely and independently make this prediction unless they are tied into an overall selection-decision strategy. This overall strategy or system requires various techniques, each contributing information segments for the decision-making process. Test scores within this system provide information about individuals which in conjunction with other information can help administrators solve problems of screening, training, transfer, and promotion. The systems approach is the only valid approach to test usage in selection and placement, as illustrated in Figure 2.

Within this systems strategy, each decision to accept or reject a job applicant is actually a prediction based on a mixture of information collected from various tools and techniques—one of which is testing. Tests "fit in" by increasing and making more objective and precise the relevant information in the mix which can serve as a guide in making a decision. Tests confirm or refute the information mixture. One can see from the systems approach that tests should not displace other selection methods, nor should other selection methods displace tests. Rather, each method serves to give breadth and depth to the sampling of an applicant's abilities.

Applicants responding to an opening are subjected to a series of information-collecting techniques which are deposited into a logical structure of an information model or data bank. Some of the tools and techniques utilized for collecting information are: transcripts, references, self-statements, biographical analysis, performance observations, appraisal ratings, critical incidents, interviews, and testing.

Human requirements	Typical jobs	Job abilities	Test accuracy
Sensory–Motor	Bus driver Waitress Laborer	Walk, lift visualize, listen, stand, bend	
Manipulative	Machinist Electrician Watch repairer	Fingers, operates, coordinates, turns dials, switches	High degree
Achievement	Technician Inspector Bank teller	Information, knowledge, techniques, experience, procedure	
Aptitudes	Engineer Lawyer Administrator	Devises, perceives interprets, analyzes, integrates, translates	
Interests	Buyer Chef Modeler	Likes, dislikes, preferences, enjoyments	Low degree
Personality Traits	Social worker Teacher Politician	Patience, dominance, aggressiveness, hostility, loyalty cooperativeness	

Figure 1.   Relative accuracy in test usage.

It is not suggested that these are the only ones; they are rather a sample of the more common ones. The information collected is compared and measured against the identified job factors required by the position. Variances both positive and negative are viewed within the model. The decision to place an individual in a job is based on the confidence that one develops from valid information which has been collected. Information in the model or data bank should be numerically weighted or ranked to determine the overall degree of match with the job requirements.

IMPORTANCE OF JOB CRITERIA AND ABILITIES

Job criteria and performance abilities are the most important part of any test procedure. Acceptable job performance is gauged by the criteria which have been established for the job. The individual's ability, knowledge, and skills must ultimately be measured against these criteria, or his predicted contribution has no utility in the organization. Since job criteria are conditions to be reached, job abilities or performance skills must be directly related to job criteria. It is the identification and validation of these abilities in an individual that form the basis for predicting job success. The strength and adequacy of job criteria form the foundation for the entire test procedure. In fact, they are the most important part of a test procedure. If these criteria are weak, the entire test procedure is weak. On the other hand, if they are strong, the test procedure is likely to be strong. Several checks can be used to maintain the adequacy of job criteria.

1. Criteria must be reliable, that is, be consistent over a period of time.

2. Criteria must be representative, that is, be relevant, necessary, and real to the job.

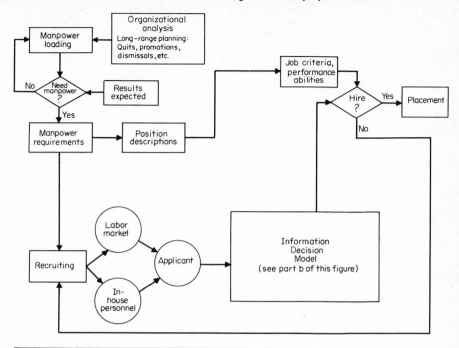

Information Decision Model										
Required job abilities: 3=High 2=Moderate 1=Low										
Information-collecting techniques	Lis-ten-ing	Coor-dinat-ing	Exper-ience	Edu-cation	Anal-ysis	Tech-niques	Devis-ing	Per-cep-tion	Inter-pret-ing	Spa-tial	Coop-era-tion
---	---	---	---	---	---	---	---	---	---	---	---
Applications		1	2	2		2			1		2
Self-statements		3		3	1	1					
References	2		3	2	1		1			2	2
Appraisal ratings		2			2	2				3	
Critical incidents			2		1			2			1
Resumes		2	3			2	3				
Transcripts	1	1	2	2				3			1
Performance observation	2					2				2	
Interviews a. single	3	1		2			2	3			2
b. multiple	2	1	2	2			3	2			3
Tests a. wonderlic					2		3	3	2		
b. SRA adaptability		1			2		2		1	2	2
c. Flanagan Dexterity		1								2	
d. Otis					2		2	1	2		
Total for applicant	10	12	14	13	11	9	16	14	6	12	13
Standard for job	9	10	12	13	14	9	11	13	9	12	14
Variance	+1	+2	+2	0	-3	0	+5	+1	-3	0	-1

Figure 2.   System approach to test usage in employment.

3. Criteria must be compatible, that is, must not conflict with other criteria.

4. Criteria must be acceptable, that is, must be accepted by management as contributing to organizational objectives.

5. Criteria must be current, that is, must change when the situation changes.

6. Criteria must be quantified, that is, must indicate how much or to what degree. Once job criteria have been established, job abilities or performance skills are identified as derivatives of job criteria. In other words, performance skills are the required abilities to achieve the results contained in job criteria. A sample of job criteria and performance skills are as follows:

Job Criteria

Sales level at x percent for y clients
Units produced at x number per hour per day
Inventory quota reduced by x per month
Occupancy ratio at minimum x percent
Reject rate less than x units
Costs to operate not to exceed x dollars
Disciplinary effects not greater than x number
Tardiness not greater than departmental average
Equipment downtime not greater than x hours
Frequency of missed delivery dates not greater than x percent
Machine setup time less than x hours
Performance budget variance not greater than x percent

Job Abilities or Performance Skills

Coordinate eyes, two hands, and one foot
Compute arithmetic without machines
Visualize assembly from layout component parts
Select parts from comprehensive list to fit assembly
Analyze diagrams and charts for information
Convey ideas in writing and talking
Devise ingenious procedures for equipment maintenance
Spot flaws and defects quickly
Interpret and reason complex specifications
Translate ideas into working statements
Analyze mechanical movements for operation
Recall names, addresses, and dates
Copy information and numbers accurately
Perceive simple patterns from complex ones
Foresee conclusions from pursuing prescribed steps
Select right word to convey idea
Accurate in making finger movements
Gain rapport and positive response from new people

Job abilities or performance skills are closely derived from the job criteria identified for the job. It is these abilities which are sought for in applicants by various techniques, the chief of which is testing.

DESIGN OF A TEST PROCEDURE

The rationale for the design of a test procedure is to compare the abilities of an unknown applicant against the known and proven abilities of many individuals in achieving the requirements of job criteria (see Figure 3). The procedure is as follows:

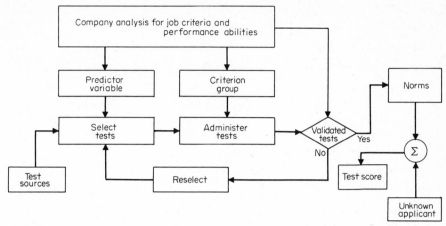

Figure 3. Design of a test procedure.

Isolate Job Criteria

Each position or groups of positions must be analyzed to identify the results that are expected from the employees. These are the conditions that must be reached for acceptable performance. Guidelines and samples of job criteria were given in the previous section.

Identify and Weight Performance Abilities

Make a list of performance abilities estimated to meet job criteria. Rank and weight the listed abilities from the most critical and significant to the most trivial and insignificant. This weighting will establish how each ability will reflect its relative contribution to the total measurement. These abilities become the predictor variables for job success.

Select Appropriate Tests

Select from test sources appropriate tests which purport to measure the predictor variables in question. Examine test manuals carefully in terms of situational validity and reliability. This selection can be made from a single test or a battery of tests. The test manuals should be useful in determining how well the test has been measured with other groups.

Select the Criterion Group

The criterion group is a group of employees already performing on the job whose ability is known. Employees are selected for both high and low degress of proficiency in the predictor variables. Various sources may be used to attest to their known levels of proficiency such as company records, production records, work observations. The employees known to have ability are ranked from high performers to low performers by their supervisors, using job results as a guide. This would suggest that line management must be involved in the development of a test procedure. Obviously, only line management can identify the two most significant components of a test procedure: job criteria and the criterion group.

Administer Tests to the Criterion Group

Give the selected tests which purport to measure the predictor variables to the criterion group, both high and low performers. It is not practical to attempt a battery of tests to measure all the identified abilities. Use judgment, and select the signifi-cant few that count.

Validate the Tests

Analyze the test scores to see if the highly successful employees received the high scores and the less successful employees received the low scores. Statistical cor-relations of these scores will provide a more precise relationship between predictor variables measured by the test and those identified by judgment and job experience. If the selected battery of tests yields high scores with high performers and low scores with low performers, the battery has been validated. If not, a reselection of tests must be made.

The entire test procedure yields a set of test scores measured by proven and known employees within a company doing a specific job. These scores are arranged into statistical norms and are used as a basis of comparison with new applicants taking the same tests. These new applicants are compared and measured with the criterion group for levels of proficiency in the predictor variables. One can see that a good test procedure depends on several factors: relevant and precise pre-dictor variables, selecting tests that discriminate levels of proficiency, and a criterion group representative of the situation. Figure 4 illustrates the systems approach in the selection of tests to meet established job criteria for an administrative engineer.

ELEMENTS OF A GOOD TEST

Test publishers provide information in their manuals as to the validity and reliabil-ity of their tests. These manuals provide tables or norms that enable the users of the tests to interpret the comparative standings of testees with those of persons tested in establishing the norms. Some standardized tests are given to thousands of employees to establish frequency and magnitude of responses with respect to pre-dictor variables. Tables are constructed and placed in these manuals to give exact percentiles in which a person making a score would fall. It should be kept in mind that six qualities are essential in a good test.

Validity

The test must measure to a high degree the identified predictor variable. The val-idity of a test is the degree of correlation between the criterion group's performance on the test and the judgment of their supervisors relative to the test factor. There are four types of validity:

Content Validity: The content of the test items correlates high with the job con-tent.

Concurrent Validity: The performance of the testee correlates high with the cur-rent requirements of the job.

Predictive Validity: The performance of testee correlates high with future require-ments of the job.

Face Validity: The content of the test items, semantics, and language looks and appears right to the job content.

Reliability

The test must have a high degree of consistency and repeatability in measuring and remeasuring the same testees. A test is reliable when a testee can take the same test or an alternate form and yield approximately the same score.

NOTE: Both validity and reliability are the chief characteristics of tests and are measured with statistical processes. Correlation is the most meaningful way to show quantitatively the strength of relationships. How the correlation coefficient (r) is computed is described in Chapter 78.

Figure 4. Systems approach in the selection of tests.

SELECTION OF TESTS

Job Title ADMINISTRATIVE ENGINEER   Date March 30, 1970

Dept. DESIGN DIVISION

Job Criteria	Performance abilities	Method of measuring competence		
		Selection indicators	Tests factors	Possible tests
Must control budget variance within 5%	Translates technical statements into financial data Arranges financial data into accounting systems Computes statistical data of performance and trends	Educational level Experiences Course in Accounting Course in statistics Engineering backgrd	Numerical reasoning Numerical ability Statistical comprehension	SNADER MATH FACTORED APTITUDE SERIES (IP) STATISTICS-ACCOUNTING*
Project schedules must not slip more than 2 weeks	Gets work completed through groups Gains rapport and cooperation from diverse groups Working knowledge of PERT/COST systems	Experiences with diverse groups People oriented attitudes Courses in human relations Course in PERT	Group empathy Attitudes Inference Planning	Watson-Glaser (CTA) How Supervise? California Psychology Inventory (CPI) Forecasting & Planning*
Responds to technical reports submitted to him without consultation	Verbal communications in technical work Perceives level and complexity of problems Analyzes diagrams and charts for needed information	Engineering background Experience Educational level Courses in language skills Courses in decision-making skills Courses in problem solving	Logical evaluation Verbal comprehension General reasoning Spatial orientation Conceptual foresight	WECHSLER (WAIS) Wonderlic OTIS

* Company developed and validated tests.

Objectivity

The test must be constructed and administered in such a way that scoring by more than one individual can be accomplished independently and arrive at the same results. Computerized scoring procedures have contributed in many ways to forcing greater objectivity in administering and scoring tests.

Standardization

The test must have been validated by enough samples to be representative of the performance norms of many groups. It is not true that the greater the validity the greater must be standardization. Obviously, a sufficient number of samples must be taken to assure this.

Culture Free

The test must discriminate between applicants who possess the performance ability from those who do not. However, cultural biases and barriers can interfere with this measurement. Title VII of the Civil Rights Act of 1964, Section 703(h), Tower Amendment states, "It shall not be . . . an unlawful employment practice for an employer to give and act upon the results of any professionally developed ability test provided such test is not used to discriminate because of race, color, religion, sex, or national origin." The law is clear. A test may be used provided it is professionally developed and has "culture-free features," that is, does not discriminate because of cultural deficiencies. Indicators of cultural biases in a test are: emphasis on academic vocabulary and language, emphasis on speed of performance, emphasis on experience elements of middle-class preparation, requirements of educational level attainment.

Supporting Manual

A decision to use a test should not be made unless a thorough examination of its manual is first made. It is the test manual that sets down important guidelines on the use of the test and its generalized validation. The following checklist of questions of a test manual would help in determining the quality of a test:

Does it clearly specify the use of the test in terms of the performance ability to be tested? This must be clearly stated.

Are there alternative forms to avoid copying and cheating?

Are the directions for administering and scoring clearly spelled out?

Are norms provided for comparing test scores?

Were the groups used to standardize the norms large enough?

Are the validity and reliability correlation coefficients included? Are they significant?

Is scoring complicated and does it require a machine?

Have correlations with other tests been made? Are they significant?

Have tables been included to convert raw scores to percentile scores for comparisons?

Is there sufficient descriptive information from which you can interpret clearly and precisely the scores in terms of the performance ability?

What is the copyright date? Is there an obsolescence factor emerging?

A good test manual should reveal positive information for the types of questions raised in the checklist.

TEST MANAGEMENT

Many of the evils attributed to testing are not inherent in the tests themselves, but are due to how, where, and why they are used. The inadequate training and semi-professional nature of some testers have contributed more to testing hazards than many would care to admit. Tests are still in the stage of development, and the art has not advanced as quickly as it should have. Users are anxious to apply tests; however there is a great need to further the art. One of the chief advantages of tests is that they are refinable and improvable. Systematic follow-up and a close working relationship between test administration and test publishers can improve their usefulness as a selection device.

POLICIES AND QUALIFYING THE TEST ORGANIZATION

If an organization has decided to employ test procedures and is committed to their effective use, it must organize by using qualified testers, setting up policies, and establishing the proper reporting relationships. Organizational guidelines and policies should be reduced to writing, communicated to those who are affected, and reviewed for changes and improvements.

Elements of a Personnel Testing Policy

Define the objectives and benefits to be reached by a testing program.

Secure the acceptance and support of top management.

Work out in conjunction with line management cooperative working relationships for implementing test procedures.

Establish functional responsibilities of the testing head and his reporting relationships.

Establish professional standards of performance for test specialists. Provide training and upgrading.

Develop limits and identify management levels for disclosing proprietary test information.

Establish testing practices which will prohibit discrimination on the basis of color, race, national origin, sex, and age.

Centralizing the Test Function

Many organizations are committed to a decentralized philosophy in their operating functions. This means separate facilities and staffs. Decentralization of the test function not only may create costly inefficiencies but will throttle the concept of selection of applicants for opportune placement. A person rejected for the machine shop may be an excellent prospect for maintenance. When the selection, placement, and development functions are centralized, the complete manpower needs of the firm are brought into proper focus. Centralization of the testing function permits professional specialists and techniques to be shared and made more effective. Figure 5 is a suggested organization structure. When an organization is not large enough to support a testing function, outside test consultants should be used. These test consultants offer a wide range of services and bring expertise into a company.

Qualification for Tests

Standard practices for professional use and security of standardized testing instruments have been established by the American Psychological Association (*Technical Recommendations Manual* 1954, pages 11 and 12). Tests must be administered according to these standards and ground rules; otherwise they would be misused and invalidated. Most test publishers abide by these standards for test usage and incorporate guidelines in their manuals.

To qualify as a test purchaser and user, an organization must meet American Psychological Association's test level conditions.

Level A. The organization must have a need and legitimate use for tests. Tests will be sold if the organization can adequately administer, score, and interpret tests

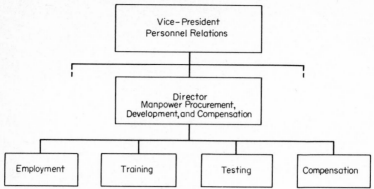

Figure 5.   A centralized testing function.

with the directions and aid of a manual.   The organization must give evidence of its general orientation to test usage.   An educational institution or training department of a company is normally oriented to test usage since it requires testing in its functions.   Examples of level A tests are achievement, vocational, and proficiency tests.

Level B.   The organization must have a qualified staff who have successfully completed courses in psychological tests and measurements or have had the equivalent experience in a test program or organization.   Tests will be sold to this qualified staff who understand the technical knowledge of test construction, statistical procedures, and guidance psychology.   Examples of level B tests are aptitude, personality, and interest inventories.

Level C.   The organization must have an individual with graduate degrees in psychology and who has had supervised experience in clinical testing and interpretation.   Tests will be sold to this individual who has substantial test knowledge and experience.   Examples of level C tests are projective tests and individual mental tests which require careful interpretations of the resulting data.

Publishers require, before furnishing tests of any level, the name of the person who is to be responsible for the use and administration of the tests.

ADMINISTERING TESTS

Applicants often get scared when they take tests.   Some tests pry into private matters that might cause fear or encourage self-stifling conformity and fake answers. Some applicants are smart enough to quickly understand what the test is seeking and produce a pattern of scores that preguess the test.   Hence, the results will be spurious.   The following suggestions should be helpful in minimizing spurious results.

Put the applicant at ease by explaining that tests alone do not decide his fate. Explain that it is the whole picture that counts.

Encourage the applicant to do his best on the test.   Explain that there are no failures or passes, only proper placement of his abilities.

Avoid the use of the terms examination, IQ, or intelligence tests.   Use the terms personnel tests, problem-solving exercises, employment tests, or just tests.

Use a testing room where there are no distractions.   The environment and furniture must be comfortable.

In administering the test, the tester should follow the manual exactly.   Directions, time limits, scoring, etc., must be followed according to the instructions in order to maintain test reliability.

Be prepared with all materials for conducting a test such as stopwatch, answer sheets, pencils, erasers.

The tester should be thoroughly familiar with the test and test manual to be ready to answer possible questions by the testees.

Give special help when administering tests to minority groups. Build into the test procedure aids that will offset poor scores. For example, provide coaching and warmup tests. Use alternate forms. Use minority examiners or interviewers. Offer a second chance. Use training as a selection device.

TEST OBSOLESCENCE—REVALIDATION

A test administrator must validate test results for his organization with a real conviction of their relevance to job criteria. This avoids using tests of low validity. He must understand how to use norms and standards. There must be an acceptable correlation with performance. However, what happens when job criteria change and there are changes in required performance abilities? Do we continue to use the same tests? The answer is "no." We must revalidate. This means that we need to test the tests regularly. Follow-up studies on criteria, test procedure, performance abilities, criterion group, etc., must be a widespread practice. Testing programs, once set up, have the tendency to be fixed in concrete. This is a great indictment of the use of tests. The use of tests under a different set of conditions than those originally intended is a practice of obsolescence. Test managers should follow up on a schedule basis to verify after placement that the selectivity of the test is accurate. He must choose the tests when job criteria have changed and then revalidate.

COST OF A TESTING PROGRAM

The value of a test procedure can be stated only in terms of the utility attached to the outcome and the cost of the strategy to produce this outcome. To define a gain and maximize its value, a test procedure must be expressed in the expected payoff. Payoff can be measured in several ways, such as changes in quit and mobility rates, weedout profile rates, accident frequency rates, performance ratios, productivity levels, percent scrap and waste, unit costs, percent utilization of capacity, mean down time, percentage of deadlines met, and performance variance against budgets. The cost of the testing procedure will take into consideration such factors as test costs, testers' salaries, research and validation time, cost of space and facilities, test time for line management and criterion group, and administrative burden.

Cost utility provides a means of making a direct comparison of payoff with costs with changes in minimum scores to qualify, as shown in Figure 6. The higher the cutoff scores to qualify, the greater the utility with attending higher costs. The lower the cutoff scores, the less the utility with lowered costs. Several approaches can be taken to increase the differential between utility and costs. Amortizing test costs over several groups with time, closer validation with job criteria, reducing test time costs, and exploiting standardized tests when and where available are but a few.

REPORTING TEST SCORES TO MANAGEMENT AND UNIONS

Line management or other non-test professionals should not be given raw scores and allowed to make their own interpretation. Raw test scores should be translated into percentiles or variances from standards or norms. A professional interpretation should accompany these numbers. Most useful to line management is relating the percentile of an unknown applicant to that of known employees already on the

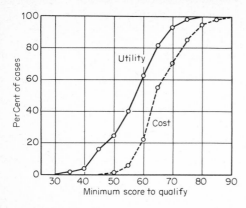

Figure 6.   Effects of cutoff scores on utility-cost profiles.

job. In this way, foremen and supervisors see how the new prospect falls above or below their own subordinates. Better still, the test manager would do well to submit test results in an information decision model, as suggested in Figure 2b. When using this decision model, each information collecting device should be properly weighted in relation to the positions to be filled.

Test information and reports to unions should be no more or no less than normal conveyance of information from interviews, résumés, transcripts, etc. In other words, companies who normally share employment information with unions when there is a mutual decision on an applicant should give the union the test results. If this is not the practice, test results must be held proprietary.

STATISTICAL CONCEPTS AND TEST TERMS

The interpretation and utilization of test scores require an elementary knowledge of statistics. This knowledge is essential for handling masses and aggregates of test scores. Much of a test procedure is statistical in nature, such as validity and reliability.

This section highlights some basic statistical concepts and test nomenclature useful in test procedures. A more detailed and extensive understanding of these concepts may be acquired from references listed in the Bibliography at the end of this chapter or in Chapter 78.

Achievement Test. A test designed to measure the amount of knowledge or skill a person has acquired usually as a result of classroom instruction.

Aptitude. The combination of characteristics both native and acquired which indicates the capacity of a person to develop proficiency in some skill or subject matter after relevant training.

Arithmetic Mean. The arithmetic average of the scores in a distribution. It is a numerical indication of where the scores of all testees tend to fall. The mean gives a standard reference line above or below which a testee's score can be seen to fall. Percentage of scores can be related to above or below this line.

Battery. A set of tests standardized on a criterion group so that results are comparable for other groups.

Concurrent Validity. A type of validation when both test scores and criterion values are obtained at about the same time.

Content Reliability. The consistency with which a test measures the performance ability. It may be estimated by a reliability coefficient based on split halves, alternate forms, and interval consistency.

Correlation. A numerical measure of the relationship between two variables. For testing purposes it relates test scores quantitatively with criterion scores. In

other words, correlation measures the degree of association between the test performance of the testee and the job performance of the criterion group. In this sense,
correlation is considered a measure of predictability. The strength of the relationship between two variables is expressed by the magnitude of the correlation which
may vary from zero (no relationship) to 1.00 (perfect relationship). The sign of the
correlation indicates the direction of the relationship. If the coefficient is positive,
as the scores of one variable increase, the corresponding scores on the other variable
tend to increase also. If the correlation is negative, as scores on the other variable
become larger, the corresponding scores on the other variable become smaller.
When the correlation is zero, changes in the scores of one variable are not accompanied by any discernible corresponding change in the scores of the other variable.

Interpretation of the correlation coefficient (r):

.00– .20   little or no predictive value
.20– .40   slight gain for prediction
.40– .60   substantial for group type predictions
.60– .80   strong and useful for group and individuals
.80– 1.00   very high for individual applications

Criterion. A standard against which a test may be validated.

Cross-validation. The process of verifying results obtained on one group by
replication with a different but similar group.

Deviation. The amount by which a score differs from a specified reference point
such as the arithmetic mean.

Discrimination value. The ability of a test item to show a difference between
high and low abilities of testees.

Equivalent Form. Any of two or more forms of a test usually standardized on the
same population. Item content and difficulty are similar so that scores on the forms
will be similar.

Face Validity. A superficial appearance of validity. Test looks as if it should
measure what is intended.

Frequency Distributions. When a collection of test scores are tabulated in an
organized fashion such as grouping by frequency of occurrence, the resulting orderly
intervals show a frequency distribution. This distribution allows computations to
be performed easily. The frequency distribution is used to give an overall picture
of the highs, mediums, and lows of the testee; to indicate where most of the test
scores fall; to give a graphic picture of testee performance; and to derive other
statistics. The frequency distribution drawn to portray the normal distribution is
a symmetrical bell-shaped curve whose properties are completely known. Scores
translated in special forms are normalized standard scores.

Item Analysis. The process of examining a test item to determine its difficulty
and discrimination value.

Key Scoring. A device or sheet containing the scored responses for scoring a test.

Norm. Average, normal, or standard for a group of specified status or characteristics.

Percentile. Any of the 99 points along the scale of score values which divide
the distribution into 100 groups of equal frequency.

Percentile Rank. A derived score stated in terms of percentage of testees in a
specified group.

Paper-and-pencil Test. Any test which required no materials other than paper
and pencil.

Performance Test. Any test involving special apparatus which requires a testee
to perform a work sample.

Personality Test. A test designed to measure some personality trait of the individual.

Profile.   A graphic representation of the performance of an individual on a series of tests or battery.

Prognostic Test.   A test used to predict future performance in a particular task.

Random Sample.   A sample drawn from a population in such a manner that each member has an equal chance of being selected.

Range.   The difference between the highest and lowest scores made on a test by a specified group.

Reliability Coefficient.   The coefficient of correlation designed to estimate a test's reliability by correlating scores on equivalent forms or matched halves.

Sample.   A selected group to represent the entire population.

Standard Deviation.   A measure of variability from some measure of central tendency such as the arithmetic mean.

Standard Score.   The number of standard deviations contained in the distance between a particular score and the mean of the distribution in which it occurs.   They are pure numbers and have no denominations.   The primary use of the standard score is to describe an individual score in the terms of the profile of the group in which it occurs.   It also serves as a basis for transforming scores in one distribution to scores in a new distribution.   An illustration of several distributions being compared with the standard deviation is shown in Figure 7.

Simulation Test.   A test designed to measure several characters operating collectively and interactively in a situation which is simulated to be "real."   Collective characteristics include attitudes, interest, achievement, personality, and intelligence.

Test Score.   A test is a sample of the totality of the applicant's ability to be measured.   A test score is a numerical approximation of the amount of this ability present in the applicant.   At best it is an indicator of the degree of ability of the testee.   Obviously, it becomes an important piece of information and should be handled as such.   It is a single value which represents a number of units measured on a score scale.

Validity.   The accuracy to which a test can measure the performance ability of a testee and the performance ability of a criterion group.

SUMMARY

Tests provide a sound and reliable way to collect information about people objectively and accurately.   Tests work well in the hands of competent and qualified users.   When used in a systems context of a selection process, many benefits are possible in recruiting, employment, indoctrinating, training, development, promotions, transfers, job enrichment, and job enlargement.   A company needs to focus on the value and utility of a testing program before its commitment.   An employer can significantly upgrade the quality of his applicants when testing procedures are valid and kept from obsolescence.

As we look ahead to the third generation of tests, we see two bright stars emerging.   The use of training as a selection and test procedure and the equally attractive situational experience that encourages "living through" with performance simulation.   Both of these approaches will require knowledge and skill in the design and implementation of test procedures.

BIBLIOGRAPHY

Albright, Lewis E., J. R. Glennon, Wallace J. Smith: *Use of Psychological Tests in Industry,* Howard Allen Publishers, Cleveland, 1963.

Armore, S. J.: *Introduction to Statistical Analysis and Inference,* John Wiley & Sons, Inc. New York, 1966.

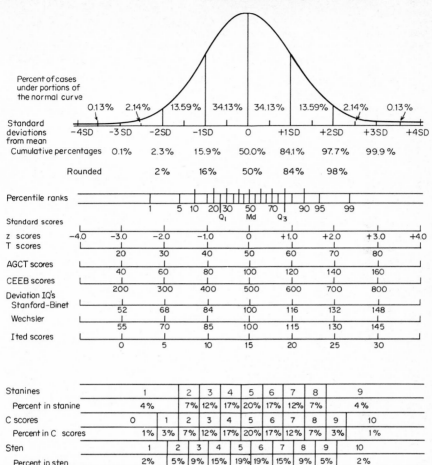

Figure 7. **Comparing several types of standard test scores.**

Barrett, Richard S.: "Gray Areas in Black and White Testing," *Harvard Business Review,* Cambridge, Mass., January–February, 1969, pg. 87–91.

—— : "Guide to Using Psychological Tests," *Harvard Business Review,* Cambridge, Mass., September–October, 1962, pg. 70–78.

Buros, Oscar K.: *Tests in Print,* The Gryphon Press, Highland Park, N.J., 1961.

Crowley, Francis J., and Martin Cohen: *Basic Facts of Statistics,* Collier Books, The Macmillan Company, New York, 1963.

Cronbach, Lee J., and Goldine C. Gleser: *Psychological Tests and Personnel Decisions,* University of Illinois Press, Urbana, 1965.

DuBois, P. H.: *An Introduction to Psychological Statistics.* Harper & Row Publishers, Inc., New York, 1965.

Gilmer, F. K.: *Industrial Psychology,* McGraw-Hill Book Company, New York, 1961.

Guion, Robert M.: *Personnel Testing,* McGraw-Hill Book Company, New York, 1965.

Gross, Martin L.: *The Brain Watchers,* New American Library, Inc., New York, 1962.

Lyman, Howard B.: *Test Scores and What They Mean,* Prentice-Hall Inc., Englewood Cliffs, N.J., 1963.

Souerwine, Andrew H.: "More Value From Personnel Testing," *Harvard Business Review,* Cambridge, Mass., July–August, 1966, pg. 79–86.

Thorndike, R. L.: *Personnel Selection,* John Wiley & Sons, Inc., New York, 1961.

Wallis, W. A., and A. V. Roberts: *Statistics: A New Approach,* The Macmillan Company, New York, 1964.

Youmans, Charles V.: "Testing for Training and Development," in Robert L. Craig and Lester Bittel (eds.), *Handbook of American Society for Training and Development,* McGraw-Hill Book Company, New York, 1967.

chapter 15

Psychological Tests:
Clerical, Mechanical, Dexterity,
and Vocational Interests

JOHN SMITH   *Associate Employment Consultant, Division of Employment, New York State Department of Labor, Albany, New York.*

In meeting the challenge of today's multifaceted manpower problems, many employers have found the need to reassess their methods of selection, transfer, and upgrading of employees.   Equal employment opportunity for minority groups and the "disadvantaged" has stressed the "screening in" rather than the "screening out" of many job applicants.   A great deal of emphasis has been focused on the use of tests in the selection and placement process; as a result, the personnel administrator has benefited from the necessity to look closely at company policies and procedures, with regard to their use.   Title VII of the Civil Rights Act of 1964, Section 703(h), provides that an employer may give and act upon the results of "any professionally developed ability test, provided that such test . . . is not designed, intended, or used to discriminate because of race, color, religion, sex, or national origin." *Guidelines on Employment Testing Procedures* issued in August, 1966, by the Equal Employment Opportunity Commission was enlarged and revised effective August 1, 1970. These Equal Employment Opportunity Commission guidelines[1] should be given attention by all who are responsible for company personnel policy and programs.

It should be clearly understood that effective utilization of the clerical, mechanical, and dexterity tests and the interest inventories presented in this chapter is

---

[1] Title 29—Labor, Chap. XIV, Equal Employment Opportunity Commission: Part 1607, *Guidelines on Employee Selection Procedures* (effective 8/1/70).   Copies of the Guidelines may be requested from the Equal Employment Opportunity Commission, 1800 G Street N.W., Washington, D.C. 20506.

predicated on the appropriateness of their selection and integration in the total assessment process.

Clerical and mechanical tests may be tests of either aptitude or proficiency (achievement) and should be used for the specific purpose for which they have been developed. An understanding of the difference between aptitude and proficiency (achievement) is pertinent to their proper application.

Aptitude tests measure potential, the ability to learn—easily, quickly, and well. They are utilized with individuals who are inexperienced in the particular occupation for which they are being considered. Properly used in total assessment, they may contribute to:

1. An increase in production by identifying potentially better workers

2. A reduction in training time and training costs by identifying those who should learn easily, quickly, and well

3. A reduction in turnover by selecting those who have the potential to learn the tasks of the job

Proficiency (achievement) tests measure the present level of skill (or knowledge). They are utilized with individuals who have had experience (or training) in the occupation for which they are being considered. Typing and stenographic tests are examples of proficiency tests, administered to ensure meeting specific job requirements, i.e., must type 60 words per minute or take dictation at 80 words per minute.

Application of Tests

Tests should always be used as an additional factor in the assessment process. The decision as to who should be tested depends on several factors. Clearly defined evidence of skill or potential does not, in most instances, require confirmation by a test. A journeyman electrician's satisfactory history of employment should be sufficient evidence of acquired skill. Habits, attitudes, etc., may be revealed in the interview that will determine the final basis for hiring or rejection. A recently employed typist or secretary whose former employer's standards are known may not necessarily require testing. However, where sufficient evidence of skill or potential is lacking on which to base a sound evaluation, testing would be indicated. Applicants most likely to require testing include inexperienced workers—trainees, those with spotty work records, reentrants into the labor market, applicants with training but no work experience.

Since aptitudes generally become stabilized by the time one reaches adulthood, aptitude tests are usually not repeated unless there is evidence that the test result may be invalid. Improper test administration, exceeding time limits, inability of the applicant to put forth his best effort due to unrecognized illness at the time of the test, etc., may warrant retesting (with an alternate form, if available). Inasmuch as skills fluctuate with practice and use, proficiency tests may be repeated provided that a sufficient time interval has elapsed to allow for a change in skill level. A typist reentering the labor market who has not typed recently and tests at 25 words per minute should not be retested until afforded sufficient time to "brush up." To test such an applicant the next day, or within one week, would be wasteful. Approximately one month should be a minimum period to allow for a change in skill level.

Applicants considered for testing should be comparable to the standardization group as to age, education, etc. It is obvious that valid test results are unobtainable from those who do not possess sufficient literacy to understand the questions. Applicants should have the opportunity to put forth their best effort. A pretest interview with the applicant is recommended to determine whether or not he can take the test under standardized conditions and to prepare him for the session. This preparation should include the reason for taking the test and indicate that it is only one factor in the assessment process. The reason for taking the test may be presented in terms of whether the applicant can master the tasks of the job. One might say to a typist, "In order to find out whether you can type fast enough for this assignment we'd like you to take a test." If the applicant raises a question about taking the test, a rejoinder could be, "We are trying to save both of us time, you don't want to begin on a job and then find you can't do it. The test is another factor to be evaluated." Appropriate explanations may be adapted for applicants for other jobs.

What Is Available

Buros' monumental *The Sixth Mental Measurement Yearbook* and *Tests in Print* cite some 32 clerical, 39 mechanical-ability, and 13 manual-dexterity tests.[2]

Surprisingly few of the tests reported on by experts in the field in the *Mental Measurement Yearbook* meet the *Standards for Educational and Psychological Tests and Manuals* prepared jointly by the American Psychological Association, American Educational Research Association, and National Council on Measurement in Education.[3] In Buros' descriptive test entries, comments such as "no reliability data," "no validity data" are frequent. Nevertheless, clerical and mechanical tests are among the most widely used in industry, and many companies have reported their use in solving personnel problems (see Examples of the Use of Tests by Employers).

Test publishers and companies from whom dexterity apparatus may be purchased are listed at the end of the chapter. Catalogs should be requested for detailed information as to current prices of tests and apparatus, who may purchase, scoring service, availability of specimen sets, etc.

The evaluation and acceptance of the validity of the tests, applicability of test norms, etc., must, in the last analysis, be the responsibility of the test user. The tests listed below vary in meeting acceptable standards but represent a sample of those more widely used. Selection should not be made solely on the basis of these brief descriptions.

CLERICAL TESTS

Minnesota Clerical Test (The Psychological Corporation). This well-validated and thoroughly studied aptitude test is used for clerical jobs involving rapid handling of numbers, letters, symbols; it consists of 200 items on each, name and number checking. Approximately 15 minutes working time.

General Clerical Test (The Psychological Corporation). This test is used in the selection and upgrading of clerical personnel. The full battery measures clerical speed and accuracy, 7 minutes; numerical ability, 23 minutes; verbal facility, 13 minutes; total, 43 minutes. Parts may also be administered separately: Booklet A, Speed and Number (checking, alphabetizing, arithmetic computation, error location, arithmetic reasoning); Booklet B., Verbal (spelling, reading comprehension, vocabulary, and grammar).

The Short Employment Tests (The Psychological Corporation). This battery of three 5-minute tests is used for selection of clerical office workers. The tests include SET-V (vocabulary); SET-N (arithmetic computation, addition, subtraction, multiplication, and division); SET-CA (clerical, locating and verifying names in an alphabetical list, and ability to read and classify the dollar amount opposite that name).

---

[2] Oscar K. Buros, *The Sixth Mental Measurement Yearbook*, The Gryphon Press, Highland Park, N.J., 1965; *Tests in Print*, 1961.

[3] *Standards for Educational and Psychological Tests and Manuals*, American Psychological Association, Washington, D.C., 1966.

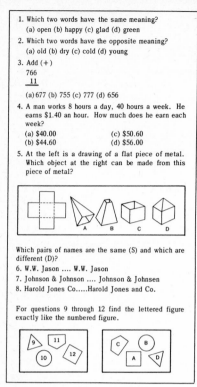

1. Which two words have the same meaning?
   (a) open (b) happy (c) glad (d) green

2. Which two words have the opposite meaning?
   (a) old (b) dry (c) cold (d) young

3. Add (+)
   766
   11
   (a) 677 (b) 755 (c) 777 (d) 656

4. A man works 8 hours a day, 40 hours a week. He earns $1.40 an hour. How much does he earn each week?
   (a) $40.00   (c) $50.60
   (b) $44.60   (d) $56.00

5. At the left is a drawing of a flat piece of metal. Which object at the right can be made from this piece of metal?

Which pairs of names are the same (S) and which are different (D)?

6. W.W. Jason .... W.W. Jason
7. Johnson & Johnson .... Johnson & Johnsen
8. Harold Jones Co.....Harold Jones and Co.

For questions 9 through 12 find the lettered figure exactly like the numbered figure.

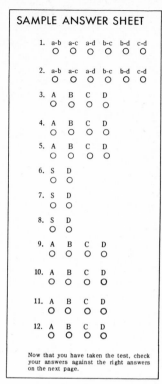

SAMPLE ANSWER SHEET

1. a-b a-c a-d b-c b-d c-d
   O   O   O   O   O   O

2. a-b a-c a-d b-c b-d c-d
   O   O   O   O   O   O

3. A   B   C   D
   O   O   O   O

4. A   B   C   D
   O   O   O   O

5. A   B   C   D
   O   O   O   O

6. S   D
   O   O

7. S   D
   O   O

8. S   D
   O   O

9. A   B   C   D
   O   O   O   O

10. A   B   C   D
    O   O   O   O

11. A   B   C   D
    O   O   O   O

12. A   B   C   D
    O   O   O   O

Now that you have taken the test, check your answers against the right answers on the next page.

Figure 1.   Sample test items.   **Figure 2. Sample answer sheet.**

Short Tests of Clerical Ability (SRA Science Research Associates, Inc.) These seven short tests (3 to 12 minutes each), approximately 60 minutes total, may also be used separately or in combination to assess aptitude for office work jobs. The tests include arithmetic, business vocabulary, checking, coding, understanding and following oral and written directions, filing, and language (grammar, spelling, punctuation).

SRA Clerical Aptitudes Test (SRA Science Research Associates, Inc.). This 35-minute aptitude battery is used for learning clerical tasks. Three subtests measure vocabulary, office arithmetic, and detail checking.

Purdue Clerical Adaptability Tests Revised Edition, Purdue Personnel Tests (University Bookstore, Purdue University). This aptitude test is used for selection and assignment of workers, emphasizing areas covered by the six scores of the battery: spelling, computation, checking, word meaning, copying, reasoning. Working time, 47.5 minutes.

Cross Reference Test (Psychometric Affiliates). This test is intended for use with applicants for clerical, shop, or warehouse positions requiring arithmetic computation. It consists of a combination of simple checking and arithmetic skills. Working time, 5 minutes.

Office Worker Test (Public Personnel Association). This 90-minute test is designed to assist in selection for a wide variety of clerical occupations including clerks and receptionists (also used with typists and stenographers). It consists of 100 multiple-choice items divided into 10 subtests, yields 11 scores: reading, vocabulary, reasoning, arithmetic, checking, filing, spelling, punctuation, usage, information, and total.

Survey of Working Speed and Accuracy (California Test Bureau). This four-part test is for use in the selection and placement of clerical workers in offices and factories; the parts are number checking, code translation, finger dexterity, counting. Working time, 20 minutes.

Turse Clerical Aptitude Test (Harcourt Brace Jovanovich, Inc.). This is an aptitude test for various types of clerical work. It measures verbal skills, number skills, written directions, clerical speed, clerical accuracy, learning ability, general clerical ability. Working time, 28 minutes.

TYPING AND DICTATION TESTS

Proficiency tests, measuring the present level of skill, are the type most frequently used in industry. Examples of what is available in this category are the following:

Typing Skills Test (SRA Science Research Associates, Inc.). This is a 10-minute test of typing speed and accuracy.

Typing Test for Business (The Psychological Corporation). Practice copy and straight copy may be used as a screening test, 10 minutes. An additional test may be given: letter, revised manuscript, numbers, and tables. Complete battery, 55 minutes.

McCann Typing Tests (McCann Associates). These are 10-minute typing tests. They yield three scores: speed, accuracy, and total.

Typist Test: Individual Placement Series (J. H. Norman). This is a 5-minute typing test.

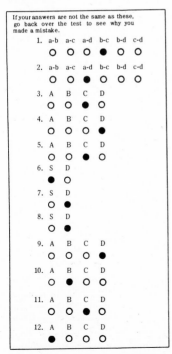

Figure 3.   Answers to test items.

Seashore-Bennett Stenographic Proficiency Test (The Psychological Corporation). This consists of a series of letters dictated at various speeds, by tape or LP record (33⅓). Dictation, 15 minutes. Transcription, 30 minutes.

Stenographic Dictation Test (McCann Associates). This test is administered verbally at 60, 80, or 100 words per minute.

Shorthand Test: Individual Placement Series (J. H. Norman). This dictation test is administered verbally or by LP record (33⅓).

For selection of trainees, aptitude tests are available.

Bennett Stenographic Aptitude Test (The Psychological Corporation)

Turse Shorthand Aptitude Test (Harcourt Brace Jovanovich, Inc.)

MECHANICAL-ABILITY TESTS

The selection of tests of mechanical ability (as with all tests) requires careful evaluation and analysis of the tasks and duties of the job and comparison with test data regarding standardization, validity, norms, etc., to ensure appropriate application. Random selection of tests and gross job specifications such as "mechanical aptitude" should be avoided. Essential aptitudes for specific jobs may vary from three-dimensional spatial aptitude which involves visualizing forms in space and understanding relationships of plane and solid objects to form perception which is the ability to make visual comparisons among various forms by observing slight differences in shapes or shadings of figures. One or the other, or both, may be the prime ingredient for job success. Occupational test validation for specific jobs should be conducted whenever a demonstrated relationship between test and job performance is lacking.

Tests of mechanical ability are most frequently associated with the more skilled occupations as differentiated from manual-dexterity tests which are utilized in selection for semiskilled jobs involving manipulative abilities primarily, i.e., packing, simple assembly, etc.

Examples of available tests of mechanical ability include the following:

Bennett Mechanical Comprehension Test (The Psychological Corporation). This test has been used as an aptitude test in the selection of workers for mechanical jobs, the selection of apprentices for construction trades, and in some instances, for upgrading of employed workers. It measures ability to understand mechanical relationships and physical laws. Approximate time, 30 minutes. Different levels and forms are available.

The MacQuarrie Test For Mechanical Ability (California Test Bureau). This test has been used in the selection of workers for mechanical jobs and of radio assemblers, apprentices (toolmakers), and calculating and adding machine operators. Approximate time, 30 minutes. It includes seven subtests: tracing, tapping, dotting, copying, location, blocks, pursuit.

The Purdue Mechanical Adaptability Test (Division of Applied Psychology, Purdue University). This 15-minute, 60-item information test covers the following areas: mechanical, electrical, carpentry, plumbing, tools, materials, and processes. It is offered as an aid in identifying applicants for jobs (or training programs) requiring mechanical abilities and interests.

O'Rourke Mechanical Aptitude Test, Junior Grade (Psychological Institute). This two-part, 55-minute test broadly covers mechanical categories, including carpentry, cabinetmaking, painting, mechanics, electricity, printing. Part I, 30 minutes, requires matching pictures to indicate which tools and objects are used together. Part II, 25 minutes, is a multiple-choice test concerning tools and materials.

Revised Minnesota Paper Formboard (The Psychological Corporation). This is a 20-minute paper-and-pencil test that requires ability to visualize two-dimensional geometric shapes into a whole design. It is used in selection of workers for mechanical jobs and of assemblers, machine operators, and apprentices in skilled trades.

Minnesota Spatial Relations Test (Western Psychological Services; Marietta Apparatus Co.; Educational Test Bureau). (An apparatus test measuring spatial relations.) The apparatus consists of four form boards. The test requires assembly of geometrical forms such as crescents, squares, and angles on each board. It is used where spatial judgment is required: in skilled trades and occupations such as automobile repair, ornamental iron workers; and in semi-skilled occupations such as assembly workers, machine operators, packers of items varying in size and shape.

MANUAL-DEXTERITY TESTS

Manual-dexterity tests involve the use of equipment such as form boards, finger-dexterity apparatus, tweezers, tools. The tests purport to measure such abilities as gross arm-hand coordination to fine finger dexterity. They may be administered individually or to groups of applicants and are often included in test batteries along with other measures.

Dexterity tests applicable for industrial use with adults include the following:

Minnesota Rate of Manipulation Test—1969 Edition (Western Psychological Services). This is a form-board test for arm-hand dexterity related to such semi-skilled jobs as packers, machine operators, wrappers, helpers. The board has 60 holes in four rows, with 15 holes in each row. The applicant is required to manipulate the disks (placing and turning) on a time trial basis. There are five separate subtests: placing, turning, displacing, one-hand and two-hand turning.

Bennett Hand-tool Dexterity Test (The Psychological Corp.). This test measures proficiency in the use of wrenches and screwdrivers. The applicant disassembles mounted bolts and reassembles them according to a prescribed sequence. This test may be used in addition to Mechanical Comprehension Test.

Stromberg Dexterity Test (The Psychological Corp.). This is a more complicated manipulative test than the Minnesota. The applicant is required to sort the disks and place each one differently by color and sequence. The manual recommends its use for general factory workers, assemblers, welders, punch-press operators, foundry molders, etc.

Purdue Peg Board (SRA Science Research Associates, Inc.). This test measures two kinds of manual dexterity: arm and hand and finger dexterity. It is related to productivity in routine manual jobs. The pegboard consists of two rows of 25 holes. The applicant places pins in holes with a 30-second time limit for each trial. Scores are obtained for each hand separately, for the sum of right- and left-hand scores, and for alternating right- and left-hand movements. A second operation requires assembly of pins, washers, and collars using both hands.

Crawford Small Parts Dexterity Test (The Psychological Corp.). This two-part test measures fine eye-hand coordination for such jobs as electrical and electronics assembly. In the first part the applicant uses tweezers to insert pins in holes and place collars over the pins. The second part requires the applicant to place small screws in threaded holes and then with a screwdriver to complete the task, driving the screws through the plate.

The O'Conner Tweezer and Finger Dexterity Tests (C. H. Stoelting Co.; Western Psychological Services). These tests measure wrist and finger dexterity related to quick and precise semiskilled jobs. They have been used with watch assemblers, radio assemblers, packers, wrappers, some electrical assembly workers. In the tweezer-dexterity test, the applicant picks up pins with the tweezer and inserts them in holes across the board, row by row. In the finger-dexterity test, the applicant picks up three pins (with his preferred hand) and inserts them in each hole.

OTHER TESTS, MULTIFACTOR APTITUDE TEST BATTERIES, VISION TESTS, "HOMEMADE" TESTS, CUSTOM TEST BATTERIES

Other Tests

Test batteries (a combination of two or more tests) are available that purport to measure several occupational areas including clerical, mechanical, stenographic, typing. Examples of this type are the following:

ETSA Tests (Educators and Employers' Tests and Service Associates). The battery consists of the following tests: 1A, General Mental Ability Test (45 minutes); 2A, Office Arithmetic Test (40 minutes); 3A, General Clerical Ability Test (20 minutes); 4A, Stenographic Skills Test (45 minutes); 5A, Mechanical Familiarity Test (60 minutes); 6A, Mechanical Knowledge Test (90 minutes); also 7A, Sales Aptitude Test, and 8A, Personnel Adaptability Test (60 minutes each). ETSA recommends administration of test 1A plus the appropriate test 2A to 8A.

The National Business Entrance Tests (National Business Education Association). Two somewhat similar series are available. The more likely one for industrial use is the "Official Testing Series" consisting of six tests: Machine Calculation Test, Typewriting Test, Business Fundamentals and General Information Test, Bookkeeping Test, General Office Clerical Test, Stenographic Test. Test administration ranges from 45 to 130 minutes.

Multifactor Aptitude Test Batteries

The use of multifactor aptitude test batteries has been confined primarily to counseling situations. Since these batteries measure several aptitudes, they may be related to a wide variety of occupations, provided that the necessary occupational validation has been completed. Although there is little reported evidence of their use in industry, their potential for screening inexperienced applicants for a number of different jobs in a single test session would appear to warrant greater utilization by employers.

The more widely known and used multiaptitude test batteries include:

Differential Aptitude Test Battery—DAT (The Psychological Corp.)

Flanagan Aptitude Classification Test—FACT (SRA Science Research Associates, Inc.)

Employee Aptitude Survey—EAS (Western Psychological Services)

General Aptitude Test Battery—GATB (United States Training and Employment Service)

While the General Aptitude Test Battery is primarily restricted for use in state employment offices,[4] it perhaps offers the most significant application for industry because of its standardization on the general working population[5] and the nature of its occupational validation. Where applicants have been tested and referred by state employment offices, employers should consider requesting an overall interpretation of the test results in terms of the applicant's potential for various jobs.

[4] Release of the General Aptitude Test Battery may be made under certain conditions, usually to nonprofit organizations, for counseling purposes.

[5] Based on the general working population according to the 1940 census.

Vision Tests

Competent, qualified personnel should be consulted when there is a question of the need for tests of this type, and they should be carefully selected for the specific situation. Vision tests include those for visual acuity, color blindness, and color discrimination. For visual acuity (and color vision), three widely used vision stereoscopes are:

AO Sight Screener (American Optical Co.)
Keystone Telebinocular (Keystone View Co.)
Orthorater (Bausch & Lomb Inc.)

Tests for color blindness and color discrimination include:

Test for Color Blindness (Ishihara) (Graham Field Surgical Co., Inc.)
AO-H-R-R Pseudoisochromatic Plates 2d edition (American Optical Co.)
Dvorine Color Vision Test (Harcourt Brace Jovanovich, Inc.)
New Test for the Detection of Color Blindness (Long's College Book Co.)
Farnsworth Dichotomous Test for Color Blindness (The Psychological Corporation.)
Farnsworth-Munsell 100-Hue Test for Color Discrimination (The Psychological Corporation; Munsell Color Co. Inc.)
Burnham-Clark-Munsell Color Memory Test (Munsell Color Co. Inc.)

"Homemade" Tests; Custom Test Batteries

So-called "homemade" tests, involving questions made up by personnel staff, employment interviewers, or foremen from their perspective of what may be significant, are to be avoided. Test development is a highly technical procedure that should be undertaken only by qualified personnel knowledgeable in the techniques of test construction, validation, and statistical method. The development of a new test, beginning with job analysis and continuing through construction and tryout of items, obtaining criterion data, standardization, and validation, can be costly and time consuming. However, the present availability of well-constructed tests offers opportunity for their combination into custom-built batteries and the establishment of company norms. This eliminates the arduous task of beginning with construction of basic test items as in the development of a new test but requires no less competence in standardization and validation techniques.[6]

VOCATIONAL INTERESTS

The subject of vocational interests has been given its share of study by psychologists and perhaps has proved to be far more complicated than anticipated. The stability of interests, degree of interests, effects of experience, influence of parents, peers, etc., and definition of the term itself are only a few of the factors involved in understanding vocational interests. Research in the area has produced several well-studied instruments which measure certain aspects of vocational interests. They have been widely used in counseling and to a much less degree in industry where their use has been confined largely (but not solely) to the selection process for salesmen. There has been reported use of interest measures in employee *placement* rather than *selection* by some companies where varied occupational assignments exist. As with the use of any type of questionnaire, the possibility of faking exists. Although this must be considered, the overall impact and the

---

[6] Examples of test items may be found on page 15—4. Questions 1 to 4 and 6 to 8 are typical clerical test items. Questions 5 and 9 to 12 are examples of those found in mechanical ability tests. Question 5 involves spatial aptitude; questions 9 to 12 involve form perception.

frequency with which faking occurs do not preclude the use of these measures in furnishing important information in the assessment process.

Two widely studied interest inventories are the Strong Vocational Interest Blank (SVIB) and the Kuder Preference Record (KPR).

Strong Vocational Interest Blank (Stanford University Press. Distributors: Consulting Psychologists Press Inc.; Institute of Psychological Research; The Psychological Corporation). Since its introduction in 1927 and subsequent revisions in 1938 (men), 1946 (women), 1966 (men), and 1969 (women), the Strong Vocational Interest Blank has become one of the most thoroughly studied psychological instruments available. Research with the Strong Vocational Interest Blank has been extensive, and published reports on its use are numerous.

The blank is applicable for use with adults and is related primarily to occupations in the professional and business areas. The current form (T399 men, 1966; TW 398 women, 1969) may be administered individually or in groups. Average time for completion of the form is 25 to 45 minutes. Few individuals require an hour or more since they are encouraged to work rapidly. The blank (T399 men) is divided into eight parts. Part I lists Occupations (100); Part II, School Subjects (36); Part III, Amusements and Hobbies (48); Part IV, General Occupational Activities (48); Part V, Type of People (47); Part VI, Order of Preference of Activities (40); Part VII, Preference between Two Items (Pairs of Activities) (40); and Part VIII, Abilities and Characteristics (30). The subject indicates whether he likes, is indifferent to, or dislikes each item, or in certain sections, selects preference among activities. (The women's blank TW 398 is arranged in a similar format.)

Results are reported on an individual profile form indicating comparison of the subject's likes and dislikes with persons employed in various occupations. Simply stated, the basic theory is that individuals successful in certain occupations tend to have a communality of interests that differentiates them from people in general.

The profile contains the Basic Interest Scales, Occupational Scales, and Non-Occupational Scales. The Basic Interest Scales identify the broad interest categories such as business management, sales, merchandising, science, mechanical. The Occupational Scales help to channel the basic interests into more specific occupations such as accounting, purchasing agent, life insurance salesman. The *SVIB Manual* (1969 Supplement)[7] recommends that the Non-Occupational Scales should be used for interpretation only by those with adequate training and experience. These scales are: academic achievement (AACH), age-related interest scale (AR), diversity of interest (DIV), masculinity-femininity (MF II), managerial orientation (MO), occupational introversion-extroversion (OIE), occupational level (OL), and special organization level (SL).

The results of the Strong Vocational Interest Blank reported on the profile form provide a systematic means for assessing vocational interests. Best use will be made by those with sufficient professional training who can integrate the profile with other test results and information about the subject.

Kuder Preference Record and Interest Surveys (SRA, Science Research Associates). First published in 1939, the Kuder Preference Record has gone through a number of revisions (1942, 1946, 1948, 1950, 1951—Vocational; 1956, 1957, 1965—Occupational). Several forms are available for use with junior high school, high school, and college students and adults. A large bibliography exists of journal articles reporting on various aspects of the Kuder's application. Administration

---

[7] David P. Campbell, *SVIB Manual 1969 Supplement,* Stanford University Press, Stanford, 1969.

time is approximately 30 to 45 minutes, and it may be given individually or in groups.

The subject is required to select one item in each set of three he likes best and one item he likes least. This forced-choice method differs from the Strong Vocational Interest Blank, where the subject indicates his like, indifference, or dislike to an individual item. Again the question of faking, deliberately or unconsciously, has been investigated. Studies show that faking can be accomplished, perhaps more easily on some scales such as persuasive and social service. All subjects do not, of course, approach the task with the intent to distort their responses. A verification scale has been developed to identify those who misunderstand the directions, answer carelessly or insincerely, or in other ways do not answer the form correctly.

The forms for general use with adults are the vocational forms (C, CH) and the occupational forms (D, DD). The results of the vocational form are reported on profiles indicating interest in ten broad areas: outdoor, mechanical, computational, scientific, persuasive, artistic, literary, musical, social service, and clerical. Tables are furnished listing specific occupations within the broad areas for further investigation with the subject. Those areas in which the subject scores at or above the 75 percentile are to be followed up, while those below the 25 percentile generally should be avoided. The tables also list occupations which include the combination of two broad categories when the subject scores above the 75 percentile in both, i.e., scientific-persuasive.

The occupational forms report the subject's interests as compared with those employed in specific occupations (Form D) and with occupational groups and college major groups (Form DD).

The Kuder is used extensively in schools and by counseling agencies. Although individual studies have been reported from time to time of its use with occupational groups, it generally has had limited application in industry. However, the Kuder (like the Strong) can furnish pertinent information in the area of vocational interest that may be integrated in the assessment process.

Other measures of vocational interest are available. In general, they have not been utilized as extensively or studied as thoroughly as the Strong and Kuder. For some, validity data are scant and reports of their use in industry are meager.

Following is a sample of the better known instruments that have been published. Careful evaluation of their applicability for a given situation should be completed prior to their use.

Study of Values: A Scale for Measuring the Dominant Interests in Personality, third edition (Houghton Mifflin Co.). First published in 1931 and known as the Allport-Vernon Study of Values, it was revised in 1951 and again in its present third edition in 1960. It has been used primarily with the college or college graduate population. Six scores are obtained that measure traits or values: theoretical, economic, aesthetic, social, political, religious. The areas are those put forth by E. Spranger as personality traits in his 1928 publication, *Types of Men.*[8] Average administration time is 20 to 40 minutes. The subject matter does not readily lend itself to use with employment applicants, which has limited its use in industry. Its application has been largely with college students, who find the content more acceptable.

Cleeton Vocational Interest Inventory Revised Edition (McKnight & McKnight Publishing Co.). This inventory was first published in 1937 and revised in 1943. There are separate forms for men and women; each yields ten scores. The men's

[8] E. Spranger (trans. by P. J. W. Pigors), *Types of Men,* M. Niemyer, Halle, 1928.

form covers the following occupational groups: biological sciences, specialized selling, physical sciences, social sciences, business administration, legal-literary, mechanical, finance, creative, and agricultural. The women's form includes: office work, selling, natural sciences, social service, creative, grade school teacher, high school–college teacher, personal service, housekeeper-factory worker, home-making–child care.

The inventory consists of a total of 700 items, 70 in each interest group. Average administration time is 40 to 50 minutes. Somewhat similar to the Strong (it has not been recommended as a substitute), its use has been mainly with school populations and in counseling facilities.

The Occupational Interest Inventory; The Vocational Interest Analyses (California Test Bureau). The Occupational Interest Inventory developed by Lee and Thorpe was published in 1943. There is an intermediate (grade 7 to adult) and an advanced (grade 9 to adult) form. Average administration time is 30 to 40 minutes. The inventory identifies six fields of interest: personal-social, natural, mechanical, business, arts, and sciences; and three types of interest: verbal, manipulative, and computational.

The Vocational Interest Analyses is a later development, devised by Roeber and Prideaux in collaboration with Lee and Thorpe, which extends the Occupational Interest Inventory information more specifically within the broad fields. Again, use has been primarily in counseling situations with school populations.

Brainard Occupational Preference Inventory (The Psychological Corporation). This inventory consists of 120 occupations depicted in sentence form to which the subject indicates his degree of preference. Broad occupational fields covered are: commercial, mechanical, professional, aesthetic, and scientific. Males respond to a sixth field, agricultural, and females substitute personal service for their sixth area. Norms are furnished for grades 8 to 12, but it is also suggested by the publisher for use with adults who have limited educational background or limited vocational possibilities. Average administration time is approximately 30 minutes.

Minnesota Vocational Interest Inventory (The Psychological Corporation). This inventory is used for measurement of interests in occupations generally not requiring a college education. Average administration time is approximately 45 minutes. It is for males only. The subject's expressed interests are compared with those employed in semiskilled and skilled occupations on twenty-one occupational scales. Also, nine area scales indicate the degree of liking for activities which may be common to several occupations.

EXAMPLES OF THE USE OF TESTS BY EMPLOYERS

The use of tests in industry runs the gamut from being the sole factor in personnel decisions to not being used at all. Unfortunately, both extremes have done disservice to potential job applicants, employees, and the company. On the other hand, there is evidence that, integrated with sound personnel practices, the proper use of tests has made significant contributions in selection, transfer, and upgrading. The following examples are offered simply as a means of providing clues for the use of tests in solving personnel problems.

Case 1 points out that testing should not be discarded on the basis of difficulty in recruiting or a tight labor market. On the contrary, rather than eliminating job applicants, testing can contribute to the most effective assignment of available workers. Case 2 illustrates the advantage of the use of tests in a seemingly simple selection situation. Cases 3 and 4 illustrate the importance of selecting the appropriate test. Case 3 shows the danger of being overselective. Case 4 demonstrates the pitfall of selecting tests solely on the basis of face validity of job requirements when other aptitudes may play an important role. Case 5 provides the groundwork for the inclusion of aptitude as a factor in upgrading.

Case 1.   Faced with difficulties in recruiting electronics assemblers, a newly opened plant in a semirural area decided to forego plans for testing, fearing it would curtail hires. After six months of operations it was found that production was poor, morale low, and turnover increasing. In spite of the tight labor market, a more selective screening program was initiated, including the administration of appropriate validated tests. Only applicants meeting test standards were assigned to assembly operation. Those who did not meet test standards, but otherwise met company requirements, were given other assignments such as inspecting or packing. Evaluation of operations after three months with the new program showed an increase in production, fewer rejects, a decrease in turnover, and better morale.

Case 2.   To combat the shortage of experienced clerical workers, Company J decided to conduct an in-plant training program. The program was opened to all employees on a voluntary basis. It was assumed that expressed interest was sufficient to learn the clerical duties involving matching identification numbers and addresses. Trainees were recruited from the packaging department. Twelve trainees moved to their new assignment after a two-week training session. Job performance was unsatisfactory, with many errors and customer complaints for receiving wrongly identified bills. Before proceeding with additional training sessions, volunteers were administered an aptitude test for clerical perception. The subsequent groups of test-selected trainees had no difficulty in performing satisfactorily.

Case 3.   Company G, a prestige employer offering good wages, experienced turnover in its mechanical assembly department. A company-wide testing program was in effect for all new hires that included an intelligence test and a test of mechanical ability. Analysis of exit interview information about employees leaving the mechanical assembly department disclosed that a high percentage of quits were due to lack of opportunity for advancement and the monotonous, repetitive nature of the assembly operation. Reexamination of the tests and test standards in relation to the tasks of the job indicated their overselectivity. Job analysis emphasized the semiskilled level of the operation calling for manual and finger dexterity. Elimination of the intelligence test and substitution of dexterity tests for one of mechanical ability resulted in selection of entry workers at a level commensurate with the job requirements.

Case 4.   A large Bank Q required teller trainees to meet high numerical standards through administration of a test emphasizing arithmetic reasoning and problem solving. With a few exceptions, trainees proved to be less than satisfactory. A clue to the problem was suggested in the finding of a high incidence of clerical errors. Reevaluation of the teller duties as performed at Bank Q indicated that clerical perception and quick computation were more important than problem solving. Utilization of a test battery that included arithmetic computation and clerical perception proved a much more satisfactory aid in the selection of subsequent trainees.

Case 5.   In Company B seniority was the basic requirement in bidding on openings in a higher classification. Due to expansion of operations, an unprecedented number of openings became available in Department X. Employees moving up encountered difficulty in learning the job. Both management and union received complaints from dissatisfied employees. Job analysis disclosed that spatial aptitude appeared to be a prime requisite for successful job performance. A recommendation was made to management and union that testing be considered as an additional factor in selection for upgrading to Department X. Management and union agreed and issued a joint statement to employees, explaining the nature of the requirements for performing the job. Subsequently, appropriate tests were selected and test standards established and incorporated in the selection for upgrading. The inclusion of the test battery contributed to a significant reduction of workers having difficulty in learning the tasks required for performance in Department X.

SUMMARY

In this chapter on clerical, mechanical, and dexterity tests and vocational interest inventories, an effort has been made to provide an overview of what is available and to indicate some of the ways in which these tests may contribute to solving certain types of personnel problems. Another objective was to present some of the cautions to be observed in their application and to emphasize their proper role in the total assessment process.

1. Clerical and mechanical tests and interest inventories should be considered as one factor in the total assessment process.

2. Aptitude and proficiency tests should be used appropriately, viz., aptitude tests with those inexperienced in the occupation, to determine potential; proficiency tests with those possessing experience or training, to measure present level of skill.

3. Tests should be selected on the basis of their validity for the occupation.

4. Subjects to be tested should be comparable to the standardization group, should be able to take the test under standardization conditions, and should be able to put forth their best effort.

5. The *Guidelines on Employee Selection Procedures* issued by the Equal Employment Opportunity Commission should be considered in the establishment of company policy on testing.[9]

Test Publishers and Companies Furnishing Apparatus

American Optical Co.
Southbridge, Mass. 01550

Bausch & Lomb Inc.
Rochester, N.Y. 14602

California Test Bureau
Del Monte Research Park
Monterey, Calif. 93940

Cardall Associates
Yardley, Pa. 19068

Consulting Psychologists Press Inc.
577 College Ave.
Palo Alto, Calif. 94306

Education Industry Services
1225 E. 60th St.
Chicago, Ill. 60637

Educational & Industrial Testing Service
P.O. Box 7234
San Diego, Calif. 92107

Educational Test Bureau
Division of American Guidance Service Inc.
720 Washington Ave. S.E.
Minneapolis, Minn. 55414

Educators and Employers' Test and Service
Associates
120 Detzel Place
Cincinnati, Ohio 45219

Graham Field Surgical Co. Inc.
32-56 62nd St.
Woodside, N.Y. 10077

Harcourt Brace Jovanovich, Inc.
757 Third Ave.
New York, N.Y. 10017

Houghton Mifflin Co.
2 Park St.
Boston, Mass. 02107

Institute of Psychological Research
34 Fleury St. West
Montreal 375, P.Q. Canada

Keystone View Co.
Meadville, Pa. 16335

Lafayette Instrument Co.
North 26th St. & 52 By Pass
Lafayette, Ind. 47902

[9] *Op. cit.* p. 2.

Long's College Book Co.
1836 North High St.
Columbus, Ohio 43201

Marietta Apparatus Company
Marietta, Ohio 45750

McCann Associates
13410 Lindsay St.
Philadelphia, Pa. 19116

McKnight & McKnight Publishing Co.
Bloomington, Ill. 61701

Munsell Color Company, Inc.
10 East franklin St.
Baltimore, Md. 21203

Norman (J. H.)
726 Austrian Way, Grand Way
Grand Prairie, Tex. 73050

Palmer Associates Inc.
4331 Winfield Terrace
Easton, Pa. 18042

Psychological Corporation (The)
304 E. 45 St.
New York, N.Y. 10017

Psychological Institute
P.O. Box 1118
Lake Alfred, Fla. 33850

Psychological Test Specialists
Box 1441
Missoula, Mont. 59801

Psychometric Affiliates
1743 Monterey
Chicago, Ill. 60643

Public Personnel Association
1313 E. 60th St.
Chicago, Ill. 60637

Richardson, Bellows, Henry & Co., Inc.
324 Balter Bldg.
New Orleans, La. 70112

Science Research Associates, Inc.
259 E. Erie St.
Chicago, Ill. 60611

Sheridan Psychological Service
P.O. Box 837
Beverly Hills, Calif. 90213

Stevens, Thurow & Associates Inc.
105 W. Adams St.
Chicago, Ill. 60603

Stoelting (C. H.) Co.
424 N. Homan Ave.
Chicago, Ill. 60624

University Bookstore
Purdue University
360 West State St.
Lafayette, Ind. 47906

Vocational Guidance Service
95 Portland St.
Buffalo, N.Y. 14220

Western Psychological Services
12031 Wilshire Blvd.
Los Angeles, Calif. 90025

BIBLIOGRAPHY

Albright, L. E., J. R. Glennon, and W. J. Smith: *The Use of Psychological Tests in Industry,* Howard Allen Inc., Cleveland, 1963.
Anastasi, Anne: *Psychological Testing,* 3d ed., The Macmillan Company, New York, 1968.
APA-AERA-NCME Joint Committee: *Standards for Educational and Psychological Tests and Manuals,* American Psychological Association, Washington, D.C., 1966.
Buros, Oscar K.: *The Sixth Mental Measurement Yearbook,* The Gryphon Press, Highland Park, N.J., 1965.
——: *Tests in Print,* The Gryphon Press, Highland Park, N.J., 1961.
Cronbach, Lee J.: *Essentials of Psychological Testing,* 3d ed., Harper & Row, Publishers, Incorporated, New York, 1970.
—— and G. C. Gleser: *Psychological Tests and Personnel Decisions,* University of Illinois Press, Urbana, 1965.
Darley, J. G., and Heda Hagenah: *Vocational Interest Measurement,* University of Minnesota Press, Minneapolis, 1955.
Dunnette, Marvin D.: *Personnel Selection and Placement,* Wadsworth Publishing Company, Inc., Belmont, Calif., 1966.
Fryer, D.: *The Measurement of Interests,* Henry Holt and Company, Inc., New York, 1931.

Ghiselli, Edwin E.: *The Validity of Occupational Aptitute Tests,* John Wiley & Sons, Inc., New York, 1966.

―――― and Clarence W. Brown: *Personnel and Industrial Psychology,* 2d ed., McGraw Hill Book Company, New York, 1955.

Guion, Robert M.: *Personnel Testing,* McGraw Hill Book Company, New York, 1965.

―――― and Wayne K. Kirschner: *Psychology Applied to Industry,* Appleton-Century-Crofts, Inc., New York, 1965.

Lyman, Howard B.: *Test Scores and What They Mean,* Prentice-Hall, Inc., Englewood Cliffs, N.J., 1963.

Nunnally, Jum C., Jr.: *Tests and Measurements: Assessment and Prediction,* McGraw-Hill Book Company, New York, 1959.

Strong, E. K., Jr.: *Vocational Interests of Men and Women,* Stanford University Press, Stanford, Calif., 1943.

Super, Donald E.: *The Psychology of Careers,* Harper & Brothers, New York, 1957.

―――― and John O. Crites: *Appraising Vocational Fitness by Means of Psychological Tests,* Harper & Brothers, New York, 1962.

Tiffin, J., and E. J. McCormick: *Industrial Psychology,* 5th ed., Prentice-Hall, Inc., Englewood Cliffs, N.J., 1955.

U.S. Department of Labor, Manpower Administration: *Doing Your Best on Aptitude Tests,* Government Printing Office, Washington, 1968 (pamphlet).

chapter 16

Psychological Tests:
Mental and Personality

J. B. STONE   *Consulting Psychologist, Hacienda Heights, California*

The major resource available to any organization is people. And the effective use of its people determines, in large measure, the health and competitive staying power of a business or company, whether large or small. This frontier of effective use of human resources looks to psychology, often, for help. Such inquiries, frequently, are concerned with clues, suggestions, assessment techniques, and other matters concerned with such key features of a person as his mental capacities and potentials and his emotional maturity and patterns.

This chapter is concerned with the assistance available in the area of psychological tests of mental ability and of personality (including emotional maturity, temperament characteristics). This chapter includes the following:

1. Mental ability tests: purposes, general nature, and selected examples
2. Personality tests: purposes, general nature, and selected examples
3. Interpretative rationales: statistical normative, prediction, individual guidance, and organizational guidance
4. Major personnel uses of such tests: hiring, placement, promotion, mobility, and training decisions, supervisory assistance, organizational analysis
5. Practical suggestions for usage

MENTAL ABILITY TESTS

Purposes

The major purposes for which mental ability tests were developed were to provide the means by which we could measure or assess capabilities and/or potentialities of intellectual (mental) functioning. Sometimes our assessment concern is with the overall or general functioning of our intelligence. On other occasions, reference is to components or special abilities relating to our intellectual process.

Knowledge of the intellectual limits and/or characteristics of a person is assumed to have value in our considerations of that person for educational contexts, vocational contexts, etc. Assumptions are frequently made that a person's intelligence plays important roles in his day-to-day life both with respect to general demands and to specific tasks or roles in which he finds himself.

The assessment of human intelligence has been of great interest to both the psychologist and the lay public. The use of mental ability tests by schools, industry, the military, and others has provided much stimulus to pure and applied research on such tests. The probabilities are that each one of us has taken tests of mental ability many times and that varied educational, vocational, or personal decisions have followed from these tests. The function of intelligence tests, then, is to provide information which is accurate and representative of our general and/or special mental skills.

General Nature of Tests of Mental Ability

Basically, all tests of intelligence provide a variety of "tasks," verbal or performance, general language or graphic, cultural or culture-free, and so on. These tasks or "items" are selected to represent and sample our intellectual development and skills.

These items are presented to us, and our responses are recorded and scored. The accumulation of our scores is reviewed to provide summary scores and/or part scores. Such scores are reflected against standards of performance previously determined on groups of known characteristics, such as age, socioeconomic level, geographical residence, vocational background, educational background.

Tests of mental ability may be classified in several ways. For this discussion, let us classify them as (1) composite tests, (2) battery tests, and (3) overall tests.

Composite tests sample a variety of intellectual processes and generate scores for segments within the total test as well as a summary score or scores. The interpretation of the score may emphasize the total score (such as the person's IQ), or a summary score (such as verbal IQ or performance IQ), or a segment score (such as reasoning, vocabulary, figure assembly).

The Wechsler Adult Intelligence Scale (WAIS), the Stanford-Binet Intelligence Scales, and the California Test of Mental Maturity are illustrative of composite tests.

Battery tests sample a variety of intellectual processes, also. Efforts are made, however, to group the items and scores within a functional context which is educationally or vocationally oriented.

We know that persons who are more gifted in verbal functions may or may not be gifted, also, in arithmetic functions or spatial perception functions, or reasoning functions. In the prediction of success in various educational and vocational contexts, it is assumed in many circles that our performance in various tests of ability has determinable relationships to our probable success in such contexts.

The battery exists, basically, as an efficient effort to assess many varied abilities in a systematic manner and against standards developed on the same samples for the several tests within the battery. It is a package of mental ability tests, designed to provide interpretations in which the person can be compared with other people *and* with himself, also. In the latter instance, we make a differential comparison, leading to such conclusions as "he is stronger in verbal than in spatial abilities," or vice versa.

Representative of the battery-type of intelligence tests are the SRA Primary Mental Abilities, the Differential Aptitude Tests, and the Multiple Aptitude Tests.

Overall tests provide a reasonably short presentation of various items which sample a variety of mental functions. The score from such tests is generally a single score indicating general or overall intelligence. The items in such tests are frequently similar to the more comprehensive composite and battery tests. However, the extensiveness of the sampling of various intellectual processes is more limited; there are fewer items, usually.

Illustrative of tests of overall mental ability are the Otis Quick-scoring Mental Ability Tests and the Wonderlic Personnel Test.

Selected Examples of Mental Ability Tests

The *Wechsler Adult Intelligence Scale* (WAIS) is an individually administered, comprehensive test of mental ability. It provides fourteen scores, grouped in two areas. The verbal score includes information (general), comprehension (knowledge of common principles), arithmetic (basic quantitative processes), similarities (perception of relationships), digit span (recall of serially presented numbers), and vocabulary (general). The performance score includes digit symbol (responding to an abstract code of symbols), picture completion (closing an incomplete picture), block design (arranging multicolored blocks to create a specific design), picture arrangement (rearranging a set of pictures to tell a story), and object assembly (rearranging the pieces to make a whole object).

The *Stanford-Binet Intelligence Scale* is an individually administered test. Its range is from early childhood to the adult level. In the latter instance a wide sampling of vocabulary, reasoning, information, spatial, arithmetical, and performance items contributes to a single score, the person's intelligence quotient (IQ).

The *California Test of Mental Maturity, Adult Level,* is group administered and scorable by machine. It provides a variety of short tests which generate the following scores: logical reasoning, spatial relationships, numerical reasoning, verbal concepts, memory, language (total), and nonlanguage (total). Scores are translatable to mental age and/or IQ equivalents. Diagnostic profiles are available for analyzing a performance.

The *SRA Primary Mental Abilities* battery is a group-administered set of tests developed from a theoretical framework designed to evaluate intellectual skills which are presumed to be basic (primary). Scores are provided in verbal meaning, number facility, reasoning, spatial relations.

The *Multiple Aptitude Tests* is a group-administered battery of tests, yielding scores for a verbal comprehension factor, including word meaning and paragraph meaning; a perceptual speed factor, including language usage and routine clerical facility; a numerical reasoning factor, including arithmetic reasoning and arithmetic computation; and a spatial visualization factor, including applied sciences and mechanics, two-dimensional spatial relations, and three-dimensional spatial relations.

The *Differential Aptitude Tests* in a group-administered battery of tests which provides several scores: verbal reasoning, numerical ability, abstract reasoning, space relations, mechanical reasoning, and clerical speed and accuracy.

The *Otis Quick-scoring Mental Ability Tests* present several forms of reasonably short group-administered tests. These tests sample a diversified array of intellectual functions, covering vocabulary, perceptual features, arithmetic, and reasoning. Usually, a total score is obtained.

The *Wonderlic Personnel Test* is an abbreviated variation of the parent Otis Self-Administering Test. The Wonderlic presents a variety of verbal, arithmetical, and perceptual items. The scoring usually provides a total score.

PERSONALITY TESTS

Purposes

Personality tests attempt, generally, to assess either a person's emotional maturity or his trait behavior. In the first instance our concern is to provide an evaluation as to whether the person is, comparatively, normal or whether his immaturities are likely to be troublesome to him or to others.

In the "trait behavior" emphasis, there is, usually, an underlying theory of personality. Such a theoretical basis will suggest characteristics or traits which, in turn, are looked at from an assessment viewpoint. Several tests referred to, below, will provide further discussion of behavior traits.

General Nature of Personality Tests

Inasmuch as personality is a very complex aspect of a person and is characterized by considerable subjectivity and general subtlety, the various instruments (tests) used to assess personality, totally or in part, are legion.

The variety is endless, as seem to be the concomitant theoretical positions. Even so, two general categories may provide an adequate basis for this discussion. One is the self-report technique; the other is the projective technique.

The *self-report technique* usually employs questions which a person answers as he feels about them. His answers are recorded and scored according to the rationale underlying the test, either as reflecting a degree of emotional maturity or stability or as reflecting development in various traits.

Projective techniques attempt to overcome certain implied biases of self-report techniques. These latter may be transparent (easily discernible); they may be easy to slant (purposely answer to your felt advantage); they may be too categorical ("always," "never," "occasionally," etc.); or they may be too ambiguous (not relatable to everyone's experiences; meanings are obscure). Projective techniques provide tests which the person responds to without knowing (or, apparently, guessing) what his responses will provide. The scoring and interpretation systems employed in projective tests are usually complex and difficult for nontrained persons to handle. Selected tests, listed below, will illustrate some of the variations presently popular among projective techniques.

Selected Tests of Personality

The *Bell Adjustment Inventory* is a group-administered, self-report questionnaire that provides six scores. These reflect a person's maturity of adjustment toward: (1) home, (2) health, (3) submissiveness, (4) emotionality, (5) hostility, and (6) masculinity.

Gough's *California Psychological Inventory* is a group-administered, self-report questionnaire that yields eighteen scores: (1) dominance, (2) capacity for status, (3) sociability, (4) social presence, (5) self-acceptance, (6) sense of well-being, (7) responsibility, (8) socialization, (9) self-control, (10) tolerance, (11) good impression, (12) communality, (13) achievement via conformance, (14) achievement via independence, (15) intellectual efficiency, (16) psychological mindedness, (17) flexibility, and (18) femininity.

The *Edwards Personal Preference Schedule* is a self-report, group-administered questionnaire that generates fifteen scores: (1) achievement, (2) deference, (3) order, (4) exhibition, (5) autonomy, (6) affiliation, (7) intraception, (8) succorance, (9) dominance, (10) abasement, (11) nurturance, (12) change, (13) endurance, (14) heterosexuality, and (15) aggression.

Schutz's *FIRO-B* is a self-report, group-administered questionnaire reflecting a person's "fundamental interpersonal relations, orientation, and behavior." Six scores are available: (1) expressed inclusion, (2) wanted inclusion, (3) expressed control, (4) wanted control, (5) expressed affection, and (6) wanted affection.

The *Minnesota Multibasic Personality Inventory* (MMPI) is a group-administered, self-report questionnaire which provides fourteen scores: (1) hypochondriasis, (2) depression, (3) hysteria, (4) psychopathic deviate, (5) masculinity-femininity, (6) paranoia, (7) psychasthenia, (8) schizophrenia, (9) hypomania, (10) social, (11) question, (12) lie, (13) validity, and (14) test-taking attitudes.

Bernreuter's *The Personality Inventory* is a self-report, group-administered questionnaire that gives six scores: (1) neurotic tendency, (2) self-sufficiency, (3) introversion-extroversion, (4) dominance-submission, (5) confidence, and (6) sociability.

Cattell's *Sixteen Personality Factor Questionnaire* is a group-administered, self-report questionnaire that yields sixteen scores: (1) reserved vs. outgoing, (2) less intelligent vs. more intelligent, (3) affected by feeling vs. emotionally stable, (4) humble vs. assertive, (5) sober vs. happy-go-lucky, (6) expedient vs. conscientious, (7) shy vs. venturesome, (8) tender-minded vs. tough-minded, (9) trusting vs. suspicious, (10) practical vs. imaginative, (11) forthright vs. shrewd, (12) placid vs. apprehensive, (13) conservative vs. experimenting, (14) group-dependent vs. self-sufficient, (15) casual vs. controlled, and (16) relaxed vs. tense.

The *Rorschach Psychodiagnostic Technique* is an individually administered projective instrument which presents a standardized set of inkblots to a person who provides his responses to what he "sees." The scoring and interpretation of the Rorschach are complex and variable; there are several scoring systems and a variety of interpretative rationales. This much-written-about test requires the assistance of a specially trained psychologist both for administration (and scoring) and for interpretation. Two derivatives of the Rorschach are described below. They are intended for more general, less sophisticated usage.

The *Holtzman Inkblot Technique* is a projective instrument which provides a wide variety of cards (inkblots) which generate twenty-two scores: (1) reaction time, (2) rejections, (3) location, (4) space, (5) form definiteness, (6) pathognomic verbalization, (11) integration, (12 to 16) content, (17) anxiety, (18) hostility, (19) barrier, (20) penetration, (21) balance, (22) populars.

The *Structured-Objective Rorschach Test* is a group-administered projective test which uses the standard Rorschach inkblots, either on cards or as slides. Responses to the test are forced choice, providing a standard 100 responses, 10 per blot. Fifteen traditional Rorschach scores are provided covering: area (whole, major detail, minor detail, white space), determinants (human movement, animal movement, good color, poor color, good form, poor form, shading), content (human, animal), and statistical (popular, original). These scores are converted to a rationale of the person which includes twelve basic categories: (1) personalism, (2) altruism, (3) rationalism, (4) social aggressiveness, (5) social responsiveness, (6) social cooperation, (7) conformity, (8) assertiveness, (9) liberality, (10) intellectual aggressiveness, (11) efficiency, and (12) purposiveness.

Murray's *Thematic Apperception Test* (TAT) may be administered individually or in groups and is a projective technique in which a variety of standard pictures (varying from blank to rather complete visual stories) are presented and the respondent writes or tells what the picture suggests to him as a story. A complex, very systematic scoring rationale is used, requiring the assistance of a specifically trained psychologist.

Rotter's *Sentence Completion Test* is illustrative of a group-administered projective technique in which introductory sentence items (beginnings of sentences) are responded to by completing such sentences. Scores are derived by reviewing the replies for indications of emotional maturity, diversity of attitudes, and variety of interests.

INTERPRETATIVE RATIONALES

The various scores obtained from mental ability and personality tests are subjected to a wide range of interpretative systems. These rationales include: (1) underlying theoretical systems, (2) statistical and scaling emphases, (3) normative bases, (4) prediction contexts, and (5) guidance emphases, both individually oriented and organizationally oriented.

The theoretical systems underlying the various tests described above are sufficiently numerous and complex to be beyond the scope of this discussion. Interested readers are directed to the manuals and related literature pertaining to any of these tests.

Statistical rationale. The scores on mental ability tests are usually converted into intelligent quotient (IQ), mental age equivalent (MA), or percentile rank (PR).

The IQ is usually thought of as the ratio of a person's mental age (determined by the test) to his chronological age. On the adult level, both ages become somewhat meaningless as components of an index of intelligence. Adult IQ tables may attempt to overcome the mental-age–chronological-age dilemma by assigning IQ equivalency in terms of comparisons with persons in broad age groups (grouped by five- or ten-year spans to accommodate for changes in mental ability influenced by age).

Percentile rank (PR) is sometimes used as a basis for comparing a person's ability with that of persons in a specified group. PR 75 indicates that a person equaled or exceeded 75 percent of the persons on whom the norms being used were developed. Similar statements can apply to any PR value. The simplicity of percentage connotations is attractive, but one often falls into the trap of interpreting comparative percentiles as if the equal arithmetical differences were absolute differences. The arithmetical difference between PR 50 and PR 60 is 10, as is the difference between PR 80 and PR 90. However, the *significance* of these apparently equal differences is that the difference between PR 80 and PR 90 is significantly greater than that between PR 50 and PR 60.

Personality tests usually develop scores that relate to percentile rank (PR), normalized standard scores (often T-scores), or stanines. The above comments concerning PR apply, also, to personality tests.

In an effort to provide a more equitable comparison of scores on personality tests, many authors use the normalized standard score. This assumes a midpoint, determined by finding the mean of the distribution, and a unit of range, determined by the standard deviation of the distribution. Scores are ordered within the normal (bell-shaped) distribution by reference to the position of each score from the midpoint in terms of degree of range above or below the midpoint. The stability of this approach for interpretation and research purposes is important. The usual score of this kind is the T-score.

Because the T-score, even though an equitable score for research and interpretative purposes, can vary from 0 to 100, an abbreviation was developed and referred to as *stanines.* Such a scale "orders" the scores into nine ranges of equal size and running from a middle (stanine 5) up to stanine 9 and down to stanine 1. The usefulness of such a scale for IBM key-punch cards and for computer treatments is important.

Normative bases. In the majority of mental ability tests, most of the norms are based on carefully selected, broadly varied samplings. A person's score on such tests is interpreted, usually, against a substantial array of persons qualifying as a general population. This broadly based normalizing makes possible substantially reliable interpretations of individual scores and of comparisons between people. Even so, a knowledge of the performance of special groups (educational and/or occupational categories) is important in order to make even more precise interpretations. Most manuals and much reported research in the literature provide such special group norms.

Most personality tests have been normalized on much narrower groups. It is important to review the characteristics of the norm group(s) of a personality test to determine the probable value such norms may have for groups we may wish to test. Gradually, more and more research data have become available on personality tests which provide special group data and/or norms as well as build the substance for more general norms.

Prediction contexts. Users of tests in business and industry usually hope to be able to predict what a person might be expected to do. Many predictive studies have been conducted, sometimes with positive results, sometimes with negative results. There are important considerations in such areas as criterion measures and research design which make prediction studies, when properly carried out, highly sophisticated tools.

It is important, therefore, to bear in mind that generalizing predictions from one context to another is a frequent error in test usage. Whenever prediction is an objective of test usage, it is wise to utilize the assistance of a person trained in the subtleties and problems surrounding prediction contexts.

Guidance of individuals. Many mental ability and personality tests are most useful, not for their conclusions or in the conclusive sense we would like to apply to prediction uses, but for the clues or suggestions that provide for "possibility."

If a person scores high on a mental ability test, he *may* do well in situations requiring a quick, alert intellect. If he has, apparently, a high score on "anxiety," he *may* work well in moderately challenging situations, but he *may* be overwhelmed by intense, demanding situations.

The use of tests in guidance is not restricted to vocational counseling. Applications to individuals in business and industry are important, as suggested above, but, one must keep in mind the "probable," the "possible," or the "tentative" and avoid the "absolute," the "for sure," or the "for certain."

Guidance of the organization. Organizations may use test data in a context of careful, considered judgment, or they may proceed expediently and impulsively. Obviously, the former attitude is preferred. It serves little purpose to invest time, money, and people in whimsical, facetious uses of tests, especially when such expenditures, appropriately made, might bear positive results.

MAJOR PERSONNEL USES

The hiring decision. Two basic questions always arise in considering a potential employee: (1) Can he do the work? (2) Will he do the work? A derivative of the first is, "Can he learn to do the work?" Test data can give broad answers to those questions. Mental ability tests may give some information on the first question (capability) and its derivative (potential). Personality tests may give some help on the second question (motivation value). Should Joe or Tom or Bill be hired? The answer may be that Tom, though not as "sharp" (intellectually) as Joe, is superior to Bill; but Tom is much more emotionally mature than either of the others; and Bill is more mature than Joe.

The placement decision. Should Tom be hired for job A or job B or job C? The probability of his succeeding in each is good. But jobs A and B lead to technically oriented, trouble-shooting assignments with far-reaching consequences. Job C, however, is challenging but not likely to be unduly difficult for Tom.

The promotion decision. Should Tom be promoted to a higher position in the line on which his job lies? Perhaps his evenness of temper will work to his advantage, but the necessity to make many quick, complex decisions might favor Harry, who, though a little more volatile, can think more creatively and with greater speed.

The transfer decision. Frequently, an organization when looking for a man searches outside the organization for him. It is possible that the man being sought is already on the payroll. But he may be overlooked because the organization is not looking for potential (which his mental ability may supply) or drive (which his personality may encompass).

The training decision. Whether the concern is for vertical mobility (promotion) or horizontal mobility (transfer), a concomitant decision may relate to the susceptibility the man has for training. Should he be encouraged to take a night school class, a college seminar, or a short-term workshop or pursue some independent study? Are there short-term assignments within the company from which he might profit, such as vacation relief or backup for another job, or committee assignments, or special projects?

Supervisory assistance. Knowledge of a man's capabilities, potential, and maturity characteristics can help a thoughtful supervisor in many ways. Such information might shed light on various developments in the probationary period. At those times when a person's efforts taper off or reach a plateau, such test data may help provide clues concerning his motivation. When problems in communication arise, they may be due in part to substantial differences in mental ability which can complicate two-way communication. They may arise from marked differences in the character of the superior and that of the subordinate. Skillful supervision can benefit from personality data, appropriately interpreted.

Organizational analyses. Implied in many of the features already discussed is the value that mental ability and personality may have in organizational development. From such data it is possible to obtain clues which can suggest the relative strength of the resources of the organization, as a whole, or of units within the organization. Within the several units of the accounting department, for example, may be some which are staffed by capable, alert, well-motivated persons. Other units may be staffed with mediocre, passive, or complacent persons. An overall view of an organization's human resources will always raise questions for which mental ability and/or personality tests may provide help.

PRACTICAL SUGGESTIONS FOR USAGE

The suggestions contained in this section are intended to help prevent many of the abuses that business and industry make of mental ability and personality tests. These tests have been subjected to a great deal of abuse or, at least, misuse. The result has been that a great many negative attitudes developed. Proper use could have avoided many of these.

Determination of purpose(s) to be served. What are the tests to be used for? Are the purpose or purposes you envision within the domain or information the test(s) can provide? Is the information you seek relevant to the context of the job you are concerned about? Mental ability tests can give either general clues or broadly specialized clues to a man's intellectual alertness and ability to learn. But they cannot guarantee that a man will use that ability. Personality tests, similarly, may suggest the degree of emotional stability a person has; but the relevance of that maturity, or of specific personality traits, to job performance may not be as important as one thinks. Congeniality, though a popular virtue, may not apply to successfulness in most jobs with uniformity and may not contribute to some job success at all. The point is that the user should have relevant purposes in mind. At least, he should have specific purposes in mind, which can be checked out as the test data are used and either validated or invalidated thereby.

Use of test data as aids to decision making. A common error in using mental ability or personality tests is to treat the scores as absolute or conclusive evidence. If you are making a personnel decision in which such test data play a part, the only legitimate use of those data is as an *aid* to you, not as the *reason* for your decision. The fact that a man has a high IQ or is substantially mature does not give you a sound basis for a decision. However, the clues that that information gives you can be weighed along with all other pertinent information to *aid* you in making up your mind. If you use scores on these tests as hurdles a man must pass, you may blithely overlook many men who would have done very well had you considered the total information available to you about them.

Adherence to standards. Test publishers provide explicit instructions for administering and scoring their tests. It is absolutely necessary to adhere to those instructions for both mental ability and personality tests. If time limits are used, they must be adhered to meticulously. If certain language is used in the instructions, one must not deviate from it. If the scoring of the test is done in a certain way, one does not make allowances in another way. When guides to interpretation are provided, it is important to stay within the limits they provide. This is particularly true in using personality tests. If you do not understand clearly the meaning of such test scores, either obtain the assistance of a psychologist who does or do not use the test(s).

Recognition of needs for research in your local setting. The fact that positive values for mental ability and/or personality tests were found in Company A or Branch B does not mean that similar values will accrue in your usage. The nature of companies or of branches is such that no two are as much alike as we might think. Practices which prove to be successful in one context may not safely be transferred to another context without checking out such applicability. This research in the local context is vital to the proper use of mental ability and personality tests. Competent professional help can aid materially in protecting you from improper interpretation of test standards, especially when they are "borrowed" from a sister branch or company.

Importance of follow-up. If you have used mental ability tests or personality tests as an aid to making your personnel decisions, be sure to follow up and see how well the man has done. Part of the skill in wise interpretation of these test scores comes from such a follow-up. Test scores are not mechanical bits of data, no matter how readily they can be processed by computers or other apparatus. Test scores are "educated guesses" about people. Like any other educated guess, follow-up is necessary to determine one's successfulness in the game of shrewd hunches, which is, after all, what these tests are all about.

Selected Publishers

Listed below are some publishers of mental ability and personality tests. Purchase of these tests is usually restricted to organizations which employ or obtain the help of persons with professional competence in using such tests. A publisher can supply you with information as to the prices, uses, etc., of his tests and the restrictions, if any, he places on purchasers.

The Bobbs-Merrill Co., Inc.,
4300 East 62 St.
Indianapolis, Ind., 46206

California Test Bureau
Del Monte Research Park
Monterey Park, Calif., 93940

Consulting Psychologists Press, Inc.,
577 College Ave.
Palo Alto, Calif., 94306

Psychometric Affiliates
1743 Monterey
Chicago, Ill., 60643

Cooperative Test Division, Educational
Testing Service
Princeton, N.J., 08540

Science Research Associates, Inc.
259 East Erie St.
Chicago, Ill., 60643

Houghton-Mifflin Co.
2 Park St.
Boston, Mass., 02107

S-O Publishers
1822 Old Canyon Dr.
Hacienda Heights, Calif., 91745

Institute for Personality and Ability Testing
1602 Coronado Drive
Champaign, Ill., 68122

Stoelting (C. H.) Co.
424 N. Homan Ave.
Chicago, Ill., 60624

The Psychological Corporation
304 East 45 St.
New York, N.Y., 10017

Western Psychological Services
12031 Wilshire Blvd.
Los Angeles, Calif., 90025

BIBLIOGRAPHY

Buros, O. K.: *The Sixth Mental Measurements Yearbook,* Gryphon Press, Highland Park,
    N.J., 1965.
Dunnette, M. D., and Kirchner, W.: *Psychology Applied to Business and Industry,* Appleton-
    Century-Crofts, New York, 1965.
Ghiselli, E., and Brown, C. W.: *Personnel and Industrial Psychology,* McGraw-Hill, New York,
    1955.
Guilford, J. P.: *The Nature of Human Intelligence,* McGraw-Hill, New York, 1967.
Guion, R. M.: *Personnel Testing,* McGraw-Hill, New York, 1965.
Kleinmuntz, B.: *Personality Measurement,* Dorsey, Homewood, Ill., 1967.
Korman, A. K.: *Industrial and Organizational Psychology,* Prentice-Hall, Englewood Cliffs,
    N.J., 1971.

chapter 17

Skills Inventories
and Promotion Systems

CARLTON W. DUKES *Industry Manager, Information Science Incorporated,
New City, New York*

As in most other human institutions, the expectations of positive contributions and
a system of reward is built into business organizations. In addition to the salary or
wage paid in exchange for employees' services, provision is usually made for monetary increases to reflect the increased value of services rendered in a particular
job. But there are those situations in which an individual demonstrates the capacity
to contribute to the organization *beyond* the level of his present job and therefore
can be considered a candidate for promotion. It is to this subject of promotion that
this chapter is directed.

DEFINITION OF PROMOTION

Promotion, in business organizations, is usually associated with the assignment of
an individual to a position of more responsibility, or to one which requires the application of his particular education or experience. Were there a sufficient supply of
promotional talent within all departments of a company or organization, then the
need for a systematic approach to promotion would be minimal. Unfortunately,
there would also be a tendency to promote only those who had been around longest,
or who had mastered the peculiarities of a particular department's practices, since
new people with different approaches or ideas applied in other departments or
companies would not be introduced into the organization.

In this context, personnel turnover can produce benefits to an organization. However, in the process, considerable inconvenience is incurred by having to define
responsibilities which change over time in almost every job context, and then having
to identify those persons who may have the attributes or skills to fulfill these responsibilities.

In order to minimize the time required in identification of the factors particular to a position, and then in the selection of the individual employee most appropriate, a systematic approach to both of these processes usually evolves in large organizations where the number of such openings is frequent, or in small organizations where the turnover is volatile.

An idealized sample promotion process can be considered as follows: Every position within the organization has a *job description* not only outlining or even detailing the duties and responsibilities of an incumbent, but sometimes even indicating the necessary experience and educational background of the incumbent. To refine further the requirements for a particular job opening, the job description can often be supplemented with a *job requisition* which may add to the education and experience requirements such items as age range and any particular personality characteristics which the supervisor of the incumbent may desire.

Then, using the position requirements as search parameters, the personnel specialist can review files containing individual qualifications (either manual or machine methods) to determine which are the individuals within the desired limits of age, experience, education, or other pertinent qualifications required on the position. Essentially, this is a quantitative search for individuals, and the qualitative aspects of personality have yet to be evaluated by other methods than those used in the file-searching process. In this context, the interview, reference checks, and appropriate counseling or testing techniques provide the necessary degree or level of qualitative information on a prospective incumbent.

Promotion as a Recruitment Source

Having considered the process of promotion in the general sense, a more detailed examination of the components of the process would first of all indicate that promotion is a recruitment source for an organization. Recruitment being defined as a new entry of an individual into an organization, the process of promotion immediately or indirectly results in an influx of one or more individuals to fill a particular position or a series of positions created by a single promotion. An example of promotion as a recruitment condition or source can occur when a general manager of marketing is promoted to vice-president, for example. This particular single move may have a chain effect, resulting in an upward movement of anywhere from one to five individuals in some cases, depending upon the depth and/or hierarchy of the organization. At one point in this chain of moves, it is quite likely that recruitment from the outside will have to occur, in that few organizations are adequately prepared to fill any and all potential vacancies, especially those in the middle or lower supervisory ranks. If there is an adequate supply of promotable talent, then the effect of the vice-presidential promotion would be confined to the internal organization and not result in recruitment. However, if, as is too often the case, there is no replacement for the junior supervisory positions, then it will be necessary to go outside the organization to obtain such talent.

This process, in and of itself, can be of considerable benefit to the organization in attempting to attract new individuals into it. A demonstrated progression path, ensuring that new talent brought into the organization *can* move upward, would be a definite plus for any person with ambition who was contemplating joining the organization. Few individuals of any talent level at all would be interested in joining an organization only to be fixed at their entry position level, rather than being able to look forward to the possibility of working themselves up to vice-president.

In fact, the ability of an organization to demonstrate a progression from the lower levels to the higher levels is more encouraging to newcomers as well as those who have spent considerable time with the organization than is a pattern whereby most, if not all, of the significant levels have been filled from the outside as such openings occurred.   In short, turnover and/or promotion can be beneficial to an organization if the promotional path to fill vacancies is oriented toward upward movement through the organization, as opposed to infusion of high-level talent from outside the organization only.   As such, this policy of promotion can be considered as a definite selling point for the organization.

Informal vs. Formal Promotion Systems

Many organizations, even those of considerable size, still depend upon an informal promotion "system" whereby a number of key managers will request the assignment of individuals to projects only from among those individuals with whom they have had previous working experience, or from those who, for one reason or another, have impressed them with their activities or presence.

As a particular example of this situation, a major petrochemical company had almost all its executive promotion activities focused upon the organization planning director who, through his some thirty-odd years of experience with the company, had managed to work his way through operational divisions to the parent company personnel function.   In the process of this experience, he gained personal insight into not only what was required as background to fill particular positions, but also the personalities of the incumbents, who carried out their duties with varying degrees of effectiveness.   Upon assuming the role of organization planning director, he had the corporate responsibility for seeing to it that position descriptions were written for all executive positions.   Under his direction, the Hay point system of evaluating executive responsibilities was installed, and having to review all position descriptions in reference to this evaluation methodology, he became even more familiar with all executive positions in terms of know-how, problem solving, and accountability (integral parts of the Hay system).

Over a period of time, other executives came to rely upon not only this director's personal experience with job levels and responsibilities, but his judgment in assessing the varying degrees of the above-mentioned know-how, problem solving, and accountability as they pertained to both new and established positions.   The evaluation system determined not only the responsibility level, but fixed, for the most part, the compensation level for the position.

Whenever an opening occurred, it became the custom, especially in establishing a new position, to consult with him, as director of organization planning.   He would analyze the component aspects of position responsibility and the appropriate level of compensation, and would also, more often than not, designate the candidate for the position from his personal knowledge of the individual's duties and performance, as well as from his thorough knowledge of comparable level or experience positions throughout the entire corporate structure.

However, as advantageous as this system was to most individuals, any prejudice toward any employee (by virtue of personality or previous errors in performance) would be reflected in the fact that the individual was seldom nominated as a candidate, and subjective comments on this individual's incompetence would be voiced in the presence of the managers who were considering this individual as a possible candidate.   The prejudice engendered by this particular director was then compounded by the presence of other members of management.   In fact, the mistaking of one man's last name for another could indeed negatively or positively affect an individual's promotion chances to a disproportionate extent.

Informal promotion systems, as exemplified above, have the minor advantage of a key man's recommendation and thorough knowledge, but can just as likely engender all the disadvantages resulting from personal error or prejudice.

Opposed to the informal or personality oriented approach to promotion, many organizations have turned to the more objective or systematic approach—either because of a large number of promotions needed, in excess of an individual's capability to adequately assess, or because of the recognized necessity to obtain more objective data than the response to "What do you think of Joe?"

A formal promotion system has two essential criteria: (1) objective evaluation of the responsibilities, duties, and level of organization significance of all positions within the company structure; and (2) insofar as is possible, an objective appraisal of the capabilities of individuals in terms of present and *potential* performance.

It should be stressed at this point that subjective measures such as personality appraisal cannot be removed from the process of considering promotional candidates. However, personality considerations in a more formal or objective system should be evaluated well *after* the comparisons between what has to be done on the job and what the individual possesses as education or experience factors to enable him to execute such duties.

When the distinction between the duties and responsibilities of a position and the person who will be in the position has been made, then it is far more easy to select an appropriate candidate who has the orientation to perform on the job than it is to attempt to tailor an individual position or set of responsibilities around the vagaries of personality. While it is true that many positions can benefit considerably from the particularities, or even peculiarities, of an individual's personality, establishing a position with only these peculiarites in mind too often results in institutionalizing some rather unpleasant characters who are the only ones suited or permitted to demand that things be done their way within the organization. Promoting such individuals out of such special niches is difficult, if not impossible, so that whatever experience could be of value to others in such a position will seldom be realized.

Most companies of any size have recognized such difficulties either implicitly or explicitly in that they have a stated policy on the subject of promotion, such as:

PROMOTIONS

We constantly seek capable people who will strive to progress as far as their abilities will take them. The opportunity for contributing new ideas, creative problem solutions and fresh approaches is essential to a research and development organization. The company hopes to help each person advance by activities such as counseling, development and education programs, job transfer opportunities and participation in technical meetings. Those who demonstrate ability to accept greater responsibility and produce effective results earn promotions. . . .

Promotions are based on recommendation of the professional staff. Promotion to Senior Technician will involve an impartial review by a committee of technical staff members. Each individual's technical knowledge, work performance, special contributions and length of service will be carefully considered.[1]

Each of these examples implies an objective evaluation of what is required on the job, and then a system whereby individuals with the ability to function within these requirements can be identified and selected.

As an example of the formal promotion system, the director of personnel research and development of a major corporation has established a comprehensive promotional system approach for executives within the corporate structure which embraces some 1,500 executives throughout the United States and overseas locations. It is his responsibility to see not only that the most qualified individual for a particular position opening is selected, but that *all* qualified candidates have been considered. This further means that no one can be hired from the outside until he gives his assurance that no such qualified individual is to be found within the organization and also that, irrespective of subsidiary company desires or delineations, individuals

---

[1] Standard Oil Company (Indiana).

identified as promotional candidates through his function must be given full consideration for the opening. If a candidate is selected and refused promotion opportunity by the subsidiary management, equal or better opportunity must be demonstrated by that subsidiary. In other words, it is incumbent upon management to provide justification for not permitting a promotion, just as it is incumbent upon the director to identify the best candidate(s) for promotion.

The Role of the Personnel Specialist

The role of this director, as the personnel specialist responsible for promotion within his organization, is not only comprehensive in its effectiveness throughout the corporation, but is understood by all levels of management, so that there is no ambiguity or lack of understanding of his area of responsibility. To ensure this completeness of understanding, he first secured a policy statement from top management stating that all executive position openings should always be scrutinized by his function, giving him sole responsibility for developing the list of appropriate candidates for any and all executive openings. This accomplished the necessary recognition of top management support of his goals and the execution of his duty to locate the most appropriate candidates, no matter where they may be within the organization.

Next, to educate middle management, he stressed the point in several management seminars that his staff would endeavor to obtain from the immediate supervisors the qualifications thought necessary for position openings. At that time, nominations for any particular candidate the supervisor had in mind were accepted without judgments being made to assure middle management that their suggestions were valued.

However, in the specifications for candidates, any purely arbitrary requirements were questioned for validity, e.g., "Will you only consider a man between forty and forty-five?" or "Would a man several years either side of those limits be equally acceptable?"

Then, reviewing these requirements as obtained from the immediate supervisor, not only were arrangements made to review personnel files with the requirements given in terms of education and experience, but also an evaluation was made on the background of any candidates nominated to determine how their backgrounds supplemented or augmented the other responsibility or education criteria.

After an appropriate list of candidates was obtained, then the director or one of his staff reviewed both the nominated candidates and all other candidates produced in conformity with the stated selection criteria and/or with backgrounds similar to those candidates previously nominated by the supervisor. In this way, all levels of management not only could feel an obligation to select the most qualified candidates for promotion, but in many instances were quite deeply involved in the actual decision-making process of determining qualifications and selection of candidates.

As a further step in the role of personnel promotion specialist, this director made it a point to counsel those individuals who were initial candidates for promotion, but who through some inadequacy in qualifications or personality were not ultimately selected, so that they might be better qualified in any future promotional searches of a similar nature.

The important point noted here is that this director as the personnel specialist responsible for promotion took considerable pains to communicate the entire process of candidate selection, from top management approval through his own evaluation efforts and the involvement of other members of management in producing candidates, to the ultimate selection of the most qualified individual, with attention being given to the development of those individuals not yet fully qualified.

It is significant, however, that without a pleasant personality and diplomatic approach on the part of this director, such efforts to communicate the promotion process might have been futile or even generated negative reactions.   Thus it might be said that the ideal personnel specialist in charge of promotion should be a logician in terms of identifying the factors most appropriate in job performance, a diplomat in recognizing the personality interfaces involved in the process, a semanticist in communicating the proper nuances of his function, and a therapist who can provide counseling and advice to those individuals not immediately qualified under the existing promotional system requirements.

Open and Closed Promotional Systems

A company that encourages an open promotion system not only considers all individuals within the organization as potential candidates, but takes specific steps to announce or internally advertise position openings as they occur.   To the extent that a company does not announce vacancies or in some way restricts the candidacy of *all* the individuals within the organization in relation to promotion openings, then it can be said that that company has a closed promotion system.

As an example of a combination of these two concepts, one major petroleum company within the United States considers positions below the executive level as open for consideration by any interested employee.   Within the executive levels, promotions to existing openings are carried out by means of consultations and conferences between the personnel function and the department management in which the opening exists.   The basic difference between these two approaches seems to be based upon the particular company philosophy that positions below the executive level are not as subject to the strictures of confidentiality in matters such as responsibility level and compensation brackets that the open posting of such position vacancies makes apparent.   In this particular organization, the relative responsibility and compensation levels are determined for executive position by a "point" evaluation system, by assigning values to various components of position responsibility and duties.   Very few individuals know their own "point" evaluation by which their relative worth to the organization is determined, much less that of their superiors or peers.

If the open posting or notification of vacancies were applied to the executive group, management evidently felt that over a period of time a series of cross comparisons between levels of responsibility (and compensation) could be drawn through noting which positions reported to whom, and thus establishing a relative hierarchy.   If a value could be fixed on any one of the positions within that hierarchy, then the relative compensation pattern for the other positions in the hierarchy could be established with some reasonable degree of accuracy.   To prevent this then, not only would the knowledge of the existence of a particular position opening be kept as restricted as possible, but those persons considered as candidates for the position would not be aware of it unless and until it was necessary to interview them in the final screening process.   In effect, many individuals considered for an executive position were only aware of it if they themselves were selected as the final candidate, especially if the position were in a location remote from their usual offices.   Of course, this was more true in the case of newly created positions than it would be of those positions where an incumbent, especially a well-known one, retired or otherwise left a well-established and recognized position.

On the other hand, for those individuals below the executive levels, and this included some managers and most of the professionals, the need for appropriate secrecy was not felt necessary.   For example, a posting of a position opening was made by having the personnel department draw up specifications relative to the open position and then displaying it on all the company bulletin boards.

Under this system, *any* employee who felt qualified to fill the position would call the supervisor whose telephone extension and department address were included in the position specifications and request an interview.

In terms of making available to the general corporate population inferences regarding the level of a particular supervisor, these could be drawn by noting the level of the opening (which was specified in the open position posting) which reported to a given supervisor or title classification.

Furthermore, the precise salary grade of all incumbents in a particular position was open for scrutiny as long as an opening existed in any department with such positions.

Management's Commitment

To embark upon an open system requires a management commitment to the notion that below a certain level (the executive level in this instance) sufficient discussion will have been carried on in any event so that there is no need for secrecy regarding the level of responsibility attached to the advertised positions themselves or to the respective supervisors of the reported vacant positions.

Another commitment which must be communicated, especially to the middle management group, is that a certain amount of toleration has to be developed in those instances where an employee who is patently underqualified for the position is using a supervisor's time to provide him with counsel so that he might be able to prepare himself to be eventually qualified.

Still another corporate commitment which must be communicated is that supervisors of employees wishing to apply for such positions should not restrict the individual from applying for such open positions, for in the restriction of what many employees regard as their rights, job dissatisfaction and perhaps even turnover can be a direct consequence of trying to "keep employees from wasting time applying for jobs for which they do not qualify."

A policy of open promotion systems leads to two other very important aspects which must also be considered: contractual obligations, i.e., unions; and legal requirements, i.e., antidiscriminatory legislation. In the case of contractual agreements, unions will be more than casually interested in a system which not only allows upward movement through the organization of any individuals so qualified, but also presents them with the opportunity to organize positions which had hitherto been unapproachable. In certain occupations or groups such as laboratory technicians and computer professionals, this upward movement of employees who were in lower level union-covered jobs moved on to positions which normally were not subject to negotiation. However, the individuals already accustomed to a union and perceiving this as an advantage have, in many instances, provided the eventual majority necessary to effect organization of professional positions.

In instances of antidiscriminatory legislation and its impact on particular jobs, the posting of position openings makes it quite easy for various rights and liberation groups to note whether or not such positions were eventually filled by members of their own particular special-interest group. The company, by its posting of positions, provides them with the necessary information which can be used in prosecuting a lawsuit should they deem it necessary. The name of the position, its level of responsibility, the supervisor's name, the approximate date during which the job was considered open, as well as those specific qualifications which were described as requirements for any candidate, are readily available through job posting.

In the instances described above, opting for a closed system might seem advantageous, but in an era of the assertion of individual rights and candor, the temporary advantages associated with not publicizing position vacancies can be more than offset by protracted legal wrangling and comcomitant bad publicity for the organization. In any event, the establishment and/or maintenance of an open position posting system might well be reviewed with the corporate legal department so that the company will be *aware* of any possible difficulties arising from adherence to, or avoidance of such a promotion system.

Salary Administration Policies and Promotion

In order to establish some standardized or reasonable approach to promotion, the salary administration function of many companies, by practice or policy, effects certain guidelines relating to promotional actions.

Many supervisors, especially those with relatively little experience, are likely to be overimpressed by the performance of a particular employee or, in order to obtain the services of still another employee, may resort to an excessively optimistic view of the individual's performance or background. Whereas it is considered theoretically possible that an individual may be well worth half again his present salary, those instances are generally so few in actual practice that a limitation on the amount of increase which can be granted either in terms of money or of job grade promotion is considered desirable to prevent personal enthusiasm from upsetting an ordered salary administration plan.

Examples of such limitations would be as follows:

Step limits: An employee may advance no more than two job grade steps at a time. For example, a grade 6 employee may not progress beyond grade 8 in a single promotion action.

Percent increase limit: In those instances where a 6 percent increase might be the norm for a performance or merit increase, a promotion action may have a bottom limit of 5 percent and an upper limit of 10 percent. In such cases, careful delineation is usually made between merit or performance increases and promotional increases.

Type limits: A promotional increase may not occur in conjunction with a merit increase, nor may it occur within a specified time limit preceding or following a merit increase.

Career path limits: Individuals may not receive indefinite promotions; i.e., no matter how proficient they may be in a given area, that particular field of endeavor has a "ceiling" of a given job grade.

However well intentioned such salary administration limits may be, care must be taken so that the process does not become institutionalized to the point that *no* individual can progress faster than the limits *suggested* by the salary administration plan. In those instances wherein an employee is drastically underevaluated at the time of hire (and such instances do still occur), it is difficult, if not impossible, to rectify the inequity, in spite of how superior an individual's performance may turn out to be. In such instances, superior performing employees may very well find they can receive the level of responsibility and salary to which they are entitled simply by going to another company.

In this respect, it is not uncommon for an individual hired from the outside, but with relatively the same qualifications as an individual already within the organization, to receive an increase over his previous salary far in excess of the maximum amount tolerated by the salary administration function for the individual already employed. There seems to be a psychological willingness to risk the performance of the outside hire, as opposed to the individual within the organization, several of whose faults may be known by virtue of his trying to get something accomplished within the organization. The peculiarity here is that a known employee with relatively few (but known) limitations does not receive the same opportunity as the individual about whom relatively little is known except his own carefully suggested references.

It is in these instances that the salary administration limitations on individuals or groups act to the detriment of the organization. Cases in point can be made almost daily in fields wherein talent is scarce and situations volatile—the electronic data processing industry is a fine example of this.

As an adjunct to this concept, lateral transfers and demotions are generally avoided too often, with most individuals and organizations psychologically attuned to upward movement. It is assumed that although not everyone can be president, everyone can try to achieve that position. However, the distribution of intelligence as well as motivational factors precludes this concept being applied in any population.

Therefore, in those instances wherein a lateral transfer is necessary for the development of the individual, or the organization, a careful counseling program must be developed in concert with such actions in order not to spread the notion that the individual affected by such action is somehow being punished for some inadequacy. It is in this respect that the previously mentioned internal advertisement of promotional chain action should be employed, with emphasis on the occasional lateral move which is made within the chain. In the case of demotions, there is little point in not telling the individual affected what the situation is, since he will very likely know in any event anyway. To ease the burdens associated with demotions, whenever and wherever possible a physical relocation to another area or even another building may be desirable. However, if possible, this should be at the option of the individual affected.

SKILLS AND INTEREST INVENTORIES

Up to this point, attention has been given to the policy aspects and organizational considerations of promotion within the company environment.

Essentially what has been covered is a summary of the *why* of promotion as well as the human considerations of *who*. However, the actual mechanics or *how* of promotion is most often thought of in terms of skills or interest inventories by which comparison is made between the skills or interests required by a position opening and the degree or extent to which an individual possesses such skills or interests. Basically, underlying this concept is some sort of an organized compilation of critical skills and pertinent educational factors which relate to most, if not all, of the openings within an organization.

Compilation of Critical Skills

To compile a list of pertinent experience or education factors involves either a very broad or a very specialized approach. The first of these, the broad approach, is one whereby a compilation of items is made which includes even those items which have only a remote chance of being referenced. In so doing the basic thoughts are that if the compilation is reasonably broad, then allowances for skills or experience background not of *current* importance may be provided for in the future.

On the other hand, if neither the time nor the effort is available to devote to determining what skills, etc., *might* be valuable to the organization, then a limited approach, confined to detailing what is *now* important, could significantly reduce the number of items to be considered as applicable.

In either event, both approaches attempt to incorporate some degree of objectivity as to what constitutes valuable skills, rather than leaving it up to the supervisor only to determine just what it is in a man's background that makes him a candidate for promotion. Attempts to confine evaluation of such candidates to only the immediate supervisor with a vested interest in filling a vacancy will, in too many cases, simply provide opportunity for reinforcement of his particular preferences and/or prejudices.

Skills and Interest Inventory Coding

Whereas there may be some value to having a personnel specialist review an individual employee's personnel folder and relevant position descriptions, as well as supervisor specifications, etc., for each and every position opening, and then make qualitative summaries of each individual's qualifications, this process is too time consuming for all but the smallest or most stable of organizations. Therefore, where a large number of individuals is involved, or a large number of job factors is similarly involved, it becomes practical to assign logically ordered series of codes to represent such skills or education factors. The basic reason for assigning codes is, of course, a timesaving measure whereby matching a four- or five-digit skill code for the desired characteristics with a similarly structured code assigned to the individual's particular background experience factor is far easier than having to analyze two separate paragraphs of material and attempt to establish a degree of relevance between them.

The use of codes requires two basic factors: the source of the items to be coded and the manner in which such codes are to be arrayed.

```
---------------------------------------------
 EXP                    EXPERIENCE OR
 CODE                   SPECIALTY NAME
---------------------------------------------
 0A003    PERSONNEL STAFF
 0A105    COLLEGE RELATIONS
 0A110    COUNSELING EDUCATION & VOCATIONAL
 0A115    COUNSELING PERSONAL ADJUSTMENT
 0A120    COUNSELING REHABILITATION
 0A125    EMPLOYEE APPRAISAL PLAN ADMIN
 0A130    EMPLOYEE BENEFITS CLAIMS PROCESSING
 0A135    EMPLOYEE BENEFITS POLICY INTERPRET
 0A137    EMPLOYEE COMMUNICATIONS-EG SPEAK-UP
 0A137    EMPLOYEE COMMUNICATIONS PROGRAMS
 0A138    EMPLOYEE - EXECUTIVE TRNG OR DEVEL
 0A139    EMPLOYEE MORALE & ATTITUDES
 0A140    EMPLOYMENT ADVERTISING
 0A145    EMPLOYMT INTERVIEWING-ADMIN EMPLOYS
 0A150    EMPLOYMT INTERVIEWING-PROF/TECH
 0A155    EMPLOYMT INTERVIEWING-PRODUCTN/SERV
 0A160    LABOR MGT RELATNS-CONTRACT DEVEL
 0A165    LABOR MGT RELATNS-CONTRACT NEGOTN
 0A170    LABOR MGT RELATNS-GRIEVANCE HANDLNG
 0A173    MANAGEMENT EVALUATION
 0A175    MANPOWER OR PERSONNEL PLANNING
 0A178    ORGANIZATION PLANNING
 0A179    PERFORMANCE EVAL. - CRITERION DEVEL
 0A180    PERSONNEL PROGRAM DEVELOPMENT
 0A185    PERSONNEL RECORDS MAINTENANCE
 0A190    PERSONNEL RECORDS SYSTEMS DEVELOPT
 0A195    PERSONNEL REPRESENTATIVE
 0A200    PERSONNEL RESEARCH
 0A205    PERSONNEL TESTS-ADMIN & EVALUATION
 0A210    PERSONNEL TESTS-CONSTRUCTION
 0A215    PLACEMENT-TRANSFERS, ETC.
 0A220    RECRUITING-COLLEGE OR TECH SCHOOL
 0A225    RECRUITING-EXPERIENCED PROF OR TECH
 0A230    RECRUITING-PH.D.
 0A235    RELOCATION ADMIN-HOME GUAR, ETC
 0A240    RETIREMENT PLAN ADMINISTRATION
 0A245    SUGGESTION INVESTIGATION
 0A250    SUGGESTION PROCESSING
 0A255    WAGE & SALARY ADMINISTRATION
 0A260      JOB EVALUATION & DESCRIPTION
 0A265      OVERTIME & PREMIUM PAY ANALYSIS
 0A270      SALARY CHANGE ADMINISTRATION
 0A275      SALARY PLANNING
 0A280      SURVEYS-CONDUC/ANAL-SALARY ADMIN
 0A888    MGMNT EXPERIENCE   PERSONNEL
 0A999    OTHER EXP. - NOT LISTED (SPECIFY)
```

Figure 1. Specific experience code or areas, relating to personnel specialities.

Code Sources

Over the past several years, IBM has devoted considerable effort to the development of personnel and skills inventories. Partly because of their own internal needs and partly because of customer needs, they have compiled a basic skills inventory of over 4,000 separately coded areas of work experience, i.e., skill items. Because of the nature of their business, these items are heavily concentrated in the experience areas of finance, accounting, marketing, product planning, electromechanical components, and, of course, the experience aspects of data processing.

However, their code categories for scientific areas or the social sciences are not as comprehensive as they might be. One company, in order to adapt the basic IBM Skills Inventory to its needs as a major petrochemical company, deleted the electromechanical components and manufacturing skills categories, and then supplemented the remaining IBM codes or skills with the National Science Foundation List of Technical Specialties. They then edited out many duplicate items, and included the National Science Foundation items into the code hierarchy, resulting in a skills inventory which was quite complete in the business and scientific or technical fields.

Unfortunately, that skills inventory did not adequately encompass the particular skills involved in the petroleum business, especially the refining processes. Therefore, detailed analyses were made of position descriptions to determine the specific areas of experience related to the processes of refining.

The combined skills inventory, i.e., IBM, National Science Foundation, and refinery skills, was reviewed with personnel specialists and operating managers who were knowledgeable in the respective skill areas. After some additions and clarifications of items, the entire skills inventory, now consisting of over 4,000 items, was put into machine-sensible form (punch cards) and then became a part of the employee information system data bank.

Other approaches apply to the development of a skills inventory data base, but considerable time and effort can be saved by adapting someone else's work to the particular needs of an organization, rather than trying to "reinvent the wheel."

Coding Structure

Not much has been made of the actual coding logic which is applied to a skills inventory, but it is important that this aspect not be overlooked.

Most of us are familiar with the controversy over all-digit telephone numbers, reminding us that some people find it easier to relate to a combination of letters and numbers rather than to all numbers. The same principle can be applied to skills inventory coding logic. Rather than all digits, a combination has the following inherent advantages:

1. A combination structure is less confusing.

2. One "column" of information with A through Z in it contains 26 categories of information instead of 10.

3. The power of multiple entries is enhanced considerably using letters, as opposed to two numbers in sequence, and then the categories in two columns is 26 X 26 rather than 10 X 10.

4. Enough previous coding has been in existence with a combination of letters and numbers so that the practice is almost familiar, e.g., license plates, drivers' licenses, some telephone numbers.

Therefore, the most comprehensive and yet comfortable coding structure for several thousand items would be one in which the first item is AA001 and the last item is ZZ999. An example of this approach can be seen in the following figures.

```
--------------------------------------------------------------
                         INDEX
--------------------------------------------------------------


INDUSTRY WHERE EXPERIENCE WAS ACQUIRED    AB TO AW    (INDEX)
MANAGEMENT EXPERIENCE LEVELS              AX          (INDEX)


SPECIALTIES & EXPERIENCE AREAS           BA TO ZE    (INDEX)
ADMINISTRATIVE SERVICES                  BA TO BM    (INDEX)
  ACCOUNTING/FINANCIAL                   BA          (INDEX)
    PAYROLL                              BC          (INDEX)
    TIMEKEEPING                          BE          (INDEX)
  ADMINISTRATIVE/CLERICAL                BH          (INDEX)
  SECRETARIAL/STENOGRAPHIC               BK          (INDEX)
  LIBRARY SERVICE                        BM          (INDEX)
TECHNICAL ADMINISTRATION/SERVICES        BP          (INDEX)


EDP SERVICES                             DA TO EZ    (INDEX)
  DP OPERATIONS                          DA          (INDEX)
  METHODS/PROCEDURES                     DC          (INDEX)


  SYSTEMS - APPLICATIONS                 EA TO EZ    (INDEX)
    ENGINEERING/SCIENTIFIC               EA          (INDEX)
    ADMINISTRATIVE - GENERAL             EB          (INDEX)
    ACCOUNTING - FINANCIAL               EC          (INDEX)
    BANKING - FINANCIAL                  EF          (INDEX)
    COMMUNICATIONS                       EH          (INDEX)
    DISTRIBUTION - PUBLICATION           EK          (INDEX)
    EDUCATIONAL                          EM          (INDEX)
    GOVERNMENTAL                         EP          (INDEX)
    HOSPITAL/MEDICAL                     ES          (INDEX)
    INSURANCE                            EV          (INDEX)
    MFG/FABRICATION/ASSEMBLY             EW          (INDEX)
    PUBLIC UTILITIES                     EX          (INDEX)
    TRANSPORTATION                       EY          (INDEX)


  PROGRAMMING - APPLICATIONS             FA TO FZ    (INDEX)
    APPLIED PROGRAMMING                  FA          (INDEX)
    SPECIAL METHODS                      FC          (INDEX)
    PROGRAMS - APPLICATION TYPES         FF TO FU    (INDEX)


GRAPHIC ARTS/REPRODUCTION                HA TO HK    (INDEX)
  GRAPHIC ARTS                           HA          (INDEX)
    INDUSTRIAL DESIGN                    HC          (INDEX)
    DRAFTING                             HF          (INDEX)
    PHOTO TECHNOLOGY                     HH          (INDEX)
    REPRODUCTION/PRINTING                HK          (INDEX)


LAW                                      JA          (INDEX)
  CONTRACTS/LICENSES/PATENTS             JC          (INDEX)


MARKETING                                LA TO LH    (INDEX)
  SALES                                  LA          (INDEX)
  RESEARCH                               LC          (INDEX)
  PRODUCT PLANNING                       LE          (INDEX)
  ADVERTISING AND PROMOTION              LH          (INDEX)


MATERIALS SERVICES                       MA TO MK    (INDEX)
  PURCHASING                             MA          (INDEX)
  TRAFFIC                                MC          (INDEX)
  MANUFACTURING ENGINEERING              ME          (INDEX)
  PRODUCTION CONTROL                     MH          (INDEX)
  MATERIALS HANDLING/TRANSPORTATION      MK          (INDEX)
```

Cont.

**Figure 2.   Computer-printed index for skills inventory, sequenced
by title items** (including blanks which come before letters or numbers).

```
-------------------------------------------------
                       INDEX
-------------------------------------------------


MANUFACTURING/MAINTENANCE                   NA TO NM      (INDEX)
     TOOL AND DIE MAKING                    NA            (INDEX)
     MACHINING                              NC            (INDEX)
     ASSEMBLY                               NE            (INDEX)
     INSPECTION                             NH            (INDEX)
     MAINTENANCE/REPAIR                     NK            (INDEX)
     BUILDING/CONSTRUCTION                  NM            (INDEX)



PERSONNEL SERVICES                          OA TO OH      (INDEX)
     PERSONNEL ADMINISTRATION               OA            (INDEX)
     MEDICAL/HEALTH                         OC            (INDEX)
     SAFETY/SECURITY                        OE            (INDEX)
     FOOD/GUEST-RECREATION SERVICES         OH            (INDEX)
SOCIAL SCIENCES - LINGUISTICS               OK TO OV      (INDEX)
     EDUCATION                              OK            (INDEX)
     LINGUISTICS                            OM            (INDEX)
     PSYCHOLOGY                             ON            (INDEX)
     SOCIOLOGY                              OP            (INDEX)
INTERDISCIPLINARY - SOCIAL                  OR TO OT      (INDEX)
     ECONOMICS                              OV            (INDEX)

SCIENTIFIC/TECHNICAL SPECIALTIES            PA TO YZ      (INDEX)
PETROLEUM - EXPLORATION                     PA TO PI      (INDEX)
PETROLEUM - REFINING                        PS TO PZ      (INDEX)



     INTERDISCIPLINARY - TECHNICAL          QA TO QP      (INDEX)



     ASTRONOMICAL                           RA            (INDEX)
     ATMO- LITHO- HYDROSPHERIC              RC TO RY      (INDEX)



     BIOLOGICAL                             SA TO SZ      (INDEX)



     RELATED BIOLOGICAL                     TA TO TP      (INDEX)



     CHEMICAL/METALLURGICAL                 VA TO VT      (INDEX)



     ENGINEERING - GENERAL                  WA            (INDEX)
     ENGINEERING - SPECIFIC                 WC TO WV      (INDEX)
         ELECTRICAL/ELECTRONIC             WC            (INDEX)
         MECHANICAL                        WE            (INDEX)
         AERONAUTICAL                      WH            (INDEX)
         INDUSTRIAL/MANUFACTURING          WK            (INDEX)
         PLANT/FACILITIES/CONSTRUCTION     WM            (INDEX)
    MFG ENGINEERING - ENGINEERING SERVICES WP            (INDEX)
         COMPONENTS - ELECTRICAL           WR            (INDEX)
         COMPONENTS - MECHANICAL           WT            (INDEX)
         INSTRUMENTS                       WV            (INDEX)



     MATHEMATICS/STATISTICS                 XA TO XT      (INDEX)



     PHYSICS                                YA TO YZ      (INDEX)



     LANGUAGE SKILLS                        ZE            (INDEX)
```

Figure 3. Computer-printed index (continued).

EXP CODE	EXPERIENCE OR SPECIALTY NAME
	(LISTING OF CODES TO BE ENTERED ON QUESTIONNAIRE)
	INDUSTRY EXPERIENCE
AB100	STANDARD OIL CONSOLIDATION EXPERIENCE ONLY
AB105	NO PREVIOUS EXPERIENCE - NEW EMPLOYEE
AC100	AEROSPACE
AD100	COMMUNICATIONS
AD105	TELEGRAPH
AD110	TELEPHONE
AD115	TELEPROCESSING
AD999	OTHER INDUSTRY EXP. (PLEASE SPECIFY)
AE100	CONSULTANTS & SERVICE BUREAUS
AE105	BUSINESS CONSULTANTS
AE110	INDEPENDENT SERVICE BUREAUS
AE112	LEGAL SERVICES
AE115	PUBLIC ACCOUNTANTS
AE999	OTHER INDUSTRY EXP. (PLEASE SPECIFY)
AF100	CREDIT UNIONS
AG100	DISTRIBUTION-CHAIN & WHOLESALE
AG105	AUTOMOBILE DEALERS
AG110	BEER-WINE & OTHER ALCOHOLIC BEV
AG115	DRUG STORES
AG120	DRY GOODS & APPAREL
AG125	ELECTRICAL GOODS
AG130	GROCERIES & RETAIL PRODUCTS
AG135	LUMBER & CONSTRUCTION MATERIALS
AG140	MACHINERY, EQUIPMENT & SUPPLIES
AG145	PAPER & PAPER PRODUCTS
AG150	RETAIL FOOD
AG155	TOBACCO AND ITS PRODUCTS
AG200	DISTRIBUTION-CONSUMER PCKGD GOODS
AG205	CONFECTIONERY
AG210	COSMETICS & SOAP MANUFACTURERS
AG215	DAIRIES/BAKERIES/BEVERAGES
AG220	FOOD PROCESSORS EXCEPT MEAT PACKG
AG225	PHARMACEUTICALS
AG230	TOBACCO MANUFACTURERS
AG300	DISTRIBUTION-PUBLISHING & PRINTING
AG305	ADVERTISING AGENCIES
AG310	DUPLICATING, ADDRESSING & MAILING
AG315	NON-PROFIT/CHARIT/MEMBERSHIP ASSOC
AG320	PRINTING/PUBLISHING & ALLIED INDUS
AG325	RADIO BROADCASTING & TV
AG400	DISTRIBUTION-RETAIL
AG405	APPAREL & ACCESSORIES
AG410	BUILDING MATERIALS & HARDWARE
AG415	CONSUMER CREDIT REPORT AGENCIES
AG420	DEPARTMENT STORES
AG425	FARM EQUIPMENT
AG430	FURNITURE & HOME FURNISHINGS
AG435	GENERAL MERCHANDISE
AG440	JEWELRY
AG445	MAIL ORDER HOUSES
AG450	RESTAURANTS
AG455	SHOES-MANUFACTURERS & STORES
AG999	OTHER INDUSTRY EXP. (PLEASE SPECIFY)
AH100	EDUCATION
AH105	AGRICULTURE/AGRICULTURAL SERVICES
AH110	LIBRARIES/RESEARCH LABS/ED SERVICS
AH115	UNIVERSITIES/COLLEGES/JR. COLLEGES
AH999	OTHER INDUSTRY EXP. (PLEASE SPECIFY)
AJ100	FEDERAL GOVERNMENT
AJ105	DEFENSE
AJ110	NON-DEFENSE
AJ115	QUASI-FEDERAL DEFENSE
AJ120	QUASI-FEDERAL NON DEFENSE
AJ999	OTHER INDUSTRY EXP. (PLEASE SPECIFY)

EXP CODE	EXPERIENCE OR SPECIALTY NAME
AL100	FINANCE
AL105	BROKERAGE HOUSES & EXCHANGES
AL110	COMMERCIAL BANKS
AL115	CREDIT ORGANIZATIONS
AL120	FINANCE COMPANIES
AL125	INVESTMENT BANKS
AL130	LAND MANAGEMENT COMPANIES
AL135	SAVINGS BANKS
AL140	SAVINGS & LOAN INSTITUTIONS
AL145	TRUST COMPANIES
AM100	IMPORT & EXPORT
AN100	INSURANCE
AN105	ACCIDENT & HEALTH INSURANCE
AN110	BLUE CROSS & BLUE SHIELD
AN115	FIRE & CASUALTY
AN120	INSURANCE RATING AGENCIES
AN125	INSURANCE SERVICE BUREAUS
AN130	LIFE INSURANCE COMPANIES
AN135	MULTIPLE LINE INSURANCE
AN140	TITLE INSURANCE
AN150	INSURANCE SALES
AN160	PERSONAL INVESTIGATION
AN165	LOSS/DAMAGE CLAIM INVESTIGATION
AN999	OTHER INDUSTRY EXP. (PLEASE SPECIFY)
AT100	STATE & LOCAL GOVERNMENT
AT105	CITIES/COUNTIES/SPECL AUTHORITIES
AT110	RACETRACKS
AT115	SCHOOLS INCLUDING BOARD OF ED
AT120	STATE GOVERNMENTS
AT125	PUBLIC TRANSIT SYSTEMS
AT999	OTHER INDUSTRY EXP. (PLEASE SPECIFY)
AV100	TRANSPORTATION
AV103	AIRLINES
AV105	AIRLINE BUSES
AV110	AUTO LEASING
AV115	FREIGHT FORWARDERS
AV120	HOTELS
AV125	MOTOR FREIGHT
AV130	PRIVATE TRANSIT LINES
AV135	PUBLIC WAREHOUSES
AV140	RAILROADS
AV145	STEAMSHIP LINES
AV999	OTHER INDUSTRY EXP. (PLEASE SPECIFY)
AW100	UTILITIES
AW105	ELECTRIC
AW110	GAS
AW115	WATER
AW999	OTHER INDUSTRY EXP. (PLEASE SPECIFY)
	MANAGEMENT EXPERIENCE LEVEL
AXO10	TECHNICAL OPERATIONS-
AXO11	PRESIDENT
AXO12	VICE PRESIDENT
AXO13	GENERAL MANAGER
AXO14	MANAGER
AXO15	SUPERVISOR
AXO16	FOREMAN
AXO17	GROUP LEADER
AX100	NON-TECHNICAL ADMINISTRATION
AX110	PRESIDENT
AX120	VICE PRESIDENT
AX130	GENERAL MANAGER
AX140	MANAGER
AX150	SUPERVISOR
AX160	ASST SUPERVISOR
AX170	ADMINISTRATIVE ASSISTANT
AX999	OTHER EXP. (PLEASE SPECIFY)

Figure 4.   Listing of industries in which experience may have been gained, with allowance for expansion of codes.

EXP CODE	EXPERIENCE OR SPECIALTY NAME
	SPECIALTIES & EXPERIENCE AREAS
BA003	FINANCE-ACCOUNTING
BA105	ACCOUNTING INSTRUCTION PREPARATION
BA110	ACCTG SYSTEMS & PROCEDURES DEVELOP
BA115	ACCOUNTS PAYABLE
BA120	ACCOUNTING DISTRIBUTION-A/P
BA125	PROCESS OR CONTROL-A/P
BA130	ACCOUNTS RECEIVABLE
BA135	ACCTG DISTRIBUTN BILLINGS/ADJUSTS
BA140	CREDIT ANALYSIS & ADMINISTRATION
BA145	PROCESS OR CTRL BILLINGS & ADJUSTS
BA150	TRIAL BALANCE PREP & ANALYSIS
BA155	AUDITING
BA160	GENERAL INTERNAL AUDITING
BA165	SPECIAL PURPOSE AUDITS
BA166	BANK TELLER
BA170	BUDGET PREP, CTRL & REPORTING
BA175	CASH BUDGETS
BA180	ENGINEERING BUDGETS
BA185	MANUFACTURING BUDGETS
BA190	OPERATING BUDGETS
BA195	CASHIER
BA200	COMMISSION ACCOUNTING
BA205	CONSOLIDATION ACCOUNTING
BA210	COST ACCOUNTING
BA211	ALLOCATION OF RESOURCES
BA212	BUDGETARY CONTROL
BA215	COST CONTROL + ANALYSIS
BA216	COST ESTIMATING
BA217	COST PLANNING + CONTROL
BA218	COST SYNTHESIS
BA220	DIRECT COSTING
BA225	JOB ORDER COSTING
BA230	LABOR DISTRIBUTION
BA235	OVERHEAD DISTRIBUTION
BA240	PROCESS COSTING
BA245	SPECIAL PRODUCTS COSTING
BA250	STANDARD COSTING
BA251	CREDIT INVESTIGATION
BA252	CUSTOMER REORGANIZATION RESEARCH
BA255	FINANCIAL ANALYSIS
BA260	APPROPRIATIONS PLANNING
BA265	CAPITAL REQUIREMENTS PLANNING
BA270	OPERATING PLANS DEVELOPMENT
BA275	PRICE ANALYSIS-POLICY
BA280	PRICE ANALYSIS-THEORY & MSMNT
BA285	PRODUCT PRICING
BA290	PRODUCT PROGRAM REVIEW & EVALUATN
BA295	REVENUE FORECASTING
BA300	FIXED ASSET ACCOUNTING
BA305	ACCOUNT MAINT OR AUDIT-F/A
BA310	PROPTY RECORD ESTABLISHMT & CTRL
BA315	STATEMENT PREPARATION-F/A
BA320	GENERAL ACCOUNTING
BA325	ACCT MAINT OR AUDIT-G/A
BA330	SOURCE REVIEW & CONTROL
BA335	STATEMENT PREP-BALANCE SHEET
BA340	STATEMENT PREP-INCOME & EXPENSE
BA345	STATEMENT PREP-SUNDRY FINANCIAL
BA350	GOVT CONTRACT FINANCE ACCTG
BA355	ACCT MAINT OR AUDIT-GOVT/ACCTG
BA360	PREP OF PUBLIC VOUCHERS
BA365	PRICE ANALYSIS-GOVT ACCTG
BA370	OPERATNS PLANNG/REVENUE FORECAST
BA375	INSURANCE COORDINATING
BA380	INTRA/INTER CO INVOICES & REQUSTNS
BA385	INVENTORY CONTROL
BA390	INVESTMENT & SECURITIES ADMIN
BA395	LEDGER PRESENTATION COORDINATION
BA400	MERGERS & ACQUISITIONS
BA405	PUBLIC ACCOUNTING-CPA
BA410	PUBLIC ACCOUNTING-NON CPA
BA415	RENEGOTIATION BOARD REPORTING
BA420	REVENUE STATISTICS MAINT OR AUDIT
BA425	SEC REPORTING-FINANCIAL
BA430	STAT REPORTING-SUNDRY GOVERNMENT
BA435	TAXES-MANAGEMENT
BA440	TAX INTERPRETATN & POLICY PLANNING
BA445	NEGOTIATION W/TAX AUTHORITIES
BA450	TAXES-RETURN PREP & FILING
BA455	FEDERAL INCOME TAXES
BA460	STATE INCOME & FRANCHISE TAXES
BA465	PROPERTY TAXES
BA470	SALES & EXCISE TAXES
BA888	MGMNT EXPERIENCE - FINANCIAL
BA999	OTHER EXP. - NOT LISTED (SPECIFY)

EXP CODE	EXPERIENCE OR SPECIALTY NAME
BC003	PAYROLL
BC105	PAYROLL ACCOUNTING DISTRIBUTION
BC110	PAYROLL AUDITING
BC115	PAYROLL PROCEDURES DEVELOPMENT
BC120	PAYROLL STATISTICS PREPARATION
BC125	PROCESS PAYROLL PAYMTS & NOTICES
BC130	PROCESSG BENEFITS PAYMTS & NOTICES
BC888	MGMNT EXPERIENCE - PAYROLL
BC999	OTHER EXP. - NOT LISTED (SPECIFY)
BF003	TIMEKEEPING
BF105	LABOR RECONCILIATION
BF110	PERFORMANCE REPORT PREP OR ANAL
BF115	DATA COLLECTN SYST 357 OPERATION
BF120	TIMEKEEPER
BF888	MGMNT EXPERIENCE - TIMEKEEPING
BF999	OTHER EXP. - NOT LISTED (SPECIFY)
BH001	ADMINISTRATION & CLERICAL - GENRL
BH003	OFFICE SERVICES/ADMINISTRATION GENL
BH105	ADMINISTRATOR
BH110	BILLING MACHINE OPERATION
BH115	BOOKKEEPING
BH120	BUDGET PREPARATION
BH125	CODING INVOICES
BH130	COMPTOMETER OPERATOR
BH140	DESK CALCULATOR OPERATOR
BH145	DOCUMENT CHECKING
BH150	DOCUMENTS COLLATING-LOGICS ETC
BH155	DOCUMENT POSTING-ORDER ENTRY
BH160	ENGINEERING RECORDS MAINTENANCE
BH165	FILING OR RECORD KEEPING
BH170	MAIL SORTING OR DISTRIBUTION
BH175	PREPARATION OF STATISTICS
BH180	RECORDS OR REPORTS CONTROL COORD.
BH185	SHIPPING AND RECEIVING
BH190	STOCK CLERK
BH195	SWITCHBOARD OPERATOR
BH200	TELEGRAPHY
BH205	TELETYPING
BH888	MGMNT EXPERIENCE - GENL ADMIN.
BH999	OTHER EXP. - NOT LISTED (SPECIFY)
BK003	SECRETARIAL-STENOGRAPHIC
BK105	COURT RECORDING
BK110	EXECUTIVE SECRETARY
BK115	LEGAL OR PATENT SECRETARY
BK120	MEDICAL OR SCIENTIFIC SECRETARY
BK125	RECEPTIONIST
BK130	SHORTHAND
BK135	STATISTICAL TYPING
BK140	STENOTYPING
BK143	TECHNICAL TYPING
BK145	TRANSCRIBING FROM DICTATION EQUIP
BK150	TYPING
BK888	MGMNT EXPERIENCE SECRETARIAL
BK999	OTHER EXP. - NOT LISTED (SPECIFY)
BM003	LIBRARY ADMINISTRATION
BM005	TECHNICAL INFORMATION
BM105	ABSTRACTING
BM110	ACQUISITIONS-LIBRARY
BM115	ARCHIVIST
BM120	BIBLIOGRAPHIES
BM125	CATALOGING
BM130	CIRCULATION-LIBRARY
BM132	CLASSIFICATION
BM135	GENERAL-CLERICAL LIBRARY
BM140	INDEXING
BM145	INFORMATION RETRIEVAL
BM150	REFERENCE-LIBRARY
BM155	SELECTIVE DISSEMINATION OF INFO
BM160	TECHNICAL LIBRARIAN
BM888	MGMNT EXPERIENCE LIBRARY/TECH INFO
BM999	OTHER EXP. - NOT LISTED (SPECIFY)
BP000	ADMINISTRATION - TECHNICAL
BP001	ENGINEERING ADMINISTRATION
BP003	LAB/SCIENTIFIC ADMINISTRATION
BP005	TECHNICAL FACILITIES-INCL PLANNING
BP007	TECHNICAL SERVICES -INCL PLANNING
BP009	INFORMATION SERVICES
BP999	OTHER EXP. - NOT LISTED (SPECIFY)

Figure 5.   Specific experience code or areas, relating to finance and accounting.

NONCOMPUTER OPERATIONS VS. COMPUTER APPLICATIONS

The use of codes implies computer usage, but computers as such are not needed unless and until the volume of records involved exceed approximately 10,000 parameters, i.e., 1,000 employees with 10 record characteristics or 100 employees with 100 characteristics. There are manual systems available which can handle the 10,000-parameter requirement, and they work quite well.

However, the heavy attention given to computer systems has made such manual systems apparently less desirable. This is less because of any inherent manual system inadequacy per se than because managers receive far more publicity about the glamorous world of electronic data processing computer systems.

Computer-oriented systems need a note of caution: they are only for those who have the need for them and who have the resources to support them. This subject is one on which an entire book can be written, but about which several topical points should be mentioned nevertheless.

1. Adequate economic justification for computerized skills inventory systems is not usually easily demonstrated. Some other joint usage of computers has to be effected, since the profit aspect of the personnel function is sometimes obscured.

2. One or more personnel specialists *must* be data processing–computer sciences sophisticated to ensure adequacy of programs as well as sympathetic understanding of machine problems. They must be able to communicate between technical and nontechnical, logical and nonlogical, and hostile and friendly management groups and specialists.

3. Input, however, is a major problem in that:
   a. All manner of non-data processing–computer sciences personnel will have to deal with unfamiliar forms, restrictive formats, and special instructions.
   b. A code control function must be established whereby data contained on input forms will be translated *properly* into data processing–computer sciences oriented codes or languages.
   c. Data must be converted eventually into machine-sensible form, i.e., punched cards, magnetic tape — an expensive process.

As an example of an approach which takes into account a form to serve as many of the previously mentioned input functions as possible, Figures 6 to 9 illustrate how to complete an input form, using a specified code *and* an English translation, both of which would be entered directly from the form into key-punch cards. A further note here is that these key-punch cards can be "listed" directly without any great effort using built-in "utility" programs, and the data will be aligned according to the categories of information (data fields) in a legible manner (see Figure 10).

ADVANTAGES AND DISADVANTAGES OF COMPUTER SYSTEMS

The most notable advantage of computer systems is their speed. On the other hand, they process errors in instruction just as rapidly as correct instructions–the result being some very expensive "garbage." If an inquiry asks for all males with characteristics X, Y, *and* Z, but only the *all* males is considered a valid instruction, then the requested report may very well contain data on all the men in the organization. Without belaboring the point, one has to be careful in structuring a request when many hundreds of individuals and thousands of characteristics are involved.

One other advantage, properly handled, is the ability to ask for ranking of records, according to "ideal limits" as well as "acceptable limits." In effect, judgment can be preprogrammed. Figure 11 conceptually illustrates a computer algorithm the author has used to select promotional candidates from a large file. Each desired

EIS — TASK

Industry Experience and Specialties

SOCIAL SECURITY NUMBER (CANADA ONLY – "C" IN BOX 10)

`1 2 3 4 5 6 7 8 9`

NAME EXAMPLE

COMPANY STANDARD
LOCATION 910 BUILDING

INDUSTRY EXPERIENCE — ENTER BELOW THE CODES WHICH APPLY TO THE INDUSTRIES IN WHICH YOU HAVE WORKING EXPERIENCE (SEE MANUAL OF CODES – AA- THROUGH AW-). NOTE: STANDARD OIL CONSOLIDATION EXPERIENCE IS DESIGNATED AS AA100, BUT OTHER PETROLEUM AND CHEMICAL COMPANY EXPERIENCE WOULD BE FOUND UNDER AP- NUMBERS. INDICATE UP TO THREE LATEST OR MOST SIGNIFICANT INDUSTRY CODES, AND THEN FOLLOW THEM WITH THE NAME OF THE INDUSTRY, AS INDICATED IN THE CODE MANUAL, USING BOTH LINES, IF NECESSARY, WHICH START WITH A BOX 42.

`4 A`   INDUSTRY NUMBER 1 `A A 1 0 0`   INDUSTRY NUMBER 2 `A P 1 3 0`   INDUSTRY NUMBER 3 `A P 1 0 5`

`S T D   O I L ,   E L E C T R O N I C S   E Q U I P M E N T   M F R ,`

USE THESE TWO LINES (DIRECTLY ABOVE AND BELOW) TO INDICATE THE NAMES OF UP TO THREE INDUSTRIES FOR WHICH YOU HAVE WORKED. FILL IN THE BOXES IN THE FOLLOWING MANNER: INDUSTRY, COMMA, BLANK, ETC. ABBREVIATE ONLY IF NECESSARY.

`4 B`   `A U T O M O T I V E   &   F A R M   E Q U I P M E N T   M F R .`

QUALIFICATIONS & SPECIALTIES — ENTER BELOW THE CODES WHICH INDICATE TWO AREAS OF EXPERIENCE YOU FEEL YOUR BACKGROUND BEST QUALIFIES YOU FOR, ALONG WITH A DESIGNATION OF THE CAPACITY SUCH EXPERIENCE QUALIFIES YOU FOR. FOLLOW WITH THE NAMES OF THESE AREAS, USING THE LINE WHICH STARTS WITH BOX 45. (CAPACITY: I – INDIVIDUAL CONTRIBUTOR; T – TEAM MEMBER; M – MANAGER; C – CONSULTANT.)

`4 C`   QUALIFICATION NUMBER 1 `D C 1 2 5`   CAPACITY `C`   QUALIFICATION NUMBER 2 `E B 7 1 0`   CAPACITY `C`   `Q U A L I F I E D –`

INDICATE BELOW THE NAMES OF THESE AREAS OF EXPERIENCE.

`M G T   I N F O   &   P E R S O N N E L / M A N P O W E R   S Y S T M S`

SIGNATURE OF PERSON COMPLETING SHEET A.N. EMPLOYEE
DATE 9/1/68

Figure 6.

EIS — TASK

Industry Experience and Specialties cont'd

SOCIAL SECURITY NUMBER (CANADA ONLY – "C" IN BOX 10)

`1 2 3 4 5 6 7 8 9`

NAME EXAMPLE

COMPANY STANDARD
LOCATION 910 BUILDING

ALTERNATE ASSIGNMENTS — INDICATE TWO OTHER AREAS IN WHICH YOU WOULD CONSIDER WORKING IF PRESENTED WITH THE OPPORTUNITY. DO NOT INDICATE YOUR PRESENT AREA. ALSO INDICATE THE CAPACITY YOU WOULD PREFER (SEE PREVIOUS CODES ON QUALIFICATIONS).

`4 D`   ALTERNATE NUMBER 1 `O A 1 7 8`   CAPACITY `M`   ALTERNATE NUMBER 2 `O A 2 0 0`   CAPACITY `M`   `A L T E R N A T E –`

INDICATE THE NAMES OF THE ALTERNATE AREAS BELOW:

`O R G A N I Z A T I O N   P L N G ,   P E R S O N N E L   R E S R C H`

WORKING EXPERIENCE — INDICATE BELOW IN WHICH AREAS OF SPECIALTY YOU HAVE ACTUAL WORKING EXPERIENCE, ENTERING THE APPROPRIATE CODE, THE TOTAL NUMBER OF MONTHS ACCUMULATED, THE LAST YEAR YOU ACTIVELY WORKED IN THIS AREA, AS WELL AS THE CAPACITY. FIRST, CONSULT THE AX— CODES TO DETERMINE THE MANAGEMENT EXPERIENCE LEVEL MAXIMUM YOU HAVE PRESENTLY OR PREVIOUSLY ATTAINED. THEN, GO ON TO SELECT THE APPROPRIATE CODES TO INDICATE THE EXPERIENCE SPECIALTIES IN WHICH YOU HAVE WORKED. IN ALL INSTANCES, FOLLOW WITH THE SPECIALTY NAMES USED IN THE CODE MANUAL.

`5 A`   SPECIALTY CODE `A X 1 4 0`   TOTAL MONTHS `9 6`   `M O S`   `M G M N T   E X P –`

NAME OF PRESENT / HIGHEST MANAGEMENT EXPERIENCE LEVEL ATTAINED

`M A N A G E R ,   N O N - T E C H N I C A L   A D M I N I S T R A T N`

`5 B`   SPECIALTY CODE `D C 1 2 5`   TOTAL MONTHS `7 2`   `M O S`   YEAR LAST USED `19 6 8`   CAPACITY `C`

NAME OF EXPERIENCE SPECIALTY

`M G M N T   I N F O R M A T I O N   S Y S T E M S   D E S I G N`

SIGNATURE OF PERSON COMPLETING SHEET A.N. EMPLOYEE
DATE 9/1/68

Figure 7.

EIS — TASK
Industry Experience and Specialties cont'd

SOCIAL SECURITY NUMBER (CANADA ONLY — "C" IN BOX 10)
`1 2 3 4 5 6 7 8 9`

NAME EXAMPLE

COMPANY STANDARD
LOCATION 910 BUILDING

5 C   SPECIALTY CODE `E B 7 1 0`   TOTAL MONTHS `8 4`   M O S   YEAR LAST USED 19 `6 8`   CAPACITY `T`
NAME OF EXPERIENCE SPECIALTY
`PERSONNEL/MANPOWER APPLICATION SYST.`

5 D   SPECIALTY CODE `0 A 1 9 0`   TOTAL MONTHS `6 0`   M O S   YEAR LAST USED 19 `6 0`   CAPACITY `C`
NAME OF EXPERIENCE SPECIALTY
`PERSONNEL RECORDS SYSTEMS DEVELOPMNT`

5 E   SPECIALTY CODE `E A 5 0 0`   TOTAL MONTHS `4 8`   M O S   YEAR LAST USED 19 `6 8`   CAPACITY `T`
NAME OF EXPERIENCE SPECIALTY
`STATISTICAL PROGRAMS - ANALYSIS`

5 F   SPECIALTY CODE `F A 4 2 5`   TOTAL MONTHS `1 2`   M O S   YEAR LAST USED 19 `6 8`   CAPACITY `C`
NAME OF EXPERIENCE SPECIALTY
`GRAPHIC OUTPUT PROGRAMMING`

SIGNATURE OF PERSON COMPLETING SHEET A. N. EMPLOYEE
DATE 9/1/68

Figure 8.

EIS — TASK
Industry Experience and Specialties cont'd

SOCIAL SECURITY NUMBER (CANADA ONLY — "C" IN BOX 10)
`1 2 3 4 5 6 7 8 9`

NAME EXAMPLE

COMPANY STANDARD
LOCATION 910 BUILDING

G   **5 Z**   SPECIALTY CODE `F G 8 1 0`   TOTAL MONTHS `9`   M O S   YEAR LAST USED 19 `6 8`   CAPACITY `I`
NAME OF EXPERIENCE SPECIALTY
`REPORT GENERATORS- MARK IV`

H   **5 Z**   SPECIALTY CODE `0 A 1 7 5`   TOTAL MONTHS `4 8`   M O S   YEAR LAST USED 19 `6 5`   CAPACITY `M`
NAME OF EXPERIENCE SPECIALTY
`MANPOWER & PERSONNEL PLANNING`

J   **5 Z**   SPECIALTY CODE `0 A 1 7 3`   TOTAL MONTHS `3 6`   M O S   YEAR LAST USED 19 `6 3`   CAPACITY `M`
NAME OF EXPERIENCE SPECIALTY
`MANAGEMENT EVALUATION`

K   **5 Z**   SPECIALTY CODE `0 N 1 4 0`   TOTAL MONTHS `8 4`   M O S   YEAR LAST USED 19 `6 3`   CAPACITY `T`
NAME OF EXPERIENCE SPECIALTY
`OBJECTIVE TESTS (INDUSTRIAL PSYCH)`

SIGNATURE OF PERSON COMPLETING SHEET A. N. EMPLOYEE
DATE 9/1/68

Figure 9.

```
123456789  1A   CARLTON, W. D.                          1934  M   5A   M   1   1   0
123456789  1B   COORDINATOR, EMPLOYEE INFORMATION SERVICES              SOCO    90084A
123456789  2B   5A   LVM   BNA      1959-1963   3.6   3.8   Q1   074421
123456789  2C   MA   INDUSTRIAL PSYCHOLOGY              UNIVERSITY OF DETROIT
123456789  2D   4B   LVH   LHA      1953-1958   3.0   3.5   Q2   074421
123456789  2E   BS   EDUCATIONAL PSYCHOLOGY             UNIVERSITY OF DETROIT
123456789  3A   7D   BFL   FF400    67    COBOL F, S/360, IBM TRAINING CENTER
123456789  3B   7D   BFA   EA475    67    VISUAL DISPLAY/GRAPHICS SYSTEMS, IBM CNTR
123456789  3C   7D   BFL   FH800    66    OS/360 COBOL INTERFACE, IBM TRAINING CNTR
123456789  3D   7D   BFA   DC125    65    MGT INFO SYSTEMS, IRC SYMPOSIUM
123456789  3E   7D   BFL   FA110    64    SPL PROGRAMMING - 1401 - IBM TRAINING CNTR
123456789  3F   7D   BFA   DC165    63    EDP FUNDAMENTALS, AMA SEMINAR
123456789  3G   7D   BFA   EB620    63    INFORMATION STORAGE/RETRIEVAL, AMA SEMINAR
123456789  3H   7B   BTL   0A138    60    EXECUTIVE DEVELOPMENT, MICH. STATE UNIV.
123456789  3J   7A   BTN   0A150    57    INTERVIEWING TECHNIQUES, GENL MOTORS INST
123456789  4A   AA100       AP130   AP105  STD OIL, ELECTRONICS EQUIPMENT MFR,
123456789  4B                             AUTOMOTIVE & FARM EQUIPMENT MFR.
123456789  4C   DC125 C     EB710 C QUALIFIED- MGT INFO & PERSONNEL/MANPOWER SYSTMS
123456789  4D   0A178 M     0A200 M ALTERNATE- ORGANIZATION PLNG, PERSONNEL RESRCH
123456789  5A   AX140       96 MOS  MGMNT EXP- MANAGER, NON-TECHNICAL ADMINISTRATN
123456789  5B   DC125       72 MOS  68 C    MGMNT INFORMATION SYSTEMS DESIGN
123456789  5C   EB710       84 MOS  68 T    PERSONNEL/MANPOWER APPLICATION SYST.
123456789  5D   0A190       60 MOS  60 C    PERSONNEL RECORDS SYSTEMS DEVELOPMNT
123456789  5E   EA500       48 MOS  68 T    STATISTICAL SYSTEMS - ANALYSIS
123456789  5F   FA425       12 MOS  68 C    GRAPHIC OUTPUT PROGRAMMING
123456789  5G   FG810        9 MOS  68 I    REPORT GENERATORS- MARK IV
123456789  5H   0A175       48 MOS  65 M    MANPOWER & PERSONNEL PLANNING
123456789  5J   0A173       36 MOS  63 M    MANAGEMENT EVALUATION
123456789  5K   0N140       84 MOS  63 T    OBJECTIVE TESTS (INDUSTRIAL PSYCH)
```

Figure 10.

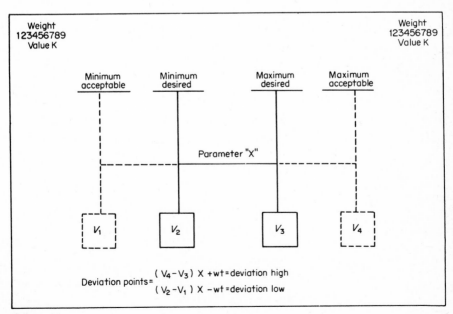

Figure 11.

characteristic was analyzed in terms of what the ideal candidate might possess in his background, but with a further realization that less stringent qualifications could still be applied. This, in effect, produced a listing of candidates who were selected and ranked by a special program. The candidates presented thereby were the "ideals" as well as the "almosts."

This system in itself brings out the most significant advantages and disadvantages of using computers. For the strong supervisor, willing to enhance his opportunities to evaluate *all* qualified candidates, the speed and convenience of a computer-produced listing was welcomed. But for the weak supervisor, either who was willing to have someone else make up his mind, or who wished to see only his favorite candidates on any list, the computer was regarded as an anathema.

No matter what system or policy is applied to the problem of promotion, whether the rules are stated or unstated, rigid or flexible, computer oriented or not, the human equation is paramount. Ultimately, it is people, not systems, who will determine proper promotion policy, practice, and procedure.

Part 5

Training and Development

chapter 18

The Training Organization

LOUIS S. GOODMAN *President, Louis S. Goodman & Associates, New Rochelle, New York, and Adjunct Professor of Management, Pace College Graduate School, New York*

TRAINING JUSTIFICATION AND POLICY

The training fuction is viewed differently in each organization, and this is a primary factor in its structure. Training can be a significant management tool in bringing about change. As an effective change agent, the training function must be systematic and orderly in providing assistance to solve organization problems and in achieving organizational goals. Increased attention is being paid to training and development activities in long-range organization planning and shorter-range, detailed manpower projections, as new and disadvantaged manpower resources are brought into the work force as hourly paid employees and as members of the management team.

During the past few years, training has become much more formalized and less haphazard. In the past, training was given the role of merely responding to the demands of line management when needs had become disastrously obvious. In some instances the mission was purely training for survival. Today there is a higher priority for training. The trend is now to predict needs and to apply appropriate training measures before consequences are felt.

There are those who believe the training function should be structured in such a way that it can serve as a leading change agent in designing corporate growth. Training, they say, might be viewed more suitably as a line responsibility instead of as a staff function. This would place it at the same level of authority as any other operating department. This reflects certain changes in organization value systems in which human skills values approach those traditionally placed on the acquisition of physical assets, such as plants and machinery.

The usual questions underlying the training mission have been: Who to train? What to train? When to train? How to train? While this still is a standard approach in some places, training policy frequently dictates a need for wider investigation. Among these broader research considerations are the following:

Need: Analysis of the organization's overall and specific training requirements in the light of total objectives

Targets: Setting the organization's training goals

Responsibilities: Formalizing the training function

Procedures: Steps to implement training policies

Staff: Selection of qualified training personnel

Review: Need for continuous controls to ensure expected results on a cost-benefits basis

Seen in this perspective, training policy has a direct relationship to job performance in terms of meeting expected standards in all employee classifications, and at all levels of management. Not all performance problems, however, are necessarily a training responsibility. Sound organization policy calls for research to determine which major problems resulting in low performance are actually due to lack of appropriate attitude, knowledge, or skills.

Other organizational indicators of possible training needs include: the cost of *not* training, losses in production, reductions in departmental efficiency, product change, excessive waste, abnormal personnel turnover, retraining requirements, increasing operational flexibility, succession and promotability needs, and future business requirements. These, then, are basic considerations in determining how the training function should be structured.

FUNCTIONAL STRUCTURE

The training structure is obviously dependent upon its *current* mission within the total organization. Ideally, it should be adaptive, maintaining a flexibility to cope with change. Practically, however, a training staff normally tends to perpetuate itself and its activities, needed or not.

Functions within the training sphere need regular appraisal to assess their results in terms of employee job performance. To meet criteria of effectiveness, training operations should be closely checked by the departments which are served. In evaluating training, certain questions will arise pertaining to function and structure, among them:

1. How will training policy be established and reviewed?
2. Should a centralized training center be established?
3. Should the organization provide purely a central consultative training service?
4. Should training be decentralized by departments and/or by geographical considerations?
5. What kinds of training personnel are needed, and what qualifications should they have?
6. What should be the reporting and feedback relationships between training and user department management?
7. How will the training budget be handled: out of "general and administrative" overhead, or on a charge-back system?

In the smaller organization, where the training function rests in the hands of one individual, he must obviously rely upon others in the organization, or on the outside, to accomplish the required training tasks. Increased growth and technological complexity resulting in greater specialization have tended to enlarge the scope of an organization's training requirements and hence its structure and staff. Today, many organizations, with overburdening responsibility in the hands of its line management, provide them with specialized training services on a staff basis. The continuing need for well-trained technical and managerial personnel has often made training a key component to organizational success.

Figures 1 to 5 indicate the wide variety of structures for the training function.

Common to nearly all training structures is the administrative responsibility for details, records, and arrangements. These may include any or all of the following: scheduling programs; attendance; use of training references, tests, and performance follow-ups; use of outside instructors and consultants; certificating and qualifying program graduates; payroll and travel expenses. These are essential duties and controls that must be properly assigned. Sometimes the importance of having administrative control over these essential functions has been the principal reason for centralization of training activities.

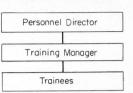

Figure 1. A small training section. In some instances, the training manager could report directly to a line department head.

In those cases where localized or divisional training competence has been well established, central training resources tend to consist chiefly of consultative and resource activities. As an organization grows, training specialists provide effective guidance throughout the organization, if they are responsive to needs and capable of applying innovative techniques. Occasionally, there are special situations in which a task approach to training, not directly responsible to the training hierarchy, can prove most effective. By using especially qualified personnel drawn from any part of the organization, as well as outsiders, the task force can provide a program of training of special value. In training structure, then, flexibility in action is a very desirable and advantageous quality.

FULFILLING TRAINING RESPONSIBILITIES

Training responsibilities should be filled in close relationship to the organization's main objectives. Rarely is it possible to fulfill all individual and group training needs simultaneously. Priority programs must be established and carried out to meet or surpass the result requirements of top management. This calls for careful prelim-

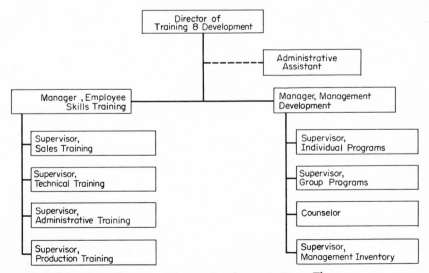

Figure 2. A training department in a national organization. The training and development unit may parallel the personnel function within the organizational hierarchy.

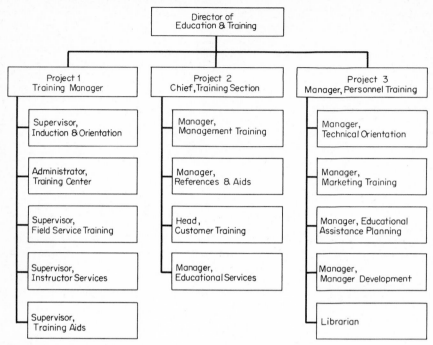

Figure 3. Functional structure of training in project management.
Upon completion of the project, its training support functions
are reduced or eliminated and the unit is disbanded.

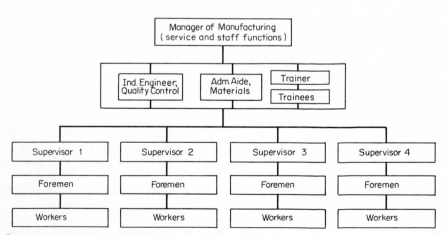

Figure 4. An integrated training function.   Administrative relationship of trainer to a training department.

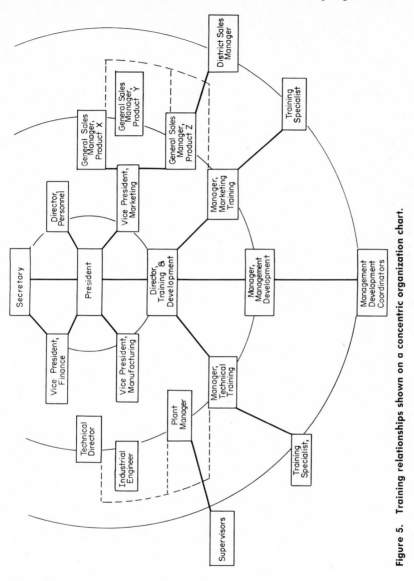

Figure 5.   Training relationships shown on a concentric organization chart.

inary determination of training needs and an ordering of priorities in cooperation with higher management.

Frequently, a department or section within an organization assumes a training responsibility on its own. Examples of this are seen most often in "sales training," "field services training," and "management development." Other indications of departmental training activities are found in supervisory coaching and on-the-job training which may be formalized or not. Such activities should be encouraged and strengthened whenever possible by the organization's training staff. Performance quality is, after all, the ultimate responsibility of line management. The role of staff services to whom training has been delegated is to develop training capabilities wherever necessary in the organization, including such abilities among supervisors and managers in line departments.

Nowhere in the broad spectrum of training responsibility is this clearer than in management development. The salient influence upon the learning of subordinates is the boss' conduct. This, by far, outweighs any other experience undertaken by the subordinate as a training or development activity. Management training can serve any or all of these purposes, assist incumbents in improving their present performance, help prepare promotable managers for higher responsibilities, forestall obsolescence, develop "high-potential" personnel, and improve total management (organizational) performance.

PROGRAM PLANNING AND PROCEDURES

The job instruction training approach, developed by training within industry for the federal government during World War II, is still a useful, effective training formula. It consists of four steps: (1) preparing the worker, (2) presenting the task, (3) trying out the worker's performance, and (4) following up on his newly developed job skill. This formula has admirably served a generation of trainers in the planning of both individual and group training programs.

Another easily remembered device for planning a program is the "ACME" approach. It proceeds as follows:

A: *Aim* of the training program
C: Its *content*
M: *Methods* to be used
E: *Execution* of the program and its *evaluation*

Figure 6 presents a training cycle that can be used in planning major training programs:

1. *Determine need.* Is this truly a training problem? Of what magnitude and relative importance?

2. *Analyze job tasks.* What are the specific tasks to be learned in order to perform the job satisfactorily?

3. *Appraise trainees.* Who will be trained, and what are their characteristics?

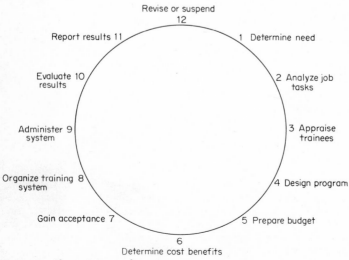

Figure 6.   The training cycle.

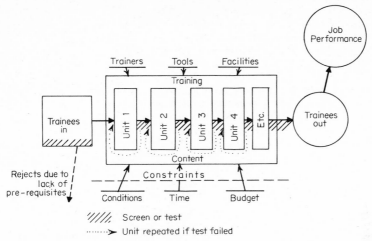

Figure 7. A training system. This diagram shows the significant factors to be considered and their relationship in the design of a typical training system.

4. *Design program.* What are the training objectives? What is the time frame? Who will conduct the training? What will be the content? What equipment, material, and facilities are to be used? What are the expected results?

5. *Prepare budget.* What will the training program cost?

6. *Determine cost and benefits.* Are the results worth the amount to be spent on training? What will indicate benefits to be derived?

7. *Gain acceptance.* Do appropriate members of management understand and approve of the program, its values, and their respective roles in support of it?

8. *Organize training system.* What are the detailed preparations necessary to implement this program (see Fig. 7).

9. *Administer system.* By whom and how will the training be handled, as to schedules, expense payments, housing and travel (if needed), training room arrangements, records, and reports?

10. *Evaluate results.* How well did each trainee learn? Is each adapting himself to his job and progressing to the satisfaction of his immediate superior? What adjustments to the training program are necessary? How can training better fit the man into the job?

11. *Report results.* Have all necessary records and reports been transmitted to appropriate management?

12. *Revise or suspend.* What changes can improve the total training process?

In the smaller organization or unit, it is important to note that all training and development functions may very well be delegated to a single person. Obviously, in such cases, his qualifications should be as well rounded as possible. As the organization or unit grows, and as demand for training assistance increases, the training specialist may find it necessary to share his responsibilities by adding staff members, by training trainers in other departments, or by farming out training assignments to outside agencies and consultants.

Among organizations generally, the role and hence the qualifications of the training and development director varies widely. This diversity of background among professionals is demonstrated in the membership of the American Society for Training and Development. The membership of this society represents the major corporations and organizations in the country and is made up of engineers, psychologists, educators, sales administrators, and others who have been attracted to the field of training and have been promoted to an administrative position. Ordinarily, the qualities and qualifications sought in a top training man or woman include an undergraduate degree, advanced study in education, psychology, business, and possibly a technology, equivalent to the master's degree. In addition, experience of at least five years, including training administration, is sought. Since training today is viewed as a profession, this experience need not be limited to the industry or field in which the individual is employed. Depending upon the makeup of the training staff sharing his responsibilities, the training director's own key qualities are his ability to establish and maintain rapport with all levels, his organizing capabilities, and his competence as an administrator.

Each member of the training staff, in his own right, must demonstrate special qualifications, if training targets within the organization are to be hit. For each, job standards and mutual acceptance of expected results offer the best delineation of the individual's responsibilities, their priorities, and their potential contribution to the main training and development mission. Since flexibility in serving the changing needs of the total organization is an invaluable asset, training specialists can, and should, be recruited from within the organization on a "loan" basis, as far as possible.

This is particularly true of instructor positions, in which specific technical knowledge is an essential factor. The technical trainer should be selected, not only on the basis of his technical knowledge and skill, but also on his desire and ability to develop these outcomes in learners. Oftentimes, selection of a second- or third-best candidate technically, but one with better transfer and rapport capabilities than the top technical man, is the superior choice for instructor. The knowledgeable technical instructor can more readily learn and apply such standard training procedures as setting learning objectives, lesson planning, test and performance measurement, and record keeping than can the educational specialist, who is a technical neophyte and must learn the required subject matter and skill.

By the same token, administrative staff training people, responsible for attendance records, class scheduling, distribution of materials and equipment, and housekeeping duties, can normally be retained for longer periods even when formal programs change. As with all other line and staff functions in the organization, the training activities should be subjected to regular audit by an independent resource to determine their effectiveness and efficiency. This audit, in turn, will reveal functional changes that will necessitate reorganization in the staff structure.

THE BUDGET

The principal management control over training is the budget. The budget for training can best be measured in terms of training effectiveness. If the results of training reduce the amount of time it takes employees to become fully productive, for example, and if training cost is lower than the cost of material waste, if employees progress is slow in reaching average production standards, and if grievances or other quantifiable specifics are reduced, then the training expenditures could be regarded as worthwhile. The development of similar yardsticks for training programs on a cost and benefits basis, wherever possible, can provide a firm, businesslike way of evaluating and justifying the various programs.

In preparing a training budget, these steps are normally followed:
1. A request is made for an overall budget estimate for the fiscal period.
2. Estimates for each training function are collected, analyzed, and evaluated.
3. A tentative budget is drawn up and submitted for approval.
4. The budget is reviewed by the organization's budget director.
5. The training chief is informed of the approved budget.

6. Unforeseen changes and variances are reviewed monthly and corrective measures taken wherever possible.

These are guidelines for administering the training budget:

1. Keep the budget realistic, in accordance with the mission and the assigned training responsibilities.

2. Changes in the budget should be made in advance and with the full knowledge of those affected.

3. Sufficient control should be exercised to maintain figures close to estimates.

4. The budget should be reviewed periodically to determine variances and potential difficulties.

5. Use a contingency fund where variables are unknown.

6. Align the budget with the specific goals of training staff members.

ASSESSMENT OF TRAINING

What are the criteria to consider in measuring the effectiveness of a training organization? Here are some yardsticks to use:

1. *Objectives.* Is there a clear target for each training program, and is this target in line with a broader organizational goal?

2. *Cost and benefits analysis.* Is the training unit in a position to justify its program by relating its monetary cost to expected dollar benefits to be derived from training?

3. *Flexibility.* Has the training group proved its ability to cope with new requirements of the organization with reasonable dispatch?

4. *Results.* In the various training functions, are key result areas specified and accomplishments indicated in quantitative and reasonable terms?

5. *Staff.* Is there an objective search procedure, including an updated manpower inventory, for staff selection and advancement?

6. *Audit.* Do all the various training functions undergo an independent audit periodically, not less than once a year?

7. *Improvements.* What feedback mechanisms are available from line operations to improve the quality, quantity, and timeliness of training?

Training and development must remain alert to trends affecting the organization economically, socially, and politically. Its leadership must be in constant touch with planned changes in the organization's products or services and the projected manpower requirements.

BIBLIOGRAPHY

Bienvenu, Bernard J.: *New Priorities in Training—A Guide for Industry,* American Management Association, New York, 1969.

Button, William H., and William J. Wasmuth: *Employee Training in Small Business Organizations,* New York State School of Industrial and Labor Relations, Cornell University, Bulletin 52, Ithaca, N.Y., 1964.

Craig, Robert L., and Lester R. Bittel (eds.): *Training and Development Handbook,* McGraw-Hill Book Company, New York, 1967.

DePhillips, Frank A., William M. Berliner, and James J. Cribbin: *Management of Training Programs,* Richard D. Irwin, Inc., Homewood, Ill., 1960.

King, David: *Training within the Organization,* Educational Methods, Inc., Chicago, 1964.

McGehee, William, and Paul W. Thayer: *Training in Business and Industry,* John Wiley & Sons, Inc., New York, 1961.

Ross, Homer C.: *The Development and Supervision of Training Programs Combined with the Instructor and His Job,* American Technical Society, Chicago, Ill., 1964.

Vizza, Robert F. (ed.): *Handbook of Sales Training,* Prentice-Hall, Inc., Englewood Cliffs, N.J., 1967.

Warren, Malcolm W.: *Training for Results,* Addison-Wesley Publishing Company, Inc., Reading, Mass., 1969.

chapter 19

Training Clerical Employees

MARKUS M. LOFTIN III   *Second Vice President, Human Resources Department, The Chase Manhattan Bank, New York, New York*

BENJAMIN ROTER   *Assistant Treasurer, Human Resources Department, The Chase Manhattan Bank, New York, New York*

The need for more efficient and effective training methods is increasingly apparent. The wide-scale use of technology has created a vast population of white-collar employees whose duties extend from the routine, manipulative tasks of the file clerk to the complex, analytical tasks of the senior credit correspondent. In addition, the traditional labor force which business could rely upon to fulfill its clerical manpower needs is continuing to decline steadily. Urban population changes, together with a drop in educational standards, have created a new labor force. For the most part, this labor force is only marginally prepared for the jobs that business will offer.

The immediate effect of these changes has been to alter the nature of clerical training requirements, and to create a somewhat new range of training and related performance problems. As a result, considerably more insight is required of the training staff in designing and developing training activities. In addition, rather than focusing initially on individual clerical duties, trainers may have to examine groupings of duties according to general performance requirement levels so as to maximize the impact of a program over a broad population in the organization.

GENERAL PERFORMANCE REQUIREMENT LEVELS

Performance requirements for clerical positions fall into three major types: knowledge, skills, and attitudes. In other words, what kind of work must the employee handle, what must he do to it, and how can he be encouraged to react positively to what he is doing? These knowledge, skill, and attitude requirements mix in varying degrees according to the following levels of clerical duties:

1. *Basic Level:*   Repetitive and routine duties with strict adherence to established rules and procedures
    a. *Knowledge:*   Modular units that define the basic unit of work, such as what is a check, what is a stock certificate
    b. *Skills:*   Manipulative, motor, e.g., machine operation; and operative, e.g., scan and search as a work-related type of reading ability
    c. *Attitudes:*   Working environment
2. *Secondary Level:*   Individualized duties involving more action and responsibility, as well as ability to choose properly between alternative procedures
    a. *Knowledge:*   Specialized units (such as drafts or promissory notes) which supplement a basic module (such as what is a check)
    b. *Skills:*   Determinative, e.g., performing a series of functions which may require discrimination among alternative procedures
    c. *Attitudes:*   Job satisfaction
3. *Senior Level:*   Duties demanding a higher degree of individual responsibility involving choice, judgment, and technical expertise
    a. *Knowledge:*   Cognitive and technical
    b. *Skills:*   Analytic and research
    c. *Attitudes:*   Career opportunities

By classifying clerical duties in terms of these levels of complexity, we can identify their corresponding performance requirements.   In so doing, we have a framework within which we can examine diverse training needs in a meaningful sequence:

	Duty Requirements	Performance Requirements	
Entry level	Repetitive, routine; strict adherence to procedures	Knowledge: Skill: Attitude:	Basic, limited Manipulative, operative Working environment
Secondary level	Moderately individualized and detailed; choice between alternative actions	Knowledge: Skill: Attitude:	Specialized, expanded Determinative Job satisfaction
Senior level	Highly individualized and complicated; wider choice judgment, technical expertise	Knowledge: Skill: Attitude:	Cognitive, technical Analytical, research Career opportunity

Figure 1 shows how training requirements could be derived from a survey of clerical duties.

GENERAL PROCEDURE FOR PREPARING TRAINING ACTIVITIES

A training activity, if properly developed, should effect a desirable change in behavior.   Since the change in behavior is measured by the attainment of performance standards, the most effective way to begin the training activity is by defining its intended results—the terminal objectives which describe desired behavior in performance terms.   The steps shown in Figure 2 outline this procedure.

These steps afford the trainer maximum amount of control throughout the preparatory process.   Since the terminal objectives (1) dictate the training content (3) and the type of training methods and media to be employed (4), the entire training effort is directed by the results it is meant to achieve.   Before this procedure is applied, however, it is necessary to define precisely the training request.

Position title	Position code numbers			Number of people (quota) on each shift				Read					Write						Speak/Listen			Arithmetic				Numerical perception				Typing				General			
				Day	Early eve.	Eve.	Night	Follow written instr.	Interpret & transform (classify)	Proofread/check	Scan/search for info.	Compare	Prepare instruct.	Ltrs./memos/reports	Wires/cables	Computer instruct.	Summarize	Dictate	Transcribe dictation	Give oral instr./adv.	Receive oral instr.	Multiply/divide	Add/subtract	Decimals / fractions	Use formulas	Identify & retain	Compare	Search	Error loca. & corr.	Copy	Forms	Layout/organize	Numeric	Filing	Prob. solving	Alpha keypunch	

Figure 1. Basic position requirements.

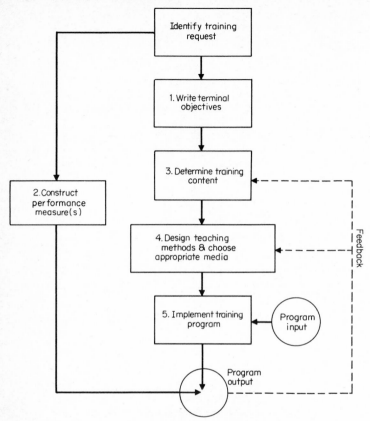

Figure 2.   **Flow chart for preparing training activities.**

FIELDING THE TRAINING REQUEST

The call for training by a department manager should not be an automatic signal for the existence of a training problem. While most managers assume that performance or related problems such as accidents, turnover, errors, and low productivity somehow relate to inadequate training, the training staff should recognize that many of these so-called problems are correctable without training. Only after training is concluded and these problems continue to exist do the unwary manager and overeager training staff understand that their efforts were premature.

As an illustration, consider the following example: The training staff was called on to teach file clerks in a bookkeeping department to file more quickly and accurately. Managers were experiencing a steady rise in customer complaints as large amounts of canceled checks were being filed by color and size rather than by account number.

Formal training would have made very little, if any, impact on this particular problem. Let us see why. The training analyst constructed a test to obtain an objective measure as to whether or not employees could perform their jobs properly. Test results showed that file clerks could file accurately and quickly if they wanted to.

The analyst followed this initial testing sequence by observing employees on the job. He observed that filing checks was often a form of punishment—as it was not only a fatiguing task but also one which, if done properly, resulted in neither intrinsic nor extrinsic benefits to the performer. At this point it was decided not to train.

The problem was solved without training by altering the clerk's arrangement of work, and providing him with an opportunity to perform more responsible tasks. In this way, outstanding performance was recognized by the supervisor who could change punishment to reward by assigning his clerk to duties other than filing checks.

This example indicates how important it is to define and analyze a training request in terms of specific performance needs before preparing a training program. A department requesting training should provide at least the following preliminary information. (A printed survey or questionnaire form, or a formal interview, could be used for this purpose.)

1. When, and how, was the problem first recognized?
2. Were attempts made to correct the problem? If so, what attempts were made and what were the results?
3. What specific cases or examples can you offer which illustrate the problem?
4. How will you know when the problem no longer exists?
5. Estimate the amount of savings you might expect if this problem ceased to exist.

These questions will define the problem and help shape a training analysis strategy from which further and more intensive study can be carried on to find the best and most economical solution. At this point, the training analyst is ready to begin the first of five consecutive phases of his work.

ANALYSIS

The analysis of any training problem begins with a statement of training needs. A need, or performance deficiency, is the difference between actual and required performance. Furthermore, as our example with the file clerks showed, performance deficiencies can result either from problems of acquisition, where employees lack certain skills or knowledge, or from problems of execution, where external job-related factors inhibit employees from doing their best.

We now know that a test which relates to the actual job or tasks involved, and which includes the same performance response, is an effective way to determine the existence of problems of acquisition. Test results will indicate specific skills or knowledge which the employee may or may not possess. If tests results are poor, training will most likely be necessary. If, however, test results are favorable, as in the case of our file clerks, a look at factors in the job environment that impact on performance may be required.

Figure 3 shows that a training analysis is concerned primarily with identifying the precise causes of performance deficiencies. As can readily be seen, this analysis format serves as a decision-making as well as a problem-solving technique. Decisions whether to train or not to train can be based on the extent to which it is shown that a performance deficiency results from either acquisition or execution problems.

Where employees are shown to have the prerequisite skills to perform properly, and yet do not do so, we may conclude that an execution (or level II) type of problem exists, and that there is no need to train.

In addition, this format can be used as a problem-solving technique, since it illustrates that job performance is contingent not only upon the acquirement of certain skills, but also upon job-related conditions which directly or indirectly influence the execution of those skills. Of course, the ideal training situation is one in which

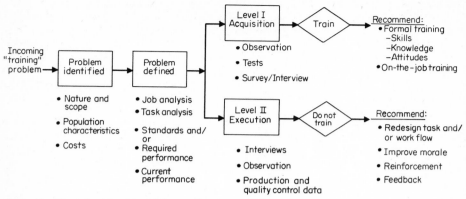

Figure 3.   Flow chart for identifying performance deficiencies.

both levels are accounted for, that is, the learner has fully acquired all necessary skills to perform his job properly, and the job environment reinforces his performance.

DESIGN

Once a problem of acquisition is identified, the objective becomes one of correcting it through an effective training design. A useful starting point for this design can be found in our earlier description of a general procedure for preparing training activities. Two of the essential components in that procedure—determination of training objectives and construction of performance measures—are examined in greater detail, and in relation to other essential components, in the schematic model shown in Figure 4.

This model represents a systems approach to training design. The overall objective or mission of the system—to effect a predetermined change in behavior or performance—defines the nature of each of its essential component parts. These are:

Input: Target population; characteristics of participants in need of training

Training activities: Teaching methods and media chosen to meet training objectives

Output: Product of training; qualifications which participants will possess upon completion of training

Actual job to be performed: The goal toward which Output is directed

Terminal objectives: Purpose of entire system, e.g., maximize production, improve quality

Measurement of actual job performance: Evaluative methods to determine that terminal objectives are being met

Measurement of training performance: Evaluative methods to determine participants' performance throughout training

An important feature of this training design is that is provides control points for measuring training effectiveness. Thus, an employee's performance during training can be related to his performance after training and on the job. If discrepancies exist between the two, the analyst can revise and improve the training process until the desired results are obtained.

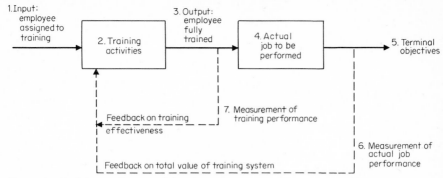

Figure 4.   Training systems model.

DEVELOPMENT

With the overall training design completed and approved by management, the analyst moves into the development phase. Having determined job requirements, formulated terminal objectives, and developed criteria or performance tests with which to evaluate training, the analyst has a basic framework for making the following decisions:

1. The kind of instructional strategy to use
2. The kind of teaching methods to use
3. The kind of presentation devices or media to use

There are no formulas for making these decisions, although there are some parameters. Essentially, the analyst is concerned with facilitating the predescribed change in the learner's behavior so that the terminal objectives in the design plan are fulfilled. Since objectives, when stated in terms of performance, imply a requirement for certain types of learning,[1] the analyst selects strategies, methods, and media which will fulfill this requirement, and satisfy the objectives as well. Thus, strategies, methods, and media used in the training situation should

- Bring about the required behavior of the actual job
- Approximate the tasks, procedures, etc., to be performed in the actual job
- Approximate the conditions in which the actual job will be performed

In addition to these considerations, the department requesting training usually imposes certain constraints. These are often in the form of costs. In making his development decisions, therefore, the analyst may have to consider the value of overcoming the problem in terms of

1. What the problem is costing
2. What the proposed solution will cost
    a. Salaries of those to be trained
    b. Salaries of instructors
    c. Developing and/or purchasing training materials
    d. Purchasing and/or renting equipment, training rooms, etc.
    e. Travel to and from place of instruction

Instructional strategies and methods can be conveniently grouped in the following manner:

---

[1] Leslie J. Briggs et al., "A Procedure for Choosing Media for Instruction," *Instructional Media*, AMI, 1967, p. 29.

Strategy	Description	Method
Self-instruction	Employee learns by himself and progresses at his own rate of speed	Job aid, programmed instruction, self-instruction material
Tutorial instruction	Employee receives assistance or guidance in one-to-one relationship with an instructor	On-the-job instruction
Group instruction	Employee participates in a training activity with others	Lecture, conference

The desirability of using any one or a combination of these particular strategies and methods depends upon the extent to which they satisfy the specifications and constraints imposed by the training analyst and the requesting department, respectively. For example, programmed instruction is considerably more effective than straightforward lecture methods for achieving participant involvement. In the straightforward lecture the participant assumes a passive role, and the instructor usually resorts to intuitive guesswork as to whether or not the participant comprehends the subject matter. Quite often the underlying assumption in the straightforward lecture—that all participants are at the same level in their achievement—makes little or no allowance for individual differences in learning ability.

Programmed instruction, on the other hand, has been shown to enhance learning effectively by presenting information in small, structured steps; by eliciting active responses from the participant; and by providing feedback, or knowledge of the correct response. Depending upon the form of the program, linear or intrinsic, the participant either will be cued to make the correct response only or will be asked multiple questions. Wrong answers would then lead to additional instruction until the correct answer is made. The lecture method, however, is eminently better suited for those who are time and cost conscious. The relatively high cost and lengthy time involved in developing programmed instruction are in part a result of extensive validation that must be carried out.

Another example of factors which would determine the selection of strategies, methods, and media should be considered. In certain clerical departments where volume of work is high throughout the day, as in large key-punch and check-processing areas, it may not be possible to use lecture or programmed instruction without upsetting the production flow. In this case, on-the-job instruction can be used. This method can provide advantages which are similar to those provided by programmed instruction. The employee receives feedback and gains confidence as his correct responses are reinforced by the instructor. An advantage that job training has over programmed instruction is that since the employee is in the actual job situation, he develops skills which are identical to those he will be required to perform when he gains proficiency. He also becomes familiar with the working environment.

Though not as costly nor as time consuming as the development of programmed instruction, the development of job training requires considerable instructor skill. For example, in teaching job procedures to a new setup clerk, the instructor would (in addition to simplifying the procedures so that the clerk could follow them) have to eliminate irrelevant or noncritical procedures which would impede progress and hamper overall training efficiency. The instructor could achieve this with a job aid constructed along the following lines:

JOB TITLE: Setup clerk.
ANALYSIS
METHOD: Breakdown.
JOB OUTLINE: (Main responsibilities)—
              1. Identify and interpret correspondence.
              2. File correspondence folders.
              3. Fill in information on account jackets.
              4. Run information through data converter.

Each of these responsibilities may be broken down further. For example, 2 might be described in detail as follows:

TASK TITLE: File correspondence folders.
MAIN STEPS: (a) Alphabetize folders according to country.
              (b) Alphabetize folders according to city in country.
              (c) Place folders in file cabinet.

After determining an instructional strategy and a teaching method, the analyst must decide on the type of media to use. There are four major types which occur in several forms:
1. Audio: taped programs
2. Visual: slides, flip charts, filmstrips
3. Audio-visual: movies, sound and slides, filmstrips
4. Printed matter: books, manuals

The location for training, the size of the population, the frequency of changes in the training materials, and the literacy level of the trainee population are all major factors to be considered. As with method and strategy, the analyst should be able to give proper justification for his choice of media.

IMPLEMENTATION

Scheduling trainees, arranging training rooms, setting up equipment, providing books and other supplies, and following up on training performance are among the administrative responsibilities performed in this phase. Though these responsibilities are often overlooked, the fact is they usually determine the success or failure of even the best conceived training designs.

These administrative responsibilities, furthermore, do not arise independently of considerations made in the previous phases. For example, the selection of an instructional strategy that is appropriate to a particular training design will determine the nature of the training facilities to be used. In choosing a group instruction strategy, the size of the group would determine whether a classroom or an auditorium is needed. A decision to use some form of self-instruction might require the design of a training facility that included individual study carrels.

EVALUATION

As organizations extend their commitment to invest in training, so the need to document the return which those investments yield in terms of improved job performance and increased profitability becomes crucial. Formal evaluation methods must be conceived to provide management with indices of overall training effectiveness from both a learning transfer and a cost point of view.

Such evaluative methods will require the development of follow-up studies, which include questionnaires, surveys, and ranking scales, the use of control groups, and the analysis of internal and external factors affecting organizational climate. The data gathered must then be translated into a meaningful evaluation report which quantifies the effectiveness of the total training effort for the client department.

Much of the success in implementing training depends upon the relationship that develops between the training staff and the requesting department. Since this phase requires a department to take specific training actions, the likelihood of resistance is small if the department was engaged actively in each of the previous phases. This cooperation requires a particular kind of line-staff accommodation. The analyst who is skeptical about the capability and sincerity of the requesting department can create problems from the outset. On the other hand, the department that decides it has a training problem even though it is presented with objective evidence to the contrary sets up the same sort of obstacle. When these problems occur simultaneously, they become insurmountable.

To meet these problems, as well as to meet the organization's real training needs, the training analyst should possess intellectual skills, a knowledge of learning theory and instructional techniques, and some competency in statistical methods and evaluation. As important, however, is his ability to communicate what he is doing and what its potential value is to the organization.

BIBLIOGRAPHY

Arzigian, Simon: *On the Job Training Costs:* An Analysis, Naval Personnel Support Activity, Personnel Research Laboratory, Washington, D.C., June, 1967.

Bloom, Benjamin S. (ed.), Max D. Engelhart, Edward J. Furst, Walker H. Hill, and David R. Krathwohl: *Taxonomy of Educational Objectives,* Handbook I, Cognitive Domain, David McKay Company, Inc., New York, 1956.

Brethower, Dale M., David G. Markle, Geary A. Rummler, Albert W. Schrader, and Donald E. P. Smith: *Programmed Learning:* A practicum, Ann Arbor Publishers, Ann Arbor, Mich., 1964.

Briggs, J. Leslie, Robert M. Gagne, and Mark A. May: "A Procedure for Choosing Media for Instruction," in Leslie J. Briggs, Peggie L. Campeau, Robert M. Gagne, and Mark A. May, *Instructional Media:* a procedure for the design of multimedia instruction, a critical review of research and suggestions for future research, American Institutes for Research, Pittsburgh, 1967, pp. 28–52.

Broadwell, Martin M.: *The Supervisor As an Instructor:* a guide for classroom training, Addison-Wesley Publishing Company, Inc., Reading, Mass., 1968.

Bruner, Jerome S.: *Toward a Theory of Instruction,* The Belknap Press of Harvard University Press, Cambridge, Mass., 1966.

Bureau of National Affairs, Inc.: *Job Analysis,* Personnel Policy Forum, Survey 79, The Bureau of National Affairs, Inc., Washington, D.C., 1966.

Cronback, Lee J.: "How Can Instruction Be Adapted to Individual Differences?" in Robert M. Gagne (ed.), *Learning and Individual Differences,* Charles E. Merrill Books, Inc., Columbus, Ohio, 1967, pp. 23–39.

Daly, Andrew A.: "Selecting and Organizing the Training Staff," in Robert L. Craig and Lester R. Bittel (eds.), *Training and Development Handbook,* McGraw-Hill Book Company, New York, 1967, pp. 507–526.

De Crecco, John P. (ed.): *Educational Technology, Readings in Programmed Instruction,* Holt, Rinehart and Winston, Inc., New York, 1964.

Ebel, Robert L.: *Measuring Educational Achievement,* Prentice-Hall, Inc., Englewood Cliffs, N.J., 1965.

Gomersall, Earl R., and M. Scott Myers: "Breakthrough in On-the-Job Training," *Harvard Business Review,* 44 (4): 62–72, July–August, 1966.

King, David: "Selection and Training of Instruction Staff," in his *Training Within the Organization,* Educational Methods, Chicago, 1964, pp. 173–181.

Lanham, Elizabeth: "Job Analysis," in her *Job Evaluation,* McGraw-Hill Book Company, New York, 1955. pp. 124–175.

Madden, Joseph M.: "Determining Training Needs," in Gabriel D. Ofiesh and Wesley C. Meierhenry (eds.), *Trends in Programmed Instruction,* National Education Association, Department of Audiovisual Instruction, and The National Society for Programmed Instruction, Washington, D.C., 1964, pp. 124–126.

Markle, Susan Meyer: *Good Frames and Bad:* A grammar of frame writing, John Wiley & Sons, Inc., New York, 1964.

Morsh, Joseph E.: "Keeping Training on Target," *USAF Instructors Journal,* 5 (2): 11–15, Fall, 1967.

Pipe, Peter: *Practical Programming,* Holt, Rinehart and Winston, Inc., New York, 1966.

Siegel, Lawrence (ed.): *Instruction: Some Contemporary Viewpoints,* Chandler Publishing Company, San Francisco, 1967.

Seiler, John A.: *Systems Analysis in Organizational Behavior,* Richard D. Irwin, Inc, and The Dorsey Press, Homewood, Ill., 1967.

Snider, Robert C.: "Selection and Use of Visual Media," in *Research, Principles and Practices in Visual Communication,* National Education Association, Department of Audiovisual Instruction, Washington, D.C., 1960, pp. 119–128.

Walrath, Donald C.: "A Systems Approach to the Training Program," *Training in Business & Industry,* 2 (1); 22–24, January–February, 1965.

Warren, Malcolm W.: *Training for Results,* Addison-Wesley Publishing Company, Inc., Reading, Mass., 1969.

chapter 20

Training Plant Employees

J. C. SMITH   *Plant Manager, The Pantasote Company, Point Pleasant, West Virginia*

The need for plant training programs becomes more important as the needs of industry change and become more complex. In the distant past, a new employee sometimes needed only a few hours of on-the-job instruction from an experienced employee to provide him training for his working life. Today, the unskilled worker and labor foreman have been virtually replaced by the technician and manager.

DETERMINING TRAINING NEEDS

"Fred," said the plant superintendent to the head of production, "Those new men are not cleaning the kettles well enough, and they are eating lunch in the chemical mixing room. They need training. See what you can do."

The first step in developing an effective training program is to determine what training is needed. Following are some of the various methods used in assessing these needs:

Observation of job performance. Much can be learned about training needs simply by getting into the work area and keeping one's eyes and ears open. The state of morale, effectiveness of communications, achievement of performance standards, and other criteria often can be measured through direct observation.

Analysis of records. Analysis of internal friction, high turnover, heavy absenteeism, material waste, and an unsatisfactory safety record can lead to fields where training is most needed. An analysis of cost records, time study reports, grievance records, records of exit interviews, and other kinds of organizational records can provide indicators of training needs.

Consideration of future requirements. Anticipated new operating equipment or introduction of a different product may require new employee skills that can be met through training. The manufacturer of the new equipment or developer of the new process is often the place to start in building a training program to accommodate the innovation.

Survey of supervision and employees. Supervisors and employees can contribute in helping determine what training is needed. This may be done individually, in groups, verbally, or through survey forms. Early participation by those to train and be trained increases the acceptance of any training program.

Study of job requirements. A comparison of the skills needed to do a job with the present skills and abilities of available manpower gauges the scope of training needs. Is there a skill shortage, real or artificial? Balanced with existing training, what additional training is needed? Is there adequate promotion material?

Goals of management. A true measure of the need for training is how well it helps solve problems that are of concern to management. Since management's goals are the basis for the organization's existence, their priorities must be determined and the training program tailored accordingly.

WHY TRAIN PLANT EMPLOYEES?

Industry demands that training be accomplished as quickly as possible through the most direct route to immediately gain:
- More production
- Higher quality
- Better attitudes
- Lower unit costs

A longer-range view shows that the best training creates within the individual the desire to learn and use the new knowledge for his own and the company's benefit. Training establishes communications on why a job is done and why it is done a certain way. Only half the job is done when arrangements are complete for carefully prepared teaching material, good instructors, suitable facilities, and equipment. Equally important is gearing the training program to the employee's total needs. The best training produces employees who are informed, trained, and motivated.

For example, a large chemical plant's safety training program was a success except for one outspoken employee who gained plant-wide attention by frequent and clever blasts at safety training. At the height of his negative influence, the man walked into a well-marked overhead pipe and suffered a severe scalp laceration. Rather than take an "I-told-you-so" approach, the company asked the injured man to recommend corrective action. He demanded that the line be raised. The company made the minor modification, allowing the man to save face, and took the opportunity to carefully sell him the idea of safety. The employee later was appointed to the plant safety committee because of contributions to the safety program.

TRAINING GOALS

The goals of training fall into one or more of these general categories:

1. Induction, orientation, and preparation to handle a new or an unfamiliar job. New-hire training and hard-core unemployed programs are examples.

2. Improved performance by present employees. Included are upgrading of skills and better motivation.

3. Retrained employees for handling a new job because of job elimination or in preparation for promotion.

In setting training goals, line and staff representatives should agree on the basis for training, what it is to accomplish, how it is to be done, and how its success will be measured. From the beginning, training goals to be accomplished are made known to all persons concerned, including the trainee. A reminder of these goals frequently is worthwhile during the training, since day-to-day problems and priorities may change the direction and effectiveness of the training program.

SELECTION OF TRAINEES

In a plant, training will involve such occupational groups as chemical operators, machine operators, craftsmen, technicians, assemblers, and janitors, among others. Selection of trainees in the case of new employees is predetermined, but choosing among established employees for training candidates can be a delicate matter. Selection aids include tests, observations of supervisors, and interviews with candidates for training. One of the common methods of selection is to have the foreman prepare a chart showing job duties and the extent to which each employee has mastered them.

TRAINING METHODS

Training can be accomplished through many methods. With the needs and goals firmly established, the required method or combination of methods should be evident. Training methods vary from actual job performance to programmed texts, with selection based on the knowledge and aptitudes of the trainees, the time allowed, the training equipment available, and the nature of the job to be taught. Below are some methods used by industry.

On-the-Job Training

By far the most common method used, on-the-job training consists of one person showing another what to do. At its worst, the employee receives help from fellow employees without an explanation of why the job is done as it is. This informal approach gets the job done, more or less, but can be expected to produce a high percentage of unsatisfactory work and high labor turnover. More formal, structured on-the-job training employs competent instructors to train on a planned basis, and it has proved highly effective. Many companies require instructor training as a part of their training program. The Job Instruction Training course developed by the Training Within Industry Service of the War Manpower Commission during World War II is one of the best and is used widely in industry.

On-the-job training emphasizes practical application of a limited amount of industrial knowledge. Focusing on the trainee, it provides maximum practice under observation. However, on-the-job training requires a large amount of attention per trainee and is best applied to small groups.

The federal government provides financial assistance for companies giving on-the-job training under the Manpower Development and Training Act. This act is usually restricted to programs involving recruitment, training, and employment of the hard-core unemployed.

Assistance is available for other manpower development programs under the Economic Opportunity Act and through the National Alliance of Businessmen. Local government employment service offices or regional manpower administrators provide information on the government-assisted training programs available.

Apprentice Training

Apprentice training traditionally has been used to prepare for work that requires a wide range of skills and knowledge, as well as seasoned experience. It requires a number of years to complete, and includes supplemental classroom instruction.

The Bureau of Apprenticeship and Training in the Department of Labor establishes standards for apprenticeship programs registered by them, and assists in maintaining the programs. The company, however, provides all the actual training. Apprenticeship programs are based on an apprenticeship agreement signed by both the apprentice and a representative of the company. Advantages of the Bureau of Apprenticeship and Training registration are:

- Gives assurance of meeting recognized training standards
- Provides permanent record of training
- Sets attainable goals for both company and apprentice

A typical apprentice program in a machine shop requires training in operation of lathe, milling machine, drill press, and benchwork. The employer outlines the training program along with requirements of proficiency levels and time intervals. The Bureau of Apprenticeship and Training assists in putting the program together according to their standards. The employer provides the instruction. The Bureau periodically inspects and guides, and finally awards the apprentice with a certificate of training upon satisfactory completion of the apprenticeship.

State employment services provide information on apprenticeship programs and will prescreen applicants.

Companies providing apprentice training often lose apprentices to other companies, however, once they are trained. Higher pay, better working and living conditions are cited as reasons for leaving.

Classroom Method

A lecture or talk given before a group to convey information is an efficient method to reach large numbers in a short time. Strong advantages of this method include the ability to use the best instructor and the best-planned material. The other half of the training experience, the trainees, may vary greatly in background and motivation, however. Provisions for questions during or after the talk help in better understanding. The showing of films is a classroom variation often used.

Simulated Operations

Actual or similar equipment is used in an area remote from the regular work site for simulated operation. Relatively large numbers of employees can be trained by a special instructional staff without disrupting normal operations. One company trains craftsmen on repair of a complicated compressor by instructing them on a spare unit; another firm built a scale-model distillation column of transparent material for use in training column operators; astronauts experience various circumstances of space flight in spaceship mock-ups.

Programmed Instruction

The material to be learned is programmed in increments of increasing difficulty, each building on those which precede. After each step, a question is asked or a problem presented for the trainee's solution. Through a logical systematic learning sequence, new knowledge is acquired. Advantages include the precise training that can be accomplished at the individual's own pace, and the generally enthusiastic reaction to programmed instruction. Some disadvantages are the high cost of developing programs and the inapplicability to certain jobs that require learning by doing. Some programmed instruction courses are available from various companies that develop them for their own use. E. I. DuPont de Nemours & Company, Wilmington, Delaware, sells courses on subjects ranging from pipefitter to chemical plant operator.

Off-the-Job Training

Welding, machine-shop, bricklaying, and other courses are offered regularly through adult education and technical schools in most areas. Classes frequently represent a cross section of employees from local industry who find it to their advantage to broaden their skills. Correspondence schools are worth considering for increasing an employee's knowledge in many plant operations. Formal off-the-job training has the advantage of commanding the trainee's full attention and not making instruction secondary to production. It also gives the employee exposure to outside ideas and generally stimulates thinking.

Instructions from Outside Plant

Manufacturers of equipment and materials offer the services of technical representatives to train plant employees in the use of their product. Manufacturers, for instance, can include in the purchase contract an agreement to instruct operators during the start-up period, and to provide operating manuals. A factory representative present during the first major overhaul can be extremely valuable as a maintenance instructor. Materials suppliers can be asked to furnish test procedures, safety information, and training of personnel on the subject of their product.

The so-called "factory schools" offer concentrated classroom and practical training in use of the manufacturer's product and have the advantage of expert instructors teaching with the actual equipment.

THE TRAINING ORGANIZATION

It must be clearly understood throughout the organization that line management is responsible for training. Every manager stands to lose if the performance of his subordinates is substandard. The training program—the organization, planning,

Figure 1. Setting up a training program.

1. Prepare job specifications
   a. Study the job
   b. Determine standards
2. Prepare selection procedures
   a. List job requirements
   b. Decide on selection methods
3. Set training specifications
   a. Identify problem areas
   b. Select training targets
4. Prepare training material
   a. Design lesson plans, outlines, tests
   b. Collect equipment and training aids
5. Perform training
   a. List responsibilities of training division
   b. List responsibilities of line management
   c. Specify role of instructor
   d. Specify role of trainee
6. Evaluate training
   a. Measure performance after training
   b. Collect feedback for future training

coordination, and evaluation—is a staff function. In a small business, both jobs will be done by one person, such as the production manager. In a large firm, a separate division may be required to direct a complex program.

SETTING UP A TRAINING PROGRAM

A training program involves elements of job specification, trainee selection, training specifications, training material, training, and evaluation. The steps involved in setting up a training program are listed in Figure 1.

The job specification specifies the tasks and performance standards for which a person is accountable in carrying out a job. Tasks for a chemical operator might include:

- Change safety disk
- Clean and inspect reactor
- Operate batch reactor

Performance standards include standards of quality, quantity, methods, equipment conditions, and records that are necessary to perform the task as a skilled operator. For instance, the standard could specify that a safety disk is changed after every seven days of service.

The job specification must be specific enough to accomplish the intended purpose, but it need not be detailed in areas where the trainee may exercise his own judgment. Also, the first-line supervisor's participation in its preparation or thorough understanding through discussion will help assure desired results later.

Selection procedures should be objective. Personnel records, tests, and foremen's records are matched with job requirements.

Training specifications note the training requirements of the job—those skills which must be learned by the trainee in addition to his present knowledge. In the case of changing a safety disk, knowledge of use of certain tools is required, as well as the safety considerations connected with the job.

Training materials can be as simple as notes outlining a new employee's job duties, or as complex as a teaching machine. Basic material includes notes summarizing the lesson for later review. Training manuals, textbooks, and programmed workbooks can be added as needed. Visual and audio-visual aids give added dimensions to training and greatly increase its effectiveness.

Figure 2. Sample job breakdown.

CHANGING SAFETY DISK

Important Steps	*Key Points*
Place scissor jack under safety valve	Seat the jack in notch to prevent slipping
Raise valve while loosening bolts in assembly flange	Use crescent wrenches, enough to free assembly
Remove one bolt, then remove disk assembly	
Clean disk assembly	Use special cleaning tool to keep from marring seats
Install new disk and vacuum support in assembly	Disk must be free of imperfections, such as dents or scratches
	Place vacuum supports on underside of disk
Reinstall	Reverse above procedure for installation

First-line management performs most of the teaching in industry because on-the-job training is used more than any other method. The type of training involved will determine who does it. Responsibilities of all participants must be clearly understood, however, so that all the parts fit together. Not to be overlooked is the role of the trainee, who needs to understand the plan and what is expected of him.

Training that cannot be evaluated is probably not needed. If safety training is given, measurable results in safety performance should be expected. Although evaluation is a final step, it has a part in the initial planning, since evaluation standards are selected early.

TRAINING THE INSTRUCTOR

Most job instruction still is done by first-line supervisors or by other supervisors who have limited training or experience in how to instruct. However, they find it is easier to tell an employee to do a job than to instruct him how to do it. On-the-job training can be excellent, since it is actual performance at the workplace, and success is measured in tangible units. But for best results, the instructor must have a knowledge of how to present a specific job, particularly from the point of view of the trainee. The practical approach called "job instructor training" was developed during World War II by the Training Within Industry Division of the War Manpower Commission and is still recognized as a leading method. It can be used as follows:

Preparation

Step 1: Have a timetable.
- How much skill is the trainee expected to have, and when? Where to start training?

Step 2: Break down the job.
- List the important steps.
- Pick key points.

Step 3: Have everything ready.
- Collect materials; have equipment ready to begin training.

Step 4: Have the workplace ready.
- Area must be clean, orderly, prepared. Employee's first impression must be best possible, and his future standard.

Instructing

Step 1: Prepare the trainee.
- Put him at ease.
- Define the job, and find what he already knows about it.
- Get him interested in the job based on what learning it can do for him. Show him why proper performance of the job is necessary, and how it affects the final product.
- Place him in correct position so that he sees the job from the position in which it will be performed.

Step 2: Present the job.
- Tell, demonstrate, and illustrate each step, one step at a time.
- Stress key points.
- Be clear, thorough, sympathetic, and friendly with trainee.

Step 3: Performance tryout.
- Have trainee do the job. Correct errors.
- Have him explain key points to you as he does the job.

- Ask questions to see if he understands. Do not ask questions that can be answered yes or no.
- Continue until certain he can perform.

Step 4:   Follow-up.
- Put him on his own, with the invitation to ask questions.
- Check back with him often. Let him know how he is doing.
- Maintain contact to control undersirable deviations.

EXAMPLES OF TRAINING PROGRAMS

Training programs vary with the employer's objectives. Some programs are a simple and direct response to an obvious need, such as making the welders acquainted with a new, semiautomatic machine. Other programs are complex, involving most of the plant's elements, and require strong staff assistance.

The following examples are not intended as recommendations, but are presented to show the experience of others. Since plant training tends to follow either trial and error, on-the-job training, or the latest fads in training, it is important that those with training responsibility carefully consider their own circumstances and design a training program accordingly.

- A power generating plant begins its training of instrument repairmen by screening all prospective maintenance personnel for suitable mechanical aptitudes. Candidates for instrument work are given a further general examination on fundamentals that shows whether instrumentation background information has been retained from casual sources. Knowledge such as the meaning of "volt" and "ohm" indicates an interest in the field. Starting as an instrument helper, the trainee works for 90 days with an experienced hand, under the direction of a foreman, while completing a self-study manual. At the end of this period, the trainee is able to demonstrate proficiency in prescribed tasks, such as changing charts, inking, and standardizing, or is returned to the maintenance pool. Passing the demonstration tests advances the man to C instrument repairman and the requirement that further demonstrations be performed before going to B, and so forth. The A instrument repairman is a master craftsman who can do any available job in plant instrumentation from changing a chart to overhauling boiler master controls. The program requires a minimum of seven years and can take longer if no job openings are available at higher levels. All maintenance specialties are developed through training processes similar to the instrument repairman.
- A small chemical plant uses an entry level utility pool for training raw manpower in plant maintenance and operations when not working as laborers. As openings occur, the trained utility men bid into permanent slots and receive additional specialized on-the-job training as needed.
- A furniture manufacturer in Appalachia trained hard-core unemployed with federal financial assistance. The local employment security office collected applications and prescreened applicants. Although craftwork was taught through on-the-job training, the primary task of the training program was motivation of trainees to want to work and identify with the plant effort. The industrial relations department had the most responsibility in training in this instance.
- Mobile classrooms are used to train specific skills in large plants, and sometimes tour a number of different plants. An instrument company presents its line to customers in a semitrailer equipped with cutaway instruments controlling simulated processes, on which training is offered to new and experienced employees.
- A wire plant assigns trainees to the best performers-teachers for training because they find that this group develops the best skills and attitudes.

Training of plant employees is not always the solution. Problems that involve employee attitude and motivation require remedies extending beyond the usual definition of training.   Current thinking applies job enrichment or restructuring in many instances where training would previously have been indicated.   However, training is extremely useful when needed and applied with planning.   The following Bibliography is offered for sources of fuller information pertaining to training of plant employees.

BIBLIOGRAPHY

American Association of Industrial Management: *Film Guide for Industrial Training*, 5th ed., American Association of Industrial Management, Jenkintown, Pa., 1965.

Bass, Bernard M., and James A. Vaughn: *Training in Industry: The Management of Learning*, Wadsworth Publishing Company, Inc., Belmont, Calif., 1966.

Bienvenu, Bernard J.: *New Priorities in Training*, American Management Association, New York, 1969.

Bureau of National Affairs, Inc.: *Policy and Practice Series*, Bureau of National Affairs, Inc., Washington, D.C.

Burt, Samuel M.: *Industry and Technical-Vocational Education*, McGraw-Hill Book Company, New York, 1967.

Craig, Robert L., and Lester R. Bittel (eds.): *Training and Development Handbook*, McGraw-Hill Book Company, New York, 1967.

Fry, Edward B.: *Teaching Machines and Programmed Instruction*, McGraw-Hill Book Company, New York, 1963.

King, David: *Training within the Organization*, Educational Methods, Inc., Chicago, 1965.

Rose, Homer C.: *The Development and Supervision of Training Programs*, American Technical Society, Chicago, 1964.

Smith, Leonard J.: *Checklist for Developing a Training Program*, Management Aids no. 186, Small Business Administration, Washington, March, 1967.

U.S. Department of Labor: *The National Apprenticeship Program*, Government Printing Office, Washington, 1965.

U.S. Manpower Administration: *How to Train Workers on the Job*, Government Printing Office, Washington, 1966.

chapter 21

Training Professional and Technical Employees

ROBERT R. REICHENBACH *Vice President, Organization Resources Counselors, Inc., New York, New York*

WHY TRAIN PROFESSIONAL, TECHNICAL, AND SALES EMPLOYEES?

There are at least three strong reasons for a company's continuing the training of professional, technical, and sales employees even though they may have a solid seventeen to twenty-one years of highly developed training behind them:

1. The skills they have developed during their formal education may need to be pointed more sharply to the company's own activities; and, over time, these skills will become out of date and will need refreshing. For example, the half-life[1] of engineers is estimated at not greater than ten years and of EDP specialists at $2\frac{1}{2}$ to 3 years. The span and degree of effectiveness in such careers can be lengthened and enhanced by continued training, bringing employees up to date on developments in their field.

2. Business skills, including managerial ones, need to be imparted to most employees with specialized technical or professional backgrounds. Even though such employees may intend to pursue the technical side of careers within the corporation, such business training will be helpful to them. Moreover, training in managerial skills is of value to professional and technical employees in their career planning. The employee who opts for a technical career early in his work life will have greater flexibility to change his mind later if he has had some management training. Also, the purely technical employee may need managerial training to carry out his im-

---

[1] The span of time in a professional or technical employee's career during which his knowledge and skill obtained in college are relevant and before his knowledge and skill begin to fall behind developments in the field is defined as the length of time it takes for 50 percent of the employee's technical knowledge to become outmoded.

mediate job.   A bench chemist in a research lab has no formal managerial responsibilities for any employees; yet, in the nature of the working relationship, various
laboratory assistants and technicians look to the chemist as their boss, and the chemist expects the lab assistants to respond to his instructions.

3. Certain policies, procedures, product knowledge, and other specific corporate
matters must be conveyed to employees from time to time.   When a new salary program is adopted, all the personnel people and the supervisors in the organization
must be trained in its application and administration.   If the company adopts a new
policy toward employment and promotion of minority employees, all appropriate
executives are trained in its meaning and application and, perhaps, exposed to training designed to make them more sensitive to the needs and problems of minority
employees.   The most pervasive need for product knowledge training is in sales.
New products are introduced; new models of existing products are developed; promotional campaigns, customer inducement programs, and the like are changed
rapidly in many companies.   All must be conveyed in a consistent manner to sales
people.   New sales employees must be trained in company sales methods; and experienced personnel must be trained to explain new models and products, to apply
new sales techniques, and to help train new salesmen.

WHO SHOULD BE RESPONSIBLE FOR TRAINING

Like many facets of personnel administration, the training function cuts across functional lines and organization levels.   Moreover, training as a general activity entails
a wide variety of skills and knowledge seldom found in one organizational unit.
Thus, the question of who should be responsible for training is not always readily
answered.

In determining responsibility for training, the format and content of the training
required must be considered.   Training format consists of the framework for the
course content, the location, the schedule, audio-visual material, teaching devices,
arrangement for speakers, etc.   The content, of course, is the subject matter presented during the program.

Depending on the content, a typical training course may involve only training
specialists or it may be a cooperative effort between training specialists and functional experts.   A course in management styles, for example, may be mounted solely
by training people because the materials presented involve somewhat abstract concepts where the manner of presentation is at least as important as the content.

On the other hand, a training course in new procedures for improving production
scheduling may be coordinated by training people who handle the format, developed
in conjunction with production scheduling experts, and by production schedulers
who develop and present the course content.   In such instances, training people
blend their skill with the expertise of functional people.

The entire training function is the responsibility of operating personnel in some
operational areas.   For example, on-the-job training of salesmen is carried out by
the local sales organization, and on-the-job training of engineers, scientists, accountants, and employees in other specialized functions is performed by those functional organizations.   In each instance, some guidance in the method of training
may be provided by the training organization.

Location of the Training Function in the Organization

Where the training function is located within the organization depends on the size
and diversity of the company and the amount of training performed.   In large, diverse companies which do a great deal of training of professional, technical, and
sales personnel, a training function is typically part of the top employee relations

executive's responsibility. Often training also is the responsibility of the divisional employee relations managers, and many sales organizations maintain their own training capability. Under such circumstances, the role of corporate training personnel is to establish broad training policies and practices and provide the divisional and functional training people with continuing support, new methods, counsel, guidance, and coordination. The corporate training function usually reports either directly to the head of the employee relations function or to a manager of training and development who reports to the head of employee relations.

In smaller, less diverse companies, and in some large companies, training tends to be viewed as a line responsibility. Actual training is designed and carried out by operating people. Such assistance as is provided by the personnel department usually comes from the personnel manager.

The growing use of video tape has enabled central training groups to conduct an increasing amount of actual training throughout the organization. Using video cameras and studio surroundings, the training staff can assemble the necessary speakers, set up the desired format, and retake the presentations as often as necessary to make them acceptable. These tapes can then be sent to field locations for training. Except that the performance is not live, this method effectively replaces the "dog and pony shows" where a team of trainers or speakers travels about the country presenting its message. Use of video tape ensures that the performance, made under favorable conditions, carries the same message and will be presented the same way to the audience. Such tapes may be accompanied by a detailed script and instructions for handling questions. The cost of using video tape equipment is relatively low compared to the cost of presenting a similar number of live performances. Equipment may be rented or purchased or the production of tape may be contracted.

TRAINING SALES PERSONNEL

Training members of the sales force can pose special problems. Often these employees work out of widely scattered locations, frequently on a nationwide basis, far removed from major company installations. To reach all these employees with essentially the same training message in the desired time frame can be quite difficult.

Ideally, new sales personnel should be sent through the same training program, preferably conducted at a single location. But the large numbers of personnel and the diverse locations where they work often make this impractical. To overcome this problem, several approaches are employed by American companies today:

1. *Programmed Instruction.* This method, basically one by which the employee teaches or trains himself, has gained increasing acceptance in recent years. It offers the advantage of reaching a large number of employees with the same instructional content at a relatively low cost and with the involvement of a minimum number of training personnel. Each employee progresses at his own pace.

It has the potential disadvantages, however, of relying almost exclusively on individual initiative, of lack of opportunity to pose questions and share experiences, of possible misinterpretation of material presented and of the need to recall outdated instruction programs and replace them with revised ones. It is essential that any programmed instruction device includes a system of feedback whereby the employees using the program can report on their success with it. Through such a system training effectiveness can be measured and necessary modifications in the program can be made.

Programs themselves vary from highly sophisticated ones using audio-visual devices to somewhat simpler ones, often no less effective, using printed booklets or manuals. Developing such programs for a particular use requires knowledge of the concepts of programmed instruction and of the subject matter being presented plus a period of experimentation to determine whether the actual program will accomplish what it has been designed to do.

Programs are divided into time frames, mechanically controlled in more elaborate programs, with broader individual options in the simpler types. At the completion of each time frame, it is assumed that a given amount of knowledge or information will have been imparted. Opportunity is provided for instant feedback so that the individual can test himself to see how much knowledge he has acquired and to determine the accuracy of his understanding of the material. Some companies use variants of this concept which require employees to complete a written examination at the end of each time frame or at the end of the course, the test then being sent to the corporate or divisional training office for grading. In most conventional programmed instruction systems, the individual is largely on his own to test his learning progress.

As mentioned above, a significant drawback present in programmed instruction may be the absence of the ability to follow up on how the trainee is progressing and, as a result, the problem of knowing whether the programmed instruction material continues to be appropriate or whether it needs to be revised. In order to avoid this problem, most successful users of programmed instruction have built-in procedures for obtaining feedback from the trainees, auditing the program's effectiveness as a teaching device, and determining when it needs updating. Feedback methods include:

a. A written examination during or at the completion of instruction,

b. An essay on what he has learned about the subject prepared by the trainee and sent to the appropriate training department,

c. Questionnaires or "tests" sent to a sample of employees who have taken the programmed instruction course during a given time period.

Results provided by any of these methods, if carefully analyzed, can provide the basis for judging the validity of the programmed instruction in use.

2. *Local Group Training Programs.* A compromise between the centralized, formal, group training session and the individual use of programmed instruction is the presentation of local training programs on a regional, district, or sales office basis, using material prepared by a central training staff. A script for the local program leader is prepared by the training specialists and reproduced for use at each location. The script usually contains fairly detailed instructions as to steps the instructor or leader should take in each phase of the program, along with verbatim scripts of remarks he or other leaders are expected to make. Guides for eliciting audience reaction, questions to be anticipated, case problems for use with small discussion groups, and other material frequently accompany the script. Visual presentations—films, video tapes, flip charts, posters, handouts—also may go with the script. How much the individual leader may deviate from the material provided him varies from company to company and situation to situation. But, since the overall purpose is to provide similar training to all, most companies discourage excessive deviation from the prepared material.

Video tape and its applications also have opened a whole new range of possibilities for bringing centrally prepared instruction and training to field organizations.

3. *On-the-Job Training.* Probably the most widespread form of training in sales organizations, in fact in all functional areas, continues to be the old standby, on-the-job training. Seldom, if ever, is a new salesman sent out alone to call on a customer no matter how careful and extensive his training. Instead, the new salesman will accompany a more experienced one or a district manager from his sales location for a matter of days, weeks, or even months, observing his techniques, how he ap-

proaches the customer, the manner in which the product and its uses are set forth, and the way the sale is closed. After a given period of time, the new salesman may have the opportunity to call on a customer, usually on a relatively simple matter, accompanied by the veteran. After his call, the new salesman's performance will be reviewed with him by the more experienced salesman or district manager. Similar calls, in increasing degrees of difficulty, will be made until the new salesman is ready to make calls on his own. Many companies use their district managers to conduct their on-the-job training because they are likely to be better trained and more experienced.

This method is virtually essential to the training of many salesmen and has proven its worth in instance after instance. However, its success hinges on the capability of the "trainer," the more experienced salesman or the district manager. If this individual's skills are sloppy, his techniques are outdated, his knowledge of the product and its potential uses is vague and imprecise, then the new salesman may be trained all right, but trained in a host of bad habits! Therefore, an ongoing program to train the older sales people is needed in order to keep the veterans', as well as the newer ones', skills sharp. Here again, it is imperative that a system be devised for regularly auditing the effectiveness and applicability of the on-the-job sales training programs.

4. *Motivational Programs.* Recognizing the need to establish a feeling of greater cohesiveness and company identification among a far-flung sales force, some sales executives hold periodic meetings which are attended by all, or a substantial part, of the sales organization. In some cases, attendance is viewed as an achievement award. The purpose is to build greater *esprit de corps* among the salesmen. Typically, such programs will include some presentations on new and forthcoming company products, new marketing and promotion plans, and overall company performance and activities planned for the future. Some organized group entertainment is often provided during nonbusiness hours. But the highlight of such sessions is the inspirational or motivational keynote speaker. A number of speakers regularly make the circuit of this type of sales meeting. They come from diverse backgrounds —business, academic, consulting, and the like. The late Vince Lombardi, Green Bay Packers' and Washington Redskins' football coach, was in great demand for this type of speech. Arthur H. "Red" Motley, chairman of the board of Parade Publications, Inc., enjoys a similar demand. Such speakers are skilled at motivating or inspiring groups of sales people to tackle goals they might not otherwise set for themselves. They have been described as the Billy Grahams and Oral Robertses of the business world. After listening to such a speaker, members of the audience may be keyed up enough to charge out of the auditorium ready to sell overshoes to Arabs.

But this form of training has its detractors as well as supporters. The former contend that improved sales performance results from continuing, careful training in selling skills, not from periodic one-shot hypos of enthusiasm, no matter how inspirational. Some sales managers stand along with training specialists in the ranks of the detractors. A major criticism leveled at this approach is that the enthusiasm generated tends to be as effervescent as champagne bubbles. A salesman may be wholly charged up after a climactic dinner speech on Saturday night, but upon arising Monday morning he remembers only his enthusiasm and cannot recall what generated it. Advocates of systematic, formal training say that this approach equips the salesman with the "why's" and "how's" and the necessary skills that stand by him when he appears at the customer's office and that these skills do not desert the salesman as does the inspiration provided by a speaker.

Each of these approaches has a place in sales training. Clearly, solid, continuing training in the fundamentals of selling is necessary. But this need not preclude periodic motivational or inspirational sessions to supplement the formal training.

Examples of Sales Training Program

Firestone Tire & Rubber Company is an example of a company that provides well-rounded training to its salesmen. Inclusion of all the material used by that company would not be practical here. However, the contents of its program and a brief description of each part is included in Figure 1 as illustrative of the various aspects of an effective sales training approach.

Figure 1.   Outline of the Firestone Tire and Rubber Company sales training program.

1. Basis of Selling Seminar
    Script provided includes company history, orientation, selling techniques, product knowledge such as features of the passenger tire, customer relations, product knowledge for retreads, light truck tires and five-point tire sales plan.
2. Self-training Guides for Firestone Wide 500 and Other Products
    Company is revising self-training guides (programmed instruction) so all passenger tires will be covered in single manual. Employee completes written, self-administered test, sends it to Sales Training Department; it is graded and, if employee passes, he receives certificate.
3. Position Training Guides
    These manuals cover elements of key jobs in company-owned stores. They cover such things as maintaining the right attitude, personal appearance, maintaining a clean service area, maintaining friendly customer relations, meeting customer needs, etc. They, too, include a written examination to be mailed to the Sales Training Department.
4. "Firestone Facts for You"
    Provides all necessary information on passenger tire construction.
5. Firestone Mileage Specialists' Handbook
    Knowledge of contents considered a must for all Firestone passenger tire salesmen. Subjects covered include elements of salesmanship, product knowledge, tire construction for the seventies, tire sizes, Firestone passenger tire line, merchandising tires, finding prospects, telephone solicitation, handling sales objections, glossary of tire industry terms, etc.
6. Firestone Store Manager Training Program
    Program is in two parts:

a. Retail sales	e. Retail sales action program
b. Service sales management	f. General store management
c. Outside sales	g. District office training
d. Operating and controls	h. Shopping competition

    One-week seminar climaxes training program. Consists of five full days (three running from 8:00 a.m. to 9:00 p.m.) of seminar sessions on such topics as:

a. Store manager responsibilities	h. Service sales
b. Personnel management	i. Passenger tires
c. Employee relations	j. Service and adjustments
d. Home and auto supplies	k. Retread sales
e. Credit	l. Customer relations
f. Operating statements	m. Many more
g. Operating and controls	

    Examinations are sprinkled liberally through each phase of the seminar.
7. Firestone Training Program for Territory Salesmen Consists of:
    a. Manual including all training and information a territory salesman needs prior to attending one-week seminar in Akron.
    b. Three-week training program in field
    c. One-week seminar in Akron

    Format similar to Store Manager Training Program with content slanted toward needs of territory salesman.

TRAINING IN JOB-RELATED SKILLS FOR OTHER PROFESSIONAL AND TECHNICAL EMPLOYEES

Training in selling skills has been covered in the preceding section. The techniques described in that section are not limited to sales training but also apply to training in job-related skills for other professional and technical employees. However, augmenting these techniques to meet specific needs often involves the use of educational and training capabilities outside the company. Continued training to upgrade the skills of scientists and engineers usually involves participation of a college or university. Increasingly, companies are granting technical and professional employees extended periods of time off for purposes of attending a college or university to pursue a higher degree or to upgrade skills.

For example, Bell Telephone Laboratories, Incorporated has a comprehensive continuing education program including a "released time" graduate tuition refund program, on-site courses taught by university professors in conjunction with rotational work assignments and courses taught by professional staff, a two-year study program at schools close to Bell Lab sites, and a "one-year-on-campus" program for a full year's study which may be at a school distant from a lab location. The last two lead to the Master's Degree. In addition, the company has a doctoral support program which permits full support and tuition refund for study one day a week and, for some, a full year's study on campus to meet residence requirements. General Dynamics has an arrangement with the University of Texas to provide faculty with college-level courses, for credit, conducted at the company's Ft. Worth, Texas plant. A consulting organization grants to staff members with seven years of service a six-month "sabbatical" for research or attendance at university classes. At least one chemical company will allow professional and technical employees leaves of absence at half pay for up to two years if the employee is seeking an advanced degree. Other companies provide shorter leaves at full pay.

As part of the ongoing effort to stay abreast of developments in scientific disciplines, a number of research departments, including those at E. I. du Pont de Nemours and Company, and Allied Chemical Company, bring university scholars to the company. Under such programs, professors from leading academic institutions visit corporate research facilities on a regularly scheduled basis. The schedule is published well in advance for those interested in what the academician has to say. In most cases, the visiting professor will present a lecture on a given subject, usually a new development or technique, and will make himself available for individual discussions with company scientists to exchange views on specific problems or questions. Many of these relationships are of long standing, and the high value of this exchange of views and information is acknowledged by most company research people who have had such experience. University–industry programs under which academic and industrial scientists exchange places for a period of time have had rather limited application but are rated highly by some research managers.

A large number of colleges and universities today offer refresher courses in many aspects of business operations. Accounting, finance, taxation, banking, employee relations, marketing, production—these and many more are the subjects of special courses, ranging from a few days to a full year, presented by academic institutions aimed at corporate employees.

Nonprofit organizations such as the American Management Association, The Conference Board, and Industrial Relations Counselors, Inc. also offer training courses in various phases of business operation. Courses of this type may be especially useful to company personnel in that they tend to be more business or operations oriented than the typical university program.

Still another method used to conduct training in job-related skills is to encourage the individual employee to take the steps necessary to improve his skills on his own.

Impetus for this activity can come from performance appraisals where the employee and his supervisor agree that a certain aspect of his work could and should be improved. Usually, the supervisor will offer suggestions as to how this improvement can be achieved; among them may be some individual action on the part of the individual, such as home study, attendance at seminars or classes, etc. Subsequent performance appraisals should take into account the extent to which the employee has improved his skills in this way. Most companies provide all or partial reimbursement to the employee for the cost of such training upon demonstration of successful completion.

TRAINING IN MANAGEMENT CONCEPTS

Although the line between training for job-related skills and managerial training may be indistinct and the distinction itself may not be too important, there are enough differences so that they can be viewed as separate although related. Each job or function requires specialized skills training related to that job. But managerial training is of broader application. Most employees in the professional, technical, and sales ranks, managers or not, need to know how to get along effectively with people, how to make themselves understood, what the overall objectives of the company are and what style it follows, how to do a better job of planning, how to keep costs down and productivity up, and many more aspects of management.

Identifying Objectives in Managerial Training

At the outset of any proposed management skills training program, needs must be determined and, from these, goals must be set. Identifying needs in the management sphere is not as precise or readily achieved as is the identification of needs for job-related training. One effective method for pinpointing management training needs employed by many firms is the survey conducted by a consultant, either an internal consultant from corporate headquarters or one from outside the company. Such surveys reveal areas in which the outlook and performance of professional and technical salaried employees may not be contributing to the overall effort of the organization. In such cases, a need for training in the various facets of accepted management often may be indicated.

Members of top management who authorize managerial training for professional employees must know what the training needs are, too. What changes does upper management wish to bring about through such training? It is the function of the appropriate personnel manager, along with his training people, to help top management clarify its thinking on this question. If it wants to lower costs through tighter cost controls, management training programs should be oriented to attain that end. On the other hand, if top management seeks more effective relationships between managers and supervisors and their employees as a means of raising productivity, the training program should be designed accordingly.

Companies usually conduct management training programs as part of a broader, continuing management development activity to accomplish a variety of objectives. No single company will be likely to strive for all these goals, but listed below are some of the objectives companies of all sizes seek through training professional employees in management concepts.

1. *Maintain the Quality of Management and Management Succession.* One of the best-run companies in the country works hard at continuous management training of its college graduate employee population. This company has excellent managers, and it is striving to ensure that this state will continue as employees move up from the professional, technical, sales, and operating ranks into management positions.

2. *Improve Specific Elements of Management Performance.* A large food proc-essing company felt that administration of its salary system was getting out of hand. An audit of this aspect of the company's employee relations activity showed that the operating divisions in this highly decentralized company were almost totally ignoring the performance appraisal aspect of the salary program. An intensive training program for all levels of management in the techniques of appraising per-formance and conducting the appraisal interview yielded highly beneficial results when coupled with some minor revisions in the salary plan itself. Other specific aspects of management and professional tasks can be upgraded through training, as well.

3. *Upgrade Overall Performance.* When a company has a market situation that does not compel it to be innovative and aggressive, members of the corporate team can become so wedded to routine and tradition that they lose their effectiveness. To introduce managers and supervisors to new and successful management tech-niques, top management may turn to broad-scale training in managerial and business concepts. Professional, technical, and sales employees may receive such training as potential managers. Training at this level contributes to the overall climate of improvement necessary to an effort of this type and sets the proper tone for future managers.

4. *Alter a Company's Direction.* When top management revises or sharpens the overall corporate objectives, moves the company to a new stance, a new product or marketing emphasis, or into an entirely new line of business, it may turn to training in management and business techniques as one means of impressing upon key em-ployees the need to use the latest methods in seeking to attain the revised goals. One company, with a protected market, found itself with a new chief executive who wanted to turn the company into a more profit-oriented organization. As one means of doing so, he appointed a multilevel task force from all functions to draw up a training course in current profit management and business techniques which would be presented to salaried personnel. The preparation and presentation of this course contributed to the "new" company's becoming much more dynamic, aggressive, and profit conscious than it had been.

5. *Convey the Company's Philosophy and Style.* Today, merger, growth through acquisition, and companies branching into markedly different industries are facts of corporate life. But some chief executives are concerned about what merger and acquisition do to the way the company does business, how the "new" employees look at the overall company. One oil company had done business under certain policies and a clearly stated philosophy for years; it wanted to keep things that way. But as more and more smaller companies were acquired by the firm, top manage-ment became convinced that the traditional way of doing business, which had pre-viously suited this company well, was becoming diffused and unclear. A series of training sessions for professional, technical, and managerial employees helped to acquaint employees of acquired companies with corporate goals, operating policies of the parent corporation, and in general, how and why it conducted its business.

6. *Build a "One-Company" Concept.* Too often, companies are so compartmen-talized that employees in one area do not even know what employees in other areas do. This makes career planning difficult. So some companies have tried to break down the walls and strive for a single company. One method used is management training for professional, technical, and managerial employees. Business games used as part of the training are effective for this purpose. Playing such a game, an accountant may find that he must decide whether or not to open another market area and determine the degree of penetration sought; a production engineer may have to float a new bond issue, etc. Employees leave these sessions with a greater understanding of interrelationships and how other functions in the company work.

Training in Management Tools

At one time, internal training courses in the various rudiments of management were conducted in many companies. College graduate employees were trained in such skills as a matter of course. In recent years, programs of this nature have fallen from style as more elaborate training topics have appeared. However, a significant number of companies still train their professional, managerial, and technical employees in such subjects as:

1. Effective report writing
2. Successful public speaking
3. Writing business letters
4. The budgeting process
5. Better planning
6. Interviewing techniques
7. Effective management of time

Here too, the capabilities of internal training people often are supplemented by outside experts such as the speech and drama professor at the local university, a consultant who specializes in the planning process, and the like.

Figure 2.   Contents of training program in management techniques for professional employees used by an oil and chemical company.

Sunday

Welcome
Objectives of the Supervisory Training Program

Monday

Basic Organization Concepts
Corporate Organization
Organization and the Role of the Supervisor
Supervisory Responsibilities
Supervisory Qualifications
Delegation of Authority
Understanding Financial Statements—Balance Sheet

Tuesday

Directing, Coordinating, and Controlling
Case Study
Motivation Principles and Techniques
Styles of Leadership
Understanding Financial Statements—Statement of Consolidated Income

Wednesday

Supervision and Employee Utilization
Job Training
Management of Time and Priorities
Supervisory Financial Management
Management Information System

Thursday

Performance Appraisal
Safety and the Role of the Supervisor
Discipline
Discipline—Case Study Discussion
Communications and the Role of the Supervisor
Budgeting

Friday

Salary Administration—Case Study
Case Study Discussion
Benefit Plans
Supervisory Clinic
Supervisor's Report
Company Management and the Future

Illustrative Training Program Contents

Outlines of material used in training professional, technical, and managerial employees in a major oil and chemical company, a large utility, and an integrated oil company are presented in Figures 2, 3, and 4.   Since the application of such programs will vary sharply, depending on the individual company's needs and goals, the illustrative material shows only the approaches adopted by these three companies for their own specific purposes.   Although the contents shown offer an idea of what such training programs might include, they are in no way intended as formats to be followed in every instance.

Figure 3.   Contents of training course in managerial skills used by a large utility company.

Topic	Speaker
I. INTRODUCTION AND BACKGROUND	
A. How Top Management Views the Management Process	Chairman of the Board
B. History of the Company	Manager of Employee Relations and Public Affairs
C. Outside Changes Affecting the Company	Independent Economist
D. Specific Impact of Change on Company	President
E. Case Problems and Discussion Groups	
II. CONCEPTS OF ORGANIZATION	
A. Basis of Planning	A Vice President
B. Basic Concepts of Organization	Outside Expert
C. Managing a Division Effectively	A Vice President
D. Flow of Authority and Responsibility	A Vice President
III. MAINTAINING CONTROLS	
A. Controlling Through Coordination	A Vice President
B. Financial Controls	Treasurer
C. In-Basket Case Problem	
D. Cost Evaluation as a Management Tool	Company Internal Auditor
E. Using the Computer to Control	Outside Expert
IV. PEOPLE AND THE MANAGEMENT PROCESS	
A. Motivating People to do the Job	An Outside Expert
B. How to Use Performance Appraisal	Manager of Organization Planning
C. Role-Play of Performance Review	
D. Leadership styles—Address and Film	Manager of Organization Planning
E. Communicating as a Leadership Tool	Manager of Employee Relations and Public Affairs
F. Preview of Coming Topics in Course	President
V. OUTLOOK FOR THE FUTURE	
A. Introduction	President
B. Anticipated Changes in the Economy	Outside Expert
C. How Management Practice Adjusts to Change	Outside Expert
D. Future of the Industry	Outside Expert
E. Case Problem on Adapting to Change	
VI. THE COMPANY'S RESPONSE TO THE FUTURE	
A. Long Range Planning	President
B. Generation and Distribution	Manager of Distribution
C. Reports on Specific Developments	Staff Experts
D. Case Problem	
E. Planning to Meet Manpower Needs	President
F. Buzz Groups on Impact of Points Presented	
G. Company's Management Philosophy for the Future	Chairman of the Board

Figure 4.   Contents of training program in management techniques for professional employees used by an oil company.

Sunday

  Petroleum Industry in a Changing Business Environment (Presentation)

Monday

  The New XYZ Oil Company (Presentation)
  "Operation Coordination" (Business Game)
  "Operation Coordination" (Discussion)
  Teamwork Motivation and Group Dynamics (Presentation and Discussion)

Tuesday

  Teamwork Styles of Leadership (Film and Discussion)
  Teamwork Conference Leadership (Skit and Discussion)
  Teamwork Conference Leadership (Film—"All I Need Is a Conference")
  Teamwork Conference Leadership (Presentation)
  Teamwork Organization and Teamwork (Presentation)
  Communications (Presentation)

Wednesday

  Delegation (Case Study)
  Delegation (Discussion) (Film—"Manager Wanted")
  Goals and Results (Case Study and Discussion)
  Goals and Results Setting Individual Goals and Appraising Results
   (Presentation) (Practice Session)

Thursday

  Goals and Results (Practice Session and Discussion)
  Goals and Results Coaching and Counseling (Workshop)
  Goals and Results Coaching and Counseling (Discussion)
  Manpower Planning (Case Study)
  Manpower Planning (Discussion and Presentation)

Friday

  Decision Making (In-Basket Case Study and Discussion)
  Decision Making (Presentation)
  The Follow-up (Presentation)
  Conclusion

INDIVIDUAL TRAINING AND ORGANIZATION DEVELOPMENT

This section has dealt with the various means of providing training in job-related skills and management techniques to professional, technical, and sales employees. Almost invariably, such training is provided in anticipation that, as a result of training, the behavior of the individual will change. Hopefully, from the company's point of view, he will perform better on the job; he will get along better with people; he will communicate more effectively.

But a word of caution which does not relate specifically to the training function is due here. Too often, in too many companies, training is viewed as a sure-fire means of altering behavior of employees in the desired manner. This is far from true! If an employee receives effective training and acquires new knowledge and perception only to find himself unable to use them because of an unfavorable organizational situation, such training will only lead to frustration. One of the deans of American training directors, the late Floyd Shannon of Western Electric Company, Inc., once observed that when an individual was removed from his work "family" situation and sent to a training course which no one else in the "family" had received, he felt fortunate if the individual's performance eighteen months after completion of training was as good as it was prior to training. He diagrammed the typical experience like this:

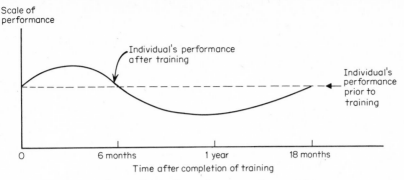

Figure 5. **Diagram of an individual's performance after training.**

This illustration points up the need for two things in relation to training:

1. Training of the individual, especially in areas of interpersonal behavior, probably will be more effective when an entire unit, group, or "family" receives the training at the same time. Various names are used for this approach: cohort training, family training, cousin training, etc. Sensitivity training, laboratory groups, T-groups, and similar behavior oriented groups lend themselves especially to this approach.

2. Often, perhaps usually, changes in the organization will have greater impact on the behavior of the individual than will training provided him as an individual. That fact is being gradually but increasingly recognized by industry trainers. Of course, bringing about significant changes in the organization, in whole or in part, represents a much more complex process than providing training to individuals. Moreover, the procedures for making such organizational changes often lie outside the training director's responsibility. How to measure the effectiveness of any training and development program is a problem confronting most training directors and personnel administrators. But many of those who assess the success of their programs intuitively have concluded that individual training cannot be divorced from improvements in the organization if it is to be as effective as desired. Organization development and individual training are mutually supportive and, as such, neither can be expected to be fully effective in the absence of the other.

BIBLIOGRAPHY

Anderson, J. J.: "Developing an In-House Systems Training Program," *Journal of Data Management,* pp. 26–31, July 1969.

Computer Systems' Analysts; Problems of Education, Selection and Training (Management Bulletin no. 90), American Management Association, New York, 1967.

Craig, Robert L., and Lester T. Bittel, eds.: *Training and Development Handbook,* McGraw-Hill, Inc., New York, 1967, pp. 474–492.

Hanam, Mack: "Ten Ways to Keep Sales Training on Track and On Time," *Sales Management,* pp. 25–74, April 10, 1971.

Hersey, Paul, and C. A. Kellner: "A Behavioral Approach to Training the Sales Force," *Training and Development Journal,* pp. 2–9, November 1968.

Long, Harvey S., and Henry A. Schwartz: "The Potential of CAI in Industry; IBM Pilot Study Report on Computer-Assisted Instruction," *Training and Development Journal,* pp. 6–17, September 1966.

Morton, J. A.: *Organizing for Innovation; A Systems Approach to Technical Management,* McGraw-Hill, Inc., New York, 1967.

National Society of Sales Training Executives: *The New Handbook of Sales Training,* Prentice-Hall, Inc., New Jersey, 1967.

O'Meara, J. Roger: "Off-the-Job Assignments for Key Employees," *Conference Board Record,* pp. 47–51, March 1968.

Training Company Salesmen (Experiences in Marketing Management no. 15), National Industrial Conference Board, New York, 1967.

chapter 22

Management Development

JOHN C. AGATHON *Director of Management Development, Celanese Corporation, New York, New York*

INTRODUCTION TO MANAGEMENT DEVELOPMENT

Why Develop Management

Organizations spend time and money developing managers because a manager cannot make it alone—he needs assistance to fully meet the requirements of his current position and even more assistance if he is going to rise to senior positions within the organization.

Andrew Carnegie could assume that someone from the rank and file, like Charles Schwab, would push his way up the managerial ladder all the way from stake driver to president of US Steel; few share that assumption today because in today's world of business:

1. The ways of business are extremely complex—broader product lines, based on changing technology, serving international markets, characterize many firms.

2. Each organization must deal with several specialized "publics": stockholders, consumers, suppliers, the financial community, governments, unions, employees.

3. There is a broadened concept of business purpose—increasing numbers of responsible businessmen are no longer solely concerned with maximizing profit; they are asking how they can be primarily concerned with profits while being socially responsible.

4. Competition is more vigorous, not only internationally but internally, i.e., within companies; plastics divisions now compete with fibers divisions of the same company, creating new major stresses which have to be understood and managed.

5. Organization charters and structures are in constant flux as companies live through radical swings in business practices caused by diversification, dispersion, and decentralization which, while solving some management problems, have created others.

6. Managers are no longer essentially "minding the store"; they are involved in a process of continuous change, only a portion of which is planned.

In most companies, therefore, management development is no longer a program but a continuing process that has significant influence on assuring manpower to achieve both their short- and long-term profit and growth objectives.

The Language of Development

Practitioners have their own language, and management development is no exception. There is much to recommend the following definitions:

Management development. This refers to career planning for increasing the effectiveness of individuals and meeting the needs of an organization. The specific development assignments of educational activities in which any manager engages are designed to enable him to reach his highest potential in the shortest time. They are designed on an individual-to-individual basis; they are not standardized, mechanical, or programmatic. Participation in management development activities is by all who can be expected to reach a higher level of performance more quickly than would be possible by job experience alone.

Management development includes systematic reviews which identify members of management who can be expected to increase their managerial effectiveness through educational and special assignments; specific career development plans are made with and for individuals; these are written down and revised on a regularly scheduled basis.

Organization development. This is a way of increasing the likelihood that the culture of a corporation is geared to excellence based upon the valid use of facts and data and here-and-now assessment of operational realities, as contrasted with reliance on the status quo. Though organization development utilizes educational methods of studying the company, it should be distinguished from management development and management training. Management training is for the purpose of aiding personnel in acquiring knowledge of a specialized subject area. Management development is geared to improving the career prospects of individual members. By contrast, organization development is designed to strengthen corporate systems by more fully integrating people into production and profit objectives of the firm.

Executive development. Early identification and development of executive talent is one approach to the more effective utilization of those judged to have a high or unlimited potential for senior corporate responsibility. It should be regarded as distinctive and separate from management development since it involves a small proportion of the organization's members and is calculated to bring the best out of the best. The system used should remain free of negative side effects such as avoiding the image of a corps of crown princes or corporate elite.

When educational efforts and special assignments, including rotation of people into areas outside their areas of initial qualification, are utilized to convert potential into general management competence, executive development is taking place.

Management's Expectations

Many top managements find it difficult to state precisely what it is they want to achieve through their organization and management development efforts. Many times objectives are stated in broad terms, such as: "develop a management team in depth," "strengthen middle management," "improve the managerial climate," "identify high-potential people," "keep all our good people," "adopt a broad management viewpoint."

The practical management development practitioner usually learns to live with the ambiguity of such statements and applies his efforts to developing realistic subgoals and a supporting climate to assure their achievement.

Prerequisites for Success

Management development will work well when it has support from all levels of management as evidenced by:

1. Statements in support of the corporation's basic philosophy of management development
2. Commitment of each organization to attain announced objectives
3. Adequate resources: time, money, manpower
4. Leadership through the personal involvement and example of the chief executive
5. Collaboration of efforts between line and staff managements
6. A value and reward system that supports attainment of management and organization development objectives
7. Making it clear that everyone in line management *has* to do it—personnel departments *cannot* do it.

Management Development Is Not a "Personnel Program"

Many operating or line managers are happy to go through life confused on this point, and unfortunately many status-hungry management development practitioners create the impression that the program is their property; they wrote it did they not?

The identification and development of qualified employees to assure a succession of management is an integral part of each manager's ongoing job responsibility. Know it or not, like it or not, he cannot delegate his accountability.

Identification of Needs

A rule of thumb is to start at the top. Determine the needs and expectations of your senior management in the area of management and organization development. If they are too busy, come down an organizational level or two to find someone who wants the help.

The professional will focus on his client's needs and not on his own; neither will he concern himself with what his department enjoys doing nor what they are most qualified to do. (How many times have you seen management development people fostering solutions which are in search of problems?) Said another way, give a little boy a hammer and he will amaze you with all the things that he finds to pound. Some little boys never grow up; they use their skills like hammers, to pound things that do not need pounding.

The balance sheet method.   One method of assessing needs is to develop a balance sheet, a display of facts and opinions that characterize the "state of the art" in an organization, for example:

Assets	*Liabilities*
1. Our replacement charts show we have backups for all key positions	1. We have recruited from the outside to fill five senior management positions
2. We have made a number of promotions from within	2. Several divisions refuse to promote outside their division
3. We have had a manpower planning program for years	3. It is a paper exercise There is no review of it with executive management and no efforts to follow plans

Now, *examine causes* behind the minus side of the ledger. A possible list might be: (1) senior management is insulated from people, or for years we have asked outside consultants and "experts" to analyze our major problems and recommend solutions; is it not natural to recruit outside when major jobs are open; (2) manpower planning and development is encouraged in profitable years and discouraged in lean years; (3) manpower, like physical assets, is regarded as an asset of the divisions; it is not a corporate resource to be optimized. General managers may therefore veto promotions of high-potential people if not in the best interest of the division.

Armed with this knowledge, the practitioner now can more effectively help identify, diagnose, and treat the major management development problems of his organization.

The force field analysis of needs. The program of any company is at all times in transition, changing for better or worse, being influenced by major forces, for success or failure.

For example, using this model a manager can maintain a perspective on the total

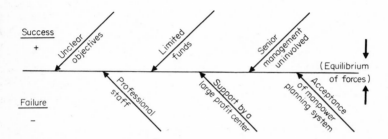

organization's needs and resources at one time. Planning and implementing change are more realistic and effective if one devotes time and effort to both reducing negative forces and increasing positive forces to attain a more favorable equilibrium and hopefully attain a greater degree of success.

The needs identification survey. Most surveys are successful when the field hears that top management endorses and is itself participating in them. Given a knowledge of the history, climate, and managerial style of a company, a survey can be a most effective method of identifying needs.

Several critical design features should be decided in advance:

Communication: Who shall announce the survey, what channels should be used; whose survey is this; what, how, and when, and why is it being conducted.

Timing: Will there be conflict with other major projects or activities, viz., the annual meeting, budget review, etc.; will we have the attention of our audience.

Cost: How much can we afford to spend (or not to spend) to define our problems and take remedial action.

Scope: Can we survey a small, statistically sound sampling; or should we avoid bruised feelings and "sell the heart out of it" by oversurveying.

Responsibility: Should we use an outside firm or inside resources, considering costs, face validity of findings, time, and talents available.

Methodology: Formal or informal; interviews, written instruments; manual or computer analysis—they all have impact on the degree of trust, openness of responses, and validity.

Commitment: Will we finish what we start, will there be realistic action plans to change those things which need changing; will we tell people why some things will not be acted upon; can we say "no."

Other proven methods of identifying needs. External consultants follow a simple and effective model with their clients; it is equally effective when used by internal consultants:

Identify the existence of a problem	Turnover
Illustrate its economic consequences	Hiring and training cost $62,000 per year
Demonstrate how it can be solved or reduced	Improved career development plan for key employees

Another model, though more elaborate, is equally effective:

1. Determine what skills and abilities are being used.
2. Appraise their effectiveness.
3. Determine what additional skills and knowledge are needed—now and in the future.
4. Arrange these needs according to priority.
5. Select methods and means to help develop these improved or additional skills and knowledge.
6. Initiate the development activities.
7. Measure results and feedback corrections to your plan.

Changing Issues in Management Development

Given a clear understanding of what your organization's needs are, it is useful to test them against the real issues and values that are seen to exist in the "outside world," i.e., in the country at large. This can be done by examining the changes that have overtaken the field in the last fifteen years.

1955	1970
Develop good programs and train the individuals by group	Develop the organization and its climate, and educate individuals for self-development within a sound culture
A happy employee is a productive employee; let good human relations training be the keystone of our program	People are still "laughing on the outside and crying on the inside"; let us find ways to accept and deal with conflict as a natural state; conflict resolution and problem-solving skills are essential
Respect for authority is the key to managerial leadership and control	Participation, mutual goal setting, and commitment are the replacements for a rigid adherence to a managerial hierarchy
Learn and respect organization traditions, precedents, and past practices	Based on broadened business values, learn to accept good and reject outmoded dysfunctional standards and practices

THE MANAGEMENT DEVELOPMENT SYSTEM

The Chief Executive's Role

Whether company president or general manager, the chief executive should be concerned with the development and maintenance of a total human resources system within the organization and the creation of a climate that will encourage this process to proceed vigorously and imaginatively. His work is best facilitated by a style of leadership which visibly encourages collaboration in those phases of planning where consensus is vital. He recognizes individual and social needs as he works toward corporate interests; he controls the intrusion of purely functional viewpoints; and he stimulates and rewards participation and contribution. Technology is less a factor of success than this power source; programs can be bought or borrowed; power cannot.

Integration with Business Planning

That well-developed systems for identifying and developing management manpower are found in many companies is well known and somewhat taken for granted, but apparently work is still needed to integrate these systems with business planning. Serious effort is required to achieve this integration on a realistic and productive basis. Unless management development relates its efforts to the achievement of organizational objectives, be it growth, profit, or service, its activities will be regarded as irrelevant, faddish, and extravagant—and ultimately unnecessary.

An Overview of Management Development

Someone in every organization has a concept of how activities relate to goals; and the more people that share this concept, the more effective the results will be. Where programs are inherited, policies fuzzy, and activities poorly executed, the cause may be in the failures of previous managements to conceptualize and communicate the essential relationships and interdependencies of what now appear to be seemingly unrelated tasks.

The effort of the management development department of one major corporation to draw all the "bits and pieces of the puzzle" is exhibited in Figure 1.

Policies and Objectives

They are both friend and foe of the practitioner. Companies without them are hesitant to act or unable to plan wisely. When they are announced, they are greeted

A strategic corporate manpower goal...	Achieve a strong, internationally oriented management team in depth						
...illuminated by a corporate management development philosophy...	The Management Development Process supports attainment of business objectives of short and long term profit and growth of the organization						
...with 7 key concepts...	Expectation is superiority	Create a proper climate	People are a corp. resource	Placement from within	Encourage self-development	Part of daily management	Relevant to personal success
...and 4 common objectives...	Establish manpower inventory control		Improve on the job performance		Provide a reservoir of talents	Develop realistic forward manpower plans	
...directed by a management team with agreed purpose and direction...	Senior management						
	Operating management		Functional management			Staff management	
	Front-line management						
...communicated to and understood by all...	Managerial and professional personnel						
...integrated with other employee functions...	Recruiting	Manpower/ organ. planning	Compensation	Information system HRIS	Medical	Research	Civil rights
...utilizing practical programs that assure attainment of objectives...	Management by objectives		Stewardship		Appraisals		
	Internal search Psychological assessment Task force assessment University courses & programs Association courses		Professional meetings Tuition refund program Company-designed courses Job rotation Planned experience		Ind. action dev. plans Coaching – counseling Reading programs Attitude surveys Comp. conferences		
embracing changes that enrich and unify our efforts...	Corporate-wide general management seminar						
...for the achievement of	Managerial superiority						

Figure 1.   An overview of management development.

Payoff	Successful job perf.	Building blocks for success in mgt. development.				
Climate	High std. of perf. by superior	Challanging opportunity to perform	Good communica-tion	Confidence between superior & subordinate	Recognition for accomplish-ment	Asst. in overcoming weakness
On-the-job activities	Job rotation	Obj. & results oriented appraisals	Special assignments	Temp. replacement for superior	Training & orientation program	Organ. changes or transfers
Company and corporate activities	University extension courses	In-plant seminars	Plant (location) visits	A.M.A. & univ. seminars	Corresp. courses	Periodic functional (dept.) meet. quality control
	City & university recruiting	Special prof. meetings	Counseling	Consultant program	Functional guidance & support	Industry shows expositions
Personal and community activities	Prof. society part.	Selected reading	Self-appraisal	Public speaking (service clubs,etc.)	Teaching	Health conservation
	Charitable works	Civic organ. & affairs (Govt.)	Business organ.	Fraternal activity	Social & recrea. (sport,hobby) activity	Family

Figure 2.   Building blocks for management development.

warmly.   However, as management changes, they can represent someone else's unrealistic expectations and unfair standards of performance.   The practitioner should collaborate in the development of policies and objectives and represent them clearly and positively to all levels in the organization.

Figure 2 is not designed to set a standard, it merely represents the resolution of this issue in one organization, at one point in time.

The Role of the Management or Organization Development Practitioner

Each function in an organization has a continuing need to renew its charter.   Its role in the organization changes, and the effect on its professional staff must be given consideration.   The traditional job description is a keystone as are standards of performance, work planning, management objectives, and other tools for estab-lishing one's congruency with his organization.

Some have found it desirable to develop guideline statements for staff that clearly state management's expectations for each major program in the system.

INTERNAL MANAGEMENT DEVELOPMENT PROGRAMS

Building Blocks for Management Development

The model in Figure 2 suggests the scope of activities available to the average orga-nization.   They have been categorized to provide a greater understanding and dis-tinction of resources available to the career planner who is willing to look to and beyond "on-the-job training" into opportunities available in the organization at large as well as in the community.

The objective is to blend desired activities into a personalized, integrated development plan that will be supported within the organizational climate.

The Importance of the Appraisal Process

The periodic review and assessment of each manager's performance and the development of an estimate of his potentiality is the heart of most "internal development programs." This is so regardless of the sophistication of other elements of the "management development system." From these data one can determine growth needs of the individual against a background of the resources that can be brought to bear on his development. These can then be summarized as group or organization needs.

Management Appraisal Variables

"By what standards and measures shall we judge managers?" The journey has been more enlightening than the destination to many who followed the long, tortuous road to finding the answers to this question. One organization uses this listing very effectively:

Learning Aptitude: To what extent does this individual compare with other managers in his ability to learn new things?

Oral Communication Skills: To what extent can he effectively present an oral report to a small conference group?

Written Communication Skills: To what extent can he effectively express his ideas in writing?

Human Relations: To what extent can he get people to perform effectively by using good human relations techniques?

Personal Impact: To what extent does he make an early impression on others? (forcefulness) To what extent does he make a likable impression on others? (likability)

Awareness of Social Environment: To what extent can he perceive subtle cues in the behavior of others toward him?

Self-objectivity: To what extent does he realize his own assets and liabilities? How well does he see himself; is it congruent with how others see him?

Behavior Flexibility: To what extent can he, when motivated, modify his own behavior to reach a goal?

Need Approval of Superiors: To what extent does he need to have his behavior approved by those he views as his superiors?

Need Approval of Peers: To what extent does he need his behavior approved by those he views as his peers?

Inner Work Standards: To what extent will he want to do a good job, even if he could get by with doing a less acceptable job?

Resistance to Stress: To what extent will his work performance stand up in the face of unusual pressures?

Tolerance of Uncertainty: To what extent will his work performance stand up under uncertain or unstructured situations?

Range of Interests: To what extent is he interested in the world around him?

Energy: To what extent can he maintain a continuous high level of work activity?

Organizing and Planning: To what extent can he effectively organize and plan his work and the work of others?

Decision Making: To what extent can he make decisions of high quality, and how likely is he to make decisions when required?

Analytical Ability: To what extent can he recognize trends and reach meaningful conclusions from numerical data?

Selecting the Right Goals and Appraisal Program

Ideally, both the individual and his supervisor have a mutual agreement on (1) what his job is within the organization, (2) what performance is expected, (3) the method of measuring and evaluating performance, (4) realistic expectations for future career growth. Appraisal programs are designed to support and measure attainment of these mutual objectives, and they vary considerably between organizations. We have been surprised to see some corporations who reject the idea of formal, written goal setting and/or appraisal programs in favor of strengthened informal plans that appear to achieve desired results. Such efforts are rare and may in part be explained more by a dissatisfaction with previous formal programs, forms, or procedures than for informality as such.

Basic Techniques for Development of the Individual

The specific development needs of the appraisee having been determined by the appraisal, the decision that must now be made is which development techniques can be used to best advantage.

Although the specific development needs of any individual will vary greatly, they can be categorized into four general areas:

1. Need to increase knowledge and ability on specific duties in his present position, in order to improve current job performance.

2. Need to increase overall knowledge and ability within the general field in which he is working, in order to prepare for a position of greater responsibility within his field.

3. Need to develop executive ability, to broaden overall knowledge and understanding, in order to prepare for a general managerial position.

4. Need to further develop personal characteristics and attitudes, in order to gain more acceptance and influence as an individual.

Since goal setting and appraisal and development are an integrated, continuing process, it is better to direct the appraisee's efforts in self-development along specific lines that represent achievable subgoals. In this regard, management development is more a series of way stations rather than one ultimate station.

Such factors as age, potential, and ability must be considered also. A development program which does not have a good chance to succeed will lead to disillusionment and discouragement, rather than development.

Early Identification of Management Potential (EIMP)

Early identification of management potential is not especially new as an idea. A large utility company has had a system for this for at least ten years, long enough for the thinking behind it to have matured as the results of the program have emerged. The focus for early identification of management potential here has been the assessment center, where men and women are given a two- to three-day stint of testing and interviews and simulations. The assessment center has been a fruitful way of finding management talent among the craft ranks. A refining company's most important talent-spotting tool is an inventory of personal and career history derived from the backgrounds and experiences of its most successful managers of the past.

Training Methods for Manager Development

Training methods are thought of as the procedures or approaches by which a person responsible for training accomplishes the training job. It is recognized that there are many opportunities for guided experience that occur every day in the normal conduct of business. These opportunities can be used from day to day by the supervisor who recognizes their developmental potentialities. In addition, there are also opportunities that can be created by the supervisor who is conscious of the needs of his people and who feels responsible for their training and development.

A variety of methods are available for the training and development of employees. The choice of methods depends on the supervisor's estimate of the needs in his particular situation and on his judgment as to which method or methods will be most effective in filling these needs.

These methods can be divided roughly into two categories. The first category includes those things which are going on all the time as a part of the daily routine in every organization. These are called the *basic* methods. The second category includes those methods which can be started or stopped at the will or the organization, as it becomes necessary to supplement the basic methods. These are called *auxiliary* methods.

Basic methods.   These basic methods are not always recognized as a means for developing people. While their primary objective is to get the job done, they account for a large share of the training and development that takes place in any organization. Consequently, one of the important functions of the management development department is to help members of supervision throughout the company to appreciate the importance of these basic methods and to make effective use of them in the day-to-day training and development of their personnel.

Training by Example.   The example set by all members of supervision in their daily activities is observed, evaluated, and in many instances, imitated by people in the lower levels of the organization. Employees, whether they are in research, production, or sales, are particularly influenced by the example set by their immediate supervisor. Every supervisor uses this method whether he realizes it or not. For instance, a supervisor who is open-minded in his dealings with those he supervises will influence them by his example to use similar approaches in their dealing with others, or the supervisor who, by his statements and actions, indicates a strong regard for safety tends to create similar feelings in those around him. His attitude regarding disadvantaged employees is particularly influential.

Development by example goes on every day. It may lend support to other more formalized developmental activities, or it may tend to counteract their effect. It is believed that the supervisor who is conscious of the effects of this method will be most careful to set a good example himself and will insist that other members of management set a good example insofar as his people are concerned.

On-the-Job Contacts.   Every supervisor has many occasions in the course of getting the job done to talk with the individuals who report to him. The contacts involve such things as giving instructions, correcting errors, handling requests, and making plans for improving or changing some aspect of the job.

The supervisor who is aware of the developmental possibilities of daily contacts will help individuals to think through the situations and problems which prompt the contacts, and to arrive at their own decisions. This method of coaching on the job is used to help individuals become better equipped to cope with similar situations in the future.

Experience has shown that most development is accomplished by this method. The salesman, research chemist, or foreman gets help at a time when he recognizes his need for help and is able to try out immediately, in a real situation, what he has learned.

Regular Meetings.   In the normal conduct of business many meetings are held at various levels in an organization. Some are held on a regularly scheduled basis, and others are called as the need arises. These meetings deal with the many matters that are important to the success of the business such as cost, competition, quality, production, and personnel. In each of these meetings, there is a training opportunity.

Regular meetings, if properly used, help those who participate to develop a better understanding of the goals of the organization, a greater sense of responsibility for the success of the business, and a feeling of really being a part of the organization.

The above three methods are the hard core of on-the-job training. The nature and extent of a person's development depend on the way these methods are used.

Auxiliary methods.   Although the basic methods are used to accomplish a large part of the training job, they have certain limitations. The process tends to be a slow one in that specialized skills cannot be easily or quickly developed. Consequently, it is necessary to supplement the basic methods from time to time with auxiliary methods which are used to accelerate the training and developmental process.

Training Meetings.   Training meetings are held specifically for the purpose of imparting knowledge, improving skills, or developing understanding. Such meetings provide opportunities to present carefully prepared material so that all members of the group get the same story at the same time. They are also a means of bringing together and reconciling many different and conflicting points of view so that participants, through exposure to the ideas of others, have a chance to modify their attitudes. They also provide a setting in which managerial skills can be developed through discussion and practice.

The subjects for training meetings cover, over a period of time, a wide range of interests and needs. Some deal with general orientation subjects such as company history, benefit plans, and policies; others deal with many of the aspects of human relations such as the superior-subordinate relationship, the handling of personnel problems, and line communications; and still others deal with more specific management subjects such as job evaluation, work simplification, and cost control. The selection of the particular subjects for a meeting or series of meetings in a work unit is based on an analysis of the needs of the individuals employed in that unit.

In many instances, the leaders for these meetings are members of line management. In other instances, leadership for some of the more formal training meetings is provided by individuals qualified by experience or training, or by staff members who are assigned to the training function. A wide variety of training techniques and training aids are used in these meetings.

Individual Discussion.   This method of developing people applies when an individual has needs which are not characteristic of other members of a group. It is individual coaching in which supervisors check lists of duties and responsibilities which they cover at regular intervals with the individuals reporting to them. Or it may mean periodic talks about different aspects of the job on a planned basis. Another approach is based on periodic reviews of performance during which the supervisor and the individual concerned discuss ways of further developing talents and of correcting deficiencies. In addition, case problems are sometimes used as a basis for such individual discussions.

Special Assignments.   Special assignments, on either a full-time or a part-time basis, are often used in the regular course of business as a way of getting nonroutine or unusual jobs done. These assignments are opportunities for the development of the people selected.

The duties assigned take the form of special studies, liaison work, or service on special committees or task forces. Special studies involve such things as cost studies, market research, quality investigations, technical problems, and sales development. Liaison work includes such things as contacts between construction and production personnel regarding the tie-in of new facilities; contacts between technical, production, and sales people regarding process and product changes; and contacts with top management regarding the handling of special events. Service on special committees involves such things as developing improved procedures, conducting fund-raising drives, and planning sales conferences or trade exhibits.

This method of developing people is most effective when supervisors select individuals on the basis of developmental needs rather than on the basis of expediency. In addition, it is a means by which an organization can find out whether individuals have capabilities and potentialities beyond those required for their normal assignment.

Job Rotation. This method of development is a planned movement of people from one assignment to another. It involves lateral transfers and promotion within an organizational unit or transfers and promotion across organization lines. People are transferred to other assignments in research, production, or sales, or from line assignments to staff assignments. Individuals of recognized potential are moved from technical assignments to manufacturing or sales. Frequently, a whole series of possible moves is worked out in advance as part of the long-range developmental plans of an organization.

Job rotation permits individuals to gain experience in various phases of the business and, thus, broaden their perspective. It also provides them opportunities to learn from the coaching and example of many members of management.

Visits to Other Areas and Locations. The use of this method involves relieving an employee of the demands of his job temporarily and allowing him to visit other areas, laboratories, sales territories, or plant locations. Such visits permit the individual to observe how others cope with their problems, to learn firsthand the importance of functions other than his own, and to see how his job fits into the overall scheme.

Visits are made to other parts of a location, to other company locations, to customers' plants, or to the company's main offices. These visits may involve the transaction of some business, or they may be arranged solely for purposes of development. In either case, the selection of individuals for such visits is made on the basis of those who need and can benefit from the experience.

Professional Society Activities. The activities of various professional societies provide opportunities for developing people. Usually an individual is chosen to attend conferences or meetings of management or professional groups with a general training objective in mind. On other occasions, the objective is to get specific information on some subject covered at the meeting. Individuals are encouraged to take part in other aspects of professional society activities, such as serving on committees, presenting talks, and working on special projects.

Participation in professional society activities permits the individuals concerned to keep abreast of new developments, to obtain new ideas, and to establish worthwhile contacts. In addition, these activities provide new experiences in dealing with people and in developing organizational skills.

Correspondence and Extension Courses. Developmental opportunities are provided by correspondence courses, extension classes, or workshops, offered by schools, universities, and management organizations. This method depends on the desire and the initiative of individuals for self-improvement. The superior's role is one of encouraging his subordinates, as their needs become apparent, to take advantage of the many opportunities available.

In general, this method is used to fill in gaps in an individual's educational background, to keep him abreast of changing technology, to provide him with a background in a new field of endeavor, or to equip him to become expert in a specialized field.

Individual Study. This method of development involves the reading and study of literature and periodicals dealing with the various areas of interest to the organization. It takes place both on and off the job. The extent to which this method is used is mainly dependent upon the desire of the individual to improve himself.

Supervisors encourage those they supervise to take advantage of the opportunities afforded for self-development by routing to them special and routine reports, copies of company publications, business magazines, national bulletin services, articles of current interest, new books that are being added to the library, and copies of pertinent talks and speeches.   Another way in which supervisors encourage their people to read and study is by discussing with them ideas contained in articles and periodicals.

Members of supervision should be encouraged to make appropriate use of these eleven methods and to treat the development of their employees as an integral and important part of their daily activities.   The supervisor who indicates to his subordinates his real interest in their growth, and who devotes time to helping them develop, creates an atmosphere which is conducive to further growth and development.

Prescription—An Individual Development Plan for John Doe

The final statement of an individual's development plan is "one of a kind"—even as you would expect his medical record to be unique; so is his development plan.

The major elements of a plan are provided in the following example:

MANAGEMENT DEVELOPMENT PROGRAM

January 1970

NAME: John Doe
POSITION TITLE: Manager, Middletown Plant
MAJOR OPERATING UNIT: Special Electronic Gadgets
TARGET POSITION: Division General Manager
DEVELOPMENT PERIOD TO ATTAIN TARGET POSITION: 5 years

1. Evaluation of present experience

Areas of Strength	*Areas of Needed Experience*
Manufacturing	Marketing or Sales
Materials	Financial operations
Production engineering	
Community relations	

2. Evaluation of managerial capability

Areas of Strength	*Areas Needing Improvement*
Job knowledge	Written communication
Planning	Controlling costs
Developing subordinates	
Oral communication	

3. Recommended Five-year Program for Development
    a. Participation in the Executive Controls Program at Syracuse University in 1972
    b. Attend AMA Workshop Seminar on Business Correspondence in next six months
    c. In mid-1973, transfer to marketing as product manager. In addition to normal responsibilities in that position, assign to pricing committee
    d. In 1974, assign as manager, educational electronics department, or as an alternative, project manager on a key defense account

International Management Development

Multinational corporations have the additional needs of integrating management development efforts throughout their worldwide network.   This involves the sensitive and delicate task of spanning geography, nationalities, and cultures.

The continued growth and effectiveness of multinational companies require an international executive force that understands and is committed to their overall company objectives and management concepts. One way of achieving this aim is to bring field executives to headquarters to stimulate an exchange of viewpoints and management skills. The focus is then on how the company operates as a coherent international system rather than on what is done by each operation and staff unit.

Blacks in Management

For historical reasons, the black man, generally, has not seen an opportunity for himself in management. The result has been that the majority of talented Afro-Americans who have the ambition and means to attend college have tended to go into the "traditional areas," preaching and teaching.

In 1964 a leading sociologist wrote that at the creeping rate of change, nonwhites in the United States would not attain equal proportional representation among business managers and proprietors until 2750.

Six years later there is strong evidence that business has turned around and is now seriously seeking to identify and promote significant numbers of blacks into all levels of management, even the highest. Until this is done, American society will not be integrated. The role of training and management development is therefore significant in this transition period.

EXTERNAL DEVELOPMENT PROGRAMS

Many companies utilize external resources to augment their in-company development programs. The most valuable activities are offered by associations, consultants, and universities and colleges, many of whom have trained literally thousands of managers.

It is very difficult to keep informed about all the courses available on all subjects; so training departments frequently limit themselves to maintaining current data on a selective basis, viz., a given number of university programs of long duration, American Management Association calendar, National Industrial Conference Board meetings, and several frequently used consultants.

Comprehensive Listings of External Courses and Programs

There are several comprehensive listings available if one wishes to use them. For example, *Sales Management Magazine* provides its readers a Seminar Calendar. Fifty-one courses were offered by 18 organizations, consultants, associations, universities, or educational companies during a three-week period in October 1970 alone. Universities are another good source.

Programs in General Management

These are usually the major programs of the institutions that offer them. Since shared experience is a major resource of these courses, participants are chosen to produce as wide a representation as possible of functions and industries and thus to add depth to the course. The subject areas cover: management as a process, the tools of the manager, and the function of the manager in an enterprise or organization. The methods of teaching may vary in each course, but the overall objective is the same throughout: to give the manager a concept of, and a sense of, self-identification in the corporate environment.

The general management programs are divided into three sections by level of management: (1) programs exclusively for senior management; (2) programs for middle managers, for middle and senior managers, and for junior and middle managers; and (3) programs that are solely for junior managers. There are no hard rules in this breakdown because the level of an executive depends to a certain extent on the type and size of the organization for which he works.

Programs in Functional Management

For our purposes, functional management may be defined as the managerial process as it is applied and practiced in one of the main areas of management: production, finance, engineering, marketing, personnel, and similar areas. These programs provide knowledge and professional skills on specific jobs and often include training in the use of these skills. The primary purpose is to upgrade manager performance on the job.

Programs in this area change more rapidly than do general management programs since they incorporate much of the changes in functional technology and expertise.

University Self-study Courses

The majority of the professional population which uses the universities, consultants, and associations services is satisfied with the results. Others find that the standard classroom with its fixed schedule of meetings and assignments conflicts with job, family, and civic responsibilities. Fortunately there are programs of self-study available with texts and journals which put the student entirely on his own. He has guides through the material, audio-visual aids, and checks in his progress. Such programs are offered throughout the country. An example of one such proven program is the Self-Study System offered by the Massachusetts Institute of Technology.

Executive Development Programs in Universities

Programs of long duration (two weeks or more). The field of university-sponsored development programs has been growing steadily since 1945 when Harvard held its first Advanced Management Program. While some new programs have appeared recently, the majority have been in existence some ten to twenty years.

The universities usually provide several non-degree programs, matched to their faculties' capabilities and the general public's needs, ranging from one-day seminars to sixteen-week programs. A summary of such programs was prepared by National Industrial Conference Board in 1969. A sample of that report, illustrated in Figure 3, shows eleven of the fifty more well-known programs.

Several consulting firms provide detailed information regarding these courses which is invaluable in selecting the most appropriate courses for any one individual.

Foremost in the field is George R. Bricker, publisher of *Bricker's Directory of University-Sponsored Executive Development Programs,* who states,

> Selection of an appropriate program for a specific individual should depend on several factors: objectives of the company, objectives of the individual, background of the individual, amount of time available, seasonable limitations on time, and budget limitations.
> It is important that a nominee be aware of why he is being chosen, and what he is expected to gain from his attendance.

Bricker provides a complete guide to more than fifty management development courses offered in the United States and Canada. For each course, two to four pages of pertinent information is detailed, such as: program title, sponsoring organization, location dates and duration of current scheduled sessions, tuition costs plus room, meals, description of living quarters; participation, such as number in group, age range, position in organizations; faculty evaluation; official contact,

Figure 3. Executive development programs in universities. Summary description of courses. *(Studies in Personnel Policy no. 215, National Industrial Conference Board, Inc.)*

Name, sponsor, and address	Duration	Approximate starting date	Established	Fee	Size of group	Accommodations
Executive Development Conference College of Business and Public Administration The University of Arizona Tucson, Ariz. 85721	2 weeks	Fall (November)	1965	$600, includes tuition, materials, room and board	15–20	Desert Willow Ranch in Tucson, single room; seminars conducted at Ranch
The Executive Program Graduate School of Business Administration 350 Barrows Hall University of California Berkeley, Calif. 94720	4 weeks	(Twice a year) Spring (April or May) Fall (October)	1959	$1,800, includes tuition, materials, room and board	35	Hotel Durant, single room; seminars conducted in Barrows Hall
Management Programs Graduate School of Industrial Administration Carnegie-Mellon University Schenley Park Pittsburgh, Pa. 15213	9 weeks	Spring (February)	1954	$2,700, includes most meals and $550–$880, depending upon type of room selected	45–50	Webster Hall, single room; seminars conducted in The Graduate School of Industrial Administration
Management Development Seminar Industrial Relations Center University of Chicago 1225 E. 60th St. Chicago, Ill. 60637	3 weeks	Summer (July)	1956	$700, tuition and materials only	45	Stanley Hotel, Estes Park, Colorado; seminars conducted in Stanley Hotel
Executive Program in Business Administration Uris Hall—Room 807 Graduate School of Business Columbia University New York, N.Y. 10027	6 weeks	(Three times a year) May June August	1952	$2,500, includes tuition, materials, room and board	60–90	Arden House, Ramapo Mountains, double room; seminars conducted in Arden House
Executive Development Program Graduate School of Business and Public Administration	6 weeks	Summer (June)	1953	$2,200, includes tuition, materials, room and board	75–85	Balch Hall, single room; seminars conducted in Malott Hall

Program	Length	Time	Year started	Cost	Enrollment	Facilities
519 Malott Hall Cornell University Ithaca, N.Y. 14850						
Institute of Modern Management College of Business Administration University of Denver Denver, Colo. 80210	3 weeks	Summer (June)	1965	$1,350, includes tuition, books, meals, and housing	25	Dormitory near classrooms, seminars conducted in the College of Business Administration Building
Advanced Management Program Graduate School of Business Administration Emory University Atlanta, Ga. 30322	6 weeks	Winter (January)	1957	$2,200, includes tuition, materials, room and board	30–35	The Cloister, Sea Island, double room; seminars conducted at the Cloister
Management Development Program Graduate School of Business Administration Emory University Atlanta, Ga. 30322	2 weeks (with one month between weeks)	(Twice a year) Spring and fall	1964	$600, includes tuition, materials, room and board	35	Ida Cason Callaway Gardens, Pine Mountain, double room; seminars conducted at Ida Cason Callaway Gardens
Management Development Conference Management Center Matherly Hall University of Florida Gainesville, Fla. 32601	2 weeks	Spring (May)	1959	$300, includes tuition, materials, and room, $50 extra for single room	20	Ramada Inn, double room; seminars conducted at Ramada Inn
Executive Development Program Department of Management Graduate School of Business Administration The University of Georgia Athens, Ga. 30601	3 weeks	Summer (August)	1953	$900, includes tuition, materials, room and board	15–30	Center for Continuing Education, single room; seminars conducted in Center

(This display is for illustrative purposes only. The sponsor of each course should be contacted for up-to-date information regarding his offering.)

including names, locations; subject matter in detail; methods of instruction in detail; special features, such as health program, membership privileges; recommendation for whom the program is most suited.

Programs of short duration.   They are part of the continuing education programs of major universities.   For the most part, they are not in residence, which allows the busy executive to schedule a day or more away from the office without seriously disrupting his business schedule.   Universities such as Harvard and Columbia supplement their public programs with special programs for associate companies, i.e., those who contribute to the financial support of the university at large and who are given the opportunity to share in the knowledge and skills created by their contributions.

Consultants

For locating consultants, many practitioners use *AMA Directory of Consultants* (1970); all American Management Association members known or believed to be full-time consultants were invited by letter to submit data on the nature of their consulting services.   A total of 921 consulting organizations responded and are listed in this edition.   The directory, like all others, does not claim to provide an exhaustive list to the needy client.

Also there are quite a number of consultants, CPA firms in particular, who in consideration of professional codes in certain fields such as public accounting and law are restricted from soliciting business or listing names.   Other good sources are *Consultants & Consulting Organizations* and *Who's Who in Consulting*, Cornell University Graduate School of Business & Public Administration.   Their references include facts about 2,612 firms and individuals conducting consultation services.

BEHAVIORAL SCIENCE APPLICATIONS

We are in the midst of a major change in our culture.   If one agrees with Marshall McLuhan that, "We must understand that a totally new society is coming into being, one that rejects *all* our old values, conditioned responses, attitudes, and institutions," then we must conclude that traditional management training and development programs and practitioners are limited in their capacity to provide the leadership required of them in this period of stress and turmoil.

Dramatic, continual social changes, ranging from technological improvements to new attitudes, have added to the complexity of every type of human system— families, schools, businesses, service organizations, churches, industry, government—and new personal and organizational problems are constantly being created.

Individuals in every role and activity are asking for help both in understanding and relating to others and in knowing and expressing themselves.   Every system in our society needs more honesty and openness in work relationships and better communication between people.   On the organizational scale, the problems of human relationships as they affect productivity for the individual and for the organization are massive and complex.

Fortunately, the behavioral sciences are providing resources—knowledge, skills, and the people competent to utilize them—to enable the traditional practitioner to engage in a continual program of self-evaluation to reexamine values and activities while promoting flexibility to select among new options and alternatives.

Organizational Development—how it differs from management development

Most management development activities (skills inventory, manpower planning, career pathing, subject matter training, human relations training, etc.) have all made valuable contributions to developing organization effectiveness.   However, they have been concerned mainly with the individual—developing the manager. Organization development includes these activities but focuses primarily on developing the work group and then attempts to link up all the subgroups toward common organization goals.

Organization development avoids the risks of sending a manager off to a seminar to learn a different, more effective way of managing only to return to a culture that has not had the benefit of his experience and often is resistant to change. As a result, he becomes frustrated, gives up, and becomes assimilated back into the old cultural norms. Such frustration with the organization climate is often characterized by such comments as, "my boss is the one that needs this training" or "this is great but in my company they say, 'we don't do things here that way'."

Problems Organization Development Attempts to Solve

Conflict of Goals. The current managerial goals may not be relevant to today's realities or to employees' goals. They may be based upon past practices or objectives which do not make sense for one's area of responsibility. Goals which are imposed gain little acceptance or commitment.

Poor Communications. There may be blockage or distortion at any level. Factual data necessary to make good business decisions may be lacking, and the quality of the data (people do not really say what they mean) may be poor. An open, problem-solving climate does not exist—real problems are ignored or kept hidden.

Suppressed Conflict. There may be a failure to confront conflict in the organization by denying its existence, or suppressing it. Conflict is not managed.

Poor Teamwork. Work groups may operate with a philosophy of competition: "every man for himself." Individuals in a work group have not developed mutual trust.

Destructive Competition. Interdependent groups (those which need each other to function effectively) have developed distrust, lack of coordination, conflicting goals, etc.

Faulty Decision Making. Decisions are based upon the authority of role or status rather than the authority of knowledge or competence. Decision making is not located close to informational sources.

Slow Response to Change. The organization is rigid and finds it difficult to change to meet a constantly shifting business and social environment. Changes in the organization are imposed, poorly planned, unrelated to objectives, etc.

Lack of Motivation. The reward system is such that it does not recognize that both the achievement of objectives (profits) and the growth of people are essential. Individuals are not positively motivated toward organizational goals; they are not committed.

MANAGEMENT RESOURCE PLANNING

While management development is proceeding on essentially an individual basis within a system, each company requires information on the total management development effort and the total results achieved. From this broad and impersonal view the issue is not whether Jones or Smith gets the job but that the one who gets the job is best qualified.

A critical responsibility therefore of a management development department is to maintain a "scorecard" of the needs of the company and the progress being made, over time, to develop managers capable of meeting those needs. The manner with which this information is secured from operating units, organized, and communicated to top management must be compatible with the style of management within the company.   The results should provide involved officials with an overall summary of management resources, both current and potential throughout the company.   The specific data developed varies so much between companies that it is hard to generalize.   The most significant factor is rate of growth—a mature company requires less assurance of strength in depth than one which plans to double its business in ten years.

Several major categories of information are usually included in a management resource planning effort.   They are:

1. The individual employee summary report
2. Replacement charts for organizations
3. Management development goals, and action plans for operating and staff units or departments or divisions
4. A consolidated organization and manpower plan audit

STEWARDSHIP
PERFORMANCE AND POTENTIAL

NAME HEIL, DONALD   DEGREE (S) bs/chemE   COMPANY   ALBA

POSITION Manager, Fiber Planning   LOCATION Charlotte

JOB LEVEL ___7___   AGE 34   YEARS OF SERVICE 8   YEARS/MONTHS PRESENT POSITION 6 months

I. PERFORMANCE RATING

DESCRIPTION	1969 RATING		1968 RATING	
OUTSTANDING — Extraordinary and exceptional accomplishments	1	BLUE	1	BLUE
VERY GOOD — Well above average results achieved	2 X	BLUE	2 X	BLUE
AVERAGE—SATISFACTORY—Accomplished all basic requirements	3	YELLOW	3	YELLOW
BELOW AVERAGE—Did not fully accomplish basic requirements	4	YELLOW	4	YELLOW
UNSATISFACTORY— Inadequate or marginal accomplishments	5	RED	5	RED

If occupied present position less than six months, no rating is required.
However, give previous position and rating here:

POSITION	COMPANY			

II. POTENTIALITY FORECAST
*INDICATES PLANNED MOVES   INCLUDE ANY LATERAL TRANSFERS FOR CAREER DEVELOPMENT

READINESS	IN PRESENT COMPANY		OUTSIDE PRESENT COMPANY		RATING
	POSITION	LEVEL	POSITION	LEVEL	
READY NOW TO 1 YEAR	Dir Customer Svc	9	Mgr Mkt Plan Intl	8	GREEN
WITHIN 3 YEARS	Dir Sales	10			BLUE
LONG RANGE	VP Marketing	15			YELLOW
REACHED HIS PEAK					RED

MANPOWER PLANNING COMMENTS Don is visable successor to Dir Customer Service. Assignments in 1969 and 1970 designed to broaden overall scope and knowledge of business. Plan to transfer to International Division as Manager Market Planning in second quarter 1971.

III. REPLACEMENTS FOR THIS POSITION — READY WITHIN 3 YEARS
+INDICATES PLANNED MOVES

NAME	READINESS	POSITION	LOCATION
R. LICATA	NOW	New Product Manager	NYO
J. MATTIMORE	2 years	Supv Ind Service	Char

APPRAISER M. Warren		APPROVED R. Hagen	DATE 9/2/70
TITLE Dir Mktg Plng	DATE 9/1/70	APPROVED G. Walker	DATE 9/5/70

Figure 4.   An individual employee summary report on performance and potential.

Individual Employee Summary Report on Performance and Potential

In Figure 4, on one piece of paper, we attempt to capture the essential information about an employee that permits those with limited knowledge and exposure to evaluate him as a corporate resource and to give him appropriate consideration in the overall manpower planning activity. It also reports the information given him about his own performance and the "individual action development plan" to which he and his manager are committed.

Occasionally, a manager will discuss potentiality with an employee, being careful to avoid creating unwarranted expectations or appearing to make promises. Identification of career goals is usually a collaborative effort as is the individual action development plan.

Replacement Chart

Management should know who is available and qualified within the company to replace the incumbent of every key position. Some firms go to the effort of describing the "backups" for every position in the company.

INDIVIDUAL ACTION DEVELOPMENT PLANS

NAME HEIL, Donald   TITLE Mgr, Fiber Planning

DEVELOPMENT ACTIVITY	DESCRIPTION NEED AREA OR DEVELOPMENT OBJECTIVE	RESPONSIBILITY	TARGET DATE
1. JOB ROTATION			
2. CORPORATE SEMINAR-WORKSHOP SERIES	General Management Seminar 2 weeks	M. Warren	9/71
3. COMPANY COURSES	1. Accounting & Finance for Non-Financial Managers	self	12/70
	2. Appraisal Techniques	self	2/71
4. OUTSIDE COURSES	Strategic Long Term Planning Boston Consulting Group	M. O'Neill functional supervisor	6/71
5. COUNSELING BY a. SUPERVISOR	to improve delegation	M. Warren	cont'g
b. OUTSIDE COUNSELOR	Psychological Consultant on Career Development	self	10/70
6. OTHER PROGRAMS			

Primary Career Goal: Vice President Marketing
Alternate Career Goal: Director Marketing Planning

PREPARED BY M. Warren 9/1/70 Date	REVIEWED with EMPLOYEE 9/2/70 Date	APPROVED R. Hagen 9/3/70 APPROVED G. Walker 9/5/70

Figure 4.   An individual employee summary report on performance and potential.   (continued)

The replacement chart is to some valuable only for the experience and learning associated with preparing it because "as soon as it is prepared, it is out of date." Other managements have dispensed with the replacement chart and work instead with a succession chart on a continuing, updated basis. Their theory is that management succession planning is a continuous activity and should be proactive, i.e., making things happen by planning, rather than being reactive, i.e., what can we do if Bud gets hit by a beer truck?

Management Development Goals and Action Plans

If one endorses the concept of planning as a way of making things happen and if there is no fear of surfacing your problems, then by all means encourage the use of written goals and action plans needed to attain excellence in management development.

The increasing number of managements who are successful in goal setting, action planning, measurement, and feedback activities describe their efforts somewhat along the lines of the following example:

MANAGEMENT DEVELOPMENT PLANS AND OBJECTIVES

We list here the major or critical management development tasks which the division faces in the next 12 to 18 months, describing also the action plan which will be implemented to meet each objective.

Objective	*Action Plan*
1. Identify potential division controller, two plant accounting managers, and manager, financial analysis, all to be ready by Sept. 16, 1972.	1. Identify potential candidate from within the division or elsewhere in the company. Evaluate and, where appropriate, modify the organization and job structures to enhance individual development and preparedness.
2. Make appropriate changes by way of departmental combinations, new reporting relationships, etc., which will expand and improve marketing planning activities.	2. Evaluate organization structures and relationships in and between division staff and profit center marketing units and develop appropriate revisions by third quarter, 1971.

EVALUATION AND MEASUREMENT OF THE MANAGEMENT DEVELOPMENT FUNCTION

If, after all, we have said that management development is a line manager's function and not just another personnel department program, then after all the appraisal interviews are completed, the forms filled out, and the reports presented to top management, each manager makes his own personal accounting regarding the worthwhileness of the effort involved and the results. This is usually done informally, sometimes alone, mostly in conversations with associates.

There is a need for each manager to be objective about his attitudes and overall performance if the total development effort is to have relevance and meaning to him, his employees, and the organization. Each management development department should provide its management assistance in this effort through both formal and informal measuring techniques.

Informal Method of Measurement—The Self-Audit of Management Development

Any self-audit helps the manager ask himself the tough questions so that he can bring reality and a greater measure of success to his efforts.

1. Of all the jobs under my direction, how many are critical to the success of the company, that is, important in meeting our major business objectives in both the short and long term? Which are they? How many of these *key jobs* can I afford to have "blocked" by qualified yet nonpromotable people? Who agrees with me? What influence does this have on the rest of our organization?

2. Do I hold myself or someone else responsible for having qualified *replacements* for each one of these jobs? Does he know and accept this? Is he accomplishing it? Am I responsible for developing candidates for my job? (Do I know why not?)

3. Who are the key *high-potential* men we are counting on to run this company both now and in the future? Who selected them? What criteria were used? Do I agree? Is there general agreement on their selection? Does senior management agree? Do the facts justify the selection? Will there always be someone better qualified?

4. Are we making real progress in our affirmative action programs for *minority employees?* Are we "playing the number game," i.e., just staying ahead of criticism? Is organization racism a reality, is key management taking risks to meet objectives, or are we "playing it safe"? Am I doing anything significant personally? How soon should we have a black executive? How many women are in management above first-line supervisory levels? What will really be different next year?

A Formal Method of Measurement—The Organization and Management Development Audit

The checklist shown in Figure 5 is a demanding test of the effectiveness of a total system of development. It is directly related to measuring performance against the management development objectives outlined under Management Development Plans and Objectives. This final exercise points out the need for using evaluation to bring goal setting and activity full circle to face the original management development imperatives established, viz:

Establishing an inventory
Improving on-the-job performance
Developing a pool of talent
Planning future manpower needs

A Concluding Rationale for Management Development

Management's current performance.   The assurance that our people perform well in their current jobs is a prerequisite to profitable operations. Periodic review is necessary since requirements for satisfactory performance change with changes in our business.

Managerial inventory.   We need to have sufficient management in depth to maintain a succession of management to operate the business. We should have a continuing capability for accurately evaluating people and their development needs before we spend valuable time and money in their training and career development. Helping to develop confidence in another manager's ratings is essential to planning interdivisional placements that make the best use of people as a corporate resource.

Management and organization development.   We require an efficient, viable process that will (1) accelerate the career development of all managers according

```
AN ORGANIZATION & MANAGEMENT DEVELOPMENT
                    AUDIT
```

division Plastics period covered Jan - Dec 1970 general manager S. Barker	
	rate performance against expectations enter ✓ and comments below
I MANAGEMENT INVENTORY	below ✓ meets exceeds

such matters as:
 	
o   accurate evaluation of individual
     manager - performance/potential
 	
o   degree to which has management strength
     in depth, i.e., replacements are avail-
     able and qualified to fill key jobs both
     within Company and within Corporation
	1. Appraisal system training has been
	only moderately successful resulting in
	lack of acceptance of both performance
	and potential ratings.
	
	2. Replacements are not available
	until 1972 for 3 plant controllers.

II MANAGEMENT PERFORMANCE	✓
such matters as: o has well qualified people in key jobs o achieves desired performance levels in all key jobs o avoids managerial & technical obsolesence	1. All managers in key positions continue to exceed objectives 2. Computer facilities are being fully utilized following recent training meetings & simulations.
III MANAGEMENT DEVELOPMENT	✓

such matters as:
 	
o   key employee groups are well defined &
     development accelerated viz Outstanding
     Potential and General Managers
 	
o   minority employee development is given
     priority
 	
o   individual Action Development Plans are
     well-planned and completed
	1. This is the first division to
	promote a black to profit center
	general manager
	
	2. Seventeen (17) hi potentials for
	general management are now on fast
	track individual development plans

IV ORGANIZATION & MANPOWER PLANNING	✓

such matters as:
 	
o   organization structure well-suited to
     meet business requirements
 	
o   key management turnover generally
     limited to planned actions
 	
o   management climate is favorable and
     supports attainment of objectives
	1. Recent attitude surveys among
	technical center employees shows
	significant improvement in six
	factors related to confidence in
	management
	
	2. Resignation of a Personnel Manager
	and two District Sales Supervisors
	with high potential

prepared by:
    W. Farnam   1/15/71
	Approved:
	    W. White 1/20/71

Figure 5.   An organization and management development audit.

to organization need and their ability, with emphasis on those with high potential;
(2) develop a corporate climate that encourages individual and group efforts and
rewards achievement in this area; (3) maintain good communications among all
levels of personnel to keep the system healthy; and (4) accelerate the development
of minority group members into middle and upper management.

   Organization and manpower planning.   By planning, we improve our chances
of having the right numbers and quality of people in place to achieve the objectives
of our long-range business plans.

BIBLIOGRAPHY

Argyris, Chris: *Interpersonal Competence and Organizational Effectiveness,* Richard D. Irwin,
   Inc., Homewood, Ill., 1962.
Beckhard, Richard: *Organization Development: Strategies and Models,* Addison-Wesley
   Publishing Company, Inc., Reading, Mass., 1969.

Bennis, Warren G.: *Organization Development: Its Nature, Origins and Prospects,* Addison-Wesley Publishing Company, Inc., Reading, Mass., 1969.

Bienvenu, Bernard J.: *New Priorities in Training—A Guide for Industry,* American Management Association, New York, 1969.

Blake, R. R., and Jane S. Mouton: *Building a Dynamic Corporation through Grid Organization Development,* Addison-Wesley Publishing Company, Inc., Reading, Mass., 1969.

———— and ————: *Corporate Excellence Diagnosis,* Scientific Methods, Inc., Houston, 1968.

———— and ————: *Corporate Excellence through Grid Organization Development,* Gulf Publishing Company, Houston, 1968.

———— and ————: *The Managerial Grid,* Gulf Publishing Company, Houston, 1964.

Bradford, Leland P. (ed.): *Group Development,* NTL Institute for Applied Behavioral Science, Washington, 1961.

Campbell, J. P., M. D. Dunnette, E. E. Lawler, and K. E. Weick: *Managerial Behavior, Performance and Effectiveness,* McGraw-Hill Book Company, New York, 1970

Craig, Robert L., and Lester R. Bittell (eds.): *Training and Development Handbook,* McGraw-Hill Book Company, New York, 1967.

Drucker, Peter F.: *The Effective Executive,* Harper & Row, Publishers, Incorporated, New York, 1967.

————: *Preparing Tomorrow's Business Leaders Today,* Prentice-Hall, Inc., Englewood Cliffs, N.J., 1969.

Glaser, Barney G. (ed.): *Organizational Careers–A Sourcebook for Theory,* Aldine Publishing Company, Chicago, 1968.

Haas, Frederick C.: *Executive Obsolescence,* American Management Association, New York, 1968.

Harris, Thomas A.: *I'm O.K.—You're O.K.,* Harper & Row, Publishers, Incorporated, New York, 1967.

Harvard Business Review, "Executive Development Series—Part I" (reprint, bound), Cambridge, Mass., 1964.

————, "Executive Development Series—Part II" (reprint, bound), Cambridge, Mass., 1967.

————, "Organizational Development Series—Part I" (reprint, bound), Cambridge, Mass., 1966.

————, "Organizational Development Series—Part II" (reprint, bound), Cambridge, Mass., 1969.

House, Robert J.: *Management Development: Design, Evaluation and Implementation,* The University of Michigan, Ann Arbor, 1967.

Kellogg, Marion S.: *What To Do about Performance Appraisal,* American Management Association, New York, 1965.

————: *When Man and Manager Talk . . . A Casebook,* Gulf Publishing Company, Houston, 1969.

Lawrence, Paul R., and Jay W. Lorsch: *Developing Organizations: Diagnosis and Action,* Addison-Wesley Publishing Company, Inc., Reading, Mass., 1969.

Likert, Rensis: *The Human Organization: Its Management and Value,* McGraw-Hill Book Company, New York, 1967.

————: *New Patterns of Management,* McGraw-Hill Book Company, New York, 1961.

Maier, Norman R. F.: *The Appraisal Interview,* John Wiley & Sons, Inc., New York, 1958.

Maslow, Abraham H.: *Eupsychian Management,* The Dorsey Press, Homewood, Ill., 1965.

McClelland, David C.: *The Achieving Society,* D. Van Nostrand Company, Inc., Princeton, N.J., 1961.

McNulty, Nancy G.: *Training Managers—The International Guide,* Harper & Row, Publishers, Incorporated, 1969.

Mesics, Emil A.: *Education and Training for Effective Manpower Utilization,* New York State School of Industrial and Labor Relations, Cornell University, Ithaca, N.Y., 1969.

Morgan, John S.: *Practical Guide to Conference Leadership,* McGraw-Hill Book Company, New York, 1966.

Moore, Larry F.: *Guidelines for Manpower Managers—A Selected Annotated Bibliography,* University of British Columbia, Vancouver, Canada, 1969.

Morrison, Edward J.: *Developing Computer-based Employee Information Systems,* American Management Association, New York, 1969.

National Industrial Conference Board: "Research Report—Executive Development Programs in Universities," Studies in Personnel Policy, no. 215, National Industrial Conference Board, Inc., New York, 1969.

———: "Research Report—Developing Managerial Competence: Changing Concepts, Emerging Practices," Studies in Personnel Policy, no. 189, National Industrial Conference Board, Inc., New York, 1964.

NTL Institute for Applied Behavioral Science: *Reading Book—Laboratories in Human Relations Training,* NTL Institute for Applied Behavioral Science, Washington, 1969.

Odiorne, George S.: *Management by Objectives,* Pitman Publishing Corporation, New York, 1965.

Reeves, Elton T.: *Management Development for the Line Manager,* American Management Association, New York, 1969.

Rowland, Virgil K.: *Evaluating and Improving Managerial Performance,* McGraw-Hill Book Company, New York, 1970.

Rush, Harold M. F.: *Behavioral Science—Concepts and Management Application,* National Industrial Conference Board, New York, 1969.

Schein, Edgar H.: *Process Consultation: Its Role in Organization,* Addison-Wesley Publishing Company, Inc., Reading, Mass., 1969.

Tracey, William R.: *Evaluating Training and Development Systems,* American Management Association, New York, 1968.

Vetter, Eric W.: *Manpower Planning for High Talent Personnel,* The University of Michigan, Ann Arbor, 1967.

Wickert, F. R., and D. E. McFarland: *Measuring Executive Effectiveness,* Meredith Publishing Company, Des Moines, 1967.

Individual Reprints—Journal Articles

Argyris, Chris: "Interpersonal Barriers to Decision Making," *Harvard Business Review,* 44(2): 84–97, March–April, 1966.

Beckhard, Richard: "The Confrontation Meeting," *Harvard Business Review,* 45(2): 149–155, March–April, 1967.

Fritz, Roger J.: "Management Development Is Your Responsibility," *Personnel Journal,* December, 1968, pp. 857–861.

Glasner, Daniel M.: "Why Management Development Goes Wrong: Five Reasons," *Personnel Journal,* September, 1968, pp. 655–658.

Herzberg, Frederick: "One More Time: How Do You Motivate Employees?" *Harvard Business Review,* 46(1): 53–62, January–February, 1968.

Levinson, Harry: "Who Is to Blame for Maladaptive Managers?" *Harvard Business Review,* 43(6): 143–159, November–December, 1965.

Tannenbaum, Robert, and Sheldon A. Davis: "Values, Man and Organizations," *Industrial Management Review,* 10(2): 67–86, Winter, 1969.

chapter 23

Orientation of New Employees

JOAN E. HOLLAND *Assistant Personnel Director, Lenox Hill Hospital, New York, New York*
THEODORE P. CURTIS *Manager—Employee Services, McGraw-Hill, Inc., New York, New York*

Orientation concerns itself with the introduction of new employees to their company, to their specific jobs and departments, and in some instances to their community. Orientation of all new employees is a must. The questions to be answered are: Who will orient the new employee? Management? Co-worker? Should it be a planned program? Why? Why not? There are two parties who have a high stake in the success of the orientation program: the new employee, who wants to learn company policies and practices, who needs to know his surroundings, and who hopes to grow in his job; and management, whose great hopes for the newcomer coincide with those of the new employee. To achieve these aims the company program, designed for him and his family, must be communicated at the right time and in the right manner.

Most companies realize that first impressions of new employees affect future job satisfaction, competence, and company loyalty. Businesses make investments of time and money in new employees and therefore want to obtain his best efforts on the job, his greatest level of efficiency in the shortest period of time, as well as his loyalty and respect. An orientation program is a critical factor in shaping the work attitude. The attitudes formed in the early days on the job tend to persist and are not easily changed.

WHAT IS GAINED FROM A RELIABLE ORIENTATION PROGRAM

A reliable orientation is achieved with a planned program involving management, recruitment, selection, and line personnel in a large company and anyone responsible for these functions in a small company. The quality of the orientation program will be reflected in the personal appearance of the employees, the degree of courtesy they show one another, and their general decorum and work performance.

The failure to properly introduce a new employee to his work situation and company policies can turn a worker with high ambition into a routine haphazard worker with low morale.   When a new employee is thrown in with a group of fellow workers to learn by trial and error, it can cause embarrassment and be discouraging to him.

A *planned orientation program* has the advantages of:
1. Making prudent use of company time
2. Proper employee induction into the company
3. Logical and natural approach to orienting a new employee

Company's Prudent Use of Its Time

The newcomer is the center of the plan.   Around him revolves the program.   The recruitor knows, for example, what is most important to the candidate: the company's growth pattern, product development, locations, financial responsibility, opportunities for growth, facilities—information developed for the recruitor's use as the circumstances demand it.   There is some overlapping between each stage from recruiting to selection and orientation.   What the recruitor gives the candidate may be picked up and further developed by the line manager or by the personnel specialist during the planned orientation.   Once the candidate accepts the line manager's offer of employment, his manager briefs him on what he will get from the orientation session.

In most cases, if properly briefed, the new employee looks forward to this program with pleasant anticipation.   This is the time for him to really get to know about the company and its policies and discuss questions leisurely in some depth.   The planned program fits in with the plans of the line manager.   He is relieved of being required to put on a professional presentation, but he is not relieved of the responsibility of being able to cope with questions arising out of the orientation program. The program is an efficient, effective method to give a good input to the new employee in terms of information and attitude development.   It is planned as a tool of management, whose interests go beyond the immediate orienting of the new employee.

Proper Induction

A planned program enables the company to teach and reteach the new employee what he wants to know in easy units, in an inspiring manner, in an order according to his needs.   It gives the newcomer a chance to see the company as it really is.

All employees need orientation.   The ideal orientation program gives each new employee confidence and pride in himself and the company he is working for.   It makes him feel part of the company team.

Co-workers will orient newcomers with or without an orientation program.   If the newcomer has the benefit of getting the facts firsthand, he has a much better chance of getting his facts right.   A co-worker's view and understanding of his company varies from one co-worker to another.   Some co-workers can give the facts straight and lend credence to all that the newcomer may have learned at an orientation session.   Others may have grievances and give a less favorable picture of the company.   Such information may be harmful to a new employee's attitude, especially if the company fails to present a reliable orientation program.   In the case of multilocation companies, it makes sense to coordinate orientation among all locations through one person to assure a consistent, effective presentation to all new employees of the company.

Logical and Normal Approach

By conducting a planned program, the company adopts a logical and normal approach to welcome the person to the organization.   It displays a sense of perception about human relations. Every human being expects to be treated in a normal, courteous way. Through a formal program the company breathes life into itself and becomes a real thing—the host greeting and welcoming his guest. The company puts the new employee at ease by furnishing him with the desired information that is of immediate interest to him about his new surroundings. This is good common sense, good employee relations, and good for the company image. An employee's feeling toward his company is of primary importance to him and to the organization, from the very beginning and throughout his career. The company fulfills its objective by giving the new employee the opportunity to have a good start. Giving the new employee a sense of his own importance makes him a confident member of the organization, who knows where he is, why, and where he is going.

HOW IS AN ORIENTATION PROGRAM DEVELOPED

When management has been convinced that orientation of new employees is inevitable and that it is wise for a company to protect its investment in employee benefits and in the new employee himself, the natural conclusion is for the company to orient its own new employees. The first step has been taken toward developing a program. The need for the program is evident.

The second step is to establish the objectives. It is necessary to decide what the orientation program should do for the employee and the company. Objectives are based on the reasons why a program is needed.

The following is a typical list of objectives:

1. To welcome the new employee, relieve his anxieties, and make him feel at home

2. To develop a rapport between the company and the new employee and make him feel part of the organization as quickly as possible

3. To inspire the new employee with a good attitude toward the company and his job

4. To acquaint new employees with company goals, history, management, traditions, policies, departments, divisions, products, and physical layouts

5. To communicate to new employees what is expected of them, their responsibilities, and how they should handle themselves

6. To present the basic information the employee wants to know: rules and regulations, benefits, payday, procedures, and general practices

7. To encourage the new employee to have an inquiring mind, show him how to learn, and assist him toward a disciplined effort in developing additional knowledge

8. To provide basic skills, terms, and ideas of the business world and help the new employee in human relations

The new employee seeks a complete knowledge of the conditions of his employment, the general rules of conduct he must abide by, and the facilities being provided for him. He strives for a thorough knowledge of the job and wants to know exactly how it is done, when it is done, why it is done, and the established standards of performance expected of him. He also seeks an opportunity to discuss his interests and aspirations, his background and attitudes so that the company can get to know him.

HOW OBJECTIVES ARE DETERMINED

Objectives of an orientation program are determined by the goals of management and the company and the needs of the company as well as the needs of the individual employees. This can be done through a committee of management and employees, through surveys, informal interviews, conferences, and a suggestion system.

The feedback provided by employee evaluations, comments, grapevine, and exit interviews are very helpful. Just plain common sense and keeping one's eyes and ears open can provide an enormous amount of insight into the company situation.

STEPS IN PLANNING AN ORIENTATION PROGRAM

With management's backing, planning an orientation program is fun and exciting. Keep in mind your objectives and the scope to be covered. Visit other orientation programs and see what is done. Involve personnel specialists because it is their job to be completely familiar with policies, rules and regulations, and benefits. They make the final decisions and are able to answer questions. They should develop the employee manual and be on hand to answer any questions. Meeting and relating to a member of the personnel staff provides an open road for a two-way communication between the employee and the company. Involve line managers or supervisors. They work closely with new employees and see more of them than anyone else. They should be familiar with the general orientation and job instruction training.

The initial introduction to the department setup and work atmosphere will probably have the most impact on the attitudes of the new employee. The general orientation may be excellent, but if the job orientation is handled shabbily, a credibility gap will be created. Since top management seems remote to new employees as well as to old ones, there is a general feeling that top men live in ivory towers and make decisions without any consideration for the needs and wants of the employee. An opportunity to meet, see, and talk to a top member of the team can create better rapport. At one company a member of administration attends the general orientation and greets each new employee personally. Such a meeting gives management an opportunity to become acquainted with the type of individual who is supplying the basic support of the company.

Decide What Is to Be Covered in Orientation Content

1. Build company identification
2. Help employees to understand themselves and others
3. Lessen anxieties and increase learning

To do this include what the new employees want and need to know. From the company point of view, include:

1. The objectives and philosophy of the organization
2. An explanation of the organization, the levels of authority, and how they interrelate
3. A brief history of the organization
4. What you expect of the new employee: attitude, reliability, initiative and emotional maturity, personal appearance
5. Job functions and responsibilities
6. Rules and regulations, policies and procedures
7. Why the organization needs the new employee
8. City, state, and federal laws, if applicable
9. Functions of management
10. Telephone techniques

From the new employee's point of view, include:

1. A welcome
2. Introduction to the department and fellow workers
3. General office practice and business etiquette
4. Skill training
5. Job responsibilities

6. Probation and performance evaluation
7. Promotional opportunities
8. Conditions of employment: punctuality, attendance, conduct, hours of work, overtime, termination
9. Pay procedures
10. Benefits: salary, job security, insurance, recreational facilities, employee activities, rest periods, holidays, vacation, sick time, leave of absence, tuition refund, pension
11. Safety and fire prevention
12. Personnel policies
13. Techniques for learning
14. Encouragement

To Attain Your Objectives

The most desirable approach is to plan what actions are required and the order in which each action should be taken. First, analyze company policies and practices, then decide on checklist contents, script content, and visual aids. Select the person who will conduct the orientation meeting.

ANALYZE COMPANY POLICIES

Look for the key topics which should be in an orientation program. Consider the company policies and practices, facilities and surroundings. The manager's manual, management policy releases, and the employee handbook are excellent sources. Once a list of items is developed, consult anyone who has a functional interest in new employees: personnel relations, top management, line management, safety and security. They are in a position to make good suggestions and have a continued interest in the program. If these people are involved in orientation, they should list their topics and their order of preference.

CHECKLIST

After the company policies and practices are analyzed, list the results and make a final evaluation of the topics, arranging them in the best order for the orientation meeting and for the supervisor's discussion after the orientation meeting. This checklist (Figure 1) serves as a reminder to the supervisor of the items he is expected to cover. There should be a provision on the checklist for the supervisor to sign the checklist after he has completed his phase of the orientation. Then he should return the checklist to the personnel representative.

The checklist outlines for the personnel specialist and the supervisor exactly what he should do. In a broad sense the checklist is the new recruit's bird's-eye view of what the company considers a prerequisite to becoming an informed member of the organization. It is an outline of the company's expectations of the employee and what the employee may expect of the organization. It is a good idea for the employee to receive a checklist of his own, that he and his supervisor both sign and return to the personnel specialist (Figure 2).

SCRIPT CONTENT

Questions come into play in the development of a script: What should be included in each topic? How are the ideas best communicated? How much time should be allotted for each segment?

The goals of the orientation program affect the approach. A sound orientation

XYZ COMPANY INC.

PERSONNEL RELATIONS DEPARTMENT

NEW EMPLOYEES ORIENTATION CHECK LIST

Figure 1.   XYZ Company orientation checklist.

NAME OF   STARTING
EMPLOYEE _____ DATE _____

DEPARTMENT_____ LOCATION_____

ITEMS COVERED BY PERSONNEL RELATIONS DEPARTMENT OR BRANCH OFFICE ON FIRST DAY OF ORIENTATION: (45 minutes)

PART I — Organization and Personnel Policies & Procedures

☐ 1. XYZ Company Organization
☐ 2. Basic Insurance Benefits *(Paid in full by the company)*
    ☐ A. Hospitalization
    ☐ B. Short-Term Disability
    ☐ C. Basic Life Insurance
    ☐ D. Travel Accident
☐ 3. Optional Insurance Benefits *(Paid for by you and the company)*
    ☐ A. Comprehensive Medical
    ☐ B. Contributory Life Insurance
    ☐ C. Long Term Disability

☐ 4. Vacations		☐ 11. XYZ Company News	
☐ 5. Holidays		☐ 12. Tuition Refund Plan	
☐ 6. Probationary Period		☐ 13. Building Facilities	
☐ 7. Compensation		☐ 14. New Building	
☐ 8. Job Evaluation		☐ 15. XYZ Company and You	
☐ 9. Medical Absence		☐ 16. Equal Opportunity Employment	
☐ 10. Personal Status Change Notice			

* * * * * *

APPOINTMENT FOR SECOND MEETING: (45 minutes)

DATE _____ *TIME* _____

       *IMPORTANT: BE SURE TO BRING THIS FORM BACK
                   WITH YOU, SIGNED BY YOUR MANAGER
                   WHEN YOU COME TO YOUR SCHEDULED
                   SECOND MEETING.*

PART II — Personnel Policies and Procedures

☐ 1. Review & Questions on Part I		☐ 7. XYZ Company Investment Plan	
☐ 2. Retirement Program		☐ 8. U.S. Savings Bonds	
☐ 3. College Gift Matching Plan		☐ 9. Employee Activities	
☐ 4. Time Off the Job		☐ 10. Suggestion System	
☐ 5. Award for Recruiting		☐ 11. Personnel Inventory	
☐ 6. Credit Union			

_____
PERSONNEL RELATIONS STAFF REPRESENTATIVE

_____
DATE

Figure 1.   XYZ Company orientation checklist.   (continued)

ITEMS TO BE DISCUSSED BY DEPARTMENT HEAD OR SUPERVISOR WITH NEW EMPLOYEE:

FIRST DAY OF EMPLOYMENT
☐ 1. Introduction to Co-workers
☐ 2. Information on Location of Facilities

A. Coat Room   D. Bulletin Board
B. Cafeteria   E. Coffee Service
C. Wash Room   F. Provision for Lunch

RULES AND POLICIES
☐ 3. Hours: starting, lunch, dismissal time, hours per week
☐ 4. Pay: when, where, and how paid — overtime policy
         (Explain deductions when 1st check is received.)
☐ 5. Holidays and Vacations in Detail
☐ 6. Probationary Period
☐ 7. Absences: Pay Policies — before and after 5 months. When and whom to phone
          Visit to Medical Dept. or Doctor's note before return to work after
          absence of 3 or more days.
☐ 8. Organization of Department
         Corporation — Division — Department — Section
☐ 9. Rules on:
         Tardiness, Telephone Coverage, Behavior, etc.

DURING FIRST TWO WEEKS OF EMPLOYMENT
☐ 10. Accident:
          Reporting accident or injury on job
☐ 11. Employee's Discount on XYZ Company products
☐ 12. Salary Check — Explanation of Deductions
☐ 13. Salary Reviews
☐ 14. Employee Appraisal Plan
☐ 15. Suggestion System
☐ 16. Reporting Change in Address, Name, Phone, etc.
☐ 17. Invite Questions and Help on Problems

As indicated by check marks, all of the above items have been discussed with the employee.

The employee has been advised as to the time and extent of 1st vacation as shown by the Table on last page of this form.

Employee has been instructed to attend the second scheduled meeting and to bring this check list with him.

```
_____
DEPARTMENT HEAD OR SUPERVISOR


_____
DATE
```

Figure 1.   **XYZ Company orientation checklist.   (continued)**

Our VACATION YEAR
begins on
JUNE 1st
and runs through
MAY 31st
of the following year.

TABLE FOR DETERMINING A NEW EMPLOYEE'S FIRST VACATION

Period in which continuous service date or date of employment falls (All dates inclusive)	Vacation to which new employee is entitled during the vacation year beginning June 1 of the year of employment	Vacation to which new employee is entitled during the vacation year beginning June 1st of the year FOLLOWING employment.
JANUARY 1st through APRIL 1st (*)	ONE WEEK AFTER FIVE MONTHS OF SERVICE	— — —
APRIL 2nd through AUGUST 1st	NONE	TWO WEEKS
AUGUST 2nd through NOVEMBER 1st (*)	NONE	ONE WEEK on June 1st . . . SECOND WEEK after 10 mos. of service
NOVEMBER 2nd through DECEMBER 31st	NONE	ONE WEEK

ON THE BASIS OF YOUR CONTINUOUS SERVICE DATE, YOUR FIRST VACATION WILL BE AS INDICATED ABOVE, CIRCLED IN RED

(*) Or the 1st working day thereafter

*FOR DETERMINING SUBSEQUENT
VACATIONS SEE YOUR COPY OF
THE VACATION CALCULATOR*

FORM 09-88400

Figure 1.   XYZ Company orientation checklist.   (continued)

NAME _____

DATE OF
EMPLOYMENT _____

DEPARTMENT _____

Complete this check list as well as you can, then take it to your supervisor who will go over it with you, and give you any additional information you may need.

JOB INFORMATION

You are expected to return this checklist (signed by your Department Head) to the Training Division within three weeks after your date of employment.

If for any reason you can not keep the appointment below, have your Department Head schedule you for another specific time.

APPOINTMENT DATE _____ TIME _____

PLACE: TRAINING DIVISION - PERSONNEL DEPARTMENT.

DEPARTMENT HEAD SIGNATURE _____

JOB INFORMATION

1. The Job of my Department is to _____

My assigned area is _____

The most important part of my job is _____

2. My Department Head's Name is _____

His/Her office is located _____

My immediate supervisor is _____

3. I receive my time card from _____

Time cards must be turned in on _____ DAY

to _____ Pay day for our
      PERSON

Department is _____

If I am out of the hospital on pay day, I can get my

pay from _____ The cashier's

office is _____ WHERE

4. If I feel ill while at work, I should _____

If I become ill while at home, I should notify my

supervisor by calling _____ HOSPITAL PHONE NUMBER
      at least one hour before I am
DEPARTMENT EXTENSION
expected at work.

Figure 2. Checklist—job information.

10. If I work with papers:

Papers I handle Daily include	They come from	When I finish they are used by
_____	_____	_____
_____	_____	_____
_____	_____	_____
_____	_____	_____
_____	_____	_____
_____	_____	_____

11. If I use equipment, I use _____

_____

To keep the equipment in good working order I must _____

_____

12. If I work with supplies, products or food - the way I handle them is important because _____

_____

---

5. My locker or checkroom is located _____

6. The hours I am scheduled to work are assigned by _____

Any change in my work schedule (days off etc.) is arranged in advance by _____

My lunch hour and relief are assigned by _____

7. Work assignments are given to me by _____

I can get help on the job from _____

8. Some of the things I do on my job are:

A. _____

B. _____

C. _____

D. _____

E. _____

F. _____

G. _____

9. In doing my work I handle the following (check the boxes)

PAPER ☐	EQUIPMENT ☐	
SUPPLIES ☐	FOOD ☐	
PRODUCTS ☐	PATIENTS ☐	

Figure 2. Checklist—job information. (continued)

13. My work helps Lenox Hill Hospital give better patient

care by _____

_____

_____

14. When I need supplies, I get them from _____
PERSON / PLACE

15. To keep things running smoothly, I should bring to my
TIME / DAY

supervisor's attention such things as:

_____

_____

_____

16. How well I do my work can be measured by _____

_____

_____

_____

_____

17. 2 Safety rules that apply in my job are:

1 _____

_____

2 _____

_____

18. I have had the most difficulty with _____

_____

19. Things I'd like to know more about are _____

_____

_____

_____

_____

_____

_____

Figure 2. Checklist—job information. (continued)

SUGGESTIONS I HAVE _____

_____
_____
_____
_____
_____
_____
_____
_____
_____
_____
_____
_____
_____
_____
_____

20. Things I like best about my job are: _____

_____
_____
_____
_____
_____
_____
_____
_____

Figure 2. Checklist—job information. (continued)

program must follow a carefully thought-out plan and adhere to a reasonable time-table so that it can:

1. Build the employee's sense of identification with the company and make him proud to work for the company
2. Impress him with the importance of the job he will do
3. Help him gain acceptance by his fellow employees
4. Enable him to fit into a smoothly functioning team operation
5. Give him a clear understandable picture of the many things he wants and needs to know

The script must be dynamic and attention getting. It should contain the key points of the subject being presented. A more in-depth discussion follows (Figure 3). In this way, the personnel specialist creates an awareness in the new employee, helps him to understand the discussion that follows. He underscores and gives support to creating a close relationship between the new employee and the supervisor.

VISUAL AIDS

The number of audio-visual aids are limitless:
1. Films, filmstrips, and slides
2. Tapes, cassettes, records
3. Charts, globes
4. Transparencies, Vugraphs
5. Flip charts
6. Video tape

Even the most expensive visual aid may not be the most suitable for your purpose. To attain active participation in an orientation program, present a combination of the communication arts. Decide how people can best be reached. An unlimited budget may be nice to work with, but it does not give you the answer as to which visual aid or combination is best for your company and your audience. List the factors that affect your selection, and evaluate each in terms of the aids available in the company and on the open market. Study the problem, and know in advance exactly what you want and why you want it.

Factors	*Evaluations*
Company with over 200 locations where new employees are oriented weekly in groups of up to 20 employees	Flip chart (Figure 4) size 15×20 does not require any expensive equipment and is a suitable device for small groups up to 20 people. It is ideal for photographing, if it is necessary to make colored slides for larger groups. Slides made directly from the charts are inexpensive.
Budget limited to under $5,000	Outside bids were $7,500 to $12,000. In-house estimates were $3,500.
Weekly use of flip chart	Rag paper was used for the pages to give long wear. Standard three-hole ring binders in pairs were mounted on an attractive hard green cover, which can be set on a table. Six-hole pages fit nicely and save the cost of a special-order ring binder.
Special use by personnel specialist	Flexibility of page arrangement for special-purpose meetings.

XYZ COMPANY AND YOU
AN EMPLOYEE ORIENTATION
PART TWO

(31) Last week we reviewed hospitalization, basic life insurance, short term disability insurance and travel and accident insurance. This is the basic program. In addition, we reviewed the supplementary optional program consisting of the comprehensive medical and contributory life insurance and the long term disability insurance. If you have any questions in regard to these benefits, this would be a good time to review them. Who has the first question? (Pause).

(32) RETIREMENT PROGRAM

(32) You may think it is a little early to talk about retirement, as a new employee of XYZ Company. However, it's not a bad idea to know at least the key points of the retirement program.

When you fulfill your eligibility, you will be invited to join the plan. The retirement program is made up of two parts — the Pension Plan and the Supplementary Retirement Income Plan. Let me tell you about each.

You are eligible to join the Pension Plan after you have been with the XYZ Company at least one year and after you have attained age 30. Employees should join at the earliest possible date after meeting the requirements, since the more years you participate, the greater will be your benefit upon retirement.

(33) PENSION PLAN CONTRIBUTION

(33) Pension Plan Contribution — The plan is a contributory plan and your share of the contribution is 2.5% of the first $7,800, plus 5% of earnings above $7,800. If your earnings increase during the year, your contribution will go up, thus maximizing your benefit when you retire. In effect, if you are earning over $7,800, you will find that this plan has been coordinated with Social Security taxes which are based on the first $7,800 of earnings. As you begin to pay 5%, you will have satisfied your Social Security tax requirements.

(34) PENSION PLAN BENEFITS

(34) Pension Plan Benefits —The formula for your annual benefit when you reach age 65 is based on contributions you made into the plan. Your annual benefit at age 65 equals 55% of all your contributions at 2.5% and 40% of all your contributions made at 5% of your earnings.

Figure 3. Orientation script.

Unless very creative people are available with experience in photography and the development of audio-visual materials, professional assistance should be secured. Initially it may seem expensive to use professional help, but if you compute the salary and time of a staff member working on such a project, the professional may seem less expensive than you expected. An amateurish production can kill your whole orientation program.

Plan your *audio-visual* aids with an eye to your objectives, audience, and budget. Movies are exciting, but expensive to produce and revise. Slides in a carousel are less expensive and can be easily changed. Cartoons are a good way to portray company rules and regulations in a favorable light. Tape recorders can be pulsed to slide carousels. Transparencies thrown on a screen explain forms. Flip charts

(35) HOW TO DETERMINE PENSION BENEFIT

(35) How to Determine Pension Benefit — This formula of 55% of all your contributions at 2.5% plus 40% of all contributions at 5% can be converted into a table, as you see here. For example, if the annual pay is $4,800, then 2½% of the figure represents $120 contributed by the employee. In terms of an annual benefit, this equals $66. If an employee paid $120 a year for the maximum of 35 years in the plan, his pension benefit at retirement would be $2,310. You can project your own pension benefit by simply working out a table in regard to your annual earnings and anticipated annual earnings using this formula.

(36) SUPPLEMENTARY RETIREMENT INCOME PLAN

(36) Supplementary Retirement Income Plan — The Supplementary Retirement Income Plan is often referred to by its initials, SRIP, which is the first letter of each word of the title. Your eligibility into the Supplementary Retirement Income Plan is 5 years of service to XYZ Company and at least age 34½. Also, you must be a member in the Pension Plan to participate in the Supplementary Retirement Income Plan.

(37) SRIP FINANCING

(37) SRIP Financing — Each year that you are in the Pension Plan you will have credited to your account your share of 2½% of XYZ Companies profits before taxes. This amount is credited each year to your account and invested in common stock by a trustee. At age 65, you will get your pro rata share of the investment, appreciation, dividend and other income.

(38) SRIP BENEFITS

(38) SRIP Benefits — No contribution is made by the employee to the Supplementary Retirement Income Plan. This plan is 100% financed by the company. In 1969, the XYZ Company News announced that, based on 1968 net earnings, the company contributed over $1,000,000 to the SRIP fund—equal to 3.637% of gross pay of each eligible member.

The retirement plan then consists of a pension pay out in fixed dollars monthly for as long as you live, and a lump sum payment at retirement, which is your pro rata share of the amount invested in common stock.

(39) COLLEGE GIFT MATCHING

(39) Company College Gift Matching Plan: For those who give to higher education, there is an opportunity to have the effect of doubling your contribution by participating in the company College Gift Matching Plan. It works like this:

Figure 3. Orientation script. (continued)

show main words and ideas to be remembered and liven up a talking presentation.

Set up a *production schedule.* Decide what needs to be done. Audio-visual aids must be produced and copy written for manuals. Plan and equip the meeting room along the lines of the type of program to be initiated.

Select the meeting facility with an eye to the presentation and comfort of the audience. Check the operation of lights and the working order of other equipment. Chairs should be comfortable and situated so that anything to be viewed will be seen by all. Ventilation must be adequate. If smoking is permitted, ash trays are needed.

(39) CONT.

First, to be eligible you must be with XYZ Company at least one year. Second, obtain a copy of the form and accompany it with your check to the school of your choice. When it is received by the school and completed, it is returned to the XYZ Company, at which time the company will mail a check in like amount.

(40) TIME OFF THE JOB
(Sickness, etc.)

(40) TIME OFF THE JOB. I discussed vacations and holidays last week but there are other occasions you need to know about.

Sickness: It is your responsibility to notify your supervisor if you are unable to come to work because of illness -- and to keep him regularly informed of your progress. It is the policy of the company to cooperate with you in providing a measure of protection against the worry and financial stress that usually accompany a siege of illness. Accordingly, if you are unavoidably absent because of illness or injury, the XYZ Company's Short Term Disability program discussed at our last meeting applies.

Death in family: If you are a permanent employee who has completed the five-month probationary period, you may be excused from work up to three days if necessary, with pay, because of the death of a member of your immediate family.

Jury Duty: If you are a permanent employee, whether part-time, full-time or probationary, and required to serve on jury duty, you are allowed time off to meet this civic obligation, and receive full pay. Women are entitled to claim exemption from jury duty. They are not required by the company to claim such exemption and will receive company pay if they are called to serve, but not if they volunteer without being called.

General Emergencies: Severe weather conditions, transportation strikes, and other wide-spread or general emergencies occasionally cause absence or tardiness. If your department head is confident that you have made every reasonable effort to get to work, he will authorize full pay at least for a time. Temporary and probationary employees are included in this policy.

Maternity: An employee should notify her supervisor within the first 3 months of her pregnancy. A pregnant employee may continue to work up to four weeks previous to the expected date of delivery, provided proper medical approval has been given to the Medical Department.

(41) TIME OFF THE JOB
(Personal Business, etc.)

(41) Personal Business: Naturally, we hope and expect personal business absences to be rare. If you must be absent or late because of personal reasons, secure permission from your supervisor in advance if at all possible. Otherwise, give him a full explanation immediately upon your return to work.

Figure 3.   Orientation script.   (continued)

Consider the cost for equipment, audio-visual aids, and manuals.   Assign different aspects of the program to members of the orientation committee, and indicate feasible deadlines.

WHO PLAYS A ROLE IN THE ORIENTATION PROGRAM?

First someone must be in charge of the program to assume responsibility and develop and coordinate the program and the people involved.   If a company has a personnel department, a personnel representative is the logical person to coordinate and con-

(41) CONT.

Tardiness: Obviously, any lateness is cause for concern. However, if, in the opinion of your department head, an acceptable reason is furnished, the chances are that such occasional lateness will be paid for.

Any repeated tardiness, however, will immediately jeopardize your remaining with XYZ Company.

Religious Observances: You are permitted to observe, with full pay, the religious holidays of your own faith. These are, of course, in addition to Christmas day and Good Friday.

Official Closings: Sometimes the Company, usually with appreciable advance notices, closes its offices to provide a long weekend or an extended holiday. In such cases full-time employees are paid for their normal working hours during the time off.

(42) RECRUITING AWARD

(42) Recruiting Award: The Personnel Relations Department is always glad to interview your friends who are seeking employment. If the applicant becomes a permanent employee, you will receive an award of $50.00. Be sure, however, that your friend enters your name on the application form.

(43) CREDIT UNION

(43) Credit Union: The Credit Union, which operates under a Federal Charter, is run by and for employees and has no connection with the Company, although the Company provides office space and other facilities.

You are eligible to join the Credit Union as a permanent employee immediately and can open up a savings account. You are not eligible to apply for a loan, however, until the completion of your 5 months probationery period.

(43.5) VOLUNTARY MONTHLY INVESTMENT PLAN

(43.5) Voluntary Monthly Investment Plan: The buying of XYZ Company stock through payroll deductions is available to all permanent full time domestic employees. The XYZ Company assumes the cost of administration of the plan and the brokerage commissions on the stock purchased with our payroll deductions.

Figure 3.   Orientation script.   (continued)

duct the program.   He orders all the required forms, keeps up to date on the changes taking place in the company, updates the orientation script and visual aids.   If the company has other locations, he would still be responsible to guide, assist, and provide the materials for the presentation of an orientation program by trained representatives at all the company's locations.

Select people to conduct the orientation meeting.   Involve the training division if there is general job training such as telephone sales training or executive development.   The financial division may wish to inform employees about getting paid, wage assignments, and garnishees.   Security might explain measures taken to pro-

(43.5) CONT.

Your participation in this plan is entirely voluntary and the availability of the program is provided only as a convenience to you. The XYZ Company does not urge your participation in any degree. If you participate, you should realize that an investment in any common stock is always accompanied by the possible risk of loss, as well as the opportunity for profit.

A booklet describing the plan may be obtained from me at the end of this meeting. The plan is administered by Merrill Lynch, Pierce, Fenner & Smith Inc., one of the largest stock brokers in the United States.

(44) U.S. SAVINGS BONDS

(44) U.S. Savings Bonds: The Company, in cooperation with the U.S. Treasury Department, offers, through regular payroll deductions, an opportunity to save toward the purchase of the United States Savings-bonds and Freedom Bond combination, as shown in the application form. If you wish to fill this out now, I'll be very happy to see that it gets to the Payroll Department. If you would rather wait till some later date, then, when you fill it out, mail it directly to the Payroll Department, Hightstown, New Jersey, through inter-office mail.

(45) ACTIVITIES

(45) Social Artistic and Athletic Activities. There are a great many employee sponsored activities at XYZ Company, including bowling teams, softball teams, a bridge club, a chess club, a dramatic club, skiing, vacation trips etc. Every year there is an Arts & Crafts exhibition in New York headquarters that is open to XYZ Company employees everywhere. You will find these activities covered regularly by the XYZ Company News.

(46) SUGGESTIONS

(46) Suggestions: The Suggestion System in the XYZ Company provides an opportunity for you to "Cash In" on any ideas you may have about improvements in the Company, the division, department, or your job. A copy of the suggestion form is among your papers. All you do is fill it out, with or without the help of your supervisor, and put it in the suggestion box or mail it to the Personnel Department. A Suggestion Committee will review and evaluate the suggestion to determine whether it merits an award and, if so, the amount.

Figure 3.   Orientation script.   (continued)

tect employees and the property of employees and the company. It is important to explain to employees how the losses of the company can affect them and to seek their assistance in preventing pilferage. The safety division should be included in general orientation and job instruction. The rising insurance rates for compensation and disability and the worker's time lost from the job can create problems for a company.

The supervisor plays a most important role in orientation. He is expected to have a complete understanding of the company's policies and practices and share his enthusiasm and knowledge with his new recruit. A good supervisory training pro-

(47) PERSONNEL INVENTORY SYSTEM

(47) Personnel Inventory System — There is one more form for you to fill out. It is called the Personnel Inventory Questionnaire. This, when completed, will help the Personnel Department to know of your interests, talents, skills and training for promotional and transfer purposes. It is one of the many ways in which you will be considered for promotional and transfer opportunities.

Naturally, the company would like to fill all of the more responsible positions by promotion or transfer. Before you complete the questionnaire, read the instructions in the Personnel Inventory booklet.

I really enjoyed being with you this morning. I hope that you found both orientation sessions helpful. I wish to thank you for coming here today and wish you success in your career at XYZ Company.

Figure 3.   Orientation script.   (continued)

gram is a must. Guidelines are needed by the supervisor as reference points for keeping himself acquainted with the policies and practices of the company. An orientation checklist is a handy tool for the supervisor. It provides an outline of the items he should cover with the new employee and can be used as a good follow-up technique. The supervisor is expected to give the recruit the information he needs when he first reports to work and to answer any questions the employee may have. He can use the orientation checklist as a means of making sure the employee has sufficient understanding of the policies and practices that he needs to know. Figure 5 is an example of a checklist for supervisors.

A program of this type helps to establish teamwork between the personnel specialist who introduces the policies and practices of the company and provides motivation toward a good work performance and the supervisor who capitalizes on the motivation by developing the employee's interest and completing the introduction period of the employee. Once this is accomplished, the supervisor can turn his major interest to the immediate training and development of his new staff member.

Every person involved in orientation needs one or two backup people in the event of sickness or vacation. It is advisable to have the backup people rotate the general orientation so that one person is not overburdened. This gives the backup people an opportunity to participate, get the feel of the program, and become acquainted with new employees. Companies with multilocations and small companies without a personnel relations department have a different source from which to select a representative to handle the orientation meeting. Usually the administrative assistant, office manager, or supervisor is assigned the job. It should be

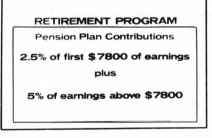
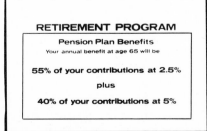

Figure 4.   Flip chart.

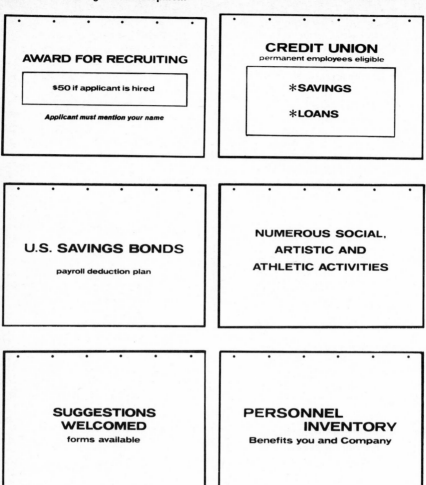

Figure 4.   Flip chart.   (continued)

someone involved with the induction process of new employees.   The headquarter coordinator or personnel relations manager is responsible for providing the guide-lines and materials.   He also maintains a mailing list of those assigned at each location and keeps them up to date on changes.   As changes occur, script books and visual aids are replaced with new ones.

The New Recruit

All employees need orientation.   Everyone likes to feel important.   The orientation meeting is the official welcome from the company.   It should be conducted with warmth and understanding.   The first days on the job are filled with doubts and fears.   The new employee needs assurance, confidence, and a nudge in the right direction until he finds his own way.

The ideal orientation program gives each new employee confidence and pride

RETIREMENT PROGRAM

Supplementary Retirement Income Plan

SRIP Eligibility

5 years of service

34 ½ years

Must be a Pension Plan Participant

RETIREMENT PROGRAM

Supplementary Retirement Income Plan

SRIP Financing

X.Y.Z. COMPANY CONTRIBUTES

2 ½% of Profits

CONSOLIDATED NET INCOME BEFORE FEDERAL INCOME TAXES

RETIREMENT PROGRAM

Supplementary Retirement Income Plan
SRIP Benefits

**BASED ON
1968 NET EARNINGS
3.637% of Gross Pay**

**COLLEGE
GIFT MATCHING**

▶ **doubles your contribution**

▶ **effective 1 year after employment**

▶ **forms available**

TIME OFF THE JOB

● Sickness
● Death in family
● Jury duty
● General emergencies
● Maternity

TIME OFF THE JOB

● Personal business
● Tardiness
● Religious observances
● Official closings

Figure 4. Flip chart. (continued)

in himself and the company he works for. It makes him feel part of the company team. The meeting, properly handled, is hardly ever forgotten by the employee. It says to him, "You are pretty important and here are the organizational tools for your use—policies and practices—not only to protect you and your family but to help you quickly settle down and become a contributing member of this organization. You, too, can help make this company a better place to work."

Most employees are interested in basic company information in terms of themselves: benefits, salary, promotional opportunities, and job knowledge.

College graduates require assistance in making the transition from the academic world to the business community. They are interested in more in-depth exposure to corporate functions and have not made definite decisions on their job futures. An in-depth orientation to various departments can help the company and the employee reach a decision.

Figure 5.   Orientation checklists for supervisors.

This checklist has been prepared specifically for supervisory personnel to complement the personnel department orientation program for all new operations group employees and those middle group employees below the division manager level.   It is part of the entire orientation process designed to acclimate the employee, to create an atmosphere in which he will learn his job quickly and well, and to acquaint him with the purposes and activities of the company.

The new employee will be taken to lunch, as a guest of the company, on the first day of employment.

Each item should be checked.   After all checklist items have been completed, please have the new employee sign in the space provided to indicate his understanding of the matters discussed.   Your signature will attest to the completion of this phase of orientation.

Please return the checklist to the *Personnel Department*—Manpower Development and Training—promptly for inclusion in the employee's file.

Employee's Name:	Discussion completed (please check *each* individual item)
I. Word of welcome	
II. Explain overall departmental organization and its relationship to other activities of the company	
III. Explain employee's individual contribution to the objectives of the department and his starting assignment in broad terms	
IV. Discuss job content with employee and give him a copy of job description (if available)	
V. Explain departmental training program(s) and salary increase practices and procedures	
VI. Discuss where the employee lives and transportation facilities	
VII. Explain working conditions: *a.* Hours of work, time sheets *b.* Use of employee entrance and elevators *c.* Lunch hours *d.* Coffee breaks, rest periods *e.* Personal telephone calls and mail *f.* Overtime policy and requirements *g.* Paydays and procedure for being paid *h.* Lockers *i.* Other _____	
VIII. Requirements for continuance of employment—explain company standards as to: *a.* Performance of duties *b.* Attendance and punctuality *c.* Handling confidential information *d.* Behavior *e.* General appearance *f.* Wearing of uniform	
IX. Introduce new staff member to manager(s) and other supervisors. Special attention should be paid to the person to whom the new employee will be assigned.	
X. Release employee to immediate supervisor who will: *a.* Introduce new staff member to fellow workers *b.* Familiarize the employee with his work place	

Figure 5.   Orientation checklists for supervisors.   (continued)

Employee's   Name:

Discussion Completed
(please check *each*
individual item)

c. Begin on-the-job training	

If not applicable, insert N/A in space provided.

Employee's Signature	Supervisor's Signature
Date	Division

Form examined for filing:

Date	Personnel Department

Company executives expect individualized orientation programs tailor-made for their needs. These programs take into consideration the executive's background and job function and help him adjust to his specific job and the departments he will be relating to.   Management and professional employees are concerned with company goals and various functions and levels of responsibility.

Today, businesses are faced with orienting the *disadvantaged employee.*   This employee may belong to a minority group, live in a ghetto, and have a poor employment record.   Many also have police records.   Most supervisors are unfamiliar with the attitudes, problems, and mores of minority people.   The disadvantaged employee is easily discouraged because so much of his life has been a failure.   He needs a great deal of counseling and coaching in even the smallest business world activities such as personal hygiene, getting to work on time, and managing money. This is where a supervisory training program is necessary to help supervisors to understand the world of the disadvantaged and how to cope with this type employee.

Common Features of an Orientation Program

In nearly every program we will find many common features:
1. Welcome and introduction to the company
2. Benefits orientation
3. Review of personnel policies and procedures
4. Discussion of physical facilities and the surrounding area
5. Checklist
6. Supplementary material
7. Special sessions
8. Programmed instructions

The contents of the program may not be the same for every division and location in the same company.   For example, a New York City location may orient its employees on how to get to work by rail, subway, or surface transportation within the city.   The same company with a rural area has an entirely different kind of message to give its employees concerning getting to and from work.   The emphasis may be on road maps, dangerous traffic areas, driver safety, rules and regulations of the parking lot, and a host of other important orientation items.

Some companies hiring large groups of employees in similar categories are willing to devote a week to orientation.   They include sessions on telephone etiquette, human relations, and how to learn.   They have a general job orientation every morning and on-the-job training under supervision every afternoon.

It is important to realize that the attention and retention ability of people is limited. The law of diminishing returns applies to human beings regarding the amount of knowledge they can acquire in a given period of time. Supplementary material which consists of fliers, schedules, applications, and booklets is a common feature of an orientation program. If the company has an Employee Handbook or Personnel Manual, it is included in the package given to each employee at the orientation meeting. The Employee Handbook or its equivalent is the primary source for the checklist items and the script content. It saves a great deal of time and avoids misunderstanding. Companies, whose supplementary material does not include an Employee Handbook, are obliged to provide written digests of the principal rules and practices. Printed material is necessary because it is impossible to tell all, and even what is told is often forgotten. A well-indexed manual serves as a ready reference to answer future questions. The employee personnel manual should include:

1. Introduction—brief history of the company and statement of its purposes
2. A general statement about cooperation and teamwork
3. Personnel policies and procedure (statement regarding discrimination)
4. Terms and conditions of employment (pay, hours, transfers, promotions)
5. Benefits (vacation, insurance)
6. Grievance procedure

Prepare information booklets in detail for life insurance, medical benefits, pension, and safety (Figure 6). Cosmetic companies publish pamphlets on good grooming. Some cities provide maps showing points of interest. Local telephone companies supply booklets on telephone courtesy. Booklets on all benefits should be included in the orientation package. Forms, such as a benefit application and a bond application, are completed at the meeting during the discussion of the particular item.

FACTORS AFFECTING ORIENTATION

Programs vary from company to company, within a company, and according to job classification. Orientation programs are affected by:

1. The nature of the business (product, service, etc.)
2. The work days (hours, shifts)
3. Frequency of hire (number of new employees per week)
4. Availability of space for the meeting
5. Availability of personnel to present orientation program
6. Plant locations and layouts
7. Behavioral objectives that have been established
8. Attitude of management
9. Budget (amount of money to expend)

Within a company, different divisions, even different operations such as production or marketing, may have different benefits and personnel policies. To the extent that this exists, the orientation program is adapted accordingly within a company and the contents are controlled by providing a separate orientation script for each type of program. If variations are minor, alternate script paragraphs may be included in a single script booklet.

Types of Orientation

It is important that some formal orientation take place the first day or week of employment. Usually on the first day of work, new employees are assembled at a designated place to participate in an orientation program. They are greeted by the personnel relations representative assigned to conduct the meeting. He intro-

Figure 6.   Information booklets.

duces himself, tells them briefly what is planned for them, and refreshments are made available.   The seating arrangement is comfortable and allows for a clear view of the speaker and visual aids.   The personnel representative presents the orientation script in an informal manner and uses visual aids.   The visual aids serve as an idea reinforcer and attention holder.   Visual aids help new employees understand the material as it is presented.

The meeting area should have good lighting, proper heat, and adequate ventilation.   Some companies use a section of the cafeteria because it is an area every employee should know about.

The personnel representative asks for questions by pausing after each topic presentation to encourage a question-and-answer period.   If no questions are forthcoming, he tries to get a discussion started by asking a few questions of his own—new employees are sometimes shy.   The agenda of the first meeting should be planned so that it lasts about 45 minutes to an hour.

Most companies divide their orientation into two or more sessions. At the first meeting the new employee receives information on the company, the rules and regulations, and what is expected of him. He gets just enough information to welcome him, relieve his anxieties, and motivate him. Many employees do not become eligible for benefits until they have completed a probationary period. The employee is more interested in the benefit when it is applicable to him. This would be the time to have an orientation session on benefits and assist the new employee in completing his forms.

A two-step orientation allows the employee to think about what he knows and what questions he would like answered at a second meeting. Many companies have the second meeting four weeks later. At the conclusion of the first meeting, the speaker announces the scheduled date and time for the second meeting. This is recorded by each new employee on his own *checklist*. The new employee presents his checklist to his department head or supervisor when he reports to work. The department head or supervisor may continue the orientation as outlined on the checklist, or he may delegate a co-worker to introduce the new employee to his co-workers and acquaint him with the facilities of the department. The co-worker helps reduce anxiety and fills the need for reassurance. However, the department head should review the rules and policies on the first day.

During the first two weeks of employment, the department head is expected to cover other items on the checklist. When the department head has completed his role in orientation, he signs the checklist and returns it to the employee. The employee gives it to the personnel specialist at the conclusion of the second meeting. By this time it is expected that the new employee can say, "I know where I am, why, and where I am going."

Special Orientations

In addition to the regular orientation meetings for all new employees, special orientation meetings may be held for specific purposes. A safety orientation program is designed and conducted where machinery is used or where there is a risk of accident. When an employer discovers the need for special emphasis in the use of a particular skill or knowledge of a basic subject, it may be necessary to develop programs on consumer education, personal habits, and the world of work disciplines. Reading, writing, and arithmetic may be reviewed in programs designed to help the disadvantaged.

Programmed Packages

Considerable interest is being shown in programmed instruction. Under certain circumstances this may be good. Companies with many locations, where a low hiring rate exists, may convert the more technical aspects of an orientation into a programmed instruction. A benefits program consisting of hospitalization, medical, life insurance, travel or accident insurance, short-term disability, long-term disability, pensions, and profit sharing are more suitable for programmed instruction than the lecture-type program. Because of its effectiveness there is a lessening of anxiety and tension for the new employee.

Case studies of supervisory situations can be used to motivate employees to discuss what will be expected of them and how they should behave toward one another. Puzzle exercises help new employees to analyze and solve problems. Picture exercises point out problems of learning, perception, and observation.

Job manuals tell employees how to do the job, step by step. Every department should have their procedures written so that new and old employees can refer to them when a question arises. A manual with good diagrams and drawings is an asset on job training.

PUBLICITY

Publicity for the program requires planning. The time, place, and date of a general orientation might be indicated on the new employee's confirmation of employment (Figure 7). A personal invitation to the employee's home makes a good impression (Figure 8). A reminder to his supervisor keeps the employee and the supervisor aware of what is going on.

FEEDBACK

Feedback is important to keep your orientation program current to meet company and employee needs.

Founded 1857

LENOX HILL HOSPITAL

100 EAST 77TH STREET / NEW YORK, N. Y. 10021 / TRAFALGAR 9-8000

CONFIRMATION OF EMPLOYMENT

TO:	______________________ Date: __________
FROM:	*Robert C. Grillo, – Personnel Director*
CONFIRMATION	We are pleased to confirm our offer of employment in the capacity of __________ (POSITION) Assigned to the __________ (DEPARTMENT) __________ (UNIT) Your Department Head's name is __________ Your Supervisor's name is __________
REPORTING DATES	Report for your Physical Exam on __________ (DATE) (TIME) (PLACE) Report for work on __________ (DATE) (TIME) (PLACE) Report for your Orientation Class on __________ (DATE) (TIME) (PLACE)
BASIC SALARY DATA	Your starting salary is __________ Per __________ Your Salary Differential is __________ Per __________ Your next salary (Increase/Review) is due on __________ Your hours of work are From ______ A.M. P.M. To ______ A.M. P.M. Total ______ Hours per week Your probationary period is three (3) months You are paid ☐ Weekly ☐ Bi-Weekly
EMPLOYMENT CLASSIFICATION	Full Time ☐ Permanent ☐ Union ☐ Exempt ☐ Part Time ☐ Temporary ☐ Non-Union ☐ Non-Exempt ☐
CERTIFICATION	I certify that the information contained on my application for employment is correct and complete. I realize that misrepresentation of facts called for on the application will be cause for rejection of my application or dismissal after employment and consequently this confirmation will be null and void.
APPROVALS	EMPLOYEE __________ PERSONNEL __________

WELCOME TO LENOX HILL HOSPITAL

EMPLOYEE

PERS 817

Figure 7. Confirmation of employment.

Figure 8.   Invitation to orientation.

23—30

Figure 9.   Program evaluation.

PROGRAM EVALUATION
1. Which section of the orientation program do you feel is most important for meeting the needs of your job:
      a. History of company _____
      b. Job opportunities _____
      c. Human relations _____
      d. Benefits _____
      e. Practices, office _____
      f. Techniques for learning _____
      g. Skill training _____
2. What were your thoughts on the company after viewing the history of the company?
_____

3. After seeing "job opportunities," what job do you think you would like to do:
      1 year from now _____
      5 years from now _____
   If you are undecided on a future job, could you please suggest a way we could help
   you _____

4. Having participated in "human relations" do you feel you are better able to:

	Yes	No
a. Handle situations or problems at work		
b. Handle situations or problems outside work		
c. Understand problems of a supervisor		
d. Realize that help is available for solving problems		

5. Which benefits that the company offers are most important to you:
      a. Pay _____
      b. Medical _____
      c. Insurance _____
      d. Training _____
      e. Employee activities _____
      f. Tuition refund _____
      g. Holiday _____
      h. Vacation _____
      i. Cafeteria _____
      j. Loan service _____
      k. Security _____
      l. Sick leave _____
6. Did your session of office practices prepare you for your job?
      Yes _____
      No _____
      Please explain _____

---

7. Was there enough time for each part of your orientation?
      Yes _____
      No _____
      Please explain _____

---

8. How would you rate your orientation leader:
      Excellent _____
      Good _____
      Fair _____
      Poor _____
      Please explain your answer _____

Figure 9. Program evaluation. (continued)

9. To what extent were you involved in the session:
   Deeply involved _____
   Interested _____
   Slightly involved _____
   Not much interest _____
   Can you explain your answer _____

10. What suggestions would you have for improving the sessions?
   _____
   _____
   _____

11. Would you refer friends for positions here?
   Yes _____
   No _____

Feedback Mechanism

To measure how well the orientation program meets its objectives, use:
   1. Testing or questionaires to see if factual material was learned
   2. The checklist
   3. Evaluation forms or opinions
   4. Discussions with immediate supervisors of newly oriented employees
   5. Personal, formal or informal, interviews during probationary periods or at the end of a month's employment
   6. Exit or terminal interviews

Design an evaluation form to provide adequate feedback and information on the reactions of new employees (Figure 9). There should be a follow-up visit between the new employee and a member of the personnel department sometime during the first two or three weeks of employment. This meeting can be casual, but it should indicate a continued interest in the new employee and how he is doing. It provides an opportunity to discuss the orientation program and its effectiveness. A record of the meeting might be filed in the employee's personnel record. The job information questionaire might be the basis of this meeting.

WHAT IS AN ORIENTATION PROGRAM?

An orientation program is the result of a plan. It takes its place as one of the personnel functions—recruitment, selection, orientation, training, and development—early in the career of a new employee. We usually think of orientation for new employees, but a company must continue to orient all its employees as change and innovation develop the need. Someone should be made responsible to take periodic inventory of what innovations have taken place and of what renewal orientation seems to be necessary and to develop special programs for this need. Group meetings, the employee house organ, a staff memo, a new policy announcement, and the updating of an employee handbook are some of the means used to keep employees informed. Orientation also continues at various stages in the career of an individual as his responsibility increases or changes occur in management, professional, creative, sales, production, clerical, or other fields.

BIBLIOGRAPHY

Arnott, W. S. A.: "Communicating Information to New Employees," *Personnel Practice Bulletin,* June, 1964.

Broadwell, Martin M.: *The Supervisor and On-the-Job Training,* Addison-Wesley Publishing Company, Inc., Reading, Mass., 1969.

Chancey, Lee: "An Orientation System for New Employees: Seven-phase Process at LTV Missiles and Space Division," *Training and Development Journal,* May, 1968.

Checklist for Orientation and Evaluation of New Employees, Humble Oil and Refinery Company, 1969.

"Formal Briefing of New Employees at Seagrams," *Employee Relations Bulletin,* Aug. 4, 1965.

Gemmell, Arthur J.: "Indoctrination Takes Time, But Never Underestimate Its True Value," *Personnel Administrator,* July-August, 1968.

"Group Presentations Reduce Cost of Orienting New Hires," *Employee Relations Bulletin,* May 3, 1967.

Himler, Leonard E.: "The Counselling Interview," in Paul Pigors and Charles A. Myers, (eds.), *Readings in Personnel Administration,* McGraw-Hill Book Company, New York, 1965.

"Informal Orientation Program Erases Negative Attitudes," *Employee Relations Bulletin,* Feb. 9, 1966.

Killian, Ray A.: "Welcome Aboard! Orienting the New Employee," *AMA Supervisory Management,* June, 1967.

Lipstreu, Otis: "A Systems Approach to Orientation," *Personnel Administration,* March-April, 1969.

Mahoney, F. X.: "New Approaches for New Employees: Effective Assimilation of Disadvantages at Humble Oil," *Training and Development Journal,* February, 1969.

McClintock, Marion, and others: "Orienting the New Employee with Programmed Instruction," *Training and Development Journal,* May, 1967.

Neidt, Charles O., and Eugene Sears: "Use of Programmed Instruction for Orienting New Employees to Company Benefits," *Personnel Journal,* June, 1967.

"Preliminary Booklet Is Effective Aid in Timing of Benefit Communications," *Employee Benefit Plan Review,* February, 1967.

Schmidt, Fred G.: "Introducing the New Employee," *Effective Communications on the Job,* 1963.

Training and Development Journal of A.S.T.D., "Training the New Hire," November, 1968; "An Orientation System for New Employees," May, 1968; "Better Orientation Training," April, 1965.

chapter 24

Other Special Training Programs

DOROTHY MOULTON *Training Director, Anchor Savings Bank, Brooklyn, New York*

The range of special training programs available to a business organization is virtually unlimited. A "special" training program is designed to fill a specific need not generally included within the usual management, supervisory, or skills training programs. Since it is impossible to discuss all such programs in a single chapter, only those which are frequently offered among a broad range of industries will be described.

Many of these programs yield immediate and tangible results; yet they can be conducted within the limits of a tight budget. Furthermore, these broad-gauged programs often provide training personnel an entry to departments and areas previously reluctant to make full use of the organization's training resources. When a special training program accomplishes its objectives and enables employees to become more effective on the job, the training department gains valuable recognition and support among line managers.

Certainly no training department can base its contribution to the organization on special training. But a broad-based training function cannot minimize or ignore the contribution special training makes to the overall effectiveness of the organization.

DETERMINING AND DEFINING THE NEED

Special training programs most often are conducted for employees who are already performing their jobs in a generally satisfactory manner. Recognition of the need to strengthen particular skills may arise either from the training department or from a member of management. A special training program is then developed to provide participants with tools which, if used consistently, enable them to become more productive on the job. Because special training programs have direct on-the-job applicability, their content should be directly work related and the transfer of training to job situations should be readily demonstrable.

Needs for such programs can be identified (1) by the training department in the course of consultation with line departments about other programs or general training needs, or by observation; (2) by specific requests from department heads or other members of management; or (3) by participants in other programs or through comments about developmental needs in the course of a manpower audit or skills inventory.

The major (and most common) drawback of special training involves the imprecise definition of objectives. Objectives often are stated as cloudy generalizations such as, "to make the participants better listeners," or "to improve the manner in which telephone calls are handled." Such objectives can lead only to "shotgun" training with buckshot hitting everything in sight—except, of course, the target. Achievement of an effective and meaningful program depends on objectives aimed like a rifle—directly at the target. Ammunition is limited, and so are the resources of a training department.

SELECTING THE PARTICIPANTS

It is one thing to know who *should* attend a program, but another to get the right people into a classroom.

Unless the need for training can be demonstrated to the prospective participants, a program's worth will be negligible.

In a telephone training program, for example, it is customary to include all secretarial employees and sometimes all clerical employees as well. The objective of such a program is to improve employee skills in using a telephone and handling calls. Some secretarial and clerical employees, however, may consider themselves already well versed in the use of the telephone, and might view the training as an unpleasant hour to be endured rather than as a learning experience. To anticipate this negative reaction at least to some extent, the training department can present the program as a review or refresher.

An alternative approach involves presenting the program only to those employees with a demonstrated need for special training. Organizations which periodically review employee performance will find this alternative most practical. The employee, in consultation with his supervisor, often will recognize his need or can be led to recognize it. The subordinate will view the training as a boost toward his personal and professional goals and as an aid toward meeting or exceeding his performance standards. Also if subordinates and superiors assess the former's developmental needs jointly, a special training program will be accepted as an integral part in developing the employee for greater responsibilities.

In organizations which have no performance review program and/or in those which attempt to evaluate only personality traits, an employee is less likely to recognize his needs. The employee's superior, in many cases, is unable to identify precisely the employee's short- and long-term needs. As a result, a department head will tend to enroll the employee in any program which comes along in the hope that one might close the gap between what the performance is and what it ought to be. The result is just another application of the "shotgun" training mentioned earlier in this chapter.

Naturally, under these circumstances, supervisor-imposed training will be perceived by the employee as a punishment or threat. He will think, "What did I do wrong now?", or "Every time I make a mistake he sends me to class," or "I thought I was doing a good job."

A third alternative (and at times the only practical one) depends on volunteers to populate training classes. This alternative can be reasonable when individual employees know their own needs.

If employees are given an option to pick and choose among programs—to enroll or not—they too often perceive the training as a fringe benefit, time away from the office, or something nice to have. Unless the employee possesses an uncommonly high degree of self-knowledge, he tends toward those programs which interest him, about which he has some knowledge, or which pose the least threat. Personal experience with this approach shows a significantly high rate of last-minute cancellations, often due to the enrollee's low rating of the program relevance to the immediate job requirements.

The trainee must bear a part of the responsibility for training effectiveness. Unless his objectives in attending the program are clearly related to the objectives of the training program, effectiveness—transfer back to the job resulting in improved performance—will be less than optimum.

The choice of training alternative depends on the training environment in the organization and the separate but related programs which support it. The trainee's recognition of training as supportive to his particular needs is an ideal. The training department must, however, assess what is practical within the limits of its resources and then work toward that ideal.

DEVELOPING THE PROGRAM

If the objectives have been set realistically—if the end results the training program will accomplish have been determined—the largest and hardest part of the developmental work is done. The task is simply to provide a means of moving the trainees from their present levels to a desired goal. Too often the "how" is determined before the "where."

As in the case of training programs generally, there are several approaches to designing special training programs.

Develop and conduct your own programs. The principal advantage to this approach obviously is its low out-of-pocket cost. It may, however, become extremely expensive in terms of staff time spent in program development. Furthermore its inflexibility is demonstrated when a degree of expertise not available among the staff is needed. For example, few training staffs include a person qualified to develop and conduct a speed reading program.

Programs tailored to an organization's special needs can be developed for almost any purpose by consultants, and can be conducted either by the consultant or by consultant-trained staff members. Such specially designed programs involve a relatively large development cost, often followed by a fee each time the course is conducted.

An approach which can be considered a compromise, or "happy medium," between the two is the purchase of a broad-based "packaged" program. Because many organizations have the same general needs, a large number of choices are available to the training department. Almost all these programs require that the program be adapted to the individual needs of the organization and allow enough flexibility for the training department to do so.

Motion pictures, filmstrips, and cassettes on a wide variety of topics are available with workbooks and leader's guides easily adapted to an industry or organization. A list of source material is included at the end of the chapter.

It is not economically feasible to use any of the above approaches when only a few employees share a particular training need. For this situation, a wide range of seminars and workshops is offered across the country. Although the cost per person is high (particularly when travel expenses are involved), the total training cost is lower than purchasing or designing a program and justifying it by enrolling a large number of people who have little or no need for it.

Supervisory, management, and skills development programs comprised of modules — self-contained units — offer a number of ready-made special training programs. A module can be extracted from a larger program and adapted for a different audience. (Sometimes the reverse route is used; a special training program meets with such success that it is incorporated into a larger program.)

EVALUATION AND FOLLOW-UP

Immediate Evaluation

At the conclusion of any course, you will want employee reactions. A simple evaluation form is most useful in assessing program content and conference leader performance. Participants may be unable, however, to predict how useful the course content will be. They must return to their jobs and apply the principles and concepts to which they have been exposed. Only then can they provide meaningful evaluation.

The evaluation made immediately after completion of the program (perhaps in the final ten minutes to ensure a 100 percent response) serves an important purpose for the conference leader. Based on feedback from conferees, he can adjust his style of delivery, can modify the program, if necessary, for future presentations.

An example is shown in Figure 1. Questions 1, 2, and 3 involve nothing more than subjective evaluations. But the responses can be compared with responses to similar questions asked at a later date.

Follow-up Evaluation

A training department often is required to justify the continuation of training programs in terms of their effectiveness. Training offers the promise of improved performance for those who participate. If the promise goes unfulfilled or unproven, management will be hard pressed to justify the expense of the programs themselves and the time away from the job for the participants.

There are two areas for possible investigation:

1. How useful has the program content been to the participants in the performance of their jobs? Were their objectives satisfied?

Figure 1.   An example of a simple program evaluation form. Questions 1, 2, and 3 involve nothing more than subjective evaluations, but the responses can be compared with responses to similar questions asked at a later date.

PROGRAM EVALUATION
Program _____ Conference leader _____
1. Please rate this program.
    Excellent _____ Very good _____ Good _____ Fair _____ Poor _____
2. What portions of the subject matter could have been excluded or expanded?
3. To what extent did you benefit from this program?
    Very much so _____ Generally, yes _____ To some extent _____
    Slightly _____ No _____ If so, how? _____
4. Please give your rating of the conference leader.
    Excellent _____ Very good _____ Good _____ Fair _____ Poor _____
Please comment on your rating _____

---

2. How well has the training department met the needs of the organization and of individual departments? In other words, how satisfied are the training department's customers?

If the training department formulated realistic objectives, if the participating departments understood and accepted the objectives, and if the program represented a reasonable means of attaining the objectives, the evaluation should be positive.

Of course, no program is perfect, and no evaluation is perfect. And so the developmental work goes on. No program is ever a final one. The entire process can be viewed as circular—each activity flows logically and constantly into the next.

The following programs are among the most commonly used.

SPECIAL COMMUNICATIONS SKILLS

Speaking, writing, listening, and reading make up a large part of a manager's job. Usually a management development program devotes some attention to each of these, but some management and supervisory personnel require more attention than a general program provides.

Courses on speaking, writing, listening, and reading are purely skills programs. Unless a person possesses greater than average discipline and strong motivation to change, a recital of rules will not improve his performance. Course content must be directly related to the job and must provide opportunity to practice the skill. Participants must recognize their deviations from the ideal, and be given opportunity to achieve the ideal.

Public Speaking

Public speaking techniques apply not only to the executive who speaks to an audience of several hundred, but also to the first-line supervisor who recommends a new procedure to his boss or informs his staff of a change. It is pointless to tell a group to organize a presentation, to use a topic sentence, supporting material, and a conclusion, and to use appropriate gestures. Each of these must be demonstrated and practiced after the basic fear of public speaking is overcome.

A generally accepted method of helping trainees overcome the fear is to have them speak extemporaneously before the group until they are comfortable. Until the trainees are at ease, little can be accomplished.

From this point, it is usual for the trainer to work with the trainees in writing a speech for future presentation, going through the mechanics—the "how to" of speech writing. A brief review of communication theory is useful. The trainer then shows how a speech is organized, including a statement of purpose, how supporting evidence is introduced, and how the talk should be presented—the "how to" of speechmaking. The trainer may even act as a horrible example, demonstrating mannerisms which reduce a speaker's effectiveness.

Where available, closed-circuit television is a valuable aid in the next step of speech training. Unless a record is available, a trainee has only the observations of his audience to build upon. Closed-circuit TV allows feedback to the trainee and gives him a chance to see himself. (An important note of caution: Do not allow the TV camera and monitor to become a plaything. Closed-circuit TV is a training tool, not a toy with which the training staff can demonstrate its Academy Award camera techniques. The television equipment can be frightening; so it should be placed as inconspicuously as possible.)

After the presentation, the trainee wants to know "How did I do?" and "What can I do to improve?" To these questions the trainer offers positive, constructive answers on how the trainees can work outside the classroom to make their public speaking more effective.

Report Writing

The writing courses most frequently offered—those which review grammar rules or restate rules, such as "Keep your writing simple"—apparently have not worked well. The truly effective programs recognize that college writing is different from business writing and do not attempt to provide more than is actually needed on the job. Writing programs are virtually useless unless the skills learned are the ones rewarded outside the classroom. An example of wasted training is one in which a manager attended a week-long outside seminar "to become a better writer." After five days of learning to write clear, coherent, orderly, concise, straightforward reports, he returned to work anxious to apply his new skills. His first memo was rejected for being too positive. He learned in less than a week that his organization did not want clear, concise writing; it wanted verbose, indefinite reports loaded with "perhaps," "maybe," and "possibly." Not only did his organization lose five days of his time and the registration fee, but it also will pay the price for an incalculable decline in his morale.

Writing training must be geared to the organization's writing style, where such a style has been established (formally or informally). And it must be practical. As in speech training, rules are useless unless trainees practice them. Editing and revising memos and reports which trainees wrote during the month before the program keep the course content work centered. It is appropriate to review the organization's report-writing manual, if one exists, and standard practices regarding such mundane matters as carbon copies. If such a manual does not exist, an outgrowth of an in-house writing program should be geared to the actual needs of the people who write reports. And the training department should capitalize on such an opportunity to reinforce training.

Reading Improvement

The major claim for reading programs is a spectacular increase in speed with maintenance or improvement in comprehension. As the pressure grows on managers to read more widely and deeply and as it becomes increasingly important to be a technical specialist and a cultural generalist, the needs for reading programs, as well as their popularity, grow.

One well-known reading program is that offered by the Evelyn Wood Reading Dynamics Institute. The program emphasizes a variety of techniques for different kinds of reading and, through drills, trains participants to accelerate their eye movements by moving their hands across the page.

Other programs, less well known, use such mechanical devices as a tachistoscope (which flashes words on a screen) or an accelerator (a sliding cover which runs down the page). Both devices train the eye to read more words in a given time.

Because of the practice time required between classes (approximately two hours a day), students need strong motivation to derive maximum benefit from any reading program. For this reason many companies require participants to pay all or part of the program's cost even when the program is conducted on the premises.

Reading programs, more often than the others discussed, are held after hours. Individuals with a need for reading improvement should investigate adult education programs in colleges, high schools, and YMCAs. The Evelyn Wood Reading Dynamics Institute will conduct a program on the premises for twenty employees at a group rate.

Listening

As in the other communications skills, listening training is most effective if it maintains a calculated balance between theory and practice—with the emphasis on practice.

By its very nature, listening training is most useful when the trainee spends the bulk of his training time listening and gaining feedback on how much of the message he comprehends. For this purpose the most practical approach is a course built around tapes or cassettes. Tests at the beginning and end of a program provide the trainee with feedback on his progress—but this progress is achieved in a necessarily artificial environment. Even so, a manager spends almost 50 percent of his work time listening. Even a small increase in his efficiency pays dividends.

Most listening programs expose trainees to the skills which make him or her a more effective listener. The better programs also include opportunities for practice and feedback. The Dun & Bradstreet Complete Course in Listening, developed by Ralph G. Nichols, is one of several courses available. Through cassettes, trainees are exposed to principles, participate in exercise, and are tested on their ability to apply the principles. Both a pretest and a posttest are administered to measure progress. A *Leader's Manual* provides material for formal training sessions, but the course also can be used individually. Several alternate presentations are possible within the basic framework, and the course can be adapted with relative ease.

TELEPHONE TRAINING

Ordinarily included as one unit of a secretarial program, telephone training is applicable generally to office personnel. Department heads and managers acknowledge readily that telephone techniques in their offices could, and should, be upgraded. Most telephone companies readily acknowledge, too, that their customers need training in telephone usage. To meet this need, the local telephone companies provide such training in a more professional and entertaining manner than most training departments could, and in many cases at little or no cost to the customer.

Specially trained telephone company representatives conduct the program and will adapt it to particular needs. A full program includes the following:

A film showing proper and improper use of the telephone, emphasizing interpersonal relations and the concept that tone of voice may convey an impression which we do not intend. Often the telephone company representative explains the technical problems of her company and demonstrates proper use of the equipment together with procedures which will save money for the user.

If the chief operator in the user's company also explains the day-to-day problems faced by the operators, the office people gain a level of understanding which should lead to better cooperation with the operators.

Further, all or some of the trainees role-play situations using practice telephones and tape recorders. Each member of the group then describes how he or she would handle the situation.

At the conclusion of the program, the telephone company representative gives each participant several pamphlets to reinforce the training.

Telephone training has substantial positive effect to the extent that management makes known, on a continuing basis, what standard must be maintained. It is more usual for a manager to express his dissatisfaction to everyone except to the employees who answer the telephones.

CUSTOMER RELATIONS TRAINING

Customer relations training tries to anticipate typical customer-vendor situations and to provide trainees with the skills needed to handle such situations. In order to represent his company effectively to the public, the trainee gains preliminary exposure to customer "complaints" under controlled conditions.

The "vestibule" approach to training, which simulates as nearly as possible the actual job situation, has gained momentum in recent years for skills training. And it has proved highly effective.

Vestibule training for public contact jobs (either telephone or face to face) emphasizes the skill areas but incorporates public relations training as well. For the customer relations aspects, trainees encounter typical situations, just as they handle actual forms and cases in the skills training phase.

Even when it is inappropriate to simulate a specific job situation, (e.g., where class members have few job tasks in common), intensive customer relations training is worthwhile.

Employees must, first, be made aware of their public relations role. Unless this point is stressed, employees might not recognize that they represent the company to its customers. They may fail to realize, too, that their actions affect company profits, and that their job depends on the impression they give to customers.

With the foundation of awareness established, the job-oriented training assumes deeper meaning. Typical problem situations, which employees will face, can be the basis for role play and discussion. With this background, employees can face on-the-job situations with greater confidence. In summary, the purpose of customer relations training is to anticipate the problems with which the employee will have to deal and to provide him with guidelines for solving them.

Customer relations training can be reinforced effectively with posters, brochures, and lapel buttons. Intensive publicity campaigns are useful in maintaining the awareness fostered by the training sessions.

New employees, however, are not the only ones with a need for this program. A review program for experienced workers reminds them of areas in which they can improve.

SPECIAL PERSONNEL TRAINING PROGRAMS

The training division often can act as support for the wage and salary, employment, and benefits areas of the personnel department. Some special training programs which might be offered on a cooperative basis include:

1. Interviewing training in cooperation with the employment division. Line managers and supervisors with hiring responsibility can make the hiring decision more objectively and with more confidence after brief exposure to, and practice in, the techniques of interviewing.

2. Attendance and punctuality control training in cooperation with the benefits division. Few supervisors are familiar with the techniques of employee counseling. If the responsibility for reducing absenteeism and lateness rests with the supervisor, however, training in counseling can provide him with a valuable tool.

3. Performance review training in cooperation with the wage and salary division. The supervisor can be taught how to use the performance or merit review system as a motivator. The training program can provide information about the system, train the supervisor to appraise, and, most important, train him to conduct meaningful appraisal interviews.

The programs not only increase the effectiveness of supervisors, but also increase the effectiveness of the personnel department. Moreover, the personnel department has the opportunity to present its philosophy and approach directly to line supervisors.

OTHER SPECIAL TRAINING PROGRAMS

As mentioned earlier, individual modules of general supervisory development programs often stand on their own as special training programs. Units on problem solving, decision making, motivation, effective supervision, and handling conflict are only a few of the many possibilities.

CONCLUSION

Be involved, involve the learner, stay involved. To achieve their full potential, special training programs must be initially realistic and subsequently reinforced. Responsibility for achievement is shared by the training department, the trainee, and the trainee's supervisor.

The training department must offer realistic, job-related programs; the trainee must participate actively in the program and apply the ideas and techniques presented; the supervisor must encourage and support the trainee's efforts to improve, and evaluate progress.

Special training programs which support and complement the more general programs of management, supervisory, and skills training contribute substantially to the overall effectiveness of the organization.

SUGGESTED PERIODICALS

Continuing Education, Pennsylvania Research Associates, Inc., Philadelphia, Pa.
Educational Technology, Educational Technology Publications, Inc., Englewood Cliffs, N.J.
Training in Business & Industry, Gellert Publishing Co., New York.
Training and Development Journal, American Society for Training and Development, Madison, Wis.

chapter 25

New Instructional Techniques for the Trainer

DR. GEARY A. RUMMLER *President, Praxis Corporation, New York, New York*

New instructional or training techniques come and go and generally make little impact on the quality of training and even less on job performance. For this reason, this chapter will not simply describe a roster of currently available instructional techniques; rather, it will discuss why some techniques have had more impact than others, present guidelines for selecting appropriate techniques, and outline a procedure for making better instructional decisions. The emphasis will be on providing the reader with a general framework for matching appropriate instructional techniques to given instructional problems.

A FRAMEWORK

The trainer is constantly bombarded with products or concepts hailed as training techniques, including programmed instruction, search-confrontation methods, overhead film projectors, audio cassettes, behavioral objectives, and the computer. Some order can be brought to the apparently random array of techniques by considering the training model pictured in Figure 1, which shows a training system as having the following components:

1. The subject-matter resources from which the information is selected to meet the instructional objectives or to fill out the course content

2. The system or means by which the instruction is presented to the trainee

3. The trainee

4. The learning environment, meaning the physical plant and trainer-trainee-classroom logistics

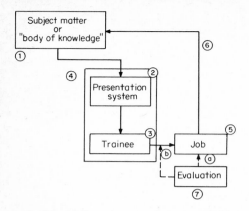

Figure 1.   A training model.

5. The performance environment (job) to which the trainee proceeds following instruction

6. The feedback from the performance environment (where the need for training occurs) to the subject-matter resources

7. Evaluation of the:

    a. Value of that learning, or its effect on the desired performance

    b. Extent of the learning transaction

This model is significantly different from the formal-educational-institution model of education (and from a great deal of formal industrial training, for that matter) in that the trainee will eventually proceed to a performance environment where the ultimate effectiveness of his training will be tested. For another, the model recognizes that there is a close relationship between the performance environment and the subject matter, the ultimate selection of subject matter depending wholly on the performance desired of the trainee in the real world.

Based on this model, there are four basic processes or subsystems that the trainer should be concerned with:

1. *The Selection of Content.*   The content is selected by examining the performance environment (job) to determine relevant instructional objectives.

2. *Design of the Instructional System.*   This process involves making learning and logistics decisions. The decisions concerned with learning are those of determining the best instructional strategies for correcting the diagnosed deficiencies and specifying appropriate methods of presenting the learning tasks, of requiring trainee response or interaction, and of providing feedback or confirmation to the trainee. From a logistical standpoint, decisions must be made on how best to deliver the instruction to the student (which depends on the location and on the number of students) and the management of the learning transaction, including scheduling, assignment, and record keeping.

3. *Design of an Evaluation System.*   This is done concurrently with the selection of content and design of the instructional system. The first evaluation point developed is *a* in Figure 1. This evaluates whether that training was of value and simply asks whether the problem that initiated the training has now been resolved. If it has not been resolved, the data gathered at this point should be specific enough to allow for a correction in the instructional system that will ultimately lead to the desired improvement.

At the second evaluation point to be developed (*b* in Figure 1), the system determines the success of the learning transaction, i.e., whether people can perform as intended. This evaluation system is usually specified at the time the instructional objectives are generated, by describing how the trainee will demonstrate mastery of the objective.

4. *Design of a Maintenance System.*   Once the trainee can perform as desired, his performance must be maintained.[1]   This is best done by establishing a system of feedback to the trainee on the quality and quantity of his performance and by structuring positive consequences to the trainee for desired performance.   This behavior-maintenance system is as important as the instructional system and must be designed and implemented with equal care if the total training system is to be effective.   (Frequently, performance problems identified in the performance environment and originally diagnosed as training problems are in fact maintenance problems.)

With this framework in mind, let us briefly review several "new instructional techniques" and see what function they perform in the training model.

Audio-tape cassettes are relevant to the transaction between the teacher and trainee components of the instructional design system.   To the extent that such a tape cassette system is used to train to objectives such as teaching salesmen to discriminate customer objections, the cassette has some *learning* (presentation-confirmation) *value*.   But when the cassette is to be distributed to the field and used to present information to salesmen while they drive from call to call, its primary value lies in the *logistical* convenience of delivery and management.   Use for this reason is quite sensible, but the technique should not be adopted for its contribution to the learning function, since listening to a tape is considerably more inefficient than reading the printed page.

The *computer* is also applicable to the transaction between teacher and trainee. It is particularly valuable in *managing* the transaction (keeping records on student performance and progress) and in delivering instruction to remote locations, i.e., any place with a terminal, which frequently is in the performance environment itself.   The current state of the art, however, limits the visual displays a computer can make and the responses a learner can make, thereby restricting the value of the computer in a *learning sense*.   The result has been generally unimpressive content in computers.   The exceptions are "games" using computers (the presentation and response made are adequate and the capability to feedback to the students uniquely appropriate) and training programs for instructing in the use of the computer terminal itself, the presentation and response requirements obviously being perfect.

Role-play is another technique used to accomplish the transaction.   Its value is strictly in the area of *learning*.   With this technique, it is possible to simulate real-world stimuli and test the trainee's responses.   Unfortunately, observers of the role-play learn more than the person in the role, since they can view his performance objectively.   In other words, the trainee in the role-play receives realistic presentation and makes realistic response, but gets very little feedback on his own performance.   The role-play technique has been made considerably more effective with the use of video-tape recording.

Video-tape recording is relevant to the transaction and has both *learning* and *logistical* advantages.   Its learning advantages include the ability to make controlled presentation of certain stimuli and record trainee response, and thereby provide important visual feedback to the trainee.   Logistically, video tapes can be distributed at relatively low cost to remote training locations.

---

[1] For a complete discussion of the importance of maintenance systems, see Karen S. Brethower, "Maintenance Systems: The Neglected Half of Behavior Change," in Rummler, Yaney, and Schrader (eds.), *Managing the Instructional Programming Effort,* University of Michigan, 1967.

Programmed instruction is concerned, in its narrowest interpretation, only with the transaction. It has both *learning* advantages (controlled presentation of highly realistic stimuli, elicitation of student response, and presentation of confirmation) and *logistical* advantages (ease of delivery to isolated trainees, administration to groups of varying size). Since programmed instruction first gained popularity, however, it has become generally considered to be a "process" of instructional design that begins by considering observed problems in the performance environment, selects subject matter for instruction accordingly, and concerns itself with how the behavior change will be maintained. Whether you interpret "programmed instruction" to mean a mode of instruction or a method of developing instruction depends on whether you are considering a specific programmed text or unit or a consultant firm of experienced programmers who will custom-design a program.

From this review of "techniques," two things should be obvious. First, the questions to ask of any proposed instructional technique are: What does it do for me? Where does it fit in the scheme of things? Does it help me select the subject matter, design a better instructional unit, evaluate the results, or maintain behavior? If it is restricted to the instructional design, what does it do for the transaction? Does it have primarily learning value (presentation, response, feedback), or is it primarily a logistical aid helping in the management of the transaction or the delivery of the instruction? Or is it just a lot of meaningless words that contribute nothing?

Secondly, it should become clear why new instructional techniques have in general had such little impact on training results. The fact is that almost all instructional innovations have taken place only in the presentation-system component or the "transaction" between teacher and learner (components 2 and 3 in Figure 1). Unfortunately, though, the greatest instructional innovation is next to worthless when the subject matter taught is irrelevant, the behavior analyzed is not maintained, and the evaluation of the entire process is too inadequate to determine whether the instructional transaction has been a success (objectives met) and the performance problem solved.

ASKING THE RIGHT QUESTIONS

The key to training effectiveness is analysis—asking the right questions—not flashy new training techniques. Until such analysis becomes the major emphasis, training will remain a field consisting of a collection of techniques in search of an application. When confronted with a supposed training need, the question trainers tend to ask is, "What training do you want?" The question that should be asked is, "What is the problem?" When one asks the former question, he is committed to engaging in some training activity. Moreover, that activity is going to be prescribed by the requestor, who will specify the content and the techniques and when to hold the session. The trainer is then left no alternative but to carry out the packaging of the activity.

In contrast, if one asks the latter question, a completely different sequence of events is likely to unfold. By additional questioning on what seems to be the problem, the trainer can guide the requestor to seeing better what the problem is, the real value of solving it, and the extent to which it can be solved by training. Now the trainer is in a position to design a course or activity that will be relevant and to know what will constitute success for the course. In the second case, then, the trainer is making a significant contribution to the organization. He is using his skill to increase the performance of persons in the organization, not just engaging in training activity for its own sake.

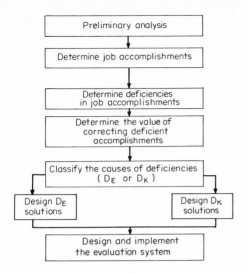

Figure 2. The process of conducting a performance audit.

THE PERFORMANCE AUDIT

The performance audit is a procedure for asking the right questions. The major steps in the procedure are summarized in Figure 2. If one assumes a model for training systems such as that put forth in Figure 1, then the performance audit is the procedure for developing all four subsystems (selecting content and designing the instructional, evaluation, and maintenance systems). The thrust of the performance audit is to continue to narrow down the problem to be attacked—always trying to get from general statements to specific examples. This is done to increase the probability of solving the actual problem, decrease training costs, and reduce educational overkill (i.e., we do not know what they need so let us give it all to them).

Each step in the procedure will be discussed in turn.

I. Preliminary analysis (What is the problem? What are the constraints on its solution?)

There are three classes of questions to ask during the preliminary analysis. The first has to do with identification of the general problem area, the second with the various expectations for solving the problem, and the third with constraints on solving the problem.

A. Problem identification
1. Why the decision to conduct training?
2. What is the stated problem?
3. Who says it is a problem?
4. How do they know it is a problem? What specific incident occurred?
5. Why is it a problem? What are the consequences of the current performance, and on whom do they fall?
6. Is it a general problem or can it be isolated by region, season, product, shift, or other factor?
7. How will you know when the problem is solved?

B. Role expectations
1. For each party concerned with the project, e.g., requestor of the training, supposed trainees, answer the following:

        a. What is the stated goal in conducting training?
        b. How will that goal be measured, short- and long-term?
        c. What are the criteria for the stated goal, short- and long-term?
        d. What are unstated needs to be fulfilled by this project, short- and long-term?
    2. Who has the most influence over the ultimate success or failure of satisfactorily solving the problem?
    3. Who (other than the trainee) stands to gain the most if this project:
        a. Succeeds?
        b. Fails?
  C. Project constraints
    1. Who is the population in question?
    2. How much change will the roles tolerate in:
        a. Time?
        b. Content?
        c. Administration and presentation?
    3. What are the general constraints on the project?
        a. Who must be talked to or included?
        b. Who cannot be talked to?
        c. How quickly must the project be done?
        d. What amount of money is available?
        e. What are the constraints on the data to be gathered?
    4. What are the general constraints on the product?
        a. Will training be acceptable?
        b. Can procedures be changed?
        c. Can jobs be redesigned?
        d. Can a feedback and/or management-information system be installed?
        e. Can the reward structure be altered?

II. Determine job accomplishments (What is expected of the performer in question?)

Once a job or position has been identified for a more detailed analysis, the performance audit begins in earnest. The next step is to specify what is expected of the performer or position in question. This consists of listing the accomplishments or job outcomes of the position being examined and the standards or requirements for each.

This step is relatively straightforward if a job is well defined. In the event it is not, there may well be some negotiation to agree on what should be expected and the standard of performance. In some cases, the current expectations for a position are totally inappropriate, and the analyst may find himself engaged in changing the expectations of the organization for a particular job.

III. Determine deficiencies in accomplishments (What is actually happening?)

Once the "expected" has been established, the analyst must determine the current level of performance. At this point, he is interested in how the expected accomplishments are *not* being met, not in the deficiencies of the performer. This information is gathered by talking with supervisors, observing performers, and examining records such as grievances, performance reviews, production records, and quality reports.

IV. Determine the value of correcting deficient accomplishments (What is the value of correcting each deficiency?)

At this point, it is necessary to determine how the deficient accomplishments "hurt" the organization and the cost of that "hurt" to the organization.

This step makes it possible to set priorities of action. It also makes it possible to assess the worth of correcting a deficiency. That is, the value *(V)* of correcting a deficiency should exceed the cost *(C)* of correcting it, or $V/C > 1$.

V. Classify the cause of the deficiency (What is the cause of the deficiency?)

Performance deficiencies can be classified as deficiencies of knowledge (D_K) resulting from the employee's not knowing what to do, how to do it, or when to do it; and deficiencies of execution (D_E) resulting from an employee's failing to perform because of factors in the work environment. Deficiencies of execution are further classified as resulting from *poor feedback* to the employee on how well he is doing and what he might do to correct his performance, from *punishment* or *insufficient positive consequences* for doing as expected, or from some form of *task interference* resulting from poor or inappropriate job design.

Distinguishing between deficiencies of knowledge and execution is a critical step in the performance analysis. Frequently, failure to make this distinction accurately results in conducting extended and expensive training to solve an execution, or nontraining, problem. In addition to being a waste of money, such training tends to reduce the credibility of the training organization with the trainee and his management. Answers to the following questions will lead to correct classification of performance deficiencies as deficiencies of knowledge or of execution:

A. What is the desired performance (job outcome)?
   1. What are the job standards?
   2. Says who?
   3. Does everybody agree on them?
   4. Does everybody (anybody) know whether standards are being met now?
B. What are the specific differences between actual and expected performance?
   1. Has anyone ever performed as required?
   2. Who?
   3. When?
C. Could employees perform properly if their lives depended on it?
   1. Did employees perform properly when they first came on the job?
D. Do deficient performers know
   1. What is expected of them?
   2. That they are not performing correctly and exactly how far they are from expected performance?
   3. How to perform correctly?
   4. When to perform?
E. What positive and/or negative consequences of performing correctly/incorrectly can employees expect
   1. From their bosses?
   2. From their subordinates?
   3. From their peers?
VI. Design D_E solutions

Deficiency of execution problems (D_E's) are basically "maintenance of performance" problems as described earlier. The process of correcting such problems will itself correct many related problems and is most certainly critical to the success of many training programs. D_E's can usually be corrected successfully and inexpensively by training personnel in conjunction with line management. The following are guidelines for developing D_E solutions:

    A. Is the deficiency due to *task interference?*
      1. Is there enough time to perform the task?
      2. Is there enough equipment to perform the task?
      3. Are there enough support people and services to perform the task?
      4. Are there competing tasks?
      5. Are there things that distract the employee from the task?
    B. Is the deficiency due to *lack of feedback* to the performer on his performance?
      1. Does the employee get information about what is right and wrong with his performance?
      2. Does the information tell the employee how to improve his performance?
      3. Does the employee get information frequently?
      4. How soon after the employee performs does he get information about that performance?
      5. Is the information such that it can be easily interpreted by the employee?
    C. Is the deficiency due to *unfavorable consequences* to the performer for performing in the desired manner?
      1. What are the consequences (positive and negative) to the individual performer for performing *as desired* (as meted out by his superior, peers, and subordinates)?
      2. What are the consequences (positive and negative) to the individual performer for continuing to perform in his present *undesired* manner (as meted out by his superior, peers, and subordinates)?

VII. Design D_K solutions

    By this time, the trainer has identified specific knowledge deficiencies of sufficient value to correct. The design of knowledge solutions should include the following steps:

    A. State instructional objectives

      The specific performance deficiencies (D_Ks) are converted into instructional objectives, the accomplishment of which can be measured.

    B. Design mastery tasks

      Each instructional objective is represented by a performance test or task that tests for mastery of the objective by the trainee. These mastery tasks become a guide for the selection of subject matter and the bases for evaluation of the instruction.

    C. Select guidance or training

      Many instructional objectives can be accomplished easily and inexpensively through the design of guidance materials (job or decision aids) that the trainee uses on the job.

    Guidance is most valuable for:
    1. Tasks that involve many simple steps.
    2. Tasks that allow instructions to be read during performance.
    3. Tasks in which small errors in performance can produce significant negative consequences.
    4. Tasks that are performed only infrequently.
    5. Tasks in which accuracy is generally more important than speed.
    6. Tasks that are assigned small instructional budgets.

    Training is desirable for:
    1. Tasks in which speed is generally more important than accuracy.
    2. Tasks where reading instructions would interfere with performance.

3. Tasks where small errors are not usually costly.
Of course, some tasks will meet criteria for both guidance and training. In those cases, the training director must weigh each criterion to choose the appropriate instructional method.

D. Develop a course plan and select appropriate instructional techniques
The general instructional sequence is specified. Then instructional techniques are selected, given the instructional objectives and logistical constraints.

VIII. Design and implement the evaluation system
The major components of the evaluation system should be developed as part of the preceding steps, and all that remains to be done now is to formalize the evaluation procedure. If performance deficiencies have in fact been identified and a value has been placed on their correction, then we have the basis for knowing whether the problem has been solved and whether it was worth solving. We can determine the value of the training. The instructional objectives and the mastery tasks are the basis for measuring whether the training has been effective.

SUMMARY

Training efforts frequently fail because they attack the wrong problem or attempt to solve the correct problem with an inappropriate instructional technique. A systematic analysis procedure such as the performance audit will aid in proper problem identification. Careful consideration of the learning and logistical requirements of the instructional system will lead to the selection of appropriate instructional techniques. The trainer's frequent task of evaluating individual instructional techniques should be done by comparing the supposed attributes of the techniques with the functions that must be performed in a total training system. It is then possible to judge whether the technique in question performs any significant function at all and, if it does, whether it does so any better than a less expensive alternative.

chapter 26

Evaluation of Training

ROBERT S. DVORIN *Consultant, Westport, Connecticut*

Training and development activities have continued to grow in business, government, and nonprofit organizations. This growth is reflected in both the range and
number of programs being offered to employees. In part it can be attributed to such
factors as the increased skills required in today's organizations, frequent shortages
of experienced and skilled manpower, and attempts to improve organizational
efficiency and effectiveness through the development of all levels of employees.
However, the growth in training and development may also be a carry-over of our
general faith and belief in the educational process. Thus, one writer, in surveying
education in general in the United States, summarized this point as follows[1]:

> The tremendous growth of mass education at all levels verifies the previous observation:
> Americans have great faith in formal education. It is good for children; it is good for
> veterans; it is good for adults; it is good for almost anyone. What it is good for is not
> always clear, but Americans approve of education.

While many of us may share this faith and belief in education, those who have
professional, management, or administrative responsibilities for the training and
development of others should operate on more than faith. We should be able to
specify what we are training for (our objectives), and we should be trying to evaluate whether or not our programs (formal or informal) are moving toward the
achievement of these objectives. Unfortunately, too often the evaluation process
is not carried out, or if it is, the bases or criteria for evaluation are unclear or inappropriate.
   In this chapter, the goals will be to (1) outline basic criteria for evaluating training
and development programs, (2) review some of the major techniques used to measure the effectiveness of training against these basic criteria, and (3) discuss briefly
the issue of reporting training results to management.

[1] Wilbur B. Brookover, *A Sociology of Education,* American Book Company, New York,
1955, p. 45.

BASIC CRITERIA

Five basic criteria for evaluation can be identified:

1. Participant's reaction. How did the participants feel about the training, the instructor and instructional methods utilized, the material, the usefulness or applicability of the training, etc.?

2. Changes in participants' knowledge and/or skills. What new knowledge or skills were acquired and demonstrated?

3. Changes in participants' attitudes. In what ways and to what degree have the attitudes of the participants (values or beliefs) been influenced by the training activities?

4. Changes in job performance. As a result of the training, do the participants perform differently in their work setting?

5. Organizational performance or results. In what way did the training contribute to achieving specific organizational goals such as reduced turnover, improved safety, higher productivity, or a decrease in employee grievances?

In the sections which follow, we shall look at each of these basic criteria and indicate techniques which will help in measuring effectiveness. Before moving on, however, it should be noted that as you move from the first criteria (participant reaction) through to the last (organizational performance or results), the evaluation involved, in general, becomes more useful from the point of view of management, but also becomes more difficult. Kirkpatrick,[2] whose breakdown of evaluation closely parallels that outlined above, highlights this point by identifying reaction, learning, behavior, and results as "steps" in the evaluation process, thus indicating the desirability of moving toward the evaluation of on-the-job performance or behavior and results.

Participant Reaction

How participants respond to a training session or program can be important in influencing its effectiveness. Certainly, if they find the sessions boring, the instructor disorganized or unqualified, or the content irrelevant, the chances of desired learning or change taking place are slight. On the other hand, it must be recognized that although a participant may have extremely positive feelings about a program, this is no guarantee that he has learned anything worthwhile or that he will apply what he has learned.

Because of the relative ease with which data can be collected on the participants' reactions, this information is often employed. While it may be of some value in assessing what has taken place and may be useful in finding some clues to improving training programs, it is a relatively inappropriate way of evaluating what has been learned or what the experience will mean in terms of individual job performance or organizational results. Thus, the training director, administrator, or manager is wise to keep in mind the nature and limitations of the data he is collecting when he applies this information.

Where participant reaction is used as part (or all) of the evaluation process, data collection is facilitated by having participants fill out a carefully designed questionnaire. The items included on the questionnaire should focus on those points which are most important to the evaluator. The form itself should be fairly straightforward and easy to complete. It can contain items which are numerically scaled, multiple-choice items, open-ended questions, or any suitable combination

[2] Donald L. Kirkpatrick, "Evaluation of Training," in Robert L. Craig and Lester R. Bittel (eds.), *Training and Development Handbook,* McGraw-Hill Book Company, New York, 1967, pp. 87–112.

of these. An important point in designing the questionnaire is to decide before-hand how the data will be analyzed, summarized, and reported. For instance, if a formal report is to be written in which a quantitative summary of the feedback is presented, the items included should be in a form which is quantifiable. Thus, open-ended questions would be avoided since, without a fairly time-consuming content analysis, responses to them would be difficult if not impossible to sum-marize in a quantitative fashion.

Figure 1 is a sample of the type of form which might be utilized. It is presented merely to illustrate some of the areas which might be covered and some of the items which might be included. While many organizations use a "standard" reaction

---

PARTICIPANT REACTION FORM

PROGRAM: _____   DATE: _____

We would appreciate your sharing with us your feelings and re-actions to this program so that we can evaluate it and, where appropriate, make changes to improve its usefulness. Please answer the questions below as frankly as possible and use the "comments" spaces provided for any additional thoughts or sug-gestions you may have.

1. Overall, how would you rate this program in terms of its value to you? (Please circle one number reflecting your feeling.)

   1   2   3   4   5   6   7   8   9
   Poor   Fair   Average   Good   Excellent

2. For each of the items below, please place an X in the ap-propriate column.

		Excellent	Good	Average	Fair	Poor
a)	How well was the program content organized?	___	___	___	___	___
b)	How well was the material presented by the instructor?	___	___	___	___	___
c)	How well did the instructor keep your interest?	___	___	___	___	___
d)	How well did the instructor respond to questions or issues raised by participants?	___	___	___	___	___
e)	How did you feel about the physical facilities (e.g., conference room, furniture, etc.)?	___	___	___	___	___

COMMENTS:

EXHIBIT I

Figure 1. Sample participant reaction and evaluation form.

PARTICIPANT REACTION FORM (cont'd)

3. Please rate the various methods or techniques used during
    the program in terms of how helpful they were.

	Excellent	Good	Average	Fair	Poor
Lectures	—	—	—	—	—
Reading Materials and Assignments	—	—	—	—	—
Films	—	—	—	—	—
General Class Discussion	—	—	—	—	—
Small Group Work Periods	—	—	—	—	—
Role-Playing	—	—	—	—	—
Cases	—	—	—	—	—

COMMENTS:

4. How would you feel about recommending this program to others?

    ___ Would strongly recommend it.
    ___ Would recommend with some reservations.
    ___ Would not recommend.

5. In what way could the program be improved?

6. OTHER COMMENTS:

EXHIBIT I (Cont'd.)

Figure 1. Sample participant reaction and evaluation form. (continued)

form or common items on a variety of forms, it is suggested that some thought be given to designing the reaction form for the particular program being evaluated.

Finally, it should be noted that obtaining participants' reactions is not limited to the end of a training program. Where there are a number of sessions in a program, reactions may be gathered periodically (or after each session) to help the trainer or instructor in making desirable modifications in content, instructional techniques, etc. Also, where one wishes to obtain information about the on-the-job application of the program content, a follow-up questionnaire may be distributed to participants say one to six months after the program. The idea here is to allow sufficient time after the program so that the participant will have had ample opportunity to apply, test out, and judge the value of his learning experience.

Changes in Participant's Knowledge and/or Skills

Included in the objectives of most training programs is increasing the participant's knowledge and/or skills in specific areas or activities. It follows, therefore, that the increase of knowledge and/or skills should be a valid criterion for evaluating training efforts. For example, if a program is designed to increase an employee's knowledge of specific office procedures, it is reasonable to expect that the employee will know more about the procedures at the conclusion of the program than at the start. Similarly, if the training is aimed at increasing the skill of a machine operator or the typing speed of a secretary, one way of assessing the training is to determine what increased skills can be demonstrated as a result of the training.

While the training activities themselves offer frequent informal opportunities for the instructor or others to observe and "get some feeling" of what learning is taking place, a more objective, structured, and quantifiable measurement of learning is usually possible and almost always desirable. Such evaluation requires two basic ingredients. First, one must have a reliable and valid way of measuring the knowledge and/or skills. Secondly, one must be able to demonstrate that any changes or learning are the result of the training. Each of these is discussed briefly below. However, the reader should be aware that proficiency in measurement and experimental design calls for knowledge far beyond what can be presented here. For those who are interested in further reading, a few specialized references in testing, measurement, and evaluation are included in the Bibliography at the end of this chapter.

Measuring knowledge and/or skills.   The two most frequently used techniques for measuring knowledge and skills are paper-and-pencil tests and performance tests. Paper-and-pencil tests are convenient for measuring knowledge, while performance tests are most often utilized for measuring skills (although it may be possible to use the latter for measuring both knowledge and skills). The development or selection of either type of test takes us immediately back to the training objectives and the early planning for the program. That is, the material included in the tests should be based upon the specific knowledge and/or skills that the program is designed to develop.

It is often argued that the tests should be prepared prior to, or at least simultaneously with, the development of session outlines and materials. For example, if it was felt that the salesmen in an organization needed training on new company products, one approach would be to prepare a list of questions that one would hope each salesman could answer about these products. Working from these questions, one could then begin to plan the most appropriate training program.

While a number of standardized tests are available, frequently they do not deal with the specific content and objectives of a given training program. As a result, the instructor or trainer will often find it necessary to write his own test. It was indicated earlier that detailed discussions of test construction and measurement were beyond the scope of this chapter. However, certain basic guidelines for preparing evaluation tests may be helpful to the reader who wishes to prepare a paper-and-pencil test in order to measure knowledge.

1. Use objective items, e.g., multiple-choice or true-false rather than essay questions.

2. Items used should be important in terms of the knowledge the participant should have. Again, items should reflect specific learning objectives.

3. Try to write items which will get at the participant's understanding of material not just rote memory.

4. Keep the reading level relatively simple so that the participant's score reflects his knowledge of the subject rather than his level of reading comprehension.

5. Make sure that there is only one correct answer in a true-false or multiple-choice item.

6. Use a random pattern of correct answers; that is, do not "give away" the answer by having a set pattern of correct answers (e.g., five true items followed by five false ones).

7. The items should vary in difficulty, a few being relatively simple, a few fairly difficult, with most somewhere in between.

8. Keep the items discrete; the answer to one item should not signal the answer to another, nor should answering one item correctly be contingent upon answering a previous one.

9. Beware of giving clues to the correct answer. In a multiple-choice item, for instance, do not "give away" the correct answer by making it clearly longer or shorter than the other alternatives.

10. Make responding to the items as mechanically simple as possible. Keep in mind that you are trying to measure the individual's knowledge of the subject and not his ability to follow complex directions.

Performance tests.   There are areas in which it is appropriate to use performance tests instead of, or in addition to, paper-and-pencil tests. Most of us have had the experience of applying for a driver's license. In addition to passing a written test to measure our knowledge of the motor vehicle laws and driving rules, acquiring a license usually involves our adequately demonstrating, by means of a performance test, at least minimal driving skills. Merely answering questions correctly does not demonstrate that we have these skills. So, too, in training programs we are faced with somehow evaluating or measuring the acquisition of skills. Can the secretary now type fifty words per minute? Can the machine operator produce a certain number of pieces in a specified time? Performance tests are used to "sample" the level of skills present.

In designing or selecting the performance test, many of the key points raised earlier apply. The test should lead to an objective measure of skills level in quantifiable terms. The test should cover those key performance or skills requirements which the training was established to develop. The test should be presented to the trainee in such a way that he knows precisely what he is expected to do rather than becoming involved with unnecessarily complex or confused directions (unless, of course, we are trying to measure his performance while he is dealing with such directions).

Measurement of certain skills (e.g., typing speed) is relatively simple. However, other skills, such as managerial problem solving and decision making, are much more difficult to measure with performance tests. As trainers become more specific in pinpointing the skills and skills standards they are attempting to develop, and as researchers evolve more sophisticated measurement procedures, more attention will be paid to evaluation by means of performance tests. Tracey[3] has neatly summarized his feelings about performance testing as he compared and contrasted it with what he calls "content measurement" (similar to the type of measurements covered under paper-and-pencil tests).

> Content measurement through testing is beginning to be replaced by performance testing. Not only are performance tests more suitable for the kinds of programs offered in the modern enterprise, but they are also more valid and reliable measures of behavioral change—change of the type training and development programs are organized to engineer. Yet even here there are problems. The design of true performance tests requires

[3] William R. Tracey, *Evaluating Training and Development Systems*, American Management Association, New York, 1969, p. 22.

a high degree of sophistication and expertise in test construction; and such tests take much more time to develop, administer, and score than conventional tests. Nonetheless, they are a necessary part of evaluation in any forward-looking program.

Assume now that suitable instruments and procedures (paper-and-pencil and/or performance tests) are available for measuring the knowledge and skills of those who take part in training programs. We are still faced with a second issue when we use as our criteria for evaluation the changes in participant knowledge and skill; we must demonstrate that it was the training program which resulted in the change.

To illustrate the importance of this issue, let us use the example of a group of thirty stenographers hired by an organization. In the employment process, all thirty were tested and just met the basic requirements of taking shorthand at eighty words per minute. Assume that the group was then divided into three smaller groups (equally skilled). Those in group A were placed in a special two-week training program in which they had a total of fifty hours of special instruction and speed drills to increase their shorthand skills. Those in group B were placed in regular stenographic positions; while those in group C were temporarily placed in clerical positions in which no shorthand was given. At the end of the two-week period, those in group A were retested and showed an increase in skill from eighty to one hundred words per minute. The most obvious conclusion might be that the training program was successful in that the participants' skill increased as indicated. This conclusion might be questioned, however, if it were also shown that those placed directly in stenographic jobs (group B) experienced a similar improvement in skill. Perhaps the training course was not at all needed or did not have to be so long or extensive. Perhaps just the practice one might get on the job is sufficient. Even further doubt would be raised if those in group C (no shorthand at all) improved their performance on the second test. While this is unlikely, it is possible that if they were more at ease and more familiar with the organization's testing procedure, higher scores could result.

In order to avoid erroneous conclusions, it is necessary to use carefully designed research-based evaluations. In the illustration given above, there was an opportunity to avoid some false conclusions about the effectiveness of the training program by comparing what happened to those who received the training (group A) with what happened to those who did not. In essence, control groups were available and could be used to check the results obtained by the "experimental group" (group A).

A number of different training evaluation research designs can be used. Basically, they are geared to assist the instructor, manager, or administrator in ascertaining whether or not the training program or activities have been instrumental in producing any measured changes. (For a brief and not too technical overview of such designs, the reader should find the discussion by Miles[4] on research training designs quite useful. While he is dealing with a limited area of training and development, the general points he makes are readily applicable to other areas.)

Before moving ahead, keep in mind that the evaluation of changes in knowledge and/or skills as discussed in this section centered around measuring such changes within the context of the training program and/or "testing sessions" closely related to the training period. This should not be confused with procedures aimed at measurements against other criteria, such as how the individual performs on the job (to be considered later).

[4]Matthew B. Miles, *Learning To Work in Groups*, Teachers College, Columbia University, New York, 1959, pp. 230–235.

Changes in Participant's Attitudes

Managers throughout organizations have become increasingly aware of the importance role attitudes may play in influencing the effectiveness of individual and organizational performance.   This awareness, coupled with related concerns about what are often called "intangible human factors" and "organizational climate," has led to training efforts aimed at changing attitudes.   Behind such efforts is the assumption that changed attitudes will result in changed and more desirable job performance, behavior, and results. While questions may be raised about the validity of such an assumption, the fact is that the goals or objectives of any particular training program may include changing "the attitudes of participants."   In some instances, fairly broad attitude change goals are indicated (e.g., "a more positive attitude toward their work and the organization").   In other instances, a somewhat more specific goal is stated (e.g., "machine operators should be more positive toward, and ready to use, proper safety equipment and procedures").   Again, the more specific the training objective, the greater is the possibility of evaluating the effectiveness of the training in reaching the objective.

The utilization of attitude change as a criterion for evaluation raises the need to understand what attitudes are, how they are formed, and what methods or approaches are useful in facilitating change.   Those who will be working in these areas are again referred to specialized references in the Bibliography.   While it is beyond the scope of this chapter to explore these issues, one important aspect should be mentioned about the nature of attitudes.   The complexity of attitudes (and their importance) can be better understood if we consider what they consist of.   One group of authors[5] has identified the following:

> 1. The *cognitive* component of an attitude consists of the beliefs of the individual about the object.
> 2. The *feeling* component of an attitude refers to the emotions connected with the object.
> 3. The *action tendency* component of an attitude includes all behavioral readiness associated with the attitude.

The reason for citing these components is to stress the point that again specificity is needed in establishing both what the training is aimed at and the criteria against which it will be evaluated.   Otherwise, it will be difficult to select proper change measurement techniques and instruments, and, eventually, it will be difficult to determine if the change was what was hoped for.   Thus, when training is initiated for attitude change, we may use and build from the three "components" to ask: "Are we attempting to change what people believe or know? Are we trying to change how they feel? Are we trying to change the way they tend to behave? The importance of these questions cannot be overemphasized. From a practical viewpoint, experience indicates that when managers call for an attitude change program they really are asking for training interventions which will lead to changes in behavior. While they may indicate concern for knowledge, belief, or feelings, the ultimate goal is behavioral. To the extent that this is true, it is wise to evaluate training in terms of "action tendency" and/or actual behavior.

Training evaluation against attitude change criteria involves the same two basic ingredients mentioned earlier: (1) a reliable and valid way of measuring and (2) the ability to demonstrate that any changes which occur are the result of the training. Since these were covered earlier, they will not be reconsidered here except

---

[5] David Krech, Richard S. Crutchfield, and Egerton L. Ballachey, *Individual in Society*, McGraw-Hill Book Company, New York, 1962, p. 140.

to remind the reader of the need to deal with these issues. (Rather than referring back to these ingredients again, it should be noted that they are also relevant and apply when dealing with evaluation of changes in job performance and changes in organizational performance or results.)

The most frequently used techniques for measuring attitudes and attitude change are of the paper-and-pencil variety. These include rating scales, disguised information quizzes, questionnaires, etc. In addition, interviews, projective techniques, and behavioral observations are employed. The Bibliography includes references which should be helpful in familiarizing the reader with the technical aspects of each of these methods as well as their advantages and limitations.

Changes in Job Performance

One of the disheartening realities of training is the fact that often there is little indication that what has occurred in the classroom has any impact on, or carry-over to, how the individual performs or behaves when he returns to his job setting. By applying the previous criteria (participant reaction, changes in knowledge and skills, and changes in attitude), we may find that people rated the training high, learned what was included in the program, and perhaps have different attitudes. However, it is as if two separate worlds existed: the "theoretical classroom" and the "work reality."

While there may be any number of reasons why the application of training does not take place, training specialists are becoming more cognizant of the need to demonstrate that job performance is positively affected by training, and line managers are becoming more demanding in having such evidence.

Three general approaches have been found useful in obtaining data about job performance and training effectiveness:

1. Study of comparative individual performance records, indices, etc.
2. Structured observations of the individual on the job
3. Evaluation or appraisal of performance by those with whom the individual works

The use of performance records and indices is contingent upon the existence of acceptable and measurable standards. In many instances, such standards exist or can be readily identified and developed. Typical of such standards would be the number of sales calls made by a salesman, the number of pieces of work completed by a production worker in a specified period of time, the frequency of complaints received, absenteeism, and tardiness. With these or similar indices, the evaluation process would, in its simplest terms, involve measuring how training influenced the individual's performance against these standards.

Use of structured observations is sometimes desirable as an alternative, or in addition, to other methods of checking employee performance. For example, consider the use of rather structured observations of an airline pilot's performance. Included in his job duties would be a specific preflight check of various parts of the plane. This preflight check has a number of purposes, including some crucial safety features. If new equipment had been introduced and supported by in-service training for pilots, one might well wish to see whether those having completed the training were now adhering to the preflight check based on the new equipment. Since the purpose ultimately may be safety, it could be argued that theoretically the important performance standards or criteria should be whether or not the pilot is or is not involved in accidents. From a practical point of view, however, what is involved is so critical that extra efforts must be taken to assure adherence to specified operating procedures before accident opportunities arise.

Some rather difficult issues are found in the observational approach, three of which should at least be mentioned in passing:

1. There is a need to carefully determine which aspects of performance are to be observed.

2. There is a need to train observers to assure their knowledge and skills in determining as objectively as possible the individual's actual performance.

3. There is the serious question as to whether or not the employee's performance is the same or different when being observed and when not being observed.

The third approach to performance involves the evaluation or appraisal of the individual by those with whom he works. These appraisals can be supplied by the employee's boss, his peers, or his subordinates. There are times when this type of evaluation is most appropriate. For example, if an organization were experiencing high turnover and had instituted supervisory training programs to assist participants in "being more aware and more considerate of the needs of their subordinates," checking with subordinates about their relationships with their supervisor and how their supervisors interact with them would be appropriate. Those interested in utilizing such appraisals or evaluations should become familiar with methods of designing, utilizing, and validating the required instrumentation.

Earlier it was stated that there may be a number of reasons why training does not result in changes in job performance. The reader is cautioned to distinguish between "poor training" and other factors which prevent desired performance changes. There are any number of instances in which it could be determined that the failure in job application is not the fault of a particular training program but rather stems from other factors in the organization. For example, an excellent program may be conducted to train mechanics or production workers in new job procedures, but if they are subsequently not supplied with the needed tools or equipment to use the new procedures on the job, it would be misleading to say that the training was inadequate. Similarly, training programs aimed at having supervisors and managers spend more time in developing subordinates will eventually fail the "performance test" if supervisors and managers continue to be rewarded for reaching short-term production goals and not for developing those who work for them.

In short, just as training programs should not be highly regarded without evidence of their effectiveness, they should not be completely downgraded when other factors or forces in the system are limiting their impact.

Organizational Performance or Results

Basically, training activities are means to attaining organizational goals and desired results. Participant reactions, learning, and even changes in job performance by individuals are of limited value to the organization if organizational objectives are not being reached. With this in mind, there is a growing trend to apply organizational performance standards and results as the ultimate criterion against which to evaluate training.

The major problem with this criterion is the fact that training per se is only one of a multitude of variables which influence the organization. As a result, it is difficult to tease out on any clear basis the part that training efforts play in terms of total organizational performance. The reader is referred to the article by Blake, Mouton, Barnes, and Greiner listed in the Bibliography for a view of some of the concepts involved and how they were dealt with in a major organization development or change program.

REPORTING TRAINING RESULTS TO MANAGEMENT

Evaluation is an integral part of every manager's responsibility and is certainly not restricted or unique to the training function. Just as management constantly needs information to evaluate production, sales, new product development, services being performed, public relations, etc., so too management needs data and information on training and training results. It is the responsibility of management to make certain that it has the needed training results data, and it is the responsibility of the training staff to supply it.

In far too many organizations, about the only training results information that is readily made available to management are figures reporting the number of programs run, the number of participants, and the number of classroom hours of instruction delivered. It is as if the training staff were primarily concerned with substantiating the fact that they are busy and that employees are "in training." If one is willing to operate on the faith in education referred to in the beginning of this chapter, perhaps this is all that would be needed, but this should be rarely acceptable in organizational life.

Probably the main reason why other results are not available is that evaluation, as discussed here, is frequently not done and, therefore, data on results are unavailable. Before one can report results, he must know what they are.

If a serious attempt is to be made at gathering and reporting data on results, it is highly recommended that the training staff begins its reporting efforts during the planning stages of the training process. More specifically, line managers should be involved in determining training and evaluation objectives, and in this process joint agreement should be reached on the evaluation criteria which will be utilized. This is not to say that line managers should become skilled in the various techniques used in evaluation, but rather that they should know, understand, and agree to what results will be reported and how.

As to the methods of reporting (formal, written, or informal) and questions concerning to whom such reports should be made, no general ground rules can be set forth here. Such procedures can be developed only within the context of the particular organization. Obviously, the pattern which would be suitable in a small company would not be applicable in a large multiplant operation.

In conclusion, the key points about reporting are:

1. Early involvement of management in setting objectives and evaluation criteria

2. The collection of required data through the use of techniques which truly reflect the specified criteria and clearly demonstrate the impact of training

3. The establishment of reporting procedures which are suitable to the organization and useful to those involved.

BIBLIOGRAPHY

Anastasi, A.: *Psychological Testing,* 2d ed., The Macmillan Company, New York, 1961.

Brookover, W. B.: *A Sociology of Education,* American Book Company, New York, 1955.

Blake, R. R., J. S. Mouton, L. B. Barnes, and L. E. Greiner: "Breakthrough in Organization Development," *Harvard Business Review,* 42(6): 133–155, 1964.

Campbell, J. P., M. D. Dunnette, E. E. Lawler, and K. E. Weick: *Managerial Behavior, Performance and Effectiveness,* McGraw-Hill Book Company, New York, 1970.

Cronbach, L. J.: *Essentials of Psychological Testing,* 2d ed., Harper & Row, Publishers, Incorporated, New York, 1960.

Engel, H. M.: "Evaluating Employee Development," in K. T. Byers (ed.), *Employee Training and Development in the Public Service,* Public Personnel Association, Chicago, 1970, pp. 253–276.

Friedlander, F.: "The Impact of Organizational Training Laboratories upon the Effectiveness and Interaction of Ongoing Work Groups," *Personnel Psychology,* 20(3): 289–307, 1967.

Harrison, R.: "Problems in the Design and Interpretation of Research on Human Relations Training," in *Explorations in Human Relations Training & Research,* No. 1, NTL Institute for Applied Behavioral Science, Washington, 1967, pp. 1–9.

Katz, D., and R. L. Kahn: *The Social Psychology of Organizations,* John Wiley & Sons, Inc., New York, 1966.

Kirkpatrick, D. L.: "Evaluation of Training," in R. L. Graig and L. R. Bittel (eds.), *Training and Development Handbook,* McGraw-Hill Book Company, New York, 1967.

Krech, D., R. S. Crutchfield, and E. L. Ballachey: *Individual in Society,* McGraw-Hill Book Company, New York, 1962. (See chaps. 5, 6, and 7 which deal with attitudes, attitude change, and attitude measurement.)

Lopez, F. M.: *Evaluating Employee Performance,* Public Personnel Association, Chicago, 1968.

Miles, M. B.: *Learning to Work in Groups,* Teachers College Press, Columbia University, New York, 1959.

Psychology Today: Communications/Research/Machines, Inc., Del Mar, Calif., 1970, chap. 33, "Attitudes and Their Change," pp. 613–633.

Scott, W. A.: "Attitude Measurement," in G. Lindzey and E. Aronson (eds.), *The Handbook of Social Psychology,* 2d ed, Addison-Wesley Publishing Company, Inc., Reading, Mass., 1968, vol. II, pp. 204–273.

Thorndike, R. L., and E. Hagen: *Measurement and Evaluation in Psychology and Education,* 2d ed., John Wiley & Sons, Inc., New York, 1961.

Tracey, W. R.: *Evaluating Training and Development Systems,* American Management Association, New York, 1968.

Part 6

Wage and Salary Administration

chapter 27

Essentials of a Sound Wage and Salary Program

WILLIAM A. GROENEKAMP   *Management Consultant, Los Angeles, California*

Wage and salary administration is an important managerial function which deals with all aspects of employee compensation. The money paid to employees in return for their services is probably the largest expenditure of an organization, while to the employee it is usually the main source of income. Therefore, proper administration of a compensation program can have a profound effect on both management and employees. It can save an organization costs involved with high turnover while attracting, retaining, and motivating capable and productive employees.

In an effort to properly use the compensation tool, many organizations have established or are contemplating the establishment of a formal wage and salary program. In either situation, there are certain fundamental elements that should be in every program.

Before exploring the development, formulation, and implementation of formalized procedures and the possible utilization of varied techniques for compensating employees, a company should examine the basic philosophy behind their payment of wages and salaries. This is usually summarized in an all-inclusive corporate policy which sets the tone for other wage and salary policies. It is characterized by many variables within a particular company and defies categorization by industry or even by a company within an industry. Factors determining policy are: management's attitude toward paying prevailing rates in a community; a company's ability to pay, influenced by its productivity and managerial efficiency; and the presence or absence of labor unions. A typical corporate policy on compensation might read:

> Company X's policy is to pay fair and reasonable salaries which will (1) allow for the recruitment, retention, and motivation of capable personnel; (2) maintain internal equity allowing employees to be rewarded on the basis of their performance and professional capabilities; and (3) further the objectives of the stockholders of the corporation.

To meet its basic obligation to employees, management must compensate them equitably for their contributions to the success of the organization. To insure this, there are several fundamental elements which must be met other than just strict adherence to the legal requirements of both state and federal governments. Management must ensure an equitable internal wage and salary structure. This implies that the duties and responsibilities of each job within a plant or company are correctly compared with the others and that employees are paid accordingly. An equitable external structure must also be ensured, which means that compensation should be competitive with the pay for similar jobs in other companies in the same industry and/or geographic area. Equally as important, a wage and salary structure should be constructed in such a manner that it provides incentive to motivate employees. If a compensation program is built around these key ingredients, the needs of employees, management, and stockholders, if applicable, will be met.

It should be evident by now that the installation or maintenance of a justifiable wage and salary program within a company is based upon a complexity of differing factors. The proper administration of these cannot be classified as an exacting science since it involves the use of human judgment. Certain tools are available to management in their application of this judgment.

INTERNAL WAGE STRUCTURE

A key element in a company's compensation program is an employee's assessment of the fairness and equitableness of the internal wage structure. He is interested in and affected by the relationship of his salary when compared with those of fellow employees. In fact, pay inequities within a firm, whether real or imagined, adversely affect an employee's morale and job performance.

The determination of equitable internal relationships can be attained through the use of certain techniques; the most commonly used is called job evaluation. Simply stated, it is a means of measuring the relative value of a job to an organization. These measurements are used as a foundation for the determination of an equitable wage structure, with the most highly valued jobs receiving the greatest pay and the lowest valued receiving the least.

The evaluation process begins with job analysis, which requires that job content be defined. This is accomplished by observing, recording, and studying the various factors which comprise a job. Included would be the inputs from job incumbents and their superiors. Abstracted from this analysis is the information which is used for a written description listing the major duties and responsibilities of each position. Since it is not possible to give a complete accounting in writing of each job, emphasis is placed on factors which will influence job worth. In addition, items such as required knowledge and skill to adequately perform in a position are also considered and recorded.

The job description is the basis for internal evaluations and comparisons which are generally conducted by a job evaluation committee composed of representatives at selected organizational levels. Each job is measured by an evaluation plan with a predetermined list of factors which are common and important to all the jobs being evaluated, such as mental effort, physical effort, and accountability. Since it is impossible to precisely determine through the use of managerial judgment the exact worth of each job based on this system of measurement, jobs are grouped into grades according to measurable differences in levels of duty and responsibility. It would be impossible to gauge the factors accurately enough to have an individual salary range for each job, and even if this were possible, it would present incredible administrative problems.

Many different evaluation plans are available with varying degrees of complexity, the most common being job ranking, point factor, and factor comparison. Regardless of the one utilized, the end result will be a ranking of jobs upon which equitable pay differentials can be determined. It is important to understand that this technique of job evaluation measures the worth of a job rather than that of an individual employee.

Once established, internal relationships between jobs should not be considered static. Technological changes can cause reevaluation of jobs, changes in job descriptions, a heightening or a lowering of the responsibility or difficulty of a job. Job reclassification occurs internally through periodic job audits or reexaminations by company job analysts. These internal changes could cause changes in a company's wage structure.

EXTERNAL WAGE STRUCTURE

The determination of internal job worth is usually followed by the task of pricing the grades or job levels into which positions have been assigned. This is influenced to a great extent by forces external to the organization itself and brought about by economics and the demand and supply of labor skills. To be competitive with the labor market, management must apprise itself of wage and salary scales outside its own company. This is done through surveying pay rates of competitors in the labor market.

Management selects and prices "key" jobs from the grades that have been established as its internal wage structure. They are chosen because their job content can be easily compared with other jobs at the same skill or value level and because they are generally the most heavily populated categories within the organization. In most cases, the key jobs are also plentiful among competitors. The secretarial classification would be a good illustration.

The surveying process can be accomplished in a multitude of ways. Written surveys are periodically conducted by many groups, including employer associations, governmental agencies, and groups of industrial firms. Often an individual organization can conduct its own survey through the use of written questionnaires, personal visits, or telephone inquiries. Whichever method is utilized for the determination of pay levels in the labor market, caution must be exercised in gathering and analyzing of data. The effects of surveys on wages should be reason enough for caution in their use.

The surveys chosen should include participating organizations which are competitors in the labor market and have jobs comparable to those within one's own firm. More than one survey should make up management's portfolio to enable checks on the surveys themselves. Surveys are usually either "industry oriented" or "area oriented." The greatest emphasis is given to surveys within the industry in which the organization is active, since jobs differ between industries as much as they do between organizations. Area-oriented surveys which are geographically limited but cross industry lines are used to supplement other wage and salary data and also to determine or develop wage movements and trends. Occasionally, speciality firms such as pen manufacturers conduct surveys within a geographic area rather than using industry-oriented surveys because their basic industry has very few competitors.

An additional point to consider in survey use is that often job titles are misleading and do not accurately define job content. Even a personnel clerk, one of the most common titles, could have differing levels of duties and responsibilities from one firm to another. Often the best way to ascertain that "apples are being compared with apples" is to personally visit the firms being surveyed and discuss job contents with the management.

The information gathered from the external labor market will offer a rough outline of wage structure for management decisions. A choice must be made by management in their use of this data to establish a wage structure whose relative level could be equal to, or higher or lower than, their competitors on the labor market. As formerly mentioned, this philosophy is generally stated in organizational policy, and its basic purpose is to recruit, retain, and motivate employees.

The complexity of a wage structure and the number of factors which influence it demand that a company be flexible in its philosophies regarding internal relationships, yet rigid enough not to completely destroy its structure, by being too strongly influenced by external factors. Companies of differing size and abilities to compensate look at these problems with varying degrees of importance. There is no clear-cut formula as to what the relationship of external factors should be to a company's internal structure. There exist market rate influences upon wage structures. The biggest management problem is to reasonably balance this influence with the internal force.

MOTIVATION

The subject of motivation is extremely broad and goes well beyond the area of compensation. Briefly, it should be noted that incentives can be built into a firm's job evaluation plan. During the establishment of the plan, jobs are priced so that each job has its own wage or salary range rather than its own flat rate. To illustrate, the range for a mail clerk might be $90 to $120 per week and that for a public relations supervisor $250 to $400 per week. These ranges allow an employee to be compensated according to the level of performance within a job. In the case of the mail clerk, an average employee would earn $105 per week, the midpoint of the range; an apprentice or below-average worker would be paid less than the midpoint; and an outstanding performer more. The proper establishment of wage ranges in this manner permits the payment of a competitive wage differential to employees based upon their individual performance.

The spread from the minimum to the maximum within ranges widens as jobs increase in complexity and responsibility and thus in compensation level. The range spread for the mail clerk could typically be 33 percent, and this spread could increase to 50 percent or higher for the public relations supervisor. This provides the broadest potential incentive to individuals in the highest level positions where the largest impact or contributions to an organization can be made. These same positions and their resultant duties and responsibilities are also more genuinely influenced by the job incumbent. The public relations supervisor would have greater opportunity to use his creativity and personal initiative than the mail clerk whose job by its very nature is more routine.

In addition to a well-developed wage and salary structure, many firms add other pay incentives to a base wage to stimulate greater productivity from their employees. These incentives take many different shapes and are formulated to meet the specific needs of the particular organization. One firm might have an individual or a group incentive plan built around piece rates (this would offer additional pay for above-normal output), and another might have a large variety of bonus plans. Regardless of which plan is proper for a specific organization, no pay plan by itself is sufficient to motivate employees. Many other items such as employee recognition, a sense of belonging, and a host of other psychological and physiological factors are also essential to a prosperous and growing company.

MATURITY CURVES

Following World War II, many organizations with growing work forces in the engineering and scientific occupational disciplines searched for methods of compensation superior to those arrived at by the traditional job evaluation plans. Their answer involved the use of "maturity curves," a compensation tool developed by Bell Telephone Laboratories. They are still in wide usage today, and use many of the same basic goals of job evaluation, previously mentioned.

Salary ranges developed through traditional means prove too restrictive for the long-term growth of professional employees, who should be judged to a great extent on personal skills rather than on job duties. The individual has a great influence on the breadth of his job because of such factors as his educational and technological training as well as the demand of his position for creativity.

Maturity curves are computed by each company to fit its own particular internal requirements. They depend on many factors, one of which might be the average years of work experience of the professional staff. They are also based on the external labor market influences as measured by salary surveys, generally on a national basis. The surveys report salaries for broad job classifications, which in most cases include a specific occupational discipline, such as programmer, or a closely allied group of disciplines, such as research and development scientists in the "hard sciences" (e.g., engineering, mathematics, and physics).

Maturity curves can be based on any of a series of measurable variables, such as chronological age, years since bachelor's degree, and/or years of experience. The last is the most common and probably the most meaningful measure of maturity in the evaluation of scientists and engineers. It provides a basis for measuring the length of an individual's professional work experience. However, there is no universal means of equating experience. For example, experience as a garage attendant would not be applicable to the job of a programmer, while years of service as a mathematical assistant might be relevant. Chronological age is the easiest measurement from the standpoint of sheer calculation, but it does not provide any determination of education and/or experience. The use of the "years since bachelor's degree" factor assumes the fallacy that all professional employees have college degrees. The question is sometimes raised as to the worth of four years of working experience versus a college degree. The surveys which are the foundation for the calculation of maturity curves give a frequency distribution for preset salary intervals for each year measured. These distributions show the statistical relationships of the salaries to whatever variables are used, allowing the establishment of curves similar to those illustrated in Figure 1.

Since the curves are calculated by and for each particular company, considering both internal and primarily external salary conditions, a job applicant's or an employee's salary determination can be made based on the maturity curve on which he is placed. As an oversimplication, a company may evaluate an applicant as a 75 percentile worker and place him on that curve, based on their measurement of maturity. This would indicate that the applicant, who might be a programmer, is considered by subjective managerial judgment to have greater potential at that particular company than 74 percent of a total programming work force. This would take into account both internal and external considerations.

Additionally, performance appraisal can be and is used which permits employers

Figure 1. Hypothetical maturity curves.

to maintain performance ratings on their employees.   These ratings coincide with maturity curves, allowing salary determinations.

Maturity curves are generally adjusted on an annual basis, and the amount of change is determined by surveys taken periodically.   They influence individual salary determination within a company and are also used to illustrate the relative position of an organization's internal salary structure to that of the external labor market.

WAGE AND SALARY POLICIES

With a knowledge of the fundamental elements of a sound wage and salary program as a base, appropriate policies can and should be developed, formulated, and implemented within the organization.   These guiding principles are established by top management, reflect their business philosophies, and create the climate for all compensation actions.   This is true for all personnel policies, wage and salary being an integral part of the whole picture.   There are many areas of integration.   Employment, for example, depends on the ability to offer competitive wages in the recruitment of new personnel.   The capacity to retain a work force and maintain a high level of morale, as well as provide incentive for promotions, is also an area somewhat influenced by the maintenance of an adequate level of compensation.   It would be misleading to indicate that proper pay policies are the sole influence in any or all of these functions.   Personnel is a complex subject with many interlacing forces, mainly since it deals with human nature and its relationships.

Poor morale, even chaos, could prevail without established corporate policies. This is true for both small and large organizations.   Lack of uniformity and consistency in the treatment of employees is probably the largest problem area.   To illustrate, a friend of the corporate president or a person who tends to aggressively complain about his salary might get larger increases than an employee who might be a high producer but tends to be less vocal about his income.   This lack of proper guidelines could play havoc with one of a company's largest items of cost—compensation.   Improper administration of salary increases could result in a probable large turnover rate.   This item has an upward spiraling effect on costs because of the expense of recruiting and training work force replacements.

The policies should be written either by a company's personnel director or preferably by the compensation administrator if the company is large enough. This person will have the responsibility for interpreting these guidelines.   To ensure their successful adoption within the organization, the policies should reflect the philosophy of top management and should be contributed to, and critiqued by, key members of supervision from various echelons.   This support is requisite since these individuals will be responsible for the success or failure of policy implementation.

The written policies should be part of a formalized program which includes the establishment of wage and salary ranges through a job evaluation plan.   The publication and distribution of this information gives supervision a framework to work within, thus allowing the planning of promotions, the fair compensation of employees for their contributions to the company, and the budgeting of employee costs.   It also lessens the possibility of misinterpretation of policies, especially if they are written in a clear and concise manner.

A formal wage and salary program is paramount in determining comparability between jobs when surveys are conducted.   Without adequate definitions, it would be difficult to obtain meaningful market data.   Informal wage and salary programs are most commonly found in smaller companies where there is not an adequate staff to formulate a more formalized program. Also, top management of small companies are admittedly not always ready to establish policies which they feel may be difficult to reverse at some future date because of changing business conditions.

Wage and salary policies should be written so that they are flexible enough to allow exceptions or slight deviations from the norm when necessary. They should never be considered static, because of changing conditions both within and outside the organization. In order to maintain the policies on a current basis, some type of periodic review should be established. One consideration is that once policies have been committed to writing, frequent changes are likely to reflect poorly on management and might create feelings of insecurity among employees. In the development and maintenance of current policies, it is essential to determine the practices of companies competitive in the labor market. When changes are made, it is best not to drastically change established practices. Since policies are broad statements governing corporate actions, it is almost mandatory to establish procedures which will detail their methods of implementation. Often procedures can be altered without subsequently changing policy. In this way, the original intent has not been altered. This type of change is often preferable.

Many different items are included in compensation policies. They range from broad guidelines which define the required ingredients of a wage and salary structure to more narrow ones explaining transfers and shift premiums. After summarizing an organization's broad compensation objectives which probably would include the requirement of paying fair and equitable compensation, an additional policy statement might read as follows:

> Equitable wage and salary ranges will be maintained on a current basis by annual comparative studies of the rates competitors pay and by periodic internal job studies to keep alert to changing job conditions.

Policies generally continue by describing the various types of increases, including probationary, merit, general, and promotional. A probationary increase might be given to wage earners in fairly routine jobs if they successfully complete an initial testing period, generally ranging from one to six months after their start with a firm. Merit increases are given only to employees who earn them by excellent performance of their duties. Differing from this is the general increase which is given to a large majority of employees of a firm because of measurable inflationary trends in the economic marketplace. This practice is not universally accepted by all organizations, but it has a strong following in unionized companies. Promotional increases are awarded to employees moving to positions requiring higher skills and/or having greater responsibilities than their prior jobs.

Policies should encompass the requirements of federal and state laws. There are many laws, and their primary purpose is to protect the employee. One law that has a great influence on almost all organizations is the Fair Labor Standards Act. It is the federal standard in the area of premium pay for overtime work and in the setting of minimum wages. Since its origin in 1938, it has been revised many times to broaden its scope of coverage to the point where it now is applicable to a majority of business enterprises and employees on a national scale. There is no question that these laws have a large influence on a company's wage and salary policies.

There are numerous other areas requiring written guidelines. Many of these are special situations which should be as carefully formulated, documented, and implemented as other company policies. A special policy may have to be established for overseas or field site allowances for organizations with employees in these situations.

Once top management has agreed to the policies, they should be published and distributed to all supervisory levels of the organization. In the communication of any or all directives, the supervisor is the key link between top management and the employee. Educating the supervisor on policies and their ramifications is important since he will interpret these guidelines to employees. Another avenue of employee communications open to management in the dissemination of wage and salary policies is the employee handbook. This is given to a new employee during his initial orientation into the company. It generally gives a broad outline of the pertinent policies without going into a great amount of detail.

Employees should be aware of their organization's policies, especially of those which directly affect them. Dissatisfaction among employees is more often found where secrecy prevails than where policies are openly discussed and fully understood. Management should remember that employees want to be informed in the vital wage and salary area since it is probably the single item of most importance in the employer-employee relationship.

In the maintenance of competitive wage and salary structure, it is advantageous to inform employees that their organization is aware of the pay practices of other companies. It will help to increase confidence in an employer and may aid in preventing the high costs of employee turnover and low morale, occasioned by idle rumors of high pay practices in other companies. The employee is primarily interested in the fact that his employer is alert to a competitor's rates; he generally will not wish to see actual survey results.

Employees often are interested in the maximum of their wage ranges. Most organizations give this information; those which do not, have kept it secret because of past corporate practices, unions, or similar reasons. If circumstances permit, it is advisable to give employees this information. In addition, they should be told that the ranges are not static and are liable to change, based on economic conditions. No employee should feel that he must stay in the same wage range during his employment with an organization. The opportunities for promotion are almost always present.

CONCLUSION

The proper administration of an organization's wage and salary program is extremely important in maintaining a good employer-employee relationship. One of the methods of retaining high morale and low turnover is to have a formal program consisting of written policies and procedures. These should be communicated to employees through supervisors and other appropriate means, such as the employee handbook. Every effort should also be made by top management to keep policies and compensation structures competitive with the outside labor market while maintaining an equitable internal structure.

BIBLIOGRAPHY

Anderson, Howard J. (managing editor): *The New Wage and Hour Law,* rev. ed., Bureau of National Affairs, Inc., Washington, 1967.

Dooher, M. Joseph, and Vivienne Marquis (eds.): *The AMA Handbook of Wage and Salary Administration,* American Management Association, New York, 1950.

Feldmeier, Joseph, and William Groenekamp: "The Profile-Ranking Method of Evaluating Fringe Benefits," *Personnel,* American Management Association, January–February, 1965.

Gray, Robert D.: *A Guide to Systematic Wage and Salary Administration,* California Institute of Technology, Pasadena, Calif., 1959.

Groenekamp, William: "How Reliable Are Wage Surveys?" *Personnel,* American Management Association, New York, January–February, 1967.

Lovejoy, Lawrence C.: *Wage and Salary Administration,* The Roland Press Company, New York, 1959.

Taylor, George W., and Frank C. Pierson: *New Concepts in Wage Determination,* McGraw-Hill Book Company, New York, 1957.

chapter 28

Job Evaluation and Pay Plans: Office Personnel

ROBERT J. KELLY *Personnel Administrator, McGraw-Hill, Inc., New York, New York*

NEED FOR JOB EVALUATION IN THE OFFICE

Whenever two or more people perform different work for a third, the need exists for some kind of job evaluation. The third person, the employer, must somehow arrive at a rate of pay for each job which will not only (1) be competitive in attracting and holding employees but also (2) be seen by them as related to the relative difficulty of their jobs. If the employer establishes pay rates which fall short of either or both of these pay goals, employee dissatisfaction with pay usually will result. Loss of good employees, inability to attract employees, low morale, and low productivity are some of the business problems which often are associated with dissatisfaction about pay.

Of the two pay goals—meeting market rates and achieving satisfactory internal pay relationships—the latter has greater priority. First, the internal pay relationships are more visible to employees. If perceived by employees as being unfair, out of line, and arbitrary, pay rates within the company can be a continual source of discontent, for employees are reminded of the internal inequities every working day. Secondly, an equitable internal pay hierarchy is a prerequisite to establishing sound and workable policies concerning pay progression for employees. Finally, a thought-out and agreed-upon set of internal relative values for jobs aids greatly in establishing an informed company posture relative to outside pay levels.

For office-clerical personnel, the need for some form of job evaluation is as important as for any other group of employees. The accounting clerk, secretary, and typist are just as concerned with pay relationships as are employees on manufacturing jobs. They ask the same questions—posed to themselves, to their co-workers, and to their supervisors—"Why is my job paid at a lower rate than that job?" "How come that easy job is paid at the same rate as my job?" "Can anyone in this company explain the rhyme or reason behind our pay scales? They just don't make sense."

Recognition of the need for job evaluation in the office followed, but slowly, the general acceptance and success of evaluation systems to rate jobs in the plant. However, as the proportion of white-collar workers to blue-collar workers has risen in the last twenty years, management's attention to pay questions in the office has markedly increased. Larger office payrolls, the growing dependence on office personnel for vital business functions, and the actual and potential growth of white-collar unions have been among the factors generating management commitments to office job evaluation, as well as recognition that job evaluation can reduce controversy and uncertainty about pay and job relationships and, thus, contribute to a more effectively functioning business organization.

PLANNING FOR AN OFFICE JOB EVALUATION PROGRAM

Usually, the need to install a formal plan for evaluating office jobs will be recognized and articulated first by the executive responsible for employee relations. It is the personnel executive who is most likely to have an overview of the pay inequities and inconsistencies resulting from uncoordinated and personal decisions about the relative worth of office jobs. In many instances, he will find acceptance and support for the general idea among line managers, but it will typically and rightfully fall to him to convince top management to undertake such a program.

Top management—the chief executive officer and the top policy makers of the organization—must give its wholehearted support to the idea. If the leaders of a company are lukewarm in their backing, any plan of action which requires the cooperation and attention of middle and first-line managers will run aground in a sea of apathy. Obviously, then, there is no step more crucial to the success of an office job evaluation program than gaining top management support. The top executives must not only want such a program, they must also be ready to commit company resources—time, effort, and money—to achieve it.

Members of top management (and subsequently, all managers) should have a firm grasp of the essentials of what job evaluation is and what it is not, what it can do, and what it cannot do. Some of these essentials might be summarized as follows:

1. Job evaluation is not a science. There are no absolute and immutable answers available to tell us the proper relative values of jobs. A job evaluation plan is merely an agreed-upon set of ground-rules for making consistent and disciplined judgments about the rank order of jobs.

2. Job evaluation cannot solve all salary problems. It is no panacea for pay disorders. It can provide a fact- and reason-based ladder of job relationships, which is a fundamental starting point for the solution of most salary problems.

3. Job evaluation is not a substitute for managerial decision making about individual salaries. It does not supplant, it can supplement and sharpen, such decisions. Job evaluation leads to a company-approved guide for the minimum and maximum pay rates for groups of jobs. It clarifies whether personnel moves are promotions, lateral transfers, or demotions. By settling questions of "job worth," it can add clarity and consistency to pay progression policies dealing with "employee worth."

4. Job evaluation is not a cost-cutting technique. It will not reduce the size of the payroll. In fact, it may add to payroll costs initially, when salaries which are found to be below minimum job rates are adjusted upward. Job evaluation leads to a more equitable distribution of the payroll. It creates a basis for equity, fairness, and uniformity in salary administration which can improve employee morale and motivation and reduce personnel turnover. Ultimately, then, job evaluation can improve the return on payroll dollars invested.

5. Job evaluation is not a one-time, nonrecurring effort and expense. It must be maintained and worked at continually; otherwise the original investment will have been squandered. If new jobs and changed jobs are not fitted into the evaluation hierarchy with the same care and judgment used at the outset of the program, inequities will multiply and employees and managers alike will rapidly lose confidence in the entire effort.

When top management has decided to go ahead with the creation of a program to evaluate office jobs, it still must answer the basic question of how best to go about it. Normally, the executive responsible for personnel administration will be charged with the leadership of a small committee of line managers whose mission will be to study, develop, and recommend a plan of action. After informing themselves on how other companies have handled it and steeping themselves in the theory and practice of evaluation as reported in a fairly wide body of literature, this group will address itself to two chief questions: What method should be used to evaluate the jobs? Who should install the evaluation program?

SELECTING A PLAN FOR EVALUATING OFFICE JOBS

There are two basic approaches to judging the relative value of jobs. One approach considers the *whole job* in comparison to a predetermined yardstick; the other considers *elements or components* of the job in comparison to a predetermined yardstick. Four basic evaluation methods or systems have evolved from these two separate approaches: the ranking system, the grading or classification system, the point system, and the factor-comparison system. Ranking and grading systems compare the whole job and are considered "nonquantitative" systems. Point and factor-comparison systems break down the job into what are thought to be compensable elements and, therefore, are considered to be "quantitative" systems. The yardsticks against which jobs are compared are another point of departure among the systems. Ranking and factor-comparison systems measure jobs against other jobs; grading and point systems measure jobs against a descriptive scale.

The system used most widely for evaluating office jobs is the point system, which does not necessarily mean it is the "best" method. No single method carries a guarantee of greater reliability or validity compared with the other systems. Any one of these systems, when applied by informed and objective evaluators, can be used to produce virtually the same set of job relationships as would be arrived at using the other systems. On the other hand, if the evaluators are permitted to make unchecked and biased judgments, any one of these systems can produce a sorry array of misaligned jobs. Furthermore, so that judgments to be made about positions will be fact based, all evaluation systems require analysis and description of the jobs to be evaluated.

It should be noted, too, that users of a selected basic evaluation method often supplement the individual plan with techniques or features of another method in order to improve or check on the consistency and validity of evaluations. Examples are factor-comparison plans which also use descriptive scales for some factors and point plans which also rely on job-to-job factor comparisons.

The Ranking System

By far the simplest and least costly to install and maintain, the ranking system also has the appeal of requiring the minimum input of time and effort. Essentially, this system consists of comparing jobs and deciding which job is most difficult and important, which is the next most difficult and important, and so on, until all jobs have been placed in rank order.

In its most elemental form, reasonably reliable results can be reached quickly for a small group of jobs by putting the title and a capsule description of each job on cards, one card for each job, and asking the raters to agree on which job should have the highest rank, which the lowest, and which one seems to represent the middle rank between these two extremes. With these three job cards displayed as reference points, the remaining jobs are compared, one by one, with the displayed jobs and are judged as belonging below or above each of the earlier ranked jobs. Each job so ranked adds another card to the display and, thus, builds a successively more detailed array of references by which to judge the rank of the remaining jobs. Some jobs may be seen as belonging on a par with other ranked jobs and will be given the same rank order. The final array is reviewed, and when agreement is reached to accept the results, the rank order of each job is recorded. A hierarchy of internal job relationships is now available for fitting into a pay structure which should reflect in dollar differentials all the significant rank-order differences.

Criteria should be agreed upon to guide raters in judging overall differences in relative worth; otherwise each rater will tend to create his own informal guides. Written guides to the factors or characteristics being considered (such as amount of training or prior experience required, complexity of duties, and responsibility for dealing with others) will help provide a common basis for discussing and resolving differences in rankings.

A number of safeguards and considerations should be built into the ranking process to improve its accuracy and reliability. One is to set the initial rankings aside and to repeat the ranking procedure several weeks later, without reference to the original results. A comparison of the two efforts may reveal different rankings for certain positions which the raters must resolve, often calling for more detailed reviews of job description information to settle the matter. Another is to ask the raters to rank the jobs on their own prior to meeting with the other raters. This step helps ensure that each rater will have done his "homework" (i.e., studying job descriptions and forming independent judgments about how he thinks the jobs should be related) and tends to lessen the chance that one rater may stampede or pressure the other raters into hasty decisions. The independent rankings should be collected, summarized, and averaged before the raters meet. These summaries will depict how close or far apart the raters are on certain jobs and focus the group's attention on resolving differences, including the option to use averaged answers or majority voting to settle ranking questions.

If the number of jobs to be ranked is large, the method of paired comparisons is a ranking technique which is recommended because it restricts the process to a judgment between only two jobs at a time. All jobs are listed so that each job is paired at random with every other job, and the rater underlines or circles his choice as to which of the two should have the higher ranking, as in the following example:

Typist-clerk	Accounting clerk
Secretary	Typist-clerk
Accounting clerk	Computer operator
Correspondent	Secretary
Computer operator	Correspondent
Accounting clerk	Secretary
Computer operator	Typist-clerk
Typist-clerk	Correspondent
Correspondent	Accounting clerk
Secretary	Computer Operator

The number of times that a job is underlined determines its rank order. Thus, in the example, the job of computer operator ranks first, followed by correspondent, secretary, accounting clerk, and typist-clerk.

The simplicity of the ranking system generates its major disadvantages:

1. It leaves no record of *why* jobs are ranked as they are, making it difficult to explain and justify rankings to managers and employees.

2. Without reasonably objective standards for weighing one job against another, ranking is easily subject to conscious or unconscious rater bias and inconsistencies.

3. Ranking can provide an order of relative job worth, but the process itself does not suggest how close or far apart that worth is from job to job.

4. As the number and diversity of jobs increase, it is less likely that raters will be familiar with all jobs being ranked.

The Grading or Classification System

This system overcomes some of the shortcomings of the ranking method by providing a defined and graduated scale of criteria against which jobs can be compared and sorted into pay grades. Grade or class descriptions are written to identify and define successively greater increments of job skills, requirements, decision making, and responsibility inherent in the type and range of jobs to be evaluated. Evaluators review each job description to decide which grade description best fits the job, a judgment which can be readily made provided that the grade descriptions are carefully written so that distinctions between grade levels are logical and clear.

Constructing and writing a scale of grade descriptions is an evolutionary process of drafting and redrafting statements which typify the nature, difficulty, and responsibility of the jobs expected to be slotted at each grade level. Before attempts are made to develop such a scale, the type and range of jobs to be measured by it must be decided. For example, when considering a grading system for office positions, will secretarial or data-processing positions be included or excluded, and will supervisory positions in any of the job families be covered? Each grade definition must be comprehensive enough to apply to each of the various office job families, and the highest grade level must accommodate the topmost jobs.

The approximate number of pay grades considered desirable or necessary should be determined in advance so that the grade descriptions can be attempted with this target in mind. The fewer the pay grades, the easier will be the task of defining distinctions from one grade to the next. On the other hand, too few grades may group jobs which employees and managers feel should be at different pay levels.

The scale of grade definitions can be developed from a preconceived notion of the distinguishing characteristics common to each grade level, based on a familiarity with the jobs to be graded. Another approach is to make a rough ranking of the jobs and to examine the jobs in each rank to identify the elements and attributes common to all. Generic statements of these characteristics must be combined to express succinctly and clearly the kind of job that belongs at each level. To add meaning and intent to key phrases, it is recommended that brief examples be cited in the grade description. Also, it is a good idea to name one or two key jobs as exemplifying the entire description.

Probably the most thorough and largest application of a classification system is the approach used by the federal government. Figure 1 typifies position classification standards developed by the United States Civil Service Commission which are used as guides for classifying the large majority of positions, white collar and blue collar, in the various agencies of the federal government. In the federal classificiation system, the primary yardstick is not a group of general grade definitions encompassing different types of positions. Instead, standards are defined for all the positions in a particular occupation, and the various classification factors pertinent to that occupation serve to guide the classifier in evaluating the position and determining the appropriate grade level.

Figure 1. Excerpt from classification standard for clerk-typist series. *(United States Civil Service Commission.)*

UNITED STATES CIVIL SERVICE COMMISSION

GS-322-1   Clerk-Typist (Trainee) GS-1   GS-322-1
                                         Clerk-Typist GS-1

Positions at this level include the performance of typing duties of the difficulty and responsibility described below either (1) as a trainee for the purpose of acquiring the typing skill and ability described at the GS-2 level or (2) as a clerk-typist performing typing work on an incidental or substantially full-time basis. Positions at this level frequently also include the performance of clerical duties classifiable at the GS-1 level.

Typing work at this level requires some degree of typing skill and ability but less than that described at the GS-2 level. The work does not require the use of initiative or judgment. Specific instructions are given by the supervisor regarding (1) the spacing and arrangement of the material typed as required by the nature of the material typed, the purpose for which it is to be used, and agency regulations with respect to format; (2) spelling, capitalization, punctuation, agreement of subject and verb, and other matters of grammar and style; and (3) all other matters involved. These instructions are given as requested by the incumbent and as indicated to be necessary by review of the work. The work is reviewed for compliance with instructions, adherence to copy, accuracy, and adequacy.

In *trainee* clerk-typist positions assignments initially involve the performance of very simple typing duties in accordance with detailed instructions and under close observation as described above. The work is evaluated periodically to determine the trainee's aptitude, competence, progress, and capacity to perform higher-level work. Assignments become progressively more difficult as competence in the work is acquired until the trainee is able to perform typing work of the difficulty and responsibility described at the GS-2 level.

In *non-trainee* positions at this level typing work may be performed on an incidental basis or on a substantially full-time basis. The typing duties are very simple and are performed in accordance with detailed instructions or in accordance with established procedures which are so specific that guidance is unnecessary. The work is reviewed for accuracy, adequacy, and conformance with instructions and/or applicable procedures.

POSITION-CLASSIFICATION STANDARDS

GS-322-1   GS-322-1

The following examples are typical of typing duties classifiable at this level:

1. Types clearly identified information such as names, addresses, identification numbers, etc., on index cards, forms and other documents, where the information is taken from clearly indicated sources which vary little or are easily located.
2. Types labels, folders, jackets, tabs, and cross-references for use in files.
3. Types lists, shipping labels, addresses on envelopes, time and attendance cards, reference slips, and other material where the information typed can be readily extracted from other forms, lists, index cards, etc.
4. Types names and addresses or other identifying data on card-size stencils for use in mechanically addressing envelopes, labels, or mailing wrappers, or for duplicating catalog cards, stock cards, etc.
5. Types straight rough drafts from handwritten or other marked copy where attention to arrangement is not required, and typographical errors, strikeovers, strikeouts, and other imperfections are permitted. The typist has no responsibility for insuring correct punctuation or grammar.

GS-322-2   Clerk-Typist GS-2   GS-322-2

Positions at this level include the performance of typing of the difficulty and responsibility described in the following paragraphs, and frequently also include the performance of clerical work which is classifiable at grade GS-1 and/or GS-2.

1. Typing (without error or correction of any kind when required) material from clean copy that is of any kind or form (e.g., printed, typed, or handwritten; in narrative, tabular, or other form; involving either specialized or non-technical subject-matter fields or foreign-language matter) provided that responsibility is limited to producing a verbatim duplicate of the copy material so that such elements as complicated spacing arrangements or foreign

Figure 1.   Excerpt from classification standard for clerk-typist series. *(United States Civil Service Commission.)* **(continued)**

---

language or specialized vocabulary knowledge are not involved.

2. Typing from material in rough draft form when the rough draft material consists of narrative material in which revisions are clearly indicated so that comprehension of the text is not required to determine proper placement in the finished copy.

3. Typing tabular material when *(a)* items and heading are preselected or specifically identified; *(b)* headings are usually single unit elements, without subdivision; and *(c)* a rough or trial draft may be prepared, whenever necessary.

The following elements are also characteristic of positions at this level:

1. The work performed requires *(a)* the application of a knowledge of instructions and procedures which specifically describe all requirements regarding matters of form involved in the kind of material which is usually typed and/or *(b)* the ability to follow specific, detailed instructions regarding material which is to be typed in other than the usual form.

2. Responsibility for using standard nontechnical dictionaries, style manuals, or other similar references to check such matters as spelling and form is usually included.

(TS 65)
December 1966

Some formidable difficulties are inherent in the grading or classification system:

1. Defining objective and meaningful grade descriptions to measure whole jobs is a deceptively simple task in concept but surprisingly difficult to execute, even when only a few types of jobs are to be evaluated by the scale.

2. As the diversity of positions increases, the difficulty of writing the scale, or interpreting the original grade definitions, becomes even greater.

3. The grading process of matching the overall job with an overall grade definition still leaves no record of *why* the job was slotted at a particular grade, and seriously limits the ability to convince others of the "correctness" of the decision.

4. A corollary to the above limitation is the possible suspicion among some managers or employees that "you merely have to use the right words in describing the job to get the grade you want."

5. Some jobs will satisfy part of the definition of one grade and also meet part of the next. Ground rules for settling such dilemmas often appear arbitrary and inconsistent to managers and employees.

The Point System

The point system offers satisfactory answers to most of the deficiencies found in ranking or grading systems, which is attested to by its widespread use. It consists of separately measuring different aspects or factors considered important and common to a group of jobs. Each job is analyzed and compared to a predefined yardstick for each factor to decide "how much" of the factor is needed or found in the job. The extent or degree to which the particular aspect is required or present in the job is measured in points. The separate point values awarded for each factor are added to get the total point value for the job. These point scores provide an index of the relative worth of the jobs and are converted into money values by assigning jobs which fall within a specified range of point totals to the same pay grade.

Because the validity, reliability, and—very important—the acceptability of rating jobs by the point method rest so heavily on the factors used, great care and effort must be invested in the selection, definition, and weighting of the factors. Some of the most important considerations are:

1. Each factor must truly operate to distinguish differences between jobs, differences that have to do with why a job should be considered more difficult, more important, worth more than another job. If it does not help to do this, a factor is superfluous and irrelevant to the job evaluation process.

2. Each factor must be common to most of the jobs to be rated, and it should exist in greater and lesser amounts so that the low to high of it can be measured.

3. Since the factors selected will not be seen as of exactly equal importance in determining relative job worth, each factor must be given a weight that will reflect its role in contributing to the overall worth of jobs.

4. None of the factors should overlap with another factor, i.e., measure the same element twice under different names, for this would give undue additional weight to the same aspect and inadvertently distort the real relationships among jobs.

5. The factors chosen and their definitions must meet the test of acceptability by employees and managers. They should be seen as a fair, natural, and complete set of criteria by which to judge *this particular group of jobs in this particular company.*

6. The number of factors used should be the minimum needed to assure a balance between completeness and simplicity in rating. Too many factors tend to blur judgments and increase the possibility of overlap. Too few factors limit the flexibility of the scale in recognizing differences among jobs.

7. The factor definitions should signify what it is that is being rated, with sufficient clarity and objectivity of language to compel the same interpretation by different raters.

The yardstick of each factor is a series of degree definitions which depict in an ascending scale the perceivable increments of that factor. The lowest and highest degree should define the least and the greatest amounts of the factor which are expected to be found within the range of jobs to be evaluated. Between these lower and upper limits, one or more gradations may be discernible. No attempt should be made to carve out distinctions which are subtle or elusive. Instead, the minimum clearly "seeable" levels should be agreed upon and defined. The number of degrees established may vary from factor to factor because the nature of each factor and the range of jobs will influence how many levels can be readily seen.

Degree definitions should be expressed in clear, concise, and objective terms, avoiding subjective language which would permit loose interpretation. The more specific and concrete the definitions are, the greater will be the consistency of ratings made by different raters. Key jobs should be selected (representative of the range of jobs to be evaluated) and compared with the degree definitions to test the clarity and aptness of the definitions. Difficulties and disagreements encountered in the testing will help reveal weaknesses and ambiguity in the definitions, which should than be reworked to achieve uniform understanding and application by the raters. Shown in Figure 2 are examples of two factors and their degree definitions taken from a plan used to evaluate office positions.

As mentioned earlier, the weighting of each factor must be determined to fix its priority in making a job difficult or important. With all the factors together representing 100 percent of the value of a job, the percentage that is thought to be assignable to each factor must be decided, pooling the judgments of those who are developing the evaluation plan. There are no precise formulas for deciding factor weights. Independent and then group judgments are necessary to rank the factors and yield an alignment of weights that seems most appropriate.

The number of points to be assigned to the first degree of each factor should be in the same proportion as the agreed-upon percentage weights assigned to the factors. Thus, in the five-factor plan outlined in Figure 3, the weights are:

1. Education required	20%
2. Experience required	25%
3. Complexity of job	35%
4. Responsibility for relationships with others	15%
5. Working conditions and physical requirements . . .	5%
	100%

Figure 2.   Two factors and their degree definitions. *(From a five-factor point plan.)*

COMPLEXITY OF JOB

Refers to amount of judgment, planning, and initiative required. Consider the extent to which the job requires the exercise of discretion and the difficulty of the decisions that must be made. It is not necessary that all qualifications noted in a degree definition be present in order to qualify for a job to qualify for that degree. The best fit is used for assigning degrees.

1st Degree   35 points
  Covers jobs that are so standardized as to require *little or no choice* of action including repetitive jobs that do not need close supervision.

2nd Degree   70 points
  Follows detailed instructions and standard practices. Decisions are limited strictly to *indicated choices between prescribed alternatives* which *detail course of action.*

3rd Degree   105 points
  Follows detailed instructions and standard practices, but, due to variety of factors to be considered, decisions require *some judgment, or planning to choose prescribed alternatives* which *detail course of action.*

4th Degree   140 points
  General instructions and standard practices usually applicable. Due to variety and character of factors to be considered, decisions require some *initiative as well as judgment and planning to choose prescribed alternatives* which in turn require use of *resourcefulness or judgment to adapt to variations* in problems encountered.

RESPONSIBILITY FOR RELATIONSHIPS WITH OTHERS

This factor measures the degree to which the job requires the employee to get results by working with or through other people. Consider the extent to which the job involves responsibility for the work of others, and for contacts within and outside the company. The primary consideration is the nature of contact. Frequency of contact is contributory only.

1st Degree   15 points
  Requires employee to get along harmoniously with fellow workers. Covers jobs with simple personal contacts within and outside own department involving little responsibility for working with or through other people, and simple telephone calls involving identification, referral of calls, taking or giving simple messages without discussion.

2nd Degree   30 points
  Requires routine personal, telephone, or written contacts with others in or out of the company involving exchange and explanation of information calling for courtesy to avoid friction.

3rd Degree   45 points
  Requires personal, telephone, or written contacts with others in or out of the company involving exchange and discussion of information calling for tact as well as courtesy to get cooperation or to create a favorable impression.

4th Degree   60 points
  Requires personal, telephone, or written contacts with others in or out of the company involving the exercise of persuasion, discretion, and tact to get willing action or consent on a non-routine level.

Point values are assigned to the remaining degrees in each factor by arithmetic or geometric progression from the value of the first degree. The degree values in Figure 3 increase in arithmetic progression by adding the value of the first degree to the value of the preceding degree to arrive at the point value of the next degree. A geometric progression would add a constant percentage to the preceding degree value to arrive at the next degree value. Either approach is effective, and both are commonly used.

Point scores for jobs are converted into pay-grade assignments by setting up constant point spreads or point ranges for each grade and placing jobs in grades

Figure 3.   Evaluation points assigned to factors and degrees in a five-factor point plan.

Factor	1st degree points	2d degree points	3d degree points	4th degree points	5th degree points	6th degree points
1. Education required	20	40	60	80	100	120
2. Experience required	25	50	75	100	125	150
3. Complexity of job	35	70	105	140		
4. Responsibility for relationships with others	15	30	45	60		
5. Working conditions	5	10	15	20		

according to their point totals. The point spreads should be determined only after a careful review of the differing job relationships which result from using different point spreads. For the point plan referred to in Figures 2 and 3, the following grade-point ranges were established:

Point Range	Salary Grade
Up to 140	1
145 to 165	2
170 to 190	3
195 to 215	4
220 to 240	5
245 to 265	6
270 to 290	7
295 to 315	8
320 to 340	9
345 to 365	10
370 to 390	11
395 to 415	12
420 to 440	13

Since the rating scales of a point system are descriptively fixed, rating judgments can be made with more consistency than in the ranking and grading systems. Why one job is evaluated higher than another can be more readily documented, a feature which is critical to the confidence that managers and employees will have in the method. The existence of this evaluation record also makes the point system less open to manipulation.

The substantial time, effort, and care required to create a point plan are its principal drawbacks. Selecting the right factors, defining clearcut degrees of each, and establishing point values call for painstaking study, development, and testing, as well as skill and insightful judgment. Also, while the process of evaluating jobs by a point system may be surer, it is slower than the ranking and grading methods because rating judgments must be made and documented for a number of factors.

The Factor-comparison System

This method combines features of the ranking and point systems to create an evaluation approach thought by many to be more precise and objective than any other system. As in the point system, factors are selected and defined, but written degree definitions are not used. Instead, key jobs are ranked under each factor, and the numerical value finally assigned to each ranked job becomes a "degree" of the given factor. With key jobs thus forming the rating scale for each factor, the remaining jobs are compared with the key jobs, factor by factor, to judge where they belong on each scale. The separate amounts of each factor awarded to a job are added to determine the total value of the job. (See Figure 4.)

Some versions of the factor-comparison system use monetary units to express the relative weights of the factors and to reflect the value of each degree. This weighted-in-money method is typical in evaluation of plant jobs, and it was the approach used in the original plan, developed by Eugene J. Benge. Because the rating scale is derived from the current rates paid to key jobs, which are thought to be correctly paid, the final evaluations made in terms of such a scale also "price" the jobs directly. However, it is more common in factor-comparison plans designed for salaried positions to assign percentages of the total worth of jobs in order to develop numerical expressions of factor weights and degree values.

The criteria for selecting and defining valid, reliable, and acceptable factors are the same as were outlined earlier for the point system. Five basic factors were used in the original factor-comparison plans: mental requirements, skill requirements, physical requirements, responsibility, and working conditions. Many of today's plans consist of factors which can be thought of as subdivisions or specific dimensions of these five generic factors.

Key jobs are selected to serve as indicators on the yardstick of each factor. Since they will become the job-comparison scale for all other jobs, the key jobs should be well-known, clearly defined, very stable positions which are representative of the type and range of jobs to be evaluated, and they should be fairly common to other organizations. The number of key jobs needed will depend on the size and scope of the installation, but usually between ten and twenty-five jobs will suffice.

The first step in building the job-comparison scale is to rank the key jobs under each factor. Before attempting this, however, the raters should undergo training or practice sessions to become thoroughly familiar with the factor definitions, the

Figure 4.   Factor-comparison evaluation of clerical bank positions.

Benchmark jobs, grade 6	Degree levels assigned								Total points
	K	J	P	S	A	D	R	W	
Advice to Receive Clerk	11	3	2	1	5	12	7	7	669
Consolidation Clerk Sr.	13	3	3	1	4	10	4	3	638
Certificate Examiner	12	1	2	1	7	14	2	5	634
Proof & Adjustment Clerk	12	2	2	1	6	14	5	6	679
Collection Clerk Sr.	10	1	2	1	4	14	6	7	602
Correspondent & Inquiry Clerk .	12	2	2	1	3	13	6	4	625
Accounting & Control Clerk	13	2	2	1	5	11	5	5	663
Special Instructions Bookkeeper .	11	3	2	1	5	13	6	6	663
New Position									
Stock Issue Clerk	10	3	2	1	8	12	3	9	661

Shown above is the evaluation of a new clerical position in a large bank, after comparing the new position with the benchmark jobs. The degree level for each factor for the Stock Issue Clerk was decided in relation to the levels already assigned to the benchmark positions. Each degree-level number represents a scheduled number of points for each factor. The eight factors and their weights are: Knowledge (30%), Judgment (15%), Planning (10%), Responsibility for Staff (10%), for Assets (12%), for Detail (9%), for Relations (10%), and Working Conditions (4%).

SOURCE: The Chase-Manhattan Bank, N.A.

key job descriptions, and the ranking process. After this orientation, the raters rank all key jobs from low to high on the first factor, then on the second factor, and so on. At first independently, and then in group sessions, the raters decide and agree on the rank order for each factor.

Next, one of several techniques should be adopted to assign weights to the factors and point values to the factor steps represented by the key job rankings. One prevalent technique is the Turner Per Cent Method by which point values for all key jobs are derived from previously determined horizontal and vertical relationships. The relative importance of each factor *within* each key job is decided, and percentages are assigned to each factor for each job to reflect this "horizontal" relationship. Then, the jobs are considered in their vertical relationships to one another under each factor. With the highest ranked job in each factor considered to be 100 percent of the factor, the other key jobs are assigned percentages to estimate the amount of the factor each requires in terms of the highest ranked job. The horizontal and vertical sets of percentages are used to compute a table of point values which merge and reflect both sets of relationships, although the resulting point values may have to be adjusted slightly to preserve the original rank order of the key jobs in each factor.

Finally, the job-comparison scales made up of key jobs are fleshed out by the addition of a secondary group of jobs. These supplementary key jobs are those which come closest, after the original benchmark positions, to meeting the criteria for key jobs. They are compared, ranked, and assigned point values under each factor in terms of their relationships to the primary key jobs. If, as is recommended, two supplementary key jobs can be added for each original key job, the resulting factor yardsticks will be well calibrated for rating the remaining positions in the organization.

The factor-comparison system goes directly to the central issue of relative value by relying on job-to-job comparisons, not semantics, and its yardsticks are always tailor made for measuring the organization's positions. Also, the rating process itself imposes a check on consistency which is not inherent in the point system.

The drawbacks of the factor-comparison system parallel those of the point system. Considerable effort and care are required to create the rating plan, and the factor-by-factor evaluation process is relatively slow.

A Market Approach to Job Evaluation

A concept quite distinct from the traditional methods of job evaluation is the guideline method developed by Smyth & Murphy Associates. Considered by some to be a fifth approach to job evaluation, the guideline method builds the realities of the labor market into the evaluation process at the outset. Considerations of internal job relationships are ignored until as many jobs as possible are surveyed to get a fix on average salaries being paid for comparable jobs in the marketplace. Each job so surveyed is assigned to a salary range in a predetermined salary structure by choosing the range whose midpoint rate is closest to the average salary paid by other employers, all midpoints being only 5 percent apart.

This tentative alignment is displayed and discussed with the responsible line executives who may modify the market relationships to meet internal needs, usually adjusting positions only one or two grades up or down. The line executives then rank and slot the remaining jobs (which could not be priced in the market) in terms of the benchmark jobs and the salary ranges already assigned to them.

Obviously, the feasibility of using such an approach depends on the availability of technically sound and sophisticated survey data to price the large proportion of benchmark positions required in the guideline method.

Tailor-making the Plan

In general, small companies with relatively few office-clerical positions would be wise to start out with a ranking approach or a simple grading plan. Larger companies would profit in the long run by choosing the point or factor-comparison method. Despite the limitations of the nonquantitative methods, on the whole they are the optimum systems for small installations because out-of-line evaluations usually can be readily recognized in a limited universe of jobs. However, whichever of the basic systems is chosen, there remains the question of whether to create a plan, to use an existing plan intact, or to adopt and modify an existing plan.

Effective use of any evaluation plan requires thorough understanding of the plan itself, and this insight is best gained in the process of creating the plan. Also, it is essential that the plan be one that is tailor-made for the company, one that fits the characteristics and operating conditions unique to that company and its office positions. Rarely will a borrowed plan meet and mesh neatly with the individual needs of a given company.

While the ideal solution is to devise and construct an evaluation plan, it is also the most time-consuming alternative. For this reason it is quite common for a company to take the middle course and alter an existing plan to serve its own purposes and needs, being careful to start with a proven plan which for the most part is already apt for the company.

USE OF CONSULTANTS AND COMPANY STAFF

For a company that has had no experience in implementing a formal job evaluation program for any other group of positions, the installation of an office evaluation program would likely require the advice or services of a management consulting firm or the employment of a thoroughly qualified salary administrator. Where no real expertise for such an assignment exists in the company, the company must go to the outside to obtain the proven competence needed to guide it at least through the creation and launching of the program. In the context of a make-or-buy decision, the company must "buy" the know-how in order to "make" this new salary administration ingredient. Complete reliance on selected company staff is not suggested unless one or more of those chosen to lead the evaluation effort have a professional background in this specialty.

Of the three possible arrangements—using a consulting firm to do the whole job, relying completely on company staff, or having consultants assist and guide company staff—the last-mentioned approach is recommended for it combines the advantages of *expert advice* and *employee participation*. Some of the benefits and pitfalls of the first two arrangements help clarify why a blend of each is usually the most successful approach:

CONSULTANTS ALONE

Advantages:

1. Consultants are technically qualified and equipped to handle the installation with efficient speed.

2. They have usually made similar installations in a number of other companies so that their techniques and solutions to problems encountered have been well tested.

3. As outsiders, they are impartial and objective.

Disadvantages:

1. Once installed, the program is left in the hands of company staff who, be-

cause of their initial exclusion, do not fully understand the concepts, premises, and technical procedures of the program.

2. Lacking a knowledge of the company, its traditions, unique operating conditions, and human relations style, consultants' efforts may appear blundering and naïve and so cast doubts on their results.

3. An inherent mistrust of "outside experts," especially those who affect pay, may lead some employees to resist or reject the results out of hand.

COMPANY STAFF ONLY

Advantages:

1. Employees identify with, and will support, a program which they have helped to create.

2. Being in on the creation and installation of the program provides them with the understanding and training required to carry on the maintenance of the program.

3. Employees are already familiar with the organization and operations of the company and the people who comprise it.

Disadvantages:

1. The program may be poorly constructed and installed because, as novices in job evaluation theory and practice, employees will lack confidence and competence in the more technical aspects.

2. The advantage of company knowledge will backfire if their objectivity is lost through biased or partial judgments.

3. If the employees cannot devote their full time to the installation, the entire effort may be slowed or deferred as business pressures limit or halt their involvement.

ANNOUNCING THE PROGRAM

Early in the preparations for implementing an office job evaluation program, the company should announce to employees that such a program is about to be installed. The first announcement and any follow-up information are important influences on how employees will react to the idea of job evaluation and the company's motives for introducing it. Timely communication about the purpose and nature of the evaluation program will help put to rest or prevent negative or erroneous speculation and rumor.

The most prevalent and recommended first step is a memorandum from the president to all staff, announcing the program, its objectives, who is in charge of it, and giving assurance that no employee's salary will be reduced because of it. (Figure 5 shows a fairly typical memorandum that was used to announce a clerical evaluation program in a large organization.) The president's announcement of the program delivers an impact of authority, commitment, and credibility which no one else in the organization can surpass. Concern about how such a program may affect him, and his current salary, will be paramount in the individual employee's reaction to the program, and this concern can be stilled or erased if the integrity and support of the chief executive are tied to the program at the outset.

Following the president's announcement, additional information may be given by conducting brief orientation meetings with supervisors and employees, as well as by publishing articles about the program in the employee newspaper or magazine. A clearer understanding of the what and why of the program should result in a surer acceptance of it.

Figure 5.   Announcement of a clerical evaluation program.

INTER-OFFICE MEMORANDUM
TO: (The Staff)
FROM: (The President)

Within the next few weeks, several committees made up of members of our own supervisory organization will begin a study of all clerical positions. This study, commonly referred to as "Job Evaluation" will analyze each position in terms of job content and will establish the relationships among all positions covered.

The primary objective of this procedure is to assure equitable salary consistency among all comparable positions within the company. It will also provide a means whereby our salary structure can be compared on a systematic basis with "going rates" in the area.

Our program has been patterned to fit our own needs. The methods to be used are quite simple and are similar to those employed in many other progressive companies. Details were developed by a Job Evaluation Policy Committee which was appointed by me some months ago. Each of the divisional committees referred to in the first paragraph will operate within that segment of the company with which its members are familiar. The Director of Personnel Relations is responsible for coordinating the activities of these groups.

The purpose of this memorandum is to give you advance notice of this project so that you need not speculate about it. I also want to assure you that *no salaries will be reduced* as a result of this program. There may be some upward revisions, but there will be no reductions.

It is anticipated that job evaluation will aid materially in maintaining our policy of paying salaries that compare favorably with those paid by other companies for the same quality of work under similar conditions.

This project will take considerable time to complete, but you will be given additional information as the work progresses.

ANALYZING AND DESCRIBING OFFICE JOBS

Before a job can be judged or measured in terms of an evaluation yardstick, the what, how, and why of the job and the demands it makes on the incumbent must be learned and recorded. The job, the thing that is to be compared and evaluated, must be understood and held still, so to speak, so that a word picture of it can be created, and this picture must reveal without distortion the presence and extent of significant features which the yardstick considers. Everything else about an evaluation program may be superbly prepared and provided for, but if the very stuff with which it is concerned is faultily understood or ineptly portrayed, the program will have been built in vain.

Job analysis for office job evaluation purposes is most effectively carried out by the interview method or, if time and staff do not permit it, by a combination of the questionnaire and interview methods. Observation of the worker, an important aspect of analyzing many plant jobs, is less pertinent in the analysis of office-clerical positions because with most office jobs there is little that can be learned by observation alone.

In the interview method, the job analyst meets face to face with the employee on the job to elicit job information, making sufficient notes about what the employee does, how he performs it, why he does it, and the know-how and skills required to do it. Prior to meeting with any employee, of course, the analyst should have discussed the evaluation program and his own role with the department manager to ensure complete understanding and cooperation. The analyst should do this, too, with each employee he interviews to clear up any misgivings or misconceptions about why the job information is being sought and what will be done with it. He must present himself as an objective seeker and recorder of facts about the *job* who is not concerned with how well the employee performs it. At the same time, the analyst should be adept at establishing an informal and easy rapport with the employee which will help make the interview a comfortable experience for the employee. Before concluding the interview, the analyst should be sure he has learned about all aspects of the job and should go back over with the employee any part which is still not clear. A thorough analysis will also include pre- and post-interview discussions with the employee's immediate supervisor to understand better the purpose of the job and its functional relationship to other jobs in the unit, as well as to clarify and verify job facts picked up in the employee interview.

Because the interview method of job analysis is so time consuming, many companies have adopted a questionnaire-and-interview method. This technique puts some of the burden of fact gathering, analysis, and description on the line organization and can provide the job analyst with a structured and condensed preview of the duties of the job and its requirements. This information is prepared in advance by the manager, or by the employee and reviewed by the manager, and is later amplified and verified by the job analyst through interview with the employee and the manager. Reliance on the questionnaire method alone, without a follow-up interview, is not recommended because the job data obtained are usually not dependable, often including vague or inconsistent job facts which will demand clarification. In addition, an interview can also provide the analyst with a "feel" for the job and an appreciation of certain nuances about it that may be important to the evaluation of the position which were not evident from the questionnaire.

The job description, the end product of the job analysis, is a written record of the job and its requirements, typically consisting of the following segments:

1. The job title, department, section, and other identifying data to distinguish it from all other jobs

2. A summary or capsule statement of the work performed and the scope and overall purpose of the job, which also helps to add perspective to the individual duties

3. The individual duties, assignments, and tasks which make up the job

4. The job specifications which bring out the requirements and demands made on the incumbent in terms of the evaluation factors

Writing a good job description is often a challenging and arduous task. The analyst is confronted with much information and detail, collected in the analysis, which now must be sifted, organized, and shaped into a clear, concise, complete, and accurate description. The time and effort which the supervisor, the employee, and the analyst invested in the job analysis will be sheer waste if the analyst cannot create from it a well-focused and meaningful report of the job. He must have a talent for factual and terse writing and be able to squeeze from a myriad of details those job facts which cast a sharp profile of the job. His target is to produce a description which, on its own, will document and support (or, if carelessly evaluated, contradict) the evaluation assigned to it.

Job descriptions are commonly written in a telegraphic style, avoiding verbiage, to get directly at what the incumbent does, how he does it, and why. Where significant, the guidance provided and the level of skill involved in the tasks are also characterized. The description follows the natural flow of work if the job consists of sequential operations. If the duties are unrelated, they may be grouped in order of their importance, the time spent on them, or the frequency of their performance.

When the analyst is satisfied with a draft of the description, he should review it with the immediate supervisor and, preferably, with the employee, too. Changes requested by either should be made in the interests of accuracy and clarity, but the addition of unnecessary, minute detail should be avoided. The final draft should then be submitted to the designated management levels for their acceptance and approval. (See job description example in Figure 6.)

Figure 6. Example of description of computer-oriented office position.

JOB TITLE	DEPARTMENT OR PUBLICATION
Computer Control Clerk	Circulation Planning & Control

REPORTS TO	SECTION
Michael Babick, Manager	Input/Output

NAMES OF EMPLOYEES ON THIS JOB
Judy Field

PREPARED BY	REVIEWED AND APPROVED BY
Name: William B. McCool	Don Page
Position: Job Analyst Date 7-7-70	Publisher or Department Head Date 7/7/70

Function: Reviews and corrects computer listings to ensure accuracy of microfilm reader input used in processing orders. Codes briefs for customer selection transactions requesting specific data. Performs miscellaneous control duties, and keeps records for control and billing purposes.

Duties
1. Receives a taped printout of scanner sheets rejected by computer because of errors. Reviews sheets to determine type of error such as invalid batch or document header symbol, improper spacing, damaged paper, improper margins or incorrect batch number. Obtains batch numbers for documents with errors from computer printouts, pulls documents, attaches scanner sheet with notation of error to documents, returns to typists for corrections. Reviews printouts to determine any unusual conditions existing in the performance of the scanner. Notifies supervisor if problems are discovered. Reviews printouts for error messages such as incorrect control number, error in variable data or missing lines. Researches source documents to resolve error; re-enters corrected data into system. Maintains an input/output schedule by weekly recording information from printouts. Maintains records of selected data, input/output counts and dates, and billing charges to clients. Balances printout totals of various reports. (30%)
2. Receives requests for customer selection reports from the Marketing System. Reviews requests to ensure completeness, including all specifications, data required and an estimate of output. Prepares coding briefs for selection transactions, following selection manual and format for different transactions and entering correct data, item code and criteria code. Receives reports from computer runs, checks against selection transaction brief to determine the validity of the output. Keeps record of each report and enters in log for billing charges. Releases reports to requisitioner. (35%)
3. Performs miscellaneous control duties, such as analysis of job control language sheets from all computer programs, checking to determine if reels being entered follow correct pattern, and reviewing certain checkpoint programs to detect any erroneous conditions before system can proceed. Maintains a monthly cycle chart to identify reel numbers and processing time for a particular program; posts information to chart to develop running times for a monthly cycle and to keep a log of all tape reels for retention purposes. Provides Electronic Accounting Machine Section with estimated output of all computer runs. Compiles from own records, tabulates and records all billing charges for jobs completed at end of each monthly cycle. Develops and maintains a retention file for magnetic tapes. Maintains records for all special cycles. (35%)

Figure 6.   Example of description of computer-oriented office position. (continued)

FACTOR	REASONS FOR DEGREE VALUES ASSIGNED	RATING	
		Degree	Points
Education required	Knowledge of mathematics, bookkeeping, and correct speech	3	60
Experience required	9 to 10 months on the job to become thoroughly familiar with source materials, manuals, and coding charts needed to correct printouts and prepare accurate coding briefs for selection reports, and the procedures for analyzing job control language sheets and maintaining various input/output records.	3	75
Complexity of job	Follow detailed instructions and standard practices. Decisions limited to indicated choices when reviewing, researching, and correcting printout errors and when coding briefs for selection reports and checking validity of output	2	70
Responsibility for relationships with others	Requires courtesy to avoid friction in frequent personal contacts with Data Processing and Electronic Accounting Machine Sections concerning performance of scanner machine and errors concerning input/output data	2	30
Working conditions	Located in a large, well-lighted office subject to noise from employees and office machines	2	10

Total - 245

RATING THE JOBS

Comparing and deciding how the described jobs relate to the rating scale is what job evaluation is all about. Obviously, the process of rating the jobs to establish their internal relative value must be carried out in such a way as to ensure the greatest practicable degree of reliability and validity in making each rating judgment, and the consistency of the judgments must be checked and verified before using the results for salary administration purposes.

A committee is usually selected and trained to do the job rating, frequently comprised of several layers of management and always including the director of the job evaluation effort. The checks and balances of a committee approach to an endeavor so dependent on judgment outweigh the administrative appeal of having only one qualified person to do the rating. Also, acceptance of the results by other managers and the employees may be enhanced if the ratings have been evolved through group judgment, especially if persons respected for their knowledge of the jobs, intellectual honesty, and objectivity are selected for the evaluation committee.

As earlier discussed, the efforts of a committee will be freer of bias or domination if ratings are attempted independently by each member prior to each meeting, with the meetings reserved to discuss and iron out differences of opinion. Detailed advice on effective ways to organize and standardize a sound procedure for rating jobs by the committee method is available in a number of texts on job evaluation, including examples of various forms for recording and checking rating judgments under each of the several evaluation systems.

The experience of those involved in rating processes where human judgment is the final arbiter, as it is in job evaluation, has been reported and repeated sufficiently to alert any prudent and informed would-be rater to the pitfalls and common errors to be guarded against in rating jobs. Nevertheless, even the most practiced and sophisticated decision makers selected to serve on the evaluation committee should be reminded of the rating dangers and deficiencies which can beset an otherwise earnest effort to make objective judgments about the relative worth of jobs. Elizabeth Lanham (see bibliography) lists some of the more common rating mistakes, as follows:

Halo effect: the tendency to rate every factor of the job high or low because the first factor rated or the most important factor to the job was assigned a high or low value, or because the general impression about the job is that it is of high or low value

Central tendency: the tendency to adhere to a middle course and rate most factors in the job neither high nor low but at midpoint on the scale

Leniency: the tendency to allow the benefit of the doubt in cases where the decision is not clear-cut, or to avoid rating jobs low on any factor or in total value

Harshness: the tendency to minimize the importance of any factor in a job or the total value of the job, or never to allow the benefit of the doubt in cases where the decision is not clear-cut

Bias or prejudice: the tendency to favor or discriminate against a job because of personal feelings

CLASSIFYING EMPLOYEES

The final step in the evaluation process is the procedure of classifying employees as to the jobs they perform. The current incumbents of the described and evaluated jobs must be identified and assigned the job titles which correctly apply to them. Proper classification of employees is as important as the correct evaluation of the job themselves, for two good reasons:

1. Errors in classification of employees, if undetected, can seriously distort the internal salary trend line and lead to a mistaken conclusion about how internal pay compares with pay levels in other companies. If employees on high-valued jobs are incorrectly classified as being on low-valued jobs (e.g., senior clerks classified as junior clerks), or vice versa, existing pay levels in the company could falsely appear to be well above or below going rates in the community.

2. Misclassified employees will be overpaid or underpaid for the work they are really doing. Such inequities destroy confidence in the job evaluation program, build resentment among employees, and, ironically, cause pay-related problems and turnover which job evaluation was designed to remedy.

The supervisors and managers of the employees, along with the job analyst, are best informed about who is doing which job and should be responsible for deciding the classification of employees. Each employee must be assigned to one of the evaluated jobs, and if none of the approved job descriptions applies to a given employee, a description should be prepared and evaluated to cover the employee. The analyst can help the supervisor to resolve classification questions, such as whether an employee should be considered as doing the junior or senior level of a basic job, and to settle such matters consistent with similar classification decisions in other departments. Also, the analyst should monitor classification decisions to guard against attempts or tendencies to classify employees on higher or lower valued jobs merely to justify their current salaries.

BIBLIOGRAPHY

Beal, Edwin F.: "In Praise of Job Evaluation," *California Management Review,* Summer, 1963.

Berenson, Conrad, and Henry O. Ruhnke: "Job Descriptions: How to Write and Use Them," *Personnel Journal,* Swarthmore, Pa., 1967.

Brennan, Charles W.: "Wage Administration—Plans, Practices, Principles," Richard D. Irwin, Inc., Homewood, Ill., 1963.

French, Wendell: *The Personnel Management Process,* Houghton Mifflin Company, Boston, 1970, pp. 311–345.

Hay, Edward N.: "Four Methods of Establishing Factor Scales in Factor Comparison Job Evaluation," *The AMA Handbook of Wage and Salary Administration,* American Management Association, New York, 1950, pp. 56–65.

Lanham, Elizabeth: *Job Evaluation,* McGraw-Hill Book Company, New York, 1955.

Otis, Jay L., and Richard H. Leukart: *Job Evaluation,* Prentice-Hall, Inc., Englewood Cliffs, N.J., 1954.

Pasquale, Anthony M.: "A New Dimension to Job Evaluation," *AMA Management Bulletin* no. 128, American Management Association, New York, 1969.

Patterson, T. T., and T. M. Husband: "Decision-making Responsibility: Yardstick for Job Evaluation," *Compensation Review,* Second Quarter, American Management Association, New York, 1970, pp. 21–31.

Scott, Walter D., Robert C. Clothier, and William R. Spriegel: *Personnel Management,* McGraw-Hill Book Company, New York, 1961.

Sibson, Robert E.: *Wages and Salaries: A Handbook for Line Managers,* American Management Association, New York, 1967.

Smyth, Richard C.: *Job Evaluation Failures,* Smyth & Murphy Associates, Inc., New York, 1965.

Terry, George R.: *Office Management and Control,* Richard D. Irwin, Inc., Homewood, Ill., 1970, pp. 769–784.

U.S. Civil Service Commission: *Classification Principles and Policies,* Personnel Management Series, no. 16, June, 1963.

chapter 29

Job Evaluation and Pay Plans:
Plant Personnel

BURTON E. BAUDER   *Vice President, Sibson & Company, Inc., New York, New York*

The use of job evaluation plans, while covered in the preceding chapter, merits some discussion in this chapter. Some of the earliest work done on the evaluation of jobs started with the study of plant or hourly paid jobs, and even today, it is possible to find examples of this original work still in use.

Many of the earliest texts written on the subject of job evaluation dealt with shop or plant jobs. It was here that the unions first started to apply their pressure for better wages. It was here that companies first recognized the need for some better method of relating the wages paid one job with respect to another. Finally, it was here that the early practitioners of job evaluation gained their experience, which ultimately was applied to office type jobs and, later, to management, administrative, and professional positions.

No one who has worked in this field for any length of time fails to recognize the early efforts of the National Metal Trades Association and the job evaluation plan developed by that organization to relate the value of hourly rated jobs; this plan was subsequently modified to use the same approach for office-clerical jobs. This plan, even in its original form, is still in use today and has served many other organizations in the development of modified or new plans. It was one of the original examples of the point system.

Today, many changes are occurring in job evaluation. A number of plans are being developed that use, as an example, less factors than were used in the original National Metal Trades Association plan. Also, unions in some industries prefer to work in an unstructured atmosphere and tend to just rank jobs, rather than go through the more formalized point system of evaluation. Pressures have come from the unskilled and semiskilled workers to obtain higher wages, with the result that many settlements are made on a flat cents-per-hour basis, rather than on a percentage basis. This can, of course, negate the effect and use of a formalized job evaluation procedure where proper differentiation can be shown between the unskilled, semiskilled, and skilled jobs. Yet, we can and do find large companies and industries, e.g., the steel industry, where a job evaluation system has been used for a number of years and is still in use today.

JOB EVALUATION

In 1947 the Department of Labor, United States Employment Service, Occupational Analysis Branch, in its paper *Industrial Job Evaluation Systems*, defined job evaluation as:

> The complete operation of determining the value of an individual job in an organization in relation to the other jobs in the organization. It begins with job analysis to obtain job descriptions and includes relating the descriptions by some system designed to determine the relative value of the jobs or groups of jobs. It also involves the pricing of these values by establishing minimum and maximum salaries for each group of jobs based on their relative values. The operation ends with the final checking of the resulting salary system.

It has long been understood that the whole technique of job evaluation is not a precise method of measurement. At best, it is a method of organizing peoples' judgment so that all jobs are examined on the same basis and with the same considerations. It is a method that is used to determine basic wage relationships, the pricing of jobs.

WAGE INCENTIVE PLAN

Just as in the case of job evaluation plans, most of the first efforts to develop incentive plans were directed to the hourly rated shop and plant-type jobs.

It will be recalled that the initial step taken in the development of any compensation program is the pricing of the jobs. This procedure establishes a price or job rate for each individual job.

Many techniques are followed in using this job rate. Some companies, as an example, move people to this job rate on the basis of time on the job, or longevity. Others just use the job rate as the wage that is paid for the job. The only time the rate is changed is when a union contract is renegotiated or when a company that is not organized determines new job rates on their own.

Still other companies compute ranges around the job rates. If a job rate is, for example, $3.50 per hour, a minimum rate is pegged at $3.00 and a maximum is set at $4.00. Thus, individuals on the same job can be paid as low as $3.00 per hour and as high as $4.00 per hour. In such instances, a form of merit rating system is developed, detailing an approach that can be used to assess the individual performance of one individual on the job with respect to another.

For a number of reasons, merit rating systems are not in wide use for hourly rated jobs. To begin, if there are ten punch-press operators, all in the same job and doing the same work, it is hard to assess differences in individual performance. Generally, the only measurable differences are variations in output of a quality standard product. Then, too, unions are hesitant to permit such programs to exist, since they usually lose control, because ratings are done by individual supervisors and are difficult to question and, at the same time, difficult to explain and justify.

Yet, companies are continually looking for ways to get greater productivity.

With the high investment necessary in machines and equipment, there is a need to obtain maximum utilization. This maximum utilization is, in most instances, dependent on the effectiveness of people, the workers on the jobs. For this reason, companies start to look for techniques to measure output, either on an individual or on a group basis. For this, a company is willing to pay extra, beyond the norm or standard production rate. The assumption is that if the company gears extra pay to extra work, each employee will tend to produce to the maximum of his or her individual ability. It is a logical assumption, as many plans have been developed for just this purpose and have been most successful. In the balance of this chapter, a review will be made of these types of plans or approaches, their advantages and disadvantages, and how and where they can be used.

TYPES OF INCENTIVE PLANS

Many plans have been developed to provide some incentive for workers to increase their output. It must be recognized that in each of these plans there is one basic principle: Employees will be more productive if the amount of their income is tied directly to the amount of work that is turned out, regardless of the amount of time that is required.

Generally, these plans are predicated on the existence of several essential conditions:

1. There must be measurable units of output that can be determined either on an individual or on a group basis.

2. There generally is a relatively continuous operation, with standardized work.

3. The quantity of output is usually directly proportional to the individual's or group's attention and effort.

4. Quality is usually of secondary concern, although offsets are sometimes prescribed in those instances where quality is of significant concern; this can vary by operations or at points in the work process.

While a number of plans were developed over the years, primarily by industrial engineering consultants, many of these are no longer in wide use. Those which will be reviewed are still in use today and will include the piecework plan, the standard-hour plan, the measured daywork plan, and the gain-sharing plan.

THE PIECEWORK PLAN

Under this plan, the employee's earnings are directly related to the number of units produced. This is one of the simplest, most easily understood, and most commonly used plans. This plan has the advantage of establishing a direct relationship between what a worker produces and what he earns.

Standards are expressed in a number of ways, generally in terms of a certain amount of money for each unit produced, that is, so much per piece, or per pound, or per dozen. Earnings thus are directly related to output. Originally, workers were paid only for their actual production, with no guaranteed minimum. However, since the passage of the Fair Labor Standards Act in 1938, employers whose employees are engaged in interstate commerce or the production of goods for interstate commerce are required to pay a minimum hourly wage. Thus, the practice today is to pay a minimum hourly wage, even if the worker has not produced enough units to meet that base.

The key to any good piecework plan is the use of a qualified industrial engineering staff. Each operation must be studied and rates set for each type of unit produced. This is not a one-time operation. Not only must rates be set originally, but they must be updated as new methods are instituted, etc.

The advantages of such a plan are readily apparent. The plan is simple and is easily understood by employees. Earnings are directly proportionate to output and thus are considered fair by employees. Minimum guarantees protect the employees during training and when production delays affect output. From a management standpoint, labor costs can easily be ascertained for output above standard.

As with any plan, there are disadvantages, the most serious being the need to change piece rates when a general increase is given. This can be a voluminous clerical chore. Here it is important to clarify the respective base or job rate and the piece rate. The job rates are established by the usual techniques that have been previously covered. Standard times, for piece rate purposes, must be determined by an objective study of the quantity of work that can be produced by a normal worker under standard conditions. Thus, it is necessary to divorce the money level and the work standard.

Piecework systems are still extensively used. They serve a useful purpose in companies where the operations tend to be standardized. They can even apply to small group units as well as to individual operators.

THE STANDARD-HOUR PLAN

This plan provides the employee with a 100 percent premium. An employee's bonus is equal to 100 percent of the savings effected by greater productivity.

This standard-hour plan is predicated on a guaranteed base rate that the employee receives, even if he fails to meet standard performance. The plan operates essentially the same as the piecework plan in that it has a guaranteed minimum. In this case, however, the standard is expressed in units of time instead of money. It is a pay plan in which the percent performance over standard is rewarded by an equal percent premium over base pay.

The plan is simple in its operation. Assume that the base rate for an individual job is $4.00 per hour. Assume further that the time standard for the selected operation is ¼ hour per unit. Using the calculation base as one day, it can be seen that an employee would earn 10 standard hours of pay, or $40.00, if 40 units are made. When the workday is 8 hours long, the worker would have earned 10 standard hours of pay, with an efficiency rate of 125 percent. When less than 32 units are produced, the employee would then be paid the base rate of $4.00 per hour, or $32.00 for the regular 8-hour workday.

This standard-hour plan is, as the piecework plan, simple to understand and communicate to employees, always a desired goal with any type of incentive plan. Here, when a change is made in hourly rates of pay, there is no effect on the standards since they are expressed in units of time rather than in units of money.

Such an approach can also be used and made applicable to groups, even when the group may include individuals on different base or job rates. In fact, since the basis of measurement is units produced rather than money, the calculations are easier to make for cost accounting purposes as well as for measurement of the individual organization segment's efficiency. Of course, there is the basic need for an industrial engineering staff to develop and maintain the standards. This is necessary in practically all plans used for incentive purposes for hourly rated jobs. This cannot be called a disadvantage.

Most people still consider this as one of the best types of plans to use for incentive purposes. It is one of the simplest to use and eliminates, to a major extent, the disadvantage of the piecework plan approach.

THE MEASURED DAYWORK PLAN

This plan does not directly relate to an incentive payoff as do the two previous plans. In effect, many question whether this measured daywork plan is an incentive plan. In this approach, a work standard is set by conventional industrial engineering techniques and the production worker is expected to meet the work quota or standard established. Whether he exceeds or fails to meet the standard, he still receives his regular rate of hourly pay.

Formerly it was the practice to review the performance of each worker quarterly for several factors, including quantity and quality of work and dependability. Those scoring highly were rewarded with a higher hourly rate of pay the next quarter. Of course, those scoring lower received a decrease in pay. Usually, a portion of the total compensation was guaranteed, e.g., 75 percent of the total rate, and the other portion would be subject to quarterly change based on performance.

Today the quarterly review procedure is infrequently applied, and measured daywork involves pay at a regular hourly rate. Worker efficiency is controlled through means of the production standards that have been established for the job. Under this variation, hourly rates are not adjusted. Instead, pressure is placed on the worker to meet the standard regularly. If the worker is at fault, disciplinary action is taken. However, care is exercised to determine that the standard is not the cause of the failure to meet the expected levels of production. In such instances, through review of the operations, either standards are changed or necessary corrective actions are taken with respect to the methods, equipment, or materials.

The advantage of this plan is that management has a better control over production and labor costs than would be the case with regular or conventional payment of hourly rates. Further, the production of an employee is assessed against measured work standards and, in this respect, he knows what is expected. It has also been indicated by some that measured daywork results in less worker reaction to new or changed methods.

At the same time, workers do not receive any direct incentive pay, as is the case with the other plans previously discussed. In the subject plan, there is only the requirement to meet production standards to receive the regular hourly rate of pay. Failure to do so can result in some form of action that is usually of an adverse nature to the employee.

THE GAIN-SHARING PLAN

This plan has been employed, in some form or other, since late in the nineteenth century. It was employed before the advent of today's industrial engineering work in conducting time and motion studies to set work standards.

In this type of plan, a standard time is established for each task or unit of work, and the employee receives a base or hourly rate of pay for production completed within the time. However, when the worker finishes the task in less than the allotted time, he receives a bonus, usually equal to about half the savings in time. The bonus earnings are usually added to the base earnings, and the earnings rate is then calculated for the purpose of computing overtime hours.

A gain-sharing plan is, as the name implies, one where the money rewards for production above standard are not in direct proportion to the increment increase in production. Here the gains are shared with the company, with the worker receiving less than a 1 percent increase in pay for a 1 percent increase in production. These plans are based on the fact that a worker will be rewarded for saving time in his work production. Thus, standards are expressed in terms of time. In some plans, 100 percent of the gain has gone to the worker; in other cases, the split has been 75 percent–25 percent. One of the best known of these plans was the Halsey 50-50 bonus plan which was designed in 1890. The standard was expressed in time per unit and was based on past performance when the employee was working for daywork wages. The split of 50-50 was designed to prevent the worker from running away with the rate since no methods analysis or time study was made and the standard was based on past performance. Thus, there was a great incentive for the worker to devise a better way to do the job.

The advantage of such a program, even when the improvements are shared with management, is the creation of better methods of doing the job, with greater productivity. Since the general practice is to base the standard time on past performance, the development costs and maintenance are less than for the other plans discussed.

At the same time, the employee often feels that the increase in pay from an increase in output is not worth the extra effort, since the results are shared with management. Thus, there is a resulting tendency to produce at a respectable, but still moderate, rate above standard. This approach is not used extensively in industry today since employees are not enthusiastic about sharing the results of their work with their companies.

Each of the plans reviewed have advantages and disadvantages. Companies that determine they want to have a wage incentive plan want to have a program that will have no weakness; in fact, they want to have a plan that will justify the continuing confidence of both employees and management.

Is it possible to have such a plan? The proponents of the use of such plans claim that it is possible, but with one very strong qualification: constant attention to the plan is necessary. The custodians of the plan must adjust and keep pace with changes. Today, companies no longer operate under a set of static conditions; rather they are part of a dynamic industrial society that is constantly changing.

WHY DO INCENTIVE PLANS FAIL?

There are a number of reasons why wage incentive plans fail, including the following:

1. The scheduling of production procedures is not geared to incentive plan requirements, resulting in an inordinate number of delays. This results in employees either having to wait for work, or having short-run jobs that require considerable time for changes in setup.

2. Maintenance of production equipment is poor. This can result in machine and/or tooling delays, requiring time-consuming servicing of equipment during regular productive time.

3. Improper and incomplete methods analysis are used. This frequently is the result of productive procedures to establish standards and, as frequently, the use of untrained personnel who are responsible for establishing such methods.

4. Finally, there is the factor of loose standards, the result of poor engineering in establishing standards, unrecorded methods changes, and lack of defined procedures for work measurement by time-study personnel. Often there is the additional pressure to relax tight standards and pressure to maintain loose standards that may be in effect.

John A. Patton, a long-time consultant in the development of wage incentive programs, stresses the need for a number of basic ingredients that must be considered before an effective plan can be established. These include the following:

Correct Base Rates. The amount of pay each employee receives each hour for performing an acceptable amount of work must be both adequate and realistic. Proper base rates can be established only by a comprehensive job evaluation approach. These can usually best be established by a competent industrial engineer. When base rates are established equitably, earnings throughout the company can be fair in relation to both effort and output.

Sound Standards. The amount of work required to earn the basic hourly rate must be realistic and clearly defined. Usually, it is the output of an average, experienced worker performing at a normal pace. If production standards are loose on some jobs and very tight on others, employees tend to work hard on jobs where it is easy to acquire extra earnings and loaf on jobs where extra earnings cannot be achieved. When performance standards are established by proper measurements, such as time studies, both management and labor can measure the output required to earn a given amount of pay.

Proper Understanding. Incentive workers as well as management representatives benefit most from a wage incentive plan when both understand how to calculate earnings and know the provisions established when unusual conditions concerning materials, supplies, or equipment are encountered. Nothing can disillusion a worker faster than to operate under a half-understood set of values, and perhaps receive a take-home pay substantially lower than he had anticipated.

Opportunity for Earnings. The successful incentive plan offers sufficient reward to inspire the worker to make an effort to increase his output, and thus increase his earnings. In order for him to do this, work flow must be well balanced. Long waits and chaotic scheduling cost a worker production which, under an incentive plan, is money. In addition to this, no ceiling should be established on total earnings; otherwise, incentive workers will peg production.

Rapport between Labor and Management. When workers and management have a high degree of confidence in each other, a wage incentive plan is off to a good start. Absence of understanding, pressures by individual groups, bargaining in poor faith, and booby-trap standards all tend to weaken the structure of an incentive plan. Most problems are caused by people and not by techniques. The people responsible for the program must realize that most human relations problems are solved by better human relations rather than by stop-watch standards and slide-rule techniques.

Finally, once the plan is in force, management must initiate and follow through with the routine legwork necessary to make the plan work. This includes training of both foremen and shop stewards and providing management officials with the ability and know-how to recognize the need for changes when and if they are required. The overall value of any wage incentive plan is only as good as the control which is exercised over it. This control is the responsibility of management.

UNION REACTIONS TO WAGE INCENTIVE PLANS

Perhaps one of the most critical aspects of any wage incentive plan is the reaction of the union. Union attitudes toward wage incentive plans vary considerably. In a general sense, unions tend to oppose incentive pay programs, with some exceptions.

Piecework in the needle trades has been generally the practice for many years. A high percentage of workers in both the men's and women's wearing apparel industry work under the piecework system, attesting to a positive acceptance by the unions. Since, in many cases, the piece rates are established through bargaining between the employer and the union, this has resulted in the general acceptance of the practice. As an example, the Amalgamated Clothing Workers Union has, for many years, favored incentives since this was the only way to increase workers' earnings without increasing labor costs. In these industries particularly, increases in labor costs in unionized firms would result in their being noncompetitive with nonunion companies. Other unions, however, have been outspoken in their opposition to wage incentive plans.

This, of course, is not unexpected, and there are numerous reasons for this union reaction to such plans. Union leaders argue that individual incentives foster competition among workers, with workers vying against one another. It becomes quickly apparent who are the best producers and who are at the low end of the scale. Management is thus in the position to judge one employee versus another. When an employer offers an employee an opportunity to make a basic living wage only by performing at above-average skills under an incentive plan, the unions will question such an arrangement. Frequently, unions will question piecework plans on the basis that such plans tend to transfer part of the risks of business ownership to the employee. It is claimed that with fixed unit direct labor costs the worker bears the brunt of production delays, inefficient scheduling, and machine breakdowns.

Questions are often raised too about inequities caused by loose or tight rates. Foreman discrimination and even favoritism can cause ill feelings. Also, inequalities of earnings can have the effect of dividing union membership. A classic situation here is where production jobs are covered by some kind of incentive plan and service units, such as maintenance, are not. Some unions will also complain about the work load of their shop stewards to process grievances resulting from the use of incentive plans. A reasonable justification can be made that plants with incentive plans need more union attention and surveillance than do daywork plants.

Even with these problems, there are many successful plans in operation. Union cooperation has been obtained, and good working relationships have been developed and maintained. Cooperation and involvement have been significant factors in arriving at positive acceptance of such plans.

KAISER–UNITED STEELWORKERS PLAN

One of the most widely publicized programs for handling difficulties associated with direct wage incentives has been that of the Kaiser Steel Corporation of Fontana, California. The plan that was ultimately evolved was to provide for the gradual elimination of direct wage incentives.

When the plan was changed in 1963, approximately 40 percent of the workers were covered by incentives. Kaiser, as was the case with many other companies, had experienced many difficulties with the operation of its incentive plan. Some rates, as is so often the situation, were loose, and the company felt that it was not obtaining the level of production for which it was paying. Employee resistance to changes in methods and rates was very great. Finally, the situation had deteriorated to the degree that many employees on low-skilled jobs were receiving more pay than were those on higher skilled jobs.

The program that ultimately resulted provided for an employee vote in each incentive unit. If incentives were voted out, employees received a sizable lump-sum payment as compensation for the loss of the usual incentive bonus. When a vote was made to eliminate the incentives in a particular unit, employees immediately started to participate in the sharing of the gains. Those who voted to retain their incentive payments were not eligible to participate in the new program. However, within three years of the new approach, about 75 percent of the former participants in direct wage incentives had voted for the change.

The Long-range Sharing Plan, negotiated between Kaiser and the United Steelworkers of America, was begun on March 1, 1963. During the 116-day steel industry strike in the fall of 1959, Edgar Kaiser, Chairman of the Board of Kaiser

Steel, negotiated a separate settlement with the union, prior to the general industry agreement. Working with David J. McDonald, then president of the United Steelworkers, a proposal was made to find a way to prevent the periodic crises and fixed bargaining positions that occurred at contract negotiations. A tripartite committee was formed, consisting of company, union, and public members. This committee was charged with the responsibility to develop a long-range plan for the equitable sharing of the company's progress with the stockholders, the employees, and the public.

It took some three years to evolve the new approach, called the Long-range Sharing Plan. It was submitted to the workers early in 1963 and was approved in a vote by a 3 to 1 margin.

The key features of the plan were as follows:

1. An employee guarantee protecting workers from unemployment as a result of technological improvements. It did not, however, protect employees against layoff resulting from a decline in the company's business.

2. A sharing of the gains plan where employees would receive 32.5 percent and the company 67.5 percent of any cost reductions realized through increased efficiency.

3. Increases in wage rates and fringe benefits that would be equal to, or greater than, those bargained throughout the rest of the industry. However, the cost of such increases would be taken from the employees' share of savings, as described above.

4. A program would be instituted that would gradually eliminate direct wage incentives.

It is interesting to note how this plan operated over the next several years. The key factor was the sharing of the gains on a 32.5 percent basis for any savings in production costs below those prevailing in 1961. The savings were distributed monthly as a cash bonus. In August 1963, the average hourly worker received a cash bonus of $39, and the next three months' amounts were $93, $70, and $64. For the three-year period of March 1963 to February 1966, the average worker received $1,560 in bonuses, or an average of $0.31 per hour worked during this same period. This bonus money was in addition to wage rates that were generally equivalent to those paid in the rest of the basic steel industry.

By 1967, the bonuses had declined to the point that there was a negative reaction on the part of the union members. As a result, a major revision in the plan was negotiated in early 1968. This revision provided that all the employees' share of cost savings would go into the monthly payments, rather than having a portion of the employees' share withheld, as before, for the wage and benefit reserve. This reserve had been originally created to provide a fund to match increases in basic wage rates and fringe benefits granted in the rest of the industry. Even with the elimination of this reserve fund in 1968, the company agreed to match other changes made in the industry, and it now counts the added expense of this matching as a labor cost in computing employees' shares.

EMPLOYEE UNDERSTANDING

The approach that was used by Kaiser was to eliminate a program of direct wage incentives and replace it with a form of profit sharing. Many companies have taken the profit sharing approach and have found it to be acceptable. At the same time, many companies are still using some form of incentive plan and new companies are going into such programs on a continuing basis. While it is axiomatic that employee understanding and acceptance be a key ingredient in any such program, this is frequently overlooked.

Installation of a wage incentive plan for workers that have not had one affects two important objectives of any worker, the amount of money earned and the amount of work that must be produced to earn that money. Such factors as working conditions, fringe benefits, and hours of work pall in comparison with these two factors. Since a wage incentive plan changes these factors, it is of primary importance that the plan be understood and accepted.

Everyone has experienced the negative reaction to change and most particularly when the purpose and/or the details of the change are not understood and often not even communicated in other than a most superficial way. Thus, it is necessary that workers have an understanding of how the new system or systems will work. They must be sold on the benefits of the change.

Obviously, the most meaningful selling points for workers is that they will have an opportunity to earn more money. Equally important, however, is the fact that they must be assured that management is not introducing a form of speedup that will require them to produce at unreasonable levels.

One characteristic that is paramount in the design of any wage incentive plan is that it must be easy to understand. A basic objective in the design of any plan is that it should be possible for a worker to calculate his own earnings. If this is not possible, or is difficult, to calculate, his motivation to produce is weakened. A complicated plan is thus difficult to explain not only to employees but also to the supervisors who must work with it.

The role of the foreman is often overlooked; to him falls the burden of getting employee acceptance. It is the foreman's responsibility to provide conditions of work that will enable the employee to perform at incentive levels. The foreman must provide work for each employee so that lost time between jobs is kept to an absolute minimum. It is his responsibility to be certain that materials, tools, and equipment are similar to those in use when the standards were instituted. At the same time, he must train new workers, promptly investigate complaints about standards, and be certain that proper records are maintained regarding downtime and work done of a nonstandard type. Failure to recognize these obligations can seriously affect the effectiveness of any incentive plan.

Many companies recognize the need to communicate and gain acceptance of new plans. There is, however, one particularly significant aspect that is often overlooked. This is the corresponding need to tell employees when method changes are instituted and new standards are set. Here again, an employee must understand, for acceptance, why such changes are made and their effect on his job and potentially his earnings.

GROUP INCENTIVE PLANS

When group incentives are used, each member of the group receives a bonus based on the output of the group as a whole. This is in contrast to individual piecework in which each worker receives a bonus based on his individual output. The group may include an entire plant or company, but it is most frequently related to the production results of an individual department or the workers who work on a single process or product. In these smaller groups, output standards are usually set by time study, in much the same way as for individual piecework.

Group piecework is particularly useful when job assignments are so interrelated that it is difficult or even impossible to measure the contribution of a single employee to the total production of the group. A small assembly line assembling and packaging toasters is an example where the group determines the speed of the operation.

The group system of incentive payments offers numerous advantages in many situations. It can eliminate, to a marked degree, the disadvantages of individual incentive plans where each man is interested in his own output and earnings. Here, there is an understandable reluctance to help new men or to perform work that is not included in incentive earnings.

Group incentives have evolved to overcome some of these problems and to still provide opportunities for incentive earnings. In group incentives, each worker shares in the earnings of the group in direct proportion to the time worked as a member of the group. Generally, it has been found that better results are obtained when the size of the group is limited. As the size of the group increases, an individual worker starts to lose sight of his own contribution and the motivation to increase production is reduced.

A number of advantages can be cited as being appropriate to use of a group incentive form of payment. These include:

1. Group piecework encourages cooperation within employee groups.

2. Since all workers in a group share in the same bonus, there is less conflict between employees on tight rates versus those on loose rates.

3. Since everyone's earnings are dependent on the group's efforts, the group may put pressure on the laggard to work harder.

4. Group incentives usually result in the need for less direct supervision.

5. Timekeeping and costing routines can frequently be simplified.

6. Newer workers are trained by those more experienced; the faster a new worker learns the operations, the faster he can be an effective member of the group.

7. Wages do not tend to fluctuate as significantly as under individual incentives, and a steadier form of income results.

As with any approach to incentives, there are some disadvantages, including:

1. It is sometimes difficult to find the right individual to be the leader of the group.

2. There is no simple way to check on individual efficiency, both good and poor.

3. There is no check on the time allowances for individual jobs.

DO INCENTIVES HAVE A FUTURE?

It is unfortunate in many respects, but still true, that many companies either have been, or are becoming, disillusioned with incentives. In part, this results from extravagant claims made in the past by those who have been actively engaged in the development and institution of such types of plans. It is for this reason that some care has been exercised in this chapter to point out both the pros and cons in the use of the various types of plans that can be used.

Many firms today continue using plans that they have had for a number of years, not so much because they are truly effective, but more frequently because the work associated with making a change is a major task. As an example, it took Kaiser Steel some three years to institute a change in their approach. When companies hesitate to make changes, they ignore the extra inspection, accounting, negotiations, and engineering costs that may be involved in continuing a plan that has outlived its usefulness or is in need of major overhaul.

However, even when unsatisfactory results are being obtained, good personnel planning can mitigate these conditions and can improve on the overall administration of the plans. Piecework has had a long history and in some industries has been quite successful, e.g., textiles. Unfortunately, modern technology with automation has reduced the close connection between individual effort and production output.

If there is any trend that is discernible, it is to the use of measured daywork. This can provide a means of increasing supervisory control and a target for measurement of an individual employee's output. Most variations of this technique consist of using systematic measurement methods to establish explicit and defined objective output goals.   Most organizations believe that output is as high under such systems, assuming good supervision, as can reasonably be expected.   There is no question that administrative costs are less.   Further, such systems usually facilitate technological changes and are not seen as a speed-up device or a technique to cut piece rates as is the case under the more traditional incentive plans.

BIBLIOGRAPHY

Bedolis, Robert A.: "The Kaiser Sharing Plan's First Year," *Conference Board Record,* July, 1964.

Benge, E. J.: *Compensating Employees, Including a Manual of Procedures on Job Evaluation and Merit Rating,* National Foreman's Institute, Waterford, Conn., 1953.

Carroll, Phil: *Better Wage Incentives,* McGraw-Hill Book Company, New York, 1957.

Healy, James J., James A. Henderson, and others: *Creative Collective Bargaining,* Prentice-Hall, Inc., Englewood Cliffs, N.J., 1965.

Industrial Relations Counselors, Group Work Incentives: *Experience with the Scanlon Plan,* New York, 1962.

Lytle, Charles W.: *Wage Incentive Methods,* rev. ed., The Ronald Press Company, New York, 1942.

Maynard, H. B.: *Industrial Engineering Handbook,* 2d ed., McGraw-Hill Book Company, New York, 1963.

Sibson, Robert E.: *Wages and Salaries,* rev. ed., American Management Association, New York, 1967.

chapter 30

Job Evaluation and Pay Plans: Engineering, Technical, and Professional Personnel

ROBERT B. PURSELL   *Director, Coloney, Cannon, Main & Pursell, Inc., New York, New York*

There is, today, probably more lack of agreement among practitioners of salary administration about how to deal with professionals than among any other employee group. Moreover, the areas of disagreement appear to be fundamental. That is, they often center around the nature of the work and the elements of motivation, as well as on the more usual questions of technique and administrative detail. For this reason it is necessary to clearly define professional[1] work and discuss the key issues in professional compensation before outlining different approaches.

DEFINITION OF PROFESSIONAL WORK

When we speak of professional employees, we speak of those who are doing professional work. This does not include others who may be "members of the profession," but who are not doing professional work. The definition of professional, then, is important, and to fully define it, one must deal with both its characteristics and range.

Characteristics of Professional Work

A number of characteristics differentiate professional work from other kinds of work in an organization. First, professional work is concerned with investigation. Professional assignments always involve conducting investigations for the purpose

[1] In this chapter, professional is understood to mean professional technical or engineering.

of drawing scientific conclusions or solving technical problems. Obtaining and recording data, making analyses and computations, and similar activities, although they may be performed by a professional, do not connote professional work. Such activities are characteristic of the work of nonprofessional technicians. Therefore, by definition, a man not directly concerned with drawing conclusions or solving problems based on his investigations is not doing professional work. The fact that such a man may, for example, have a technical degree is not relevant. Nor does the lack of such a degree preclude someone from doing professional work.

Another characteristic of professional work is its requirement for individual contribution. A professional worker is primarily concerned with the execution of technical work himself, and secondarily with planning, organizing, and directing work carried out by others. Even though he may be the leader of a team or group attempting to reach a common objective, he will nevertheless be making a substantial part of his contribution in an individual fashion. In such a case, the other team or group members, both professional and nonprofessional, act as extenders or multipliers of the leader. In other words, a professional technical employee is employed to carry out engineering or scientific assignments, and any team or group that he heads or coordinates is brought together primarily to assist him. In this way, he differs from a managerial employee, technical or otherwise, whose position exists for the prime reason of organizing, directing, and controlling the work of others.

A third characteristic of professional work is that it is not routine or repetitive. It does not follow a pattern or cycle; nor does it consist of specified duties and responsibilities as does the work of managerial or administrative positions. Professional work consists of a series of assignments, each having a definite beginning and end; and in most cases each is quite different from the others with respect to the steps taken in carrying it out and in the end results achieved. Therefore, the professional position is neither defined nor limited by reporting relationships, responsibilities for the utilization or development of resources (human, physical, financial), and the like. Rather, it is defined and limited by the technical nature of the assignments carried out.

These characteristics of professional work point up the fact that each professional position is unique. A professional is hired to apply his *individual* technical knowledge and skill *to solve problems and/or develop new knowledge* on a *variety of different assignments*. This is in sharp contrast to the work of hourly clerical and managerial employees where specific fixed duties, responsibilities, and/or activities can be identified.

Range of Professional Work

Professional work covers a wide range of difficulty or complexity. Conceptually, this range can be defined at one end by the type of assignment one might give to a beginning, inexperienced engineer or scientist and, at the other end, by the most complex and advanced assignment given to a professional employee. Between these extremes, of course, lies a continuum of increasing complexity.

An individual professional employee, and in a sense his position, will move through this range gradually as his level of competence increases. For example, although a scientist or engineer may remain at the same bench and in the same organizational slot over a period of years, he may be asked to carry out assignments of increasingly greater complexity. During this period, he may even reach the point of exploring the frontiers of his field. In such a case, the man has grown and, at the same time, his position has grown in value to the company. In other kinds of work, individual growth can be recognized by moving to successively higher organizational levels or to larger positions at the same level, but a professional can grow like a tree, staying in the same spot for a long time and branching out.

Another pertinent facet to the concept of range of work is that the professional may not always be working at his identified level, but the managerial employee always is (at least in theory). Said another way, a production superintendent is always doing superintendent's work (so long as he is so designated—he cannot escape it). However, a "senior engineer" is not always carrying out "senior" assignments. In fact, he may go months, even years, without any such assignments because of the random nature of assignments to be made and his availability to be assigned.

ISSUES IN PROFESSIONAL COMPENSATION

It is clear that professional positions are substantially different from managerial positions. Many also believe that the personnel who hold these positions, the professionals, are also different from those in managerial positions. Such differences have caused many to raise serious questions concerning the viability of applying the same position evaluation and pay plan to both managerial and professional employees. At issue are three fundamental aspects of salary administration:

Motivation
Position evaluation
Performance measurement

Motivation

Salary administration plans are based on the implicit assumption that man has an inherent, strong economic drive. Yet, practically all research on this subject (primarily attitude surveys) shows overwhelmingly that the professional, especially the scientist, regards pay far down his list of motivations.

Every attitude survey taken among professionals shows challenging, stimulating work assignments as the most important motivational element. Such surveys indicate that a professional is apt to put up with shortcomings in his work situation if provided with increasingly challenging and important work—to the point where he feels a continuing sense of accomplishment and contribution to his field. On the other hand, when work assignments become less demanding, other elements become proportionately larger. According to this thesis, it is only when the professional is bored that he tends to place greater emphasis upon the need for technicians, secretarial help, space, equipment, status symbols, and increased compensation. He may even leave for a better paying job, but in most cases it is not the desire for more money that triggers the search, but rather the professional's feeling that his assignments do not match his capability. Such turnover, of course, takes place among those professionals an organization can least afford to lose.

The essence of the argument is that for the professional, pay is not a positive motivation. That is, the promise of reward in terms of more money will not, by itself, influence the professional to work harder or perform better. It is also held that pay can be a negative assessment of his accomplishments and growth.

Position Evaluation

The second, rather basic, issue centers around the difficulties of evaluating professional positions, particularly with respect to managerial positions. This issue manifests itself in a variety of ways, some of which are discussed below.

Regardless of how it is expressed, economic impact is an important factor in position evaluation. By and large, the greater the impact or influence a position has on profits, sales, costs, etc., the higher it is evaluated, hence paid. Many argue, however, that economic impact cannot or should not be a consideration in evaluating professional positions. A number of reasons are given for this point of view:

1. The economic impact of professional assignments is, to a great extent, fore-ordained (although often unknown) by management through the process of technical program development and project selection. Thus, the greatest part of the economic consequences (plus or minus) can and should be attributable to managerial, not professional, work.

2. Two technical assignments can be carried out with the same degree of skill, creativity, insight, expertise, etc.; yet, one may result in a correct conclusion to terminate a line of investigation, thus leaving no economic impact; while the other might result in a product of enormous economic consequence.

3. Ordinarily, the results of a technical investigation (professional work) pass through so many hands (process scale up, production, marketing, etc.), before the economic impact can be judged, that it is impossible to tell how much is due to the professional work. In theory, at least, a mediocre technical achievement could have a significant economic impact if followed by outstanding marketing, for example. On the other hand, an outstanding technical breakthrough could have limited economic impact due to ineffective marketing, or market research which mistakes market need at the outset.

A second stumbling block to position evaluation is that managerial positions are viewed differently from professional positions. Managerial positions are perceived, hence, compared with each other in tangible, mainly quantitative terms (i.e., sales, costs, number of personnel, investment, etc.). However, professional positions are perceived in largely intangible, qualitative terms (i.e., the need for creativity, independence of action, knowledge of the field, etc.). Thus, when both types of positions are evaluated, using a common plan, one usually suffers. Most observers believe it is the professional position that suffers because the majority of position evaluation plans are developed, calibrated, and administered by management, rather than professionally oriented personnel.

A third problem, in some ways related to the second, arises because of differing points of view regarding organizational relationships. In evaluating managerial positions, it is axiomatic that the organizationally superior position is evaluated higher than those subordinate to it. However, some professional positions can, and should, be evaluated on a par with, or higher than, an organizationally superior position. This apparent paradox has given rise to the use of "dual ladder" approach to position evaluation (see Figure 1). The dual ladder is a special case of the classification approach to position evaluation discussed below.

The final dimension of this issue is the lack of sharp distinction between professional positions such as exist between managerial positions. The movement from grade to grade in management positions is almost always clear and immediate. Therefore, for the most part, the limits of a grade (in terms of what jobs are in it) can be sharply defined. However, a professional, in a way, slides from grade to grade. His movement does not happen in an obvious and immediate way. Thus, the limits of a professional grade are necessarily vague. The question, "How can I tell he is really in that grade?", is often raised regarding a profession, but (assuming that the evaluation system is sound and is followed) is hardly ever raised regarding a management position. As a result, there is almost always an unconscious pressure on keeping professionals from advancing to higher grades when a common plan is used.

Performance Measurement

Almost all pay plans for exempt personnel are based on a pay for performance or "merit" principle. That is, a salary increase and/or position in a salary range is

Illustration of Dual Ladder
Classification for Professional Employees

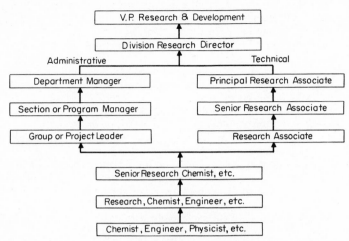

Figure 1. Dual ladder classification for professional employees.

dependent upon performance relative to objectives (standards) or other employees in the same grade.

Proponents of separate plans for professional personnel feel that traditional approaches to merit plans are inappropriate for professionals. Their reasoning is as follows: for most jobs, and especially for creative scientific jobs, performance differences are hard to measure. For example, they say, "How could anyone, even an expert in the field, objectively appraise the relative performance of two competent geophysicists working on two different projects, even if the projects were of the same level of difficulty?" The question becomes more perplexing when we realize that, in most cases, the projects will not be at the same level. And, if one feels this presents a problem, they continue, who will tackle the job of measuring the performance of a geophysicist relative to a biochemist, relative to a materials engineer, etc. Thus, it is concluded that appraisals of individual performance beyond that of differentiating between acceptable and unacceptable are highly subjective, unreliable, and have systematic biases.

Because of the obvious lack of objective performance criteria, professionals tend to shy away from merit ratings and pay systems that are based upon them. The general feeling is that to give differing rewards to personnel purely on the basis of subjective judgments as to degree of acceptable performance will have more of a negative than positive effect. The awareness of these difficulties in making accurate appraisals of performance underlies the popularity of career or maturity curve plans which relate pay to professional growth and accomplishment rather than to performance as such.

EVALUATION AND PAY SYSTEMS

The special character of professional work, coupled with questions raised regarding professional compensation, has led to the development of widely differing pay systems. This part of the chapter describes a number of them in sufficient detail to guide their installation and use. The final section of the chapter outlines the factors that should be taken into consideration in choosing one or another.

TRADITIONAL SYSTEMS

Traditional systems comprise that group of factor comparison and point plans generally and traditionally used to deal with all exempt[2] positions in an organization. While such plans come in many forms and have a variety of names, virtually all are developed by ranking a sample of positions using, in every case, the same fundamental determinants of position value. These fundamental determinants are:

1. What a man has to know to do his job—labeled knowledge and skill or know-how in some plans—often subdivided into education and experience or technical knowledge, negotiating skills, supervisory skills, etc.

2. The tasks to be carried out in the position—labeled scope and impact or accountability in some plans—often subdivided into impact on, or accountability for, personnel resources, markets and products, physical resources (equipment, processes, etc.), financial resources, etc.

3. How a man uses knowledge and skill to carry out his assigned tasks—labeled problem solving, decision making, or creative and analytical ability in some plans—often subdivided into independence of action (degree of supervision) and level of difficulty.

Since these plans are not intended to be exclusively used for professional personnel, and are covered in detail in another chapter, we shall be concerned here only with how professional positions should be handled when using them.

Benchmark Positions

The first step in installing a traditional pay plan is choosing a representative cross section of positions to serve as benchmarks for developing or calibrating factor scales. Such scales are developed or calibrated by comparing these benchmark positions with each other and placing them in a rank order. Therefore, when professional positions are involved, they must be compared not only with other professional positions but directly or indirectly with each managerial position. The problems inherent in making such comparisons (outlined above) can be eased somewhat by selecting a large enough sample of professional positions to establish a frame of reference with managerial and administrative positions in most functional areas (sales, production, maintenance, etc.). ·Most agree that a sample representing 15 to 20 percent of all supervisory, managerial, and administrative positions is sufficient for developing or calibrating factor scales. However, a sample of 30 to 40 percent of all professional positions may very well be required to adequately represent them.

The large sample is necessary, not only because professional work spans a wide range of importance or difficulty, but because it can occur in a variety of fields and encompasses a number of activities. Thus, provided they occur, the cross section should include a sample of (1) professionals in each field, such as chemistry, physics, biology, electrical engineering, industrial engineering; (2) those associated with each different activity, such as basic research, product development, process development, design, systems analysis, production trouble shooting and problem solving, methods development.

Position Descriptions

The next step is the preparation of position descriptions for the selected positions (and ultimately for all positions to be included in the plan). Such descriptions, whether prepared by the incumbent or an analyst, call for, among other things, a

---

[2] Supervisory, managerial, administrative, and professional.

listing of duties or responsibilities of the position (i.e., a statement of what is done in the job).

For professional engineering and scientific positions, this section of the job description should be modified to call for a listing of assignments and a brief, yet definitive description of how the incumbent carried out the one or two considered to be most significant. Such information can be valuable, not only in comparing one professional position with another, but in establishing a frame of reference for comparing a professional with a managerial position. If this modification is not made, professional position descriptions tend to be so generalized and vague that they become virtually useless as a basis for comparison of one position with another.

Ranking

The key step in developing or calibrating a traditional plan is factor ranking. The usual and preferred way this is done is by a committee of managers, each one of whom represents and is familiar with a segment of the positions in the sample. Typically, the committee is headed or coordinated by a consultant or analyst, whose role is to guide them in making judgments on relative job value.

Although there are a variety of "ranking techniques" based on the number of ranks, the use of closed or open-end scales, predefined versus free form scales, forced ranking versus grouping, etc., the fundamental act is the same in each case. The committee compares each position with others in the sample with respect to a given factor until it reaches agreement on the order or rank of the positions. The process is repeated using the next factor and so on until all factors are considered.

The important thing to ensure when ranking professional positions is that they are considered for ranking in a sequence that provides a ready frame of reference for comparison with managerial positions. Then, somewhat of a family approach should be used. For example, one might organize the ranking so that production supervisory and managerial positions are considered first. These could be followed by ranking those professional positions which deal with production problem solving and trouble shooting, then professional process development positions followed by process research, research management, product research professionals, product development, design, technical service, marketing management, etc. Such a sequence would provide smooth transition from one group to another and ensure a good frame of reference for making comparative judgments.

CLASSIFICATION SYSTEMS

Classification systems differ from what we have labeled "traditional systems" in that the grades or levels are defined first; then a position or individual is slotted into the grade having the most appropriate definition. No comparisons with other positions are made, and the work or position is not broken into elements or factors for evaluation purposes.

Defining Grades

In establishing a classification system, it is wise to provide for the total range of professional work (see above) even if it is unlikely that it is represented in the organization at the time the system is installed. This range, in a sense, is continuous, and establishing grades breaks it into discrete steps. However, there are no conceptual or theoretical guidelines as to how many steps (grades) there should be. The issue must be resolved on purely pragmatic grounds, considering such things as:

1. What survey information will be used to establish grade ranges? For example, the American Management Association presents professional compensation data using six groupings or levels, whereas the Bureau of Labor Statistics uses eight.

2. Is it desirable to relate to range structures established for managerial positions? If it is, one need only establish dollar values for the extreme professional grades (starting salaries at one end, the highest data in the survey used at the other end). Once this is done, the number of grades to be used will be obvious when the extremes are compared with the managerial structure.

3. How many grades can be used before creating a burdensome and arbitrary classification and reclassification process?

The pragmatic approach is also best in developing grade definitions. Since a number of sets of definitions have been developed, a simple and satisfactory method is to start with such a set and modify it to suit the needs of the organization. An example of one such set is presented below.

PROFESSIONAL GRADE DEFINITIONS—CHEMISTS

Chemists perform professional work in research, development, interpretation, and analysis to determine the composition, molecular structure, and properties of substances; to develop or investigate new materials and processes; and to investigate the transformation which substances undergo. The work typically requires a B.S. degree in chemistry or the equivalent plus experience.

Chemist I

General characteristics.   This is the entry level of professional work requiring a bachelor's degree in chemistry and no experience, or the equivalent (to a degree) in appropriate education and experience. A chemist I performs assignments designed to develop his professional capabilities and to provide experience in the application of his training in chemistry as it relates to the company's programs. He may also receive formal classroom or seminar type training.

Direction received.   He works under close supervision. He receives specific and detailed instructions as to the required tasks and results expected. His work is checked during progress, and is reviewed for accuracy upon completion.

Typical duties and responsibilities.   He performs a variety of routine tasks that are planned to provide experience and familiarization with the chemistry staff, methods, practices, and programs of the company. The work includes a variety of routine qualitative and quantitative analyses; physical tests to determine properties such as viscosity, tensile strength, and melting point; and assisting more experienced chemists to gain additional knowledge through personal observation and discussion.

Responsibility for the direction of others.   Usually he has none.

Chemist II

General characteristics.   At this continuing developmental level, a chemist II performs routine chemical work requiring selection and application of general and specialized methods, techniques, and instruments commonly used in the laboratory and has the ability to carry out instructions when less common or proposed methods or procedures are necessary. The chemist II requires work experience acquired in an entry level position, or appropriate graduate level study. For training and developmental purposes, assignments may include some work that is typical of a higher level.

Direction received. The supervisor establishes the nature and extent of analysis required, specifies methods and criteria on new types of assignments, and reviews work for thoroughness of application of methods and accuracy of results.

Typical duties and responsibilities. He carries out a wide variety of standardized methods, texts, and procedures. In accordance with specific instructions, he may carry out proposed and less common ones. He is expected to detect problems in using standardized procedures because of the condition of the sample, difficulties with the equipment, etc. He recommends modifications or procedures, e.g., extending or curtailing the analysis or using alternate procedures, based on his knowledge of the problem and pertinent available literature. He conducts specified phases of research projects as an assistant to an experienced chemist.

Responsibility for the direction of others. He may be assisted by a few aids or technicians.

Chemist III

General characteristics. A chemist III performs a broad range of chemical tests and procedures utilized in the laboratory, using judgment in the independent evaluation, selection, and adaption of standard methods and techniques. He may carry through a complete series of tests on a product in its different process stages. Some assignments require a specialized knowledge of one or two common categories of related substances. Performance at this level requires developmental experience in a professional position, or equivalent graduate level education.

Direction received. On routine work, supervision is very general. Assistance is furnished on unusual problems, and work is reviewed for application of sound professional judgment.

Typical duties and responsibilities. In accordance with instructions as to the nature of the problem, he selects standard methods, tests, or procedures; when necessary, he develops or works out alternate or modified methods with his supervisor's concurrence. He assists in research by analyzing samples or testing new procedures that require specialized training because (1) standard methods are inapplicable, (2) analytical findings must be interpreted in terms of compliance or noncompliance with standards, or (3) specialized and advanced equipment and techniques must be adapted.

Responsibility for the direction of others. He may supervise or coordinate the work of a few technicians or aids, and be assisted by lower level chemists.

Chemist IV

General characteristics. He is a fully competent chemist in all conventional aspects of the subject matter or the functional area of the assignments. A chemist IV not only (1) plans and conducts work requiring mastery of specialized techniques or ingenuity in selecting and evaluating approaches to unforeseen or novel problems, but (2) has the ability to apply a research approach to the solution of a wide variety of problems and to assimilate the details and significance of chemical and physical analyses, procedures, and tests. He has sufficient professional experience to assure competence as a fully trained worker; or, for positions primarily of a research nature, completion of all requirements for a doctoral degree may be substituted for experience.

Direction received. He independently performs most assignments, with instructions as to the general results expected. He receives technical guidance on unusual or complex problems and supervisory approval on proposed plans for projects.

Typical duties and responsibilities. He conducts laboratory assignments requiring the determination and evaluation of alternative procedures and the sequence of performing them. He performs complex, exacting, or unusual analytical assignments requiring specialized knowledge of techniques or products. He interprets results, prepares reports, and may provide technical advice in his specialized area.

Responsibility for the direction of others. He may supervise a small staff of chemists and technicians.

Chemist V

General characteristics. A chemist V participates in planning laboratory programs on the basis of specialized knowledge of problems and methods and probable value of results. He may serve as an expert in a narrow specialty (e.g., class of chemical compounds or class of products), making recommendations and conclusions which serve as the basis for undertaking or rejecting important projects. Development of the knowledge and expertise required for this level of work usually reflects progressive experience through chemist IV.

Direction received. Supervision and guidance relate largely to overall objectives, critical issues, new concepts, and policy matters. He consults with his supervisor concerning unusual problems and developments.

Typical duties and responsibilities.   These include one or both of the following:

1. In a supervisory capacity, he plans, organizes, and directs assigned laboratory programs. Independently he defines the scope and critical elements of the projects and selects the approaches to be taken. A substantial portion of the work supervised is comparable to that described for chemist IV.

2. As an individual researcher or worker, he carries out projects requiring development of new or highly modified scientific techniques and procedures, extensive knowledge of his specialty, and knowledge of related scientific fields.

Responsibility for the direction of others. He supervises, coordinates, and reviews the work of a small staff of chemists and technicians engaged in varied research and development projects, or a larger group performing routine analytical work. He estimates manpower needs and schedules and assigns work to meet the completion date. Or, as an individual researcher or worker, he may be assisted on projects by other chemists or technicians.

Chemist VI

General characteristics. A chemist VI performs work requiring leadership and expert knowledge in a specialized field, product, or process. He formulates and conducts a systematic attack either on a problem area of considerable scope and complexity, which must be approached through a series of complete and conceptually related studies, or on a number of projects of lesser scope. The problems are complex because they are difficult to define and require unconventional or novel approaches or have other difficult features. He maintains liaison with individuals and units within and outside his organization, with responsibility for acting independently on technical matters pertaining to his field. Work at this level usually requires extensive progressive experience, including work comparable to chemist V.

Direction received. The supervision received is essentially administrative, with assignments given in terms of broad general objectives and limits.

Typical duties and responsibilities.   These include one or both of the following:

1. In a supervisory capacity, he plans, develops, coordinates, and directs a number of large and important projects or a project of major scope and importance. Activities under his leadership are of such scope that they require a few (three to five) subordinate supervisors or team leaders, with at least one in a position comparable to chemist V.

2. As individual researcher or worker, he determines, conceives, plans, and conducts projects of major importance to the company. He applies a high degree of originality and ingenuity in adapting, extending, and synthesizing existing theory, principles, and techniques into original combinations and configurations. He may serve as a consultant to other chemists in his specialty.

Responsibility for the direction of others. He plans, organizes, and supervises the work of a staff of chemists and technicians. He evaluates the progress of the staff and the results obtained, and recommends major changes to achieve overall objectives. Or, as an individual worker or researcher, he may be assisted on individual projects by other chemists or technicians.

Chemist VII

General characteristics. A chemist VII makes decisions and recommendations that are recognized as authoritative and have an important impact on extensive chemical activities. He initiates and maintains extensive contacts with key chemists and officials of other organizations and companies, requiring skill in persuasion and negotiation of critical issues. At this level, individuals will have demonstrated creativity, foresight, mature judgment in anticipating and solving unprecedented chemical problems, determining program objectives and requirements, organizing programs and projects, and developing standards and guides for diverse chemical activities.

Direction received. He receives general administrative direction.

Typical duties and responsibilities. These include one or both of the following:

1. In a supervisory capacity, he is responsible for an important segment of a chemical program with extensive and diversified scientific requirements. The overall chemical program contains critical problems, the solution of which requires major technological advances and opens the way for extensive related development. He makes authoritative technical recommendations concerning the scientific objectives and levels of work which will be most profitable in the light of company requirements and scientific industrial trends and developments. He recommends facilities, personnel, and funds required.

2. As an individual researcher and consultant, he selects problems for research to further the company's objectives. He conceives and plans investigations in which the phenomena and principles are not adequately understood, and where few or contradictory scientific precedents or results are available for reference. Outstanding creativity and mature judgment are required to devise hypotheses and techniques of experimentation and to interpret results. As a leader and authority in his company, in a broad area of specialization, or in a narrow but intensely specialized one, he advises the head of a large laboratory or company officials on complex aspects of extremely broad and important programs. He has responsibility for exploring, evaluating, and justifying proposed and current programs and projects and furnishing advice on unusually complex and novel problems in the specialty field. Typically, he will have contributed innovations (e.g., techniques, products, procedures) which are regarded as significant advances in the field.

Responsibility for the direction of others. He directs several subordinate supervisors or team leaders, some of whom are in positions comparable to chemist VI; or, as an individual researcher and consultant, he may be assisted on individual projects by other chemists and technicians.

Chemist VIII

General characteristics. A chemist VIII makes decisions and recommendations that are authoritative and have a far-reaching impact on extensive chemical and related activities of the company. He negotiates critical and controversial issues with top-level chemists and officers of other organizations and companies. Individuals at this level have demonstrated a high degree of creativity, foresight, and mature judgment in planning, organizing, and guiding extensive chemical programs and activities of outstanding novelty and importance.

Direction received.   He receives general administrative direction.

Typical duties and responsibilities.   These include one or both of the following:

1. In a supervisory capacity, he is responsible for an important segment of a chemical program with very extensive and highly diversified scientific requirements, and which is of such complexity and scope that it is of critical importance to overall operations and includes problems of extraordinary difficulty that have resisted solution.   He decides the kind and extent of chemical programs needed to accomplish the objectives of the company; he is responsible for choosing the scientific approaches, for planning and organizing facilities and programs, and for interpreting results.

2. As an individual researcher and consultant, he formulates and guides the attack on problems of exceptional difficulty and marked importance to the company and/or industry.   Such problems are characterized by lack of scientific precedents and source materials, or the lack of success of prior research and analysis so that their solution would represent an advance of great significance and importance. He performs advisory and consulting work for the company as a recognized authority on broad program areas of considerable novelty and importance.   He has made contributions such as new products or techniques or development of processes which are regarded as major advances in the field.

Responsibility for the direction of others.   He supervises several subordinate supervisors or team leaders, some of whose positions are comparable to chemist VI or individual researchers, some of whose positions are comparable to chemist VII and sometimes chemist VIII.   As an individual researcher and consultant, he may be assisted on individual projects by other chemists or technicians.

The above set of definitions can be modified to fit other disciplines or expanded to more closely represent the work done in a particular organization by research or engineering management.

Assigning Grades

The process of assigning individuals to grades in a typical classification system is, by its very nature, subjective.   Conceptually, it is an attempt to judge where a given individual is on the spectrum of professional growth at a point in time.   Thus, the line of demarcation between position evaluation and performance evaluation, which is fairly distinct in traditional systems, becomes blurred.

Most companies using a classification system consider grade assignment and salary action (within a grade range) at the same time.   Where feasible, reviews are made by a salary committee or a series of committees made up of technical managers.   Generally, such committees consider one individual at a time, reviewing his performance record in terms of possible movement to a new grade (or in the case of a new employee, initial assignment in a grade).   Most companies impose a discipline of reviewing an individual in relation to each part of the definition, considering specific examples or incidents in each area.   Referring to the grade definitions above:

1. Specific assignments are reviewed to determine which General Characteristics statement is most appropriate.

2. The amount of direction necessary is discussed until agreement is reached as to which statement best fits.

3. Specific incidents are cited to substantiate the appropriate duties and responsibilities definition.

Generally, the individual has to satisfy the grade definition in all three areas to be assigned to that grade. For example, if a given chemist fits two of the three definitions for grade IV, but only the grade III definition in the third area, he is generally assigned to grade III.

ASSIGNMENT ANALYSIS

The lack of clear distinction between position evaluation and performance measurement has led to the development of the assignment analysis approach to evaluating professional technical positions. The conceptual argument supporting this approach is as follows:

1. The range or spectrum of professional work is one of increasing complexity or difficulty. Thus, there is a direct relationship between a professional's ability to handle assignments of increasing complexity and his growth in competence, hence value, to the organization. Analysis of successfully completed assignments in terms of complexity, then, would represent a more objective, work-oriented basis for position evaluation.

2. Professional positions are evaluated by analyzing the assignments each employee carries out and relating them to predefined grade specifications, which include definitions of level of assignment complexity along with listings of characteristic activities.

The following paragraphs define these "levels of complexity," list the steps in evaluating a professional position, and outline some of the guidelines followed in the evaluation process.

Defining Levels of Complexity

The first step in defining levels of technical complexity is to differentiate between two broad categories of technical assignments: problem and project. These categories are defined as follows:

1. *Problem:*   An assignment with narrow limits and a clearly recognizable objective, normally requiring an effort of less than one-half man-year and generally confined to a single area of investigation (i.e., a type of compound, a specific product characteristic or improvement, a specific piece of equipment, etc.)

2. *Project:*   A longer term assignment made up of a group of related problems normally requiring an effort of more than one-half man-year and involving several areas of investigation

Generally, a project assignment is more complex than a problem assignment, primarily because the interrelationships among problems present added difficulties. However, a wide range of complexity exists within each category. It is necessary, then, to define levels of problem and project complexity.

There are three elements of problem assignments that account for differences in complexity. First, and probably most significant, is the degree to which the problem is isolated and defined when the assignment is made. An assignment to improve the quality of an off-grade product is an example of a problem which is *not isolated*. If, on the other hand, when the assignment is made, the location of the trouble is specified but not the exact cause, the problem is *isolated but not defined*. If both location and exact cause are specified, then the problem is *isolated and defined*. It is, of course, obvious that a problem which is *not* isolated is considerably more complex than one which is. In the former case, the individual must first determine what he is attempting to solve before he can proceed. On the other hand, a problem is relatively simple when it is not only isolated but defined well enough to proceed with little or no prior investigation or study of alternatives.

Next, the number of variables or elements involved in a problem will affect its complexity. Other things being equal, a problem involving many variables or elements is more complex than one involving few or several.

Finally, the approach or technique required in carrying out a problem assignment influences its level of complexity. If a new or unusual approach is required, the assignment is inherently more complex than if a known approach can be applied.

As in problem assignments, there are three elements that account for differences in the complexity of project assignments. However, they are somewhat different. In project assignments, the most significant element appears to be the number of problems to be solved. Problems within a project are almost always interrelated; thus, as the number of separate problems increases, project complexity increases at an even faster rate.

In addition to the number of problems, the difficulty of problems affects project complexity. Other things being equal, a project in which most problems require original solutions is more complex than one in which only some problems require original solutions.

Finally, the amount of information available in the field of a project influences its complexity. It is evident that a project becomes more complex if it is in a field where little previous work has been done and limited information is available rather than if it is in a field that has been studied and documented sufficiently to indicate a clear course of action.

Figure 2 specifies levels of professional work in terms of complexity of problem and project assignments and the elements of each which account for the differences. This exhibit expresses, in tabular form, the definitions of assignment complexity for each professional grade specification. Figures 3 and 4 are examples of two such grade specifications.

Assigning Professional Positions to Levels

The following steps are taken in evaluating a professional position:

1. The assignments carried out during the past year are reviewed, and the one or two assignments that are indicative of the highest level of complexity are chosen for analysis.

2. Each assignment chosen is analyzed to determine whether it falls into the problem or project strategy.

3. Assignments in each category are analyzed on the basis of three measures of complexity, as shown in accompanying tables:

	PROBLEM ASSIGNMENTS	
Degree of definition	Number of variables or elements	Approach
Isolated and defined	Few	Known
Isolated, not defined	Several	New
Not isolated	Many	

PROJECT ASSIGNMENTS		
Number of problems	Number requiring original solutions	Amount of information available
Few	Some	Limited
Several	Most	Much
Many		

4. These judgments, combined, indicate the complexity level, as shown in Figure 2.

Figure 2.   Levels of technical assignment complexity.

Level	Problem assignments			Project assignments		
	Degree of definition	Number of variables or elements	Approach	Number of problems	Number of problems requiring original solutions	Information available in project area
I	Isolated and defined	Few	Known			
II	Isolated and defined	Few	New			
	Isolated and defined	Several	Known			
III	Isolated, not defined	Few	New			
	Isolated, not defined	Several	Known			
IV	Isolated, not defined	Several	New			
	Isolated, not defined	Many	Known	Few	Some	Much
	Not isolated	Few	New			
	Not isolated	Several	Known			
V	Not isolated	Several	New	Few	Some	Little
	Not isolated	Many	Known	Few	Most	Much
				Several	Some	Much
VI	Not isolated	Many	New	Few	Most	Little
				Several	Some	Little
				Several	Most	Much
				Many	Some	Much
VII	. . .	. . .	. . .	Several	Most	Little
				Many	Some	Little
VIII	. . .	. . .	. . .	Many	Most	Little
IX						

5. The position is reviewed against the grade specifications for the indicated level and the specifications for the grades immediately below and above. In doing this, it should be borne in mind that the grade specifications are cumulative, that is, each includes all lower grade specifications. By this process, then, each position is assigned to a grade level.

6. After a position has been evaluated, the assignment chosen for analysis, along with the judgments made in determining its complexity level, is described in writing. This record then serves both as documentation for the evaluation made and as a point of reference for subsequent reviews.

Guidelines for Evaluating Positions

The following guidelines should be observed in administering an assignment analysis system:

1. Because individual progress in professional work is gradual, it is necessary to analyze professional assignments and review grade assignments at least once a year.

Figure 3.   Grade III.

NATURE OF ASSIGNMENTS

Isolated but *not* well-defined problems involving several variables or elements and the application of known techniques or approaches; or involving few variables or elements but requiring a new or unusual approach

CHARACTERISTIC ACTIVITIES

On problem assignments, independently determines the significant variables or conditions, selects an approach to be followed, designs and carries out the necessary experiments, and draws conclusions from his work

Establishes and drafts standard laboratory, analytical, and/or process instructions

Works independently with production and engineering management or scientists outside his department in the solution of assigned problems

Coordinates the work of one of more technicians where instructions must be given, work planned, and data observed, logged, collated, and reported

Prepares periodic and final progress reports for high-level review

---

Figure 4.   Grade V.

NATURE OF ASSIGNMENTS

Problems that are not isolated involving several variables or elements and requiring a new or unusual approach

or

Problems that are not isolated involving many variables or elements and the application of known techniques or approaches

or

Projects consisting of few problems, some of which require original approaches, in an area where little previous work has been done and limited information is available

or

Projects consisting of few problems, most of which require original solutions, or consisting of several problems, only some of which require original solutions, in an area studied and documented sufficiently to indicate a clear course of action

CHARACTERISTIC ACTIVITIES

Works independently outside the laboratories in the solution of customer application or utilization problems

Designs and carries out projects subject to periodic review by a more experienced professional to be sure the project is proceeding satisfactorily

Directs the transition of new developments from laboratory to production equipment when new or modified processes or techniques are involved

Makes frequent oral reports to management personnel

Trains and develops less experienced chemists

Gives advice and consultation in his field to production and sales personnel on the technical aspects of operating and customer problems

Provides sound and original suggestions for new areas of investigation in his field

Recognizes the significance of experimental results from both the theoretical and the applied points of view

---

2. Judgments of assignment complexity must be made by technical managers who are close to, and familiar with, the work itself. The role of the personnel staff is to question these judgments and require substantiation. However, technical managers are the only ones in a position to make these judgments.

3. Evaluation judgments *must* be made on the basis of assignments *carried out*, not on the basis of an individual's ability to carry out an assignment *if* given to him. This guideline in effect limits the grade assignment of any professional to the level of work done in his department or field within the company.

4. Because the professional assignments available at any given time will not encompass the total range of complexity, the individual professional may not always be performing assignments of the highest complexity of which he has shown himself to be capable. This, however, is a problem of personnel utilization, and the professional must be evaluated according to his highest *demonstrated* level of accomplishment.

5. It cannot be expected that every professional employee will continue to grow in his ability to handle more complex assignments. Each will "level out" at a certain grade. When this occurs, the tendency to evaluate a man higher just because time has passed must be resisted. This tendency can be controlled by concentrating exclusively on the work being done and requiring specific examples of assignments as a basis for a change in grade.

(NOTE: For the approaches discussed above, salary structures and ranges are developed as they would be for any other employee group. Since establishing wage and salary structures is the concern of Chapter 33, the subject has not been covered here. However, since the final two approaches, which follow, represent significant departures from practices applied to other groups, material dealing with establishing salary guidelines is included.)

CAREER OR MATURITY CURVES

During the late 1940s, a new type of technical pay plan evolved. The approach, refined to a large extent by the University of California's Los Alamos Laboratory but stemming from an approach used by Bell Telephone Laboratories during the 1930s, is labeled in a variety of ways, but most commonly as the "career curve" or "maturity curve system."

The career curve approach is quite different from those discussed above in that no direct reference is made to position responsibilities or specific assignments. Its underlying assumption is that the individual technical employee is a productive resource whose contribution increases with experience. However, the rate of increase depends upon his native ability and drive (as manifested by performance) and the amount of training he has been given. Therefore, the curve approach relates salary to the variables of maturity or experience, relative on-the-job performance, and educational attainment.

Curve Derivation

The key step in utilizing the curve approach is obtaining or deriving a family of curves. Figure 5 illustrates a typical family of curves. From an operational point of view, the curves substitute for a salary structure or series of ranges.

The process of developing a family of curves is conceptually simple. A survey is conducted or used to provide individual salaries and experience (usually reported as years since first degree). Frequency distributions of salaries, according to experience, are then developed, and the desired statistical parameters are determined for each year. The most usual parameters are 10th,[3] 25th, 50th (median),

---

[3] The 10th percentile means that 10 percent of the data in the distribution falls below it.

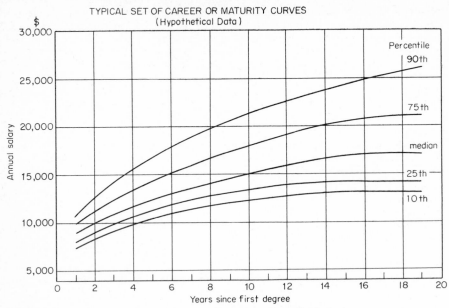

Figure 5.   Typical set of career or maturity curves (hypothetical data).

75th and 90th percentile.   Each curve, as shown in Figure 5, is constructed by smoothing the appropriate parameters using the least-squares or other appropriate statistical technique.

The difficulties of deriving a family of curves lie with the survey.   Conducting a reliable survey is time consuming and expensive.   Therefore, when possible, existing surveys should be used.   The survey conducted, until recently, by the Los Alamos Laboratory was probably the most comprehensive and well known for research personnel.   However, a number of others are available for particular industries and fields.   Obviously the more a survey reflects the subject population (in terms of field, type of activity,[4] and degree level), the more appropriate it will be as a basis for a family of maturity curves.   The key issue is balancing the degree of fit of an existing survey against the costs of conducting a special survey.

Using Maturity Curves

In practice, maturity curves are used in two different ways: first as a frame of reference for individual salary determination, and second as a basis of assessing the competitive level of the group as a whole.

In the first instance the curves provide similar guidelines for salary action as those provided by grade salary ranges in a classification system.   The basic premise is that the position a given individual's salary should occupy in the distribution for his degree and experience group correlates with his performance relative to his peer group.   Thus, a method of peer group ranking is required.   Generally, such a ranking is done by a committee utilizing performance observations of the members, reports submitted by the supervisor, or both.   Most often a committee will rank members of a peer group on a number of factors,[5] add the rankings, and reorder

[4] Basic research, development, application engineering, etc.
[5] Figure 6 lists the performance factors used by one company.

Figure 6.   Factors for evaluating the performance of technical personnel.

FORMULATING PROBLEMS AND HYPOTHESES

This area stresses creative or imaginative behavior, emphasizing alertness to deviant or unusual phenomena suggesting new problems, and ingenuity in proposing explanations for such phenomena. It includes seeing and exploring new problems areas, clearly delimiting the precise problem to be investigated, and proposing systematic hypotheses to fit the available facts. Consider:
- Identifying and exploring problems
- Defining the problem
- Setting up hypotheses

PLANNING AND DESIGNING THE INVESTIGATION

In this area are subsumed all the planning functions concerning the technical investigation of the problem or hypothesis selected. This area includes setting up a logical and systematic sequence of steps, considering existing information in the problem area and making assumptions, evaluating the relative importance of factors in the problem and taking precautions for accurate collection of data, judging the effectiveness of available methods and foreseeing the course of the investigation and attendant difficulties. Consider:
- Collecting background information
- Setting up assumptions
- Identifying and controlling important variables
- Developing systematic and inclusive plans
- Developing plans for the use of equipment, materials, and techniques
- Anticipating difficulties
- Determining the number of observations

CONDUCTING THE INVESTIGATION

The emphasis in this area is on general technical competence in conducting the active phases of a research study as planned. The area should measure the ingenuity and resourcefulness with which the scientist devises, chooses, or modifies techniques, materials, or procedures to fulfill his plans or to adjust to changes in conditions; his understanding of techniques and principles as shown by his application of them during the course of the investigation; his awareness of the need for checking details and seemingly insignificant occurrences; his care in recording data and the progress of the investigation, and his analysis of the data. Consider:
- Developing methods, materials, or equipment
- Applying methods and techniques
- Modifying planned procedures
- Applying theory
- Attending to and checking details
- Analyzing the data

INTERPRETING RESEARCH RESULTS

This area is confined to the logical and deductive abilities of the research worker as demonstrated in the interpretation of the results of his investigation of a problem. It includes consideration of all the data or phenomena observed, the effect of the experimental design on the data, and the final conclusions as to the valid meaning of the results. It includes, also, insight into the implications of his findings for further work or application to related work, and the extending of conclusions from the specific data on hand of more general conditions or problems. Consider:
- Evaluating findings
- Pointing out implications of data

PREPARING REPORTS

This area concerns the manner in which reports are prepared. It includes describing and illustrating work in a clear and understandable fashion; reporting only those facts and details necessary for a thorough understanding of the work; explaining the background of the problem, the relations of the problem to other work, and the meaning of the results; including sufficient information about the material, conditions, and equipment used in the problem to

Figure 6. Factors for evaluating the performance of technical personnel. (continued)

support the conclusions reported and to permit the reader to draw his own conclusions; reporting work in logical sequence and in a form which the reader can follow; using simple language which conveys its meaning to the reader; and presenting oral reports in a clear and interesting manner. Consider:

- Describing and illustrating work
- Substantiating procedures and findings
- Organizing the report
- Using appropriate style in presenting the report

ADMINISTERING RESEARCH PROJECTS

This area concerns the scientist's ability to administer a research project and the various duties entailed by administrators in dealing with their subordinates. It includes: selecting, training, and placing personnel; dealing with subordinates; planning and coordinating the work of groups; making decisions and taking action based on those decisions; fostering cooperation between groups. Consider:

- Selecting and training personnel
- Dealing with subordinates
- Planning and coordinating the work of groups
- Making administrative decisions
- Working with other groups

ACCEPTING ORGANIZATIONAL RESPONSIBILITY

This area emphasizes the attitudes of the scientist toward the organization for which he works. It includes acceptance of his share of responsibility for completing the work of the group; cooperation with others in the work situation; subordination of personal interests to those of the group; and contribution to the efficiency of the group. Consider:

- Performing own work
- Assisting in the work of others
- Subordinating personal interests
- Accepting regulations and supervision

ACCEPTING PERSONAL RESPONSIBILITY

This area concerns the attitudes of the scientist toward his associates as reflected by his interaction with associates, his reactions to job demands, and his behavior concerning matters of ethics. It should indicate how the scientist adjusts to his co-workers, and to difficulties in meeting standards of his assigned job; how he reacts to constructive criticism; how he fulfills personal promises and commitments. It also includes activities that reflect honesty and fairness in his dealings with others and in his own work. Activities not directly related to assignments which indicate interest in his work are also included. Consider:

- Adapting to associates
- Adapting to job demands
- Meeting personal commitments
- Being fair and ethical
- Showing interest in work

---

the totals. In this way an individual's salary can be compared directly to the family of curves on the basis of his performance rank position. For example, the salary of a person ranked at or near the 75th percentile in the distribution of his experience group is compared with that indicated by the 75th percentile curve at the appropriate experience value. In this way the maximum increase he could receive is determined.

The second and more common use of maturity curves is to guide salary action for the technical or professional group as a whole. A number of organizations develop internal maturity curves and compare them to the survey to determine their competitive position.   Others use survey curves as a basis for determining salary bud-gets.   This is done by measuring the year-to-year growth resulting from an added year of experience on the curve, plus the upward movement of curves due to eco-nomic and inflationary factors, averaging their movement, and statistically weighting it by the organization's technical population for each year of experience.   The result is often used as a budget or limit of increases for the population as a whole.

TRACK SYSTEM

The newest approach in the field, labeled the "track system," was devised initially for professional firms, consulting engineers, for example.   These firms need to, rather quickly, align compensation levels with contribution to the work of the firm[6] among a group of engineers hired at widely differing salaries.   This fact, along with the difficulties of obtaining comparable compensation data covering the full range of work levels, prompted the development of the track system.

Overview of System

The track system is most often used to administer both salary and bonus, and we will develop the exposition of the system on this basis.   The track, which serves a function similar to the traditional salary range, is a function of two variables. The independent variable is how long it should take a given engineer to advance to a designated level, project manager, for example.   The dependent variable compensation is influenced by this time dimension.   The following, then, are the key elements of the system:

1. Peer groups (similar to professional levels[7])are established below the objective level (in this illustration, project manager).   For each of these groups (engineer, senior engineer, and principal engineer, for example) performance standards and advancement criteria are developed.   Figure 7 is a statement of standards for senior engineer as defined by one firm.

2. A target compensation value is established for the objective level (project manager) in terms of a salary (a flat-rate figure, not a range) and a normal bonus percentage.   This is the only salary figure that needs to be established from com-petitive data for the system.

3. A professional's performance is appraised against the appropriate standards on each assignment and periodically summarized.   The summary aims at answering the single question, "How fast will he be advanced to project manager?": (a) faster than normal, (b) at a normal rate, (c) slower than normal, if at all.

4. Salary changes are then determined by calculating the annual rate of increase required (when applied to the individual's present salary) to reach the target salary for project manager at the time he is expected to be advanced to project manager.

The following paragraphs discuss these elements in more detail.

Establishing Target Salaries and Normal Bonuses

To arrive at a target salary, data such as that illustrated below, taken from a com-pensation survey of professional firms, are used:

---

[6] Many professional firms feel they cannot keep engineers (or other professionals) who do not progress at a satisfactory rate, at least to the project manager level or its equivalent.   This gives rise to what often is called an "up-or-out" policy which, in a sense, underlies the track system.

[7] See Fig. 1.

Title	Average		High	
	Salary	Bonus	Salary	Bonus
Project manager .	$20,534	10.2%	$30,000	25%
Design (research)				
associate	17,500	15.0	35,000	40

In this illustration a target salary of $25,000 was established along with a normal bonus of 30 percent. Also, using the normal 30 percent bonus as a point of reference, the following bonus schedule was developed:

Title	Expected bonus		
	Slow track	Normal track	Fast track
Principal engineer .	10%	17.5%	25%
Senior engineer . . .	5	10.0	15
Engineer			

Figure 7. Senior engineer standards.

Performance area	Required proficiency	Advancement criteria
Problem solving: 1. Develop hypotheses and/or identify issues	1. Identify, independently, several key issues through research, analyses, and interviews; develop one key hypothesis in depth	Attainment of required proficiency in every aspect of problem solving
2. Determine data necessary	2. Identify required facts and/or areas of examination necessary to resolve issues or test hypotheses	
3. Gather data	3. Collect and organize data under minimal supervision	*and*
4. Draw conclusions	4. Relate facts to issues or hypotheses in such a way as to yield creditable, practical conclusions	
5. Develop recommendations	5. Develop alternative recommendations and rank, in order of priority, by clearly and accurately assessing pros and cons of each alternative	Demonstrated ability to guide others in problem solving
Client action: 1. Address client's concern	1. Build confidence to the point where client personnel raise issues and present ideas they would be reluctant to reveal to others *or* Identify opportunities where problem solutions may be improved by application of special techniques and/or creative design	Attainment of required proficiency in every aspect of client action *and* Demonstrated ability to "take the lead" in inducing client acceptance and implementation

Figure 7.   Senior engineer standards.   (continued)

2. Establish climate for acceptance of recommendations	2. Test alternative hypotheses during discussions with client executives and accurately judge impact of, and reaction to, tentative recommendations	
3. Implement client relations strategy	3. Establish solid working relationships with key client executive; take lead in resolving minor conflicts	
Team performance: 1. Plan within time and cost restraints	1. Plan segment of project within technical area to meet time and cost deadlines set by project director	Clear demonstration of leadership within technical area
2. Provide guidance for other engineers	2. Provide leadership in technical area for work on project	
3. Establish environment encouraging free team communications and creative problem solving	3. Communicate overall progress of assigned portion of study to team and encourage generation of new ideas and free discussion by drawing out those who are reluctant to participate fully	
Communications: 1. Prepare documents and/or presentations	1. Structure the whole of major reports in technical area with little guidance. Preparing text and renderings or layouts with a good grasp of correct tone and major theme(s)	Demonstrated ability to prepare and deliver client communications, within technical area, effectively
2. Respond extemporaneously to questions in discussions 3. Make prepared presentations	2. Make good exposition verbally and graphically of conceptual points, ad hoc 3. Give major parts of prepared presentation in technical area with ease and full command of material	
Staff development: 1. Identify individual developmental needs	1. Work with project manager to diagnose development needs of others; continue to accurately assess own needs	Demonstration of interest in and involvement in the development of *other* associates
2. Provide on-the-job training	2. Lay out engineer's assignment in a way that will allow or force him to focus on development needs; provide ongoing feedback	

Thus, an engineer, which every new hire is regardless of past experience, is rewarded by salary increases only. He receives a bonus when he is advanced to senior engineer, a higher bonus when he becomes a principal engineer, and a still higher bonus when and if he is advanced to project manager.

Track Definition

In most cases, initial track definition is largely subjective. However, some firms have records sufficient to make an objective analysis. A typical set of definitions appear below:

EXPECTED ELAPSED TIME

Track	From entry as engineer to advancement to project manager	From advancement to senior engineer to advancement to project manager	From advancement to principal engineer to advancement to project manager
Fast	3 years	2 years or less	2 years or less
Normal	5 years	4 years	3 years
Slow	7 years or more	6 years or more	5 years or more

Administrative Procedure

Using the above parameters, then, compensation administration would proceed along the following lines:

1. New men are recruited and brought into the firm as engineers with no significant increase in compensation.

2. The "engineer" group is reviewed (all at the same time) for salary action twice a year: near the end of the year and in the middle of the year. Prior to each review, "track charts" are prepared for each man. Figure 8 illustrates two such charts.[8] Once the performance data are analyzed, and the track is selected, the new salary is taken directly from the chart. For example, if it is decided that A should be on a fast track, then his new salary would be $13,500 (the point on the salary scale when the fast track line intersects the appropriate point on the tenure scale). If B, on the other hand, were judged to be on a slow track, his new salary would be $14,500.

At year end, advancement to senior engineer would also be considered. Those advanced would receive a bonus equal to 10 percent of their salary at the time of advancement (i.e., before the salary increase) and be eligible for full participation in the bonus program as a senior engineer during the ensuing year.

3. Senior engineers are also reviewed for compensation action, but only once a year: at year end. Track charts are based upon expected elapsed time from advancement to senior engineer to advancement to project manager. At the same time, advancement to principal engineer is considered. Those who qualify and are advanced are paid a 17.5 percent bonus (based on the salary before it is increased).

4. Principal engineers are reviewed for compensation action as a group at year end. However, the compensation decisions proceed in a somewhat different manner. The first consideration is advancement. Those who are advanced to director are automatically raised to $25,000 and paid a 30 percent bonus for the past year. Track charts are then prepared for the balance of the principal engineer group, using the expected elapsed time for advancement from principal engineer to advancement to project manager. Once the appropriate track is determined, new salaries are taken from the track charts and bonuses awarded accordingly.

[8] The charts are plotted on semilog paper so as to result in constant percentage change.

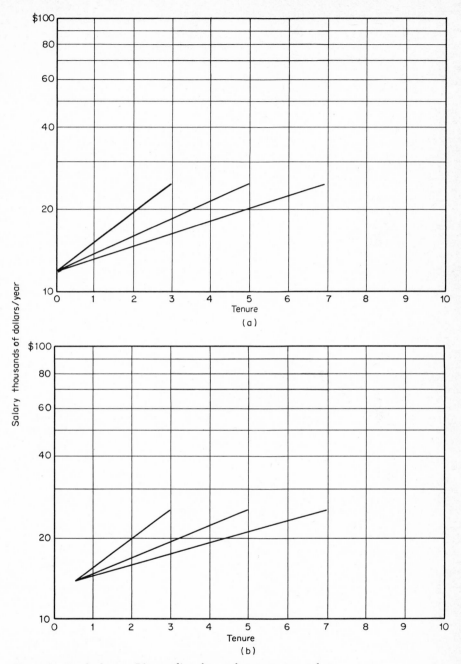

Figure 8.   Track charts. Lines radiate from salary at tenure at last increase to $25,000 at 3, 5, and 7 years tenure. *(a)* Salary $12,000, tenure 6 months. *(b)* Salary $14,000, tenure 1 year.

FACTORS INFLUENCING THE CHOICE OF A SYSTEM

It is fair to say that there is no "best" system.   On the other hand, it is evident that under certain conditions one system will tend to work better than another.   The two most important aspects to consider when choosing an approach to professional pay are:

1. The size of the professional group relative to other employee groups
2. The likelihood of transfer into and out of the professional group

As a general but simple guide to dealing with the system selection issue, the systems presented in this chapter ranked below that deemed most appropriate for relatively small groups with a high probability of movement in and out (traditional systems) to that probably best suited for large groups with virtually no possibility of transfer to other functions (track systems):

Traditional systems
Classification
Assignment analysis
Career curves
Track system

chapter 31

Job Evaluation and Pay Plans: Sales Personnel

IAN E. McLAUGHLIN *Director of Sales Training, Del Monte Corporation, San Francisco, California*

POSITION EVALUATION

The position of salesman within a company is seldom differentiated by classifications of the job. Unlike many positions, such as clerk-typist, which may have a junior, an intermediate, and an advanced classification, "A salesman is a salesman is a salesman," as Gertrude Stein would say.

In a company having several different sales forces covering different divisions, each sales force could employ a different compensation plan. Within one division, however, the pay scale of each sales position should be similar to every other one. True, under a straight salary plan some salesmen would receive more pay than others, but the factors governing the difference are not inherent in the job or work, but exist rather because of assignment (the salesman is covering the largest customers; so he is paid more), or longevity (the salesman has been with the company longer; so he is paid at least more than the average), or personal production (he is the top producer and rates top pay). In the case of straight salary, a stated policy for handling salesmen's compensation should be clearly defined to field managers and enforced by them. Without such a policy, the managers tend to go their own ways, with the result that compensation conditions are almost chaotic.

In commission plans, the man's earnings are his job evaluation for pay purposes.

In combination plans, both influences are present.

Although classifications within the sales job are rare, some companies have various types or levels of jobs within the selling organization, each with its own pay scale. For example, some companies have junior salesmen. These jobs are essentially training spots. The job classification is separate and distinct from that of the salesman. Its compensation is at the entry level of sales work for the company. This is a short-term, temporary assignment. Some companies might have a regular salesman covering a geographical territory and also have a national account salesman covering the "house accounts" or major purchasers. This latter assignment would, again, be different from a regular sales position and be paid on a different basis, generally at a higher level and closer to first-line managers' salaries.

In evaluating what to pay these different kinds of salesmen, the next section of this chapter which deals with determining levels is applicable.

Several organized plans can greatly assist in evaluating sales positions. The Hay plan, mentioned later, is one such plan. Most management consultants have developed ways to help evaluate positions, but the basis of all of them is internal judgment of the relative value of the position to the company, the law of supply and demand, and the activity required of the job.

Actually very little is done in evaluating gradations of sales jobs. The final evaluation of results achieved by the individual is the most frequently used position evaluation.

PAY PLANS FOR SALES PERSONNEL

There are many different opinions on equitable compensation for salesmen among consultants and company officials. When approaching this subject, one must realize that there are more variations in ways to pay salesmen than there are ways for paying any other single job or position in industry. For this reason, the use of caution, extreme care, and diligent research into an individual company's needs is the best way to proceed.

Any treatise on salesmen's compensation should always refer the reader to that in-depth, detailed work *Salesmen's Compensation* by Harry Tosdal and Waller Carson, Jr.[1]* Although dollar amounts change as we go through inflation and recessions, the principles enunciated in that work are still applicable. Many of the findings are used by compensation experts. Many of the thoughts expressed in this chapter originated in the application of these findings to actual practices we have employed.

In 1970, the National Industrial Conference Board in its study of incentive pay plans[2] brought out the point that many managers are themselves not completely satisfied with their present compensation plans. It would seem, therefore, that the perfect compensation program for salesmen has not yet been designed, and it is not the purpose of this chapter to attempt to do this.

What it will try to do is to present the various methods of paying salespeople. It will discuss the pros and cons of each method, both from the salesman's and from the company's point of view. It will cover ways to determine the levels or amounts that should be paid.

Compensation for salesmen covers not only the monies paid for services rendered, but also the extras that are inherent in sales work, such as the automobile provided by the company. Common today, of course, are the fringe benefits of a company. Paid vacations, retirements, hospitalization plans are all forms of compensation. Other chapters will cover these indirect forms of compensation; so this chapter will restrict itself to the monies paid directly for services rendered by salespeople.

A sound plan, equitable to both the individual and the company, is of paramount importance to any business organization. Its purpose is to provide compensation which is competitive in order to reduce turnover and which is objective oriented in order to increase sales.

---

*Superior numbers refer to Reference at the end of one chapter.

Money may not be the "end all" for salesmen, but it is a big factor in their drive stimuli. Salesmen, as a group, however, also have a high-level need for satisfying what the behavioral scientists call their "psychic income." Factors which comprise this psychic income—recognition, sense of achievement, prestige—are all available in the sales situation if the sales manager will make use of them. A sales manager should not expect that more money will necessarily solve sales problems such as turnover, poor results, poor morale—problems which could result from poor psychic income rather than inadequate monetary income.

On the other hand, even the best sales manager cannot long achieve optimum sales results using good psychic income factors without an adequate money plan to back them up. In order to have satisfied, successful salesmen, a sales manager must use a good compensation plan as well as these motivational forces.

Elements of a sound compensation plan are:

1. It should make the salesmen work *enthusiastically* toward company goals by means of proper pay for satisfactory work performance and further monetary reward for outstanding performance. Salesmen are, by nature, entrepreneurial. When they work harder than the next salesman, they want recognition for this. When salesmen are truly enthusiastic in their work, due to proper pay and recognition of outstanding performance, the results they achieve are better than those of a poorly motivated group, and thus help to fulfill corporate goals.

2. It should aid in recruiting by attracting the type of salesperson that will get the desired results for the company.

3. It should be easily understood by the salesmen.

4. It should be easy to administer.

5. It should encourage proper treatment of customers.

6. It should keep good salesmen.

These objectives can be met by any one of the three basic forms of salesmen's compensation: straight salary, straight commission, and combination plans. Each has advantages and disadvantages, both from the salesman's and the company's point of view.

What type of compensation is most frequently used? In recent years the trend is to choose combination plans as the method of salesmen's compensation. According to studies made by the National Industrial Conference Board,[3] in 1946, 48 percent of the 443 manufacturing firms surveyed used combination plans. In 1966, the percentage had increased to 65 percent of a total of 665 firms surveyed. Further illustration of the trend toward combination plans as the method of payment is contained in Figure 1 from an article, "Salesmen's Compensation: A Survey of Company Practices," published in 1969.[4]

Recent surveys indicate salesmen themselves prefer a combination plan of compensation.

Let us look at the three basic plans first, then discuss the multitude of variations possible under combination plans. We shall also examine the many problem areas that arise with both combination and commission plans. These problem areas are the variable conditions that occur during the operation of a plan.

THREE BASIC COMPENSATION PLANS

STRAIGHT SALARY

Advantages:

1. It is a fixed total cost (but not a fixed cost to sell). You know what your payroll cost is. You do not know how much you will get in return for these dollars.

2. There is good control of sales activity by the company. For example, when

Figure 1.   Payment methods (by percentage of companies, 1969).

Method	Consumer products	Industrial products	Other commerce and industry	All industries
Straight salary	20.1	25.6	56.5	27.6
Straight commission	2.1	1.3	2.2	1.5
Draw against commission	7.5	1.3		2.4
Salary plus commission	19.2	21.1	13.0	20.1
Salary plus individual bonus	21.3	18.0	8.7	17.7
Salary plus group bonus	8.5	4.4	6.5	5.4
Salary plus commission plus individual bonus	7.5	5.3	2.2	5.4
Salary plus commission plus group bonus	1.1	0.6		0.6
More than one method of payment	12.7	22.4	10.9	19.3
Total	100.0	100.0	100.0	100.0

SOURCE: *American Management Association Compensation Review,* vol. 1, no. 4, fourth quarter, 1969.

jobs require a great deal of prospecting and researching preliminary to making a sale, you can insist on this work being done because you are paying for it.

3. The plan is easily understood by salesmen.   Salesmen know the amount of their income.

4. This plan is good for starting new salesmen.   They can concentrate on learning rather than earning.

Disadvantages:

1. Salary is not related to results.   In many cases it is the salesman's longevity with the company that counts.   He not only gets the higher salary because of regular increases, but he often gets the largest accounts because of his seniority, whether or not his performance deserves it.

2. There is little incentive for the individual to work harder.   As long as the sales manager is satisfied, so is the salesman.   More work will not get him more pay.

3. Selling costs are not related to sales volume.

4. A weak or ineffectual manager can pay more than is necessary to achieve results or, as often happens, respond to cost-cutting pleas from headquarters by paying salesmen inadequately.

5. The high-producing salesman may feel he is carrying the weak ones, and so become frustrated.   This can lead to increased turnover in salesmen or reduced sales activity by the top producers.

Variations:

The only variation possible in a straight salary plan is that which you add in the form of reward for specific results.   One company provides a more luxurious car for salesmen who exceed their annual goals by a set amount.   Travel awards are common when certain levels of performance are reached.   Contests of both short and long duration provide opportunities for recognition and reward for outstanding performance.   Commonly the reward takes the shape of prizes or some form of credits that can be exchanged for merchandise.

By avoiding the use of monetary prizes there is little danger of getting into a situation where the compensation plan is inadvertently switched from salary to combination.   Contests and award systems can be changed or discontinued as conditions change, with little effect on morale.   On the other hand, a change in compensation can be very upsetting, particularly if something is taken away.

STRAIGHT COMMISSION

Advantages:

1. It pays for results (sales), and only for results.
2. It rewards the salesman who produces, according to his individual results.
3. It is a fixed cost to sell.
4. It does not require readjustment as frequently as a salary plan.
5. It attracts men who want the opportunity for top money.

Disadvantages:

1. Salesmen tend to push the easier to sell items and the high-volume items. They may neglect some items in the line.
2. Management has little control over the activities of the individual.
3. Salesmen tend to be less company oriented and more money oriented. Turnover is increased by constant job hopping in many industries.
4. The level of income for salesmen fluctuates.

COMBINATION PLANS

Advantages:

1. The company can direct the activities of the salesmen: "Your salary is being paid in return for the following activities. . . ."
2. Salesmen have a floor to their earnings; so they have fewer worries about their family's maintenance.
3. Provision is built-in for rewarding the individual for superior performance.

Disadvantages:

1. These plans can sometimes become very complicated and serve as a frustration to the salesman because of misunderstanding.
2. The cost to sell varies because the base (salary) part is paid regardless of sales results.
3. Combination plans include elements of both salary and straight commission plans, and so present some of the problems of each.

Variations:

The variations in combination plans are almost limitless if you count the differences in percentages of commission and salary, or the ways in which bonuses are computed, or all the combinations of the variations. There are four basic combinations:

1. Salary plus commission: This is the most common plan of the combination type. There are as many formulas for this type of plan as there are sales managers or compensation experts. The plan may vary from a minimum salary, just enough on which to subsist, combined with an opportunity to make a good living by commissions, to the other extreme of a high salary, with just enough commission to stimulate more than routine work.

The commission paid under a combination plan can either start with the very first sale or not begin until a certain predetermined level of results is reached. This level is generally set to pay off after the salary portion of the compensation has been "earned." There appears to be more motivation for each sale, however, if the payoff is for every sale.

2. Commission plus drawing account: This plan is almost straight commission. The difference is that the salesman has money on which to operate, even when sales are low. The most common variations of this plan are:

   a. The salesman must repay from earnings.

b. The salesman must repay, but in difficult times he is allowed to wipe the slate clean under certain conditions.

EXAMPLE: During designated periods the salesman does not have to repay a basic amount of draw if his earnings do not cover it. In effect, the company is guaranteeing a minimum income. This is generally referred to as a "guaranteed draw."

One benefit of a guaranteed draw plan is that the company can adjust the amount upward or downward without too much reaction from the salesmen. Commission salesmen, while counting on guaranteed draw as a backstop, do not necessarily consider it part of their income.

3. Commission plus bonus: This plan basically pays a man for his own effort and, in addition, rewards him for certain directed activities. To some extent, commission plus bonus gets around the straight commission drawback of having the salesman decide what he is going to sell and when. The bonus can be set up to pay for:

a. Extra results on certain product lines.

b. Certain nonproductive but necessary work, such as customer service, administrative work, training new men. It is possible to award credits or points for these activities; then the payoff is based on these.

c. Extra effort on the product line as a whole. The bonus can be set to pay off only if a certain level of sales is first reached (minimum overhead is met).

Bonuses can take the form of a share in the profits of the company. This is quite common in smaller companies that use straight commission. The bonuses can be predicated on gross sales of the company. They can be based on the individual's gross sales.

There are some negative factors to watch for in designing such a plan. It can become so complicated that administrative costs exceed the value and the salesmen are frustrated, resulting in poor morale.

Any type of plan featuring commission plus another factor requires more checking than a straight commission plan. The company which utilizes any combination plan must be certain it is getting the work for which it is paying.

4. Salary plus bonus: This is the reverse of the commission plus bonus. In the commission plus bonus plan, the salesman starts by having to produce his own income (his commissions). He earns extra income for doing certain things the company wants. Theoretically, his income (commissions) is limited only by his own capabilities.

In the salary plus bonus plan, the salesman's income (salary) is set and predetermined by the company. His extra income (bonus) is controlled by the plan and not entirely by his own efforts. Here, again, the variations are many. The salary can be a barely livable wage with the bonus being a high percentage; the salary can be at the going rate with the bonus being a small part of the salesman's annual income.

This type of plan gives the company much more control over all the salesman's activities than do other combination plans.

Many companies have suggested that a combination plan which affords a top performing salesman commissions which will amount to 25 to 35 percent of total income will maximize the advantages of each type.

VARIABLES IN COMMISSION OR COMBINATION PLANS

In commission or combination plans there are many variables that could become problems unless definitions are formed and rules inculcated before situations arise.

Windfalls

The first of these variables is that of windfalls. A windfall is an extra-large order that is the result of circumstances rather than selling effort on the part of the sales-

man. Should he get full credit? It could be argued that he received the order because of his past favorable performance with the customer. In this case, he has
earned the benefits because of his work. On the other hand, it could also be stated
that the product or the company's unique service influenced the customer to place
the order with that salesman. In this case, the company "earned" the order.

The plan for handling windfalls could be either a maximum percent payment per
windfall or a maximum or ceiling on earnings for any one month (or other specified
period of time). Ceilings tend to reduce salesmen's output, however, as will
be shown later. On the other hand, some companies feel that if windfalls occur
only rarely, the salesman deserves all the rights and benefits pertaining to the
windfall.

Split Commissions

Another problem is that of split commissions. In some industries, the buying is
done in one location and the goods are used in another. The second location frequently has the responsibility for maintaining customer contact, trouble shooting,
and related customer service activities. If services to the customer in the field location are not properly handled, reorders may be nonexistent. How to properly recognize the contribution of each salesperson in the combination plan format becomes
an important decision.

There is no easy formula for this situation. A careful weighing of the time involved for each salesman and his contribution to the orders must be made. As with
windfalls, the method of handling split commissions must be decided before they
occur. The salesmen should know what they must do and what return they will
receive for their activity.

According to the National Industrial Conference Board's 1970 report on incentive
pay plans,[5] there are three commonly practiced methods for handling this situation:
1. Setting a schedule. Apparently a 50-50 percent split is most frequently used.
2. Using historical practices to decide each case on an individual basis.
3. Giving full credit to the order-taking salesman for the first year, and after the
first year crediting orders to the servicing salesman.

Promotions and Transfers

When a man is promoted or transferred, how are his earnings to be calculated under
a commission or combination plan?

The common practices are:
1. Pay to the date of move under each category or position.
2. Pay a prorated sum, based on the time in each position, if an annual bonus is
involved.
3. Pay to the nearest completed incentive period—quarterly, monthly, etc.
4. Pay according to the rate of the position in which the individual spent the
longest period of time. This method is mostly used for annual bonuses, etc.

Retirements, Leaves of Absence, Military Leaves

Most frequently the payoff is on a prorated basis for these.

Eligibility

The time at which the salesman becomes eligible to participate in earnings under
combination plans should be clearly stated at the time he is hired. Many companies
have a probationary period, such as:
Eligible starting with next full quarter
Eligible after six months of employment
Eligible after first year of employment

Deaths

Under commission or combination plans, the amount paid to survivors in the event of the employee's death should be specifically stated. One example would be: "Beneficiaries will receive prorated award based on the man's share at the time of death."

Payments to beneficiaries should be made as soon as possible after the employee's death, not delayed until the plan's normal payoff date.

Terminations and Resignations

Companies vary in their handling of payoffs in cases of termination or resignation. Where a year-end bonus is concerned, it is not awarded if the man has already left the company. When the payoff date is for a set period of time (e.g., quarterly), many companies pay if the man is on the payroll on the closing date. The exception here is in the case of an employee "terminated for cause." Any such plan, however, should be approved by the company's legal department and careful consideration given to current civil rights rulings. In group-earned plans, payoffs for terminations or resignations can be sticky. The men remaining do not feel that the person who left deserves any portion of the compensation. If he was terminated, the feeling among the others is that he probably was not a good producer and therefore not deserving of any payment; if he resigned, he was deserting them. The fact probably is that if he resigned he was one of the better men—it seems that only the good men leave voluntarily. It comes down to a case of business ethics. Did the man earn a portion of the group award? If so, he should be paid.

New Products and Test Markets

The term "new products" should be defined and rules definitely stated concerning payments to salesmen. The salesmen are required to expend a major effort in launching a new product. Should they be rewarded for this? Is an additional quota to be given, based on marketing hypotheses? Is a separate payoff to be made? (This could cause the men to neglect their selling efforts on other products.)

Some companies in the retail field do not pay for new products placement, but do for reorders. Some have an introductory period with no payoff and use sales figures for this period as a basis for quotas.

In the case of industrial products, such as machinery with its "one-time sale," either a straight arrangement to pay off with the first sale or a plan to start paying after a given level of sales is reached could be equitable both to the salesmen and to the company.

In any case, the rules must be set when a new product is announced. Most companies do not pay for results in the test-marketing stage.

House Accounts

The rules for handling house accounts should be carefully worked out and worded specifically if the company is operating under a commission or combination plan of compensation. When does an account become a house account? What share, if any, does the salesman earn? In some cases, the salesman must service the account even though the sale is made by the house. To solve this, the salary part of a combination plan can be stated as payment for servicing, or it can be worked out so that a minimum percent is paid for all business received in return for proper servicing.

Government and Other Special Customers

Some products are sold to government agencies on bids. Here the salesman has little or no control over securing the business. Some companies have ruled that this class of business is excluded from their plans for commission or combination payments. Others have salesmen whose sole job is to handle national accounts or government business. In these latter cases, the pay plan for these special representatives is different from that for the regular territory salesmen.

Ceilings on Earnings

Where a salesman is paid under a commission or combination plan, should his earnings have a ceiling? Under a straight salary plan he does have a ceiling. Under a "pure" commission plan he does not. He can earn as much as he wants. The life insurance industry is a good example of this. There are no limitations as to territory, customers, or earnings in most life insurance companies.

The idea of a salesman earning more than his manager or even more than the president of the company is abhorrent to many people. Yet this is happening in some companies. Ceilings on earnings occur mainly in the combination type of plan.

The principal benefits of instituting a ceiling are:

1. There is maximum exposure for selling costs. Results of windfalls can be controlled in a limited way.

2. The average producer does not see the star producers outstripping him to the point of his dissatisfaction, discouragement, and frustration.

The negative side of having a ceiling on earnings is obvious. When a top producer hits the maximum he can and does tend to coast. In the same National Industrial Conference Board study referred to earlier,[6] one comparison indicates that a ceiling can have a depressing influence on efforts of the top stars.

Figure 2. Comparison of incentive earnings of high-producing salesmen under plans with and without earnings ceilings.

	Type of plan					
	Has earnings ceiling			Has no earnings ceiling		
	Total earnings	Base salary	Incentive as a percent of salary	Total earnings	Base salary	Incentive as a percent of salary
Median*.........	$14,950	$12,000	20%	$16,800	$12,000	30%
Range of middle 50%:						
Low..........	11,500	10,000	13	14,400	9,000	20
High.........	15,960	13,000	30	20,350	15,000	50

*Based on earnings data supplied for 48 plans with an earnings ceiling and 37 plans with no earnings ceiling.

SOURCE: *National Industrial Conference Board, Studies in Personnel Policy,* no. 217, 1970.

Compensating Team Selling Efforts

As discussed earlier, many sales jobs in today's highly specialized technical world are part of a team effort. In setting up compensation plans for this kind of sales activity, the trend is to straight salary or a combination format. Seldom is straight commission used.

Salary plan. In a salary plan for compensating team selling efforts, job evaluation is frequently used to determine the levels of pay for each member of the selling team. Sophisticated plans like the Hay system take into account the various parts of each job and weight them in accordance with such factors as personal initiative, judgment, and difficulty.

Combination plans.   There are various forms of combination plans for compensating group effort. The easiest to administer is one in which everyone receives an equal share of the incentive. The incentive is generally designated as a "district pool." In a pool earned by the group but distributed on an individual basis, there are several factors on which distribution can be based:

1. Salary. The feeling here is that the relative importance of each job to the total project has already been decided by the variance in salary. The drawback to this method is that the man with the highest salary is not always the top producer or even the hardest worker on the team; he could be just the one with the most seniority.

2. Annual appraisal. Such factors as achievement of objectives, overall contribution to group tasks, and customer relations are considerations in these plans.

3. Managerial judgment of the individual's contribution.

In the National Industrial Conference Board study,[7] one-third more of the companies compensating for group efforts used subjective measurement instead of solely objective measurement in determining incentive awards. It appears that this is done when the quantitative input for the results is not exactly measurable for each individual.

Figure 3.   Determination of incentive awards by objective and subjective measurement, by type of selling activity.

Measurement	Total plans	Type of selling activity		
		Sales engineers	Direct contact	Promotional selling
Objective measures:				
Only	62	16	28	18
Individual plans. .	44	11	23	10
Group plans.	18	5	5	8
Subjective measures:				
Also used.	38	17	12	9
Individual plans . .	12	3	8	1
Group plans.	26 *	14	4	8

*Five plans base the bonus share solely on subjective measures of performance. Three of these plans are for engineer sales forces: two are in effect for promotional salesmen.

SOURCE: *National Industrial Conference Board, Studies in Personnel Policy,* no. 217, 1970.

As mentioned earlier, the simplest team effort plan is a division of any bonus pool equally among all team members. It has some advantages in the team effect of total effort and discipline by team members.

Contracts with Salesmen

Salesmen compensated under a commission plan often have a contract with the company. Salaried salesmen seldom do. In combination plans, a contract is infrequent.

The basis for a contract should include the following:

Term of the contract
Territory
Exclusions, such as house accounts
The rate of pay, with restrictions, if any, such as ceiling and windfalls
Expenses: who pays what, conditions
Car arrangements: allowances, etc.
Timing of payments

Conditions for arbitration
Conditions of termination
Benefit plans: vacations, hospitalization, etc.; who pays for what, etc.

Frequency of Payoffs for Combination Plans

The National Industrial Conference Board survey[8] showed that 40 percent of the companies surveyed paid off annually. These were mostly companies which utilize a year-end bonus type of incentive. Another 43 percent paid off quarterly or monthly. Most of these companies were those having plans geared to objectives, quotas, etc.

Figure 4. Frequency of payments, by type of selling activity.

Practice	Total companies	Type of selling activity		
		Sales engineers	Direct contact	Order taking
Payments are made:				
Annually.	40	20	13	7
Semiannually. . . .	17	2	6	9
Quarterly	34	7	18	9
Monthly	9	4	3	2
Total.	100	33	40	27

SOURCE: *National Industrial Conference Board, Studies in Personnel Policy*, no. 217, 1970.

From a motivational standpoint it is desirable to pay off as frequently as possible, yet at periods extended enough to make the payoff amounts noticeable. The same holds true for salary plans involving contests, etc., as incentives. In "salary plus" plans, where the salary is the larger part of the income and the commission is less than 25 percent, a quarterly payoff could be used. It would make the payoff a large sum, but not so large that the lack of it for three months would constrict the man's standard of living, and it would offer the advantage that it would not simply become an expected part of money available for monthly living expenses (which would relegate it to the maintenance factor). Conversely, if the salary is minimal and the commissions are the major portion of the salesman's income, monthly payoff periods should probably be considered maximum.

SELECTION OF A COMPENSATION PLAN

No matter which type of compensation plan is being considered, the following basic factors should be kept in mind when choosing a plan: tradition, competition, and the selling activity.

Tradition. Tradition, to a large extent, governs the method of payment. Each industry has a traditional way of compensating salespeople, and salesmen apparently select their type of industry as much for the method of payment as they do for interest in the type of product or customer.

Those men who prefer working on a straight commission plan seldom stay with jobs based on straight salary, and vice versa. One industrial psychologist calls this the "law of natural selection." "Men tend to gravitate to the type of work where they enjoy both the work and its perimeters." In other words, in an industry that traditionally pays a straight commission, a company with a straight salary plan would not be likely to attract experienced, aggressive salesmen with a background in that industry. There might be a chance of getting such men under a combination plan.

The best method, however, would be to follow the industry and compensate sales-men under a straight commission plan.

Does this mean that the company has no control over the method to be selected? Not at all. Even straight commission has variations, as mentioned earlier.

Competition. A sales talent is just like any commodity. It follows the law of supply and demand. This means that the level of payment, just as the method of payment as previously shown, is governed by the competitors' payment for the same talent or experience.

As with almost anything in this world, it also means that the company gets what it pays for. There are excellent means to offset top money. Opportunity for ad-vancement, a chance for ownership participation through stock options, a thorough training program, a more luxurious car are among the compensations various com-panies offer to offset not being able to outbid competitors monetarily for sales per-sonnel. In general, however, a mediocre pay scale will attract mediocre men. If the pay is tops, the chances for hiring top performers will be greater.

The Selling Activity. With the growth of technology, the traditional salesman has changed in many industries. He is an engineer selling a whole system. He is a subject expert counseling a client. He is a problem solver working on his cus-tomers' problems. With these changes a third ingredient must be introduced in designing a compensation plan. The type of activities that will be required must play a major role in deciding which type of compensation is best.

The person who is more oriented to the job, to the point of acting as consultant where the sale is almost incidental—engineer, scientist, architect—is more likely to need and respond to a salary plan than to a commission plan. His interest in doing the research, developing custom-tailored solutions, and servicing the account gives him his job satisfaction and motivation drives. To put on the pressure of "earn money or do not eat," such as would occur through payment of straight commission, could, in many cases, be frustrating and demoralizing.

On the other hand, a sales activity that is primarily one of cold calls, quick closes, one that is primarily selling, is quite conducive to a straight commission plan.

As more and more companies adopt the marketing concept, it becomes more and more necessary that the sales force's efforts support these marketing goals. No longer can the salesman decide where his effort should be placed, based on personal likes or easy-to-sell items. He must exert effort to further the company's goals. Combination plans seem the best way to ensure this for most companies, since it is possible under such plans to direct the efforts of the salesman toward specific activities or results.

All good modern selling has service to the customer built into the job. A really professional salesman thinks first of his customers and how he, the salesman, can help them. But in different industries and in different sales jobs within industries there is a variance in the way a company wants the salesman to spend his time and effort. All sales positions are designed to get sales results. It is the way that the company dictates how this effort is to be made that is referred to above. So, in determining which plan or what percent of a combination plan should be paid through salary or commission, this activity must be a deciding factor.

The basis for determining the plan to be used could be illustrated as shown below. If the job is aimed mainly at getting volume, the plan could be mostly

commission. If the work required a large amount of customer service and research, and selling is the end result of many other activities, then a salary plan is indicated. If the requirements of the job's time and effort were plotted on the scale, it would indicate the percentages for a combination plan.

Thus, if the optimum expenditures of time and effort for a position were:

Servicing present customers. 10%
Developing system application plans. 10%
Prospecting for new accounts. 15%
Selling to present customers. 50%
Selling to new accounts 15%

the results would be as shown below.

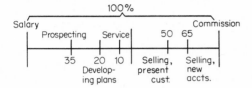

It would then appear that a combination plan of 35 percent salary and 65 percent commission would be suitable. Obviously, these job factors would have to be carefully analyzed. The above is greatly simplified, but it illustrates the point.

Several companies have developed a systematized approach toward putting together these three factors of tradition, competition, and selling activity and coming up with an acceptable answer. One of these companies is Edward N. Hay and Associates, who have developed what they call the Guide Chart-Profile Method of determining compensation. They start with a detailed appraisal of the job. They then use a point system to weight the principal parts of the job, these being job know-how, problem-solving requirements, and accountability or measured effect of the job on end results. By using a standard weighting scale, they can compare a given sales job with similar jobs within like industries and with sales jobs in general. There are rarely two sales jobs which are identical, even within the same industry. Because companies add to or subtract from factors of their job assignments, the Hay system weights these differences. After analyzing these factors again, the next step is to bring out where the job fits within the industry, or externally, and where it fits within the company, or internally. From this comparison the existing salary practice can be visualized, and if needed, a new policy can be developed to properly compensate sales personnel.

This system can be used in three major areas:

1. Determining what monies should be paid for the job within the company or how it fits competitively.

2. Weighting the variances in territories or customer class. In some territories it is more difficult to sell an identical product than in others, and this system tends to take these factors into consideration.

3. Providing a base for acceptable payment of team members in a selling team situation. It can weight the contribution of the salesman, applications engineer, and service man in a given sales situation.

In addition, the Hay system could be used to determine the relative payoff for those in a team situation in the incentive part of the compensation plan. In total, this program takes into consideration the competitive situation, what other companies are paying, and the activities as defined by the particular company for the particular job. What further factors should be weighed in choosing the method and level of payment?

These are some things to be considered:

1. A company with a sound training program can pay about average for the particular industry and still get good men.

2. A company which does not have a training program and which needs experienced salesmen must pay for them. This means paying above average for the industry. Most small companies find that this is necessary to get fast starts of new men (no training) and competent salespeople.

3. If it is possible for a company to start men with little or no experience, the entry level of compensation can be paid.

4. The more the product is promoted, advertised, and known by brand, the more likely it is that the company will use a straight salary plan and average pay level.

5. Conversely, the less the product is promoted and advertised, the greater the need for personal selling, the more the compensation levels tend to be above average.

6. The more the sale is a result of a team effort—engineers, estimators, plus salesmen—the more likely it is that compensation will be on a straight salary plan.

7. The more strong personal selling is required to close, the more often a commission plan is utilized.

Remember, the above are only guidelines. Indeed, this whole chapter is one guideline after another, one conclusion after another, based on generalities and averages. Each company must take its own situation, analyze it within its own needs, and decide what plan and what variations of that plan will best suit its marketing needs. There is no compensation formula that is as perfect as a geometric theorem.

STEPS IN DESIGNING A COMPENSATION PLAN

1. Study the industry.
   a. Find out the leading company's method and level of payment. Study the up-and-coming companies, even though they might not be the largest. One source of information on competitive salaries might be the industry's trade associations. This research should establish both the prevailing scale or *levels* and the most common *method* of compensation.
   b. Find out which companies the customers feel have the best salesmen.
2. Determine the company's economically feasible maximum cost to sell. This establishes a ceiling—it is not, and should not, be the answer which will necessarily be used.
3. Determine company goals and the sales department's specific objectives to support them.
   a. Is the goal growth in a share of the market? This will mean lots of prospecting and developing new accounts, and the company must plan to pay salesmen for this activity.
   b. Is the goal in unit or dollar volume increase? Some plan that will reward extra results should then be considered.
   c. Is it company policy to promote from within? If so, then a plan will be required that will attract promotable men and will also hold them with the company.
4. Write a position description for the sales job. This will reveal what parts of the work required do not result in immediate sales, such as servicing an account.

5. Design a proposed plan that meets the requirements of tradition, competition, and job activity, and then pretest it.
   a. This can be done by applying the new plan to a sampling of salesmen's results for the past few years. A survey of this type enables the company to see if the plan is feasible. It also shows the salespeople how much they will be earning as a direct comparison with their previous earnings.
   b. If the company is new, then a paper test should be made—"If the salesman meets goals, he will get this amount; if he exceeds goals by 5 percent, this amount"—to help salesmen to visualize what income they can expect.
   c. Any time a change is instituted or a new company starts up, the company should state at the beginning that the initial period of the plan is to be a test and that after the test period, adjustments might be made. In any case, salesmen should know the range of pay for the work expected.
   d. An experienced company that is switching plans could use one or two districts to test the new plan. In this case, it is best to guarantee the salesman no loss of income during the test.
6. Set up administrative details for handling the plan.
7. Announce the new plan to the sales force.
   a. This is best done with small, informal meetings, such as a field district group or, better still, a small group meeting followed by individual conferences.
   b. Explain why the company is changing.
   c. Show the men a comparison between plans, outlining both the good points and the weak points.
   d. Show a comparison between present earning and expected earning under the new plan.
   e. Set and state a deadline for review of the plan.
8. Review the plan after it has been in force for a time, and change it if necessary.

MARKETING OBJECTIVES AND SALESMEN'S COMPENSATION

With the advent of the marketing concept there has been a change in the traditional thinking as to the basis for the salesman's payoff. Straight commission, in its commonest and oldest form, pays off for volume. Straight salary pays off for the easy route of sufficient volume to keep the boss satisfied. Neither method in its basic form concerns itself with the goals or profits of the company.

Marketing executives are more and more turning to sales executives and asking, "What is the sales force doing to achieve our goals?" And now, in addition, "What is the sales force doing to contribute to profits?"

Day and Bennett[9] make a case for the practicality of designing a plan that not only rewards the salesman for his efforts, but also directs activity toward satisfying the company's goals and specifically contributing to profit. Here, again, many variations are possible.

In a salary plan, contests, prizes, or other incentive rewards could be based on the profitable items in a line. The traditional volume goal could be the qualifying level if the need for volume per se were there. Points could be given for various groups of products and, by giving extra points for the more profitable items, cause more effort to be expended on those items.

In a combination plan the above ideas could be used. In addition, the base or salary part of the plan could be used to obtain the necessary volume and the commission paid only on the profitable items after a base volume figure had been attained. Varying commission rates for varying profitability of items or groups of items could also be used. This would also work for straight commission plans.

In any case, care must be taken to be sure that profit alone is not the determining factor in the payoff. There are certain items in many companies' product lines that "pay the rent." Their very volume covers the overhead even if their profit contribution is small.

There are two main considerations then in this approach: (1) contribution to overhead and (2) contribution to profit. Both of these factors could, after study, be weighted in a compensation plan so that marketing objectives would be met. Such a plan would increase the salesman's decision requirements for his sales activities, in other words, give him more responsibility for the success of the company.

Behavioral scientists have determined through their studies that increased responsibilities increase interest in the job, and increased interest results in increased production. This approach, a form of management by objectives, appears to warrant more attention than it presently receives.

SUMMARY

There are three forms of salesmen's compensation: straight salary, straight commission, combination plans. Each has advantages and disadvantages for both the salesman and the company.

In deciding which plan to use, three determinants should be considered: tradition, competition, and sales job activity. The trend is toward combination plans. The majority of companies are using one variation or another of this type of plan.

The elements of a sound plan are that it should:

Make salesmen work to achieve company goals

Attract good new hires

Be easily understood by salesmen

Be easy to administer

Ensure good customer relations

Keep good salesmen

Salary plans give the greatest control over the salesmen. They are frequently best when customer service or long intervals of cultivation are necessary, or when selling is chiefly repetitive orders from established customers.

Commission plans have the best fixed cost to sell. They are a very real stimulator of results, and they are simplest to administer.

Combination plans can do the same as either salary or commission plans, and many other things. However, they can have the problems of complexity, frustration for the salesman, and failure to accomplish their objectives if improperly designed.

This chapter has dealt with the various compensation plans primarily from a company's point of view. It is just as important to consider the receiver of such plans, the salesman. Modern behavioral scientists have done much research on the needs and drives of workers. When you hire a salesman you also "hire a family," and scientists' findings have shown that the need for the security, safety, and well-being of his family will motivate a salesman to work. The need for recognition and for the esteem of his peers will cause him to work harder. A plan should therefore carefully consider building in elements that will compensate a salesman for doing the routine or "duty" parts of his work and, in addition, will reward him for doing the extras, the unpleasant parts, such as "cold calls." The plan should also incorporate ways of capitalizing on the entrepreneurial nature of salesmen by rewarding them for results and work "above and beyond the call of duty."

A carefully thought-out plan that has considered both the salesman's needs and the company's needs will have a higher probability of success than one that is based only on "We've always done it that way." All in all, compensating salesmen is one of the most difficult parts of the sales management job, but one for which the rewards can be great in results and in morale.

REFERENCES

[1] Tosdal, Harry R., and Waller Carson, Jr.: *Salesmen's Compensation,* vols, I and II, Division of Research, Graduate School of Business Administration, Harvard University, Boston, 1953.

[2] Weeks, David A.: *Incentive Plans for Salesmen,* 1970 National Industrial Conference Board, Studies in Personnel Policy, no. 217.

[3] *Ibid,* p. 3.

[4] Reen, Jeremiah J.: "Salesmen's Compensation: A Survey of Company Practices," *American Management Association Compensation Review,* vol. 1, no. 4, Fourth Quarter 1969.

[5] Weeks, *op. cit.,* p. 86.

[6] *Ibid.,* p. 80.

[7] *Ibid.,* p. 57.

[8] *Ibid.,* p. 67.

[9] Day, Ralph, and Peter D. Bennett, "Should Salesmen's Compensation Be Geared to Profits?," *Journal of Marketing,* vol. 26, no. 4, October, 1962.

chapter 32

Compensation Plans for Executives

PHILIP H. DUTTER *Director, McKinsey & Company, Inc., New York, New York*

The problem of compensating executives and managerial personnel is no different in many respects from the problem of compensating any other group of employees. Certainly the basic objectives are the same: an organization needs to pay whatever is required to attract and retain executives and managers of the caliber it needs, just as it needs to pay whatever is required to attract and retain salesmen, engineers, secretaries, and production workers. In addition, compensation and the way it is administered can affect the morale and motivation of executives and managers just as it affects the morale and motivation of other employees. Thus, the key requirements for effective compensation administration for all groups are: (1) compensation should be competitive with what other employers are paying for similar skills on similar jobs; (2) compensation paid various individuals in an organization should *reflect the comparative value of their respective contributions* to that organization; and (3) compensation decisions should be made and communicated in a way that is perceived as *rational and fair*.

Beyond these basics, executive compensation is different in several ways. First, compensation practices at the executive and managerial level tend to set the tone for compensation practices at lower levels. If the chief executive's compensation is low compared with the chief executives of similar companies, compensation for down-the-line personnel is likely to be depressed. If compensation for executives and managers is determined by whim or in response to individual pressure, these executives in turn are likely to deal in a similar manner with the compensation of people reporting to them.

A second significant difference is that executives and managers typically have greater latitude to "make their own jobs" than personnel at lower organization levels. The chief executive's job grows as his company grows, whether by internal expansion or by acquisition. Heads of divisions or departments become more important as the operations they direct expand as a result of their efforts. Staff executives become more important and influential as they gain acceptance through demonstrated ability.

A third difference is that the results achieved by the company as a whole or by a profit center within the company are more likely to accurately reflect the personal contributions of higher level executives or managers than those of employees at lower levels. And higher level executives are more likely to accept the concept that their compensation should be tied to business results. Thus, a variety of incentive bonus plans has been developed; and in some industries most managers and executives are compensated through a combination of base salary and annual incentive award or bonus.

A fourth important difference is that the compensation of higher level executives and managers is subject to much higher personal income tax rates than the compensation of lower level employees. Thus tax considerations become a much more significant factor in compensation planning, and as a result, a variety of compensation forms such as stock options and deferred compensation has become popular at executive levels.

A fifth difference is that the personnel department often plays a more limited role in dealing with compensation for executives and managers than with compensation for other groups. In some companies, executive compensation has been considered so sensitive a matter that the personnel department has had little involvement. However, as the need for sophistication has increased and executive compensation programs have become more formalized, personnel departments, at least in larger companies, have played an increasingly larger role in all aspects of executive compensation.

This chapter will focus on those aspects of compensation planning and administration which are of particular importance at the executive and managerial levels. It will cover:

1. Position evaluation
2. The salary structure
3. Performance appraisal
4. Incentive bonus plans
5. Supplementary forms of compensation

POSITION EVALUATION

The compensation any employee is paid represents the value the organization's management places on him and the contribution he has made or can make to that organization. This value, of course, is influenced by outside competitive forces, i.e., compensation levels that management finds have to be paid to attract and retain people with the desired backgrounds and skills. On the other hand, the market is an incomplete and sometimes unreliable guide. The market value of an executive or manager is not always easy to determine. Some skills are more marketable than others. Managers and executives who have spent their entire careers with the same company are often worth more to that particular company than they are to any other.

Does this mean that these men should be paid less than executives who are more marketable, even though losing them would hurt the company more? A big factor to consider in any such situation is that most people are motivated by recognition, and that compensation is a highly tangible form of recognition, a kind of managerial scorecard. Words of commendation may well have a hollow ring if a contrary message is conveyed by compensation decisions. Furthermore, the resulting negative impact at the executive level can have repercussions throughout the organization. Thus, a heavy penalty is paid if decisions on executive and managerial compensation appear to be inequitable or capricious.

The process of setting compensation levels for executives and managerial personnel implies some kind of evaluation of each man's worth to the organization. This inescapable fact needs to be recognized and faced up to by top management. Once it is recognized, two questions need to be answered:

1. How should this evaluation be made?

2. How should the basis for compensation decisions be communicated to the executives concerned?

Answers to these questions depend mainly on the size of the executive and managerial group and on the chief executive's depth of exposure to all members of that group. If the executive-managerial group is small (no more than twenty or thirty) and the chief executive works closely with all members of that group, the chief executive will be able to make compensation decisions based on his perceptions of each member's individual contribution as well as his market value. On the other hand, if the executive-managerial group is larger, and no single person is in a position to objectively compare the contributions of all the members, some means must be found to evaluate individual performance and equitably compensate the executive for his contribution—a task made more difficult by the fact that some executives are inclined to be more enthusiastic than others about their subordinates' performance and more generous in rewarding it.

The basic approach used by most large companies to assure some degree of equity among various divisions and departments is to classify all positions into a series of grades, to which a series of salary ranges is attached. The basic premise underlying this approach is the same as that underlying job evaluation for other types of personnel: it is possible to determine the upper and lower limits of what a particular position should be worth based on comparisons with competitive compensation levels and with other positions in the company and then to recognize differences in individual capabilities and performance within that range.

There are some objections to this approach, or at least to the way such programs are administered in many companies. These objections are sometimes expressed in simplistic terms, such as: "I don't like the idea of putting people into slots," or "We don't want the system to determine what our people will be paid." Regardless of the words, such statements reflect a serious concern, often justified, that the cure for compensation inequities may be worse than the disease, that it stifles or deemphasizes recognition of individual performance and contributions.

However, in a large organization the alternative to establishing position grades and salary ranges is generally far from satisfactory. Usually, it involves reviews of salary increase recommendations by one or more committees, few of whose members are in a position to evaluate the recommendations. Therefore the reviews are frustrating for committee members and meaningless as a control procedure. Since the committee members have no reliable information on comparative responsibilities or performance, factors such as age and tenure often loom large in the discussion of whether a proposed increase is reasonable. If the committee goes beyond rubber-stamping the recommendations, the executives whose recommendations have been modified resent the apparently arbitrary "second-guessing." If the committee assumes a more passive posture, other executives are left wondering whether they have been too conservative in estimating what the committee would have been willing to accept.

Thus, while granting the pitfalls and limitations of the position evaluation salary range approach, it seems the most practical route to achieving a balance between the need to recognize individual contributions and the need to achieve some degree of equity among the various divisions and departments of a large organization. It also provides a means of involving a substantial number of people in the compensation decision-making process in an orderly and meaningful way.

If we then conclude that positions should be evaluated formally and that salary ranges should be established, the next questions are:

1. Who should do the evaluating?
2. How should the evaluations be made?
3. When and how often should positions be evaluated?

Who?

A cardinal rule in evaluating positions, particularly executive and managerial positions, is that no position should be evaluated without the participation of someone directly familiar with it who also has authority over a broad spectrum of positions. While it is worthwhile to prepare position descriptions of what the individual is responsible for doing and why, such descriptions rarely are adequate as a basis for comparison. This is particularly true in regard to high-level staff positions, where the old adage that "the man makes the job" applies most aptly.

Given this principle, the evaluation of any significant number of positions requires a committee, and in some organizations may involve several committees. A possible alternative is to make an internal staff group or an outside consultant responsible for the evaluation. One difficulty with an internal staff group is that someone has to evaluate their positions too. More fundamentally, turning the whole job over to an internal staff or to outside consultants is likely to encourage the feeling that compensation decisions have somehow gotten away from the line organization's control, that the "system" or the staff has taken over.

Some participation on the part of all key executives in the evaluation process is vital. The role of the staff or consultant should be one of structuring line participation to make it more meaningful and less time consuming than committee reviews of individual salary recommendations.

How?

Over the past twenty-five years, there has been an inordinate amount of fascination with position-evaluation techniques. More recently, this aspect of personnel management has come to be viewed in a more balanced perspective. More and more people are recognizing and accepting the fact that there simply is no way of evaluating positions so that the results are unassailably "right." Perceptions of each position vary from one person to another as do opinions on the criteria that should be used, their relative importance, and how they should be interpreted. The best that can be realistically expected from a formal position-evaluation program is that everyone concerned will develop increased confidence that all positions have been evaluated as thoughtfully and objectively as is humanly possible.

One approach to position evaluation is simply to rank the positions in relation to each other, grouping those which are of equal value. Hopefully, the ranker attempts to take into account all the factors that have a bearing on a position's worth, such as its potential impact on business results, difficulty in performing the task, and requirements for special knowledge and skill. He also has to balance the relative importance of these factors in arriving at an overall judgment. This approach works reasonably well with a single ranker and a limited number of positions (twenty to thirty). It has the virtue of simplicity, and the results rarely differ significantly from those the ranker obtains when he uses a more complex method.

In dealing with a committee and a larger number of positions, however, the overall ranking-classification method leaves much to be desired. It is not particularly helpful as a means of pinpointing, narrowing, and resolving differences of opinion among committee members. Furthermore, the method is less likely to produce rigorous, analytical consideration of all pertinent facts than a more highly structured approach. The latter typically involves identifying and defining the criteria to be considered in evaluating positions, evaluating the positions with regard to each criterion, and combining the ratings on all criteria to arrive at an overall evaluation. In some evaluation systems, degrees of difference and scales of point values are defined in advance for each criterion; positions are then assigned to one degree or another, based partly on interpretations of these definitions. In other systems, positions are compared directly with each other, one factor at a time; the number of degrees of difference established under each factor depends on the number that can be clearly distinguished by the committee.

Three basic factors or criteria are generally used in evaluating executive and managerial positions. These are:

1. The scope of the position and its potential impact on business results, long term and short term

2. The complexity, difficulty, and creative demands of the position

3. The requirements of the position in terms of knowledge and skill

These basic factors are often split into a number of subfactors in order to facilitate making meaningful comparisons. However, the dangers of an overly complex system are becoming increasingly recognized. There is a certain artificiality in any piecemeal look at job values, and the process can become so complex and mechanistic that it appears to become an end in itself. When this happens, the overly complex, time-consuming system itself stands in the way of developing the desired understanding on the part of key line executives.

To reduce the amount of executive time required in the position-evaluation process, a high-level committee may be used to establish a broad framework by evaluating a limited number of "bench-mark" positions representing all major functions, departments, and divisions in the company. Lower level committees can then relate other positions to the bench-mark positions.

When and How Often?

One of the problems with formal position evaluation is that the evaluations quickly become dated. This is particularly true of executive and managerial positions since organizational shuffles, which occur with surprising frequency in many companies, often cause shifts in position responsibilities. Also a change in a position's incumbent may result in a surprising change in the nature and importance of the position.

Any position-evaluation plan should be sufficiently flexible to reflect any clear-cut change, such as creation of a new position, when it occurs. In addition, all positions should be reevaluated every two or three years to take account of more gradual shifts in values that reflect variations in individual performance or a change in the nature and requirements of a company's business.

In some companies, position evaluations are reviewed annually in connection with the determination of salary increases. The problem here is that the linking of position evaluation to salary review leads to recommending position reclassification only for those individuals whose salaries are near the range maximums. Thus, the classification and range tend to become regarded as a justification for whatever salary is desired rather than as a guide to help determine what that salary should be.

THE SALARY STRUCTURE

Once positions have been evaluated, whether in terms of point values or a simple ranking, it is necessary to translate these evaluations into dollars of compensation if the evaluation is to be of any use for compensation administration purposes.

Let us assume that 200 executive and managerial positions have been evaluated and that current salaries paid the incumbents range from $15,000 to $100,000 annually. It is very likely that these 200 positions might fall into some 50 to 100 different ranks in the evaluation process, which is unwieldy for administrative purposes. Furthermore, establishing fine gradations of difference among positions implies greater precision in evaluation than actually exists. Therefore, the usual practice is to group positions of similar value into a series of grades—typically, some ten to fifteen grades will cover a range of salaries from $15,000 to $100,000 (see Figure 1). The key consideration in determining how many grades to establish is the desired salary difference between grades. This difference should be on the order of 10 to 15 percent. If the salary differential between two successive grades is less than 10 percent, the implication is that the difference is so slight that it is hardly worth making the distinction. On the other hand, a differential of more than 15 percent suggests that there may be significant differences in position value within the same grade that are not being recognized. If the increment from one grade to the next is in the 10 to 15 percent range, there usually is little doubt that a move from a position in one grade to one in the next higher grade is in fact a promotion, while a move to one in the same grade is a lateral transfer.

Since one of the primary objectives of an executive compensation program is to attract and retain people who are well qualified to carry out their responsibilities, it is vital to take competitive compensation levels into account in setting the salary structure. For most companies, the *Top and Middle Management Compensation Services* published by the American Management Association will provide information on a dozen or more positions similar to those in the company. This number of comparisons should be adequate to check the general competitiveness of the salary structure, although occasionally special surveys are worthwhile to check key positions not included in the American Management Association services.

At the executive level, particularly near the top, compensation tends to be closely related to the size of the company measured in terms of sales. Thus, comparisons at this level should take into account the size of the companies with which comparisons are made. One technique for accomplishing this is to plot on a graph (see Figure 2) the compensation paid for a selected top-level position, such as chief execu-

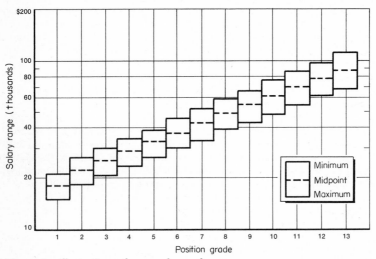

Figure 1. Illustrative salary grades and ranges.

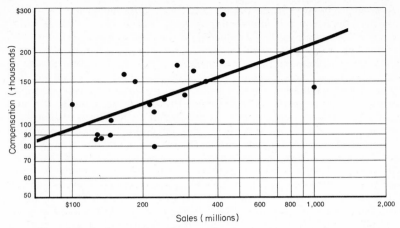

Figure 2. 1968 chief executive compensation in nineteen apparel companies—sales vs. compensation.

tive, against the sales volume for each comparable company. A line of best fit can then be constructed, and the point at which this line intersects the sales volume for any company will be a reasonably good indicator of the industry norm for a company of that size.

In addition, surveys show significant differences in executive compensation levels among industries. For example, banking, insurance, air transport, railroad, and public utility industries tend to pay less for the same sales volume than the chemical, department store, automotive, steel, textile, and appliance industries. Therefore, comparisons should be limited to organizations in the same industry.

Occasionally, the relative value of positions indicated by surveys does not conform to the relative value indicated by the positon-evaluation process. Such discrepancies can be resolved only by reexamining both the external and internal comparisons and using the value that seems to be most solidly based.

Total cash compensation for executive positions in many industries is likely to consist of a combination of salary and incentive bonus. Both the proportion of total cash compensation paid in the form of bonuses and the number and types of positions covered by bonus plans vary widely from company to company. Because of this, it is best to look at total cash compensation in assessing competitive compensation levels. The next step is to decide what position your company wants to maintain vis-à-vis any particular set of competitors. Determination of what this position should be will partly depend on the amount of cash compensation that is paid in the form of bonuses and how sensitive the bonus is to fluctuations in business results. If a company expects its executives to take greater compensation risks than those expected by its competitors, management may be well advised to aim at higher-than-average total compensation levels. On the other hand, if it pays straight salary while most of its competitors pay part of total compensation in the form of incentive bonuses, management may be well advised to continue to pay salaries somewhat below the average total compensation of its competitors. In any case, the company's desired competitive position vis-à-vis its competitors in terms of total compensation and the proportion that will normally be paid in the form of bonuses should be determined.

The next step is to deduct the amount of the normal bonus from the desired total compensation levels in order to set the midpoints for salary ranges. Normal bonus amounts typically range from 15 to 50 percent of salary, with higher level positions typically paying a higher proportion of compensation in the form of a bonus. In a few companies, bonuses are paid only for outstanding performance and thus are the exception rather than the rule. If this is the company's philosophy, salary ranges should be set on the assumption that there normally will be no bonus payment.

Regardless of whether a bonus plan exists, the salary range for each position should be broad enough to recognize differences in individual performance, but narrow enough to provide a useful guide in decision making. Theoretically, the midpoint of the range represents the salary that a fully qualified individual with entirely satisfactory job performance should receive; the minimum is the least that will be paid for someone who fully meets the position requirements; the maximum is the most that will be paid an incumbent who has demonstrated outstanding performance over a period of time. For managerial and executive positions, the range maximum typically exceeds the minimum by 40 to 60 percent. Frequently a 40 percent spread is used at the $10,000 to $15,000 level, and is graduated upward to 50 or 60 percent at the highest salary grades. Such a pattern recognizes that the range of differences in individual performance in the same job is likely to be greatest in the highest level positions.

It is important that the overall compensation structure be anchored at the top by establishing a competitive range for the chief executive position, since this is the position most readily compared with other companies. Furthermore, the chief executive's compensation inevitably has an effect on the compensation of the officers reporting to him. Thus, a company is unlikely to maintain its desired competitive position at lower levels if the chief executive's compensation is sharply at odds with its stated policy.

One key question that needs to be faced if formal position grades and salary ranges are established is whether each person should be told what his grade and range is. If the individual is not informed of the salary range for his position but knows that such a range exists, his confidence in the equity of the compensation program may be shaken. On the other hand, he can easily misinterpret the significance of the salary range or attach more importance to it than it deserves. Generally, managements that communicate most effectively concerning their salary administration programs do advise each individual of his salary range but focus on what he can do to increase his compensation through merit increases and advancement to higher level positions.

PERFORMANCE APPRAISAL

If a compensation program is to serve as a positive motivational force, the most difficult, and at the same time the most critical, requirement is to relate compensation to individual performance. Virtually all salary programs and most incentive bonus plans for executives and managerial personnel require some judgment of individual performance as a key ingredient in compensation decisions. Too often these judgments are superficial or even haphazard. In many companies, in fact, status and seniority may carry more weight than performance. In other companies, recognition given to individual performance may not be soundly based, or it may not appear to be soundly based, which is equally important.

Performance appraisal as a formal process has been the center of a great deal of controversy over the years. The practice of rating employees on a standardized set of traits or characteristics, an approach which had never been widely used for executive and managerial employees, has come to be regarded in recent years as counterproductive for other groups of employees as well. The trend has been toward defining individual performance standards in the form of individual objectives or goals. This approach, commonly known as "management by objectives," serves a number of purposes. In some companies, it has been introduced as part of an effort to improve the development of executives through feedback and counseling. In others, it has been seen as a tool for identifying people with high potential for advancement. In still others, it has been viewed as part of an overall business planning and control process aimed at channeling effort in desired directions and achieving improved communication and coordination among managers whose activities are interrelated. In a number of companies, management by objectives has been introduced as a tool for improving compensation administration, i.e., for making salary and bonus decisions that reward individual performance.

According to one school of thought, if the performance review is directly linked to compensation, its usefulness in providing feedback to an individual in a way that will contribute to his development is substantially diminished.[1] When compensation is at stake, the theory goes, the individual receiving feedback is likely to be more sensitive and defensive than he otherwise would be. His attention is so focused on the compensation decision and his emotions are so affected by it that he is unlikely to view constructive criticism with anything like an open mind.

While there are undoubtedly negative aspects to linking a decision on compensation with a detailed discussion of individual performance and development needs, the fact is that the compensation decision calls for some kind of explanation. If none is forthcoming, the decision is likely to be viewed as capricious. If the explanation has nothing to do with individual performance, it is unlikely to have any positive motivating force. If the decision seems inconsistent with what the individual has been told about his performance, the effect is likely to be demotivating.

The negative consequences of tying compensation reviews directly to performance appraisal feedback noted by some observers may largely be the result of inconsistencies between the message contained in the performance appraisal and the message contained in the compensation decision. One test of the effectiveness of an executive compensation program is the extent to which executives are convinced that their performance does in fact have a bearing on their compensation.

Developing and maintaining a positive relationship between performance and compensation is not easy in a large organization or in one in which there are few positions where individual performance is clearly apparent in the results achieved. In either of these situations, a formal program requiring written objectives or performance standards against which evaluations can be made is helpful since it tends to build confidence that compensation decisions are not made arbitrarily. If top-level executives exercise care and discipline in applying this program, they establish a pattern that is likely to be followed with similar discipline and good faith at lower levels in the organization.

Too often managements devote a great deal of attention to evaluating positions in a logical, organized way and then do little or nothing to emphasize the importance of evaluating individual performance. This imbalance often gives rise to position-evaluation "gamesmanship" since position evaluation is seen as the major means of controlling compensation. Establishing a formal position-evaluation program virtually requires a formal performance-evaluation program, if the importance of individual performance is not to be diminished. If incentive bonuses, as well as salaries, are to be based partly on judgments of individual performance, the need for a formal appraisal program becomes even more critical. Without it, bonus decisions are impossible to justify and the bonus program is more apt to be a bone of contention than a motivational tool.

---

[1] H. H. Meyer, E. Kay, and J. R. P. French, Jr., "Split Roles in Performance Appraisal," *Harvard Business Review,* January–February, 1965.

INCENTIVE BONUS PLANS

In the manufacturing and retailing fields, where year-to-year results are largely a reflection of management performance, it is common for executive and managerial personnel to be compensated partly in the form of a base salary and partly in the form of a year-end bonus. Among banks, petroleum, utility, and insurance companies, where year-to-year results tend to be less closely related to management performance, bonus plans are far less common.

Incentive bonus plans take a great variety of forms. Basically, they can be divided into three broad categories, depending on whether the bonuses are

1. Determined by formula
2. Discretionary but based on a formula
3. Purely discretionary

At the top executive level, the second type of plan is the most common. The first type is used most often to compensate district and regional sales managers, store managers, and profit center heads, where annual results and individual performance are closely related. The third type is the least used of the three.

Bonus plans based on a formula use either a permanent formula or one that is determined annually. As the name implies, the permanent formula remains the same year after year unless the plan is revised. It is often used with district sales managers and store managers and has the distinct advantage of providing an incentive to strive to improve results in the future as well as in the current year. On the other hand, continuous formula plans often produce serious problems. Typically these problems arise from the fact that changes in external conditions or internal operating patterns are not reflected in the formula; so it gradually becomes obsolescent. As time goes on, the manager may find that changes over which he has no control have made it either more difficult or substantially easier to achieve the same results as in yesteryear. Or he may find that policy decisions over which he has no control can dramatically improve or worsen the results on which his compensation is based. This, of course, can lead to bad feelings concerning the equity of the plan. Perhaps, more important, a fixed formula can result in assigning personnel on the basis of "what the territory or division will pay," rather than on the needs of the situation and the individual's opportunity for development. When this happens, operations that have been doing poorly tend to get worse and those doing well tend to get better.

To avoid these kinds of problems, in some companies the formula for determining the incentive bonus is subject to review and adjustment each year. Typically, this review is carried out in connection with establishing the annual operating plan and budget. In many plans the annual adjustment takes the form of adjusting a profit, sales, or return on investment objective, which is used as a basis for determining the amount of the bonus. In some plans, the adjustment may be in the percentage or percentage scale used to determine the bonus. Often this approach involves establishing a "target" total compensation figure, assuming that certain results are achieved, deciding how much of that should be paid in the form of salary and how much in bonus, and then calculating the factor likely to generate the desired bonus amount.

While the annual review and adjustment of the formula avoids the major pitfalls of a permanent formula, its weakness lies in the fact that incentive payments are based exclusively on short-term results, possibly at the expense of building for the future.

The most widely used approach to top-level executive bonus plans is to relate the bonus to both overall corporate results (generally using a continuing formula) and individual performance (generally based on a judgmental performance appraisal).

Typically, a corporate incentive bonus fund formula is established with the approval of the directors and shareholders.   A common approach is to stipulate that the total incentive awards granted will not exceed a certain percentage of profits either before or after taxes after deducting a "set aside" based on average capital invested. The percentages depend on: (1) the company's profit and return on investment goals and expectations, (2) the size and number of bonuses management would like to pay for achieving expected results, and (3) the extent to which it is considered desirable for bonus payments to increase or decrease if results are greater or less than expected.

This form of bonus plan has the potential for providing a group incentive, since the amount of money available for distribution depends on overall results achieved by the company.   It also acts as an incentive to improve both immediate and longer term results since (with a fixed formula) the size of the fund will grow as results improve.   Finally, rewards can reflect individual, as well as group, performance. However, such a bonus plan is extremely difficult to administer effectively, particularly if a large number of executives is involved.

In decentralized companies it is customary to divide the fund among subsidiaries or divisions, based on divisional results, before determining individual awards. Even so, the process of tying together recommendations for individual awards based on performance appraisals and adjustments in the amount available for distribution based on company and divisional results is necessarily complex.   Usually a "normal" bonus award is established, based on the executive's salary and position grade. (See Figure 3 for an illustration of "normal" awards.)   This normal award is then adjusted twice: first, to reflect company and divisional results and, second, to reflect individual performance.   Since a number of factors can affect the amount of the bonus, the reasons why a particular bonus is paid are often unclear to the executive receiving it.   This is particularly true when there is reluctance to interpret bonus decisions in terms of individual performance.

The decision of whether to install an incentive bonus plan for executives and, if so, what kind of plan to install should not be made lightly.   On the one hand, a bonus is a more immediate and flexible form of compensation than salary and thus has greater motivational potential.   On the other hand, a bonus plan that is poorly conceived or administered can have a negative motivational impact.

Two questions need to be answered before deciding whether to install a bonus plan:

1. To what extent do operating results reflect the current performance of management?   To what extent are they affected by uncontrollable factors or by actions taken in the past?

2. What decisions have the greatest impact on results?   Who makes these de-

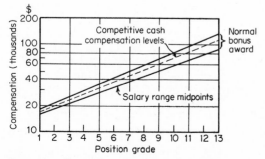

Figure 3.   Illustrative normal bonus awards.

cisions? Do the company's management processes encourage or permit individual decision making and risk taking, or are they largely committee run?

If a bonus plan seems appropriate, careful attention should be paid to what kind of plan would be most effective. Whether the plan should be of the straight formula type or whether it should have discretionary features is mainly a matter of weighing how tough-minded and disciplined top management is likely to be in evaluating and rewarding individual performance. Even in the same industry, the approach that is best for one company might not fit the management climate and style of another.

Beyond these fundamentals, there is a whole host of issues that needs to be considered in designing an incentive bonus plan:

1. Who should be included in the plan? Should the key criterion for determining eligibility be status, organizational level, nature of responsibilities, position grade, salary level, individual performance and potential, or some combination of these factors?

2. What proportion of those eligible should receive bonuses? All? All except those whose performance has been unsatisfactory? Only outstanding performers?

3. What proportion of total compensation should be paid in the form of bonuses? Most people feel that a bonus that amounts to less than 15 percent of salary is hardly worth the bother. Typically, the bonus-to-salary ratio is substantially higher at higher executive levels. For example, a $100,000 executive is likely to receive a bonus in a normal year amounting to 40 to 100 percent of his salary, while it is rare for a $30,000 executive to receive a bonus in excess of 50 percent of his salary (normally it will be in the 20 to 40 percent range). This is not only because higher paid executives can better afford to have a larger proportion of their compensation deferred and "at risk," but more importantly because they typically have greater responsibility for results and, therefore, can logically expect greater participation in the rewards and penalties directly related to the results.

4. How should results be measured for purposes of determining bonuses or an incentive fund? Should only one measure be used or a combination of measures? If profits and invested capital are used, how should they be defined? How will tax and accounting anomalies be handled? Will adjustments be made for changes in uncontrollable conditions? If so, on what basis?

5. What impact will the bonus plan have on salary levels and on salary increase decisions? Will salaries be reduced when it is installed?

6. In what form or forms will bonus payments be made?

7. In what detail will the plan be communicated to employees who are eligible? To those who are not eligible?

SUPPLEMENTARY FORMS OF COMPENSATION

At all employee levels noncash forms of compensation, such as contributions to pension plans, life, medical, and disability insurance, deferred profit sharing and savings plans, have become increasingly significant elements of the total compensation program. In most large companies the cost of these "fringe" benefits amounts to 15 to 25 percent of total salary costs.

At the executive level certain forms of compensation have special interest and significance because of their tax implications. If an executive's cash compensation is more than $50,000, his personal income tax rate is likely to be more than 50 percent, even with the reduction in tax rates in the 1969 Tax Reform Act.

Two main approaches have been used in compensating executives so as to reduce the impact of high personal income tax rates:

1. Stock options or "phantom" stock plans which provide opportunities to accumulate capital and take capital gains at lower tax rates.

2. Individual deferred compensation arrangements which defer compensation until after retirement. (Pension and profit sharing plans, of course, are forms of deferred compensation. However, these plans may not discriminate in favor of executives if company contributions are to qualify as federal income tax deductions.)

With the reduction in personal income tax rates, these two approaches are likely to be somewhat less popular in the future than they have been in the past twenty-five years. This is particularly true of stock options since the tax rate on any capital gains realized as a result of stock option grants will be higher than was previously the case. Still, these forms of compensation will have significant advantages for some executives, depending on their personal financial needs and circumstances.

Increasingly, companies are adopting plans that provide some opportunity for individual choice both in the form and timing of compensation. For example, some bonus plans offer the bonus recipient the option of choosing whether he would like the bonus in cash or in company stock and whether he would prefer to be paid immediately or to have all or part of the payment deferred until after retirement. This flexibility seems particularly appropriate if personal financial planning assistance is made available, enabling the executive to make choices that are most advantageous to him. Obviously, the form of compensation most attractive to a forty-five-year-old executive with three children in college is likely to be quite different from the form that will be most attractive to a sixty-year-old executive whose children are self-supporting.

Beyond the tax implications, stock bonuses and options have special significance in some companies because they are used to build a sense of proprietary interest into the thinking of the top management team. This is particularly relevant when the company operates in an industry that is in a state of flux, where simply "doing more of the same" will not enable the company to grow and prosper, and where a strong motivation to effect change is important to serve the best interests of the shareowners. Unfortunately, many stock option plans have simply enabled some executives to make a quick profit while other plans have led to disappointment when share values declined due to general stock market conditions. Even so, stock ownership can be and has been a powerful long-term motivating force in a considerable number of companies.

Both deferred compensation arrangements and stock options or stock grants often have restrictions that are intended to serve as "holding devices" since the executive forfeits compensation he would otherwise receive if he leaves the company before the restriction lapses. The value of these holding devices is a moot question. One school of thought holds that such devices are more likely to create resentment than to build loyalty and positive motivation.

Unfortunately, very little research has been conducted among higher level executives to probe deeply into the relationship between various forms and methods of compensation and motivation. Clearly, compensation is only part of a larger pattern of factors that influence executive behavior. By itself, its influence may not be significant. But the approach taken to executive compensation also influences other practices and conditions that make up the executive environment. Therefore, executive compensation demands careful thought and attention if it is to reinforce, and not detract from, management's efforts to maintain the kind of leadership that is essential for an organization's continued growth and vitality.

BIBLIOGRAPHY

Compensating Executive Worth, American Management Association, New York, 1968.
Crystal, Graef S.: *Financial Motivation for Executives,* American Management Association, New York, 1970.

Kraus, David: "Ahead in Executive Pay—More Cash, Fewer Options," *Commerce,* June 1970.

Lewellen, Wilbur G.: *Executive Compensation in Large Industrial Corporations,* National Bureau of Economic Research, 1968.

Patton, Arch: *Men, Money, and Motivation,* McGraw-Hill Book Company, Inc., 1961.

Smyth, Richard C.: *Financial Incentives for Management,* McGraw-Hill Book Company, Inc., 1960.

Winstanley, N. B.: "Management 'Incentive' Bonus Plan Realities," *The Conference Board Record,* January 1970.

chapter 33

Establishing the Wage and Salary Structure

JAMES F. SHERIDAN *Director of Compensation & Benefits, Bristol-Myers Products, New York, New York*

After establishing the internal relationship between jobs through evaluation, the next step in developing a wage and salary program is to translate these point values into monetary values. This can be done in three steps: establishing pay grades, or levels, pricing them, and setting up pay ranges.

ESTABLISHING PAY GRADES

A pay grade is simply grouping jobs of approximately equal difficulty as determined by job evaluation. There are no set rules as to the number of grades in any job structure. However, keep in mind these basic points:

1. Certain jobs should be grouped because of their relationships or similarities in evaluation.

2. Some jobs should be recognized as of higher or lower value than others to reflect the progression of skill and experience levels.

3. A promotional hierarchy should exist to allow for a reasonable program of worker advancement and growth.

First, list the jobs from low to high, according to their evaluated points. Examine this list carefully to determine natural cutoff points and groupings as mentioned above. Common practice is to establish grades of equal width or point spread. Random widths are difficult to justify. Be flexible at this time, for it may be necessary to go back and examine the evaluation and make some changes. Plotting the jobs on a chart may be of assistance in determining the grades. Whether the data represent hourly or salaried jobs, a flat trend line would permit wide point spreads, and a steep line would call for narrow point differences. Large numbers of employees are affected by manipulation of pay grades; therefore great care and fairness must be exercised. Time spent here will minimize complaints later.

PRICING THE PAY GRADES

There are many factors that affect company pay policies, and certainly the most important one to consider is what competing companies pay their workers. This can best be determined by a wage survey. To accomplish this, decisions must be made on four basic questions: what companies should participate, what jobs should be included, what information should be obtained, and how should the survey be conducted?

Selection of the companies is the most critical part of the survey, for depending on whom you compare yourself with, you can prove or disprove any conclusion you want. High-paying industry leaders could make your rates appear low, and by the same token the opposite could also be true. In selecting the companies, these factors are important:

1. Is the company a competitor?
2. Does the company have a formal wage and salary program? If not, their rates may be a meaningless hodgepodge and you may be forced to discard them in the analysis stage.
3. Is the company large enough to make the survey meaningful, and are their operations similar, so that comparable jobs will exist?
4. Is the company in the same labor market, do you draw employees from the same area, and have you perhaps lost employees to this company in the past?

If carefully selected, ten to fifteen companies should be sufficient.

Next, select the key or bench-mark jobs, one or more from each pay grade. A key job is one in which the duties are clearly identified, circumscribed, and defined. It is desirable also that its content be reasonably stable, for upon it you will base your wage structure. The key jobs selected should be representative of all levels of job worth covered by the system, from the lowest to the highest, and they should also be found in other firms in the community. Prepare descriptions that differ from those used in the company. Make them shorter, and avoid terminology peculiar to the company or industry as much as possible. Explanations of requirements or qualifications, such as high school graduate, no experience, or completion of full apprenticeship, are helpful in establishing comparability. Standard practice is to use a separate sheet for each job, as shown in Figure 1. This could easily be condensed by listing all wage data on one sheet and job descriptions on separate sheets.

Other information which should be included is the number of employees, changes in the structure made recently, method of progression from minimum to maximum, wage incentives, if any, and some idea of the indirect pay (or fringe benefits) provided, indicating the cost to the employee.

The best means of collecting the data is by the interview method. A thorough, trained interviewer can do a great deal to increase the accuracy and applicability of the data to be collected. He can also ask pertinent questions about job content to the point where he is satisfied that comparability exists. The disadvantage is the time and cost involved.

The other basic method is the questionnaire. The advantage of this method is that data can be collected from a large number of companies at a comparatively low cost. The disadvantage is that the accuracy and applicability of the reported data depend on the degree of interest and care exercised by the company representative

Figure 1.   Bench mark-position, salary survey.

CONSOLE OPERATOR

FUNCTION: Sets up, operates, and controls electronic data-processing equipment; also prepares and sets up peripheral equipment with paper, card, tape, or disk files.   Operates console typewriter and takes necessary corrective action.

QUALIFICATIONS: High school education or equivalent knowledge plus special training in the operations of EDP equipment.   One to two years applicable experience.

REMARKS: Note any significant differences in qualifications or duties.

YOUR DATA

STRUCTURAL RANGE Min. _____ Max. _____

PROBABLE STARTING RATE OR RANGE_____

No. of employees									
$ per week									
No. of employees									
$ per week									

completing the questionnaire.   Even the most diligent are subject to misunderstandings and fail to report the information properly.   Be prepared for follow-up telephone calls as the deadline approaches.

When good comparability is established by visiting each company surveyed, follow-up mail surveys will suffice.   Record the participating company's job titles to save time in future surveys.

Each participating company should receive a coded summary of the survey, including a digest of the findings.   The name of the companies involved should be included, together with the name of the person supplying the data.   Each participant should be able to identify his data and those of the company conducting the survey.   Participants in the survey are then free to call and exchange codes if they wish (see Figure 2).

The next step in establishing a pay structure is to determine statistically the best relationship between evaluation points and grades, and the survey rates of pay. Use graph paper, and place evaluation points on the y axis from low to high and range of pay on the x axis.   Then plot the survey data or the average rate for each

Figure 2.   Coded summary, salary survey.

CONSOLE OPERATOR

Company Code	Number of employees	Average paid rate, weeks	Structural ranges	
			Minimum	Maximum
F	7	156	138	204
K	3	152	135	185
Q	6	150	137	168
R	5	148	116	160
C	11	145	129	190
A	4	137	100	160
P	9	136	125	165
L	3	132	102	133
E	4	132	124	154
I	4	119	98	159
Mean. . .		142	120	167

grade according to the evaluation points of the key jobs. Establish a trend line for these data in either of two ways:

Inspection.   Draw the line freehand, using a ruler or string as a guide

Least-squares or Second-degree Curve.   These techniques may best indicate the trend of the data. The formulas can be found in any statistics text. If you have access to a desk computer, it is possible to determine the trend line in a few minutes.

NOTE: Be sure the trend line is drawn correctly and that it reflects the data (see Figure 3).

The location of the midpoint depends on the method of movement within a grade. If an employee is allowed to move through the range, receiving automatic increases to the maximum, as in most hourly jobs, the range must be narrow. If the upper half of the range is reserved for superior employees, the spread should be greater.

Next, repeat this procedure by preparing another scatter chart reflecting the rates paid to company employees and compare this with the survey line.

At this time we come to one of the basic issues of a formal program. Where does the company want to be in relation to the area or community average? As mentioned earlier, many factors influence this decision, chief among these being competitive conditions and, certainly, ability to pay. Most companies want to be equal to the area, and some want to be 2 to 5 percent above.

Based on this policy decision, adjust the company trend line and determine the costs involved in implementing these changes. Use caution in making too great a change at one time. You may find it best to bring your rates in line over a six- to twelve-month period.

Once the trend line is fixed, ranges can then be established.

ESTABLISHING PAY RANGES

The minimum of a grade should reflect the amount necessary to hire a person with minimum qualifications. The average minimum for each grade from the wage survey will be helpful in determining this amount. The midpoint should be a fair rate of pay for average performance and is usually matched up with the company trend line. The maximum is difficult to set, and there are no scientific means of determining where it should be placed. Theoretically, it is the maximum amount of money the company is willing to pay for the performance of a given job. Again, the survey maximum can be used as a guide. If a "follow-the-leader" approach is

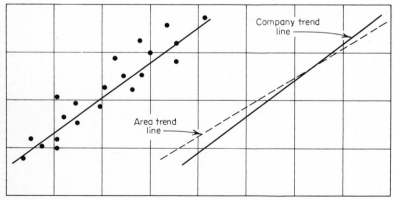

Figure 3.   Evaluation points, wage rate. *(a)* Company trend line.
(b) Comparison of company and area trend lines.

being pursued, and the midpoint or company trend line is equal to the community average, perhaps the company is willing to pay 5 or 10 percent more. However, the line must be drawn somewhere.

The amount above and below this trend line determines the width of the range. The amount from one midpoint or minimum to another is the spread between grades, and should remain constant. The following guidelines will help.

Type of job	Width of range percent, min to max	Spread between grades percent, min or midpoint
Hourly	10–20	5–7
Salaried nonexempt	15–35	7–10
Exempt	35–50	8–15

Common practice at this point is to have two separate structures, one for hourly and the other for salaried, exempt and nonexempt (see Figure 4).

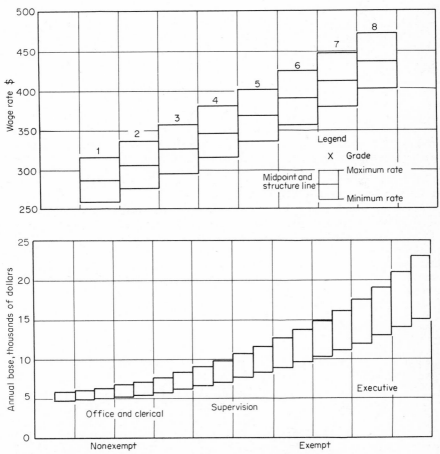

Figure 4. Evaluation points. (a) Hourly structure. (b) Salary structure.

ASSIGNING EMPLOYEES TO THE STRUCTURE

The rates of pay for most employees will fall within the range established for their grade; however, some will fall below the range minimum. Little question exists as to the appropriate action to be followed in these cases. They must be brought to the minimum of the range either immediately or in one or two steps. Two would be preferable if the person is more than 8 to 10 percent below minimum.

The other extreme is the employee whose rate is above the maximum, a red circle rate. Opinion varies here because of the morale problem involved. The most common solutions are the following: (1) freeze the rate until structure changes or general increases bring it into line; (2) transfer or promote the employee to a job that will carry his rate; (3) eliminate the differential immediately or over a period of time. Overpayment is not the fault of the employee, and any solution to this problem that involves a reduction in pay will surely appear unfair to the incumbent and to the entire work force.

MOVING EMPLOYEES THROUGH THE RANGES

Ranges provide a means whereby a company can recognize differences in performance, ability, and seniority of individual employees occupying positions in the same level. This requires a system for assigning a rate to each person and for moving an employee from the starting rate to the maximum.

Automatic Progression

Some companies divide their structure into a series of steps in each range. This is common where differences in job performance are not great enough to justify a merit approach. Increases are automatic, each six, twelve, eighteen, or twenty-four months from the date of hire. The number of steps will depend on the width of the range. They should enable an employee to realize increased remuneration for service and experience on the job and should permit him to reach the upper limit within a reasonable length of time. One approach is to have the steps relate to other grades, or to "interlock," to provide a smooth transition for promotional opportunity and reduce the number of rates in the structure (see Figure 5).

This automatic-increase policy is justifiably criticized as an inflexible approach to wage and salary administration because it removes the merit approach to pay decisions. The outstanding employee is treated the same as the average, and mediocre performance by the majority is often the end result. Many companies proudly state that they have a merit program when in actual practice supervisors grant fixed increases at regular intervals and really unofficially practice an automatic-increase policy rather than make the evaluative judgments necessary for a merit system.

Figure 5.   Interlocking pay structure.

INTERLOCKING PAY STRUCTURE								
Interval, months	Step	Grade I	Grade II	Grade III	Grade IV	Grade V	Grade VI	Grade VII	Grade VIII
24	7	3.14	3.34	3.56	3.78	4.00	4.22	4.46	4.71
18	6	3.04	3.24	3.45	3.67	3.89	4.12	4.34	4.58
12	5	2.94	3.14	3.34	3.56	3.78	4.00	4.22	4.46
9	4	2.85	3.04	3.24	3.45	3.67	3.89	4.12	4.34
6	3	2.76	2.94	3.14	3.34	3.56	3.78	4.00	4.22
3	2	2.67	2.85	3.04	3.24	3.45	3.67	3.89	4.12
Start...	1	2.58	2.76	2.94	3.14	3.34	3.56	3.78	4.00

Merit Progression

The procedure used by most companies to determine merit increases is a formal "performance review and evaluation program." This review should take place periodically, usually on a semiannual or annual basis, because it assures the employee that he has not been overlooked, and it obviates the need to ask for a raise. The vociferous employee who pushes for an increase is often not the best performer.

There are several kinds of performance review procedures used, from ranking to goal setting, elsewhere in this Handbook. From a compensation standpoint it is important that increases based on performance be consistent throughout the company. Some argue that to impose restrictions in a merit program defeats the basic purpose of the system. This criticism must be weighed against the need to budget and control increases and to prevent some supervisors from awarding a merit increase of only 2 to 3 percent to an exceptional performer. On the other hand, some give increases so large that in a few years the employee is at the maximum and the request for reclassification has been submitted. Merit increases must vary with performance, but should be within limits and should take into account promotional potential and position in the range.

Guidelines should be issued and refined in terms of the specific evaluation program in use. A range of 4 to 12 percent for merit increases should be broad enough to cover most situations.

BIBLIOGRAPHY

Belcher, David W.: *Wage and Salary Administration,* Prentice-Hall, Inc., Englewood Cliffs, N.J., 1962.

Otis, J. L., and Richard H. Leukart: *Job Evaluation,* Prentice-Hall, Inc., Englewood Cliffs, N.J., 1954.

Gibson, R. E.: *Wage and Salaries: A Handbook for Line Managers,* American Management Association, New York, 1966.

chapter 34

Maintaining a Wage and Salary Program

JOHN K. MOYNAHAN   *Consultant, Towers, Perrin, Forster & Crosby, Inc., New York, New York*

The establishment of a corporate wage and salary program is a time-consuming and demanding task which, once completed, can provide the mechanism for accomplishing corporate compensation objectives.   Unless the program is kept current and is maintained properly, its usefulness declines rapidly.   The functions involved in maintaining a wage and salary program are directed toward continued compatibility with those corporate objectives the program is intended to serve.

It is important to recognize that a newly established wage and salary program cannot instantaneously create a totally equitable internal and external compensation pattern, except under the most extraordinary circumstances.   Rather, the achievement of an optimal wage and salary system is an evolutionary process, resulting from a series of planned "fine-tuning" adjustments and periodic updatings.   The principal reasons why wage and salary programs must constantly be reviewed are:

1. If a new wage and salary program is established for an existing group of employees, there probably will be some whose pay cannot immediately be adjusted (either upward or downward) to bring it into line with the demands of external and internal equity.

2. Even the most scientific wage and salary program requires management judgment and subjective interpretation; these skills become sharper as the executive becomes familiar with the program and its administration.

OBJECTIVES

The activities required to maintain a sound wage and salary program on a current basis fall principally into two general categories:

1. Maintaining (or establishing) external equity
2. Maintaining (or establishing) internal equity

Those charged with maintaining the program are responsible for assuring the following:

1. Adherence to overall corporate policy in terms of level of wage and salary payments
2. Reduction of employee turnover due to inadequate compensation levels
3. A compensation environment which is conducive to motivation
4. Adaption of the wage and salary program to changes in corporate organization structure, or to such external factors as labor market conditions, compensation trends in particular industrial and/or professional groups, and requirements of federal and local governments

EXTERNAL EQUITY

The most important factor affecting the ability of a wage and salary program to meet its objectives is the establishment of competitive rates. "Competitive rates" may be defined as pay levels or rates paid by competing employers. Both "people" competitors and "product" competitors must be considered. People competitors include companies who draw from the same general labor pool, such as geographical neighbors, or companies requiring similar technological skills. Product competitors are companies who are involved in the same industry, but who may not be directly competitive for personnel on a continuing basis. At executive levels, product competitors' rates are particularly important, given the high degree of mobility of today's executives. In arriving at a "going rate," the particular job will suggest the appropriate emphasis between people and product competitors. At a lower level job, the competition may be strictly other local employers, in any industry. In highly specialized positions, the employment market may not be entirely local, but may include organizations in the same industry. At top executive levels, both people and product competitors should always be included.

A corporate compensation philosophy regarding the level of competitive rates should be established. For example, if it is corporate policy to pay "average" wage rates within the geographical area, then the company's competitive wage rates should cluster about the 50th percentile when compared with rates paid by competing companies.

In fact, different pay objectives may be established for different employee groups. For example, the company may wish to pay only average compensation to clerical personnel, but outstanding compensation to its engineers. These objectives should reflect management's judgment as to the relative importance of various employee groups in meeting the organization's profit objectives. For example, a stock brokerage firm might perceive its professional research staff as the most vital group, and have a 90th percentile objective for its analysts, while paying intentionally average compensation to its clerical staff.

Naturally, a compensation philosophy cannot be established without looking at company performance. Outstanding compensation is justifiable only if outstanding performance is realized from its recipients. In fact, a company which pays outstanding compensation relative to its competitors without realizing outstanding performance relative to the same competitors could force itself out of business.

Corporate policy regarding wage and salary objectives should be reviewed at least every five years. Reviews may be necessary more often if any of the following circumstances exist:

1. The labor market is exceptionally tight.

2. Significant changes have been made in the nature of the business or its organization structure.

3. The company is experiencing unfavorable employee turnover in critical areas or generally.

4. The company is losing key executives.

Surveys

To keep wage and salary rates competitive, a firm must pay continual attention to the compensation marketplace. Surveys, therefore, are used extensively to obtain the basic compensation data.

For executive compensation practices, two of the most frequently used surveys are the *American Management Association Executive Compensation Series* and *Project 777*, a private survey of key executive positions in a variety of industries. Both of these provide a wealth of useful statistical data for comparing company pay rates with broad-based averages. But both also have disadvantages:

1. They are available only to subscribers.

2. They include a wide variety of companies, with individual subscribers having no control over the number of participants. These inclusions may produce meaningless results for many companies since the final averages include other organizations with whom a subscriber is in no way competitive for executives.

Published clerical, hourly, and salaried employees' surveys are available from such sources as the chambers of commerce and federal agencies. These surveys have the advantage of being comprehensive, broad-based samples of compensation data. Assuming that they show timeliness and careful job matching, they are useful in checking clerical, hourly, and salaried levels.

In considering surveys, the wage and salary administrator should keep in mind three questions:

1. In which surveys should the company continue as a participant?

2. What criteria should be applied in deciding whether to accept an invitation to participate in a new survey?

3. Under what circumstances is it desirable to conduct a survey of your own?

A company should review its participation in surveys every two or three years; otherwise it may be participating in an ever-increasing number of surveys, some of which may be of dubious value. In many cases, the survey results may not justify the staff time consumed. Answers to the following questions are useful when judging whether to participate in a survey:

1. Does the survey include a number of positions which are closely matched by positions in the company?

2. Is the job matching controlled through periodic personal visits?

3. Does the survey deal with positions in the local or regional market?

4. Are other participating companies a good representation of people and/or product competitors?

5. Will the reporting of the data be timely enough to be useful?

6. Will the data, in fact, be used in evaluating the competitiveness of pay rates, or is it really unnecessary?

Periodically, a company will be asked to participate in new salary surveys. These surveys may be conducted by competitor companies, associations, or consultants. Participation in a well-designed and controlled survey can often provide a considerable amount of useful information at very little expense. Therefore, invitations to participate should be reviewed carefully. Assuming that the survey is conducted by a reputable organization and that the confidential nature of the data will be observed, the same questions may be applied as those used to determine whether to continue participation in existing surveys.

At times, the wage and salary administrator may believe that the presently available survey data are not sufficient, and may decide to conduct his own wage and salary survey. However, conducting a salary survey can be an expensive and often unrewarding process—even for a small number of jobs. In deciding whether to conduct a private survey, he should consider:

1. What companies should be involved and are they likely to accept the invitation? Some of the following factors might affect their decision whether or not to participate:

   a. Is it a common practice within the industry to exchange compensation information directly with competitors, or are such exchanges normally made through a third party?

   b. Are the wage and salary administrators promising output which will be interesting and useful to survey participants?

   c. Is the number of jobs being surveyed small enough, say twenty-five to thirty or less, so that companies will not find it too time consuming to participate?

2. Is the present staff adequate and qualified to conduct the survey? In determining this, two questions must be resolved:

   a. Does the staff have sufficient expertise to control job matching and thus assure the validity of the data?

   b. Does the staff have the time to make personal visits to the participating companies? As a rule of thumb, allowing one day for each participating company is probably reasonable.

3. Does the staff have the time and expertise to prepare a comprehensive questionnaire, contact prospective survey companies, follow up on nonrespondents, and prepare a useful detailed report to survey participants? (And do they have the time to do all this while still fulfilling their normal responsibilities?)

In many cases, the answer to one or more of the questions is no. However, the survey is still essential. If so, it may be desirable to have an outside firm conduct the survey. The use of an outside firm can help gain participation from companies who may be reluctant to exchange compensation data with direct competitors. They may, however, be willing to supply the data on a confidential basis to an outsider who would not divulge specific compensation data of individual companies. The use of an outside consultant also has disadvantages: first, because of possibly greater expense and, second, because of the missed opportunity to develop skills of the wage and salary staff who ultimately will have to work with the output of the survey.

In summary, a company's policy toward wage and salary surveys should be determined by the quality of the survey information it receives or wants rather than by the number of surveys in which it can participate. To assure the success of this policy, survey practices should be scrutinized every two or three years.

Inflation and Productivity

While surveys help a firm to keep track of prevailing rates for particular positions, they are also useful in measuring the inevitable escalation of general wage rates. Salary ranges are normally established in the expectation of continued inflation and increases in productivity. Therefore the minimums and maximums of the salary ranges should be reviewed periodically.

Both productivity increases and inflation influence the amount of escalation which is appropriate; the amount of real (or productivity-related) increase in the wage structure equals the escalation factor less inflation. In the late 1950s and early 1960s, when inflation averaged 1 to 1½ percent per year, wage rates typically increased about 3 to 3½ percent per year, thus indicating some real dollar growth for the employee. As the rate of inflation increases, the rate of salary escalation also tends to increase, but not necessarily as fast. For example, if inflation was 3 percent per year, average salary increases might be 4½ percent. In rapid inflation such as 6 percent, the entire escalation in a wage structure generally just about keeps up with inflation.

Range Escalation

Range escalation involves an upward adjustment of salary grade minimums, maximums, and intermediate point dollar amounts by the use of some predetermined factor or set of factors. Unless the rate of inflation in the American economy becomes considerably more rapid, an annual review of salary ranges is sufficient. In selecting such factors, the following information should be taken into account:

1. Survey results, particularly for those positions which were identified as bench marks in setting the structure originally
2. Increases in the cost of living
3. Negotiated increases in pertinent union settlements
4. A structure should remain competitive for at least a year (In this connection, escalation factors selected could be those permitting competitiveness six to nine months from the effective date, to allow for further assumed increases in general wage rates.)

Annual consideration should be given to range escalation, to assure continued anchoring of the wage and salary structure to the marketplace. A review of the specific pay rates incorporated in the structure should always be accompanied by a review of the method in which the structure is being used. Specifically, this should include a review of merit policies and current positioning in the ranges (both are described in more detail later in this chapter under Maintaining Internal Equity).

Types of Increases

It is virtually axiomatic in modern personnel administration that wage and salary rates always go up, never go down, and only temporarily stay the same. Therefore, the questions facing the wage and salary administrator are:

1. What types of increases are appropriate (general increases, merit increases, promotional increases)?
2. How often should the increases be given?
3. How large should the increases be?

Each of the questions should be answered separately for each category of personnel: executive, professional, clerical, and hourly. While the questions should be asked and answered separately, the answers, particularly in today's environment, may often be the same. For example, the disadvantages associated with general across-the-board increases, while usually justified on the basis of counteracting increases in the cost of living, are similar for all employee groups:

1. No distinction is made between outstanding and poor performance. In fact, the company is sometimes put in the embarrassing position of giving a pay increase to someone about to terminate, or to be terminated.
2. Any inequities in present internal relationships will be magnified.
3. They undermine the motivational advantages of a wage and salary system.

When a wage and salary system is devised, specific guidelines should be developed to govern policies on merit and promotional increases. These policies should dictate both the frequency and the amounts of increases permitted. Examples of such a policy might include:

1. Merit increases may be granted no oftener than every twelve months, and shall not exceed 10 percent of the individual's current pay rate.

2. Promotional increases may be granted at any time and may not exceed the greater of 15 percent of the individual's current rate, or an increase sufficient to bring his pay to the minimum of the range in which his new job is placed.

In conducting merit and promotional increase policy reviews, the following questions should be raised:

1. If, for example, 10 percent is the maximum merit increase, is this enough to enable the company's compensation package to remain competitive?

2. Are employees being considered for increases frequently enough to enable the company to remain competitive in an inflationary compensation market?

The frequency with which merit and promotional increase policies (as distinguished from actual increases themselves) should be reviewed probably decreases as the value of the job decreases. For example, executive merit and promotional policies should be reviewed every one to two years. For lower level employees, every three to five years is probably sufficient. Individual organization characteristics are more important in determining the frequency of merit and promotional policy reviews than any general guidelines. Management judgment should always prevail in this area. For example, if the company is not maintaining its desired competitive compensation posture, more frequent reviews may be appropriate.

Red Circle Rates

When a wage and salary program is established, there inevitably will be individuals whose current rates of pay do not conveniently conform to the ranges and guidelines established. For example, an incumbent in a position might be paid above the maximum of the range established for his salary grade. Alternatively, the upgrading of a position could result in the incumbent's pay rate being so far below the minimum of the range that it could not be increased to the minimum without violating the constraints of maximum merit increases. The existence of red circle rates represents a violation of the objectives of internal and external equity. Therefore, it is advisable to eliminate them as quickly as possible, consistent with the following guidelines:

1. The salary of an incumbent who is paid above the maximum of his range should generally not be reduced. However, he should be informed that his rate will not be increased until one of the following occurs:
   a. His position is upgraded.
   b. His range is escalated sufficiently to place his present pay rate back within the range.

2. Individuals whose pay rates are below the minimum of the range should be brought up to the minimum as quickly as possible. In theory, the correction process should take place quickly at all levels of the structure. In practice, however, the rate at which the individual is increased to his range minimum will be heavily influenced by the pressures of the external compensation marketplace. In the case of an executive showing satisfactory performance, his pay should be increased to at least the minimum of his range in no more than two steps, preferably within one year. Failure to do so will jeopardize the company's ability to hold the executive against outside offers. In the case of lower level personnel, the same principles apply. In all cases, it should be communicated to the individual that the increase exceeds the normal limits of company policy and that this magnitude should not be expected in the future. In other words, he should be told that an exception is being made in his case.

MAINTAINING INTERNAL EQUITY

While wage and salary programs should enable the employer to pay rates which produce the desired relationship with the external market, it is also vital that the proper internal pay relationships be maintained. Periodic reviews and necessary adjustments can be accomplished through the following:

1. Job evaluations
2. Position descriptions
3. Salary structure
4. Relation of actual pay rates to the structure

Review of Job Evaluations

If a formal system of job evaluation was used for the initial positioning of jobs in salary grades, the initial factor values or rankings should be examined periodically. For executive jobs, this review should be performed biannually. For clerical and hourly employees, every three to five years is probably sufficient unless organizational changes dictate more frequent reviews.

Preparatory to the review of the actual factors, position descriptions should be carefully updated. A system should be established for continual review and updating of position descriptions. It is especially vital that this process be reviewed, preferably as the result of individual discussions and agreement with incumbents just prior to the reassessment of the factor values assigned.

Systems of job evaluation and position slotting can become obsolete over a period of time. The system itself should be reviewed every five years, preferably by impartial outsiders, or by a committee of knowledgeable company executives who are detached from the day-to-day use of the position evaluations and the salary administration process.

Two corollary aspects of position evaluations should evolve as a normal outgrowth of this review process:

1. When a review of a position's responsibility suggests that a change in classification should be made, it is necessary to reevaluate all positions whose value may tend to move in tandem with the position in question. Additionally, it is necessary to review two other types of positions as well:
   a. Positions which incumbents perceive to be "peer" positions to those being upgraded.
   b. Positions which are immediately above the one being upgraded, particularly if there is a superior-subordinate relationship involved; this is to assure that compression problems do not occur.
2. The Fair Labor Standards Act sets forth criteria for determining exemptions from the overtime provisions of the Federal Wage and Hour Act. Positions meeting the tests of executive, supervisory, or administrative activity do not require the payment of overtime. Exempt positions should be verified at least every two years. Reviews should be conducted more frequently if marginally exempt positions are filled by individuals who are working significant amounts of overtime and are being paid less than one and one-half times the base hourly rate.

Review of Structure

The internal mathematical relationships of the salary structure (as distinguished from the dollar values of the minimum and maximum paid to the various grades) should also be reviewed, at least every three years. The purpose of the review is to assure that the program's structural characteristics do not inhibit the company's ability to pay competitive compensation rates. This review should include the width of ranges and midpoint differentials.

An illustration of the need to coordinate the range escalation process and the structural characteristics reviews is the case of one major company which, over a period of years, increased its salary ranges by 5 percent each year. However, this company also had a policy stating that merit increases in excess of 10 percent were considered exceptions, available under only the most unusual circumstances for outstanding performance. Because its salary ranges had a width of 50 percent, this combination of policies evolved into a situation where an above-average performer could mathematically progress from the minimum to the maximum of his salary grade in about thirty-three years.

One test that can be applied annually, particularly in an inflationary environment, involves examining the positioning of actual pay rates within the range. The distribution of actual pay rates within each quartile of each range should be observed; in an inflationary environment, it is not unusual for a majority of the rates to be in the lower half of the range; however, this situation could be a warning that the individual pay increases are not keeping pace with the range escalation. Thus, the company's actual pay rates can become less competitive even though the structure itself is properly updated.

An additional test can be applied by correlating range positioning with length of service. Theoretically, there should be a high correlation between performance and relative positioning in the range, with length of service being no more than an intervening variable. While there is normally some positive correlation between length of service and positioning in the range, this correlation is similar to the one observed between college grades and success in business: positive but statistically not very significant. Examination of the correlation between length of service and positioning in the range can reveal two possible danger signals:

1. If there is a near perfect correlation between length of service and positioning in the range, this is an indication that longevity, rather than performance, is being used to determine amounts of pay increases.

2. Occasionally, the reverse is true. Shorter service employees can be positioned higher in the range than longer service employees. In such a situation, the company may be meeting external competition when forced to hire from the outside, but failing to adhere to its stated policy when reviewing pay rates of present staff members.

Use of Incentives

Executive and salaried incentive compensation plans are complete subjects in themselves and are covered in Chapter 32. However, just a note should be included here on incentives for lower level employees. Any piecework or other incentives included in a wage and salary program should be reevaluated as often as the salary structure itself. All incentives tend to become obsolete, and, increasingly, what is an incentive today becomes routine tomorrow. If no real structural changes are made in the salary administration program over a five-year period, original incentives likely will have lost their incentive value. They, therefore, ought to be critically reviewed, probably modified, and possibly replaced.

Responsibilities

Executive compensation policy decisions are typically made by a committee of corporate officers. For top executive compensation, or for changes in programs requiring significant expenditures of funds or company stock, the committee ordinarily submits recommendations to the chief executive officer, who in turn submits them for review by a compensation committee comprised of outside directors. Recommendations are then acted upon by this outside committee, subject to the approval of the board and/or stockholders. A salary committee of corporate officers typically reviews and approves pay policy questions affecting middle management levels and those lower down, based on recommendations from the staff personnel function.

Within the personnel function, specific (although not necessarily different) individuals should be charged with the following aspects of maintaining the wage and salary program:

1. Conducting annual or other periodic reviews of
   a. Job evaluations
   b. Position descriptions
   c. Positioning of pay rates in ranges
2. Formulating overall company compensation policy
3. Approving exceptions to policy
4. Internal communication of policy
5. Surveys
6. Record keeping
7. Assuring consistent understanding of corporate policy by supervisors making salary recommendations
8. Reviewing such recommendations to assure consistent application of the policy

Communication

The question of how much information to communicate on wages and salaries is a perplexing one. In lower level jobs, of course, pay rates are known as a result of publicized union settlements. For the majority of salaried employees in industrial organizations, however, salary information has customarily been treated with the utmost secrecy. In establishing the wage and salary program, decisions of course will have been made as to what salary information to communicate, and to whom.

In the communication of information on salaries, one extreme is to disclose all salaries to everyone. Such an approach certainly enables management to document its performance evaluations, and let the superior performer know that he is recognized. It can be argued that even for the poorer performer the knowledge will not be harmful, since the unknown is often perceived as being more distasteful than the actual facts. However, given prevailing attitudes toward the confidential nature of salaries, it is probably inadvisable for any company to go as far as to communicate the actual salaries to all employees.

Between the extremes of total secrecy and total disclosure, there are several intermediate possibilities which could be advantageous, particularly to a company which is confident that its structure is sound and that its rates are competitive:

1. Inform the employee of the minimum and maximum of his own range. This information illustrates the growth potential available. It also requires that the company accomplish and maintain range positioning which is justifiable on the basis of performance.

2. Inform employees of the maximums and minimums of all ranges, and the ranges in which individual jobs are positioned. This information can resolve not only continued competitive placement in the range, but also natural, defensible slotting of jobs in ranges.

If a company is proud of its salary system and pay rates, some advantage can be gained from partial communication. Some companies have communicated competitor information to certain groups of employees, e.g., engineers. Periodic reports on the relationship of company salaries to those of its competitors were made. Questions concerning the company's salary administration program were encouraged. The company's attitude was that if the questions could not be answered satisfactorily, the system probably should be altered. Thus, the communication of certain salary information was viewed not only as a motivator, but also as a source of ideas for possible improvement in the system.

Any communication, of course, requires that the company has a defensible position. If the wage and salary system is out of date, or if pay rates are low relative to competition, the company is well advised to maintain as much secrecy as possible.

CONCLUSION

The most finely constructed wage and salary administration program produces at best momentary competitiveness. More likely, some inequities exist from the day the program is adopted, and will become magnified quickly in the absence of proper maintenance. Keeping a wage and salary administration program equitable and up to date requires simultaneous development of administrative skills, exercise of judgment, resolution of inequities, and adherence to original objectives in a dynamic and usually inflationary wage and salary environment.

BIBLIOGRAPHY

Belcher, D. H.: *Wage and Salary Administration,* Prentice-Hall, Inc., Englewood Cliffs, N.J., 1962.

Brennan, Charles W.: *Wage Administration; Plans, Practices and Principles,* Richard D. Irwin, Inc., Homewood, Ill., 1959.

Crystal, G. S.: *Financial Motivation for Executives,* American Management Association, New York, 1970.

Dooher, J. Joseph, and Vivienne Marquis (ed.): *The AMA Handbook of Wage and Salary Administration,* American Management Association, New York, 1950.

Lovejoy, Lawrence C.: *Wage and Salary Administration,* The Ronald Press Company, New York, 1959.

Part 7

Employee Benefits

chapter 35

The Scope
of Employee Benefits

HARRISON GIVENS, JR.   *Second Vice President, The Equitable Life Assurance Society of the United States, New York, New York*

Let us begin by defining an employee benefit program as the collection of private employer-sponsored plans that provide protection on a mass basis against the financial requirements that usually accompany

Retirement
Death
Disability
Medical care

We thereby exclude all governmental programs, whether at the federal level, e.g., social security, or at the state level, e.g., workmen's compensation, and focus on the areas in which employers and employees have the freedom to select their goals and the benefit plans that will best achieve those goals.

Notice also that by dealing with mass plans we mean to exclude consideration of individually tailored benefits for selected, highly compensated personnel, known by various names such as deferred compensation, split dollar plans, stock options.

Further, by dealing with "mass" plans, we are implicitly assuming that the employer has a sufficiently large number of employees that he can no longer deal individually with each employee but must provide employee benefits more or less uniformly for all employees.

Employee benefits are commonplace today, and it is the rare employer that does not have some benefit plan for each of the major financial contingencies under discussion. In the aggregate, employee benefit programs accumulate and disburse enormous sums, and are highly significant to the investment and financial community. They are increasingly the subject of major legislative studies and proposals at the federal and state levels. They are discussed here, however, because they are, or potentially are, important and useful instruments of a company's personnel and social policy.

Benefit programs are generally expensive. When well conceived, they are an important means toward specific employer objectives. These objectives should be explicit, they should be reasoned, they should be consistent with other major company objectives, and they should be understood by operating management. If such guidance and direction exist, the benefit program is not fixed and arbitrary, but changing and evolving as circumstances change, while always retaining its basic objectives. Those responsible for employee benefit programs can then assure a timely flow of pertinent data to top management on present program operations; they can evaluate new developments in this complex and expanding field; and they can initiate recommendations for changes that will maintain the objectives of the program.

Because the employee benefits field has grown rapidly in recent years, stimulated powerfully by numerous complex and often conflicting forces, many employers have not reached a clear-cut statement of the reasons and objectives for their own programs. Nevertheless such a philosophy may well exist. Present benefit programs reflect certain policies and, probably, certain objectives. The missing link may be only a clear-cut top-level policy statement that will enable others responsible for benefit management to appraise and revise the program, or its various parts, when necessary.

This chapter is a guide to identifying the various company objectives and viewpoints that an employee benefit program can reasonably hope to serve. Much of the guide is in the form of questions. There are no right or wrong answers to the questions. Companies differ widely in their attitudes toward the various subjects. Similarly, executives within a company will view certain questions differently. This chapter aims to help develop a consensus as to what the benefit objectives should be.

It is important to understand that the objectives may change from time to time, as the company's circumstances change. Such a change does not, however, make the objectives for a given period any less valid for that period.

The following topics are discussed:
1. General attitudes
   a. Single or multiple programs
   b. Objectives for benefit levels
   c. Allocation of responsibilities
   d. Financing of benefit plans
2. Attitudes toward sharing in company success
3. Attitudes toward union employees
4. Attitudes toward employees acquired through merger or acquisition
5. General design considerations
   a. Averages
   b. Duplications
   c. Measuring adequacy

GENERAL ATTITUDES

Single or Multiple Programs

What differences in treatment, if any, are appropriate for different groups of employees? For example, should office employees be treated differently from production employees?

Should organized employees be treated differently from those who are not organized?

How might the answer to the above vary because of hazard area (old age, death, disability, medical care)?

What are the reasons for any differences?

Examples.   Some alternatives are to have

1. All employees of the company in one program
2. All executive personnel of the company in one program, and all office and production employees in another program
3. All executive employees of the company in one program, office employees in another program, and production workers in still another program
4. All nonunion employees in one program and all union employees, either presently or in the future, in a separate program

Other combinations or alternatives will readily come to mind.

Considerations.   The principal considerations for most companies are as follows:

Advantages of a single plan:

1. Simpler administration
2. Simple and more effective communications
3. Fewer tax and governmental troubles
4. Possible long-range personnel advantage through treating everyone similarly from the standpoint of benefits
5. Absence of discrimination
6. No complication or impediment to the transfer of employees from one payroll group to another

Advantages of separate plans:

1. The company can make changes affecting certain groups of employees independently of other groups.
2. Each plan can be separately considered, providing greater adjustability to the needs and desires of different groups.
3. Each plan permits different emphasis in communication.

Disadvantages of separate plans: ·

1. There is the risk that separate group consideration may eventually result in overall escalation, through a "whipsaw" effect.
2. Complications of administrative, tax, and financing mechanics may result.
3. Transfers between groups are more difficult.
4. Personnel problems may arise because all employees are not treated alike.

Objectives for Benefit Levels

1. What general principles should guide the determination of your company's benefit levels?

Doing what other companies are doing (in the area? in the same industry?)

Replacing some proportion of income lost (how much is needed?)

Meeting minimum employee needs (how measured?)

To what extent might these attitudes vary by hazard area (i.e., old age, disability, death)?

2. To what extent should employees participate in the determination of benefit amounts, the form of payment, or the time of payment? How might the attitude vary by group?

Allocation of Responsibilities

To what extent is employee security the responsibility of the company? The individual employee? The government?

What statement seems most appropriate?

1. The individual has ultimate responsibility for his own security. The company's job is to use its knowledge and group buying power to make available the best "buys" as a means to help the employee help himself.

2. Between the company and the government, resources should be provided that give only basic or minimum security to the employee. His individual role is to supplement this security to the extent he wants.

3. The company believes it should provide all, or nearly all, of the common benefit needs of individual employees and their dependents.

4. The company does not willingly accept any responsibility beyond paying compensation for work performed, but it provides what benefits it must to stay competitive.

5. The company is willing to provide basic benefit levels, including government-sponsored programs, as the price it must pay to maintain an effective work force. Any additional benefits provided represent a general employee desire to expend a certain portion of total compensation.

Financing of Benefit Plans

1. In considering its total compensation, what does the company attempt?
   To be a leader
   To be up among the leaders
   To be competitive with industry and area practice
   To be as independent as possible, substantially ignoring what others do

2. What is the company's attitude toward financing benefit plans?
   The company should pay as little as possible.
   The employees and the company should share costs on some predetermined basis.
   The company should pay a specific dollar amount or percentage of pay, the employee paying the balance.
   The company should pay for basic or minimal levels of protection; the employee should have the opportunity to supplement.
   The company should pay a larger proportion or all costs.

3. The principal considerations for most companies are as follows:

Advantages of noncontributory plans:

a. Company dollars (tax deductible) provide larger benefits than the same amount of employee dollars (not tax deductible).

b. Administration is simplified.

c. There is a greater degree of flexibility and variation in establishing benefit levels, in administration, and in financing.

d. The company may obtain substantial employee relations value compared with the amount that could be recovered through employee contributions.

Advantages of contributory plans:

a. Employees may place more value on the plan.

b. Employees ought to provide for their dependents and for their own retirement income.

c. Larger benefits are available.

Disadvantages of contributory plans:

a. Practical considerations limit the amount of such contributions and the ratio of company-employee contributions.

b. The company may ultimately pay the entire cost, at higher cost, if wages are increased to offset employee contributions.

c. If the plan is mandatory, employees may be resentful if contributions are substantial.

d. If the plan is voluntary, the benefit objectives are still unmet for those who do not participate.

e. Employees contribute from earnings *after* individual income taxes.

f. Employees may have little financial ability to contribute after deductions for federal income tax, social security tax (which will be increasing in the future), state and city taxes, bond drives, union dues, etc.

4. Consideration might be given to the combination of a noncontributory basic plan and a supplementary voluntary contributory plan. Such a combination is often used because it meets basic needs for all and accommodates savings and thrift for those who value a voluntary discretionary participation.

5. Does the attitude toward financing benefit plans vary by group covered, by hazard area?

EXAMPLE   In reference to long-term disability benefits, the protection of future earning power may be more properly the responsibility of the individual employee, particularly one with short service.

ATTITUDES TOWARD SHARING IN COMPANY SUCCESS

Which statements below are appropriate?

1. It is not appropriate for any employee to share in the success of the company other than through normal compensation and job stability.

2. It is not appropriate for the general run of employees to share in the success of the company, but it is suitable for those management employees whose effectiveness makes a direct and significant contribution to company success.

3. Sharing in the success of the company should apply for most employees, thus providing a means of increasing, in relation to the company's performance, the moderate pay scales required by irregular and perhaps uncertain profits.

The primary purpose for sharing of company success should be:

1. To provide incentive compensation now, thereby motivating employees currently and repetitively.

2. To build a long-term accumulation, as a reward for service? A curb on turnover? A substitute or supplement for a retirement plan?

If the sharing of company success is appropriate, which statement best characterizes the company's attitude?

1. All regular employees help create success and have an influence on it by their daily activities. Therefore, all regular employees should share.

2. Certain groups are more responsible than others for creating success. Therefore, such groups should have a larger share.

3. Only certain employees are responsible for creating the company's success. Therefore, only certain employees should share in it. If this is true, which classification or classifications of employees should be included?

To what extent should individuals control the time and manner of receipt of the amounts shared? What limitations, if any, should be applied?

If sharing in company success is considered a reward for outstanding group effort, and if it is considered an advantageous form of pay, what part of that pay should an employee receive upon termination for other than retirement?

1. All of it because . . . .
2. Part of it because . . . .

If a sharing program is used as an incentive, the amount to be shared should be geared to profit or some other measurement of success, e.g., cost savings. If the amount is related to profit, it should be geared to:

1. A *fixed* proportion of
   a. All profit
   b. Profit above a minimum level
   c. All profit after certain minimum profit levels are attained
2. A *variable* proportion, increasing with
   a. Dollar profit performance
   b. Performance related to some other variable

If variable amounts are to be shared, should they
Increase proportionately?
Increase in some other way?

ATTITUDES TOWARD UNION EMPLOYEES

Which statement best characterizes the company's attitude with respect to employees who have elected to be represented by a union?

1. All employees have the same status regardless of whether they are unionized.
2. Employees who have elected to negotiate as a group on relationships with the company have decided to be regarded as apart from nonunion employees, and have chosen a particular instrument (the bargaining process) to express their different objectives.
   a. The company has therefore a greater obligation toward nonunion employees, who rely only on the company to do what is fair.
   b. The company has the same degree of obligation for all employees, and is willing to make available to union employees any plan available to nonunion employees, but with due allowance for the compensation value of all such plans.

ATTITUDES TOWARD EMPLOYEES ACQUIRED THROUGH MERGER OR ACQUISITION

The company will strive to have such persons

1. Maintain close identification with the former employer?
2. Become identified with the parent company as quickly as practical?

Does this attitude vary by group covered?
Where benefit plans are related to service, should parent company plans recognize

1. All service with the former employer?
2. No service with the former employer?
3. As much service as necessary to have such employees become eligible for parent company plans?

What differences exist because of various plan provisions, i.e., eligibility to participate, eligibility for vesting purposes? Do these attitudes vary by groups covered?

GENERAL DESIGN CONSIDERATIONS

Averages

Employee benefit programs by our definition are mass plans, designed for employees as a class and with little room for sensitive adjustment to the particular circumstances of the individual employee. They have to be relatively simple and uniform in order to avoid undesirable administrative complexity and expense. But benefit plans generally aim for the common needs of all employees, so uniformity of design does not often seem to present a problem.

Employers have, of course, frequently varied benefit plans between groups of employees, e.g., a salaried plan and an hourly paid plan. Now employers are increasingly interested in some variation within a group of employees, primarily salaried employees. It is more and more often recognized that no one is an "average" employee. The following are some principal areas of variation.

Earnings. Most benefits are keyed to the amount of the employee's income. Should the relationship be uniform?

If a single sum death benefit of twice the annual salary is "right" for the $10,000 employee, is it still right for the $50,000 employee? If not, which should get the higher multiple?

If a 50 percent pension is right for the career employee at the $10,000 level, is it still right for the $50,000 employee? If not, which should get the higher percentage? Is the situation the same for disability income?

Family status. Benefits for medical expenses typically recognize family status—simply by covering the expenses of dependents—and have little or no relationship to earnings. Earnings-based benefits, however, are thought of like salaries, and rarely recognize family status.

Is it sensible to provide the same single sum death benefit whether the employee has a family or is single? Does the answer depend upon the proportion of employees who are single? Who are male?

Should disability income be larger for the family man than the single employee? Is the answer the same for pensions?

Service. Pension and profit sharing benefits are generally heavily weighted for service. Other benefits generally ignore service except as a minimum requirement for eligibility.

Where service is now important, should there be a maximum to the number of years recognized? Which years should be counted? Are all years of service of equal value?

Where service is not now important, should it be? Should the duration of survivor income benefits, for example, reflect the length of the employee's sevice?

Duplications

Internal. Most benefit programs are what they are because of their history. They did not appear suddenly in the current form; they grew. Benefit areas were added at different times. The original scale of benefits, set cautiously, has been expanded several times. As a result, duplications are common. Disability income benefits are the most frequent example:

1. Salary continuance plans
2. Insured short-term disability benefits
3. Long-term disability benefits
4. Disability provisions under group life insurance policies
5. Retirement plan benefits (explicitly for disability, or general early retirement provisions)

Do the several sources properly reflect their separate purposes? Do they duplicate? Do they leave gaps? Are there too many vehicles?

External. Other benefit sources are increasingly important and widespread,
and may duplicate or overlap a company program:

1. Death and disability benefits under social security
2. Death and disability benefits under workmen's compensation
3. Medical expense benefits for the employee as the dependent of a spouse working elsewhere
4. Medical coverage under governmental plans, e.g., workmen's compensation,
Medicare, verteran's benefits

Can the duplication be ignored? Should it be avoided by providing no benefits
at all where there is duplication? By reducing benefits? If benefits are reduced,
should this be done in a broad way, or by individual calculation?

Measuring Adequacy

Years ago, when employee benefits, and their costs, were more modest, no one had
to worry about excessive benefits. But benefit areas have proliferated, and aspirations have risen. Now it is possible to find plans producing payments that are remarkably large in comparison with any visible need. This is a questionable use of
funds available for benefit purposes. But how can one know how much is enough,
or too much?

Single sum payments

Distributions from profit sharing and thrift plans: Are there too many small
accounts? Too many large accounts? Does the plan have the right financial
emphasis in relation to other employee benefits, or are some starved in relationship to others?

Insured death benefits: How far do they go beyond burial needs? Last illness
costs? Is the single sum payment a simple approximation to the need for family support, and payable even if there is no family?

Income payments. When earnings cease because of death, disability, or retirement, what portion should be continued if the employee, or his family, is to maintain
the same standard of living?

What is the effect of a different tax status? The tax status of the income benefit?
Other sources of benefit? Changed expenses?

Does this depend on the particular hazard?

Inflation. Should income benefits be increased to recognize the effect of inflation? If so,

1. How should inflation be measured?
2. Should inflation be recognized only if it is "large enough"? Should there be a
maximum on the escalation?
3. Does this depend on the particular hazard?

Wage levels generally rise somewhat faster than the cost of living. The differential produces gains in the *standard* of living.

1. Should income benefits be increased to recognize this, too?
2. How can it be measured?

CONCLUSION

This chapter identifies the principal considerations common to employee benefit
programs as a whole. There are many additional considerations, treated in the following chapters, that relate to specific hazards. The company that has thought
through an overall benefit philosophy will find it again and again an indispensable

guide to constructive and consistent choices among the alternatives available for particular benefits and to clear employee communications of the resulting benefit program.

BIBLIOGRAPHY

Chamber of Commerce of the United States, Economic Analysis Study Group: *Employee Benefits,* 1967.

Deric, Arthur J. (ed.): *The Total Approach to Employee Benefits,* American Management Association, New York, 1967.

Eilers, Robert D., and Robert M. Crowe, (eds.): *Group Insurance Handbook,* Richard D. Irwin, Inc., Homewood, Ill., 1965.

McGill, Dan M.: *Fundamentals of Private Pensions,* 2d ed., Richard D. Irwin, Inc., Homewood, Ill., 1964.

chapter 36

Holidays, Vacations, Accidents, Sickness, Long-term Disability, and Other Time off the Job

J. E. SHEA *Division Vice President, Industrial Relations, Union Tank Car Company, Chicago, Illinois*

Pay for time not worked cost American industry and business over 39 billion dollars in 1968. This compares to 5.9 billion dollars paid in 1949. The average employee receives approximately $1,719 annually in so-called "fringe" benefits, or about 26.6 percent of the employer's total labor costs. These are substantial costs which should be understood and controlled.

ESTABLISHING A POLICY

The application of a particular benefit to any given industry is really a value judgment. A company must decide why a given benefit should be granted, what is the purpose of the benefit, and if the cost is commensurate with the good derived. What may be a good benefit in one industry, such as an extended vacation plan, may be frowned upon in another industry. Is a day of holiday a better benefit than an extra day of vacation? In making choices between paid time off alternatives, we demonstrate the nature of our system.

Our society is a mixed capitalistic system. Most decisions made by management or bargaining units in the area of paid time off are conditioned, but not necessarily determined, by both federal and state laws. Sick pay, supplemental unemployment benefits, military pay, and other paid time off benefits are all affected by unemployment compensation, social security, workmen's compensation, and military service laws. However, the laws and administrative rulings of the federal government have not set indelible patterns for paid time off such as those established in Sweden or even in Canada.

Laws regarding compensation are not new to the Anglo-American system. As early as 1349 an Ordinance of Laborers was passed in Great Britain fixing wage rates and requiring employees to refrain from seeking employment elsewhere. In 1741, the first strike in this country was reported when the bakers protested the federal government's establishment of a bread price. Each of these laws interfered with the mechanism of a free market economy.

Thus, the Wagner Act, the Walsh Healey Federal Contracts Act, and several of the statutes mentioned in this chapter are not the first to interfere with the wage-price mechanism of a free economy. Part of their intent is to correct inequities arising from structural problems of a mixed economy. Within the legal framework, management, unions, and employees attempt to arrive at the best compensation mix of wages, paid time off, insurance, medical protection, and retirement income that will serve the best interests of all the contributor claimants of a given enterprise. The manner in which certain industries have done this is shown in Figure 1. This chart clearly shows the variance between industries, both in the aggregate and in the arrangement of their compensation plans.

We can now see that the levels of paid time off benefits are largely determined by the nature of the industry, and the personal preferences of the employees of a given firm. These factors all operate within the parameters set by law, out of which emerge the benefits found in an individual firm. The oldest of these benefits is a holiday from work.

Figure 1.   Paid time off expressed as a percent of total compensation for selected industries.

Compensation practices	Mining	Finance, insurance and real estate	Meat packing and processing	Basic steel	Electric and gas utilities	Wholesale groceries	Taxicab
Vacations. . . .	2.7	3.4	3.8	7.2	4.4	3.0	1.7
Holidays.	1.0	2.4	2.1	2.2	2.5	1.9	0.3
Sick leave. . . .	0.3	1.0	0.7	0.4	1.7	0.4	*
Civic and personal leave. .	*	0.2	0.1	0.1	0.3	*	*
Social security.	2.2	2.0	2.3	2.1	2.0	2.3	3.1
Unemployment compensation.	1.1	1.0	1.3	1.2	0.6	1.1	1.7
Workmen's compensation.	2.6	0.2	0.9	0.5	0.4	1.0	1.7
Severance or dismissal pay and/or supplemental unemployment benefit funds.	0.2	0.1	0.1	0.6	*	. . .	0.1
Total.	10.1	10.3	11.3	14.3	11.9	9.7	8.6

*Less than 0.05 or $0.005.

SOURCE: *Handbook of Labor Statistics 1969,* U.S. Department of Labor, Bureau of Labor Statistics, Government Printing Office, 1969, pp. 268, 270, 271, 276.   Base period 1960–1965.

HOLIDAYS

The word "holiday" itself comes from a Greek root indicating a feast or day of merriment. As time passed, the word took on religious connotations and became holy days. Whether for holidays or holy days, American firms observed many of these days but paid for few of them. Prior to World War II, only 12 percent of manufacturing companies provided compensation for hourly employees on these days.

To observe eight paid holidays is now the most prevailing practice in manufacturing, although seven days is quite common. Certain service industries, such as finance, traditionally observe many additional holidays. The retail trade and wholesale trade tend to have the least number of paid holidays. In a recent survey made by the federal government, only 8 percent of all labor agreements had ten or more paid holidays. Geographical areas show clear preferences as to holidays. In the New England and Middle Atlantic regions, more than 20 percent of the agreements provided ten paid holidays as contrasted with the Mountain states where no one reported ten holidays.

The ethnic group covered by the holiday pay plan often dictates the particular holidays observed. The New York Retail and Wholesale Bakery Workers Agreement, for example, provides the following:

In retail shops the following holidays shall be paid holidays regardless of the day on which said holiday falls:
New Years (January 1)
January 30th (Franklin D. Roosevelt's birthday)
May 1st
Two days Rosh Hashana
One day Yom Kippur
Thanksgiving Day
Christmas Day
In the event the employer operates an Orthodox shop, that is, a shop which is kept closed on Saturday and religious holidays, then, in that event, all employees in such shop shall be paid for the following days instead of the holidays listed above:
Two days Rosh Hashana
One day Yom Kippur
Four days Succoth
Two days Shevuoth

The area of the country in which one is employed may also influence the days observed. For example, certain rural regions observe the first day of the deer season.

The trend is toward an increasing number of holidays and the observing of these holidays either preceding or following the weekends. In 1971, holidays became mini-vacations under the Federal Monday Holiday Law which shifts the observance of certain holidays to Monday. These are Washington's Birthday, Memorial Day, Columbus Day, and Veterans' Day.

Holiday Pay Eligibility

The typical union negotiating committee, and many other employees, feel that a holiday is a negotiated benefit and thus an employee may not properly be deprived of it. They see holiday pay eligibility conditions as methods of depriving employees of legitimate benefits. Managers look upon eligibility requirements as assurances that holidays will not be extended so that work may continue in an orderly manner.

In addition to standard eligibility questions, the company might determine in advance what will happen if work is not scheduled the day before or the day after a holiday, what happens if only a partial day is worked, or what happens if a layoff occurs subsequent to a holiday in a manner to disqualify an employee who is otherwise eligible for holiday pay.

Computing Holiday Pay

Holiday pay is computed in a variety of ways. A salaried employee receives his base salary. To compute holiday pay for an hourly employee, one must first determine the hourly rate to be used. He may receive his regular hourly rate for a preceding time period, his current incentive earning, or his average incentive rate. All this can be complicated by the inclusion or exclusion of shift differential and overtime premium rates into an average rate computation. Having found the proper hourly rate, the hourly rate multiplier must then be considered. How many hours shall he be paid for on each paid holiday? Does the employee receive eight hours pay or some other amount, such as the average number of hours worked per day in the last pay period?

Overtime Pay on Holidays

About 95 percent of all labor agreements provide for additional compensation if a represented employee works on a paid holiday. In the case of salaried employees, companies normally provide for additional compensation, but often tie this to having worked on all other scheduled workdays in that particular week.

The typical salaried policy provides for overtime over forty hours, with eight hours credited work for a holiday not worked. As an illustration, if the holiday worked is Monday and the individual is absent Tuesday, he would receive forty hours pay for the week. Under such a policy, if no work is performed on the holiday (Monday), Tuesday is not worked, but the employee works Saturday, he would still earn forty hours unless his company pays Saturday overtime as such. Any company holiday policy must also consider what compensation is to be given when work is done outside the normally scheduled hours of work on a paid holiday. For example, an employee scheduled to work from 8 A.M. to 4 P.M. during his regular workweek reports to work on a holiday at 5 P.M. and works to 10 P.M. Should he receive his regular holiday pay plus five hours at the applicable premium rate, or should he receive five hours at a straight time rate and eight hours of holiday pay?

One last question on holiday pay relates to vacations. The normal practice is to provide an additional day of vacation if a holiday falls within the vacation period, or to provide an equivalent amount of compensation without the additional day of vacation.

VACATIONS

A rest from work is considered beneficial both mentally and physically for the typical worker. Paid vacations are a time-honored institution in American government but a relatively new benefit in business and industry. The traditional military and governmental service practice of thirty days annual leave has been well known but largely ignored in the private sector. The sabbatical leave common in education has been completely ignored. Before World War II, the practice of granting unpaid vacation to hourly workers and short paid vacations to salaried employees was quite common. However, few hourly workers received paid vacations.

In 1940, only about 25 percent of all workers covered by collective bargaining agreements received some form of vacation. The National War Labor Board encouraged paid vacations and granted them, by administrative order, to most defense workers. The length of vacations increased in the post–World War II years. In the mid-fifties a fourth week of vacation after twenty-five years of service was not uncommon.

The sixties saw a compression of the eligibility schedules so that only twenty years are usually needed for four weeks of vacation. A recent survey of the length of service and vacation granted indicates that 69 percent of all industries grant one week of vacation after one year, 76 percent grant two weeks after five years, 53 percent grant three weeks after ten years, and 37 percent grant four weeks after twenty years. However, the maximum vacation available in a typical vacation plan is still four weeks. The early seventies will show an increased emphasis on vacation pay greater than vacation time off. This will appear in the form of vacation bonuses or extra days of vacation pay. In addition, the granting of five weeks after thirty years will be in vogue.

Vacation Pay and Vacation Trouble Spots

Computation of vacation pay presents all the problems found with holiday pay. In essence, employees are compensated in the same manner as if they had worked. In collective bargaining it is wise to compute holiday and vacation pay in the same manner and cross-reference this in the labor agreement.

Some typical questions arise in relation to the problems associated with vacation eligibility requirements. For example, is vacation eligibility determined on the employee's anniversary date or as of a fixed date such as January 1 of each year? If an employee terminates prior to his next eligibility date or his anniversary date, does he get a prorated vacation or a full vacation? Does he accrue next year's vacation this year so that if he retires or quits he is eligible for a vacation the year after he quits or retires? Is an employee eligible for a vacation during a sick absence? Does he accumulate service for vacation purposes while on a prolonged disability from which he is expected to return?

Vacation scheduling is a major problem. Many manufacturing operations now adopt a standard shutdown period in which at least two weeks of each employee's vacation is scheduled. If an employee has less vacation than the plant shutdown, he simply does not work and is not compensated. Most states require a one-week waiting period in order to be eligible for unemployment compensation. Thus the employer has little additional cost if the employee is laid off or considered laid off during the vacation shutdown. Most vacation plans require that the employee take the actual vacation. He may not receive pay in lieu of time off. This practice is questionable since many people do not require long vacations from a physiological viewpoint. In many instances, managers, executives, and other key personnel simply lose their vacation because they work through it.

Extended Vacation Plan

The extended vacation plan is found primarily in the steel and aluminum industries. Figure 2 shows the history of vacation development in the steel industry. This history is typical of industries in general. It shows a compression of the eligibility requirements and an increase in vacation cost per hour worked, even when the eligibility requirements remain the same. This cost creep is caused by the maturation of the employee group involved and the increase in wages upon which the vacation pay is computed. It is a basic rule that when the wage rate increases the vacation cost per hour will also increase, even without any additional vacation time off being granted.

New ground was broken in the field of employee benefits in October 1962 when the United Steelworkers of America won extended vacations, or "sabbaticals," as the result of contract negotiations with the American Can Company. Although

Figure 2. Length of paid vacations and service requirements for vacations in the steel industry, and vacation cost per hour worked 1937–1968.

Year Negotiated	Weeks of paid vacation				Vacation cost per hour worked in the industry
	1	2	3	4	
	Years of service required				
1937	5	. . .	. . .	. . .	¶
1941	3	15	. . .	. . .	$0.018
1944	1	5	. . .	. . .	0.022
1947	1	5	25	. . .	0.051
1952	1	5	15	. . .	0.099
1956	1	5	15	. . .	0.126
1958*	1	5	15	. . .	0.190
1962 †	1	3	10	25	0.224
1963 ‡	1	3	10	25	0.240
1965	1	3	10	25	0.343
1968 §	1	3	10	25	0.376

*One-half week extra pay for those with 3 to 5, 10 to 15, and more than 25 years of service.
†Single week vacation benefits effective Jan. 1, 1963.
‡Extended vacation plan negotiated, effective Jan. 1, 1964.
§Vacation bonus. For each week of regular vacation in 1969, 1970, and 1971, other than regular vacation included with an extended vacation, the employee will receive an added payment of $30.
¶Not available.
SOURCE: Edward Robert Livernash, *Collective Bargaining in the Basic Steel Industry,* U.S. Department of Labor, Government Printing Office, 1961, pp. 233–306. "Wage Trends in the Iron and Steel Industry," American Iron and Steel Institute, New York, April, 1969, pp. 2–3.

longer than usual vacations had been negotiated by other unions somewhat earlier, this was the first time that vacations as long as thirteen weeks were provided. Similar terms were agreed to by the basic steel industry in the next year. Following acceptance of the extended vacation plan by the eleven major steel producers, which bargain as a group, the rest of the steel industry fell into line. The aluminum industry later negotiated an extended vacation with the Steelworkers in which all employees were eligible for extended vacation.

The extended vacation is one of the most complicated benefit programs ever negotiated in American history, designed to give about 10 percent of the employees a maximum vacation of thirteen weeks every five years. To determine who gets an extended vacation, the company first determines the size of its work force, and lists its work force in order of seniority for the total corporation. The list is then divided into two equal parts, with the older service employees called the "senior group" and the second half shown as members of the "junior group." Each employee is then notified of his position in the senior or junior group. Those in the senior group are eligible for an extended vacation in the five-year cycle.

Because benefits accrue on a corporate basis, they are distributed primarily in the older plants, and the young men in Chicago and Gary see the old-timers in Youngstown and Pittsburgh getting extended vacations that few of the new breed can qualify for. As a result, the younger workers have been dissatisfied and the companies have had scheduling problems and shortages of skilled labor. However, on balance the plan has been well received by the older men and has had no adverse mental or physical effects on them.

Other Vacation Ideas

Only two other vacation variations are worth considering. The first involves the use of funds allocated to vacations not taken. In this concept the employee may "bank" his vacation money with the company, where it accumulates interest and is withdrawn at the time of his retirement or termination, whichever is earlier. At least one West Coast local of the Operating Engineers uses vacation monies to buy shares in a credit union.

The second innovation relates to incentive vacation plans. Extra weeks of vacation may be given in recognition of outstanding performance or for extraordinary longevity. For example, an employee with forty years of service may be given an extra week or two of vacation on his fortieth anniversary.

UNEMPLOYMENT COMPENSATION, SUPPLEMENTAL UNEMPLOYMENT BENEFITS, AND FEDERAL INCOME SUPPLEMENTS

When a employee is available and able to work, should he be paid for not working? In a surprising number of cases the answer is yes. This payment may take the form of four hours pay guaranteed for call in or report to work. It shows itself in paid lunch periods and paid coffee breaks. Most of these items are now taken for granted and are well known.

Workers have been traditionally concerned not only with the wage rate but with job security. Unions have long recognized the importance of what Dr. A. A. Blum of Michigan State University calls the "belly" issues rather than the "soul" issues. To maintain income they have pushed for the guaranteed annual wage and have settled for supplemental unemployment benefits and, in a few cases, for guaranteed work. The longshoremen in the Atlantic and Gulf ports have contracts providing up to 2,080 hours of pay or work a year. Such guarantees are rare. There are, however, certain major payments made directly or indirectly by the employer that deserve review. The three areas to be covered are unemployment compensation, supplemental unemployment benefits, and federal income supplements.

Unemployment Compensation

All states have unemployment compensation acts. They provide for weekly benefits ranging from $5 minimum to $88 maximum. The maximum time the benefit is paid out is twenty-six weeks, but with federal assistance it may continue up to fifty-two weeks.

All states provide for initial unemployment compensation benefit eligibility determination by a state agency with the right of appeal by either the employer or the employee. An individual laid off for lack of work is normally considered eligible for payments. A person is not eligible in most states if he quit without good cause, if he refuses a suitable position, or if he is discharged through misconduct. Some states have attempted to eliminate the lockout as a management bargaining device. They provide compensation to an employee if he is locked out from his job. The state of New York assumes that any labor dispute lasting forty-eight days or longer is a lockout. The employees then become eligible for compensation.

The funds for payments are obtained from individual employers both by taxing and by experience rating. The unemployment compensation taxes are levied on the wage base of an employee up to a set maximum wage amount. His total compensation is not taxable for unemployment compensation in most states. In some states, employees also contribute to the fund.

Supplemental Unemployment Benefits

Supplemental unemployment benefits are transfer payments provided for in many collective bargaining agreements. These payments are normally granted to eligible employees to provide for three contingencies: layoff, reduced workweeks, and relocation.

Supplemental unemployment benefits plans are normally found in heavy manufacturing operations, particularly in those with bargaining units represented by the United Automobile Workers and the United Steelworkers of America.

A typical United Steelworkers plan provides for twenty-six hours of straight time pay plus a dependency allowance which is payable up to fifty-two weeks a year. The recent United Automobile Workers plans provide for benefits payable at 95 percent of the employee's weekly after-tax pay minus $7.50 work-related expense. In both plans, state unemployment compensation is deducted from the weekly benefit amount, as is compensation from other gainful employment. Income received by an employee under a supplemental unemployment benefits plan is taxable and is subject to tax withholding.

In a typical case, a worker earns $3.54 an hour, or $141.60 for a forty-hour week, and takes home $120.74 after social security, federal, state, and city income taxes. He would get $107.20 a week if he did not work at all. If he loses only one or two days of work, the employee is paid for 80 percent of the time not worked. If he is permanently relocated, he gets a set amount to cover moving costs. This amount is reflected on a schedule based on distance moved and his family size.

The cost of supplemental unemployments benefits may continue for a firm even though few employees are laid off. The plan may call for either "hard" or "soft" funding. In "hard funding," the employer's contribution is at a fixed rate, normally between 5 and 7 cents per hour worked, and the contribution continues even though no one is on layoff. In "soft funding," the employer's contribution is sufficient to keep the fund within certain fixed limits and normally has a maximum contribution rate of 12.5 cents per hour.

The union views the plan as a method of maintaining the purchasing power of the employee. To employers the plan is viewed as a wage cost. The sociological view requires maintaining a careful balance between wages as an incentive to work and wages as income. If the income is too low, the employee and his family may suffer. If the amount paid to an employee approaches his weekly net income less related work expenses, the employee has no incentive to look for work elsewhere.

Supplemental unemployment benefits adversely affect the economy by reducing labor mobility. They have a positive effect by maintaining consumer expenditures.

Stated as a value judgment, the amount of supplemental unemployment benefits transfer payments should be a positive function of both area unemployment and the employee's average propensity to consume. The higher the unemployment rate in a community, the higher the money to be paid as supplemental unemployment benefits. At best, the willingness of people to relocate to labor areas with a shortage of workers is not elastic. People wish neither to sell their homes nor to lose the friends and neighbors of a lifetime. They prefer to wait and hope.

A general analysis indicates that transfer payments designed to maintain consumer expenditures at a high level should not exceed the recipient's average propensity to consume, as determined on a sectoral basis. When income declines, consumption is not likely to decrease in the short time run.

Federal Income Supplements

Interwoven with the income maintenance provisions of unemployment compensation and supplemental unemployment benefits is the overall question of poverty and welfare. One in every 200 persons in this country receives welfare payments.

In 1968, a total of 11 million people received aid. In the same year, 25 million persons were considered to be in poverty.

The official poverty line of the United States government in 1968 was $3,553. A 1970 estimate is approximately $4,000. These figures assume a nonfarm family of four people. To maintain a lower living standard in 1967 in a metropolitan area required an income of approximately $6,000. The U.S. Department of Labor has established standard family budgets of three types: a lower living standard, a modest living standard, and a higher living standard. The dollar requirements for the latter two are $9,243 and $13,367.

It becomes apparent that a family receiving unemployment compensation will normally fall either below the subsistence level or certainly below the modest and lower living standard. If this is true, then the family group may very well be eligible for funds from the federal welfare system.

A proposed federal plan guarantees a certain income level by family size to support the no-income family. As the income rises, the federal supplement decreases, but only by a portion of the increase in income. Such a plan provides a financial incentive to work. Those who work will always have more income than those who do not. This plan can be administered through the social security administration, the Treasury Department, or local unemployment offices.

In one such plan, the working poor would be guaranteed a basic annual income of $1,600 a year. The first $750 of earnings could be kept without any reduction in the $1,600 subsidy. For every dollar earned above $750, the $1,600 federal subsidy would be reduced by 50 cents.

For example, a family earning $2,000 would receive $975 in federal funds; a family earning $3,000, $475 in federal funds; a family earning $3,920, no federal funds.

This plan would have a break-even point at which time income supplementation would cease. The plan described above has a reduction rate of 50 percent in earnings. The wage earner can thus earn up to twice his guaranteed income before federal supplementation ceases. The incentive to work is retained in such a plan.

If this 50 percent plan without the $750 deduction were applied to various income levels, we could determine the break-even level at which federal subsidies would cease and the approximate aggregate national cost of such a plan. This information is shown in Figure 3. To provide a subsistence income based on a break-even income of $6,000 for everyone in the United States would cost over 20 billion dollars.

It is not without possibility that unemployment compensation per se could be eliminated, and all welfare systems eliminated, if the amounts forthcoming under the federal income supplementation plan were increased to maintain at least the subsistence level of existence.

Figure 3.   Federal guaranteed income break-even income level by 50 percent reduction rate; net cost by guarantee level, family of four.

Guarantee	Break-even income	Net cost, billions	
		Universal	Families with children
$1,600	$3,200	$ 2.5	$ 1.8
2,000	4,000	4.8	3.4
2,400	4,800	4.8	6.1
2,800	5,600	13.6	10.0
3,200	6,400	20.7	15.5

SOURCE: Robert Harris, "The Negative Income Tax and the Welfare System," *Business Economics*, vol. 1, pp. 1966–1969, January, 1970.

WORKMEN'S COMPENSATION

The subject of workmen's compensation and safety is more fully treated in other parts of this handbook.   This section is concerned with financing arrangements and payment of workmen's compensation claims.

Workmen's compensation payments replace employee loss of earning capacity due to occupational injury.   However, there are no short-cut ways of determining what this could cost each company.   The laws are not uniform, and thus the costs are not the same.   Do not assume that a valid workmen's compensation claim in one state is a valid claim in another state.   Each state law needs to be studied to determine the extent to which an employee is covered.   The coverage will determine the risk to be financed and the amounts that may be paid out.

General Rules of Compensation Payments

Most states require a one-week waiting period before benefits begin.   Limitations are placed on the maximum and minimum benefits payable each week and the total number of weeks for which the benefit is paid.

Workmen's compensation payments are computed in one of two ways:

1. As a lump sum.   For example, a fatality costs $49,000 in Michigan but only $12,000 in Georgia; a permanent partial disability through the loss of a great toe costs $3,943 in Wisconsin but only $625 in Maryland.
2. As the number of weeks of disability.   This weekly benefit figure is computed as
   a. A percentage of the employee's weekly wage
   b. A flat rate set by the state

The weekly maximum amount paid is set somewhat less than take-home pay to discourage malingering.   Weekly pay amounts are paid out in accordance with the schedule of benefits for that class of injury.

Fatalities.   Each state values a human life at either a set dollar figure or on the years of gainful employment that would have remained to the deceased.   This method often has a maximum dollar limit, such as 80 percent of wages for balance of expected working life (age sixty-five minus current age).   Benefits payable in the event of fatal injuries comprise slightly over 10 percent of all compensation benefits in any given year.   Funeral expenses, subject to a maximum dollar limit, are normally paid by the employer.

Temporary and permanent disability payments.   Where there is permanent total disability, most states provide payments extending through the employee's lifetime.   The wage replacement percentage for either temporary total or permanent total disability is the same.   However, in permanent total disability cases the time limits tend to be longer and the maximum dollar amount tends to be higher than in cases of temporary total disability.   Some states provide additional amounts for dependents, medical expenses, rehabilitation services, and other benefits.

In most states all medical expenses are borne by the employer.   The employee normally has the choice of physician.   Medical benefits amount to nearly 35 percent of all workmen's compensation benefits.   In some forty United States jurisdictions and in all Canadian provinces, unlimited medical benefits are provided either specifically by statute or by administrative discretion.

Rehabilitation is considered an integral part of complete medical treatment.   It also may include vocational training or other items.   Rehabilitation is provided in all states even if unspecified in the law.   The Federal Vocational Rehabilitation Act is operational in all states.   It provides federal funds to aid states in vocational rehabilitation of the industrially disabled.

Second-injury funds.   Second-injury funds were developed to take care of problems arising when a preexisting injury is combined with a second to produce disability greater than was caused by the original injury alone. "Second-injury" employers pay compensation related primarily to the disability caused by the second injury alone, even though the employee receives a benefit relating to his combined disability; the difference is made up from a second-injury fund usually financed by taxes on all employees.

Temporary disability laws. California, Hawaii, New Jersey, New York, Puerto Rico, and Rhode Island have laws providing for temporary disability benefits. These benefits provide protection for the employee who is unable to work because of an illness or injury not covered by workmen's compensation. With the exception of New York, the disability benefits laws are administered in connection with the state unemployment compensation laws. All employees covered by the unemployment insurance laws are also covered by the temporary disability benefits provisions.

The state disability benefit laws vary considerably. In general they are state plans for which an approved private plan may be substituted. The employee pays most of the cost. The employer usually pays nothing or enough only to assume benefits. One quirk of the law in California is that benefits are payable for absences due to pregnancy, twenty-eight days after termination of the pregnancy. Benefits have a maximum duration of twenty-one weeks.

Determination of Benefit Levels and Eligibility for Benefits

The state agency empowered with the enforcement of the workmen's compensation laws determines both the eligibility for payment and the applicable benefit level. The agency first asks, Is the company in a covered industry? Does it have the minimum number of employees required under the state law? If both answers are yes, then the company is responsible for providing those benefits set forth in the statute. The state agency then finds out if the injury is work related. If the answer is affirmative, it will determine the nature and extent of the benefits. Each state, however, has certain exceptions to the above which deny benefits to an employee. In some jurisdictions, intoxication or violation of safety rules precludes the individual from receiving compensation. In other states, an employer may list with the state those individuals with certain preexisting physical limitations. Should these individuals be injured as a result of the preexisting condition, the employer has no liability. Certain states provide exceptions for specific industries and occupations, such as farm workers, while other states stipulate a minimum number of employees before the firm is covered.

Disagreements in either eligibility or the level of payment may be appealed by the parties. Both the employer and the employee, in a timely manner and without counsel, may appeal the initial determination through the state administrative hierarchy. Some states provide for court review if either party desires this. Most court reviews result from the employee moving the action to the court in the hopes of recovering benefits in excess of those provided for in the statute. This can be done if he proves gross negligence on the part of the employer.

Financing Workmen's Compensation

Financing of workmen's compensation is normally handled in one of the following manners:

1. Self-insurance. The employer is prepared to pay all costs and to grant the benefits required under the statute.

2. Private insurance. A carrier is paid to handle the administration and bear the financial risks related to compensation claims.

3. State insurance. The premium is paid to the state rather than to an insurance company.

4. Flat payroll tax. This method covers administrative costs of workmen's com-

pensation and shares the workmen's compensation cost burden in a more egalitarian way.

These four methods are normally combined in some manner. The most common is the flat payroll tax plus state insurance. The payment to the state for insurance is determined by the experience rating of either the firm or the industry.

Experience rating merely qualifies how good an employer is at furnishing a safe working environment. There are three ways of making this judgment:

1. Schedule rates assign a standard risk for a classification of work or industry.

2. Experience rating is based on the three-year safety record for the plant or company being rated.

3. Retrospective rating extrapolates the previous year's cost to the current year.

All three of the merit rating techniques are little more than semisophisticated guesses as to what workmen's compensation will cost a particular firm in a given year.

Suggestions for the Practitioner

Before the injury

Develop a method of emergency aid to the injured employee, including evacuation methods.

Train people in first aid and disaster control.

Become a self-insurer only if you have an adequate staff to police malingerers, make intelligent board appearances, and if your premium costs have been relatively steady.

Welcome state inspections, do not be afraid of them.

After the injury

Find out what happened and why.

Keep careful records; send out reports *on time* to meet the state schedule, not that of your insurance carrier.

Be sure the waiting period, if any, is observed before benefits begin.

Make sure the workmen's compensation administrator and the employee benefits administrator talk to each other; otherwise you may pay for the same injury under two plans.

Social Security Disability Payments

Permanent disability for social security purposes requires the individual to be disabled from any sort of substantial work for pay because of physical or mental disability. The disability must last or expect to continue for not less than twelve months.

To be eligible for benefits the employee must offer medical proof of disability by a doctor, hospital, or clinic where he has had treatment.

If an individual becomes entitled to disability benefits, he will not be paid those benefits if, without good cause, he refuses counseling, training, or other services offered by the state vocational rehabilitation agency.

There is a waiting period of six months after disability begins before an individual can collect disability benefits. On the other hand, benefits are continued for three months after recovery to allow time for the individual to find a job. Once the employee has gone back to work, if his disability recurs within five years, he can again receive benefits without another six-month waiting period, provided that his second occurrence of the disability is expected to last twelve months or more.

The amount of monthly benefit is the same as the amount of retirement benefit an employee would get if he were already sixty-five. Payments received as military disability are not offset against social security benefits. However, combined workmen's compensation and social security benefits cannot go above 80 percent of an employee's total yearly earnings before he became disabled.

LONG-TERM DISABILITY AND OTHER PAID SICK TIME

So-called health and welfare programs cover a wide spectrum of employee benefits ranging from medical insurance to pay for sick absences. Paid sick time provides for income maintenance in both the short and long run. In the short run most salaried employees receive their salary for one- or two-day absences. This is now beginning to spread over into the hourly area. In the 1970 General Electric settlement, sick pay is provided for two days' pay with five years' service, three days' with ten years, four days with fifteen years, and five days with twenty-five years. The chief disadvantage of paid sick leave is in the short-run period where employees tend to take all the allowed sick time in a given period. These absences will coincide remarkably well with weekends, holidays, and personal business.

On the other hand, long-term sick payments are seldom abused because they concern illnesses verified by a physician. Such protection against income loss during a period of illness becomes greater as the employee's service increases. For example, the U.S. Steel Corporation in its agreement with the salaried employees, represented by the United Steelworkers of America, provides for salary continuance for the balance of the pay period for employees with up to eight weeks of service. The schedule is graduated until with service of twenty years and over the employee would receive the balance of the pay period and thirteen additional pay periods at full salary.

In addition to long-term sick pay, many companies provide for long-term disability. This protection is granted after one or two years' service. Total disability is defined as the continuous inability to engage in any occupation or employment for which an individual is reasonably qualified by education, training, or experience. In most companies he will be considered to be totally disabled if he is unable to perform the duties of his regular occupation, or if he is not engaged in any other occupation or employment for which he is qualified. The essential difference between disability as defined in social security and disability as defined by most employers is that in the former the individual is disabled from all work; but in the latter he is disabled from doing his work or work of a comparable nature within his corporation. Some plans provide as much as 66 percent of the employee's salary for the total period of disability, even when the disability will be for life.

MISCELLANEOUS ABSENCES

There are countless other ways of providing pay for time not worked. A few of the more common ones will be considered.

Funeral Leave

Bereavement pay typically provides for three days time off for a death in the family. In forming a policy, one must carefully define who is a family member, and whether or not the paid time off must be taken concurrently with the funeral and on consecutive days. Better than 60 percent of all employers provide such time off.

Civic Leave

Paid time off for jury duty, jury selection, summer military encampment, and riot duty are common civic duties that are paid for by companies. Banks, insurance companies, and manufacturers tend to grant these benefits, while retailers and small manufacturers often do not. A smaller percentage grant paid time off for witness duty. The majority of those providing paid time off do so for witness duty in criminal cases. Few, if any, provide paid time off in civil cases. Many states require an employer to release employees for voting, even though the employees could do so during normal poll hours and still work a full day.

Charity Drives

Many labor agreements, especially in the federal service, provide for paid time off to conduct charity drives. It is not unusual in private industry to support activities such as the United Fund and the Red Cross by releasing both salaried and hourly employees to solicit funds or attend meetings.

Personal Time Off

Banks and utilities traditionally provide salaried employees paid time off because of illness in the family or to keep medical and dental appointments. Time off for marriage of an employee is granted to more than 70 percent of bank employees. Very few manufacturing companies provide hourly employees with paid personal time off.

Other Paid Time Off

A brief listing of other types of paid time off includes:
  Check-cashing time (longer lunchtimes on payday)
  Coffee break
  Credit union activities
  Grievance processing pay
  Heat fatigue recovery time (for example, a "catcher" in a hot strip mill)
  Lunch period
  Personnel office visits
  Portal-to-portal pay
  Rest-room time
  Union duties
  Wash-up time
  Wet time (paid time off for inclement weather)

Leaves of Absence

In concluding this section, special attention must be given to leaves of absence. This term should be used exclusively in connection with absences over which the employer may exercise his discretionary judgment. All other absences should be prefaced by the word "absent," such as "absent—sick" or "absent—maternity." The term "leave of absence" denotes permission to be off and provides some guarantee of protected reemployment and benefits. The term should be used with great discretion. The use of the term in connection with a leave of absence to attend school, or leave of absence for personal business, or leave of absence for unpaid vacation might be appropriate. This term should not be applied to sickness, military, or maternity absences. In the latter two cases, the federal law provides for certain guarantees of reemployment. In the case of sickness, the company benefit plan usually spells out reemployment and insurance rights in some detail.

LEGAL ASPECTS

Vacation Pay

Some periods of paid time off are covered by statutes. They are social security disability payments, unemployment compensation, federal welfare payments, and in certain states, jury duty pay, and voting time off pay. The Equal Employment Opportunities rulings and the national policy on military service will naturally impinge on items such as maternity absence pay and military pay allowances. The employees vested interest in most paid time off has been considered by the courts.

In certain cases involving bankruptcy, federal courts have said vacation pay constitutes additional wages. In the *Wil Low* and *Public Ledger* cases it has been held that if the the conditions precedent to earning a vacation have been met, the vacation pay is the same as wages earned but not paid. *In re Wil Low Cafeterias Inc.*, decided by the United States Court of Appeals in New York in 1940 (III F. 2d 429), the court said:

> A vacation with pay is in effect additional wages. It involves a reasonable arrangement to secure the well being of employees and the continuance of harmonious relations between employer and employee. The consideration for the contract to pay for a week's vacation has been furnished, that is to say, one year's service had been rendered prior to June 1, so that the week's vacation with pay was completely earned and only the time of receiving it was postponed. If the employer had discharged the employee wrongfully after the latter had done the work necessary to earn a vacation he could not be deprived of the benefits due him. . . . It can make no difference whether the discharge is due, as here, to a cessation of business by the employer, or was wrongful. In either event an amount earned would be a valid expense of administration.

However, where an employee has been terminated and he has not fully qualified for vacation pay under the terms of the labor agreement in effect, or in terms of the written company policy, it is unlikely that he would be eligible for even a pro rata vacation, much less full vacation pay.

Reemployment after Workmen's Compensation Award

Can an employee who has received a 50 percent permanent partial disability award because of injury to his back be denied his old job? In the light of several arbitration cases, the answer may well be no. An employer has a right to discharge an employee who is injured and unable to perform his job. The employer must demonstrate the employee's inability to perform his job as a separate issue, and may not rely exclusively on payment of workmen's compensation as prima facie evidence of inability to do the job. Physical ability to perform a specific job and the degree of permanent partial disability are two distinct issues which must fall or rise on their own merits. The doctrine of collateral estoppel does not ban the claimant from seeking both his old job back and a substantial award from workmen's compensation.

IMPLICATIONS FOR THE FUTURE

Social scientists such as Maslow tell us that once a man fulfills his subsistence needs he turns to his social needs. In America, most employees appear to earn better than a subsistence wage, and are concerned with their social needs more than their work. The worker has elected more and more paid time off as one way of satisfying his social needs.

However, some paid time off provisions do provide protection for the employee's subsistence needs during periods of unemployment. The employee is concerned with having maintenance of income during periods of rest from work, illness, following industrial injury, and while unemployed through no fault of his own. His concern with these forms of security will lessen in the seventies as wages received for nonworked time will approximate his disposable income had he worked. Work will become less and less of a means to an end and, therefore, must be made more desirable as an end result. In short, the employee will be able to live whether he works or not. The quality of his life style will depend on his desire to work. Often, the desire to work will depend on the quality of the working environment.   Workers will become more concerned with pensions, early retirement, etc.   Today's leaders have their expectation levels conditioned on the hard times of the thirties and the tensions of the forties.   Today's workers, and tomorrow's leaders, are conditioned on the prosperities of the fifties and sixties.   Their expectations move on a different, much higher schedule.   The children in schools and colleges today have expectation levels of such height as to be unperceivable by most adults.

Today's compensation ceilings are tomorrow's floors.

BIBLIOGRAPHY

Public Documents

U.S. Bureau of Labor Statistics: *Handbook of Labor Statistics 1969*, Bulletin 1630, July, 1969.
—— : *Paid Vacation and Holiday Provisions*, Bulletin 1425–9.   June, 1969.
—— : *Severance Pay and Layoff Benefit Plans*, Bulletin 1425–2, March, 1965.
—— : *Supplemental Unemployment Benefit Plans and Wage-Employment Guarantees*, Bulletin 1425–3, June, 1965.

Books and Pamphlets

Analysis of Workmen's Compensation Laws: Chamber of Commerce of the United States, Washington, 1969.
Becker, Joseph M.: *Guaranteed Income for the Unemployed*, The Johns Hopkins Press, Baltimore, 1968.
Dirio, Arthur J.: *The Total Approach to Employee Benefits*, American Management Association, New York, 1967.
Dunlop, John T. (ed.): *Automation and Technological Change*, Prentice-Hall, Inc., Englewood Cliffs, N.J., 1962.
Lewis, H. Gregg: *Unionism and Relative Wages in the United States; An Empirical Inquiry*, University of Chicago Press, Chicago, 1963.
Time Off with Pay: National Industrial Conference Board, Inc., New York, 1965.

Articles and Periodicals

"Fringe Benefits: Their Cost Now," *U.S. News and World Report*, vol. 65, no. 15, p. 100, Oct. 7, 1968.
Harris, Robert: "The Negative Income Tax and the Welfare System," *Business Economics*, vol. 5, no. 1, pp. 66–69, January, 1970.
Masse, Benjamin L.: "Fringe Benefits," *America*, vol. 120, pp. 168–169, Feb. 8, 1969.
Morton, W. A.: "Trade Unionism, Full Employment and Inflation," *American Economic Review*, vol. 40, pp. 13–19, March, 1950.
Schultz, G. P., and C. A. Meyer: "Union Wage Decisions and Employment," *American Economic Review*, vol. 40, pp. 362–380, June, 1950.
Wachter, M. L.: "Cyclical Variation in the Interindustry Wage Structure," *American Economic Review*, vol. 40, no. 1., pp. 75–84, March, 1970.

Unpublished Material

Feinberg, I. Robert: "Do Contract Rights Vest?," address to National Academy of Arbitrators.

chapter 37

Pension Plans
and Social Security

DOUGLAS J. KENNEDY *Director of Employee Benefits Administration, The Greyhound Corporation, Phoenix, Arizona*

PENSION PLANS

The word "pension" is defined as a fixed amount other than wages paid at regular intervals to a person or his surviving dependents in consideration of his past services, age, merit, poverty, or an injury or loss sustained. A retirement pension is further defined as an allowance, annuity, or subsidy. Today's pension plans are far removed from the days when the wealthy took it upon themselves to pay a pittance to a faithful servant too old to care for himself any longer, or of government pensions paid to inhabitants of old soldiers' homes, in order to provide them with tobacco or other small comforts.

Company pension plans date back to the early 1900s, with the U.S. Steel Plan, dating from 1911, as a forerunner. The development was slow, and it was not until the early 1920s that insurance companies first made pension contracts available.

Strange as it may seem, the enactment of the Social Security Act in 1935 stimulated the growth of pension plans, rather than retarding them. As a result of the Great Depression, the public had a need for security, and as an added measure to social security, pension plans began to take greater importance in people's minds. It was not until the early 1940s that trust companies entered the pension field and initiated the potential for noninsured plans as opposed to the annuity plans provided by the insurance companies.

Pension plans did not become a notable part of industrial relations until the 1940s. Negotiations for fringe benefits, including pension plans, became increasingly popular as a result of wartime restrictions on wage increases, and this development was encouraged by the National War Labor Board as a means of deferring compensation in order to maintain a better balance between wages and prices in the wartime economy.   After the close of World War II, the courts ruled in the Inland Steel case (1949) that pension plans were a proper subject for collective bargaining.   In today's economy, pension plans are the rule rather than the exception, and are an important factor in attracting personnel in the competitive labor market.

Benefit Structure

A satisfactory pension plan is, simply, one that meets the needs of the group it covers within the budgetary limitations of the employer.   If the group is primarily involved in nonphysical work with a minimum of job-connected accident potential, then the plan should be designed to provide maximum benefits at a normal retirement age. If, however, the group is engaged in physical work, possibly with machinery, with greater accident exposure, then some of the weight should be transferred from normal retirement benefits to provisions for disability retirement.   If the work is extremely taxing either mentally or physically as the employee ages, then consideration should be given to adequate early retirement benefits.   Provisions for early retirement benefits are also important when company mergers or mechanization reduce the work force requirements.   All these and other factors related to the covered group must be taken into consideration in tailoring a successful plan; it is also important to structure the plan so that it is flexible enough to allow revisions in order to meet the changing requirements of the group, without excessive cost to the employer.

Eligibility

When should a pension plan be offered to a newly hired employee?   The factors to be taken into consideration are years of service, age, or both.   Whether the plan should be extended only to regular full-time employees or to all employees is a question that must be given consideration.   Enrolling employees at a relatively young age or with limited amounts of service can, particularly in trust type plans, benefit the plans through a high turnover rate factor.   However, it can result in unnecessary capital being tied up in the pension plan when such money could be used more efficiently by the company to meet other needs.   Many plans have a common enrollment date of once each year, at which time employees are enrolled after completing one year of service, and/or having reached age 25.   This plan, to a great extent, removes from consideration the younger employee who has not yet found his niche, and is still searching for work with which he will be satisfied.   The inclusion of part-time employees in a pension plan, while possibly desirable from some points of view, causes many administrative problems not found in plans which are confined to regular full-time employees.

Vesting

Determination must be made as to when an employee shall earn irrevocable benefits in the pension plan payable at normal retirement, even though such employee might leave the company prior to reaching retirement age.   For example, a plan which requires contributions from both the employee and the employer might specify that if the employee leaves the company before completing 5 years of service, he has no vested right in the plan, and must withdraw his contributions, which are returned to him with accrued interest.   This same plan would then provide for employees leaving the company after completion of 5 years of service a pension payable at age 65, representing amounts purchased by all the employee's contributions, and all or a part of the contributions made by the company in his behalf.

Let us assume that the employee is leaving the company with more than 5 years of service but less than 10.   The plan could provide that a pension would be paid to him at normal retirement age based on an actuarially determined amount purchased by his contributions, and 25 percent of the company's contributions. If he left with more than 10 years of service but less than 15, his contributions again would be used to provide a pension along with 50 percent of the company's contributions, and after completing 15 years of service, the full amount of both the employee's and the company's contributions would be used for the purchase of a pension to be payable at normal retirement. In all such cases, however, the employee retains the right to withdraw his contributions regardless of length of service in lieu of any accrued pension benefits.

In many plans, however, the employee is not allowed to withdraw his contributions or discontinue participation in the plan so long as he remains an employee. Organized labor is a strong proponent of immediate vesting, using the argument that contributions to a pension plan on behalf of an employee are amounts paid in his behalf in lieu of wages earned by him. The unions further are insisting more and more on portability provisions in pension plans, which would allow an employee moving from one company to another to carry his accrued pension benefits with him. To date, the portability provisions are more generally found in the construction industries. There are many area pension plans maintained by union trustees which are participated in by a number of employers and their employees belonging to a particular industry, and so long as the worker remains in that area, he can move from job to job and company to company without disturbing his accrued pension benefits.

Plan Benefits

The basic ingredient of the benefit structure of a pension plan is an amount paid to the employee at retirement with no other provisions, and which is known as the "single life" pension provision. Such a provision could provide, for example, a pension of $1\frac{1}{2}$ percent of the individual's career average earnings, i.e., the average of all his earnings for all the years of his service, times the number of years of service. Assuming that an employee began work at a rate of $500 per month and retired 20 years later at a salary of $1,500 per month, and the pension plan provided $1\frac{1}{2}$ percent of career average earnings times years of service, we could assume that his average career salary was $1,000 per month, which would provide a pension of $300 per month ($1,000 times $1\frac{1}{2}$ percent times 20).

There is, however, a current tendency to get away from the career average formula, inasmuch as it does not give necessary weight to cost-of-living increases and/or inflation. There is a greater trend to base the pension on an average of earnings of the later years of employment, rather than the entire career. Using the same example as previously, we could assume that a plan which provides $1\frac{1}{2}$ percent pension based on the last 5 years of earnings, or $1,300 per month, would produce a monthly pension of $390 per month ($1,300 times $1\frac{1}{2}$ percent times 20). Other plans make provision for using the average salary of a set of the highest years of earning such as 5, and still others provide an option for electing one established year, such as the year in which the employee reaches age sixty-three.

Lump Sum Distribution

There are plans which provide that at retirement an employee can elect, in lieu of regular pension benefits, a lump sum payment which would equal the actuarially determined value of the pension he had earned to date. To reduce this provision to its simplest elements, we could assume that at retirement an employee would be eligible to receive a pension of $300 per month. His life expectancy is 13 years, and you would normally expect to pay him until death a total of $46,800. The lump sum paid to the individual, however, would be less than that amount, inasmuch as consideration must be given to earnings lost from the pension plan on that sum due to interest and other factors.

Integration Provision

Many plans contain a provision that an employee will receive a percentage of his salary in the form of pension benefits together with social security benefits. Such a provision might contain advantages to employees in the higher salary brackets where the amount paid the employee as a percentage of his pension, plus social security, could be less than a higher percentage amount paid to him including social security. Assuming that the earnings of an individual provide a pension based on an average annual salary of $40,000, under a plan paying 1½ percent of the average after twenty years of service, such plan would provide him with an annual pension of $12,000; and further assuming that his social security benefits amounted to $200 per month, he would have a total income from pension and social security of $14,400. If the pension plan were to contain a provision that the employee could elect a pension of 40 percent of average earnings including social security, he would receive a total income of $16,000 per year, of which $13,600 would be provided by the company pension plan, and $2,400 from social security. It should be noted, however, that the Internal Revenue Service is imposing tighter restrictions on plans of this nature to the point where a plan, to be qualified, must apply something less than the full social security benefits in the use of the integration formula.

Variable Annuities

Another form of pension income is the variable annuity, wherein a portion of the contributions to the plan on behalf of an employee are invested in equities, and the balance is used to purchase a fixed pension amount. Upon retirement, the employee receives a fixed pension amount, and additional amounts resulting from the stock investments in accordance with the fluctuation of their market values. The theory upon which this plan is founded is to attempt to attune the amount of pension to cost of living. It is not effective during periods when the stock market is down and inflation continues.

Stepup Plans

Some plans have given consideration to equalizing the total retirement benefits of higher paid employees, inasmuch as social security benefits are paid only on the first segment of the employee's income as established in varying amounts since the inception of social security. For example, a plan was established at a time when the maximum amount of earnings to which social security benefits could be applied was $4,800. This plan provided for retirement benefits based on average earnings of 1 percent of the first $4,800 of earnings, and 2 percent of earnings in excess of $4,800. Thus, all employees received accelerated pension benefits on earnings over $4,800 to compensate for the lack of social security benefits in the higher bracket. In establishing such a provision, however, it is important to ensure that the percentages tend to equalize rather than discriminate in favor of the higher paid employees. In other words, the percentages applied to earnings over the maximum covered by social security must not be excessive.

Optional Benefits

Many employees at retirement wish to make some provision for continued benefits to be paid to a dependent in the event of the retiree's death. There are two primary forms in general use. One is known as the "certain and continuous annuity option," which provides that the pension will be paid for the balance of the retiree's life, or for a set number of years from date of retirement, whichever is longer. In order to obtain this option, the single life benefit normally paid is actuarially reduced or discounted.

Under such an option an employee could, at retirement, in lieu of receiving a monthly pension under the single life provision of $500 a month, elect to receive a pension reduced to 70 percent or $350 per month, under a "certain and continuous 20-year option" which would be paid for the balance of the employee's life. If, however, the employee died after 5 years of retirement, the $350 per month would be paid to his designated beneficiary for the balance of the 20-year period, or 15 years.

The other form is known as the "joint annuitant option," and this allows the employee at retirement to elect a reduced pension with the provision that after his death his designated beneficiary will receive all or a portion of that pension for the balance of the beneficiary's life. Using the same figures as in the previous example, an employee normally eligible to receive pension benefits of $500 per month could, upon retirement, elect an option which would provide that his wife who is age 60 would receive one-half of the pension benefit payable to him for the balance of her life, in the event she outlives her husband. In order to provide this provision, the single life pension of $500 per month would be reduced to 80 percent, or $400 per month payable to the retiree for the balance of his life. In the event of his death prior to the death of his wife, she would then receive one-half of that amount, or $200 per month for the balance of her life. The payments of these benefits cease upon the death of the retiree and his beneficiary, whereas under the certain and continuous option previously described, the payments would be continued for the stipulated number of years, even though both principals had expired. The amount would be paid to a contingent beneficiary, or to the estate of the deceased.

Portability

Portability, or the right to retain accrued pension benefits in moving from one company or plan to another, was included in the discussion of vesting. This feature was not contemplated when pension plans were initiated, inasmuch as the original reason for a pension plan was to encourage employees to stay with a company until retirement, in other words, to encourage career employees. With the evolution of family-owned firms into the modern-day large corporations, this feature has greatly diminished. The trend today, particularly among the management ranks, is for movement from one company to another as greater opportunities present themselves, and the portability provision has become important in salaried plans as well as in those involving trade unions.

Death Benefits

Originally, the only death benefit related to pension plans was found in contributory plans wherein the employee's contributions plus interest were returned to his beneficiary upon his death. If the employee died after retirement, any excess of amounts contributed by him over what had been paid to him in pension benefits were returned to his beneficiary. There is now, however, a trend to add other provisions, particularly in the form of "spouse's benefits." Such benefits can take the form of providing a pension payable to the spouse equaling the amount of pension benefits accrued to the date of the employee's death. Other plans carry provisions for employees who die prior to retirement, but after the employee has reached a certain age (usually the age for which early retirement is available, such as age 55). In the event of the death of the employee, the provisions of the plan assume that he retired on the day before he died, and would pay his widow one-half of what his monthly early retirement would have been. There are a number of variables in this option, but the foregoing is the primary one, and can be used as a basis for other alternatives as required.

Disability

Many plans make provisions for preretirement pensions paid to disabled employees, for to allow an employee to continue to work at a less-than-standard rate of efficiency will adversely affect production. On the other hand, to merely cast out such an employee without making some provision for his welfare will adversely affect employee morale. Many plans provide for disability payments to the employee to age 65, at which time they are discontinued in favor of social security and, possibly, normal retirement benefits payable under the pension plan. Care is usually taken to ensure that the disability benefits do not exceed the normal retirement benefits. Some plans provide for a flat percentage of salary upon disability retirement, regardless of years of service; whereas others are scaled upward to a maximum amount in accordance with the number of years of service.

It is important that disability provisions in a pension program make a distinction between those employees disqualified for a particular job and those employees disqualified for any type of gainful employment. It is unfortunate if a pension plan is saddled with a provision where employees disqualified for a particular job can draw disability benefits while still physically able to perform other types of work. This will lead to employees working full time for other companies, while at the same time drawing a full pension from the original company's pension plan. This, of course, defeats the purpose of disability provisions which were intended to provide an income for disabled employees who are not capable of performing work for pay. This situation is more prevalent in industries where it is necessary to maintain high safety standards for employees. For example, a truck driver might be disqualified from driving because his vision does not meet safety regulations, although it is good enough for him to perform many other forms of work at comparable pay levels. For these reasons, disability provisions in pension programs should contain differentials in proportion to the degrees of disabilities involved.

Contributions

The merits of contributory plans where both employees and employers contribute to the funds as opposed to noncontributory plans involving contributions only by the employer provide room for much discussion pro and con. The advocates of the contributory plans feel that the employee has greater regard for a plan in which he is a joint participant with the employer. It is also felt that greater benefits can be purchased with less drain on the employer's resources through joint contributions.

Another argument which has been advanced in favor of contributory plans is based on the conclusion that pension contributions made by employers are fringe benefits provided in lieu of wage increases. Many employees, therefore, would prefer to continue contributing and take the wage increase so that the pension benefits will be based on the higher earnings amount. This feeling is most prevalent among older employees nearing retirement age.

The proponents of the noncontributory formula point out the tax advantages where the employee is not taxed on the amount of employer contributions made on his behalf. He is not subject to federal income tax on these amounts until he begins to draw them in the form of pension payments, which is normally at a time when his income is reduced and his tax bracket is relatively lower. It is also pointed out that additional monies contributed to pension plans, rather than added to gross pay, are not subject to deductions for various taxes, and therefore the employee receives more actual value for his money on the noncontributory basis.

Financing

The means used for financing pension plans can be divided into two general categories: (1) by contracting with an insurance company to insure the benefits under an annuity or insurance form of contract, and (2) through the establishment of a trust fund wherein the accumulation, earnings, and appreciation of the fund will furnish the plan benefits.

Group deferred annuities. This formula, which comes under the heading of the insured type of plan, involves a contract between the employer or trust and the insurance company to purchase annuities for the employee as each year of service occurs. To illustrate, if the employee who is a member of the plan earns $10,000 during the current year and the plan provides for an annuity to be purchased equaling 1 percent of earnings, a $100 annual annuity is purchased for that employee at a cost stipulated by the insurance company to be paid the employee for life beginning with normal retirement age, usually 65. If the employee's salary is $11,000 during the next year, an annuity of $110 is purchased to be paid him for life beginning at the normal retirement age. As employees leave the company through severance or death, with accumulating vested interests or subject to reduced vesting, the company will receive proportionate refunds in the form of experience credits, or such amounts can be used to reduce future contributions.

Normally, insurance companies impose a minimum annual premium payment, and also require a minimum percentage of employee participation, usually 75 percent if the plan is contributory.

Group deposit administration. The principal feature which distinguishes the deposit administration contract from the deferred annuity contract is that the contributions are not used to immediately purchase individual annuities. Instead, the funds are accumulated with interest added at a guaranteed rate until such time as each employee retires, and the annuity is then purchased for him. By removing the necessity for maintaining individual annuity contracts under this second plan the amount of administrative work involved is reduced. This plan also differs from the group annuity plan in that the requirements of participation previously mentioned under the group annuity plan do not apply. Because of the nature of this plan, it does not require a fixed normal retirement age.

Group permanent life insurance. In its simplest form, this plan provides life insurance coverage to retirement age, with cash values providing a fixed amount of monthly retirement income (normally $10 of monthly retirement income for each $1,000 of life insurance). It provides the advantage of allowing ample insurance coverage for an employee under a group plan during his active years, which is then convertible to retirement income at the required age. There are many variations to this plan, such as making provisions for survivors' benefits by virtue of reduced base rates of income, and also optional adjustments where additional benefits can be purchased independent of the life coverage, in order to bring the retirement benefits up to a more desirable level.

Individual contract pension trust. This type of plan is geared to meet the needs of a small group of employees not of sufficient size to allow the use of a group annuity or group permanent life insurance contract, inasmuch as the cost would be prohibitive. Under this plan, money is placed in a trust fund from which individual insurance and annuity contracts are purchased. Because of its small size, the individual records can readily be maintained by the trust with relatively low administrative costs. In many instances insurance companies will not issue straight retirement annuities, but will require the purchase of life insurance for a small additional cost, which often involves $1,000 of life insurance coverage for each $10 of monthly retirement income.

Ordinary life with supplemental fund.   Under this plan, the trust purchases individual policies for the participants, which are held by the trust.   Life insurance coverage is maintained until retirement, and is then used to purchase a part of a pension allowance, with the balance supplemented from funds accumulated in the trust.

Trust, self-administered.   A trust agreement must be established in order to operate an uninsured or self-administered pension plan.   Contributions are made to this trust which can be administered by the employer, or an appointee designated by the employer, or the employer and the representative union.   It can also be placed under the direction of a salaried administrator who, in turn, is usually under the direction of a board of trustees either appointed by the company or, if the union is involved, made up of an equal number of company and union-appointed members. It is a normal practice to appoint a bank or an investment counselor either to handle the investments of the trust monies in bonds, stocks, etc., or to advise the trustees in making such investments.   It is the responsibility of the board of trustees to direct the administration of the plan, to make rulings within the terms of the plan provisions, to interpret such provisions, and to take the necessary means to measure the performance of the investment media.   In some cases the trust may be too small to function as an individual investment medium, and many of the smaller funds participate in a common trust with other funds of similar size in order to gain the advantage of investments on a larger scale.   The amount of contributions required in order to provide the established level of benefits for a trust is determined by an independent actuary.   Monies contributed to the trust by the employer are not revocable until such time as the plan or trust is dissolved and all commitments to retirees, employees, and other involved parties have been satisfied.

Funding Methods

An orderly and realistic procedure must be established for the adequate funding of any type of plan.   The type of funding to be used, of course, is best determined through the use of an independent actuary.   There are a number of acceptable procedures which are briefly highlighted in the following.   The allowable space does not permit detailed descriptions.

Terminal cost method.   This method requires the determination of the present value of future benefits payable to pensioners, and the deduction from this amount of the actuarily determined value of the present assets in the fund.   There is then added to the fund the amount needed to keep the assets on hand at least equal to the value of pension benefits payable to the employees now on pension.   To simplify, as each employee retires, there is added to the fund an amount equal to what is assumed will be paid to him for the entire period of his retirement, and the individual pension liability is not determined and funded until the employee actually retires.

Unit cost method.   This procedure requires that the normal cost for a year be determined as the total for the entire group of employees, which is made up of the single premiums for the unit benefits accruing during the year for each member. For example, a unit of pension, which could be a specified percent of salary, is assumed, and a contribution is made equal to the value of that unit of the pension.   As the employee grows older and consequently has less years left to retirement, the annual cost for each unit will increase.

Entry age normal method.   Two cost factors are computed under this method. One gives recognition to service of the employees prior to the inception of the plan, which is known as the "past service benefits."   The other factor takes into consideration the expense applicable to pension costs for the current year.   The current cost necessary to pay the amount of pension earned that year is determined and paid into the plan. In addition, the unfunded expense for past service prior to the inception of the plan is recognized, and a percentage of one year relating to the total years over which the cost is to be funded is deposited in the fund. For example, after the amount for the current year is determined and deposited, it is calculated that the unfunded liability for past service is $100,000. The assets or amounts set aside to cover this past service liability amount to $20,000. The amount to be funded over 20 years, therefore, is one-twentieth of the difference of $80,000, or $4,000, which is to be deposited to the fund for the current year. It should be noted that Internal Revenue Service regulations limit contributions for past service in any one year to 10 percent of the total unfunded liability amount.

Level cost method. Under this method the total pension cost for each participant is determined, and an equal amount is set aside each year so that when the employee reaches retirement age, the total amount necessary to pay his total pension benefits will have been contributed to the fund.

Aggregate cost method. Under this formula, it is necessary to determine the present value of the total future benefits. The amount of accumulated funds on hand to date is deducted from this figure, after which the present value of all future salaries is ascertained, and the first figure is divided by the second figure, which provides a percentage of salaries required to be contributed to the plan for the current year.

The Evolution of a Company Pension Program

The initial plan was founded as an insured plan for all employees of the company, both union and nonunion, with the company retaining unilateral rights of administration. It was an insured plan, with each employee contributing 2 percent of his salary, and the company making up the difference necessary to buy a monthly annuity equal to 1 percent of the employee's annual salary. In the event of death or severance prior to retirement, the employee's contributions plus interest were returned to the employee or his survivor. In due time, the benefits of the plan became subject for negotiations, and a formula was gradually developed which provided pension benefits of 1¾ percent for each year of service for the first 20 years, and ½ of 1 percent for each year of service thereafter. Early retirement benefits were established, and a provision for the payment of disability benefits was inserted into the plan. The early retirement benefits exceeded the levels provided under the insured annuity plan, and a trust was established which paid the pensioner the difference between the annuity benefits and the amounts guaranteed under the plan. There was no provision for the payment of disability benefits under the annuity plan, and the full amount of these benefits was paid by the trust until the employee reached age 65, at which time his accumulated annuity benefits became payable. The trust and the insured plan eventually evolved into three trusts: one for the salaried noncontract group, and the others for two union groups. Improvements to the plan were continued, and finally it was decided to make them noncontributory plans with the full costs borne by the employer.

The conclusion was then reached that in order to more efficiently fund each of the three plans, they must become trusts, and agreements were made with the insurance company wherein specified reserves were retained by the insurance company to guarantee the payment of the annuities purchased prior to the inception of the trust. Any excess amounts were transferred to separate accounts established for investment purposes, with all income from these investments reverting to the trust. Payments to pensioners were made by the trust, with the insurance company reimbursing the trust for the portion of such payments representing the annuities held in the insurance company's reserve accounts. All company contributions made from the date of the inception of the trust were paid into the trust's investment accounts for investment in stocks, bonds, and other income-producing media. As the required insured amounts of reserves decline due to severances, deaths, etc., the excess funds are transferred from the reserve accounts to the separate accounts as additions to funds available for investment.

In order to give greater recognition to service, an additional retirement formula was developed which provided a pension equal to 1½ percent of the employee's average salary for the last 5 years of service, or for the 5 years in which his salary was the highest, times the number of years of service, to a maximum of 50 percent at age 60 or above. For example, an employee joining the company at age 26 will, at age 60, have accumulated the necessary service years (34) to provide full retirement benefits, although retirement is not mandatory at age 60. The employee may, if he wishes, continue to age 65, or any age between 60 and 65, without any increase in the percentage, but a potential increase in final average earnings on which to base that percentage. The mandatory retirement age is 65, and there are provisions for early retirement beginning at age 55, with proportionate discounts for each year under age 60. The plan and the contract with the insurance company provide that in the event of the dissolution of the plan, the insurance company will use the reserves on hand to repurchase annuities for all participants, and will be responsible for the payment of those annuities to active employees upon retirement and to current retirees.

Tax Advantages to Pension Plans

The Revenue Act of 1942 legislated favored tax treatment for plans meeting the required standards for nondiscrimination in favor of executives, owners, stockholders, or high-paid employees. In other words, a plan, in order to be qualified by Internal Revenue, must prove to be one for the general benefit of all employees, and not just a favored few. Some of the tax advantages are as follows: The earnings of a qualified trust plan are exempt from federal taxes. Likewise, earnings on pension reserves held by the insurance company under an insured plan are exempt from such tax. The employer's contributions to a qualified or approved plan are, subject to certain limitations, legitimate tax deductions. The employee also benefits, inasmuch as he is not taxed on contributions made on his behalf by the employer, but only on the benefits received as the result of employer contributions; as previously mentioned, this usually occurs during a period when the employee's income is in a lower tax bracket and subject to a lower tax percentage. Therefore, each dollar contributed in the employee's behalf today is not taxed at the current tax rate of possibly 20 to 30 percent or more, but at a rate based on the employee's gross income at the time he receives the pension benefit. In addition, death benefits of up to $5,000 are excluded from taxable income, and the proceeds from the plan are generally exempt from state taxes.

Other requirements for favored tax treatment are: the plan must be maintained within the United States; it must be for the exclusive benefit of the employees; it must be irrevocable, that is, monies contributed to the plan cannot be refunded to the employer; it must be maintained on an actuarially sound basis; it should cover 70 percent or more of the employees, and if 70 percent are eligible, 80 percent of that group must be covered. The plan cannot extend the waiting period for enrollment beyond the first 5 years of employment, and any age limits imposed are to be superseded by service restrictions. In other words, if the plan says an employee must be 35 years of age before joining it, and such employee accrues 5 years of service before reaching age 35, he must be allowed to join the plan. Finally, there can be no discrimination in the payment of benefits. In other words, set percentages must be established to apply equally to all employees.

Summation

The growth of pension plans over the last 20 years has fulfilled a great need, and the evidence is apparent today when we see so many of our "golden-agers" actively enjoying life, maintaining good health, and living in pleasant surroundings. The days of cleaning out the spare bedroom so that grandma or grandpa can waste away their declining years away from the mainstream of family life is rapidly disappearing, and for this we can be thankful. We hear many cries today about making the world over for the young; there must also be room for the *old* to live their lives in decency and with dignity. Pension plans play a large part in providing these means.

SOCIAL SECURITY

The Social Security Act was passed in 1935, and provided retirement benefits at age 65 ranging from a minimum of $10 to a maximum of $85 per month. It required contributions for covered employees of 1 percent each from the employer and the employee of the first $3,000 of the employee's annual earnings. Since that time, there have been substantial changes in the types of coverage, benefit structure, contribution rates, and eligibility requirements, along with an expansion of the occupations covered. The plan presently provides benefits for retired and disabled workers, their dependents, and the survivors of deceased workers. There are, also, hospital insurance benefits and medical insurance benefits available to retirees age 65 or over under the Medicare provisions of the program. We will deal only with retirement benefits in the space allotted for this material.

Current regulations require contributions equally from the employer and the employee of 4.8 percent of the first $7,800 of the employee's annual wages. Under the present law, the percentage will be subject to periodic increases to a maximum of 5.9 percent in 1987. A self-employed person eligible for social security and Medicare is presently required to pay a tax of 6.9 percent, which will gradually increase to 7.9 percent in 1987. His benefits and those of his family are computed in the same manner as those of the wage earner.

To be eligible for old-age benefits, a worker must be age 62 or over and fully insured. The determination as to whether he is fully insured depends upon the number of "quarters of coverages" he has accumulated at retirement age of 62 or later. A quarter of coverage is determined as each quarter of the calendar year in which the worker received a minimum of $50 in wages. In order to make this determination, he must count the number of years after 1950 or the year he became 21, whichever is later, and ending with the year prior to the year in which he will be age 65. The maximum amount of earnings on which benefits can be computed for this period are:

```
1951–1954:   $3,600
1955–1958:   $4,200
1959–1965:   $4,800
1966–1967:   $6,600
1968–1969:   $7,800
```

For this example, we will assume that he earned in excess of those amounts in all years, and we will compute his average earnings on the maximum amounts. His total earnings for the period were $93,600. He is allowed to deduct 5 years' earnings from this amount, which would be the years with the lowest earnings, or 1951 through 1955, which would leave a balance of $75,000, which divided by 168 months would produce average monthly earnings of $446 (only even dollar amounts are considered). It is then necessary to refer to the benefit table (used in lieu of any computation formulas) which shows that the primary insurance benefit based on average wages of $446 to $450 per month would be $189.80 per month. His spouse, if also age 65, would receive one-half of this amount, giving them a total monthly benefit of $284.70 per month.

Had this worker decided to retire at age 62, his benefits would have been reduced by 20 percent, based on the same average earnings as those computed for retirement at age 65.

It should be noted that the wife of an insured worker is entitled to receive the wife's insurance benefit at age 62, even though her husband has not yet retired. The benefit will be 75 percent of what her normal benefit would have been had she waited until age 65.

Some benefits under the social security program require that the worker be fully insured as previously described. Others require only that the worker be "currently insured." This means that the worker must have at least 6 quarters of coverage in the 13-quarter period insured to qualify himself or his dependents for the following types of benefits:

Retirement benefits

Retired worker, 62 or over
Wife, any age if caring for child (except student 18 to 21), entitled to benefits
Child under 18 (18 to 21 if student) or any age if disabled
Dependent husband, 62 or over

Survivors benefits

Dependent widower, 62 or over
Dependent parent, 62 or over
Widow or dependent, divorced wife
He can qualify for the following types of survivors benefits if "currently insured" or "fully insured":
Widow or surviving divorced mother any age caring for child (except student 18 to 21) entitled to benefits
Child under 18 (18 to 21 if student) or any age if disabled

There are many ramifications involved in the Social Security Act, too many to describe in any detail here, but we believe that the foregoing has provided an outline which can be used as a guide for further research. Personal guidance is available at local social security offices, and should be used in making exact and individual determinations.

BIBLIOGRAPHY

Pensions and Profit Sharing, 3d ed., Bureau of National Affairs, Inc., Washington, D.C., 1964.
Pension and Profit Sharing Service, (Bi-Weekly Service), Prentice-Hall, Inc., Englewood Cliffs, N.J.

chapter 38

Group Life and Health Insurance Plans

E. G. SHERMAN *Manager Employee Benefits, Honeywell Inc., Minneapolis, Minnesota*

Group life and health insurance plans provide financial security to the members of the group in case of death and illness. While such a group usually consists of the employees of a company, it may also be made up of members of a fraternal, social, religious, or other association-type organization.

The basic financial concept of group insurance is that a group of persons can generally purchase life and health insurance coverage at a lower cost than if the same group of persons separately purchased individual insurance contracts.

GROUP LIFE INSURANCE

The objectives of group life insurance can generally be viewed from two points, that of the individual, or employee, and that of the provider, or employer. From the individual's point of view, group life insurance provides low-cost financial security for beneficiaries in case of the employee's death, and may also do so for the employee, in case of his total and permanent disability. Through some group insurance plans the employee may also secure life insurance to cover certain members of his or her immediate family. The objectives of the provider, or employer, include the following:

1. Assisting employees to purchase life insurance at low cost
2. Securing and maintaining an efficient work force
3. Meeting a feeling of moral obligation to provide some financial security to the beneficiaries of an employee in the case of the latter's death

Types of Group Life Insurance

Term insurance. This is the most widely used form of group life insurance. Term insurance does not build up a cash value over the life of the policy as do the conventional forms of regular individual life insurance. The insurance contract is between the insurance company and the provider, or employer. Each person in the group is usually issued an insurance certificate which summarizes the principal provisions of the actual contract.

A term insurance contract provides the amount of insurance for all members in the group according to a uniformly applied formula. The amount of insurance may be related to pay, age, years of service, or a combination of such factors; or the amount might be a flat sum; or in more recently developed plans, the benefit may be related to the type and number of dependent survivors.

For example:

1. Insurance related to annual pay may provide two times annual pay.
2. Insurance related to age may specify:
   Age up to 35:   four times annual pay
   Age 35 to 45:   three times annual pay
   Age 45 to 55:   two times annual pay
   Age 53 to 65:   one time annual pay
3. Insurance related to service may provide:
   Up to 1 year service: $1,000
   1 to 5 years service: $4,000
   5 to 10 years service: $7,000
   10 to 15 years service: $10,000
   15 years and over: $15,000
4. Combination of age and earnings may provide insurance for a group member equal to:
   10 percent times annual rate of pay multiplied by years remaining to age 65
5. A flat amount of insurance may provide $10,000 of coverage for each employee.
6. A survivor benefit may provide a monthly annuity equal to:
   20 percent of monthly pay for spouse, plus 10 percent of monthly pay for each child under 18 with a maximum of 50 percent of pay

On the death of the participant the face amount of term insurance may be paid to the beneficiary in installments with interest, usually over a 5-, 10-, or 15-year period, or it may be paid in a lump sum amount. In older group policies the amount of insurance in force could be paid off for total and permanent disabilities occurring prior to age 60. If such disability occurred on or after age 60, the insurance would be continued without further payment of the premium. Policies currently issued are more apt to provide total and permanent disability provisions only on the basis of a premium waiver rather than a cash payment.

The cost of term insurance varies from one insurance company to another and is primarily dependent upon the makeup of the participating group. Factors having an effect upon the premium rates include:

1. Size of group
2. Age makeup of group
3. The formula determining the amount of insurance
4. Whether a total and permanent disability feature is included
5. Whether insurance is continued into retirement for an employee group

The cost of group term insurance is absorbed by many employers. It is quite common to have an employer provide a nominal amount of term insurance such as $5,000, or one-half to one times annual pay, at no cost to the employee. The employee is then permitted to voluntarily purchase by payroll deduction an additional amount of term insurance based on one of the formulas previously discussed.

Cost of the participant paid portion of the insurance may be expressed in various ways, such as in the following examples:

1. 1 percent of monthly base pay
2. 60 cents a month per $1,000 of insurance
3. Up to age 25:   40 cents per month per $1,000
   Age 25 to 40:   50 cents per month per $1,000
   Age 40 and over: 60 cents per month per $1,000
4. $X per month toward the cost of the life insurance coverage

Paid-up life insurance.   Insurance plans of this type are used by a few employers. This type of group insurance is used in a program which provides a combination of term insurance and ordinary life insurance, the latter accumulating paid-up cash values.   Usually the plan provides that the employee pays for the paid-up portion and the employer pays for the term insurance.   As the cash value of paid-up insurance increases, the amount of term insurance decreases.   Thus, the objective of this approach is to allow an employee to build up an equity in life insurance which he has available at the time of retirement, or can take with him when he terminates his employment.   Since the amount of term insurance gradually decreases, the cost to the employer also decreases as the amount of paid-up insurance increases.

The total amount of insurance, paid-up and term, is usually related to the employee's annual pay.

The overall cost of this type of program is higher than that of one providing only term insurance because a portion of the premium goes to the purchase of paid-up insurance.

Upon the death of an individual, the face amount of the paid-up insurance and the term insurance are paid to the beneficiary in the form of monthly payments or in a lump sum.

Group ordinary life insurance.   Group insurance of this type is similar to ordinary life insurance which a person buys on an individual contract basis.   This type of plan is usually provided as a supplement to a group term insurance plan.   In this type of group plan, however, the individual usually can buy only a specific amount such as one times annual pay, or perhaps a flat sum such as $10,000 or $15,000. The premiums are paid through payroll deduction.

The cost of this form of insurance is based on the individual's age at the time he enrolls in the plan, and the cost remains level for as long as he pays the premium.

Group ordinary life insurance builds up cash values in the same manner as does paid-up life insurance.   Thus, upon retirement, the insurance can be used for retirement income, or upon termination of employment, the individual can retain the policy and continue paying for it.

Accidental death and dismemberment insurance.   Such coverage is an inexpensive form of specialized insurance which pays the face amount upon an accidental death, or a part of or all of the face amount in the case of defined loss of eyesight or certain limbs.   This type of insurance is usually written as a supplement to other forms of group life insurance previously covered.

The amount of insurance coverage for a participant can be determined in different ways:

1. It may be equal to or a portion of the amount of the group life insurance for a participant.
2. It may be a multiple of the person's annual pay, such as one times, or two times, base pay.
3. It may be a flat sum such as $10,000 or $15,000.

4. It may be in multiples of sums such as $5,000 units up to a maximum level related to the person's annual rate of pay.

Upon an accidental death or dismemberment, the beneficiary, or participant, is paid the insurance in a manner such as the following:

Death.	Face amount
Loss of two legs.	Face amount
Loss of two arms.	Face amount
Loss of one leg and one arm. . .	Face amount
Loss of two eyes.	Face amount
Loss of one limb or one eye. . .	One-half face amount

The cost of this type of insurance is relatively inexpensive compared with other forms of life insurance. This results from the fact that the rate of incidence of accidental death or dismemberment is much lower than that of death from all causes. Accidental death and dismemberment insurance costs vary somewhat by the size of the group, but it usually ranges from 5 to 10 cents per month per $1,000 of insurance.

Travel accident insurance. Travel insurance is a specialized form of group insurance providing death benefit coverage for an individual while he is traveling. Many employers purchase this form of insurance for their employees without any cost to the employee. In many respects, this type of insurance is similar to accidental death and dismemberment coverage, but it is more restrictive because the face amount of the insurance is generally paid only if the employee is actually traveling in the course of his employment.

There are three common forms of travel accident insurance:

1. "All accident coverage" which pays the benefit regardless of the accident cause provided that the person at the time of the accident is in the state of travel away from his usual place of work

2. "All conveyance coverage" which pays the benefit only when the accident involved a form of conveyance such as automobile, bus, train, aircraft

3. "Common carrier coverage" which pays the benefit only when the accident involves a carrier for hire such as a taxi, bus, train, or aircraft

The method of specifying the amount of insurance coverage available to a group is very similar to that used for the conventional accidental death and dismemberment insurance explained previously. However, some employers may provide a larger sum for officers and a smaller amount for lower paid employees such as:

Officers: $100,000
Managers: $ 50,000
Others: $ 10,000

A travel accident insurance policy generally specifies that the face amount of the policy will be paid in the case of death or total and permanent disability. The insurance amount paid is usually in addition to any benefits the employee is entitled to under a workmen's compensation law.

The cost of this form of coverage is inexpensive and usually less than accidental death and dismemberment insurance. This is due to the fact that the incidence of such events occurring while in the course of employment is less than that of those occurring in nonemployment situations.

Group life insurance may take a variety of other forms. The insurance industry is continuing to develop many sophisticated group programs to meet the needs of employee groups. A number of the forms of insurance discussed on previous pages may be combined in a package arrangement to give an employee group a comprehensive death benefit program.

Sources of group life insurance. Life insurance companies, both stock and mutual, and casualty insurance companies usually have group departments which specialize in the underwriting, administration, and claim processing of group insurance contracts.

Plan development. This is the process by which an organization seeking or altering coverage determines the design, administration, cost, communication, and installation of a group insurance plan. Outside resources available to assist a company in its development of a plan include:

1. Consultant: a company which, for a fee paid by the employer, provides consulting services in the design and development of a group insurance plan.

2. Insurance broker: a company which provides consulting services, secures insurance company cost bids for a group plan, and receives its compensation for service in the form of commissions from the insurance company.

3. Insurance company: a company which underwrites insurable risks and processes claims in accordance with the provisions of insurance contracts. Its overhead costs are included in the premium charges.

Plan administration. Two primary means are used in administering group life insurance plans.

The insurance company is capable of performing all the administrative functions

1. Develop a plan
2. Provide insurance contract and certificates
3. Produce participant communication items and provide enrollment assistance connected with a group life insurance plan. It can
4. Process claims
5. Provide claims analysis
6. Furnish annual financial reports
7. Provide insurance conversion procedures for terminating participants

A few employers self-administer group life plans. Using internal resources, including computer facilities, they can

1. Develop their own plan
2. Produce communication and enrollment materials
3. Process claims
4. Produce their own claims analysis

In either situation, the insurance company is responsible for underwriting the risk, producing the final insurance contract and certificates, providing insurance conversion facilities for terminating employees, and preparing annual financial reports.

Retiree life insurance. Large employers usually provide for a basic amount of insurance after an employee retires. The basic objective of this coverage is to provide a lump sum amount of insurance to cover burial and final expenses of the deceased person. However, some employers feel that this coverage should also provide additional income to a surviving dependent.

The amount of coverage usually is a flat sum, such as $1,000 to $3,000, or an amount based on the coverage the person had prior to retirement. In the latter case, for example, the amount of retiree life insurance may be 20 percent of the preretirement insurance, with a maximum of $10,000 insurance. Many companies reduce the preretirement insurance on a gradual basis over a period of several years. For example:

Age 65:   80 percent of preretirement coverage
Age 66:   60 percent of preretirement coverage
Age 67:   40 percent of preretirement coverage
Age 68:   20 percent of preretirement coverage

Retiree insurance also can be provided by paid-up life insurance, previously discussed. The cost of the paid-up life insurance has been paid for by the employee prior to retirement.

The cost of term insurance for retirees may be paid for by the employee over the course of his working career and in retirement, or by the employer when the claim is incurred. One of the principal reasons for continuing only a modest amount of retiree life insurance is the high cost of such coverage.

Most employers in planning the extent of retiree life insurance take into account that retirees and their dependents are apt to receive income benefits from social security, from a company retirement plan, and from personal savings. Thus, group life insurance generally is not considered as a principal source of monthly income for a retiree.

Trends. A few trends are developing in group life insurance which include the expanded application of the survivor's benefit concept. Such a plan provides monthly annuity benefits directly related to the type of dependent beneficiaries such as spouse and dependent children up to age eighteen.

Another form of coverage being developed by many insurance companies is to offer a plan which provides a modest amount of group term life insurance for the employee's spouse and each dependent child under age eighteen. The amounts of insurance may be similar to the following:

Spouse. . . . $2,000
Each child. . $1,000

The objective of this family coverage is to provide for a burial fund. The cost is low and is usually paid for by the employee.

GROUP HEALTH INSURANCE

The objective of group health insurance for an individual is to provide him financial protection against unpredictable medical expenses and maternity expenses incurred for himself and his immediate family dependents.

An employer's objectives for providing such insurance to his employees include the desire to secure and maintain an effective work force in a competitive labor market and a recognition that group buying of health insurance is less costly for an individual than if he purchased it by a separate arrangement.

The customary practice for an employer is to provide the same general type of health insurance coverage to all his employees. The level of benefits payable under a plan may differ from one city to another. Such differences reflect variations in medical costs.

Types of Group Health Insurance Plans

Health insurance plans are designed to provide a specific set of benefits payable to meet the expenses incurred by the participants of the group. The most common forms of health insurance plans are described in the following paragraphs.

Basic hospital, surgical, medical insurance. This is the most common type of health insurance plan. Its major features include benefits payable for:

1. Hospital board and room charges for a specific number of days
2. Hospital ancillary expenses
3. Surgery charges
4. Medical expenses, such as
   a. Doctors' visits to the hospital
   b. Outpatient emergency care
   c. Diagnostic laboratory and X-ray services
   d. Ambulance fees

An example of the typical benefits for this type of plan would be as follows:
1. Semiprivate board and room charges for 180 days per disability
2. 100 percent of hospital ancillary charges
3. Usual and customary surgical charges
4. Doctors' visits to the hospital—$5 per visit for 180 days
5. Hospital outpatient emergency care within 48 hours of an accident
6. Diagnostic laboratory and X-ray charges to a maximum of $100 per year
7. Ambulance charge—$15 per call

The cost of this type of plan varies according the benefits covered and the geographic location of the participant group.

Major medical insurance. The objective of this type of plan is to meet the catastrophic or extremely high medical expenses resulting from long-term or very serious illnesses or accidents. The plan supplements the benefits paid under a base hospital-surgical-medical plan. It has certain characteristics which include:
1. A corridor, or deductible, amount paid by the participant, on a calendar year or per disability basis, prior to benefits paid by the plan
2. A coinsurance feature which indicates the percent of eligible medical charges to be paid by the plan and the participant
3. A maximum dollar benefit on a lifetime or disability basis

The types of charges covered by this type of plan include:
1. Hospital and surgery charges not paid by the basic plan
2. Private duty nurses
3. Doctors' home and office calls
4. Qualifying preventive medicine care
5. Drugs
6. Prosthetic devices

The types of expenses not usually covered include:
1. Routine physical examinations
2. Routine dental care
3. Eye examinations and glasses
4. Expenses covered by workmen's compensation and other governmental type plans

An example of typical benefits in this type of plan would be as follows:
1. $100 calendar year deductible
2. Plan pays 80 percent of eligible charges
3. $25,000 lifetime maximum

Figure 1 shows that portion of expenses usually paid by a major medical plan.

The cost of a major medical plan is dependent upon its level of benefit features, the level or the basic hospital-surgical benefits, and the sex, age, and earnings make-up of the participants in the plan. In general, the cost of this type of plan may be as little as one-tenth of the cost of the basic hospital-surgical-medical plan.

Comprehensive medical insurance. The objective of this form of coverage is to combine into one plan the general features found in a basic hospital-surgical-medical plan and a major medical plan.

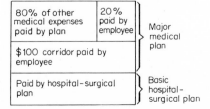

Figure 1. Major medical insurance plan expense reimbursement.

The characteristics of this insurance vary considerably from one plan to another, but the following items represent commonly found features:

1. Hospital: Plan pays first $1,000 of expenses and 80 percent of the expenses thereafter.

2. Surgery: Benefits are paid according to a schedule, and then 80 percent of charges in excess of the schedule.

3. Other Medical Expenses: Participant pays $50 deductible; plan pays 80 percent of charges.

Figure 2 shows the extent to which medical expenses are paid by a comprehensive type medical plan.

The cost of a comprehensive medical insurance plan is based on the specific features of the plan and the sex, age, and earnings makeup of the participants in the plan. In general, the cost would approximate the total cost of the basic hospital-surgical plan and the major medical plan.

Prepaid group health insurance. The objective of this type of plan is to provide a person and his dependents complete health care protection. The plan provides for hospital care, surgery, preventive medicine, regular physical examinations, prescription drug service, dental care, and eye care.

There are a number of plans of this type in operation in the United States. Included among them are the following:

Kaiser Foundation Health Plan, Inc.

Harvard Community Health Plan

Health Insurance Plan of Greater New York

St. Louis Labor Health Institute

Group Health Cooperative of Puget Sound, Seattle, Washington

Dental care insurance. This type of plan provides benefits to cover a portion of the cost of both routine dental care as well as orthodontia and dentures. This form of coverage is relatively new when compared with other group health insurance programs.

Since dental care insurance is new, its format of benefit features may vary widely. However, a common type of plan would cover the following expenses:

1. Routine oral examination

2. Basic dental work including fillings, crowns, extractions, bridges, and periodontal treatment

3. Orthodontia

4. Dentures

Plan pays 80% of excess charges	Employee pays 20% of excess charges	Plan pays 80% of excess charges	Employee pays 20% of excess charges	Plan pays 80% of charges over deductible	Employee pays 20% of charges over deductible
Plan pays first $1,000		Benefit paid according to surgery schedule		$50 deductible paid by employee	
Hospital charges		Surgery		Other medical expenses	

Figure 2. Comprehensive medical insurance plan expense reimbursement.

The extent to which the above expenses are covered vary considerably from one plan to another. However, a typical plan may include:

1. A $25 deductible per calendar year per participant
2. Payment of 80 percent of allowable expenses for oral examination, fillings, extractions, and X-rays
3. Payment of 50 percent of allowable expenses for crowns, dentures, gold inlays, and orthodontia
4. $5,000 maximum lifetime benefit
5. $1,000 maximum annual benefit
6. $500 maximum lifetime benefit for orthodontia

Benefits such as the above may be underwritten separately or incorporated as part of a regular basic hospital-surgical-medical plan, a comprehensive or major medical plan, or a prepaid group health plan; or they can be obtained from a local dental service organization.

The cost of dental insurance is dependent not only on the benefit features of the plan, but also to a great extent on the dental condition of the participants in the group. Claim experience in the earlier established plans was much higher than predicted. Thus, strict eligibility provisions and cost controls were built into subsequent plans. An organization which contemplates a dental insurance plan on a group basis should carefully review cost estimates of providing such benefits to assure that they are as realistic as possible.

Prescription drug insurance.   This form of coverage provides benefits to cover a portion of the cost of regular prescription drugs. Such expenses have been reimbursable for many years through comprehensive and major medical health insurance plans. With the expanded use of prescription drugs, some organizations provide a drug reimbursement program. Such plans are not yet very common, but are growing in number, primarily through collective bargaining agreements. The characteristics of such a plan commonly include:

1. A deductible, such as $2.00, for each drug prescription
2. Payment of the balance of the druggist charge
3. Use of a plastic type identification card
4. No maximum benefit
5. Certain controls on prescription reissue

A prescription drug insurance plan can be incorporated as part of regular medical insurance plans, similar to dental insurance.

The cost of drug insurance is dependent upon the basic costs of drugs, the administrative costs, and the usage of the plan. Simplification of claim processing and the use of generic drugs may assist in controlling the cost of such a plan.

Vision care insurance.   This plan provides benefits to cover periodic eye examinations, refractions, and glasses which are required for the individual to correct his vision. Eye care coverage may be offered by group insurance plans, prepaid group health plans, or prepaid vision care plans through optometrists; or it may come from direct use of funds created for such programs.

Other forms of group health insurance provide benefits for an increasing number of situations, conditions, or groups, such as

Nursing home care
Psychiatric care
Persons age sixty-five and over

Sources of Group Health Insurance Coverage

Group health insurance is underwritten by different types of organizations which are summarized as follows:

Life insurance company. Such companies write group health insurance plans. They are usually able to provide a wide range of benefits to both local and nation-wide organizations. Insurance contracts providing health insurance benefits are written as indemnity contracts in which the insurance company guarantees to pay a fixed amount toward a charge for which a premium has been paid. Most insurance company group contracts are experience rated, a technique by which the amount of premium paid by the policyholder is related to the loss experience and expenses of the group covered.

Casualty insurance company. This type of company provides group health insurance coverage as a natural extension or part of disability income insurance. Many contracts provide a combination of health and disability income plans in one contract. Such companies provide indemnity type contracts similar to those of life insurance companies. Casualty insurance company contracts are usually written on an experience-rated basis.

Blue Cross—Blue Shield organizations. These types of organizations were created to provide for the prepayment of medical expenses: Blue Cross for hospital expenses and Blue Shield for physician expenses.

Each of the two organizations in its own area is able to provide for a wide range of benefits. Both Blue Cross and Blue Shield units have expanded the types of expenses covered by their plans and have gradually moved from a community rating form of underwriting to experience rating for the group purchasers of their contracts.

Blue Cross and Blue Shield organizations are established on a locally autonomous basis. They operate in most states under special legislation covering nonprofit prepayment plans. With the development of health insurance plans by nationwide corporations, both Blue Cross and Blue Shield have developed special arrangements to service nationwide accounts.

Prepaid group health plans. Such plans have grown in numbers, and are becoming a more significant part of the entire group health care system. They fall into three general categories. (1) Community type plans, such as the Kaiser Foundation Health Plan or the Health Insurance Plan of Greater New York, have been created in large communities to provide comprehensive health care. (2) Joint labor-management type plans, such as St. Louis Labor Health Institute, have been developed to meet the health needs of employees in certain industrial groups. (3) Private group clinics are being created by small groups of doctors to provide health care services in a community for a variety of employee groups.

Taft-Hartley welfare funds. Funds of this type have been created by some companies and unions through collective bargaining. The income for such plans is usually received from employers who contribute a number of cents per hour per employee or a percent of payroll into a specific trust fund which may be administered by a bank, an insurance company, or a group of trustees appointed by the employer and the union.

Self-insurance plans. A few large companies underwrite group health insurance plans through self-insurance. Such organizations retain the risk, since it is a recurring one without wide fluctuations.

Self-insurance generally implies self-administration of the benefit plan, including claim processing. Consulting organizations are able to advise employers of the practical administrative and financial planning which must be accomplished before a decision is reached as to whether to use this form of underwriting.

State insurance plans. The state of California provides for hospitalization benefits for employees through its California Unemployment Compensation Disability Benefits Act. This act was adopted in 1946. It provides for unemployment, disability, and hospitalization benefits. In 1963, regulations governing the plan were adopted which, for all practical purposes, eliminated group disability income plans in California. Since hospitalization benefits also are paid out of the state plan, employers have integrated the state benefits with those paid by their group health insurance plans.

Retiree group health insurance. Many employer organizations in years past continued group health insurance for their employees who retired. The retiree benefits for such coverage were continued either at the same or at a lower level. If retirees were not retained in the employer's group health plan, they were usually afforded the opportunity of converting their policy to one written by the health insurance company on a bill-direct basis. Thus, the retiree was for the most part able to have some health insurance coverage.

Social Security Medicare coverage which became effective in 1966 changed the extent to which employers provided health insurance for their retirees. Many companies altered their plans to provide supplemental benefits not payable by Medicare. Others retained their old plans and reduced their benefits by those paid by Medicare. Still others eliminated retirees from their group health insurance plans, feeling that Medicare provided adequate hospital-medical coverage for this group of citizens.

Group life and health insurance conversion. Group life and health insurance contracts have a feature which permits a person, who is no longer eligible for the coverage because his employment was terminated, is no longer in the eligible group, or has retired, to convert his insurance to a nongroup policy offered by the insurance company without evidence of insurability. In the case of group life insurance policies, such a contract provision is generally required by the state laws. The states are not as stringent in requiring a similar provision in group health insurance contracts.

The employee, to take advantage of this privilege, must apply for conversion with the insurance company within thirty-one days after termination of employment. He must prepay the premium for the insurance policy for which he applies.

Since the person who applies for conversion can do so without evidence of insurability, the insurance company makes a charge on life insurance conversions against the employer for each conversion. The amount of these charges is reflected in the experience rating formula.

Communications. Group life and health insurance plans are usually communicated to members of the group by two principal methods.

First, an insurance certificate is provided members of the group. The certificate is a summary of the principal provisions of the contract between the insurance company and the employer, or other purchasing organization. The insurance company provides the certificates to the employer, who in turn distributes them to the group members.

Second, some form of narrative summary of the plan and its benefits is given to each group member. Many employers provide this information in attractive multicolor booklets. Consultants and insurance companies provide resources in preparing attractive booklets describing employee benefit plans.

Other forms of communications include posters, newspaper articles, payroll stuffers, slides and movies, and computerized annual reports.

Evaluation of Group Insurance Plans

Periodically, perhaps every two or three years, employers should review their life and health insurance plans to assure that they still meet the objectives for which they were originally established. This process includes the following steps:

1. Identification of areas of financial protection not covered by group insurance plans.

2. Collection and evaluation of employee attitudes regarding the present forms and levels of benefits.

3. Collection and analysis of group insurance plans and practices in other organizations with which the company competes for manpower.

4. Determination of areas in which present benefits do not equal standards adopted by the company as reasonable benefit levels.

5. Solicitation of comments and suggestions from consulting and insurance organizations used by the company.

6. Identification of problem areas, if any, to be corrected.

7. Development of alternative approaches to solve problems. This step should include the laying out of advantages and disadvantages, cost information, and consequences for each alternative.

8. The selection and installation of the best alternative to solve the problem area.

BIBLIOGRAPHY

Brecher, Ruth, and Edward Brecher: *How to Get the Most out of Medical and Hospital Benefit Plans,* Prentice-Hall, Inc., Englewood Cliffs, N.J., 1961.

Deric, Arthur J.: *The Total Approach to Employee Benefits,* American Management Association, New York, 1967.

Eilers, Robert D., and Robert M. Crowe: *Group Insurance Handbook,* Richard D. Irwin, Inc., Homewood, Ill., 1965.

Follmann, J. F., Jr.: *Medical Care and Health Insurance,* Richard D. Irwin, Inc., Homewood, Ill., 1963.

Foundation on Employee Health, Medical Care and Welfare, Inc.: *Pros and Cons of Insurance and Self-Insurance of Health and Welfare Benefits,* New York, 1960.

Gregg, Davis W.: *Group Life Insurance,* 3d ed., Richard D. Irwin, Inc., Homewood, Ill., 1962.

———— : *Life and Health Insurance Handbook,* Richard D. Irwin, Inc., Homewood, Ill., 1964.

Somers, Herman M., and Anne R. Somers: *Doctors, Patients and Health Insurance,* The Brookings Institution, Washington, 1961.

chapter 39

Profit Sharing, Bonuses, Stock Purchase, Stock Option, Savings, and Thrift Plans

BERNARD MANDEL   *Partner, Terrell, Williams and Salim, Cleveland, Ohio*

Employee benefits are instituted by employers for various reasons, primarily however to stimulate employees to greater loyalty and efficiency. Another prevalent reason is to remain competitive in the labor market. The end results desired may be obtained by a variety of methods.

A company should first determine if it is in a situation where it must reduce employee turnover or increase employee efficiency and loyalty, or if its labor competitors are outdistancing it in the employee benefit area. If the determination is in the affirmative, the next decision to be made is how to remedy the situation. The company should decide which type of benefit plan is best for them, taking into consideration (1) a good balance of its total salary and benefit structure, (2) its type of business (i.e., whether it is a high physical risk type of business in which employees would benefit from higher death and disability benefits), (3) cost, (4) the employee relation benefits which the company will obtain from the various benefits, and (5) existing benefits.

Subsequent to choosing the benefit areas to be dealt with, the next determination is the method of providing the benefit. Should the plan be insured? Should the employees contribute to the plan? Should the plan be paid out of pocket or funded? Numerous other questions will have to be answered, depending upon the benefit.

The most common of all employee benefit plans are pensions, which are covered in another chapter; however, numerous other types of benefits are available. A discussion of these follows.

PROFIT SHARING PLANS

In the late 1930s there were approximately 30 known profit sharing plans. In the late 1940s the figure had grown to over 6,000 plans, and in the late 1960s a 60,000 figure was attained. Why such a rapid growth? During the war years some companies were able to use this method of deferred payment in lieu of salaries which were frozen. As the use of profit sharing grew, its benefits became more widely known. It became the method of choice for providing employees with security for retirement and for disability, temporary loss of income, and emergency cash requirements. A further advantage is that the cost of the plan can be determined in relation to employer income. Flexibility of benefits and contributions also makes this an extremely attractive type of benefit.

Because employees' accounts are credited with proportionate shares of the company's contribution to the profit sharing plan, and because the company's contribution in most instances is determined by earnings, the hope of every company having such a plan is that it will foster greater efficiency and make each participant employee earnings conscious. The preface in a certain employee handbook explains that the plan for employees means an opportunity to participate more fully in the company's earnings and develop security. For the company, it further explains that the added incentive offered by the plan is capable of stimulating greater efficiency and growth. Another company points out to its employees that they now have a "direct" personal interest in profits and should strive to keep expenses down, recommend customers, and make suggestions to improve operations.

Eligibility Provisions

Each plan must set forth the conditions which must be met by an employee in order that he may become eligible for participation in the plan. The first requirement usually found is that he must be a full-time employee. The term "full-time" *must* be defined and should state a minimum number of hours worked per week and/or months per year.

Although many plans allow full-time employees to participate from the date of hire, in most instances an employee must first complete a definite period of service. A recent study indicated that the greatest number of plans had a one- to two-year waiting period, which may be measured to the anniversary of date of hire or in full "plan years." For example, a plan may defer participation of an employee until the first anniversary date of the plan following one year of employment, or it may allow participation after the employee has completed service with the company during one full plan year.

Why make employees wait to participate in the plan? The primary reason, of course, is because of employee turnover. The larger the company, in terms of employees, and the larger the turnover rate, the greater will be the administrative expenses connected with setting up participants' accounts and then removing them. The turnover problem should determine the waiting period, but the company should also consider the purpose of the profit sharing plan. If the company does not have a pension plan, and the profit sharing plan is to be used for retirement security by the employee, the company may wish either a relatively short waiting period or no waiting period in order to allow a maximum accumulation of contributions.

In addition to service requirements, every plan may cover either all employees or only certain groups of employees. In many instances, plans cover only salaried employees, the union employees participating under their own plan, which may be either profit sharing or pension. It is important to note that if a company desires a profit sharing plan qualified by the Internal Revenue Service so as to take advantage of the tax laws, the plan cannot discriminate in favor of stockholders, high salaried persons, officers, or any other preferred group.   It would be well for any company contemplating installing a profit sharing plan to have legal counsel thoroughly investigate the Internal Revenue Service guidelines.

In determining participation eligibility, often age, both minimum and maximum, is considered.   Ages twenty-one, twenty-five, and thirty are popular minimum ages, and a number of plans provide that employees at, or over, age sixty-five cannot participate.   If the plan provides for employee contributions, then participation may, if the company wishes, be limited to those employees who contribute.   If a company has a plan integrated with social security, the plan may include employees with earnings at or above a certain base, with contributions distributed on earnings over the base.   Eligibility may be limited to employees in specific plants or divisions. Many companies have identical, or similar, plans for various subsidiaries and divisions.

Although there is, or appears to be, an infinite number of variables for determining eligibility for participation, caution must be used.   Do not discriminate against any preferred groups unless there is some compensating benefit to other employees. Do not discriminate against union employees, or either of the sexes, or any race, or anyone because of age.   Provisions of benefit plans are scrutinized not only by the Internal Revenue Service but are also areas of interest to the Equal Employment Opportunity Commission and the National Labor Relations Board.

Allocating Employer Contributions

Once a contribution is made to the plan by the employer, it is allocated among the participants.   There are a great number of allocation formulas from which an employer can choose; one must keep in mind, however, that a formula must not result in a discriminatory allocation favoring prescribed groups.   The only other requirement for allocations is that there must be an objective allocation formula.   It must not be discretionary.

The allocation of contributions to individual employees may be based upon compensation, service, age, or several other criteria or a combination of these.   The most prevalent methods are:

1. *Percentage of compensation.*   Under this method each participant receives a portion of the total contribution in the same ratio as his compensation bears to the total compensation of all participants.   If total compensation of all participants is $500,000 and employee X's compensation is $10,000, he would receive 2 percent of the total contribution, $500,000 divided by $10,000.

2. *Compensation and Service.*   This method gives recognition for employee loyalty and long service.   The usual method of allocating the contribution under this method is to credit each participant one unit for each full $100 of compensation and one unit for each year of service.   If employee X had 20 years of service, he would be credited with 20 service units plus 100 units for his $10,000 compensation. He would then receive that portion of the total contribution in the same ratio as his units bear to the total units of all participants.

3. *Employee Contributions.*   In plans requiring employee contributions, often the company contribution is allocated in the same ratio as each participant's contribution bears to the total employee contribution.   If employee X had contributed $1,000 and the total employee contributions amounted to $100,000, employee X would be allocated 1 percent of the company contribution.

4. *Integrated with Social Security.*   Under this formula a breaking point is established.   (The Internal Revenue Service has established a formula for minimum breaking points.)   A company can allocate none, or a lower percent, of the contributions on the basis of compensation up to the breaking point and a greater percentage based on compensation in excess of the breaking point.   The intent of this method

is that, since all employees receive social security benefits, in order for higher salaried employees to receive the same percent of their compensation in retirement benefits as lower salaried employees, no benefit is related to the earnings up to the social security breaking point. Since social security benefits and bases are changing, the Internal Revenue Service has, through a complicated formula, established a changing schedule which can be incorporated into any plan. For example, assume that a plan has a $6,600 breaking point. You may allocate none of the contribution up to the breaking point and up to 6.818 percent on compensation in excess of the breaking point. (It is important to note that if a company has an integrated pension plan it cannot use an integrated formula for a profit sharing plan.)

The current trend in formulas is for compensation only. Until recently the compensation and service formulas were equally popular. One factor in favor of compensation only is that theoretically compensation normally increases with length of service; therefore reward for long service is built in. A factor against the compensation plus service method is that this method favors lower salaried employees.

With regard to matching percentage of employee contributions, a number of companies use a combination of this plan and another, such as allocating a portion of the total contribution by this method and the balance by one of the other methods. The attempt in the employee contribution method is to encourage employee savings.

In determining credited compensation for purposes of the contribution allocations, some definitive decisions must be made as to what compensation to include. Credited compensation can be straight time earnings, salary including overtime, commissions and bonuses. It is important at the outset to determine whether to include sick pay. A number of companies base credited compensation upon taxable earnings.

The allocation formula is one of many variables the company can use to its greatest benefit, and it should be determined only after analysis of the potential participant makeup and desired results.

Vesting

Vesting means that a participant obtains an irrevocable right to certain portions of his account balance. It is important to precede any discussion of this subject by mentioning that the government has been active in this area. Mandatory vesting within ten years will eventually be the outside limit of all plans. An employee's account must be fully vested at retirement and is usually fully vested at death. Employee contributions are always fully vested.

Vesting is most frequently based upon length of service or length of participation in the plan. A plan designed to grant full vesting after ten years of service with 10 percent granted each year means that a participant who terminates employment after his second anniversary of date of hire would be entitled to 20 percent of his balance. If employee X was 20 percent vested when terminated and his balance was $1,000, he would receive $200. If the plan was a contributory one and employee X had contributed $500, in addition to the $1,000 employer portion, he would receive $200 plus his own $500 in full.

Many plans have liberal vesting provisions and allow vesting in less time, some immediately. Some plans have more strict vesting provisions, such as no vesting for the first five years then 20 percent per year for the following five years.

Vesting is one method an employer can use to control the end result of installing a profit sharing plan. Liberal vesting gives an employee immediate motivation; a strict vesting plan is conducive to a plan for retirement and to reducing rapid turnover of personnel.

It is important in designing a profit sharing plan to have counsel investigate the current Internal Revenue Service regulations in this area.

Forfeitures

Forfeitures, sometimes referred to as reversions, are those nonvested amounts left in the plan when a participant terminates. The company in drafting a new plan must determine how these forfeitures are to be applied. Some companies use these amounts in their contributions formula to arrive at their annual contributions liability. The most common disposition is to allocate the total reversions to the participants, and this may or may not be done by the same formula as contributions; however, any other method may be used. Again the employer must guard against any discriminatory allocation of these amounts in favor of some preferred group. The allocation of reversions or forfeitures to participants is a graphic example to the participants that the company plan is for them. The psychology is of affirmative value.

Loans or Withdrawals

Shall an employee receive the benefits of his profit sharing balance while still actively employed? The employer must review the philosophy of the plan to decide. If the plan is geared for retirement benefits, the employer should hesitate to allow employees' accounts to be depleted prematurely. If, however, the plan is a supplement to retirement benefits, then the employer may benefit from the knowledge that an employee has a place of last resort from which to obtain funds in a crisis. About half of all profit sharing plans contain provisions allowing participants to obtain at least a portion of their accounts. Once again the versatility of the profit sharing plan may be shown here. Of those plans which allow premature use of funds, most employ the loan method.

Although a participant may usually withdraw his own contributions, such a withdrawal may affect his future participation. He may be precluded from contributing to the plan for a specified time. If the plan requires employee contributions as a condition of participation, the withdrawing participant may be given a specified waiting period before being allowed to return to the plan, or he may be allowed to withdraw his own funds but not the earnings which accrued on these contributions; many other methods are also possible.

With regard to participant's accounts accruing by reason of employer contributions, plans allowing withdrawals do so only up to the amount of the participant's vested interest. Thus, if an employee was 50 percent vested and had a balance of $8,000, he could withdraw $4,000.

Most plans allowing use of funds by employees do so by means of loans. Participants are generally allowed to borrow against their vested interest. The participant is usually allowed to borrow less than 100 percent of his vested interest as a hedge against devaluation of the accounts. Thus where an employee had a $4,000 vested interest and was allowed to borrow 75 percent, he could borrow $3,000. Where loans are available and an employee can make voluntary contributions, he should first withdraw his own funds as a prerequisite for making a loan.

It is extremely important to note that rulings of the Internal Revenue Service indicate that loans will be treated as taxable distributions if there is a tacit understanding that the loans do not have to be repaid. Loans therefore should have maturity dates and bear interest, and a participant should not be allowed to continue borrowing without some repayment.

Loans are normally left to the approval of a loan committee. Some plans allow loans or withdrawals only for specific purposes such as medical emergencies, purchase of a home, or education.

Employer Contributions

The term "profit sharing" connotes a sharing of the employer's earnings with the participants of the plan. How much will be shared is to be determined by the employer. The Internal Revenue Service sets a maximum allowable for tax deductions by the employer at 15 percent of the total compensation of all participants.

The amount of employer contributions may be discretionary or in accordance with a fixed formula or scale or a combination of both. The fixed-formula method is the most prevalent. The advantage of a fixed formula is that it is conducive to projecting net earnings for the year. In certain instances, if a company has a fixed liability prior to its year end, the amount can still be deducted for the year if paid by the time that the company files its tax return. The fixed-rate method facilitates this deduction. For employee relations, the incentive may be greater if the employee knows how much he will receive when measured against the company's profits.

Some examples of fixed rates are (1) 5 percent of net earnings before taxes, (2) 8 percent of profits, before taxes, in excess of $10,000,000, or (3) nothing if earnings after taxes are below 5 percent on capital funds, 3 percent of participants' compensation if the 6 percent figure is attained, and proportionately increased up to a maximum of 15 percent of compensation as the return of capital increases.

When the discretionary method is used, a precedent may be set in distributions to the plan, and the employer, by legal action, may be required to continue making payments. This method, however, is favored by companies wishing to control contributions in accordance with changing economic climates and money availability. Companies using this method should be advised by counsel of changing requirements in order to satisfy the U.S. Department of Labor under the Fair Labor Standards Act.

The percent of contributions is a peculiarly individualized matter. A company must consider its own situation, taking into consideration its earnings history, its shareholder relations, its other employee benefit plans, and its own employee relations problems.

Employee Contributions

Some plans require employee contributions, as indicated in the discussion concerning eligibility, but many plans allow voluntary employee contributions. Slightly more than one-half of all plans are estimated not to have employee contributions of any kind.

There are a number of pros and cons connected with employee contributions. Mandatory contributions are usually limited by the Internal Revenue Service to a maximum of 6 percent, and voluntary contributions to a maximum of 10 percent.

Why should an employee be required to contribute? One reason is that it is a forced savings. Another reason is that if the company's contributions are insufficient to provide for retirement, then the employee's own contributions will provide a minimum benefit. Voluntary contributions offer an employee the opportunity to save and take advantage of professional investment counsel, diversification of investments, and a trustee's custodial and accounting services. All employee contributions share in a common tax advantage in that earnings on the contributions are not taxable to the employee until distributed.

The disadvantages, and there are some, are that a mandatory contribution can be burdensome to some employees; employee contributions are made with after-tax dollars and while it is a savings for the employee, he relinquishes control of the investment. Although the advantages may far outweigh the disadvantages, employee contributions are rarely favorably accepted by employees.

Investing the Funds

We now have funds held under a plan, what do we do with them? The company has a vast responsibility to keep funds properly invested. In today's financial market, this burden can be shifted to professional investment counsel or to a corporate trustee. All too often, however, the employer feels that his responsibility ends there.   A conscientious employer will measure investment results against some standard indicator and, if required, seek new investment counsel if the results warrant a change.

After retaining investment advisors, a full analysis should be made of objectives. A sufficient amount of liquid assets should be retained to provide immediate cash for disbursements, and a proper mix of fixed-income and equity securities must be determined.

Some plans allow a participant to invest his account in various funds, usually equity or fixed income.   Some of these plans require investments in the more secure fixed-income funds if loans have been obtained by the participant against the interest.

Another possible investment is insurance.   Insurance may be purchased for participants so long as less than 50 percent of the contributions for those participants are used for premiums.   This should be considered where a company does not have adequate death benefit or disability plans.

Administration

A profit sharing plan requires a vast amount of administration regardless of the number of participants or the amount of money involved.   The profit sharing plan requires day-to-day administration in most instances.   Investments must be constantly reviewed, income collected and accounted for, and such procedures as annual allocations to participants' accounts, revaluations, participant withdrawals, filing of governmental forms, and communicating with employees must be carried out.

Improper administration can lead to a total voiding of any benefits which should be derived from the plan.   For this reason it is wise to seek professional help.   The trust department of any bank can discuss the ways in which they can help you to make the plan a success, and the cost is relatively small.

Communication

To obtain the full measure of employee relations benefits from a profit sharing plan, the company must communicate to its employees exactly what the plan means to them.   The Internal Revenue Service requires that each employee be advised of the plan provisions.   This, however, is not enough.   Prepare a booklet or pamphlet or for smaller plans a letter setting forth in lay terms what the plan means, what its objectives are for the company and the employees, and how it will work.

Annually thereafter, subsequent to the revaluation of the plan and the company's contribution, each participant should be sent a certificate or letter indicating his beginning balance, the addition to or reduction from this, and the ending balance. Figure 1 shows a sample of a profit sharing certificate.   At the time that this is forwarded to the participant it would be proper to remind him of the plan provisions and how it is working.   If in fact the value of the fund has increased by reason of investments, take advantage of this to point out how this plan is helping the participant.

Communication with the employee is of importance in order to derive the greatest employee relation benefits from the expenditure of funds by the company for the benefit of its employees.

SAVINGS AND THRIFT PLANS

Savings and thrift plans are relatively new in the development of employee benefit devices.   These plans are in actuality forms of contributory pension, profit sharing, or stock bonus plans, and for Internal Revenue qualification they must be classified as one of these.   The difference to the employer, however, is cost.

Savings and thrift plans are used, not as a substitute for pension plans, but usually to augment them, with respect to both benefits to employees and employee relation benefits to the employer.

Employer cost, when measured against other types of benefit plans, can be extremely low. For instance, if the average employee contribution is 5 percent of compensation and if the company matches employee contributions to the extent of 50 percent, then the cost to the company could be as low as 2½ percent of compensation, with administrative costs offset by forfeitures. A profit sharing plan, depending upon the formula, can run as high as 15 percent of compensation.

A savings and thrift plan encourages thrift in employees by matching a substantial proportion of the voluntary savings of employees. It is an attractive way for an employee to prepare to meet unforeseen emergencies or to ultimately accumulate a personal estate in order to provide additional funds for retirement.

Another general benefit which may be obtained through savings and thrift plans is to have employees become investors in the company through stock ownership on a dollar-cost-averaging basis. This is unlike a standard stock purchase plan where an employee must commit himself to buy a fixed number of shares within a fixed period of time.

The savings and thrift plan has become an important tool in designing overall employee benefit packages as well as an important factor in attracting and retaining competent personnel. It is a good means of stimulating employee enthusiasm for the welfare of the company and to increase profits. Psychologically, a pension plan, in the mind of the employee, is in the future. An employee may leave the employ of the company and not be eligible for any pension benefits. Even pointing to the future security of a pension plan and indicating how much the company is spending for the future security of the employee will evoke the query, "But what have you done for me lately?" A savings and thrift plan may be the answer, providing the most in employee relations for the least cost.

In essence, the typical savings and thrift plan is a profit sharing plan which has mandatory employee contributions, and which is used to encourage thrift in employees while giving employees a share of company profits. It give employees an opportunity to amass a personal estate with professional administrators, no administrative expenses, and certain tax advantages. Its attractiveness to employers is its relatively low cost and high return in employee relations.

Eligibility Requirements

As in other types of employee benefit plans, a savings and thrift plan must not discriminate in favor of any preferred group of employees. This discrimination is limited not only to those patently discriminatory provisions, but also to those which may be discriminating by operation of the plan, such as allowable contribution rates where the maximum could be easily reached by high-salaried people but would be a burden to middle- or low-salaried people.

With this in mind, the first consideration in setting up a savings and thrift plan is to determine which employees will be covered. In order to be effective, the broader the coverage, the better, and for this reason most companies have a savings and thrift plan in which participation is offered to all employees without exception. In an extensive study released by the Bankers Trust Company of New York in 1967, of 132 qualified plans reviewed more than 65 percent covered all employees. However, they indicate a trend toward covering only salaried and nonbargaining unit employees. If a company wishes to exclude union employees, it must be done carefully. It is an unfair labor practice to specifically exclude union employees only; however, you may exclude them unless their collective bargaining agreement specifically provides for plan participation.

Groups eligible for participation are subject to other exclusions. Sometimes, in an attempt to enforce the feeling that the plan was adopted for the "average" employee, plans have been designed to exclude such groups as those earning above a certain salary, company officers, and perhaps employees who are eligible for certain other benefits such as a stock bonus, stock options, or other bonus plans.

After determining the group to be covered, all employees, salaried employees only, salaried employees and nonunion, hourly only or any particular variation thereof, the eligibility requirements as to the individual employee should further be defined. Generally, the age and service requirements are extremely liberal, and most plans have requirements of one year or less for service and no age requirement or, at most, age twenty-one. Restrictions on age or service are used to eliminate some administrative costs in high turnover groups of employees. It must be remembered, however, that a savings and thrift plan should have a large participation in order to reap its full potential.

Employee Contributions

The essence of a savings and thrift plan is to encourage thrift in employees through a systematic savings program of payroll deductions. How much an employee contributes is determined by his individual needs and requirements. Plans usually express employee contributions as a percent of compensation (an employee can elect to contribute 1, 2, or 3 percent, etc.) which amount, after a percent is determined by the employee, is deducted by the company from the employee's salary.

The maximum contributions to most plans range from 2 to 10 percent; the median is 6 percent (according to the Bankers Trust study). The 6 percent figure is the most prevalent, because where contributions are allowed in excess of this amount on an employee matching basis, the Internal Revenue Service may require the employer to show that the high rate is not advantageous in practice to high-salaried persons. If the plan allows contributions of 10 percent, but if only high-salaried persons can and do contribute the maximum, it may be determined that the plan is discriminatory, which may jeopardize the qualification status of the plan.

Some plans allow for a graduated increase in the maximum allowable contribution, either with age or length of service. The basis for this is (1) that as an employee nears retirement age, it is more important for him to save for retirement; (2) that with longer service, the employee's salary usually has increased so that he can afford a larger contribution; and (3) a reward for faithful service. It must be remembered, however, that this may lead to discrimination difficulties.

A number of plans impose a limitation on the contributions which may be made. For example, contributions may be made on compensation up to $25,000, or a maximum contribution of $100 per month. This effectively reduces maximum contributions which can be made by highly compensated employees.

There is still another facet to employee contributions. We have discussed employee contributions which are used as a basis for employer contributions. There are, however, a few plans which allow contributions in excess of the employee contribution, but which are not matched in whole or in part by the employer. Such plans allow the employee, among other things, to take advantage of the preferential tax treatment given to these plans.

Employer Contributions

What is it that makes a savings and thrift plan attractive to employees? Primarily, it is the employer contribution which is related to employee contributions. Employer contributions may vary from very little up to 100 percent of employee contributions or even greater. The most prevalent rate is 50 percent of employee contributions. This simple basic formula has been varied in many ways.

Some plans vary the percentage payable by the employer with the length of service of the participant or with the participant's years of participation: some plans vary the rate with the percent contributed by the participant.

An important variation is to relate the employer contributions, in total or in part, to earnings of the company. Most plans that use this variation used a fixed matching contribution formula and supplement this either with discretionary amounts or with a fixed-formula related to the company's earnings. A company thus may have a matching rate of 25 percent of employee contributions and then be required to contribute additional amounts so as to increase the rates to perhaps 50 percent. One advantage, of course, is to give the participant added incentive. Another is to make the employer's obligation less when earnings are low.

Some plans, although very few, limit the employer contributions to fixed dollar ceilings for each participant, or, in the aggregate, reduce the matching contributions, or eliminate them depending upon company earnings.

In summary, the company adopting a savings and thrift plan can, to a large measure, control the cost of the plan. If, for example, a 6 percent maximum contribution rate is available to all employees and the company is obligated to match this at a 50 percent rate, the cost would be 3 percent of total compensation, provided, of course, that all employees were eligible for participation and did participate at the maximum rate. Administrative costs could be offset in whole or in part by forfeitures.

Investments

We now have a fund amassed through a combination of employee and employer contributions. What should be done with the money? First, the employer must decide whether to allow the participant the right to direct how his money shall be invested. The vast majority of plans allow participants to elect the investment medium for their share of the fund, or at least a part of it. What options can and should be offered? The types available are usually (1) company stock, (2) savings bonds, (3) equity securities, or (4) fixed-income securities. Each employer must review the purpose and philosophy of his particular plan in order to determine the options to be allowed.

Investment in company stock was mandatory in two-thirds of the Bankers Trust survey plans, and an available option in an additional 22 percent of the plans. Investment in company stock is used by companies which desire to promote employee investment in the company as a means of fostering employee loyalty and incentive. To ask an employee to invest his present and his future in the fortunes of one company may, however, have an adverse psychological effect. For this reason, it would probably be preferable to offer this investment as an option only for at least the employee's voluntary contributions.

If the company wishes to provide a vehicle for savings coupled with maximum safety, it may offer an option to purchase United States savings bonds.

A company may want to offer the participant an opportunity to take advantage of the fluctuations of the stock market as a hedge against inflation, and so it may offer an opportunity to invest in units of an equity stock fund. All the funds of all employees so electing would then be invested in highly mobile common stocks, and the participants would buy units, or shares, in the common fund.

Another type of common fund is a fixed-income fund. This is similar in operation to the common stock fund, except that investments are made in more secure fixed-income investments such as bonds, preferred stock, and even mortgages.

It is probably advantageous to offer more than one option. When an employee is asked to save 6 percent of his earnings, he is being asked to give probably all, or the greater part, of his savable income. It would be proper to allow him to have some voice, even if it is a limited one, in how his money is to be invested.

Vesting

When does a participant attain an irrevocable interest in his savings and thrift plan balance? The more liberal the vesting provisions of the plan, the more attractive it is and the larger the employee participation rate. There are several standard methods for determining vesting.

Some plans grant immediate vesting, that is, as soon as the company contribution is made, it vests in the participant. This, of course, is the most liberal and most attractive to the participant.

A second, and the most prevalent, method is to graduate the vesting. A plan may grant, for example, 20 percent vesting for each year of the plan participation, so that after five years of participation the participant reaches full vesting.

A third method, and almost as prevalent as the graduated method, is commonly known as a class method. This method provides that a participant receives 100 percent vesting upon the lapse of a specified period of time after the company contribution is made. For example, if a three-year period is used, then three years after the company contribution is made, the participant becomes fully vested in that particular contribution amount. With this method, a participant can never obtain full vesting.

It is possible, of course, to tailor any of these methods to a company's needs; for example, class vesting can be graduated during the intervening years. Some plans provide for loss of vesting if voluntary withdrawals are made. All employee contributions, needless to say, are always fully vested.

All plans usually provide for full vesting upon retirement, death of the participant, or total disability. Here again it is possible to vary and add other contingencies allowing full vesting, such as involuntary terminations, being drafted into the armed forces, or plant shutdowns.

Vesting is an important area to consider in designing a plan in that it is one which has a dramatic effect on the rate of employee participation.

Withdrawals

The mere fact that a participant has a vested interest in his plan does not allow him to withdraw the funds in his account. It is one thing to give an employee the right to funds and another to let him use them. In designing a plan it is essential to take into consideration, first, the company's aim and, secondly, the tax ramifications. In a qualified plan there is a tax advantage to employees in that company contributions are not taxable to employees when made; nor does the employee pay taxes on earnings attributed to the invested funds. It takes careful planning to preserve the tax advantages, and an attorney should be consulted when drafting a plan.

Distributions of the entire participant account, including employer contributions and accrued earnings, are made upon the death, retirement, permanent disability, or termination of a participant. In the first three instances, the full amount in the participant's account is paid, but in the event of termination, the amount paid is governed by the vesting provisions of the plan.

There are two other instances where distributions may be made; these are under plans which provide for (1) voluntary withdrawals or (2) periodic distributions.

Almost without exception, savings and thrift plans permit employees to withdraw all or part of their own contributions, and most allow employees to withdraw at least a portion of their vested employer contributions. In most plans, however, a penalty is imposed if there is a voluntary withdrawal. The purpose of the penalty is not as a punishment for the withdrawing participant. The fact is that unless some penalty is attached to voluntary withdrawals, the Internal Revenue Service would probably rule that each contribution made by the company is constructively received by the participant when made and, therefore, immediately taxable. Of course, the fact that a penalty is imposed will also tend to discourage withdrawals and, hence, further the thrift concept of a savings thrift plan. The penalty is commonly in the form of a restriction against the participant making any further contributions for a specified period of time. This penalty can be made sterner by requiring the withdrawing participant to start accruing vesting again or to meet the eligibility requirements again.

Periodic distributions are usually found in a class plan (see under Vesting) and refer to regularly scheduled distributions to participants, while still actively employed. A plan using this method will usually stipulate that, at the end of a certain period after contributions have been made, the participant will acquire a vested right to that year's contributions. Most plans do not require the participant to withdraw the funds, while others provide that the participant will receive the funds unless he declines. Some plans of this type allow the participant to elect to withdraw his funds within a specified period after a contribution becomes vested, and his failure to do so precludes withdrawal of that particular year's contributions until the participant terminates employment.

Some plans make provisions for withdrawals in emergency circumstances only. It is important to remember that the aim of a savings and thrift plan is to encourage long-term thrift, and plans should be designed to discourage constant withdrawals by participants.

Forfeitures

When a participant withdraws, forfeiting a portion of the funds held for his benefit, what happens to the funds remaining in the plan? Most plans apply the forfeitures to reduce required future company contributions. Some allocate the forfeitures to the remaining active participants in proportion to their balances or the current contributions.

Miscellaneous Provisions

There are numerous variations which may be included in a savings and thrift plan. For example, loans can be provided for, although this is seldom done.

If employees are allowed to purchase company stock, provisions for voting the stock should be set forth. The plan can provide either that the employee have the right to direct the voting or only vote vested shares, or the plan can provide for a trustee to vote the stock.

The company should determine if it will administer the plan itself or engage a corporate trustee. Companies with large plans should consider the latter since the day-to-day activity of administration can be considerable.

In addition to the provisions of the plan, good communications with employees is essential. They must be made aware of the provisions of the plan in simple language. Annual certificates should be rendered to each participant to graphically illustrate how his account is accumulating.

Summary

The savings and thrift plan is a fast-growing vehicle for evoking employee loyalty and enthusiasm. It is less costly than other types of plans and is highly popular with employees. The Bankers Trust study indicates that in two-thirds of the plans 81 percent or more of the eligible employees elected to participate, and only in 8 percent of the plans did less than 50 percent of the eligible employees participate.

The plan promotes employee participation in company stock ownership. Its advantages seem to make this an attractive employee fringe benefit to both employers and employees.

STOCK OPTION PLANS

Many corporations attempt to strengthen the management ties of its executives and key employees through a program of employee stock ownership. The is done by adopting a "qualified stock option" plan, a plan which gives favorable tax treatment to employees purchasing the company's stock. There are generally two basic types of employee stock options: those which are nonstatutory, are not subject to preferred tax treatment, and do not necessarily have to be issued pursuant to a plan of any type; and qualified stock option plans. We are concerned here with the latter type.

The Plan

Employee stock option plans were introduced into the Internal Revenue Code in 1950, and the code provisions pertaining to or regulating them were amended in 1954, 1958, and 1964. The latter amendment set forth rigorous requirements, and plans meeting these requirements are called "qualified stock options." In order for employees to take full advantage of the preferential tax opportunities afforded optionees under a qualified stock option plan, the plan must meet these conditions:

1. It must be approved by the shareholders within twelve months before or after the corporation adopts the plan, and it must indicate the aggregate number of shares issuable and the class of employees covered. The class may be designated as "key employees" or "salaried employees."

2. The options must be granted within ten years of the first to occur of stockholder approval or adoption by the corporation.

3. The option must be exercised within five years after it is granted.

4. The option price generally must be at least the fair market value of the stock on the day the option is granted.

5. The option may not be exercised while any qualified stock option granted to the employee earlier with a higher option price is outstanding.

6. The option must be nontransferable, except by disposition at death of the employee, and must be exercisable by the employee only during his lifetime.

7. Generally, the optionee may not own 5 percent or more of the voting power or value of all classes of stock of the employer, its subsidiary, or parent corporation.

Tax Treatment

Taxable income does not result to the employees upon the granting of any option, but is deferred until the stock is sold, and then, if the stock is held for three years prior to the sale, it is taxed at capital gains rates. In the event that the option stock is sold within the three-year period, the difference between the value of the stock on the day the option was exercised and the option price is deemed to be income as of the day the stock is sold, and the excess, if any, between the value on the day of the exercise of the option and the sales price is treated as a capital gain. If the stock is sold at less than the option price, there is no ordinary income and there is a loss. If ordinary income results from a premature sale of the stock, then the corporation may take a corresponding deduction.

In order to take advantage of the preferential tax treatment, the optionee must be an employee of the company or subsidiary three months prior to exercising the option.

Where the option is exercised after death of the employee, the overall gain or loss upon the final disposition of the stock is to take into account the value of the option on the date of death. Thus, if at the date of death, the value of the shares have increased and the difference between the option price and value as of the date of death is $20 per share and if the final sale is $100 per share and the option price is $60, then the gain is only $20 ($100 minus $60 minus $20).

Plan Provisions

Who shall the plan cover? The prime objective of qualified stock option plans is to encourage officers and key personnel to acquire an ownership interest in the company, thereby stimulating their efforts toward the success of the company. A recent study indicated that although there is great pressure within the corporate structure to grant options to executives who influence corporate earnings, only 10 percent of the plans studied restricted option plans to top company officials. More than 30 percent of the plans included middle management, and the most prevalent type of plan included managers earning approximately $17,000 per year. After the class of employees is chosen, the typical plan provides for an administrative committee to award the options to employees within the class.

The next problem is to determine how much stock to offer. The common plan states a maximum number of shares any employee is entitled to buy, with the exact amount of each option left to the committee. Some plans set forth a schedule of shares which may be purchased related to salary brackets. In the aforementioned study, it was determined that the employee earning between $20,000 and $35,000 was generally allowed to buy stock equal to one year's salary. The option for employees earning $35,000 to $50,000 ranges from two to three and one-half times the salary, and the option for those earning $50,000 or more comes to three, four, or even five times the annual salary.

After an option has been awarded, a problem may arise as to when the employee must pay for the shares. To afford employees the opportunity to purchase stock, but then to have them in a position where they cannot exercise their option for want of the purchase price would frustrate the fundamental precepts of the plan. Some plans provide for payment in full at the time the option is exercised, but the optionee need not exercise the full option at one time. Some plans allow the option price to be paid in installments, and even payroll deductions may be offered as an alternative.

Other provisions of the plan deal with option prices, the terms of the option, the period within which an option may be exercised, how options are to be exercised, the rights of the optionee as a shareholder, and other statutory requirements. Legal counsel should be sought when developing a plan because of the rapidity with which new Internal Revenue Service requirements are continually interposed.

Effect on Company

The company, in adopting a qualified stock option plan, hopes to encourage the loyalty of its key employees and officers, the decision makers, the profit creators and to encourage continued employment of these employees. On the other side of the ledger, addition to outstanding shares will dilute the equity of the shareholders and perhaps deflate prices, and the company may be required to take additional capital when other methods of obtaining funds may be more feasible at the time.

The use of this type of plan as an incentive, however, is growing. In the study which was mentioned earlier, of the 179 companies questioned, 75 percent of those listed on the New York Stock Exchange granted stock options to key employees.

This growth has occurred in the face of continuing Internal Revenue Service controls and whittling away at the preferential tax treatment. Option plans appear to be a good motivator and a status symbol for employees.

STOCK PURCHASE PLANS

A qualified stock option plan attempts to stimulate employees to greater loyalty and production through stock ownership, but is usually aimed toward middle management, executives, and in general, key personnel. Some companies, however, desire to broaden the scope of employees' stock ownership and have adopted stock purchase plans. There are three basic types of such plans, namely, (1) deferred payment plans by which employees purchase shares which are then pledged as security for the installment payments of the purchase price, (2) current payment plans by which the employee buys shares as he pays for them, and (3) plans by which an employee is given an option to buy shares at a certain price and within a certain period of time. It is important that the employer be aware of a major pitfall to a very liberal, broad-based plan which, unlike a qualified stock option plan, is not geared to high-salaried persons and in which there is the danger of allowing an employee to undertake a financially disastrous obligation. Most plans, therefore, limit the number of shares an employee can buy, and many concern themselves with the method of payment.

Current Payment Plans

Current payment plans usually provide that an employee may request a certain amount be deducted from his pay each payday. The company then remits the aggregate amount of all employee participants to a custodian, usually a bank or stockbroker, who on a certain day each month purchases company shares at the current market price. The custodian then credits each participant's account for the number of shares to which he is entitled, including fractions. Dividends are similarly divided and may be reinvested. The employee's shares may be delivered to him when he accumulates a specified number, or the plan can provide for immediate distribution on request only.

This type of plan offers little incentive to the employee, and since he is still making purchases at market value, all he is saving is brokerage commissions and the administrative expenses paid by the employer.

In order to make the plan more attractive, therefore, some companies make contributions, usually based upon a percentage of the employee's contributions. Some companies go further than contributing cash, and deposit stock. Company contributions result in taxable income to the employee and a deduction for the company.

Note that in current payment plans there is no commitment by the participant to purchase shares. He purchases as he contributes, with a resultant dollar averaging since the purchases of stock are at the market value each month.

Deferred Payment Plans

Under the provisions of a deferred payment type of plan, the employee becomes the immediate owner of the number of shares he is entitled to and elects to purchase, and the stock is held as security for the payment of the full purchase price. The balance owed is usually then made by payroll deductions. The participant, as a shareholder, is entitled to all dividends and must pay the tax thereon, but the dividends are usually applied toward the unpaid balance. Interest, if charged by the employer, is usually low and usually is well offset by dividends.

The advantage of this type of plan over the current payment plan is that the participant receives the benefits of immediate stock ownership and financing at low or no charge.

It is extremely important to beware of possible state security statutes which require that all stock when newly issued must be fully paid for and cannot be paid for by incurring a liability; therefore, it may be necessary to use treasury stock.

Option Plans

The basic premise of the option type of plan is to extend to the employee an option to purchase at a certain specified price. This can be done by allowing the participant a period of time within which to exercise an option to purchase a certain number of shares, and the price is then deducted from his salary in installments. The participant does not acquire the rights of a shareholder until the subscription is paid.

Options issued pursuant to an employee stock purchase plan may qualify for preferential tax treatment, if they meet the following conditions:

1. The plan must provide that only employees may be granted options.

2. The plan must be approved by the shareholders within twelve months of its adoption by the company.

3. The option price may not be less than 85 percent of the market price at the time the option is granted or exercised.

4. The option must be exercised within five years of the grant where the market price is not less than 85 percent at exercise, or if the option price is less than 85 percent, the option cannot be exercisable after twenty-seven months after the grant.

5. With certain exceptions, the option must be offered to all employees.

6. No employee may be allowed to purchase more than $25,000 of stock in a calendar year.

7. The option may not be transferable.

8. All employees must have the same rights and privileges, except that the amount of stock may be geared to compensation.

9. Owners of 5 percent or more of the voting stock may not be granted options.

If stock is acquired pursuant to a plan meeting the above requirements after being held for the required period, the optionee will have ordinary income to the extent that the fair market value on the date of exercise exceeds the option price. The sale price in excess of this is treated as a capital gain. If the stock is sold within two years of the grant or within six months after the exercise of the option, ordinary income is recognized to the extent that the market value on the *date of exercise* exceeds the option price. The employee must also meet employment requirements similar to those required for a qualified stock option plan.

Under an option type plan, an employee is usually given the right to cancel his subscription prior to payment in full.

Provisions

The plan itself must be drafted to meet the particular desires of the employer. Eligibility must be clearly defined, as well as how options are to be exercised, requirements for company contributions, if any, rights of participants as shareholders, disposition of dividends, rendering of statements, and so on.

In constructing a plan, it is important to be mindful of the philosophy of these plans, namely, that their greatest benefit is derived from the granting of a proprietary interest in the company to the greatest number of employees. This type of benefit can cost an employer very little and can be a source of great employee relation benefits in the form of incentive for profit seeking.

BONUSES

Deferred profit sharing plans, savings plans, employee options, and the like have been developed throughout the years and have become important tools in shaping employer-employee relations, but constant throughout the years has been the employee's desire for immediate benefits, immediate reward for loyal service— "do something for me now." The aforementioned plans are usually designed so as to defer benefits while retaining the loyalty and enthusiasm of the employee. For this reason, many companies pay a cash bonus to employees or to certain classes of them.

Executive bonus plans are not uncommon in both large and small companies and are based upon specified formulas based on the income of the company or simply on an informal plan. Employee bonuses may be allocated to employees by length of service, or on a percentage of salary, or based upon the employee's productivity. A number of companies couple what amounts to a current bonus with a profit sharing plan, by allowing the participant to elect to receive 50 percent of the company contribution in cash and to have the remaining 50 percent deposited to his credit in a profit sharing plan; this may be done without jeopardizing the qualification of the profit sharing plan.

Some companies, but very few, pay bonuses with shares of the company's stock. The trend in this area is toward profit sharing or savings and thrift plans. If a stock bonus trust is used, the employee's deduction for income tax purposes is limited to a maximum of 15 percent of compensation.

SUMMARY

In this chapter we have attempted to outline several types of employee benefit plans. Whether a company should have any plan is a decision to be resolved based upon the company's need to reduce employee turnover, to increase employee production and loyalty, to meet the competition in the labor market, and on the ability of the company to bear the costs of the plan.

The specific type of plan to be installed depends upon the total picture of employee benefit needs. Is the pension plan adequate, or should it be supplemented? It is important to analyze the total picture. Subsequent to deciding on the type of benefit to be installed, the provisions of the plans must be adopted to fulfill the ends which the company seeks.

It is important to remember that governmental requirements are constantly changing, and prior to designing a plan, counsel should be sought. Attorneys, banks, or professional consultant firms should be used.

A last, but important, piece of advice is that a company installs an employee benefit plan in order to derive a benefit from it. To do this, it must be communicated to the employees and communicated well. This should be done through the use of booklets, certificates, and employee meetings. Employees must be told often, and well, what is being done for them and how it will affect their lives.

Part 8

Employee Appraisal and Assessment

chapter 40

Principles and Techniques
of Assessment

KENNETH F. HERROLD *Professor, Department of Psychology, Teachers College, Columbia University, New York*

The term "assessment" has many meanings in the world of work. It is associated with a variety of concepts, programs, and procedures. Assessment includes measurement, evaluation, correlation, and prediction with one or many variables, criteria, and standards of performance.

Advocates of assessment rarely observe the same guidelines or initiate appraisals with the same basic assumptions. Criteria and methodologies are often inadequately described. Comparisons of the results are rarely reliable or useful. Programs and practices seem often to have been haphazard, inconsistent, ritualistic, and at times even suggest violations of human rights. It is, however, encouraging to find a developing literature produced in a responsible and disciplined manner.

Different forms of assumptions underlie the planning and implementation of appraisal or assessment programs and procedures. Assumptions, expressed or implicit, can be humorous (Maslow, 1963). Others appear to be unjustified or indefensible (Fiske and Pearson, 1970). Many assumptions are not disclosed or are so diaphanous as to defy definition despite the copious documentation and statistical "fills" presented in a manner that is more "scientistic" than scientific. Columns of numbers seem to be too often used to defend fuzzy rationales and abstract theories rather than to demonstrate the relevance and utility of a critical variable or attribute performance thereto.

JUSTIFICATION

Principle 1. The description, measurement, and evaluation of the nature and significance of a human resource should be directed toward the achievement of meaningful personal and system goals.

40—3

It is usually assumed that an established assessment process has been instituted to select an employee, review performance, prepare for advancement or a change in position requirements, or to confirm the need for terminating employment. Certain general conditions are desirable. (1) The underlying assumptions regarding the need for assessment should be clear to all persons involved. (2) The human attributes and operational criteria should be relevant, valid, and reliable. The establishment of validity is essential. (3) The output of the assessment should be regulated in a manner that is positively directed, relevant to the critical need for assessment, and practical in terms of tangible or meaningful contributions to the employee and to the employing system. (4) The output or products of assessment should be immediately useful as inputs to individual-personal, group, or system planning and to problem solving to cope with recognized and meaningful issues, wants, needs, or difficulties. Longer range predictions are less dependable because they involve certain undetermined interventions of variables that are perhaps not yet recognized or precisely defined. (5) The employing system should be sufficiently accommodating in its assessment procedures to emergent controllable and uncontrollable factors that may modify the significance of any particular assessment process or product. (6) The desired products and processes should be anticipated and provided for in such a manner that will provide a bridge to related subsequent assessment and development activities.

MANAGEMENT OF ASSESSMENT

Principle 2.   The authorization, control, and regulation of personnel assessment should reside in the system management to assure responsibility and credibility within the organization.

Historically, assessment has been conducted to satisfy the needs of persons who, when technically competent, were not always sufficiently aware of the actual performance requirements. The assessment products under these conditions cannot be useful or trustworthy to decision makers in management or operations. In other instances, assessments have been made by persons who have been highly subjective in their judgments. The assessor is at times too "close" to the work, and although he may have opinions as to what is required based on long practical experience, he is not able to describe precisely, for effective measurement and evaluation, what is required, nor to determine in a reliable and valid manner the competency of an individual or work group to perform what was required, nor to make dependable predictions of future performance. It is also often true that what was essential in the past may not be essential in the future. Social, economic, and technological changes can invalidate the relevance of present or past experience.

The most commonly observed errors of assessment, on the practical scene, are those which have to do with four conditions. First, there is the condition wherein the assessment is for very practical reasons conducted upon the assumption that performance requirements are relatively stable. Second is the condition present when it is thought that what is true in a large number of similar work situations must be true for any particular situation. It would seem evident that the operant individual in a dynamic situation will be perceived with a potential for greater degrees of error in judgment and that corrections should be provided for in abstracting inferences regarding his value to a system. Third, there are "pressure situations" wherein it often appears that any available measure or measurement procedure should be used to deliver "here and now" assessments. There is a tendency to believe, in such an action-oriented situation, that it is better to do something than to do nothing. The fourth condition exists when the assessment process is initiated with the assumption that the person to be appraised cannot be involved in the process and that it is better, more objective and scientific, to have the assessment conducted by an unrelated "other" person. In fact the management of the system invests the other person with a blind faith that his judgments are valid and reliable. Organizations have delegated recruitment, selection, promotion, and other personnel functions to persons and organizations that have had neither the training nor the experience to be so responsible. They desire to economize or to abdicate the assessment responsibility to such other persons who may be only slightly, if at all, capable of understanding the actual demands of the work to be performed, but, cannot possibly relate the work demands to significant and relevant human attributes or to work patterns they are competent to measure and evaluate. These are conditions and issues for which the management of any system must be directly responsible.

Employees and the employing system must both be accountable in their own way. It should be clear why, for what reason, and for whom any assessment procedure is conducted. Organizations have been engaged with ever-increasing vigor and diversity in efforts to assess people, performance, work procedures, system adequacy, organizational change, and development. There are times when such preoccupations can represent ways of avoiding the responsibility for a more personal face-to-face familiarization with work and people. Persons responsible for assessment or measurement programs and procedures who are too academically oriented can suffer a credibility gap with the operations personnel. The "organization assessor" who has little or no professional training when pressed will borrow concepts, techniques, and procedures (from the academician or from another company) in an effort to be "practical," "useful," "economical" in responding to a directive to conduct some type of performance review. Under these conditions it is easy to neglect or avoid the critical search for, and examination of, the theoretical, research, or field-testing foundation upon which a sound assessment procedure should be established. Many such homespun "evaluators" engage in assessment that is often technically invalid, unreliable, and dangerous. This type of irresponsible activity can convey the appearance of authentic authority and responsibility. It can impress a naïve management that becomes an ally, by delegation, in an unjustifiable program of personnel assessment.

There is an obligation to provide for accountability in every product or service delivery system. Management and competent professionals have an obligation to be responsible to each other. Neither should place the other knowingly in jeopardy. Together they can work to eliminate the communication and the credibility gaps that prevent effective reciprocity. Neither unproductive nor imcompetent assessment is defensible. Management and the persons responsible for assessment need to be mutually supportive in efforts to cope with the basic problems of criterion definition, of reliable and valid measurement procedures, and in the establishment of realistic standards of performance and prediction of future capabilities. It is encouraging to note in recent reports that such collaboration is being more often pursued.

> *Principle* 3. Measurement and evaluation of personal or system performance (behavior) should be a part of a continuous and integrated growth facilitating process for both the employee and the employing system.

It is essential to understand fully the interaction effects of personal attributes and work environment characteristics (Thompson and Van Houten, 1970). It is no longer defensible to attribute every inadequacy or failure, by a process of reductionism, to individual-personal inadequacies when the cause may primarily reside in inadequately organized (structured) and/or deprived work systems and environments (Cumming and Cumming, 1962; Hersey and Blanchard, 1969; Riesman, 1954; Stein and Cloward, 1958; and Von Bertalanffy, 1968).

Today, assessment decision making must be system oriented, and although "systems thinking" may be pursued as the "in thing" in a management science department, there may be a concurrent application of traditional "individual-oriented" measures and procedures in a personnel or operations department unrelated to the system-management policy and planning. This practice seems to be quite indefensible. Such inconsistent and uncoordinated assessment procedures can jeopardize the organizational proficiency and credibility; they may even destroy the career potential of talented individuals inappropriately held accountable for inadequacies that are primarily system derived. Management can hold an individual exclusively responsible for an inadequacy only when he has control of all the conditioning factors influencing his performance. When management has taken all possible steps to assure that the individual employee with the necessary attributes and experience has been placed in a work environment, with well-defined subsystems, wherein he has a reasonable opportunity to succeed, then a reasonable and relevant form of assessment of his response can be implemented. There is a need for the management decision makers, the responsible parties, to assure that there is internal consistency in the allocation of responsibility, the pursuit of causation, and the institution of the appropriate interventions.

Principle 4.   The interaction of personal and system attributes renders many estimations of an employee's responsibility difficult and often impossible.

There should be established a clear and relevant linkage of the attributes of the employee as a person to the attributes and activities of other members of any work force, and to the impersonal policies, structures, functions, and procedures that constitute the work environment. An inadequate organization or work procedure can result from the choice of patterns in the decision making by central persons in interlocking subsystems of an organization. It is rarely possible to control, individually or collectively, all the inputs into such decision-making processes. It is, therefore, difficult to fully determine the success or the failure of any aspect of a large complex system exclusively in terms of one employee's intelligence, initiative, creativity, or performance. Multiple-assessment programs do gather more and different data, but if these data elaborate only the individual employee's attributed characteristics, and neglect the characteristics of his primary subsystem, related subsystems, or the nature of the total organization, the interaction phenomena are neglected.

Principle 5.   Change requires the regular review of criteria and standards of performance to determine their relevance and priority.

Society and its component systems will shift the focus of concern from the pursuit of a mastery of the physical environment to the pursuit of social justice. The concepts, criteria, and methods of determining accountability, in product or service systems, will be influenced by the accelerating attention to this national priority.

Crisis management in product and service delivery systems is often a wonder to behold. Where there is a great demand for goods or services, expansion-directed growth and change, there seems to be less concern with the need for critical and careful assessment. When the demand for service and profitability diminishes, the management is inclined to respond with unplanned, haphazard, impulsive efforts to control, or eliminate, the threat of real or imagined destructive factors and forces associated with individuals or groups. There is an apparent need to maintain or recover confidence and to engage in a variety of rituals. Each new age brings with it more complex and elaborate rituals. "Reduction in force" is one of these rituals in "hard times." Impulsive decisions are made to reduce costs. The assessment decisions, as to who is useful and who is expendable, may be on the basis of who is visible, known, politically "in or out," and hopefully on some basis of competencies. In two instances with which we are acquainted, some of the most talented individuals were expelled by reductions in force during recessions only to result in a deprivation of succession leadership within a decade.

Assessment models are always a reflection of how management thinks and to what it is committed. Some practices are "accidents" or desperate efforts to cope with economic, political, or social crises. These crises often come in bunches. Title VII of the Civil Rights Act of 1964 provided new employment opportunities, and shaped the conditions of employment during the late sixties, for the minority group members. When inflation initiated a growing financial crisis, and system inadequacies were exposed in an urban public school system, the management regressed to the traditional "seniority system" approach in the reduction of personnel. The minority group members who were predominant in the group last to be hired were the first to be discharged. A new social and economic crisis thus was created in the pursuit of social justice. The way this management would think and act in a crisis was demonstrated. That system and its management now have a new crisis of confidence, in addition to a dollar crisis, and there is a rapid deterioration of the system's capability to provide education in a competitive manner.

The disposition of management, at any given moment under any given set of conditions, will determine the policies and procedures that shape the criteria and methods management uses to maintain its performance and existence. The "informal" communication network, the "grapevine," of the organization or system can usually be relied upon to reveal whether or not assessment activities have the serious support of the recognized authority or authorities. If they are supported, they represent to the employee something worthy of serious attention and respect. Authentic concerns of top management are most respected. Vendettas or campaigns for power through the threat associated with assessment and performance review techniques, harassments, and "housecleaning reductions in force" may provoke anxiety and system-destroying fear that will impair morale and productive performance upon which the "power seekers" thrive. In the end, all are debilitated or destroyed.

> *Principle* 6. The value of membership and the respect attributed to the norms and traditions of any system shape its influence in the measurement and evaluation of individual or group performance.

The changing competition for manpower will need to be seriously considered in assessment assumptions, criteria, techniques, and procedures. In a period of recession, with talk of unemployment, and of long-term automation, it is easy to assume that manpower can be taken for granted. Talented manpower is essential for profitability, full service, and coping with complex social problems; it is critical in other transactional relations where a job, a subsystem, and the total work environment interface with each other and with society as the enveloping context of work and being.

The rapid and diverse social, economic, technological, and political changes throughout the world reflected in every human system have tended to invalidate many of the principles and practices of assessment before they are fully refined and tested. A few years ago, while working in the aerospace program to reduce human error, we found that technology was advancing so fast and in such diverse ways that product prototypes were modified before job descriptions, criteria, and standards of performance could be completely prepared. Consequently, they were rendered obsolete by new designs, requiring new production procedures, unique competencies, and standards of performance. It has become apparent that the principles, methods, and procedures of assessment must be continuously reviewed and modified or replaced to maintain relevancy, reliability, and validity, and more difficult possibly, the respect of the employee, supervisor, and management.

Principle 7.   Assessment strategies and the management thereof should facilitate growth by means of relevant continuous bridging from one state of any assessment and development process to the next.

It is helpful to remember that experience and research indicate that there is little justification for "episodic" or "opportunistic" approaches to measurement and evaluation insofar as they concern human beings.   The principles and the techniques of measurement, evaluation, and control should, indeed must, maximize the desirable consequences of future acts to assure continued maneuverability and creativity on the part of the employee, and to develop an organizational or system capability to respond effectively to the persistent need to change.

In the design and implementation of any measurement and evaluation process or program, it is essential to provide for the effective prevention and reduction of destructive conflict among persons and between the person and the system. This form of "preventive management" of assessment programs is sometimes facilitated by anticipatory planning, in process sensitivity and a reasonableness that confront the need for prompt innovation of appropriate modifications in the use of criteria, procedures, and products of the anticipated or instituted program and/or processes of measurement and evaluation.

TECHNIQUES OF ASSESSMENT

Certain decisions determine the nature of assessment data gathering.   The features of a job or position have to be described and then ordered in terms of relevant priorities of performance requirements.   These job attributes must then be related to appropriate attributes of a person.   It is from this matching process that selection criteria, measurements, procedures, and qualifications are developed. The pitfalls, uncertainties, false promises, and the risks of faith in unreliable and invalid decisions are always present.   Qualifications, selection, and job requirements determine the criteria and standards of performance used in performance reviews, career planning, promotion decisions; or they determine changes of employment.   The data available to be gathered for such decisions depend upon the organization and the technical competence of the personnel responsible for the administration of programs and techniques of appraisal.

The full service personnel assessment program provides for the reliable and valid collection, storage, analysis, and interpretation of the present and future implications of the employee's work history, education and training, interests, aptitudes, abilities, personality attributes, and interfacing capabilities with people and work situations.   It is how this information is gathered and used that determines how well the assessment program estimates the employee's ability, or technical knowledge; competence and proficiency; planning and direct action; organizing, coordinating, and integrating sensitivity and skill; leadership mode and style; responsibility for his work organization and personnel; and in all of these his judgment and communication.   It is appropriate to recognize the efforts of many investigators who have identified critical attributes and provided responsible practitioners with advances in concept and technology (Campbell, 1970; Flanagan, 1951; Hemphill, 1960; Kay, 1959; and others).

There is little support for the belief that a person behaves in such a consistent manner as to guarantee the predictive value of any assessment datum, however carefully identified.   There is little justification to believe, with all the contextual and environmental variations and their impact on the person, that it is possible to equate behaviors mediated by different variations.   Neither are we able to assume that any given performance has the same meaning for every demonstrative employee (Block, 1968).

The literature abounds with reports of testing, interview, and observation efforts to define and classify human traits or states. This can be done, but not in any general or simplistic manner. The potential for permutations and combinations, associated with success or failure on the job, suggests that any simplistic classification will be useless for the personnel officer who must engage in practical assessment programs (Zuckerman, Persky, and Link, 1967).

The third technical caution for the practitioner concerns the comparative value of statistical and clinical judgments.

"Clinical judgment" is a term used to describe the judgment of a line officer when he states, "I know a good man when I see one." Sawyer (1966) and Pankoff (1968) challenge the infallibility of even the most perceptive and highly trained clinical judgment. Computerization of assessment inputs will most certainly have an influence on future practice and lead toward more objective and less subjective evaluative and predictive forms of judgment.

The principles and techniques of assessment are directed to obtain, analyze, interpret, and use the most valid and reliable information about general ability, specific abilities, proficiencies, interests, and personality attributes essential to the fulfillment of present or anticipated position responsibilities.

The techniques used in a variety of procedures and contexts essentially include observation, self- and other reports, performance testing, personality measurement, and interface assessments. In this brief introduction to selected principles and techniques, it is impossible to review in detail all the basic methods of data gathering. Each deserves at least the space and consideration devoted to all the topical areas suggested for this chapter. The history of work and training, observation of performance, and self- or other reports may be gathered by many different techniques that are essentially dependent upon the same data-gathering procedures. Fiske and Pearson (1970) provide sobering cautions for the use of these products by the zealous investigator. Nevertheless, these basic data-gathering procedures frequently appear in the following or similar forms in assessment programs:

Observation Techniques	*Self- and Other Reports*
Historical records	Interview
Direct personal	Questionnaire
	Inventories and tests

Performance Testing	*Personality Measurements*
On the job	Self-description
Simulation	Tests of judgment
Decision	Tests of affect
In basket	
Case study	

Interface Appraisals
Interpersonal relations
Placement fit
Environmental assimilation

The techniques listed above should be used in a responsible manner according to the principles described earlier in this chapter. All impose considerable demands for sophistication and skill upon the technical director of such activities.

It has been emphasized earlier that these and other techniques of assessment should be

1. Goal and results oriented
2. Conducted under the surveillance of a responsible management and the best available professional knowledge and skill

3. Consistently pursued throughout the organization

4. Designed to include the interaction of personal and situational variables

5. Regularly reviewed and modified when required

6. Used to reinforce commitment to, and satisfaction with, organizational membership and employment

7. Designed to provide for a continuity of relationships from one assessment stage to the next

Finally, selected constraints should be respected in the use of all techniques. It is necessary to recognize that there are real and serious

1. Limitations in the generalization potential in the outputs of any techniques

2. Limitations in simplistic classifications of human beings any time and in any situation

3. Limitations of subjective clinical judgment when compared with statistical judgments

In concluding these observations, it is useful to examine the concepts considered to this point in terms of selected methodological conditions and in terms of certain emerging social conditions.

METHODOLOGICAL ISSUES

There is a need for important changes in the focus of attention of the advocates of criterion validity and reliability and of the advocates of practical job-oriented assessment of individual differences that influence the use and value of human resources. Guion (1967) described four kinds of change requirements that are needed. (1) There is a need to be more realistic about the limitations of description of human ability when no evidence of predictive value is available. (2) While professionals are beginning to recognize that they have greater responsibility than they sometimes have assumed, there is a need for the development of a more relevant scientific foundation for competent professional practice in the areas of measurement and evaluation of personnel attributes in work situations. (3) A force for change is derived from the fact that measurement and evaluation developed in its early stages from the measurement of educational achievement and from the appraisal of production related to the motor skills of semiskilled and skilled workers. The human rights movement has forced everyone to consider many aspects of the total human existence that have been previously ignored or unrecognized. (4) The academic-professional concept of validity has been both ridiculed and viewed as sacrosanct by many practitioners in the world of work. Validity as a concept is being reexamined to determine the possibility of defining and using different concepts of validity. There is a dearth of scientific undergirding for almost every phase of measurement and evaluation insofar as they relate to the world of work. If there are to be any of the much-needed improvements in the measurement and evaluation of the attributes of employed personnel—assessment—then more support and incentive will have to be generated if competent professionals are to invest their energy, knowledge, and skill in a resolution of these issues. There is no cheap short cut to significant achievement in this area of knowledge.

SOCIAL CONDITIONS

Owens and Jewell (1969) note certain conditions that will continue to influence basic and applied concepts and methods.

The proprietary right of an employer to subject an applicant, or employee, to any type of measurement, evaluation, prediction, or classification that may satisfy the employer's needs has been challenged. Lockwood (1966) and Ward (1965) have described such difficulties in studies of compliance with fair employment practices. When there are different patterns of validity, predictions will have different meanings. Measurement, on the other hand, has in some ways facilitated respect for human rights. Dudek (1966) and Ash (1965) found that few complaints about employment appraisal had been submitted to state Fair Employment Practices Commissions. In fact, deep-seated culture-wide discriminatory attitudes are more troublesome than the use of testing. Lopez (1966) found in toll collectors' test-criterion correlations that it was the white who performed less well. These results seem to suggest fresh perceptions of white-black test performance abilities.

A further development is the increased sensitivity of all people to invasions of privacy. This issue is related to the ethical use of personal information. McGhee (1964) clarified the obligation of the "assessor" to provide clear explanations of his measures and procedures. The employer has an increasing responsibility to use the results of appraisals only for the appropriate purposes mutually agreed upon by the employee and the employer. The employer, or his agent, is expected to recognize the limitations of instruments and procedures of assessment and to avoid invasions of privacy on the job that professionals and academicians have had to observe in consideration of the rights of human beings. The ignorance of people and employees of their rights has probably delayed many legal confrontations. Freedman (1965) has examined this issue in very realistic terms.

One other constraint is more subtle and less publicized than the above. It is the growing demand of the employee that his capabilities be fully used in any employment situation. The traditional selection-rejection approach will be the object of increasing criticism and the subject of drastic modification in the years ahead. It is impossible here and now to speculate on how extensive the impact of this human right will be in the years ahead.

CONCLUSION

Selected principles and practices of assessment have been examined, with special attention to the promise, the doubts, and the dangers in this form of measurement and evaluation. There is little reason to be confident in many of the present assumptions, the data gathering, and the utilization of the products in the world of work. Progress has been made. Rapid and diverse social changes concerning human rights foretell the need for new and higher standards in the assessment of personnel.

BIBLIOGRAPHY

Annette, J., C. W. Golby, and H. Kay: *Quarterly Journal of Experimental Psychology,* 10: 1–11, 1958.

Ash, P.: *American Psychologist,* 20: 797–798, 1965.

Block, J.: *Psychology Bulletin,* 70: 210–212, 1968.

Campbell, J. P., M. D. Dunnette, E. E. Lawlor, and K. E. Weick: *Management Behavior, Performance, and Effectiveness,* McGraw-Hill Book Company, New York, 1970.

Cumming, John, and Elaine Cumming: *Ego & Milieu,* Atherton Press, Inc., New York, 1962.

Dudek, E. E.: *Industrial Psychology,* 2, 3: 51–53, 1966.

Fiske, Donald W., and Pamela H. Pearson: *Annual Review of Psychology,* 21: 49–86, 1970.

Flanagan, J. C.: *Education, Psychology, Measurement,* 12: 151–155, 1951.

Freedman, M. H.: *American Psychologist,* 20: 877–879, 1965.

Guion, Robert M.: *Annual Review of Psychology,* vol. 18, 1967.

Hemphill, J. K.: *Dimensions of Executive Position: A Study of the Basic Characteristics of the Position of Ninety-Three Business Executives,* Bureau of Business Research, Ohio State University, Columbus, Ohio, 1960.

chapter 41

Appraising Office and Plant Employees

GLENN FISCHBACH *Director of Engineering Services, American Association of Industrial Management, Melrose Park, Pennsylvania*

In discussing the subject of appraising office and plant employees, there is a risk of repeating some basic principles and philosophies appearing in chapters devoted to the appraisal of employees in other types of classifications. However, this limited repetition may serve a useful purpose in emphasizing the value of appraising individual performance in any endeavor, and of compensating employees accordingly. If individual performance is not given consideration, one must then have only a single rate of compensation. Obviously, a single rate can be logically defended only in those instances where quality and productivity are controlled mechanically and the employee's contribution becomes a constant.

TERMINOLOGY

Employee appraisal is known under a number of different names. A few of these are "merit rating," "performance rating," "employee rating," and "efficiency rating," but in any of these programs the purpose is to measure and evaluate as fairly as possible the variable results brought about by the employee's individual contribution. The problem then becomes (1) proper determination of the ways in which the employee can contribute to improved results, (2) a proper weighting of the potential value of the maximum contribution in each area, and (3) a means for making a fair appraisal of the extent to which the employee approaches the maximum possible contribution.

The appraisal, or rating, of employees is beneficial in several ways:

1. It is invaluable in making wage or salary adjustments, determining whether an employee deserves an increase, and preventing unwarranted inequalities in rates of pay.

2. It can be used effectively in appraising new employees during the probationary period and for determining whether their performance warrants retaining them.

3. It provides a factual basis for decisions as to transfers, promotions, layoffs, or dismissals.

4. It can be used as a guide in developing training programs where certain weaknesses are apparent in a number of cases.

5. Individual ratings can be used to stimulate interest in self-improvement where the rating shows an unsatisfactory performance. Ratings should be used in such cases in a friendly, constructive way to point out shortcomings.

PLANS IN EFFECT

There are several general types of systems or methods in common usage in American industry today:

1. Written appraisal
2. Field review
3. Critical incident
4. Adjective type
5. Forced choice
6. Graphic rating scale

The first two are infrequently used, and the fourth is of little value in maintaining consistency among raters. To have terms such as excellent, good, average, fair, and poor mean the same to each person in a group of raters is manifestly impossible.

The third type, the critical-incident method, involves maintenance by the supervisor of a card or folder for each employee in his department or section. Each time an employee does something noticeably favorable or unfavorable, an entry is made on the card or inserted in the folder. This record is then used as a basis for the subsequent periodic ratings. The critical-incident method is better used in conjunction with the graphic rating scale method than as an independent application.

The fifth type, the forced-choice method, is the most objective of all the various systems. Briefly, the forced-choice method is a series of statements pertaining to job proficiency or relevant personal qualifications. There are four statements to each group and probably in the neighborhood of twenty-four groups, or as many as needed until the overall requirements of the job are adequately covered. Two of the four statements are favorable in import and two, unfavorable. One of the favorable statements indicates performance or behavior found only among high-performance employees, while the other may be found just as frequently among lower performing employees as among the former. The terms differentiating and nondifferentiating favorable statements are applied to this category of statements. In like manner, the two unfavorable statements are also classified as differentiating and nondifferentiating unfavorable statements, where one is characteristic only of low-performing employees, and the other is applicable to employees at all proficiency levels. No rater has knowledge of which statements are the differentiators. Only the scorer has access to this information.

The main detriments to this method are that (1) it cannot be used for counseling employees and thereby loses an important feature of employer-employee communications, (2) it is extremely difficult to explain and sell to supervisors due to their lack of knowledge of the statements and is particularly disliked by shop foremen, and (3) it cannot be obtained as a packaged deal. As far as we know, so far each installation has been statistically developed and pretested in the plant or office. From this it can be readily realized that the installation is extremely costly and out of range of the smaller companies.

Probably the most widely used method in American industry comes under the graphic rating scale, further characterized as a statement type, point system plan. These plans have shortcomings in that in many cases the concentration of ratings through pressure may be toward the upper end, and that a tendency toward bias may unconsciously affect the results of ratings. However, with proper control and provisions for "rating the rater," good administration can be achieved. A plan of this type can be defined as a method to appraise, on the basis of specific factors and statements, the employees' performance on the job for use in determining pay rates, prospects for promotion, leadership qualities, and transfers. It provides the factual means of appraising the performance of employees fairly and tends to eliminate management's arbitrariness in the matter. As indicated by the name, each factor contains a number of statements carrying certain point values. The linear values should be psychologically determined and the value of each factor to the overall rating statistically developed and validated. While this approach would be costly to the individual company in developing its own plan, packaged plans (e.g., the American Association of Industrial Management plans which provide the exhibits shown here) have been so determined and made available. Under such plan, the rater does not actually rate the employee, but compares his (her) performance with statements that have predetermined values. However, the main features of any plan can be categorized as follows:

1. It should be thoughtfully prepared.
2. It definitely should be easily understood.
3. It must be easy to operate, i.e., the form must be simple and easy to fill out, and it should not be necessary after initial training to conduct additional courses at every rating period.
4. It should be consistently applied. The rater should be rated to make sure the ratings are free from unconscious bias or prejudice and the level of determination is equal among all raters.
5. The factors should be few. In many conferences held throughout the country, the consensus was five to eight factors.

The important criteria are reliability and validity. Is the plan reliable in that it gives an accurate picture of the employee, and is it valid in that the rating measures what it claims to measure? In applying and using a plan, sound administration may be divided into three phases:

1. The reporting phase
2. The evaluating phase
3. The effectuating phase

THE REPORTING PHASE

Some companies desire to give merit increases if due on the anniversary date of the employee. They then give a reporting form (Figure 1) to the rater several days prior to the event and when returned score the sheet and thereby determine whether a merit increase is warranted. The trouble here is that management is confused in that the program is geared only to the third phase, and no control or consistency is obtainable. The better procedure is to rate an entire department at one time. All the clerical work should be done prior to sending the rating forms to the raters, the forms for all employees on the same job should be together, and the lowest rated job should be placed on top and then in inverse order so that the highest rated job is on the bottom. This psychological approach assures due consideration of each employee.

The rater must be familiar with the content of every job over which he is exercising supervision. Therefore, unless accurate job descriptions have been prepared and a copy has been placed in possession of the rater, the program cannot be success-

EMPLOYEE RATING REPORT
FORM A

for

NON-SUPERVISORY

Office, Clerical, Engineering and Professional Personnel

EMPLOYEE

OCCUPATION

DEPT.   DIVISION

RATER

RATER'S POSITION

DATE

FACTOR	
A	
B	
C	
D	
E	
TOTAL	

A HOW ADEQUATE ARE HIS KNOWLEDGE AND SKILL FOR THE REQUIREMENTS OF HIS PRESENT POSITION?

☐ Meets the usual requirements satisfactorily.

☐ Well trained and skillful in most phases of his position.

☐ Neither noticeably deficient nor superior in this respect.

☐ A better-equipped person would be hard to find.

☐ Possesses only minimum qualifications for the job.

☐ Has ability superior to most employees in similar positions.

☐ Exceptionally well informed, resourceful, efficient.

☐ Does his job well, and is improving.

☐ Able to do fairly well the regular duties.

☐ Does well what he understands, but knowledge limited.

☐ I have insufficient basis for judgment.

B HOW EFFECTIVELY DOES HE FUNCTION IN THE PERSONAL CONTACTS WHICH HIS WORK REQUIRES?

☐ Handles routine contacts with fair success.

☐ He's all right when you get to know him.

☐ Somewhat lacking in tact or considerateness.

☐ Handles personal relations with better than ordinary tact and discretion.

☐ Difficult for most people to get along with.

☐ Patient and effective in all ordinary personal contacts.

☐ Neither outstandingly superior nor deficient in this respect.

☐ Exceptionally effective in all personal contacts.

☐ Has a tendency to rub people the wrong way.

☐ Most people prefer to deal with him rather than others.

☐ I have insufficient basis for judgment.

Figure 1. Employee rating report form. (*American Association of Industrial Management.*)

HOW EFFECTIVE IS HE IN PLANNING AND ORGANIZING HIS WORK?

C

☐	☐	☐	☐	☐	☐	☐	☐	☐	☐	☐
Little aptitude or inclination for devising better means for accomplishing objectives.	Displays some ability for devising practical techniques and procedures for solving problems.	Capable of assuming independent responsibility.	Needs supervision a little more than should be necessary.	Discriminates well between important and unimportant matters.	Resourceful in practical adaption of means to ends.	Contributes some practical suggestions for improving details.	Neither conspicuously deficient nor superior in this respect.	Is a good starter but a poor finisher.	Plans his work, but his judgment isn't always good.	I have insufficient basis for judgment.

HOW MUCH APTITUDE FOR LEARNING DOES HE SHOW IN THE FIELD OF HIS WORK?

D

☐	☐	☐	☐	☐	☐	☐	☐	☐	☐	☐
Distinctly superior in intelligence.	Able to apply rules and procedures to fairly varied types of situations.	Learns routine operations better than general principles.	Rather slow or erratic in comprehension.	Readily adapts himself to new circumstances.	Handicapped by intellectual adaptability.	Exceptionally quick and sound judgment on new or emergency problems.	Neither noticeably deficient nor superior in this respect.	Needs fairly specific rules and instructions.	Fair judgment on new problems if they're not exceptionally complex.	I have insufficient basis for judgment.

HOW SATISFACTORY ARE HIS ATTITUDES TOWARD HIS WORK AND HIS EMPLOYER?

E

☐	☐	☐	☐	☐	☐	☐	☐	☐	☐	☐
Office would get on much better without him.	Not easily distracted from his work.	Attitude more satisfactory than that of most employes.	Attitude toward work and employer as desirable as could be wished.	Disturbs and interrupts other employes unnecessarily.	Attitude satisfactory as a rule.	Inclined to be lazy.	Imperturbable and diligent even under annoying circumstances.	Outside interests or troubles interfere with his efficiency.	Does his work well enough but without wholehearted loyalty.	I have insufficient basis for judgment.

Figure 1. Employee rating report form. (*American Association of Industrial Management.*) (**continued**)

SECTION II

Could individual handle a better position?
In your opinion is employee qualified to handle a better position?
What   type?

Yes _____

_____

_____

Possibly _____

_____

_____

No _____

_____

_____

SECTION III   ADDITIONAL COMMENTS

_____

_____

_____

_____

_____

_____

_____

_____

_____

_____

SECTION IV (OPTIONAL)

(A) Attendance Adjustment

$\dfrac{\text{late and absent x}}{\text{Hours}}$ .... _____

(B) Attendance   Score ....

Rating Score ___ *Rating Group* ___

Name ___ *Occupation* ___ *Division* ___ *Dept.* ___

Figure 1. Employee rating report form. *(American Association of Industrial Management.)* **(continued)**

ful. Once the rater has the job and the employees' performance in mind, he should mark the appropriate statements for all factors. It is true that some plans have different colored forms for each factor and request that all employees be rated on one factor before proceeding to the next, but to have a rater keep orienting and reorienting himself to the job and man is cumbersome and subject to the loss of objectivity. The consistency of factor relationships should be obtained in the next phase of the program, namely, the evaluating phase. After all employees have been rated, the forms are returned to the place of origin.

Figure 1 is a reporting form used for office employees. A similar form for plant employees might list factors such as

1. Quality of work
2. Quantity of work
3. Adaptability
4. Job knowledge
5. Dependability
6. Attitude

together with appropriate statements and assigned point values.

THE EVALUATING PHASE

Upon receipt of the marked rating forms, the necessary clerical work is performed. The point score of the statement or statements marked for each factor is usually obtained from a scoring mat and totaled. A departmental summary sheet (Figure 2) should then be prepared, with the highest scored employee on top and in descending value to the poorest or lowest scored employee. The summary form should have columns for each factor used, one for the total score, another for the group slotting as well as the initial columns such as clock number, name of employee, and name of job. Some of the better controlled installations include a column relative to the deviation from the average rating.

At this point, only the point score for each factor is posted beside the employee data, and the summary sheet is returned to the rater for review and comparison of factor relationships for consistency. Each man's rating is compared on a man-to-

DEPT.__________ DATE__________

Employee No.	Name	Position	Class	Knowledge Skill	Personal Contacts	Planning Organizing	Learning Aptitude	Attitudes	Supervision	Total Points	Group	Dev. from Average	Attendance Score	Adjusted Group

Figure 2. Employee rating report summary sheet. *(American Association of Industrial Management.)*

man basis regardless of the job to obtain the necessary consistency. After the return of the summary sheet by the rater, the balance of the data such as total points, group number (for wage administration purposes), and the deviation from average is determined and posted.

It is at this point that the successful installation is controlled. Here is where the rating of the rater takes place. The departmental averages are compared with the plant average, and the deviation from average is obtained. This immediately points out the high and/or low raters, which means only those supervisors having such low standards that everyone in the department is a "genius" or those having such high standards that no one can meet them and all are therefore slotted in the "moron" category. Unless there is some unusual reason which should be apparent, the chance is that the mix in all departments will be similar, and this is true regardless of seniority. Through discussions with the raters or through conferences, the standards of the high and low raters are brought in line. Length of service, per se, has no place in sound employee rating and should never be a factor in a rating plan. Performance and only performance should be the determination.

The next step is to set up a master grade rate range on a plantwide and/or departmental basis to determine the within-grade employee distribution. Where deviations from normal distribution are indicated, further breakdowns by individual grades can be made to pinpoint the areas for investigation. The range should be divided into four, five, or six intervals depending upon the spread, and as a guide, the distribution should conform with a Gaussian or "bell" curve (see Figure 3). The group column on the reporting form refers to the intervals used in dividing up the grade rate range. With these applications and naturally the backing of top management, subjectivity or the "horns or halo" effect is reduced to a minimum. If a wage or salary administration committee is established, this is the time for them to review the results.

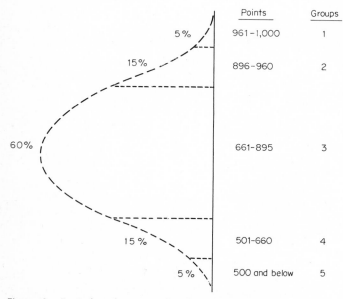

	Points	Groups
5%	961–1,000	1
15%	896–960	2
60%	661–895	3
15%	501–660	4
5%	500 and below	5

Figure 3.   Typical performance distribution curve.

SOC. SECURITY NO.	EMPLOYEE NAME	DIV.	DEPARTMENT	WK. LOC.	DATE OF HIRE
ENTER POSITION TITLE: ____		HOW LONG UNDER YOUR SUPERVISION? ____	POSTPONE THIS APPRAISAL UNTIL (DATE):____		

CHECK APPROPRIATE RATING FROM APPRAISAL SCALE
FOR EACH CATEGORY BELOW. ENTER TOTAL.

RATING SCALE

1. KNOWLEDGE OF JOB	10	8	6	4

R A T I N G S

1. KNOWLEDGE OF JOB .... 10 | 8 | 6 | 4
2. QUALITY OF WORK .... 15 | 12 | 9 | 6
3. QUANTITY OF WORK .... 15 | 12 | 9 | 6
4. ATTENDANCE AND PUNCTUALITY................ 10 | 8 | 6 | 4
5. ATTITUDE .... 10 | 8 | 6 | 4
6. JUDGMENT.................................. 10 | 8 | 6 | 4
7. RELIABILITY .... 15 | 12 | 9 | 6
8. FLEXIBILITY ● ADAPTABILITY .... 10 | 8 | 6 | 4
9. PERSONAL CHARACTERISTICS .... 5 | 4 | 3 | 2

ENTER TOTAL
APPRAISAL
SCORE HERE

T R A I N I N G   A N D   D E V E L O P M E N T

YOUR COMMENTS ARE SOUGHT CONCERNING TRAINING AND DEVELOPMENT NEEDS OF THIS EMPLOYEE. THE PERSONNEL DEVELOPMENT SECTION WILL NOTE YOUR SUGGESTIONS AND BASE PLANS FOR TRAINING PROGRAMS AND ANY OTHER TRAINING ASSISTANCE UPON THE NEEDS RECOGNIZED AND RECORDED.

A. ESTIMATE YOUR GENERAL EVALUATION OF THIS EMPLOYEE'S POTENTIAL FOR EVENTUALLY REACHING TOP QUALITY PERFORMANCE IN HIS PRESENT POSITION:

☐ EXCELLENT POTENTIAL   ☐ FAIR POTENTIAL
☐ GOOD POTENTIAL   ☐ POOR POTENTIAL

B. WHAT ARE YOU DOING NOW, OR PLANNING TO DO, TO IMPROVE THIS EMPLOYEE'S PERFORMANCE, OR TO REALIZE HIS POTENTIAL? ____

C. IF THE FOLLOWING TRAINING PROGRAMS WERE MADE AVAILABLE, CIRCLE BOXES OF THOSE YOU WOULD RECOMMEND THE EMPLOYEE ATTEND:

13 Business Writing & Editing   18 Advertising & Marketing   23 Grammar & Spelling   28 Telephone Techniques
14 Copy Editing & Proofreading   19 Promotion   24 Shorthand Refresher   29 Receptionist Training
15 Copy Writing   20 Research & Statistics   25 Starting Shorthand   30 Supervisory Training
16 Make-up & Production   21 Business Math   26 Typing Refresher   31 Other - specify:
17 Graphics, Art & Design   22 Correspondence   27 Starting Typing   ____

D. IF THIS EMPLOYEE CAN ASSUME GREATER RESPONSIBILITIES, TO WHAT POSITION OR TYPE OF WORK COULD HE BE PROMOTED?

32 IN YOUR DEPARTMENT ____
33 ELSEWHERE IN MC GRAW-HILL ____

E. IF THIS EMPLOYEE IS NOT DOING THE JOB FOR WHICH HE IS BEST SUITED, TO WHAT POSITION OR TYPE OF WORK COULD HE BE TRANSFERRED?

34 IN YOUR DEPARTMENT ____
35 ELSEWHERE IN MC GRAW-HILL ____

DO YOU PLAN TO DISCUSS THIS APPRAISAL WITH THE EMPLOYEE?   ☐ YES   ☐ NO

NOTE: IF NEEDED, PLEASE ENTER ANY ADDITIONAL REMARKS ON REVERSE SIDE.

APPRAISED BY:____   DATE:____
APPROVED BY:____   DATE:____

PLEASE RETURN APPROVED APPRAISAL FORM TO YOUR PERSONNEL MANAGEMENT ADVISER.

Figure 4. Office employee performance appraisal record.
(McGraw-Hill, Inc.)

Figures 4, 5, and 6 show reporting forms used in other types of employee appraisal or performance plans. In these instances, an evaluating phase similar to the one previously described must, of course, be employed in recording, comparing, and grouping as a means of maintaining consistency on the part of the raters.

Figure 5. Performance review form. *(New Holland Group, Sperry Rand Corporation.)*

THE EFFECTUATING PHASE

The methods of putting the results of the rating in effect vary considerably in different plants. Where the company desires to grant a merit increase when due on the anniversary date of the employee, that is perfectly satisfactory. If other companies want to establish a fixed time such as January 1 and July 1 or a different date for each department, that too is satisfactory. However, the company should definitely determine and publish its policy to the employees so as to have an orderly procedure. There does not have to be any direct relationship between the reporting and effectuating phases. Many companies rate employees anywhere from two

EXCELLENT	GOOD	AVERAGE	FAIR	MINIMUM	UNSATISFACTORY		

WORKING RELATIONS: ABILITY OF INDIVIDUAL TO GET ALONG WITH OTHERS   REMARKS

1. Attitude toward fellow employees
2. Attitude toward management
3. Attitude toward staff and service functions
4. Attitude toward company procedures and policies
5. Willingness to accept change
6. Overall working relations rating

HEALTH & PHYSICAL MAKE UP: ABILITY TO DO ASSIGNED WORK CONSISTENTLY   REMARKS

1. Attendance — Tardiness
2. Productivity — works up to his ability (physically)
3. Energy and endurance
4. Overall health and physical make up rating

SAFETY: ABILITY AND DESIRE OF AN INDIVIDUAL TO AVOID INJURY TO HIMSELF   REMARKS
OR OTHERS WITH WHOM HE WORKS

1. Attention to safety of others
2. Attitude toward safety work rules
3. Recognizing and reporting unsafe conditions or actions
4. Following procedures established to promote safety
5. Reporting injuries and following procedures for medical attention
6. Housekeeping (orderliness and cleanliness of his work area)
7. Overall safety rating

OVERALL RATING

Discussed this review with employee on _____

(DATE)   (EMPLOYEE'S SIGNATURE)

SUPERVISOR'S REMARKS (to be completed before employee signs form) _____

EMPLOYEE'S COMMENTS (to be completed by employee) _____

SUPERVISOR	DATE	DEPARTMENT HEAD	DATE
GENERAL MANAGER	DATE	WAGE AND SALARY ADMINISTRATOR	DATE

Figure 5.   Performance review form.   *(New Holland Group, Sperry Rand Corporation.)*   **(continued)**

to four times yearly but make only one adjustment in wages or salaries, if merited. Probably the most common frequency in rating is three times a year for plant employees and twice a year in the office.

USE IN WAGE ADMINISTRATION

Employee appraisal is a wage policy relative to within-grade progression. Its use is usually in conjunction with a rate range and not a single rate structure. A rate range provides an incentive for dayworkers. It is not an incentive for incentive

	Performance Ranges				

PRODUCTIVITY

Performance Ranges: V IV III II I

Operations: Level of performance in producing tangible results for his area of responsibility (sales, production, maintenance, accounting, etc.)

Costs: Effectiveness in controlling costs and in using manpower.

Safety: Effectiveness in carrying out his responsibilities safely, both himself and thru others.

Overall Productivity Rating

KNOWLEDGE

Basic: Knowledge required to carry out his primary responsibilities.

Related: Knowledge of other areas helpful in his performance.

Application: Effectiveness in applying his knowledge to the job.

Overall Knowledge Rating

PROBLEM SOLVING

Recognition: Ability to see problems and the opportunity for their solution.

Analysis: Ability to gather and evaluate pertinent facts.

Judgment: Quality of recommendations or actions taken.

Creativity: Evidence of original thinking applied to his job.

Overall Problem Solving Rating

DEALING WITH PEOPLE

Subordinates: Effectiveness in selecting, coaching and motivating subordinates.

Other Company Personnel: Evidence of cooperation with his associates.

Others: Effectiveness in representing the Company in his relationships with customers and the public.

Overall Dealing With People Rating

ADMINISTRATION

Planning: Effectiveness in anticipating needs, setting up objectives, and establishing time schedules.

Communication: Effectiveness in getting across to others, both orally and in writing.

Execution: Effectiveness in holding to objectives, interpreting progress, and taking corrective actions.

Organization: Effectiveness in distributing work and delegating responsibility.

Overall Administration Rating

OVERALL PERFORMANCE RATING

Considering all of the foregoing factors, with greatest emphasis on those most closely applicable to his present position.

Name: _____ Period ending _____ Date _____

Position: _____ Grade _____ Organization _____

Figure 6.   Performance appraisal form.

workers. The objective criteria which are the heaviest weighted factors in an employee rating plan are the same as those inherent in any sound wage incentive plan. Therefore, to use a rate range for incentive workers is pyramiding and unfair to the dayworkers. Further understanding can be obtained if we recognize that an employee rating plan is an indirect means of measuring performance, while a formal wage incentive plan is a direct means of measuring performance. Both are not applicable at the same time. However, an employee who is not fully covered by incentive should be rated to determine his personal rate when on daywork and for holiday and vacation pay.

Where a five-interval structure is in effect, all employees slotted in group 5 should be paid the job rate or the minimum of the rate range. Those slotted in group 4 should be paid the intermediate job rate, or the low intermediate of the rate range; those in group 3, the maximum job rate, or mean of the rate range; and those in groups 2 and 1, the bonus rate, or high intermediate of the rate range, and the premium rate, or maximum of the rate range, respectively. Naturally, once an

Details Of Performance

Under the appropriate heading provide specific examples of performance which caused you to rate any
factor on the other side in Range I, II, IV, or V.

PRODUCTIVITY

_____
_____
_____
_____
_____

KNOWLEDGE

_____
_____
_____
_____
_____

PROBLEM SOLVING

_____
_____
_____
_____
_____

DEALING WITH PEOPLE

_____
_____
_____
_____
_____

ADMINISTRATION

_____
_____
_____
_____
_____

Discussion of Performance with Individual

You are reminded that under Company Policy you must discuss this appraisal with the employee in
detail after it and the salary recommendation have been approved.

Figure 6.   Performance appraisal form.   (continued)

employee is placed in the rate range, he should maintain or better that position.
Failure to do so will necessitate penalties if the plan is to be sound and fair to all
employees.

Today there are two means of obtaining this latter phase of the wage administration program. The first is to reduce the pay of the employee, but only after a warning has been given and the employee has failed to attain his former position. The
second is to consider his rate as a "blue circle" rate. This is to distinguish it from
a "red circle" rate which is a rate paid in excess of the maximum of the rate range.
A blue circle therefore is a rate paid to an employee within the rate range but for
a group in excess of that indicated by the actual employee rating. As the entire rate
range is subject to inflationary and deflationary impacts on our economy, a blue
circle rate remains stationary while the rate range moves up until it reaches the level
of the rate paid.

CONCLUSION

It should be remembered always that within a grade progression should be based on performance only. Length of service, economic changes, and the profit or loss statement of the company have nothing to do with the application of this policy. Theoretically, such progression should not increase unit or manufacturing costs for, like a direct wage incentive system, improved performance should absorb the cost.

Administration along the lines indicated herein will not eliminate all grievances, but it should reduce them to a minimum. It will also pinpoint the grievances and confine them mostly to the most inefficient personnel. Without appraisal and recognition of performance, grievances are more prevalent among the best producers because there are little or no differentials in pay.

BIBLIOGRAPHY

Bryson, J. F.: "A New Approach to Merit Rating," *Supervision*, February, 1962, pp. 4–6.

Greisman, Bernard (ed.): *J. K. Lasser's Business Management Handbook*, McGraw-Hill Book Company, New York, 1960.

Lopez, Felix M., Jr.: *Evaluating Employee Performance*, Public Personnel Assn., Chicago, 1968.

Luck, Thomas Jefferson: *Personnel Audit and Appraisal*, McGraw-Hill Book Company, New York, 1955.

Personnel Management—Principles, Practices, and a Point of View. Walter Dill Scott, McGraw-Hill Book Company, New York, 1961.

Tibbin, J.: "Six Merit Rating Systems," *Personnel Journal*, January, 1959, pp. 288–291.

Wolf, William B.: *Merit Rating as a Managerial Tool*, College of Business Administration, University of Washington, 1958.

These publications and numerous others, as well as articles appearing in personnel and trade periodicals, deal at length with varying methods and philosophies employed in the process of employee appraisal. Space allotted to this chapter does not permit detailed discussion of each of the variations involved.

chapter 42

Appraising Supervisory Employees

ROBERT B. PURSELL *Director, Coloney, Cannon, Main & Pursell, Inc., New York, New York*

It could be said that appraising supervisory performance is the application of management's most controversial process to its most controversial level. Yet because the first-line supervisor is "management" to the majority of employees, how the process affects him has profound impact upon the success of the organization. Achieving a positive effect, however, is not merely a question of technique, forms, procedures, etc. Rather, it depends upon an overall approach that:

1. Distinguishes among the key elements of the process
2. Clearly identifies specific purposes of appraisal in light of these characteristics and differences
3. Recognizes the special characteristics of, and differences among, first-line supervisory positions

This chapter discusses each of these points in detail, then outlines a model process based upon them.

KEY ELEMENTS OF THE PERFORMANCE APPRAISAL PROCESS

A major shortcoming of performance appraisal, at any level, can be the failure to clearly separate the two major phases of the process: measurement and evaluation. Because they consist of the same three basic elements: (1) a series of performance judgments, (2) feedback, and (3) action, measurement and evaluation are often considered as being the same thing. Adding to the difficulty is the fact that most formal appraisal programs are "once a year" propositions, making distinctions between these two phases a virtual impossibility. Yet measurement and evaluation are quite different, and clarification is essential to a viable performance appraisal process, particularly at the first-line supervisory level.

Performance measurement is an objective process that goes on without, or in spite of, a formal appraisal process. It is an integral step of the management process; if anything is managed, performance is measured. Moreover, it is the performance of people that is measured; one cannot, of course, manage an abstraction like production or inventory, only the actions of people. Any budget system, for example, incorporates performance measurement and in a very objective sense:

Standards or objectives are set.

Results are reported and judgments made.

Results and judgments are "fed back" to those concerned.

Some action (or reaction) takes place, usually some change in operations.

Evaluation of performance, as the name implies, values the measurements. Here we are dealing solely with subjective judgments made against a preestablished frame of reference. The frame of reference may be others in the group, results in the previous period, the idealized supervisor, etc. Although evaluations are constantly being made in any human relations system, they are usually specifically called for only when "personnel" actions, such as salary increases, promotion, or staff reduction, are contemplated. In most cases, formal performance evaluations are called for once a year, as opposed to usually shorter time spans for performance measurements. But the process looks much the same:

Results (or observations) are reported and judgments made.

Results and judgments are "fed back" to those concerned.

Some action takes place; almost always this is a "personnel" action.

Figure 1 summarizes the key differences between performance measurement and evaluation, as discussed above.

Figure 1.   The key differences between performance measurement and evaluation.

	Performance measurement	Performance evaluation
Frequency	Monthly, often weekly	Usually yearly
Type of judgment used	Objective	Subjective
Frame of reference	Implicit in management system	Must be made explicit to be meaningful
Purpose	To control or improve performance results	To take administrative action

PURPOSES OF PERFORMANCE APPRAISAL

It is generally accepted that performance appraisals serve one or more of the following purposes:

1. To bring about better operational or business results

2. To meet some of an individual's developmental needs

3. To provide information useful for manpower planning by identifying men with potential for advancement and men with abilities not currently being used

4. To provide a basis for compensation action

Each of these purposes suggests a somewhat different approach to the appraisal process. Thus the relative importance of each must be consciously taken into account when devising an approach. What is, or can be, their relative importance, however, depends upon the special characteristics of the first-level supervisory position discussed in detail below. Here we shall comment briefly on what is suggested by each purpose and why.

Improved Performance

If improved performance is a key objective of the appraisal process, as it almost always is said to be, a "job-centered" appraisal process is mandatory. Improvement can come about only if specific targets (objectives, goals, standards, etc.) are established, plans are formulated as to how they can be achieved, and frequent measurements are made to determine what change in plans, if any, need to be made. Such a process is fact based, result oriented, and objective, with relatively short measurement intervals.

Experience has shown that a participative process is best. There are two reasons for this. First, the individual in question is in the better position to know what can be done and how best to do it, although his superior may be in a better position to recognize improvement opportunities. Second and equally important, participation of an individual in establishing his own objectives and devising ways of attaining them creates a sense of commitment that is difficult to achieve in any other way. There is, of course, no question but that some negotiation is involved in establishing objectives in this way. However, if importance and feasibility of achievement (to avoid wheel spinning) are the criteria for objective setting, rather than degree of difficulty or opportunity for development, optimum improvement will most likely be attained. In other words, if the system aims at maintaining an overall high level of, or improvement in, job performance, it probably will not result in "fully equitable" objectives for positions at the same level.

Development Needs

When individual development is a purpose of performance appraisal, the process must go beyond performance measurement against targets. Evaluations are needed with respect to methods and approach, using performance measurements as raw material. Such evaluations require consideration of a longer time span than measurements, and must be made within a specific frame of reference, i.e., the individual's past record in relation to the requirements of his current position. Subjective judgment is involved, but it can be rudimentary, e.g., "A development need exists or it does not." Feedback of this judgment should be made only if a need exists, and then in terms of a program designed to help the supervisor "measure" better against his targets.

Figure 2 is an illustration of the format used by one company to structure the evaluation of development needs. It is appropriate for first-line supervisors as well as for higher level ones, so long as one realizes that the questions posed are not to be taken literally. Rather, they are illustrative of the *kind* of question the evaluator should pose to himself, as he reviews individual performance measurement data. Here an outstanding category was included to facilitate, when possible, the development of programs to capitalize on particular strengths, as well as to meet development needs.

Manpower Planning

To deal with potential for advancement, the appraisal process needs to go considerably beyond measurement of current job performance. If providing "potential" and other manpower planning information is to be a purpose, a set of subjective judgments needs to be made against skill-centered, as opposed to job-centered, criteria. Although performance measurements represent input, the evaluator must be admonished to recognize that job performance alone does not necessarily correlate with potential to do higher level work. He must infer this from performance results and other indicators.

Figure 2.   A sample of the format used by one company to structure the evaluation of supervisory development needs.

A performance judgment should be made for each relevant item in this section. In some cases, an item will not be relevant or so unimportant that its consideration will unduly influence more important aspects of the individual's job. When this occurs, check the box headed N/A.

The following questions are presented as a guide in evaluating performance against each element.

	Outstanding	No improvement needed	Development needed	N/A
1. Utilization of resources	[ ]	[ ]	[ ]	[ ]

Personnel: Did you review the goals he set for his subordinates? Were they demanding but realistic? Were they reached? Does he make judicious use of overtime? How often are his subordinates singled out for praise or promoted? Is his safety record one that can be improved? How?

Capital: Were new investments needed? Did he recognize the need and propose the required investments? Were his proposals supported by evidence necessary for an evaluation? What contributions did he make to the management of inventories or receivables?

Expense fund: Did he recommend a budget for his operation? Did he meet it? Do you know of specific costs he cut below budget? Do you know of volume increases due to his efforts? Did he define accurately his needs for supplies and services? Did he go beyond his forecasts? Can you identify specific savings he made?

Materials: Did he plan his requirements in materials? Did he exceed his forecasts? Do you know of cases where he reduced consumption of material by reduction of waste and/or off-grade product?

Facilities: Did he get optimum output from the equipment under his jurisdiction? Was maintenance adequate and timely? Do you know of any instances where he was primarily responsible for an increase in production or improvement in quality?

Technology: Did he improve his own technical knowledge? How did he personally train his subordinates in technical skills? Did he suggest any new or improved techniques? What were they? Did he deal with any new areas of technology? How quickly did he pick it up? Did he fully utilize the know-how available in his group? '

	Outstanding	No improvement needed	Development needed	N/A
2. Reaction to unforeseen events	[ ]	[ ]	[ ]	[ ]

Did unforeseeable changes in the competitive situation, new production processes, labor trends, or other largely uncontrollable factors make it more difficult for him to reach his goals? Was he prepared for them? Was he able to counteract their effects?

	Outstanding	No improvement needed	Development needed	N/A
3. Planning, objective setting	[ ]	[ ]	[ ]	[ ]

Did he set targets for his unit? Were they based on sound analysis? Were they ambitious but attainable? Did he plan the activity of the unit effectively to reach these objectives?

	Outstanding	No improvement needed	Development needed	N/A
4. Problem solving	[ ]	[ ]	[ ]	[ ]

Figure 2.   A sample of the format used by one company to structure the evaluation of supervisory development needs.   (continued)

Identification: What were the toughest problems he faced?   Did he recognize them? Soon enough?   Did he solve any of them?   Which ones remain?
Analysis: What analytical problems did he face?   Costs, prices, or margins?   Location of a piece of equipment, a warehouse, or a sales territory?   Analysis of market trends— overheads, quality, chemical usage, etc.?   Were his analyses complete?   Accurate?
Creativity: What steps did he take to encourage creativity in his unit?   Has he brought about specific improvements?   Do you know of costs he reduced, techniques he developed or improved, systems or procedures he improved?   What ideas did he contribute to the R&D program?

	Outstanding	No improvement needed	Development needed	N/A
5. Decision making	[ ]	[ ]	[ ]	[ ]

Basis: Did he consider alternatives in making important decisions?   Did he dig behind the obvious?   Did he request special information or analyses?
Speed: Did he face any unexpected problems or opportunities?   What was the result? How fast was his reaction in dealing with a new problem or opportunity?
Quality: Has he made important decisions or presented recommendations in the course of the year?   Did he present well-founded recommendations?   Were they realistic and was their implementation feasible?   Do you have confidence in him when he makes a recommendation?   Do his decisions conform to company policy and objectives?
Follow-through: Did he communicate his decisions well?   Did he lay out the necessary actions?   Did he follow up to ensure that the appropriate action was taken?

Figure 3 is a potential evaluation format used by a number of organizations which is particularly appropriate for use with first-line supervisors.   It illustrates a number of facts about potential evaluation.   First, although subjective judgment is used, no more than a yes or no answer is needed.   Generally, if there are more than occasional nos, potential for advancement is unlikely.   Second, it is critical that management know the individual's career ambitions.   Without such knowledge, feedback from the process could be damaging.   Third, a suggested action program is required to be prepared for each person evaluated.   These programs could range from a counseling plan designed to bring his career aspirations in line with his evaluation, or present evidence that will change the evaluation, to a plan incorporating both on- and off-the-job management training.   Finally, it is advisable to have the evaluation made by someone at least one level removed from the individual, for his perspective is greater and his personal involvement is less.

Compensation Action

Many performance appraisal programs are instituted specifically for salary administration or incentive bonus purposes.   The more successful of these expand the objective-setting element of the process to provide a sound basis for evaluating performance measurements.   For example, instead of a simple objective of 3 percent rejects, a scale of ranges are established such as:

Over 3.5 percent	Unacceptable
3.2 to 3.5 percent	Acceptable
2.8 to 3.2 percent	Target
Under 2.8 percent	Superior

Figure 3. A sample form to evaluate potential for advancement.

1. Assessment of skills	Yes	?	No	N/O[1]
a. Personal				
Does he complete all his assignments: well?	[ ]	[ ]	[ ]	[ ]
On time?	[ ]	[ ]	[ ]	[ ]
Without close supervision?	[ ]	[ ]	[ ]	[ ]
Does he have a high personal drive and capacity for work?	[ ]	[ ]	[ ]	[ ]
Does he work well under pressure?	[ ]	[ ]	[ ]	[ ]
Is he prepared to make sacrifices of personal time to advance?	[ ]	[ ]	[ ]	[ ]
Is he always looking for better ways to do his job?	[ ]	[ ]	[ ]	[ ]
Is he sensitive to the people he works with as well as to supervisors?	[ ]	[ ]	[ ]	[ ]
Is he mature and stable in his approach to unexpected problems?	[ ]	[ ]	[ ]	[ ]
Does he fully understand the nature and economics of the business?	[ ]	[ ]	[ ]	[ ]
b. Managerial				
Does he plan and organize his work well?	[ ]	[ ]	[ ]	[ ]
Do subordinates respect him?	[ ]	[ ]	[ ]	[ ]
Does he delegate and follow up well?	[ ]	[ ]	[ ]	[ ]
Can he get peers to readily accept his leadership on team or joint problems?	[ ]	[ ]	[ ]	[ ]
Does he express himself persuasively in group meetings?	[ ]	[ ]	[ ]	[ ]
Is his advice solicited when not required by protocol?	[ ]	[ ]	[ ]	[ ]
c. Technical and professional				
Does he apply his theoretical knowledge to his work?	[ ]	[ ]	[ ]	[ ]
Does he keep up to date in his specialty?	[ ]	[ ]	[ ]	[ ]
Is he readily accepted at all necessary levels in the organization?	[ ]	[ ]	[ ]	[ ]
Can he get others to act by either persuasion or authority of knowledge?	[ ]	[ ]	[ ]	[ ]

2. Career ambitions

   a. Is he satisfied with the present direction of his career and his rate of advance? _____

   _____

   b. Where does he see himself 5 to 10 years from now? _____

   _____

   _____

   c. What does he believe he and/or the company must do to realize his potential? _____

   _____

   _____

3. Potential rating
   a. Promotable: immediate [ ], in   year(s) [ ]
        To higher professional level [ ], management position [ ],

   [1] No opportunity to form a judgment.

Figure 3.   A sample form to evaluate potential for advancement.   (continued)

In same function [ ], other function [ ] _____
(specify)

Same division [ ], other division [ ] _____
(specify)

Ultimate level he could reach _____
  b. Not promotable: well placed now [   ], in wrong position—needs transfer [   ],
      over his head [ ], should be replaced in job but kept in company [ ],
      should be terminated [ ]
  c. Near retirement (within 7 years): better utilization could be made of him [   ], valuable
      where he is [ ], performance is slipping [ ], should consider early retirement [   ]
4. Suggested action program

_____

_____

_____

_____

Rated by: _____   Date: _____

Discussed with immediate superior: _____   Date: _____

Reviewed and approved by: _____   Date: _____

Moreover, uncontrollable conditions which could swing performance off target are identified and referred to when the performance result is evaluated.   In the above example, such conditions could be ambient humidity, raw material quality, etc.

If this purpose is to be served well, it is also considered important to fix the frame of reference.   The individual should know how much of a contemplated increase or bonus will stem from the appraisal of his performance and whether such amounts will be awarded on an absolute or relative basis; i.e., will his reward depend only upon what he does or what he does relative to what others do.

THE FIRST-LINE SUPERVISORY POSITION

The elements of performance appraisal and its purposes, described above, ordinarily cannot be applied to first-line supervisory positions in the same way they might be to higher echelons of management.   This is due to both the special characteristics of first-line supervisors and their differences from function to function.

Special Characteristics

Because it is the first step on the management ladder, first-line supervisory positions have two special characteristics that need to be carefully considered in any performance appraisal program.

The first is that, regardless of functional area, most first-line supervisory positions are filled by men "up from the ranks." As this is probably the most difficult transition to make in management, short of moving to chief executive, initial development and performance improvement needs tend to be great. At the same time, primarily due to inadequate selection procedures, the failure rate, although not often admitted, is relatively high. In terms of compensation, the individual's frame of reference tends to be that of the group he left rather than "other managers." For example, the production foreman tends to compare his pay and pay increases with those of the worker he supervises. Likewise, the research group leader looks more to what other members of his profession are paid than to what supervisors in other functional areas are paid.

A second and equally important characteristic is that first-line supervisory positions tend to be tightly prescribed. Thus, their direct influence is limited to relatively few result areas and short time spans. Even within these limits, there are more factors uncontrollable by the first-line supervisor that can affect results than at any other management level. As a result, there is not a great deal of tangible difference between acceptable and outstanding individual performance. Moreover, most management information systems cannot, at any reasonable cost, generate the data necessary for measuring the performance of many first-line supervisors. Consider, for example, rotating shift foremen. Most information systems will provide data by department or shift, but not by foreman. A final significant point with respect to the prescribed nature of the first-line supervisory position is that it is unlikely to hold the interest of a high-potential employee for very long. A superficial appraisal approach can result in interpreting boredom and frustration as merely poor or undesirable performance, rather than what it often is: a sign that a man is overdue for greater responsibilities.

Differences among First-line Supervisory Positions

There are, of course, considerable differences among first-line supervisory positions which also require consideration in designing a performance appraisal program.

One difference is the degree to which the first-line supervisor becomes involved in doing, as opposed to supervising, the work of the unit. This can range from the production foreman who cannot, as specified in most labor contracts, do any "work" to the research group leader who is expected to do as well as supervise bench work, or to the sales supervisor who is supposed to make the transition from doing (selling) to supervising, but often finds it extremely difficult to do so.

A second difference is found in the nature of the work of the unit supervised. One end of the spectrum can be illustrated by the work of a production unit in a process plant and the other by the work of a process engineering group. In the former case, work is highly structured and to a great degree cyclic or repetitive, giving rise to performance standards and established (usually by a budgeting system) regular review[1] periods. In the latter case, however, the work is of a project nature, hence far less structured, and if performance is to be measured at all, objectives must be set for each project. In addition, the review period varies with the length and nature of the project.

The final difference to be considered relates more to individuals rather than the job. In the past, the first-line supervisory position was, without question, the beginning position in management. Over the years, however, it has become, for many, a terminal position. In a number of industries, for example, second-level production supervisory jobs are being filled by men from technical staff functions rather than by the "up from the ranks" first-line supervisor. Also, for a variety of reasons, some companies have found it convenient to "create" supervisory positions as rewards for

---

[1] Performance measurement and feedback.

especially productive sales or technical personnel, who then experience a constant parade of personnel being promoted around, or moved in above, them. This "ambivalent" nature of the position, which can and does occur in all functional areas, more than any other single factor, precludes dealing with first-line supervisors in a uniform way.

PROGRAM MODEL

All evidence leads to the conclusion that the approach to performance appraisal for first-line supervisors should be a good deal more flexible and in some ways quite different from that for other groups. To achieve this, to the extent that it is feasible in a given organization, depends more on timing, emphasis, and technique than on forms and procedure. Recognizing this, the outline below is presented as a conceptual model which, along with some of the preceding illustrative material, can serve as a design framework for a viable program.

  I. Measurement phase
    A. Perspective. This is the most critical phase of the appraisal process because (1) it is the way in which first-line supervisors are managed and through them control is exercised over operations and (2) it provides all the information for subsequent evaluations and personnel action. Clearly, if this phase is not executed well, it makes little or no difference how subsequent steps are handled. The balance of the outline for this phase suggests how each element in it might be approached with respect to first-line supervisors concerned with three different types of work:
      1. Cyclic work (typical of production groups).
      2. Project work (typical of technical groups).
      3. Combination cyclic and project work (typical of sales groups).
    B. Performance criteria
      1. Cyclic
        a. Standards, stemming from position description, in critical areas such as:
          Output
          Waste
          Quality
          Safety
        b. Usually stated in quantitative terms, as a single figure or range.
        c. Suggested by staff groups; agreed to by supervisors concerned.
        d. Usually not changed unless conditions change, e.g., new equipment, different materials.
      2. Project
        a. Objectives, stemming from nature or purpose of specific project, supported by project work plan indicating check points.
        b. Often stated in qualitative terms, e.g., acceptable results within agreed-upon time frame.
        c. Jointly developed by first-line supervisor and his organizational superior for each assignment.
        d. Will differ from project to project, but will usually not change during a project.
      3. Combination
        a. Objectives of two types:
          (1) Those stemming from position description, e.g., sales, expense ratios.

      (2) Those stemming from special projects, e.g., new product intro-
duction.

    b. Usually stated in quantitative terms (ranges preferably) supported
by plans as to how objectives will be achieved.

    c. Developed by supervisor, approved by higher management echelons.

    d. Reset for each measurement period.

  C. Measurement time span

    1. Cyclic: the normal accounting or budget period, usually 1 month.

    2. Project: the agreed-upon check points for each project.

    3. Combination: the "natural" period dictated by the characteristics of the
market, e.g., seasons; if no natural period is present, then every 3 to 6
months.

  D. Feedback

    1. Cyclic: results and coordinated action plan to correct unfavorable vari-
ances.

    2. Project: critique of progress and review of plan for next interval.

    3. Combination: review of results, analysis of changes in the environment,
and setting of objectives for ensuing period.

  E. Administrative action. In each case, recording of results for future use in
evaluation phases.

II. Interim evaluation phase

  A. Perspective. Because of the relatively high failure and/or frustration
rate at the first supervisory level, it is desirable to provide a periodic
evaluation of performance for the specific and exclusive purposes of determining the need for a development program and/or job counseling.
Experience has indicated that a more reliable evaluation can be made if
compensation and other issues are not considered at the same time. Moreover, it seems advisable to make such evaluations more frequently than
is necessary for these other purposes: hence, the "interim" evaluation
phase.

  B. Procedure. Evaluations ordinarily should be made jointly by the next
two higher line managers (with personnel department assistance if available), using measurement data as the basis.

  C. Evaluation time span. At least twice a year but out of phase with "annual" evaluation.

  D. Feedback. Communication of the evaluation to the individual is made
only if some development program or counseling is called for, or if such a
program is in existence, to review the progress that has been made.

  E. Administrative action. Where required, the formulation and implementation of a development or counseling program.

III. "Annual" evaluation phase

  A. Perspective. The annual evaluation phase serves two purposes: to identify
potential and to provide information for compensation action. The relative importance of these two purposes will depend, to a large extent, upon
a company's compensation and manpower planning programs. However,
at the first supervisory level, there are several fairly good reasons for
minimizing the impact of performance evaluation upon compensation
action.

    1. Except in extreme cases, variation in performance above an acceptable
level among first-line supervisors has little impact upon results. Moreover, controls are usually tight enough at this level that such variations
below a very narrow range of acceptability will not be allowed to exist
for long. Finally, results at this level are so influenced by conditions

beyond the supervisor's control that most evaluations could be seriously challenged, again except in extreme cases.

2. Salary actions are dictated at this level, in almost every case, by a variety of factors other than performance, such as tenure, cost-of-living changes, maintenance of differentials, potential for advancement, and competitive salary levels. In most situations, the budgetary realities are such that not enough can be added to reflect more than the extreme case (1 or 2 percent of salary).

3. Those first-line supervisors who are likely to recognizably respond to an "above expected" increase (recognizing the impact of such response is limited by the constraints of the job) are most likely also the ones with potential for advancement. In such cases, more mileage might be gained by relating "above expected" increases to potential. On the other hand, there is no evidence that indicates that a "poor" supervisor will show any improvement by receiving a "less than expected" increase. The best action in either case, if clearly recognizable, is movement out of the first-line supervisor job, obviously up in the former case and down in the latter.

B. Feedback. Following from the perspective above, feedback of the "annual" evaluation should probably focus on career aspirations and planning.

C. Administrative action

1. Input of potential and career planning information to the manpower planning system.

2. A recommendation for salary action.

3. A recommendation for change of job action, if appropriate.

BIBLIOGRAPHY

Periodicals

Kelly, Philip R.: "Reappraisal of Appraisals," *Harvard Business Review,* May–June 1958.

Kindall, Alva F., and James Gatza: "Positive Program for Performance Appraisal," *Harvard Business Review,* November–December 1963.

McGregor, Douglas: "An Uneasy Look at Performance Appraisal," *Harvard Business Review,* May–June 1957.

Meyer, Herbert H., et al.: "Split Rates in Performance Appraisal," *Harvard Business Review,* January–February, 1965.

Neiman, Robert A.: "Measuring Supervisory Performance," *Personnel,* January–February, 1962.

White, James M.: "Appraising the Work of Supervisors," *Advanced Management,* vol. XXVI, July–August, 1961.

Books

Busse, Frank A.: *Three Dimensional Foremanship,* The American Management Association, 1969.

Patten, Thomas H. Jr.: *The Foreman, Forgotten Man of Management,* The American Management Association, 1968.

chapter 43

Appraising Sales Employees

WESLEY S. CALDWELL   *Program Director, Porter Henry & Co., Inc., New York, New York*

Consider the salesman. His job requires him to see and talk with people, but in spite of these many personal contacts the job is a lonely one. More often than not he has little contact with the other salesmen in his company and sees his immediate supervisor only infrequently. Small wonder then that the process of appraisal can be even more important to him and his superior than it might be in many other kinds of supervisor-subordinate relations.

If the salesman is to succeed in his work and develop his abilities, there are six things he needs to know, and all of them are closely related to appraisal and counseling.

SIX THINGS A SALESMAN NEEDS TO KNOW

What to do. The salesman needs a job description. More than a simple description of *what* is expected of him, he needs to know and understand *why* he is expected to perform these functions. His understanding of the job should match closely that of his supervisor.

How to do it. He needs certain knowledge and certain skills. Some of this knowledge and some of these skills he can be expected to acquire on his own initiative, but much will come to him through training. Many of the functions on his job description will be accompanied by "standard operating procedures." Training will also be instilled through written materials such as manuals, bulletins, correspondence courses, and programmed instruction. He will gain knowledge and skill through periodic group meetings. Much of his development, however, will be through on-the-job training. Headquarters may provide programs and materials, but the prime responsibility for on-the-job training rests on the shoulders of the supervisor, among whose important tools are appraisal and counseling.

What is par?   What are the performance standards? A track coach does not tell a high jumper to "jump" without giving him some mark to shoot at. Neither should sales management do that to a salesman. The salesman should know the "par" for the course he is playing. He should know how many accounts he is expected to open, how many service calls he is expected to make, what dollar volume and what product mix he is supposed to sell. Furthermore, he will work more effectively if he has had some voice in the setting of the performance standards.

How am I doing?   Depending on the job itself, the salesman may have many or few clues as to how he is doing. The orders he writes give him clues, but he needs more: he needs regular feedback from his company, from his supervisor. This may come in the form of computer printouts or other statistics, but even more important it should come to him through conversations with his supervisor—again the appraisal and counseling process.

How can I improve?   Showing a man how he is doing is not enough. If the supervisor is to fulfill his function of developing his men, he must help each one to build on his strengths and overcome his weaknesses. Again, among the important tools are appraisal and counseling.

What's in it for me?   Why should the salesman accept the training and work harder to produce more? Why should he be motivated? Motivation is too broad a topic to discuss in this chapter, but certainly the supervisor in the appraisal-counseling situation can have a motivating or demotivating effect on the salesman.

APPRAISAL AND COUNSELING DEFINED

In the review of the six things a salesman ought to know, the words "appraisal" and "counseling" keep recurring. Since many people may have many definitions, let us define these terms as they apply in this chapter.

The supervisor (whose title may be sales supervisor, field sales manager, territory manager, district manager, branch manager, or any of dozens of others) is constantly appraising his men, whether or not his company has supplied an appraisal form and an appraisal procedure. It may sometimes be a casual, shallow appraisal—"Pete's sales seem to be slipping a bit lately"—but nevertheless appraisal is taking place.

Every time the supervisor makes a call with his salesman, he is appraising; if he discusses the call with the salesman afterward, he is counseling (although "coaching" is more often the term used in this day-to-day situation).

Most of the suggestions made in this chapter apply also to these frequent coaching opportunities, but primarily we are discussing periodic, formal, scheduled appraisal and counseling.

Appraisal precedes counseling. Counseling, the personal interview between salesman and supervisor, is based on the appraisal. "Counseling" is often referred to by other names, including "development review interview" or "appraisal interview."

APPRAISAL OBJECTIVES

There may be many different objectives for having an appraisal program for salesmen. One, for example, may be to provide one more piece of paper to stuff into a salesman's home-office personnel file jacket. Another might be to satisfy a marketing vice-president's desire to feel that he has close personal contact with what is going on in the field. In addition to such questionable objectives, there may be as many as a dozen perfectly valid ones for having an appraisal program. Of these the most important have to do with:

Raises

Promotions and transfers

Training needs

Man development

The important fact to be taken into account is this: no form has yet been devised that can accomplish all four of these objectives simultaneously. If such a form could be devised, it is unlikely that a supervisor could be developed who could fill it out with such perfect objectivity that it would effectively accomplish all four objectives.

Picture the situation: you are a field sales manager; you have been asked to fill out an "annual development review" form on Bill Bronson, one of your salesmen. If this same form is to be used to help develop Bill in his job and also to justify the raise you feel he deserves, is it likely that you can be completely factual and objective when you fill it out?

For what you consider to be good, solid management reasons you want Bill, a "good" man, to get a raise. But you know that the company is only awarding raises, at this time, to "exceptional" men; so you paint an "exceptional" word portrait of Bill Bronson. In such a case the form and the procedure lose their utility as development tools. Moreover, if headquarters people are also using the form to obtain information on training needs of the salesmen in the field, they will get no clues from Bill's appraisal. In your zeal to get him a raise, you have painted a picture of a man who has no training needs; he is great; he knows everything he ought to know —he deserves a nice fat raise.

Let us consider the matter of promotions, and the closely related matter of transfers. For development purposes, the appraisal should limit itself to developing the man in his *present* job; it should concern itself with how the man can better perform the work he is doing *now*. To appraise a man for this purpose on the same form and at the same time that you make an assessment of promotability tends to cloud the issue while it clouds the thinking of the manager and salesman alike.

It is a well-recognized fact that the best salesman is not necessarily the best candidate for promotion into the ranks of first-line sales management. A less-than-best salesman may have far greater potential for management. Let us suppose, then, that you have a merely "good" salesman who has excellent potential for management. Your best estimate is that he will be ready for the next step up in twelve to eighteen months. Meanwhile his development in his present job should continue to move forward. To present both these situations on the same appraisal form is not practical.

If these remarks are in conflict with some established procedure that a sales supervisor is required to follow, then he must, of course, follow the instructions and procedures issued by his management. If, on the other hand, his company allows him full flexibility in how he handles appraisals, he would be well advised to keep the different kinds of appraisals widely separated.

WHO MAKES THE APPRAISAL?

Some appraisal procedures have been set up so that everyone in the sales-management hierarchy is involved. The first-line sales manager makes the original appraisal (in whatever form). Then the paper is passed on up the line. At each level the appraisal is read and comments are added before it is passed upward to the next level. In extreme cases, even the president of the company may get to add his comments before the form finally comes to rest in the salesman's personnel jacket. Of course, appraisals having to do with salary recommendations, training needs, or promotability might well go through many levels of management before reaching the point where action will be taken. In a particular sales organization, there may even be good reason for moving a man-development appraisal through all levels of sales management. However, since the prime responsibility for developing a man rests with his immediate boss, the development appraisal should originate at that point and be limited in how much farther up the line it goes.

(In the balance of this chapter, the word "appraisal" will be used to refer to an appraisal made with the intent of developing the salesman, that is, improving his performance in his present job. Where we mean "salary recommendation" or "promotability prognostication," we will say so.)

Who makes the appraisal? The salesman's immediate supervisor, the first-line sales manager, whatever his title may be. One important reason for not letting the higher levels of management add their comments is that they are not in close enough contact with the salesman. No one can make a meaningful appraisal of a salesman's work unless he has meaningful knowledge of that salesman's work.

It is important to note that even the man's immediate boss should avoid appraising the man he "does not know." Suppose, for example, that you are a district sales manager. In your group you have a number of men you know well and have worked with many times; you also have a man who has been with you for only a few months; you have not yet had a chance to get to know him very well. When you fill out his appraisal form, fill out the blanks only on those items you can appraise honestly. Do not feel impelled to turn in a "completed" form; leave blanks; make "do not-know" entries—appraisals should not be guesswork.

Having established that the immediate supervisor, because of his greater knowledge of the salesman and his work, makes the appraisal, we now come to the problem of how much farther up the management line the written appraisal should progress before coming to rest.

Most managers agree that the appraiser should review his appraisals with his own manager before conducting the counseling interviews with his men. Any steps beyond this will not usually result in any positive contribution to the appraisal and counseling process; they can be useful only as control steps to ensure that the procedures are being followed.

(For convenience, let us call the first-line manager the "district manager" and his boss the "zone manager.")

In the usual case, the zone manager knows the salesmen in the district manager's district fairly well. In the discussion with the district manager, it is likely that he may be able to make some positive contribution. Of course, it is not his purpose to second-guess the district manager, but because he is one step removed he should be able to ensure that the district manager's appraisals are objective and fair to the salesmen. Furthermore, if the salesman knows that the appraisal has been discussed by the district manager and the zone manager (and he should be made aware of that fact), he will have a greater appreciation of the importance of the appraisal and the appraisal interview.

THE SALESMAN'S ROLE IN THE APPRAISAL

The salesman should be given a blank appraisal form well in advance of the counseling interview. He should be asked to fill it out as objectively as possible and bring it with him to the counseling interview. In the event that the appraisal is in the form of a narrative report, then he should be given the criteria and asked to write a narrative appraisal of himself. In this way he is made aware of the criteria used in the appraisal; furthermore his effort at rating himself will better prepare him for the interview.

Part of the self-appraisal will deal with hard data (sales volume, number of new accounts opened, etc.); these are facts not subject to interpretation. Beyond this area, the degree of objectivity the salesman is capable of will vary greatly depending on the climate that has been created by the company and the manager. If the salesman suspects that his self-evaluation may be misused, he will be unwilling to confess to any weaknesses. He might be willing, for example, to admit to a need for help in prospecting if he knows that it will be a problem that he and his supervisor can work on together. If he suspects, however, that his self-appraisal might find its way into his permanent record at headquarters, he will tend to color it "excellent."

It can be useful to both the manager and the salesman to have the salesman's self-appraisal include a brief statement of what he thinks were his one or two major accomplishments during the appraisal period.

At the interview the supervisor can review the salesman's self-appraisal first. If some of his self-ratings correspond closely with those of the district manager, then the district manager can spend interview time more profitably on those items which do not correspond so well.

(It is suggested that the actual self-appraisal "document" remain in the salesman's hands after the interview — his to file or dispose of as he sees fit.)

FREQUENCY OF APPRAISAL

As stated earlier in this chapter, appraisal takes place continuously — the supervisor cannot avoid making appraisals as he works with the man and as he reads his reports and sees the orders he is writing. However, the supervisor may or may not discuss his appraisals with the salesman. Much depends on the frequency of the supervisor's contacts with the salesmen and on his willingness or reluctance to counsel with them.

The more formal development reviews are usually scheduled on a semiannual or annual basis. An appraisal and counseling plan would in most cases be more effective if the salesman's progress toward development goals were reviewed more frequently — quarterly is probably ideal. With a quarterly plan the annual development review could still be the major milestone, but the interim progress appraisals and interviews tend to make development move smoothly forward on a continuing basis.

Experience in many companies shows that managers do not always view the appraisal and counseling aspects of their jobs with great enthusiasm. They are often reluctant to appraise and even more reluctant to conduct the appraisal interview. Top management may recognize the desirability of leaving the development review form out in the field where it will do the most good, but in order to ensure compliance they choose to impose deadlines: "Completed appraisal forms must be on the desk of the general sales manager by June 1." Then, although the procedure clearly calls for the form to be mailed *after* the counseling interview, the company finds that many field sales managers are electing not to conduct the interviews. Salesmen working for such managers are often quite unaware that there is such a thing as an appraisal procedure.

When the appraisal is scheduled on an annual basis, perhaps this reluctance to counsel is understandable. The annual event comes as an interruption of "normal" routine. The supervisor now has to find time to do something he has not done for a year, and each salesman has to steel himself for what may turn out to be an unpleasant experience.

Greater frequency of the "periodic development reviews" will not automatically improve the skills of a manager who is a poor appraiser and a poor counselor. It could, however, help to avoid making the appraisal a once-a-year traumatic experience for man and manager alike. A formal annual appraisal could be quite enough if the salesman and manager get together for effective coaching and counseling at fairly frequent intervals throughout the year.

WHAT TO APPRAISE

In this chapter we have used the expression "appraisal form" on several occasions. This form, usually developed at a management level somewhat higher than first-line sales management, may or may not be a good one. Some companies do not use a form but depend on a narrative written report instead (although they usually supply some guidelines on writing the report).

This chapter includes three actual forms used by actual companies (Figures 1 to 3). Let us talk about some of the basic principles involved in designing good appraisal forms.

As a starter here is an excerpt from a form (author unknown):

Overall Performance

Leaps tall buildings with a single bound (5)	Must take running start to leap tall buildings (4)	Can leap short buildings only (3)	Crashes into buildings when attempting to leap them (2)	Cannot recognize buildings (1)

Communications

Talks with God (5)	Talks with the angels (4)	Talks to himself (3)	Argues with himself (2)	Loses those arguments (1)

This is amusing because, like most humor, it has its basis in fact; it has a very familiar ring to it.

Real forms of this genre, although less common than they once were, are still in use today. They may run to many pages and rate a man on everything from "appearance" ("Always well dressed, faultless linen, shined shoes, etc.—rate 5") to "zeal" ("Always in the forefront, a self-starter, lives for his work—rate 10").

"Appearance" and "zeal" and many other qualities, such as "creativity," "wears well with customers," "shows leadership qualities," may all affect a salesman's results. And Boy Scouts are not the only ones who are better if they are trustworthy, loyal, friendly, helpful, and so on. The problem is to find a reliable way to rate these qualities. If salesman Sam were rated by two different supervisors, the ratings might be widely (and honestly) different. What we have to do is develop more reliable criteria.

If we are going to rate a man on what he is doing, then we should be rating him on standards of performance that are based on what his job description says he is supposed to be doing. If our appraisal standards are to be useful, then the job description has to be useful.

The job description must specify the functions to be performed: "covers the territory, makes regular calls, opens new accounts, handles complaints, services regular customers." Unless terms like "regular" are defined in performance standards, the salesman has no bench mark as to how well he is expected to perform each function.

A performance standard, by the usual definition, is a "written statement of conditions that exist when a job is well done." It follows this kind of pattern: "This function is being performed satisfactorily when all class A accounts are being called on once a month, all class B accounts are being called on once in three months, and all class C accounts are being called on once in six months."

Figure 1.   A typical "traits" form.

The closer we can come to putting numbers on these standards of performance, the more reliable they become in the appraisal process.   Job functions like these translate easily and directly into standards of performance: "Open an average of six new accounts per month; sell a product mix in the proportion of $6,000 in bulk goods, $3,000 in package goods, and $1,000 in specialties for a total of $10,000 in monthly sales."   Such standards are measurable and therefore reliable; they are a matter of record and leave little room for disagreement.

However, even with the numbers to help him, the supervisor still has a problem. Numbers can be deceptive.   One salesman's territory may be growing well in spite of his lack of devotion to duty; another salesman may be working intelligently and

B | Instructions

Suggestions:

Review the individual's job responsibilities to develop a current list of all his functions and responsibilities. These are job functions for which the individual is held accountable.

Next, select and list only the major job responsibilities which are the PRIMARY functions of the individual's job.

At the year-end review the manager should analyze the individual's overall performance on the primary responsibilities, write his appraisal in the space provided and then discuss it with the individual.

B. PRINCIPAL JOB RESPONSIBILITIES

1. Implement key wholesaler and dealer concept, specifically integrating National Accounts.

2. Operate within financial budgets and work BPI.

3. Protect and keep up company records and properties.

C | Instructions

Select the specific job targets (Projects, programs, assignments) the individual is expected to accomplish. The targets should be specific, mutually understood and agreed upon. Also, to the extent possible, indicate priorities, completion times, and results expected. If a target is complex or requires a prolonged period for completion, break it into phases showing when certain elements or parts will be completed.

During the year, the manager should meet at least quarterly with the individual to:

1. Review his progress towards target completion.

2. Discuss any help or assistance he needs to achieve the targets.

3. Make any changes necessary to current targets; add new targets if workload permits.

Also, the manager should indicate in the space provided, what action was taken on each target.

At year-end, the manager should evaluate the results accomplished in the column provided, noting the quality and quantity of the work done. This should then be discussed with the individual.

C. SPECIFIC JOB TARGETS | 1st Quarter Review

1. Complete Anytown retail audit by 1/1/71.

2. Program Anytown's dealer organization.

3. Get Hugh M. Woods Lbr. chain as programmed dealers.

4. Key retailers file, with work schedule.

5. Increase accessory volume on portables 50% over same period one year ago.

D | Instructions

This part is to be completed at the year-end review. This section is not to be completed in advance.

The manager should:

1. Analyze the other critical factors which in your judgment have interfered with the individual's performance through the year, e.g., knowledge the man brings to the job, technical and managerial skills, and personal characteristics.

2. Select those factors which have MOST adversely affected his performance last year, describe and give examples in the space provided.

3. These factors should be considered when the individual's personal targets (Part A, #3 and #4) are established next year.

D. OTHER FACTORS AFFECTING JOB PERFORMANCE

1. Until end of fiscal '69, had always worked in conjunction with senior man.

2. Previous lack of detail organization.

3. High degree of affibility and integrity, poise, and golden-rule business sense.

Figure 1. A typical "traits" form. (continued)

effectively only to have his sales figures slipping because of factors beyond his control.

Then, too, criteria should not be selected simply because of ease of measurement. For example, a computer printout may provide you with an automatic figure for total monthly dollar sales volume. In a certain kind of business it might be an excellent index of performance; in another kind of business it might be a lot less than desirable as an indicator of good sales performance. Product mix, or profitability, or number of new accounts opened, or the sales-to-calls ratio might be more meaningful, even if it may be more difficult to ascertain.

So we see that goals, or targets, or objectives should be capable of being appraised

HOW WELL DID HE PERFORM?

1. Accomplish with excellent results.
2. Accomplished with good results.
3. Good accomplishment.

2nd Quarter Review	3rd Quarter Review	4th Quarter Review	Results
			1. Working on same when transferred to Bigtown.
			2. Accomplished programming prior to transfer.
			3. Unsuccessful - as no special monies available.
			4. Organized.
			5. Transferred middle of time period.

DESCRIBE AND GIVE EXAMPLES

1. Came to abrupt halt as Bill Short transferred to Towson, and Joe moved to Bigtown. Has met the challenge head on, and is stepping right along and proving himself.
2. Leaving the bachelor ranks at the beginning of this period, Joe got better at accomplishing this job.
3. Was well accepted immediately by his new accounts, most knowing of him prior Bigtown takeover.

Figure 1. A typical "traits" form. (continued)

reliably—the more numerical, the better. On the other hand, in trying to help the salesman to improve "the numbers," the supervisor will usually have to dig for the roots. He will have to look beyond the numbers to ascertain the causes. If, for example, the salesman is failing to open enough new accounts, there could be many possible reasons. He has so many other "more important" things to do that he has no time for new-account calls? He is uncomfortable and unsure of himself when he makes new-account calls? He does not know how to find potential new accounts? If, for example, he is losing too many old accounts, can it be that he does not in fact "wear well with customers"?

If the numbers are not right, the manager will have to find out why. Are there

E Instructions

To be completed by the manager:

1. Check the statement which best describes the individual's overall job performance.

2. Then support this performance rating by giving a word picture of the individual's performance.

3. Review the individual's career aspirations on page one. Then, based on present performance and overall growth potential, recommend a career path or future jobs you feel the individual is capable of achieving. It will be helpful to consult with other managers in other divisions for their opinions about the individual's performance and potential.

NOTE:
All factors in this overall performance appraisal should be considered when preparing next year's targets for the individual.

If the individual or the rater's superior would like to comment on this appraisal, attach his statement to the completed Work Sheet.

E. OVERALL PERFORMANCE SUMMARY

1. HOW WELL DID HE MEET STANDARDS OF JOB PERFORMANCE?

____ FAR EXCEEDS: Outstanding Performance in Present Assignment in practically every respect.

_X_ EXCEEDS: Above Average Perfomance in Present Assignment in most respects.

baseline performance level

____ MEETS NORMAL REQUIREMENTS: Average or Satisfactory Performance in PRIMARY FUNCTIONS, JOB TASKS and MANNER.

baseline performance level

____ MEETS MINIMUM REQUIREMENTS: Acceptable but does not meet average performance in the majority of primary functions, job tasks and manner.

2. EXPLAIN IN DETAIL:

Joe has highly developed analytical powers, and can size up a situation fast! Got pants put on him fast upon moving to Bigtown - not that he wasn't wearing some in Anytown. He inherited a much more aggressive territory where programming of bigger accounts was a necessity, and did an outstanding job on Winter-Spring, as evident by sell-in orders received. The sell-thru is all set and is taking place as evidenced by repeat stock orders, plus D/S orders received. He was working well with Tom Lightman and both of them are real "chargers". There is room for improvement in Joe's performance along the lines of getting experience with certain customers, shows, etc., as to more definite directions in the future and pacing self on same. Any time a change of territories is made, there is bound to be a period of separating the grain from the chaff.

3. CAREER PATH RECOMMENDATIONS:

Do good job in Bigtown first.
Then -- Staff Training Department.

SIGNATURES:
Individual Rated: Typical — Date: 2/24/71
Rater: I. M. Manager — Date: 2-24-71
Rater's Superior: ____ Date: ____

☐ SEE ATTACHED STATEMENT

Form No. 2283

Figure 1. A typical "traits" form. (continued)

circumstances beyond the man's control? Maybe he is not making enough calls; maybe he is failing to ask for the order; maybe he is not as cheerful, brave, clean, and reverent as he ought to be. The supervisor has to uncover the "why" and then do something about it.

Some appraisal systems attempt to assign numerical values to selling skills. The form lists separate selling skills, such as prospecting, selling benefits, handling objections, closing, and the manager is to rate the salesman on each of these skills, using a numerical scale. A typical scale might be something like this: excellent, 5; very good, 4; good, 3; fair, 2; poor, 1. Perhaps the principal value of such a scheme is that it forces the supervisor to do some serious thinking.

```
                    SALES TRAINEE EVALUATION REPORT
         ━━━━━━━━━━━━━━━━━━━━━━━━━━━━━━━━━━━━━━━━━━━━━━━━━━━━━━━━━

   TRAINEE                              DIVISION

   DATE        MARCH 20, 1970          PHASE        FIVE

   LOCATION OF TRAINING                INCLUSIVE DATES   MARCH 9-13, 1970



   1. To what extent has the Trainee acquired the knowledge and skills listed in this phase of his training?

        The Trainee has gained a basic knowledge and an overall understanding
        of      manufacturing.



   2. What characteristics of this man will contribute most to his success as a Salesman?

        Intelligence, brightness, excellent personal appearance, easy to talk
        to, very personable, a variety of interests, past experience.



   3. What characteristics of this man will limit his success? To what extent?

        He shows nervousness by obvious physical movements. If this were
        pointed out to him and he concentrated to correct it, there would be
        no problem.



   4. What caliber of Salesman do you think he will become? Why?

        Pat will become a very good salesman because of his intelligence,
        appearance, and obvious interest in what he is doing.



   5. Fill out the following rating form.
```

Figure 2.   A detailed performance report.

The most useful numbers in the appraisal are those which are tied directly with the numerical aspects of the performance standards, which in turn are tied directly to the individual job functions on the job description. In making the appraisal, the supervisor should make an evaluation of each of the performance standards, giving attention first to those which have definite number values (sales volume, number of new accounts, product mix, etc.). Did the salesman achieve the goals? Exceed them? Fall short?

Then the supervisor appraises the effectiveness with which the salesman has carried out each of the other not so easily measured job functions (implement company policy, develop the product knowledge of distributor salesman, etc.).

Listed below are the personality traits which the Training Program aims to develop in the Trainee. Rate the Trainee on these traits by *placing an "X" in the appropriate squares.*

		OUT-STANDING	GOOD	FAIR	POOR
Appearance:	Clean-cut, well-groomed, good physique, appearance of good health, makes good impression.	X			
Self-expression:	Distinct voice, good vocabulary, clear expression of ideas.		X		
Intelligence:	Thinks quickly and accurately, comprehends readily, analyzes with good reasoning, uses good judgment.		X		
Ambition:	Keen interest in self-development, intense desire for maximum accomplishment on the job, and to advance to the level of his greatest potential; a desire to sell and to grow in the organization.		X		
Aggressiveness:	Self-starter, enthusiasm, initiative, and self-assertion.		X		
Maturity:	High sense of responsibility, can make up his own mind, a clear idea of his short- and long-range goals, self-discipline, realistic.		X		
Sincerity:	Natural firmness and directness in manner and expression, unpretentious, trustworthy, honest, leaves the impression that he means what he says.		X		
Persuasiveness:	Prompts respect and interest from others, convincing in content and manner of speech, makes a personal impact on others, can influence others.		X		
Stability:	Makes plans and carries them out; has positive attitude toward life and work.		X		
Friendliness:	Prompts a kindly reaction in others, establishes good rapport quickly with others, pleasant to talk with.	X			

OVER-ALL RATING: *Outstanding* ☐   *Good* ☐   *Fair* ☐   *Poor* ☐

PHASE SUPERVISOR

The foregoing report has been discussed with me and I wish to make the following comments:

....

....

....

                                             Trainee ....

Figure 2.   A detailed performance report.   (continued)

On the theory that even superlative performance can be improved, and on the assumption that no salesman can have a long list of weaknesses and still be on the payroll, the manager decides on one or two things that might be singled out to be improved as part of the continuing development of each of his men.   If the supervisor has a major development goal for a man, minor areas which need correction can be covered in subsequent coaching sessions.

In making his appraisal, the supervisor is guided by sales report forms, sales figures provided by headquarters, and so forth; these are the "numbers," the hard data.   But when it comes to the salesman's traits, selling skills, etc., the supervisor had better be prepared to supply the salesman with "for instances."   In the inter-

PERFORMANCE REVIEW

I. VITAL STATISTICS

NAME		PRESENT POSITION		AGE
DISTRICT/REGION		TIME IN PRESENT POSITION		TIME WITH COMPANY

II. SALES PERFORMANCE
A. Sales Results (Jan. — Dec. 1969)

CATEGORY	1968	1969	$ INCREASE	% INCREASE
Total Direct Sales				
Total Hospital Sales				
Prorated Sales				
Total All Sales				

B. Sales Performance Versus Quota (Jan. — Dec. 1969)

AVERAGE $ VOLUME INCREASE						
	TERRITORY	DISTRICT	REGION	DIVISION	Terr. Quota	$
Total Sales					Terr. Quota Attainment	
Hospital Sales					Dist. Quota Attainment	
					Reg. Quota Attainment	
					Div. Quota Attainment	

C. Special Sales Programs (Jan. — Dec. 1969)

CATEGORY	TOTAL $ VOLUME	% ATTAINMENT
Habit		
Medicinal Contest		
Summer Savings Program		
1st Anniversary Promotion		

Figure 3. *(a)* **Performance review, sales representatives.** *(b)* **Selection and evaluation summary.**

view the supervisor might say something like this: "We've made quite a number of calls together, George, and it seems to me that your sales would improve if you could be a little stronger in closing." He might be quite right, but his case will fall apart if he is not prepared to give at least a couple of examples that George will recognize. The only way to be sure of having the right examples is to keep some kind of records.

KEEPING RECORDS

Keeping a "little black book" may have a less-than-beautiful sound about it, but it is a rare manager indeed who can prepare for a periodic appraisal while relying only on his memory. Some of the needed facts will be readily available in statistics and

SELECTION AND EVALUATION SUMMARY	NAME OF APPLICANT		
	ADDRESS OF APPLICANT		TELEPHONE NO.
	POSITION		

"CAN DO" FACTORS	WELL-QUALIFIED	ACCEPTABLE	QUESTIONABLE
APPEARANCE AND MANNER	☐ CONSERVATIVELY DRESSED, IMMACULATE	☐ NEAT, WELL GROOMED; NO SEVERE DISFIGUREMENTS	☐ FLASHY DRESSER, DIRTY, UNKEMPT, ETC.
AGE	☐ 24-32	☐ 21-40	☐ UNDER 21/OVER 40
PHYSICAL CONDITION AND HEALTH	☐ EXCELLENT	☐ GOOD	☐ MARGINAL ☐ POOR
EDUCATION	☐ COLLEGE DEGREE IN BASIC SCIENCE	☐ 2-3 YEARS OF COLLEGE	☐ LESS THAN 2 YEARS OF COLLEGE
EXPERIENCE IN THIS FIELD	☐ SUCCESSFUL SALES RECORD	☐ NO SALES EXPERIENCE	☐ MARGINAL SALES RECORD
BASIC ENERGY LEVEL	☐ EXCELLENT	☐ GOOD	☐ MARGINAL ☐ POOR
"WILL DO" FACTORS			
CHARACTER TRAITS (BASIC HABITS)			
STABILITY, MAINTAINING SAME JOBS & INTERESTS	☐ GOOD	☐ EXCELLENT	☐ MARGINAL ☐ POOR
INDUSTRY, WILLINGNESS TO WORK	☐ EXCELLENT	☐ GOOD	☐ MARGINAL ☐ POOR
PERSEVERANCE, FINISHING WHAT HE STARTS	☐ EXCELLENT	☐ GOOD	☐ MARGINAL ☐ POOR
LOYALTY	☐ EXCELLENT	☐ GOOD	☐ MARGINAL ☐ POOR
ABILITY TO GET ALONG WITH OTHERS	☐ EXCELLENT	☐ GOOD	☐ MARGINAL ☐ POOR
SELF RELIANCE, STAND ON OWN TWO FEET, MAKING DECISIONS	☐ EXCELLENT	☐ GOOD	☐ MARGINAL ☐ POOR
LEADERSHIP	☐ EXCELLENT ☐ GOOD	☐ MARGINAL	☐ POOR
MOTIVATION			
SECURITY	☐ DEFINITE	☐ STRONG	☐ SLIGHT
RECOGNITION	☐ STRONG	☐ DEFINITE	☐ SLIGHT
RESPONSE, SENSE-BELONGING	☐ DEFINITE	☐ STRONG	☐ SLIGHT
NEW EXPERIENCE AND GROWTH	☐ DEFINITE	☐ STRONG	☐ SLIGHT
EMOTIONAL MATURITY			
DEPENDENCE	☐ SLIGHT	☐ DEFINITE	☐ STRONG
SELFISHNESS	☐ SLIGHT	☐ DEFINITE	☐ STRONG
PLEASURE MINDEDNESS	☐ SLIGHT	☐ SLIGHT	☐ DEFINITE ☐ STRONG
DISREGARD FOR CONSEQUENCES	☐ SLIGHT	☐ SLIGHT	☐ DEFINITE ☐ STRONG
WISHFUL THINKING	☐ SLIGHT	☐ SLIGHT	☐ DEFINITE ☐ STRONG
SHOW OFF TENDENCIES	☐ DEFINITE	☐ SLIGHT	☐ STRONG
LACK OF SELF-DISCIPLINE	☐ SLIGHT	☐ SLIGHT	☐ DEFINITE ☐ STRONG
DESTRUCTIVE TENDENCIES	☐ SLIGHT	☐ SLIGHT	☐ DEFINITE ☐ STRONG

IMPORTANT: DO NOT ADD OR AVERAGE THESE FACTORS IN MAKING THE OVER-ALL RATING. MATCH THE QUALIFICATIONS OF THE APPLICANT AGAINST THE REQUIREMENTS OF THE POSITION.

STRONG POINTS FOR THIS POSITION _____

WEAK POINTS FOR THIS POSITION _____

RATED BY	OVERALL RATING		RECOMMEND TO EMPLOY	DATE
	1 2 3 4		☐ YES ☐ NO	

Figure 3. *(a)* **Performance review, sales representatives.** *(b)* **Selection and evaluation summary.** **(continued)**

reports, but others will have to come from some kind of personal records kept by the supervisor himself.

Part of the appraisal will have to be based on things the supervisor observed when he worked with the salesman. After working with Charlie Brown for a week in his territory, the supervisor should certainly carry back with him some notes on Charlie's performance to guide the coaching on the next trip and to aid in making the next appraisal. Many managers would make it a point to send Charlie a note following such a work-with period. The note would serve as a reminder to Charlie of what is expected of him, and the carbon copy goes into the manager's file as against the day he needs its help in making an appraisal. An alternative is to ask Charlie to mail the manager a summary of the discussions and decisions.

III. SALES ACTIVITIES (Jan. — Dec. 1969)

CDP PHYS. CALL AVG. DAY			PRODUCT DETAILED/CALL			T/O %		
TERRITORY	DISTRICT	REGION	TERRITORY	DISTRICT	REGION	TERRITORY	DISTRICT	REGION

IV. SELLING ACTIVITIES

	E	G	F	D
A. Product Knowledge				
B. Proficiency in use of selling skills				
C. Proficiency in utilization of material				
D. Quality of Details				
E. Utilization of samples				
F. Pre and post call analysis and recording				
G. Adherence to programs				
H. Quality of hospital coverage				
I. Territory organization				
J. Adherence to itinerary				
K. Accuracy in classification of CDP				
L. Implementation and follow-up to special programs				
M. Quantity of returns				
N. Utilization of stock package requisitions				
O. Awareness of competition				

V. ORGANIZATION – ADMINISTRATION

	E	G	F	D
A. Use of sales and activity reports				
B. Implementation of program				
C. Promptness, accuracy and completeness of reports				
D. Follow-up on special requests and programs				
E. Contribution to meetings				
F. Written and oral communications				
G. Expense control				

Figure 3. *(a)* **Performance review, sales representatives.** *(b)* **Selection and evaluation summary.** **(continued)**

Many field sales managers, in keeping their records of a salesman's progress, make use of the "critical-incident" technique. The theory behind this technique is that much of the work done by a "good" salesman is similar to much of the work done by a "poor" salesman. The difference is to be found in the critical incidents involved in each man's work. Inattention to a service problem causes the loss of a good account—critical incident. A creative solution helps a customer to solve a sticky problem—critical incident. Particularly good handling overcomes a difficult objection—critical incident. By keeping track of this kind of information the supervisor will be provided, at appraisal time, with meaningful material on which to base his appraisal.

The supervisor should be careful not to allow some critical incident showing poor sales behavior or judgment to outweigh many "good" but perhaps less critical incidents. Similarly, he should not allow some recent happening to color a salesman's appraisal just because it is fresh in his mind. Keeping records and reviewing them before making the appraisal will avoid this kind of warped judgment.

VI. SUMMARY

What significant progress has this man made this year; in what areas has he shown improvement/development? What is his greatest strength?

1969 OVERALL PERFORMANCE RATING IN DISTRICT			
EXCELLENT	ABOVE ADEQUATE	ADEQUATE	DEFICIENT
SIGNATURE OF REPRESENTATIVE			DATE
REVIEWED BY		APPROVED BY	

Figure 3. *(a)* **Performance review, sales representatives.** *(b)* **Selection and evaluation summary.** **(continued)**

COUNSELING (THE APPRAISAL INTERVIEW)

For tips on coaching an effective counseling interview, see Chapter 40. The interview with the salesman is conducted on the same principles as any other appraisal interview. In one respect, however, there can be a difference. The salesman who is separated from his supervisor by geography may present a more difficult interview problem. When the supervisor is in contact with a salesman on a daily basis, he gets to know him and his work quite well. He has frequent opportunity to counsel with him on an informal basis. In such cases the formal, periodic appraisal interview is just a somewhat more important link in a long chain of counseling interviews. The salesman in an outlying territory, on the other hand, may see his boss only infrequently. In such a case, the supervisor should make a particular effort to appraise fairly and to set up an interview atmosphere that is friendly and permissive.

BIBLIOGRAPHY

Black, James M.: *Assignment Management,* Prentice-Hall, Inc., Englewood Cliffs, N.J., 1961.
Brown, Ronald: *From Selling to Managing,* American Management Association, New York, 1968.
Davis, Robert T.: *Performance and Development of Field Sales Managers,* Harvard University, Boston, Mass., 1957.
Herzberg, Mausner, and Snyderman: *Motivation to Work,* John Wiley & Sons, Inc., New York, 1962.
Kellogg, Marion: *What to Do About Performance Appraisals,* The Macmillan Company, New York, 1965.
Maier, N.R.F.: *The Appraisal Interview,* John Wiley & Sons, Inc., New York, 1958.
McGregor, Douglas: *The Human Side of Enterprise,* McGraw-Hill Book Company, New York, 1960.
Newgarden, Albert (ed.): *The Field Sales Manager,* American Management Association, New York, 1960.
Schleh, Edward: *Management by Results,* McGraw-Hill Book Company, New York, 1961.
Tonning, Wayland A.: *How to Measure and Evaluate Salesmen's Performance,* Prentice-Hall, Inc., Englewood Cliffs, N.J., 1964.
Vizza, Robert F.: *Measuring the Value of the Sales Force,* Sales Executives Club of New York, 1963.

chapter 44

Appraising Technical Employees

RICHARD CROOK   *President, Selling Systems, Inc., Lake Forest, Illinois*

SETTING APPRAISAL OBJECTIVES

"What are we looking for?"

This should be the first question asked before setting the appraisal machinery into motion. As it does take time and effort to develop a workable system, it is important that thought be given to the objective of the system prior to the development stage. This objective should be well defined as it might well dictate the methods and tools of the system itself.

Consider the following objectives:

1. Making a compensation review
2. Exploring weakness in job performance for the purpose of future training
3. Evaluating on-the-job relationships for future management candidates

In each example specifics are being sought which are not necessarily related. Our first example might be a comparison of job performance, in which actual performance is measured against management expectation. In our second example areas of job performance are sought which can be improved through training. This type of appraisal can be highly motivating and productive, as it is positive in nature. Our third example is concerned with management potential in terms of control, planning, setting objectives, and behavioral relationships.

Once the objective has been defined and agreed upon, we are ready to consider the standards of measurement.

SETTING THE APPRAISAL STANDARD

An appraisal standard is best defined as "a job profile consisting of two factors." The first factor concerns the key functions which make up the job. These are usually listed in general terms in a job description. The second concerns the behavioral relationships which affect the performance of the job. These are often referred to as the "maintenance" phase of the job. For the most part, we would not be concerned with maintenance factors unless the technician was a supervisor, or was being considered for management promotion.

As mentioned, a job description offers an ideal starting place for the development of the job profile. If job descriptions are not available, another system can be used with equal effectiveness.

Using 3 by 5 in. file cards, list all the job functions to be appraised. Be sure to *list only one function* to a card. By doing this, you can soon have all the functions under your direction catalogued in a workable form. If you tend to be lazy, have your technical personnel fill out the cards. A sample card might look like Figure 1.

This information clearly defines the specific responsibility charged to the employee being appraised. We are now in a position to evaluate specific functions within the job and not the job as a whole. This method has been successfully used by corporations of all sizes, including the Buick Division of General Motors who used it to set up job descriptions within their car dealerships.

No matter what method is used to isolate the job functions, it is important that the appraisal be made on the functions which are directly the responsibility of the employee. This procedure will provide a fair evaluation for the employee as well as establishing sound ground for the appraisal.

Developing a profile for the "maintenance," or behavioral, phase of the job presents a greater challenge to the manager. The following examples might serve as the basis of a meaningful maintenance listing:

Attitude: Objective, open-minded, and cooperative (enthusiastically relating to fellow employees)

Sociability: Friendly, tactful, courteous, considerate, persuasive, interacts with others

Thinking: Analytical, orderly, able to see relationships and to reason out problem situations

Expression: Able to present ideas in a clear manner, fairly and forcefully, but not monopolize communications situations

Listening: Able to comprehend and to interpret the views of others, aware of what others say

Productivity: Makes overall contribution to the total work accomplished by the group

As with our job functions listing, each of the profile items should relate to the individual being appraised.

When all functions have been clearly identified, we can put them into a semblance of order. This might call for the design of an appraisal form if the company does not provide one which is suitable. The form would list functions to be evaluated, and it would have a section for an overall evaluation and a planning section which would provide for a realistic corrective action.

The functions should be listed in two sections: The first should include functions which are concerned with *knowledge and job skills;* the second section should be concerned with functions relating to *behavioral relationships.*

Figure 1.   Sample card of job function.

FUNCTION: COMMUNICATION
Responsibility
To record daily test results into the Drug Book in
a clear, meaningful manner.

Figure 2.   Function example, showing weighted system.

WEIGHTING THE FUNCTIONS

Having defined the functions of the job, we are now ready to develop a method of comparison.

The following "weighted" method offers many advantages with a minimum of difficulties. Figure 2 shows how our first function example might look when using the weighted method. In using this method, it is important that everyone concerned with the appraisal fully agrees to the definitions of the appraisal terms.

APPRAISAL TERMS

Performance Levels

1. Marginal. . . . . .   Borderline—questionable. Frequently falls short of achieving expected results.

2. Acceptable . . . .   Adequate—fair. Usually achieves expected results. Seldom exceeds and sometimes falls short of achieving them.

3. Good . . . .   Achieves expected results. Occasionally exceeds and occasionally falls short of achieving expected results.

4. Very   good . . .   Consistently achieves expected results. Sometimes exceeds but rarely falls short of achieving expected results.

5. Superior . . . . . .   Always achieves and often exceeds expected results. Seeks out opportunities to improve results on his own initiative.

Management can further implement the appraisal by having the manager who has made the appraisal justify all ratings below a 3, or good. This will cause some in-depth consideration as to the reasoning behind the rating, as well as providing an opportunity for the manager to consider how the function might best be improved.

After rating all the functions which make up the individual's job responsibilities, we are ready to consider his *overall* performance. Figure 3 illustrates how this important end step might look. You will note that we again ask for the reason behind any rating less than a 3, or good.

MAKING THE APPRAISAL

All too often the appraisal process stops at this point. Once the appraisal has been completed and the form signed by the manager, it is filed for future reference. This is a waste of the time of all parties involved with the system. We may have taken care of our corporate obligation; however, we have failed to fulfill our responsibility to the employee who has been appraised. This can never happen if a worthwhile objective has been set for the system.

Consider some of the readings that a manager might make with a well-defined objective and, in turn, some of the decisions that might result from the reading.

For example, a new technician reporting to you qualifies for a final appraisal of 3, or good. This might be most satisfactory to the company and might point to

SECTION C – OVERALL PERFORMANCE

Place an "X" in the area that best describes the employee's overall performance.
If rating is less than Good (3) Explain:

MARGINAL	ACCEPTABLE	GOOD	VERY GOOD	SUPERIOR
1	2	3	4	5

SECTION D – PERFORMANCE IMPROVEMENT

Consider what the employee can do to improve and what you and the Company can do to assist him.

	What should be done	By whom?	When?
1.			
2.			
3.			
4.			

SECTION E – COMMENTS (to be made by reviewer and/or reviewer's supervisor)

Figure 3. Scale for evaluating overall job performance and performance improvement recommendation.

future potential. However, what if the employee has been with you for ten or fifteen years? Would you still feel satisfied with the performance, and would you be willing to invest in training for increased value to the company?

Here are some factors which should be considered in evaluating the final appraisal.

Age. With the many changes taking place in our technology, it is essential that corporations continually upgrade their technical personnel. This need for an increase in knowledge and skill can be costly. Age becomes an important factor at this point. Is it a good investment to spend time and money training older employees who exhibit limited potential of present skill, or would it be wiser to invest in younger staff members who have greater potential?

This is a decision that must be made by the department manager and often presents internal problems that are difficult to cope with.

Time. It takes effort and patience to improve on-the-job performance. A manager must continually match his overall objective against the time that he has been allotted to accomplish it. If a rating of 3, or good, is not adequate to satisfy a departmental objective, how much time should be made available to bring the individual's rating up to a 4, or even a 5? In some situations several years might be required for the desired change.

It might well be that the individual being appraised cannot contribute to the departmental objective due to the time and effort required to bring out full potential. In this case, the manager might be forced to find another technician who could participate to a greater degree.

Limited ability. Dismissal should always be a reality in the mind of the manager making the final appraisal. We must honestly recognize that there are some employees who, due to their limitations, tend to block the overall productivity of the technical team. A realistic appraisal will pinpoint the areas of weakness. If, in the mind of the manager, little can be accomplished by training, or by closer supervision, dismissal should be a prime consideration.

One of the true values of a sound appraisal system is finding low-potential employees before the company investment is too great to make a change. If the employee is involved in the appraisal system, he is fully aware of his on-the-job weakness and is in a better position to accept the conclusion of management. Dismissal is never easy; however, it is greatly simplified with an acceptable appraisal system.

The overall appraisal reflects the manager's evaluation of the individual's performance of specific job functions as compared with an acceptable job standard. In making such an appraisal we eliminate the dangerous technique of comparing one technician against another, ignoring the important individual considerations of age, time, and ability.

The final overall appraisal should clearly indicate a course of action. It is here that our objective becomes important. If we know what we are looking for, we can soon evaluate what must be done to reach our goal.

The next section of the appraisal is the sole responsibility of the manager. He should make specific recommendations to improve the job performance of the technician being appraised.

Figure 3 shows an example of a simple, but effective, layout for this corrective step. It illustrates the three key considerations that must be made if something positive is to happen.

SELECTING THE APPRAISAL SYSTEM

Having defined the appraisal objective, identified the key job factors to be appraised, and assembled the appraisal guidelines into a workable form, we are now ready to consider an appraisal system to fit our need. Due to the varied systems and confusing semantics, the selection of the right system often becomes a challenge. By removing the many variations available, we can narrow the selection down to two basic systems.

The first system is primarily a one-way communication in which the manager has the sole responsibility for making the appraisal. He then attempts to sell his conclusions to the employee being appraised. With this system, the employee is allowed little or no participation in the appraisal process. The *second* system utilizes the thinking and participation of the manager as well as that of the employee being appraised. The thought here is that if the employee can participate in the appraisal system, he will be more likely to accept the conclusions reached in the final evaluation.

In this second type of appraisal, both parties use an identical appraisal form which covers the specific job functions under consideration. They then discuss their personal evaluations and arrive at a mutually agreed-upon appraisal. If we consider the environmental conditioning of the technician, we can readily accept this system as the one having the most merit.

Due to the nature of his job, the technician has come to accept weekly job discussions pertaining to the specific job assignment. For the most part he looks forward to this review as it will implement his own thinking, and it provides him with an opportunity to discuss work-related problems. He has grown accustomed to an honest evaluation of his assignment progress and has adapted his thinking to this relationship with his manager. The review also provides a sharing of experience which further adds to his job knowledge. This rapport establishes the ideal climate for the mutual discussion of the technician's job appraisal. Several weeks prior to the appraisal interview, the technician and his manager fill out duplicate copies of the appraisal form. The technician evaluates his performance as he sees it, while his manager considers the same factors from his vantage point.

Many times the manager is saved from the embarrassment of reporting a low rating to an employee because of the equally low rating made by the employee himself. We often tend to rate our own job performance lower than our boss will rate it. This might indicate that most people strive to be honest in evaluating their own performance; in fact, they might lean a little farther in the area of recognized weakness.

Each of the participants in the appraisal brings his evaluations to the appraisal interview where they will serve as guides for the appraisal discussion. During the interview each of the listed job functions is discussed in detail. This discussion leads to mutual understanding of why specific ratings were arrived at and to the degree of proficiency reached during the period being appraised. As we are talking about a weighted evaluation, the system provides ample opportunity of being flexible in the final evaluation. Adjustments can be made during the interview in a rather painless manner if complete understanding can be reached by both parties.

Points to Remember during the Interview

1. Try for a positive climate. The manager should communicate a positive attitude about the appraisal. He should give every indication that the basic objective of the appraisal is to improve the job relationship of the technician. This, however, might depend on the objective of the appraisal program; whatever the purpose, it is important that an optimistic feeling exist in the relationship.

2. Mutual discussion. It is important that both parties in the interview have ample opportunity to express their opinions of the factors under consideration. The technician will find greater acceptance of the final conclusions if he can participate in the process. Participation is the key to acceptance.

3. Limit discussion to the listed factors. The listed job factors provide the manager with a discussion guideline. If he ignores the guideline, or stresses points outside the job, he may well run into a personal discussion that might become emotional.

4. The corrective action. Once the areas of weakness have been defined, it is important that a corrective step be undertaken. The step in most cases is of a positive nature. However, there might be situations that could end in an employee termination. A more positive interview would clearly define the corrective action to be taken and a time schedule which is acceptable to both parties.

MANAGEMENT FOLLOW-THROUGH

No matter how well we have planned, we must always face the possibility that the appraisal system may fail when put into practical use. When this happens, the failure can usually be traced to ineffective management support. A weak manager might endanger the system by contributing some of the following problems:

He might *eliminate, or ignore, the appraisal interview.* He could simply fill out the appraisal forms and file them away for future reference. By doing this, he has taken the effective two-way system and converted it into an ineffective one-way communication process. The technician is kept in the dark as to how he relates to his job performance, and management has lost the opportunity of gaining employee acceptance of the system.

He might try to *sell his own conclusions* to the technician. In this situation the manager takes advantage of the system by selling his own ideas and concepts. This is easily done if the manager ignores the technician's evaluations and directs all discussion to those of his own. As the technician fails to be involved in his job review, he soon loses interest in the procedure and little is accomplished.

The manager *modifies the agreed-upon action.* This is easily done following the interview. Changes made might represent the thinking of the manager while ignoring the feelings of the technician. At a later date the technician might be held accountable for conclusions reached by his manager and not reflected in the thinking of the technician.

The manager might *ignore the completed appraisal* and agreed-upon follow-up measures. This seems to be the one most common failing with any appraisal system. Little can be accomplished if the action phase is overlooked and neither party is held accountable for any agreed-upon conclusions. It soon becomes apparent to both parties that they are involved in a management game that has no real meaning to either one of them.

The manager might try to *motivate the technician with his personal motivating factors.* Motivation is a key factor if the manager is to create any change in the existing situation. If nothing happens, the system has failed, and time has been wasted with little result. A sincere manager, in his concern to create change, might ignore the motivating factors of the technician and force his own in a fatherly manner.

One of the advantages of the two-way appraisal system is the opportunity that presents itself to the manager to gain insight into his personnel. This insight might reveal the technician's motivating factors, which in turn can be used to create the desired change in the technician's job performance.

These typical "pitfalls" can be avoided if allowances have been made for a feedback system to management. This accountability factor tends to keep all parties "honest," and the system then becomes an effective management tool. The requirements for the feedback process should include information on the technician's overall performance evaluation, salary recommendations, and aspects of promotability.

Overall Evaluation

This is a recapitulation of the appraisal interview data. It provides management with a clear, yet concise, evaluation of the technician's job performance. If this performance falls below the grade of 3, or good, the manager must supply his reasons for the evaluation.

Salary Recommendations

This section of the report provides management with salary data relating to the appraisal. It should provide a concise picture of the situation, including the present salary and reflecting any adjustments recommended by the appraising manager.

Promotability

This might be the most difficult feedback assignment made by the appraisal manager. Due to the nature of a technician's job philosophy, he might express little interest in progressing up the management ladder. It is for this reason that care must be taken in the appraisal manager's judgment in this area.

A simple "yes" or "no" statement should be avoided as it communicates little to management. It is important that the manager supply his reasons for any statements which might affect the corporate fugure of the technician. Figure 4 illustrates how these key areas might be assembled into a management reporting form. You will note that in every case the appraisal manager is asked for the reasons behind his expressed judgments.

In summary, a good appraisal system for technical employees should have the following requirements:

1. An objective which is both realistic and obtainable
2. An evaluation system based on the specific functions of the technician's job
3. An opportunity for the technician to become part of the evaluation process
4. An opportunity for the technician, and his manager, to openly express their opinions and feelings about the job performance being appraised
5. A reporting channel to management so that the appraisal system has built-in accountability

SECTION A — OVERALL PERFORMANCE

Place an "X" in the area that best describes the employee's overall performance.

MARGINAL	ACCEPTABLE	GOOD	VERY GOOD	SUPERIOR
1	2	3	4	5

If your overall rating is less than Good (3) indicate your reasons.

_____

_____

_____

SECTION B — SALARY RECOMMENDATIONS

Is this employee eligible for an increase?

☐ Yes (If yes, indicate how much $ _____ per month.)

☐ No (If no, indicate why not below.)

_____

_____

_____

_____

SECTION C — PROMOTABILITY

1. Is this employee promotable to a more responsible position?

1
☐ Promotable in less than 6 months

2
☐ Promotable in more than 6 months but less than 2 years

3
☐ Promotable in more than 2 years

4
☐ Promotability Questionable

5
☐ Not Promotable

Figure 4. Performance and promotability guide.

BIBLIOGRAPHY

Heyer, Carl: *Appraising Executive Performance,* American Management Association Handbook, 1958.

Kindall, Alva: *Personnel Administration,* Richard D. Irwin, Inc., Homewood, Ill., 1958.

Laird, Donald A., and Eleanor C. Laird: *Sizing Up People,* McGraw-Hill Book Company, New York, 1951.

Maier, Norman: *The Appraisal Interview,* John Wiley & Sons, Inc., New York., 1958.

McGregor, Douglas: *The Human Side of Enterprise,* McGraw-Hill Book Company, New York, 1967.

Odiorne, George, *How Managers Make Things Happen,* Prentice-Hall, Inc., Englewood Cliffs, N.J., 1962.

Rating Employee and Supervisory Performance, American Management Association, 1964.

chapter 45

Appraising Managerial Employees

CHARLES L. HUGHES   *Director, Corporate Industrial Relations, Texas Instruments Incorporated, Dallas, Texas*

An effective managerial performance appraisal system begins with the fundamental assumption that a manager is responsible for achieving predetermined organizational goals. His job exists to aid the organization in identifying its objectives and subsequently developing a system for allocating and managing resources in the accomplishment of those objectives. This concept can be applied universally to any organization and stands as a definition of a managerial employee. The overall framework of a management by objectives system is a fundamental prerequisite to meaningful managerial appraisal. The objectives and goals of the organization and its subunits structure the corporate system for identifying targets and criteria for organizational performance. The appraisal of the performance of individual managers is intimately involved with the appraisal of the performance of the organization for which they are responsible. Consequently, a workable managerial appraisal system is a dependent variable and a subset of the broader organizational planning, control, and evaluation system.

Appraisal systems in this context, therefore, focus their attention primarily upon the contribution of a manager's efforts toward the realization of preset business goals. To the extent that it can be interfaced realistically, a managerial appraisal system can be a valuable asset in the achievement of organizational performance criteria. There are two additional applications of appraisal through management by objectives: identification of managerial talent and individual career enhancement, both of which focus upon the manager as an organizational asset and resource to be evaluated and enhanced to the maximum possible extent as a managerial function of the leadership at higher organizational levels. Under this concept it is the individual's responsibility to assess and develop himself within the boundaries and framework of the management by objectives system. The appraisal system aids him in developing himself and directing his motivation toward the simultaneous accomplishment of organizational goals and individual career goals.

In the broader view, the appraisal of managers begins with the concept of the organization and its purpose in society as a system for providing useful products and services to that society. Consistent with the free-enterprise concept, the organization has responsibilities to return value to the social system in the form of furthering the goals of the society through its products and services, returning investment to the shareholders through dividends, and providing entrepreneurial opportunity and self-development of the individual manager through career opportunities and compensation. For the individual manager, there is a duality to his role as a member of the organization conceptualized as *the achievement of personal goals through the achievement of organizational goals.* It is therefore the function of the appraisal system to maximize both aspects through a meaningful integration of organizational performance planning and evaluation with individual performance planning and evaluation.

MANAGERIAL APPRAISAL SYSTEM

The appraisal of managerial employees will be most effective as part of the overall management system if it integrates several subsystems for management decisions: goal setting and planning, compensation, job evaluation, selection and placement, the individual's history and track record, and individual development planning. The integration of these subsystems requires an overall managerial appraisal system.

The diagram shown in Figure 1 describes a managerial appraisal system designed to integrate data from four sources into an information matrix which is the input to management appraisal decisions on three factors: compensation, selection and placement, replacement and staffing forecasts. As the system diagram also illustrates, there are three additional features: estate and tax planning, individual development planning, and manpower analysis. Each of the twelve phases will be described.

Integrated Information

Information needs to be integrated from several sources, specifically performance evaluation, individual history, performance review goals and accomplishments, and a company planning system related to business objectives and individual goal setting related to job objectives. First to be addressed in this system would be the organizational planning system and individual goal setting with respect to a manager's own personal work assignment.

Goal Setting and Planning

The basic philosophy of this integrated approach is the achievement of personal goals through the achievement of organizational goals. In many cases organization and individual goals will be identical, based on the degree to which the individual has had the opportunity for involvement and participation in the organization planning process. The greater the opportunity for the manager to align his personal goals with those of the organization, the greater will be the motivation to achieve organizational goals. The need for heavy participation in the planning process cannot be overemphasized. Only through such an approach can the goals of a manager's job be made meaningful and measurable. Organizational goals will be preset, and consequently individual job goals will be preset before the manager embarks upon his attempts to achieve those objectives.

A goal setting and planning wórksheet should be provided (Figure 2) which can be used as part of an iterative and consultative process in which the individual man-

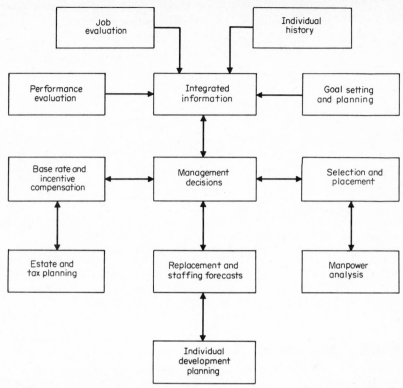

Figure 1.   Managerial appraisal system.

ager interacts with the organizational planning system through the media of his superior in the organizational hierarchy. Each goal or project should be clearly identified by a working title which denotes the main thrust of the manager's efforts. He will be assigned as the individual responsible for the achievement of those goals, and he makes a documented psychological contract to achieve a certain end result within the specified time frame and resources. In this way he is not only identifying what he is going to do for the organization, but also verifying that he understands the personal commitment that is required from him and the trust placed with him.

There may be more than one goal or project for which an individual manager is responsible, but such goals are probably limited to a very few key important objectives for the future. These may be identified as long-range goals (one to five years in the future) or short-range goals (one month to one year in the future). An individual manager's goals should be rank ordered by their importance to the organization in terms of the impact upon billings, growth, return on assets, market share, and other relevant organizational criteria. A superior who has several managers reporting to him who are all involved in the goal setting and planning process will combine the rank orders into a single ranking based upon the same organizational criteria of impact on organizational performance.

Goals are the key factor in the planning process and define the specific results to be achieved in behalf of the organization, the measurements to be applied in terms of relevant criteria, the target dates by which goals will be accomplished, and the several projects or programs in support of these goals. Each manager will

```
GOAL/PROJECT TITLE _____    RANK NO. _____
                                                                ☐ LONG RANGE GOAL
INDIVIDUAL RESPONSIBLE _____ DATE _____      ☐ SHORT RANGE GOAL
GOALS: (Specific results to be achieved, measurements, target dates, projects)




PLANS: (Action programs, who, what, when, key events and activities, barriers to overcome)




BENEFITS: (Value to organization, tangible & intangible)


ALTERNATIVES AND CONSEQUENCES: (Other means of accomplishing goals & effects of not achieving)


RESOURCES REQUIRED: (Capital & expense $, man-hours/days, assistance needed, space, equipment)
```

Figure 2.   Goal setting and planning worksheet.

define his goals to be accomplished during the measurement period (ordinarily cycled annually with the fiscal year). It will be necessary for the superior to have an extended dialogue with each of his key managers until there is full understanding and agreement about the goals and to assure that there is no misunderstanding or miscommunication, and further to assure that the goals are set realistically for maximum impact and achievability.

Plans are the second step in the goal setting process. These outline the action programs required to accomplish the goals and specify who is going to do what when. Key events, checkpoints, and activities to be carried out will also be identified at this time. Also important to the goal setting process are the barriers to be overcome that otherwise may stand in the way of achieving the goals. Steps for overcoming these barriers and the resources required to do this must be identified.

Benefits of the goals in terms of their value to the organization, both tangible and intangible, must be specified. The benefits may be in terms of increased billings or market share, reduced manufacturing cost, return on assets, and other tangible measures; but they may also include employee attitudes, customer relations, and other important or difficult to quantify items.

Alternatives and consequences are the fourth step in goal setting which identify the backup plans, that is, other means of accomplishing the same goals and the effects upon the organization of not achieving the meaningful and desirable objectives. This section is critical because it spells out other actions that may be necessary in the future to reach the goals and the negative impact of failure to perform in the managerial assignment. This step will be useful at a later stage when performance evaluation is done and the individual's performance is reviewed with him by his superior.

Resources required round out the final part of the goal setting and planning process by identifying the resources that must be committed to this manager's assignment in order to accomplish the goals desired. Capital and expense dollars, man-hours or days required on the project, and assistance needed from other parts of the organization and other functions and, most importantly, from the manager's superior are part of the resource package. In addition, space and equipment necessary to execute the plan should be detailed and related to the value of the goals to the organization in order to determine if asset utilization is in keeping with the payoff returned from the investment.

The interaction of the individual manager with the planning system and the presetting of his goals, plans, and resources from the first input to the integrated information of the appraisal system will be used later as the criteria for performance evaluation and the guide to the performance review goals and accomplishments feedback loop of the system.

Two-phase Evaluations: Job and Performance

The goal setting and planning phase just described will be applied as part of the criteria used in the evaluation of managerial jobs and individual performance. The goals of the individual will define his job content and must be translated into a company-wide standardized job evaluation scheme. A number of good job evaluation techniques are available, and for our purposes here we will use the Guidechart System developed by Edward N. Hay Associates of Philadelphia. Job descriptions developed from content only will not be useful in realistic managerial appraisal; descriptions of jobs should be developed which are based upon the goals to be achieved because these represent the only true value of a manager's job to the organization.

Job Evaluation

The E. N. Hay Guidechart System develops three factors, each having three dimensions of measurement. These factors should be evaluated early in the performance cycle so that anomalies in the job content, goals, and performance expectations can be identified and worked through. The same factors will serve as a basis for determining compensation, base rates, and incentives later in the appraisal process. Figure 3*a* shows a form for restating the plans and goals for which the individual is responsible into the format applicable to the Guidechart System.

The first step is to evaluate the *know-how* required to accomplish the goals in terms of three factors (Figure 3*b*):

1. Specialized know-how: knowledge of practical procedures, specialized techniques, and scientific disciplines

2. Management breadth: know-how of integrating or harmonizing diverse functions through the management process; may be exercised consultatively as well as executively

3. Human relations skills: (*a*) basic effectiveness in dealing with others; (*b*) important (understanding and influencing others); or (*c*) outstanding (motivation of others is critical and the position cannot function without this emphasis on human relations skills)

A point score of the know-how required to accomplish the goals of the job will be derived from an evaluation of these factors.

The second step in managerial job evaluation under the Hay Guidechart System (Figure 3*c*) is *mental activity* which is the utilization of know-how and is expressed as a percentage of the know-how required to do the job that is actually applied in its execution. It includes the innovating, analyzing, planning, evaluating, creating,

PERFORMANCE EVALUATION

Name_____ Date_____

Organization_____

Title_____ Job Grade_____

Evaluated by_____ Approved_____ Approved_____

Evaluation Factors	KNOW HOW				MENTAL ACTIVITY				ACCOUNTABILITY				TOTAL POINTS
	SPEC	MGRL.	HR	PTS	FDM	COMP	%	PTS	FDM	MAG	IMPCT	PTS	
Job Evaluation													
Percent Performance													
Performance Evaluation													

Instructions to Rater:
Evaluation Factors are the E. N. Hay Guide Chart factors used to evaluate managerial jobs and their relationships.
Job Evaluation is the current approved evaluation on the individual's job and defines his opportunity to impact performance.
Percent Performance is your percent rating of the degree to which the individual met the performance opportunity and expectations defined by his job.
Performance Evaluation is your percent multiplied into the Job Evaluation points.
Refer to the three included guide charts in percent performance decision making and for documenting key factors.

Plans & Goals: Past Year & Next Year

Figure 3a.   Performance evaluation form.

reasoning, and decision making required in doing the job. Mental activity has two aspects:

1. Freedom to think, within the limitations imposed by policy, procedures, and supervisory review;

2. Complexity of the thinking required in utilizing know-how. By working from a definition of the preset goals defined by the goal setting and planning phase, know-how can be converted into a point rating score for mental activity;

The third step in managerial job evaluation is *accountability* (Figure 3d). This is the effect of the job on the organizational goals. It has three aspects:

1. Freedom to act in pursuing the desired financial results

2. Dollar magnitude of the end result which the job most clearly affects

3. The directness of the job impact on end results, that is, remote, contributory, shared, and primary

A point score is derived for each of these three factors.

The sum total of the job evaluation points taken from each of the three sections of the three evaluation factors must trace very clearly back to the definition of the goals established on the goal setting and planning worksheet (Figure 2). While the Edward N. Hay Guidechart System has been used here as a model, any job evaluation technique which attempts to relate the value of the job to be accomplished against the goals to be achieved can serve the same purpose.

Performance Evaluation

The key in this phase of the managerial appraisal system is to convert the goals and plans into a numerical rating system which will be useful in assessing the degree to which performance criteria have been met. Once goal setting and planning and

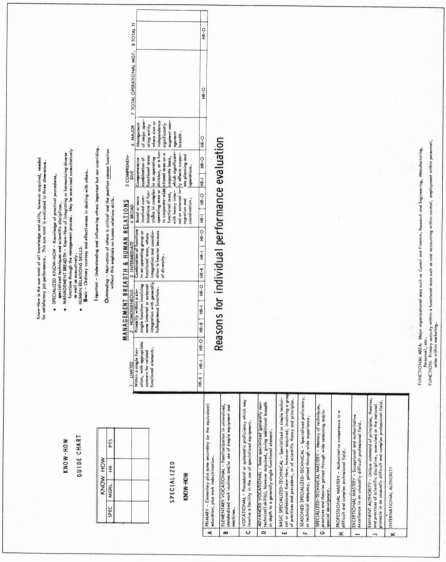

Figure 3b. Know-how guide chart.

45—7

MENTAL ACTIVITY
GUIDE CHART

Mental Activity is the utilization of Know-How, and is expressed on this chart as a percentage utilization of Know-How. Mental Activity includes the innovating, analyzing, planning, evaluating, creating, reasoning and decision-making required by the job. It has two aspects:

o Freedom to think – consider limitations imposed by policy, procedures and supervisory review.

o Complexity.

MENTAL ACTIVITY			
FDM	COMP	%	PTS

COMPLEXITY

	1 SELECTIVE MEMORY Uninvolved choice of learned things in simple situations.	2 PATTERNED Choice of learned things in situations which conform to clearly established patterns and modes.	3 INTERPOLATION Interpolation of learned things in somewhat varied situations.	4 ADAPTIVE THINKING Analytical, interpretative, evaluative and/or constructive thinking in variable situations of manufacture, market and the like.	5 CREATIVE THINKING Novel or nonrecurring pathfinding situations requiring the development of new concepts and imaginative approaches.

FREEDOM TO THINK

A STRICT ROUTINE
Activities covered by detailed rules, instructions and/or rigid supervision.

B ROUTINE
Activities covered by standard instructions, and/or continuous close supervision.

C SEMI-ROUTINE
Activities with minor diversification, covered by well-defined procedures, precedents and supervision.

D STANDARDIZED
Somewhat diversified activities, covered by established procedures, standards, and general supervision.

E DIRECTED
Activities covered by established practices or policies, and direction as to execution and review.

F GENERALLY DIRECTED
Activities covered by broad or functional policies and objectives, and general direction as to means and results.

G GUIDED
Activities within general policies, principles and objectives, and guidance as to means and results.

H MINIMUM GUIDANCE
Activities covered only by general company principles and objectives within a framework of cultural standards and business philosophy.

Reasons for individual performance evaluation

Figure 3c. Mental activity guide chart.

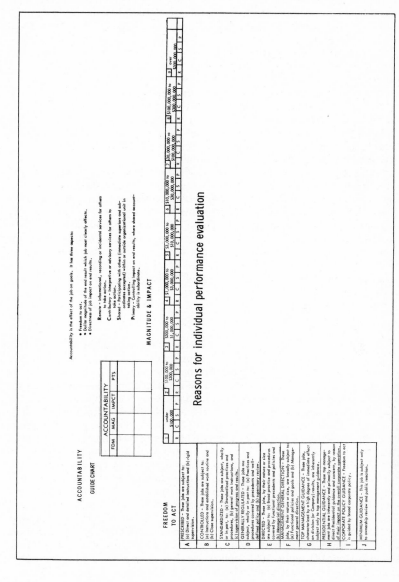

Figure 3d. Accountability guide chart.

the job evaluation phases have been completed, the supervisor is now ready to compare the standards of performance expectations to perceived actual performance. Performance evaluation may be initiated at the time results were expected and target dates were to have been met or at the end of the fiscal year planning cycle.

The performance evaluation approach is parallel to job evaluation. The same Guidechart factors and points used for job evaluation will be applied to measuring performance. For example, the know-how actually used in performing the job will be compared with the know-how required to do the job. Know-how points will be judged by the superior in evaluating an individual manager's performance in the same manner as job evaluation (see Figure 3a). The ratio of job evaluation to performance evaluation is converted to a percent performance index. Performance in the case of a perfect match between performance and job evaluation will be 100 percent. In most cases the performance evaluation will be less than the know-how indicated by the job evaluation; so the score will be less than 100 percent. It is also conceivable that actual performance will exceed the know-how required on the job and derive a performance score in excess of 100 percent. The same steps will also be carried out for mental activity and accountability.

As Figure 3a indicates, we then have an *evaluation of the relationship between the job evaluation*, which was derived from the statement of the goals to be achieved, *and the performance evaluation*, which is derived from the performance against the preset goals; these in turn are converted to points and to a percentage performance score for each of the evaluation factors. These will then be combined with other inputs to integrate information for the managerial appraisal system. This same analysis of job evaluation versus actual performance in comparing the on-target, over-and-under performance areas will also be applied later when management decisions are made in selection and placement of the individual, identifying replacement and staffing forecasts, determining base and incentive compensation, and individual development planning.

Individual History

The fourth input to the managerial appraisal system is individual history (see Figure 4). Individual performance data need to be supplemented by the history of the individual's work experiences and identifying background. Educational data describing the level and type of training can be combined with a skills inventory. Many organizations attempt to maintain up-to-date records of skills and the series of significant work assignments of the individual but often find these difficult to keep up to date. The tendency to obsolescence of data is often caused by the lack of integration of the individual's work history with other aspects of the decision process. Integrating the history as part of the regular integrated information system and bringing it in as a key of data into the management decisions should make this information more meaningful and give rationale for maintaining up-to-date files.

As with job evaluation and performance evaluation data, individual history data can often be manipulated more easily and accurately through a data-processing system. This will also facilitate the combination and correlation of various evaluation, history, and other records into a meaningful on-line integrated information system. The individual history record will be a summation of the key factors from the individual's personnel file and would replace it (as most personnel files are full of more irrelevant than relevant material).

Integrated Information

The information available for integration for the purposes of the management decisions now consists of *individual goal setting and planning,* the performance requirements of the individual job and the specifics of the organizational goals and work

INDIVIDUAL HISTORY

PERSONAL DATA

EMPLOYEE NO.	EMPLOYEE NAME	SEC.	SEX	AGE	DEPEND.	MARRIED	STATUS	EMPLOYMENT DATE	COST CTR.	DIVISION

PREVIOUS SIGNIFICANT EMPLOYER	YEARS	PRESENT JOB CLASSIFICATION	JOB GRADE	JOB CODE

EDUCATION DATA

LEVEL	CODE	MAJOR DESCRIPTOR	COLLEGE	YEAR	OTHER EDUCATION AND TRAINING

SKILL DATA

NO.	CODE	SKILL DESCRIPTOR	YEARS	NO.	CODE	SKILL DESCRIPTOR	YEARS
1				6			
2				7			
3				8			
4				9			
5				10			

SIGNIFICANT WORK ASSIGNMENTS

SUPERVISOR OR EMPLOYER	PROJECT/ASSIGNMENT OR CUSTOMER	PRODUCT/SERVICE OR CREW	LEVEL AND FUNCTION	JOB GRADE	TIME (MOS.)	LAST ACTIVE YEAR	LOCATION

Figure 4.   Individual history form.

goals; *job evaluation,* a measurement of the dollar worth of the job specified during the goal setting and planning phase; *performance evaluation,* based on a comparison of actual performance versus goals using the same techniques applied in job evaluation; and *individual history,* the track record of the individual in terms of assignments, education, and past performance.   This information is now integrated into a single format, as shown in Figures 3*a, b, c,* and *d* and Figure 4.   In addition to these sets of data, it will be useful to integrate information on other individual managers in a summary form so that man-to-man comparisons can be made among individual managers.   This will permit management decisions on selection, placement, base rate, and incentive compensation appropriate for an individual relative to his peers and their job level and performance on preset goals.

MANAGEMENT DECISIONS

All the individual managers within an organizational unit should be working toward the same ultimate management objective, even though each of their individual goals will vary with the content and responsibilities of their assignment.   The different job assignments will have different values to the organization and its business objectives, and additionally there are likely to be differences among managers in the performance levels within their areas of assignment and responsibility.   Essentially the management decision process is to apply a criterion of managerial performance, which may be stated as a *contribution to the achievement of the organizational goals during the year.*

The difference in managerial performance would be represented by a *rank order*

Figure 5. Managerial appraisal rank order.

Rank	Employee name	Function	Rate			Percent increase	Incentive
			Current	Proposed	Increase		
1	Johanning, Earl W.	Manager	$2,600	$3,000	$400	15.3	$15,000
2	Riggs, Karl A.	Manager	2,350	2,700	350	14.8	10,000
3	Donley, Lowell M.	Manager	2,700	2,940	240	8.8	10,000
4	Herbert, John F.	Manager	2,300	2,650	350	15.2	7,500
5	Shaw, Robert J.	Legal	2,050	2,300	250	12.1	7,500
6	Parker, Donald R.	Manufacturing	2,000	2,300	300	15.0	7,500
7	Petty, Samuel B.	Manager	1,700	1,950	250	14.7	5,000
8	Pressman, Hilary E.	Research	2,200	2,410	210	9.5	5,000
9	Childress, Wilfred L.	Control	1,680	2,000	320	19.0	3,500
10	Whiteside, Thomas K.	Engineering	2,000	2,250	250	12.5	2,000
11	McCall, Dan A.	Personnel	2,100	2,300	200	9.5	2,000
12	Coe, Arthur W.	Manufacturing	1,800	2,020	220	12.2	1,000

which can best be achieved by using a judgment technique known as "paired comparison." Paired comparison compares each individual manager with each other manager, two people at a time. In each case the criterion is applied to the pair, and the individual manager contributing the most to the success of the organization is selected. The number of times an individual is selected determines his position in the rank order, with the individual receiving the most paired selections against the criteria receiving rank one, and the one with the second greatest number of selections among the pairs, the next rank order position, and so on, from the relatively highest contributor down through the relatively lowest contributor. Figure 5 shows an example of a *rank order display* resulting from the paired comparison and some of the relevant data that are added to the rank order for the purposes of decision making on compensation and job assignment. By using the rank order of *contributors,* decisions on base rate and incentive compensation can then be made within the policy framework of the compensation scheme.

To aid in the decision process on compensation and selection for increased job assignment, *scattergrams* are often useful.

There are several different scattergrams which can apply. Figures 6a, b, and c are examples of the basic information that could be compared.

1. Managerial rank order versus proposed compensation, the annual base rate and possibly including incentive or discretionary bonus for a total annual compensation (Figure 6a)

2. A manager's job evaluation points, which determine his opportunity to make a contribution, identified during the job evaluation versus the rank order of all managers (Figure 6b)

3. Proposed compensation versus job evaluation points (Figure 6c)

These three scattergrams display in visual format the three key factors in the decision process of the managerial appraisal system:

1. The opportunity to make a contribution to the success of the organization as specified by the job evaluation versus the actual contribution as determined by a position in rank order

2. The actual contribution versus the compensation value of that contribution as determined by rank order versus pay

3. The opportunity to make a contribution versus the compensation value of that contribution.

In a perfect relationship between opportunity, performance, and compensation, managers would fall along a line represented by the diagonal of the scattergram. Perfect correlation in the relationships will not always be found, but the majority

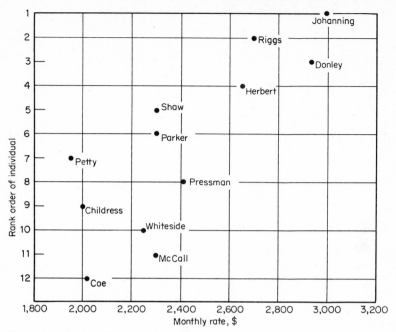

Figure 6a. Rank order versus monthly rate.

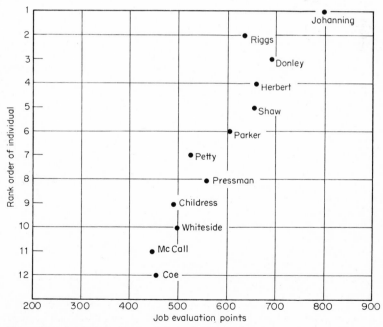

Figure 6b. Rank order versus job evaluation points.

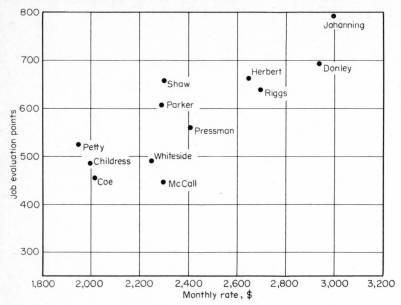

Figure 6c. Job evaluation points versus monthly rate.

of managers would be located on the scattergrams in a cluster around the line of best fit. Certain anomalies will also appear which indicate some error in the judgment process. For example, an individual may be ranked high in contribution but low in compensation, indicating either too high a ranking or too low a reward. We may also find anomalies in terms of high in job evaluation, indicating a significant opportunity to make an impact on the company performance, but a relatively low rank order, indicating either that the job is overevaluated in the expectancies for impact or overstated or that actual performance has been misjudged. Ranking, evaluation of opportunity, and compensation variables must be iterated until most individuals fall very close to the best fit diagonal line through the scattergram.

Replacement and Staffing Forecasts

The decisions reached on managers provide an input to establishing replacement tables for future organization growth as key managers are elevated, reassigned, or lost. The strengths and weaknesses of the organization as a total entity will give an indication of where immediate staffing requirements are necessary so that in the future the proper kind of managerial talent will be available to balance the team. Replacement and staffing forecasts can be made by taking the present organizational structure and identifying the people who are likely to be moving up or out of that particular organization with an indication of the time available to produce a replacement and the lead time necessary for the acquisition of new talent so that suitable experience can be gained.

Future organizational structures will need to be compared with present ones so that the anomalies and gaps in the capabilities of the managerial talent pool are identified for long-term selection and placement of individuals and replacement and staffing forecasts for the total management team. Derived from the long-range projection of the organization and the type of management capabilities that will be necessary for growth will be an individual career planning system.

Individual Development Planning

Individual development planning for career purposes and for the future needs of the organization are often disconnected from the overall managerial appraisal system. The question that usually arises is, "development for what?" If the personal goals of the individual are to be achieved in such a way that they enhance the achievement of the long-range organizational goals, it is particularly critical that the individual and his superior address specifically the question of his individual development. Particular emphasis should be placed upon the reasons why he was evaluated in performance the way he actually was. There should be a candid discussion of the performance which brought him up in the rank order as well as the performance limitations which held him back from being in a higher rank. Also the forecast of the individual's future capabilities and contribution that were made during the replacement and staffing forecast phase should be brought forward so that there is sufficient lead time for the individual to identify assignments which will develop experience as well as education and training which will supplement on-the-job skill acquisition.

This phase of the appraisal system should be approached with the same degree of depth in planning and goal setting as in the work goal setting and planning phase, and the same form (Figure 2) that was used is also applicable for individual development planning. The goals of career development should be specified along with plans and target dates for the accomplishment of education, training, and experience. The benefits to the individual and the alternatives and consequences of success or failure in his personal development efforts should be prestated along with the resources required in terms of assistance and the capital and expense investment in the manager as a human asset of the organization. Training and experience and change of assignment may be kept on a human asset balance sheet basis, with development capitalized as an investment in a manager's future and the expectancy of a return on that investment.

Manpower Analysis

One of the outputs from the managerial appraisal system that is derived from individual selection and placement decisions is the opportunity for manpower analysis, that is, the identification of the strong and weak points among the managerial work force and an identification of the key individuals who can be placed in significant positions as well as those who need reassignment or retraining to be more effective.

Certain functional areas may be over- or underrepresented among the key contributors. For example, a number of marketing managers may appear very high in the rank order, while accounting as a function may have no managers among the key people near the top of the evaluation. The first case indicates a strong marketing managerial supply of talent (or a decision bias), but with no people coming up through the ranks who are developing experience and capability for future assignments. The case of accounting may indicate that accounting as a function does not have the strength that marketing has, showing again either in the process or in the selection and placement of people with accounting capabilities. Both of these represent a problem and an imbalance in the organization's capabilities.

At this point we can go back to the job evaluation and determine whether accounting jobs have been structured with enough scope to permit an impact by this function; if so, this gives us an indication of the type of organizational change necessary to make a fully effective managerial team. We can also go back to the goal setting and planning phase and determine whether the accounting staff is thinking broadly about the type of impact they should have upon the total organizational performance. In future goal setting and planning stages the accounting management should be permitted and encouraged to enhance their impact upon the achievement of organizational objectives.

We may also investigate the individual history records of the accounting organization to see whether the proper kind of talent is being introduced into the corporation. Of course we should look at the performance evaluation stage to see whether it is simply a bias in disfavor of people in accounting functions. The results of such analyses will help to improve the management decision process as well as enhance the talent pool available within each organizational function.

Estate and Tax Planning

An additional feature of the managerial appraisal system ties into base and incentive compensation and provides the chance to maximize the after-tax income of individuals. Since people have varying estate goals, investments, and tax situations, a useful service can be provided through data-processing systems constructed around Internal Revenue Service regulations which minimize tax liability. After compensation is determined for a manager, he can then compare his tax alternatives and select how and when he receives his compensation (cash, stock, deferred income, etc.) to his greatest after-tax advantage.

The reverse can also be done with individual factors held constant and the organization's alternatives on the forms of compensation programs provided maximized to the advantage of both the individual and the organization.

SYSTEM SUMMARY

The managerial appraisal system is organized on the principle of goals and management by objectives. Management decisions on performance utilize several integrated inputs: goals and plans, job evaluation, performance evaluation, and individual history. Comparisons of individual goals and relative achievements yield decisions on compensation, selection and placement, and replacement and staffing forecasts. Additionally, information on the management team permits manpower analysis, individual development planning, and estate and tax planning. This concept permits and motivates managers to achieve personal goals through the achievement of organizational goals.

BIBLIOGRAPHY

Forrester, Jay W.: "A New Corporate Design," *Industrial Management Review,* vol. 7, no. 1, Fall, 1965.

Edward N. Hay & Associates: *Men & Management* Series, 1970.

Hughes, Charles L.: "Assessing the Performance of Key Managers," *Personnel,* January–February, 1968.

———: "Goal Oriented Approaches to People and Job Measurement," *Handbook of Wage and Salary Administration,* sec III, chap. 13, McGraw-Hill Book Company, New York, 1972.

———: *Goal Setting—Key to Individual and Organizational Effectiveness,* American Management Association, 1965.

——— and Donald L. Wass: "Promoting Goal Seeking Behavior in Managers," presented to Task Management Symposium, Management Research Center, University of Rochester, November, 1968, published in *Symposium Proceedings.*

Lewellen, Wilbur G.: *Executive Compensation in Large Industrial Corporations,* National Bureau of Economic Research, Columbia University Press, New York, 1968.

Likert, Rensis: *New Patterns of Management,* McGraw-Hill Book Company, New York, 1961.

Myers, M. Scott: "Conditions for Manager Motivation," *Harvard Business Review,* January–February, 1966.

Thompson, Paul H., and Gene W. Dalton: "Performance Appraisal: Managers Beware," *Harvard Business Review,* January–February, 1970.

Winstanley, N. B.: "Management 'Incentive' Bonus Plan Realities," talk delivered at annual conference of Eastern Region of the American Compensation Association in Montreal, *The Conference Board Record,* January, 1970.

Part 9

Employee Services, Safety, and Health

chapter 46

Recreational Programs

ROBERT L. BAUER *Activity Advisor, Armco Association, Armco Steel Corporation, Middletown, Ohio*

"What a man does with his working hours determines what he has—what he does with his leisure time determines what he is," said George Eastman of Eastman Kodak. And it seems a modern company has a role to play in what its employees *are*, if we can judge from the number of American companies that are beginning or expanding recreation programs for employees. At the beginning of the seventies more than fifty thousand of America's businesses and industries have some form of recreation program.

Why a Company Recreation Program?

Growing along with the number of picnic groves, club activities, physical fitness programs, and softball teams is the *philosophy* of industrial recreation. Recreation is absolutely essential to the development of a human person. Recreation is part of life. But why should a steel mill provide a basketball league? How does a golf course fit into the purpose of a television manufacturer or the policies of a soap producer? What advantages does the company gain by having a recreation program?

In general, a recreation program follows from any company policy to "promote the general well-being of the employees" or to provide opportunities "so that each individual may reach his or her highest potential." But management will want some kind of visible results to justify bowling teams and clubhouses, especially when these make few entries into the credit side of the ledger, and often appear as very large numbers on the debit side.

Henry Ford II has called the benefits of a company recreation program "intangible." "They cannot readily be measured in dollars and cents. But," he continued with confidence, "I am sure they are substantial indeed."

The recreation program does have substantial, discernible benefits in terms of employee loyalty to the company, the cooperation of employees, and the development of leadership and creativity among employees. The employee finds it easier to identify with the company that helps satisfy his off-the-job human needs; he identifies with the company where his fellow workers become teammates and buddies "after hours"; he identifies with the company where he is an occasional golf partner of the vice president and can meet his supervisor at a square dance; he identifies with the company that offers his children summer movies and peewee football and his wife a bridge club and swimming lessons; he identifies with the company that gives him a chance for recognition of a particular talent, a chance to exercise his competitive instinct and to express himself, and an opportunity to stay in contact with the company after retirement.

Studies also show that physically fit employees have better productive capabilities and have fewer problems in their relationships with their co-workers. Robert S. Oelman, Chairman of the Board, National Cash Register Company, sees the recreation program as a help in "attracting outstanding people to the company and inducing them to stay." Finally, as wage increases reach their limits, a recreation program can be included in the "benefits package" that is an ever greater part of union contracts.

With confidence in the benefits, more and more companies commit themselves to recreation programs. What we must treat now are the practical considerations: (1) what activities to include in the program, (2) where to hold these activities, (3) how to organize and administer the program, and (4) how to pay for it.

I. WHAT ACTIVITIES SHOULD BE INCLUDED IN A COMPANY RECREATION PROGRAM?

An effective company recreation program is directed to the employee and his family and is based on three fundamental principles. First, the program provides the greatest opportunity for the greatest amount of participation by the greatest number of people.

Second, it must understand, therefore, that recreation is more than *play;* recreation includes not only softball and golf, but also coin collecting, dancing, theater parties, picnics—all activities a person engages in during his leisure time to refresh, relax, and develop himself.

Third, the program must be flexible, so it can change and grow as new needs and activities arise.

With these principles in mind the program selects, arranges and schedules activities by considering (1) the interests of the employees, (2) the availability of facilities, (3) the existence of activities in the community.

The interests of the employees will give the program a core of activities such as golf, softball, picnics. But there are many other interests in any group of people, and activities can even be initiated "from the top." Often there is a great deal of hidden interest that needs only the opportunity to arise. In fact, Dr. Jackson M. Anderson of the University of Minnesota believes that in recreation programs "we've got to make a more careful study of the people with whom we work and, little by little, we have got to try to inject into our programs the things we need."

In building a program on interest, we must be wary of fads and small special-interest groups. In six months or eighteen months, when the fad passes, the program could be stuck with an unused go-cart track or several hundred hulahoops. And should a recreation program make a large investment in time and money for the benefit of the few people interested in sky diving?

Finally, a program built on interest requires interested *leaders,* people with some knowledge of the activity, who are willing to take responsibility for it. Leadership is a major factor in the success of a recreation program or any particular activity in the program (see below).

Determining the "availability" of facilities for an activity begins by considering the geography and climate where the company is located. For example, is it practical for a company in Phoenix to invest in a ski slope for the company park? If the activity is reasonable in your area, you will consider whether ball fields or activity rooms are already available or can be acquired, and whether the activity is financially "available." (These two points will be covered in detail below.)

Recreation opportunities already existing in the community are our third consideration. Should the company build a golf course when most employees can play at the country club? Should the company compete with (and possibly undermine) the fitness program at the Y?

Four General Categories of Activities

It is thus impossible to list activities that are equally suitable for a small company in Boston, a large manufacturing unit in Wyoming, and a middle-size fabricator in the Midwest. However, a balanced recreation program has some activities organized into each of four general categories: *social activities, cultural activities, team and individual physical activities,* and *intercompany leagues and tournaments.*

Social activities include all the less structured activities the employee can enjoy in his leisure time with his family, his fellow employees and other friends. Such activities have no regular schedule and include picnics, Easter egg hunts, dances, theater parties, group attendance at sports events, fishing, boating, and golf.

Cultural activities involve particular hobby or interest groups and provide an important outlet for creative expression. These activities usually require few company funds to operate, very little supervision, and usually only a place to meet. Included in this category would be art shows, bridge clubs, stamp or coin clubs, railroad clubs, and group travel plans.

The physical, team sports traditionally hold the most interest among employees and should be considered basic to any program. The essential feature of these activities is the involvement of people throughout the company, though most of these sports also have spectator interest. By their very nature these activities require good leadership, supervision, and adequate funds to ensure their success, which will stimulate the entire recreation program.

There is a danger, however, that team sports will be dominated by a few younger, more athletic employees and limit the interest throughout the company. In order to avoid this and to ensure the fullest participation of everyone interested, there must be an imaginative approach to the development of leagues and classifications, and certain limits must be placed on participation by an individual.

There have always been men's leagues and women's leagues. But also try basketball leagues for those over thirty-five years of age, for those under six feet tall, for fast-break leagues and slow-break leagues are other possibilities. In softball try a league for those over thirty-five. Handicapping in golf and shooting sports allows the greatest participation.

Keeping the competition as even as possible is essential to sustained interest. Therefore, it is wise to have departmental teams, to prevent all the "good" players from being on one or two teams. Also there can be limits on the number of times a particular player can play during a week, and each person can be limited to membership in only one league.

Finally, *competition between different local companies* should be included in the program, as well as participation in community, state, and national tournaments. Today this is a much smaller part of the recreation program than it was ten to fifteen years ago, when companies were represented in national competitions by semi-professional teams. Team sports now stress individual participation by employees more than spectator value, and intercompany leagues and tournaments should give the employees a chance for recognition, as well as foster the company reputation.

In weighing the various parts of a company recreation program, however, these intercompany activities have the lowest priority. They require a considerable expense, often as much as 20 percent of the recreation budget, and should be the first activities affected by economy measures.

Recognition and Awards

One of the valid goals of a recreation program is to recognize excellence, which can be done by trophies, awards, and banquets. In league competitions, a roving trophy is a good idea. Each year it goes to the championship team or department, with a provision that it is retired after perhaps three consecutive wins by the same team.

Nonetheless, individual recognition is also necessary. For example, a small trophy or perhaps a championship jacket can be given to each member of a championship team. Jackets are also a popular way to recognize members of company representative teams who have won intercompany leagues or competitions. Plaques might be used to recognize employees who, in a general way, have made outstanding achievements in the recreation program.

The manner in which the trophy is presented often gives as much recognition as the award itself. That is why many companies have an awards banquet held annually—or, in larger companies, held seasonally for each sport or group of sports. The banquet can be structured in many ways. It can be open to all personnel in the company, to those who participated in the activities programs, or to the champions, officials, directors, volunteers, and supervisors from departments with winning teams.

Successful banquet programs include a good speaker, usually a significant sports figure, the presentation of the awards by a high-ranking member of management or the president of the association, and a social hour with the opportunity for employees and management to meet the speaker and one another.

II. WHERE SHOULD COMPANY RECREATION ACTIVITIES BE HELD?

The availability of facilities interacts with employee interests to determine the company recreation program. Company-owned ball diamonds and company parks and halls facilitate program planning and guide the selection of activities. However, the company without such facilities—especially the smaller company—should not feel handicapped. A lively program can develop without company investment in special recreation areas.

First, every community has public facilities such as school gymnasiums, municipal auditoriums and meeting rooms, community ball fields, and golf courses. These can often be used without charge, or for a small cost or user's fee. Second, look to the commercial facilities in an area, such as bowling lanes and theaters. Finally, use existing company property such as cafeterias, meeting rooms, parking lots.

The Company Park

A growing number of companies, however, do have special recreation facilities or parks, which take many forms. A 1967 survey by Owens-Illinois showed that company parks range in size from two to seven hundred acres, and average over one hundred acres. Ninety percent of these have softball diamonds; the majority also have meeting rooms, picnic groves with tables, horseshoe pits, a clubhouse, restrooms, and paved parking areas. Fewer than 25 percent have their own bowling alleys, golf course, or swimming pool, either indoor or outdoor.

One example and model of what a company park can be is the expansion and development of the Armco Steel Corporation park at Middletown, Ohio. The park is a 750-acre recreation complex, including a twelve-acre lake for fishing, which is being expanded for small boats and swimming. There are golf courses, a driving range, miniature golf, and an outdoor theater. Over one hundred acres is given to picnic areas with shelters, playground equipment, shuffleboards, and horseshoe pits. Lighted tennis courts and athletic fields allow for extended use.

A company park can aid the recreation program and be a matter of prestige and distinction; but it is not necessarily the place to begin. Creative and imaginative recreation programs can be developed with the use of facilities already available in the community and the company.

III. WHO RUNS THE COMPANY RECREATION PROGRAM?

The administration of a company recreation program reflects who pays the bills. In any company there are three possible ways to organize and finance the program. At one extreme is the program completely run and paid for by the company, and at the other is the recreation program completely supported by the employees.

A Plan for Mixed Responsibility

The third possibility, which will be discussed more fully here, is the mix of responsibility and financing between the company and the employees. The first step is to establish an operating base and identity for the recreation program by forming a club or association whose members are the employees and managers of the company. In order to get as much participation as possible, the employees should have responsibility for the operation and advancement of the program. Yet, since the association bears the company name and is in fact a unit of the company, it is best that the company through its management be in a position of ultimate authority.

A concrete attempt to interrelate the role of the company and the employees is the Armco Association. The final authority for the program lies with the *management advisory committee* of four members, including the vice president of personnel relations as chairman. This committee makes recreation decisions for the company; it approves the final budget for the program; advises on new programs, facilities, and policy; and represents the company at meetings and social functions of the directors.

Authority for the activities of the association, however, lies with the *board of directors,* who are elected by their fellow employees. Where possible, the directors should be elected as representatives of the departments or divisions of the company, rather than at large. At Armco each of the fourteen directors represents five hundred to seven hundred employees. In smaller or larger companies this proportion can be adjusted to achieve a board of eight to twenty directors, which seems to be the optimum working size. Some companies' programs have as many as sixty directors, but this tends to be unwieldy. To ensure continuity and experience, it is also best to have the board members serve two-year or three-year terms, with only part of the board being elected each year. Also directors should be ineligible for reelection, so that more employees can serve in the association's leadership.

The board elects its own officers, as needed. At Armco the officers are president, vice president, and secretary. (The duties of treasurer are performed by the activities adviser.) Regular board meetings are essential, and these should be announced and open to all employees.

The board as a whole has authority to formulate the policies, rules, and regulations of the association and to determine the budget, new programs, and operations of the association (subject to the advice of the management committee mentioned above).

Because of the variety of activities in the recreation program, it is best to have committees to handle individual activities. The committees should be formed from the board members, according to their interests in specific activities. Depending on the number of directors and the number of committees, service on more than one committee may be required. However, it may be better to have directors act as chairmen of the committees and to select other employees to serve on the committees.

The Activities Adviser or Director

The execution of the recreation program should be in the hands of a special administrator, an *activities adviser* or *recreation director*. Ideally the adviser devotes his full time to the recreation program. However, if he has other functions, for example, in the personnel department, he should have part of his schedule specified for work on recreation, so that the program does not suffer by default.

In some companies the adviser is hired by the directors of the association and responsible to them. However, it seems best that he be responsible to the management advisory committee and to the vice president or director of personnel.

The recreation adviser coordinates and administers the recreation program; he serves as treasurer to the board of directors and represents the management committee to the association board and the board to the committee. He advises the board on company policy, budget, program selection, and new trends; and he must motivate leadership within his organization.

Though company management and employees must work together to have a good program, the real key to an alive and exciting program is the recreation adviser, and care should be given to his selection.

The recreation adviser must have a broad cultural background. He must be interested in people and understand them. He must be thoroughly familiar with his company's policies, as well as familiar with the field of recreation. He should know the theory and philosophy of recreation and be able to impart it to others, and he must be able to coordinate the special services and skills embraced within the recreation department. Finally he should understand the problems of the community in relation to recreation.

The recreation director should be paid by the company, and his salary and status should be on a par with the heads of other employee services in the company. A recent survey shows that the annual salaries of recreation advisors in 279 companies range from $8,000 to $15,000, plus benefits such as the use of a company car.

Additional Staff and Occasional Leadership

In large companies and programs additional recreation staff will be necessary. Among the possibilities to be considered are the use of part-time personnel during busy seasons, and the employment of a resident park manager, who may or may not be accountable to the recreation adviser, depending on the status of the park in the program (see below).

A successful recreation program depends on a competent and qualified staff. However, a large measure of the success also depends on the efficient employment of occasional leadership. First there are volunteers who serve in short-duration activities, such as one-day tournaments and special events.

A second group of occasional leaders are the league directors and secretaries.

This leadership is used in team sports and league-type activities, where control, records, and safety are factors. These leaders receive a standard remuneration, such as $10 per team per year in a league like baseball, or $1 per participant in leagues such as bowling.

These directors or secretaries administer the leagues under the supervision of the recreation adviser. The leaders arrange for the necessary scorekeepers and referees. They are responsible for association equipment, they make schedule changes, and they keep records of team standings. They enforce rules and regulations and report accidents and unsportsmanlike conduct. They also report scores and outstanding happenings to the local newspapers and radio stations.

IV. HOW IS THE COMPANY RECREATION PROGRAM PAID FOR?

In recreation programs run totally by the company or totally by the employees, the responsibility for financing is clear. In programs, however, where the administration and cost are divided between the company and the employees, there are many questions of who pays for what.

One widespread practice is to help support the recreation program by the profits from the candy, soft drink, and coffee vending machines. Another practice, when the recreation program is organized as a club or association, is to charge employees membership dues. At Armco, there are no dues for participation in the association activities, but employees do pay dues for the use of the park facilities (see below). The employees also assume part of the recreation costs by paying users' fees and making as-you-go payments.

Social activities are usually a minimal expense to the program. The company provides the facilities, such as picnic grounds and a horseshoe pit, while dances and theater parties are paid for by the participants.

Cultural and club expenses are also paid by the participants. The company provides a meeting place and a minimal budget of $50 for operating expenses.

The most costly part of the program, of course, includes team sports and leagues, and there are many formulas for sharing the costs between company and participants. In team activities of the Armco Association, for example, the company provides the facility and the team equipment such as bats, balls, bases; employees pay half the cost of uniforms. In activities with a user's fee, such as bowling, golf, or trapshooting, the participants pay these fees.

In outside tournaments and league play, the company pays the expenses of travel and uniforms for company representative teams.

However financial responsibility is shared, the budget of a company recreation program will include the following items: (1) administration; salaries for the adviser, other staff, and officials; office costs (this is usually the largest item in the budget); (2) cultural and social activities (these usually require a minimum allotment); (3) team sports and league activities, with special provisions for (a) equipment, (b) uniforms, (c) awards, trophies, banquets; (4) representative teams and intercompany tournaments; (5) community projects and public relations (see below on sponsorship of activities such as Little League baseball teams).

Separate Maintenance of the Park

At Armco the park is incorporated as a club distinct from the activities program, and there are dues for membership. The membership card entitles the employee, his family, and a limited number of guests to use the facilities. The dues money provides for some of the park maintenance, such as rangers, utilities, game equipment, and special picnics. Facilities which require added maintenance and operating help, such as the golf course, driving range, miniature golf, snack bar, and pro-shop are supported by the fees levied against employees using these facilities. Remaining expenses are paid by the company.

In determining the dues, a club or association must consider factors that might affect the amount of money available, such as taxes. For example, until January 1, 1966, club dues in excess of $10 were subject to a 20 percent federal excise tax; the Armco Park dues were therefore set at $9, since a $10 fee would have cost the employee $1 additional, yet given the park $1 less for operations.

At the present time, club dues and users' fees pay 40 percent of the park's day-to-day operating expenses, and the company pays 60 percent.

V. HOW IS THE COMPANY RECREATION PROGRAM EVALUATED, AND HOW ARE PROBLEMS DEALT WITH?

As in every company venture, there are some risks and some problems in even the best recreation program. These should not deter the company from sponsoring the program, but the alert manager is aware of the dangers and takes corrective steps.

The first problem is that the company recreation dollar cannot reach *all* employees. Of course, any activity taking a disproportionate amount of money to service few employees should be discontinued. However, a diversified program with good leadership and promotion will reach as many as possible. It is then the employee's fault if he does not use his opportunities. Second, sports activities can pull employees away from their families, and some employees are not interested in competitive sports. These problems can be met by a diversified program, and especially by ample family activities.

Since team and league sports are the biggest part of a recreation program, they can occasion many problems. Cheating and unsportsmanlike conduct should be handled by an employee committee for this purpose. The committee should have the authority to take appropriate action such as suspending offenders from the program.

In sports activities, injuries are a constant danger, and the program must stress safety and have a ready first-aid procedure. Normally the insurance a company provides for its employees at home or on the highway also covers participation in the recreation program.

When the company has a park, littering, vandalism, and speeding become problems. Numerous litter barrels and signs reminding the users "This is your park; keep it clean" will help. Some littering must be expected, though, and is remedied by adequate maintenance crews. Vandalism can be minimized by the use of roving rangers and other security personnel. Traffic control devices such as humps in the road, as well as security rangers, help alleviate the speeding problem.

Particular problems can arise, such as drunkenness on company facilities or at company functions, and parking and necking. Alcoholic beverages can be restricted to certain areas, the park can be closed at dark, except for certain areas, and security patrols can enforce good order.

Norms For Positive Evaluation

Besides a procedure for problems, the recreation program must also include ways to positively evaluate its success. Clearly formulated goals make evaluation easier. If the goal is to have the greatest participation by the greatest number, we can judge the program on the number of participants and the number of activities they participate in. We can credit the program if there is a high degree of participation, if there is a high degree of family participation. We should also be able to see leadership developing.

A high injury rate, many cases of unsportsmanlike conduct, and a high cost per participant indicate a weak program.

Evaluation of the program and of each activity should be an ongoing practice, and there should be careful records of the participants and the costs. There should also be an annual review in which costs and the number of participants, the problems, and the benefits are considered, to make future long-range plans and program modifications.

Program evaluation can use at least three methods to gather information. The first, observation, is undoubtedly the best method, and it is the duty of the committee chairmen to make analyses of their activities and report to the board at the monthly meetings. Management observations, especially on the team sports and park use, are very important. Some of the best suggestions for improvements come from the second method, the individual interview. Third, questionnaires can be used to determine successful programs and activities. This method can especially be used when there is evidence of lack of interest, or when excessive sportsmanship problems arise.

VI. HOW CAN THE COMPANY RECREATION PROGRAM SERVE THE COMMUNITY?

In developing a recreation program, the company should consider its place in the community as a whole. The company need not duplicate community opportunities that adequately serve the needs of employees, nor should the company run unnecessary competition with community programs. Remember that employees are members both of the company and of the community they live in. It is only good business to avoid the duplication and competition that can mean unnecessary costs or can destroy existing community programs.

The recreation program might also be the structure through which the company engages in many community projects. For example, the sponsorship of Scout troops, Little League teams, and Junior Achievement could be part of the recreation program. The use of company facilities, such as a park, for community activities is another way of exercising responsibility toward the community at large. In some companies the involvement in once-a-year activities such as United Appeal is a function of the recreation program.

VII. WHERE CAN A COMPANY GET HELP ON ITS PROGRAM?

In developing a company recreation program it is never necessary—and usually foolish—to "go it alone." There are professional associations, schools, seminars, regional organizations, and consulting services all eager to help your program— usually with more efficiency and at less cost than if you did it by yourself.

Professional associations offer excellent opportunities for the recreation adviser, the personnel director, and the whole program. Two such organizations are the NPRA (National Park and Recreation Association, 1700 Pennsylvania Ave., Washington, D.C. 20006) and the NIRA (National Industrial Recreation Association, 20 North Wacker Drive, Chicago, Ill. 60606).

Of the two, the NIRA concentrates more of its efforts on promoting and assisting industrial recreation programs. Its main services include reviews of new developments and ideas in all phases of industrial recreation, and the publication of "how-to" manuals which are particularly helpful in starting new programs. NIRA also publishes the monthly *Recreation Management* and occasional special bulletins. It conducts research, sponsors regional conferences and an annual national conference, and has programs of certification for both the professionals (certified industrial recreation administrators) and the volunteers (certified industrial recreation leaders) in your program.

There are also several *schools and seminars* to help the recreation advisor. Both the NIRA and the NPRA conduct regular workshops, and particular mention should be made of the executive development school for park and recreation administrators and the revenue source management school (information can be had from NPRA).

Further help can be gained from membership in *regional organizations,* such as the Dayton Industrial Athletic Association, to which Armco belongs, or the excellent Milwaukee Industrial Recreation Council. These organizations allow for an exchange of ideas and provide a framework for intercompany tournaments and league competitions. They also bring together management from member companies on common goals and let employees from member companies meet one another. A full listing of such regional organizations can be obtained from NIRA.

Your recreation program can also be helped by the many professional *consulting firms* that can be recommended by NIRA or NPRA. Special consultation is particularly helpful when building a park or major facilities such as a golf course, lake, swimming pool, or clubhouse, or when lighting a field or park area. The expense of the consultant will be offset by the efficiency of the facility.

A NONCONCLUSION: WHERE IS THE COMPANY RECREATION PROGRAM GOING?

A discussion of modern industrial recreation really has no conclusion. There is so much development, change, and imaginative planning that today's statements can only survey the current situation and hint at the future.

However, the following trends will surely become more prominent and will guide the future of company recreation programs.

1. Programs designed to include the employee's whole family will continue to grow in importance, and imaginative new programs will reach individual members of the family.

2. Recreation programs will give more emphasis to fitness and education. There will be special exercise and conditioning programs directed especially toward executives and others who get little exercise on their jobs. There will also be programs to teach special physical skills, mental health, and preparation for retirement.

3. The movement will continue toward more elaborate facilities, such as employee country clubs with golf courses and other supporting recreational facilities. And since we are now a mobile society, these new facilities will be some distance from the plant, allowing for the development of larger tracts of land and the maintenance of remote and natural environments.

4. Recreation programs will become more important in labor-management contract negotiations, as part of the "benefits package," especially as the workweek shrinks and employees have still more leisure time.

Industrial recreation is in a period of exciting development, and a company will have to show imagination and progress in this area to be considered among the leaders of business and industry in the future.

BIBLIOGRAPHY

Anderson, Jackson M.: *Industrial Recreation,* McGraw-Hill series, 1955.

Athletic Institute: *Sports Techniques—Instructional Aids,* 805 Merchandise Mart, Chicago, 1971

International City Management Association: *Municipal Recreation Administration,* 1140 Connecticut Ave., N.W., Washington, D.C., 1959.

National Park and Recreation Association: *Guide to Books on Recreation* (annual publication), 1700 Pennsylvania Ave., Washington, D.C.

Olin-Mathieson Corp., Winchester-Western Division, East Alton, Ill.: various publications on shooting and conservation.

Recreation Management (monthly magazine), National Industrial Recreation Association, 20 N. Wacker Dr., Chicago.

Various publications on health and physical fitness, available from Superintendent of Documents, U.S. Government Printing Office, Washington, D.C.

chapter 47

Financial, Educational, and Other Aids to Employees

MURIEL E. MERKEL *Staff Communications, Personnel Department, The Port of New York Authority, New York, New York*

The number of ways in which companies can compensate employees—other than in wages or salaries—changes with the times and with theories of employee relations. The company's own philosophy is paramount; some organizations believe that so long as they provide equitable pay and first-rate working conditions, the rest is up to the individual employee. His private life and problems are his business, provided they do not interfere with his job, and realization of his potential is his concern. Any employee aid or support is regarded as paternalistic. Other companies believe that they employ the whole person, not just thirty-five or forty hours per week of him, and that assistance and support are well within the company's purview. They are convinced that in this complex, impersonal world, the employee may find it difficult to know where to turn or whom to ask for advice if he does not want to be trapped in a mediocre job or a frustrating personal life.

In this chapter, therefore, we shall consider two policies: the first, which can help the individual employee develop his potential through extra education, and the second, which can help him cope with the problems inherent in everyday living and working.

TUITION AID PLANS

Under tuition aid programs, the company pays all or part of the cost of tuition (and perhaps other expenses as well) for eligible employees who attend outside schools or colleges and pursue courses that meet company standards. These plans take a variety of forms and cover a variety of employees but share this common objective: assistance to the employee who contributes his own time and effort to seek extra learning or skills.

Why Tuition Aid?

Tuition aid programs had their beginnings early in this century, but until compara-tively recently, only a few companies provided these plans, and employee participa-tion tended to be restricted. However, rapid technological progress, particularly since World War II, has focused attention on industry's need for knowledge and skill—the knowledge and the skill of its employees who can contribute to indus-trial progress by devising new products, services, and methods, or by improving old ones.

As in other fields, knowledge in industry becomes obsolete far more speedily than in the past. The professional employee out of college only ten years finds that his learning has lost its luster; newly minted graduates have more up-to-date knowledge and may be considered more valuable to the company either as prospects for employ-ment or as candidates for promotion. When the labor market is tight and competi-tion for graduates heavy, companies are more aware of the necessity for updating the learning of their staff members. Moreover, the employee already on the staff who has proved his competence and loyalty may be considered a better investment than the newcomer. To both the organization and the individual the quest for fur-ther education is a mutually desirable goal.

Note: At some organizations, on-the-job training programs or leaves of absence to study full time are viewed as the answer to the need for additional education and training. Tuition aid plans can easily be combined with these other programs.

The purpose of most tuition assistance programs is to permit employees to get further education and improve their skills so that the company will have a reserve of fully qualified staff members to meet present and anticipated needs. More re-cently, some organizations have broadened their policies on educational aid to meet current concepts which hold that education is desirable in and of itself and that employees should therefore be encouraged to pursue additional education and should be given financial aid whether or not the additional study is a direct benefit to the company. Some organizations have used their tuition aid plans as a means of attracting new recruits. They reason that the higher the educational level of em-ployees, the better for the company.

Who Should Be Eligible?

The extent of employee participation depends on the company's view of tuition aid. If the additional training is considered necessary only when it relates directly to the organization's needs, then eligibility may be limited to employees who need to im-prove performance in their present positions or who are being prepared for pro-motion. Companies extend assistance to such groups as:

Management and professional personnel
Salaried employees
Nonunion employees
All full-time or permanent employees

The trend is to open tuition aid to all employees, regardless of their position or level of education. Usually, however, a length-of-service condition is imposed. Obviously, some service requirement gives the employer an indication of whether the employee's job performance and conduct are satisfactory. This consideration is another standard that employees may be required to meet—satisfactory perform-ance. The reason, of course, is the practical one that no employer wants to invest in an employee who may be a candidate for discipline or discharge rather than for educational assistance. The plan may specify that the employee have a satisfactory appraisal or an endorsement from his supervisor before being permitted to apply for assistance.

Schools and Colleges

A desirable condition to include in any educational aid program is that the employee must attend an approved or accredited school or college. Accrediting is granted by one of the regional college associations. "Approval" may be understood to mean licensing by a state department of education or endorsement by a professional society. Licensing, approval, and accreditation all are indications that the courses offered meet standards, that the instructors are qualified and that the diploma or certificate granted has value.[1]

By requiring that the institution of learning be acceptable, the company protects the employee from exploitation by unethical or unscrupulous operators who are interested in the student's cash and not in his career, who offer worthless courses, and who issue useless diplomas.

An approved institution of learning may be a college or graduate school, or a trade, technical, or business school. Increasingly, companies are permitting and even encouraging non–high school graduates to go back to school and qualify for a high school diploma or equivalency certificate.

The boundaries of what is considered an approved institution may be extended to include reputable organizations such as trade or professional associations that conduct seminars and workshops on subjects directly related to work. For example, a local YMCA or Chamber of Commerce may offer programs in supervisory training or labor-management relations. Other special schools may teach speed reading or public speaking, courses that employees may find directly connected with their job responsibilities.

A recent development that a company should consider in formulating or revising its tuition aid plan is the TV college credit course. Students who view these programs and want to receive credit for them must do assignments and pass examinations just as if they were attending a lecture course on campus. A tuition charge is made for credit courses (otherwise, anyone is welcome to watch them, free), and companies are generally accepting these charges as legitimate tuition costs under an educational assistance plan.

Correspondence schools and courses also may be viewed as acceptable. Usually, the requirement is that these schools be accredited by the National Home Study Council.

What Is an Acceptable Course?

The greatest variety in company policies is found concerning the kinds of courses or programs of study that are approvable for tuition aid. The standards set depend, of course, on the company's philosophy on tuition aid.

Where the company conviction is that extra education paid for by the company should be geared to company needs, the obvious standard is that the course be job-related. Most companies do require a demonstrable relationship between the course and the company's objectives. Thus an acceptable course may be designed to improve the employee's performance in his current position or to ready him for advancement to the next position on the job ladder.

A middle ground is favored by companies that emphasize the job-related aspects of a course but are liberal in interpreting this standard, especially for professional or managerial employees seeking advanced degrees. For instance, a company might grant aid to a chemist studying for his doctorate, even though he does not require a doctorate to advance in that particular company.

[1] For a list of nationally recognized accrediting agencies, write to: Accreditation and Institutional Eligibility Staff, Bureau of Higher Education, U.S. Department of Health, Education, and Welfare, Washington, D.C. 20202.

Other organizations stretch the standards considerably and are inclined to approve almost any course that has some relation to the company. In this group are the companies that encourage high school graduates to get their college degrees at company expense, or that encourage high school dropouts to get high school equivalency certificates. These companies operate on the assumption that a company's needs or an individual's job future cannot be charted absolutely, that at some point in the future the employee can put his learning—and his trained mind— to uses that also will help the company achieve its goals.

Virtually all organizations, however, attempt to identify—and reject—courses that an employee wishes to take to prepare himself for a job elsewhere or for extra work on his own time. An exception to this would be instances where the employee is about to retire and the company policy is to help him prepare for a retirement where he can either supplement his income or enjoy a more purposeful leisure. As the retirement age gets lower and lower—and as the cost of living gets higher and higher—organizations may want to take a positive view of tuition aid plans designed to help the prospective retiree.

Similarly, educational aid may be offered as rehabilitation opportunity to employees whose physical restrictions or handicaps prevent them from continuing in their present positions.

No matter what the company policy, what is important is that the company develop guidelines and make them known to employees. Clear policy statements will make it easier for the company to administer its plan fairly and consistently.

Educational Guidance

Employees may request guidance in deciding what school to attend or what course to take. If at all possible, they should be directed to a qualified guidance counselor. Usually the school or college has counseling service available.

If the company has professional counseling services (discussed elsewhere), employees can get the necessary advice from the company staff member. A counselor will use his judgment about administering a battery of tests or using other methods, including in-depth interviewing, to determine aptitudes and interests in terms of the individual employee.

Otherwise, it is the rare personnel man or manager who has the training and the skill to provide proper vocational guidance (discussed elsewhere). What the supervisor or the personnel man can do is explain, factually, what is needed to qualify for a specific position—skills, years of experience, physical requirements, promotion system, and so forth. When an unqualified individual tries to give career or vocational guidance, he may do the company a disservice and the employee damage. For example, at one organization a bright new personnel staff member told a forty-year-old employee in search of tuition aid to forget it—"At your age, you wouldn't be interested in more education."

What a company representative can and should do, however, is caution the over-enthusiastic employee that participation in tuition aid is not an automatic guarantee of promotion. The employee's expectations should not be dealt with lightly, nor should false hopes be raised.

One word of caution should be given the employee-student: Do not attempt too heavy a program. Each hour actually spent in a classroom may require up to two hours more of reading, studying, and preparation of assignments. The employee who signs up for too many courses may find it difficult to complete them all successfully and also handle the job competently—not to mention home responsibilities that he may have.

How Much Aid?

Company policies on the amount of aid run the gamut—from 100 percent to varying percentages or to fixed dollar amounts; any number of combinations are reported too, with amounts based on grades, length of service, kind of course taken, and so on. The reasons given for each payment plan are as varied as the plans, since they usually reflect the view of the men at the top and may be based on personal opinion and experience rather than pure logic.

A universal requirement is that the employee complete the course satisfactorily. At some companies, the amount of tuition aid depends upon the grade attained, for example, 100 percent aid for a grade of A or its equivalent, 80 percent for B, 70 percent for C. Other companies argue that this is not equitable. A married man of thirty-five with four young children may have to put in more time and effort to earn a C than does a young unmarried employee just out of college, used to the study habit and without the family responsibilities. Moreover, some instructors are notoriously low markers; a C from one of these may be the equivalent of the B+ earned from the easy instructor.

Payment plans based on grades may be impractical too with the current trend toward marking students either "pass" and "fail" or "satisfactory" and "unsatisfactory." Similarly, minority group students who find it difficult to make high grades for reasons that have nothing to do with their innate intelligence and ability may resent getting less tuition aid than their white colleagues whose cultural backgrounds make taking courses easier for them.

Other Expenses

In addition to tuition, other costs are involved in the pursuit of extra education: registration fees, laboratory fees, books, supplies, etc. The company should decide precisely what it will pay for and inform its employees accordingly. The most common policy now seems to be to include registration, tuition, and laboratory fees but to exclude all other costs. This makes sense, since the major expenses are covered and the costs of books, supplies, and other items can vary according to the student's economy—buying used books, for example.

Other Funds

Another determination to be made in drafting or revising policy is to decide whether the company will pay costs where the employee has other sources of income for education, such as the G.I. Bill, scholarships, grants-in-aid, special awards.

Some organizations seek to keep their costs down by requiring the student to use other income before applying for tuition aid. For example, a man entitled to G.I. benefits must use them first. If assistance under the G.I. Bill does not cover all costs, the company will make up the difference.

Other organizations hesitate to require an employee to exhaust a scholarship or grant before applying for educational assistance. They take the view that the employee gifted or diligent enough to win an award or scholarship should not be penalized but rather should be permitted to enjoy the fruits of his intelligence and effort and get tuition aid on the same basis as his less gifted co-workers.

Conditions for Refund

When tuition and other costs are refunded after satisfactory completion of the study program, the employee must show evidence of this accomplishment as well as receipts for the costs he has paid.

Where tuition assistance is given in advance—and this is a minority practice—receipts may be all that is required to show that the student actually used the money for the intended purpose.

In addition to satisfactory completion of the course, the company may require that an employee agree to remain in the company employ for a stated period of time. Sometimes the employee must remain for a period of time equal to the amount of education required at company expense; for instance, if he completed the credits equivalent to two years of college, he must stay with the company two years.

Refunding the Refund

Naturally, cases arise in which the employee who was given his tuition in advance fails the course or does not complete it. The usual practice is to require him to refund to the company all or part of the aid he received. An exception may be made if the employee's failure to complete his study was due to a circumstance beyond his control—getting drafted, for example, or becoming ill. Generally, these questions can be resolved on an individual basis.

Public Relations for Employees

Tuition aid is a substantial benefit, one that may have long-range returns for both company and employee, and no company providing such generous assistance should keep its program secret. Employees should have both a basic brochure or statement of policy and periodic reminders that the plan is available to them. Articles in the employee publication can point up the utilization of the plan; stories about employees who have participated in the program and achieved both educational and career goals should be publicized. New employees should receive information about educational assistance as part of their orientation program.

The brochure, pamphlet, or statement of policy need not be elaborate. It should, however, be clear and easy to understand. As many definite guidelines should be given as practical. Employees ordinarily will be suspicious of any policy statement couched in such broad general terms that it means little to them as individuals.

Evaluating Tuition Aid

Most companies like to have a balance sheet of sorts on their personnel programs. Is a policy worth the staff time and effort? Is the money poured into a particular benefit bringing any return at all? Tuition aid is no exception, and yet few companies make any attempt to evaluate this benefit. Although no accounting method is adequate to measure a benefit that raises the company-wide educational level and that may have results which defy computation, management may still be able to arrive at a judgment about the worth of a plan.

How many employees participate? What job levels do they represent? What length of service? What education levels have they achieved? What kinds of courses are they attending? What on-the-job achievements have resulted, that is, what success stories have resulted? How do employees view the plan? What changes would they suggest?

These are just some of the basic questions management might consider in evaluating the value of educational assistance—and in designing or redesigning plans.

EMPLOYEE COUNSELING SERVICES

The term "counseling" covers a wide variety of situations ranging from professional counseling to routine information giving. For purposes of this chapter, counseling will be considered under these general headings:

1. Psychological counseling by a qualified professional of employees with emotional or mental problems.

2. Vocational guidance by a qualified individual of employees who wish advice on careers or vocations. (Often this is given in conjunction with psychological counseling.)

3. Information giving by a supervisor or other staff member on questions concerning the company or the job.

4. Information on community resources given by a trained staff member to assist employees with personal problems. (This may be given in conjunction with psychological counseling.)

Health counseling, which is considered the province of medical services, may also include psychological counseling.

Psychological Counseling Services

The burden on the company of the psychologically handicapped employee and the suffering the individual may experience are both impossible to estimate. A psychological handicap may range from chronic mental illness to a temporary disturbance triggered by an emotional upset, with stops at every point in between.

Reams have been written on the mentally ill employee—recognition of his illness, treatment, dealing with him on the job, and so forth. Many sophisticated training programs include advice for supervisors and management on how to recognize signs of mental illness and how to handle the employee who is ill or who returns to the work world after having been ill.

However, severe mental illness usually is easier to recognize and to deal with and may be less of an industrial problem than the less serious emotional illness or mental problem that, unfortunately, is not easy to identify and may be accepted or explained away as "peculiarity" or "temperament." These ills come to management's attention only if they cause some other problem in the work situation. Yet absenteeism, alcoholism, turnover, and grievances may all have their roots in someone's emotional disturbance. Nor is the rank-and-file employee the only person prone to these problems. Supervisors and members of management with emotional ills cause a considerable amount of damage to the other human beings in their work environment, and their needs should not be overlooked.

Because a few farsighted companies have long understood the need for psychological counseling, others have become convinced, and counseling services of this nature are accepted as a valuable form of employee assistance. These services can deal with the employee who already has become a problem, and can identify and take preventive measures for individuals whose behavior threatens to pose a problem.

Qualified Professional Staff

The chief requisite—besides the obvious policy decision that psychological counseling is desirable—is that the service be headed by a competent professional. The size of the company, its location in a community, and the availability of other resources will help determine whether that professional is a full-time psychiatrist or a part-time psychiatrist retained on a consulting basis. The company may also, with advice from a psychiatric consultant, decide that a qualified psychologist can supervise its counseling services and deal effectively with the day-to-day operations, referring employee-patients to a psychiatrist or other qualified therapist as the need dictates.

What is of paramount importance is that the psychiatrist or psychologist be qualified. A psychiatrist is a physician who has specialized in psychiatry. An organization seeking his services should first make certain that he is indeed qualified in this specialty, that he is affiliated with reputable institutions and programs in the field, and that he has genuine interest in occupational mental health. The qualifications of the psychologist should also be carefully investigated. A doctorate in psychology is not necessarily evidence of qualification. What is evidence is a license. Most states license psychologists, and this certification is evidence that the individual has the education and the clinical experience necessary to provide effective counseling services in an industrial organization.

Sometimes this emphasis on a professionally qualified staff is questioned. Cannot any mature, intelligent staff member do counseling? Not so. True counseling requires some very special skills, some very special training, and some very special insight. Commonsense advice, which the untrained dispense so easily, often has no bearing on a problem that is emotional in nature. Talking out a problem with a sympathetic listener may help, but it does not necessarily resolve the problem unless the listener is trained to hear not only what is said but what is left unsaid, to evaluate what he hears, and to offer perceptive suggestions and, where indicated, therapy.

The industrial psychiatrist or psychologist will counsel individual employees on a short-term basis. Long-term counseling or therapy ordinarily is not undertaken by a company staff member, since this would be time-consuming and prevent his active involvement in all the programs that constitute company service. The company counselor, however, should have the contracts necessary to make outside referrals of employees whose problems require lengthy treatment.

Other areas that should involve the company psychiatrist or psychologist include executive evaluations, assessments of college recruits, supervisory training programs, and programs for control of alcohol and drug addiction. The qualified professional can offer valuable guidance in many areas; his full potential is not utilized if his services are restricted only to counseling or treating the employee with problems.

Referrals

The psychiatrist or psychologist should be available to any employee who believes he has a problem and wants to seek professional help. When an employee requests assistance or counseling voluntarily, whatever is discussed in his counseling sessions should be kept confidential unless the employee gives written consent to release specified information. The entire relationship and the effectiveness of counseling will be destroyed if the counselor is required, through company policy, to reveal the reasons why an employee voluntarily sought help and what the nature of the problem or the treatment is. Members of management will be more likely to seek counseling for themselves when their confidence is respected.

The issue of confidentiality is different when an employee is directed to report for counseling because of his conduct, attitude, attendance, and so forth. When management makes a direct referral, it has the right to expect feedback. Moreover, the feedback can help management or the supervisor to deal with the employee since the psychiatrist or psychologist can provide the necessary clues and guidelines.

At this point, it might be well to note that employees with problems or employees who seek professional counseling are not necessarily one step removed from a breakdown or mental illness. Indeed, it may be the mark of good mental health for an individual to realize that he requires professional assistance to solve his problems effectively.

A major requisite for a successful psychological services program is the acceptance of the psychiatrist or the psychologist as a member of management—without apologies or excuses. The psychologist or the psychiatrist who is accepted as a respected colleague and included in the managerial circle can be much more effective than the one who is regarded as an outsider who deals only with peculiar employees.

Vocational Guidance

Counseling employees about their careers requires professional competence. A well-meaning personnel staff member usually is not equipped to give advice and information that may influence an individual's educational choice and vocational future.

On the other hand, a supervisor or a personnel man or woman should be competent to provide information about the jobs in a company—what the requirements are, how the promotion system operates, and so forth. However, if an employee doubts that he is in the right career or wishes to switch careers completely, or if a young employee is undecided about the direction he should take, vocational guidance is in order.

If the company provides psychological counseling services, this evaluation or assessment should be available; otherwise, the employee should be referred to an assessment center or vocational guidance counselor. Assistance can be sought from a local university or college since most have guidance counselors on their staff.

It should not be overlooked too that a request for vocational guidance may indicate that the individual really wants psychological assistance. The person who hesitates to ask for psychological aid finds it easier to tell himself that it is career guidance he needs. Moreover, emotional disturbance may be manifested by distaste for the current job or the company and an expressed desire to change jobs or careers. For this reason, an occupational psychiatrist or psychologist is the person best suited to deal with career guidance at the company.

Information Giving by the Supervisor

The emphasis in the preceding paragraphs on the need for qualified professionals to do employee counseling does not preclude supervisors from giving information. In fact, it is desirable for supervisors to be the source of information about the company—its policies, procedures, rules, products or services, history, personnel, and the like. The importance of the supervisor's role in providing such information should not be underestimated. He represents the company; he is the company so far as his people are concerned. Management, therefore, should provide him with the tools he needs to carry out his information-giving role effectively.

For the supervisor to gain or retain credibility as a source of company information, the communications system should ensure that he get information well in advance of its general release to all employees. Also, the supervisor must be able to reach an authoritative member of management quickly when he himself requires facts to deal with an employee query or emergency. To be completely effective too, the supervisor must be told the "why" of every action or policy, not only the "what".

No supervisor, however, should be expected to counsel employees with personal problems, whether emotional or mental. This kind of counseling requires experts such as the psychologist. A supervisor is not, by virtue of his age, experience, or rank, a qualified counselor on marital problems, delinquent adolescents, emotional stress, or mental illness. The untrained supervisor may, indeed, do the employee and the company a great deal of harm if he assumes the role of counselor.

Nevertheless, a supervisor can be an invaluable ally of the professional counselor when he is able to recognize the warning signs of stress or mental illness and refers the employee to the professional counselor promptly. Many companies give their supervisory staff special training to enable them to identify the employee who needs help. This kind of training can be conducted by the psychiatrist or the psychologist on the staff.

Taking this training a step further, some organizations have had their psychological services staff select supervisors with the interest and the willingness to undergo thorough training in counseling. This enables these supervisors to deal with some counseling situations themselves, thus relieving the professionals of a portion of their work load and leaving them free to concentrate efforts and attention on the employees with critical problems.

The absolute necessity for giving supervisors additional training that will provide insights into the part that emotional ills play in industry is underscored in company programs to control alcoholism and drug addiction. No such program can succeed fully without the cooperation and understanding of informed supervision.

Information on Community Resources

Another kind of counseling that some companies provide concerns community resources—where to turn for a variety of aids. For example, an employee with a retarded child may need to know what special institutions are open to him, or a woman with a physically handicapped youngster may want information about a summer camp. Employees may need welfare assistance in emergencies. Widowers with small children may require information about housekeeping services. An employee with a chronically ill relative may ask help in finding a nursing home. A father or mother may request professional assistance for a child with a behavior problem. An employee with a wife dying of cancer may have exhausted his funds paying for private nurses and need access to other help.

Any time an employee is beset with these or similar worries and does not know how to cope with them, his physical and mental health and his job performance will be adversely affected. A host of public and private agencies stand ready to assist, but the average employee does not know about them and does not know how to go about enlisting their help.

For this reason, some organizations have designated a staff member whose business it is to learn all the resources the community has to offer and to help employees utilize these resources. (Where psychological counseling services are provided, this information should be available there.) The amount of time saved, the worry avoided, and the easing of the burden from the employee's shoulders may have a positive effect on employee relations as well as a demonstrable effect on the troubled employee's attendance and job performance.

Another situation in which company aid can be most helpful is when a death in the family occurs. Some organizations make it a practice to send a staff member to assist the bereaved family in making arrangements, helping with phone calls, assisting with errands, and so forth. Help may also be provided in filing insurance and social security claims. This on-the-scene assistance can save the remaining relatives a substantial amount of expense. The presence of a reasonable and uninvolved third party is likely to act as a restraining influence and prevent extravagant and needless expenses.

Preretirement Counseling

A counseling service may be provided as part of the entire program for prospective retirees. Preretirement counseling involves many professional disciplines and should include psychological counseling where necessary, vocational guidance where desired, information about community resources, and advice on real estate, investment plans, insurance, and health services. (Counseling programs of this kind are discussed in Chapter 71.)

ADDITIONAL EMPLOYEE SERVICES

Some other aids that companies provide to ease the burdens of modern life for their employees include:

Credit unions—to encourage thrift

Legal and tax services—to help unsnarl red tape
Loans and welfare funds—to tide over emergencies
Discount buying services—to help the employee get the most out of his dollar
Parking facilities—to speed the journey to and from work
Day-care centers—to assist working mothers

CREDIT UNIONS

Credit unions have grown at an astonishing rate—and this growth holds true even in metropolitan centers where other banking institutions abound, are conveniently located, and offer a wide range of services.

Perhaps the clue to the widespread popularity of credit unions lies in their very definition. Credit unions are cooperative associations. Employees organize them, employees serve as directors and officers, and employees perform all the myriad tasks necessary to operate their own banking institution. This knowledge that they are the decision makers in a responsible financial institution which promotes thrift and provides loans for provident purposes may be one reason for the popularity of the state or the federal credit union. Other reasons include the dividend rate, which usually is high, the interest rate on loans, which usually is low, and the comparative ease with which loans can be obtained.

Federal credit unions are chartered and supervised by the National Credit Union Administration. State credit unions are chartered and supervised by the various states. Thus credit unions, like banks, are either state or federal institutions.

A credit union may be sponsored by the company (particularly when the union is new and struggling for a foothold) or solely by the employees. All credit unions, however, must operate within prescribed fields of memberships (defined in their charters) and under established rules and regulations.

Members of the credit union buy shares (usually at $5 or $10 each), elect officers, manage the affairs and enjoy the ensuing benefits, in particular the ability to borrow money at interest rates that generally are lower than those charged by finance companies or levied on installment accounts.

Typical organization of a credit union is along these lines (for a federally chartered union): A board of directors is elected by the members (usually a five-member board); it must meet once a month. A credit committee (usually having three members) is also elected. This committee reviews and passes on all loan applications. A supervisory committee is appointed by the board of directors. This committee is required to make a comprehensive annual audit and a semi-annual audit of the treasurer's books and records. In addition the supervisory committee must verify members' accounts with the treasurer's records at least once every two years.

Officers of the credit union are elected by the board of directors. Only the treasurer may be compensated for his services; other officers serve without compensation. All persons handling funds are bonded.

The advantage for members, besides systematic savings, is the privilege of making loans for approved purposes with a minimum of red tape. After all, a credit committee composed of employees should be familiar with all the other workers and can make an intelligent decision based on the character of the borrower. The loss rate on loans, by the way, is extremely low. Moreover, recent legislation makes it possible for federal credit unions to apply for federal insurance coverage on members' accounts, so members have further protection, just as in a bank.

So far as a company is concerned, a credit union can keep employees out of the hands of loan sharks or finance companies that charge high interest rates, can cut down on garnishments, and can negate the need for a company to make loans to employees. A credit union gives many employees a chance to exercise skills that may not get full scope on the job. Management often is surprised to see the managerial skills demonstrated by its employees in the operation of their own credit union. (Incidentally, credit union membership is not necessarily limited to rank-and-file employees; many members of management are staunch supporters of the company credit union.)

So highly do some companies regard the credit union that they give it substantial support, including providing office space, equipment, and services such as utilities and janitors.

The checklist below gives the essential information about setting up a credit union. Further detailed information can be obtained by writing to CUNA International, Inc., Box 431, Madison, Wisconsin 53701.

FEDERAL CREDIT UNION CHECKLIST

At least seven people must sign incorporating papers.

Papers must be notarized.

Credit union must have at least 100 potential members.

Certificate of incorporation must be presented for approval to a supervising director appointed by the National Credit Union Association.

Upon approval of the charter, a $25 fee is paid.

Each members pays a 25-cent fee.

Records are checked by the federal credit union inspector at the end of each fiscal year.

LEGAL AND TAX SERVICES

The company that wishes to provide legal and/or tax services for its employees must tread carefully. The organization may have excellent professional talent on its staff, but if an employee requests and receives advice that does not work out in his favor, he may well blame the company.

What a company can do is restrict its free legal service to specified cases. For example, employees may be permitted to bring in leases, sales contracts, and the like to get a company lawyer's opinion about whether they are in order or whether they contain pitfalls. Then, if legal service or action is required, the employee will be advised to consult his own attorney.

The legal staff of a company should be knowledgeable about free or low-cost legal services that are available in many communities so that employees can be referred to them when necessary. Likewise, if an employee needs the services of a legal specialist, the company staff should be able to provide sound advice on how to locate and retain one.

Another method of providing legal and/or tax assistance for employees is to do it on a general group basis. For example, a member of the legal staff might address an employee meeting or conduct a seminar-type session on common legal problems involved in buying a house, making a will, obtaining proper insurance coverage, and the like. These sessions can be extremely worthwhile for employees, and yet they avoid the danger of having a company attorney giving legal advice to an individual employee.

Likewise, it frequently proves helpful, around income tax time, to have a company tax expert available to speak to employee groups about tax problems and changes in the law, and to give information about filling out the various forms. This minimizes the hazards inherent in having an employee ask the company tax specialist for advice in his own particular situation—advice that could backfire.

Companies that have relatively unsophisticated work forces may want to make a positive effort, via their legal talent, to educate employees about unethical sales methods and about various fraudulent schemes that can trap the unwary. A company might also forget the hands-off rule if employees are duped by unscrupulous salesmen and end up with defective merchandise—or no merchandise at all—or become the victims of inequitable sales contracts and salary garnishments. Often all that it takes to make an unethical merchant or salesman back off or remedy a situation is a call from the company's attorney. An attorney can also advise an employee on how to seek redress through a complaint to the Better Business Bureau or other reputable trade association, the state attorney general, the Police Department, or the U.S. Post Office, as appropriate.

EMERGENCY LOANS AND WELFARE FUNDS[2]

The availability of bank loans has to a great extent curtailed the need for a company to lend money to employees. Also, where an employee credit union exists, it is relatively easy for an employee to obtain a loan.

Nevertheless, emergency situations do arise in which an employee needs money immediately and cannot obtain it through a bank or credit union. Rather than have an employee go to a finance company and have to pay a high rate of interest or to a loan shark and pay a usurious rate of interest, a company may make loans—or salary advances—available to employees.

An emergency may involve an illness, accident, or death. For example, even though an employee is covered by health insurance, he may find that a hospital requires a cash deposit before it will admit a patient. Ambulance or oxygen services may require immediate cash. An accident or death in the family may give rise to any number of situations in which cash is required immediately and the employee literally has no time in which to apply for a bank or credit union loan, or he may already have received a loan up to the limit and be unable to take out another loan.

Another circumstance that makes employee loans desirable in the case of an employee who has suffered a loss through a catastrophe such as fire or theft. For example, an employee may cash her paycheck and then have her pocketbook stolen. If she has no savings account and no checking account—and faces a weekend with no cash—a company loan can tide her over.

An employee may come home from work to find that his apartment has been burglarized. In urban areas, these robberies may leave an employee bereft of major appliances such as TV sets, stereo equipment, and such items as cameras, jewelry and clothing—anything that can be sold quickly or pawned—and even the furniture and other possessions may be ruined by vandals. If the employee is still paying off a loan that he made to buy his appliances or if he is still paying for them on the installment plan, his loss is double. A company loan, interest-free, can be a lifesaver.

Similarly, an employee whose home has gone up in smoke may need cash to assist him until the insurance claims are settled and paid for.

A company loan, interest-free, can protect an employee from disaster. Arrangements can be made to have the employee repay the loan through salary deductions. Moreover, unlike a bank or finance firm, the company can delay repayment until the employee has had a chance to get back on his feet.

Should a company decide to make interest-free loans available to help employees meet emergencies, it should establish broad general guidelines for the members of management who will have the authority to recommend or approve loans and to

[2] This section is concerned only with emergency loans, not with formal loan plans under which employees are lent money to purchase homes, finance home improvements, or pay for college tuition for their children.

arrange for repayment. Usually, it is wiser to make loan determinations on an individual basis rather than to attempt to cover all contingencies with detailed rules.

Welfare Funds

At some organizations, the whole issue of loans to aid employees is handled through a welfare fund. The fund may be sponsored and underwritten by the company or it may rely entirely on sums raised by employees through bridge and theater parties, entertainments, etc. One organization, which has food vending machines at various locations, contributes the profits from vending machines to the employee welfare fund.

These funds generally are administered by an employee committee. Cases are handled on an individual basis, and confidentiality is respected. One advantage of a welfare fund is that the committee may decide whether to grant a loan, which must be repaid, or whether, in view of the employee's situation, to make an outright grant which need not be repaid.

DISCOUNT BUYING PLANS [8]

Everyone loves a bargain, and discount plans of one kind or another often are made available to employees and are viewed by them as a distinct benefit. At present, three kinds of plans are in use:

1. Sales of company products or services at a discount
2. Sales of other products or services at a discount
3. Discount buying plans or services (including group travel plans)

Company Products or Services

If a company manufactures a product or provides a service that employees can utilize, it usually enables them to make purchases or use the service. Common examples are the airlines, which have travel plans for their employees' use, and the automobile companies, which have purchase plans.

Manufacturing companies may sell seconds, irregulars, or obsolete, discontinued, or surplus merchandise to their employees. Selling imperfect items to employees, may impress the employees with the company policy that only first-rate products ever are sold to the general public. Also, selling imperfect or discontinued items provides a practical and logical way for companies to dispose of the merchandise and also give their employees a benefit.

Other organizations sell only first-quality merchandise to their people. They comment that the word-of-mouth advertising of employees really pays off; also, where the product is new, the feedback from employees can be most helpful.

Eligibility

At most companies, only current employees are eligible to take advantage of this kind of discount buying (the privilege usually is extended to retired employees too). Some firms report that they permit widows of employees to participate — that is, until they remarry. Others restrict the privilege to permanent staff members. Temporary or part-time employees are not eligible. Employees should have a means of identification to indicate that they are entitled to the buying privilege.

The Price Tag

No general rule can be cited about how items are priced. To some extent, the cost to employees depends on the kind of item sold and the company's marketing practices.   Various pricing plans include selling at cost, below cost, at the wholesale price, at the distributor's price, or at any percentage or amount below these levels, or at a percentage below the retail price.

Frequency of Purchase

Another consideration is: How often shall the employee be permitted to make a purchase?   The kind of product or service influences this determination.   When a company manufactures such products as TV sets, it may well restrict employee purchases on the theory that any employee who wants to buy a number of sets must be running his own little business on the side.   For this reason, some companies state how often a particular product may be purchased or allow additional purchases only at certain times of the year—Christmas, for example—or for special occasions—wedding gifts, anniversary presents, etc.   Sometimes companies require the employee to sign an agreement or statement that the product is for personal use.

Where the company product is a relatively low-cost consumer item, no restrictions ordinarily are imposed.

Payment and Pickup

Usually the employee pays cash for his purchases.   However, when the expenditure is a major one, companies generally arrange for payment via payroll deductions. Similarly, the responsibility for arranging to transport a large item is the employee's. In some instances, however, when the employee makes the purchase through a dealer or distributor, delivery is made at a nominal cost.

Sales of Other Products

Where a company sells items other than those it manufactures itself, the products tend to be limited to such merchandise as safety equipment, articles made from company products, vitamins, special items at Easter or Christmas, and so forth. A common service provided is ticket service—tickets to the circus, athletic events, fairs, shows, and other special events.   Usually the company buys a block of tickets at a low price and makes them available, at cost, to employees.   Producers of these entertainments believe that the free advertising via word of mouth is worth the reduction in price to the company.

Where and When

A factor to take into account is the location of the company "store" and the hours at which employees will be permitted to make purchases.   A frequent choice of location is a display area in the company cafeteria or lounge.   Other companies have more elaborate arrangements and actually set aside space for a store.   Some companies keep the "store" open only during working hours; others will have it open even on Saturday or holidays.   Administrative responsibility varies—the personnel department or the purchasing department, for example, may carry on this activity.   Any company that undertakes a sales operation, however, must be prepared to provide staff to handle the transactions.

Discount Buying Plans

A company benefit that has come into prominence in recent years is the provision of an outside discount buying service.   This relieves the company of a considerable amount of work and responsibility and provides employees with a wide variety of merchandise that they can purchase at substantial savings—ranging from automobiles to electric toasters.

The discount service may consist of a store or group of stores that will provide worthwhile discounts on purchases by employees. Or the buying service may simply provide the employees with a list of stores and dealers in specified localities that will, upon proper identification, give the employee a substantial discount on brand name merchandise.

The prime consideration for a company in arranging for a discount buying service is to select a reputable organization, one that will supply dealers and stores in locations convenient for employees and that will also guarantee that the dealers and stores will make refunds and exchanges when necessary. The best way to choose a buying service is to ask. Ask other companies what buying service, if any, they use and what their experience has been. Frequently, a buying service will contact your company. Ask for names of other companies that it serves and check them out to see if they are satisfied with what it provides. Although regular discount stores and chains are to be found almost everywhere, a discount buying service should provide even more savings, especially on major purchases such as furniture and appliances. Employees ordinarily appreciate having this particular benefit made available, especially if the company is located far from a shopping area.

In recent years, another discount service has proved popular with employees. This is the travel plan. Travel agencies and airlines can and do make special trips and tours available to employee groups at rates lower than what an individual must pay. As in the case of the discount buying service, the best way to check on quality of the packaged tours and the service is to ask other companies that are already offering such plans to the employees what service they utilize and how the tours have been working out.

PARKING FACILITIES [10]

A company located in an urban area usually has one advantage over its rural neighbors: its employees can use public transportation, and parking facilities may not be needed. Nevertheless, some companies located in buildings with garages pay for parking space for the cars of a limited number of staff members, usually officers of the company or top management, and for visitors' cars. Where a building has no garage, the company may arrange with a nearby parking lot or garage to provide space for a stated number of company cars. Frequently, the company will agree to pay for parking, but only for weekday use, not for weekends.

In areas where public transportation is not available or is inadequate, a company must provide parking space for its employees. Here are the major points to consider:

Number of Cars

A questionnaire to employees will help determine the number of cars to be accommodated. Reminder: Where there are multiple shift operations, accommodations must take each shift into consideration. Also, it is a good idea to find out whether the cars are compacts or standard models. Space planners require this information.

Amount of Space

When the company planners know how many cars to provide for, they can figure out the space requirements to fit current needs, to accommodate visitors, and to anticipate future expansion.

Kind of Space

To a great extent, only the company with enough space to expand operations or the company planning a new facility has much choice about the kind of parking facilities it will provide—open-air lot, underground garage, rooftop parking, or any combination of these. An already established company may have no space available, and it may have to lease or purchase a lot or garage. (Although space in parking lots generally is provided free of charge, a company may require that a nominal fee be paid for special parking facilities, such as in a garage.)

Surface; Arrangement of Space; Entrance and Exit

Engineering advice and assistance is needed for the physical layout of the parking facility.[3] Expert counsel will cover such items as the kind of surface, the advantages and disadvantages of various materials, the parking space arrangement, entry to and exit from the facility, whether traffic signals are necessary, and safety of vehicles and pedestrians.

In arranging parking space, for example, the car models help determine the amount of space. A compact car needs space about 7 by 14 feet; a standard car needs at least 8 by 18 feet. Engineers will recommend whether parking should be straight, at an angle, etc. Likewise, they will recommend the means of entry to and exit from the facility, and decide whether local authorities should be contacted about traffic signals (which is essential when the facility is on a busy highway).

Safety and Security

Obvious requirements for a parking facility are that both people and automobiles be protected and that unauthorized persons be prevented from entering or using the lot or the garage. Fences, gates, and proper lighting will contribute to safety. In addition, guards or attendants may be required to protect the property against thieves and vandals and to protect employees from personal injury. Another safety consideration is to provide adequate walkways or paths for employees going to and from their cars.

Identification

To prevent unauthorized persons from using the company parking facility, employees may be given seals to affix to their cars or identification cards to show. (These may be reissued each year as an additional security device.) Needless to say, all means of identification should be carefully accounted for, and employees should be required to return them upon resignation or dismissal.

Reserved Space

At some companies, each employee is given a specific parking space; at other organizations, it is impractical or unnecessary to do this. However, it is common practice to provide reserved space for certain members of the staff, such as officers or top management. The specific list of individuals given reserved parking privileges is up to the company to decide.

Rules and Regulations

The rules governing use of a company parking facility should be publicized. The best method for assuring that the rules be taken seriously and observed is to pro-

[3] Information can be obtained from the Institute of Traffic Engineering, 2029 K Street, N.W., Washington, D.C.

vide for disciplining employees who violate them. Violators of these regulations should be subject to discipline just as they would be for infraction of any other company rule.

DAY-CARE CENTERS

As more mothers become working mothers, interest in day-care facilities for preschool children increases, even in industry. Companies where working women make up a substantial portion of the work force know that mothers will have attendance problems because of their obligations to the children. Even when women work part-time, they may have child-care problems.

As this is written, there are about 11.6 million working mothers. About four million of these mothers have children under six years old. Current social trends indicate that the percentage of women in the work force will grow, and that the number of working mothers with preschool children will increase accordingly. Since industry is dependent upon the skills of women as well as men, and since women have become much more articulate about their desire to hold jobs, the day-care center as an employer-provided benefit will gain acceptance.

In urban centers, the company day-care center may not be a necessity and may not become a widespread service. Working mothers will tend to prefer community or neighborhood centers, since it is scarcely desirable to subject young children to the discomfort and the vicissitudes of rail, subway, or bus travel during weekday rush hours. Companies may, in the interests of their women employees, consider furnishing financial support to day-care centers in communities from which they draw employees. A company can help to sponsor a center, can provide the funds needed to establish a center, or can agree to provide a specific amount of financial support at regular intervals to enable a center to maintain itself and so provide facilities for the children of working mothers. At present, some government funds are available for centers, but the sums are inadequate even for current needs, the number of day-care centers is insufficient, and the prospect is that the demand for these facilities will consistently outstrip the supply. Companies that require women workers may find it practical to support government and local movements towards day-care facilities.

In other areas, such as towns and cities where women can walk or drive to work, it can be a distinct advantage for the company to provide its own day-care center for preschool children.

Establishing a day-care center requires a suitable location, proper equipment, a qualified staff, and strict compliance with the local laws governing such facilities.

Licensing

Usually, a licensing procedure covers day-care centers and nursery schools. The first step is to find out precisely what the local law requires, what agency or bureau is involved, what the standards and the conditions are for a center — space, equipment, safety and sanitation measures, staffing, insurance, and so on. Once these basic requirements are satisfied, the company can take an additional step and add what is desirable to what is absolutely essential.

Eligibility of Children

Another consideration is the age of the children who will be accepted. Will infants be accepted or only children of nursery school age? The age standard will help determine staffing. If infants are cared for, the services of a registered nurse or a licensed practical nurse will undoubtedly be necessary.

Custody or Learning Experience

Another decision is whether the children will receive only custodial care—be kept safe and happy—or whether they will also be given a learning experience, as in nursery schools or kindergartens where toddlers are prepared for grade school. The current trend is to provide a genuine preschool learning experience.

Staffing

Staffing, of course, depends on the age of the children and the kind of care they will be given. At a minimum, the services of a licensed teacher to direct staff effort are required. Although additional full-time staff members are necessary, assistants can include young men and women who are majoring in education or an allied field (child psychology, for instance) and who would welcome part-time employment. Retired employees, both men and women, who enjoy children might like to supplement their pensions by working part-time as aides in their company's day-care center. Wives of employees can provide another source of nonprofessional staff members, and in some cases, wives who have been licensed teachers might wish to return to part-time work.

Food Service

In addition to providing play and educational experiences for the youngsters, the company must feed them. Snacks and lunch must be provided. The company with a food service must prepare to accommodate children's needs; a dietician or nutrition specialist may be needed.

Some organizations find it helpful to permit the working mothers to lunch with their children. This can be a considerable aid to the staff, and mothers usually appreciate this arrangement.

Health

An important consideration in child care is the availability of medical attention. The licensing requirements may spell this out in detail, but in any event, a company should provide for this contingency. Whenever a group of children are together, the possibility of an outbreak or spread of contagious disease exists. The day-care facility should have provisions for dealing with situations where Susie is suspected of having the mumps or Billy seems to have contracted measles. The agreement with the mothers should specify the procedure that will be followed if a child is ill and must be referred for treatment or taken home.

Finally, the company and the mothers should come to an agreement on visiting privileges. Ordinarily, having mothers drop in anytime, during their coffee breaks, for instance, tends to be disruptive. It is more orderly and makes more sense to permit the mothers to visit only during lunch hours or other specified times.

REFERENCES

[1] Calhoon, Richard P.: *Personnel Management and Supervision*, Appleton-Century-Crofts, New York, 1967.
[2] Ferguson, C. A., J. E. Fersing, A. T. Allen, N. P. Baugh, G. A. Gilmore, J. W. Humphrey, F. E. McConnell, J. W. Mitchell, J. W. Sauer, and F. J. Scott: *The Legacy of Neglect*, Industrial Mental Health Associates, Fort Worth, Tex., 1965.
[3] Jucius, Michael: *Personnel Management*, 5th ed., Irwin, Homewood, Ill., 1963.
[4] Levinson, H., C. R. Price, K. J. Munden, H. J. Mandl, and C. M. Solley: *Men, Management and Mental Health*, Harvard University Press, Cambridge, Mass., 1963.
[5] McLean, Alan, "Occupational Mental Health," *American Journal of Psychiatry*, March, 1966.

[6] McLean, Alan (ed.): *To Work Is Human*, Macmillan, New York, 1967.

[7] National Credit Union Administration, *Annual Report of the Federal Credit Union*, Washington, D. C., 1969.

[8] National Industrial Conference Board: *Discount Privileges for Employees*, Studies in Personnel Policy, no. 207, New York, 1967.

[9] National Industrial Conference Board: *Employee Tuition-aid Plans*, Studies in Personnel Policy, no. 221, New York, 1970.

[10] National Industrial Conference Board: "Handling Employee Parking Problems," *Management Record*, New York, June, 1961.

[11] National Industrial Conference Board: "Loans to Employees—When and How," *Conference Board Record*, New York, June, 1965.

[12] National Industrial Conference Board: "When an Employee Dies," *Management Record*, New York, February, 1961.

[13] Yoder, O.: Personnel Principles and Policies, 2d ed., Prentice-Hall, Inc., Englewood Cliffs, N.J., 1959.

[14] Yoder, Dale, H. G. Heneman, Jr., John Turnbull, and C. Harold Stone: *Handbook of Personnel Management and Labor Relations*, McGraw-Hill Book Company, New York, 1958.

chapter 48

Employee Safety

JAMES E. GARDNER   *Training Manager, Fieldcrest Mills, Inc., Eden, North Carolina*

Safety men who take an objective look at where we stand currently in our accident prevention efforts will recognize the inappropriateness of complacency and will see the need for finding better solutions for persisting old problems and new answers for the emerging new problems.

To an appreciable extent, the safety movement is at a crossroad. The earlier optimistic view, as expressed by Heinrich in 1959, that accident prevention has progressed to "an effective, practical, scientific approach" [1], has been confirmed in only a limited way by measurable results. We have moved forward, to be sure, but that movement in recent years has not been fast enough or far enough and certainly has not reached the point where we are prepared to face the formidable new challenges of the 1970s.

Howard Pyle, President of the National Safety Council, stated flatly in June of 1970 that "for ten years there has been little or no improvement in occupational accident rates" [2]. Consequently, he announced a new NSC campaign, entitled "Zero In on Safety" and designed to provide motivational and promotional help which, it is hoped, will contribute to a resurgence of progress. The statistics for 1969 give support to Pyle's statement and to his plea for stronger countermeasures. Work accidents resulted in 14,200 deaths in 1969, representing a decrease of 100 (a drop of only 1 percent) from the 1968 total. For the sixth consecutive year we experienced an increase in the all-industry frequency rate; this time it was a 10 percent rise. Severity declined by 4 percent. (For comparable employers, those reporting in both 1968 and 1969, the frequency rate rose by 3 percent and the severity rate remained virtually unchanged [3].)

The federal government's record is equally unimpressive. Its "Mission Safety-70" program set as its objective a 30 percent decrease in accident frequency among federal employees in the five-year period ending in 1969; it achieved a drop of about 10 percent [4].

Assuming that the figures reflect more than a tightening of reporting requirements and an improvement in the reporting of accidents (which may indeed exert some influence), why has recent progress been slow? Pyle attributes the lessened pace to "a failure to stay ahead of new demands" represented by increased production, a shrinkage in the supply of trained workers and supervisors, and the new materials and more highly sophisticated manufacturing techniques involved in the making of new products. Other safety professionals point to employees' lack of self-discipline, personal responsibility, and respect for the leadership of supervisors; the ambiguous position of safety in the organizational structure; labor shortages and the resultant lowering of hiring standards; the use of supervisors untrained in safety; technological changes; and heavier production demands (and light emphasis on safety) [5]. One may also speculate that part of the answer is that we do not know enough about accident causation. Perhaps the benefits we have reaped in the past have come largely through the establishment of organizations and procedures for combating accidents and through the promotion of safety awareness. These processes have apparently brought results, and we should continue to strengthen them; but in the absence of a strong base of accident-causation knowledge, they may have moved us to a stage of diminishing returns.

Research in industrial safety has not been strong in terms of the number of studies, adequacies of samples, or experimental design.

Ironically, at a time when our success in the prevention of accidents is being seriously questioned and we are critically examining the effectiveness of our measures in this sizable but limited endeavour, we are faced with even broader problems; and safety men are confronted with an accompanying increase in responsibility and with the need for wider professional skill. Specifically, accident hazards from relatively new and somewhat esoteric sources (radiation and laser) are progressively demanding more attention in industry, new chemical substances are being used or processed in greater numbers, and the work force is changing. Moreover, in a significant development in social consciousness, the government (federal and state) is evincing a growing concern for the general well-being of employees at work, for their protection against diseases as well as injuries, for their protection against harmful effects of the work environment—as evidenced by the 1969 amendment, dealing with hearing protection, to the Walsh-Healey Public Contracts Act.

While complacency is hardly the sentiment a safety man can confidently carry into the new decade, he is certainly not without resources. As Seaton, Stack, and Loft remind us, "Out of the accumulation of reasoning, experience, and evidence, certain facts and opinions have filtered down" and can serve as useful guides for our safety efforts [6]. Among these, Seaton cites the need for investigations of any accident for determination of causes (he sees the inevitable involvement of human factors in causation) and the profit in studying "environmental conditions that are questionable" and "human conditions that are questionable." We have learned a great deal about protective equipment and machine guarding, about safety promotion and the maintenance of employee interest in safety. We have developed procedures for making safety inspections and for investigating and reporting accidents. We are learning to keep the sort of score that validly measures performance. We are moving toward a more realistic concept of safety training and are beginning to get a sighting on that most elusive of targets, safety motivation.

The challenge of the seventies is not to begin anew but to improve on what we already know; to strive for new discoveries (particularly in regard to accident causation); to so enlarge our professional competence as to enable us to cope with the growing dimensions and responsibilities of the safety job; and to learn to live with a certain amount of frustration since chance and unpredictability, in spite of our best efforts, cannot be entirely eliminated from our lives—on the job or off.

THE SAFETY JOB

One need only review a comprehensive list of functions and responsibilities of an industrial safety job to appreciate its size and complexity and, in the light of new developments and requirements, to envision the probable reshaping—in terms of expanded activities and new directions—which the job will undergo.

The broad functions of the professional safety position are seen by the American Society of Safety Engineers as the following:

1. Identification and appraisal of accident and loss-producing conditions and practices, and evaluation of the severity of the accident problems;
2. Development of accident prevention and loss-control methods, procedures, and programs;
3. Communication of accident and loss-control information to those directly involved; and
4. Measurement and evaluation of the effectiveness of the accident and loss-control system, and the modifications needed to achieve optimum results [7].

Simonds and Grimaldi [8] have provided a summary (cited here with slight modifications) of the work of a safety department which serves to translate safety responsibilities into terms of job duties: developing and administering the company safety program, making inspections for unsafe conditions or practices, investigating accidents, seeing that corrective action is taken, maintaining and analyzing accident records, preparing reports, making hygiene studies, acting as adviser to management on safety matters, publicizing safety materials, supervising the procurement and distribution of personal protective equipment, checking on company compliance with safety regulations (federal, state, and local), acting as executive secretary of major safety committees, checking on or helping in safety aspects of training. Other functions, depending on the assignments in the particular company, may also fall within the safety man's jurisdiction: first-aid provisions, administration of workmen's compensation insurance, fire prevention and other plant security measures, promotion of off-the-job safety.

To carry out his responsibilities, the safety director serves almost invariably in a staff capacity and reports typically (though not in the majority of cases) to the director of industrial relations. Many safety men regard this position in the corporate structure as an uncomfortable one and not conducive to maximum effectiveness, and would prefer to report to a line executive such as production manager or works manager.

There is a merit on both sides of the argument. The industrial relations director, if he is skilled, can provide the coordination required for effective joint activity among the safety director and other members of the personnel department (in the medical, benefits, and training sections, for example) involved directly or peripherally in safety matters. The production executive has the advantage of direct authority, with its power of enforcement, over the line supervisors who must carry out the safety programs. The case for reporting to a line executive can be a strong one, but only if the executive has a genuine concern for employee safety. Otherwise safety is likely to be neglected when its economic advantages are outweighed by the economic gain possible through higher production. Safety can have monetary value, but it cannot compete with production goals on an economic basis alone.

Whatever reporting relationship emerges, the safety man will continue to function in a staff capacity with its limitation on his power to initiate or carry out a program or phases of it on his own authority. The safety man, like other staff men, will grouse about the operating peoples' failure to carry out his recommendations and will express, at times of frustration, the wish to compel action. Actually, he is in a somewhat special position, not having line authority, to be sure, but not being as helpless to enforce action as staff members in other departments. Policy in many instances will give him power, along with the unique and often fearful consequences of ignoring safety policy. Even without specific policy statements, certain of the safety director's recommendations carry weight by their very nature. These are recommendations arising from inspections and relating to hazardous machinery or materials and imminent danger to employees. Again, the possible consequences of ignoring such warnings exerts a strong influence on supervisory action. In particularly hazardous operations, there is little question about it; the safety director does speak with the voice of authority. He is given the power in some companies to delay or stop operations.

Finally, as the safety function becomes more complex and specialized, the obvious need for expertness somewhere in the organization provides the safety man with the opportunity to wield greater influence. As the line supervisor comes to see that common sense is not an adequate answer to his mounting safety and health problems, he tends to place increased reliance on the expert. The safety director and his staff can become a source of such unique skills and knowledge as to assume the role of true experts—a role which has "clout" no matter what the organizational chart says.

As all staff men come to know, the establishment of satisfactory personal and working relationships with line and staff personnel, involving mutual respect and confidence, is the key to accomplishment within any organizational structure. It pays to work on the building and maintenance of such relationships rather than to fret about structure.

The question arises: How does the safety director acquire the expertness which he needs in order to carry out his current and expanding functions? This is a question arousing serious discussion among safety men and organizations, notably in the American Society of Safety Engineers. Obviously the day is long past—if it ever existed—when a bright, personable young fellow with no relevant background of experience or education could qualify, after a few quick courses, as a competent safety man. In varying degrees a safety man must know his way around in mechanical engineering, industrial engineering, chemistry, psychology, training, and certain aspects of medicine, accounting, and law.

If the safety functions are to reside in a safety director or safety department (which appears preferable to dispersing them), the appropriate degree of competence in this broad array of disciplines must be developed in safety men. One proposal is for a four-year college curriculum leading to a B.S. degree in industrial safety and graduate degrees at the master's level in industrial safety, industrial hygiene, systems safety engineering, and human factors engineering [9]. Some movement has already occurred, of course, in the development of college courses and degree programs. The 1969 survey of the American Society of Safety Engineers, involving contacts with 1,200 colleges, revealed that five schools offered bachelor's degrees and fourteen offered graduate degrees in some aspect of safety [10]. A total of 975 courses were listed in eleven major subject areas. More than half of the courses were in safety education and driver or traffic safety.

The unquestioned need for a strengthened program to train safety professionals will probably result in a continuing increase in course offerings and in further attempts to construct comprehensive curricula from such courses.

THE SAFETY DEPARTMENT

A safety "department" may include anything from a personnel man or line supervisor handling safety as a part-time responsibility and relying upon the insurance carrier's safety man for expertise, to a safety director supervising a staff of assistants or inspectors and exerting control (usually indirect) in safety matters over hundreds of line supervisors and a network of committees. The size of the staff will depend upon the size and structure of the company (number and types of units, whether centralized geographically or dispersed, etc.), the type of business, and the extent of the commitment the company is willing to make to safety in terms of financial expenditures. No rule of thumb can be relied upon, although there is some support for the view that a full-time safety man is justified when a company employs as many as 2,000.

Since the safety man, by rather common agreement, works primarily through the line supervisors, the building of an empire within the safety department itself is a somewhat dubious procedure. The safety director does need to establish the means, through committees and procedures, by which the line personnel can perform certain activities which they are in the best position to perform. By organizational and administrative methods and the establishment of relationships, the safety man multiplies his effect. On the other hand, the safety staff must include enough members to provide line supervisors adequately with guidance, training, and monitoring in those aspects of safety which the line organization best performs and to take direct steps in those aspects which only a safety professional can handle competently, as, for example, the determination of hazards in new equipment and new material, the conducting of genuinely comprehensive inspections and investigations, the designation and purchase of appropriate gear, the safeguarding of machinery, the updating of programs to comply with new statutory requirements.

Safety committees, which often represent the safety "intrastructure" in an industrial plant, come in a variety of shapes; and a major problem is to sort out the various safety functions which can be performed satisfactorily by committees and allocate them accordingly. Obviously, the consideration of corporate safety policy is properly the concern of an executive committee. A review of the safety indices relating to large units—plants or the entire company—and discussion of proposals for company-wide programs are likewise appropriate functions of the "top" or "central" committee. Supervisors, whether under the guise of a committee or not, will periodically get together to review safety performance in the plant or department, report on actual accidents and accident investigations, discuss corrective measures, review progress (or lack of it) in ongoing programs, submit to or engage actively in "educational" presentations, and resolve to improve. Safety committees on which employees hold membership may assist with periodic departmental or plant inspections and with accident investigations, may review reports of injuries, may make recommendations relating to physical hazards and unsafe work procedures or job methods, and may assist with the publicizing and promotion of programs among employees. In some companies, the union is represented on safety committees.

Many companies report satisfactory experience with committees. Committees which include employees have often served as a link of communication with employees generally and as a means of involving employees to a larger extent in safety matters and of maintaining employee interest. They are often a fertile source of accident-prevention ideas because of the employees' continuing contacts with the equipment and their familiarity with its operation and "peculiarities." Committees, however, do present certain difficulties and do require tactful handling. For example, the supervisor may tend to turn over his safety responsibility to his committee; but unfortunately, committees cannot be held accountable. In addition, care must be taken to use the committee in functions it can perform with competent knowledge. When the cause of the accident is complex and particularly when personal factors are involved, a committee is likely to arrive at naïve and unfounded conclusions.

Without disparaging the empirical basis for evaluation of employee safety committees, one would feel more comfortable about advocating them if their motivational value were confirmed by research investigation; they have largely escaped research scrutiny. The use of safety awards—another popular motivational tool—has been subjected to a recent study in a large corporation. No significant differences were found in costs or in frequency and severity rates between plants with award plans and those without, although fewer cases were referred to doctors in the former [11].

Companies with widely dispersed manufacturing units, such as the so-called conglomerates, present a special problem in safety organization and administration. The difficult objective is to administer corporate policy and exercise control from a central source (and give the professional guidance that should go along with it) while at the same time providing for prompt attention to local situations [12]. The safety organization of one conglomerate includes a safety office in the corporate headquarters and safety directors in each division. The latter have some autonomy over local programs, but the corporate office sets broad goals, recommends means of achievement, requires extensive reporting, controls training materials and safety analyses, and holds annual planning seminars.

PREVENTIVE AND CONTROL MEASURES

Preventive measures can be taken against the accident itself or against injurious consequences of the accident.

The examination of new equipment and machinery and materials prior to putting them into production, the ongoing inspection of machinery and equipment for unsafe conditions, and the observation of employees to detect unsafe behavior are measures basically intended to anticipate possible occurrences of a type which could cause damage or injury and intended, in effect, to prevent the untoward event from happening.

This is a tall order. It is one to which the practitioners of "systems safety" in our space program have been addressing themselves. The purpose of systems safety is to take action before an accident occurs through a "systematic approach to identify and correct hazards continually from the early conceptual stage of a project right on through detailed design and operation" [13].

The concept of system as a man-machine combination has been a useful engineering approach for a number of years. And man-machine research studies have produced findings conducive to safety as well as efficiency in regard to the perceptibility or readability of visual displays (dials, control panels, signals, scales), direction of movement of control handles or rotational direction of knobs in relation to the machine or vehicular movement being controlled (to avoid conflict with the operator's expectation or normal directional orientation), etc.

The questions to be raised in the design of the system or its modifications relate to the performance of the machine and the requirements which the operation of the machine places on the individual. In the latter aspect, the system should not place a demand on an operator—should not demand certain perceptions, for example—which he cannot fulfill. Although care must be taken, in the use of this approach, to give enough weight to differences in capabilities among individuals and to variations in an individual's performance from one time to another, it does encourage, in its application to safety, a broad look at preventive measures encompassing various causative factors rather than a view of factors in isolation.

For purpose of safety analysis, emphasis is being increasingly placed on the environment as a major component along with the machinery (or equipment) and operator. The interaction of machine and operator is an obvious source of hazards, but the less apparent effects of temperature, humidity, air pollutants, and noise on the equipment or employee must be taken into account in analyzing hazards.

As expressed in "systems terms" by Levens, the components are "in continuous, dynamic interaction with one another within some predetermined limits of variability. If these limits of variability are exceeded, then the system may be incapable of operating or become damaged. It may deteriorate too fast. It may perform its mission poorly, or someone may get hurt" [14].

The characteristics of man require analysis in relation to assigned tasks in order to predict the occurrence of stress leading to human error. These characteristics include physical dimensions, perceptual and motor capabilities, learning capability, sensitivities, and variability. The possible human errors themselves need to be defined.

The best way to deal with possible stress and malfunctioning within the system is through adequate testing prior to placing the system into operational use. Where pretesting is impossible or excessively costly, an intensive analysis may serve to uncover hazards. The analysis may proceed from element to undesirable outcome or, perhaps more effectively (if the experience of the aerospace industry is borne out), from the undesirable outcome to the system elements that may influence or contribute to the unfavorable occurrence—the so-called "fault-tree analysis." If the sources of stress can thus be identified beforehand, then the system can be redesigned to eliminate the stress or to protect against its bad effects.

Also to be taken into account beforehand, as one of the interacting elements in industrial operations, is the material being processed or used in the processing, especially chemicals. Stability, flammability, and toxicity are the three major characteristics to be investigated. Wood has proposed the following framework for analysis of various aspects of these characteristics [15]:

Stability	Flammability	Toxicity
Oxidizers	Flash point	Oral toxicity
Head sensitivity	Ignition temperature	Skin-absorption toxicity
Shock sensitivity	Ignition energy	Skin irritation
Reaction with water	Polymerization tendency	Eye irritation
Corrosiveness	Vapor density	Inhalation toxicity
	Flammable limits	Carcinogenicity

Wood emphasizes the need to know the chemical itself and to think ahead concerning various contingencies—its reaction with other material in the environment, what happens if the electric power fails, etc.

Of course, the search for hazards or "hazard potential" must be a continuing procedure once the equipment is in operation and the material is being processed in the normal manufacturing routine. Whoever does the inspection must be knowledgeable about the processes. A checklist may be helpful in directing his observation, but he should be aware of the full significance of the items, must realize that "static things" in themselves are not hazards (that interactions are required), and that the list is never complete. It is useful to discuss hazards with the employees, particularly the near misses, to increase their insight into the changes that occur, because the hazard usually lies in the unusual occurrences that throw the system out of equilibrium. In his observation of employees he must make sure that his sampling of their behavior is adequate to provide reliable information on performance in the different job tasks so that the various occurrences of interaction with other elements come under scrutiny.

Although the supervisor must be depended upon to do most of the inspecting, it is obvious that he will not be prepared to do the full job. He brings a strong knowledge of the processes into the inspection, but he may not always apply it. He may have developed a perceptual blindness to hazards in his own department. If he has lived with them for a long time he tends to relegate them to the background so that they fail to present the unusual aspects that facilitate perception. And he may simply fail to see what he does not want to see—the conditions requiring action on his part which may be a troublesome addition to the many problems he is already facing. These are common bases for errors or failures in perception, to which a supervisor is certainly not immune. To avoid them or to minimize their effect, it is often helpful (1) to provide the supervisor with a checklist [16] to direct his observations and establish a conscious intent and (2) to help him set up a schedule and routine by which the intent can be carried out in a practical way. In this regard, there is special merit in the use of a knowledgeable committee or supervisors from other departments to help with the inspection; a more comprehensive and objective list of findings may emerge.

Even when a supervisor avoids perceptual pitfalls, he needs training from the safety expert and the help of the expert's own insightful observations. A reasonable distribution of the inspection chores is to depend upon the supervisor, with guidance, to carry out the frequent periodic inspections in his department but to bring the safety man into the act at certain intervals. The type of manufacturing would dictate the optimum schedule.

A few precautions are in order. First, a supervisor should keep an eye out for hazards in his regular routine of supervisory activities day by day rather than restricting his safety observations to the scheduled time of inspections. Second, he should take prompt steps to correct hazard potentials he does uncover, including the unsafe practices of his employees. Finally, the help he gets from the safety professional—in terms of guidance of the supervisor's observations and the safety man's inspections—will not serve him well if the professional takes a simplistic view of what to look for, if he is committed to a narrow definition of unsafe conditions and unsafe acts and does not assign enough importance to interactions and changes.

To assume that all hazards can be eliminated and all events predicted or controlled is unrealistic, of course. Protecting the employee from injury becomes the primary objective of safety efforts when accident potential remains. Machine guards and lockout procedures are useful for this purpose, and provisions for such protective devices fall within the safety man's responsibility. Of major and increasing importance as a protective technique, against threats to employees' health as well as against injuries, is the use of personal equipment and gear. Personal protective equipment comes in a variety of forms and serves numerous purposes:

Head protection, principally with helmets

Eye and face protection, with goggles, face shields, and spectacles

Hearing protection, with muffs and inserts

Respiratory protection, with air-purifying devices such as filter respirators and gas masks and with air-supplying devices:

Hand protection, with gloves

Foot and leg protection, with safety shoes, boots, guards, and leggings

Body protection, with garments such as suits, aprons, jackets, and coveralls

There is the recurring need to update and make specific the standards for protective equipment (a function performed by the American National Standards Institute) and to set new standards applying to new types of hazards, such as for eye protection against laser radiation. To illustrate the effort necessary for establishment of standards, the Z41.1 standard, a general standard primarily for footwear for the purpose of protection of toes, is being supplemented by standards applying to metatarsal protection, conductive and nonconductive shoes, and electrical hazards [17].

In the case of the individual company and its safety man, there are the imposing tasks of deciding (1) what needs exist for personal protective equipment, (2) what are the best kinds for the particular types of hazards and exposure, and (3) how to see that the employees wear the gear.

Hand protection will serve as an illustrative case. Injuries to hands and fingers accounted for one-fourth of all disabling work injuries in 1969. Hand protection is obviously needed in a great many jobs. But an all-purpose glove to provide protection against all types of hazards is not available. Gloves must be chosen to meet the specific need for protection in the particular job. The hands may have contacts with many types of objects or substances and be in proximity to energy sources of different kinds. Does the worker need protection against abrasion, cuts, punctures, heat, electric shock, or what? Does he at the same time, in order to perform the job tasks, need a considerable degree of tactile sensitivity and tightness of grip? The ultimate question needs specific answers: What types of gloves, with what types of coating, are needed for safe and effective performance of the specific job duties? The manufacturers' representatives may help in the analysis of needs, but the final decision about selection and purchase is usually up to the safety professional. He has also another major responsibility: assuring, through line supervision and by means of workable procedures for initiating and maintaining the program, that employees wear the gloves.

ACCIDENT INVESTIGATIONS

Accident investigations, in order to be useful in identifying sources of the specific accident and in the compilation of useful statistical data, should follow a logical procedure and employ a meaningful system for classifying information. The ASI standard 16.2 method for recording accident information directs the inquiry through a series of steps involving various factors in accident occurrence:

1. Nature of injury—the type of physical injury incurred, such as cut, bruise, burn, fracture

2. Part of body—the part of the injured person's body directly affected by the injury

3. Source of injury—the object, substance, exposure, or bodily motion which directly produced or inflicted the injury

4. Accident type—the event which directly resulted in the injury, such as struck against, struck by, caught in, fall, slip, overexertion, contact with extreme temperature, inhalation

5. Hazardous condition—the physical condition or circumstances which permitted or occasioned the occurrence of the accident type

6. Agency of accident—the object, substance, or part of the premises in which the hazardous condition existed

7. Agency of accident part—the specific part of the agency of accident that was hazardous

8. Unsafe act—the violation of a commonly accepted safe procedure which directly permitted or occasioned the occurrence of the accident event [18]

Effective measures of correction can evolve from such investigation, particularly if an unsafe mechanical or physical condition is validly identified as a source of the accident.

Investigations tend to be a weak basis for corrective action when they:

1. Take too limited a view of the environmental and agent factors beyond the

machine itself or superficially conceive the environmental hazards to consist of obvious work-area hazards (such as water on the floor) which can be cured by improved housekeeping. Gibson has proposed the classifying of environmental hazards in terms of the various sorts of physical energies which may be interchanged in an accident: mechanical, thermal, radiant, chemical, and electrical [19]. Such a classification system injects a fresh and clarifying view of accidents into investigative and inspecting procedures which in some firms tend to follow a hackneyed and narrow course.

2. Do not go far enough in tracing the development which culminated in the accident but treat the accident as a "now" event which can be fully explained in terms of what happened at the precise time of the occurrence. Causation is not so simple as to be tied to the time-and-place terms by which we define accidents.

3. Do not come to grips with the unsafe act by neglecting to get behind the employee's inadequate performance to find the basis for his failure. We need, then, to take a searching look at the employee and to reject as causes the simple description of the act (such as failure to perceive, carelessness, inattentiveness, haste) immediately related to the injury. We need to consider attitude and motivation, social and cultural factors, training, and physiological factors. If the search for sources leads to the host, causation becomes much more difficult to pin down and will require more than the amateurish efforts of work committees and untrained supervisors.

Gardner has indicated the necessity for supervisors to look behind the employee's unsafe act to determine whether lack of training or misdirected motivation or a conflict in motives (reflected in the sacrifice of safety to satisfy other needs) may be an underlying cause [20]. But he has emphasized the importance of adequate safety motivation and training for the supervisors themselves if they are to perform such a function effectively. Bird and Schlesinger have advocated an emphasis on safe acts, citing the advantages of positively reinforcing safe acts (rather than punishing unsafe acts) by increasing the satisfactions associated with working safely [21].

Since the quest for causes is such a difficult one, it would appear unwise to allow the investigative function to reside exclusively within the production department or to foreclose further investigation beyond the first brush. The supervisor is usually required by his employer to complete an accident analysis form promptly if an injury occurs; in this process he usually secures a statement from the injured employee (if practical) and information from witnesses. In addition, his report usually requires him to draw conclusions about causes and possible preventive measures on the basis of the data he uncovers. In many cases, the result is a superficial analysis and a poorly supported course of action or a course of action aimed strictly at symptoms (such as "Instruct the employee to take more care"). If the safety director accepts the reports at face value and merely serves as a compiler of statistics, the accident investigations are not likely to pay off in improved safety.

The supervisor needs training and help in analyzing accidents. If he must play a primary role in accident investigation, as appears most practical, he must be prepared by the safety professional to assume it. But severe and complex accidents especially require the direct attention of the safety director. And where personal factors are involved, the safety director and line supervisors are well advised to consult with staff members in the organization who are expert in psychological and medical matters.

Close surveillance—including personal investigative actions—of accidents by the safety man has the advantage of placing accident data in the hands of the individual who is in the best position to judge its application in the plant or company to future possible situations involving other individuals with similar characteristics or involving similar machinery and conditions. While a safety man should guard against overgeneralizing the findings from single accidents, he would be remiss in his responsibility if he did not make whatever applications of findings his informed judgment directed. In short, the safety man must do what he can, with the expertness and common sense he possesses, to deal with specific situations as they arise and to absorb and apply what they can teach him, even if the data are somewhat fragmentary. He would be better able to carry out his responsibility, of course, if he could lead from a stronger suit, that is, from well-established research findings on accident causation.

The use of data-processing equipment in the compiling and analysis of accident information, a recent development, has some genuine advantages for large companies in focusing attention quickly on the where, what, and possibly the why of accidents and in providing quick summaries and statistical manipulation of data. A commonplace worth keeping in mind is that the computer does not improve the validity of the basic data; investigations must produce accurate input data. In addition, if the computer is to be used for research purposes, adequate research designs are needed for the selection and handling of data and the interpretation of output. One must be wary of an impressive numerical pursuit of single variables which obscures the dynamics of accident situations and the interplay of factors.

SAFETY TRAINING

Safety training of employees, as it is often conducted, has apparently been more effective in arousing a safety "consciousness" than in teaching safe job skills. If a distinction can be made, we appear to have expended more time and effort on "educating" employees than on "training" them. That is, we have told them about safety but have often failed to incorporate safety as an intrinsic aspect of the method by which they perform their jobs.

DeReamer in 1958 pointed to the necessity for going beyond "mass training" (or a group educational treatment of what the hazards are) to give the employee "personalized" training in identification and avoidance of hazards [22]. He cited earlier studies reported by Fugal in 1950, studies which found that group training is helpful in maintaining employee awareness of safety but does not become effective until the employee knows the hazards of his job and the means of avoiding them.

Gardner more recently has attempted to tie safety securely to job skills by integrating safety with the basic pattern of motions and perceptual feedback in the task analysis for job training and by assuring that the prompting, guidance, and reinforcement are adequate to build the safe pattern into habitual performance and to maintain it [23].

The manager of the National Safety Council's Training Department, L. C. Smith, has advocated a combining of safety training with job training, specifically recommending that "job safety analysis" (a statement of hazards and safe procedures related to job sequence steps) be tied to the four-step Job Instruction Training procedure [24].

Although it is unwise to stint in our efforts to elicit safety awareness, the training of employees in safe job performance is apparently moving toward a closer amalgam with job skills training and toward the accompanying necessity for the use of effective job training arrangements and techniques. In this latter connection, safety and training men would be well advised to look beyond the simplistic approach of JIT and to consider the use of the somewhat more sophisticated techniques now emerging in the training literature. But, at the least, there appears to be agreement among safety men that safety performance of employees does respond to sound training techniques and is not a uniquely untrainable behavior. Strong training efforts in safety will be required in the seventies to meet the needs of the changing work force (especially young employees, minority group members, and women) whose exposure to industrial hazards and whose indoctrination in industrial safety have been minimal.

The safety training of supervisors has in many instances suffered from the same lack of attention to the matter of "doing" as employee training. That is, we have tended to tell supervisors about safety matters over and over again, to "educate" them in safety without developing their safety skills in any organized or systematic way. We have tended to leave the applications up to them. Certainly they need to conduct inspections and investigations and to train and motivate and correct employees, but even in these essential expressions of supervisory responsibility we have often assumed that a periodic film or safety talk would serve.

What do supervisors need to know and do? We need to make an analysis of the safety aspects and requirements of the individual supervisor's job to find out. Some needs are common to all departments; others are peculiar to the department. We must then be as careful in training the supervisor to perform the indicated functions as we are with hourly employees. Prompting, coaching, and reinforcing are pertinent at any level of training.

Again, the importance of safety awareness is not to be minimized. But beyond such awareness, specific and successful activities must evolve; we must take explicit steps to direct and expedite this development.

An overriding objective in supervisory safety training is to convince supervisors that accidents are avoidable to a great extent and that safe behavior in employees is trainable. Such conviction is the necessary foundation for the training of supervisors in specific techniques and approaches.

It is pertinent to remember that the expanding safety and health programs have the effect of enlarging the supervisor's functions as well as those of the safety man himself. Since the safety professional must depend upon line supervision in the execution of programs involving or affecting employees, he needs to expand his training of supervisors to encompass the new programs, to enlarge the understanding and activities and skills of supervisors so that the changes can genuinely take hold where they must—among employees at the workplace.

ACCIDENT RESEARCH

Accident research has not been strong, especially research dealing with industrial accidents—partly because of the nature of the subject (manipulative research in safety presents some obvious problems, for example) and partly because our efforts have been inadequate and fragmentary and lacking in good research design.

In 1955 Larson and others pointed out that the design and conduct of research studies into human causes of industrial accidents must take into account special considerations [25]. In the decade that followed we apparently made little progress in grappling with these considerations [26]. In 1964, Haddon, Suchman, and Klein saw a formidable number of deficiencies in behavioral research in accidents:

1. Lack of hypotheses clearly formulated in a form which permits reasonable proof or disproof.
2. Poorly defined concepts both of causal factors and of the kinds of accidents being studied.
3. Use of second-hand reports and data sources of unknown representativeness, reliability, and validity, which, in addition, often yield samples of inadequate size.
4. Absence of adequate controls for matching accident and nonaccident groups on such crucial variables as degree of exposure and background characteristics.
5. Excessive reliance upon respondents' subjective reports of accident sequences. . . .

6. Insufficient attention to the dynamics—the how and why—of the accident studied. . . .

7. Inadequate statistical methods.

8. Absence of necessary qualifications to findings and overgeneralization of results.

The authors concluded that accident research from the behavioral science point of view "had not come of age" [27].

While such criticism was justified then and is still justified—research has certainly not yet come of age—we are not completely in the dark. As suggested in the excellent Haddon, Suchman, and Klein review itself, the general literature of the behavioral sciences—psychology, sociology, and anthropology—provides us with useful hypotheses for accident research [28]. The conclusions we have reached in regard to motivation, learning, and perception from sound psychological research, moreover, do not become suddenly invalid because we are dealing with industrial safety. The "safety behavior" of employees does not follow a unique set of psychological laws. Nor is it lawless, fortunately. Our general knowledge of human behavior, derived elsewhere, can help us understand safety behavior and can lead us, if only darkly, into the sort of accident research which may give us a greater control over accident events.

In addition, the specific accident research studies recently conducted, although relatively sparse, have not been unrevealing. They have at least discouraged some of our blind-alley pursuits (after proneness characteristics, especially) and have pointed us in new and more hopeful directions. If the reader will excuse an intermixture of hypotheses, findings, and personal speculations, here is at least part of what research has revealed or suggested:

1. To our advantage, we seem to be equipped with certain safeguards against environmental changes, as evidenced by an infant's ability to discriminate between short and great depths and our sensitivity to objects "looming" toward us [29].

2. There are forces on the other side. We have a basic exploratory drive which may expose us to danger. We seem to have a sense of invulnerability ("It can't happen to me") which impersonal statistics cannot dispel and which leaves us unaware of possible dangers and not on the alert to avoid them. And our culture places a value on risk taking, endowing the daredevil with the mantle of the hero. There is a suspicion that the amount of risk taking remains fairly constant no matter what improvements are made in environmental hazards, although a driving study did indicate that the amount of risk taking may be altered by training (the more experienced drivers tended to take less risk) [30]. Much more study needs to be done on risk taking and margin of error.

3. Causation is probably much more complex than our earlier somewhat exclusive preoccupation with unsafe acts and unsafe conditions may have led us to believe. We need to take account of the entire framework—including host, agency, and environment and the interactions and evolving situations among them. And because the host factors especially are so varied, we must be wary of generalizations based on behavioral findings from specific studies, even if the findings are statistically significant.

4. Our tendency in accident investigations to concentrate on what happened at the exact time of the accident, though a necessary investigative procedure and important in compensation matters, may obscure the importance of activity preceding the accident. If our behavioral research is to have the latitude it needs, the accident is better seen in its developmental aspect and the injury as the end of a sequence of behavior.

5. Although there may be differences involving the host between accidents and near accidents (unexpected events not producing injury), the value of studying non-

injury cases appears to be gaining acceptance. The point can be argued that an accident happens if an event is unexpected or unplanned whether an injury occurs or not. The essential mark of an accident, then, is its unexpectedness; the essential problem is our lack of control. If our objective in accident prevention is to increase predictability and control, then near injuries are a legitimate field of study [31]. In addition, the inclusion of such cases enlarges our samples to the point where rigorous statistical procedures make sense, and significant relationships and differences have an opportunity to emerge.

6. There have been studies showing relationships between accident frequency and certain physical, psychological, or psychophysical factors such as reaction time, visual acuity, perception, age, physical impairment, certain diseases, sensorimotor abilities, and intelligence. But to make generalized statements from such findings is a highly questionable practice since such factors do not exert influence in isolation but must be related to specific job demands and conditions and placed in the context of the interactions among host, agent, and environment. Certainly, we must use common sense; we would not hire a blind man as a railroad brakeman.

The search for determinants of accident proneness in personality characteristics has proved somewhat frustrating, although certain states or characteristics have been ascribed to accident-susceptible people in a number of studies. The catalog of such characteristics, taken from Iskrant and Joliet's summary of studies [32], includes egocentricity, impulsiveness, feelings of insecurity, conflict with authority, pessimism, low morale, introversion, aggressiveness, social irresponsibility, emotional instability, fatalism, unstable employment record, negative attitude toward employment, tension, anxiety, unconscious wish for self-injury.

In attempting to associate accident proneness with personality characteristics, we have perhaps placed too much emphasis, in our exploration, on permanent or lasting characteristics. A somewhat more promising view of accident susceptibility —and one which is gaining support—is the view that the susceptible employee is more likely to be the normal individual subjected to temporary emotional disturbances which "may contribute to inattentiveness or poor judgment, thereby causing accidental injury" [33]. Kerr has stated, in this connection, that "What often appears at first to be constitutional accident proneness may be shown very clearly upon more careful examination to be the operation of temporary stress factors" [34]. The adjustment stress theory he suggested holds that liability to accidents is increased by unusual and distracting stress imposed on the individual by internal or external environment.

Our skepticism about accident proneness as a proved and workable basis for accident prevention should not blind us, however, to the importance of psychological factors in accidents nor discourage the continuing search. After citing accident proneness studies, Haddon, Suchman, and Klein hopefully see a positive good emerging:

> The foregoing studies indicate that accident proneness is a psychological abstraction based upon a statistical frequency. As often happens when a statistical distribution is given theoretic significance, the concept quickly assumed much more meaning than was originally intended. The unacceptability of the concept of accident proneness in a technical sense should not, however, be taken to mean that personal factors do not play an important role in accidents. In fact, rejecting the concept of accident proneness, with its implications of a global personality trait, forces one to search for many different psychological factors and their significance in given environmental circumstances [35].

7. Kerr offers the interesting second theory that accidents represent "low-quality" work behavior which can be improved by the sort of rewarding climate which will raise the employee's level of alertness [36]. The suggestion of a tie-in of safety

behavior with other aspects of an employee's job performance is eminently worth further study.

8. The possible social or cultural bases of certain identified personality or attitudinal factors associated with safety need to be taken into account. A simple illustration of such need, evident to all safety men and supervisors, is the obvious unreadiness of naïve work groups, new to the labor market, to face industrial hazards.

The emphasis on behavioral research in this cursory review of accident research and, indeed, the concentration on behavioral factors in much of our accident research should not obscure the importance of research into environmental and engineering factors. Indeed, as Haddon, Suchman, and Klein suggest, these latter factors, because of their greater susceptibility to change, may be the more fruitful subjects of accident research than the psychological [37].

But a nibbling disquiet remains. Even with developing insights, will our research efforts really be sufficiently effective to make drastic cuts in the accidental death and injury list unless we attack on a truly wide front? As operating men in industry, we can engage in our necessarily limited endeavors at finding answers. It would be comforting to know, as we struggle along, that something truly significant was stirring in other quarters. The epidemiologic and interdisciplinary approaches to accident prevention have much to recommend them.

SAFETY EVALUATION

The most commonly used statistics for the evaluation of safety programs are frequency and severity rates. In order to provide a valid comparison with a company's past record, with records of other companies in the same kind of manufacturing, and with records of the industry as a whole, a standard code of charges (the Z16.1 standard) is employed.

Both the frequency and the severity rates give a measure of disabling injuries only. Frequency is concerned with the number of such accidents, severity with days lost. The frequency rate represents the number of disabling accidents per million man-hours worked; severity, the number of days lost per million man-hours worked.

Since actual days lost vary widely from company to company and plant to plant for the same kind of injury and are therefore a shifting basis for comparisons, the Z16.1 code applies fixed charges of days for various types of permanent partial disabilities. (Examples: 100 days for loss of the distal phalange of the index finger, 3,000 days for loss of hand.) There is also a fixed charge, 6,000 days, for permanent total disability or a fatality. The use of actual days lost is restricted to temporary total injuries; these cases are so extremely variable in kind and degree of injury that fixed charges are impractical.

There are also accounting evaluations based on medical costs and compensation claims paid [38]. If a company uses an insurance carrier, a low loss ratio (ratio of payments to premiums), favorable experience ratings, and a downward modification in premiums serve as signs of good safety performance. A self-insuring company can use as indicators of performance: (1) the comparison of actual expenditures from year to year (making proper allocation of unclosed cases carried over) and (2) the comparison between what costs were and what they would have been with a commercial carrier.

Major criticisms of these types of evaluations have been voiced:

1. They do not reflect indirect (uninsured) costs.

2. They are not sensitive or diagnostic enough for accident control purposes.

Uninsured costs—costs not covered by medical and compensation payments—are numerous. As listed by Simonds and Grimaldi [39], they include: (1) cost of wages for working time lost by workers who were not injured, (2) net costs to repair, replace, or straighten up material or equipment that was damaged in an accident, (3) cost of wages paid for working time lost by injured workers, other than workmen's compensation payments, (4) extra costs due to overtime work necessitated by an accident, (5) cost of wages paid supervisors while their time is required for activities necessitated by the accident, (6) wage cost due to decreased output of injured worker after return to work, (7) cost of learning period of new worker, (8) uninsured medical cost borne by the company, (9) cost of time spent by higher supervision and clerical workers on investigations or in the processing of compensation application forms, (10) miscellaneous unusual costs.

Simonds and Grimaldi propose a formula for total costs which takes into account the insurance cost, number of lost-times cases, number of doctors' cases, number of first-aid cases, and number of no-injury cases [40].

Thomas H. Rockwell, in a presentation before the 1969 National Safety Congress, stated, "The present measures of evaluation of accident prevention programs are based on safety performance measures that are vague, unstable, insensitive, and of limited reliability." He proposed an evaluation method combining the critical-incident technique and sampling of behavior and environment [41].

The critical-incident technique, as applied to safety, uncovers unsafe conditions and practices by means of questions addressed to employees, asking them to recall critical incidents that resulted in injury or property damages or could have had such results. A modification of this technique, called incident recall, concentrates on near misses; the supervisor asks a random sample of employees to recall all incidents which could have produced injury or damaged property [42]. Such a technique can serve a dual purpose of auditing unsafe practices and conditions—an evaluative function—and pinpointing potential sources of accidents.

The gross indices of frequency and severity rates, while useful in making comparisons between large manufacturing units and in indicating monthly and yearly trends in such units and as a reporting device for the information of plant managers and company executives, is of limited value as a means of safety control within a production department. Such control is exercised chiefly by the production supervisor, and these large and relatively infrequent indices (usually issued monthly) do not adequately serve to provide him with feedback information on the effectiveness of his own safety-control activities. As measures, they are not immediate or specific enough to reinforce his effective efforts or to redirect his ineffective efforts. They operate largely outside his control. The indices do not tell him specifically what works and what does not. They teach him very little.

Of course, one cannot find fault with the indices for failing to serve a purpose for which they were not intended. The point is that the purpose of reinforcement must be served by some indices or other, and we must find appropriate ones if we are to teach and motivate our supervisors to engage in activities which are likely to pay off. Intermediate measures or indicators more directly under a supervisor's control or ability to influence are often at hand or can be readily devised, such as the number of hazards corrected and unsafe acts uncovered and dealt with, the extent to which safety training is given to employees, the findings from audits and surveys of departmental adherence to established safety policies or programs, and, as discussed above, the results from employee interviews in which accidents or near accidents are recalled.

Indices of safety performance, even if focused on the supervisor's operation, still need to be carefully chosen. For example, the number of first-aid cases has often been proposed as an index and is certainly a direct count of a type of safety activity. But there are serious objections to its use as an indicator. First of all, the record is hard to interpret. Is an increased number good or bad? In addition, there is apprehension, perhaps justifiable in the light of our experience, that in an effort to avoid worsening the record the supervisor will not encourage employees to seek first aid and the employees themselves may be reluctant to seek it. In regard to more serious injuries, stories of extreme and often absurd efforts to minimize time lost have been making the rounds for years, and instances are still being cited in which the application of the current Z16.1 standard has been less than strict [43].

The danger in "fudging" or distorting the statistics is the tendency it often generates in an organization to "beat" the record by means other than an improvement in the performance the record is supposed to reflect.

The playing of such juvenile games is of no genuine or long-lasting advantage to a safety man. Instead, a professional will discourage it since invalid records tend to mask genuine problems which should be brought into the open and confronted and to lead the reviewing executives to expect the attainment of unrealistic goals. Beating the game is only a temporary triumph.

Yet, the company executive himself may encourage the numbers game if he overrates the Z16.1 statistics and gives little or no attention to other indices of safety performance. Many safety men see executives as reading too much into the frequency and severity rates or as failing to place these rates in perspective [44]. Again, the safety men themselves may stimulate efforts to play the statistics game among line management if they saddle such management personnel with negative incentives, such as mock awards for the poorest record. Finally, the Z16.1 standards themselves may be seen as unfairly weighted in favor of light industry and large plants and therefore as justification for "taking the benefit of the doubt."

There is no serious movement to discard the Z16.1 standards. The more common position is to use these standards (along with the revised Z16.1 Serious Injury Index) as general or rough indicators of safety performance in large units but to supplement them, for purpose of accident control, with measures that are more sensitive and more reinforcing.

SAFETY LEGISLATION

Although workmen's compensation is discussed as a separate subject elsewhere in this volume, it merits at least a brief comment here in the context of statutory requirements and trends and their effect on the safety job. The trends are significant; they point to greater employer liability—in matters of employee health as well as injury—and an enlarged role for the safety man as this liability is translated into programs and activities. In addition, the federal government is entering more actively into the legislative field.

State workmen's compensation laws, as first instituted about sixty years ago, were addressed to work injuries. The more recent tendency, through court interpretation and legislative action, has been to expand disability coverage to include occupational diseases; thirty-seven acts give full coverage and the others cover "schedule" (listed) diseases [45]. The emergence of new diseases from radiation has resulted in much new legislation.

In general, the bars to compensation in injury cases have been diminishing. The newer emphasis on occupational diseases has presented the safety man (if he acts as claims administrator) with new questions concerning compensability. Milton Dunn offers this advice concerning allergic dermatitis cases:

> It is recommended that before a case decision is made, the law be carefully investigated. Some states require that trauma be present at the time that the material or substance in question was first introduced into the skin before a "resultant allergic dermatitis" can be legally declared. In other states, the trauma is not required. There are various interpretations as to specific cause and aggravation, and in most states the law has been carefully worded to include all of the usual circumstances [46].

It would appear that the accident requirements established for injuries, with the emphasis on trauma and a definite time and place of occurrence, have been stretched somewhat unrealistically to apply to occupational diseases. A redefinition of the latter may be in order. In this connection, the then Secretary of Labor George Shultz was asked the following question in 1969 by the editors of *Environmental Control Management:* "Should the courts in their interpretations apply the accident theory of compensable injury or should they broaden their interpretation to include any injury or disease which is work related?" Shultz replied, "This should not be left to interpretation by the courts; rather, the statute should make it clear that any work-related injury or disease is covered by the law [47]." This is the direction—defining compensability in the legislation itself in terms of any injury or disease related to work—that workman's compensation is very likely to take.

RECENT FEDERAL LEGISLATION

In a major revision of the Walsh-Healey safety standards (applying to employers having federal contracts of $10,000 or more) effective May 20, 1969, a new standard was established for the purpose of protecting the hearing of employees. The legal basis of the Walsh-Healey standards resides in the federal government's role as awarder of contracts.

The provisions governing occupational noise exposure state that the employee shall be protected against the effect of noise exposure if (1) the employee continuously for eight hours is exposed to a level of 90 dBA (90 decibels measured on the A scale of a sound level meter) or (2) the employee is exposed to impulsive or impact noise exceeding 140-dBA peak sound pressure level.

When these levels are exceeded, the employer is required to use feasible administrative or engineering controls. If these controls fail to reduce the level to an acceptable point, the employer must provide personnel protective equipment. Engineering controls would include such measures as enclosing the noise-making machinery, vibration control, and soundproofing; an administrative action might involve revisions of work schedules to reduce the periods of exposure. The two most common types of protective equipment are earmuffs and ear plugs.

A hearing conservation program requires a multiplicity of administrative, engineering, and medical decisions and procedures, and it illustrates the added complexity which employee protection assumes when it goes beyond safety to encompass aspects of employee health.

First, a sound-level survey is required in order to locate those areas where exposure is excessive. Where the decibel level must be reduced, the means must be devised, starting with a consideration of the possibilities and practicality of engineering controls. Such investigation is more than a cursory gesture. If protective equipment must be used, the decision must be made as to type, a decision which takes into account such factors as the degree of noise reduction obtained, comfort and convenience of the device, possible physical side effects (irritations or infections), cost, and difficulties of monitoring. The device ideally should protect hearing but permit the required communication through conversational sounds and the perception of those sounds which the employee must pick up to run his job effectively, as, for example, the sounds of machine malfunctioning which a repairman must detect.

The program must be instituted with extreme care. Supervisors should be thoroughly briefed and should set an unvarying example by wearing the devices themselves. Employees need an explanation containing strong positive statements on the benefits of wearing the device so that they will not come to regard the program as a punitive action against them or an unwarranted imposition. The requirements of the Walsh-Healey hearing protection provisions should be explained in simple terms against the background of the legislation's larger positive intent: to protect the safety and health of employees. The damaging effect of noise on hearing should be explained, again in laymen's language and advisedly by a physician; being recognized as an expert in medicine is an advantage to anyone attempting to sway attitudes in medical matters. The reference to sound levels should not deal with numbers alone but should relate the decibel levels to familiar sounds; motion pictures are available for such purpose. A tryout period of several weeks should be allowed so that the employees can become accustomed to the device, but the employees should be told what to do with the device (when to wear it, how long, etc.) during the tryout period, and an effort should be made to see that they do not arrive at the mandatory date without the trial experience which adjustment depends upon. Adequate provisions must be made for storing, ventilating, cleaning, and replacing the worn devices or parts and for monitoring and enforcing their use. The equipment must be individually fitted, again preferably by medical personnel or with their assistance.

Audiometric testing, by medical personnel or under medical supervision, is a vital part of the ongoing program. Employees must be tested at the beginning of the program (or when hired) to measure their hearing and thereafter (yearly intervals appear suitable) to detect any changes.

A safety professional is equipped to carry out much of this procedure for instituting a hearing conservation program, but he needs the help of medical personnel, as stated above, and should arrange to work cooperatively with them in the planning, installing, and maintaining of the program.

In another federal legislative action in 1969, the Coal Mine Health and Safety Act was passed. In addition to strengthening the mine safety standards, this act established the first health standards for coal miners and provides compensation for victims of pneumoconiosis (black lung) or their widows.

Additional federal legislation is imminent in the field of safety and health. The main thrust of proposed legislation is clear:

1. To extend federal safety and health protection to a greater number of people—specifically to workers of employers engaged in interstate commerce. Legislation enacted on such a basis would have virtually blanket coverage of industrial employees. The National Safety Council has urged, in a statement of position, that the standards established by federal legislation be national consensus standards [48].

2. To give emphasis to employee health, even though most of the standards will probably apply to safety. The concern for employee health evident in the Walsh-Healey amendment and the coal mine act will apparently be extended to the larger work population [49].

The legislative signs—state as well as federal—point clearly to the new decade as a period of rapid and significant changes in legal requirements. The safety man will necessarily be the instrument for carrying out such changes, for working them into practical, ongoing, effective programs in his company. Legislation is merely the start, as our short experience with hearing conservation has taught us. Safety in the seventies is no place for the well-meaning amateur.

REFERENCES

[1] Heinrich, H. W.: *Industrial Accident Prevention*, 4th ed., McGraw-Hill Book Company, New York, 1959, p. xi.

[2] Pyle, Howard: "Zero In on Safety," *National Safety News*, vol. 101, no. 6, pp. 34–35, June, 1970.

[3] For statistics on 1969 deaths and frequency and severity rates, see *National Safety News*, vol. 101, no. 3, pp. 174–175, March 1970, and vol. 102, no. 2, pp. 32–33, August, 1970.

[4] "The Safety Panorama: A View from the Nation's Capital," *Occupational Hazards,* p. 34, February, 1970.

[5] See "Has Safety Progress Ended?" in *National Safety News,* vol. 100, no. 4, pp. 38–47, October, 1969, for the comments of Pyle and other safety men.

[6] Seaton, Don Cash, Herbert J. Stack, and Bernard I. Loft: *Administration and Supervision of Safety Education,* The Macmillan Company, New York, 1969, pp. 4–5.

[7] See Vernon, Ralph J., and Adil M. Mayyasi: "Education for Occupational Safety and Health Professionals," *Journal of American Society of Safety Engineers,* vol. 15, no. 5, p. 10, May, 1970, for the listing of four functions of the professional safety position in connection with a discussion of education for the position. The list originally appeared in the booklet *Scope and Functions of the Professional Safety Position,* published by the American Society of Safety Engineers in 1966.

[8] Simonds, Rollin H., and John V. Grimaldi: *Safety Management,* Richard D. Irwin, Inc., Homewood, Ill., 1963, p. 67.

[9] Vernon and Mayyasi, op. cit., pp. 16–17.

[10] "Safety Education Survey," *National Safety News,* vol. 101, no. 1, p. 77, January, 1970.

[11] Stresau, Ann: "Do Safety Award Plans Pay Off?" *Journal of American Society of Safety Engineers,* vol. 14, no. 3, pp. 17–18, March, 1969.

[12] "The Conglomerate: What It Means to the Safety Manager," *Occupational Hazards,* pp. 47–49, February, 1970.

[13] Lederer, Jerome: "Systems Safety," *Best's Review,* vol. 71, no. 1, p. 50, May, 1970.

[14] For Ernest Levens' discussion of systems (on which these comments are largely based), see the fourth installment of "Search 1," *Journal of the American Society of Safety Engineers,* vol. 15, no. 5, pp. 19–21, May, 1970.

[15] See William Wood's discussion of materials in the third installment of "Search 1," *Journal of the American Society of Safety Engineers,* vol. 15, no. 4, pp. 23–26, April, 1970.

[16] For example of a safety inspection checklist, see *Supervisors Safety Manual,* 3d ed., National Safety Council, Chicago, 1967, p. 16. Whatever items are used in a department or plant should be pertinent to the particular operation.

[17] Stuffing, W. Eugene: "The Protective Footwear Story," *National Safety News,* vol. 101, no. 3, pp. 128, 132, 134, March, 1970. This issue of the *National Safety News* is devoted to a coverage of various types of personal protective equipment.

[18] Elroy, Frank E. (ed.): *Accident Prevention Manual for Industrial Operations,* 6th ed., National Safety Council, Chicago, 1969, pp. 270–273. For example of supervisor's accident report form (using questions related to accident factors) and of first-aid form, see pp. 244, 246–247. Many safety forms and checklists, especially useful in investigating and analyzing accidents and in conducting inspections, are presented and discussed in this NSC manual.

[19] Haddon, William, Jr., Edward A. Suchman, and David Klein (eds.): *Accident Research Methods and Approaches,* Harper & Row, Publishers, Incorporated, New York, 1964, pp. 296–298.

[20] Gardner, James E.: *Safety Training for the Supervisor,* Addison-Wesley Publishing Company, Inc., Reading, Mass., 1969, pp. 17–19.

[21] Bird, Frank E., Jr., and Lawrence E. Schlesinger: "Safety Behavior Reinforcement," *Journal of the American Society of Safety Engineers,* vol. 15, no. 6, pp. 16–24, June, 1970.

[22] DeReamer, Russell: *Modern Safety Practices,* John Wiley & Sons, Inc., New York, 1958, pp. 46–47.

[23] Gardner, op. cit., pp. 20–30.

[24] Smith, L. C.: "Let's Wed JIT and JSA," *National Safety News,* vol. 101, no. 1, pp. 75–77, January, 1970.

[25] Larson, John C., and others: *The Human Element in Accident Prevention,* New York University Press, New York, 1955, pp. 70–74.

[26] For a comprehensive listing of studies of human factors from 1950 to 1962, with related commentary and questions, see Brody, Leon: *Human Factors Research in Occupational Accident Prevention,* American Society of Safety Engineers and Center for Safety Education, New York University Press, New York, 1962.

[27] Haddon, Suchman, and Klein, op. cit., pp. 280–281.

[28] Ibid., p. 285.

[29] Ibid., pp. 302–303.

[30] Ibid., p. 345.

[31] Ibid., p. 278.

[32] Iskrant, Albert P., and Paul V. Joliet: *Accidents and Homicide,* Harvard University Press, Cambridge, Mass., 1968, pp. 46–47.

[33] Ibid., p. 53.

[34] Kerr, Willard, "Complementary Theories of Safety Psychology," in Edwin A. Fleishman (ed.), *Studies in Personnel and Industrial Psychology,* The Dorsey Press, Homewood, Ill., 1967, p. 655. This article appeared earlier in *Journal of Social Psychology,* vol. 45, pp. 3–9, 1957.

[35] Haddon, Suchman, and Klein, op. cit., p. 444.

[36] Kerr, op. cit., p. 653.

[37] Haddon, Suchman, and Klein, op. cit., p. 286.

[38] For a detailed discussion of insurance and insurance costs, see Bowen, Gordon L., and Donald C. Whytock: *Economics of Safety,* Prentice-Hall, Inc., Waterford, Conn., 1964, pp. 17–26, 70–71, 74–75.

[39] Simonds and Grimaldi, op. cit., pp. 86–91.

[40] Ibid., p. 112.

[41] See "They Came to Speak for Safety," *National Safety News,* vol. 100, no. 6, pp. 52–56, December, 1969, for an account of the proceedings of the fifty-seventh National Safety Congress (1969); the measures for evaluation of safety programs came under close and critical scrutiny at the congress.

[42] O'Shell, Harold E., and Frank E. Bird: "Incident Recall," *National Safety News,* vol. 100, no. 4, pp. 58–63, October, 1969.

[43] "Z16.1 — Do the Figures Lie?" *Occupational Hazards,* pp. 44–46, September, 1969.

[44] Ibid., p. 46.

[45] For a detailed discussion of workmen's compensation from the point of view of claims administration, see Carter, Neil: *Guide to Workmen's Compensation Claims,* Roberts Publishing Company, New York, 1965. For a summary of workmen's compensation laws, see the U.S. Department of Labor (Bureau of Labor Standards) publications: Bulletin 161, rev. 1969; and Labor Law Series, no. 10, January, 1970.

[46] Dunn, Milton S.: "Allergic Disease in Industry," taken from *Dangerous Properties of Industrial Materials* by Irving N. Sax. Copyright © 1968 by Litton Educational Publishing, Inc. Reprinted by permission of Van Nostrand Reinhold Company.

[47] For an account of the interview with George Shultz, see *Environmental Control Management,* pp. 24–25, 42, October, 1969.

[48] For the full statement, see "National Safety Council Position on the Proposed Occupational Safety and Health Legislation," *National Safety News,* vol. 100, no. 6, pp. 38–42, December, 1969.

[49] Federal legislation was passed by the 91st Congress late in December, 1970.

chapter 49

Employee Health

BERNERD BURBANK, M.D.   *Medical Director, McGraw-Hill, Inc., New York, New York*

WHY A HEALTH PROGRAM?

Every company—large or small—runs into health problems and must have some way to handle them:

A girl falls unconscious to the floor of the office.

A 35-year-old man who works with several other employees in a crowded office comes down with hepatitis.

An executive due to retire in two years learns that the man he has trained to succeed him has developed heart disease.

A company salesman, traveling in South America, develops a high fever and is hospitalized in a small town in Brazil.

A woman with seventeen years of service shows changes in behavior and work performance, and office rumor suggests drugs or alcohol.

Although every one of these situations can be handled by somebody, medical problems are best handled by competent professionals: doctors, nurses, industrial hygienists.

WHAT CAN A MEDICAL PROGRAM DO FOR A COMPANY AND ITS EMPLOYEES?

1. Treat on-the-job accidents and medical emergencies occurring at work, and arrange for follow-up care.

2. Help select applicants for employment who are free of significant health prob-

lems, evaluate handicaps and disabilities, and advise placement in jobs safe for the applicants and for fellow employees.

3. Evaluate employees before transfers to jobs having different physical requirements; evaluate employees before foreign travel or residence, before participation in company-sponsored sports, and before returning to work after an illness or injury; and evaluate employees who are exposed to physical or chemical hazards in their work.

4. Maintain and improve the health of the work force by conducting periodic examinations; immunizations; group surveys for diabetes, cancer, tuberculosis, glaucoma, etc.; health education; and by assisting with personal and family problems with referral to proper treatment and rehabilitation agencies.

5. Advise and assist managers with problem employees who are not performing satisfactorily because of health or emotional problems, prolonged illness, excessive absenteeism, drug addiction, or alcoholism.

6. Advise management about health hazards associated with handling and use of the raw materials used in manufacture, and about potential hazards to the consumer from the company's products.

WHAT TYPE OF PROGRAM?

The choice of plan, the size of the medical unit, and the number and type of personnel to staff it will depend on:

1. The company's philosophy and what it wants to do about the health and welfare of its employees

2. The type of industry; physical and chemical hazards in the manufacturing processes and final products

3. The number and kind of industrial accidents and illness (In industries with a large number of accidents, on-premises treatment is usually more satisfactory and less expensive than outside referral.)

4. Size of the company, number of employees, and geographic distribution of company units

5. Local customs

6. Availability of private and community health resources

If the company decides to install a health program, it can be accomplished in one of three ways:

1. Consult a local physician or appropriate industrial health specialist as problems arise.

2. Maintain a well-trained industrial nurse on the premises who has access to a specific local physician familiar with the company and its manufacturing processes, and who will come in to the plant for emergencies and whenever necessary.

3. Establish a medical department regularly attended by a nurse and physician who have special training and an interest in the health problems of the company and its personnel.

Small Company

If a company has under 500 employees, few accidents, and no unusual health problems, and if it is near private medical facilities, there is no need for a medical unit:

1. Assign responsibility for handling medical emergencies and accidents to three or four competent individuals trained in first aid (through American Red Cross, a local hospital, or a private physician).

2. Arrange emergency care with one or two local physicians and with the emergency department of the nearest hospital.

3. Engage a physician trained and interested in occupational health who will

make regular visits to the plant or office often enough to become familiar with the layout, manufacturing processes, and at least the key personnel. Besides responding to accidents and emergencies, he can do necessary medical examinations and advise management on day-to-day health matters. He should arrange satisfactory substitute coverage when he is unavailable. He will develop greater interest if he is considered a "part" of the company and is invited to some of the company functions. He should be paid a monthly retainer in addition to fees for specific services.

4. Post in a conspicuous place an "emergency plan" with up-to-date procedures; addresses and telephone numbers of hospitals, ambulances, and physicians to be called; fire and police departments; management personnel to be notified; and transportation to be used if other than ambulance.

5. Purchase and regularly replenish first-aid supplies including bandages, splints, a wheelchair, a stretcher, a small tank or container of oxygen (with clear instructions on how it is to be used), and a flashlight with fresh batteries. Drugs and medications of all kinds are of little use and possibly dangerous unless ordered by a doctor or nurse. The list should be approved and supplemented by the physician.

6. The plan must provide for emergencies occurring after hours, during night shifts, and on holidays.

7. Use and support community facilities such as hospitals, the volunteer ambulance corps, service clubs, blood banks, and local health projects, and participate in programs aimed at detecting diseases like diabetes, tuberculosis, and glaucoma.

Medium-sized Company

If there are 500 to 1,500 employees, a company should give strong consideration to employing a nurse, engaging a physician on a retainer basis, and maintaining a small medical department of three or four rooms (and separate toilet).

The company may require a nurse on a part-time or full-time basis, or one for each shift. She must have access to and professional guidance from the physician at all times. She should report administratively to the first or second level of management or to the executive in charge of personnel. Full responsibility for the professional care of employees must be given to the nurse if the physician is not present.

Large Company

Companies of 1,500 employees or larger will need at least one or two industrial nurses—adding a nurse for each additional thousand employees—and a physician several hours a week. Companies of 1,500 to 3,000 employees will probably require a physician full time. Expanded medical programs and industries with many accidents will require additional personnel.

The Occupational Health Survey

In considering whether or not to initiate a medical program, what its costs and benefits will be, and how to go about it, a company can get expert advice from a physician with experience in occupational medicine. If a local physician or the County Medical Society cannot suggest a suitable consultant, the Executive Director, Industrial Medical Association, 150 North Wacker Drive, Chicago, Illinois 60606 (with a national membership of about 3,800 physicians interested and trained in occupational health) can furnish names of physicians available for consultation.

Staffing

Doctors and nurses working in industry must have congenial personalities and get along with each other, members of management, and employees at every cultural and educational level. They must have adequate professional qualifications as well as an interest in the company and the type of problems to be encountered.

The part-time physician's office should be reasonably near the plant. He must hold a license to practice medicine in his state, be in good standing with his medical colleagues, and in some states be approved to treat industrial accidents by the Workmen's Compensation Board. Staff membership in a local hospital with the privilege of admitting patients may be necessary. He may be a specialist certified by the American Board of Preventive Medicine or an internist, surgeon, or general practitioner with a special interest in industrial medicine. He will need some knowledge of administration, statistics, preventive medicine, sanitation, occupational illness and injury, workmen's compensation law, industrial hygienics, toxicology, and common diseases, and will have to become acquainted with the chemicals, materials, and methods which are used in the plant and which may be harmful.

Availability for emergencies, substitution by a colleague when he himself is not available, hours to be spent at the plant, parking facilities for his car, whether or not he should accept employees as private patients, and remuneration should be discussed and agreed upon.

He may be paid a salary for regular hours, or a fee for each service rendered plus a monthly retainer. In either case the arrangement should include adequate compensation to encourage the physician to take an interest in the health and safety of the company and its employees, and not merely to handle industrial accidents when they occur.

The nurse can make or break the entire program. In a very real sense she is the central figure: She screens every employee who comes to the department, decides which ones must be seen by the physician, gives treatment to the majority of patients, and handles many of the problems between management and employees.

She must have a unique blend of warmth, tact, and competence. Graduation from an accredited school and registration in the state are required. Besides knowledge of general nursing techniques, it is helpful if she has additional training and experience in occupational and public health nursing. She must know or be willing to learn first aid and how to handle the type of illnesses and injuries to be seen in her plant, and she must have a basic knowledge of workmen's compensation law, medical record keeping, and the company's medical, hospitalization, and disability insurance plans; and she must acquire knowledge of her community's health and welfare agencies. Her salary and benefits should compare favorably with those of nurses in other local industries and local hospitals.

Limitation of Nurse's Responsibility: Standing Orders

The nurse should never be expected to make medical decisions or render treatment beyond her training, ability, and legal limitations. To protect the employees and the company—as well as herself—she should operate strictly within a list of "standing orders," prepared jointly by her and the physician, which should state explicitly the extent and limitations of her professional actions. These standing orders should conform to the standards of the community and be signed by the physician to whom she is responsible. The nurse must have access to the physician at all times for professional guidance.

Other Staff

In large medical departments a full-time medical director may need additional full-time or part-time physicians, nurses, laboratory and x-ray technicians, and clerical help. Some companies with special circumstances and expanded programs employ radiologists, dermatologists, psychiatrists, gynecologists, surgeons, dentists, physiotherapists, health physicists, and industrial hygienists on either a part-time or a consultant basis, depending on the particular health problems encountered in the industry and on the extent to which a company becomes involved with the health of its employees and the consumers of its products.

Outside Consultants

All physicians require occasional consultations with outside experts in special situations and should have the authority to arrange them.

Keeping a Good Staff

In addition to better-than-average financial compensation, the doctor and nurse will appreciate benefits and privileges accorded executives of the company, good medical facilities and equipment, close contact with and support from upper levels of management, and inclusion in pertinent management meetings. They need regular briefing on management-union negotiations, proposed changes in manufacturing processes, acquisitions and mergers, and any changes which will affect the health, safety, or morale of company personnel. They should be encouraged to maintain their competency by attending professional meetings at company expense. Full-time nurses and medical directors can become insulated and grow stale unless they spend part of their regular working hours caring for patients at local hospital clinics, or attending some outside professional activity.

Layout

The medical unit, large or small, should be centrally located and accessible to all employees, some of whom may have to be transported in and out by stretcher and wheelchair. Doorways, ramps, and elevators must permit quick exit to an area accessible to ambulances.

The rooms should have comfortable temperature and humidity and should be quiet, free of vibration and noxious odors, and soundproof enough so that private conversations cannot be overheard.

The simplest medical unit should have at least three or four small rooms—a waiting room, an examination-treatment room, a room with a bed or cot, and a lavatory-toilet. A second examination-treatment room and a consultation room will provide faster and more efficient care if space is available.

Large medical departments will require 5,000 to 10,000 square feet or more, depending on the number of employees and the extent of services offered, and may include rooms or areas for these purposes: waiting patients, medical records, receptionist-secretary and other clerical staff, examination and treatment, rest and recovery, consultations, clinical laboratory examinations, taking and developing x-rays, cleaning instruments, physiotherapy, taking electrocardiograms, a medical library, staff dressing rooms, and storage space for medical records, x-ray films, medical supplies, secretarial supplies, and the stretcher and wheelchair.

Building or renovating a medical department requires close cooperation among the architect, the company's office planning staff, and the medical director and nurse. It should be laid out for the functions to be performed, and most medical departments have three main functions:

1. Consultation and minor treatment
2. Treatment of more seriously ill patients, serious accidents, and emergencies
3. Examinations with laboratory tests and x-rays

These functions can be diagramed in a flow chart, drawing a plan which places the rooms consecutively according to function but keeping the major functions somewhat separate, and at the same time planning so that the staff can care for patients with a minimum of unnecessary walking back and forth. In developing such a flow chart it is a good idea to trace the movements of each category of patient and of each staff member through each procedure to develop an orderly traffic flow.

The medical department should be clean and as attractive as any unit of the company. Floor covering should be quiet and, in most rooms, washable. Treatment and examining rooms require sinks with controlled-temperature water supply. Toilets should be adjacent to examining rooms for the partly dressed patient who may have to use them during special examinations like pelvic examinations and proctosigmoidoscopies. A second exit door is desirable to facilitate moving sick or injured patients in and out of the department without going through the waiting room.

Budget

The medical director with the authority and responsibility for operating the medical department should prepare and administer an annual budget. It should include salaries and other professional fees, rent and utilities (if this charge is allocated to the department), telephones, drugs and medical supplies, medical instruments and equipment, secretarial and office supplies, office furniture, alterations and maintenance of the medical department, periodicals for the waiting room and professional journals and books for the medical library, dues and membership fees to professional societies, laundry and uniforms (the company should provide uniforms for nurses and others who are required to wear them), depreciation, expenses for attendance at professional meetings, and the estimated cost of any projects the director plans, after discussion and approval by management.

RECORDS, FORMS, AND LICENSES

A medical department must operate under a written company medical policy. It also needs a manual of department procedures including the nurses' standing orders, a daily log listing all patients who are examined or treated, and a confidential medical record on each patient including details of examinations, consultations, and treatment—and particularly accurate and complete notes about any industrial accidents. Other forms can be developed by the medical director as needed.

Some basic statistics should be kept because of their value in providing data for analysis and study of occupational hazards and accidents, illness trends, and to provide reports to management showing the medical department's activities, problems, and accomplishments.

Even though it is not a medical report, the Employer's Report of Injury (Workmen's Compensation) may be initiated in the medical department since all injuries are referred to the medical department at the time of the accident.

LICENSES AND INSPECTIONS

License and certificate requirements vary according to city and state laws. For the medical department itself licenses may be required to operate a medical bureau (treat Workmen's Compensation cases), to operate a clinical laboratory, and to operate an x-ray machine. For the doctor, nurse, and laboratory and x-ray technicians, current renewals of state licenses to practice, and licenses to perform medical laboratory examinations and to take x-rays must conform to local law. Doctors are required to have a current federal tax stamp to purchase and use narcotics in treatment.

The medical department may be subject to inspection by city and state departments of health, labor, and Workmen's Compensation.

CONFIDENTIALITY OF RECORDS

Everyone is entitled to some privacy, and the exact definition of what constitutes "privileged and confidential information" is not always clear. In an organizational setting where people work closely together, it is especially important to shield individuals from embarrassment and invasion of privacy. For this reason, as well as to avoid possible legal action by a patient for unauthorized disclosure, actual medical details of illness cannot ordinarily be given to other persons, including supervisors, without authorization by the patient. Consequently, medical records must be kept in the medical department under the personal care of a doctor or nurse and should be given to no one without express consent of the employee or under court subpoena. And the medical files should be locked. If there is no medical department, these records should be kept in the office of the physician.

This policy should not handicap the medical department's ability to help management with work-related problems. Medical reports stating the work capability and specific limitations of an employee can be given to the supervisor without violating the employee's confidence or disclosing details of his illness. If such details are pertinent to the situation, the doctor or nurse can almost always get the patient's permission to discuss them with the supervisor.

In the long run, knowledge throughout the company that a person's privacy is recognized and respected will engender a confidence in the medical department that will greatly enhance its effectiveness to the company and its employees.

SCOPE AND SERVICES OF A MEDICAL DEPARTMENT
Emergency Treatment

Emergency treatment for injuries and illness occurring at work, with referral to the next proper treatment facility or hospital, has to be carried out with the highest level of medical skill. Employees injured or stricken at work may feel that they are "at the mercy of the company medical department," and nothing can more seriously undermine the stature of the company's medical program than a medical emergency poorly handled. Good up-to-date medical equipment, organization and readiness for handling various medical emergencies, and an equal mixture of efficiency and warmth are the ingredients of good medical care.

Ambulances ordered by the medical personnel should be paid for by the company (unless covered by insurance), and not by the patient. Otherwise the decision to use or not to use an ambulance may be influenced by a concern over the patient's finances rather than on medical judgement alone.

Preemployment Examinations

These examinations establish the groundwork for every medical program. Their primary purpose is to place an applicant in a job for which he is medically suited. They are more valuable to the applicant and the company when done by in-plant medical personnel than by a physician who has less knowledge of the company and working cond:tions, and who is not likely to have any future responsibility for care of these employees.

Benefits to the company may be greater from examination of the skilled and managerial worker likely to remain with the company than of the clerical or young female group where turnover is greatest.

"Preemployment" examinations done *after* employment are of little value in placement and can pose major problems if serious medical or surgical conditions requiring prolonged treatment are discovered at the examination—problems which may not only prevent the new employee from working for several weeks but which may oblige the new company to assume obligations to pay medical expenses and disability payments—particularly if the employee has already severed connections with his former employer, given up his medical insurance coverage, sold a house, and relocated to the new area.

Preemployment examinations may vary in extent from a questionnaire evaluated by the nurse or doctor to a complete examination with special laboratory tests—depending on the health and age of the candidate and on the hazards and specific work requirements of the job. From them the examining doctor can:

1. Advise management of an individual's capacity to perform work satisfactorily, free of significant health problems, and without adding excessive cost to the company's insurance and benefit programs.

2. Find remediable medical problems which can be improved by prompt referral and treatment, thereby lessening future disability and medical expense.

3. Record health status and details of existing conditions, information that may be valuable in treating subsequent emergencies, and that may be helpful in establishing a fair adjudication after subsequent industrial accidents.

Rating systems. From a medical examination the doctor tries to put his assessment of the candidate into a meaningful statement. Although details of a confidential nature disclosed at a preemployment exam cannot be ethically disclosed to anyone, a person forfeits the legal right to confidentiality when the examination is required and paid for by a company as a condition of employment. Practically, however, there is little value in disclosing such details, unless the prospective employee has some condition like epilepsy, severe diabetes, or some definite limitation that the supervisor must be aware of in the employee's own best interest—and it is rarely difficult for the doctor to get his permission to discuss it with the supervisor.

Rating systems are not perfect, but they are helpful. It should be remembered that the medical department can only make recommendations, based on the applicant's medical history and an examination: Management must make the final decision whether or not to hire an applicant—based on these recommendations. Here is an evaluation system that can be modified to suit particular needs:

1. Medically recommended for the specific job for which the applicant is being considered, or one of similar physical requirements and hazards or exposures. Transfer to a job of different characteristics requires reevaluation. Includes the healthy, and those with stable handicaps or limitations compatible with the job. (Can do the job; should have average longevity and be free of health problems; predict average attendance.)

2. Applicant has or may have health problems or psychological attitudes which will interfere with average attendance or work efficiency and will require special consideration by management. (Examples: History of regular absenteeism; "doesn't feel well" often and stays home; suspected alcoholic or emotional problems.) This category may include chronic conditions which, even with good medical care, may cause an increase in absenteeism.

3. Applicant has health problems which should be corrected before he can work safely and productively. (Examples: contagious disease, needs glasses badly, back sprain, hernia, unknown diagnosis needing further evaluation, needs surgery, drug addiction, definite alcoholism, and more severe emotional states.)

4. Applicant is below average health risk for long-term employment and will probably develop permanent disability. (Examples: progressive diseases—cancer,

serious high blood pressure, leukemia, multiple sclerosis, severe psychoneurosis or psychosis.)

5. Physically or emotionally unable to work. (Rare, rehabilitation unlikely.)

Very few applicants need be refused employment because of physical findings. The main health problems preventing employment are these:

1. Contagious disease (usually of brief duration)
2. Incurable progressive disease leading to disability
3. Complex emotional problems

Other Examinations

Other examinations designed to protect employee health and minimize risk:

Transfer examinations before transferring an employee to a job that requires different physical abilities or subjects the employee to other hazards or exposures.

Examination after illness or injury to determine whether the employee may safely resume work and whether he is free of contagious disease.

Examinations for foreign travel and residence. Employees and their families intending to travel or reside abroad on company business should have medical evaluations at company expense to disclose any conditions that require treatment or might be aggravated by travel or be potentially dangerous in areas away from home and good medical care. Proper immunizations and advice on health and sanitation of the area to which they are going can be given. Special medications, extra eyeglasses, and a dental checkup may be advised.

Special periodic examinations are advisable for employees exposed to chemical and physical agents, including radiation and noise; for employees participating in company-sponsored athletic teams; for operators of vehicles, aircraft, and some types of machinery; and for food handlers to see that they maintain good hygiene and are free of transmissible disease.

Periodic or health-maintenance examinations are a fundamental part of any company health-maintenance program. They should be offered to all employees if possible, the periodicity depending on age, previous health history, and exposure to occupational hazards.

Beginning the program with management personnel is traditional, and yet everyone's health is of equal importance to himself; and from a company's investment point of view, a good draftsman may be as difficult to replace as a vice president. Soon it should be extended to all key employees, then to all employees starting with those over age forty-five (yearly), to those from age thirty-five to forty-five (every two or three years), and finally to younger employees (every five years or more often).

Since only 10 percent of people are estimated to have regular examinations by their own physicians, these examinations are valuable to both the employee and the company. By prompt treatment of early disease, costs and disability can be definitely reduced. The exams should be voluntary, and done on company time; the results should be confidential and have no effect on job security. No one besides the patient and his private physician should get a report.

The extent of the exam will vary with the patient's age and health, the doctor, and the money available for the program; but the usual periodic exam includes history taking, a physical examination including special procedures such as tonometry for glaucoma, proctosigmoidoscopy for rectal cancer, pelvic examination and pap smear for cervical cancer (females), chest x-ray, electrocardiogram, and blood and urine tests. If some of these tests are not available under the company's program, or if additional tests or examinations are required, they can be done by the employee's private physician at personal expense.

An important part of the examination is a clear discussion of the results at the end of the examination. Reassurance of good health is good medicine. If abnormalities are found, the employee is referred to his own doctor for treatment.

In the absence of a medical department, the local company medical adviser, a clinic specializing in employee health examinations, or the employee's private physician may do them at company expense.

OTHER HEALTH PROMOTION

Other services to promote good health among employees include mass health surveys and multiphasic screening techniques which offer all employees examinations or tests for one or several conditions such as cancer, vision abnormalities, glaucoma, diabetes, and lung disease; immunizations for tetanus and epidemic diseases; discussion of health, emotional, and family problems of employees; counseling and referral to private physicians or community agencies; health education, talks, and films; reading racks; and special organized groups to control weight, smoking, etc.

FOOD SERVICES

Company-sponsored food services should maintain high standards of cleanliness and sanitation. Although local health authorities may inspect and regulate the facilities, the medical director ought to determine that proper methods of refrigeration, dishwashing, and food preparation are being used. Food handlers should be regularly examined with particular attention to the hands for innocent-looking skin conditions that can carry disease, and to serve as a reminder that cleanliness is a large factor in preventing food sickness. Bacterial cultures of foods and food handlers can be made if problems arise, or to reinforce the importance of cleanliness.

SAFETY AND INDUSTRIAL HYGIENE

Manufacturing methods, chemicals and raw materials, and finished products all too often produce sickness and injury before the cause is discovered. By assuming its obligation to protect its employees and the handlers and consumers of its products, industry will at the same time reduce Workmen's Compensation payments and the size of legal settlements. If a stronger incentive is needed, the recently enacted Occupational Safety and Health Act of 1970 will cause every company to reappraise its occupational health and safety standards and bring them to safe levels preparatory to federal inspection and control. The health and welfare of employees require good sanitation, good drinking water, adequate toilets and washing facilities; proper ventilation, humidity, lighting, and control of dust and excessive noise; and safe working conditions effected by proper study and control of physical and chemical agents used in manufacture. All new processes and materials to be used should be reviewed, screened, and maximum permissible exposures determined. Controls should be established and maintained. Regular plant and office inspections should be made by the person best qualified to make them, and his findings and recommendations should be made to a member of management who has the desire and authority to improve or eliminate unsatisfactory or unsafe conditions. If there is a safety engineer or a safety committee, the medical director should function as an adviser. Where there are physical hazards or toxic chemicals, plants should consult or employ an industrial hygienist. Records of accidents and injuries should be analyzed to find common causes and a plan invented to reduce or prevent them.

BLOOD BANK

The blood bank in some companies may rightly be an administrative function of the medical department. The blood collection is often made by a community agency such as the American Red Cross, collections are pooled with other organizations in the area, and paper transactions are made whenever an employee or a member of his family receives blood in a hospital. This is primarily an administrative process to provide partial reimbursement for medical expense and can also be handled by some other department, or by an employee committee.

SPECIAL PROBLEMS

Alcoholism and Drugs

Alcoholism and drug abuse are illnesses, or symptoms of illness, and are problems of the social system of which industry is a part and for which industry must shoulder some responsibility. Firing alcoholics or drug addicts without some attempt to salvage them sacrifices employees who are, or once were, valuable to the company, and throws upon the streets of society individuals who will now have much less chance of recovery.

The company must have a policy to deal with these problems. It should be something like this: "An employee who is abusing drugs or who has a drinking problem must be referred to the company physician and be given a reasonable opportunity for rehabilitation before he is considered for termination." The situation should be handled on the basis of job performance whenever possible, leaving to the physician the medical aspects of diagnosis, treatment, or referral to outside rehabilitation agencies. This job-leverage technique has already been valuable in rehabilitating many individuals with drinking problems. Close cooperation among the supervisor, the personnel adviser, and the company physician are essential. Supervisors and foremen must be trained to recognize early signs of these afflictions and to realize that they are doing their employee a disservice to temporize and allow such a condition to progress to the point where treatment becomes hopeless. Drug and alcoholic problems rarely disappear spontaneously.

Emotional Problems

Many emotional problems of a transient nature respond well to sympathetic listening by a skilled supervisor. Serious personality disturbances, feelings of persecution or depression, and suicidal thoughts, however, are difficult to treat under the best of circumstances and should be referred immediately to the medical department for evaluation and appropriate treatment or referral. Although complex emotional disease can affect attendance and performance, many employees with "severe mental illness" function quite well if given adequate supportive therapy.

Absenteeism

Sickness is sometimes used as a socially accepted reason for being away from work, while the real reason may be something entirely different. An astute supervisor can recognize this and deal with it. But repeated absences associated with illness should always be discussed with the medical department. Sometimes an evaluation of the employee will disclose physical or emotional conditions that can be substantially improved by proper treatment.

Contagious Diseases

Employees with fever, rash, and contagious diseases like measles and mumps should be referred to the medical department before being sent home and again before returning to work so that further spread of disease can be prevented. Many of these diseases are reportable to local health officials by law. Medical personnel can also help allay unfounded fear and the panic that sometimes occurs in a department when an employee develops a contagious disease.

Venereal Diseases

Venereal diseases (with the possible exception of crab lice—which are more of a nuisance than a disease) cannot be transmitted to other employees through use of toilet seats and rarely present any problems at work. It is imperative that the patient receive correct diagnosis and prompt treatment for his own welfare.

Homosexuality

The homosexual employee—like the heterosexual employee—is never a problem in industry unless he creates a problem. We are now recognizing that there is no absolute norm for sexuality. Viewpoints on homosexuality are changing and becoming more tolerant. With the possible exception of a few cloak-and-dagger jobs where threat of exposure and blackmail could create a security risk, homosexuality in itself is not likely to be a significant factor in hiring or retaining an employee.

Maternity

A pregnant woman with no medical complications may work at her regular job as long as she feels able, provided she is under regular medical observation and that her attending physician has stated limitations to her activities, if any. Because of concern that she might fall or have an accident causing complications to herself or the baby with attendant liability under the Workmen's Compensation Law, and also because of the unlikely possibility that she may deliver her baby in the plant, many companies limit employment to the seventh or eighth month of pregnancy.

Body Odor

Perhaps body odor is not a medical matter, but a medical department can usually handle it more effectively and with less embarrassment than a fellow employee or supervisor. Even people who bathe daily can have a strong unpleasant odor. Causative factors are some of the clothing textiles, unsatisfactory or infrequent dry cleaning, and eating foods containing volatile substances which are carried from the stomach through the blood to the pores of the skin. Besides attention to these factors and regular bathing, underarm shaving and use of a nonirritating deodorant are helpful.

HIRING THE HANDICAPPED

Disabling conditions may be stable or progressive. Most stable "handicaps" imply loss of a part of the body or of a function. Many persons with amputations, cerebral palsy, learning problems, loss of sight or hearing, and other disabilities, have learned to compensate and if properly placed in a suitable job can perform extremely well.

Progressive diseases, on the other hand, ultimately lead to further, and perhaps total, disability. Ideally a job can be tailored to suit the physical ability of the applicant on a day-to-day or week-to-week basis for as long as he can do productive work.

Epilepsy

Most persons with this disorder lose little time from work and can work well if they are under regular medical care. They should not climb ladders or scaffolding, or operate vehicles or machines that would be dangerous if unconsciousness occurred.

Having an attack at work is uncommon; for the average epileptic it occurs perhaps once in several years. A convulsion is not in itself dangerous, but observing it is unpleasant and requires maturity and understanding among co-workers.

Workmen's Compensation

A medical department can do several things to improve a company's accident experience:

1. Screen candidates at preemployment examinations to ensure proper placement of candidates, and record preexisting disabilities and scars to protect the company from unwarranted excessive claims arising from subsequent accidents.

2. Advise management of physical and chemical hazards which can be corrected.

3. Treat injured employees promptly with a genuine concern for their welfare, and provide or arrange treatment of highest quality. Perhaps the attitude displayed by the medical personnel is the most important single factor in reducing disability and preventing ill will between a company and its employees.

4. Support and assist rehabilitation of the employee if it is indicated. The company's responsibility does not end when the medical or surgical treatment is finished but when the worker has been retrained to live and work with what he has left.

Except in cases where an employee elects an option to seek treatment from a physician of his own choice, a medical department can treat most industrial accidents right at the plant, saving time and in many cases reducing medical and hospital expenses.

The Second-Injury Law

Most states have a provision under the Workmen's Compensation Law called the "Second-Injury Clause." This legislation was enacted to encourage employers to hire persons who have a partial disability or handicap from a previous injury, at the same time protecting the new employer from excessive liability which might occur following a subsequent or "second" injury. In New York State, for example, this law states that if an employer knowingly hires an individual who has a partial disability, the employer will be limited in his liability in the event of a subsequent injury causing further disability to the employee. The employee is not penalized, however, since if further payments are necessary, they are paid to him out of a special "second-injury fund," sustained by all employers in the state.

To take advantage of this provision an employer may have to prove that he was aware of a preexisting condition when he employed the person—a reason for keeping careful records of scars and disabilities found at the time of the preemployment physical examination.

Determination of Disability

Disability may be partial or total, and either of these can be temporary or permanent. Estimation of an employee's disability depends on a comparison of the employee's physical and psychological capacity to work with the requirements of the job—or of any job the employee could reasonably be expected to do. The plant physician, being familiar with the job requirements, can make a good estimate of disability after examination of the employee and discussion with the employee's attending physician. Many employees try to return to their job before they have sufficiently recovered from their accident or illness. Others, consciously or subconsciously, seem to have greater disability than objective evidence would substantiate. If such problems cannot be solved by discussion and examination of the employee's attitudes, a psychiatric consultation may be helpful—and it should be done promptly.

COSTS AND VALUE OF A MEDICAL PROGRAM

A medical program cannot be judged solely on the basis of the number of examinations done or the number of treatments given, nor by an attempt to equate the cost of the program with savings in insurance and decreased absenteeism rates. Measuring costs per employee or trying to determine the effect of a medical program on the morale of the employees, or on the company's net profits, is as difficult as assessing an advertising campaign or the value of fringe benefits. It does seem logical that selection of healthier candidates, proper job placement, limitation of liability for preexisting disabilities, and earlier diagnosis and treatment for all types of health problems should result in less total expense to the company—and a healthier, more productive work force.

MANAGEMENT, THE PERSONNEL ADVISER, AND THE MEDICAL DEPARTMENT: A TEAM

Every manager is confronted with department problems involving morale, illness, or absenteeism, or with employees whose performance or behavior defies the usual analysis. Discussing these problems with the personnel adviser and the industrial nurse or physician often generates a workable solution.

BIBLIOGRAPHY

"A Management Guide for Occupational Health Programs," *Archives of Environmental Health,* vol. 9, pp. 403–413, September, 1964.

Council on Occupational Health of the American Medical Association, Henry Howe, M.D., Chairman, "The Role of Medicine within a Business Organization," *Journal of the American Medical Association,* vol. 210, no. 8, Nov. 24, 1969.

"Guide to the Development of Company Medical Policies," *Archives of Environmental Health,* vol. 11, pp. 729–733, November, 1965.

Hadden, Samuel B., M.D.: "Newer Treatment Techniques for Homosexuality," *Archives of Environmental Health,* September, 1966.

Leavell, Hugh R., M.D. and E. Gurney Clark, M.D.: *Preventive Medicine for the Doctor in His Community,* 3d ed., McGraw-Hill Book Company, New York, 1965.

Levinson, Harry: *Emotional Health: In the World of Work,* Harper & Row, Publishers, Incorporated, New York, 1964.

"Scope, Objectives and Functions of Occupational Health Programs" (revised 1960; also currently under revision), *Journal of the American Medical Association,* vol. 174, pp. 533–536, Oct. 1, 1960.

Shepard, William P., M.D.: *The Physician in Industry,* McGraw-Hill Book Company, New York, 1961.

Teplow, Leo: "New Dimensions for Management in Occupational Safety and Health," *Management Memo,* Organization Resources Counselors, Inc., New York, 1970.

Part 10

Government Controls

chapter 50

Federal and State Labor Laws

PETER A. DAVIS *Partner, Hooper, Hathaway, Fichera, Price & Davis, Attorneys at Law, Ann Arbor, Michigan*

SECTION X. CHAPTER 1. CATCH
FEDERAL AND STATE LABOR LAWS

> *"That the labor of a human being is not a commodity or article of commerce."*
> Section 6 of the Clayton Antitrust Act.

INTRODUCTION

In 1806, in Philadelphia, a handful of shoemakers organized a club and tendered a demand for higher wages to their employers. It was America's first labor case and the shoemakers were indicted by a grand jury, tried, convicted, and imprisoned for criminal conspiracy. Thomas Jefferson was then President, and Lewis and Clark were completing their overland journey west.

More than a century passed before workers could safely organize and strike for higher wages. To rectify certain antilabor abuses of the Sherman Antitrust Act of 1890, President Woodrow Wilson, in personally writing Section 6 of the Clayton Antitrust Act of 1914, recognized that human labor was an intangible product and workers should be allowed to combine to offset an employer's natural bargaining advantage. Anyone who has ever labored for a paycheck knows the tremendous inequality that can exist between employer and employee—indeed, for hundreds of years we referred to that relationship as master and servant.

In the half century following the Clayton act, our labor laws multiplied enormously, so that in all areas of employer-employee relations the government became, if not an active participant, a silent participant. The purpose of these laws is not to render the employee equal to the employer, but to render him less unequal.

Because modern personnel administration is the orchestration of human energies, just as in music there are certain well-settled rules which must be observed if the end result is to be harmonious. An employee now enters the marketplace under an umbrella of government protection, and it is important that the employer understand the nature and extent of that protection.

This chapter is divided into three parts. Part One surveys the various federal and state labor laws which may apply to most employers and briefly describes them so that the reader should be able to reliably determine how many of them apply to his business. Parts Two and Three deal exclusively with the National Labor Relations Act and the Fair Labor Standards Act since they have the greatest and broadest impact on modern personnel management. Part Two discusses the administration of these federal laws, and the machinery for their enforcement. Part Three explains, in practical terms, how they operate, what they mean, and how to comply with them.

A working knowledge of these laws will aid the employer in his day-to-day relations with his employees and will help to ameliorate those problems not otherwise prevented by sound employment practices. In other words, this chapter is intended to show the employer how to practice preventive labor law.

PART ONE: A SURVEY OF FEDERAL AND STATE LABOR LAWS
I. The Federal Labor Laws

National Labor Relations Act (NLRA). The principal federal labor law was adopted in 1935 and has been amended from time to time, most notably by the Taft-Hartley Act of 1947. Its stated purpose is to "diminish the causes of labor disputes" by guaranteeing the *choice* of employees to organize and bargain collectively with their employers.

Its coverage extends to industries involved in or substantially affecting interstate commerce.

To ensure that each side treats the other fairly, the NLRA has vested the National Labor Relations Board (NLRB) with extremely broad powers to investigate disputes and prevent persons from engaging in "unfair labor practices."

Fair Labor Standards Act (FLSA). Adopted in 1938, the FLSA is intended to maintain "minimum standards of living necessary for the health, efficiency and general well-being of workers" by regulating hours and wages and by outlawing oppressive child labor. As amended by the Equal Pay Act of 1963, the FLSA also condemns sex discrimination ("equal pay for equal work").

The FLSA is not as extensive in scope as the NLRA in that the reach of the FLSA is limited to industries engaged *in* commerce or in the production of goods *for* commerce, and does not reach activities merely affecting the flow of commerce.

The Secretary of Labor enforces the FLSA through the Wage and Hour Division of the Department of Labor and has power to apply civil and criminal sanctions.

Garnishment Provisions of the Consumer Credit Protection Act of 1968. Uniform restrictions on wage garnishments were imposed by Congress because garnishments frequently result in the loss of the debtor's job, causing the disruption of employment and production, and constituting a substantial burden on interstate commerce.

Under the statute only 25 percent (*or* that amount by which his take-home pay exceeds thirty times the prescribed federal minimum wage, *whichever is less*) of an employee's take-home pay (earnings less amounts required *by law* to be deducted) in any given work week may be subjected to garnishment. In addition, no employer may discharge any employee because his earnings have been subjected to garnishments for any one indebtedness. Usually one indebtedness is satisfied only through several garnishments; and, under the 25 percent limit, the number of garnishments necessary to cancel a single debt will increase. The statute does not prohibit discharge for garnishments upon a second indebtedness.

The garnishment restrictions do not apply to (1) court orders for support, (2) bankruptcy orders, or (3) state or federal tax debts.

The Wage and Hour Division of the Department of Labor enforces the new garnishment law, and criminal penalties exist for its violation. While the statute is designed to set minimum national restrictions, any state can set more stringent restrictions if it so desires.

It is doubtful that the federal limit on garnishments will seriously affect employer paperwork in the long run, as one of the apparent purposes of the restriction, and of the Consumer Credit Protection Act as a whole, is to reduce the free and easy granting of credit in this country, and the rather shocking collection practices that it fostered. Garnishment will be less useful to those imprudently extending credit, the very people who abused it in the past, and ultimately will be seldom used.

The United States Supreme Court, under due process principles, recently outlawed the use of wage garnishments by any creditor unless the creditor first obtains a court judgment against the debtor-employee.

Walsh-Healey Public Contracts Act of 1936. Manufacturers and dealers who furnish more than $10,000 in supplies to or for the federal government must observe certain working conditions and must pay the prevailing minimum wage as determined by the Secretary of Labor. (See Part Three.)

Davis-Bacon Public Works Act of 1931. Employers involved in federal construction, alteration, repair, painting, and decorating, where the contract exceeds $2,000, must pay their employees weekly at the prevailing minimum wage as determined by the Secretary of Labor. (See Part Three.)

Work Hours Act of 1962. All employees engaged on any federal project, or on any project financed in any part by federal loans or grants, are entitled to overtime payments at time and a half. Thus, any employer subject to the Davis-Bacon act also would be subject to the Work Hours Act. (See Part Three.)

Copeland Public Works "Kickback" Act of 1948. The Copeland act provides criminal penalties for any person who induces another to give up any compensation to which he is entitled for work on any public building or project which is financed in any part by federal loans or grants.

Welfare and Pension Plans Disclosure Act of 1958. All employers engaged in or affecting interstate commerce are required to register, report, and disclose employee welfare and pension benefit plans with the Secretary of Labor if the plan covers more than twenty-five persons.

Landrum-Griffin Labor-Management Reporting and Disclosure Act of 1959. Many employers overlook that while this well-known statute was enacted as a bill of rights for the union member, in that it was designed to clean up certain notorious practices of union leaders, it also has provisions that apply to the employer. Fiscal year reporting to the Secretary of Labor must be made by any employer who (1) makes certain payments or loans to any labor organization or officer, agent, or steward; (2) makes any payment to, or reimburses the expenses of, any employee for the purpose of causing him to influence other employees with respect to their right to organize and bargain collectively, unless such payment or reimbursement also was disclosed to such other employees at the time; (3) makes any expenditure with intent to interfere with his employees' rights or to obtain information concerning organizational activities, *except* for use in conjunction with certain proceedings, such as representation elections; (4) hires a labor relations consultant to persuade his employees with respect to their organization and bargaining rights, *except* in conjunction with certain proceedings, such as representation elections.

Reemployment of Veterans Provisions of the Selective Service Act of 1967. This statute guarantees reemployment rights to any person who is required to leave other than a temporary job for military service or training. In order to protect his rights such person must seek reemployment within ninety days after termination of his military duty (or hospitalization if such does not continue for more than a year after discharge). If still qualified to perform the duties of his old position, he must be restored to that position or to a like position with the same seniority, status, and pay. If he is not still qualified, by reason of disability sustained during military service, his employer must restore him to any other position for which he is qualified with seniority, status, and pay equal to his old job or approximately the same, consistent with the circumstances of the case. Alternatively, say the courts, a returning veteran would be entitled to severance pay. The act also forbids discharging or denying promotion to any person because of any pending military obligation.

In a suit against his former employer (or successor) to enforce his rights to reemployment, the employee has the burden of proving his old job was not temporary, but note that the employee is entitled to have the United States District Attorney represent him in his suit.

Labor Provisions of the Federal Civil Rights Act of 1964. This law, which is discussed more fully in Chapters 53, 69, and 70, forbids discrimination in hiring and employment conditions based on race, color, religion, national origin, or sex, and is administered by the Equal Employment Opportunity Commission (EEOC). An exception is made about the latter three criteria where it can be supported by a "bona fide occupational qualification." A 1965 amendment to the Civil Rights Act adds age (between thirty-five and sixty) to the criteria, requiring a bona fide occupational qualification to permit job discrimination. These laws apply to all employers of twenty-five or more persons.

II. The State Labor Laws

State labor relations acts. For industries not involved in or substantially affecting interstate commerce, the several states have enacted their own labor relations acts. These statutes generally are patterned after the NLRA with respect to both procedural requirements and substantive provisions.

State minimum wage acts. Most states have wage and hour legislation equivalent to the Fair Labor Standards Act and the Walsh-Healey and Davis-Bacon acts. They apply to smaller employers than do the federal laws and specifically require that the employer not be subject to the FLSA.

State pay period statutes. All states have laws regulating the length of pay periods. Normally these laws make it a crime to withhold wages due, except under compulsion of legal process (e.g., garnishment). Under most of these laws it is improper to dock an employee's wages on the assertion that he damaged company property, did not give his best efforts while on the job, etc.

State Sunday closing laws. Sunday closing laws may be archaic, as they are rapidly eroding in most states, but they do affect personnel practices, particularly in large retail stores where Sunday laws prohibit the sale of some but not all merchandise. If only a few departments are required to close down, the employer must decide how to treat the affected employees vis-à-vis those who will work on Sundays.

State juvenile employment laws. The states have their own laws prohibiting the employment of minors (usually under eighteen years) in hazardous or morally injurious occupations, and regulating their employment in other occupations (excepting farming, domestic work, family businesses, summer camps, etc.) through the issuance of work permits. See Chapter 53.

State fair employment practices acts. This subject is treated more fully in Chapters 53, 69, and 70, but it is pointed out here that, unlike application of other labor laws, in this area state law takes precedence. The Federal Civil Rights Act of 1964 provides that federal agencies will not act unless state law is invoked first. If an alleged unlawful employment practice occurs in a state which has its own law prohibiting the unlawful employment practice alleged, and the state has established a body to deal with such practices, no charges may be filed under federal law until sixty days after state proceedings have been commenced, unless the state proceedings are terminated earlier adversely to the charging party. Furthermore, when federal charges are filed the EEOC is required to notify the appropriate state authority and then wait at least sixty days for the state agency to take prior action.

Special state labor laws.   There may be special labor laws that affect personnel management in a particular state.   As a rule of thumb every employer who feels there is some question about a projected line of activity ought to consult with the company attorneys and obtain clearance beforehand.

California, for example, has a law establishing minimum wages and working conditions for apprentices.   (There is also a 1937 federal law authorizing the Secretary of Labor to develop labor standards to safeguard the welfare of apprentices.)   North Carolina, Washington, and Wisconsin have similar laws.

Michigan has had a statute on the books since 1903, making it a misdemeanor to induce a person to leave his home locality to work elsewhere, except under clear written contract.   That statute also provides for civil damages to the full extent of an employee's injury in the event of employer misrepresentation of the job's conditions, whether that misrepresentation is written or oral.   Obviously, all traveling salesmen are covered by the act, and it may well be true that the little-used statute would protect those members of our highly mobile population who find Michigan jobs, for example, and then move there to find the jobs were not quite what they expected.   The law is a throwback to the lumbering days when sawmills sent their men deep into the woods to carve out a living; but its terms bear vitality today and we often hear about an ancient law being used to vindicate modern rights.

Indiana has a contrary law of dubious constitutionality which makes it a misdemeanor for an Indiana employer to go outside the state and contract for alien labor to come into Indiana to work.

Both Indiana and Missouri require employers to give all departing employees a "service letter" or letter of recommendation, upon request.

Every personnel manager should make it a point to obtain copies of all state and municipal labor laws in effect in his area.   State trespass laws may have application when union organizers invade company premises.

Unemployment Compensation Laws—A Joint Federal-State Program

Unemployment compensation insurance is available in every state as a joint federal-state program.   The federal government pays the costs of administration of the program which is administered by the state governments.   Federal funds for this program are obtained by the Federal Unemployment Tax Act (FUTA) which is imposed on virtually every employer.

In order to qualify for unemployment benefits the former employee must comply with the procedural steps outlined by state law as to filing deadline, employment duration and wage, waiting period, availability for work, and so forth.   The employer may have valid defenses which will prevent an employee from receiving benefits at all, or for a period of time, usually six weeks.   Those individuals who voluntarily quit without employer cause, who are discharged for theft, fighting, misconduct, or intoxication, who lose their jobs due to imprisonment, who fail to report for new work upon notification, who are pregnant, or who fraudulently obtain benefits, will be disqualified from receiving benefits for at least six weeks. An employee who falsified an employment application form generally will be disqualified from unemployment benefits for the appropriate statutory period.

Needless to say, the job application form is an important document and always should be referred to when a former employee applies for unemployment compensation.

Leaves of absence also serve to disqualify for the period of the absence when they are obtained at the request of the employee. In some states employees will be entitled to unemployment benefits even when their plant is closed for a nonpay "vacation" period pursuant to a collective bargaining agreement. This is so because the employer voluntarily executed the contract and the resulting unemployment is attributable to him, despite the employees' bargaining representative's consent to the vacation period provision in the contract.

Unemployment resulting from a labor dispute, or a plant shutdown caused by a labor dispute, in which the compensation applicant was involved, will serve to bar the applicant from unemployment benefits for the entire period of the dispute. In situations where employees are discharged for participating in wildcat strikes, however, the employees generally will be entitled to benefits, after the statutory disqualification period.

In view of the limited disqualification periods some employers may feel it is not economical to contest a compensation claim. The short answer to this is that the ordinary person will find other work before the six-week or so disqualification period expires; no one likes to live on unemployment compensation benefits. And if several employees are affected by the same defense it could very well be uneconomical not to rely on available defenses and contest their claims in a single proceeding.

As in all other areas of labor relations employer fairness will be rewarded. No employer should want the reputation of being hard-nosed, and neither should he want a soft-hearted reputation. It is possible to keep your employees at arms' length and still be able to shake hands.

PART TWO: ADMINISTRATION OF THE FEDERAL LAWS

I. The Expansion of Federal Labor Laws

The federal labor laws and the capsulized one-paragraph annotations of court decisions interpreting them have now expanded to approximately four thousand pages spread out over five volumes of the United States code. In addition, the full texts of thousands of court decisions would fill many more volumes. And this says nothing of the countless decisions of the National Labor Relations Board, presently filling 191 large volumes, and growing by several volumes a year; or the more than fifty volumes of arbitration decisions. No lawyer in general practice can master this tremendous mountain of material—and neither can that modern-day specialist, the labor lawyer.

Certainty in labor law is a fleeting thing. Indeed, the National Labor Relations Board itself cannot always agree on a consistent and uniform application of the law. Apart from the sheer size of the statutory and decisional law, there are two reasons for the vagaries and fluctuations of labor doctrines. First, the board is composed of five members who are appointed by the President for five-year terms, the expiration dates being staggered so one member's term expires each year. Thus, each full-term President appoints at least four NLRB members during his term of office. These appointments are more political than judicial appointments, and the politics of labor always influences the direction in which a particular board may lean. Second, the board has broad discretion to interpret the National Labor Relations Act in accordance with *changing industrial experience,* and is not bound by either its own prior decisions or the decisions of United States courts. Each case coming before the board must stand or fall on its own facts, and no two cases are ever completely alike.

II. The Machinery for Administration of the Federal Labor Laws

National Labor Relations Board (NLRB). The NLRB cannot enter into a labor dispute unless it is requested to do so by individuals, employers, or unions. Once it enters a dispute it has two powers which it can exercise and these powers are separated by the NLRB's parallel vertical organization. Its investigative powers are exercised by the Office of the General Counsel while its adjudicative or quasi-judicial powers are exercised by the five-member board.

Both of these powers are used conjointly in pursuit of the NLRB's two main functions under the statute: (1) to prevent and remedy unfair labor practices by either employers or labor organizations, and (2) to conduct secret ballot elections to determine whether workers wish to have unions represent them in collective bargaining. Unfair labor practice cases are referred to as C cases because they are instituted by the filing of a *charge*. Election cases are referred to as R cases because they are instituted by the filing of a *representation petition*.

The NLRB has thirty-one regional offices where cases are filed. C cases are investigated by the regional office staff and about 65 percent of such cases are dismissed or withdrawn as being without merit. The other 35 percent go to the regional director who attempts to get the parties together in voluntary settlement. Unsettled cases are heard by a trial examiner on formal written complaint issued by the regional director, and on answer filed by the opposing party. Trial examiners are authorized to conduct formal hearings, much like court trials, and issue decisions in the form of recommended orders. The parties may then appeal such decisions to the five-member board in Washington. Of the C cases originally filed, not more than 5 percent ever reach the board in Washington. In fiscal 1969, for example, 18,651 C cases were filed at the regional level, but the Board was called upon to decide only 732 of them.

It is apparent that in C cases the thirty-one regional directors wield the NLRB's investigative powers. In R cases, however, they also exercise the board's adjudicative powers. Utilizing these powers, the regional directors decide the appropriateness of employee bargaining units, order elections to be held, conduct the elections, and certify the results. Hearings are held in R cases as they are in C cases, but by a hearing officer and not by a trial examiner. These hearings are not adversary as are C hearings, and the hearing officer does not have power to decide issues by recommended order. The transcript of the hearing conducted by the hearing officer is submitted to the regional director who renders a decision. In some few cases the decision of a regional director in an R case is reviewable by the five-member board. When it is not, and an employer wishes to contest the appropriateness of the bargaining unit, the procedure is for him to refuse to bargain with the employees' representative after the election, wait for a C case to be started for the unfair labor practice of refusing to bargain, and then contest the appropriateness of the unit in the C case proceedings.

Generally, the parties to a dispute voluntarily comply with the board's orders. Where they do not the board will ask a United States Court of Appeals to enforce its orders. So, too, any party to a dispute who feels aggrieved by a board order may seek review in a Court of Appeals. During 1969, the ten circuits of the Court of Appeals decided a total of 363 NLRB cases, affirming the board in whole or in part in 82 percent of them.

Insofar as the appeal of labor cases is concerned, both within the NLRB and beyond to a federal court, corporate management should decide to exercise its appeal rights only after careful consideration of the policy ramifications, apart from the legal implications which are the responsibility of its counsel. The expense of the appellate procedure must be weighed against various competing factors, including

(1) the likelihood of prevailing on appeal, (2) the economic advantages to be gained, (3) the effect on corporate goodwill among employees, the union, and the community, and (4) the effect on those governmental agencies charged with administering the labor laws, before whom the employer will have numerous future dealings.

In the past many employers resorted to use of the appellate machinery only to gain time, without regard to the merits of their cases. Just recently the board began fining employers (e.g., $500 plus heavy costs) who take frivolous appeals from recommended orders of its trial examiners in unfair labor practice cases, and some Circuit Courts of Appeal have coupled enforcement orders with suggestions that fines be levied for wasting the court's time with dilatory appeals from board orders.

Federal Mediation and Conciliation Service (FMCS). A product of the 1947 Taft-Hartley amendment of the National Labor Relations Act, the FMCS has none of the powers of the NLRB, being strictly an independent agency geared to assist in resolving labor disputes of major national proportions. The FMCS may, on its own motion or on request of one of the parties, offer its services in settling disputes which threaten to cause substantial interruptions in commerce. Experience has shown that where communications break down between two disputing parties, a third voice is often useful in restoring a reasoned approach to solving the dispute, without further widening of the gulf.

Once the FMCS accepts the task of mediating and conciliating major disputes, the parties must cooperate and attend meetings called by the FMCS and must embark on a good faith effort to resolve the matter. The failure or refusal to do so would constitute a refusal to bargain, subject to investigation and adjudication by the NLRB.

If the FMCS cannot get the parties to agree within a reasonable time, it must attempt to get them to try other means of settlement without resort to strike or lockout. Among the "other means" suggested by theTaft-Hartley Act is the employer's submission of his "last offer of settlement for approval or rejection in a secret ballot." This is the only area within the federal labor laws where an employer is authorized to submit what is tantamount to a take-it-or-leave-it offer. Normally that kind of offer, as opposed to a "best offer," is an unfair labor practice because it suggests a refusal to bargain further at a point when a refusal is without economic or good faith support.

The statute states that the services of the FMCS are intended as a last resort in exceptional cases.

National Labor-Management Panel. Also established by the Taft-Hartley Act, the panel has twelve members appointed by the President, half of whom are management-oriented and the other half labor-oriented. The panel is an advisory body designed only to advise the director of the FMCS in the avoidance of industrial disputes with particular reference to controversies affecting the general welfare of the country.

Presidential Board of Inquiry. The Taft-Hartley Act authorizes the President to appoint an *ad hoc* Board of Inquiry to inquire into the issues involved in disputes which imperil the national health or safety.

Presidential injunctions. Upon receipt of a report from a Board of Inquiry, the President, through the Attorney General, may obtain an order from the appropriate United States District Court enjoining a threatened strike or lockout for sixty days. The awesome powers of a Presidential injunction are provided for by the statute only in case of national emergencies; that is, only when the District Court finds that the actual or threatened strike or lockout affects an entire industry or a substantial part of an industry engaged in interstate or foreign trade, commerce, transportation, transmission, communication, or manufacturing, *and* if such strike or lockout will imperil the national health or safety if continued.

When the District Court issues the injunction the President must reconvene the Board of Inquiry. At the end of the sixty-day injunction the board must report the current positions of the parties to the President, who must make the report public. At that point the NLRB has fifteen days within which to conduct a secret ballot of the employees to determine whether they will accept the final offer of settlement made by their employer. After the results are certified by the NLRB the President is required to submit a full report to the Congress which can take further action if necessary, by way of special legislation.

Department of Labor. First established in 1888, the U.S. Department of Labor was elevated to cabinet level status and placed under the control of the Secretary of Labor in 1913. The statutory purpose of the department is to "foster, promote and develop the welfare of the wage earners of the United States, to improve their working conditions, and to advance their opportunities for profitable employment."

The department has the following eight offices under its jurisdiction and supervision:

Advisory Committee on Construction Safety and Health
Bureau of Employees' Compensation
Bureau of Labor Standards
Bureau of Labor Statistics
Division of Public Contracts
Employees' Compensation Appeals Board
United States Employment Service
Wage and Hour Division
Women's Bureau

Personnel management in most companies should be familiar with two of these offices:

1. *The Bureau of Labor Statistics.* Comprehensive data, including copies of many collective bargaining agreements, can be obtained by the public from the bureau. Any employer, employee, or union has a right to obtain *all* bureau data which may aid in the settlement of any labor dispute, whether that dispute is under the NLRA or the FLSA.

2. *The Wage and Hour Division.* Although the division is within the Department of Labor, the President rather than the Secretary of Labor appoints the all-important administrator of the division. Minimum wages and maximum hours are established for various industries upon analysis and recommendation of industry committees.

The administrator of the Wage and Hour Division is empowered to investigate and gather data regarding the wages, hours, and other conditions and practices of employment in any industry subject to the act, and a wage and hour investigator may enter upon company premises and do any of the following:

Inspect the company property.

Inspect and copy company records regarding wages, hours and other conditions and practices of employment.

Question employees.

Make such investigation as he may deem necessary or appropriate.

Utilize personnel of state labor agencies to assist him.

Record keeping is of crucial importance and the administrator prescribes by regulation or order the type of records which must be kept, how long they are to be kept, and what reports an employer is to file.

Any employer who violates the FLSA shall be liable to any employee affected by the violation in the amount of his unpaid minimum wages, or his unpaid overtime compensation, and in an additional *equal* amount as liquidated damages. Any employee may bring suit on his own behalf, or the Secretary of Labor may sue on his behalf. Injunctive relief and criminal penalties of six months of imprisonment and fines up to $10,000 also are provided for by the act. Orders of the department are subject to court review.

American Arbitration Association. Collective bargaining agreements provide for grievance adjustment by arbitration. Normally a three-member arbitration board is selected, with each side supplying one arbitrator and the third arbitrator being selected by a process of elimination from a list of names furnished by the American Arbitration Association. A majority vote of the three-member arbitration panel, or grievance board, decides. There is no appeal from an arbitration award and no procedure for setting aside such an award, unless fraud on the part of the arbitrators can be shown. An arbitration award may, however, be enforced in state or federal court.

Many collective bargaining agreements provide for arbitration by a single arbitrator, selected in accordance with American Arbitration Association rules, and this is the preferred procedure because it is the neutral arbitrator in the three-man panel who is the "swing man" and decides the dispute. Two members of the three-man panel would therefore seem superfluous.

The American Arbitration Association has many top-flight labor arbitrators available, and some of their awards are cast in the form of opinions which are published and may be cited, not necessarily as precedent but as good reasoning, in subsequent labor hearings of one type or another. The NLRB, however, is not accustomed to giving much weight to prior arbitration awards.

PART THREE: OPERATION OF THE FEDERAL LABOR LAWS

I. The National Labor Relations Act (NLRA)

Jurisdictional scope of the NLRA

1. *Interstate Commerce Concept.* Although some state and some federal labor laws apply to all businesses, no business will be simultaneously subject to both the National Labor Relations Act and a state labor relations act: they are mutually exclusive.

Application of the principal labor law hinges on a determination of the scope of an employer's business. If the company is engaged in interstate commerce, or if its business substantially affects interstate commerce, it will be subject to the National Labor Relations Act. Businesses engaged in intrastate commerce, and which have no substantial impact on interstate commerce, will be subject to the basic state labor law. Where there is a close question, and both state and federal agencies claim jurisdiction, the state must defer to the federal agency. In fact, the parties to state proceedings may petition the NLRB for an advisory opinion on whether the pending labor dispute should really be before the federal rather than the state agency.

2. *The Federal Law in Theory.* Theoretically there are two independent grounds for asserting jurisdiction under the NLRA: the *in-commerce ground* and the *affecting-commerce ground.* Most industries engaged in interstate commerce come within the purview of the NLRA, with the exception of railroads and airlines which fall under the coverage of the Railway Labor Act of 1926. Those industries *affecting commerce*—and all do to some extent—will be subject to the NLRA only if their impact is great enough.

In determining whether enough impact on interstate commerce exists to give the federal agency jurisdiction, the statutory test is whether a work stoppage would impede the free flow of interstate commerce. For instance, a company which is wholly located in one state and which sells only to customers in that state will, nonetheless, be subject to federal law if it purchases a substantial amount of its raw materials or other goods originating from out of state. This is so because a strike of its employees presumedly would impede the free flow of its supplies across state lines. "Substantial amount" here does not mean a large percentage but means a large dollar volume. (Note that a large percentage, almost no matter what the volume, would put the business *in* commerce and not require application of the affecting commerce test.)

3. *The Federal Law in Practice.* Because application of the theoretical test is cumbersome and time-consuming, the National Labor Relations Board has developed a set of practical yardsticks by which it determines whether to assert jurisdiction over an enterprise affecting commerce. The current jurisdictional standards are as follows:

Nonretail businesses will be subject to the NLRA if they have an annual outflow (sales) or inflow (purchases) across state lines of at least $50,000. It does not matter whether this traffic is direct or indirect; that is to say, a local businessman who buys $51,000 in goods from a local supplier will be subject to the act if the local supplier fills the order from out of state.

Retail businesses will be subject to the act if their gross annual sales are at least $500,000, even though all of the sales may be "local."

Different jurisdictional standards are used for certain other businesses:

Office buildings—Total annual revenue of $100,000, of which at least $25,000 is derived from tenants who meet any of the jurisdictional standards except the indirect outflow-inflow standard for nonretail businesses.

Public utilities—At least $250,000 total annual volume of business, or $50,000 outflow-inflow, direct or indirect.

Newspapers—At least $200,000 total annual volume of business.

Radio, television, telephone or telegraph companies—At least $100,000 total annual volume of business.

Hotels, motels, or residential apartment houses—At least $500,000 total annual volume of business.

Private hospitals operated for profit—At least $250,000 total annual volume of business.

Private nursing homes operated for profit—At least $100,000 total annual volume of business.

Private nonprofit colleges—Gross annual revenue of at least $1 million for operating expenses.

Transportation enterprises, links and channels of interstate commerce—At least $50,000 total annual income derived from interstate passenger and freight transportation services, or $50,000 derived from services performed for customers meeting any jurisdictional standard other than the indirect outflow-inflow standard for nonretail businesses.

Transit systems—At least $250,000 total annual volume of business.

Taxicab companies—At least $500,000 total annual volume of business.

National defense industries—All businesses whose operations have a substantial impact on national defense, whether or not their operations satisfy any other of these standards, will be subject to NLRB jurisdiction.

Associations—Regarded as single employer with the annual business of all of its members being totaled to determine whether the association itself will be subject to the NLRA.

Enterprises in the District of Columbia—All businesses in the District of Columbia are subject to the act. Business in United States territories are measured by the other jurisdictional standards, as applicable.

Satisfaction of any of these standards also must be coupled with some evidence that the business in fact has the requisite effect on interstate commerce. Generally speaking, the NLRB will decline jurisdiction over employers not meeting any of the above standards. But it should be remembered that these standards do not fully measure the extent of the board's discretion or the breadth of the National Labor Relations Act. While the above standards were in effect in 1971, new standards will be developed for other and new businesses, and some of the old standards may be changed.

A word of caution: any employer who refuses to divulge economic data in accordance with the applicable standard will be presumed to fall within the ambit of the federal labor laws—his is a special jurisdictional pigeonhole. It is never wise, in this or any other area of labor law, to withhold information from a governmental agency.

Employee rights. The heart of the National Labor Relations Act is Section 7, which guarantees employees certain rights:

> Employees shall have the right to self-organization, to form, join, or assist labor organizations, to bargain collectively through representatives of their own choosing, and to engage in other concerted activities for the purpose of collective bargaining or other mutual aid or protection, and shall also have the right to refrain from any or all of such activities except to the extent that such right may be affected by an agreement requiring membership in a labor organization as a condition of employment.

These rights are protected and implemented by Section 8 of the act, prohibiting certain enumerated unfair labor practices by employers or unions, and by Section 9, establishing election procedures for employee choice of a collective bargaining representative.

The last clause of Section 7 has reference to union security clauses—contained in most collective bargaining agreements—requiring all newly hired employees to join the union after thirty days of employment as a condition of continued employment.

Despite the universality of union security clauses the Section 7 right to refrain from organized activities is an important right and guarantees, among other things, the choice of nonunion employees to continue working while union co-workers are striking their place of business. Nonstrikers who choose to continue working are entitled to free access to the plant to do so.

Similarly, union rules which are intended to limit production need not be obeyed by union members, and the union may not fine them for violating such rules in exercise of their Section 7 rights.

Employer unfair labor practices. Section 8 of the act condemns six types of employer conduct as unfair labor practices:

1. *Interference with Employee Rights.* An employer may not interfere with, restrain, or coerce employees in the exercise of their Section 7 rights. Threats of reprisals for engaging in union activity, or promises of benefits for refraining therefrom, are illegal. The limits for permissible employer conduct are more fully explained by way of example in the discussion of representation election campaigns below.

2. *Employer Domination of Union.* It is an unfair labor practice for an employer to dominate or interfere with the formation or administration of any labor organization, or contribute financial or other support to it. Where two unions are competing to organize a company's employees, the employer must not indicate which union he prefers, or which union he would least like to meet at the bargaining table. Company-formed unions, often called "safety committees" or some such euphemistic term, are illegal. By the same token, it would constitute illegal

assistance to a union for an employer to pay wages to a union steward who does no work for the company.

3. *Discrimination for Union Activities.*   An employer must not encourage or discourage membership in any union by discrimination in regard to hire, tenure, or any other term or condition of employment.   Discharge for union activities is the most common unfair labor practice—and the one most easily avoided by the employer.   In a proceeding for such a violation the NLRB has said it will want answers to these six questions:

   a. What reason did the company give the employee for its action against him?

   b. Did the company take the same action against other employees for the same reason?

   c. Was the employee warned at any time before the company took its action?

   d. Did the company know before its action that the employee was a union member or was active in union affairs?

   e. What was the employee's work record—efficiency ratings, wage increases, promotions, supervisor praise, etc.?

   f. What was the company's attitude toward unions, and toward the employee's union in particular?

4. *Discrimination for NLRB Activities.*   Obviously it is not only bad practice but it is illegal to discharge or otherwise discriminate against any employee who files charges or gives testimony under the NLRA.

5. *Employer Refusal to Bargain in Good Faith.*   The statutory language makes it an unfair labor practice for an employer "to refuse to bargain collectively with the representatives of his employees" as to "rates of pay, wages, hours of employment, or other conditions of employment."

   The duty to bargain includes the duty to bargain *in good faith* over all mandatory bargaining subjects.

   Good faith in this context does not mean that the employer has to like the union representative or enjoy any stage of the negotiations.   It means simply that he intends to comply with the laws and intends to use every resource and skill available to him to reach an acceptable agreement within those laws.   ("Hard bargaining" as opposed to "surface bargaining.")   More fully:

   He must meet to bargain at all reasonable times.

   He must make *some* offer, even if it consists of continuing the present wages, hours, and working conditions.

   He must disclose economic data to support his position on wages, if he claims he cannot go higher because of the company's economic position.

   He may be required to furnish economic data to the union to enable it to formulate its own position.

   He must bargain to an impasse, if necessary, on those subjects which the law deems mandatory bargaining subjects.

   No employer should reject a union offer without at least indicating what would be an acceptable offer.   Concessions are not required however.

   Mandatory bargaining subjects are those within or directly related to the statutory phrase "wages, hours, and other terms and conditions of employment."   A suggestive list of directly related subjects would include, but not be limited to: seniority, retirement, pensions, supplemental unemployment benefits, grievance procedures, fringe benefits, vacations, bonuses, employee housing, prices in employee cafeterias, health insurance, plant removal or relocation, union shop clauses, dues check-off clauses, safety rules not required by state law, discipline and discharge, and job classification.

   Permissive bargaining subjects are those which are neither mandatory nor prohibited (such as closed shop clauses), but on which the employer may bargain if he chooses to do so. Permissive subjects can be used to advantage in collective bargaining by employers who are willing to use them in exchange for union concessions more desirable to the company.

The employer should *never* bargain over his management rights. Without a collective bargaining agreement that contains a management rights clause, labor-management relations will easily break down. The right to direct the work force; to determine its size, to schedule hours, overtime, and shifts; to set training programs; to determine what products will be made and at what cost; to promulgate shop rules for absenteeism, behavior, and discipline; to subcontract work; and to generally *manage* the business, are all management rights and should not be bargained away.

6. *Hot Cargo Agreements.* The sixth statutory employer unfair labor practice outlaws agreements to cease handling another employer's products, or to cease doing business with another, except in the construction industry with reference to on-site subcontractors and in the garment industry with reference to on-premises jobbers or manufactures.

Union unfair labor practices. There are eight union unfair labor practices defined by Section 8 of the act, three of which (1, 3, and 8) are equivalent to employer unfair labor practices (1, 3, and 6):

1. *Union Restraints on Employee Rights.* The word "interference" is not used in that section of the statute proscribing union restraint or coercion of employees in the exercise of their Section 7 rights, as it is used in the comparable section on employer conduct. The omission is deliberate because, as explained by a proviso clause, unions are authorized to prescribe their own rules of membership and such rules necessarily interfere with individual rights, as do all majority rules from time to time. The following are types of union conduct that have been found to restrain or coerce employees' exercise of their Section 7 rights:

Mass picketing in such numbers that nonstriking employees are physically barred from the plant.

Acts of force or violence on the picket line.

Threats to employees who indicate disagreement with union goals or methods, whether strikes or other activities.

Threats to workers who do not wish to sign authorization cards.

Racial discrimination, as in refusing to process black employee grievances.

Procuring discharge of maverick union members for failure to wholeheartedly support the union.

The same subsection of the act declares that it shall be an unfair labor practice for a union to restrain or coerce an employer in the selection of his representatives for collective bargaining or in the adjustment of grievances. Therefore, no union has the right to insist that the employer's bargaining team include the company president, or that a particular individual not liked by a union agent be kept out of the room, or, indeed, that the negotiators have final authority. An attempt to get the employer to favor one of two competing unions is also a union unfair labor practice.

2. *Causing Employer Discrimination.* A union may not cause, or attempt to cause, an employer to discriminate against employees as a means of encouraging or discouraging union membership. Union attempts to secure a closed shop violates this subsection of the act, as does union insistence that the employer hire only members of the union, or persons approved by the union (without regard to union security provisions giving a new employee thirty days to join the union after hire).

3. *Refusal to Bargain in Good Faith.* The same bargaining obligation imposed on employers is imposed on unions. Union insistence on an unreasonably long

contract duration, or insistence upon any illegal contract provisions (closed shop, discriminatory hiring hall) is a refusal to bargain.

4. *Strikes and Boycotts for Certain Purposes.* It is an unfair labor practice for a union to engage in, or induce others to engage in, any strike or other concerted activity when an object of such strike or activity is: (*a*) to force or require any employer or self-employer to join a union or enter into a hot cargo agreement; (*b*) to promote a so-called secondary boycott (i.e., to force or require a person to stop dealing with products or services of another person); (*c*) to force or require an employer to recognize or bargain with the union when another union has been certified; or (*d*) to force or require an employer to assign particular work to employees in a particular union rather than to employees in another union, unless such employer is failing to observe a board-determined appropriate bargaining unit as to such employees.

Under a proviso clause, it is lawful for any person to refuse to enter the premises of another employer whose employees are legally on strike.

5. *Excessive Initiation Fees.* A union may not require employees to pay excessive or discriminatory fees in order to join the union. The board has sole discretion to determine what constitutes an excessive or discriminatory fee.

6. *Featherbedding.* Any union causing, or attempting to cause, an employer to pay or deliver (or agree to do so) anything of value for services not performed, or not to be performed, shall be guilty of an unfair labor practice. There are very few cases where the board has found a union demand to constitute an exaction for unperformed services, or featherbedding, no matter how outrageous the proposal may seem to the employer.

7. *Picketing for Certain Purposes.* Basically, there are three types of picketing: informational, organizational, and recognitional.

Informational picketing, sometimes called advisory picketing or advertising picketing, is intended to inform the unorganized public that a labor dispute exists and is permissible activity provided the picket signs are truthful and the picketers are peaceful. If this type of picketing has the effect of stopping or seriously interrupting deliveries or pickups by third parties, then it is illegal.

Organizational picketing is illegal when its primary purpose is to force or require employees to select the union as their bargaining representative *and* where any of these three situations exists: (*a*) another union has been lawfully recognized by the employer, (*b*) a valid representation election has been conducted by the NLRB within the preceding twelve months, or (*c*) such picketing has been conducted without an election petition being filed within a reasonable period of time not to exceed thirty days from the commencement of such picketing.

Recognitional picketing is illegal if its primary purpose is to force or require the employer to recognize the union as bargaining representative of his employees, *and* if any of the three situations described under organizational picketing also exists.

8. *Hot Cargo Agreements.* See employer unfair labor practice number 6, above.

Unfair labor practice cases generally

1. *Time for Filing.* The charge must be filed with a regional office of the board no later than six months from the date of the alleged unfair labor practice. An exception is made for employees prevented from filing due to military service: they may file within six months from date of military discharge.

2. *Procedure.* Unfair labor practice charges are investigated by field examiners. Charges generally are disposed of during this investigation by adjustment, withdrawal, or dismissal; or they may be modified. Formal complaint is issued by the regional director if he finds the charge well-grounded and the case unsettleable. Answer to the complaint is filed and a public hearing is held before a trial

examiner who makes findings of fact and prepares a recommended order which is sent to the NLRB in Washington. Unless one of the parties objects (files written exceptions to the order) the trial examiner's recommended order becomes the order of the board. Cases excepted to are reviewed by the board on written briefs, and sometimes oral argument. Decisions of the board may be reviewed by a federal court. See the discussion of NLRB machinery in Part Two, above.

3. *Remedies for Unfair Labor Practices.* The ever-growing list of remedies which the board fashions to prevent and adjust unfair labor practices speaks for itself:

Back-pay orders plus interest.

Reinstatement of discharged employees, with seniority.

Order to bargain collectively and sign a contract if agreement is reached; this order may be entered in some cases even though no election has been held and even though a true majority of employees may not want a union.

Dissolve a company-dominated union.

Order a new election.

Order to abrogate employer agreements with third persons, such as agreements to contract out work.

Offer reinstatement and moving expenses to employees of runaway plants.

Furnish the union with economic data and lists of employee names and addresses.

Grant the union access to the plant premises and bulletin boards, or equal time to respond to employer captive-audience speeches.

Order employers to post notices or give speeches of apology to employees.

The board may also seek federal court injunctions to enforce the NLRA.

Free speech. An important right given employers and unions alike is the right to free speech, against which oral and written expressions in unfair labor practice cases and representation cases must be weighed. The statute provides that:

> The expressing of any views, argument, or opinion, or the dissemination thereof, whether in written, printed, graphic, or visual form shall not constitute or be evidence of an unfair labor practice under any of the provisions of this Act, *if such expression contains no threat of reprisal or force or promise of benefit.* [Italics supplied.]

Application of the employer's free-speech right is best illustrated with reference to permissible and impermissible employer conduct during representation election campaigns, discussed below.

Employee representatives and elections. Section 9 of the act governs the selection of employee representatives for purposes of collective bargaining, and the determination of the unit of employees to be so represented.

There are three types of elections provided for in the act:

Representation elections, in which the employees vote to determine whether they wish to be represented in collective bargaining. Such elections are held upon petition of a union, or of the employees, or of the employer.

Decertification elections, in which the employees vote to determine whether they wish to get rid of an incumbent union. Either the union or the employees can petition for this type of election.

Deauthorization elections, in which the employees vote to determine whether the authority of their representative to make a union-shop contract should be revoked. Only the employees can petition for such an election.

No election of any type can be held in the unit if any type of valid election has been held in the preceding twelve-month period, or if there is a present *valid* contract (contract bar rule), as to the employees involved.

Representation elections. When a petition for an election is filed, the board's regional director is required to determine forthwith the unit of employees appropriate for collective bargaining and to direct an election in such unit.

1. *The Appropriate Bargaining Unit.*   A bargaining unit must consist of at least two employees under federal law.   State laws generally allow one-man units.

There may be several appropriate units in any given case, but the *most* appropriate unit is that unit which shall assure its members the "fullest freedom" in the exercise of their Section 7 rights.   While the statute refers to "the employer unit, craft unit, plant unit, or subdivision thereof," those terms have been interpreted to allow multiplant units (same employer or craft) and multiemployer units (same craft or plant).   The board is bound by three statutory prohibitions:

a. A single unit may not contain both professionals and nonprofessionals, unless a majority of the professionals vote for inclusion.

b. A craft unit shall not be deemed inappropriate on the ground that a different unit was established by prior ruling, unless a majority of the craft employees vote against separate representation.

c. Guards shall not be included in units composed of other employees against whom the guards enforce plant property or safety rules.

The extent to which employees have organized must not be given any weight by the board in determining the appropriate bargaining unit.   In practice the board pays little more than lip service to this provision of the act, since it is generally presumed that employees who have enough community of interest to organize together have enough community of interest to be represented together in the same bargaining unit.

The community-of-interest test is broken down into at least three parts:

a. The similarity of skills and working conditions.

b. Prior unit and bargaining history.

c. The desires of the employees.

A present member of the board, in a 1969 speech, said that a separate and identifiable community of interest can only be determined in light of constantly changing circumstances; and that the structure of the industry, the content of jobs, and the impact of changing technology, all will affect the board's unit determinations.

Sometimes the board will find a joint-employer or multi-employer bargaining unit.   This is especially common in the retail field.   Modern retail and discount stores often have many departments which are staffed and operated by other companies under license or lease agreement.   The board has said in these cases that all selling employees in such a store may be an appropriate unit even though their nominal employers may be different companies: because the store is seen as a single enterprise, there is a single, strongly identifiable community of interest, and usually one employer dominates.

As evidence of changing board rules in this area, the insurance industry for seventeen years was required to be organized on a state-wide basis only.   In 1961 the board reversed itself and permitted local single-office organization.

A unit determination is never final: it may be subject to review by a clarification petition, or by a union claim that certain outside employees ought to be included on the theory that they have become "an accretion to the unit."

2. *Authorization Cards.*   A labor organization or individual seeking representation rights by election petition must show that at least 30 percent of the employees sought to be organized have indicated their support of such representation (but this is not required where a representation election is sought through proper recognitional picketing).   The customary method of obtaining and showing this support is through the use of authorization or membership cards.

An employer may petition for an election simply by showing that some union is courting his employees; he need not show that any percentage favor or disfavor representation.

Authorization cards must be dated—although ofttimes employees sign them in blank, without dating them or reading what they are signing—and cannot be more than twelve months old to be valid support for an election petition. Union organizers have been known to collect cards over a period of years and then update them when ready to rely on them. For these reasons one federal court has said that authorization cards are a "notoriously unreliable" means of showing union support.

Non–English-speaking employees can validly sign cards that have been explained to them.

The board has said that union organizers' oral representations to employees in soliciting signatures on authorization cards are sales talk or "puffing," and union agents can say that "practically everyone" has signed when in fact that is not true.

The cards must show, however, that the signers desire a particular union to represent them. They cannot merely indicate a desire to union representation.

It is important to remember that authorization cards can be used for two purposes: first, cards signed by 30 percent of the claimed unit can get an election, and second, a numerical majority of the cards can be used to support a demand for bargaining without an election, as an election presumably would be useless if a majority had already signed up.

Union organizers who obtain signatures by promising employees that the cards will be used for an election, and then do not petition for an election but demand bargaining on a claim of majority status, will be guilty of an unfair labor practice, voiding the demand for bargaining. Proof of this conduct, and its effect on employees, is extremely difficult, however.

When a union approaches a company and demands to bargain upon the strength of a majority of the cards, the employer should *never* call this bluff and ask to see the cards. If he does and the union has a majority, it will be an unfair labor practice for the employer to refuse to bargain. If an inspection reveals that the union has miscounted and does not have a majority of the cards, the union can demand an election, having more than 30 percent; if the union loses, it can claim the employer's postinspection activities dissipated the union's majority status; and if successful in this claim, the union can obtain a bargaining order even though it lost the election.

When faced with a card-based bargaining demand the employer should immediately petition for an election if he is confident of winning, and gain labor peace for another year under the twelve-month rule. He must, however, have a *good faith doubt* that the union has gathered a majority of signatures. Should the employer have *independent knowledge,* gained perhaps from talks with employees and observation of the number of striking employees, that the union does have majority status, it is an unfair labor practice to reject a card-based bargaining demand.

If the employer is not confident of winning but does have a good faith doubt about majority status (formed, for example, on the basis of voluntary employee statements that they know the union has stale cards, or has double-talked employees into signing), he should refuse the bargaining demand and wait for the union to file an unfair labor practice charge. The board can then consider the validity of the cards if a majority are presented.

Also, if the employer ever takes a look at the cards, sees who has signed any of them, and later on discharges a signed-up employee, the employer may be faced with an unfair labor practice charge that he knew the employee had signed an authorization card and the employer's antiunion animus was the real reason for the discharge.

The odds of an employer winning the authorization cards game are worse than in blackjack. If you take a peek the dealer will probably win.

3. *Representation Election Campaigns.* Undeniably unions have more "free speech" during election campaigns than do employers. This is so because a union, trying to organize from the outside, has a harder row to hoe. The employees are easily reached by the employer and, more importantly, the employer is the fellow who writes the paycheck and has the power of hire and fire; these superior powers are always considered in measuring employer conduct and speech because they affect meaning and impact. The board refers to this silent force as "the economic realities" of the employer-employee relationship. In other words, the form of the employer's message carries a persuasive meaning independent of the substance contained in it.

It is well to keep this factor in mind when formulating employer campaign strategy. There are a number of general rules for campaigning which should be used as a foundation before using the special rules to be discussed later.

General rules for campaigning

The employer's campaign begins as soon as the union petitions for an election; but it must not be an antiunion campaign, it should be a proemployer campaign.

If the employer has every confidence and expectation that his employees will reject the union in the election, he should do little or nothing.

The converse proposition is *not* that an employer who expects to lose should do everything he can to win. Rather, he should exercise moderation, politeness, and courtesy. A clean and honest campaign just might win the election for him, while the no-holds-barred approach will not only lose it, but will seriously damage his future relations with his employees and their representative. The board has said that an election should be held under "laboratory conditions." No matter what the temptation, do not engage in mudslinging.

Supervisors and foremen are on the firing line and it is their words and conduct, however well-intentioned, that lose the bulk of representation elections for employers. They must be thoroughly educated as early as possible about the specifics of the employer's campaign, their roles in it, and the ground rules for lawful conduct.

Copies of every scrap of union propaganda of every kind should be saved in a separate file as a history of the union's campaign, together with notations of union conduct, pinned down by date and observer or source.

The employer's campaign should be documented, too, with copies of all speeches, letters, and other propaganda being preserved. Speeches always should be given undeviatingly from prepared texts.

Business should continue normally. If employees are scheduled for raises or promotions, they should be given as usual. Unscheduled raises or promotions, or working condition improvements, or lower production quotas, should *never* be made at this time. There is only one exception to this rule: discharges should be made with an excess of caution since the employer may unknowingly discharge a union kingpin. Obviously employees whose rule-breaking conduct is flagrant must be treated as in the past, and discharged if customary.

Do not form employee committees, "safety" committees, or any other employer-built organization during this period of time, if they might be construed or used as vehicles for campaigning against the union, or as company unions.

Talk with other companies in the same geographical area who might have election campaign experience with the same union local.

Remember that while the fundamental prohibition of the statute is against threats of reprisal or force for voting for the union, or promises of benefits for voting against the union, the employer's conduct will be judged in its totality. A string of activities found separately lawful in the past might be found collectively unlawful when viewed in the light of the "economic realities" of the situation.

Have a healthy respect for union organizers: they are sharp and are not to be underrated.   Remember, they do this every day for a living.

Special rules, or guidelines, can be supplied from actual cases.   Some of these rules are named after the cases in which they were announced by the board.   They are divided into categories, described below.

Special rules and guidelines for campaigning

Speeches to Employees

The Peerless Plywood rule of 1953 prohibits an employer from making campaign speeches to massed assemblies of employees on company time within twenty-four hours of a scheduled election.   In one case six employees were deemed a "massed assembly."   Speeches made during that period are presumed to be coercive, and the election will be set aside if the union loses.   As extended in 1966 the rule also prohibits employer-conducted question-and-answer sessions with groups of employees within the twenty-four-hour period.   However, campaign speeches can be made in this period on or off company premises if the employees voluntarily attend on their own time.   "Workbench visits" with *individual* employees at their work stations is permitted at any time.

The employer may say he is opposed to the union and will use every lawful means to defeat it, but he may not say that the union is his enemy, or that its officers are Communistic or racist (even if they are).

Relevant economic considerations may be suggested to the employees.   The employer may advise that, if the union is elected, so much per week will come out of their paychecks for union dues, that there will be an initiation fee, and that the employer believes these employee expenses will be a waste of money.   The employer may also say that if the union secures wage raises the company *might* find itself in an economic pinch and have to cut down on overtime.   It is obviously improper for an employer to intimate wage or seniority cuts if the union wins, or prophesy improvements if it should lose.   In a 1970 decision the NLRB held unlawful an employer's remark that if money was the reason why employees were organizing then the union was unnecessary; in this case the speech contained an implied promise of more money for rejection of the union and stood out in the context of a fairly bitter campaign.

Employees may be informed of actual experiences of other plants after organization (what the union got through bargaining; strikes; plant relocation, etc.), or of conduct of the union in question, but such information must not be used to impart threats of retaliation.

An employer may caution his employees to be careful about what they sign and consider what it might mean to them, their families, and fellow employees.

Otherwise questionable speech might be redeemed by emphasizing the employees' freedom of choice and the employer's willingness to bargain and negotiate benefits with the union if it were elected.   When in doubt, consult company counsel in advance and clear the content of proposed speeches.

Interrogation or Polling of Employees

Interrogation of employees is not a per se violation of the act but is generally regarded as unlawful when of the the third-degree variety, or when coupled with other borderline conduct.

The place for employer interrogations must be at the employee's workbench or on "neutral" territory.   It may not lawfully take place at the employee's home, private office, or delivery route.   Neither can it occur in a supervisor's office or in any "locus of managerial authority."

Group meetings of various employees may be held, but the employer must be sure not to isolate a few employees so as to create a special treatment atmosphere.

An employer may not mail questionnaires to his employees as a means of interrogating them.

Successive interrogations of the same employee should be avoided as they may inspire fear in the employee.

Any employee who voluntarily comes to the employer to report on the union's organizing drive may be interrogated on the nature of his information.

Employees who voluntarily request advice on how they can get their authorization cards returned or how they might indicate their loyalty to the employer may be counseled in this regard.

Under the recently revised Blue Flash rule an employer may poll his employees if (1) the purpose of the poll is to determine the truth of a union's claim of majority, (2) this purpose is communicated to the employees, (3) assurances against reprisal are given, (4) the poll is by secret ballot, and (5) the employer has not engaged in unfair labor practices or otherwise created a coercive atmosphere.

Letters to Employees

A well-drafted employer letter, approved by company counsel, is a highly effective means of carrying the employer's campaign to the employee. It is something he can review at his leisure and take home to his family who may aid him in his decision. There are two schools of thought about who should sign the letter: (1) the company president signs because, if he does not, the employee thinks the company is not sufficiently interested in him, or (2) the general manager or a key line officer signs because he is the one the employees see the most, and what he writes will be most believable. If it is a large company and the president has no day-to-day contact with the employees it could appear contrived for him to suddenly write the employees a letter. Careful consideration should be given to this point.

The most important use of the campaign letter is (1) to summarize the employer's past generosity, (2) to point out how little the particular union local has gained for its members elsewhere in a particular plant, and (3) to show how much union membership will cost in dues and initiation fees, and also in strike assessments.

Employer letters may enumerate the employer's rights under the act and advise the employees that the statutory course will be followed.

Such letters may lawfully express the hope that the union will be rejected and the hope that the employees will distinguish between promises the union can and cannot carry out.

Letters do not fall within the Peerless Plywood prohibition and may be distributed or mailed within the twenty-four-hour preelection period.

Countering Union Solicitation

Unions generally solicit membership or election support by buttonholing employees on or near company premises. This activity may be restricted to some extent by company rules against solicitation.

No-solicitation rules may not be adopted and posted after the union begins its organizing drive, and existing rules may be invalid depending on the circumstances. The NLRB classifies such rules as presumptively valid or presumptively invalid. In either case the presumption is rebuttable: a presumptively valid rule may be held invalid if applied discriminatorily, and a presumptively invalid rule may be held valid if the employer can justify it by special circumstances.

A rule prohibiting solicitation by employees during nonworking hours on company property is presumptively invalid. But the employer may enforce such a rule against the solicitation of union strike funds on company property at any time.

A rule prohibiting solicitation during working hours, whether by employees or outside organizers, is presumptively valid. However, if the employer has allowed solicitation for other purposes during working hours (such as solicitations for charitable contributions), he may not discriminate against unions by enforcing the non-solicitation during working hours rule.

A rule prohibiting solicitation by nonemployees at any time on company property is presumptively valid. But if the union cannot reasonably reach the employees elsewhere, or if other outside solicitors are allowed on the premises, the rule will be regarded as invalid.

A no-solicitation rule that purports to apply to employees during their nonworking time is unlawful as it interferes with their Section 7 rights to discuss self-organization among themselves.

The retailer has the right to maintain a "privileged no-solicitation rule" prohibiting solicitation during nonworking time in working areas, because such solicitation might offend customers and disrupt business. But if the employer gives an antiunion speech during this time he must grant the union equal time and allow outside organizers to come into the store to talk to the employees in nonworking areas during nonworking time, unless the union has adequate means of assembling the employees in the immediate area (which is unlikely).

Where the retailer has a number of distinctly separate stores he may forbid employees to solicit in working areas in stores other than the specific ones in which they were hired.

The manufacturer need not give equal time after an antiunion speech if his no-solicitation rule simply prohibits solicitation during working time, and the organizers have access to the plant to solicit during free time.

Union off-premises solicitation and distribution is facilitated if the union knows who the employees are. Consequently, under the so-called Excelsior rule, the employer is obligated to furnish the regional director with a list of the names and addresses of all eligible employees in the unit within seven days after an election is directed or a consent election agreement is executed. The regional director shall then furnish the union with the list.

Countering Union Distribution

A company may not forbid distribution of union literature by employees during nonworking time on nonworking areas of company property. However, special circumstances may justify an exception to this rule if, for example, the company can show that such distribution impedes production or impairs discipline.

No employer should be forced to remain passive while outrageously libelous handbills are being distributed on his property.

Nonemployee organizers found distributing materials on company property (including private company parking lots) during working hours perhaps may be ejected as trespassers under applicable state laws. Many states allow company-owned parking lots which are open to the public, such as shopping malls, to be used by nonemployees for distribution of organizational materials; but this distribution must not interfere with shoppers or traffic safety. Littering probably is an insufficient ground for prohibition.

Employees cannot be warned to refuse handbills.

An employer may not help employees distribute "Vote no" cards, or permit employees to distribute proemployer materials of any kind during working time.

The distribution of gifts or money is improper, whether by union or employer, but the board has allowed a union to distribute orchids to female workers, and has allowed an employer to distribute fortune cookies containing the message "He who votes 'Yes' puts his destiny in another man's hands, vote 'No'."

A no-distribution or no-solicitation rule which is recognized and articulated in a valid collective bargaining agreement may be enforced if other means of union communication are available. In view of the intended use of Excelsior lists, at-home means of communication will be available in virtually all cases except where the work station is widely itinerant or located in a remote or isolated place (ships at sea, offshore oil rigs, lumbering camps, traveling shows or events, etc.).

Use of Bulletin Boards, Buttons, and other Media

If an employer has permitted employees to use plant bulletin boards in the past for notices not relating to company affairs, he must permit them to post organizational notices.

The fifty-foot rule prohibits posting notices within a fifty-foot radius of the polling place within twenty-four hours of the election. This applies to union and employer notices. Any such material should be removed by the employer with notice to the board's regional office and to the union, and should be preserved in the event of a challenge to the election results. The fifty-foot rule has commonsense flexibility, is subject to discretion of the regional director, and may be increased in smaller shops. If the employees must pass through a narrow corridor, for example, no twenty-four-hour posting should be permitted anywhere along the corridor, however far it may be in feet from the polling place.

Prior to the election the NLRB will send the employer a "notice of election" containing a sample official ballot for prominent posting. Once posted, the employer has a duty to prevent defacement of either the notice or the sample ballot. The board also sends a preliminary notice, in advance of the mandatory-posting official notice, which is to be posted only at the discretion of the employer. Depending on the circumstances, it is recommended that this optional notice *not* be posted because the employer would broaden his duty to prevent defacement. The marking of a sample ballot, or what purports to be a sample ballot, with an X in any square interferes with the employee's free choice, and the election will be set aside. An employer may use a facsimile ballot which is patently different from the official sample ballot, and mark an X in the appropriate box with the legend endorsed below, "This is the way to mark your ballot."

It is an unfair labor practice to show employees the notorious film "And Women Must Weep," or any other acted or nondocumentary films depicting strike violence. But the board has sanctioned the showing of a true documentary of strike violence in another of the same employer's plants.

A company cannot prevent employees from sporting campaign buttons, badges, pins, or insignia. An exception can sometimes find support if three conditions are met: (1) they detract from the dignity of the business, (2) customers have voluntarily complained in writing, and (3) there is a marked diminution in business. They may be limited in size if too distracting and if the nature of the employer's business demands total concentration in order to prevent, for example, enormous waste of material in the manufacture of delicate and intricate precision parts.

Management personnel (including supervisors and foremen) may wear dignified campaign buttons. In one case the board allowed the company's election observer to wear a "Vote no" sticker on his hat in plain view of arriving voters. Nonunit employees may not wear buttons to take sides.

"Don't be a scab" or similar scurrilous buttons can be absolutely prohibited.

In one case an employee who endangered machine shop operations by bandaging himself with as many union stickers as his clothing would allow was rightfully discharged.

Stickers can be removed from plant property (excepting bulletin boards under circumstances as already noted), and employees can be appropriately disciplined for defacing machinery or other property with difficult-to-remove stickers.

The board held it unfair for an employer to give an otherwise legitimate speech the day before the election and place a canister of "Vote no" buttons near the door of the meeting room, because this constituted an implied request to wear the buttons in an atmosphere where an employee's actions would disclose his wishes.

Payroll Strategy

Unions today are big business, and it takes money to make them run. As the employees support them with a part of each paycheck there are a number of gimmicks to make them aware of the sometimes tremendous cost of union membership. But keep in mind that payroll strategy should be formulated with full attention to fairness and accuracy—there are few electioneering techniques more successful, or more infuriating to unions.

Propaganda leaflets may be included in pay envelopes even within the 24-hour Peerless Plywood ban, provided of course that such leaflets are substantially accurate in their message and contain no implied threat or promise.

The paycheck may have the exact amount of the union dues deducted and enclosed as a separate, for example, five-dollar bill, along with a note such as "This five-dollar bill is the amount a 'Yes' vote means in union dues," or "Why reduce your paycheck by $5 in union dues?"

The full paycheck may be accompanied by play money to the same effect with a note, "You cannot spend play money and you cannot spend the five dollars which will be deducted for union dues."

The NLRB held that an employer interfered with an election by distributing cloth bags of 105 pennies representing the average cost per employee hour for fringe benefits, coupled with a notice to vote "No" for job security. This conduct not only contained an implied threat but constituted an unlawful gift of $1.05 to each employee.

An excess of caution would suggest that payroll leaflets contain a statement that the employer would bargain under the law if the union should win, but that whatever the union gains for its members, union dues come off the top.

Miscellaneous Practices

Employer surveillance of union or employee activity is unlawful. Common forms of unlawful surveillance run the gamut from the use of detective agencies or employee informers to photographing distribution of handbills or having a supervisor drive by a union hall to see which employees might be observed going inside.

Eligible employees may be transported to the polls by the employer (1) if they ask for transportation and (2) if the employer offers to transport all similarly situated employees, regardless of their voting intentions.

An employer has a positive duty to disavow antiunion newspaper articles or speeches made by local town officials or by retired plant personnel, or by members of Chambers of Commerce, etc. In one-industry towns the observance of this duty may be very difficult as local figures often join in the campaign on the side of the company.

Preelection parties are often illegal because a party fosters camaraderie and might convey promises of benefits for voting against the union. They can be held if carefully divorced from partisan electioneering. It is an unfair labor practice to give an employee money with instructions to buy beer for other employees and urge them to vote against the union, despite the fact that unions customarily hold tavern parties without incurring board censure.

II. The Fair Labor Standards Act (FLSA)

Jurisdictional scope of the FLSA. Contrasted with the administrative standards set by the NLRB for acceptance of jurisdiction under the NLRA, the Fair Labor Standards Act has built-in statutory standards for determining whether businesses are required to observe its provisions, and little room for discretion exists.

1. *Included Enterprises.* Any enterprise which has employees engaged in

interstate commerce or in the production of goods for commerce, including employers who handle, sell, or work on goods which already have moved in or have been produced elsewhere for commerce, will be subject to the Act if any of the following additional tests are met:

It is an enterprise with an annual gross volume of sales made or business done in the amount of at least $250,000 (less retail excise taxes).

It is engaged in laundering, cleaning, or repairing clothing or fabrics.

It is engaged in the business of construction or reconstruction or both.

It is engaged in the operation of a hospital, other health-care institution, school, or institution of higher education (regardless of whether the same is profit or nonprofit).

The only businesses which are specifically exempted from compliance with the act are those where *all* employees are of the owner's immediate family.

2. *Employees Excluded from Both Wage and Hour Provisions.* There are numerous statutory exemptions from the wage and hour provisions for certain types of employees. These are broadly stated here, although the statute should be consulted if in doubt:

a. Bona fide executives, administrators and professionals.

b. Certain outside salesmen as defined by the Secretary of Labor.

c. Employees of any retail or service establishment if more than 50 percent of the establishment's annual dollar volume of sales is made within the state (except laundries, hospitals, schools, and construction enterprises).

d. Employees of amusement or recreational enterprises open not more than seven months a year.

e. Employees engaged in fishing, lumbering, or forestry enterprises.

f. Agricultural employees only if (1) employer did not use more than 500 man-days of agricultural labor in any calendar quarter of preceding year, (2) employer and employee are in same immediate family, (3) employee is hand-harvest laborer paid on piece-rate basis, commutes daily to work from his home, and did not so work more than thirteen weeks in preceding calendar year, (4) employee is age sixteen or under and is hand-harvest laborer paid on same piece-rate basis as those over age sixteen, and is employed on same farm as parent or guardian, *or* (5) employee is principally engaged in range production of livestock. A "man-day" is defined as any day on which any employee worked at least one hour. (Under these tests most agricultural employees are included under FLSA coverage.)

g. Employees of newspapers having less than 4,000 daily circulation in localized area.

h. Employees of motion picture theatres.

i. Switchboard operators of independent telephone companies having not more than 750 stations.

j. United States seamen on foreign vessels.

k. Cigar tobacco-growing employees.

l. Others as determined by the Department of Labor.

m. Independent contractors (exempted under the statutory definition of employee).

3. *Employees Excluded from the Hours Provisions Only.* Further exemptions exist from the hours requirements:

a. Employees subject to jurisdiction of the Department of Transportation.

b. Employees of railroad, bus, and truck carriers which are subject to ICC regulation.

c. Employees of all air carriers subject to the Railway Labor Act.

d. Employees engaged by fish canneries and packers.

   e. Outside buyers of poultry and raw dairy products.
   f. Seamen.
   g. Drivers, operators, and conductors of state or locally regulated public transportation lines.
   h. Employees of hotels, motels, or restaurants, and resident employees of nursing homes.
   i. Announcers, news editors, and chief engineers of radio and television stations in smaller towns.
   j. Employees engaged in selling or servicing motor vehicles, farm implements, or aircraft if employed by nonmanufacturers.
   k. Local deliverymen and their helpers if paid by the trip.
   l. Agricultural and most related-enterprise employees.
   m. Taxicab drivers.
   n. Food preparation and service employees.
   o. Bowling alley employees if paid overtime for more than a forty-eight-hour work week.
   p. Other employees as determined by the Department of Labor.
   Limit of employer liability. Enforcement experience with the FLSA showed that some employers were being faced with double-damage back-pay orders and suits of staggering size because there was no cutoff date for liability. Consequently, the Portal-to-Portal Act of 1947 was adopted as a statute of limitations on claims for unpaid minimum wages, unpaid overtime compensation, or liquidated damages, whether under the FLSA, the Walsh-Healey Act, or the Davis-Bacon Act.
   As amended in 1966, the Portal-to-Portal Act requires an employee to bring his claim for back pay within two years after it accrues, or within three years for willful violations of the law. A separate claim "accrues" on each separate payday, and not only on the first of several paydays on which the employee was underpaid.
   The practical effect of this is to limit an employer's liability to two years' back pay, plus an equal liquidated sum. An employer who knowingly underpaid an employee would be guilty of a willful violation and would have his exposure increased an extra year. Although no court decisions have been rendered fully interpreting the statutory language, it would seem that an employer who unwittingly underpaid an employee for a period of time and learned that he had done so before the expiration of two years but did not then voluntarily offer the amount due would be guilty of a willful violation. An employer who has a good faith doubt or question about a suspected underpayment would not be guilty of a willful violation.
   Substantive provisions of the FLSA
   1. *Minimum Wages.* The 1966 amendments of the FLSA became effective February 1, 1967, and set different minimum wages, with some annual gradations, for different classes of employers. Employees who became subject to the act in 1966 with respect to all or part of their employees are treated differently. Because the 1966 amendments were extensive and complicated, any employer who is doubtful about his status should consult his attorneys.
   For all employers subject to the FLSA in 1966, the minimum wage for their nonexempt employees was not less than $1.40 an hour from February 1, 1967, through January 31, 1968, and not less than $1.60 an hour thereafter.
   Employees engaged in nonexempt agricultural employment were entitled to not less than $1.00 an hour from February 1, 1967, through January 31, 1968, $1.15 an hour from February 1, 1968, through January 31, 1969, and $1.30 an hour thereafter.
   For all employers who became subject to the FLSA by virtue of the 1966 amendments, the minimum wage for their nonexempt employees was not less than $1.00 an hour from February 1, 1967, through January 31, 1968, $1.15 an hour from

February 1, 1968, through January 31, 1969, $1.30 an hour from February 1, 1969, through January 31, 1970, $1.45 an hour from February 1, 1970, through January 31, 1971, and $1.60 an hour thereafter.

2. *What Is Included in Wages.*   Wages paid an employee includes the reasonable cost, as determined by the Federal Wage and Hour Administrator, of employer-furnished board, lodging, or other customarily furnished facilities, provided the same is not excluded from an applicable collective bargaining agreement.

Employees who receive customer tips may have up to 50 percent of their minimum wage contributed to by such tips.   However, as interpreted by the courts, there must be an express agreement between employer and employee that tips are to be considered as compensation in computing the minimum wage.   The employer should insist that the employee keep accurate records of all tips (as he is required to do anyway under the Internal Revenue Code) so that a wage and hour investigation will confirm that the employee does receive 50 percent of his compensation in the form of tips.

Unless reflected by reliable records, it will be presumed that the employer did not pay the minimum wage.

3. *Maximum Hours.*   Under the 1966 amendments the maximum hours any nonexempt employee may be paid straight-time compensation is forty hours per work week.   Employers who became subject to the act under the 1966 amendments must observe the following limits with respect to their nonexempt employees: 44 hours from February 1, 1967, through January 31, 1968, 42 hours from February 1, 1968, through January 31, 1969, and 40 hours thereafter.

These limits do not apply to compensation for excess hours for any employee subject to a collective bargaining agreement under which no employee shall be employed more than 1,040 hours during any consecutive twenty-six-week period, *or* under which no employee shall be employed more than 2,240 hours and shall be guaranteed not less than 1,840 hours (or not less than forty-six weeks at no less than thirty hours per week) and not more than 2,080 hours of employment for which he shall receive compensation for all hours guaranteed or worked at rates not less than those applicable under the agreement, and overtime for all in excess of the guarantee which are also in excess of the statutory maximum work week applicable.

Neither do these limits apply to employees engaged for not more than fourteen work weeks in seasonal employment.

As to all of the foregoing exemptions, overtime must be paid for more than twelve hours in any one workday or for more than fifty-six hours in any one work week.

A work week consists of any seven consecutive days, and may begin at any hour of any day.   The employer sets the work week unless it is set by a collective bargaining agreement.   However, once the employer fixes the work week, he may not change it temporarily—the change must be permanent and without intent to evade statutory overtime requirements.

4. *What Is Included in Working Hours.*   Common sense controls the determination of what is working time, both for computing hours subject to payment at regular rates, and for overtime compensation.

Waiting time may be working time if due to machinery breakdown, or if requiring the employee to continue wearing cumbersome and uncomfortable employer-supplied workclothes, or if the employee is subject to call.

Lunch time may be working time if the employee is required to eat in a company cafeteria and must pay for his own lunches, or if he is subject to call, etc.

Sleeping time, or idle or recreational time is not usually compensable, but may be if the employee is on call and is required to observe stringent company rules during those periods so that in actuality those periods belong to the employer.

Clock time is not compensable unless the employee is required to be on the premises during that time.

Travel time is compensable if travel is on company premises from gate to work station *and* involves physical or mental exertion (as in coal mines) or requires some attention to the employer's business.

5. *Overtime.*   Payment of 1½ times the employee's hourly rate is required for all work in excess of the maximum hours prescribed for any work week, without regard to whether those hours are worked on a weekday, weekend, or holiday.   An employee paid by the week, for example, is paid overtime at a rate arrived at by dividing his weekly rate by the number of hours worked and multiplying by 1½. Piece-rate workers are paid overtime according to a formula set by Labor Department regulations.

The regular rate, or straight time, paid an employee does not include Christmas or other gifts; payments for vacations, holidays, illness, travel, or like occasional periods; sums paid as reward for service, not based on or measured by hours worked, production, or efficiency; sums paid at sole discretion of employer without reasonable employee expectation of regularity; profit-sharing payments; or like payments. Neither can these payments be construed as part of overtime rates.

6. *Child Labor.*   Children below age 16 may not be employed except as models, actors and performers, in newspaper delivery, in the making of pine wreaths in home enterprises, and on family farms. See Part One (II.) above.

General guidelines for compliance.   There are a number of guidelines an employer can follow to protect his position in the event of a wage and hour investigation or an employee claim:

Keep complete records of all wages paid and all hours worked for every employee.

If the wage includes an amount for employer-provided board, lodging, or facilities, keep accurate records showing the employer cost of such facilities.

Be sure that all employee understandings respecting wages and hours are in writing.

Have independent contractors performing the work of employees acknowledge their independent status in writing.

Make periodic reviews and corrections.

Keep current on Department of Labor regulations.

In doubtful cases either consult company counsel or pay the minimum wage.

If the employer is engaged in handling goods produced by others for movement in commerce, the employer will be liable for transporting them if the manufacturer has not complied with the FLSA.   To avoid this liability obtain written assurance from the manufacturer that the goods were manufactured in compliance with the FLSA.   The form of this assurance is suggested by Labor Department regulation.

BIBLIOGRAPHY

I. Suggestions for a Working Library

It is possible to build a useful, working library of labor materials at nominal cost:

NLRB materials of a wide variety are available from the Division of Information, National Labor Relations Board, Washington, D.C. 20570.   Write the division and ask to be placed on its mailing list for its free "Weekly Summary of NLRB Cases."   This mimeographed summary contains excellent descriptions of every decision and order of the board, as well as notations on every decision of its trial examiners and directions of elections by its regional directors. Upon receipt of the summary each week, review the descriptions of board decisions and write the division for copies of the full texts of the decisions of particular interest.   They will be furnished free while the supply lasts.   Once you are on this mailing list you will receive other materials from the board, including copies of important labor speeches and quarterly reports on case developments. The division may also supply you with free copies of its printed annual report, rules and regulations and the labor laws, even though those documents are otherwise for sale by the U.S. Superintendent of Documents.

U.S. Department of Labor materials are available on the same basis; and the department has twenty-five different types of mailing lists, including the monthly Consumer Price Index, with a special index for your geographical area. You cannot always rely on the cost-of-living figures published in newspapers and magazines.

State labor materials, including copies of full texts of state laws, can be obtained without cost from various agencies of your state government.

Superintendent of Documents, U.S. Government Printing Office, Washington, D.C. 20402, can supply a free price list of labor publications (Price List 33), containing a vast assortment of useful publications available at nominal cost. An example is *Veteran's Reemployment Rights Handbook,* published by the U.S. Department of Labor.

Labor Grievances and Decisions, New Series (1970), by Morris Stone, is a most instructive manual available from the publisher, the American Arbitration Assocation, 140 West 51st Street, New York, N.Y. 10020.

Labor Law Summary, a weekly pamphlet containing summaries of all types of federal and state labor and arbitration cases, and notations of new and changed labor laws, available from the publisher, Commerce Clearing House, Inc., 4025 W. Peterson Avenue, Chicago, Ill. 60646.

II. Major Labor Law Publishers

There are three major publishers of labor materials, and the employer should write each of them for descriptive literature and price lists:

Bureau of National Affairs, Inc.
1231 25th Street, N.W.
Washington, D.C. 20037

Commerce Clearing House, Inc.
4025 W. Peterson Avenue
Chicago, Ill. 60646

Prentice-Hall, Inc.
Englewood Cliffs, N.J. 07632

III. Resource and Reference Library

GENERAL LABOR MATERIALS

Bureau of National Affairs, Inc.: *Labor Relations Reference Manual,* 73 hardbound volumes of annotated federal and state labor decisions since 1935, and 10 loose-leaf volumes of current material.

Commerce Clearing House, Inc.: *Labor Cases,* 61 hardbound volumes of full texts of selected federal and state labor decisions since 1937, and 11 volumes of current material.

Prentice-Hall, Inc.: *American Labor Cases,* hardbound volumes of decisions since 1947, with loose-leaf service, not quite as ambitious as either of the two preceding items.

Superintendent of Documents, Government Printing Office: *Decisions and Orders of the National Labor Relations Board.* As of 1970 the government was three years and 20 volumes behind in publishing the board's decisions: 166 volumes, through August of 1967, were available.

FAIR LABOR STANDARDS ACT MATERIALS

Bureau of National Affairs, Inc.: *Wage and Hour Cases,* 19 volumes, texts of all court and administrative tribunal opinions from 1941 to date.

Prentice-Hall, Inc.: *Wage-Hour Guide,* one volume.

UNEMPLOYMENT COMPENSATION MATERIAL

Commerce Clearing House, Inc.: *Unemployment Insurance Reporter,* thirteen volumes containing federal laws (social security, Medicare, FUTA) and regulations, all state unemployment compensation laws and regulations, and reports of decisions.

Prentice-Hall, Inc.: *Social Security and Unemployment Compensation,* seven volumes.

ARBITRATION MATERIALS

Bureau of National Affairs, Inc.: *Labor Arbitration Reports,* 53 volumes containing texts of important arbitration awards, court decisions, and statistics since 1945.

Commerce Clearing House, Inc.: *Labor Arbitration Awards,* 23 volumes containing texts of selected awards since 1960, with loose-leaf volume of current awards.

Prentice-Hall, Inc.: *American Labor Arbitration Awards,* 13 volumes containing texts of selected awards since 1944.

MISCELLANEOUS MATERIALS

Goldberg, Arthur J.: "Management's Reserved Rights—A Labor View," *Management Rights and the Arbitration Process,* Bureau of National Affairs, Inc., Washington, D.C., 1956.

Jenkins, Joseph Alton: *Labor Law,* 3 vols. by a former member of NLRB, Anderson, Cincinnati, 1968.

Keller, Leonard A.: *The Management Function: A Positive Approach to Labor Relations,* Bureau of National Affairs, Inc., Washington, D.C., 1963.

Robert's Dictionary of Industrial Relations, Bureau of National Affairs, Inc., Washington, D.C., 1966.

Schlossberg, Stephen I.: *Organizing and the Law,* Bureau of National Affairs, Inc., Washington, D.C., 1967.

Silverberg, Lewis G.: *How to Take a Case Before the National Labor Relations Board,* Bureau of National Affairs, Inc., Washington, D.C., 1967.

State Fair Employment Laws and their Administration: An Operations Manual, Bureau of National Affairs, Inc., Washington, D.C., 1964.

Stessin, Lawrence: *Employee Discipline,* Bureau of National Affairs, Inc., Washington, D.C., 1961.

chapter 51

Workmen's Compensation

ANN DAVIS *Employee Benefits and Workmen's Compensation Administrator, The J. L. Hudson Company, Detroit, Michigan*

ORIGIN OF WORKMEN'S COMPENSATION

The Industrial Revolution and the establishment of the factory system in this country created a sharp increase in the number of work-connected accidents. The injured worker had few, if any, common-law remedies for his injuries, and a seriously disabling accident often meant destitution for him and his family. Workmen's Compensation is a system of social legislation that developed from the need to take care of victims of industrial accidents. The underlying philosophy of such legislation is social protection and support, not righting a wrong between adversaries. Its basic principle is that an employee is automatically entitled to certain benefits whenever he incurs an injury arising out of and during the course of his employment.

The granting of Workmen's Compensation benefits to an injured worker is regulated by the statutes and administrative rules established by each state. Typically, the administration of Workmen's Compensation is handled by state administrative commissions. The primary role of such commissions is the settlement of disputed claims, but they have the whole compensation procedure under their supervision. Neither the employee nor the state contributes toward the support of the system. Employers are completely responsible for supplying the required benefits and must secure their liability through private insurance carriers, through state-fund insurance in some states, or by qualifying as "self-insurers."

When protection is purchased from a private insurance carrier, the carrier acts for the employer in making compensation payments, furnishing medical care, and directing the progress of a particular case. A "self-insurer" is in effect his own insurance carrier and assumes the responsibility of paying compensation, providing proper medical care, etc. Each state's jurisdiction has varying requirements established by its Workmen's Compensation Act and Rules of Practice for the reporting of employee accidents by employers. Therefore, specifics with regard to any forms and/or reports that an employer must submit to the state when an injury occurs and during the course of an employee's disability are not discussed in this chapter. In general, most states require that either the insurance carrier representing the employer, or the employer as a self-insurer, file various reports with the state's administrative office for Workmen's Compensation according to a prescribed procedure. Such reports are really completed and forwarded by the insurance carrier unless the employer is self-insured. In a few states, reports of injury are sent directly to the state by the employee since the commission administering the law is also the body which administers the insurance fund against which claims are made.

WORKMEN'S COMPENSATION BENEFITS

Workmen's Compensation benefits fall into two major categories: monetary and medical. When an employee sustains a work injury that results in his death or inability to work, most statutes require that the employee be paid a cash wage benefit to prevent destitution. The amount of this benefit is based on the employee's prior earnings and usually is from one-half to two-thirds of his average weekly wage. Quite often, there is a schedule of minimum and maximum benefits imposed on the basic computation. Thus, two-thirds of an employee's average weekly wage may be $100, but if the employee has only one dependent and the maximum rate payable in that category is $80, the employee will receive $80 and not $100. The majority of the states set the duration of cash wage benefits according to the nature of the employee's disability. If the employee is partially or temporarily disabled from work because of his injury, as for a minor fracture, he will receive a wage benefit until it is established that he has recovered and can return to work. Should an injury result in permanent and total disability for the employee, most statutes provide that Workmen's Compensation benefits be paid for a specific period of time. In Michigan, for example, payments are continued for 800 weeks and may be extended under special circumstances. When death results from a work injury, the employee's dependents receive Workmen's Compensation benefits for an established period of time from the date of death. In some states, the employer also may be required to pay a portion of the burial expenses.

When an injury causes a specific loss, such as the loss of a finger, toe, hand, or leg, the employee is entitled to Workmen's Compensation benefits for a period of time established in a statutory Schedule of Losses. These benefits are continued to the injured employee even though he may return to work prior to the expiration of the time period. Thus if the Schedule of Losses entitles the employee to thirty-three weeks of compensation payments for the loss of a second finger and the employee returns to work after an absence of three weeks, he still would be entitled to thirty weeks of benefits in addition to his regular earnings. The employer is responsible on a continuing basis for an employee's condition resulting from a work injury. Consequently, an employee may return to work from an absence following an injury to his back, but, if during the next year or any time thereafter he has further problems with his back that can be attributed to his original injury, the employer is again liable for providing Workmen's Compensation benefits.

Typically, there is a waiting period during which compensation benefits are not available. Some states have provisions making compensation retroactive to the date of the injury if the disability lasts longer than a certain period. The most common waiting period is seven or so days. Absence from work for part of a day for treatment is not considered "disabling." To be counted as "disabling" an injury must either have caused some permanent impairment or made the person unable to work at a regularly established job for at least one full workday after the day of injury.

In addition to providing cash wage benefits during an injured employee's inability to work, the employer must furnish or cause to be furnished medical, surgical, and hospital services and medicines or other treatment needed by the employee. The injured employee also is entitled to dental service, crutches, artificial limbs, eyes, teeth, eyeglasses, special shoes, garments or belts, or any other appliance or prosthetic device that may be expected to reasonably relieve the effects or appearance of the injury. The employer's liability often includes such miscellaneous expenses as transportation costs to and from medical appointments, and the cost of educational or rehabilitation courses necessary to get the employee back to work.

DEFINITION OF A COMPENSABLE INJURY

A compensable injury is any injury that is determined to have arisen out of and in the course of employment, and which results in death, permanent impairment, or temporary total disability. The employee does not relinquish or waive his right to Workmen's Compensation benefits because of his own negligence or fault while on the job. Contributory negligence or assumption of the risk does not lessen the employer's liability. Thus, the question of compensability is not decided by the employee's real relation (fault) to an event but the relationship of the event to his employment. For example: An employee working on a loading dock is required by his employer to wear safety shoes. His toe is broken when a heavy carton drops on his foot on a day that he is not wearing the required shoes. The employee's failure to wear safety shoes as instructed by the employer does not waive his claim to Workmen's Compensation benefits, nor his employer's responsibility to provide them.

An injury may be deemed compensable not only if it is directly related to the employment activity, as when an employee is injured by broken machinery, but also if it arises out of the nature, conditions, obligations or incidents of the employment when viewed in any of its aspects. Therefore, the employer is liable for such obvious traumatic personal injuries as cuts, puncture wounds, and broken bones, and also may be liable for the following:

1. *Traumatic Neuroses:* Should an employee develop a traumatic neurosis following a work injury, the employer usually is liable. A truck driver who could no longer drive because of his severe anxieties after an accident on the expressway would be compensated.

2. *Psychogenic Symptoms:* Much has been written about the employee who will subconsciously cause an accident because the resultant injury can be used as an excuse for or solution to his life problems. Such individuals are especially prone to retain their symptoms of pain and distress despite the lack of medical findings. Since it is often difficult, if not impossible, to medically prove that a patient's symptoms are wholly psychogenic, the employer may find that he is liable for what really amounts to psychogenic symptoms following an injury and not for a proven anatomical disability.

3. *Occupational Diseases or Conditions:* When the nature of an individual's employment causes him to develop a disease, he is said to have a personal injury, even though it would be medically classified as a disease. A hospital worker who contacted tuberculosis from exposure to infected patients would therefore be compensated.

4. *Wear and Tear:* The deterioration of an individual's physical state resulting from the conditions or nature of his employment may be considered compensable.

Most employees who develop hernias from years of lifting are compensated even though there is no identifiable incident of injury.

5. *Aggravation of Preexisting Conditions:* Employers take their employees as they find them.   The employer is as responsible for the aggravation of a condition which the employee had prior to his employment as for a new injury.   Hence, if a kitchen employee who suffered from rheumatoid arthritis of both wrists prior to her employment became disabled because her hands were in and out of water all day, the employer would be liable for providing Workmen's Compensation benefits.

6. *Property Damage:*   Most statutes provide that if an employee breaks his eyeglasses, teeth, etc., in an accident or damages his clothing, the employer must replace the damaged item.   If a secretary falls down while on the job, injuring her knee and tearing her stockings, the employer is responsible for replacing her stockings as well as for taking care of her knee.

7. *Neutral Risks:*   This is one of the most controversial areas of compensability in the law today.   A neutral risk is one that is not clearly attributable to employment as when an employee is struck by lightning or a stray bullet.   However, the view may be taken that the conditions of the employment put the employee in a position to be injured by the neutral risk, and the employer may be held liable on that basis.   A good illustration of this type of compensable injury is found in a Michigan compensation case where an employee of a resort hotel on Mackinac Island was injured after work while on a bicycle sightseeing tour of the island. The State Workmen's Compensation Appeal Board held that but for his employment on an attractive island, which the employer would reasonably expect his new employee to tour, the injury would not have happened and was thus so work-related as to be compensable.

RECORDS OF EMPLOYEE WORK INJURIES

It is essential that even the smallest employer maintain a high standard of record keeping with regard to work accidents.   Such records serve to protect both the employee and the employer and should be kept for even minor injuries in case the injury develops into something more serious.   They are a critical part of every claim file and may have an effect on the employee's medical treatment, company accident prevention, or on legal interpretation.   In addition, under the provisions of the Federal Occupational Safety and Health Act, most employers are required to keep detailed records and to submit comprehensive reports of occupational injuries and illnesses occurring after July 1, 1971.

Every employer whose business "affects commerce" is subject to the act and must maintain on a calendar year basis a log-type record in the detail provided for on the prescribed form (Occupational Safety and Health Administration Form OSHA No. 100) for all occupational injuries and illnesses that are classified as nonminor by federal regulations (recordable injuries).   In addition to the log, every employer must maintain supplementary records of each recordable injury in the detail prescribed by Occupational Safety and Health Administration Form OSHA No. 101. Workmen's Compensation, insurance, or other internal reports are acceptable alternative records if they contain the information required by Form OSHA No. 101. The employer is further required to prepare at the end of each calendar year an Annual Summary of Occupational Injuries and Illnesses Form OSHA No. 102 from the information contained in the log.   A copy of the summary must be posted in a conspicuous place where notices to employees are customarily posted.   Under this law, Labor Department Inspectors have the right to examine an employee's records at any time to see that they are being properly maintained.   Employers should contact their Regional Director of the Bureau of Labor Statistics for further information on these requirements and to determine whether or not their internally maintained records and reports will be accepted by the Department of Labor as alternative records. Most state jurisdictions also require that all employee accidents be reported by employers to the commission, board, agency, or office that administers the statute.

All accident reports or combination of reports should identify the injured employee by name, occupation, and department and should provide the answers to these questions:

When did the accident happen: time and date?
Where did it happen?
How did it happen?
What was the employee doing when it happened?
What injury or injuries to what part of the body resulted from the accident?
Why did the accident happen?
Who saw the accident happen?
What treatment was given to the injured employee?

Management should educate its employees on their responsibility for reporting all accidents, no matter how minor, to a specific individual, such as their immediate supervisor, or to a specific office, such as the medical department. When an accident occurs, the first consideration is, of course, the employee's well-being, but after the necessary treatment or first aid has been administered, an accident report should be completed. A good time-tested example of an employee's report of injury form is shown in Figure 1. It should be completed at the time the accident is reported since delay oftentimes dims an employee's recollections. The accident report should be made out by the employee in his own handwriting; otherwise the employee's statement can be recorded by a nurse or other responsible individual, and then preferably read and signed by the employee. If only first aid was administered by an attendant, or if emergency first aid was given before the injured employee was referred to a hospital emergency room or company medical department, it is important that those particulars be fully recorded.

The statement at the bottom of the form in Figure 1, regarding the necessity of obtaining authorization from the employer before medical expenses will be reimbursed, can be particularly important. Many employees will see their own physician following a work injury and then expect their bills to be paid by the employer. In most states, the employer is responsible, at least initially, for the direction of the employee's medical treatment, and unauthorized treatment is at the employee's own expense. The statement also gives the employee instructions about the medical followup required. It can be torn off and given to the employee. Again, it is very important for an employer to have evidence that the employee received specific instructions concerning injury procedure, since in many states the employee's failure or refusal to cooperate with the employer's instructions regarding the direction of his medical treatment can be used as a basis for disputing an accident claim. It should be pointed out here that the employee's failure to complete an accident report does not waive the employer's liability for compensation. Although most compensaction acts require that injured employees give notice of injuries to their employers, this requirement may be excused on several grounds.

When there is a company medical department or first-aid facility, a formal record of the treatment administered should be kept. An example of a form used for this purpose is shown in Figure 2. The nurse or member of the medical department filling in the information should make sure that all the employee's complaints are recorded and that the injury is described in maximum detail. The employee

EMPLOYEE'S REPORT
OF INJURY

349 5/68

INSTRUCTIONS:
Two copies are to be completed by the employee
whenever treatment or first aid is administered as a
result of a work incurred injury. One copy is retained by the Store Hospital or Personnel Office. One
copy is forwarded to the Workmen's Comp. Admin.

P
R
I
N
T

Last Name	First Name	Number	Store	Dept.
Job Title		Home Phone		Dept. Ext.

Date of Injury	Time	a.m.
		p.m.

Describe the cause and manner of your injury. Tell what happened and how it happened.

What did you hurt?

When did you first notice this? (Answer only if report was not completed on date of the injury)

Employee Signature	Date

Complete If First Aid Was Given Elsewhere Than In A Store Hospital

First Aid Given

Applied By

TO THE EMPLOYEE:

Hudson's will pay the medical expenses relating to an injury determined to be work
incurred only when such medical expenses are authorized by the Store Hospital in
stores 1, 2 or 3 or by the Personnel Office in other locations.

Unauthorized medical care is at the employee's expense, unless it is on an emergency
basis. Report any emergency treatment administered to the Store Hospital or Personnel
Office immediately.

On the first day of any absence due to a work injury you must call your supervisor to
report the absence and in addition call _____ on ext. _____
In order that we can give you proper treatment for the injury you have reported today,
we are asking you to:

☐ Check back with us if you have any further difficulties.

☐ Report to the Store Hospital

☐ Report to Approved Medical Facility

Date
Time

Figure 1. Employee's report of injury form.

should be examined for other injuries in addition to those he can describe specifically. During this procedure, the employee's reaction to the accident should be
observed. If he seems highly emotional or overly disturbed, an attempt should be
made to determine what events occurred prior to the accident, such as an argument
with the supervisor or another employee. Additional information of this type
should be noted on the report. In such instances, employees should be encouraged

MEDICAL REPORT
OF
EMPLOYEE INJURY

INITIAL ☐   PROGRESS ☐
Report   Report

INSTRUCTIONS:
Two copies are to be completed by the Store Hospital or Store Medical Facilities whenever an employee receives first aid or medical treatment for a work incurred injury. One copy is retained by the Store Hospital or Personnel Office. One copy is forwarded to the Workmen's Compensation Administrator.

Employee's Last Name	First Name	Number

Store   1 ☐ 2 ☐ 3 ☐ 4 ☐ 5 ☐ 6 ☐ 7 ☐ 8 ☐ 9 ☐ 10 ☐ 60 ☐   Dept.   Dept. Ext.

Date of Injury	Time	a.m. p.m.	Date employee first reported injury	Time	a.m. p.m.

Place of accident

Nature of injury (specify part of the body affected)

Treatment administered

Were x-rays taken Yes ☐ No ☐	If yes, by whom	Results of x-rays

Signature of person administering treatment	Date

DISPOSITION OF EMPLOYEE

☐   Hospital

☐   Return to regular duty

☐   Return to regular duty with the following restrictions: _____

☐   Off duty estimated length of the absence _____

☐   Return visit needed   NO ☐   YES ☐

Date _____   Time _____

WORK
TIME
LOST

496 5/68

Figure 2. Medical report of employee injury.

to talk and fully express their feelings since many cases result in litigation because of an employee's rancor against the company and his desire for revenge. Of course, the nurse or individual attending the employee should always soothe and reassure him.

When the medical report of injury is completed by a nurse or first-aid attendant, a diagnostic opinion never should be indicated, such as "Employee seems to have ruptured cervical disc." *Only* the employee's complaints should be recorded. The employee's treatment should be described in detail, and any medication dispensed should be identified. Complicated medical terminology should be avoided when words understandable by the layman can be used. Offhand opinions such as "This condition is not compensable" should not be made without medical substantiation and documentation. The individual administering any treatment should sign the form. The disposition of the employee following treatment should also be indicated. If the employee was referred to an outside medical facility, the means of transportation should be noted—ambulance, cab, car—as well as the identification of anyone who may have accompanied the employee. Any work restrictions imposed upon the employee's return to work should be clearly explained by the physician. Both the employee and the employee's supervisor should be informed of the nature of the restrictions, the length of time they are to be in effect, and the date they are to be reviewed. A form that can be utilized for this purpose is shown in Figure 3. Since complete medical records are the most important part of any compensation claim file, the concerned employer will make sure that members of the company's medical department receive proper training in record keeping.

EMPLOYER INVESTIGATION OF ACCIDENT CLAIMS

A well-organized system for the investigation of accident claims is essential to the successful control of Workmen's Compensation benefits. This is true whether the employer has secured his liability through an insurance carrier or is self-insured. Employers represented by an insurance carrier can help their carrier control claims and thereby possibly reduce their own insurance premiums by prompt and thorough investigation of an accident claim as soon as the employee gives notice of injury. While most accidents and work injury claims are bona fide, there are doubtful cases in which the employer may wish to dispute his liability. An illustration of a form that can be utilized for investigative purposes is shown in Figure 4. While an employer may not wish to require an investigative report for all injuries, it is recommended under the following conditions:

1. Whenever a work injury causes an employee to be absent from work for one or more days.

2. Whenever the accident resulted in a head, leg, back, or knee injury or a hernia.

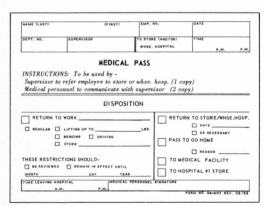

Figure 3.   Medical pass.

SUPERVISOR'S REPORT
OF
EMPLOYEE INJURY
512 5/68

INSTRUCTIONS:
Complete two copies of this form. Forward
both copies within 3 days to the Store Hospital
in stores 1, 2, & 3 or to the Personnel Office
in other locations.

P R I N T	Employee's Last Name	First Name		Number	Classification
	Job Title		Store	Dept.	Extension

Date of Injury   Time   a.m.   p.m.

Was the employee sent to the Store Hospital or other approved medical facility?   Yes ☐   No ☐

Did the employee lose any work time as a result of this injury?   Yes ☐   No ☐   If "YES", how much time was lost?

Describe how the injury occurred.

_____
_____
_____
_____

Was the employee doing part of his regular job when injured?

Did Anyone See The Accident Happen	Name of Witness		Number
	Name of Witness		Number

Did the employee violate any safety rules or perform an unsafe act?   Yes ☐   No ☐

If "YES", explain.

What agency was involved in the injury? (Be Explicit: Slippery floor, Faulty equipment, Clothing unsuitable, Bad weather, Etc.)

_____

Was it a preventable accident?

_____

What are your recommendations for preventing a recurrence of this type of accident?

_____
_____
_____

Date	Supervisor's Signature

IMPORTANT: Company liability in employee injury cases extends to paying all expenses incurred by the employee and weekly compensation if the employee is absent beyond seven days. Whenever an employee calls in absent and claims his absence is due to a work incurred injury, it is important for you to notify your Store Hospital or Personnel Office on the day the absence is first reported to you.

Figure 4. Supervisor's report of employee injury.

3. Whenever there has been a continuing problem that has caused previous accidents, such as a slippery floor.

4. Whenever an injury is very serious.

5. Whenever outside medical expenses were incurred in treating an injury, as when a company's medical department refers the employee to an outside medical facility or specialist.

6. Whenever the employee's claim seems questionable because of the circumstances surrounding the accident, the way in which it was reported, or the employee's personality.

An important aspect to accident investigation is the identification of any witnesses to the accident. The names of any witnesses should be recorded, and in serious or doubtful cases they should be asked to give their testimony of what happened and how it happened. The questions on the form in Figure 4, regarding the employee's violation of any safety rules, have no bearing on waiver of employer liability, but they serve to alert supervisors to careless employees. Such employees should receive special supervisory attention concerning proper work methods and safety responsibilities.

Finally, the information regarding any recommendations for accident prevention may be helpful to the employer in determining hazards and causes or unsafe working conditions. Most of the larger insurance carriers have departments that work with their policyholders in the promotion of safety and accident prevention programs, and this is the kind of information that is valuable to them. In very serious or doubtful cases, the investigative report should be supplemented by a personal investigation and interview.

The following are examples of cases in which the facts discovered in the claim investigation may cause the employer to contest his liability for compensation:

1. The accident was not reported within a reasonable period of time. An employee claims in September that his back hurts from delivering a piano in May of the previous calendar year. He did not report the injury at the time of the alleged accident, nor did he mention it to his helper or anyone else in his work area. An employer may wish to contest liability in a case of this type because of the length of time elapsed between the injury and the report.

2. There is conflicting testimony concerning the accident claim. A supervisor referred an employee to the company medical department because the employee claimed to have hurt her finger at home and it was swollen. The employee told the medical department that it was a home injury. She was referred for an x-ray but was told it would be at her own expense since it was a home injury. When the employee received the bill for the x-ray two weeks later, she went to the medical department and completed an accident report claiming to have injured her finger at work. Such a claim of course would be seriously questioned because of the conflicting testimony.

3. There was proven horseplay involved in the accident. While on his lunch hour, an employee accepted a dare from another employee to hurdle a fence in the company parking lot. In attempting the hurdle, the employee fell over the fence breaking his leg. The employer may wish to dispute his liability for injuries arising from this type of accident involving proven horseplay.

4. It is questionable that the time or place of the accident is work-connected. An employee slipped and fell on the ice on his way to work. The fall occurred two blocks from his place of employment. The place of the accident is not work-connected, and the employer may wish to contest the claim.

5. There is no causal relationship between the nature of the accident and the employment. Prior to her starting time, a secretary in a department store stopped in the cosmetic department and used perfumes and hand lotions on the counter available for use as testers in selling to customers. As a result, she developed a rash on both arms. Liability in this case could be contested on the basis that no causal relationship exists between the injury and the individual's employment. Although the condition occurred in her place of employment, the employee is a secretary and her work is unrelated to the sale of cosmetic products or contact with such products.

CESSATION OF COMPENSATION BENEFITS AND THE ADVERSARIAL POSITION

Once an employer or insurance carrier has accepted an accident claim and compensation benefits have been provided, they may be terminated for several reasons. When there is a scheduled award of a specific amount payable for a definite number of weeks, compensation may be stopped when the employer or carrier regard the full amount of the award as having been paid. When compensation is being paid to the dependents of a deceased employee, payments may end when the dependency of the survivors is determined to have ended. In most states, compensation may be stopped if the employee refuses or fails to cooperate with the prescribed medical treatment. The employer or insurance carrier may terminate compensation when it is medically determined that the employee has recovered sufficiently from the disability and is able to return to work.

When an employer provides to the injured employee all the benefits required under the state's Workmen's Compensation Act, the employee and his dependents give up their right to sue the employer. A third party may be sued if his negligence caused the injury, but the proceeds are applied first to the reimbursement of the employer or his insurance carrier. However, once the employer ceases to provide compensation benefits for any of the reasons previously discussed, an employee may engage an attorney to represent him in contesting the decision. The employee's role then changes from that of worker to plaintiff. It is at this point that referral is made to a Workmen's Compensation "case" and both the employer and employee assume adversarial positions. In the case of a deceased employee, the surviving dependents can commence litigation against the employer.

Of course, employees for whom benefits never were provided because their accident claim was denied also can contest the decision through the litigative process. For the most part, the plaintiff's attorney in Workmen's Compensation cases is interested in "redeeming" the case for a lump-sum settlement. Once a case has been redeemed, the employer or insurance carrier is divested of any further liability for the employee's condition. In cases where redemption is not the goal, a plaintiff's attorney may seek to force the employer to resume compensation payments and the provision of medical treatment. Such motivation, however, is not typical. The effectiveness of the adversary system in settling contested claims has been seriously criticized because in order to achieve redemption it emphasizes the claimant's retention of disability and not his recovery from it.

RETURNING THE INJURED EMPLOYEE TO WORK

During the course of a disabling injury, the attitude of those having contact with the injured employee can be most important in the recovery process. Contact should be maintained with the absent employee to avoid having the individual feeling like a "forgotten man." The employee should have some association with a sympathetic person not necessarily connected with the medical aspect of the injury. This could be the employee's supervisor, or a member of the company's personnel or Workmen's Compensation department.

If there is no company medical department, and/or when outside physicians are used to treat injured employees, the employer should establish good communication with the attending physician. The physician should be made aware of the physical requirements of the employee's job and should know of the employer's interest in getting the employee back to work.

When an employee has been seriously injured, the employee's supervisor and co-workers should be encouraged to visit him. Employees should have a thorough explanation of how and when their cash wage benefits will be paid and how their medical treatment will be handled. The injured employee needs a great deal of supportive concern and attention to maintain his image of himself as a worthwhile person. Recently so much has been written about the accident-prone employee or psychologically motivated injuries, that there is sometimes a tendency for those in contact with the employee, such as representatives of the employer or insurance carrier or attending physicians, to regard the employee's disability as invalid. The legitimately injured worker with legitimate symptoms will quickly sense any intimations that he is a malingerer and this will not help the recovery process. Although there is always the possibility that an employee will "use" his symptoms as an excuse for his life problems or to obtain a cash settlement, it is best to proceed as if the symptoms are bona fide. When an employee does return to work, he should be expected to perform the job assigned within the limits of any restrictions that may have been imposed. Supervisors should be advised not to baby an employee but to exercise good judgment. It would be unreasonable, of course, to expect an employee just returning from a hernia repair to begin lifting washing machines or other heavy appliances. While the purpose of Workmen's Compensation benefits, as stated at the beginning of this chapter, is to prevent the destitution of the injured employees, such individuals can become social destitutes if they are not returned to productive work. The employer's final goal in handling Workmen's Compensation therefore always should be the recovery and rehabilitation of the injured employee, and his restoration to a productive role in society.

BIBLIOGRAPHY

Association of Casualty and Surety Companies, *Digest of Workmen's Compensation Laws of the United States and Territories,* 16th ed., annotated, New York, 1961.

Blair, Elmer H.: *Reference Guide to Workmen's Compensation (A Quick Retrieval Handbook),* Thomas Law Book Co., St. Louis, Mo., 1968.

Commerce Clearing House, Inc.: *Workmen's Compensation Law Reporter,* 4025 W. Peterson Avenue, Chicago, Ill. 60646. Single-volume loose-leaf service reporting on current decisions of federal and state courts pertaining to workmen's compensation, occupational diseases, and employers' liability, with summaries of the statutes of all states.

Hirschfeld, Alexander H., and Robert C. Behan: "The Accident Process," *Journal of the American Medical Association,* vol. 186, pp. 193–199, 300–306, Oct. 19 and 26, 1963. An excellent two-part study on the causation and treatment of industrial injuries.

Larson, Arthur: *The Law of Workmen's Compensation,* 4 vols. including forms, Matthew Bender & Co., New York, 1968, serviced by annual supplements.

State administrative decisions are usually available in mimeographed form at nominal or no cost. Hearing referees or examiners in compensation cases pay more attention to the published decisions of their administrative appeals tribunals than to decisions of the state appeals courts which hear cases appealed from the administrative tribunal. It is very useful to be able to quote an administrative decision in support of your position at a compensation hearing, and the employer should try to obtain copies on a regular basis.

State statutes and regulations are generally available free of charge in each state in pamphlet form. Every employer should have a complete set of the laws for his state. The various written forms which each state uses to process workmen's compensation claims are also available without charge. The self-insured employer should be particularly careful to keep current on the compensation laws of his state, noting that the regulations adopted pursuant to statute may undergo periodic changes.

chapter 52

Wage Stabilization

N. T. PHILLIPS   *Corporate Compensation Manager, Midland-Ross Corporation, Cleveland, Ohio*

WAGE STABILIZATION

Wage stabilization is a term that can be defined as an attempt to hold the line against upward pressures on wage levels and prices.

LEVEL OF WAGES

The level of wages has always been a difficult problem of wage and salary administrators. If too low, turnover rates tend to turn upward to undesirable levels and recruitment programs meet with little success. If extremely low, companies may have difficulties with state and national regulatory bodies administering minimum wage laws and prevailing wage laws. Also, such an organization may be the target of concerted organization drives if no union is present, or of pressing wage demands where a union does exist.

When wage levels are too high, the competitive position of the firm may suffer. Low turnover may result and the organization may tend toward inflexibility and stagnation. Also, if during periods of wage control by federal authorities wage and salary levels are too high, there may be problems arising from these administrators.[1]

COMPANY CONTROLS

The usual approach to supervising wage costs is to develop rough standards by which measurements of performance can be made and necessary corrective action indicated. Such performance standards might include budget direct labor costs, in-

---

[1]David W. Belcher, *Wage and Salary Administration,* Prentice-Hall, Inc., Englewood Cliffs, N.J., 1958, p. 31.

dices of direct to indirect labor costs ratios, or direct labor cost per unit production. These methods permit an acceptable approximation of the relative status of wage costs and can therefore be of value in control.

Better controls are possible through proper use of information, primarily available from job evaluation data. These wage controls also permit a number of related benefits [4].

WAGE INFLATION

Currently wage levels have been increasing far in excess of gains in production, causing wage inflation. The administration in Washington has been fighting inflation by orthodox methods of monetary and fiscal restraint. These attempts have slowed the rate of increase but not nearly as much as they had planned. Business, labor, and politicians have been recommending direct wage and price controls.

GOVERNMENT CONTROLS

The most recent instance of United States government mandatory price controls occurred in 1950, shortly after the United States became involved in Korea. On September 8, 1950, the Defense Production Act of 1950 was passed. Title IV of that Act was concerned with price and wage stabilization.

World War II wage and salary controls were authorized by the Stabilization Act of 1942. They froze wages and salaries at their September 15, 1942, levels. The controls were lifted in September, 1947.

The following is a review of the controls on wages and benefits under Title IV of the Defense Production Act of 1950 and the Stabilization Act of 1942. This review outlines the scope of government control practices and their effect on personnel policies, procedures, and programs.

World War II Controls

In comparison with the controls that were put into effect during the Korean "police action," World War II controls were less detailed in the *direct* compensation area and substantially less restrictive in the employee benefits area with the exception of profit sharing plans.

Direct compensation. A significant regulation during this period sanctioned across-the-board-increases of 15 percent above rates that existed on January 1, 1941, to cover cost-of-living increases between 1941 and 1942.

Merit, length of service, and promotional increases were allowed without prior approval if job classifications were clearly defined, individual merit increases were not given more than twice a year, no more than 50 percent of the employees in a job classification received merit increases during the year, and individual length-of-service increases were not given more than four times a year. The employer had to choose between granting merit and length-of-service increases; he could not give both to the same employee within any one year.

Prime and subcontract "war suppliers" could not pay employees premium pay for Saturday or Sunday unless it was the sixth or seventh day in a regularly scheduled work week. There were other restrictions on premium pay.

Insurance and pension benefits. Most employee benefit increases, were limited to 5 percent of payroll.

Profit sharing plans. These plans were subjected to very specific controls. Profit-sharing plans established prior to October 2, 1942, were permitted to continue cash distribution. Employer contributions to these plans did not require approval as long as they did not exceed those for the year before October, 1942.

Those established after October, 1942, banned new current cash distributions. New plans were approved if their earliest distribution date was ten years after the establishment of the plan, and at a rate of 10 percent per year after that period. Otherwise, distributions were payable only in the event of death, total disability, sickness, termination of employment, or normal retirement.

Korean Controls

Wage and salary controls went into effect on January 26, 1951, and ended in April, 1953. The government was much more definitive in setting rules governing compensation, in the benefits area as well as in the direct compensation area.

Controls first froze all compensation at January 25, 1951, levels. They were relaxed one month later to permit general increases in wages, salaries, and other compensation of up to 10 percent, reduced by direct compensation increases given since January, 1950.

Base salaries. Stabilization of base salaries was the primary concern. Most of the regulations dealt with formal pay structures and informal arrangements. Initially, new employees could not be hired at rates higher than those in effect on January 1, 1951.

Companies with formal pay structures in existence before January 25, 1951, could continue merit and length-of-service increases without approval if the plan was either part of a collective bargaining agreement or a written statement of policy in operation on January 25, 1951; it contained job classification rate *ranges* with clearly defined maximum rates and increases fell within the rate range maximum.

Companies without formal arrangements could grant merit and length-of-service increases if the employee had not received a merit or length-of-service increase during the last twelve months, the number of employees receiving increases in any month was not proportionately higher than the average number receiving increases during 1950, and no employee was raised beyond the highest rate paid for the job on January 25, 1951.

In September, 1951, merit and cost-of-living increases in total were restricted to 6 percent of base salaries.

Promotional increases were permitted if they were in line with formal pay structures or collective bargaining agreements in operation on January 25, 1951. Where there were no formal plans or agreements, the increases had to be determined by 1950 standards.

Pay rates for newly hired employees, where a formal plan existed, could not exceed the job's established rate. If no formal arrangement existed, the new employee could receive only the minimum rate paid to any employee doing similar work on January 25, 1951.

Cost-of-living increases could be given if they were part of a written agreement made prior to January 25, 1951, even if the increases when combined with others went beyond the 10 percent limit. Tandem increases such as an automatic increase to salaried employees in conjunction with a union increase could be given if they were traditional and consistent, and could also go beyond the 10 percent limit.

Additional direct compensation. The 10 percent limitation did not apply to wages which were made up of a combination of hourly pay rates and incentive wages; the 10 percent rules applied only to the original hourly pay base. The piece rate had to be established for a new production item or when an hourly rated job was placed on a piece-rate basis and the company had an incentive wage plan, or the pay rate was altered because of a design, or natural or technological change, and the new incentive wage change continued the same percentage relations to base earnings as before.

The new rates had to be set in accordance with engineering principles or procedures or a written wage agreement in effect on January 25, 1951, or they were set by estimates or negotiations, and maintained the historically established relationship between earnings and job content.

Bonus and incentive compensation. On July 27, 1951, bonus payment plans with predetermined formulas could continue if the plan had been in operation since January 25, 1949, or it was part of a collective bargaining agreement, or it had been communicated to employees prior to January 25, 1951.

Bonuses in excess of 25 percent of base salary were reviewed. In August of 1951 a new regulation restricted pre-1951 plans with predetermined formulas from changing the formula upward and it held individual bonuses in plans without predetermined formulas to 1950 award levels.

Formal plans established after January, 1951, required approval for every phase of their operation.

Cull-out pay, overtime premium pay, and shift differential allowances were originally included in the 10 percent increase limit, but by July, 1951, the regulations had been relaxed to permit increases which were within the prevailing area or industry levels. Paid vacations and holidays were also given this leeway. Payment in lieu of accrued vacation was never considered a wage increase, but safety awards, suggestions awards, and travel expenses were subject to the 10 percent limit.

Stock option and stock purchase plans. These plans represented deferred compensation and were not a major consideration. No approval was required for restricted stock option plans where the employee could qualify for full capital gain treatment. Approval was necessary if the plan provided for ordinary income tax on the difference between 85 percent (to 95 percent) and 100 percent of market value and treated the difference between 100 percent and the market value at the time of exercise as capital gains; and approval was granted only if the employee had a reserve to write off the difference between the option price and 95 percent of market value.

The same rules applied to stock purchase plans, but there were special rules for employers who provided employees with loans to make stock purchases. This was to ensure that the loans were not indirect compensation.

Benefit plans. The initiation of new pension and deferred profit-sharing plans and improvements in existing plans went through three cycles. They were at first frozen, then brought under the 10 percent rule, and finally given a self-administration status. Existing group life, medical, and disability plans were unaffected by the controls.

Pension plan benefits were included in the 10 percent limitation until February, 1952, when they were also given a self-administration status. The self-administration guidelines called for a normal retirement age of sixty-five for men and sixty or older for women, a proportionate reduction of benefits for early retirement, and an actuarial reduction for early retirement, with benefits, except for death benefits, payable at least over the lifetime of the employee and deferment of termination benefits until normal retirement date.

Pension benefit formulas had informal guidelines which permitted formulas that provided per year of service benefits up to 1 percent of the first $3,600 of earnings and up to 1½ percent of the excess. In May, 1952, trusteed plans were permitted to provide $1,000 of life insurance for each $10 of retirement income.

Deferred profit sharing plans. Deferred profit-sharing plans were also included in the 10 percent limitation until February, 1952. During this period, plans which operated on a discretionary share basis were required to set up formulas for distribution, by fixing the distribution as either a definite amount or a certain percentage of profits.

After February, 1952, new or amended deferred profit-sharing plans could be established on a self-administration basis if they paid benefits only in the event of retirement, total and permanent disability, death, or termination of employment; if the benefits would not be paid for at least ten years after the employee entered the plan; and if the benefits were to spread out over a ten-year period after the initial ten-year waiting period.

No lump-sum benefits were permitted except in the case of an employee's death. The ten-year membership requirement was later removed in cases of normal retirement (sixty-five for men, sixty for women) or total disability.

Group life insurance, medical and disability insurance. New plans also went through the three-stage cycle. They were removed from the 10 percent limitation in December, 1951, and "review criteria" were established for each type of plan.

Group life plans were approved if the employees contributed at least 40 percent of the plan's costs or the average death benefit did not exceed the greater of 85 percent of average annual earnings or $1,500. In either case, death benefits for retirees could not exceed the greater of 40 percent of active coverage of $1,000, and group Accidental Death and Dismemberment benefits could not exceed group life benefits.

New group hospital surgical and medical plans were approved if employees contributed at least 40 percent of the cost or no "unusual" benefits were provided, the surgical schedule did not exceed a standard $200 schedule or a medical association prepaid schedule, in-hospital medical expense coverage did not go beyond $5 a day for seventy days, no home or office visits were covered, at least 40 percent of dependent coverage was paid for by the employee, and the dependent coverage was within employee limits.

Disability income coverage was permitted if the employee contributed 40 percent, if the cost of the benefit did not exceed 60 percent of the employee's average weekly pay, and if it was not paid for more than twenty-six weeks after a seven-day waiting period. In June, 1952, more liberal benefits were approved than had previously been allowed.

EFFECT OF WAGE STABILIZATION REGULATIONS

As outlined in the preceding pages, wage stabilization regulations affect not only the wage and salary policies but also employee benefits and the entire personnel program in a company.

Management must be prepared for possible wage and price controls at all times with formal policies and procedures. During periods of government control, the companies with approved programs will be able to grant wage increases and maintain competitive wage levels. The other companies will lose their employees to the companies that can offer higher compensation.

REFERENCES

[1] Backman, Jules: *Wage Determination,* D. Van Nostrand Company, Inc., Englewood Cliffs, N.J., 1958.
[2] Brady, Robert A.: *The Citizen's Stake in Price Control,* Littlefield, Adams and Co., Totowa, N.J., 1952.
[3] Committee for Economic Development, Research, and Policy, *Price and Wage Controls,* December, 1951.
[4] Craig, Robert: "How to Control Wage and Salary Levels," *Industrial Engineering,* February, 1970.
[5] Defense Production Act of 1950, Title IV, Sections 2102 (a) and (b).
[6] Galbraith, John Kenneth: *A Theory of Price Control,* Harvard University Press, Cambridge, Mass., 1952.

[7] Harris, Seymour E.: *Inflation and the American Economy,* McGraw-Hill Book Company, New York, 1945.

[8] *Price and Related Controls in the United States,* McGraw-Hill Book Company, New York, 1945.

[9] McMillan, S. Sterling: *Individual Firm Adjustments under OPA,* Principia Press of Trinity U., San Antonio, Texas, 1949.

[10] *New Salary Freezing Regulations,* Prentice-Hall, Inc., Englewood Cliffs, N.J., 1952.

[11] Stabilization Act of 1942.

chapter 53

Equal Employment
and the Employment
of Minors and Women

WILLIAM H. BROWN III   *Chairman, Equal Employment Opportunity Commission, Washington, D.C.*

INTRODUCTION

Women, by law, may not be treated differently than men in employment (with certain narrowly defined exceptions). Minors, on the other hand, *must,* by law, be treated differently than the rest of the work force. This chapter, is, therefore, divided into three parts.

The first part, Equal Employment, presents an overview of the law as it applies to all groups affected by the specific regulations on the employment of women and minors. This section also discusses the administrative machinery for the enforcement of the law.

The second part, The Employment of Women, and the third part, The Employment of Minors, deal with the specific provisions applying to these two groups.

EQUAL EMPLOYMENT
What Is Discrimination?

The more familiar form of discrimination is called "unequal" or "disparate" *treatment.* This means treating people of different groups in different ways, giving one an advantage over the other.

A second form of discrimination is not so readily apparent. The company or labor union that discriminates is often entirely unaware of the practice. This is called "disparate *effect.*" This occurs when any personnel policy or practice, even though administered equally to all, has the effect of discriminating against a particular group.   The courts have now recognized that merely *neutral* treatment is not enough to meet the requirements of the law.

What Is Equal Employment?

The U.S. Equal Employment Opportunity Commission (EEOC) has stated that, as a general rule, all jobs must be open on an equal basis without regard to race, color, religion, sex, or national origin.   While there are certain exceptions—hiring only women for jobs which only women can perform, such as models for women's clothes —the EEOC and the courts have found that the exceptions are rare.   Accordingly, as a general rule, a job cannot be closed to all men or all women as a class; it can only be denied to an individual man or woman because he or she individually does not have the qualifications or cannot perform the job.

What Are the Regulations on Equal Employment and Who Administers Them?

Title VII of the Civil Rights Act of 1964, Equal Employment Opportunity, prohibits discrimination because of race, color, religion, sex, or national origin, in hiring, upgrading, and all other conditions of employment.   It became effective on July 2, 1965.

Title VII established the Equal Employment Opportunity Commission, an independent, bipartisan agency, composed of five members appointed by the President and approved by the Senate.

The Commission is concerned with discrimination by three major groups: employers, public and private employment agencies, and labor organizations.   Title VII applies to: (1) employers of twenty-five or more persons, (2) labor unions with twenty-five or more members, or which refer persons for employment, or which represent employees of employers covered by the act, (3) employment agencies dealing with employers of twenty-five or more persons, and (4) joint labor-management apprenticeship programs of covered employers and unions.

The Commission receives and investigates charges of employment discrimination. Individual commissioners may initiate charges if they receive information suggesting that the law has been violated.   If the Commission decides, after investigation, that reasonable cause exists to believe that a violation of Title VII has occurred, remedy is sought through the process of conciliation.   If conciliation fails, the individual charging party is usually notified of his right to file suit in federal court.   Class actions are permitted and are frequently employed.   In certain cases, where it is determined that a pattern or practice of discrimination exists, EEOC may advise the Justice Department, and the Attorney General may file suit in a federal court.

In addition, the Commission promotes programs of affirmative action by employers and labor organizations to put the principle of equal employment opportunity into practice.

Legislation is currently before the Congress which would give EEOC enforcement powers and would broaden its coverage of employers and workers substantially. As this is written, Congress has not taken final action.   Personnel administrators should check with EEOC to determine the latest statutory requirements.

Title VII makes it unlawful:
For Any Employer to Discriminate in:
- Hiring or firing;
- Wages, terms, conditions, or privileges of employment;
- Classifying, assigning, or promoting employees or extending or assigning use of facilities;
- Training, retraining, or apprenticeships;

For Any Employer or Employment Agency to:
- Print, publish, circulate, or cause the printing, publishing, or circulation of advertisements or any other statement or announcement relating to employment expressing any specifications, limitations or preferences based on race, color, religion, sex, or national origin;
- Discriminate in receiving applications or classifying or referring for employment;

For Any Labor Organization to:
- Exclude or expel from membership; discriminate against any individual; limit, segregate, or classify membership, refer or fail to refer for employment on the basis of race, color, religion, sex, or national origin; cause or attempt to cause an employer to discriminate;

For Any Employer, Employment Agency, or Labor Organization to:
- Discriminate against or take any retaliatory action against any person because he has opposed any unlawful employment practices or because he has brought charges, testified, or participated in any action under Title VII. EEOC generally gives highest priority to any violation of this section.

Title VII Exemptions

Among those *not* covered are local, state, and federal government (but state employment agencies *are* covered), government-owned corporations, Indian tribes, and educational institutions where the employee performs work connected with the institution's educational activities. *Note:* These exemptions may be changed by pending legislation.

Related Federal Agencies

Other federal agencies also have authority to assure equal employment opportunity.

The *National Labor Relations Board* can prohibit certain discriminatory practices by labor unions and employers.

Office of Federal Contract Compliance, U.S. Department of Labor

OFCC is responsible for implementation of Executive Order 11246 and the amended portion—Sections 201, 205, and 211 (commonly known as Order No. 4)—which prohibits job discrimination and requires affirmative action on the part of federal contractors and subcontractors.[1] Sex discrimination in employment is also prohibited by Executive Order 11246, as amended by Executive Order 11375. Neither those orders, nor the federal government in enforcing them, makes any distinction

---

[1] Generally speaking, the no-discrimination requirement of Executive Order 11246 applies to all government contracts for more than $10,000. (The limit is set by the Secretary of Labor, not by the executive order.) For every formally advertised supply contract of more than $1 million, the government checks the compliance status of the prospective contractors prior to awarding the contract. Executive Order 11114 prohibits discrimination in all federally assisted construction; that is, for all contracts paid for *in whole or in part* with funds obtained from the federal government or borrowed on the credit of the government pursuant to a grant, contract, loan, insurance, or guarantee. This means that the no-discrimination requirement not only covers construction contracted for directly by the federal government, but also construction insured or guaranteed by the government, such as housing insured by the Federal Housing Administration or the Veterans Administration.

Note: The amount of the contract, not the amount of federal assistance, is the controlling factor.

Executive Order No. 4 applies to nonconstruction contractors and subcontractors with fifty or more employees and a contract of at least $50,000.

in the end result sought between sex discrimination and discrimination based on race, religion, color, or national origin.

New guidelines on sex discrimination were issued by the Labor Department in June, 1970, to provide new requirements of and guidance to government contractors in eliminating the barriers to equal employment opportunity based on sex.   Order No. 4, on the other hand, was issued to eliminate, primarily, race and color barriers to equal employment opportunity.   Both documents are directed to the same result, and both require affirmative action programs on the part of government contractors to attain that result.

These programs are intended to produce results in terms of increased employment, increased promotional opportunities, and increased job security for minority citizens and women.

An acceptable affirmative action program must have goals and timetables.   Once the goals and timetables are set up, then what is required is a good-faith effort to meet them.   The best evidence of good faith is, of course, meeting the standards in terms of people hired, people promoted, revised seniority systems, increased transfer and promotion opportunities, and upgrading of skilled workers to supervisory and management positions.

What about compliance reviews?   Executive Order 11246 states "The Secretary of Labor may investigate the employment practices of any Government contractor or subcontractor, or initiate such investigation by the appropriate contracting agency, to determine whether or not the contractual provisions . . . have been violated. . . ."   The Secretary may also investigate complaints by employees or prospective employees of a government contractor or subcontractor which allege discrimination.

Sanctions and penalties.   The Secretary of Labor or the appropriate contracting agency may publish the names of contractors or unions which have complied or have failed to comply with the provisions of the order; recommend to the Department of Justice that, in cases in which there is substantial or material violation of the provisions, appropriate proceedings be brought to enforce those provisions; recommend to the Equal Employment Opportunity Commission or the Department of Justice that appropriate proceedings be instituted under Title VII of the Civil Rights Act of 1964; cancel, terminate, or suspend any contract, or portion thereof, for failure of the contractor or subcontractor to comply with the nondiscrimination provisions of the contract; provide that any contracting agency shall refrain from entering into further contracts with any noncomplying contractor until the contractor has established and carried out personnel and employment policies in compliance with the order.

OFCC is now developing a system of priorities to determine the order in which reviews should be conducted.   These priorities will be based on the likelihood that a compliance review will produce the maximum impact for equal opportunity either in promotions or new hires.   From a contractor's point of view this means that if his work force appears to have a reasonable minority or women component in *all* job categories, the likelihood of his having an in-depth compliance review is significantly reduced.

In addition, the Labor Department is moving to standardize the concept of a compliance review.   For the immediate future *all* compliance reviews conducted by all agencies will be the same.   The department's concept of a compliance review is one in which the employer, prior to an on-site interview, will submit a standardized set of facts and information to the office conducting the review.   Only after the compliance review officer has evaluated this information will he make the on-site review.   In this way, it is hoped to save time for contractors and government personnel.   When the reviewer arrives, he will check the records to confirm the accuracy of the report, and then discuss the requirements of the Executive Order as applied to the facts of the situation. This process will be helped by the affirmative action plan which the contractor previously prepared in accordance with the requirements of Order No. 4.

OFCC is implementing its responsibility to provide technical help to assist contractors meet their compliance requirements and will soon publish a model recruiting program that can be used as a guide. It will be general and flexible enough for adoption by a variety of industries. There will be two other model programs available soon—one that suggests ways to open up promotion and transfer opportunities and another to help contractors identify those minority or women employees who are eligible for promotion to supervisory slots.

In May, 1970, OFCC and EEOC issued a Memorandum of Understanding to reduce duplication of compliance activities and to facilitate the exchange of information in the equal job opportunity field.

The agreement reduces duplication of compliance activities by:

1. Having OFCC check with EEOC prior to beginning an investigation
2. Having OFCC handle broad, company-wide compliance reviews, and EEOC handle complaint investigations

The effect of the agreement is not to diminish the jurisdiction of either agency. On the contrary, the only distinction the memorandum intends is between complaint investigations and compliance reviews. While these are technically different kinds of inquiries, the difference rests on method rather than scope. EEOC will continue to seek remedies on as broad a basis as possible.

The *wage-hour administrator in the Department of Labor* administers both the Equal Pay Act, which prohibits unequal pay for substantially similar work because of sex, and the Age Discrimination in Employment Act, which protects persons between the ages of forty and sixty-five from discrimination because of age. These two acts amend the Fair Labor Standards Act.

Guidelines on employee selection procedures. EEOC has issued guidelines on employee selection procedures, specifically testing. These comprehensive guidelines are most specific about what screening devices may be used by employers. They are "must reading" for personnel administrators. These guidelines are available upon request to EEOC, 1800 G Street, N.W., Washington, D.C. 20506.

What happens if a charge of discrimination is filed with EEOC? If the charge appears to be within the jurisdiction of the Commission, an investigator will gather all the facts in the case from the charging party and the party charged with discrimination (respondent). A copy of the charge will be given to the respondent.

If the Commission finds that the facts do not support the case, the charge will be dismissed and both parties will be notified. (The charging party may still file suit in federal court.) Should the Commission find reasonable cause to believe that there has been discrimination, it will attempt to conciliate and reach an agreement satisfactory to the charging party and the respondent. If an agreement is not reached, the charging party has the right to file suit in federal court.

Where the charging party resides in a state which has an enforceable fair employment practice law, and the means to enforce it, the Commission will defer the case to the state agency for a period of sixty days. Both parties will be notified if this is done. Unless there is a satisfactory resolution of the case on the termination of state proceedings, or after sixty days have passed, whichever comes first, EEOC will begin processing the case. (For a list of states to which the Commission will defer, contact the nearest office of EEOC.)

If conciliation is unsuccessful. Title VII provides two methods for bringing matters before a federal court in the event that conciliation efforts should fail. If the case is of general public importance, the Commission will discuss with the Department of Justice the possibility of the Attorney General bringing suit. A prerequisite to such suits is a determination that a "pattern or practice" of discrimination exists. Otherwise, the Commission will notify the charging party of his right under Section 706 of Title VII to maintain a civil action to compel compliance. EEOC has not only the right, uniformly recognized by all courts, but the duty to participate in such litigation where participation will tend to effectuate the policies of the act.

What are the sanctions if the court finds the respondent guilty of an unlawful employment practice? Under Section 706(g) of the 1964 Civil Rights Act,

> If the court finds that the respondent has intentionally engaged in or is intentionally engaging in an unlawful employment practice charged in the complaint, the court may enjoin the respondent from engaging in such unlawful employment practice, and order such affirmative action as may be appropriate, which may include reinstatement or hiring of employees, with or without back pay (payable by the employer, employment agency, or labor organization, as the case may be, responsible for the unlawful employment practice). Interim earnings of the person or persons discriminated against shall operate to reduce the back pay otherwise allowable. . . .

Under Section 706 (i):

> In any case in which an employer, employment agency, or labor organization fails to comply with an order of a court issued in a civil action brought under subsection (e), the Commission may commence proceedings to compel compliance with such order.

Under Section 706 (k):

> In any action or proceeding under this title the court, in its discretion, may allow the prevailing party, other than the Commission or the United States, a reasonable attorney's fee as part of the costs, and the Commission and the United States shall be liable for costs the same as a private person.

Investigatory powers. The Commission has the power, enforceable in federal courts, to compel from respondents the production of documentary evidence related to the charge under investigation. The courts have construed this power broadly. Federal courts have held that EEOC is entitled to all data that is relevant to the charge. They have said that EEOC has investigatory powers analogous to other investigatory agencies such as the National Labor Relations Board.

Compliance process. The goals of the Commission in conciliation are to obtain specific relief for the charging party; to remedy the practice of the respondent which led to unlawful discrimination against the charging party; and, where necessary, to modify other employment practices to achieve compliance with Title VII. Thus, successful conciliation nearly always results in direct benefits not only to charging parties but to other persons similarly situated.

A fully successful conciliation results in the respondent signing a formal agreement that provides redress to the charging parties and revises employment policies or practices to meet the requirements of Title VII. The agreement generally includes pledges of affirmative action to remedy present discriminatory effects of past discriminatory practices.

What happens after a conciliation agreement is reached? In order to ensure the long-term effects of conciliation agreements, the Commission utilizes a system of compliance reviews.[2] Compliance review officers examine the manner in which respondents conform with the provisions of the conciliation agreement.

---

[2] EEOC compliance reviews are not to be confused with OFCC compliance reviews. OFCC, on its own initiative, periodically reviews the records of federal contractors and subcontractors to make sure they are complying with the equal employment regulations under Executive

Consequently, respondents are put on notice that the Commission views its conciliation agreements as binding. Compliance officers check to ensure that the "immediate action" provisions are implemented, and also that those requirements calling for ongoing remedial action are met.

In preparation for the review, the officer secures information regarding subsequent charges and decisions involving the respondent. The charging party is then contacted and the compliance officer ascertains the charging party's views of the agreement as it relates to him and to the members of the affected class.

In addition to reviewing the conciliation agreement with the charging party and the respondent, the compliance officer secures printed copies of relevant labor agreements to study any changes related to Title VII. The compliance review presents an opportunity to correct discriminatory practices before they become entrenched company procedure.

Required Forms

Employer Information Report EEO-1 (Standard Form 100) is required to be filed annually by all employers who have 100 or more workers and are covered by Title VII or by Executive Order 11246.

Joint labor-management apprenticeship committees must file annual reports (EEO-2) if they have five or more apprentices, and at least one employer sponsor with twenty-five or more employees, and at least one local union sponsor which operates a hiring hall or which has fifty or more members.

Local unions covered by Title VII must file annual reports if they have 100 or more members. The report form is Local Union Equal Employment Opportunity Report EEO-3.

Questions on EEO-1, EEO-2, and EEO-3 reporting provisions should be addressed to: Equal Employment Opportunity Commission, Employment Surveys Division, 1800 G Street, N.W. Washington, D.C. 20506.

Required poster.   Employers are required by law to post in a conspicuous place a notice setting forth summaries of the law and information about the filing of complaints. A $100 fine is provided for willful failure to post the summary. Copies of the poster may be obtained by writing to EEOC.

Voluntary Action

The Equal Employment Opportunity Commission is involved in a number of cooperative programs to assist employers, labor unions, employment agencies, and joint labor-management apprenticeship programs in attaining equal employment opportunity. One of these programs is the following:

Affirmative Action

EEOC encourages and assists compliance by employers, unions, and employment agencies through affirmative action programs.

Such programs are designed to help business, union, and community leaders achieve the goals of equal employment opportunity through recruiting and job upgrading. The Commission offers guidance in the development of these programs through its technical assistance specialists.

Guidance is provided in open recruiting, in creating a climate for integrated work forces, in obtaining federal funds for training projects, and in intergroup employee relations.

Order 11246. OFCC may conduct such reviews whether or not it has received complaints against the contractor. EEOC conducts compliance reviews only pursuant to a conciliation agreement which has resolved a complaint.

Where Can I Get Current Information on Employment Regulations?

Keeping informed on the latest rules and regulations on employment is a time-consuming, but necessary, task.   There are several labor reporting services and government agencies—such as the Bureau of National Affairs, Commerce Clearing House, Prentice-Hall, Equal Employment Opportunity Commission, Wage and Hour Division, Office of Federal Contract Compliance of the U.S. Department of Labor, and the state fair employment practice commissions—whose publications will help bring you up to date.   Some of the private labor reporting services are rather expensive but worth the price for the personnel administrator who needs to be well informed.

Federal agencies will supply you with free information upon request.

EMPLOYMENT OF WOMEN

> Most intangible, but by no means least telling, of recent changes is one in the general attitude toward women's participation in the various aspects of American society.   It is a change which includes the attitudes of men toward accepting women as colleagues and employees, the attitudes of both toward the creation of a society whose aim is the well-being of people—not of men alone or of women apart—a society of diverse talents used to their fullest.
>
> "American Women, 1963–1968," report of the Interdepartmental
> Committee on the Status of Women

Highlights of Laws Governing Women's Employment and Status[3]

Minimum wage.   Women workers in forty-one states are covered by some form of minimum wage legislation.   Provisions of the law vary considerably and change often.   Personnel administrators should consult appropriate state agencies for latest information.   Women employed in business affecting commerce must be paid the prevailing federal minimum wage.

Equal pay.   Thirty-one states have equal pay laws; five states and the District of Columbia which have no equal pay laws have fair employment practices laws that prohibit discrimination in rate of pay or compensation based on sex.   The federal Equal Pay Act of 1963 prohibits employers from providing unequal compensation for substantially similar work.

Sex discrimination.   Fifteen states and the District of Columbia prohibit discrimination in private employment based on sex.   Employers and unions with at least twenty-five employees or members are covered under Title VII of the Civil Rights Act of 1964, the federal law prohibiting discrimination in private employment based on sex as well as race, color, religion, and national origin.

Executive Order 11375, amending Executive Order 11246, explicitly prohibits discrimination on the basis of sex in federal employment and by federal contractors. These orders are administered by the Civil Service Commission and the Department of Labor.

Hours of work.   Forty-one states and the District of Columbia regulate daily and/or weekly working hours for women in one or more industries; twenty-five states and the District of Columbia set maximum hours of eight a day, or forty-eight or less a week, or both. (See Overtime.)

Night work.   Eighteen states and Puerto Rico prohibit and/or regulate the employment of adult women in specified industries or occupations at night.

---

[3] Many state laws making distinctions based on sex are currently under legal attack, and some have been declared invalid by state attorneys general.   Many employers are legitimately confused by apparent contradictions in state and federal law.   Personnel administrators should consult legal counsel when such questions arise. (See State Protective Laws.)

Industrial homework.   Nineteen states and Puerto Rico have industrial homework laws or regulations.

Employment before and after childbirth.   Six states and Puerto Rico prohibit the employment of women immediately before and/or after childbirth.

Occupational limitations.   Twenty-six states prohibit the employment of adult women in specified occupations or industries or under certain working conditions considered hazardous or injurious to health.

Age discrimination.   Discrimination in employment against men and women forty to sixty-five years old by employers, employment agencies, and labor unions subject to the Fair Labor Standards Act is prohibited by federal law.

Jury duty.   All states, the District of Columbia, and Puerto Rico permit women to serve on all juries.   Women are eligible for federal jury service in all jurisdictions by virtue of the 1957 Civil Rights Act.

Married women's rights.   All states recognize a married woman's legal capacity to contract her personal services outside the home.   Married women generally have control of their own earnings, however, in four of the eight community property states, the wife's earnings are under the complete control of the husband.

Equal Rights Amendment.   At this writing it does not appear that Congress will soon pass the current version of the amendment which reads: "Equality of rights under the law shall not be denied or abridged by the United States or by any state on account of sex."   If this amendment should be passed by Congress in the near future, it would probably be several years before it took effect.

Guidelines to bar sex discrimination on Government contract work.   These guidelines were issued by the U.S. Department of Labor in 1970.   Covered contractors must maintain written personnel policies expressly indicating that there shall be no discrimination against employees because of sex.   Collective bargaining agreements on conditions of employment must be consistent with these guidelines.

The Equal Employment Opportunity Commission and the courts have set precedents which focus on some of the main issues of sex discrimination under Title VII. The following section reviews those of broadest concern.

Availability of Jobs for Both Sexes

As a general rule, all jobs must be open to both men and women.   Jobs must be open to both sexes unless the employer can prove that sex "is a bona fide occupational qualification reasonably necessary to the normal operation of that particular business or enterprise."   The term—"bone fide occupational qualification"—is narrowly defined by the Commission and the courts, with the burden of proof that sex is a bona fide occupational qualification for the job in question falling on the employer (or union or employment agency) involved.   Following are some examples of preferences, limitations, specifications, and restrictions that are legitimate under Title VII and some which are not.   Jobs may be restricted to members of one sex:

For reasons of authenticity (actress, actor, model)

Because of community standards or morality or propriety (restroom attendant, lingerie salesclerk)

In jobs in the entertainment industry for which sex appeal is an essential qualification

Jobs may *not* be restricted to members of one sex for any of the reasons listed below:

Assumptions related to the applicant's sex; e.g., some or most of the members of one sex are unable or unwilling to do the job.

Preferences of co-workers, employers, clients, or customers.

The job was traditionally restricted to members of the opposite sex.

The job involves heavy physical labor, manual dexterity, late-night hours, overtime, work in isolated locations, or unpleasant surroundings.

The job involves travel, or travel with members of the opposite sex.

Physical facilities are not available for both sexes. (Only in cases where the expense of providing additional facilities is totally unreasonable can this be used as a legitimate excuse.)

The job requires personal characteristics not exclusive to either sex such as tact, charm, or aggressiveness.

Conditions of Employment

All employees are entitled to equality in all conditions of employment including:

Recruitment, hire, layoff, discharge, recall

Opportunities for promotion

Participation in training programs

Wages and salaries

Sick leave time and pay

Vacation time and pay

Overtime work and pay

Medical, hospital, life, and accident insurance coverage

Optional and compulsory retirement age privileges and pension benefits (Employers may be permitted to effect gradual adjustment of certain plans that provide for earlier optional retirement of women since the immediate removal of the earlier retirement option would be unfair to women close to retirement.)

Rest periods, coffee breaks, lunch periods, and smoking breaks

With respect to *maternity leave*, EEOC has taken the position, that, as a general rule, female employees are entitled to maternity leave of absence, with the right of reinstatement of the other benefits and privileges of employment.

Specific Employer, Employment Agency and Union Obligations under Title VII

The employer, the union, and the employment agency are responsible for seeing that the law is obeyed. Collective bargaining contracts may not discriminate on the basis of sex. Employers and unions cannot contract for a system which establishes separate job classifications, wage rates, or seniority lines which discriminate on the basis of sex except in the few instances where sex may be a bona fide occupational qualification for the jobs involved.

One area of importance regarding employer obligations relates to state "protective" laws, such as those that limit the number of hours that women may work or the number of pounds that they may lift while on the job. In a series of cases the Commission has decided that such laws cannot justify the limitation of work opportunities for women. In other words, the existence of a state protective law does not establish a bona fide occupational qualification for a job. Again where state laws may prescribe certain minimum wages or overtime pay for women, that is no justification for refusal to hire women, and the same benefits must be available to male employees.

A union may not:

Restrict its membership on the basis of sex

Classify its members on the basis of sex

Discriminate on the basis of sex in its referral of individuals for employment, its representation of employees, or its operation of apprenticeship or other training programs

Cause an employer to discriminate

Under Title VII, "Employment Agency" refers to private employment agencies, the U.S. Employment Service, and state employment services.

An employment agency may not:

Refer only members of one sex to a particular job unless sex is a bona fide occupational qualification for the job;

Restrict its services to members of one sex unless it limits its services to furnishing employees for jobs (such as model, actor) for which sex is a bona fide occupational qualification

Classified Ads

EEOC guidelines provide that help-wanted advertisements may not specify any preference, limitation, specification, or discrimination based on sex unless sex is a bona fide occupational qualification for the job advertised.

EEOC has interpreted this provision to mean not only that the *content* of classified ads must be free of such preferences to conform with Title VII but that the *placement* of ads in separate male and female columns, when sex is not a bona fide occupational qualification for the advertised job, is in violation of Title VII.

The rationale behind EEOC's guideline regarding ad placement (which became effective January 24, 1969) is quite straightforward. There are relatively few occupations for which sex is a bona fide occupational qualification; those jobs which have traditionally been restricted to men (or to women) are much more numerous.

If job vacancies are listed in separate columns headed by "Male" and "Female" designations, the effect is first to exclude one sex from learning about the opportunity (since few women read the "Help Wanted—Male" column, and vice versa); and, second, to discourage applicants from pursuing the opportunity even if the ad is read, because of the implied employer preference for an applicant of the opposite sex.

Thus the Commission position simply rules out baseless "feelings" on the part of employers (or employment agencies, or unions) that certain jobs are men's jobs and certain are women's jobs. Only if such "feelings" are based on a bona fide occupational requirement are they justifiable; and if this is the case, the advertiser's right to solicit applicants of one sex or the other is still recognized and protected.

Other Federal Agencies

There are other federal agencies as well as state agencies which have jurisdiction over discrimination based on sex. Among them are:

The state or municipal fair employment practice commissions

The state agency which administers the state equal pay statute

The U.S. Labor Department in Washington, D.C., or the local U.S. Labor Department office which administers both the Equal Pay for Equal Work Act and Executive Order 11246 (See Equal Employment, below.)

The U.S. Civil Service Commission, which administers the Executive Order prohibiting sex discrimination in federal government employment

The National Labor Relations Board in Washington, D.C., or one of its regional offices which handles certain unfair labor practice complaints based on sex discrimination

Penalties for Violations

See Equal Employment and Employment of Minors.

Equal Job Opportunity for Women in Government Contract Work

On June 9, 1970, the Department of Labor issued new guidelines to assure equal job opportunity for women on federal contract work. The guidelines apply to employment with government contractors and subcontractors covered by Executive Order 11246.

Under the guidelines, contractors must maintain written personnel policies expressly indicating that there shall be no discrimination against employees on account of sex. Collective bargaining agreements on conditions of employment must be consistent with the guidelines.

The new guidelines also prohibit covered employers from:

Making any distinction based upon sex in employment opportunities, wages, hours, or other conditions of employment.

Advertising for workers in newspaper columns headed "Male" or "Female" unless sex is a bona fide occupational qualification.

Making any distinction between married and unmarried persons of one sex unless the same distinctions are made between married and unmarried persons of the opposite sex.

Denying employment to women with young children unless the same exclusionary policy exists for men.

Penalizing women in their conditions of employment because they require time away from work for childbearing. Whether or not the employer has a leave policy, childbearing must be considered a justification for leave of absence for a reasonable length of time.

Maintaining seniority lines or lists based solely upon sex.

Restricting one sex to certain job classifications and departments.

Specifying any difference for male and female employees on the basis of sex in either mandatory or optional retirement age.

Denying a female employee the right to any job that she is qualified to perform in reliance upon a state "protective" law.

The guidelines also specify that covered employers shall take affirmative action to recruit women to apply for those jobs where they have been previously excluded.

The guidelines point out that "women have not been typically found in significant numbers in management" and that "traditionally, few, if any, women" have been admitted into management training programs.

The guidelines will be used by federal contracting agencies in their compliance activities under the supervision of the Office of Federal Contract Compliance (OFCC).

State Protective Laws

Numerous states have laws, commonly referred to as state protective legislation, which restrict the employment of women regarding such terms and conditions as the type of jobs they may hold, the hours they may work, the weights they may lift, and minimum and overtime pay. The result of such restrictions is the labeling of certain jobs or job categories as "male" and others as "female." The employer then has separate lines of progression, structured on the basis of sex and based on the assumption that not all women (or men) can, should, or prefer to do certain kinds of work. For example, if a particular female employee disputes this assumption by asserting that she both wants to perform and is capable of performing a prescribed job, she is specifically prohibited by several state laws from getting the job she wants. *Such laws have been superseded by federal law.*[4] EEOC guidelines provide:

> The Commission believes that such State laws and regulations, although originally promulgated for the purpose of protecting females, have ceased to be relevant to our technology or to the expanding role of the female worker in our economy. The Commission has found that such laws and regulations do not take into account the capacities, pref-

---

[4] See, for example, the decision of a federal district court in *Caterpillar Tractor Co. v. Grabiec*, 63 LC ¶0522, 2 FEP Cases 945 (S.D. Ill. 1970).

erences and abilities of individual females and tend to discriminate rather than protect. Accordingly, the Commission has concluded that such laws and regulations conflict with Title VII of the Civil Rights Act of 1964 and will not be considered a defense to an otherwise established unlawful employment practice or as a basis for the application of the bona fide occupational qualification exception. [5]

Women with Children

The EEOC has said that an employer may not refuse to hire married women or women with children, legitimate or illegitimate, unless it has a similar policy for men. Similarly, an employer may not discharge female employees because of marriage or parenthood unless the same policy applies to men.

In its first sex discrimination decision under Title VII, *Phillips v. Martin Marietta Corporation,* [6] the Supreme Court held unanimously that the law forbids "one hiring policy for women and another for men" when both are parents of pre-school age children.

Overtime

In December, 1969, the Equal Employment Opportunity Commission ruled that an employer cannot deny overtime to female employees despite a law limiting women to working no more than eight hours per day and forty-eight hours per week. The Commission called the 1914 District of Columbia statute "inconsistent with Title VII of the Civil Rights Act of 1964" and said that the discriminatory provisions of the District of Columbia law were, in effect, "repealed by the subsequent enactment of Title VII."

The Commission has made similar rulings in the past concerning state "protective" laws which limited female work hours. In those cases, the Commission ruled that hour limitations on females ignore the capacities, preferences, and abilities of individual females, tend to discriminate, and thus conflict with Title VII. Several federal courts have agreed that Title VII supersedes conflicting state "protective" laws, and the Commission expects that its decision on the District of Columbia Hours Laws will be similarly affirmed.

Department of Justice Action

On July 20, 1970, the Department of Justice for the first time filed suit under Section 707 of Title VII to give women equal employment rights with men. The suit charged a major glass manufacturer and its employees' union with violating the Civil Rights Act by a policy of restricting women production workers to one of five nearby plants, of assigning them to the less desirable and lower-paying jobs with the least opportunity for advancement, and of subjecting them to a high frequency of layoffs.

The complaint asked the federal district court to issue preliminary and permanent injunctions against the company and union requiring that women be given equal opportunities with men in hiring, assignment, transfer, promotion, training, working overtime, advancement to supervisory positions, and seniority.

In addition, they would be required to make compensatory payments to discriminatorily rejected women job applicants and discriminatorily assigned women employees who have suffered economic loss as a result.

The case, which is pending at this writing, had been referred to the Justice Department by the Equal Employment Opportunity Commission following unsuccessful efforts at conciliation.

[5] Rules and Regulations, Equal Employment Opportunity Commission, part 1604.1(b)(2).
[6] *Phillips v. Martin Marietta Corp.,* U.S., 91 S. Ct. 496 (1971) forthcoming.

Judicial Support of Administrative Guidelines

Victims of sex discrimination have experienced a high rate of success in litigating federal administrative agency guidelines in the courts. For example, in 1969 the Seventh Circuit Court of Appeals held that, in factory jobs of a strenuous nature, an employer may not refuse to consider women on grounds that the job required the lifting of 35 pounds or more. The court held, in *Bowe v. Colgate Palmolive Co.,*[7] that female employees seeking jobs must be judged on their individual ability to perform the work.

The court also held that all female employees who had been damaged by Colgate's illegal job-assignment, layoff, and seniority policies were entitled to recover back pay and seniority credit on an individual basis regardless of whether they had (1) previously filed charges with EEOC or (2) participated as plaintiffs in the law suit.

Equal Pay Act

This act prohibits an employer from discriminating on the basis of sex by paying employees of one sex at rates lower than he pays the opposite sex, in the same establishment, for doing substantially equal work, performed under similar working conditions. This act is administered by the Wage and Hour Division of the U.S. Department of Labor. (For further information, see Chapter 50.)

On the state level, there are state and municipal fair employment practice commissions and state agencies which administer state equal pay legislation.

EMPLOYMENT OF MINORS

It has been said that progress can be measured by the extent to which children's rights are safeguarded. In the United States we uphold the value that our children are our richest resource. This was not always true. From the broad perspective of history, it was not too long ago that the work of young children in factories, mines, and fields was not only condoned but approved.

In earlier days, children often worked alongside a parent as "helpers." Employers favored families with many children. Poor or orphaned children were "bound out" or indentured as apprentices and sent to the factories by their families or by the almshouses in which they lived. . . .

Most people believed in child labor as a righteous institution, regarding it as economically necessary and morally desirable. . . . Other factors were the need to foster domestic manufacturing, the scarcity and high cost of male labor, whose use in agriculture was essential, and the desire to prevent poor children from becoming public charges. Employing young children, however cheaply, was looked upon as a form of philanthropy, and approved by employers, public officials, and parents.

The past century has seen a complete reversal in point of view. People of the United States now look upon unregulated child labor as incompatible with our way of life. But attitudes change slowly. . . .[8]

In the early part of the present century numerous efforts were made to secure the passage by Congress of a Federal child-labor law. The first bill was introduced by Senator Beveridge in 1906 but it was not until 1916 that Congress enacted a Federal child-labor law. This law was later declared unconstitutional by the U.S. Supreme Court as was the Child Labor Act of 1919.

Because of these decisions, it was believed that an amendment to the Constitution would be necessary. A proposed Child-Labor Amendment to the Constitution was

---

[7] 416 F.2d. 711 (7th Cir. 1969).

[8] "Child Labor Laws Historical Development," U.S. Department of Labor, Washington, D.C., 1968.

adopted by the Congress in 1924; however, the amendment was never ratified by the required number of States. . . .

In 1938, however, the Federal Fair Labor Standards Act, containing child-labor provisions was enacted. With the decision by the U.S. Supreme Court in 1941 upholding this act (*United States v. Darby*, 312 U.S. 100), the constitutional validity of Federal child labor legislation dealing with interstate industries is now firmly established. . . .[9]

What Are the Regulations?

The Fair Labor Standards Act, in addition to its basic minimum wage and overtime provisions, contains provisions relating specifically to the employment of minors.

These provisions set a basic minimum age of sixteen years for general employment and hazardous agricultural occupations (if not contrary to state or local law, young people of this age may be employed during school hours, for any number of hours, and during any periods of time); eighteen years for nonagricultural hazardous occupations; and fourteen years outside school hours in various nonmanufacturing, nonmining, and nonhazardous occupations for limited hours and under specified conditions of work. These provisions apply when the youth are working in interstate commerce, producing goods for commerce, or in an enterprise engaged in interstate commerce.

The Public Contracts Act (PCA) minimum age of sixteen for both boys and girls (the previous minimum age of eighteen years for girls was amended to sixteen in April, 1969) applies to establishments with government contracts in excess of $10,000 for materials, supplies, articles, or equipment.

The purpose of these standards is not to keep young people from working, but rather to be sure that the jobs in which they work do not adversely affect their physical development, expose them to physical injury, or interfere with their opportunity to obtain an education.

Not all young people under sixteen years of age are covered by these child labor standards because of specific exemptions; i.e., the parental exemption (children under sixteen years of age employed by their parents in agriculture or in nonagricultural occupations other than manufacturing or mining occupations or occupations declared hazardous for minors under eighteen, the exemption for newsboys, performers in theaters, and on radio and television, and exemptions from certain hazardous occupations in agriculture.

What Are the Regulations for Minors Under Sixteen?

Employment of fourteen- and fifteen-year-old minors is limited to certain occupations under conditions which do not interfere with their schooling, health, or well-being.

1. Fourteen- and fifteen-year old minors may *not* be employed:

   a. During school hours, except as provided in paragraph b;

   b. Before 7 A.M. or after 7 P.M. (7 A.M. to 9 P.M. from June 1 through Labor Day)

   c. More than three hours a day on school days

   d. More than eighteen hours a week in school weeks

   e. More than eight hours a day on non-school days

   f. More than forty hours a week in non-school weeks;

2. In the case of enrollees in work training programs conducted under Part B of Title I of the Economic Opportunity Act of 1964, there is an exception to the requirement of paragraph 1a. If the employer has on file an unrevoked written

[9] "History of Federal Regulation of Child Labor," leaflet no. 5, U.S. Department of Labor, Washington, D.C., 1959.

statement of the administrator of the Bureau of Work Programs or his representative setting out the periods which the minor will work and certifying that his employment confined to such periods will not interfere with his health and well-being, then he may be employed. The statement must be countersigned by the principal of the school which the minor is attending with his certificate that such employment will not interfere with the minor's schooling.

Permitted occupations for fourteen- and fifteen-year-old minors in retail, food service, and gasoline service establishments. Fourteen- and fifteen-year-old minors *may be* employed in:

1. Office and clerical work (including operation of office machines)
2. Cashiering, selling, modeling, artwork, work in advertising departments, window trimming and comparative shopping
3. Price marking and tagging by hand or by machine, assembling orders, packing, and shelving
4. Bagging and carrying out customers' orders
5. Errand and delivery work by foot, bicycle, and public transportation
6. Clean-up work, including the use of vacuum cleaners and floor waxers, and maintenance of grounds, but not including the use of power-driven mowers or cutters
7. Kitchen work and other work involved in preparing and serving food and beverages, including the operation of machines used in the performance of such work, such as, but not limited to, dishwashers, toasters, dumbwaiters, popcorn poppers, milk shake blenders, and coffee grinders
8. Work in connection with cars and trucks if confined to the following:
   Dispensing gasoline and oil
   Courtesy service
   Car cleaning, washing, and polishing
   Work listed in items (1) to (7)
But not including work involving the use of pits, racks, or lifting apparatus or involving the inflation of any tire mounted on a rim equipped with a removable retaining ring
9. Cleaning vegetables and fruits, and wrapping, sealing, labeling, weighing, pricing, and stocking goods when performed in areas physically separate from areas where meat is prepared for sale and from outside freezers or meat coolers

Permitted occupations for fourteen- and fifteen-year-old minors in any other place of employment. Fourteen- and fifteen-year-old minors *may be* employed in any occupation *except* the excluded occupations listed below:

1. Any manufacturing occupation
2. Any mining occupation
3. Processing occupations (except in a retail, food service, or gasoline service establishment in those specific occupations expressly permitted there in accordance with the foregoing list)
4. Occupations requiring the performance of any duties in workrooms or workplaces where goods are manufactured, mined, or otherwise processed (except to the extent expressly permitted in retail, food service, or gasoline service establishments in accordance with the foregoing list)
5. Public messenger service
6. Operation or tending of hoisting apparatus or of any power-driven machinery (other than office machines and machines in retail, food service, and gasoline service establishments which are specified in the foregoing list as machines which such minors may operate in such establishments
7. Any occupations found and declared to be hazardous
8. Occupations in connection with:

    a. Transportation of persons or property by rail, highway, air, on water, pipeline or other means

    b. Warehousing and storage

    c. Communications and public utilities

    d. Construction (including repair)

Except office or sales work in connection with these occupations (not performed on transportation media or at the actual construction site)

    9. Any of the following occupations in a retail, food service, or gasoline service establishment:

    a. Work performed in or about boiler or engine rooms

    b. Work in connection with maintenance or repair of the establishment, machines, or equipment

    c. Outside window washing that involves working from window sills, and all work requiring the use of ladders, scaffolds, or their substitutes

    d. Cooking (except at soda fountains, lunch counters, snack bars, or cafeteria serving counters) and baking

    e. Occupations which involve operating, setting up, adjusting, cleaning, oiling, or repairing power-driven food slicers and grinders, food choppers and cutters, and bakery-type mixers

    f. Work in freezers and meat coolers and all work in preparation of meats for sale (except wrapping, sealing, labeling, weighing, pricing, and stocking when performed in other areas)

    g. Loading and unloading goods to and from trucks, railroad cars or conveyors

    h. All occupations in warehouses except office and clerical work

Hazardous Occupations

The Fair Labor Standards Act provides a minimum age of eighteen years for any nonagricultural occupation which the Secretary of Labor "shall find and by order declare" to be particularly hazardous for sixteen- and seventeen-year-old persons, or detrimental to their health and well-being.

    A sixteen-year minimum age applies to any agricultural occupation that the Secretary of Labor "finds and declares" to be particularly hazardous for the employment of children under sixteen.

    Determination of hazardous occupations is made after investigation by the Department of Labor's Bureau of Labor Standards of the occupations to be included within the scope of the investigation. A preliminary report is prepared on the basis of the investigation and is submitted for comment and suggestion to a technical advisory committee appointed from the ranks of employers, associations, trade unions, and experts in the particular field under consideration. After comments and suggestions have been received from the advisory committee, the report is revised and a proposed finding and order, if justified, is prepared.

    Upon the issuance and publication of the proposed finding and order, opportunity is given for any interested party to make objection to or to suggest revisions in the order at a public hearing. Objections and suggested revisions are considered and, if they are found to be justified, the proposed order is revised. Thereafter, if warranted, the order is adopted and issued by the Secretary of Labor. Once issued, the orders have the force of law, and a violation of their provisions constitutes a violation of the child labor provisions of the Fair Labor Standards Act.

    The seventeen hazardous occupations orders now in effect apply either on an industry basis, specifying the occupations in the industry that are not covered, or on an occupational basis, irrespective of the industry in which found. Investigations and procedures followed in determining hazardous occupations in agricultural employment are similar to those described in connection with industry.

Hazardous Occupations Orders in Nonagricultural Occupations

Those occupations declared to be particularly hazardous for minors between sixteen and eighteen years of age (also for minors fourteen and fifteen) are included in the seventeen Hazardous Occupations Orders listed below:

1. Occupations in or about plants or establishments manufacturing or storing explosives or articles containing explosive components

2. Occupations of motor-vehicle driver and outside helper[10]

3. Coal-mine occupations

4. Logging occupations and occupations in the operation of any sawmill, lath mill, shingle mill, or cooperage-stock mill

5. Occupations involved in the operation of power-driven woodworking machines

6. Occupations involving exposure to radioactive substances and to ionizing radiations

7. Occupations involved in the operation of elevators and other power-driven hoisting apparatus

8. Occupations involved in the operation of power-driven metal forming, punching, and shearing machines

9. Occupations in connection with mining, other than coal

10. Occupations involving slaughtering, meat-packing or processing, or rendering

11. Occupations involved in the operation of certain power-driven bakery machines

12. Occupations involved in the operation of certain power-driven paper-products machines

13. Occupations involved in the manufacture of brick, tile, and kindred products

14. Occupations involved in the operation of circular saws, band saws, and guillotine shears

15. Occupations involved in wrecking, demolition, and ship-breaking operations

16. Occupations involved in roofing operations

17. Occupations involved in excavation operations

Exemptions. Nonagricultural Hazardous Occupations Orders Nos. 5, 8, 10, 12, 14, 16, and 17 contain exemptions for apprentices and student-learners provided they are employed under specified conditions. For further details see "A Guide to Child Labor provisions of the Fair Labor Standards Act," U.S. Department of Labor Bulletin No. 101, page 8.

How to Hire Teenagers

Contact your local state employment office and tell them what kinds of jobs you have available and how many young people you can hire.

Also, contact officials at all your local schools, colleges, and community organizations; advertise in community, neighborhood, church and school papers; advertise on local radio and TV stations.

What about Wages?

If teenagers' jobs are covered by the Fair Labor Standards Act (FLSA), unless otherwise exempt, they must be paid the federal minimum wage and time and a half for all overtime as established by the act.

---

[10] Subject to certain specific exemptions. See "A Guide to Child Labor Provisions of the Fair Labor Standards Act," Child Labor Bulletin No. 101, U.S. Department of Labor, Washington, D.C. p. 11.

All employees covered by the minimum wage must receive $1.60 an hour and time and a half for all hours worked over 40 hours in a week, unless a specific exemption is applicable.

Minimum wage and summer jobs. If your company is in the retail or service industry, or in agriculture, there are special minimum wage rates for full-time students. Those students who attend an accredited school full time and who would work only during hours when they are not attending classes or during school vacations may be paid 85 percent of the applicable federal minimum wage by employers who qualify for a special authorization certificate.

For more information contact your local office of the Wage and Hour Division of the U.S. Department of Labor.

What about Proof of Age?

An employer can protect himself from unintentional violation of the minimum age provisions by obtaining and keeping on file an age or employment certificate for each minor employed, showing the minor to be of the age established for the occupation in which he is employed. Employers should obtain such a certificate and have it on file before the minor starts work. Most state child labor laws require that such a certificate be obtained by the employer.

Age or employment certificates, sometimes called work permits or working papers, issued under state child labor laws are accepted as proof of age in forty-five states, the District of Columbia, and Puerto Rico. Special arrangements for proof of age have been made in Alaska. In four states—Idaho, Mississippi, South Carolina, and Texas—federal certificates of age are issued by the Wage and Hour and Public Contracts Division, U.S. Department of Labor.

Age certificates have the twofold purpose of (1) protecting minors from harmful employment as defined by the child labor provisions of the FLSA; and (2) protecting employers from unintentional violation of the minimum age provisions of the act by furnishing them with reliable proof of age for minors employed in their establishment. This protection is specifically authorized by the act.

To make sure that the minors in their employ are of legal age under the act, employers are urged to obtain an age certificate for every minor claiming to be under eighteen years of age before employing him in any occupation, and for every minor claiming to be eighteen or nineteen years of age before employing him in any of the nonagricultural occupations declared hazardous.

The age certificate protects the employer only if it shows the minor to be of the legal age for the occupation in which he is employed.

To obtain an employment or age certificate, give the teenager you are about to hire a written promise of employment showing hours of work and the occupation. The teenager takes your statement, along with evidence of his birth date, to a person who issues the certificates—usually the local school or the state Department of Labor or Education.

If an employer has any difficulty in obtaining age certificates for minors he wishes to employ, he should notify the nearest office of the Wage and Hour and Public Contracts Divisions, U.S. Department of Labor, or the Bureau of Labor Standards, U.S. Department of Labor, Washington, D.C. 20210.

What Are the State Laws?

Every state has a child labor law, and most have a compulsory school attendance law. Whenever a state standard differs from the federal standard, the latter must be observed. For further information on your particular state laws, contact the state Department of Labor or Education.

Compliance Procedures of the U.S. Department of Labor

The Wage and Hour Division, Workplace Standards Administration, is responsible for the administration and enforcement of the following federal laws with certain standards for women and minors:

Fair Labor Standards Act

Equal Pay Act

Public Contracts Act

Age Discrimination in Employment Act

The Fair Labor Standards Act and Public Contracts Act contain child labor standards in addition to minimum wage, overtime, and equal pay standards which apply to all employees—men, women, and children.

When an investigation is made by a compliance officer, regardless of the particular act being enforced, the procedures are similar. Also, the Wage and Hour Division representative generally checks on all the applicable federal standards, in the laws outlined above, in a given establishment.

Investigations are made for a variety of reasons: Some are based on complaints; some because of other information that an establishment may not be complying; some to correct improper practices found in a particular industry; and some because of a general plan to get around to see as many covered employers as possible within the limits of available staff.

If the Wage and Hour Division has received a complaint, the compliance officer's instructions require him to treat the complaint as confidential.

Investigation procedures. In the usual case, a prior arrangement has been made with the employer for the visit of the compliance officer. The compliance officer discusses with the employer or his designated representative the records needed and how he plans to go about his work. He will also ask permission to conduct private interviews with some of the employees in the establishment.

The employer will be asked to make work space available for him and to indicate some person in the organization who can help him, should he have questions about the records and payroll system.

The compliance officer will ask to see certain records necessary to decide what laws apply and what, if any, exemptions are available. For example, records of government contracts, records showing interstate commerce, or records showing annual dollar volume of business.

Payrolls, time records, records of dates of birth, occupations, and hours of work for minors under nineteen will be reviewed, and any necessary notes or transcriptions will be made. Information obtained during the investigation will not be revealed to any unauthorized person.

Certain employees will be privately interviewed. Generally, the purpose of such interviews is to confirm payroll or time records and to ascertain duties in sufficient detail to decide what, if any, exemptions apply. There also are other reasons, such as to check on possible discrimination based on sex or age, and illegal employment of minors.

When all the fact-finding steps have been completed, the compliance officer will confer with the employer or his representative about what he found. If he discovered no violations, he will tell the employer so; if he found violations he will tell him what they are and how to correct them. If the employer owes back wages, the usual procedure is to ask him to compute and pay the amounts due. If there are child labor violations, the employer is asked to put the minor in an occupation for which he is old enough and to correct hours violations if they existed.

Enforcement remedies. While most employers inadvertently violate the law, and when advised of their errors are anxious to rectify mistakes and comply in the future, there are some who deliberately violate statutes and refuse to rectify their mistakes. For this latter group the "teeth" in the law provide:

An employee may bring his own suit to recover back pay and an additional sum, up to the amount of back pay, as liquidated damages, plus attorney's fees and court costs

The Secretary of Labor may bring suit for back pay upon the written request of an employee;

The Secretary of Labor may also obtain a court injunction to restrain any person from violating the law, including the unlawful withholding of proper minimum wage and overtime compensation;

The act provides in cases of willful violation for a fine of up to $10,000; or for a second offense committed after the conviction of the person for a similar offense, for a fine of not more than $10,000 or imprisonment for not more than six months, or both.

These penalties are applicable for violation of any of the provisions of the Fair Labor Standards Act.

For violation of the child labor provisions of the Walsh-Healey Public Contracts Act, liquidated damages of $10 a day for every day the minor was illegally employed may be assessed.

Inquiries about the Fair Labor Standards Act will be answered by mail, telephone, or personal interview at any office of the Wage and Hour Division of the U.S. Department of Labor. Offices are listed in the telephone directory under the U.S. Department of Labor in the U.S. government listing. These offices also supply publications free of charge explaining the provisions of all the laws administered and enforced by them.

REFERENCES

[1] U.S. Equal Employment Opportunity Commission, various publications and reports on employment discrimination based on race, religion, color, sex, or national origin—most of which are available free of charge. Write to EEOC, 1800 G Street, N.W., Washington, D.C., 20506.

[2] U.S. Department of Labor, various publications, reports, and Executive Orders on employment discrimination based on the above categories—most of which are available free of charge. The Office of Federal Contract Compliance has jurisdiction over Federal contractors. The Wage and Hour Division has jurisdiction over the Equal Pay Act, Age Discrimination in Employment Act, Fair Labor Standards Act (child labor laws), and the Public Contracts Act (child labor laws). The Women's Bureau also issues many publications on the employment of women. Write to the appropriate office, U.S. Department of Labor, 14th and Constitution, N.W., Washington, D.C., 20210.

[3] National Labor Relations Board, various publications dealing with unfair labor practices and collective bargaining—most of which are available free of charge. Write to the NLRB, 1717 Pennsylvania Avenue, N.W., Washington, D.C., 20570.

[4] State Departments of Labor, State Fair Employment Practice Commissions, State Human Rights (or Civil Rights) Commissions also have publications and reports on equal employment within their respective States.

[5] Bureau of National Affairs, Fair Employment Practices Guide publishes decisions on equal employment. The FEP Guide is available by subscription. Write BNA, 1231 25th Street, N.W., Washington, D.C., 20037.

[6] Commerce Clearing House publishes material on equal employment which is available by subscription. Write CCH, 425 13th Street, N.W., Washington, D.C., 20004.

Part 11

Labor Relations

chapter 54

Collective Bargaining
and Union Contracts

JAMES J. BAMBRICK* *Labor Relations Representative, The Standard Oil Company (Ohio), Cleveland, Ohio*

EARLY HISTORY OF LABOR

Soon after the American Revolution, trade unions composed of shoemakers, tailors, carpenters, printers, bakers, and other skilled workers were organized. These early unions did not engage in collective bargaining as we know it today by meeting with the employer to work out terms and conditions of employment. Instead, they posted the prices and conditions under which they would work. The employer either met these conditions or faced a refusal to work. A forerunner of the union business agent grew out of the need to check on shops to see whether they were adhering to the union wage scale. The early "tramping committees" and unpaid representatives later led to specialized, paid agents known as "walking delegates." Gradually, however, an end came to the unilateral posting of prices when the idea of bargaining by employers and union leaders over the terms and conditions of employment took hold.

In the early 1830s, idealistic union reformers came into vogue. Robert Dale Owen, for example, wanted to set up a "utopia" where everyone would work for the good of all—a sort of heaven on earth. The realities of labor's needs soon separated Owen and his followers from the more practical men of labor. The great depression of 1837 brought a rapid decline in the few unions then in existence. After this, the intellectuals never again made any serious inroads on American labor unions.

With the 1840s came the impact of the industrial revolution. The middle nine-

* Any opinions expressed are the author's and do not necessarily reflect the opinion of the company for whom he works.

teenth century saw the rise of large factories, the concentration of wealth, and the widening of the gap between employees and employer. Unions of this period, however, were not aimed at organizing the expanding mass of unskilled workers. They appealed to the highly skilled worker. In 1852, the International Typographical Union, which still flourishes today, was founded. In the next dozen years other "craft unions," such as the Stonecutters, Hat Finishers, Molders, Machinists, and Locomotive Engineers, were established.

Rise and Fall of the Knights of Labor

In 1869 one of the more interesting organizations on the American scene was formed. Several tailors met in Philadelphia and formed the Noble Order of the Knights of Labor. Its purpose was to unite all workers under one banner, regardless of race, nationality, or creed. The order was, at first, a secret society, as were many early labor unions. Because of the terroristic activities of some other secret groups (particularly the Molly Maguires which attempted to secure social justice by murdering company officials) secrecy was, for the Knights, a liability.

In 1879, Terrence V. Powderly became head of the Knights of Labor, his title being "Grand Master Workman." Insisting that secrecy be abolished, Powderly won approval of the Roman Catholic Church for his organization. With the end of secrecy, the Knights grew rapidly.

To a large extent, any organization is a reflection of its leader. Powderly, a genial Irishman, had a keen sense of social justice and a firm belief in the American system of private property. Many of the figures around him were of a more radical bent, however, and under the constitution of the Knights they held the ruling hand.

The Knights of Labor attempted to weld together all the elements of the working classes. To do so, it permitted craft unions to join directly with its general assembly, or national organization. It also organized local groups, called "mixed assemblies," which took in workers on any basis under which they would enroll. In some cases these came on a craft union basis—while in other cases, the local group would take in all workers in an industry, making no distinction between crafts. The Knights were thus one of the first large unions to attempt what is known as industrial unionization.

The Knights of Labor grew rapidly. In 1885 membership reached 100,000. As a result of a strike in 1886 against the Wabash, Missouri-Kansas-Texas, and Missouri Pacific Railroads, Jay Gould, the financier who controlled these railroads, was forced to grant the Knights recognition. This helped to skyrocket the membership. In one year, 1886, they grew to 700,000 members.

The decline of the Knights was rapid as their ascent. They lost a number of strikes. Chief of these was a defeat when for the second time they struck the Missouri Pacific Railroad. They also lost many craft unionists to a new labor organization, which was later to be known as the American Federation of Labor. In 1888 the Knights declined to 222,000 members, in 1890 to 100,000, and in 1893 to a scant 75,000. Twenty years later, when they finally dissolved, they were a paper organization.

Samuel Gompers and the American Federation of Labor

In 1881, Samuel Gompers and Adolph Strasser of the Cigar Makers Union helped form a group known as the Federation of Organized Trades and Labor Unions. In 1886 several craft unions left the Knights of Labor to form their own organization. After meetings with Gompers and Strasser, however, they decided to amalgamate their new organization with the Federation of Organized Trades and Labor Unions to form a new organization to be known as the American Federation of Labor.

The American Federation of Labor reflected Samuel Gompers' philosophy of trade unionism. He believed that skilled workmen should not submerge themselves in a mass labor movement such as the Knights of Labor. He believed that such skilled craftsmen should form their own craft unions. As a result of this philosophy, AFL unions were "craft" unions.

Samuel Gompers set the American trade union movement on an entirely different road than the European trade union movement. Unlike European Socialist, Communist, and Syndicalist union leaders, he did not believe that unions should try to achieve their goals through revolutionary upheaval. Rather, he believed that American unions should try to achieve their goals on a gradual basis. He felt that instead of looking forward to a socialist utopia, American unions should strive for 5 cents an hour more in the pay envelope, an hour less per day of work. His motto for the American trade union movement was "More, now." AFL co-founder Adolph Strasser accurately described the AFL's goals when he declared, "We have no ultimate ends. We are going on from day to day. We are fighting on for immediate objects. . . . We are all practical men."

Samuel Gompers was unlike European union leaders in another respect. He did not believe that American unions should be the tail of any political party's kite or get embroiled in splinter-party politics. His motto for the American workingman was "Support your friends and punish your enemies" in America's major political parties. Except for one year when a Socialist was elected AFL president, the AFL has always been headed by men who essentially believed in the American system of free, competitive enterprise.

The American Federation of Labor under Gompers grew slowly but steadily. Under its constitution, the national unions in the AFL were strictly autonomous, and had full control of their internal affairs. Rules for governing the AFL were made at yearly conventions, the organization being governed between conventions by a full-time president, secretary, and executive board. This board varied from five to thirteen members, and under the constitution held considerable power.

Except for a one-year period (1894–1895), Samuel Gompers served as AFL President from 1886 until his death in 1924. The highest point of AFL membership under Gompers occurred in World War I, when its ranks shot up to 5,500,000. Immediately after the war, labor union membership declined due to a number of factors, chief of which were (1) a postwar depression, (2) a change in national administration, and (3) a personnel program by employers to provide directly what the unions promised the workers. By 1923 union membership declined to 3,500,000 members.

Upon the death of Samuel Gompers in 1924, United Mine Worker President John L. Lewis secured the election of Mine Worker Secretary William Green as president of the AFL. Under William Green, the AFL did not gain membership during the increased employment of the Roaring Twenties prosperity. Instead, unions either held their own or declined in membership. In 1929, at the height of prosperity, unions had no more members than they had in 1923. The Great Depression following the 1929 stock market crash brought further union membership losses. By 1933, union membership had declined to 2,973,000.

Early New Deal

In 1933, during the early days of the Roosevelt administration, Congress enacted the National Industrial Recovery Act, one section of which granted to labor the right of self-organization without employer interference (see Labor Legislation). At that time John L. Lewis's United Mine Workers had but few members and was practically broke. He gambled on Section 7(a) of the act that gave unions protection in their organizing activities. He took the last bit of money in the union's treasury, hired scores of organizers, and assisted by the new law signed up mine workers by the thousands. Other unions followed Lewis's example and conducted union organizing drives at this time. Among them were the International Ladies Garment Workers, the Amalgamated Clothing Workers, the Oil Workers, and the Building Service Employees.

Rise of CIO

AFL craft unionism left large groups of workers in the mass production industries untapped by unions. Pressure for membership drives among such workers led to discontent in AFL circles. To pressure for unionizing on an industrial union basis, John L. Lewis of the Mine Workers, David Dubinsky of the Ladies Garment Workers, Sidney Hillman of the Amalgamated Clothing Workers, and leaders of oil, textile, and metal unions formed within the AFL a Committee for Industrial Organizations, which the newspapers shortened to CIO. The governing body of the AFL, the Executive Council, ordered this committee disbanded. When the CIO member unions refused to disband the committee the AFL Executive Council suspended the unions affiliated with the Committee for Industrial Organizations. These unions never showed up at the 1936 AFL convention, which voted to expel them.

The CIO unions that were expelled changed the name of the committee to Congress of Industrial Organizations and elected John L. Lewis as president. The CIO conducted whirlwind organizing drives in automobile, steel, meat-packing, and other mass production industries.

In organizing the steel industry the CIO used as forums to sell the CIO's brand of unionism the independent unions established by the companies in the early twenties and thirties. By January 1937, the CIO's Steelworkers Organizing Committee had largely unionized the big Carnegie-Illinois Steel plant of the United States Steel Corporation. Through the good offices of the White House, John L. Lewis and Myron Taylor, then board chairman of the U.S. Steel Corporation, met and signed a contract for U.S. Steel's many plants. Heading up the Steelworkers Organizing Committee was Phillip Murray, who held the job of vice-president of John L. Lewis's Mine Workers Union.

In organizing the automobile industry, the CIO's United Automobile Workers union conducted at General Motors and Chrysler a series of "sitdown" strikes during which striking workers stayed inside the plant but refused to work or permit management personnel or strikebreakers to enter the buildings. Both these companies recognized the Automobile Workers union in 1937. Ford held off the union that year, but signed a contract after a strike in 1941. This union succeeded in organizing the rest of the automobile industry and also organized a number of aircraft and agricultural implement companies.

Other CIO unions succeeded in organizing the "Big Three" rubber companies, many of the meat-packing companies, and the big producers of electrical appliances.

One of the basic weaknesses in the CIO organizing campaigns, however, was that John L. Lewis permitted the Communist party to supply organizers. While the Communists were effective union organizers, Mr. Lewis soon found that they had captured large CIO unions.

In December of 1940, John L. Lewis resigned as president of the CIO. The CIO elected as president Phillip Murray, vice president of the United Mine Workers and president of the United Steelworkers of America. Mr. Murray, after some delay, began a campaign to wean away the leadership of Communist-dominated unions and bring them into the anti-Communist camp. Under his leadership, the CIO in 1949 expelled the following unions on charges of Communist domination: (1) United Electrical, Radio and Machine Workers of America, (2) United Office and Professional Workers, (3) Food, Tobacco, Agricultural and Allied Workers, (4) Mine, Mill and Smelter Workers Union, (5) Farm Equipment Workers, (6) Fur and Leather

Workers, (7) United Public Workers, (8) International Longshoremen's and Warehousemen's Union, (9) National Union of Marine Cooks and Stewards, (10) American Communications Association, (11) International Fishermen & Allied Workers. Of these expelled unions only the Electrical Workers and Longshoremen still survive as independent, unaffiliated unions. The other nine unions have either merged with other unions or disbanded.

In the fall of 1952, AFL President William Green and CIO President Phillip Murray died. As Mr. Green's death occurred shortly after the AFL's convention, the job of picking his successor devolved on the AFL Executive Council. They elected George Meany, who the following year was elected by convention vote.

As Mr. Murray died a week before the scheduled CIO convention, his successor was chosen by convention vote. The two nominees were the heir-apparent Allan Heywood, CIO executive vice-president, and Walter P. Reuther, president of Automobile Workers. After a heated floor fight, Walter P. Reuther was elected CIO president by the slimmest of margins.

Immediately after his selection as AFL president, George Meany announced his determination to reunite the divided labor movement. Abortive attempts at reunification of the AFL and CIO had been made in 1937, 1939, and 1942. These were resumed in 1947 and 1952, but it was under Meany, on December 5, 1955, that the AFL and CIO were once more together.

AFL-CIO ATTEMPTS TO CLEAN HOUSE

In the December, 1955, merger convention, the AFL-CIO wrote into the new constitution Article 8, Section 7, which provided: "It is a basic principle of this Federation that it must be and remain free from any and all corrupt influences and from the undermining efforts of Communist, Fascist or other totalitarian agencies." Under this provision, the AFL-CIO executive council was given power:

1. To investigate corrupt unions.
2. To give clean-up directions to unions involved.
3. To suspend upon two-thirds vote, if the clean-up directions are not followed. The suspended union may appeal to next AFL-CIO convention, but the executive council's decision stands until that time.

Hearings before Senator McClellan's Senate Subcommittee on Improper Activities in the Labor or Management Field, running from 1957 to 1959, revealed widespread corruption in AFL-CIO unions. At the AFL-CIO convention in December, 1957, unions indicted by the AFL-CIO executive council were heavily dealt with, following revelations of corruption and undemocratic practices. The Teamsters' Union, the Bakery Workers, the Distillery Workers, the Laundry Workers, the United Textile Workers, the Brewery Workers, and the Jewelry Workers were all either expelled or suspended. Leading the fight for Teamster expulsion was Automobile Worker President Walter P. Reuther.

In 1959, with James R. Hoffa's Teamsters' Union threatening to become the nucleus for a new federation, the AFL-CIO executive council decided to abandon recourse to expulsion. They decided that unions were not strong enough on their own to wipe out all corruption and that what was needed was a law.

The Labor-Management Reporting and Disclosure Act of 1959 introduced government control of unions to a greater extent than union proponents of reform had anticipated. It sought to protect employees and the public from breach of trust and corruption by placing restrictions on union officers. A digest of this law, which covers management as well as labor, is given in the labor legislation section of this chapter.

ALLIANCE FOR LABOR ACTION

The new federation that the AFL-CIO sought to avoid came into being in 1968. Following a long series of policy disputes between AFL-CIO President George Meany and United Automobile President Walter P. Reuther, the UAW formally disaffiliated from the AFL-CIO in July, 1968. The event marked the first major schism in the labor movement since 1957, when the AFL-CIO had expelled the Teamsters and two other unions, charging corrupt practices.

Shortly after the Automobile Workers disaffiliated from the AFL, Walter P. Reuther and Acting Teamster President Frank E. Fitzsimmons teamed up to form the Alliance for Labor Action, to coordinate their efforts toward organizing, bargaining, community action, and political goals. They were soon joined by the International Chemical Workers Union. When other labor organizations were invited to join the new group, the AFL-CIO charged that they were attempting to set up a rival federation, and warned its affiliated unions that supporting or joining the ALA would be grounds for suspension.

The UAW-Teamster–sponsored Alliance for Labor Action held its first convention in Washington, D.C., May 26 and 27, 1969. The delegates adopted a constitution and elected an executive committee, naming UAW President Walter P. Reuther and Acting Teamster President Frank E. Fitzsimmons as co-chairmen. Fitzsimmons, who was elected Teamster president in July, 1971, was named chairman of the ALA organizing committee. Work of the ALA is financed by a 10-cent levy from the monthly dues of ALA union membership.

The eighth bicentenial convention of the AFL-CIO, held in October, 1969, voted to expel the 90,000-member Chemical Workers Union, which had joined the Alliance for Labor Action despite AFL-CIO warnings of expulsion.

The founding of the ALA was attended by a great deal of publicity, but the organization really never did get off the ground. The sudden death of Walter Reuther in a private plane accident in the summer of 1970 and the succession of Leonard Woodcock to the presidency of the United Automobile Workers Union raises further question about the continuance of the Alliance for Labor Action.

TYPES OF UNIONS

There are two types of unions: industrial unions and the craft unions. Industrial unions take in all workers in a plant or industry from top to bottom. For this reason they are called vertical unions. The same industrial unions, for example, may bargain for unskilled production workers, highly skilled craftsmen, and clerical workers.

Craft unions, on the other hand, take in only members of a particular craft no matter where they are working in the local unions's area. An International Association of Machinists' local union, for example, may take in as members and bargain for one to a dozen maintenance machinists at each of several hundred plants in an area. Since they bargain for only a thin strata of workers at each plant, they are called horizontal unions.

In the building and construction trades, local craft unions frequently control employment in their area. Thus, for example, when the contractor reaches the stage in building that he needs bricklayers, he calls the Bricklayers Union hiring hall for the required number. As soon as the bricklayers are finished, he sends them back to the union hiring hall where the process is repeated again and again with other contractors. This is the spigot concept of labor: the union controls the pool of skilled labor and doles it out on an as-needed basis. Unions in such situations take on many characteristics of employers, and employers become subcontractors of labor.

LOCAL UNIONS

When one talks about unions in a labor relations situation, he is generally talking about local unions. The unions may be small locals limited to one plant and containing but fifty members. They may be giant, one-plant locals such as Ford Local 600 at River Rouge with about fifty thousand members. Or they may be area-wide organizations, such as Service Employees Union Local 32B in New York's Manhattan with about fifty-five thousand members.

Locals Based on Racial and Nationality Lines

Some local unions are based on nationality or racial lines. The founding of unions along these lines is an outgrowth of the successive waves of immigration that have swept across the United States.

There was and is continuing, for example, a wave of Italian immigration into the Eastern seaboard. A large number of Italians went to work in the ladies garment industry. They stuck together and spoke Italian, not English. The already established local Garment Unions were largely Jewish as a result of a previous immigration wave. When Italians went to local union meetings they found the members lapsing into Yiddish, which they did not understand.

To meet this situation, the officers of the International Ladies Garment Workers Union organized an Italian-American Dressmakers' Union. Now, if a member finds at a membership meeting that he cannot find the right English word, he lapses into Italian and everybody at the meeting understands him.

Local unions founded on racial and nationality lines are fairly common. The International Typographical Union, for example, has the Yiddish-American Typographical Union in New York, whose members set type for the Yiddish-language papers. In a number of Midwestern cities, there are German-American, Polish-American, and Swedish-American local unions.

STRUCTURE OF AFL-CIO

The United States Bureau of Labor Statistics estimates the number of local unions chartered by national and international unions at approximately eighty thousand. More than two-thirds of the locals are in AFL-CIO affiliates.

The AFL-CIO resulted from a merger of the American Federation of Labor and the Congress of Industrial Organizations in December, 1955. The structure of the AFL-CIO is set forth in the organization chart shown in Figure 1. As can be seen from this chart, the principal member organizations of the AFL-CIO are:

1. The affiliated national and international unions, which, in turn are made up of local unions

2. City federations of labor and state federations of labor, also made up of local AFL-CIO unions

3. Departments composed for the most part of a group of national or international unions in a particular trade or industry

4. Local trade unions and local industrial unions directly affiliated with the AFL-CIO and not chartered by any national or international union

The supreme governing body of the AFL-CIO is the biennial convention. Each union is entitled to convention representation according to the membership on which the per capita tax of 10 cents a month has been paid. Between conventions, the executive officers, assisted by the executive council and the general board, direct the affairs of the AFL-CIO.

The functions of the two top officers and of the two governing bodies are as follows:

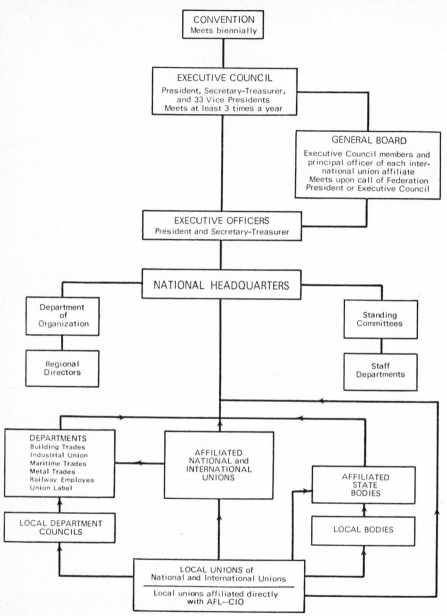

Figure 1.   Structure of the AFL-CIO (United States Department of Labor).

Executive Officers

The AFL-CIO has two executive officers, president and secretary-treasurer.   The president is the chief executive officer.   He has authority to interpret the constitution between meetings of the executive council, and to direct the staff of the federation.   The secretary-treasurer is responsible for all financial matters.

Executive Council

The executive council consists of thirty-three vice-presidents and the two executive officers. It is the AFL-CIO's governing body between conventions. It meets at least three times each year on the call of the president.

Among the duties of the executive council are proposing and evaluating legislation of interest to the labor movement and keeping the federation free from corrupt or Communist influences. To achieve the latter, the council has the right to investigate any affiliate accused of wrongdoing and, at the completion of the investigation, make recommendations or give directions to the affiliate involved. Furthermore, by a two-thirds vote, the executive council may suspend a union found guilty on charges of corruption or subversion. The executive council is also given the rights:

1. To conduct hearings on charges that a council member is guilty of malfeasance or maladministration, and report to the convention recommending appropriate action

2. To remove from office or refuse to seat, by two-thirds vote, any executive officer or council member found to be a member or follower of a subversive organization

3. To assist unions in organizing activities and charter new national and international unions not in jurisdictional conflict with existing ones

4. To hear appeals in jurisdiction disputes

General Board

This body consists of all thirty-five members of the executive council and a principal officer of each affiliated national union and department. The general board acts on matters referred to it by the executive officers or the executive council. It meets at least once a year. Unlike members of the executive council, general board members vote as representatives of their unions, with voting strength based on per capita payments to the federation.

Trade and Industrial Departments

The AFL-CIO constitution provides for six trade and industrial departments: (1) building trades, (2) industrial union, (3) maritime trades, (4) metal trades, (5) railway employees, (6) union label. Affiliation with the AFL-CIO departments is open to "all appropriate affiliated national and international unions." The department per capita tax which affiliates are obligated to pay is determined by the number of their members coming within its jurisdiction.

Department of Organization

To further the union organizing activities of the AFL-CIO, the constitution established a separate department of organization to operate under the general direction of the president. The director of the department is appointed by the president, subject to approval of the executive council. The department has its own staff and other resources necessary to carry out its activities.

UNION MEMBERSHIP

Membership of national and international unions with headquarters in the United States was 20.2 million in 1968, according to the United States Department of Labor. Of this total, 15.6 million are in unions affiliated with the AFL-CIO, and 4.6 million are in unaffiliated national and international unions. Total membership in the United States—that is, excluding Canadian membership—was 18,774,000 in 1968.

These figures account for the membership of national and international unions with headquarters in the United States. However, they exclude members of unaffiliated unions which confine their activities to a single employer or a single locality. The United States Bureau of Labor Statistics estimates this membership to be about half a million. Using this estimate for single firm and local unaffiliated unions, the 1968 total membership in the United States (as distinct from membership in national and international unions with headquarters in the United States) is 19,423,000. It is arrived at this way:

Membership of national and international unions in the United States.	18,774,000
Add membership of federal labor unions and local industrial unions and unions directly affiliated with AFL-CIO.	48,000
Add estimate of membership in single firm and local unaffiliated unions.	475,000
Total union membership in the United States.	19,297,000

This tabulation does not account for certain categories of workers, such as the unemployed, retired, and those on strike, who, though still attached to unions, were exempted from dues requirements and hence were excluded by certain unions in their reports to the United States Department of Labor.

After a more than twofold increase between 1937 and 1944, national and international unions made slow but steady gains and reached a peak of 17.5 million members in 1956 (exclusive of Canada). They subsequently lost one million members during the 1957–1961 period. Since 1961 union membership in absolute numbers has been slowly gaining each year.

Union membership has not kept pace with the growth in the work force since 1956, as the data in Figures 2 and 3 illustrate.

FIGURE 2.   Union Membership as a Proportion of the Labor Force, 1956–1968

Year	Total membership excluding Canada	Membership exclusive of Canada as a percent of—			
		Total labor force		Employees in nonagricultural establishments	
		Number (thousands)	Percent union members	Number (thousands)	Percent union members
1956.	17,490	69,409	25.2	52,408	33.4
1957.	17,369	69,729	24.9	52,894	32.8
1958.	17,029	70,275	24.2	51,363	33.2
1959.	17,117	70,921	24.1	53,313	32.1
1960.	17,049	72,142	23.6	54,234	31.4
1961.	16,303	73,031	22.3	54,042	30.2
1962.	16,586	73,442	22.6	55,596	29.8
1963.	16,524	74,571	22.2	56,702	29.1
1964.	16,841	75,830	22.2	58,332	28.9
1965.	17,299	77,178	22.4	60,815	28.4
1966.	17,940	78,893	22.7	63,955	28.1
1967.	18,367	80,793	22.7	65,857	28.0
1968.	18,916	82,272	23.0	67,860	27.9

SOURCE: U.S. Department of Labor.

WHITE-COLLAR UNION MEMBERSHIP

Of the 35.5 million white-collar workers, there are approximately 27.8 million in nonmanagerial jobs. Of these, unions have organized 3,179,000, or 11.4 percent.

FIGURE 3. White-Collar Union Membership as a Percentage of Nonmanagerial White-Collar Work Force, 1958–1968 (In Thousands)

Year	White-collar workers except managers, officials, and proprietors*	White-collar union members	Percentage
1958	20,042	2,184	10.9
1960	21,449	2,192	10.2
1962	22,226	2,285	10.3
1964	23,416	2,585	11.0
1966	25,662	2,810	11.0
1968	27,775	3,179	11.4

* Includes all professional and technical employees, not just unionizable occupations.

SOURCES: Bureau of Labor Statistics, National Industrial Conference Board.

This 11 percent figure is fairly constant for the past ten years, as is shown by Figure 3.

The 11 percent of the white-collar work force that unions have organized is not a uniform 11 percent. It ranges from practically zero for banks, insurance companies, and company home offices, to over 90 percent of railway white-collar employees who are members of the AFL-CIO Railway Clerks International Union, which has some 350,000 members.

In the telephone field between 50 and 70 percent of the white-collar force is represented by unions. The principal union in this field, the Communications Workers of America, claims a quarter of a million members.

In the basic steel industry, about 50 percent of the white-collar workers in offices directly connected with plants are organized by the United Steelworkers of America. The Steelworkers union, however, has not organized the main offices of the steel companies.

A high degree of white-collar unionization exists in the entertainment field. The American Federation of Musicians has a quarter of a million members, though many of the members work in this field on only a part-time basis. In Hollywood and on Broadway, unionization is the rule rather than the exception.

LEGAL BACKGROUND OF COLLECTIVE BARGAINING

Because of recent experience with the New Deal and the Fair Deal and because of recent British experience with Labor government there is a tendency to think of government as decidedly prolabor, to think that government is the first place to which labor historically turns. Nothing could be further from the truth. If one looks back on labor history he finds that government has for hundreds of years been decidedly antilabor.

Conspiracy Doctrine in England

America gets its main body of law from English common law. Common law held labor unions to conspiracies in restraint of trade. One of the English laws held to apply to unions is the Statute of 1305 (Edward I) entitled "Who Be Conspirators." One of Britain's early queens established a law making it a crime for workers to combine for the purpose of raising wages.

During the 1700s the English Parliament passed with clocklike regularity laws against conspiracies in restraint of trade. These laws were one-sided. As Lord Jeffrey said in 1825: "A single employer could lay off his whole work force of 100 or 1,000 at one time if they would not accept his offer. Yet it was an offense if the workers walked out." Employers had at that time what Adam Smith referred to as "tacit but constant combinations of employers to depress wages, but these could not be reached by law." Baron Passfield (Sidney Webb) wrote: "During the whole period, while thousands of union members were fined and jailed for the crime of combination, there is no case on record in which the employer was punished for the same offense."

Conspiracy Doctrine in America

In picking up English common law, America picked up the conspiracy doctrine lock, stock, and barrel. The earliest example of this is the Philadelphia Cordwainers (which means shoemaker) case of 1806, in which the court held that unions were illegal conspiracies against the public and employers.

This continued until 1842, when in *Commonwealth v. Hunt* the test became whether the action sought by the union combination was legal or illegal. Everything hinged on "motive" and "intent." Thus, one judge would say all strikes are bad and enjoin all strikes and another might say that a strike's purpose was primarily for a beneficial purpose and refuse to grant an injunction.

In one broad injunction during a railroad strike, the barber usually patronized by railroad workers was cited for contempt for hanging a sign in his window that no scabs were wanted as customers. If an injunction was found to be unfair, it was too late, for the union was out of existence.

The First Law—Sherman Antitrust Act

One of the things to keep in mind is that in America during all this time there was no law on labor relations. Rather it was court rulings on the basis of English common law.

The earliest law that affected labor relations was the Sherman Antitrust Act, passed in 1890. This law was supposed to be aimed at big business trusts. But a brilliant lawyer, Walter Gordon Merritt, applied it against unions. This he did in the well-known Danbury Hatters strike.

To win this strike, the Hatters union asked all union men not to buy the struck Danbury hats. Merritt claimed that this boycott was violation of the Sherman Antitrust Act. The United States Supreme Court upheld Merritt's contention.

The Supreme Court said the union's boycott was a "combination in restraint of trade or commerce among the several states." The result was that the United States Supreme Court ordered the union and the workers individually to pay the triple damages that the act provided as penalties. This broke the strike. The union was cleaned out of every cent in its treasury, and the workers were sued individually by the firm for damages caused by the strike.

Thus the first law to be applied in labor relations hit unions very hard. But the Danbury Hatters case became a cause célèbre among unions. They put on a campaign to raise money to pay off the court judgment in the case, which they finally did.

More important, they started a campaign to amend the Sherman Antitrust Act so that unions could not be sued under it. They succeeded in this, the act being amended by the Clayton Antitrust Act of 1914. This amendment was supposed to aim the act strictly at big business and not in any way at unions. But when the courts finished interpreting the Clayton Antitrust Act, unions again found that they could be sued. After these two experiences, old-time AFL union leaders like John L. Lewis, Sam Gompers, and Andrew Fureseth shied away from laws dealing with labor relations. They said: "No law is the best labor law."

Yellow-dog Contracts

From the time of the Clayton Act (1914) to 1932, no important federal laws governing management-union affairs were passed. But during that time, the courts were issuing injunctions against strikes by unions.

In 1917, the U.S. Supreme Court in the *Hitchman Coal and Coke* case upheld the so-called "yellow-dog" contracts, in which a worker promised his employer that he would not join a union. The high court held that the courts could issue injunctions that would stop union organizers from trying to organize workers who had signed such contracts.

Perhaps the best way to understand the import of a "yellow-dog" contract is to give an actual example, as follows:

> I am employed by and work for the X Company with the express understanding that I am not a member of the United Mine Workers of America and will not become so while an employee of the X Company, and that the X Company is run non-union and agrees with me that it will run non-union while I am in its employ. If at any time while I am employed by the X Company I want to become connected with the United Mine Workers of America, or any affiliated organization, I agree to withdraw from the employment of said company, and agree that while I am in the employ of that company I will not make any effort amongst its employees to bring about the unionizing of that mine against the company's wish. I have either read the above, or heard same read.

The U.S. Supreme Court said that such a contract was legal. Moreover, it said that a union in trying to organize workers who had signed these contracts was trying to get them to break their contracts. The court said that the employer could get an injunction against the union to prohibit them from trying to organize workers who had signed these contracts.

Norris-LaGuardia Anti-injunction Act

In 1932, a Republican Senate, a Democratic House, and a Republican President, Herbert Hoover, got together on a law that spelled the end of an era. This law was the Norris-LaGuardia Anti-injunction Act, a law that is still on the books. The act did the following:

First, it limited use of injunctions. Under the act the courts were not permitted to issue injunctions which would stop:

1. Concerted refusals to work
2. Membership in, or support of a labor organization
3. Peaceful urging of others to leave work

Second, it required employers who come to court for injunctions:

1. To have clean hands, that is to have done nothing that provoked violence
2. To prove that local police could not handle dispute

Third, it banned yellow-dog contracts as being against public policy.

BLUE EAGLE DAYS

The year 1933 ushered in Franklin Delano Roosevelt and the National Industrial Recovery Act's Blue Eagle days. That act contained the Section 7a that for the first time since World War I gave workers the right to designate representatives of their own choosing, and required employers to deal with the unions the workers chose.

WAGNER ACT

On May 27, 1935, the Supreme Court found the National Industrial Recovery Act unconstitutional in the *Scheckter Sick Chicken* case. Shortly thereafter, in 1935, Congress passed the National Labor Relations Act, better known as the Wagner Act.

The Wagner Act changed the whole relationship of employers and unions. Its sponsors said that it was not meant to be balanced law but rather to be a balancing law. Their view was that the weight had been on management's side of the collective bargaining seesaw. The law's objective was to place weight on union's side of the seesaw to balance things in the union's favor. In its own words, it sought to redress the "inequality of bargaining power between employees who do not possess full freedom of association or actual liberty of contract and employers who are organized in corporate or other forms of ownership association."

The basic philosophy behind the Wagner Act was:

1. It was desirable that collective bargaining between management and labor unions resolve the terms and conditions of employment.

2. Workers should organize into unions, and bargain collectively through their own representatives.

3. Since employers, if not prevented, would hinder the above, employers should be restrained from carrying on coercive practices against unions.

The Wagner Act provided no unfair labor practices for unions. In fact its backers assumed that unions were so weak and puny that it was virtually impossible for them to commit any unfair labor practice that would be consequential.

Employer Unfair Labor Practices

The Wagner Act restrained employers by setting up employer unfair labor practices. The same unfair labor practices are in the Taft-Hartley Act, and are in effect today. They are as follows:

1. The employer may not interfere with his employees' right to bargain collectively. It is clearly illegal for him to:
   a. Set up a spy system
   b. Threaten his employees for joining a union

2. The employer cannot interfere with the formation or administration of a union. The means that the employer cannot solicit membership for the union or participate in running it. For example, in the *Virginia Electric Light and Power* case, the NLRB and the Supreme Court upheld the employer domination charge because the company gave office space free of charge to the independent union and let it use its addressograph and mimeograph facilities.

3. Forbade the employer from discriminating against an employee for filing charges or testifying under the act.

4. Forbade the employer from refusing to bargain with the legal representative of his workers.

5. Forbade the employer from encouraging or discouraging union membership except where a closed shop was agreed upon. (The Taft-Hartley Act changed this to union shop.)

Established Exclusive Representation

The Wagner Act also established a procedure for setting up bargaining units. It said that the representative of the majority of the employees in appropriate bargaining unit should be the exclusive representative of workers in unit. This is just the opposite of the system used in many European countries. In Italy and France, for instance, several industrial unions may exist side by side in a plant and speak only for their own members.   One union may be Communist, one Socialist, and the other Catholic.   In short, America has exclusive representation, and some European countries have concurrent representation.

Wagner Act Inequities

The Wagner Act was a boon to unions.   It resulted in a tremendous growth of unions.

The act was also strongly attacked as inequitable in that: (1) It favored unions over management.   (2) It gave employers no protection against a union's unfair labor practices.   (3) It afforded no protection to individuals and the public from union actions.

TAFT-HARTLEY ACT

The year 1946 saw a tremendous wave of strikes hit the United States.   In that year, there were 116 million man-days lost due to strikes.   What particularly incensed the public was John L. Lewis's dictatorial "public be damned" attitude in his coal strikes.   The wave of strikes, coupled with public reaction against OPA rationing and price controls, led to the election of a Republican Congress.

The happy days for union officials that accompanied the New Deal were over. On June 23, 1947, the Labor-Management Relations Act of 1947 was passed by Congress over President Truman's veto, by an overwhelming majority—a majority of Democrats and Republicans.   This law is more commonly known as the Taft-Hartley Act.

Taft-Hartley Purposes

The goals of the Taft-Hartley Act are set forth in the Declaration of Policy of the act.   The purposes are fivefold and are taken directly from the act.

1. To prescribe the legitimate rights of both employers and employees in their relations affecting commerce.

2. To provide orderly and peaceful procedures for preventing the interference by either with the legitimate rights of the other.

3. To protect the rights of individual employees in their relations with labor organizations whose activities affect commerce.

4. To define and prescribe practices on the part of labor and management which affect commerce and are inimical to the general welfare.

5. To protect the rights of the public in connection with labor disputes affecting commerce.

Taft-Hartley Union Unfair Labor Practices

The Taft-Hartley Act did something that the Wagner Act never did.   It established unfair labor practices for unions.   In the hearings that went on before passage of the Taft-Hartley Act, there were thousands of pages of evidence showing union abuses against the public and against individual members.   The unfair labor practices for unions were aimed at correcting these abuses.

The unfair labor practices for unions set forth in the Taft-Hartley Act are as follows:

1. The first of these unfair labor practices appears in Section 7 of the act.   It says in effect that unions may not interfere with a worker's right *not* to participate in collective bargaining.   It was aimed at unions that use strong-arm methods for organizing.

2. A second unfair labor practice for unions was that they could not engage in secondary boycotts.   A secondary boycott is a device whereby a union that has a

dispute with employer A puts pressure on employers B, C, and D not to do business with employer A in order to get employer A to capitulate to the union.

3. Unions may not "refuse to bargain collectively with an employer." This was aimed at unions that have contracts printed up beforehand and demand that each employer sign them without any privilege of bargaining. As one employer said in congressional testimony: "This is not collective bargaining; it is collective bludgeoning."

4. The fourth union unfair labor practice was to forbid unions to charge excessive initiation fees. This was done in Section 8 (b) (5) which says:

> It shall be an unfair labor practice for a labor organization or its agents to require of employees covered by an agreement authorized under subsection (2) (3) the payment, as a condition precedent to becoming a member of such organization, of a fee in an amount which the Board finds excessive or discriminatory under all the circumstances. In making such a finding, the Board shall consider, among other relevant factors, the practices and customs of labor organizations in the particular industry, and the wages currently paid to the employees affected.

Let's see how this section worked out. The NLRB in a case involving motion picture operators said that an initiation fee of $1,000 was not excessive. If a $1,000 fee is not excessive, what is? The answer seemingly is that nothing is excessive, and this section has become a dead letter.

Antifeatherbedding Section

A fifth union unfair labor practice is attempting to induce employers to make featherbedding agreements. This is prohibited under Section 8(b) (6) which says:

> It shall be an unfair labor practice for a labor organization or its agents to cause or attempt to cause an employer to pay or deliver any money or other thing of value, *in the nature of an exaction,* for services which are not performed. [Italics supplied]

At the same time Congress passed the Taft-Hartley Act, it also passed the Lea Act. The antifeatherbedding section and the Lea Act were aimed at:

1. Standby musicians: Let us say that a radio or television station was going to have a high school band play over the air. The musicians union would have the station pay an equal number of union musicians to stand by while the high school band played.

2. Extra driver or $8: At New York and other large cities, over-the-road trucks were met by local Teamster agents at bridges and tunnels. The over-the-road drivers were told, "Let us drive the trucks in the city or give us $8."

Both the Musicians and the Teamster cases went to the courts. The courts hinged everything on the words "in the nature of an exaction." They held that requiring standby musicians was not an exaction as the musicians were willing to play. They held that the required $8 fee for over-the-road trucks was not an exaction as the business agent offered to drive the truck.

These court decisions pretty well killed the Lea Act and the antifeatherbedding section of the Taft-Hartley Act.

Taft-Hartley Union Shop

The sixth union unfair labor practice is that unions may not cause employers to discriminate against nonunionists, except under legal union security agreements.

The Taft-Hartley Act says that unions may not cause an employer to encourage or discourage union membership. It then permits a special type of union shop provided the union is certified. Under this type of union shop the employer agrees that all workers must belong to the union to keep their jobs. He can hire whom he wants but new workers must join the union not later than thirty days after employment.

The second union security restriction is that the employer cannot discharge a worker for nonmembership if:

> . . . he has reasonable grounds for believing that membership was denied or terminated for reasons other than the failure of the employee to tender the periodic dues and the initiation fees uniformly required as a condition of acquiring or retaining membership.

This is meant to protect the union member at a union meeting who asks: "Mr. President, I would like a report on our treasury," and who then is expelled from the union and his job on the pretext that he disrupted a union meeting.

Section 8(a)(3)(A) and (B) in effect makes the Taft-Hartley union shop a "union dues" shop.

State "Right-to-work" Section

There is one other union security restriction in the Taft-Hartley Act. This is Section 14(b), the right-to-work section, which says:

> Nothing in this Act shall be construed as authorizing the execution or application of agreements requiring membership in a labor organization as a condition of employment in any state or territory in which such execution or application is prohibited by State or Territorial law.

This means that in the nineteen states that prohibit union shop contracts under their right-to-work laws, the state law is supreme.

Unions are trying to repeal the right-to-work laws in the nineteen states by repealing Section 14(b). If that section is eliminated from the act, then only federal labor law will apply in the union security field, and the state laws will be dead letters. The last attempt to repeal Section 14(b) failed in Congress in 1968. There undoubtedly will be other attempts.

Foremen Part of Management

A section of the Taft-Hartley Act is aimed at removing foremen from the threat of being swallowed up in a bargaining unit consisting of his own employees, and against his own wishes. At the time the Taft-Hartley Act was passed, unions were going hot and heavy to force unionization of foremen. And this drive had its salutary effects. The forgotten man became the well-remembered man, and many basic reasons for foreman unionization disappeared.

The Taft-Hartley Act first defined supervisors. It then says that the term employee shall not include any individual employed as a supervisor. This means that employers shall not be forced by the NLRB to deal with a union claiming their supervisors.

LABOR-MANAGEMENT REPORTING AND DISCLOSURE ACT

On September 14, 1959, President Eisenhower signed into law the Labor-Management Reporting and Disclosure Act of 1959. This is popularly called the Labor Reform Law, or the Landrum-Griffin Act. Most of its provisions affect labor. But, many also affect management.

Bill of Rights for Union Members

The new law sets up a bill of rights for union members. This is popularly called the McClellan Bill of Rights. It does the following:

1. It guarantees to union members equal rights and privileges to nominate candidates, to vote in union elections, to attend, speak freely, and vote at union meetings, to meet with other members, and to give their views on candidates for office.

2. It specifies that unions cannot increase union dues, initiation fees, or assessments except as the law provides.

3. It grants union members the right to sue union officers to stop them from violating union rights or misusing union funds.

4. It safeguards union members against improper disciplinary action by specifying that they cannot be fined, suspended, or expelled unless they have been told the specific charges against them and have been given a full and fair hearing.

5. It gives every member the right to get copies of a union contract that directly affects him or her as an employee.

6. And last, but not least, it requires all unions to inform their members of their rights under the act.

If a worker's union doesn't give him these rights, he is given the right to go to federal court to get them.

Financial Reports by Unions Required

The second thing that the Landrum-Griffin Act does is to require detailed financial reporting by all unions. Among the things they have to file are all receipts, expenditures, salaries, and loans to people on the union payroll. The act requires every union officer and employee to file a report on all financial transactions made by him or members of his family with firms with which the union deals. It requires union officers and employees to report any money received from labor relations consultants. The act says unions are forbidden to make loans to officers and employees that result in a total indebtedness to the union by the borrower in excess of $2,000.

Reports Are Public Information

The law makes these reports public information. Interested citizens may inspect and examine these reports on request. They are furnished copies, on request, on payment of a service charge of 25 cents for each page.

Reports may be examined and copies made at the U.S. Labor Department's Office of Labor-Management and Welfare-Pension Reports, Washington, D.C. 20210, or from the nearest of the following area offices:

1371 Peachtree St. N.E.
Atlanta, Ga. 30309

J. F. Kennedy Building Government Center
Boston, Mass. 02203

121 Ellicott St.
Buffalo, N.Y. 14203

219 S. Dearborn St.
Chicago, Ill. 60604

1240 E. Ninth St.
Cleveland, Ohio 44199

1416 Commerce St.
Dallas, Tex. 75201

821 17th St.
Denver, Colo. 80202

234 State St.
Detroit, Mich. 48226

1833 Kalakaua Ave.
Honolulu, Hawaii 96815

911 Walnut St.
Kansas City, Mo. 64106

300 N. Los Angeles St.
Los Angeles, Calif. 90012

51 S.W. First Ave.
Miami, Fla. 33130

110 S. Fourth St.
Minneapolis, Minn. 55401

801 Broadway
Nashville, Tenn. 37203

1060 Broad St.
Newark, N.J. 07102

423 Canal St.
New Orleans, La. 70130

233 W. 49th St.
New York, N.Y. 10019

Ninth and Market Sts.
Philadelphia, Pa. 19107

1000 Liberty Ave.
Pittsburgh, Pa. 15222

450 Golden Gate Ave.
San Francisco, Calif. 94102

1200 Ponce de Leon Ave.
Santurce, Puerto Rico 00907

506 Second Ave.
Seattle, Wash. 98104

1520 Market St.
St. Louis, Mo. 63103

1111 20th St. N.W.
Washington, D.C. 20210

Rules for Union Elections

The Wagner Act and the Taft-Hartley Act said nothing about how unions were to hold their elections. Unions were considered private organizations free to make up their own rules.

Most unions run clean elections. But over the years it has been shown that some do not.

The Hod Carriers, Building, and Common Laborers Union, for example, did not hold a convention for a period of thirteen years. This is not a small union: it has over 300,000 members.

In some unions, men who ran for office against the incumbents were expelled, lost their jobs, and were physically intimidated. In other cases nobody ever ran against the incumbent for periods ranging up to thirty years because they knew it was impossible to ever reach the membership. Only the incumbent had the membership list.

The act attempts to correct these abuses. It requires that every national and international union must elect its officers no less than every five years, either by secret ballot among the members in good standing or at a convention of delegates chosen by secret ballot.

Every local labor organization must elect its officers not less than once every three years by secret ballot among the members in good standing.

To give candidates running against the incumbents a fair shake, the act says: A union may not discriminate among candidates with regard to distribution of campaign literature to members. Every bona fide candidate shall have the right to inspect lists of all members who are subject to an agreement requiring membership as a condition of employment. Union funds may not be used to promote the candidacy of any particular person.

To put teeth into this provision, the act says that if the Secretary of Labor finds, after a hearing, "probable cause" to believe that a violation has been committed, he is authorized to press suit to void the election.

Abuses of Trusteeship

The abuses of trusteeship are dealt with in the act. During the McClellan Committee hearings many witnesses told how their local unions were put under international trusteeship and that they and the members had absolutely no rights for periods ranging from five to twenty-five years. It was shown that one-fifth of all the locals in the Teamsters were under trusteeship and that delegates from such locals voted in a block for Hoffa.

The law tries to do away with the abuses of trusteeship. It specifies that national unions that exercise trusteeships must report to the Secretary of Labor on the reasons for the trusteeships within thirty days of its establishment and then every six months thereafter. It says that a trusteeship that is properly established will be assumed valid for only eighteen months. After eighteen months the presumption will be that they are invalid, and the onus is on the national union to prove that the trusteeship must continue.

At national union conventions and elections it is required that the votes of delegates from trusteed locals not be counted unless the delegates were chosen by secret ballot vote. The act also specifies that dues and other funds of trusteed locals may not be transferred to the parent organization.

The Secretary of Labor may investigate complaints and sue for injunction if he finds probable cause that a violation of the act's trusteeship provisions has been committed.

Union Officers Fiduciarily Responsible

The act makes union officers fiduciarily responsible for the handling of union funds and property. The embezzlement of union funds or property is made a federal crime with a penalty of a $10,000 fine, or imprisonment of not more than five years, or both. Union officers who handle funds or other union property in excess of $5,000 must be bonded.

Extortionate Picketing

The act covers extortionate picketing by making it unlawful to picket an employer for the purpose of personal profit or enrichment of any individual "by taking or obtaining money or other thing of value of such employer against his will or with his consent." This is a federal offense and the penalty is very stiff: Up to $10,000 fine or twenty years in jail, or both.

Employer Reports

The act requires employers to file reports with the Secretary of Labor. Employers have to file:

1. If they made any payment (except wages) or loan to any official or employee of a union.

2. If they paid any money to any employee or committee of employees for the purpose of causing employees not to exercise their right to organize and bargain through a union of their own choice.

3. If they made any expenditure where the object was, first, to interfere with, restrain, or coerce employees regarding their right to organize and bargain collectively or, second, to obtain information on a union that is involved in a labor dispute with the employer. The act specifically exempts expenditures for arbitration or court procedures from the reporting requirement.

4. If they had any dealings with a labor relations consultant for the purpose of influencing employee on labor relations matters. The only exception is if they had dealings with a consultant on arbitration or court procedures.

Secondary Boycott and "Hot Cargo" Banned

The section against which many unions fought hardest was the secondary boycott section. A secondary boycott is a device whereby a union that has a dispute with employer A puts pressure on employers B, C, and D not to do business with employer A in order to get employer A to capitulate to the union.

As previously covered, the Taft-Hartley Act set out to make such activity both an unfair labor practice and illegal. In the twelve-year history of the Taft-Hartley Act, however, it was found that there were many loopholes in the act's prohibition against secondary boycotts. It got so bad that, for all practical purposes, the secondary boycott sections were close to useless.

The Labor-Management Reporting and Disclosure Act attempted to plug these loopholes by rewriting the secondary boycott section of the Taft-Hartley Act.

Hot cargo is closely akin to secondary boycotts. The best way to describe it is to give an example.

Down in Texas there was a trucker whose employees did not want to join the Teamsters union. In an NLRB election they voted overwhelmingly against joining. The Teamsters union said that he had to sign a contract and have his employees join anyway. This he refused to do. The Teamsters union therefore declared anything that he carried in his trucks "hot cargo."

Generally a trucking line does not run across the United States covering each and every state and county in the country. They have regular runs which are covered by the Interstate Commerce Commission regulations. What they do is deliver their cargo to central terminals in major cities, and the cargo is then picked up and shipped by other trucking firms to its final destination. When the Teamsters union declared the cargo of this trucker as "hot," it meant that Teamsters throughout the country would refuse to handle it. Therefore, none of this trucker's cargo could get to its destination.

The Labor-Management Reporting and Disclosure Act makes such refusal to handle hot cargo an unfair labor practice and says that union contracts that contain hot cargo clauses—that is, one in which the employer agrees that his employees won't handle such hot cargo—are unenforceable and void.

Collective Bargaining Legislation Summary

The Labor-Management Reporting and Disclosure Act of 1959 represented the last important overall piece of federal legislation on collective bargaining at the time of writing in 1971. It introduced government control of unions in order to protect union members and the public from breach of trust and corruption. Federal law thus had a voice in the realm of internal union affairs. For decades, beginning in the thirties, the unions had enjoyed all the advantages of two legal worlds. Statutory authority bolstered their bargaining and organizing power, on the one hand, while as voluntary nonprofit associations they still held privileged status. In 1959, Congress decided that internal union affairs could not be closed to regulation or inspection.

WRITING THE UNION CONTRACT

Once the National Labor Relations Board has certified a union as the collective bargaining representative of the majority of the employees in the bargaining unit, the law imposes on the employer and the union an obligation to bargain in good faith with respect to wages, hours, and other terms and conditions of employment. It also requires the execution of a written contract incorporating any agreement reached, if requested by either party.

To aid the parties in writing contract clauses covering points of agreement, a number of organizations have published books, services, and pamphlets. The United States Bureau of Labor Statistics, for example, has published and is publishing a series of booklets giving examples of various types of collective bargaining provisions. They are generally referred to as the Major Collective Bargaining Agreements series. These may be secured at a nominal cost per booklet from the Superintendent of Documents, Government Printing Office, Washington, D.C. 20225.

A number of commercial firms publish services designed to aid those engaged in collective bargaining. The Bureau of National Affairs, Inc., of Washington, D.C. publishes a loose-leaf service called "Collective Bargaining, Negotiations and Contracts". Similiar services are published by Commerce Clearing House of Chicago and by Prentice-Hall, Inc., of Englewood Cliffs, N.J.

Collective bargaining is a complex subject with many legal ramifications. It is therefore best to confer with a competent labor relations attorney during negotiations and particularly before signing a union contract.

Union Security and Checkoff

One item that generally comes up early in negotiations is a union demand for union security and checkoff provisions. A key point to remember here is that under such provisions the employer agrees to become an agent of the union in getting and keeping members and in collecting union dues. The various types of union security and checkoff provisions are set forth in Figure 4.

Figure 4.   Union Security and Checkoff Provisions

TYPES OF UNION SECURITY

CLOSED SHOP   Employer agrees that all workers must belong to the union to keep their jobs. He further agrees that, when hiring new workers, he will hire only members of the union. This generally means that the union has complete say about employment in the industry. The closed shop is illegal under the Taft-Hartley Law. But many "off-the-record" closed-shop clauses exist.

UNION SHOP   Employer agrees that all workers must belong to the union to keep their jobs. He can hire whom he wants; but the workers he hires must join the union within a specified time (usually thirty days) or lose their jobs. The union shop is permitted under the Taft-Hartley labor law.

MODIFIED UNION SHOP   Employer agrees that all present and future *members* of the union must remain in the union for the duration of the contract in order to keep their jobs. (*Present* workers who are not in the union and who do not join the union in the future can keep their jobs without union membership.) The employer further agrees that all *new* employees must join the union within a specified time (usually thirty days) or lose their jobs.

AGENCY SHOP   The employer and the union agree that a worker shall not be forced to join or stay in the union to keep his job. The worker has the choice of joining or not joining. But if he elects not to join he must pay to the union a sum equal to union dues. This sum represents a fee charged him by the union for acting as his agent in collective bargaining and in policing the union contract.

MAINTENANCE OF MEMBERSHIP   Employer agrees that all present and future *members* of the union must remain in the union for the duration of the contract in order to keep their jobs. (Workers who are not in the union and who do not join the union in the future can keep their jobs without union membership.) In most cases, the clause does not say anything about employees who are nonmembers; but, under maintenance of membership, nonmembers do *not* have to join to keep their jobs.

PREFERENTIAL HIRING   Employer agrees that in hiring new workers he shall give preference to union members.

HIRING HALL   Employer agrees that he shall get all his new workers from the union's hiring hall.

TYPES OF CHECKOFF

VOLUNTARY IRREVOCABLE   Employer agrees to deduct union dues and other monies from the worker's wage only if the worker signs a form authorizing him to do so. This generally requires that the worker's authorization shall not be irrevocable for more than one year or beyond the termination date of the contract, whichever is sooner.

YEAR-TO-YEAR RENEWAL   Employer agrees to deduct dues and other monies from the worker's wages if the worker signs a checkoff authorization. If the worker does not revoke his authorization at the end of a year or at the contract termination date, it goes into effect for another year.

Figure 4. Union Security and Checkoff Provisions (continued)

VOLUNTARY REVOCABLE Employer agrees to deduct union dues and other monies from the worker's wages if the worker signs a form authorizing him to do so. The worker can revoke this authorization any time he sees fit.

AUTOMATIC Employer agrees automatically to deduct dues and other monies from the worker's wages and turn the money over to the union. This type of checkoff does not provide an authorization form and is illegal under the Taft-Hartley Act.

INVOLUNTARY IRREVOCABLE Employer agrees that to secure and keep his job a worker *must* sign a form authorizing the employer to deduct union dues and other monies from his wages.

SOURCE: J. J. Bambrick, "Union Security and Checkoff Provisions," *Studies in Personnel Policy,* No. 127, National Industrial Conference Board, New York, 1952.

SENIORITY

Seniority is the right of one worker over another because of length of service, because of union office, because of the sex of the worker, because of place of residence, because of disability, or because of any reason specified in the union contract. The key words are a "right of one worker over another."

SUPER SENIORITY FOR UNION OFFICIALS

Many contracts give super seniority to union officials and shop stewards. Thus a union officer with one-year's service has greater seniority than a man with twenty-five-years' service. It is theoretically possible, and has happened where a management has not provided safeguards, that after a large layoff the entire remaining work force were union officials.

Some contracts also provide that a man who leaves to take a paid union office accumulates seniority during this leave. Some recently signed contracts provide the same thing for those who take political office. Thus a man who left twenty years ago could come back and have top seniority. This is a case of having your cake and eating it, too.

Like many things in labor relations, there originally was good reason for having these provisions. In the early days of unionism, holding union office meant that one might be fired or be the first to be laid off; and if he ever accepted paid union office he might be blacklisted throughout the country, and could never get another job in his industry.

To protect the officials who were put in this hot seat, the workers insisted that contracts provide that these officials would be the last—and not the first—to be laid off, and that if they took paid union office they would have a job to come back to.

Since passage of the Wagner Act in 1935, however, the nation's law provides widespread protection for union activity. Though the original reason for the super seniority for union officials has ended, the clause still appears in contracts. Why? This leads to the second reason for such provisions. A union contract is an agreement between two parties, the employer and the union, for the benefit of a third party, the employees. The danger here is the human tendency of the union officials doing the bargaining to take care of Number One—themselves. Hence they are tempted to insist upon provisions that give them seniority rights over and above all other workers.

Experienced company negotiators try to protect employees against the abuses of super seniority for union officials. Some say that if the union committee's objective is to negotiate a layoff provision that is fair, then they must negotiate one that is fair to all. These firms insist that the contract's regular layoff procedure apply to all alike—both rank-and-file employees and union officials. They refuse to negotiate contracts that give union officials super seniority over rank-and-file employees in layoff.

SENIORITY VERSUS MERIT IN PROMOTIONS

When it comes to the use of seniority in promotions there is a great deal of disagreement between management and unions.

When a promotion is available the unions invariably urge that it be given to the employee with the greatest length of service, rather than the employee with the greatest merit. In answer, management says that if this were done neither the employee with greater service nor the one with lesser service would have any incentive to gain the promotion; the employee with greater service would get the promotion whether he tried or not; and the employee with less service could not have it regardless of how hard he tried.

Many people regard this management stand as a "just" position.

But here again we have to go into the background of labor relations to find out why unions want seniority and not merit to be the basis of promotions. When we do so, we find that it was lack of sound management policy that originally caused this union demand. In many firms prior to unionization there was no clear-cut personnel policy on promotions. Too often promotions were given through nepotism and favoritism.

When the union came in, the men wanted to see promotions given on a fairer basis. The basis that the union leaders seized upon was seniority. Unions are mass movements. As such they need to have mass standards and not individual standards. To their mind time makes all men equal.

Personnel management, on the other hand, puts its emphasis on the individual person. Its techniques are aimed at measuring differences among individuals so that individuals with the greater ability get the promotions.

The type of clause that the union leaders insisted upon and sometimes got reads this way: "The job sequence for promotion and demotion of hourly paid employees is set forth in Appendix . . . annexed hereto. Job seniority shall govern in cases of promotion and demotion. In the event that job seniority is equal, departmental seniority shall prevail."

Job Bidding and Job Posting Required

Some contracts go one step further. They require the company to post all vacant or promotional jobs. Then everyone has an opportunity to bid on the job. The man with the highest seniority who bids on the job automatically gets the job. Now, of course, the man's old job is open, and another round of job posting and job bidding starts all over. Thus for one opening, there have been as many as ten rounds of job posting and job bidding, the promotion in each and every case being determined by seniority.

"Ability is Equal" Clause

The most frequently found clause is the famed "Ability is Equal" clause. An example of this type of clause reads:

Seniority is defined as the length of an employee's service with the company from his latest employment date and shall apply in all cases of promotion or increase or decrease of forces. However, the factors listed below shall be considered and where factors (b) and (c) are relatively equal, length of continuous service shall govern:

(a) Length of service.
(b) Ability to perform the work.
(c) Physical fitness.

This clause seems to be a simple, fair enough clause that one might sign without worrying. The joker here, however, is that in numerous arbitration cases where a clause says that where ability is equal, seniority shall prevail, the arbitrator in effect rules that seniority shall be the sole basis of promotion.

Clauses that Stress Ability

Management negotiators fight hard against clauses that state "where ability is equal, seniority shall prevail in promotion". Instead they fight for clauses that put the emphasis in promotion on a definite showing of ability. One such clause requires that the employee show "experience on the job with another company, experience with his own company that would qualify him for the job, or that he present satisfactory evidence of schooling or training."

To prove that opportunity for promotion is equal, another clause provides that "a qualified person for promotion shall be one that has passed the examination for the job." The contract then goes on to spell out the help that the company shall provide employees who take the examination. This strikes one as a "just" arrangement that eliminates nepotism, and stresses the concept of "an equal opportunity for promotion."

HOW MANAGEMENT CAN MAINTAIN AND REGAIN FLEXIBILITY

One of the manager's more important labor relations duties is to take the steps necessary to maintain and regain the flexibility his company needs to operate efficiently and profitably. To do this he must be committed to the need for flexibility.

Society puts a grave responsibility on the individual members of management. It makes it their duty to develop and put into effect in their businesses the latest in scientific techniques, technologies, and innovations.

This duty is "built in" to the manager's role. If a union leader were to change sides and take a manager's job, he too would have to accept the role of innovator and the responsibilities which that implies. If this duty is shirked, it is done at great sacrifice, not only to the enterprise, but to its employees. Union leaders have said time and again that the worker's worst enemy is the employer who fails to keep up with the times and must go out of business.

Many people have the idea that a firm or plant must actually lose money before the decision is made to go out of business. That is not necessarily so. A critical point in the decision to continue or discontinue a business is reached when the rate of return on money invested in the enterprise falls below the rate which would be obtained if it were invested elsewhere. There is competition not only in the production and sale of goods and services, but for the money invested in the enterprise.

The ways management can maintain and regain this needed flexibility are as follows:

First, it can set down clearly defined objectives and specific goals in the area of management flexibility. It is not enough to use a generalized approach that "We must have more flexibility." What is needed is a plant-by-plant and department-by-department approach to the specific consolidations, work realignments, and other changes that will have to be made. A significant part of this approach is a timetable for the achievement of these flexibility goals.

Second, the management organization can be realigned to achieve flexibility. Here is a specific example. At one location, maintenance supervisors were on a craft basis. Rather than continue them on a craft basis, they were put on an "overall job" or "area" basis. Thus, in getting and giving work assignments the foremen thought in terms of the overall job to be done instead of strictly along craft lines. The company that did this feels that in making this management organizational change they took a big step towards developing flexible, all-round mechanics.

Third, supervisory training can emphasize management flexibility. To change a man's title from worker to foreman does not in itself make him management oriented. Supervisory training is aimed at reorienting his thinking. He must be able to see that the exception he makes can, through precedent and practice, become the rule. He must be encouraged to ask in each case, How would this exception affect the company if it became the rule?

Fourth, a management audit of practices that go beyond the contract and militate against management flexibility can be instituted. In many organizations there are two agreements. One is the written contract. The other is a series of verbal understandings that go far beyond anything that management would ever knowingly permit. At the negotiations table the company's negotiators fight hard to retain management's rights under the contract. But during the contract term, supervisors and middle management may give away these same rights through oral understandings and side agreements with union stewards and committeemen.

Fifth, a policy can be established to live strictly by the contract and to set aside as null and void any oral side agreements that restrict management's flexibility.

Sixth, management can develop new precedents and practices conducive to management flexibility. What a contract does not specifically prohibit, it permits. This leaves vast areas wherein management can attempt to achieve its flexibility objectives and goals. It is management's duty to take the initiative. It is the union's duty to object when it feels management has gone beyond the contract. Certainly, some actions will go to arbitrations. But for every action that does, there will be other unchallenged management actions which will establish a new body of precedent and practice aimed at creating a living, vital, competitive organization.

Seventh and last, but by no means least, there can be contract repair. Particularly fruitful areas to examine are clauses that may require the company to hire or keep more workers than are needed. Examples are:

1. Full crew clauses and manning tables setting forth all the positions that must be filled before work can start.

2. Clauses calling for a craft mechanic and a helper for all jobs, whether the extra man is needed or not.

3. Clauses saying that "work peculiar to a classification" shall be done solely by workers in that classification. The danger here lies in the fact that "work peculiar to a classification" builds up over a period of time through precedent and practice. The supervisor's exception becomes the rule.

4. Negotiated job duties. As is well known, job duties are continuously changing. However, once they are negotiated they are frozen for the life of the contract, and they are difficult to change from contract to contract.

5. Prohibitions against supervisors doing any kind of work at any time.

6. Prohibitions against, or penalties for, schedule changes necessary to meet the needs.

HOW MANAGEMENT'S OWN ACTIONS LOSE FLEXIBILITY

Management cannot blame the unions for the full extent of its loss of flexibility. It must accept some of the blame itself.

First, in many cases it insists on maintaining outmoded management organization when it adopts new equipment and technology. For example, a number of companies have spent millions of dollars building new integrated processing units that take raw material in at one end and turn out finished products at the other. Such continuous flow-processing units are perhaps the most advanced examples of automation in the world.

Yet, in instance after instance, examination of the organization charts before and after installation of this automated equipment shows that while the equipment is "new," the management organization is "old." The companies spend millions of dollars to bring in integrated units and then fail to change their management organizations to reflect the new concepts that come with extended integration. They thus fail to realize the full potential of the combination of brilliant innovation and substantial capital investment.

Second, management loses flexibility because the worker's craft consciousness is sometimes encouraged by supervisors who may foster the same type of limited craft thinking. It is not uncommon to find supervisors fighting with other supervisors about which craft should do which work.

Third, management loses flexibility because its supervisors, acting as "good Joes," permit the exception that becomes the rule through precedent and practice. Let's take a specific example. In one company, management granted a liberal sick leave clause on the basis that no employees would receive paid time off except for personal illness. One supervisor, however, permitted several of his long-service employees time off for reasons such as going to court on a traffic violation, or visiting a sick relative. He was convinced that this was not a bad thing to do. In fact he felt it was a good thing to do, because he didn't want these long-service workers to suffer loss of pay. This went on for almost a year before his management found out about it. When the practice was discovered it was ordered stopped.

The union protested the company's order canceling the supervisor's ultraliberal practice and eventually took the matter to arbitration. They not only wanted its return in the supervisory area involved, but demanded an extension of the practice to all employees. Their contention was that the practice had been permitted for a substantial period without management's objection, that to discontinue it now was unfair, and that failure to extend it to other departments was discriminatory. This view was upheld by the arbitrator.

There is a more common example. We all know of cases of supervisors who, trying to be "good Joes", gave light work to a worker who suffered some misfortune, only to have the same worker later refuse to do any other work on the basis that the light work was his job.

PREPARATION FOR POSSIBLE STRIKES

Strikes are anything but a happy experience for the individual employee, for the company, and in many cases for the union.

One may therefore well ask, "Why strike?" The answer lies in the fact that the union in bargaining says, in effect, to management: "It would be cheaper for you to give us this or that demand than to take a strike."

And at some point the company, in effect, will say: "In this bargaining we have given all we can give. We will take a strike and the losses you will suffer through striking will outweigh anything you might gain over and above our last offer."

Usually the above process results in a new agreement. But sometimes the union wants something management cannot give; or the management may want something the union will not give. In either case there is a strike.

If a group of labor leaders get together for any length of time they will invariably discuss strike strategy. This is natural, as labor relations is the prime responsibility of union leaders. It is their lifeblood.

Strike strategy is discussed by labor leaders as often and in much the same way that military leaders discuss battle strategy. And it is discussed for the same reason. For a military leader to lose a battle is a disaster. For a labor leader to lose a strike may mean the end of his political life as a labor leader.

To prepare for strikes practically all unions levy on their members some kind of strike assessment. In some cases the strike assessment is a special one and may be quite high. The Automobile Workers collect $5 a month strike assessment over and above regular dues for several months. The other way unions collect strike money is by setting a certain portion of dues money to go into the strike fund. In this way the unions build up big funds.

The primary purpose of paying strike benefits from these funds is to increase the staying power of the strikers so that the strike will not collapse. Another purpose is to make members less hesitant to strike by assuring them beforehand that they will have some financial assistance. The third purpose of paying strike benefits is to share the cost of striking among nonstriking members in other establishments who may benefit if the strike results in an advantageous pattern-setting agreement.

The paying of strike benefits also gives the International union greater control over local unions. First, it puts teeth in the union's strike authorization procedures by giving the national officers power to pay strike benefits if they authorize the strike, and conversely to withhold strike benefits if they do not authorize the strike. Second, this ability to authorize or not authorize a strike gives weight and power to collective bargaining negotiations to the union's international representative in his dealings with both employers and the local union officials.

Strike benefits are not given just as soon as the strike starts. Most of the time there is a waiting period of two or more weeks. The theory behind this is that strikers must live off their own savings the first two weeks. They also figure that since most strikes do not last more than two weeks they are preventing depletion of their strike funds.

If the strikes last a long time the unions also make arrangements for the strikers to get assistance from public and private social service agencies. A number of unions have put the procedure for getting health and welfare assistance from public and private social service agencies into their strike assistance manuals.

As has been seen, union leaders give a great deal of time and thought to strike preparation. For people in management, however, a strike represents an entirely different thing. They are so busy with their many management responsibilities that they have little or no time to think about how to prepare for a strike until it is upon them. It is something they are ill-prepared for.

In the last 20 years there has been an awakening among management executives to the idea that just as a union can win a strike, it can also lose a strike. It is necessary to point out an important distinction in nomenclature. One can say that management lost a strike, but with rare exceptions it is almost impossible to say management won a strike. Management does not initiate a strike. The union does. The initiator of any action is the one who either wins or loses his objective. Management's position almost invariably is that of a defender who is either overrun or turns back an assault.

Strike Manuals

As has been seen, unions prepare in great detail for possible strikes. Many of them put this detail in strike manuals.

Some companies have set up committees whose job it is to think out in advance all the arrangements that will lessen the effect of the union's shutdown attempt. These arrangements are put into a manual of procedures for strikes. If the strike occurs the company officials automatically put into effect the procedures called for by this manual.

These strike manuals are of two types: first, those prepared by companies who continue operations during a strike; and second, those prepared by companies whose business is such that they can shut down operations during a strike.

The manuals of public utilities, which must continue in operation, strike or no strike, furnish examples of the first group. These manuals are very complex. Some are several volumes long and give in detail the entire operation of the company. They specify operation jobs to be performed by practically every executive and supervisory employee. Training for these jobs is no last-minute improvisation. Rather it begins months or years before a strike appears imminent. It may require an executive to retrain in a job he graduated from years previous and report to a foreman several ranks below him.

The second type of manual covers firms that can shut down if necessary. These manuals are generally very short. They are concerned not with how to operate during a strike but with how to ride out a strike with the least damage to the company.

Details of what is covered in company and union strike manuals are set forth in *Preparing for Collective Bargaining*, vol. 2, Studies in Personnel Policy, no. 182, National Industrial Conference Board, New York.

The Wildcat Strike

In addition to union-authorized strikes called at contract expiration or during wage reopenings, there is another type—the wildcat strike.

The wildcat strike differs considerably from authorized strikes. In the first place, the wildcat generally comes as a complete surprise, while management is usually notified well in advance when an authorized strike is to take place. A second difference is that a wildcat is usually of short duration—sometimes only a few hours— while the authorized strike generally lasts much longer. In the third place, unlike authorized strikers, wildcat strikers do not have the right to strike. They do so in violation of their own union contract, and management under that contract has the right to discipline them for such unauthorized work stoppages.

When a wildcat looks likely, most companies instruct foremen to emphasize to employees that the contract's grievance and arbitration machinery is the only proper way to secure redress of grievances. They are also instructed to bring the wild-catters' attention to the contract's no-strike clause and the penalties for unauthorized walkouts.

Some companies instruct the foreman to speak directly to the union's representative in the plant. Other companies, however, feel that at this stage a foreman–chief steward meeting might be too heated, and might even widen the area of controversy and precipitate a plant-wide walkout. Therefore, these companies' procedures provide that the plant's union representative is to be contacted by someone one step removed from the immediate controversy, such as the industrial relations manager or the plant manager.

Once the walkout starts, the foreman's main job is twofold: to prevent the wildcat strike's spread; and to put into writing information that would support the company's discipline of wildcatters as set forth in the grievance and arbitration procedure. To avoid the wildcat strike's spread, foremen should (1) prevent workers from gathering together in the work area: and (2) prevent them from gathering in the locker room.

The second point is to establish who are the leaders of the wildcat strike and who are actually out on strike.   To this end supervisors make a time card check and immediately make a full report while events are fresh in their minds, covering who, what, where, and when.

When Authorized Strike is Over

Once an authorized strike is over the main concern of companies is a speedy return to normal working relations.   Sometimes this is difficult to achieve, especially if there has been a long strike or if the union officials seem bent on taking reprisals against nonstrikers.   To help supervisors get through this difficult period, which is totally different from the strike period, a number of firms issue instructions to their supervisors about how to conduct themselves.   These instructions cover such items as:

1. How to meet returning employees.
2. How to prevent being baited into useless discussions of strike issues.
3. The need for being always available and ready for sympathetic understanding of the individual worker's problems; and how, through company channels, to secure proper handling of these problems.
4. How to avoid charges of being partial to "strikers" or "nonstrikers"—particularly how to avoid being overfriendly with either group.
5. Danger signs the supervisor should be alert to are:

    a. Refusal by strikers to work with nonstrikers, and instructions about what to do in such cases

    b. Snide remarks or insults to either himself or fellow employees

    c. Congregating anywhere in departments or washrooms

    d. Physical contact such as shoving by strikers

6. Instructions to supervisors about how to protect themselves, as for example:

    a. In handling grievance or controversial problems, always have another supervisor present.

    b. Always be the last to leave the department for a month or two after the strike.

BIBLIOGRAPHY

Bambrick, James J.: *Union Security and Checkoff Provisions,* National Industrial Conference Board, New York, 1952.
——— and Albert A. Blum: *Unionization among American Engineers,* National Industrial Conference Board, New York, 1956.
——— and George Haas: *Handbook of Union Government, Structure and Procedures,* National Industrial Conference Board, New York, 1955.
——— and Wade Shurtleff: *Foremanship under Unionism,* National Foremen's Institute Division of Prentice-Hall, Inc., Englewood Cliffs, N.J., 1952.
Bloom and Northrop: *Government and Labor,* Richard D. Irwin, Inc., Homewood, Ill., 1963.
Bok, Derek C., and John T. Dunlop: *Labor and the American Community,* Simon and Schuster, New York, 1970.
Bureau of Labor Statistics, *Brief History of the American Labor Movement,* bulletin no. 1000, U.S. Department of Labor, Washington, D.C., 1970
———: *Directory of National and International Unions in the United States, 1969,* U.S. Department of Labor, Washington, D.C., 1970.
Cartter, Allan M., and F. Ray Marshall: *Labor Economics: Wages, Employment and Trade Unionism,* Richard D. Irwin, Inc., Homewood, Ill., 1967.
Commons, John R., and associates: *History of Labor in the United States,* The Macmillan Company, New York, 1936.
Cormier, Frank, and William Eaton: *Reuther,* Prentice-Hall, Inc., Englewood Cliffs, N.J., 1970.

Goldberg, Arthur J.: *AFL-CIO: Labor United,* McGraw-Hill Book Company, New York, 1956.

Gompers, Samuel: *Seventy Years of Life and Labor,* autobiography revised and edited by Philip Taft and John A. Sessions, E. P. Dutton & Co., Inc., New York, 1957.

Hutchinson, John: *The Imperfect Union: A History of Corruption in American Trade Unions,* E. P. Dutton & Co., Inc., New York, 1970.

Labor Law Course, 20th ed., Commerce Clearing House, Inc., Chicago, Ill., 1970.

Perlman, Selig: *A History of Trade Unionism in the United States,* reprinted by Augustus M. Kelley, Publishers, New York, 1950; copyright 1922.

Shultz, George P., and John R. Coleman: *Labor Problems: Cases and Readings,* 2d ed., McGraw-Hill Book Company, New York, 1959.

Taft, Philip: *Organized Labor in American History,* Harper & Row, Publishers, Inc., New York, 1964.

———: *The AFL in the Time of Gompers,* Harper & Brothers, New York, 1957.

Velie, Lester: *Labor USA,* Harper & Brothers, New York, 1959.

Webb, Sidney, and Beatrice Webb: *History of Trade Unionism,* Longmans, Green & Co., Ltd., London, 1935.

Young, Dallas M.: *Understanding Labor Problems,* McGraw-Hill Book Company, New York, 1959.

chapter 55

Union and Nonunion Employees

DR. JOSEPH P. YANEY *Associate Professor of Management, The Ohio State University, College of Administrative Science, Columbus, Ohio*

I. BASIC ORIENTATION

Two very basic and important policies need to be a part of every modern personnel manager's thinking:

1. That there will be unions, but that their impact can be treated as one more constraint.

2. That the fever of the seventies is toward equality of opportunity and treatment.

In short, there is a need to examine the present personnel policies to see if management is given the needed flexibility and that the company is in the step with social changes in the population.

II. UNION VERSUS NONUNION POLICIES AND PROCEDURES

A. Overview

Many companies maintain two sets of standards regarding their union and nonunion employees. The reasoning behind such actions is that the collective bargaining agreement imposes certain additional obligations toward those members in the bargaining unit. More precisely, the collective bargaining agreement imposes limitations and sets forth specific procedures which are contractually required. The case of discipline is a key example and will be contrasted in example one.

Case Example One

Objective: Maintain a work force under conditions to maintain productivity and protect the life and property of those in the work area.

1. *Nonunion approach.* There may exist in the personnel handbook given to all new employees a statement about progressive discipline and the need for the employees to conform to certain basic standards. In operation, this policy may

involve the layoff or discharge of some employees and the mere warning of others. To some employees this will seem fair, to others it will smack of favoritism.

2. *Union contract disciplinary procedures.*   There will probably be a statement about the need for discipline and the right of the employer to maintain order.   The key difference is that specific steps and penalties will be included and time limits for action imposed.   For excessive absenteeism the procedures may call for an oral warning, a written warning, and finally a three-day layoff without pay.

3. *Comment.*   The intent of both policies is the same.   The procedures are different.

B. Specific Functions

The focus of the following sections will be on specific personnel functions and what differences are suggested due to union constraints.

Recruiting and Selection

1. *Procedures.*   The objective of any recruiting and selection program is to bring qualified personnel into the organization.   To make an optimum use of resources, the company's policy should match the skills and potential of the individual with the requirements of the job.

To do this there needs to be a manpower function assigned to one personnel officer.   In this function jobs will be studied for their characteristics and for the type of skills needed to be successful.   Inventories of skills of the employees may be kept in the individual personnel files or perhaps on magnetic tape in a large installation.   This bank of data will assist in answering the question of who is needed and when.

Most personnel officers use the following indicators to determine the success of their efforts:

   a. The average number of vacancies in relation to the total work force

   b. the average length of time needed to fill requests for personnel

   c. the turnover index for different categories of jobs (in this regard it is better to compute many individual job indices rather than use a macro "company turnover" figure which tends to obscure the trouble areas).   An example here would be to divide the number of men in one job category by the number of regular positions

$$\frac{\text{Men employed in one year}}{\text{Number of positions}} = \text{turnover index}[1]$$

Turnover ratios of 1.05 are considered good in most companies, which is computed by taking say 105 men employed in a job position over 100 opening for an assembler position, $105/100 = 1.05$.

2. *Union Constraints.*   Most union contracts allow the employer to make the initial selection of the employee according to company standards.   In fact, both the company and the union are restricted in the policies affecting prospective employees.   The national labor law says that it is unlawful to favor a man because he either is or is not a union member (with some exceptions given to hiring halls which may continue to supply manpower if nondiscriminatory).

The main union constraint comes after the man is hired, not before.   Under many contracts there is a bidding procedure for advancement to new positions where preference must be given to a union man qualified by skill or potential

---

[1] Since there are many turnover ratios discussed in the management literature, the reader must find out what formula is used in order to compare numbers or values objectively.

skill and seniority. If this is so, the personnel department must project any new employee not only into the entry level job, but also into more skilled positions. Example two illustrates this situation.

Case Example Two. During the tight labor market almost anyone was hired in the entry-level maintenance jobs. When additional job openings became available the union pointed to the contract and wanted the present employees to be upgraded; the company refused, saying they are not qualified. At arbitration, the arbitrator read the contract and found that the probability that some of the employees would be slower in learning the higher-paid jobs was not sufficient reason to deny them those jobs.

3. *Alternatives:*

a. Under such contract conditions there is a great deal of pressure to hire people who are more than qualified for the initial job so that they will be able to progress. The short-run result is a partially dissatisfied employee who is more than capable of handling the entry-level position.

b. Attempt to negotiate the provision that the present employees must pass an aptitude test in order to qualify for additional training or promotions. This is, of course, not something the union leadership will give automatically. An attempt to handle this problem is seen in the operations of the Southfield office of Michigan Bell. Located on the top floor are student work stations where the employee is given a set period of hands-on training to determine whether he has the mental and physical abilities necessary to learn the more sophisticated techniques. This approach is of course an attempt to give the individual a full opportunity and also protect the company in filling its manpower needs with qualified people.

4. *Commentary.* It is clear that the changing social forces plus national legislation are pointing the way toward an almost equal opportunity for both union and nonunion employees, both in initial employment and in later promotional opportunities. New legislation such as the Civil Rights Act of 1964 (see Title VII), State Fair Employment Practices Laws, and the National Labor Relations Act, as amended, all are reducing the gap in treatment of different groups of employees or potential employees.

Compensation of Union and Nonunion Employees

The key principle in this very touchy area is as follows: Provide equal pay for comparable quantity and quality of work produced under comparable conditions. The employer is on his best economic and legal ground to state and follow a policy of paying for the value of the output, regardless of the union status. This implies that the personnel and industrial engineering staffs are faced with the responsibility of determining the value of the output of individual jobs or crews. Without this economic data, the wage-setting process is a guess. The second step in the overall wage-setting procedure is determining the company's competitive position in the labor market. Hence, the final pay rate offered will be a mix of economic output and market forces. Unions represent an important force in the manpower market.

1. *Union Pressures.* In a unionized operation there will be pressures which are beyond pure economics. Each employer faces the test of negotiating as the present contract expires. If there is an increase it may be a combination of cost of living, fringes, a general across-the-board percentage, plus some individual adjustments.

2. *Impact on Nonunion Employees.* There is a tendency to grant all union increases to the nonunion employees without modification. In some cases this is an appropriate move; in others it will further complicate the compensation system.

3. *Alternatives.*   The alternatives are a mixture of reacting to new economic pressures and making adjustments for management policy reasons.   An example of the economic adjustment is the voluntary granting of cost-of-living increases if the geographic community has in fact undergone such changes.   If the jobs are almost exactly the same, one unionized and one nonunionized, it would seem clear that unless the nonunionized position is granted the same wage, the union organizers will be in a far better position to expand the bargaining unit.

There are some jobs which may not deserve such increases because of their prior rate.   For instance, if a company has had to pay computer programmers far and above the contribution they make due to the tight labor market, it would be possible in a less tight market to give them less of an increase in order to adjust their compensation in line with market realities.

In considering the policy issues, some companies feel that the supervisor, a nonunion employee, should always receive more than any of the men in his unit. Under such a policy, the answer is probably to grant the same increases to the supervisory personnel, especially in the bargaining unit area.   Behavioral research supports the contention that the supervisor must have some differential in pay to maintain his organizational status as a member of management.

4. *Merit Increases:*

   a. *Union Members.*   Merit increases represent a mandatory bargaining item for the union and the company.   In this regard whatever the final agreement is, most arbitrators have stuck to the language of the contract and have required actual "meritorious service" which is something more than seniority.   In a recent survey it was found that 11 percent used only merit increases, while the majority had some mixture of base rate, seniority, and merit pay.

   b. *Nonunion Members.*   Granting a merit increase is a management right. It would seem necessary to establish measurable criteria for such increases in order to protect the company from charges of favoritism or discrimination.   The clearest data to support such increases would be production records or instances of specific work which resulted in a known advantage to the company.

One legal qualification is necessary.   It is clearly illegal to grant regular or merit increases to employees in order to cause them to reject a union organizational effort.   In such cases an illegal motive is inferred, and the employer may be found guilty of interference under the National Labor Relations Act.   In an organizational drive by a union, the refusal of the company to grant a customary and normal increase to its people may be interpreted by the National Labor Relations Board as a threat or an attempt to restrain its employees.   When union organizational efforts are at hand, legal counsel should be consulted promptly.

5. *The Nonunion Company Paying above the Going Rate.*   Some firms pride themselves on paying above the going rate.   In reality this means that their average compensation line is above the community average for most of their positions. Making this decision can be part of a clear economic move to hire the most capable men who will then be more productive.

If a firm quickly changes its approach from average wages to above average wages, there is the hint that this might be for antiunion reasons.   If so, the problem relates to a direct attempt to interfere with the employees' right to join or organize a union.   The best evidence to offset such claims consists of clear productivity data and economic information relating to the firm, its wage policy, and a clean record when facing possible unionization efforts.

6. *Trends.*   Many personnel men are talking about job enlargement and job enrichment.   This refers to the approach of increasing the job responsibilities in order to give the man greater satisfaction and improve overall productivity.   If

this trend continues, it would seem likely that wages could increase because productivity goes up. Such increases would have a firm economic base and would probably be acceptable even in the face of potential unionization overtones.

Different Working Conditions for Union and Nonunion Employees

In general, working conditions represent part of the reasons why employees may be more or less satisfied with the total employment situation. While working conditions alone will not produce a successful company, it is well known that poor working conditions will cause greater turnover, tardiness, and attempts to avoid the working place such as abusing the sick leave privilege.

1. *Alternatives.* For nonunion employees the management has the full right within the minimum state law on sanitation and health to provide as good or as poor conditions as possible. The key question involves cost versus the positive impact on productivity, through better working conditions. Such features as air conditioning are becoming expected. A firm without such features faces the possibility of losing ground in the employment market.

2. *Union Considerations.* Working conditions represent an item of mandatory bargaining with the union. In most cases the company must provide the union with information such as the number of BTUs in the cooling system, air purity, and temperature ranges.

The situations which cause the most problems relate to union and nonunion personnel doing the same work, but under quite different circumstances. To favor the nonunion employees in facilities is probably just an invitation for hard bargaining over this issue at the next negotiations.

If it is not a matter of entirely different work locations—such as an administration building separate from the plant or manufacturing units, and there is a systematic sorting of union and nonunion employees, this probably is unlawful discrimination by the employer. Such a discrimination policy is quite shortsighted in that it will probably eventually be the subject of a grievance, or an unfair labor practices charge, or a civil rights charge. The net result for the employer is poor employee and community relations.

3. *Future Trends.* More and more new installations are being engineered for employee comfort. New techniques such as "office landscaping" represent a trend toward pleasant and efficiently organized work stations which help the individual be more productive. If the economics of the firm permits it, such changes should be made as soon as possible.

Different Hours of Work for Union and Nonunion Employees

Having different working hours has been a long-standing custom in many industries. The most typical example is having two or three production shifts with an administrative staff which works from eight to five. Where such differences exist, the employees have probably come to expect such schedules. The more sensitive issue is trying to operate with union and nonunion employees doing essentially the same functions, but working different hours.

1. *Alternatives.* Since the matter of hours is a mandatory bargainable item, there should be strong technical or production reasons for treating the employees differently. Without such reasons it is clear that in the next bargaining session the matter of hours will be covered.

In some operations, say retail department stores where the doors are open for ten or more hours, there is the question about how to arrange the overlapping shifts. In such operations the management can: (a) use rotating shifts to balance the early and late times, (b) examine the jobs for occupational qualifications which necessitate specific assignments (an example might be that the credit clerks must work during the day whereas most of the maintenance staff will work before or after formal store hours), or (c) allow the employees to indicate their preferences when management is essentially neutral.

2. *Union Considerations.*   Hours of work is one of the most tangible working conditions.   Union efforts to share the decision making in this area are to be expected since employees for various reasons will express strong preferences for certain day or night hours.   Because it is a key issue management needs to have developed a sensible rationale which focuses on the technical jobs requirements and to avoid any appearances of separating individuals for the purpose of interfering or restraining employees in their rights to act jointly.

3. *Future Trends.*   The requirement for equal treatment is an obvious legal and social trend of modern times.   The employer who attempts to manipulate conditions of work which are *not* based on legitimate occupational requirements will find it increasingly difficult to operate in the community.   Employees are among the first to recognize *legitimate* differences and the requirement to work unpleasant third shifts or holiday hours.

The existence of shift differentials indicate that employees see certain daytime hours as the most desirable, and the agreement to work the second and third shifts is conditioned upon such an extra pay differential.   If the trend continues for more personal and leisure time, the pay differential might be increased to purchase additional employee time during the less desirable hours.

Another future trend is the possible use of group participation in planning for mixed shift work.   Under such a plan the employees would have a significant voice in deciding when they will work and how the less desirable times will be allocated.

Performance Appraisal Systems

In any compensation or manpower plan, a key item is the performance appraisal system.   This is the control device to indicate how well the men are performing the tasks assigned.   A second important use of the appraisal technique is in changing behavior and helping the employees grow in their job performance.

1. *Alternatives.*   Many different performance appraisal systems have been used, and many work well because of the personnel administrator's persistence, in spite of possible flaws.   One of the options is a system which emphasizes personality traits such as honesty or aggressiveness.   This information might be quite important in determining who could be selected for a security guard or for a foreman trainee.   Other systems rely more heavily on performance, such as management by objectives or management by results.   The latter two techniques involve the establishment of mutual goals by superiors and subordinates.   This planning document then becomes the basis for evaluation of performance in the next quarter or other specified time period.   Many companies have evolved an appraisal form which includes both current performance and the question of what positions the men will be qualified for in the future.   This additional information might then go into a manpower system inventory.

2. *Union Considerations.*   The unions have been aware of the key role of the evaluation system in determining future and present work opportunities for their members.   Bargaining about the appraisal system is a mandatory issue since it does involve pay, promotions, and working conditions.   Early union pressures against piecework systems were sometimes based on actual technical complaints against inaccurate determination of the wage rates.   Even when the rates are seemingly fair, there are union pressures for more uniformity in wages or even using day-rate pay procedures.

In a nonunion department which is part of a work force that is partially organized, it is apparent that the employees will compare the equity of the two systems. Management must expect this comparison and should plan from the very beginning to have standards of evaluation which are precise, workable, and fair. If the nonunion employees are evaluated and paid under an easier system, there is the danger of an unfair labor practices charge if intentional discrimination can be found. The lesson is clear: in this area engineering and technical information need to support the plan in all possible areas. In the areas of judgment—say in recommending a man for promotion—every effort is needed to remove any bias on the part of the supervisory staff completing the appraisals.

3. *Future Trends.* There is a great deal of interest in appraisal systems in terms of controlling the employees and improving the profit picture. The key limiting factor is the inability of most managements to be able to measure the value of the man's output. Due to this inability, the appraisal plans become very suspect, though few are discarded. Of all the plans, the management-by-objectives system seems to offer the most hope for the future.

III. THE ASSESSMENT OF EMPLOYEE ATTITUDES

1. *Research-based Efforts.* Employee morale studies were first conducted by university researchers interested in behavioral science. Later came the management interest in human relations and the factors affecting employee satisfaction. During this same human relations era the unionism drive developed and many of the research tools were used to determine employee sentiments concerning potential union organization. The motives for such studies were mixed and it should be expected that the employee would have approached these studies with mixed emotions, also. In the current era many companies such as Sears, Roebuck and the General Electric Company have devoted much time and money to positive programs to determine present and future employee attitudes on a wide range of variables.

2. *Alternatives.* The two best-known techniques involve the structured interview and the mail questionnaire. In the interview approach trained interviewers talk to a representative sample of the work force in an effort to determine their general attitudes and emotions. The questions asked may reflect the specific problem areas of concern to the company (e.g., the evaluation system) or general indicators such as job satisfaction. In the second approach, the mail questionnaire, the employees may receive the questionnaire with an introductory letter explaining the reasons for the survey and instructions on how to comply with the requests. The interview offers a greater chance to probe for reasons while the questionnaires seem to offer more protection for the individual who wishes to express negative feelings about the management.

3. *Evaluation of the Data.* While collecting the data may be a time-consuming task, the key aspect of the entire project is the evaluation of the data.

   a. Sample size. Many managers are concerned about how representative the sample is. There are statistical techniques which will produce the specific sample size needed. In general, the idea is that with a greater amount of variance a larger sample will be needed to ensure a high degree of reliability. In short, it is expensive to be sure that the sample is representative. For this reason some companies prefer to take a few in-depth or structured interviews and try to emphasize the analysis of the limited data as opposed to the manipulation of a greater deal of information.

   b. The norm and base line. Raw information can be quite misleading. For example, one personnel executive commented that his plant had a questionnaire response showing that 46 percent of the people were dissatisfied with their pay. Unless you knew that this was about normal for this plant on this questionnaire, you might have suggested something of a radical change in compensation policies. Companies which have conducted surveys have the advantage of being able to establish a "base" or "normal" for their groups of employees. To complete the example, the executive also mentioned that while 46 percent said they were dissatisfied with their pay, the turnover rate was less than 1 percent annually. Putting the two facts together adds a great deal of light to the interpretation of the raw data.

c. *Emphasizing differences.*   While the macro information about all the employees is helpful, it is often useful to compare reactions by grade or pay level. This more sophisticated analysis might reveal greater dissatisfaction in the night shift or perhaps in one manufacturing department. Statistical techniques are very well developed in this area for determining whether the differences between the groups are significant or due probably just to chance. Analyzing the data for differences is directly tied to the management programs to help correct deficiencies. In this case specific complaints by departments or groups are reviewed to see what alternatives management has.

d. *A timetable.*   Every six months or less is the recommended interval for using the questionnaires or interviews. There are many factors which will be a part of the management decision, but the lesson to note is that very sporadic surveys lose much of their value because they are less comparable and probably are seen by the employees as something of a crisis measure.

4. *Improving Behavioral Techniques.*   As more behavioral scientists assist business management there is growing sophistication in the administration and the interpretation of the data. For example, when survey data seemed quite discouraging managers often felt compelled to try something out of desperation. Now with additional measures of the employee's behavior as well as their words, the risk of overreacting is reduced. Observation studies should accompany the interview studies to see if the men act in a way consistent with the questionnaire or interview data. For example, a high dissatisfaction score may be tempered by an observation study indicating high interaction among the employees and much apparent social satisfaction present on the job.

IV. UNION ORGANIZATION: LEGAL AND MANAGEMENT ISSUES

Union representation of a substantial segment of the labor force is an accepted part of the United States economy. From the current indications, more professional and technical employees are finding the union structure useful and beneficial. If so, there seems to be a continuing need to understand the labor laws and what they allow or disallow regarding employer and union behavior. Section 7 of the National Labor Relations Act as amended sets forth the issue clearly:

> Employees shall have the right to self-organization, to form, join, or assist labor organizations, to bargain collectively through representatives of their own choosing, and to engage in other concerted activities for the purpose of collective bargaining or other mutual aid or protection, and shall also have the right to refrain from any or all such activities except to the extent that such right may be affected by an agreement requiring membership in a labor organization as a condition of employment as authorized by Sect. 8(a) (3). (49 Stat. 452,29 U.S. Code, Sec. 157, as amended by P. L. 101, 80th Cong., 1st Sess.)

This set of rights is broad and to most personnel managers, it represents a very complicated structure. Many owners or managers make a sincere effort to provide equal or better wages and benefits to the employees than those promised by the union organizations. The fact that the union organizer finds receptive listeners is a function of the total employment situation—not just the level of pay.

A. Factors or Conditions which May Support a Union Organizational Effort

There is no precise formula for predicting the success or failure of a union organizational drive. There are, however, some key areas of concern which seem to contribute to producing a work force which is ready to consider unionization. The sad part of the analysis is that it often takes a unionization drive before management will correct abuses or slack procedures.

1. *Working Conditions.* This is a key factor in producing dissatisfaction among employees. In earlier years, the working conditions were dangerous as well as undesirable. Today the employee expects a safe and reasonably comfortable work environment. Much of the industrial engineer's efforts should be in arranging the work situation both for efficiency and for the health and safety of the employees.

2. *Dull Jobs.* Hospitals are facing the push for unionization. In many cases their housekeeping and dietary positions are dull, degrading jobs. Management needs to be constantly examining new work techniques in order to upgrade the job and the people performing the job. Arguing that dull jobs have to be done in any regard is only a partial answer; there needs to be more job enlargement and job enrichment.

3. *Weak or Inconsistent Supervision.* Supervisors who fall into the traps of favoritism or inconsistencies are key targets for the union organizers. The men may have legitimate grievances, and there may be no formal system for airing them. The suggestion that a union contract will bring with it a grievance procedure to handle these problems is then quite attractive.

4. *Promotions on Unclear Grounds.* While promotions or the lack of a promotion may mean a difference in pay, it also means a great deal in terms of motivation. The employees are disturbed by higher management's apparent sanctioning of supervisors who act to promote their friends, rather than on the basis of job performance.

5. *Unjust Disciplinary Procedures.* Every organization needs some ground rules for discipline. Most employees agree with this idea. What they do not agree with is the highly punitive techniques some supervisors favor, and they are especially disapproving when discipline is not administered consistently. The union organizer has every right to recommend his grievance system as a requirement in order for the men to protect themselves from management. If your attitude survey reveals that many men feel that discipline is unfair, there is a dangerous head of steam building toward unionization.

6. *Unkept Promises to Employees.* Employees do not like to be considered children who can be put off by promises of better times in the future. Making such promises weakens the management communication links and shifts the attention of the men toward a maybe world instead of considering the present problems and possibilities.

7. *Automation's Influence on the Employee.* You might read the economist's statement about the positive expansion effect of automation, but the individual employee may be quite concerned about what is going to happen to him and his job. Part of this fear comes from a lack of information about management plans. Part of the fear also stems from some self-appraisal where the man admits that his own skills are limited and maybe obsolete. One way of protecting his job is with the help of the union. Management may consider these fears irrational since they have retraining programs, but to the man such programs may seem unreachable or too abstract.

8. *Lack of Training for Advancement.* Training in today's society is not a luxury —it is a requirement to adjust to the changing technology. An employee who is used by the company and later disregarded can hardly be a candidate for the sat-

isfied worker list. The work force needs the motivation of seeing its members being trained and upgraded, and receiving more pay and recognition. A stagnant outlook to a man convinces him that joining a union is really a very small risk since the company is not doing anything on his behalf. It should be noted again that even if the management has some type of a training plan, it is important that the men perceive it as in their interest, too.

B. Political Factors in an Organizational Effort

The above listing of potential trouble areas may indicate potential targets for the union organizational campaign. At the same time there may be a company which is facing a union movement even though they have done everything as recommended. In this case the company may be a political choice due to its strategic position in the industry or because of its reputation. If this seems to be the case, management can concentrate its efforts on meeting the challenge in every legal and ethical manner.

V. LEGAL MEASURES DURING THE ORGANIZATIONAL CAMPAIGN
A. Overview

To say that the area of labor law is both complicated and uncertain is an understatement. Legal counsel is a must and the sooner the better. The events which begin the first hint of a union organizational effort through the time when both sides are attempting to influence the employees, and finally into the election phase represent a complex chain. The material presented in this section will follow the same approximate time pattern of events in a typical union-management encounter. Each section will specify the major issues and make suggestions for management actions which are appropriate and legal. The specific facts of each situation make generalizations dangerous, and this is another strong reason for listening to counsel.

B. The Prerepresentation Hearing Phase

This is the period which is the most explosive in terms of emotions and angry actions. This period includes the time when the union is attempting to marshall support and the company is trying to substantiate its claim that the men would be better off without such union organization.

   1. *No-solicitation Rules.* A common way of spreading union sentiments is by soliciting employees to sign authorization cards. The process of getting signatures is more difficult outside of working hours than during working hours. Since both sides know this, there is constant friction over the issue of management's right to restrict solicitation. The general legal position is that the company can restrict soliciting during working hours if it interferes with production and/or safety and if management has been consistent in this policy toward other unions and other community groups (e.g., United Fund, etc.). At the same time it seems clear that during nonworking hours (coffee breaks or lunch) solicitation is permitted. These rules must be made more liberal for the union organizer if he is able to show that no reasonable alternative method of contacting the men exists. Such an issue will probably be decided by one of the field staff members of the National Labor Relations Board.

   2. *Physical Interference with the Organizers.* Actual physical interference with the union organizers or any employee exercising his rights is clearly illegal. Such actions will usually receive instant negative publicity by the press, and the net result is a clear loss for the personnel staff. A threat or actual violence is illegal.

   3. *Observation and Surveillance.* Top management and its supervisors are able to observe and record what changes are happening. They are not allowed to install

listening devices or other surveillance devices for the purposes of an antiunion campaign.

4. *Unfortunate Assistance from Third Parties.* During a heated campaign there may be third parties (neither employees nor a part of management) who attempt to influence the employees and their thinking about the union issue. Peaceful attempts to persuade, and coercive or threatening actions may be traced back to management. If management allows or condones such coercive third-party actions, they are accepting these third parties as agents and, therefore, share their liability under the law.

5. *Stating Management's Position.* During the campaign many words will be exchanged. The key question is the total impact of the management communications. If the National Labor Relations Board examiner determines that there was no intimidation or reprisal communicated, the employer will generally be protected. The test that will probably be applied concerns itself with how the employees reacted subjectively to the employer's speech. Legal counsel should review such statements and recommend specific language to the executive staff. It should be noted that it is not the personal motivation of the executive making the speech, but rather the total set of facts and words which will be considered. In a very tense situation, for example, management would probably be advised to choose its words very carefully and to be rather conservative in stating the facts and its position.

The employer can express his ideas on the economic position of the employees after the election or perhaps comment on the possibility of rising labor costs forcing greater automation. Again, the line is hazy between a free-speech statement and a veiled threat to the employees. During this same period the union has the same obligation to represent the facts though it can be expected to paint a brighter picture. The employer has the legal right to question such union statements and he may argue that they are such a departure from the truth that the impact of the words could not but have had a significant influence on the employees. If the National Labor Relations Board examiner or regional director agrees, the election may be set aside and other legal steps taken to correct the situation.

6. *Interrogation of the Employees.* Often the management will want to find out how the employees feel toward the union campaign. The general trend has been to provide the individual employee with more safeguards. In this regard it is probably unlawful to call an individual employee into a supervisor's office and ask him what he thinks of this union or any union. The new guidelines for obtaining information from the employees seem to be as follows: that the employees know why the poll is being conducted, that there are assurances against any reprisals because of the outcome, that something similar to a secret balloting procedure be provided, and that during this period the employer has not been guilty of other coercive acts.

7. *Protection of the Employees during the Campaign.* Under federal law the employees have the right to organize or not to organize. There is a constant problem of protecting those employees who are not in favor of the current union from coercive acts by the union. The package of protection is a mix of labor, civil, and criminal law which would be administered on the local level. For example, the employee is to be free from threats during this tense period. The line between threats and forceful persuasion is hazy, and it should be expected that the employees will have a certain degree of anxiety. Obvious cases of violence against the employee or his property should be documented and the local authorities notified of the incidents. If there is violence or the threat of violence at the plant entrances, the employees have the right to protection by police and plant security forces.

A more complex issue involves picketing. According to the statutes, there is a ban against organizational or recognitional picketing when the plant is already organized, if there has been an election within the preceding twelve months, or if no petition for election procedures has been filed within thirty days. The difficulty arises in separating organizational and recognitional picketing from free-speech or informational picketing. Once again legal counsel is needed to help interpret the facts and their full impact on the situation.

8. *Disciplining or Discharge of Employees during an Organizational or Recognitional Campaign.* Each employee is protected in his right to advocate the presence of this union or any other union. At the same time the employee has a duty to meet the performance standards which are ordinarily applied to his position. Disciplining or discharging employees during this uncertain period requires very clear records of poor performance or a violation of written disciplinary rules. Without such evidence, there is a strong possibility that these actions will be interpreted as antiunion and that the man will be ordered reinstated will full back pay. Worse than the dollar amount involved is the total psychological impact of having a federal agency make such an adverse finding during the campaign period. In extreme cases, the employer may be ordered to bargain with the union without the intermediate step of having a secret ballot.

C. The NLRB-sponsored Representation Hearing and Election

The basic objective of the representation procedure is to ensure that the employees have a free and unhampered opportunity to vote. The technical procedures before, during, and after the election require legal counsel.

1. *Filing a Petition for Election.* When the employer or the union makes a petition for an election (NLRB form 502, shown in Figure 1) the formal process is started. Filing this petition causes the regional director of the NLRB to examine the situation and assign a hearing officer if the facts seem to indicate that substantial issues are present.

2. *The Representation Hearing.* All parties concerned will receive copies of the Notice for Representation Hearing (NLRB form 852, shown in Figure 2) which states a time and place for the hearing. At this hearing an officer of the regional board will hear arguments concerning whether there is sufficient reason to hold an election and, if so, what is the appropriate bargaining unit, and which employees should be eligible to vote. The results of this hearing go to the regional director for a decision (unless this case has been marked for action by the full board in Washington).

3. *Information to the Employees.* During the period when the petition for a representative election has been made the employees are formally made aware of this fact by the posting of NLRB form 666, shown in Figure 3. This forms says that the election may be held and briefly describes the employees' rights. Additional information may be given to the employees for the employer and union pursuant to the regional director's request for the names and addresses of the persons eligible to vote. Literature may then be mailed to their home address.

4. *The Formal Election.* If the regional director or the board in Washington decides that an election should be held, a date will be set, and the federal agency will arrange for the ballots, the boxes, and some appropriate polling place on the company premises in the usual case. Balloting must be secret, and there should be no conversation by the observers to the employees. This restriction on communication extends from twenty-four hours prior to the election through the election period. Ballots may be challenged or the procedure may be challenged. The regional director or the board will make the final determination on any challenges or issues concerning the election. In any event the NLRB will certify the tally of ballots and the decisions reached.

5. *Legal Appeals.* The law provides safeguards for all parties and for appeal procedures throughout the representation and election phases. Legal counsel will advise management on its rights during this period.

Form NLRB-502
(11-64)

UNITED STATES OF AMERICA
NATIONAL LABOR RELATIONS BOARD

PETITION

Form Approved
Budget Bureau No. 64-R002.14

DO NOT WRITE IN THIS SPACE

CASE NO

DATE FILED

INSTRUCTIONS—Submit an original and four (4) copies of this Petition to the NLRB Regional Office in the Region in which the employer concerned is located. If more space is required for any one item, attach additional sheets, numbering item accordingly.

The Petitioner alleges that the following circumstances exist and requests that the National Labor Relations Board proceed under its proper authority pursuant to Section 9 of the National Labor Relations Act.

1. Purpose of this Petition *(If box RC, RM, or RD is checked and a charge under Section 8(b)(7) of the Act has been filed involving the Employer named herein, the statement following the description of the type of petition shall not be deemed made.)*

(Check one)

☐ RC–CERTIFICATION OF REPRESENTATIVE—A substantial number of employees wish to be represented for purposes of collective bargaining by Petitioner and Petitioner desires to be certified as representative of the employees.

☐ RM–REPRESENTATION (EMPLOYER PETITION)—One or more individuals or labor organizations have presented a claim to Petitioner to be recognized as the representative of employees of Petitioner.

☐ RD–DECERTIFICATION—A substantial number of employees assert that the certified or currently recognized bargaining representative is no longer their representative.

☐ UD–WITHDRAWAL OF UNION SHOP AUTHORITY—Thirty percent (30%) or more of employees in a bargaining unit covered by an agreement between their employer and a labor organization desire that such authority be rescinded.

☐ UC–UNIT CLARIFICATION—A labor organization is currently recognized by employer, but petitioner seeks clarification of placement of certain employees. *(Check one)* ☐ In unit not previously certified ☐ In unit previously certified in Case No. _____

☐ AC–AMENDMENT OF CERTIFICATION—Petitioner seeks amendment of certification issued in Case No. _____

Attach statement describing the specific amendment sought.

2. NAME OF EMPLOYER	EMPLOYER REPRESENTATIVE TO CONTACT	PHONE NO

3. ADDRESS(ES) OF ESTABLISHMENT(S) INVOLVED *(Street and number, city, State, and ZIP Code)*

4a. TYPE OF ESTABLISHMENT *(Factory, mine, wholesaler, etc.)*	4b. IDENTIFY PRINCIPAL PRODUCT OR SERVICE

5. Unit Involved *(In UC petition, describe PRESENT bargaining unit and attach description of proposed clarification.)*

Included

Excluded

(If you have checked box RC in 1 above, check and complete EITHER item 7a or 7b, whichever is applicable)

6a. NUMBER OF EMPLOYEES IN UNIT

PRESENT _____

PROPOSED (BY UC/AC) _____

6b. IS THIS PETITION SUPPORTED BY 30% OR MORE OF THE EMPLOYEES IN THE UNIT?*
☐ YES ☐ NO
*Not applicable in RM, UC, and AC

7a. ☐ Request for recognition as Bargaining Representative was made on _____ *(Month, day, year)* and Employer declined recognition on or about _____ *(Month, day, year)* *(If no reply received, so state)*

7b. ☐ Petitioner is currently recognized as Bargaining Representative and desires certification under the act.

8. Recognized or Certified Bargaining Agent *(If there is none, so state)*

NAME | AFFILIATION

ADDRESS | DATE OF RECOGNITION OR CERTIFICATION

9. DATE OF EXPIRATION OF CURRENT CONTRACT, IF ANY *(Show month, day, and year)*	10. IF YOU HAVE CHECKED BOX UD IN 1 ABOVE, SHOW HERE THE DATE OF EXECUTION OF AGREEMENT GRANTING UNION SHOP *(Month, day, and year)*

11a. IS THERE NOW A STRIKE OR PICKETING AT THE EMPLOYER'S ESTABLISHMENT(S) INVOLVED? YES ___ NO ___	11b. IF SO APPROXIMATELY HOW MANY EMPLOYEES ARE PARTICIPATING?

11c. THE EMPLOYER HAS BEEN PICKETED BY OR ON BEHALF OF _____ *(Insert name)* _____ A LABOR ORGANIZATION, OF _____ *(Insert address)* _____ SINCE _____ *(Month, day, year)*

12. ORGANIZATIONS OR INDIVIDUALS OTHER THAN PETITIONER (AND OTHER THAN THOSE NAMED IN ITEMS 8 AND 11c), WHICH HAVE CLAIMED RECOGNITION AS REPRESENTATIVES AND OTHER ORGANIZATIONS AND INDIVIDUALS KNOWN TO HAVE A REPRESENTATIVE INTEREST IN ANY EMPLOYEES IN THE UNIT DESCRIBED IN ITEM 5 ABOVE. (IF NONE, SO STATE)

NAME	AFFILIATION	ADDRESS	DATE OF CLAIM *(Required only if Petition is filed by Employer)*

I declare that I have read the above petition and that the statements therein are true to the best of my knowledge and belief.

_____ *(Petitioner and affiliation, if any)*

By _____ *(Signature of representative or person filing petition)* _____ *(Title, if any)*

Address _____ *(Street and number, city, State, and ZIP Code)* _____ *(Telephone number)*

WILLFULLY FALSE STATEMENT ON THIS PETITION CAN BE PUNISHED BY FINE AND IMPRISONMENT (U.S. CODE, TITLE 18, SECTION 1001)

GPO 886-477

Figure 1.   NLRB Form 502, petition.

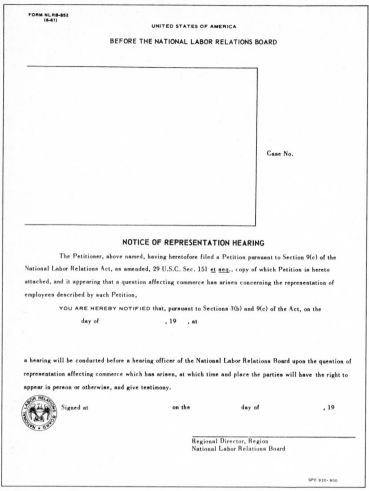

Figure 2.   NLRB Form 852, notice of representation hearing.

BIBLIOGRAPHY AND SOURCE MATERIALS

The nature of the industrial relations sector requires that reference materials be current. Little which is set forth in older texts should be accepted without technical review. For this reason, it is suggested that the personnel manager consult one or more of the loose-leaf references listed below, for the most current and accurate information in this dynamic field.

Basic Sources with Weekly Updating

1. Commerce Clearing House, Inc., Chicago, Ill.
2. Bureau of National Affairs, Washington, D.C.
3. Prentice-Hall, Inc., Englewood Cliffs, N.J.

These three sources are among the best known in the industrial relations field.

Form NLRB 666
(9—66)

★NOTICE TO EMPLOYEES

FROM THE

National Labor Relations Board

A PETITION has been filed with this Federal agency seeking an election to determine whether certain employees want to be represented by a union.

The case is being investigated and NO DETERMINATION HAS BEEN MADE AT THIS TIME by the National Labor Relations Board.   IF an election is held Notices of Election will be posted giving complete details for voting.

It was suggested that your employer post this notice so the National Labor Relations Board could inform you of your basic rights under the National Labor Relations Act.

YOU HAVE THE RIGHT under Federal Law

- To self-organization
- To form, join, or assist labor organizations
- To bargain collectively through representatives of your own choosing
- To act together for the purposes of collective bargaining or other mutual aid or protection
- To refrain from any or all such activities

It is possible that some of you will be voting in an employee representation election as a result of the request for an election having been filed.   While NO DETERMINATION HAS BEEN MADE AT THIS TIME, in the event an election is held, the NATIONAL LABOR RELATIONS BOARD wants all eligible voters to be familiar with their rights under the law and wants both labor and management to know what is expected of them IF it holds an election.

You are therefore advised that the Board applies rules which are intended to keep its elections fair and honest, and which result in a free choice.   If agents of either labor or management act in such a way as to interfere with your right to a free election, they will risk the possibility of having the election set aside by the Board.

NOTE:

The following are examples of conduct which interfere with the rights of employees and may result in the setting aside of the election.   Where appropriate the Board provides other remedies, such as reinstatement with backpay for employees fired for exercising their rights.

- Making threats of loss of jobs or loss of benefits by a party capable of carrying out such a threat
- Firing employees or causing them to be fired in order to encourage or discourage union activity
- Making promises of promotions, pay raises, or other benefits, to influence an employee vote, by a party capable of carrying out any such promise
- Making threats of physical force or violence to employees to influence their vote in the election
- Making misstatements of important facts where another party does not have a fair chance to reply
- Making campaign speeches to assembled groups of employees on company time within the 24-hour period before the election
- Inciting racial or religious prejudice by inflammatory appeals
- Exerting repeated pressures by persons or groups not themselves involved in the election which tend to create fear of job loss, violence, or other trouble

Please be assured that IF AN ELECTION IS HELD every effort will be made to protect your right to a free choice under the law.   Improper conduct, a few examples of which appear above, will not be permitted.   We expect all parties to Board elections to cooperate fully with this agency in maintaining basic principles of a fair election as required by law.

NATIONAL LABOR RELATIONS BOARD
an agency of the
UNITED STATES GOVERNMENT
Cincinnati, Ohio 45202
Telephone: 684-3634

THIS IS AN OFFICIAL GOVERNMENT NOTICE AND MUST NOT BE DEFACED BY ANYONE

U.S. GOVERNMENT PRINTING OFFICE : 1967 O - 240-882

Figure 3.   NLRB Form 666, notice to employees.

Part 12

International Personnel Management

chapter 56

Staffing the Overseas Unit

FRANKLIN R. ROOT and **DAVID A. HEENAN**   *Wharton School of Finance and Commerce, University of Pensylvania, Philadelphia, Pa.*

Responding to the twin challenges of market opportunities abroad and competition at home, American corporations are joining the ranks of international companies at an astounding rate. Many are already on the way to becoming truly multinational companies with global strategies encompassing far-flung operations in scores of countries. This transformation from domestic to multinational enterprise is crucially dependent on the availability of management talent to staff burgeoning foreign operations.

What are the staffing requirements of international companies? What is the nature of the overseas assignment? How does the international company recruit and develop manpower for overseas management? What is the role of local nationals in overseas management? How do governments influence the staffing of the overseas unit? These are the principal questions addressed by this chapter.

STAFFING REQUIREMENTS OF INTERNATIONAL COMPANIES

Multinational companies are attaching increasing importance to the effective use of management in overseas operations. Traditionally, United States companies have placed a disproportionate burden on their own nationals for the staffing of overseas subsidiaries. This pool of foreign-assigned nationals or "expatriates" is estimated to number 40,000 or, including dependents, 150,000. In aggregate terms, overseas Americans are increasing (with expanded levels of United States direct investment abroad) but at a decreasing rate (owing to the strategic advantages of host-country and third-country nationals). At the company level, however, a general decline in expatriate representation overseas can be observed. One senior oil company executive notes:

> For example, twelve years ago we had 78 expatriates and 17 third-country nationals assigned to our Indian refining and marketing company. Today, there are four expatriates

and two third-country nationals. The Government has given us till the end of this year to get down to a maximum of two foreign nationals in India. This trend is typical world-wide.[1]

While the direction is one of more fully utilizing local nationals to staff overseas affiliates, it is anticipated that the core of United States expatriates will still maintain important responsibilities for the management of the foreign operations of United States companies.

Perhaps a more significant trend is the shortened tenure of overseas assignment. The days of the extended foreign service career for the expatriate manager are abruptly ending with today's emphasis on abbreviated, more meaningful assignments, generally of either a trouble-shooting variety or of a temporary nature conditional on the evolution of a skilled local management team.

> Old China hands are being phased out of our company as rapidly as possible. The corporate equivalency of a foreign service corps is unrealistic in view of the times. Firstly, we're now able to attract effective, and less expensive indigenous managers for key subsidiary jobs. And, second, the aggressive, self-directed American businessman of this era will not tolerate an open-ended (undefined) lifetime abroad.[2]

Nevertheless, as international business tends to generate increasing levels of total corporate sales and profitability, senior executives generally concur that some exposure—usually ranging from two to ten years—to overseas operations is mandatory for the manager's appropriate career development. Some companies, for example, have standing policies that automatically block a manager's advancement beyond a certain level if he lacks overseas exposure of an operational variety. That tomorrow's executive, at least in Standard Oil of New Jersey, would necessarily be "a man for all countries" was pointed out by Michael Haider: "Our future managers, if they are to measure up to the requirements of their jobs, will have to spend a part of their careers living and working abroad. International and domestic jobs will be thought of as virtually interchangeable."[3] Thus, the overseas assignment—although more infrequent and of shorter duration—will serve as an integral part of the career development of tomorrow's manager.

NATURE OF OVERSEAS ASSIGNMENT

A Group-oriented Decision

A significant difference area between domestic and foreign activity staffing relates to the family-oriented nature of the latter assignment. The importance in providing appropriate incentives for the expatriate's wife and other family members is well-recorded. In describing "The Pretty Americans," Dr. Harland Cleveland, President of the University of Hawaii, identifies three major fears that confront the foreign service wife: (1) threat of disease, (2) absence of adequate schooling for children, and (3) cross-cultural barriers. His advice to the prospective family venturing abroad: "Decide whether you really want to go and stay for a long enough time to be effective. Otherwise stay home."[4] Gonzales and Negandhi, citing the mystic "Factor X" which makes for successful work abroad, further isolated "wife and family adaptability" as the key variable.[5]

[1] Personal interview.

[2] Personal interview.

[3] Michael Haider, "Tomorrow's Executive: A Man For All Countries," *Columbia Journal of World Business,* Winter 1966, pp. 112–113.

[4] Harland Cleveland, "The Pretty Americans," *Harper's Magazine,* March 1959, pp. 31–35.

[5] Richard F. Gonzales and Anant R. Negandhi, *The U.S. Overseas Executive: His Orientation and Career Patterns,* Michigan State University Graduate School of Business Administration, East Lansing, Michigan, 1967, chap. 2.

Accordingly, today's international personnel manager carefully scrutinizes the family element in the overseas setting. W. R. Jeeros, Director of Overseas Operations, Parke, Davis and Co. suggests: "Equally important, we attempt to assess the attitude and suitability of the candidate's wife for living abroad."[6] Mobil's four-hour environmental interview of the prospective overseas manager and his wife has been a major breakthrough in the acknowledgement of the group-nature of the foreign service assignment.

Environmental Differences

The environment confronting the overseas manager has been described as one consisting of three interactive components: (1) physical or spatial, (2) sociocultural, and (3) technical. Successful adaption overseas depends on the ability of the expatriate and his family to reconcile such components.

Physical distance provides the overseas employee with his introduction to the foreign setting. The expatriate and his family may be exposed rather abruptly to markedly lower living standards, inadequate medical and public-health facilities, inferior educational institutions, climatic irritations, and occasional physical dangers. One major shortcoming of foreign service is the discomfort of living far from home, conflicting with the family's need for communal security.

The remoteness of home will be felt differently by individual family members. For the businessman, separation from headquarters reduces his visibility and possibly his career advancement; he believes he is deprived of opportunities more readily available to his contemporaries back home. For other family members, removal from friends and familiar environs may yield somewhat different problems. A common reaction is "separation anxiety," which ultimately impairs on-the-job effectiveness and family morale.

On the whole, the hardships of physical separation are fairly obvious and easier for the international employer to remedy than is the second environmental component: an unfamiliar society. In addition to isolation and mundane living problems abroad, the expatriate and his family are exposed to a network of cultural patterns frequently at odds with their own system of values and patterns of thought. The newcomer's natural lack of shared experiences and historical perspective suggests that overseas assignments should be given only to those persons who can adapt easily to a new cultural environment. Further, intercultural competence implies not only a facility in languages, but more importantly, a certain sensitivity to, and empathy with, the local people.[7]

The difficulties of adjusting to a new culture cannot be overstated. An estimated 15 percent to 20 percent of overseas turnover results from the inability of the individual or his family to empathize with a foreign setting. Cultural ambivalence or "ethnocentrism" can destroy the basis for successful communication among persons of widely different backgrounds and severely handicap the competence of an expatriate team.

The need for the expatriate to perform in a foreign business setting may deepen his sense of alienation. Operational variations may exist, such as scaled-down plant and equipment, differing standards of productivity, nonavailability of credit, inefficiency of internal distribution, restricted selection of communications media, and the like. At times, the foreign-based manager, when exposed to countries in varying stages of economic development and industrialization, may see the technical differences as insurmountable.

[6] "Recruiting, Selecting, and Developing Personnel for Foreign Operations," *Management Record,* December 1959, p. 249.

[7] David A. Heenan, "The Corporate Expatriate: Assignment to Ambiguity," *Columbia Journal of World Business,* May–June 1970, p. 36–39.

In some overseas countries where political and economic centralism runs high, the government's involvement in business makes it necessary for the foreign-based executive to be able to evaluate the government as a co-negotiator (along with unions in labor relations), as a supplier (where public utilities are state-owned), as a competitor (in the form of the quasi-public enterprise), or even as a marketer (when distribution facilities are government-owned). Accordingly, international companies are best served by a foreign-service contingent capable of meeting such differences in commercial conduct with responsive policies.

A further problem is the degree to which the alien business setting is open to participation by outsiders. A frequent complaint of young managers on overseas assignments is that they tend to be excluded from meaningful decision-making. One young marketing manager, recently returned from the Swiss subsidiary of an American multinational, complained:

> Although the setting was beautiful and the standard of living very high, I just couldn't get untracked in our Swiss company. Because of my age, I was excluded from many key strategy sessions. Also my being a nonengineer and a basic sales-type left me at the bottom of the ladder statuswide. My counterparts back in the States certainly don't have problems of this variety or intensity.[8]

Furthermore the foreign-based manager must recognize not only the manner but also the setting in which local business is conducted. Since in many societies business negotiations are quasi-social and occur after normal working hours, the overseas manager must adjust his schedule accordingly. Many expatriate managers have failed to acknowledge this social dimension. One Regional Director (Southeast Asia) of a major pharmaceutical company states:

> Larry, our best trained, most knowledgeable domestic production manager, was assigned to the same position in the Philippines. While his on-the-job performance was exceptional, his workday terminated at 6 P.M. regularly in a business environment that placed a heavy emphasis on social responsibilities. After six months, a crippling strike hit the subsidiary which was eventually traced to Larry's inability to extend normal social courtesies to local union officers. Larry was recalled to New York and replaced by Bill, a much less promising manager. Yet, Bill realized the importance of maintaining close off-the-job relationships and, through scheduled socializing, has developed the highest degree of union-management harmony in our entire Asian theatre.[9]

All foreign-based employees, when exposed to host-country pressures, try to minimize environmental threats. Some managers' behavioral patterns become those of the host culture. From an initial state of shock and, perhaps, sense of alienation, the expatriate plunges totally into the foreign environment. In other words, he "goes native."

On the other hand, the expatriate may defend himself by being chauvinistic. Overwhelmed by the milieu of unfamiliarity, the expatriate and his family completely shun associations in the host country. Any number of manifestations can occur: overt prejudice, social isolation, and possibly even direct conflict with the local citizens. Although aware he is jeopardizing his job, the "ugly American" engages in a war with the feared environment. One point is certain: since the employee is usually assigned overseas in at least a middle-management position, such defensive tactics will have far-reaching effects within the local company.

Job Dissatisfaction

Many of the problems of expatriate adaptation can be prevented or minimized by the international employer. When appropriate motivation exists, the problems of managerial assimilation can be resolved. Historically, multinational enterprises

[8] Personal interview.
[9] Personal interview.

have attempted to minimize expatriate problems by offering inflated salary and benefit programs for foreign service.   John Vivian, an internationally known consultant in the area, has described the expatriate as "overpaid but under compensated," noting: "Compensation means more than pay.   It also includes psychological satisfaction that comes from doing a job well and enjoying the monetary rewards achieved.   Unfortunately, many expatriates lack such compensation, either in their work or the foreign environment in which they live."[10]   Evidence substantiates this lack of psychological support in international employment.   Spencer Hayden, analyzing the anxieties and complaints of 1,200 American managers and technicians abroad, identified eight major causes of distress in the following order of frequency: (1) isolation from opportunities, (2) language problems, (3) insufficient technical or staff support, (4) overall dependence on the company, (5) professional staleness, (6) family separation, (7) social obligations, and (8) legal and political problems.[11]

Job Motivations

Why, then, does the manager accept or seek a foreign-based assignment?

Since today's international assignment is visualized as an integral part of one's worldwide career development, the majority of managers accept overseas positions for their advancement possibilities.   Gonzales and Negandhi define the circumstances that influence the manager's decision to accept a foreign assignment.[12]

Factors Influencing Overseas Assignments

Factor	Percent
Opportunity for advancement and recognition . . .	37
Desire to live abroad with wife and family	31
Desire for an overseas career	13
Financial rewards	13
Others	6
Total.	100

Although a wide diversity of opinion was observed in identifying the positive features of an overseas assignment, the following advantages of a foreign service career were noted:[13]

Advantages of Foreign Assignments

Factor	Percent
Higher pay	17
Broader experience and responsibility	16
Learning about people and customs.	15
More rapid advancement	14
Self-accomplishment	11
Travel	9
Other	18
Total.	100

[10] John Vivian, "Expatriate Executives: Overpaid But Undercompensated," *Columbia Journal of World Business,* January–February 1968, p. 30.

[11] Spencer Hayden, "Problems of Operating Overseas," *Personnel,* Vol. 45, January–February 1968, p. 17.

[12] Gonzales and Negandhi, p. 107.

[13] *Ibid.*

An interesting paradox can now be seen. Many of the key shortcomings of the international career are often viewed as its major sources of satisfaction. Two general areas of job satisfaction/dissatisfaction exist—environment and organization. By providing appropriate rewards, the international manager can minimize the difficulties of organizational hardships (lack of visibility, reduced authority, etc.). To reduce environmental problems, on the other hand, careful attention must be placed on the recruitment and selection process for potential overseas candidates.

RECRUITMENT AND SELECTION

The environmental difficulties encountered by Americans stationed abroad call for a greater degree of personal resourcefulness and self-reliance than is necessary for managers living in their native surroundings. Accordingly, the following variables seem to be most important in identifying the successful overseas manager:

1. *Sensitivity to foreign environment.* John T. O'Connor, former Secretary of Commerce, points out that the successful expatriate is a "highly emotional human being with highly developed humanitarian instincts." Willingness to learn the local language and an overall cultural empathy are included under "sensitivity."[14]

2. *Profit-oriented.* Robert McElfesh, a senior executive of Ford International, insists that "the ideal international manager is profit-minded; he never lets his profit-mindedness become overshadowed by secondary considerations."[15]

3. *Flexibility.* Robert C. Zuehlke, Personnel Manager, Standard Fruit and Steamship Company, advises the need for "an open-minded, unprejudiced attitude towards other people. Flexibility is a highly desirable—if not essential—quality in an (overseas) candidate."[16]

4. *Motivation to work abroad.* Contrary to Swedes and the Dutch, Americans have typically been reluctant to spend a significant portion of their business careers abroad. In recent years, the viewing of international operations as "fast track" has reduced this risk to some extent. Nonetheless, the international personnel manager must construct a comprehensive career-pattern, clearly identifying the purpose and tenure of overseas assignments. Failure to provide organizational incentives will result in recruitment of a less-than-desirable managerial corps for overseas operations.

5. *Proper family support.* William J. DeGenring, Manager of Employee Relations, Cynamid International, suggests the policy of interviewing wives whenever possible: "It has been my experience that the most frequent reason for an American's lack of success in a foreign career has been because of his family's, principally his wife's, inability to adjust to the foreign situation."[17] A recent study by Business International further revealed: "There is reason to think that a wife's hostile attitude to a foreign environment is a determinant factor that must be included in the appraisal report on any executive who is to be groomed for international management."[18]

---

[14] "What It Takes to Be a Successful International Manager," *International Management,* Vol. 14, August 1963, p. 49.

[15] *Ibid.*

[16] "How to Hire Employees for Foreign Work," *International Management,* Vol. 20, January 1965, p. 68.

[17] William J. DeGenring, "How to Minimize Overseas Recruiting Risks," *Management Review,* LVI, March 1967, p. 13.

[18] "Developing Management for the Worldwide Enterprise," *Business International,* New York, 1965, p. 23.

6. *Age.*   The general age range of twenty-eight to forty-five years is recommended for initial foreign service assignments.   DeGenring suggests: "Aim for youth.   Without reservation young married people are far better risks for their first-time overseas career than older people."[19]   While youth usually insures the flexibility and sensitivity requirements of overseas assignments, there are dangers of transferring employees abroad with less than three to five years of significant domestic experience of an *operational* variety.   Since most foreign billets are at a midmanagement level, functional expertise should accompany the overseas American.   Foreign subsidiaries are not the place for on-the-job training and corporate teeth-cutting.   Young managers proposing assignments abroad without the proper experience patterns do themselves a disservice.

Although the above traits are critical for the success of overseas managers, interviews indicate that, at present, the international selection process is unsystematic. One senior personnel executive described his company's overseas recruitment and selection process as "a no-systems system."[20]   Gonzales' substantiated this, remarking: "It is more accurate to say that there is a non-selection process . . . to fill foreign corporate positions."[21]   This lack of carefully defined international manpower programs has been a major reason for the high turnover rate of foreign service assignments and the general disenchantment of many managers for overseas postings.

MANPOWER DEVELOPMENT

Intensive development programs are particularly necessitated by the following characteristics inherent in the international career:

1. An overcentralization of operational decisions by the international headquarters company.

2. An information gap between overseas subsidiary and headquarters.

3. A requirement for overseas-seasoned managers to reenter regional and headquarters activities for executive duties at a later time.

4. A trend for accelerated development of local nationals in not only the subsidiary but also in parent and regional organizations.

Headquarters controls, as communicative devices, enable the international organization to bridge the gap between the head office and its overseas subsidiaries. They also insure an appropriate measure of uniformity and consistency among local affiliates.   However, overextensive controls in global corporations far too often exist, tending to deny operational authority to subsidiary management teams.   Instead of overcoming the obstacles to international communications, elaborate control systems may impede the development of expatriate managers.

Overcentralized decision-making is inconsistent with the requirements of the overseas business environment.   If the manager's authority is visibly constricted, his chances for establishing and maintaining effective relationships with his local associates are lessened.   Host environments which attach special significance to authority quickly withdraw recognition from these overseas managers.   Even in cases where reduced autonomy is visible only to the manager and his co-workers, the problem of status inconsistency often occurs for the overseas executives whose plush home and social surroundings may significantly outweigh his day-to-day work responsibilities.

[19] DeGenring, p. 14.

[20] Personal interview.

[21] Richard F. Gonzales, "The Expatriates," *MSU Business Topics,* Vol. 15, Spring 1967, p. 73.

Another aspect of organizational centralization has been described by Cameron McKenzie of Standard Oil (N.J.):

> (The foreign-based manager) may regard his role as undefined, dysfunctional, and too expensive in terms of personal stress and noninvolvement with the company. His waning enthusiasm may often lead to even more company controls, which in turn will seem to verify his incompetence. Thus, with the passage of time, increasing centralization of overseas operations which will appear to be self-fulfilling, will prove to be a self-defeating mechanism.[22]

Furthermore, the level of foreign technological competence at which the overseas manager must function can militate against his own development. Generalized skills nurtured in small-scale subsidiary operations are less transferable to a scene in which specialized abilities are at a premium. As a result, professional staleness, obsolescence, and immobility in the firm may characterize extended overseas assignments.

Besides the limitations on autonomy and job content, there is a tendency for headquarters to overlook the need for communication with its overseas personnel. The subsidiary manager's exclusion from the mainstream of corporate life makes informational support all the more necessary to lessen the many uncertainties that cloud the overseas career. Described as "the information gap" by Dimitris N. Chorafas, this phenomenon is characterized by (1) a failure to inform executives abroad about activities at home and (2) a lack of understanding among corporate executives about the differences between conditions abroad and at home.[23] The international firm's inability to structure an ongoing dialogue with its expatriate corps obstructs the employee's need for personal recognition and increases the difficulty of adaptation.

Development of personnel is often the responsibility of headquarters executives, many of whom are probably biased by ethnocentrism. Home-country-biased manpower standards that have little relevance to conditions at the subsidiary level have also been utilized. Accordingly, in many instances, an unresponsive personnel mechanism has severely frustrated the foreign-based manager.

In addition, the interests of the international organization and its expatriate employee conflicts with respect to the length of overseas assignments. Since the appropriate degree of environmental assimilation and facility within a foreign commercial setting involves a significant time commitment, the overseas manager's greatest value to the company is realized only as long as he remains abroad. The time element, however, may run counter to the individual's personal objectives of returning to the parent company to catch up professionally and to make up for lost visibility.

Perhaps a more important problem confronting the international personnel manager is that of expatriate reentry to headquarters for assignment. One senior executive warns:

> Very often our most successful subsidiary managers have turned out to be flops as area executives, staff managers, or what-have-you in the parent organization. Aside from the problem of adequate compensation adjustment, we think the major anxiety confronting the returning manager is status deprivation. Overseas, he was a big fish in a small pond. Here, at headquarters, he's just on a level with maybe twenty peers; many are his superior. Further, his external life—maids, limousine service, entertaining in a diplo-

---

[22] Cameron McKenzie, "Incompetent Foreign Managers," *Business Horizons,* Spring 1968, pp. 83–85.

[23] Dimitris N. Chorafas, *Developing the International Executive,* AMA Research Study 83, American Management Association, 1967, p. 4.

matic circle—are replaced with a relatively shallow existence. This works tremendous hardships on him and, in particular, his wife. In the last six months, two new regional directors have resigned requesting reassignment to the field. This happens all the time.[24]

Appropriate developmental safeguards in the form of systematic career scheduling must be taken to minimize the reentry problem.

Finally, the necessity for expanded representation by foreign nationals at the subsidiary and headquarters level has demanded more comprehensive development strategies. Increasing reliance on accelerated company development programs and regional educational institutions (such as IMEDE, CEI, and INSEAD) can be expected over the next decade.

A recent study conducted by Warren Harrop of the Wharton School with the co-operation of Towers, Perrin, Forster, and Crosby indicates that only 60 percent of all United States firms maintain international management development programs to assist overseas managers in overcoming the above difficulties.[25] These programs typically consist of formal company development courses, university programs, short informal company programs, sensitivity training, and on-the-job training. Generally, positive evaluations were conveyed by most program participants. Programs deemed most valuable were formal company development courses and on-the-job experience. Accordingly, it is suggested that worldwide developmental efforts be expanded.

Evaluation by Managers of Development Programs

Programs	Excel-lent	Good	Fair	Poor	Total	Per-cent
Formal company development program	21	8	1	—2	28	38
Formal university development program	6	4	1	—1	10	13
Short informal company program	3	6			9	12
Sensitivity group program	6	2		—1	7	10
Job rotation and experience program	18	2			20	27

STAFFING OVERSEAS UNITS WITH LOCAL NATIONALS

As indicated earlier, international companies are demonstrating a strong preference for staffing their foreign operations with local nationals. In a recent Conference Board survey, only two out of 254 company executives expressed a definite preference for Americans over local nationals in overseas management positions.[26] The representative United States international company today depends on expatriate managers only for temporary assignments and a small number of key jobs while the vast majority of its overseas managers are nationals of the countries in which they work. For instance, 99 percent of the 84,000 employees of IBM World Trade are local nationals.

Why Staff with Local Nationals?

Several factors have encouraged international companies to use local nationals in managerial and technical positions.

[24] Personal interview.

[25] Warren Harrop, "The Manager's View: International Development," Wharton School, University of Pennsylvania, Philadelphia, 1969 (Unpublished MBA Thesis).

[26] The Conference Board, *Foreign Nationals in International Management,* New York, 1968, p. 3.

The local national has a native's understanding of the host country, especially its people and their culture. The ability of a local national to communicate effectively with his fellow nationals whether they be customers, suppliers, government officials, other businessmen, or the general public can seldom, if ever, be matched by an expatriate manager. The many problems of environmental adaptation that bedevil the expatriate manager and his family are irrelevant to the local national, enabling him to focus his energies on the management job.

Hiring local nationals for middle and top level management in a company's foreign subsidiary can go a long way toward appeasing nationalistic demands, especially when it is not forced by government policy. One executive of an international mining company bluntly stated: "We employ the most nationals possible to head off trouble in advance."[27] Apart from nationalism, local nationals can often deal much more effectively with government officials in matters ranging from taxation to import permits.

The expense of local-national managers to the parent company is less than the expense of American expatriate managers who are not only paid salaries at United States levels but also receive generous allowances for foreign assignment, cost of living, housing, education, and other purposes. Although the differential between American and European executive pay scales is narrowing, it is usually very substantial in less-developed countries.

Another reason for the widespread use of local nationals is the shortage of management resources in parent companies. Spokesmen of international companies frequently cite their inability or unwillingness to make permanent overseas assignments of managers who are badly needed at home. The following statement by an executive of an international mining company is typical:

> We simply do not have the surplus of talent available to export large staffs overseas, and maintaining them is extremely expensive. Moreover, there is a natural desire in the host nations to see their own citizens reaping the benefits of employment in enterprises established on their own soil.[28]

The Continuing Need for Expatriate Managers

Although there is a powerful tendency to staff overseas operations with local nationals, most international companies must continue to rely on expatriates (including third-country nationals) to fill some management jobs in those operations. The principal explanation of this situation is the scarcity of qualified local managers. When local managers are not available, the next-best alternative for most companies is to send an American or third-country national on a temporary basis (usually two or three years) with firm instructions to train a local replacement.

Even when qualified local nationals are available, parent companies often want a few expatriate managers in their foreign affiliates in order to maintain effective control. It is commonplace for companies to secure a continuing American "presence" by appointing an American as local general manager or chief financial officer. A few companies secure control by placing expatriate managers only in regional headquarters while staffing local operations entirely with nationals.

International companies that have adopted a global strategy may wish to assign Americans overseas as part of their executive development. E. S. Groo, Vice-President of IBM World Trade Corporation, says in this regard:

> In recent years there has been an increasing interdependence of the country operations, one upon the other, and a growing set of interrelationships between the operations abroad

---

[27] Personal interview.
[28] Personal interview.

and the activities of the company in America. More and more, the countries share common programs and services with each other and with the United States. We have, therefore, become increasingly preoccupied with multinational goals and interests. So our selection and training of managers has been focused not only on the needs for local subsidiary management but equally on management at international levels.[29]

Spokesmen of multinational companies commonly assert that their choice of managers with international responsibility is based on merit regardless of national origin.

Aside from the general scarcity of local management talent, the need for headquarters' control, and the requirements of executive development programs, factors that are specific to an individual company may support the use of expatriate managers. The *newness* of a foreign operation is important: the newer the operation, the greater the need for expatriate managers and technical personnel to build a profitable, on-going business. The *nature* of the operation is a second specific factor. An operation, such as petrochemical plant, that demands a sophisticated technical staff and experienced management is more likely to need expatriate personnel than (say) a warehouse or assembly plant.

The Scarcity of Qualified Local National Managers

Although the scarcity of local managers is most intense in the less-developed countries, it also extends to European and other advanced countries. The Conference Board found that engineers and manufacturing managers are in shortest supply in the less-developed countries of Asia, Africa, and Latin America while sales and marketing people are in shortest supply in the industrial countries.[30] Expatriate employment patterns reflect the high scarcity of indigenous management in the less-developed countries. For instance, although less than twelve percent of GM's overseas employment is in Latin America, nearly forty-two percent of its expatriates are located in that region whereas Europe has seventy-five percent of GM's overseas employment but only forty-six percent of its expatriates.[31]

American managers cite many deficiencies in local national managers, as indicated by these findings of the Conference Board:

Shortcomings of Local National Managers[32]

(Frequency of typical citations)
Unfamiliar with U.S. business practices. 78
Lack of education or technical competence 50
Lack of initiative or aggressiveness. 19
Inadequate or difficult communication 19
Reluctance or failure to delegate 18
Failure to plan adequately. 17
Not sufficiently profit-oriented 16

All these factors generate management and communication gaps between headquarters and local nationals in their affiliates that must be overcome to achieve satisfactory performance levels.

[29] National Foreign Trade Council, Inc., *Transnational Personnel Session,* New York, 55th National Foreign Trade Convention, November 18, 1968, p. 79.
[30] The Conference Board, *op. cit.,* p. 10.
[31] National Foreign Trade Council, Inc., *op. cit.,* p. 75.
[32] The Conference Board, *op. cit.,* p. 18.

Recruitment of Local Nationals for Management

To meet the shortage of local managers, international companies have devised several recruiting strategies. Some companies have "bought" local managers through acquisitions or participation in joint ventures. Recruitment has also made use of techniques first developed in the United States. In Europe, for example, United States companies interview students at graduate business schools (notably the one at Fontainebleau), employ executive search firms, and also practice the time-honored method of piracy. Some companies also interview foreign students in the United States for assignment in their home countries.

Development of Local Managers

For the most part, international companies cannot recruit experienced local managers; they must develop them. Most of this development is informal, on-the-job training within the subsidiary. Expatriate managers play the dominant roles in this training, supplemented by visits of headquarters managers. Top-level local nationals are also frequently brought to corporate headquarters in the United States for periods long enough to give them an understanding of corporate policies and a "feel" for the company as a whole. Periodic international management conferences at home or abroad are also used to bring about face-to-face contacts between local managers and the headquarters staff.

Ordinarily, training outside the company in universities and other institutions is minimal. In training local nationals, the emphasis is on work experience guided by expatriate managers and corporate visitors.

The more sophisticated international companies have integrated local management training programs into corporate-wide executive development programs. These companies follow international personnel policies that offer opportunities for advancement throughout the corporation that are the same for foreign nationals and Americans.

The Lack of Specific Guidelines

This review of local nationals in international management points to a simple conclusion: there are no specific guidelines for the hiring of foreign nationals. Much depends on the individual company: its business philosophy; its degree of internationalization; the nature of its production, product line, and markets; and its management resources. Much also depends on the particular countries in which the company carries on its business. Nonetheless, the broad movement toward the greater use of local managers is unmistakable, and it is likely to accelerate in the future. And some companies are now moving beyond the traditional distinction between expatriate and local managers to create a corps of multinational executives who are available to fill management positions at headquarters or in affiliates without regard to their national origin.

GOVERNMENT CONSTRAINTS ON OVERSEAS STAFFING

Host government constraints on the staffing of overseas units are most commonly experienced by international companies in the less-developed countries. Motivated by strong, nationalistic drives for economic development, many governments attempt to persuade or compel international companies to replace expatriate managers and technicians with local nationals. When qualified local nationals are not available, these pressures can create serious staffing problems.

Staffing constraints take many forms, including administrative holdups in the granting of work permits, work permit quotas, work permits of limited duration, specific national staffing requirements to be met now or in the future, and limitations on the compensation paid to expatriate personnel.

The most frequently encountered constraint is bureaucratic delay in the issuance of work permits. International companies can minimize this constraint by presenting local government officials with a detailed explanation of the need for expatriate personnel (with an estimate of their probable length of stay) and by submitting their requests for work permits well in advance of actual need. At times, a quota may be imposed by the host government, as in the following instance cited by one executive: "We sometimes need a license to bring in American personnel. In Nigeria, for example, since it is a recent operation we have a quota for 25 Americans out of 800 employees. Eleven of the Americans have temporary permits."[33] Ordinarily, however, work permits are obtained for expatriates on an individual ad hoc basis. Serious difficulties arise only when government officials are dogmatic.

A few governments have detailed staffing regulations that may place international companies in an awkward position. The Pakistan government promotes a policy of full "Pakistanization" that requires all Pakistani enterprises with foreign participation to achieve the following staffing arrangements five years after production start-up: 100 percent Pakistani in salary groups under 1,000 Rs, 75 percent Pakistani in salary groups 1,000 Rs to 2,500 Rs, and 50 percent Pakistani in salary groups over 2,500 Rs. Brazil has a "two-thirds law" that requires two-thirds of a foreign subsidiary's payroll to be paid to Brazilians. However, the effect of this law is moderated by the exclusion of foreign specialists from the foreign payroll base if local substitutes are not available.

International companies that have already placed local nationals in high-level jobs seldom have major problems in bringing in expatriates. A top executive of a United States extractive company put the matter this way: "Nations have become less resentful of expatriate managers for two primary reasons. First, locals hold many of the important jobs in the firm; therefore, expatriate managers are not seen as a group of men coming into their land. Second, most expatriate managers stay for only a short period of time. The firm uses very few career overseas men any more. Because the people know that the outsider is bringing the needed technical knowledge and because they know that he is going to remain for only a short time and is therefore not replacing local people, they welcome and in most cases encourage the importation of short-term management."[34]

In conclusion, host government staffing constraints are rarely serious deterrents for international companies that actively recruit and train nationals for technical and management positions in their local affiliates. Most governments are willing to cooperate with international companies toward that end.

BIBLIOGRAPHY

Baker, James C., and Ivancevich: "The Job Satisfaction of American Managers Overseas," *MSU Business Topics,* Summer 1969.

Chorafas, Dimitris N.: *Developing the International Executive,* AMA Research Study 83, American Management Association, Inc., New York, 1967.

Duerr, Michael G., and James Greene: *Foreign Nationals in International Management,* The Conference Board, New York, 1969.

Gonzales, Richard F., and Anant R. Negandhi: *The United States Overseas Executive: His Orientation and Career Patterns,* Michigan State University, East Lansing, Michigan, 1967.

Hayden, Spencer J.: *The Personnel Job in a Changing World,* AMA Report No. 80, American Management Association, New York, 1964.

[33] Personal interview.
[34] Personal interview.

Heenan, David A.: "The Corporate Expatriate: Assignment to Ambiguity," *Columbia Journal of World Business,* May–June 1970.

Lovell, Enid Baird: *The Changing Role of the International Executive,* The Conference Board, New York, 1966.

National Foreign Trade Council, Inc., *Transcript of Transnational Personnel Session,* New York, May 15, 1969.

The Conference Board, *Foreign Nationals in International Management,* Managing International Business, No. 2, New York, 1968.

Vivian, John, "Expatriate Executives: Overpaid But Undercompensated," *Columbia Journal of World Business,* January–February 1968.

chapter 57

Compensation of
Overseas Personnel

ALFRED J. FIGLIOLA *Assistant Vice President, International Banking Group Personnel, Salary Systems Development and Research, First National City Bank, New York, New York*

Compensation of overseas personnel for the multinational organization concerns itself with three categories of staff. These are United States expatriates, third-country nationals, and local nationals. Compensation for the third-country national and local national will be covered briefly later in the chapter. As concerns the United States expatriate, varying practices reveal that compensation for these employees is essentially developed along almost identical lines by different employers and usually results in the payment of base salary, foreign service premium, and other appropriate allowances which are designed to offset costs higher than those in the United States.

Any compensation plan, of course, must be sensitive and responsive to changing overseas conditions relating to housing and living cost differentials plus all the other equally important factors which make up the "compensation package." Most important, the plan, once devised, must be simple to understand and maintain, no matter how soundly it is conceived, if it is to achieve the recognition and support of all those covered by it.

Some considerations which should be kept in mind in the development of the expatriate compensation plan are: (1) consistency, (2) competitiveness, (3) motivation, and (4) control of costs.

Finally, the plan must be kept up to date. Conditions in the home country relating to changing salary levels, tax changes, housing, and cost-of-living movements versus the overseas location affect all the elements of any compensation plan.

UNITED STATES EXPATRIATE COMPENSATION

An expatriate employee, by definition, is a person who resides and works outside his country of origin for temporary and indeterminate periods of time without the intent of giving up his citizenship.

Compensation of the United States expatriate is designed: (1) to grant the expatriate a net income at least equal to that of the individual in the home country performing similar work and of like financial status and (2) to provide a cash incentive or premium as a reasonable financial inducement to work and reside abroad. This involves payment of a base salary, foreign service premium, and differential housing and living allowances. When not combined with the foreign service premium, a separate hardship or "cultural shock" allowance is also paid. In addition, the expatriate is protected against excessive income tax liability and, whenever appropriate, is provided with an allowance for education costs. In essence, these considerations represent the variable factors which are normally calculated for each country or area of assignment. They give recognition to the differences in the desirability of various places because of climatic or other permanent conditions, and are designed also to facilitate transfers of personnel by eliminating or minimizing the effect on employees of differences in the variables to be encountered in different areas or countries of assignment. The total cost in addition to base salary to maintain a United States expatriate overseas can be as much as 50 percent greater than prevailing base salary at home.

These and other factors making up the overseas "pay package" will be discussed separately throughout this chapter.

BASE PAY

Compensation paid to the United States expatriate employee begins with the base salary. The question often asked is whether the base pay for an overseas position occupied by the employee should be determined by a salary scale separate from the domestic pay structure. The practice among multinational organizations is payment of a salary related to the domestic salary structure for positions of comparable value and responsibility exclusive of any consideration for payment of other environmental allowance and incentives for overseas work. This is commonly referred to as the "domestic equivalent" salary. For purposes of salary administration, a salary range, i.e., minimum and maximum salary, is developed for each position. The related domestic base salary scale, therefore, when adjusted for competitive or other economic reasons, also affects the pay rates for positions of like scope overseas.

Because pay is keyed to the United States domestic structure, a base-pay gap usually exists between the United States expatriate and the local and/or third-country national counterpart. Although this is a source of discontent among other nationals working side by side with the Americans, the principle of "equal pay for equal work" unless coincidental is not valid when you consider that payment of base salary is related to different base-country economic conditions.

FOREIGN SERVICE PREMIUM

The foreign service premium is paid (although there is an increasing trend in the feeling that it is superfluous) to motivate employees to accept overseas assignments and to remain in foreign service. Additional to exposure to new laws and customs and the necessity to conduct business in a foreign language, the premium is also paid because of related cultural changes. It is a pay incentive expressed as a percentage added to the base salary. The foreign service premium may be fixed or variable for each country or geographical area of assignment. In practice some companies grant the same amount of premium to all employees overseas irrespective of area. Other organizations vary the amount by country.

Calculating the foreign service premium on a sliding percentage of salary rather than as a fixed percentage of base salary is a relatively standard practice—e.g., 20 percent of the first $5,000, 15 percent of the next $10,000 and 10 percent of the next $20,000. A ceiling on the amount of foreign service premium to be paid on the base salary is practiced primarily to maintain the salary differential between the base pay plus premium within "reason" without making it difficult for the employee or employer to make the transition to domestic service upon repatriation to the home country.

Many organizations, as previously indicated, combine the hardship allowance with the foreign service premium and thereby establish variable premiums to recognize environmental and other social and political considerations. However, when this allowance is paid separate from the foreign premium and the latter has a maximum salary cutoff—e.g., $30,000 @ 20 percent = $6,000—the same principle should apply to the hardship allowance. See Figure 1, Summary of Compensation Practices, which illustrates practices among major international organizations on types and sizes of foreign service premium paid.

The variation in the size of the foreign service premium as noted in the survey is related to intangible factors existing between countries, ranging from the difficulty of maintaining an American standard of living and a pleasant environment to unpleasant climate, altitude, isolation, exposure to danger, and other like considerations in practice. The premium is not made subject to United States federal, state, or municipal taxes by the employer. Thus it is always maintained at 100 percent.

The foreign premium is normally paid effective on the date of departure from the home country to accept employment with a foreign affiliate. Payment continues uninterrupted, including periods of home leave and other bona fide absences from the area of assignment. It is discontinued upon date of transfer to domestic service.

When employees are transferred between countries or areas having a different foreign service premium, the premium should be changed effective with transfer date. When employees are transferred from a high premium area to a low premium area during the tour of duty, the amount of premium paid during home leave should be calculated by prorating the total home leave in the same proportion as the amount of service spent in each area during the tour of duty. Normally, a lump-sum payment is made in this situation to cover the amount of premium in excess of the rate in effect at the time of home leave.

Employees transferred to a higher premium area should be compensated on the basis of the higher premium in effect at the time the leave is taken.

DIFFERENTIAL COST OF LIVING ALLOWANCE

This allowance is the main equalization factor in the overseas compensation package. It is paid to equalize the difference, if any, in the cost of purchasing goods and services between the country of assignment and the home country. No allowance should be paid in any location where the cost of living is equal to or less than that in the home country. Normally, the official rate of exchange is used to convert the amount of allowance into local currency.

The difference in the cost of living in a particular foreign city is usually determined by employing the services of outside consultants or relying on data submitted

FACTORS	Surveying Co.	1	2	3	4
PART I					
BASE SALARY	Head Office Salary Scale	Head Office Salary Scale	Head Office Salary Scale	Head Office Salary Scale	Head Office Salary Scale
FOREIGN PREMIUM 1. % of Base 2. Paid in Canada / Puerto Rico	1. 20% all areas – $5M maximum 2. Yes – 20% / Yes – 20%	1. 25% all areas – No maximum 2. Not applicable / Not applicable	1. 15% all areas – $3M maximum – $1200 minimum. 2. Not applicable. / Yes – 15%	1. 35% first $18M, 20% next $18M Latin America 30% India 25% Japan 20% Australia 15% Europe – No maximum 2. No / Yes – same as Latin America	1. 25% first $18M – Indonesia, Nigeria 20% first $9M, 15% next $9M – all other areas except 10% first $18M – Bahrain, Lebanon, South Africa, New Zealand, Australia, South Rhodesia, Europe. 2. Not applicable / Not applicable
HARDSHIP (POST) ALLOWANCE 1. Stated locations (Expressed as % of base)	15% Bombay 10% Djakarta 15% Karachi 5% Quito 15% Monrovia 5% Maracaibo 10% Guayaquil 5% Santo Domingo	1.25% Bombay 25% Djakarta 25% Karachi 20% Quito NA Monrovia NA Maracaibo 25% Guayaquil 25% Santo Domingo	1.0% Bombay 25% Djakarta NA Karachi NA Quito 25% Monrovia 15% Maracaibo NA Asuncion 20% Santo Domingo NA Guayaquil	1. No allowance in Maracaibo; other locations not applicable.	1. No
DIFFERENTIAL COST OF LIVING ALLOWANCE 1. Source 2. Applied to Spendable Income 3. Percent of base (Married Employee) considered Spendable Income 4. Negative allowance if index below 100	1. State Department 2. Yes 3. Base % / Base % / Base % $7500 70.0 / $20M 51.3 / $35M 40.0 10M 65.0 / 25M 46.0 / 40M 38.1 15M 60.0 / 30M 42.5 / 45M 36.6 4. No	1. State Department 2. Yes 3. Base % / Base % / Base % $7500 95.0 / $20M 53.0 / $35M 53.0 10M 87.0 / 25M 50.0 / 40M 50.0 15M 70.0 / 30M 50.0 / 45M 50.0 4. No	1. State Department 2. Yes 3. Base % / Base % / Base % $7500 75.0 / $20M 37.5 / $35M 21.4 10M 75.0 / 25M 30.0 / 40M 18.8 15M 50.0 / 30M 25.0 / 45M 16.7 4. No	1. State Department 2. Yes 3. Base % / Base % / Base % $7500 62.2 / $20M 54.4 / $35M 45.8 10M 60.0 / 25M 51.0 / 40M 43.3 15M 58.2 / 30M 48.7 / 45M 41.4 4. Only when index falls below 90.	1. State Department 2. Yes 3. Base % / Base % / Base % $7500 72.0 / $20M 37.0 / $35M 21.1 10M 54.0 / 25M 29.6 / 40M 18.5 15M 46.0 / 30M 24.7 / 45M 16.4 4. No
CHILD ALLOWANCE	Yes – State Department scale – $60–$120 per child	No	Yes – State Department scale – $60–$120 per child.	No	No
HOUSING ALLOWANCE 1. Rent and utilities limit 2. Employee charge	1. Established through field surveys 2. 20% first $5M of Base 15% next $5M Flat – $4465 over $30M	1. Actual rent – no limit 2. According to salary on graduated basis – $1200 ◆ $5M, $200 ◆ $18M and over.	1. State Department or set by senior man in foreign area. 2. 15% of base – $3M maximum	1. Rent line constructed to cover 100% rent of 85% of employees based on State Department data. Utilities and maintenance covered separately. 2. 15% of base up to $12M declining in straight line to 12% at $40M.	1. State Department plus own adjustment. 2. No fixed charge. Employee may be required to pay excess rent and utilities over allowance.
U.S. INCOME TAX 1. Taxes charged 2. Deduction used in determining tax 3. Tax on earned income exceeding exclusion 4. Tax on unearned income 5. Fee for tax consultant service	1. Federal, State, City on base plus cash profit sharing 2. U.S. tax – 10% Base, no maximum; State $1M maximum 3. Reimbursed 4. Not reimbursed 5. Not reimbursed	1. Federal on base. 2. 10% of base – $1M maximum 3. Reimbursed 4. Not reimbursed 5. Not reimbursed	1. Federal on base 2. 10% base – no maximum 3. Reimbursed 4. Not reimbursed 5. Reimbursed – reasonable cost	1. Federal on base 2. 15% up to $15M, 14% up to $25M, 13.5% over $25M 3. Reimbursed 4. Not reimbursed 5. Reimbursed – limit on type of service only.	1. Federal on base. 2. 10% of base – no maximum. 3. Not reimbursed 4. Not reimbursed 5. Not reimbursed
FOREIGN INCOME TAX 1. Tax reimbursement basis 2. Tax on unearned income	1. Total compensation 2. Not reimbursed	1. Total compensation 2. Not reimbursed	1. Total compensation 2. Not reimbursed	1. Total compensation 2. Not reimbursed	1. Total compensation 2. Not reimbursed

	Company 1	Company 2	Company 3	Company 4	Company 5
EDUCATION ALLOWANCE 1. Grades covered 2. Amount reimbursed	1. Through grade 12 2. State Department "At/Away from post" is maximum. If not appropriate establish own maximum. Reimburse up to maximum for those costs provided free under U.S. Public School system.	1. Through grade 12 2. Actual tuition of an accredited school.	1. Through grade 12 2. Reimbursed up to $500 at post. Excess paid by employee.	1. Through grade 12 2. If State Department approved school available, reimburse up to maximum of $2M per child. If not available, will provide up to $2M per child for U.S. education.	1. Through grade 12. 2. At local designated school employee pays first $150. Excess covered cost reimbursed. At nearest designated boarding or home country high school (grades 11 and 12) company pays 75% to maximum reimbursement of $1500.
LOCAL BENEFIT SCHEMES 1. Employee contribution reimbursed 2. Benefit refunded to company	1. Yes 2. Yes	1. Yes 2. Yes	1. Yes 2. Yes	1. Yes. If no benefit received. 2. Yes. If full benefit received, not reimbursed for contribution.	1. Yes - usually. 2. Yes - if reimbursed for contribution.
PRESERVATION OF BASE SALARY AND/OR FOREIGN PREMIUM 1. Base salary offset against negative factors 2. Foreign Premium offset against negative factors	1. No 2. No	1. No 2. No	1. Yes 2. Yes	1. Yes 2. Yes	1. No 2. No
PERQUISITES Provided in addition to allowances	Yes. Club membership, occasionally cars for Senior Management. Periodic Economy Class t/t transportation from some hardship areas for local leave.	Yes. Club membership.	Yes. Club memberships.	No	No formal policy. Club membership, representation allowance provided in some areas on individual basis.
PART II **EXPENSES PAID** 1. For cancellation of lease 2. Prior to departure from U.S. 3. Upon arrival at foreign assignment 4. Upon reassignment to U.S. 5. In connection with housing abroad	1. Yes. Usually 2 months rent. 2. Yes. Normally 1 week to 10 days. Reimbursed difference between normal living costs and hotel expenses. 3. Yes. Normally up to 2 weeks full expenses. Thereafter full hotel rent and difference between living cost in hotel and normal living costs. 4. Yes. Same as #3 above. 5. Yes. Electrical conversions, recutting drapes and rugs, cleaning of home interior, etc., normally up to $1000 actual expenses.	1. Yes 2. Yes. Reimbursed for hotel, meals and laundry. 3. Yes. No maximum time. Hotel, meals and laundry. 4. Yes. 30-90 days. Hotel, meals and laundry. 5. Yes. All expenses paid.	1. Yes 2. Yes. 1 week full expenses. Thereafter charged 15% of base as share of rent and pays 1/3 food cost. 3. Yes. Same as #2 above. 4. Yes. Same as #2 above. 5. Yes. Basically conversion of appliances only. Will protect on sale of minor appliances if loss sustained.	1. Yes 2. Yes. For minimum period. Usually only while movers occupy house. 3. Yes. 30 days full expense less "at home" savings. Management discretion beyond 30 days. 4. Yes. Same as #3 above. 5. Yes. Up to 5% yearly foreign salary (base plus foreign premium).	1. No formal policy. Individual consideration. 2. Yes. Maximum 2 weeks but may allow longer depending on circumstances. 3. Yes. 30 days actual reasonable living expense. 4. Yes. 2 weeks actual reasonable living expenses. 5. Yes. Individual consideration.
TEMPORARY ASSIGNMENT AT HEAD OFFICE 1. Foreign Premium paid for periods 6 months or less 2. Foreign Premium paid for periods over 6 months up to 1 year 3. Expenses	1. Yes 2. Reviewed on individual basis. 3. Yes. Difference between hotel for employee and family and employee charge for N.Y. housing. Per diem for other expenses. Determined on individual basis.	1. Yes 2. No 3. Yes. Rent subsidy.	1. No 2. No 3. Yes. Rent in excess of 15% of base salary plus utilities only.	1. Yes 2. No 3. Yes. Actual costs less "at home" savings.	1. Yes 2. No 3. Yes. Reasonable expenses up to 6 months; over 6 months 1 month base salary plus $100 p.m.

Figure 1. Summary of compensation practices.

FACTORS PART I	5	6	7	8	9
BASE SALARY	Head Office Salary Scale	Head Office Salary Scale	Head Office Salary Scale	Head Office Salary Scale	Head Office Salary Scale
FOREIGN PREMIUM 1. % of Base 2. Paid in Canada / Puerto Rico	1. 25% first $20M, 15% next $10M, 5% next $20M – maximum $7500 – all areas except 20% first $20M, 10% next $10M – Europe – maximum $5M 2. No Yes – same as for "all areas" above.	1. 35% Iran 25% Tehran 20% all other areas. No maximum. 2. No No	1. 20% – Ghana, Thailand, India, Pakistan. 10% – So. Cent. America, South Africa, Australia, Rhodesia, Japan. 5% – Europe. No maximum. 2. No Yes – 10%	1. 20% all areas – No maximum. 2. Yes – 10% Yes – 20%	1. 40% India, Africa – maximum $5M; 25% Asia – maximum $4M; 20% Hong Kong, Central America – maximum $3400; 15% Europe – maximum $2800; 10% U.K. – maximum $2200. 2. No No
HARDSHIP (POST) ALLOWANCE 1. Stated locations (Expressed as % of base)	1. Djakarta – $1500. Other locations not applicable.	1. Considered in foreign premium.	1. Considered in foreign premium.	1. Locations not applicable. Where applicable. State Department post differential.	1. No
DIFFERENTIAL COST OF LIVING ALLOWANCE 1. Source 2. Applied to Spendable Income 3. Percent of base (Married Employee) considered Spendable Income 4. Negative allowance if index below 100	1. State Department most areas. Special pricing at some. 2. Yes 3. Base / % : $7500 : – / $20M : 47.7 / $35M : 37.4 10M : 66.6 / 25M : 42.5 / 40M : 35.9 15M : 54.4 / 30M : 39.4 / 45M : 35.1 4. Yes. To extent it can be offset against positive housing allowance.	1. State Department 2. Yes 3. Base / % : $7500 : 63.8 / $20M : 44.6 / $35M : 37.5 10M : 58.0 / 25M : 40.4 / 40M : 33.2 15M : 50.5 / 30M : 38.6 / 45M : 29.5 4. No.	1. State Department 2. Yes 3. Base / % : $7500 : 60.0 / $20M : 50.0 / $35M : 40.0 10M : 60.0 / 25M : 40.0 / 40M : 40.0 15M : 50.0 / 30M : 40.0 / 45M : 40.0 4. No.	1. State Department 2. Yes 3. Base / % : $7500 : – / $20M : 38.0 / $35M : 21.7 10M : 76.0 / 25M : 30.4 / 40M : 19.0 15M : 50.7 / 30M : 25.3 / 45M : 16.9 4. No.	1. State Department 2. Yes 3. Base / % : $7500 : – / $20M : 52.5 / $35M : 47.1 10M : 66.0 / 25M : 51.6 / 40M : 41.3 15M : 62.0 / 30M : 51.0 / 45M : 36.7 4. No.
CHILD ALLOWANCE	No	No	No	Yes – State Department scale – $60–$120 per child.	Yes – State Department scale – $60–$120 per child with minor adjustments.
HOUSING ALLOWANCE 1. Rent and utilities limit 2. Employee charge	1. Adjusted State Department or own studies. 2. Varies from 16% at $12M to 13% at $56M and above.	1. Employee reimbursed 80% of excess over 15% base to maximum $3600. 2. No charge. See #1 above.	1. State Department adjusted as appropriate. 2. 15% of base for salaries less than $15M; 12% of base for salaries $15M to $25M; 10% of base for salaries $25M and over (no revision in charge subsequent to initial assignment).	1. Employee reimbursed 80% actual rent (ex. utilities) in excess $1200. No limit if rent considered reasonable for location. 2. Employee pays first $1200 plus 20% of excess plus all utilities.	1. State Department costs projected for all salary levels. 2. 15% of base.
U.S. INCOME TAX 1. Taxes charged 2. Deduction used in determining tax 3. Tax on earned income exceeding exclusion 4. Tax on unearned income 5. Fee for tax consultant service	1. Federal on base. 2. 14% of base – no maximum. 3. Reimbursed 4. Not reimbursed 5. Not normally reimbursed.	1. Federal on base. 2. 10% of base – $1M maximum. 3. Not reimbursed 4. Not reimbursed 5. Not reimbursed	1. Federal on base. 2. 10% of base – $1M maximum. 3. Not reimbursed. 4. Not reimbursed. 5. Not reimbursed.	1. Federal on base. 2. 10% of base – $1M maximum. 3. Reimbursed 4. Reimbursed to extent tax on earned and unearned income exceed hypothetical tax on base plus unearned income. 5. Reimbursed – not beyond consultants standard charge.	1. None 2. Not applicable 3. Reimbursed only if U.S. and foreign taxes on total comp. exceed U.S. tax on base plus foreign premium. 4. Not reimbursed 5. Reimbursed $50 one consultation.
FOREIGN INCOME TAX 1. Tax reimbursement basis 2. Tax on unearned income	1. Varies by location. 2. Reimbursed only to extent tax may exceed taxes on unearned income if in U.S. at same base.	1. Total compensation 2. Reimbursed – no limit.	1. Total compensation 2. Not reimbursed	1. Total compensation 2. Reimbursed – same basis U.S. unearned income.	1. Not reimbursed 2. Not reimbursed

	Column 1	Column 2	Column 3	Column 4	Column 5
EDUCATION ALLOWANCE 1. Grades covered 2. Amount reimbursed	1. Through grade 12. 2. 100% of tuition and fees at Co. designated adequate local school. If no adequate school, allowance for "regional" school set at 75% of cost tuition, room and board, and required books or 75% same costs U.S. boarding school, both within maximum based on competitive practice and median U.S. boarding school costs.	1. Through grade 12. 2. Normally, actual expenses.	1. Through grade 12. 2. 80% of cost at post or location nearest where schools are considered adequate.	1. Through grade 12. 2. Reimburse tuition, fees, books, local transportation, insurance, medical costs in excess $50 per child. Room, board, laundry in excess $250 per child where boarding necessary.	1. Through grade 12. 2. Actual costs at work location or third country.
LOCAL BENEFIT SCHEMES 1. Employee contribution reimbursed 2. Benefit refunded to company	1. Too many variables to answer yes or no. 2. Too many variables to answer yes or no.	1. Yes 2. Yes	1. No 2. No	1. Yes 2. Yes	1. Yes 2. No
PRESERVATION OF BASE SALARY AND/OR FOREIGN PREMIUM 1. Base salary offset against negative factors 2. Foreign Premium offset against negative factors	1. No 2. No	1. No 2. No	1. No 2. No	1. No – except for tax equalization. 2. No – except for tax equalization.	1. No 2. No
PERQUISITES Provided in addition to allowances	Yes. Limited to certain employees and as duties require.	Yes. Club membership.	No formal policy. Varies by location. Cars, club memberships to some members of top management.	No. Except cars provided Managing Directors of subsidiaries.	Not generally. Exceptions such as Japan (family club membership).
PART II					
EXPENSES PAID 1. For cancellation of lease 2. Prior to departure from U.S. 3. Upon arrival at foreign assignment 4. Upon reassignment to U.S. 5. In connection with housing abroad	1. Yes 2. Yes. Up to 7 days. Full reasonable hotel/motel expenses. 3. Yes. Up to 30 days full reasonable hotel/motel living expenses. 4. Yes. Same as #3 above. 5. Yes. Flat amount 1 month's overseas base salary. Not accounted for.	1. Yes 2. Yes. 7 days prior to departure. 3. Yes. 30 days. 4. Yes. Same as #2 and #3 above. 5. Yes. $1000 maximum. Adapt electrical equipment, install plumbing, electrical wiring, outlets, curtains, drapes.	1. Yes 2. Yes. Approximately 30 days. All reasonable expenses. 3. Yes. Up to 60 days. All reasonable expenses. 4. Yes. Same as #3 above. 5. Yes. $500 for alteration of rugs and drapes, connection of utilities, legal fees, closing expenditures.	1. Yes 2. Yes. Food, lodging, laundry for reasonable period (individually considered). 3. Yes. Up to 30 days meal, lodging, laundry. Thereafter only lodging, in excess $150 p.m. (30 day period may be extended if furniture not available). 4. Yes. Same as #3 above. 5. Yes. Reasonable cost to reinstall carpets, drapes, conversion and reinstallment of major appliances.	1. Yes 2. Yes. See #3 below. 3. Yes. Total #2 and #3 – 28 days reasonable room, meals, personal service, car rental, laundry. 4. Yes. 56 days. Same expense as #3 above. 5. Yes. Reasonable cost to reinstall carpets, drapes, conversion and reinstallment of major appliances.
TEMPORARY ASSIGNMENT AT HEAD OFFICE 1. Foreign Premium paid for periods 6 months or less 2. Foreign Premium paid for periods over 6 months up to 1 year 3. Expenses	1. Yes. No tax protection on foreign premium. 2. Yes. No tax protection on foreign premium. 3. Yes. If single status elected, expense account. If accompanied, expenses up to 7 days, cost of furnished housing over housing charge, $600 (accountable). Provision made for loss on sale of car abroad (assignment of 6 months or more only) or car rental if retained abroad. Net cost of retained housing abroad, local storage of car and household effects and other unavoidable continuing cost abroad duplicated in U.S.	1. Yes 2. Probably no. 3. Yes. Per diem for employee only.	1. Yes 2. No 3. Yes	1. Consider individually for very short period only. 2. Not applicable 3. Each case considered individually.	1. Not applicable – returns for business trips. 2. Not applicable 3. Not applicable

Figure 1. Summary of compensation practices. (continued)

by United States embassies and consulates abroad from which an index is compiled and issued by the U.S. Department of State through the National Foreign Trade Council. The index issued by the State Department is usually adapted by most organizations to allow for special company situations. The amount of allowance is calculated by applying the index over 100, expressed as a percentage, to spendable income, i.e., that portion of income which is available for the purchase of commodities and services after allowing deductions for housing and utilities, taxes, insurance, savings, and other contributions. For example, an individual earning $25,000 with a spendable income of $11,500, assigned to an area where the cost of living index is 125 versus 100 in the home country, would be paid an allowance of 25 percent of $11,500 or $2,875 per year. The $11,500 spendable income varies with salary level, decreasing as the salary rises (see Figure 2).

Revaluation of a local currency causes an index to increase since fewer monetary units are obtained for the same amount of money than formerly; devaluation causes a lower index since more units are obtained. Allowances also fluctuate because of differences in the cost of living in the area of assignment versus the United States.

Problems with the cost of living index have their greatest impact in those unusual economic areas where problems exist which give rise to rapid or extreme fluctuations in the cost of living. Moreover, increases in the cost of living in a foreign area may not require an adjustment in the allowance if an offsetting increase has occurred in the cost of living in the home country. Should the increase in the cost of living in the home country exceed the increase in the cost of living in the foreign area, a decrease in the allowance is effected.

Figures 3, 4, and 5 illustrate typical situations which affect the cost of living allowance.

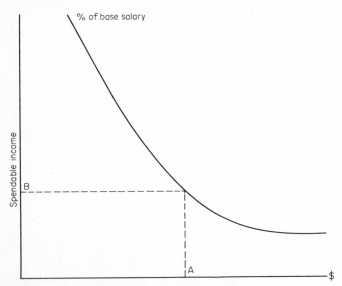

Figure 2. Spendable income as percentage of base salary in home country of overseas employee. The proportion of income for commodities and services varies with income level; hence, the percentage of income that goes for all goods and services is different at each salary level. The portion for goods and services is spendable income and it rises with income, but at a slower rate.

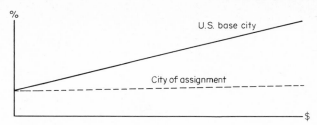

Figure 3.   Living costs in overseas city of assignment lower than United States base city—no allowance paid.

Cost of living allowance is normally paid effective as of the date the employee establishes permanent housing in the area of assignment, and it remains in effect on a continuous basis. Some employers discontinue the allowance during periods of home leave or reduce the allowance proportionately to account for absence during home leave.

SEPARATE MAINTENANCE ALLOWANCE

Separate maintenance allowance is a payment made to employees who must maintain dependents outside the area of residence for reasons beyond the control of the organization. Usually when the payment is made, it is not intended to cover the entire expense of maintaining an employee's family during the period of separation.

Separate maintenance allowance may be granted for reasons such as war, civil commotion, or related hazards which are recognized as sufficient to make it inadvisable or undesirable for the family to reside in the area to which the employee is assigned. Other considerations for payment of separation allowance are lack of family housing, delays in securing visas, medical reasons.

Payment of this allowance is not made at the option of the employee. When effected, payment begins on the date the family departs the area of assignment and is discontinued on the date they depart to rejoin the employee.

BALANCE SHEET APPROACH

This is a method by which the multiple factors of total compensation are broken down into component parts. In this manner the plus and minus factors of the compensation package are combined to ensure that there will be no losses or gains for the expatriate. A savings made by the expatriate in a low cost of living area might be offset by higher taxes in the same foreign location.

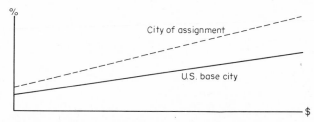

Figure 4.   Living costs in city of assignment higher than United States base city—allowance paid. Also living costs increasing faster than in United States—allowance increased.

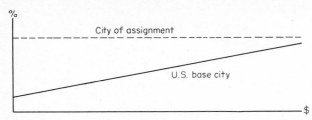

Figure 5. Living costs in United States base city increasing faster than in city of assignment—allowance reduced accordingly.

Cost of living, tax equalization, and housing are most frequently included in the balance sheet approach. Reimbursement for education costs is also included by some employers.

In many countries employees are required to make contributions to local benefit schemes such as social security. In these instances they should be reimbursed for such contributions. In the event that monetary benefits accrue to employees as a result of such socially legislated contributions or that they are in receipt of locally mandated bonuses, allowances, or other payments, administration can be facilitated by deducting equal amounts from that portion of salary paid at the home office.

Effecting plus and minus calculations in the individual components facilitates adjustments to reflect changes in local conditions, transfers between countries, and repatriation. Moreover compensating adjustments avoid "windfalls."

Where rental and tax equalization policies are utilized by an employer, the "windfall" element is eliminated since all employees are assessed hypothetical charges equal to normal home country costs, developed according to income level. Federal taxes, as well as state and municipal taxes, where applicable, are also assessed hypothetically in the same manner. In both instances the employer absorbs the excess costs incurred by the employee.

A typical balance sheet format is illustrated in Figure 6, for a married employee with two children earning a United States base salary of $20,000 per annum.

HOUSING ALLOWANCE

Consideration for housing assistance is significant in relocating personnel overseas to ensure that an employee and his family are established in suitable accommodations. Employers should share in the cost of housing to the extent that the foreign

FIGURE 6. Balance Sheet Approach to Overseas Compensation (for Married Man with Two Children)

1. Gross base salary	$20,000
2. Minus hypothetical United States, federal, and city taxes	4,648
3. Minus United States housing element	3,115
4. Minus other mandated income paid abroad	300
Total	$11,937
5. Plus foreign service premium @ 20% of base salary	$ 4,000
6. Plus hardship allowance @ 15% of base salary	3,000
7. Plus housing differential over United States cost	2,385
8. Plus differential cost of living allowance over United States cost (index 107.5)	1,025
9. Plus foreign tax	1,000
Total net compensation	$23,347

costs exceed those rental costs the employee would be expected to pay in the home country based on family size and income level. Housing assistance paid by the employer then is designed to offset the higher actual rental costs, including utilities, in the foreign location where the costs for like housing exceed those prevailing in the home country. Normal housing costs may be determined by establishing a sliding percentage scale or by expressing the normal United States cost as a flat percent of salary. In the case of flat percentage, the most common figure is 15 percent for a married individual and 10 percent for a single person. Other employers state the cost of housing for single employees as 75 percent of the married employees cost. As concerns the use of sliding percentage, the figures vary. Typical policies (also see Figure 1) used by some organizations are indicated below:

1. 15 percent of base to $12,000 declining in straight line to 12 percent at $40,000

2. 16 percent of $12,000 to 13 percent at $36,000 and above

3. 20 percent of first $5,000, 15 percent of next $6,000, 13 percent next $19,000

Figure 7 illustrates median housing charges of one company at stated salary levels using fixed and sliding percentages compared to other companies. In this illustration rental charges from $30,000 and above levels off.

Figure 8 illustrates that at the same income levels the amount spent for housing decreases in terms of percentage of salary.

To simplify administration, the employer should pay the total rental cost locally in the area of assignment. The employee's share for rent based on a formula or other company policy is then subtracted from his salary paid at corporate headquarters.

Foreign housing costs are best determined by the resident management in the area after consultation with landlords, realty, and other international employing

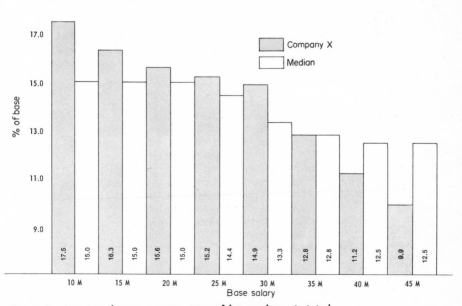

Figure 7. Housing charge as percentage of base salary at stated salary levels.

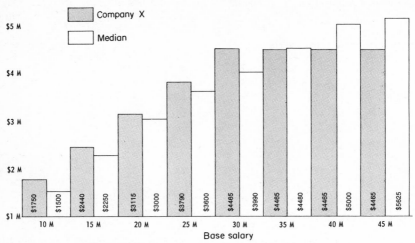

Figure 8.   Housing charge in dollar amounts at stated salary levels.

organizations.   The Quarters Allowance Guide published by the Allowances Division of the U.S. Department of State is another source of reference.

Whenever an employee incurs rental costs less than his normal United States costs the employer should subtract or charge the lesser of the two figures; e.g., if the actual rental cost in the area of assignment is $3,000 per annum and company policy requires an assessment of $3,600, the employee should not be penalized for paying the lower rent while abroad.   His charge, therefore, should not exceed $3,000.

Reimbursement for housing costs continues during absences on home leave, during vacation taken in or within the area of assignment and for other valid absences from the area.

UNFURNISHED QUARTERS

Employees having no basic furnishings might have to rent furniture.   This usually applies to employees who have been transferred from an area where furnished housing had been provided by the employer or where the employee has been specifically requested to go to an area without major household effects.

Reimbursement for rental of necessary furniture in amounts not in excess of a certain percentage of the actual rental cost is widely practiced.   Many employers allow up to 25 percent of the actual rental cost for this purpose.   Arrangements can also be made with furniture stores to rent furniture with an option to buy with the rental cost applying toward the purchase price.

COMPANY LEASED OR OWNERSHIP OF HOMES

Rental assessments should be levied based on community practices for company provided owned or leased housing.   Companies owning homes should charge employees an amount equal to the charge under their rental equalization policy as it relates to the income level of the employee.

PURCHASE OF HOMES

Purchase of homes by expatriates except for top overseas management should be discouraged. Financial arrangements are involved and complex. Also home ownership tends to immobilize the expatriate. Employees purchasing their own home, however, should be considered for some housing allowance assistance on the assumption that home ownership includes maintenance and other costs sometimes approximating rental costs.

SALARY SPLIT

Salary splitting is a practice whereby a specified portion of the expatriate's salary is paid in the country of current employment. The balance is paid in another country usually where the corporate headquarters are located. In some countries, it may be inadvisable to have employees accept a portion of their salary locally. Conversely, legal requirements in some areas specify stipulated percentages of salary to be drawn locally. In any case, employees are indemnified should nontransferable balances accrue related to portions of salary paid locally.

A portion of the expatriate's salary must be disbursed in the home country because employees maintain equity in their home country and require currency to make payments for mortgage, savings, tax, insurance, and even participation in company benefits plans. Foreign exchange controls and devaluation of currency also make it practical to have portions of pay received outside the country of assignment. Certain tax benefits might also be derived by both the expatriate and the employer. Some considerations involved in the split payment of salary to expatriate personnel are discussed below.

A. Total Salary Paid in Foreign Currency

Payment of entire salary could, depending on country of assignment and prevailing tax laws, generate more tax liability for the employee versus United States tax. For employers utilizing a tax equalization policy, payment of salary in local currency would, of course, result in a higher foreign tax reimbursement to the employee as opposed to tax liability incurred if some or all of the total compensation were paid outside the country of assignment.

B. Total Salary Paid in United States Dollars

This may not be entirely feasible because of many considerations attendant to transfer of salary charges, including the possibility of not being able to take a deduction on the corporate tax return and the unavailability of home country dollar currency to maintain personal obligations.

C. Salary Paid Partly in United States in Dollars and Partly in Foreign Currency

Of the three methods discussed, this type is perhaps the most convenient and popular approach practiced since it allows for a proportional amount of money to be paid in the country of assignment as well as in the home country. This does not necessarily mean that tax advantages will result because of the lower income declared locally. In many countries, where world-wide income must be declared, for instance, no tax benefit accrues to either the employer or the employee.

Another consideration is that the portion of salary paid locally can be kept in line with salaries paid to local employees.

In the determination of split compensation, it is difficult to establish any "pay formula" on the ratio of dollars to local currency. Such situations should be determined based on the requirements of individual employees and employers and their affiliates and subsidiaries abroad and establish whatever is deemed appropriate and feasible under given situations. In any event, tax equalization, if practiced, would limit employee tax liability to the equivalent of federal, state, city, or municipal tax if it were part of the employer's policy.

INCOME TAXES

All United States citizens residing abroad must file federal income tax returns and report income earned outside the United States notwithstanding the fact that income may be exempt from tax because of bona fide residence or physical presence without residence status in a foreign country or countries for at least 510 days during a continuous eighteen-month period.

Prevailing practice among international employers reveals that expatriates are reimbursed for payment of foreign taxes to the extent they exceed the taxes they would have been subject to pay on the base salary in the home country. The intent of the tax policy is to reimburse employees in the amount that their income tax on total remuneration, consisting of salary inclusive of foreign service premium and allowances, exceeds the equivalent tax on base salary in the home country.

The practice among international employers requires expatriates to pay income taxes on total remuneration in compliance with applicable tax laws and regulations. Therefore, it is the personal responsibility of each employee to determine his status under the tax laws and regulations and to fulfill all obligations. Employers should keep employees informed concerning applicable tax regulations. Employers have two options: the employee pays the tax and is reimbursed by the employer; or, the employer subtracts a hypothetical income tax from base salary and then pays the foreign tax due.

The most advantageous method of applying tax policies to minimize pyramiding of tax on tax is best determined and accomplished consistent with local tax laws and regulations.

The decision to include or exclude state or other municipal taxes when calculating the hypothetical tax is dependent on the location of the home country office and also on maintaining tax equity between the overseas and domestic employee.

Current foreign resident exclusion for tax purposes is $20,000 or $25,000 on total remuneration depending on foreign residency status of under or over three years respectively. Earned income as opposed to unearned income (non-employment-derived) exceeding the residency exclusion is subject to reimbursement for the portion of tax on the amount of salary exceeding the exclusion attributable to foreign residency.

Reimbursement for taxes on unearned income or for tax consultant services is normally not made since like consideration is not afforded to home country staff. However, complete exclusion is not suggested and should be considered whenever appropriate.

EDUCATION ALLOWANCE

This is a non-pay-related allowance since it represents an occasional or one-time payment as distinguished from the continuing other pay-related allowance differentials.

The purpose of the education assistance allowance is to help expatriate employees in providing their children with elementary and high school or preparatory school education generally comparable to that normally available in their home country.

Expatriate staff required to send their children to private primary including kindergarten and secondary schools due to lack of adequate free schooling at the area of assignment should be assisted in the payment for educational expenses for their children. Moreover, in the absence of adequate private schooling, an employee should be allowed to send his child to another area with reimbursement provided up to designated maximum amounts. The decision about what is adequate should be considered in the light of acceptance at higher grade levels in the home country.

Financial assistance covers tuition, room and board, books, uniforms, and laboratory equipment. Transportation charges are also reimbursed. Reimbursement for schooling costs is usually limited, through the twelfth grade. Additionally, schooling policies should also consider economy transportation to either the parent or the child for reunions, including unmarried dependent children attending college. Such transportation should be additional to and not in lieu of normal home leave travel entitlement.

Guides for schooling costs are developed by the employer or may be obtained from other private sources or the U.S. Department of State.

Reimbursement for education expenses is usually claimed by the employee by submitting expense reports supported by receipts from the school and/or such places as a child may be boarded, if other than at school. Normally, reimbursement is made in the currency of the country in which the employee is assigned.

HOME LEAVE

Employees residing and working abroad accrue vacation or leave time designed to give them a period of rest and relaxation away from the job which is taken upon completion of the tour. Leave time accrued may range from one to three months depending on length of tour, which may run anywhere from one to two years, and area of assignment.

Below is the formula used by one employer in calculating home leave using the following basic factors:

D = number of days actually served in the area

730 = number of days in twenty-four-month normal tour

72 = number of days of home leave earned for a twenty-four-month period in an area with three days per month accrual rate

$\frac{D}{730} \times 72$ = accrued home leave

Home leave accrual commences with the employee's arrival date in the area of assignment and continues until the employee departs from the area of assignment.

Reimbursement for overseas housing costs is continued assuming the employee is returning to foreign service, as is continued payment of foreign service premium and other appropriate allowances.

HOME LEAVE TRAVEL ALLOWANCES

Transportation costs and related expenses for an expatriate and accompanying family members are paid by the employer within certain stipulated provisions relating to approved routes and class of travel. The latter considerations usually cover the mode and route of travel as authorized by the company, e.g., tourist class via the most direct air route. Employees electing other official means of travel are reimbursed up to an amount equal to tourist travel by most direct air route.

LIVING EXPENSES IN TRANSIT

These expenses are paid by employers for the employee and family members for reasonable periods prior to departure after arrival in the area and during any time spent at headquarters which may range upwards of several weeks. Other employers grant fixed per diem living allowances to take care of transit situations, with amounts stipulated for the employee, wife, and accompanying family members.

THIRD-COUNTRY NATIONAL

The TCN, by definition, is an expatriate national of another country employed by a United States firm who resides and works in a country other than his own with a United States expatriate and local national. A German employed by a United States firm in Italy would be a TCN. In another sense, this type of expatriate, meaning the TCN, is also referred to as an "internationalist" or "globalist." This is a term used to define a category of employees (including United States expatriates) who are paid on an equal basis, irrespective of country of origin, for like or similar work performed. They receive identical allowances, benefits, and perquisites, and in some instances, pensions, although the latter are normally related to the TCN's country of origin since it is more than likely that is where his retirement will take place.

The designation of a TCN and the manner of compensating this type of expatriate really depend on what is best for the employer or employee in terms of maximizing manpower utilization and thus broadening availability of personnel opportunities for a given organization in its overseas network of operations. The basic considerations and alternatives involved are:

1. United States terms—same as those for United States expatriates except perhaps for pension.

2. Host country terms—host country salary, if higher, with cash premium inducement, tax protection, and differentials for costs exceeding home country expenses for living and housing plus education.

3. Home country—same as host country approach except base pay related to home country and not host country even though latter scale is higher.

4. Combinations of any of the above.

Most employers utilize approaches 2 and 3 listed above. However, a growing trend toward compensating this type of employee in a manner equal to the United States expatriate is making its presence felt. Obviously, this creates higher costs; however, the compensation gap between the TCN and the United States expatriate in developed and underdeveloped parts of the world where managerial skills are scarce are beginning to parallel and even exceed United States salary levels.

Whenever the TCN cannot be maintained in the pension program of his country of origin, guarantees should be established to ensure that he will accrue pension benefits at least equal to those he would have earned in his home country. Consideration pertaining to "split salary" applies equally to the third-country national.

LOCAL NATIONAL

This is an employee residing and working in his country of citizenship. Because of the great demand for quality management talent, particularly in the underdeveloped countries, international organizations are likely to offer this type of individual a higher salary than the local business organization. The foreign national is paid a salary commensurate with the prevailing local market requirements. However, because salary practices in some countries other than the United States where taxes are higher resort to perquisites and other forms of noncash compensation, salary differences are equalized for local nationals by the purchase of club memberships, automobiles, housing, and deferred compensation (usually diverted into pension schemes). Employers will also resort to "split payments" for local nationals under the same principles discussed previously.

REFERENCES

Caltex Petroleum Corp., Home Office, New York, N.Y.
First National City Bank, Home Office, New York, N.Y.
Mobil Oil, Inc., Home Office, New York, N.Y.
National Foreign Trade Council, Inc., 10 Rockefeller Plaza, New York, N.Y. 10020.
National Industrial Conference Board, Inc., 845 Third Avenue, New York, N.Y. 10022.
Organization Resources Counselors, Inc., 1270 Avenue of the Americas, New York, N.Y. 10020.
Standard Oil Company of New Jersey, Home Office, New York, N.Y.
U.S. Department of State, Washington, D.C.

chapter 58

Employee Benefits
and Special Policies

LOUIS M. ELLISON   *Director of Employee Relations, United Utilities, Inc.,*
Kansas City, Kansas

Company policy must be defined prior to adopting an employee benefit program
for expatriates. Decisions about (1) centralization or decentralization of the plan,
(2) installing one international plan or separate plans in each country, (3) repro-
ducing United States benefits at foreign operations, (4) eligibility requirements
for coverage, and (5) selection of a funding method, will be determined by this
policy. After company policy is approved, the basic parameters of the plan should
be developed to meet certain objectives, such as (1) being competitive on costs, (2)
meeting operating needs, (3) ensuring equitable treatment, (4) promoting employee
understanding, (5) simplifying administration, (6) attracting and holding high-
caliber employees, and (7) meeting requirements of varied income levels. It is
the general practice that expatriates continue to participate in the benefit programs (specifically pensions and group insurance) sponsored by their United States
employers.

DOMESTIC PENSION PLAN

The pension plan of a United States company may be designed to provide for leaves
of absence for foreign assignment in order to preserve the retirement benefits of
expatriates. For the purpose of accruing retirement benefits on behalf of expatriates, the pension plan should recognize base salary only (see Figure 1). The
exception to this rule is the expatriate whose assignment overseas will last for
the greater part of his career with the company. In this situation, base salary plus
expatriation premium may be used.

  If a pension plan does not accommodate leaves of absence for foreign assignment

Figure 1.   The "leave of absence" provision in the IMC salaried pension plan permitting temporary assignments to subsidiaries.

Leave of Absence: A participant's absence from active employment by reason of leave of absence granted by his Employer because of disability, military service, *temporary assignment to a subsidiary corporation,* attendance at a school or training program at the request of his Employer, government service in a civilian capacity, jury duty, lay-off, or personal hardship, pursuant to a policy of his Employer uniformly applied in all similar circumstances.   A leave of absence shall not be deemed to interrupt the participant's period of employment, and, to the extent such absence does not exceed three years, shall be treated as a period of service, provided he returns to active employment with his Employer within the time specified in his leave or, if not specified therein, within the time hereinabove prescribed, his service shall be considered terminated as of the date on which his leave began.   If the participant is not compensated by his Employer during any such absence, his salary during such absence shall be deemed to be the same as immediately prior to such absence.

The participant's absence from service because of compulsory engagement in military service shall be considered a leave of absence granted by his Employer and notwithstanding any provision of the first paragraph of this section shall not terminate his service if he returns to active employment with an Employer within thirty days following the period of time during which he has reemployment rights under any applicable federal law.

---

or limit the length of such leaves, any loss of benefits may be replaced through an insured annuity.   However, an annuity under these circumstances need not be purchased until such time as the employee terminates employment or retires and is entitled to receive benefits from the pension program.   Extending coverage under the parent company's qualified pension plan to expatriates will assure (1) accrual of retirement benefits that are not interrupted; (2) security of benefits in the employee's mind; (3) no adjustment, up or down, in the level of benefits when an employee is placed on a foreign assignment; (4) elimination of the purchase of "makeup" annuities; (5) that costs are not affected, and (6) that at retirement, the employee is not faced with unusual or extraordinary tax problems.   Administration and record keeping, resulting when expatriates are retained in the parent company's pension plan, are not substantially affected.   Transfers between foreign subsidiaries and to different countries do not affect the employees' status in the plan.

LEGAL CONSIDERATIONS RELATIVE TO INTERNATIONAL PENSION PLANS

In designing an international retirement plan for expatriates, the Revenue Act of 1964 (Sections 406 and 407) must be considered.   Prior to installing or even designing a retirement plan for expatriates, it is advisable to seek the aid of tax and pension plan experts.   Actuarial firms can provide the legal, tax, and actuarial expertise required in developing a pension plan.

The expatriate's social security participation should continue through the period of foreign service, provided the parent company has entered into an agreement known as the "3121 Agreement," which ensures coverage to all United States citizens working abroad.   In the process of hiring an expatriate or assigning overseas service, the employee's citizenship should be ascertained to avoid the danger of future social security claims from employees who do not contribute (see Figure 2).

FUNDING PENSION PLANS

An international plan for expatriates can be funded or unfunded.   A *funded plan* offers the following advantages:

1. Costs to provide pensions are met during the active employment years of participants.

2. Pension benefits are more secure, as viewed by employees.

3. Investment income meets some of the cost.

4. Costs can be equitably allocated between foreign subsidiaries.

In the event that the future of foreign operations is uncertain, or that the number of expatriates is small, an *unfunded* international pension plan would meet the objectives of providing a retirement program. It would have the following advantages:

1. Flexibility; changing to a funded plan is possible.

2. The level of benefits can be altered without restriction.

3. There are no monetary exchange control restrictions.

4. Cash for funding is retained by the company, and will earn a yield equivalent to the marginal return on invested capital.

It is important to keep in mind that unfunded plans cannot handle employee contributions, do not accommodate cost accruals and allocations, and provide no guarantee for pension payments.

FOREIGN SOCIAL SECURITY

In almost all foreign countries, expatriates, nationals, and employers contribute to the social security scheme of that particular country. However, keep in mind that the expatriate will generally never qualify for foreign benefits—and this eliminates in most instances any dual benefits that could be forthcoming. Therefore, any required contributions by an expatriate to a foreign government program should be reimbursed as part of an income tax adjustment. When overseas income taxes and other required taxes are in excess of what the expatriate would pay in the United States, based on comparable income, he may be reimbursed for the taxes paid over comparable United States taxes.

GROUP INSURANCE—HOSPITAL, SURGICAL, AND MAJOR MEDICAL

Unless prohibited by law or local custom, the expatriate and his family should continue as participants in the United States company's group plan at the level commensurate with earnings or position comparable to his counterpart in the United States, or in the foreign country assigned, whichever would provide the higher coverage. In situations where medical coverage is provided to all residents

Figure 2.   The definition of a "participant" in the IMC salaried pension plan that provides coverage to employees on leave to foreign companies.

Participant: Any salaried employee of an Employer who was a participant in the old plan on December 31, 1969 and any other salaried employee of the Company or any other Employer named in Section 1.4, who as of any January 1 subsequent to 1969 shall have completed three years of service, except those age 60 or older on date of hire. *Any person employed by a foreign corporation shall be deemed to be an employee of the Company* during his period of employment by such foreign corporation if (i) not less than 20% of the voting stock of such foreign corporation is owned by the Company; (ii) the Company has entered into an Agreement under Section 3121 (1) of the Internal Revenue Code which applies to such foreign corporation; (iii) the employee is a citizen of the United States; (iv) contributions under a funded plan of deferred compensation are not provided by any other person with respect to the remuneration paid to such person by such foreign corporation.

under government programs, the domestic plan should provide supplemental coverage so that total benefits are at least equal to those of the parent company.

Coverage against occupational illness or injury is extended by most foreign governments to all residents employed in the country. In many instances, foreign coverage is more liberal. Where it is deficient, some companies will provide coverage for occupational illness or injury equal to that provided in the expatriate's home state or state of residence just prior to his overseas assignment.

DISABILITY INCOME BENEFITS

Short-term disability income benefits, whether occupational or nonoccupational, are most generally identical to domestic plans. This type of benefit is commonly self-insured and based on years of service. A guideline to follow in the case of occupational disabilities is to provide disability income of half to full pay for up to six months.

To provide protection against loss of income resulting from disabilities in excess of six months, whether occupational or nonoccupational, many companies extend coverage to expatriates under their domestically insured long-term disability plans. These plans generally provide disability benefits of 50 to 60 percent of base salary, integrated with social security and disability programs sponsored by the employer, with benefits beginning after six months and continuing to age 65.

LIFE, ACCIDENTAL DEATH, AND DEPENDENT COVERAGE

Expatriates should be continued as participants in the company's plans of group term life insurance, accidental death and dismemberment, and business travel (see Figure 3). Special attention should be given to insurance contracts, to make sure that the area of assignment for expatriates is not excluded from coverage.

SPECIAL BENEFIT PLANS

Special programs of coverage such as personal accident or dependent group life, sponsored by the company whether contributory or not, can continue to cover expatriates. Continued participation in the company's benefit program while on foreign assignment is common and provides flexibility in reassignment.

Figure 3.   Two excerpts from group insurance contracts (providing coverages for accidental death and dismemberment) illustrating provisions for (a) **worldwide coverage for employees and** (b) **dependent coverage while traveling to and from assignments outside the United States.**

With respect to Coverage C:
Insurance provided under this coverage includes riding as a passenger or as a pilot or crew member in, including boarding or alighting from, any aircraft being used for the transportation of passengers.

TERRITORIAL LIMITS
Worldwide

CLASS VI —Each lawful spouse of an Insured Employee transferred to or from the continental limits of the United States is insured hereunder as Class VI Insured Persons.

CLASS VII—Each dependent child of an Insured Employee transferred to or from the continental limits of the United States is insured hereunder as a Class VII Insured Person.

ARRANGING EXPATRIATES COVERAGE

Trusted retirement plans can be designed within the parameters of the Internal Revenue Service regulations to accommodate leaves of absence to foreign assignments. Your legal department or actuary represents the best source of information on this subject. Insured retirement plans can be designed or amended to include expatriates, but the insurance carrier underwriting the plan must approve. Group insurance plans in the United States are not always flexible enough to provide benefits for expatriates. Here, too, check with the insurance carrier and have the contract amended to provide coverage for employees transferred to a foreign country. In the case of self-administered or self-insured health plans where benefits are paid by the employer, arrangements can be made with the expatriate during the indoctrination period, just prior to overseas assignment, to pay health claims directly to his United States bank account.

HOW DOES THE EMPLOYEE PAY FOR BENEFITS WHILE OVERSEAS?

Where the employer maintains contributory benefit plans, the same schedule should apply to expatriates as to domestic participants. Expatriates should maintain a United States checking account and make their contributions by checks written on this account. Contributions could be sent on a quarterly or semiannual basis to the personnel department. Changes in the level of contributions should be communicated to expatriates by one department assigned this responsibility.

HOME LEAVE POLICIES FOR EXPATRIATES

The purpose of home leave is to provide overseas service employees the opportunity to visit the United States at periodic intervals for vacations, as well as to provide the opportunity for consultation and reorientation in company policies and practices.

The frequency of home leaves and their length is company policy. The trend today is to grant such a leave at least once every twenty-four months for the expatriate and his dependents. The home leave would be considered part of the annual accrued vacation time, and if leaves are scheduled every twenty-four months, regularly accrued vacations in the year in between would be based on the vacation policy of the United States company. Pay in lieu of home leave or local vacations is not recommended. Home leave can be thirty to forty calendar days, excluding travel time. A more elaborate schedule could be devised, depending upon the country in which the employee is assigned. For example:

A schedule for expatriates assigned in the United Kingdom, France, Switzerland, Puerto Rico, and Mexico would generate 1½ calendar days for each continuous calendar month of assignment in that country.

For expatriates assigned to countries such as Africa and India, two calendar leave days for each calendar month of overseas assignment could accrue for their home leave.

Additional days of home leave could be added based on years of continuous employment with the United States company.

Home leave includes round-trip transportation, provided by the company, to the home office of the United States company. Air travel should be on economy tourist jet, via the most direct route, unless otherwise altered by a corporate officer. Voluntary stopovers should be considered as leave time. The time spent on company business during the course of a home leave visit should be added to the total home leave. For each day the employee is required to conduct company business he and his family should be reimbursed for all out-of-pocket expenses. During home leave the employee's compensation should consist of base salary. Where a housing allowance is granted and the employee continues to incur the expense of an overseas residence, this allowance should continue during the home leave. All overseas service· allowances, except housing allowances where permitted, should be discontinued at the time of departure from the overseas location and not resumed until the employee returns to the overseas location.

VACATIONS AND HOLIDAYS

Expatriates should be covered by their normal company vacation policy. This vacation is granted during the years they do not exercise their home leave privileges.

Expatriates should observe legal holidays which are traditionally observed by Americans in that locality, either by law or custom.

EMERGENCY OR SICK LEAVE

Emergency leave is generally granted to the expatriate in the event of serious illness or dealth in the immediate family. It is advised that such circumstances be reviewed on an individual basis and the leave approved by both the United States company and the foreign subsidiary.

EDUCATIONAL ALLOWANCE FOR DEPENDENT CHILDREN, GRADES 1 TO 12

Expatriates may be reimbursed for tuition and reasonable transportation costs for the education of their dependent children when available public schools do not provide the education curriculum and service which meets the U.S. State Department's test of adequacy; i.e., can the child, upon completion of an elementary grade or high school semester in the overseas school, enter the next highest grade or semester in the United States? The employee should be reimbursed for the actual cost of room, board, travel, and tuition for each dependent child attending primary or secondary schools in the country of assignment. Where all schools in the country of assignment are inadequate by State Department standards, employees with children who remain in the United States for their education and who are eligible to attend grades 1 through 12 should be reimbursed in accordance with a definite schedule. A typical schedule follows:

Expatriate employees, with children attending grades 1 through 12 in the United States, will be reimbursed for 75 percent of the direct costs, which include registration fees, tuition, textbooks, etc., up to a maximum of $650 per year, per child.

Such children could also be provided one annual round trip from the area of school attendance to the location of the employee's assignment by economy tourist jet, for the purpose of visiting the parents. During the years the employee enjoys home leave, transportation of children attending United States schools is not generally provided.

EDUCATIONAL ALLOWANCE FOR DEPENDENT CHILDREN IN COLLEGE

When an expatriate has one or more children attending a college or university in the United States, the employee could be reimbursed for one direct round trip annually, per student, to the assigned overseas location at economy tourist jet passage. The years the employee enjoys home leave, such transportation of United States college students is not generally provided.

The expatriate could also be reimbursed for the amount of tuition incurred in excess of the tuition normally paid by residents of his home state, i.e., the state in which the expatriate and his family resided prior to acceptance of the overseas assignment. This differential is not generally applied for students attending a state university outside their prior state of residence, or for a private college or university—including all other educational institutions of the college or university level, outside the United States.

BOARDING SCHOOLS OVERSEAS

Excellent information regarding the schools suitable for American children can be obtained from the U.S. State Department, Overseas Schools Advisory Council. A good source of information pertaining to elementary and secondary schools, including costs, in Europe, Africa, the Middle East, and part of the Far East is the International Schools Service, 392 Fifth Avenue, New York, N.Y. 10022. Information about schools in Latin America can be obtained from the Inter-American School Service, American Council of Education, 1785 Massachusetts Avenue, N.W., Washington, D.C. 20036.

RELOCATION EXPENSES

The United States company usually pays for the moving of household goods, which includes packing, shipping, insurance, and other related factors (with no weight limitations), but should exclude automobiles or other unusual or bulk items. When it is deemed advisable not to ship household goods to an overseas location, the expatriate may be reimbursed for the actual cost of packing, shipping, and storage in the United States, for the duration of the foreign assignment. If the expatriate elects to sell his household goods before reporting to his foreign assignment, the company could reimburse him in an amount equal to the estimated cost of packing and shipping, including storage, up to a maximum of three years. Some companies provide each employee assigned overseas with a lump-sum payment to assist in defraying the supplemental cost normally incurred in moving household goods to a new location, such as appliance conversion, telephone installation, alterations in draperies, carpeting, and other miscellaneous moving costs. As an example, the allowance could be 25 percent of base monthly salary with a minimum of $300 for an expatriate without dependents, and 50 percent of base monthly salary with a minimum of $600 for an expatriate with one or more dependents.

DISPOSAL OF UNITED STATES HOUSING

If the expatriate chooses to rent his home during the period of overseas assignment, he should be responsible for all transactions related to the house rental. If the employee chooses to sell his home, the company may then apply the same policies in this instance as it does for employees transferred within the United States. Exceptions to the housing disposal policy should be approved at the corporate level.

BIBLIOGRAPHY

American Management Association: *Europe*, vol. 1, 1967, and *Selected Countries of the World*, vol. 2, 1968, in *Sourcebook on International Insurance and Employee Benefit Management*, New York.

Greene, Mark A.: "International Levels of Employee Benefits," *Journal of Risk and Insurance*, March, 1968, pp. 1–15.

Industrial Relations Counselors Service, Inc.: *Personnel Practices and Compensation in Overseas Operations,* New York, 1967.

National Foreign Trade Council, Inc.: *Foreign Service Personnel Compensation,* New York.

O'Meara, J. Roger: "Relocation Allowances for Employees Transferred Overseas," *The Conference Board Record,* pp. 39-44, April, 1969.

Organization Resources Counselors, Inc.: *Personnel Policies and Compensation in Overseas Operations,* New York, 1970.

U.S. Internal Revenue Service: *Tax Guide for U.S. Citizens Abroad,* Washington, D.C., annual.

U.S. Social Security Administration: *Social Security Programs throughout the World,* U.S. Government Printing Office, Washington, D.C., 1967.

Business Insurance, Crain Communication, Inc., Chicago, Ill.

Part 13

Acquisitions and Mergers

chapter 59

General Personnel Considerations

CHARLES H. FROST   *Vice President—Employee Relations, USLIFE Corporation, New York, New York*

In considering the people part of acquisitions and mergers, one should first recognize that there are at least four different ways to view the matter:

1. The view of the company being acquired
2. The view of the company doing the acquiring (or the company that thinks or says it is doing the acquiring)
3. The sale (or spin off) of a part of a company which requires special separate considerations from the view of the acquiring company
4. The special and separate considerations from the view of the company that is selling one part of its operation

There are also many sub-parts within each of the above. The thrust of this chapter is based on general personnel considerations of the acquiring company.

Just how much weight do personnel factors carry in an acquisition? Of perhaps greater significance is the question, "How much weight *should* they carry?" Why is there a continuing and increasing concern about personnel considerations when one company acquires another? How many acquisitions have failed, and how many of these failures are due to the improper meshing of the human element? Finally, just how often has this human element been the difference between the success or failure of an acquisition?

For the purpose of discussion one should accept the premise that to buy a business is to buy people. Assuming this, how does this blending and complementing of the human element before, during, and after the acquisition result in the difference between profit and loss, success and failure, growth and stagnation? Further, if we accept the view "that you never really know a person until you have lived with him," we must recognize that this is most certainly true in an acquisition situation. There is also the matter of the pragmatic acceptance of change. No matter how one initially faces the situation, there is *always a change* when one organization is acquired by another. Circumstances will indeed be different after the acquisition. Take, for example, the instance of the president of a company which has been acquired who tells his people that no matter what the buyers say, things will be different after the merger—a big company (in this case, the buyer) must have different administrative procedures—otherwise there would be turmoil. When the buying company says that the operation will be separate and autonomous, just as it had been before, it is just impossible. The acquired unit must tune in to the parent and live according to its rules.

Here is what one author says about change[1]:

> A common representation made during negotiations for the acquisition of a company is, "There will be no changes in your policies and programs. You will continue to operate exactly as you did before. The only difference is that we, rather than others, will own the stock in your enterprise." Unfortunately such a representation is not true. It cannot be true. Even the least amount of financial control is a change, and the eventual changes may range from minimum financial control to complete overhaul and reorganization of the acquired operations. Owners and managers considering the sale of their enterprises to others must realize that this is an inevitable result of the transfer of ownership.
>
> The representation of continuing and unimpaired independent operations was described by one acquiring president as "being in the category of substantial honesty. You cannot be completely honest in the negotiations because if you are, nobody will ever sell to you. The best you can do is to be substantially honest and then rely upon faith and wisdom in administering changes to make the acquisition successful, both for the acquirer and for the acquired."

We should recognize that people are often the only variable between the success and failure of an acquisition. We should also recognize that there are probably fewer absolutes for personnel administration than in any other areas of operating a business. In this chapter we will try to cover some of the many personnel problems which occur when one company acquires another.

SPECIFIC CONSIDERATIONS

Consideration of the following questions should enable the personnel administrator to better evaluate the problem:

1. What jobs will be involved, and who are the people who will be performing them?
2. Will there be centralized control of the unit, or will it be decentralized?
3. What is the community environment?
4. What is the industrial environment?
5. Is there a principal personality in the company being acquired?

The foregoing questions indicate the need for realistic evaluation of the human factors long before making the decision to acquire. The real goal here seems to be: (1) obtaining the facts, (2) recognizing these facts for what they really are, and (3) evaluating such facts in a meaningful manner.

There are also many important considerations in the compensation area: What is the acquired company's compensation philosophy and policy? Are employees at various levels receiving high, low, or middle-of-the-road pay? What is the method of compensation? Are the compensation pieces the same in the company being acquired as they are in the acquiring organization? Does the company grant a higher level of noncash compensation and a lower level cash compensation than the acquiring company? What is (as best can be determined) the absolute level of compensation? What is the proper posture if the total cost of the compensation

---

[1] Myles L. Mace and George G. Montgomery, Jr., *Management Problems of Corporate Acquisitions,* Division of Research, Harvard Business School, Boston, 1962, pp. 258–259.

package is about the same as the acquiring company, but the direct dollar effect on the employee does not reflect the total program's value to all the employees? What are the costs of other benefits, such as company cars, expense accounts, and club memberships? How much of an unfunded pension liability is there? Is the group life insurance experience rated? (*Note:* The technical details and impact of employee benefits are covered in another chapter. They are mentioned here since they are a part, and an important part, of the total compensation package.) How does the acquired company approach control of wages and salaries? How are wages and salaries administered? Are the controls and administrative systems of the two organizations compatible? Will changes be necessary? How much, how many, and when should they be made?

Finally, the multitude of labor relations considerations must be given an early and thorough evaluation and analysis. What is the union relations history? What unions represent the employees? How many strikes? What is the grievance and arbitration caseload? Is the company a pattern setter or follower in contract negotiations?

BEFORE THE ACQUISITION

It is practically impossible to anticipate all the many people problems which might occur as the result of an acquisition. Likewise, it is almost impossible to compile an all-inclusive checklist of actions to be covered by which these problems could be anticipated or prevented. However, to try and minimize these potential problems, an organized research of the subject is possible. To aid the acquiring company in considering the human problems before taking on the responsibility for the people involved, a checklist is most useful. If the checklist is approached in the form of a series of questions, it will be helpful in identifying problems.
Employee Benefits[2]

1. Pensions
   a. What is the future service cost?
   b. What is the past service cost?
   c. What is the method and rate of funding?
   d. What is the unfunded past service liability, if any?
   e. If the plan is contributory, what percentage of the cost is paid by the employee?
2. Group insurance
   a. Is the plan contributory? Is it experience rated? If so, are the dividends retained or distributed to the employees?
   b. What has been the experience for the past two or three years?
   c. What is the real cost of the plan?
3. Savings or similar plans
   a. What is the company cost?
   b. What percentage of the eligible employees participate?
   c. Is there any obligation on the part of the acquired company to deliver its own securities to the participants at some future date?
4. Sick leave, vacation, service award, and similar plans
   a. What are the details of each plan?
   b. What is the annual cost of each?

The answers to these questions provide the key to making a reliable estimate of the cost of balancing benefit plans. It is not appropriate here to detail the steps involved in estimating such costs. However, with this information one can make a

---

[2] These are covered in greater detail in Chap. 60.

good estimate of the costs, which should then be reduced to a percentage-of-payroll figure. Such a cost analysis is a basic ingredient in any merger recipe.

Answers to the following questions are also necessary in order to make a meaningful evaluation:

1. What are the specifics as to employees, numbers, jobs they hold, sex, age, and service?

2. What is the turnover in the work force? High or low; why?

3. Where are the principal sources from which the company obtains its employees?

4. What is the labor relations history?

5. What are the principal unions involved?

6. Where is the thrust of the union management relationship?

7. Is there a heavy grievance caseload? If so, why?

8. Do the labor contracts reveal an unrealistic attitude on the part of the union or the company?

9. What is the basis on which new labor contracts are generally determined? Industry pattern, area pattern, competition?

10. Is the company a pattern setter or pattern follower in contract negotiations?

11. If it is nonunion, why?

12. If it is nonunion, what unions appear to be most likely to be candidates for organizational attempts?

13. What is the labor climate in the area of the company's locations?

14. Is there an incentive plan? Who is covered? What does it cost? How does it work?

15. What is the ratio of labor costs to sales?

16. What is the ratio of total payroll cost to sales?

17. What is the experience rating for state unemployment compensation?

18. What is the experience rating for workmen's compensation? If not experience rated, why not?

19. How is the personnel function organized as to (a) management, (b) salary administration, (c) employment procedures, (d) benefit plans, (e) training and development, (f) labor relations, (g) community relations?

20. What are the major strengths of the personnel department?

21. What are its major weaknesses?

22. How does it compare with the personnel function in the acquiring company as to status in the organization and level of contribution?

23. What is the assessment of the management of the acquired organization?

24. What is the anticipated structure of the new organization? Which positions will be upgraded? Which ones downgraded? Which ones eliminated?

25. What is the policy (or what will be the policy) on termination, termination payments, and/or early retirement for those employees whose positions will be eliminated? For those who will be demoted? For those who will be transferred?

26. What is the best way to go about a careful, personal explanation to each employee who will be affected as a result of the acquisition? Those to be terminated, transferred, retired, promoted, demoted?

27. How do the answers to the preceding questions fit in with and compare with the personnel policies of the acquired company?

28. What should be done to change the personnel policies in the acquired company to fit those of the acquiring company, or vice versa?

In an article on the people part of acquisition planning, the role of the personnel manager in preacquisition evaluation was questioned. In the survey, which formed the basis for the article, several chief executive officers were asked to state which members of their staff had participated in the preacquisition evaluation, other than the chairman, president, or executive vice-president. Results showed that the principal personnel executive was consulted less frequently than was the principal finance or legal executive. Fewer than 40 percent of the acquiring companies top managements consulted with their principal personnel executive before the acquisition.

In the same survey, the same chief executive officers were asked about the need for analysis of various personnel factors during the preacquisition stage. Their replies confirmed the need to thoroughly examine the many personnel considerations. Included among the items they said should be examined were: depth of management talent, top-management talent, compatibility of the acquired company organization structure with that of the acquiring company, and employee benefit programs.

Since there was need for secrecy during the acquisition evaluation by the acquiring company, the examination process was necessarily restricted to a few top executives. How this requirement is balanced by the need for more in-depth personnel information and evaluation at the preacquisition stage is the subject of a deeper and more specific study of the "real role" of personnel executive in the preacquisition process.

AFTER THE ACQUISITION

As most problems concerning people arise after the acquisition, we should thoroughly examine the post-merger difficulties concerning management and other salaried and hourly paid personnel. Many corporate procedures and checklists for acquisitions tend to overemphasize the money aspects of the matter and forget the people factor. Most top managers know the importance of the people side of the business—but, at the same time many acquiring companies completely ignore it. After the deal has been closed, the tendency is to pass the acquisition over to operating management with the directive, "Make it run better for us than it did for them." If operating management stumbles, staggers, or sinks in the mass of the complexity of the people readjustments, everyone wonders what happened.

Of course, the significance of people considerations is more basic than shown by this brief description. People are the catalyst (or the inhibitor) in the acquisition process. If the number of employees that an acquisition will affect is considered, it is obvious that many problems will follow. However, just because the human element is complex, there is no reason for trying to think away the problem behind the profit and loss statement and the balance sheet. The study of human reactions is a matter of psychology. Few businessmen are academically trained psychologists, and they use what they know as "common sense"—but which is actually practical applied psychology.

The people consideration route in an acquisition should be objective patience. Patience induces confidence and respect, and it permits the needed time and consideration for the integration of the people problems involved. The limits of patience obviously must be determined by the related factors involved in the final management decision.

For the balance of the discussion, let us assume that we are considering the role of the personnel department of the acquiring company in an organization with several decentralized autonomous divisions. A major staff responsibility for implementing people considerations in the acquisition in a timely manner rests with the chief personnel executive of the acquiring company. Before there is any analysis of the acquired company, it is essential that the personnel executive of the parent company establish good relationships with all the officers, including his own counterpart, of the newly acquired company (division). Visits are much more effective than memorandums.   Without first establishing such good relationships, it will be difficult, if not impossible, to identify the real problem areas.

Often it is difficult for an acquired company's second and third level of management to accept the fact that their new organization has lost some, or much, or all, of its old identity and independence of action.   Of even greater concern to the management group of the acquired company is the uncertainty of their own future.   After good working relationships have been established, analysis of policies and programs can proceed under favorable circumstances.   Recommendations and actions growing out of such a study will, of course, be guided by many different factors in each organization.

Although the corporate personnel staff is concerned with all aspects of the newly acquired unit's personnel operation, efforts must be concentrated in those areas in which the problems are most acute.   The adage to make haste slowly is good counsel.

In addition to analysis of the new unit, the corporate personnel staff can encourage exchange of experiences of the personnel organizations in the various divisions, especially that of the new unit, with one another.   For example, group meetings or visits of divisional training, employment, or labor relations managers develop a knowledge of, and a pride in, the company which can be achieved in no other manner.   Such meetings are of immeasurable help in promoting understanding.   The success or failure of any acquisition will in a large measure result from the degree of harmony in the relationships developed between the acquiring and acquired company.   Those engaged in the personnel function—whether called human relations, employee relations, industrial relations, or personnel—can make a major contribution to the success of an acquisition by bending every effort to establish those most necessary good relationships with the newly acquired unit.

COMMUNICATIONS

The communications framework can well be the single most important factor for smooth integration in an acquisition.   With effective communications, the acquiring firm can develop a climate of confidence and, hopefully, eliminate much of the friction which frequently occurs.   The acquiring company in the preacquisition phase should obtain samples of internal reporting systems and evaluate them carefully.   Usually, the acquiring company will want such systems to parallel its own.   During the period immediately following the acquisition, however, the amount of such reporting may vary, depending on the differences between the two companies.

Good communication is an essential part of good human relations.   The timing and setting of communications are as important as, and sometimes more important than, what is actually said.   The best time to start the program is before the acquisition talks begin.   A communications program is like a reputation: you cannot press a button to start improving it today; you have to start, in a sense, from the beginning and build it just as you would a reputation—each individual move adds to the total.

The effect and meaning of what is said to employees are of prime importance.   The need is to start the process as soon as the idea of an acquisition is first mentioned.   Remember, rumors and half-truths travel faster than the facts.   One company handled the rumor problem by saying: "Let us know the rumor, and we will put out the facts."   To combat rumors of the sale of the company, they announced that their management had indeed had some discussions with another about merging, but that they had been terminated.   This direct and frank approach greatly increased the respect of the employees for their top management.   There are really only a few problems that cannot be solved by seeing that everyone gets the information needed to do his job.   It is necessary, of course, that information be screened to ensure that it is factual and that the distribution is effective. In the same way that doing nothing is a form of business decision making, so is keeping quiet a form of communication. Premature leaks on acquisitions can lose the battle before it begins. The basic objective is to inform employees about an acquisition as quickly as possible. We have to build from within the acquired company the most important of assets—the people themselves—so that they can contribute and grow with the new company.

Top management, to an extent, communicates through formal channels, but it does not by any means control all the means of communication. We must realistically accept that employees talk to each other, to their union leaders, to the press, television, and radio. If we do not make an accurate statement at the right time, facts are replaced by rumor and speculation. We also have to be ready to try and answer the employee's questions. Typical questions are:

"Will I keep my job?"

"Do I get a new boss?"

"Who owns and controls the company?"

Questions on wages, benefits, personnel policies and practices must also be answered.

Acquisitions and mergers are a fact of corporate life. Since there are sound reasons for acquisitions, they will probably continue at a rapid rate, and employee communication aspects in future mergers, as in previous ones, will present many and varying challenges.

Although the success of an acquisition can depend on maintaining good employee morale, too many companies unfortunately continue to direct communications efforts during acquisitions or mergers at the financial community—an interesting paradox.

SUMMARY

One of the most helpful and thorough summaries was contained in a report[3] which, among other matters, listed the topics that companies have found to be of most concern to the employees as the affected individuals in an acquisition process. The following questions were asked by employees in acquired companies. Answers to these would appear to form a real basis for helping the personnel executive to do his job during an acquisition of another company.

1. Reasons for the merger. Why is the change necessary? What does his company expect to get out of it? (It is a truism that people resist change and find it upsetting, also that they can accept it more readily if they understand why it is proposed.)
2. Facts about the company with which his organization plans to merge.
   a. What does it make, or what services does it sell? Are its products or services similar to those of his own company?
   b. What about the quality of its products or services?
   c. How efficient is the company? What is its profit-and-loss record?
   d. What are its sales figures? (Of particular interest to the sales force, but also to rank-and-file employees as a measure of company strength and prominence.)
   e. How old is the company? How well is it known?
   f. Where are its headquarters? How many plants? Where are they located?
   g. How many employees does it have?
   h. How is it organized? (Particularly in comparison with the employee's own company. For example, does the merging company have its own sales force, or does it sell through manufacturers' agents? Does the company have its own advertising

[3] Geneva Seybold, "Communicating with Employees about Mergers," *Studies in Personnel Policy*, no. 211, pp. 51–52, The Conference Board, Inc., 1968.

department or use an outside agency? The interest here is in duplication of function and how the employee sees himself fitting into the merged structure.)

   i. What is the company's philosophy in dealing with unions?

   j. What is the general reputation of the company in regard to treatment of employees? Is it known as a good place to work?

3. General changes that might result from the merger.
   a. What will be the name of the new company? Will his own company lose its identity?
   b. What changes will be made in organization structure and management?
      (1) What will be the place of his company in the new organization? (Example: A division? A subsidiary?)
      (2) Who will head the new company?
      (3) Will his own company be represented on the board of directors?
      (4) Will any of the present officers of his company be officers of the new company?
      (5) Will any functions now represented in the organization of his company be subtracted? Any added?
      (6) Will authorities and responsibilities of executives of his company be changed?
   c. Are there plans for decreasing the total number of employees after merger?
   d. Are there plans for de-emphasizing products his company is making?

4. In terms of his specific job and income
   a. Will he keep his job? What is the possibility of layoff or dismissal?
   b. Will his duties be the same?
   c. Who will be his boss? In reporting relationships, will he be farther from the top after merger?
   d. Will he keep his title, or be given one of less distinction?
   e. Will he suffer other loss of prestige? (Will he keep his office on the top floor? His carpet? Use of a company-owned car? His liberal expense account?)
   f. Who will be his immediate associates? (The employee may especially enjoy working with his present associates, or have established personal contacts that make his work easier.)
   g. Will he be forced to transfer? Move to another city?
   h. How will the merger affect his present compensation? (Basic? Overtime? Bonus?)
   i. How will the merger affect employee benefit plans? (Vacation, group insurance, retirement, profit sharing, sick leave, stock purchase and thrift plans, continuing education and professional development)
      (1) Will he be able to keep the benefits he now enjoys?
      (2) Will he become eligible for any new benefits as a result of the merger?
      (3) Will length of service established in his company count in qualifying for benefits after merger?
   j. In what ways is the union contract under which he works affected?
   k. Will company policies, in general, be the same after merger?

5. In terms of future responsibilities and compensation
   a. How will the merger affect his chances for promotion? (Are promotions likely to be as frequent as now, less frequent, or more frequent?)
   b. What will the wage or salary schedule be? (The range)
   c. What are business prospects for his unit after merger? (With the thought that prosperity of the company may be reflected in employees' compensation)

6. Stock exchange arrangements in the merger (Especially when the employee is a participant in an employee stock purchase plan or executives' stock option plan)

These questions, of course, are of concern to the employee. Some are more important to top management than to hourly paid employees. While some may appear insignificant, experience has been found to the contrary. A department head's concern over the moving of his office, for example, has served to cause more than one morale problem at the time of an acquisition.

All questions cannot be answered during the early stages of the acquisition process. For example, the specifics as to how employee benefit plans will be changed may not have been decided at the time that shareholders of the merging companies approve the agreement. Decisions on such matters are often made later, in some instances many months, or years, later.

Regardless of the size of the company that is acquired, it is possible to state a few more or less uniform principles. Although these principles are not new, they are, in the long run, the most important.

1. *Know the People.* This cannot be done by long-distance telephone calls. Go out and visit the new people; get to know them and to understand their problems. In trying to evaluate attitudes of newly acquired employees, some companies have used an informal employee survey. Many others feel that direct contact is much more helpful.

2. *Do Not Rush.* This is more difficult. In spite of the pressures that tend to force uniformity at an early stage, a persuasive argument can be made for a gradual transition. The people who are new to the company will soon learn of those personnel policies which are more liberal than the ones of the acquired company; let them develop an appetite for them. Then, when the total personnel programs are integrated, it will be much easier for employees to accept the less desirable part of the change.

3. *Train and Sell.* Best results appear to be obtained when the personnel staff and others from the acquired company are thoroughly trained and indoctrinated in the total personnel program of the acquiring company. Also, best results are obtained when the personnel staff and others from the acquired company then go out and sell and explain these programs to their own people. The importance of informative group meetings which make use of visual aids cannot be overemphasized.

The technical and financial considerations should not overshadow the "human element" of the acquisition. People are the muscle of any company. Just like the body of a trained athlete, they have a natural rhythm which can be severely injured by improper handling.

There is usually only one chance in any one situation to pursue people problems properly. If the approach is considerate and well planned in advance, the handling of these problems can result in growth and profit. Bad handling at the start may lead to countless problems which may last for months or for years—or perhaps forever.

BIBLIOGRAPHY

Books

Mace, Myles L., and George G. Montgomery: *Management Problems of Corporate Acquisitions,* Division of Research, Harvard Business School, Boston, 1962.

Periodicals

Boland, Richard J.: "Merger Planning," *Personnel,* March–April, 1970.

Butler, John J.: "Maximizing Personnel Potential in a Merger," *Mergers and Acquisitions,* Fall, 1965.

Riggs, Thomas J.: "Mergers and People," Mergers and Acquisitions, American Management Association, Management Report 4.

Roalman, A. R.: "Communication Makes the Merger," *Public Relations Journal,* September, 1969.

Schoonmaker, Alan N.: "Why Mergers Don't Jell: The Critical Human Element," *Personnel,* September–October, 1969.

Spelfogel, Evan J.: "Labor Considerations in Corporate Acquisitions and Mergers: The NLRB's Successor and Accretion Doctrines," *Law Notes: American Bar Association,* vol. 7, pp. 15–17, October, 1970.

Wytmar, Richard J.: "The Impact of Mergers on the Executive," *Business Horizons,* December, 1969.

"Employee Policies Play a Role in Mergers and Acquisitions," *Employee Relations Bulletin,* February, 1969.

"The Successor Employer's Duty to Arbitrate: A Reconsideration of John Wiley and Sons, Inc., V. Livingston," *The Harvard Law Review,* vol. 82, p. 418.

"WU, CSC Terminate Merger Proposal," *Western Union News,* no. 18, August, 1968.

Miscellaneous

Finkel, Stanley M.: *Selling the Merger to Personnel,* American Management Association, Management Report 75.

Hawn, John L.: *Fringe Benefit Policy and the Merger,* American Management Association, Management Report 75.

Pitt, Gavin A.: *Mergers and Acquisitions: The Personnel Department's Responsibility for Analysis and Action,* American Management Association, Management Report 173.

Scheu, Edward M., *Organizational Problems after the Merger,* American Management Association, Management Report 75.

Seybold, Geneva: *Communicating with Employees about Mergers,* Studies in Personnel Policy 211, The Conference Board, Inc., New York, 1968.

Towers, Perrin, Forster, and Crosby: *Mergers and Acquisitions,* Philadelphia, 1965.

chapter 60

Merging of Employee Benefits

RICHARD A. WAMBOLD *Director of Benefits and Personnel Services, Tenneco Inc., Houston, Texas*

INTRODUCTION

There are many questions to be answered and many points to be resolved in dealing with employee benefit plans when two companies merge or when one company is acquired by another. Will pension plans merge? Discontinue? Will new ones be created? What, if anything, is to happen to existing plans: short-term disability, long-term disability, group life insurance, medical care plans, profit sharing, thrift, or other savings plans?

Many possible answers can be given to these questions. But just as no two mergers are exactly alike, neither are there any pat answers to the treatment of benefit plans that can be stereotyped or "canned" and followed time after time in each merger situation. Each merger and the benefit problems it presents must be considered unique, and specific solutions to the problems presented will ultimately be tailored for each situation.

Therefore, because of the multiplicities involved, and the impracticability of dealing with each in an adequate way in this brief chapter, this discussion will be concerned with the employee benefits considerations that ensue from the most common business "marriage," e.g., when one corporation is dominant as the result of its stockholders being in control after the acquisition of another corporation.

Before proceeding further, one point should be mentioned. The success of the merger is the important consideration. From it should ensue an organization with synergistic potential: one plus one adding up to three. All efforts must be in support of this proposition.

The specific postmerger treatment of employee benefit plans is one such supportive effort, involving the economic well-being of the employees involved, as well as an activity which will have its effect on the corporate profit and loss statement.

It follows then, that effective treatment of benefit plans will be most adaptive to the success of the merger if clear-cut employee benefits objectives are established and agreed to by both parties to the merger.   If these are set in advance of the merger or acquisition itself, so much the better.   Much needless postmerger employee benefit negotiation between the two companies can be avoided if mutually understood and agreed-upon objectives are established early in the proceedings.

PREMERGER CONSIDERATIONS

While concentration in this chapter is on the postmerger treatment of employee benefit plans, it is important that prior to the merger the acquiring corporation review the employee benefits program of the corporation to be acquired for a number of reasons.

First, it should be determined in advance whether any benefits problems exist which might of themselves present impediments to the merger.   Second, it should be determined whether any factors are present which might bear on the value of the corporation to be acquired and thus affect the purchase price.

In this aspect of the study, special attention should be given to the pension program (including the plan or plans for union employees).   Eligibility for participation, vesting conditions, and the amounts of benefits provided should be compared to those of other companies in the same industry and/or geographic areas, and this comparison should extend to comparable elements in the acquiring company's pension plan (or plans).   If, for example, the quality of the union pension plan is markedly below the standards generally prevailing in the industry, it may reasonably be anticipated that future negotiations with the union will yield improvements at higher costs which will affect net income.[1]   Similarly, if the acquiring company's pension plan is to be the surviving plan for all employees, and it is more liberal than that of the acquired company, this too will affect future costs.   The status of funding of the pension plan(s) is also meaningful, and should be investigated carefully.   An analysis of the actuarial assumptions used to arrive at company contributions to the pension fund should be made to determine whether they are realistic.   The interest assumption is particularly vital.   For instance, it is a generally accepted actuarial premise that an increase of $\frac{1}{2}$ percent in the interest assumption will tend to reduce employer contribution requirements by 10 percent.   This is particularly relevant since such costs flow directly through to the bottom line of the profit and loss statement.

An unfunded past service pension liability will also significantly affect the value of the corporation to be acquired.   Provision for amortizing this liability over succeeding years will represent an abnormal pension expense during the amortization period, which should be appropriately reflected in the price to be paid for the acquired company.[2]

In addition to the financial reasons for premerger investigation and study of employee benefit plans, there are the people reasons.   Merging companies together is at best an unsettling experience for the employees involved, especially those of the acquired company, and the psychological impact must not be overlooked.   Much

---

[1] The United Auto Workers in their 1970 negotiations with the "big three" made a pension demand which General Motors asserted would double its present annual pension expense of $255,000,000.

[2] Conversely, if the acquired corporation's pension plan is overfunded (perhaps through good fund investment results), and less than normal pension fund contributions are anticipated over future years, this will also have a bearing on its real earning power, and thus should increase its asking price.

can be done to allay any feelings of insecurity, with resultant loss of efficiency, that may accompany such a move, if careful thought and planning is given in advance to anticipated employee reactions. It should be a point to let employees know promptly how they are to be affected by the merger or acquisition and of any particular changes that may take place.

This need not be communicated to employees in definitive terms, and in fact rarely is. Such detail in a merger agreement or management announcement is unlikely (and at merger time, probably impossible). The consummation of mergers seldom hinges on employee benefit plan considerations. Moreover, principals to mergers or acquisitions are more apt to deal with the subject in general terms.[3]

What is desirable is to issue a sufficiently informative statement to employees, satisfactory to both companies, that will counter any feelings of apprehension employees may have.

ESTABLISHING THE OBJECTIVES

Where it is expected that there will be a close working relationship between the people in the two organizations, a reason for the standardization of benefit plans becomes compelling. On the other hand, if an acquisition results in two companies whose activities are completely unrelated, and where the two groups of employees are geographically separated, there is less need for comparable plans.

Most companies do, however, desire personnel homogeneity within the overall organization to promote teamwork.

Some of the specific management considerations in establishing employee benefit plan objectives[4] are:

Advancing the corporate image within the organization: How important is it to the dominant corporation that the employees of the acquired company feel a close sense of identification with the parent company?

Cross-fertilization: The ability to most effectively utilize employees, particularly those at the management level, and to facilitate transfer between companies without loss of seniority and benefits is an important consideration.

Costs: If it will increase costs to standardize benefits, are the results to be obtained worth the additional expense?[5]

Operational autonomy: What effect, if any, will installing parent company benefit plans have on the managerial autonomy of the operating divisions?

Apart from cost, which is the basic consideration against which all others are measured, the other points given above are philosophical, and do not lend themselves to positive measurement. They do, however, bear directly on a company's attitude toward its employees, and are an intrinsic part of corporate character.

A CASE HISTORY

It has been previously noted that there is no completely consistent way of treating employee benefit plans in mergers and acquisitions.[6] Let us therefore assume a

---

[3] This can be the wiser course, as it leaves some latitude to unravel knots, or seek later accord between the two companies on employee benefits problems which may not be apparent during the complicated negotiations which precede the merger itself.

[4] Emphasis on one consideration or another is apt to vary greatly depending upon the particular circumstances of the merger, the nature of the companies involved, etc.

[5] This presupposes that for practical reasons any standardization of benefits will result in upgrading.

[6] The exception to this would be if each acquired company has no employee benefits at all and the acquiring company extended its plans on a uniform basis.

situation where one company is acquired by another,[7] with both companies retaining their respective corporate identities and separate managements. Let us also build into this assumption problems of sufficient scope to bear an identifiable relationship to most of those that will be generally encountered in the joining of two separate corporations' benefit plans into one viable program.

A suitable name that we may use for the acquiring company—the dominant corporation—is "principal employer." This designation is frequently used to avoid redundant use of overlong corporate names, and this identification is that which is most often used[8] in plans, trusts, insurance contracts, etc., with which benefit plan administrators work.

The acquired company will be referred to as the "company."

The employee benefits objectives established by the principal employer are as follows:

1. To place the principal employer's pension plan and employee savings plan in effect with the company.

2. To achieve uniformity with respect to other benefit plans in effect in the two companies as will facilitate the intertransferability of employees.

3. To make all changes to employee benefit plans effective January 1, 1972.[9]

Analyzing the Work

Should it happen that the acquired company does not have either a pension plan or an employee savings plan, then placing the principal employer's plans in effect becomes relatively simple. Concentration here would be given to communicating the provisions of these plans to new groups of employees, enrolling those who are eligible, and establishing administrative procedures. However, in this day when such plans are in common use, it is rare to find neither a pension plan nor a savings plan of some sort in effect; frequently both will be, and let us assume this to be the case of the acquired company.

With this predication, the first problem is to decide what to do with the existing plans of the company and, as a corollary, how the principal employer's plans are to replace them.

Employee benefit plans and related insurance contracts, trust agreements, etc., are often difficult to read and interpret. This is especially the case with those of older vintage. Therefore, before any changes to the plans and related documents are attempted, these instruments together with any explanatory booklets, handouts, and so forth, should be meticulously studied.

During this study, the principal employer should prepare a list of any possible problems and questions which may arise. The company should do the same with the principal employer's plans.

Following these separate studies, a conference between the principal employer and the company, lists in hand, should be held to assure agreement between the two parties on the problems that exist, and to iron out any differences. This may appear to be a needless procedure, especially when one considers that positive objectives have been set and are being observed. Nevertheless, such a conference will almost surely surface matters that may be obscure or of seeming irrelevance to one party

---

[7] The technique of acquisition can be an exchange of securities, or the outright purchase of voting stock, in addition to other methods. The technique used, however, is not germane to this discussion.

[8] Particularly when the principal employer controls many subsidiary companies.

[9] A good practice is to effect no major changes to plans until a reasonable time has elapsed following the consummation of the merger. This "settling down" period will allow normal work to flow unimpeded and will permit problems to surface.

but quite meaningful to the other, and which must be resolved with some flexibility, consistent with the basic objectives, in the interest of a harmonious blending of the plans.

As examples, a pension plan may really be functioning as a savings plan, and it is not unusual to have an employee savings plan whose ultimate basic purpose is to provide income to its participants following retirement.

PENSION PLANS

The objective already having been established that the employees of the company are to participate in the principal employer's pension plan, the next step to be taken is to formally authorize it. A resolution of the principal employer's board of directors to accomplish this purpose would read:

> WHEREAS, the principal employer's pension plan provides that a subsidiary company desiring to adopt said plan shall, as a condition thereto, first be designated as eligible to adopt the plan, and
> WHEREAS, the principal employer's pension plan also provides that continuous service with a subsidiary company may, with the approval of the principal employer, be recognized for purposes of eligibility to participate therein,
> NOW, THEREFORE, be it and it hereby is
> RESOLVED, that the principal employer designates the company as a subsidiary company eligible to adopt its pension plan, such adoption to be effective January 1, 1972, and it is further
> RESOLVED, that continuous service as an employee of the company shall be given full recognition for purposes of meeting the eligibility requirements of principal employer's pension plan.

With this accomplished, a part of the principal employer's objective has been met. The principal employer's plan has been made available to the company, but steps must now be taken so that it in effect replaces the company's existing pension plan. This is a function of the company's board of directors, which must not only adopt the principal employer's pension plan, but also take the necessary steps to preserve the benefits which have thus far accumulated in its pension plan.

There are two possibilities for such treatment:
1. Discontinue the company's pension plan.
2. Continue it in amended form.

Effect of Discontinuance

A pension plan that has been "qualified" under the provisions of the Internal Revenue code and which is subsequently discontinued, must provide full vesting rights[10] to the participants in the benefits that each had accumulated up to the date of discontinuance.

Since vesting under these conditions can encourage early retirement, which may not be desirable from an employer viewpoint, and also rules out any possibility of future reductions in pension expense which arise from forfeitures of benefits by employees whose employment terminates prior to completion of the vesting pe-

---

[10] The New York State Insurance Department defines vesting as ". . . an employee's right, on leaving employment before retirement, to receive all or a part of the benefits purchased in his behalf by the employer's contributions." A more colloquial understanding, generally accepted, is the circumstance or conditions of a pension plan, which when satisfied by the employee, irrevocably entitles him to a pension benefit paid for by the employer, usually payable at the employee's normal retirement date, whether or not he is then employed by the employer.

riod,[11] and therefore will result in some added expense to the company, discontinuation of a pension plan under these circumstances will usually not be a prudent course to follow.

Discontinuance should not be ruled out automatically, however. If, for instance, the pension plan has been in effect for a relatively short period of time, and the accrued nonvested benefits are nominal, or conversely, if the pension plan has been in effect for a long while and most of the employees are already fully vested, discontinuation of the pension plan may be the simplest and least expensive thing to do.

Neither of these circumstances is probable. More than likely the population of the company's pension plan is such that fairly substantial expense would be incurred as the result of the accelerated vesting made necessary as the consequence of the pension plan's discontinuation.

Effect of Continuation of the Company's Plan in Amended Form

The most logical way to handle the company's pension plan when it is being superseded by the principal employer's is to "freeze" it. In this process the plan is kept alive for the sole purpose of providing the benefits that had been accumulated under it before it was replaced. This must be done in such a way that is easy for employees to understand (a paramount requirement for any employee benefit plan), economical to maintain, and convenient to administer. The technique used is to amend the company's plan so as to make its provisions inactive (in this case) after December 31, 1971, by replacing these provisions with those of the principal employer's pension plan. When such a method is used, in effect, to stop one plan and start another with unbroken continuity of participation, it becomes much simpler to communicate. The employees need not be presented with a lot of technical mumbo jumbo; all that is necessary is to tell them that the pension plan has been changed, and in what manner.

But regardless of the way in which the company's pension plan is to be amended ultimately, a useful preliminary device for clarifying and defining the scope of the amendments necessary is the preparation of a comparative listing of the more important elements of both the principal employer's and the company's pension plans. (Presumably this would be put together during the initial analysis study and finalized at the preamendment conference.)

From examination of the data in Figure 1, it will be seen that the principal employer's and the company's pension plans differ in both concept and operation. The more important differences, and those which must be reconciled, are commented on briefly below.

Participation Requirements

The principal employer's plan requires a one-year waiting period before enrollment in the plan, and does not recognize the first year of employment for benefit accumulations. It does, however, afford participation to anyone who has not attained age sixty-five. The company's pension plan recognizes the entire period of employment, but does not permit participation on the part of anyone who is fifty-eight years of age or older when first employed.[12]

---

[11] Contributions made by an employer to a pension plan "qualified" under the provisions of the Internal Revenue code, may not be recovered by an employer unless the pension plan is funded in excess of its obligations as the result of actuarial error. However, excess funding resulting from nonvested employee turnover can be used to reduce future employer contributions.

[12] It can be argued, and with some logic, that permitting the start of participation in a pension plan to employees of advanced age, and therefore with relatively few years of employment left before mandatory retirement, is costly to the employer and will not produce a sig-

Benefits Formula

The essential characteristic of the principal employer's plan is that benefits are based on "career average" compensation, e.g., benefits are directly related to the employee's pay throughout his entire period of participation. The company's plan, on the other hand, is a "final pay" plan, with earnings in the early years of participation (usually the low earnings) being disregarded, and compensation earned in the later years providing the base for the benefit.[13] It may be observed here that it is customary in final pay plans to use an estimate by which compensation will increase over ensuing years (the salary progression estimate) when projecting probable pension benefits. Frequently the estimate used is 4 percent per year. This is statistically supportable. Over the last forty years wages in the United States have increased at an average annual rate of 3.9 percent.

Normal Retirement Date

Although age sixty-five is the normal retirement date in both cases, the company's plan requires ten years of continuous service.

Vesting

The plan of the principal employer requires ten years of participation at termination of employment for the employee to have an earned right to a deferred annuity. The company's plan requires ten years of continuous service and attainment of age forty for the same right. (See footnote 10 for more detailed information on vesting.)

PENSION PLAN AMENDMENTS

With all preliminary studies completed, and agreement having been reached in principle on the amendments that are necessary, the actual job of amending the company's pension plan may now begin.

The following resolution of the company's board of directors will be appropriate for this purpose:

WHEREAS, the company has been designated by the principal employer as a subsidiary company eligible to adopt the principal employer's pension plan, and

WHEREAS, the company desires to adopt said pension plan for the benefit of its employees in the manner in which authorized by the board of directors of the principal employer, and

WHEREAS, the company has in effect a pension plan for its employees wherein participants have accumulated benefits which are to be preserved, and

WHEREAS, for the purpose of preserving accumulated benefits of participants accrued through December 31, 1971, but for no other purpose,

NOW, THEREFORE, be it and it hereby is

RESOLVED, that the company amends its pension plan for employees in its entirety effective January 1, 1972, by adopting the provisions of the principal employer's pension plan, which provisions will replace and supersede those of the company's pension

---

nificant pension, when the pension benefit is based in part on service. It has its advantages, however, both to the relatively few employees who will benefit under such an open plan and to an acquisition-minded company for its psychological value.

[13] It is interesting to note that in using similar denominators, e.g., a starting salary of $450 per month, a 4 percent annual salary progression, and twenty-five years of participation, the principal employer's pension plan will provide a monthly straight-life benefit of $334 in comparison with a monthly benefit of $278 from the company's plan.

Figure 1.   Comparison of Pension Plans

	Pension plans	
	Principal employer	Acquired company
Participation requirements. . .	All full-time employees under age 65 will be enrolled on the first day of any month after one full year of continuous employment.	All full-time employees are eligible for participation on the date employed provided age 58 has not been attained.
Benefits formula.	An annuity credit for each month of participation will be provided in accordance with the following formula: 1¼% of the first $350 of monthly base compensation, plus 2¼% of monthly base compensation in excess of $350. The total of all annuity credits is normal annual retirement income.	1¼% of average annual compensation received during the 15 years before attainment of age 65, or the year before actual retirement, if that is earlier, multiplied by years of participation.
Normal retirement date.	First day of month following 65th birthday.	First day of month following 65th birthday, and completion of ten years of continuous service.
Early retirement requirements.	Attained age 55 and completed 14 years of participation.	Attained age 60 and continuously employed for at least 10 years.
Vesting rights at termination of employment.	Employees whose employment is terminated after 10 years of participation and who do not qualify for normal or early retirement benefits, are eligible for a deferred retirement allowance commencing on normal retirement date.	Employees whose employment is terminated after attained age 40 and completion of 10 years of continuous service, but before normal or early retirement benefits, are eligible for a deferred retirement allowance commencing on normal retirement date, or reduced benefits at or after age 60.

plan in effect prior to this amendment in all respects, except as specifically stated below as follows:

1. Continuous, uninterrupted service and/or participation in the pension plan, as amended, before and after January 1, 1972, shall be recognized as being unbroken for all vesting purposes and requirements.

2. Benefits accrued for service through December 31, 1971, shall be preserved for participants hereunder, and shall be payable in accordance with the terms and conditions of the plan as amended January 1, 1972. The accrued normal retirement benefit for each participant shall be calculated as follows[14]:

A. For employees who have completed fifteen or more years of service at December 31, 1971: Actual average compensation for the fifteen years of completed service at Decem-

---

[14] "Final pay" pension plans such as the company's do not lend themselves readily to establishing "accrued benefits." The two approaches generally recommended by actuaries in this type of situation are to either determine the benefit that can be provided by the reserve established, or to prorate the expected end benefit based on the actual years of participation to the number of expected years of participation. The latter is considered to be the more equitable approach and is the one used in this discussion.

ber 31, 1971, multiplied by 1¼ percent, multiplied by the percentage ratio that the number of actual years of service at December 31, 1971, bears to the total number of anticipated years of service to normal retirement date.

B. For employees who have completed less than fifteen years of service at December 31, 1971: Average annual compensation for the actual number of years of completed service at December 31, 1971, multiplied by 1¼ percent, multiplied by the percentage ratio that the number of actual years of service at December 31, 1971, bears to the total number of anticipated years of service to normal retirement date.

It is not suggested that the foregoing pension plan treatment be considered in every case to the exclusion of possible other methods. To reiterate what has been said earlier, no two mergers and resultant employee benefit plan problems are the same, and each must be approached with flexibility in keeping with basic objectives.

PROFIT-SHARING AND EMPLOYEE SAVINGS PLANS

There are many different kinds of supplementary compensation schemes in use by business, most of which are generically classified as profit-sharing plans or employee savings plans.[15] Within these classifications, however, plans will differ widely from one another in concept and operation. There are though, certain basic characteristics which identify each of these types of plans which are summarized in the following paragraphs.

Profit-sharing Plans

In the conventional profit-sharing plan a part of the company's profits before provision for federal income taxes is set aside each year after profits have been determined. The amount can be a preset specified percentage of profits, or may be determined from year to year by the board of directors. This is then credited to accounts of participants in the plan, usually on an allocable basis related to current salary. The formula also frequently takes into consideration length of service, and sometimes also includes the employee's previously accumulated account balance. Funds deposited to the plan are ordinarily invested under the direction of a company-appointed committee, but this may be done through an independent adviser who may be the trustee of the plan or someone designated by him. Distribution of funds to employee-participants is generally made following termination of employment, though it is not uncommon to make some allowance for interim distributions of limited sums in hardship cases. Essentially profit-sharing plans are noncontributory, but some plans do permit employees to make additional voluntary contributions. Apart from the savings aspect, the attraction for making voluntary contributions is that earnings which may accrue on them are not taxable until distribution is made to the employee, and then usually on a preferential long-term capital gains tax-rate basis.

The purpose of a profit-sharing plan is to encourage a direct involvement in the profit-making potential of the company on the part of the employees who participate in the plan.

Employee Savings Plans

Employee savings plans are established to encourage thrift on the part of employees, on the theory that an employee with a personal financial reserve will make a better, more stable, more dependable employee. Almost all such plans are contributory,

---

[15] As differentiated from other forms of supplementary compensation such as incentive compensation plans, bonus plans, and the like, which normally are applicable to limited groups of people.

with the incentive to participate being in the form of supplementary contributions made by the employer. Characteristically, these plans require that all employees contribute a definite percentage of salary within certain specified limits, with the employer contributing a percentage of the amount contributed by the employee. For instance, it is common among many oil companies where savings plans have been in effect for decades, to permit employees to contribute a flat 6 percent of compensation, with the employer contributing an amount equal to 50 percent of the employee contribution. Other employee savings plans tie employee contributions levels to length of service, such as 2 percent for the first three years and an additional 2 percent each year thereafter until a maximum permissible contribution of 8 or 10 percent has been reached. In some of these plans employers match the employee's contributions dollar for dollar.

Investment of the funds deposited to employee savings plans may be made in the same manner as in profit-sharing plans, but it is not uncommon for some plans to allow limited investment discretion to participants.

The distribution provisions of employee savings plans tend to be less restrictive than those of profit-sharing plans. Usually participation for a fixed period of time, say five years, will make the employee eligible to withdraw a portion of his account without penalty.

In preparing to follow the objective set forth by the principal employer in our case history, the company, which has a profit-sharing plan, shall adopt the principal employer's employee savings plan, and some of the procedures which were observed in the merging of the two pension plans may again be used. These are important enough to reiterate them here briefly:

Each corporation should study the other's comparable plan carefully.

A side-by-side comparative listing of the essential features of each plan should be prepared (Figure 2).

A conference between the two companies should be held to assure common agreement on the problems involved and their reasonable solutions.

As Figure 2 shows, the profit-sharing plan of the company and the employee savings plan differ substantially in important respects. These differences and proposed methods of treatment are described as follows:

Participation Requirements

The participation requirements of the profit-sharing plan may be viewed as a condition of employment in the minds of those who are not present participants but expect to be following the six-month eligibility period. Even though the principal employer would have no legal responsibility to observe this, since the right to change the plan rests with him unilaterally, he may as a gesture of "good faith," and in the interest of good employee relations, make a special provision for these people to enter the amended plan (which requires a one-year waiting period) at the conclusion of the six-month period.[16]

Employee and Employer Contributions

Employee contributions to employee savings plans are mandatory in order to obtain employer contributions, whereas employee contributions to the company's profit-sharing plan, though permissible, are not required in order to share in the allocation of profits. This may be viewed negatively by those in the profit-sharing plan as being a forced savings situation, but may be somewhat offset by the fact that profits credited to the profit-sharing plan are conditional, uncertain, and arbitrarily set,

[16] Latitude for flexibility is most useful in merging benefit plans. Broad objectives can be observed and good employee relations maintained if there is room for some judgment.

Figure 2.   Comparison of Employee Savings Plans

	Employee savings plan of the principal employer	Profit-sharing plan of the company
Participation requirements. . .	One full year of continuous employment.	Six months of continuous employment and annual salary of $4,800 or more.
Employee contributions.	2% for first three years of participation, not more than 4% for next two years of participation, not more than 6% for next two years of participation, not more than 8% thereafter.	Participants may make voluntary contributions up to 10% of compensation.
Employer contributions.	Employer matches employee contributions 100%.	Not less than 3% nor more than 10% of net profit before federal income tax.
Investment provisions.	Participant may invest in: a. Life, endowment, or annuity contracts. b. Cash held at interest. c. Securities of the employer.	An investment adviser appointed by the company invests the fund.
Vesting requirements.	Participants vest in company contributions at the cumulated rate of 20% per year during first five years of participation.	Vesting in company contributions commences following three years of employment at $12\frac{1}{2}$% each year thereafter until fully vested after ten or more years of employment.
Distribution of account balances.	At the election of the participant after completion of ten years of participation; otherwise at termination, death, or retirement.	Termination, death, or retirement.

whereas the employer's contributions to the employee savings plan are fixed by schedule.

Investment Provisions

This presents a unique problem in that the employee savings plan provides no operational apparatus for a managed fund such as that of the profit sharing plan. Two alternatives are possible:

1. Liquidate the profit sharing plan over a reasonable period of time, crediting each participant with his share in cash, which can then be reinvested at the participant's direction in accordance with the investment provisions of the employee savings plan.

2. Continue the managed fund of the profit sharing plan "as is" for present participants only, without making any further contributions to it.

Since the forced sale of securities is an undesirable circumstance, particularly in a "down market," this should not be required for purely administrative reasons, and therefore continuation of the profit-sharing fund, though the assets therein may be incorporated with the corpus of the employee savings plan, is the better arrangement in this case. However, this will require that the principal employer's employee savings plan be amended to provide investment authority for this limited purpose to the plan administrators.

OTHER EMPLOYEE BENEFIT PLANS

Pension plans, profit sharing, and employee savings plans have received the bulk of attention in the preceding pages. Properly so, for these plans usually cost the most money and certainly present the most complex problems. Moreover, continuity of participation with its vesting implications is more than just desirable, it is in practically every case a necessity. Also, such plans are almost without exception subject to the stringent "qualification" requirements of the Internal Revenue Service,[17] which must be met and continuously observed in order for the employer's contributions to be tax deductible.

With regard to other employee benefit plans, the principal employer has set an objective "to achieve such uniformity . . . between the two companies as will facilitate intertransferability of employees." If there are no compelling reasons which dictate comparability, this objective should be pursued with caution on the basis of "all other things being equal."

It is entirely possible, for instance, that the principal employer will find out after the acquisition is completed that the employee benefit program of the company acquired is substantially better than its own. The company may have a medical plan which pays 100 percent of all medical bills, or perhaps even very costly dental care insurance. Viewed realistically, it is next to impossible to reduce any employee's benefits, and if comparability is to be achieved in this case, the principal employer's benefits must be improved. This problem is further compounded, of course, if the principal employer has acquired other companies in the past and has raised their levels of benefits to correspond to its own.

If the principal employer's insured benefits are substitute for the existing insured plans of the company, and if this involves a switch in insurance companies, the main consideration becomes one of determining the best circumstances under which the existing insurance policies are to be canceled.

For the larger company, insured employee benefits are really a cost-plus arrangement. The insurance company uses the company's funds to pay claims and charges a fee for its service. Often it holds substantial reserves for the payment of future claims. These reserves are generally set as high as possible by the insurance company for two reasons, (1) they desire to have sufficient money on hand to pay potential claims under any foreseeable circumstances, and (2) earnings on these reserves, if credited at all in rate analysis determinations, are usually discounted below actual earnings. When a contract is canceled with an insurance company, most will contend that this money belongs to them. The point is, that there is usually no policy provision requiring them to return the money to the employer.[18]

The insurance company should be requested to provide an analysis of the current experience under the contract, and the reserves held carefully measured against possible future claims. If this review indicates probable excessive reserves, the retention should be negotiated with the insurance company in advance of the cancellation of the policy.

SUMMARY

No two mergers or acquisitions are exactly alike. Neither is the treatment of employee benefit plans uniform following such business marriages. The complexities ensue not from the mere extension of the acquiring company's employee benefits

---

[17] It has been presumed throughout the discussion that those who work on such matters have a thorough working knowledge of the pertinent provisions of the Internal Revenue code.

[18] There is no reason, however, why such a policy cannot have a contingency cancellation provision setting forth specifically how reserves held are to be treated in this eventuality.

program to the acquired company, or vice versa as is sometimes the case. Most of the problems arise from the tying together of some plans, canceling others, and changing still others, all in a way which is understandable and satisfactory to the employees involved, consistent with corporate objectives, and with due consideration for the expense.

From the corporate point of view, one may think of the treatment of benefit plans described in this chapter as being the effective use of a common bond to unite the employees of the multicompany organization, giving each a stake in the success of the enterprise.

BIBLIOGRAPHY

American Management Association, Finance Division: *Corporate Mergers and Acquisitions,* New York, 1958.

Anderson, Harry C.: "Insurance Problems in Mergers and Acquisitions," *Business Insurance,* vol. 4, p. 21, Aug. 17, 1970.

Kwasha, H. Charles: "Benefit Programs after the Merger," *Employee Benefit Plan Review,* no. 6, p. 12, December, 1969.

Parsons, Robert Q., and John Stanley Baumgartner: *Anatomy of a Merger,* Prentice-Hall, Inc. Englewood Cliffs, N.J., 1970.

Strong, Jay V.: *Employee Benefit Plans in Operation,* Bureau of National Affairs, Inc., Washington, D.C., 1951.

Davis, R. E.: "Compatibility in Corporate Marriages," *Harvard Business Review,* pp. 86–93, July–August, 1968.

Commerce Clearing House, Inc.: *Pension and Profit-sharing Plans and Clauses,* Chicago, Ill. 1957.

MacDougal, Gary E., and Fred V. Malek: "Master Plan for Merger Negotiations," *Harvard Business Review,* pp. 71–82, January–February, 1970.

Part 14

Special Personnel Problems

chapter 61

Absenteeism and Tardiness

C. J. STERNHAGEN, M.D. *Medical Director, Kerr-McGee Corporation Oklahoma City, Oklahoma*

THE INCIDENCE OF ABSENTEEISM AND TARDINESS AMONG EMPLOYEES

The United States Department of Labor defines absenteeism as "the failure of workers to report on the job when they are scheduled to work—that is, when they are actually 'on the payroll.'"

Throughout the world, absence from work has, generally, been considered on the increase even though many companies have positive programs attempting to control absenteeism and tardiness. The percentage of employed persons absent from work on an average day due to illness has varied from country to country, from a high of 5.7 percent in West Germany to a low of 1.1 percent in Canada. The incidence of illness absence in the United States generally has ranged in the neighborhood of 2 percent to 4 percent or more depending on the type of industry.

The problem of absenteeism is far more serious than that of tardiness although the two are inherently related since the tardiness-prone individuals are usually the same as the absence-prone individuals. Also, many instances of tardiness are simply stretched into absences by chronic absentees. Therefore, by concentrating on the problem of absenteeism, it is possible to simultaneously cover the essential aspects of tardiness.

The incidence of absenteeism increases in the situation where physical working conditions are poor. Environmental stresses or distractions such as excesses of temperature, unpleasant noise, fumes, inadequate light and ventilation, and unhappy work associates can significantly affect attendance to a greater degree than the attitudes toward the company, the pay, or the work itself.

Absenteeism also increases when workers have relatively poor relations with their immediate supervisors. The worker who feels that the supervisor is unfair or unfriendly tends to have poor attendance records.

It is also highly significant that older employees do generally maintain a better average attendance record than younger employees. When jobs are plentiful and employment is high, there is usually some increase in absences even though less than 1 percent are job-related. The incidence of absenteeism is higher under the age of thirty, after which it generally levels off.

The ratio of absence proneness is similar in all age groups, which indicates that it is the small group of around 5 to 10 percent of the employees (the chronic absentees) that causes 50 percent or more of the absences, generally. The incidence is also higher in women than men, 30 percent higher in married than unmarried women, about 50 percent higher in nonmanagement positions, and higher under female supervisors.

The absence rate rises as the number of personnel reporting to one supervisor rises.

THE COST OF ABSENTEEISM AND TARDINESS

In spite of absence control programs, absentees continue to hurt corporate profits severely. For example, the cost was $20.73 per $1,000 payroll from 1957 to 1963 in one company that spent $10 per employee annually on its occupational health program.

By counteracting this cost, another company has stated that the average return was from $4 to $25 for every dollar invested in health promotion and services, explaining that the major portion of this return was felt to be from the significant reduction of absenteeism by the emphasis on medicine and the causation of health.

In general, the absent rate indicates the relative cost to a given company because production workers simply cannot produce as much annually when absent rates are high as they can when absent rates are low. Company managers begin to understand the astounding and staggering cost of absenteeism when they realize that, for example, a 4 percent absent rate means that in twenty-five years the entire work force was completely absent for an entire year! It is also of profound importance to recognize that by relatively simple, inexpensive measures, the incidence can be cut as low as possible, thus saving the major proportion of the productivity that would be lost due to absenteeism without requiring stringent economy moves, greater industrial achievement, or expensive advertising campaigns.

No company can afford to allow the incidence of absenteeism to eat up these hard-earned corporate profits. In marginal companies, the presence of excessive absenteeism becomes an extremely critical one which, in fact, is a significant factor in the ability of the company to persist on a sound financial basis in the competitive market.

THE NECESSITY OF DATA

The few employees causing most absences may be difficult to spot without accurate statistics. Therefore, in order to analyze absenteeism and tardiness, it is absolutely essential that exact and complete scientific records be established and maintained in order to have accurate data for statistical analysis. Small companies sometimes have sufficient esprit de corps and personal supervision to keep absenteeism to an absolute minimum without accurate data. However, as company size increases, the need for stronger organizational control of absences increases in proportion to size. Similarly, the need for absence data must also increase since supervision and company loyalty are more difficult to maintain at optimum levels as growth continues due to a relative depersonalization of the work force in progressively larger groups.

ABSENCE RECORDS

Absenteeism from all causes, excused or otherwise, can be studied thoroughly by measuring these four standard rates annually at the end of the year.

(1) Total absent rate
(Absences from all causes or total frequency rate) $= \dfrac{\text{total absent days}}{\text{total personnel}}$

(2) Sickness absent rate $= \dfrac{\text{sick days}}{\text{total personnel}}$

(3) Severity rate $= \dfrac{\text{disabled days}}{\text{sick days}}$

(4) Disability rate $= \dfrac{\text{disabled days}}{\text{total personnel}}$

The total absent rate is the number of absences due to all causes per employee, while the sickness absent rate is the number of sick days per employee. As used here, "absent rate" is synonymous with "frequency rate." The severity rate is the number of disabled days per sickness absence.

The disability rate equals the sickness absent rate multiplied by the severity rate:

$$\text{Disability rate} = \frac{\text{sick days}}{\text{total personnel}} \times \frac{\text{disabled days}}{\text{sick days}}$$

$$= \frac{\text{disabled days}}{\text{total personnel}}$$

In addition, it is very helpful to use the percentage absent per day and the percentage disabled per day since these standard percentages are easily computed during the year providing a daily measure of absence and disability:

$$\text{Percentage absent per day} = \frac{\text{personnel absent}}{\text{total personnel}} \times 100$$

$$\text{Percentage disabled per day} = \frac{\text{personnel disabled}}{\text{total personnel}} \times 100$$

Then at the end of the year, the average percentage can be calculated for the year:

$$\text{Average percentage absent per year} = \frac{\text{man-days lost}}{\text{man-days scheduled}} \times 100$$

$$\text{Average percentage disabled per year} = \frac{\text{total disabled days}}{\text{man-days scheduled}} \times 100$$

Absence and tardiness records may be kept accurately and easily by using the calendar system. Each employee's supervisor should maintain a calendar attendance record form using marking pencils of different colors indicating the amount of time of each tardiness and encircling the calendar date. The absences are recorded similarly using a different color coding. Then, at the end of each month, a summary analysis of absences and tardiness is placed on each calendar form.

This will result in a very simple but extremely accurate and complete absence and tardiness record which can then be added to the company composite for producing very thorough records of absence and tardiness at quarterly and annual intervals with several years recorded per form.

Although holidays and nonscheduled days should not be recorded as absences when they occur at the beginning or end of absence days, they should be marked for purposes of analysis with a slash in a different color than the absence color code being used. Absences of less than a full day should be recorded as half days; and the morning, afternoon, or evening shift should be so designated in order to indicate the exact work shift missed for future records.

Along with the calendar record of absences and tardiness, a simple additional sheet should be maintained which includes the investigation and action taken following an interview with the employee exploring the reason for the absence or tardiness. The reason for the absence as stated by the employee should be given in the employee's own words using simple, basic terminology. The investigation and action should be recorded in sufficient detail to include all significant and pertinent information such as medical visits, family problems, or underlying psychosocial problems that frequently are mentioned by employees when such interviews are handled in a serious and sincere fashion by the supervisor. The supervisor must sign and date each interview, and the note should be in his own legible handwriting. This is not a job to be relegated to anyone else but must be done by the immediate supervisor of the employee incurring the absence.

THE ANALYSIS OF ABSENTEEISM AND TARDINESS
Identifying Absentees

Chronic absentees are largely immature malcontents who may not have had the opportunity to mature properly or simply have not yet learned or accepted the lesson that true happiness and satisfaction in life come mostly from conscientious work performed to the best of one's ability.

Since the supervisor acts as the absentee's counselor, it is necessary to become completely familiar with the underlying causes in order to have sufficient background to be properly prepared to handle absentees in a poised, professional manner.

Underlying Causes

A. Lack of social pressure. Sociologists demonstrate social pressure with the classic example of a small community where people traditionally go to church faithfully. The church absentee is visited, the cause is investigated, and positive help (or negative gossip) creates pressure to return. In contrast, today many people do not stay in one community social group long enough to establish deep roots and to feel social pressures. Positive social pressure is relatively absent today, and family pressure is also decreasing, much of which is ineffective, negative criticism. Such negative pressure is of little value without strong, positive leadership example also being present in the home so that children can better identify with the positive attributes that are too easily overshadowed by attitudes that cast a negative pall on the home environment. Everything feasible must be done to help employees from inadequate homes to adjust to their environment and become rehabilitated.

Today, the individual and his personal rights and selfish concerns often seem more important everywhere, and group interests are, for the most part, secondary. Team effort, even in some sports, is gradually giving way to special attention to key individuals whose presence or absence is credited with the victory or defeat. Similarly, superstars in industry have staggering motivating pressures, but those in less glamorous positions require special motivation to keep on the job faithfully for less glory and less pay in their supporting roles.

The health team has been defined as the physician, the patient, and allied health professionals. To that definition might be added the co-worker, the supervisor, and the family, so that with each case a new ad hoc team is formed and tailored to the specific needs of that case. The *goals* of the health team should be to *make every employee feel wanted* by positive efforts and to *make every reasonable effort toward rehabilitation.* This is essentially the same goal of the "family team" where each child should be wanted and all activities should serve the best interests of everyone.

The frequent travel required by some employees and the poor attendance habits of other chronic absentees may provide poor attendance examples for novices, who often misinterpret the facts and are adversely influenced and later imitate others' apparent bad habits. Union attitudes may back up the wayward absentee, making it even more difficult for management to control absences. These narcissistic attitudes are on the increase nationwide and are largely responsible for high tardy and absent rates. Chronic absentees may demonstrate their scornful attitude by abusing weak or indefinite management policies which have loopholes regarding detection, recording, and control.

B. The new work force. Another major factor is that both government and industry have joined in giving more jobs to those who would otherwise be relatively unemployable or who are occupationally inadequate to some degree. The absent rate of "unemployables" will always be higher than the rate present in better trained, motivated, and experienced groups of more mature and better adjusted employees. The older workers apparently give the impression of having better physical health and resistance, as well as emotional stamina, since their absence records usually surpass those of younger workers. The attitude of getting to work in spite of borderline feelings or symptoms of indisposition paradoxically seems to be a characteristic of older workers who experience those feelings more often, rather than of their younger, more buoyant colleagues.

However, a high degree of constitutional strength is seldom seen in those who have a family history of unemployment, lack of education, and lack of proper medical attention. The emotional consequences of these handicaps are well known, and some employees from this stratum feel secure knowing they can make about the same income from charity, unemployment, or welfare payments as they can by actually working. This attitude is partially due to the diminishing social stigma attached to the jobless. This group is particularly hard to inspire with company loyalty and job devotion. The problems they present are basically related to their immaturity.

C. Space age stress. Technological changes, recurring local and world crises, and the everthreatening possibility of world catastrophe from nuclear war have created a confusing, stressful environment. This causes chronic underlying worries which inevitably lead to more widespread emotional illness. Employers, supervisors, and parents are harried by these worries as much as, if not more than, the employee or child, since they carry the burden of looking after their subordinates. These fears and uncertainties are subconsciously or consciously transmitted to others so that tension is reinjected and reinforced in the anxiety cycle. Persons from maladjusted families contribute greatly to this by perpetuating their poor patterns.

D. Immaturity. Absenteeism may be correlated with the size of emotionally immature employees' medical records, which may have hundreds of entries. The tragic and sordid tales of these absentees are countless variations on the main theme:

immaturity. If immaturity could be eradicated, most "person" problems would be eliminated leaving much more time for everyone to concentrate on solving "thing" problems.

The Menninger criteria for maturity are: (1) having the ability to *deal constructively with reality,* (2) having the capacity to *adapt to change,* (3) having a relative *freedom from symptoms* that are produced by tensions and anxieties, (4) having the capacity to *find more satisfaction in giving than in receiving,* (5) having the capacity to *relate to other people* in a consistent manner with mutual satisfaction and helpfulness, (6) having the capacity to *sublimate,* to direct one's instinctive hostile energy into creative and constructive outlets, and (7) having the *capacity to love.*

For supervisors to avoid overreacting while remaining objective, tolerant, helpful, and understanding, it must be remembered that absentees may have simply had insufficient examples and opportunity to become mature.

E. Overemphasis on health.   While the main purpose of medicine is to promote health, overemphasis on health in the mass media frequently results in hypochondria.   The hypochondriac employee may erroneously believe that previous physicians who treated him were wrong in their diagnoses, and he may abuse the patient-doctor relationship repeatedly until mutual disenchantment sets up a cycle of doctor changing.   This infringes on work time, and absences increase without health improvement.   Hypochondriacs must be taught to distinguish serious from minor symptoms, but this is obviously no easy undertaking.   In movies, TV plays, and advertisements, symptoms are indiscriminately described in a worrisome fashion.

The medical team handling the company medical problems or the personal medical problems of the employee should put more emphasis on the fact that activity is a large part of recuperation and that work may be safely performed during a re-cuperation period.   Arbitrary orders by physicians to stay home for minor illnesses must be avoided in absence control programs.   To prevent iatrogenic absenteeism the physician must avoid communication errors by using persuasive return-to-work policies in all cases, especially with malingerers.   *Tolerating abuses perpetuates them.*   These policies must be laid down quietly without any emotional overlay or additional obstacles arise.

F. Health benefit abuses.   The health industry today is the third largest employer and is still growing fast.   Customs and legislation may leave no alternative to providing broader health programs for all, including "younger" workers, who may be classed as those born after World War II, and the "middle-aged" born during World War I, the Depression, or the early 1940s.   Middle-aged workers have the motivation of experiencing those eras that were directed at production, employment, and personal devotion to job and country to such a degree that being a responsible, mature worker became a national issue.   Proper work habits were vital to national security and family survival.   The sight of jobless fathers during the Great Depression left indelible scars witnessed profoundly, or suffered traumatically, by most children who now are that middle-aged group of steady workers aiming for achievement or retirement rewards and who want and need to maintain good work records. The bad impression created by a minority of today's immature reactionaries does not give proper credit to the great contributions by those mature young workers constituting the majority who possess responsible attitudes.

Public welfare and industrial benefit programs have mushroomed.   Sick leave is often undifferentiated from vacation in the minds of absentees.   The burgeoning health industry itself may be indirectly responsible for some of the abuse of sick leave benefits.   The paternalistic attitude in this more socialized era is also demonstrated by the too lenient attitude of some parents, schools, and physicians.   Such *overpermissiveness is an abandonment of responsibility.* Prevailing attitudes reflect shocking weaknesses compared to the optimism of rugged pioneers who left secure lives—gambling on their power to overcome the dangers of opportunity and adventure. Thinking patterns are deteriorated by any movement which weakens the concept that individuals have maximum rights and are masters of the government. Some forget that liberty must be loved, guarded, and defended, and that, as a group, there is no freedom for the weak.

This socialistic trend shows effects in England and Europe where absence is rising alarmingly, yet less than 1 percent is job-related! This is attributed to a crisis in motivation and responsibility where individuals are letting the work team down while tolerating the same in co-workers. The situation is considered even worse in France and Germany than in England, and represents a major communication break between management and labor. Absenteeism is prevalent and expensive everywhere but is still much worse in Europe than the United States.

Sick benefits reduce the incentive for chronic absentees to get to work when they are only slightly ill or tired or when work is simply an inconvenience. This kind of malingering can be identified quickly by analyzing absences and medical records around holidays, the opening days of hunting and fishing seasons, extracurricular community or family events, and morning versus afternoon absences.

The chronic absentee often does not categorize benefits accurately, nor does he feel any need to be honest about reporting the exact reasons for his absence, since he foresees no harm to others by his actions. Chronic absentees frequently argue defensively that they contribute heavily to benefit plans and so feel justified in using benefits in any way they can. One company has successfully reduced absences by reducing the upper limit of sick leave. Another company found that the extreme measure of allowing no time off for sickness at all was necessary to cut the absence rate.

G. Outside distractions. Supervisors must become familiar with the frequent reasons for chronic tardiness in employees. Moonlighting, TV watching, and other outside activities that infringe on rest are bound to lessen the normal drive to get out of bed in the morning and get to work on time. Being chronically tired out in the morning, the employee uses a variety of imaginary illnesses as excuses to his supervisor or the company physician. It takes great patience and understanding to deal with this situation since the employee brings the fatigue upon himself, but he really does not feel well.

This behavior often starts in school and can be checked before employment by examining absence and tardiness records. Actually, it is not laziness, but it is a form of disorganized living. Many disorganized persons have a tendency toward frequent tardiness, but, since they are "allowed" so many "sick" days per year, they consciously or subconsciously stretch their tardiness into an absence. This is an attempt to change an embarrassing situation of tardiness into a "legitimate" situation of absence.

H. Poor motivation. Up to a point, it is not unreasonable to expect that time off the job should be spent getting recharged for better work performance, because, after all, work consumes the better part of every normal person's daily life. But, what if his work is not really "the better part" of the employee's daily life? What if he is dissatisfied with his job?

There are many reasons for dissatisfaction, of course, and most of them seriously impair motivation. For example, if anticipated opportunities for worthwhile achievement or meaningful progress either slow down or are eliminated, the individual becomes touchy and sensitive and starts to find fault with the employer.

On the other hand, if he is given a challenging job with the possibility of responsibility, growth, achievement, and advancement to satisfy his need for recognition, he will enjoy coming to work and performing to the best of his ability. The supervisor ordinarily provides these conditions and the ways to maintain motivation, but, occasionally, he requests assistance from the physician in health problems. The physician then must be capable of accepting the referral from the supervisor and also must have a good understanding of people so he can communicate effectively with all levels of employees, but especially with the front-line supervisors, who most often represent management to the employee.

Having discussed some general environmental and social elements in the absenteeism problem, we might turn to specific medical problem areas of concern to the company. Of these, psychiatric disorders are responsible for nearly all correctable absenteeism.

1. Alcoholism. Alcoholism is an age-old social, physical, and environmental problem, but today it is generally considered a psychiatric one. In any case, it is estimated that it causes an average of 3 percent of industrial absenteeism.

By 1966, thirty-four of the top 100 companies in the *Fortune* list of 500 had alcoholism programs, and such programs in industry are increasing steadily in number.

Actually, mental problems may not be the underlying cause of alcoholism since nonalcoholics often have the same apparent mental problems as alcoholics. Nevertheless, alcoholism creates "lost weekends," increases marital flare-ups, destroys physical health, brings financial crises, and causes crime and other antisocial behavior. All of this sooner or later catches up with the employee, and he has to lose work time because he is strapped to a vicious, downhill treadmill. For alcoholics, there is simply not enough time available to drink, to create these problems, to solve them, and to keep working as steadily as they could before alcoholism set in. The chronic alcoholic may subconsciously feel that work itself is one of his problems, and that all these problems interfere with his drinking, which is his only solace.

This brings us to the all-important medical fact that nearly everyone tries to dodge: *whenever drinking consistently interferes with the job, the physician is obliged to call it alcoholism.* The job suffers long before the onset of absenteeism, but as a rule, everyone, including co-workers, supervisors, family, friends, and physicians, tries to protect the alcoholic in any way possible until their patience for the alcoholic is exhausted.

Co-workers often ignore the deficiencies of alcoholic employees or hide complaints about them, but so do their supervisors. Supervisors are in a critical position, since they are personally responsible for placing production stress on subordinates, which may worsen alcoholism, and at the same time are vulnerable to criticism from management for excessive absences.

The incidence of alcoholism among supervisors themselves and among executives is another serious problem, but it is difficult to assess because of inconsistent policies and data on their absences. Even without data, though, a diagnosis may still be made by observing certain general characteristics of alcoholism, such as emotional distress and inappropriate changes in appearance, ability, coordination, use of authority, attitudes, and adaptability. Specific characteristics include the dilated facial vessels, particularly around the cheek bones and nose, which are usually present in chronic alcoholics. These skin changes and tremors are usually late changes, however, and the importance of identifying alcoholics as early as possible cannot be overstressed.

The three important predisposing factors to alcoholism are hereditary sensitivity, personality disorders, and the widespread practice of social drinking. These three combined are too much for the potential alcoholic once the habit begins.

Somehow, the usual cycle of ten to twenty-five years of alcholism must be broken or the alcoholic will become physically defeated and financially and ethically bankrupt.   Meanwhile, since absences due to alcoholism are beyond the untreated, hardened, and unaware alcoholic's ability to control, it is the responsibility of industry to step in and help its employed alcoholics.   The influence of alcoholics on the habits of other absentees is very great, and therefore, their true total effect on the absent rate is probably much higher than recorded.

J. Nonmedical drug problems.   The current explosion of nonmedical drug usage has again become a true personnel problem, as was the case with morphine addiction after the Civil War—which was then aptly called "the soldiers' disease."   Today it is not only the minority of returning veterans from the Vietnam War but persons of all age groups who are causing an influx of personnel into the labor market who range from total abstainers to hard-core addicts.   A much greater number of people of all ages are becoming involved in the abuse of drugs.   A new awareness of this hazard has resulted in both governmental and private groups working toward the proper solution of the continuing problem.   Nevertheless, nonmedical drug abuse is a growing cause of absenteeism and will require expert management or it may someday supersede alcoholism as a cause of absenteeism in this country.

K. Handling other emotional problems.   Mental health training and rehabilitation should be directed toward the development of Gomberg's five ideals: a realistic appraisal of self, self-respect, capacity for growth, resilience in the face of stress, and regulatory autonomy over one's behavior.

The emotionally healthy person has adequate mechanisms for controlling anxiety, hostility, and guilt.   This ability comes primarily and almost exclusively from the home, where children identify with their parents and imitate them consciously and subconsciously.   But if parents do not or cannot provide reassuring and edifying adult behavior, the child rarely succeeds in learning to handle emotions properly— unless other wholesome adult contacts with strong influence are at hand—and narcissistic or other self-centered behavior disorders can be anticipated, which are primarily responsible for the failure to respect appointments and work hours.

Those who enjoy their work seldom neglect it, but emotionally troubled employees have considerable difficulty enjoying anything.   By studying their psychiatric backgrounds, the supervisor and company physician usually find the causes of the chronic absentee's defective habits.

L. Physical illness.   The primary medical causes of absenteeism are psychiatric, but some physical causes are so frequent they deserve mention: the common cold, migraine headaches, flu, menstrual disturbances, diarrhea, ankle sprains, and back injuries.   These are largely unpreventable, but a sound home background philosophy and medical support usually keep them from becoming major causes of absenteeism.

The control of physical problems related to serious chronic physical disabilities is a problem of rehabilitative medicine.   The absences they bring about are unpreventable but are ordinarily not detrimental to work habits.   The handicapped worker usually has a commendable attendance record, but serious chronic diseases, such as severe diabetes, may cause higher than average absence rates.

CONTROLLING ABSENTEEISM AND TARDINESS

The best method of controlling absenteeism and tardiness is by preventing them from occurring.   This can be done in several ways, all of which may become necessary in order to rehabilitate chronic absentees.

Company Policy, Management Support, and Direction

As a matter of company policy the control of absence must be promulgated as a serious endeavor for each company.   This requires the complete understanding and support of management if it is to be controlled. All supervisory personnel must be made aware through company policy statements that the control of absence is the direct responsibility of management, the employees, and the medical department, and requires the best possible interpersonal relationships between managers and their employees. Top management should set forth this company policy and establish the supervisory responsibilities necessary for controlling absenteeism.

Company attendance policies should state that:

Each employee was hired as an important and necessary person to fulfill the objectives and obligations of the company, and therefore each person is needed every day he or she is supposed to be present on the job. If this were not true, then the employee would not have been hired by the company.

Sick leave is offered by the company only for *illness emergencies* which might result otherwise in excessive worry, hazardous work performance, and financial burden to good employees. All employees, including all management employees, should be aiming for perfect attendance records. Everyone is expected to stay in as good a state of health as when hired insofar as reasonably possible. Perfect attendance can be achieved by living and working safely at all times whether at home or at work, taking timely preventive measures against sickness and injury, and never allowing minor illnesses or other minor problems to prevent work attendance at the proper time.

The company is forced to recognize any absence as significantly detrimental by weakening the company's goals, services, and productivity. No one in the company is exempted from the need to strive for perfect attendance, and therefore good attendance is one of the most important criteria of employability. In fairness to other employees, the company will be required to terminate anyone who does not comply with company attendance policy.

The supervisor is directly responsible for the promotion of good attendance, and most employees respond to positive demonstrations of appreciation and recognition for their excellent attendance by verbal commendations or by letters or certificates of appreciation and recognition from management.

For employees with chronic absentee or tardiness records, the supervisor must be capable of detecting irregular attendance quickly and be able to efficiently get to the bottom of the problem in order to rehabilitate such employees before they incur significant losses to themselves, the company, or the community. The supervisor should use a thorough method such as the calendar-type form and must be capable of accurately knowing the incidence, the quantity, and the reasons for absences or tardiness if rehabilitation is to be as effective as possible. When dealing with a true, chronic absentee, it is essential for the supervisor to maintain a close guard on all types of absences from normally scheduled work, including excused absences, personal leave, and any other type of absence that may occur. This is because many chronic absentees have developed rather sophisticated methods for finding "legitimate" ways of getting out of work which show up as excessive "excused" absences.

Controlling Absence by Supervisory Action

The disciplinary action taken may be divided into several stages:

1. *The First Absence.* Initially, the supervisor will record the absence and check with the employee regarding the cause and the condition early on the first day of his return. This information should be recorded both on the calendar attendance record and on the investigation and action taken form regarding absence and tardiness records. At this stage, it may be necessary to refer the patient to the medical department or to counsel the employee regarding his reason for absence. During the interview, it is important to review the company policy regarding attendance

with the absentee and to document this discussion on the investigation and action taken form.

2. *Occasional Recurring Unexcused Absences.* If absenteeism continues, the supervisor is required to bring the matter to the attention of higher management after which another interview with the employee is held. During this discussion, the employee should be clearly warned that his future employment and position are now both at stake if unexcused absence occurs again. This should be fully documented on the investigation and action form including the remarks of the employee as well.

3. *The Final Warning.* If absenteeism then continues, the management is obliged to inform the employee that this, in fact, is the *last chance* prior to termination from the payroll. This should be done in writing by the appropriate official in management.

4. *Termination.* If another unexcused absence then occurs, the employee is terminated.

Whenever the supervisor becomes aware of a physical or psychiatric problem underlying the absence, the employee should be immediately referred to the medical department for rehabilitation during any stage prior to termination.

MEDICAL TREATMENT AND CONSULTATION SERVICES

Since absenteeism is at least a symptom of disease, and perhaps a form of disease itself, the proper approach is basically the same as that used in treating any occupational disease. The philosophy behind medical policy should be to establish the best possible rapport with all employees from the time of preplacement examinations on, by devoting sufficient time and energy to the cultivating of sincere patient relationships by every member of a highly motivated health team.

Since employees tend to confide personal information to the members of the medical team, it is necessary for the medical workers to be well trained in psychiatric procedures so that they do not show condescension to the chronic absentees, many of whom are relatively difficult patients to handle at this stage. If the medical department cannot meet the patient's needs, then they should be referred efficiently and discreetly to the proper place.

The medical approach to absence control is naturally directed at each individual medical cause, but primarily at the reduction of mental causes, the most fruitful area for improvement.

The consulting physician must endeavor to improve insight by gently assisting absentees in completely understanding why they came to have these habits, while pointing out the personal benefits to be derived from a better attendance record. The disciplining of absentees is completely beyond the medical approach, although the physician must be prepared to explain the firm alternatives supervisors may be forced to use if absentees continue to abuse the system. This keeps the lever in the picture but avoids alienating absentees, once they realize that it is the *system* which rightfully must be obeyed by all, with no exceptions. Company medical policy aims and programs similarly should be formulated and stated publicly.

By instituting a modern absence control policy and program with the complete backing and support of all levels of management, including the proper use of medical services, industry can expect to significantly lower the absent rate. By lowering the absent rate in this way, the additional benefits will be: (1) improved attitude and productivity, (2) protection against hazardous workers (who create work hazards), (3) longer and more productive employability of workers, (4) lower disability and compensation costs, (5) fewer lost-time accidents, (6) lower accident frequency and severity rates, and (7) lower turnover.

The monetary benefits to each industry can then be measured with reasonable accuracy by comparing company productivity per employee which should increase directly proportional to the man-days saved by the absence control program.

PROGNOSIS

By proper identification of the underlying factors and the use of "absence control" programs, the rate of absences should eventually decline. Current practices will continue to result in the employment of many with relatively inadequate personalities who lack physical and mental strength and endurance. However, if a proper absence control program is established in *all* companies, some of the predisposing factors will diminish nationwide since immature employees will be receiving similar maturity training wherever they work.

BIBLIOGRAPHY

Bews, D. C.: "A Medical Program to Assist Management in the Control of Absenteeism," *Journal of Occupational Medicine,* vol. 5, p. 243, 1966.

Blumberg, M. S., and J. A. Coffin: *A Syllabus on Work Absence,* American Medical Association, Chicago, 1956.

Bond, M. B., et al.: "An Occupational Health Program," *Archives of Environmental Health,* vol. 17, p. 408, 1968.

Cole, E. N.: "Industry's Increasing Dependency upon its Medical Departments," *Journal of Occupational Medicine,* vol. 12, p. 641, 1966.

Felton, J. S.: "Emotional Health in Industry," *Journal of Occupational Medicine,* vol. 9, p. 439, 1967.

"International Occupational Health," *Journal of Occupational Medicine,* vol. 4, p. 194, 1966.

Johnstone, R. T., and S. E. Miller: *Occupational Diseases and Industrial Medicine,* W. B. Saunders Company, Philadelphia, 1960.

Leavell, H. R., and E. G. Clark: *Preventive Medicine for the Doctor in his Community,* 2d ed., McGraw-Hill Book Company, New York, 1958, pp. 222–259.

Pell, S., and C. A. D'Alonzo: "Sickness Absenteeism of Alcoholics," *Journal of Occupational Medicine,* vol. 12, pp. 198–210, 1970.

Pelnar, P. V.: "Occupational Health in Europe," *Journal of Occupational Medicine,* vol. 2, p. 53, 1967.

Sternhagen, C. J.: "Medicine's Role in Reducing Absenteeism," *Personnel,* American Management Association, New York, November–December, 1969.

Thorpe, J. J.: "Attendance Motivations," *Industrial Medicine and Surgery,* vol. 24, p. 450, 1955.

Trice, H. M., et al.: "The Alcoholic and His Steward: A Union Problem," *Journal of Occupational Medicine,* vol. 9, p. 481, 1966.

Wright, H. B.: "Examining the Individual in Relation to his Environment," *Journal of Occupational Medicine,* vol. 8, p. 397, 1967.

chapter 62

Personnel Turnover

JOSEPH C. AUGUSTINE *Personnel Administrator, Medical Center Personnel Office, The University of Michigan, Ann Arbor, Michigan*

PERSONNEL TURNOVER: WHAT IS IT?

Turnover refers to the termination of employees and the hiring of other employees to replace them. These actions are broadly divided into accessions and separations. Accessions are additions of staff while separations are terminations of staff.

Accessions include new hires and call-backs. Separations include quits, discharges, and layoffs for normally more than seven consecutive days. Temporary employees and transfers between jobs, shifts, departments, and buildings are not considered terminations or additions in calculating overall organizational turnover.

Turnover is often categorized as voluntary or involuntary and avoidable or unavoidable. Voluntary separations are initiated by the employee while involuntary terminations are initiated by the employer. Avoidable separations are ones the employer has control over such as wages, benefits, hours, and working conditions. Unavoidable separations are ones the employer has no control over such as illness, retirement, death, and pregnancy.

The Turnover Problem

Most employers recognize that a serious and ongoing problem of great concern is personnel turnover. This is a costly problem with one authority noting that it costs American industry 11 billion dollars a year. This figure includes such items as recruitment, hiring, and training.

A recent U.S. Department of Labor study indicated that in the twenty to twenty-four age group, the average worker will change his job 6.6 times during his lifetime. Those in the twenty-five to thirty-four age group will change jobs 4.8 times. Those in the forty-five to fifty-four group can expect to change jobs 1.4 times before retirement.

Controlled turnover can be healthy as it clears out deadwood and brings new blood and fresh ideas and approaches to an organization. All too often, however, the ones who leave are not the ones management wishes would leave.

While most employers recognize the seriousness of the problem, they all too often fail to attach a dollar value to the loss. Failure to connect turnover and reduced profits often results in little being done to reduce the problem. If the same dollar expenditure were for scrap, much would be done to attack the problem. It seems strange then that people—our most important and costliest asset—receive less attention.

Considerable time, effort, and money are poured into attracting and selecting employees, but all too little of the same are directed toward keeping them.

Some employers brush the problem aside and take comfort in the fact that their problem is not worth worrying about because their competition has a turnover rate twice as high. Another typical response is that it is a complex problem and nothing much can be done about it.

If we are sincere about reducing turnover we must first recognize and admit that it is a soluble, though admittedly, complex problem. Recognizing that the stated reasons for terminations are often not the real reasons, we have to develop techniques to get at the real reasons, and efforts are therefore directed at the problems and not the symptoms of the problems.

Measuring Personnel Turnover

The most generally accepted formula for calculating "gross" turnover is the number of separations per hundred employees in the work force during a month or year.

$$\text{TR (turnover rate)} = \frac{S \text{ (separations)}}{\text{AWF (average work force)}} \times 100$$

The average work force is the total number of employees at the beginning and end of the month or year divided by two.

Variations of the above formula are possible if one wants to calculate turnover based on such factors as voluntary quits, dismissals, avoidable separations, and unavoidable separations. Avoidable turnover is something an employer has control over so efforts to reduce turnover could be profitably directed at this group of terminations. The formula for computing avoidable turnover is

$$\text{TR} = \frac{\text{TS (total separations)} - \text{AS (avoidable separations)}}{\text{AWF (average work force)}} \times 100$$

and is often referred to as a "refined rate."

Determining Turnover Costs

The dollar cost of replacing employees varies significantly depending on the job and the education and training required to perform that job. Employees filling non-skilled jobs might be added to the staff at little direct cost while highly trained or educated employees may cost several thousands of dollars.

In determining turnover costs, one must consider both direct and indirect expenditures. Direct expenditure would include such costs as advertisements, agency fees, interviews, tests, reference checks, medical examinations, and training time. Indirect expenditures might include reduced production, work disruption, increased scrap, and overtime for other employees in order to meet deadlines. One study indicated that a rule-of-thumb generalization is that the minimum direct cost of replacing a competent worker probably ranges from 300 to 700 times the hourly pay rate for that position.

A simple form listing direct and indirect expenditures down the side and type of positions (office, technical, professional, hourly, etc.) across the top can be used in estimating and dramatizing the financial impact of employee turnover. These figures can often be used in convincing management that turnover is not only a significant problem but a costly one.

If there are 500 terminations with an average replacement cost of $500, turnover has cost $250,000. Commitment of only a portion of this amount could provide for the addition of a capable professional to the personnel office staff to devote full-time effort toward identifying the real causes of turnover and working toward solutions to the problem.

In addition to the financial cost, terminating employees who leave with a bad feeling often influence the attitudes of others toward the employer. The result may be additional turnover and difficulty in recruiting good employees.

Why Employees Are Terminated

Employees are discharged for two basic reasons: inability to perform and unwillingness to perform. Termination for inability should come only after the employee has had proper training and reasonable opportunity to perform satisfactorily. The unwillingness or attitudinal cases might include absenteeism, tardiness, failure to observe rules and regulations, and insubordination.

Why Employees Resign or Quit

Employees voluntarily terminate for a host of reasons that can be listed as avoidable and unavoidable. The list might include but is not limited to better opportunity elsewhere, lack of challenge, lack of promotional opportunities, unfair or unequal treatment, poor supervision, interpersonal relationships, unsatisfactory pay, unpleasant working conditions, inability to perform, moving, return to school, pregnancy, illness, retirement, and death.

Communicating the Problem

Little can be done to attack the problem if management and supervision are either unaware of it or unaware of facts and statistics related to it. Communicate the rate of turnover, the cost of turnover, a profile of the people that are leaving, and the areas or departments that are experiencing the greatest rate of turnover.

Meetings held with top management and then supervision are a must in communicating the problem and gaining the support required if serious effort is to be devoted to attacking the problem.

Turnover and the Higher-pay Myth

Terminating employees often indicate they are leaving to accept a position with "higher pay." From the employee's standpoint, this is an acceptable reason for leaving. Unfortunately, many supervisors and employers either accept this as the real reason or find comfort in the explanation when they know the real reason is a reflection on their supervision or on unfavorable conditions existing in the department or organization. The fact is that more money is seldom the real reason an employee leaves, but if it is, it is usually accompanied by other reasons as well. The other reasons usually involve fundamental job dissatisfaction for a variety of reasons. When an individual is hired he is aware of the starting salary and has voluntarily accepted a position knowing that salary. Inasmuch as most turnover takes place within the first hours, days, weeks, or months of employment the explanation of higher salary when terminating is often a whitewash.

COLLECTION OF TURNOVER DATA

Addressing ourselves to the turnover problem first requires that we know the nature and magnitude of the problem.

Personnel Records

A method of gathering data on a systematic basis is the first step in the process. Normally a central point such as the personnel office is the best place to consolidate and compile the data. A form should be designed that will record specific information about terminating employees such as name, department, classification, work shift, age, sex, marital status, education, length of service, and reason given for leaving. It is best to break down identifiable information into the lowest possible denominator since any single part of it may prove to be significant. The material can always be reassembled if the more detailed breakdown is of no use.

Exit Interviews and Questionnaires

The exit interview is an attempt by the employer to find out why a person is leaving, what he liked and disliked about his job and the company, and what suggestions he might have that would make the department and the employer a better place to work.

While the immediate supervisor and the department head might conduct an exit interview of their own with the terminating employee, the personnel department generally has this responsiblity. Where problems have existed, the employee will normally be more willing to speak honestly and openly with a personnel staff member.

The interview is often conducted on the last day of work with the hope that the employee will be more willing to discuss his real reasons for termination. This is to be weighed against the potential of salvaging the employee by talking with him as soon as the resignation is known.

Great skill in interviewing is required if the interviewer is to gain the confidence of the employee and obtain the desired information. The interview generally goes from direct nonthreatening questions to a more nondirective approach as rapport is established. Care must be taken not to display surprise, pass judgment, or justify management action in response to what the employee says.

To be an effective and accurate tool, exit interviews should be conducted with all terminating employees, and the results or summary should be written up immediately after the interview.

A questionnaire designed to get at the same information may be used where interviewing time is not available or where it is impossible to meet with a terminating employee.

Postexit Questionnaires

Recognizing that they might be thought of as troublemakers and given a poor evaluation when seeking another job, many employees are reluctant to give their real reasons for termination while still employed.

The postexit questionnaire, designed to find out why employees left and what suggestions they might have, can be sent out any time after a person terminates. Generally the time span varies from two weeks to three months after termination, with a month being the most common.

The primary advantages of this system are minimal cost and increased likelihood of honest answers. The disadvantages are the normally poor return and the extreme variation in response tending to indicate that those responding were very pleased or very dissatisfied.

An interesting and significant point is that stated reasons for termination at the time of termination will often differ from reasons given after termination.

Telephone Interviews

A personal telephone call to the home of an employee who has left may be fruitful in getting specific information about the reason for leaving. Waiting a few weeks or even months until the employee is settled in a new position so he does not have to worry about a reference check will increase the likelihood of meaningful information. The fact that someone was interested enough to call him at home combined with the opportunity to express one's self without a face-to-face meeting will often evoke excellent cooperation and results.

Random Sampling Interviews

Recognizing that every employee has certain attitudes about his job, his supervisor, benefit programs, ways to improve the system, etc., members of management should establish an objective of getting out into the work areas to talk to employees to learn more about their attitudes. Each member of management could have specific areas of responsibility where he would be expected to randomly select an employee each day that he would approach unannounced and proceed to initiate conversation about that employee and his feelings and recommendations. Such a system would assist management in assessing the pulse of the organization while demonstrating to employees a real interest in what they think and feel. Problem areas are more likely to surface early when this attitude prevails.

Attitude Surveys

Unlike the exit interview and the postexit questionnaire, attitude surveys are normally conducted with employees who are still on the rolls. Properly constructed, they should get at a wide range of work-related attitudes including why employees stay, things they are happy with, areas of concern, and suggested improvements.

Survey questionnaires can and do take a variety of forms. Many are prepared and even conducted by professional social scientists specializing in such activities. Others that may be equally as effective can be done by the employer himself if care is taken and a few pitfalls are avoided.

While the survey is usually in the form of a written questionnaire, it should get as specific as possible regarding attitudes, location or position, type of position, etc. without revealing the identity of the respondent unless he desires to sign his name.

In addition to specific questions that might be asked, open-ended questions should be included to give respondents an opportunity to express what is on their minds and to comment on items the survey failed to ask about.

Carefully analyzed, the results of the survey should prove helpful in pointing out strengths that can be capitalized on and weaknesses that are worthy of attention.

ANALYSIS OF TURNOVER DATA

Inasmuch as there is no standard and uniformly accepted formula for recording statistics and computing turnover, there is limited value in comparisons of one company with another. The greater value is an internal one in working to reduce the figure on a monthly and over a yearly basis.

Gross turnover figures, while helpful, are misleading in that they fail to identify high turnover versus low turnover areas. Comparing departmental figures will help identify organizational trouble spots. In reviewing the data collected it is generally obvious that the rate of turnover varies significantly from department to department.

There should be the expectation that turnover will be higher in those areas having the larger number of entry level positions, unskilled workers, and younger workers. It is not uncommon for many organizations or departments to have more than 100 percent turnover in a given year. While this is a serious matter, we do not know whether the figure means that every person turned over or some positions turned over several times. We must analyze the figures by asking questions such as:

1. Is turnover equally distributed in the organization or is it significantly higher in certain departments?

2. Where turnover is high in a particular department, is there a concentration in a particular kind of job or under a particular supervisor?

3. Are terminations from a particular age group, sex, shift?

4. Is there a common reason for termination?

Where high turnover concentrations are identified, efforts need to be directed to identifying reasons so corrective measures might be taken.

AN ALL-OUT PROGRAM TO REDUCE TURNOVER

The question is often asked, "Where do I start, in attacking the turnover problem?" Recognizing the complexities of the problem, it is fair to say that turnover is normally caused for a variety of reasons rather than for any one single reason. Serious efforts must be directed to an examination of the entire process affecting employees from the day they are recruited through the day they leave. The review should include such items as recruitment, selection, training, salary and wage programs, fringe benefits, working conditions, and supervisory practices. Many of the factors are related, and dissatisfaction with one may lead to dissatisfaction with another.

Establish Updated and Realistic Job and Man Requirements

Review the job duties to be sure they are complete and up to date before attempting to recruit for the job. Consider the requirements *necessary* to perform the job as opposed to the desired qualifications of education, experience, specialized training, physical effort, etc. Recognize that not everyone will become the company president and do not require more than is necessary to perform the specific job unless rapid promotion can be assured. Underutilization of overqualified personnel is a major source of dissatisfaction. Avoid stereotypes and artificial barriers that stand in the way of employing qualified personnel.

Improve Recruitment and Selection Procedures

Recruitment is the positive attempt to attract applicants, while selection is the process of eliminating applicants in an attempt to match the qualifications of the individual with the requirements of the job. Good selection is the right person in the right job.

1. Employment interviewers must be trained and skilled in their work. Do not put rejects in personnel as it is no longer just the health and happiness department.

2. Interviewers should know position requirements, work areas, supervisors, and the peculiarities of these.

3. Be honest with the applicant. Tell the bad as well as the good so applicants know the full truth and will not be turnover statistics because the job was not honestly represented.

4. Show the applicant the work area, show him where he will be located, and introduce him to people he will work with.

5. Provide as much lead time as possible for personnel to recruit so they can refer the right person for the job.

6. Medical examinations, reference checks, and testing, where appropriate, can help screen out potential turnover.

Effective Promotion From Within

Every employer boasts of a program of promotion from within. Many times this stated philosophy is not much more than that, however, as higher-level positions are filled by new employees rather than through promotion of current staff members with excellent work records and performance appraisals indicating they are capable of increased responsibility. While new blood needs to be brought into the organization, it must not be at the expense of good staff members who will read this as a sign that there is no future for them, causing them to look for employment opportunities that will recognize and reward their ability and performance.

It is essential that the promotion-from-within philosophy be supported by top management and well understood by everyone in the organization. The personnel office must establish a systematic means of reviewing the performance appraisals of every employee and consider them for promotions as they become available.

Job posting is an effective means of letting employees know what opportunities exist so they can make their interests known. An equally effective and possibly easier system is "dial-a-job." This is a telephone number that can be called at any time by both employees and applicants interested in learning what opportunities are available. The system allows the employer to record and change the message as often as he likes. Either system has the advantage of allowing employees to let their interests be known, and combined with a systematic review by the personnel office, should provide an effective promotion-from-within program.

Effective Orientation Program

We know that turnover is highest during the early stages of employment. As the period of employment increases, turnover decreases. It is important to see that employees' needs are met early in order to increase the likelihood of their continued employment.

All too often employees are hired and put to work without proper orientation. Other times we try to cram too much in at once when employees are already nervous about starting a new job. Consider spreading the orientation out over several days, weeks, or months so the employee can absorb more and can ask meaningful questions along the way. Rather than have a continuous orientation program before putting the person to work, integrate it with the duties to be performed. An integrated orientation and training approach will assist the employee to adjust to the requirements of the new job on a more gradual and comfortable basis.

Employee Training

Training takes place whether we formally provide for it or not. A formalized program is far superior to the informal haphazard approach of letting employees get things on their own the hard way and often incorrectly.

1. Designate responsibility and accountability for the training function.
2. Develop a list of items to be covered.
3. Demonstrate as well as explain the tasks to be performed.
4. Explain the relationship of the specific job to that of the department and the organization as a whole.
5. Watch the employee perform the assigned tasks.
6. Follow up to see if there are questions or problems.

7. First-line supervisors must be given sufficient time to see that employees are properly trained rather than always being concerned about meeting production standards.

8. Training is not a one-shot effort; be sure it continues.

Supervisory Training

The attitudes and actions of supervision are a major influence on the seriousness of the problem of turnover. Supervisors are generally well-intentioned and desire to do a good job, but all too often, despite their technical knowledge, they lack the necessary training of how to supervise. Often they have come up through the ranks, having been promoted because of outstanding performance.

It is imperative that supervisors be given training as soon as they become supervisors or even before they assume supervisory responsibility. The training should address itself not only with "what" to do, but "how" to do it, as well. It should include human relations skills or sensitivity training that will assist supervisors to be more sensitive to the needs and feelings of those they supervise.

Competitive and Equitable Salary and Wage Program

Develop and maintain a program that offers a competitive salary and provides for internal equity and a systematic salary review for all persons on a fair and appropriately timed basis. Employees should be aware of their classification and the salary range for that classification. Competitive starting salaries with appropriate increases at reasonable time intervals generally provide greater long-range satisfaction than the higher starting salary with smaller increases over longer intervals between increases. As stated previously, more money is seldom the real reason an employee leaves.

Attractive and Competitive Fringe Benefit Program

Employees seldom join or leave an employer because of the fringe benefit program alone. Where salary is comparable, fringe benefits may make a difference however.

Performance Appraisals

Performance appraisal systems, properly constructed and conducted should let an employee know how he is performing his particular job in relation to what is expected of him. Without getting into the middle of the debate over the results or goal-oriented system versus the all too common personality assessment approach, suffice it to say that the system should evaluate performance against preestablished and mutually agreed-upon objectives while taking into account how this was accomplished.

If a supervisor is doing his job properly, what is said in the formal appraisal or review process should not be a surprise to the employee, but rather a summary of earlier discussions. As such, formal appraisal systems must be endorsed by top management, and more than that, carried out from the top on down. Further, it should be required that reviews be discussed with subordinates, as a completed review that has not been discussed is of no value in informing the subordinate where he stands and what is expected of him.

As part of this program, employees should be expected to complete a form annually that would encourage them to indicate their degree of satisfaction with their present job as well as to indicate what types of positions they might aspire to and what type of additional training they would find helpful.

The completed supervisory appraisal and employee interest form together would be useful to the personnel department in identifying persons for internal promotion and transfer as well as identifying desired training needs.

Effective and Responsive Complaint Procedure

It is imperative that a formal and effective complaint procedure exist so that employees can express their concerns and expect to have them reviewed and responded to.

Union contracts normally contain a grievance procedure that often includes arbitration as a final step when employees feel they are wronged.

A procedure for non-bargained-for employees should provide for a hearing beginning with the immediate supervisor, with one or two intermediate steps, before it is heard by a top member of management.

It is essential that the specific complaint be investigated carefully and completely to ensure fair treatment of the particular employee who has filed the complaint. Recognize also that the complaint may point out a fundamental problem deserving of attention and correction.

Repeated complaints from a particular department or involving a particular supervisor may point up an area or a person in need of assistance.

Dial-a-complaint

Employees are sometimes reluctant to ask questions or voice complaints directly because of fear of reprisal. A "dial-a-complaint" telephone system can be established with a special telephone line that will record the comments of the caller. The number can be called anytime of the day or night which provides the advantage of allowing employees, particularly timid ones, to say what they want when they want. Each day the personnel office can listen to the comments recorded. In some cases, responses to general questions and problems might be published in the house organ. When the caller is willing to leave his name and the number where he can be contacted, the personnel office can call that number to respond to the question or complaint. This system will encourage employees to get things off their chest and will provide information that will be investigated with the goal of ironing out legitimate complaints and problems that are called to attention. This approach can be particularly helpful in locating problem areas and potential problem areas early.

Consistent Application of Policies and Procedures

It is important that policies and procedures be known by employees if they are to perform their jobs successfully. It is essential that supervisors enforce them on a consistent basis to ensure equal treatment and to avoid hard feelings leading to job dissatisfaction and termination.

Corrective Disciplinary Process

When our automobile or a piece of work equipment breaks down we usually try to diagnose the problem and have it repaired before we consider replacement of the item. It is strange, but true, that we often do less than this for our human resources when they have problems. All too often we look to termination as the solution to a problem without making an honest effort to salvage an employee. When we consider that a man works about forty years, and if we were to estimate an average salary of $10,000 over that period of years, we have an investment of $400,000. Such an investment should be worth some effort before disposing of it.

In initiating corrective action, we must first consider whether the problem is one of attitude or inability. If the problem is inability every attempt should be made to transfer the employee to a position where he can perform satisfactorily. Good selection is the right person in the right job. Personnel and the department must share in the responsibility if a poor placement is made. Transfers of this type will usually appreciate what has been done for them, and a sense of loyalty will be created that will be conveyed to friends and relatives and co-workers about the organization.

If the problem is one of poor performance because of attitude, the employee must be informed of this and told what he must do if he wishes to continue his employment. The process should be corrective in nature beginning with verbal warning and ending in termination with written warning and layoff usually included in the process.

Many employees can be salvaged if we are willing to meet problems honestly and head-on.

Restructure Jobs

Many jobs are often very monotonous and lack challenge while others may be so physically demanding that employees quickly throw in the towel. Where jobs fall into these categories, attempts should be made to provide relief by possibly having two work groups that would alternate assignments on an appropriate basis such as every four hours.

At the same time equipment, supplies, and methods can also be modified to accommodate the worker if they are a serious problem resulting in turnover.

More imagination and flexibility should be demonstrated in the use of part-time help in areas where monotony and physical strain and effort are a problem.

The idea of job enlargement and job enrichment has had considerable attention in recent years. The efficiency, contrary to what some believe, usually increases where the restructuring has been well planned. Where added challenge can be provided, it is reasonable to expect a marked improvement in morale and job satisfaction and a reduction in turnover.

Employment of the Handicapped

Generally, the handicapped are the last hired and the first fired. Employers of the handicapped find that most of them are among their best workers and their rate of turnover is less than for the work force as a whole. Physically handicapped persons, properly placed, will ordinarily perform as well as or better than the person with no disability.

The mentally retarded or handicapped can often be employed in routinized or simple kinds of jobs that would often bore other employees because of their repetitive nature or lack of challenge.

Increased Use of Part-time Help

In most cases too little has been done to accommodate the part-time worker. Through lack of imagination or unwillingness to break from tradition, we continue to insist on the full-time worker.

Many persons, particularly mothers with children in school, are anxious to work part-time if they can see their children off to school and be home to meet them on their return from school. Most bring a maturity and desire and often previous experience that employers welcome. Often there can be a cost saving in employing them, for in many jobs they produce as much on a part-time basis as the full-time employee who has to pace himself. Where the job requires coverage for a full shift, two persons can often share the job.

The accommodating employer will find an almost untapped reservoir of high-quality part-time personnel available to him. Studies have demonstrated that turnover is usually much less in the part-time employee.

Employee Participation

Where possible, employees should be encouraged to assist in determining how departmental goals might be achieved. Given the job to be accomplished and the date by which it must be completed, the group can often help plan on how to proceed to meet these goals in a manner that is acceptable to both the employer and the employees.

Greater Recognition of Human Needs

Through years of improvement in wages, benefit programs, and job security, the biological or survival needs of most employees are being met reasonably well. The depression years and related problems are unknown to many of today's workers. In the future we must devote increasing efforts to meeting the needs that every person has for recognition and acceptance.

A study of telephone company employees indicated that full appreciation of work done, feeling "in" on things, and sympathetic help on personal problems were all more important than job security and good wages.

More and more, people want to do their own thing. It is becoming increasingly important to allow greater freedom in appearance, dress, etc. There seems to be more of a social consciousness, particularly in the young workers, and they want personally and for their employer to help improve the world in which they live.

Review of Absenteeism

Analysis of absenteeism rates and turnover rates generally indicates a direct correlation between the two. Absenteeism, particularly the single-day variety that often coincides with Monday, Friday, or the normally scheduled days off, is often a predictor of turnover. This absence from work is often an indication that there are problems and is used as an escape. Identification of these employees and discussion with them might help pinpoint problem areas that encourage absence from work. Another result should be an improvement in attendance.

Improved Communication

Efforts devoted to keeping employees informed will ordinarily lead to improved morale as nearly everyone has a desire to know what is happening and why.

Weighted Application Blank

Development of a weighted application blank can be a useful and predictive tool in selecting successful employees and long term employees.

This procedure can be developed by examining the many items included on the employment application of unsuccessful and terminated employees as opposed to currently successful and long-tenure employees. Individual items such as education, age and marital status begin to take on significance where there is a concentration of employees with that same characteristic. Once "significant" items are isolated, numerical weights can be assigned to them and a cutoff point can be established to predict success versus failure and long tenure versus short tenure.

The weighted application blank can best be developed where there are relatively large numbers of employees performing the same kind of work. It is important to review the weights on a regular basis because they change in value for a variety of reasons. Interestingly, there may be no explanation of why certain characteristics predict success or long tenure.

Staff Counselor

Many problems that employees have are personal problems rather than work-related problems. Recognizing that outside problems can and do affect work performance, the addition of a trained counselor may be able to assist employees directly or through referral so that a possible termination can be avoided.

CONCLUSION

Efforts to reduce turnover can be likened to raising children. When children turn out to be "good" there is no simple answer or no one thing that the parents did that resulted in their being good. Love, patience, understanding, encouragement, discipline—all these and more are usually present. In the same way, turnover control is a complex problem that requires an interest and concern for many variables if the problem is to be attacked. While there is no panacea, there are variables over which an employer has control. Proper attention to all of them will result in an improvement in performance, morale, and job satisfaction, and a corresponding reduction in costly turnover.

chapter 63

Automation

JULIUS REZLER *Professor of Economics, Loyola University of Chicago, Chicago, Illinois*

INTRODUCTION

Automation, this latest phase of technological change, emerged in the American scene hardly twenty years ago. But even within this rather short period of time, it has exerted a major influence not only on the technique and organization of production but also on the people involved in the production process. First, it engulfed the blue-collar group, particularly the unskilled workers. Then it reached the offices and created manyfold problems for the clerical work force. In the past few years, it has become obvious that even managers are no longer immune to the effects of automation. It is ironic that managers who initiated and introduced automation in their plants and offices may themselves be affected by this new technology.

Of all functional groups of management perhaps none has a greater stake in the changes caused by automation than personnel management. It is true that, in its initial phase, automation is primarily a technological problem. But once it is introduced it transforms not only the technology of production but also the nature of work and the relationships existing among the people in the firm. It is the duty of personnel management to recognize the new organizational relations, to reexamine the personnel policies and programs to determine whether they are still relevant to the new conditions, and to offer bold solutions for the emerging problems in order to make automation an effective tool of management.

The purpose of this chapter is to assist personnel managers in dealing with problems in automated situations. The author intends to call their attention to major changes in the business organization and in the personnel functions, and to suggest alternative actions for the solution of these problems.

At this point, a few qualifying remarks are in order. First, one should keep in mind that automation is still in an emerging stage, and its impact on organizations and people cannot fully be realized yet because there is a gap between technological change and the subsequent reaction of organizations and the people involved. Consequently, findings concerning problems and solutions should be considered as preliminary. Second, limited space makes it impossible to discuss all the ramifications of automated technology. Emphasis will be placed, therefore, on the basic problems associated with automation and having relevance to personnel management. Third, academic and management experts are sharply divided on the evaluation of automation's effects as well as on the possible solutions to the problems resulting from it. In view of the highly controversial nature of the subject, an attempt will be made to present both sides of the issues discussed in this chapter.

Definition and Types of Automation

Before the organizational and functional problems are considered, the meaning of automation has to be defined. A conceptual clarification is in order because of the confusion surrounding the term "automation," both in the literature and in everyday usage. This confusion may be attributed partly to the tendency to use such terms as "technological change," "mechanization," "cybernation," and "productivity" synonymously. The basic difference in these terms therefore will be briefly indicated: *Technological change* is a term of the broadest meaning comprising any change in the organization and the process of production from time immemorial. *Mechanization* is a type of technological change, the application of machinery to tasks formerly performed by human and animal labor. *Automation* is the latest phase of mechanization, and *cybernation* means the application of computers. *Productivity* indicates the efficiency of production which is usually increased by automated equipment.

For the purpose of this discussion, automation is defined as the latest phase of technological change in which human functions of operating and controlling equipment, collecting information and making decisions concerning the production process have been replaced by mechanical and electronic devices.

Experts frequently refer to automation as if it were a single and simple concept. Some of them fail to recognize that it is a collective name for a complex technological phenomenon. Actually, three basic types of automation exist and are utilized in the business organization: (1) automatic transfer mechanism, (2) continuous flow process, and (3) computers.

The first basic type, also known as the Detroit type because it was first adopted in the automobile factories of that city, links together already highly mechanized individual operations by automatic transfer devices. This type of automation is adopted by industries that use hard substance for raw material (metals, wood, plastics, etc). The continuous-flow type has been developed and used in industries processing liquid and gaseous materials. The emphasis is on the automatic control of the flow, and on the immediate and steady transmission of information concerning all phases of the productive process. Finally, the third type of automation is constituted by computers. There are two kinds of computers: digital and analog. While the two other types of automation are applied to the fabrication of "hard" and "soft" substances, computers process information either in numerical or verbal forms [11, pp. 7–8]. In the last few years, new types of automation, the so-called "super systems" have come into being. These second- and third-generation systems have resulted from the combination of the three basic types. For example, the superimposition of computers on the Detroit type has created the numerically controlled machine tool complexes.

I. AUTOMATION'S IMPACT ON THE BUSINESS ORGANIZATION

Managerial economists and organizational theorists have become increasingly aware of the interrelationship existing between the technology of production and its organizational framework. Charles Perrow pointed out that "A good deal of the variance in the structure of the organization can be explained by the technology they employ . . ." [19, p. 156]. The majority of organizational theorists are in agreement with Thomas Whisler who contends that "Technology is related systematically to task content, authority structure, departmentation, skill structure, cultural values, and the personal characteristics of organizational participants" [19, p. 202]. Findings of an empirical study conducted by the AMA appear to support the previous general observations. Of the companies participating in the survey, more than one-fifth reported organizational changes caused by automation [7, p. 12].

Because of the relatively short period of time that has passed since the introduction of automated technology, its particular impact on the structure of the business organization could not yet be mapped and detailed in its entirety. But on the basis of a number of empirical and analytical studies, it is possible to recognize the direction of changes and the impact areas. It may be concluded that automation appears to affect the following areas of the organizational chart:

1. The hierarchy of the organization. (Application of computers will flatten the traditional pyramidal hierarchy.)

2. The distribution of authority. (The process of decentralization has been reversed and the organization is being recentralized.)

3. Interrelationship among the units. (Data-processing systems are cutting across departmental lines and eventually may break down the traditional departmental form of the organization.)

4. Interrelationship among managerial levels. (Basic change takes place between upper and middle management.)

5. Emergence of new organizational units. (A new department to handle the EDP function is usually added to the existing structure.)

6. Restructuring of existing units. (The efficient use of computers requires the reorganization of certain departments.)

The above changes in the organizational structure will naturally have derivative effects on personnel management. Any shift in man-machine relations and any subsequent change in the organization will definitely create serious human problems which, unless they are solved satisfactorily and without much delay, would endanger the overall efficiency of the organization.

The improvement of human relations is one of the basic functions of personnel management. In order to perform it efficiently, they must be aware of the major changes occurring in the organization during the introduction of automation. Limited space precludes discussion in detail of all the organizational implications of automated technology listed previously. But the following structural changes which are of particular importance to personnel managers will be examined briefly: (1) the distribution of authority (decentralization versus centralization), (2) interrelationship between managerial levels (the effect of automation on middle management), (3) the organization of the computer function.

Distribution of Managerial Authority

One of the major controversies presently reigning among organizational theorists revolves around the question of how the use of computers will affect the distribution of authority in the corporate organization. Will the process of decentralization continue or will it reverse itself and give way to a recentralization of decision making at the top executive level? Three major views appear in this controversy. Members of the first school of thought believe that decentralization of authority in the past was a matter of necessity for the majority of executives, though its principle went against the grain of their business philosophy [15, p. 74]. But with the horizontal and vertical dispersion of the organizational units and information, they had no choice but to delegate authority to the level where the information was available in sufficient quantity and in due time.   The present revolution in information technology, however, has largely eliminated the reasons which previously required the delegation of authority to lower managerial levels, and top management can retake its full control.

A minority of management experts represents the second school of thought according to which computerization of the business organization would actually promote decentralization.   A spokesman for this viewpoint feels that "The anticipated advances in information technology . . . can strengthen decentralization in those businesses that have adopted it and will encourage more management to experiment with decentralization philosophy" [5, p. 124].

Finally, the third school is made up of those students of managerial organization who feel that the computer itself is a neutral factor in shaping the organizational structure and there is no reason why it should lead to centralization of decentralization [8, p. 193].   Taylor and Dean refer to a survey conducted by the consulting firm, Booz-Allen-Hamilton, which concluded that there is "no evidence of relationship between the effectiveness of computer usage and centralization or decentralization" [18, p. 104].

Actually, a centralized computer system in itself does not require recentralization of authority, but it does make this process feasible.   In the final analysis, the philosophy of top management will determine whether they wish to take advantage of this opportunity.   Empirical studies surveying changes brought about by computers in the organizational structure, however, strongly indicate a trend toward centralization of authority.   According to an AMA survey, more than one third of the companies in the sample said that they had centralized the corporate structure; an additional 10 percent of the companies reported centralized controls; and another 10 percent reported other forms of centralization.   Only 5 percent of the companies suggested that electronic data processing has improved their decentralization [7, p. 12].

Middle Management in a Computerized Company

Of all managerial levels, middle management appears to be most seriously affected by the organization changes caused by computerization.   Just as middle management benefited most from the process of decentralization, it may suffer most from recentralization.

Two aspects of middle management are currently subject to a heated discussion: the effect of computers on its job content and on its number.   As to changes in the job content, two major views have emerged.   Members of the first school contend that the job of middle managers is being upgraded because of computers for the following reasons: repetitive tasks are eliminated; less time is spent with controlling operations; there is an increase in the planning function with expanding responsibilities; it considerably increases the need for communications with both the supervisors and the subordinates [14, p. 175].

Those few who believe that the middle management function will be downgraded argue along these lines: the computers have taken over certain functions in such areas as accounting, production scheduling, inventory control [8, p. 195]; the kind of activities that now characterize middle management will be more completely automated than the others [17, p. 47]; in the past, middle management had a monopoly of gathering and evaluating information, and in a modern company this function will be done by the computer.   Similar differences in opinion appear concerning the evaluation of the computer's effect on the number of middle managers. A few experts suggest that there will be no change in their numerical strength; for the long run their number might even increase.   They usually refer to company reports indicating little change in the overall number of middle management jobs during the sixties. But other experts are inclined to conclude that, even if the job of middle managers will not be downgraded, their number has decreased. Executive officers of such companies as Gulf Oil, Westinghouse, General Electric, have reported a decline either in the absolute number of their middle managers or in their number relative to output [1, p. 6].

The controversy over the impact of computers on the numerical strength of middle management should be settled on the basis of observing trends during the current recession. The introduction of computers coincided with one of the longest prosperities in the American economic history. During such periods little effort is made to economize. Recently, however, companies have made strenuous efforts to cut out "deadwood" and eliminate waste from their organization. A survey of middle management positions at the end of the current recession would truly reveal the real impact of computers on their number.

While there is an apparent disagreement concerning the impact of automation on the content and number of middle management jobs, there is no doubt in the minds of the experts that computerization has created grave psychological and organizational problems for the middle management group. They feel threatened by the computer for such reasons as fear of losing certain responsibilities and status; unfamiliarity with computer technology; facing changes in job content; no rapport with the specialists who man the computer center [3, p. 107]. As a result, many middle managers have developed a resistance to the introduction and use of computers, thus impairing their efficiency and their blend with the organization.

Personnel management has valid reasons for being interested in the problems of middle management. First of all, personnel management is considered an integral part of middle management, and therefore anything that happens to the middle management level may have serious implications for personnel management, too. Second, personnel managers are expected to play a major role in solving the human problems resulting from computerization for middle management.

There are several approaches that personnel managers may take to alleviate the fears of middle managers and overcome their resistance. First, personnel managers should recognize that the most critical period for the middle manager in his encounter with the computer is during the phase-in of the latter [3, p. 42]. This is the time when they need as much assistance as they can get. To reduce the tenseness of this period, middle managers should be kept informed about the timetable of computer installation. They should also know about the areas where computers will be used. Personnel managers may also be helpful in straightening out the personal problems arising between the computer specialists and middle managers. The last, and perhaps the single most important, thing personnel managers may do for their colleagues is to help them to obtain the skill and knowledge necessary to understand the implications and operations of the computer. Specialized workshops offered in the planning and phase-in periods would do much to attain these objectives.

Organization of the Computer Function

The most direct impact of the computer on the organizational structure has resulted from the necessity to organize this new function and integrate it with the already existing units of the organization. Several major problems have emerged in connection with the organization of the data processing function: (1) The form of organizing this function, (2) the responsibility for this organization, (3) the relationship between the computer staff and other members of the management team.

The success of computerization may depend to a large extent on the way in which this function is related to the total organization. According to an AMA study, "There is a very real relationship between the location of the computer complex within the organization and its effectiveness in meeting company needs" [10, p. 22]. A survey of major companies reveals three major patterns in organizing electronic data processing (EDP). Originally, this function was either decentralized or became a part of the financial department. As its importance grew, data processing has become more centralized and autonomous, and moved upward in the organizational structure. At present, the majority of data-processing systems are operated either as autonomous service centers or as independent departments on an equal level with other functional units of the organization.

Once the computer function is organized the question that arises is: To whom should the manager of the unit report? Canning and Sisson recommend that "The function should be headed by a man at least capable of operating at the third organization level—that is, reporting to a vice-president" [6, p. 52]. Apparently top executives recognize that the efficiency of the EDP unit depends partly on the organizational level at which it operates and the manager of the unit is increasingly supervised by one of the executives. According to a recent survey, almost 75 percent of EDP managers report to presidents, executive vice-presidents, vice-presidents, controllers, secretaries, or treasurers of their respective companies [7, p. 35].

Staffing the new computer center represents a novel task as well as a challenge for personnel management. It is a novel task because computer programmers, designers, and systems analysts who make up the staff of the center constitute a new brand of specialists whose training and job classification is still ill-defined and who frequently differ from the typical corporate manager. It is a challenge because the personnel manager must compete with hundreds of other organizations which are in the process of staffing their own computer center and are determined to get the best men in the market.

Since staffing an EDP center is a relatively new game, there are few established rules to follow and the personnel manager is frequently left to his own devices and improvisations. But a few preliminary observations may be of some help to personnel managers faced with staffing a center. There are two sources of data-processing personnel: promote and upgrade people from within the organization, and hire trained men from outside. As to the first method, experience shows that usually young, junior-level people are selected for positions with the computer center, because older, more experienced men often consider it beneath their dignity to accept such a job [6, p. 14].

Programmers are mainly selected from within the organization usually through a programmers' aptitude test. According to a survey, 70 percent of the organizations used such tests in selecting programmers. The test most frequently used was the IBM Programmer Aptitude Test. There is some doubt, however, about the validity and reliability of these tests. Using supervisors' ratings as a measure of job performance, aptitude test scores correlate about 0.1 to 0.4 with these supervisors' ratings, a relatively low correlation. Also these tests have not yet been validated [6, p. 65].

In the case of a blue-chip pharmaceutical company, the majority of the programmers have been promoted from the clerical personnel of the data-processing center. They were selected on the basis of intelligence, interest, and skill. Only 20 percent of its programmers have a college degree.

Outside hiring is used mainly to obtain the services of systems analysts, the majority of whom have college degrees. For this or for other reasons, they usually keep apart from the programmers and neither have programming experience nor are interested in acquiring it [6, p. 61].

Antagonism between the staff of the computer unit and line managers which may reach the degree of hostility is a side effect resulting from the novelty of the data-processing function and from the different orientation of the specialists who perform this function. The reasons for such conflict situations between these two groups was recognized by a comprehensive study: "Differences in personality, age and experience between the computer specialist and the old-line manager are accentuated by a reciprocal naïveté about their functions" [1, pp. 30–31]. The specialist is sometimes unfamiliar with the organization of the company and with the information needs of line management. On the other hand, line managers view with suspicion these members of a new breed of specialists who are immersed in technicalities and seem to disregard the human problems associated with their operations.

Personnel managers may contribute to the reduction and the eventual elimination of this controversy and tension by considering the following policies: On one hand, management trainees who will become the future line managers should be selected and trained in such a way as to obtain an education compatible with modern information technology. They should know something about statistical analysis and systems design. On the other hand, the computer specialists, whenever possible, should be selected from existing management ranks so that they will be familiar with the operational problems of the company. Also the use of integrated teams to head the major computer programs could develop some understanding and mutual respect on both sides [1, pp. 32–33].

II. AUTOMATION AND THE PERSONNEL FUNCTION

Computers and other types of automated equipment, although sometimes of frightening proportions, are only tools and devices used by people. Changes in the man-machine relations and the problems resulting from it, in the final analysis, are the business of personnel management, and therefore, affect its functions.

It should be noted that while the previously discussed changes in the organizational structure of the enterprise have been primarily caused by the computer type of automation, the personnel function is affected by all the three types of automated technology. This is because personnel management administers not only the managerial and clerical personnel that are primarily exposed to computers but also the work force of the plant. The latter is involved in processes to which either the Detroit-type or the continuous-flow type of automation may be applied.

A function of personnel management is affected by the various types of automation in two distinct ways: indirectly and directly. The installation of automated equipment in various organizational units other than the personnel department has an indirect effect on the personnel function. Change in the technology of those units will also cause a corresponding change in the quality and quantity of the manpower required to operate the new equipment. Such development, in turn, will cause personnel management to alter or modify its methods and procedures used previously to perform its functions [12, pp. 76–77].

As these changes have actually originated in other departments of the organization and spread to the personnel department in a derivative manner, their effects should be considered as indirect in nature. But there is also a second way in which automation may directly hit personnel management, namely the personnel department itself could be automated by applying computers to some of its own functions such as personnel record keeping, skills inventory, recruiting, etc. The computerization of the personnel function is examined in Chapter 79, and therefore this part will deal entirely with the indirect effects of automation on the personnel function. For the purpose of this discussion, the so-called industrial relations function will be considered as a part of the overall personnel function.

A major technological change like automation would affect many aspects of the work force. Again space limitations forbid us to cover all the ramifications, and instead, a few developments of automation which have exerted a profound impact on the work force, and indirectly on the personnel function, will be discussed in the following pages.

Automation and Employment

Of the various effects of automation none has caused deeper concern among employees and managers alike than its real or alleged impact on employment. To save on direct labor costs is one of the main reasons for the adoption of this technology. Once an automated equipment is installed, it usually eliminates jobs and displaces workers. Displacement, however, is not the same as unemployment. Although the displaced worker loses his previous job, he may retain his employment in another department or plant of the same company. But there have been quite a few cases in which the company was not able to absorb workers displaced by automation, and they were permanently separated from the work force and became technologically unemployed.

The effect of automation on the volume of employment varies from company to company. Beaumont and Helfgott have examined thirty-one case studies for a comparison of employment before and after the introduction of automation. They found that in twenty cases employment declined by as much as 15 to 45 percent, in four cases it remained unchanged, and in seven cases there was actually an increase in the number of jobs [2, p. 26].

In the majority of other case studies published by the Bureau of Labor Statistics, a considerable number of blue-collar workers were displaced; at the same time, the number of technical and other white-collar jobs has increased. In most cases, however, with the notable exception of the meat-packing firms, the displaced blue-collar workers were not disemployed because they were transferred to the non-automated operations of the same company [11, p. 30].

Nevertheless, the effects of automation on employment may represent a major problem for the personnel manager as the administrator of the work force, unless he plans and acts well in advance. As soon as he learns about pending automation of the company, he should make plans for adjusting the work force to the requirements of the new technology. He should begin with surveying the impact of automation on other companies of the same industry, and learn from their lesson. A study published by the U.S. Department of Labor [20] would provide him with a possible pattern to be expected in his own industry. Within the industry itself, however, each company may represent an individual case. Whether or not automation will cause a major reduction in the work force of a particular company will depend primarily on two factors: the labor savings effect of the automated equipment in terms of jobs eliminated, and the growth rate of the company in terms of new jobs to be created. The net balance will indicate the extent to which automation will affect the volume of employment of the firm.

If the rate of reduction due to automation is offset by an increase in employment because of growth, then personnel management will have less to do with layoffs and separations and more with transfers and retraining. On the other hand, if the automated equipment will drastically cut employment, the personnel manager will be required to perform the unpleasant task of separating surplus labor from the work force.

In any case, the personnel manager must act long before the new equipment is installed. First, he should give an advanced notice to the affected employees and their union of the forthcoming automatization. At the same time, they should also be informed about the policies of the company to deal with displacement and possible disemployment. If the company is in the position to absorb the workers to be displaced, they should be reassured and should learn about the transfer procedures. If the reduction of the work force appears to be unavoidable, the personnel manager should plan an orderly procedure of separation and, if possible, use attrition to cut the work force to the desired size. If, for any reason, the policy of attrition cannot be pursued and layoffs will be required, the workers to be separated should learn of the severance payment provisions, if any, or of the possibility of an early retirement. In all likelihood, in unionized companies, such procedures are regulated by collective agreements.

Once the adjustment of the work force to automated production is completed, the personnel manager can expect less fluctuation in employment than before automation. According to several case studies, employment in automated companies achieves a relative stability and will not fluctuate much with changes in capacity utilization [11, p. 31].

Changes in the Occupational Composition of the Work Force

Automation does not affect only the volume of employment but also its composition, thus creating some additional problems for personnel management. The work force of a company is composed of various occupational groups which are quite sensitive to technological changes. Displacement of workers in one occupational group and their forced or voluntary migration to another, has been generated by the following effects of automation: the creation of new jobs, the change in content of some existing jobs, the elimination of several jobs, and the fact that new skills are required because existing skills have become obsolete [11, p. 53].

A major controversy has developed concerning the effects of these changes on the quality of the work force. Three views are discernible among the discussants. One group contends that the impact of automation on the occupational structure is upgrading the work force; another group does not notice any qualitative change; and a third group feels that downgrading may result from automation.

In the majority of case studies it has been found that, following the introduction of automation, the work force of the company is upgraded. This process may take place in two different ways. First, the content of jobs may be changed so that they require higher skills. But the upgrading of the work force may also result entirely from a shift in the relative shares of the various occupational groups in the total work force. For example, North-American Rockwell has reported recently that "During World War II about 80 percent of our employees were so-called blue-collar personnel; today about 36 percent are" [9, Vol. VI, p. 219]. It is generally assumed that a decline in the blue-collar category and a subsequent increase in the share of the white-collar group means an upgrading of the work force.

Changes in the occupational structure of employment has serious implications for manpower planning. It should strengthen this personnel function that has been either neglected in the past or practiced on a temporary basis when manpower shortage created a crisis situation. Presently, the reduced need for unskilled and semiskilled labor and a growing demand for skilled workers, technicians, and certain categories of white-collar workers require personnel management to plan actions in order to have adequate supply of these occupational groups when and where they are needed. To perform the manpower planning function successfully, personnel management must do the following things: (1) consider manpower planning as a continuous process, (2) anticipate trends in the work force and in the labor market, (3) be aware of the changes occurring in the technology of production and in the structure of the work force, (4) be able to project future manpower requirements of the company, and (5) develop a long-range program which would take all the previous aspects into consideration.

As a further result of changes in the composition of employment, the whole orientation of personnel management has to be reexamined. At present, personnel policies and techniques are mainly designed to deal with the employment problems and needs of the blue-collar workers who for many years constituted the majority of the work force. With the number of the blue-collar workers steadily declining and the number of the better-educated white-collar workers increasing, the existing personnel policies should be revised and readjusted to the requirements of the latter group [8, p. 34]. In the absence of such reorientation serious morale and motivational problems may arise.

Changes in Job Content

The content of production and clerical jobs is made up of a series of tasks and functions that the employee is expected to perform. Obviously, there is a significant relationship between the job content and the technology of production. Changes in the tools and equipment of operation will cause subsequent changes in the job requirements. The introduction of automation has eliminated certain tasks and modified others, thus causing a change of varying magnitude in the job itself. Depending on the intensity of automation's impact on their content, jobs may be divided into three categories. The first category includes those jobs in which automation makes all or most of the tasks obsolete (e.g., machine tending, materials handling, and materials processing). Jobs in the second category are those that have been recently created by the requirements of automation, such as equipment design, coordination of highly integrated mechanisms, and systems analysis. Finally, in the great majority of existing jobs, modifications caused by automation have not gone so far as to change their identity entirely. These jobs have retained their former title but with a more or less different content [11, pp. 83–84].

There are certain job factors or requirements which have been seriously affected by automated technology. Skill is one of them. In some exceptional cases skill has been downgraded. In a number of cases, either the skill requirements are not affected by automation or a different skill at the same level as the previous skill is demanded. In the majority of jobs associated with automation, however, skill requirements have been raised, sometimes considerably.

Besides skill, other job factors have also been affected by automation, though to lesser extent. In general, physical efforts have been considerably reduced; but at the same time, there is a greater demand for mental efforts. Responsibility for equipment, quality, and maintenance has also been raised by automation. On the other hand the safety factor is improved in automated plants because of mechanized materials handling, and reduction of the number of people involved in direct production [11, pp. 86–90].

What are the implications of these changes for personnel management? First of all, its training function will be enhanced because of the impact of automation on the skill factor. Parallel with the installation of automated equipment, personnel management is expected to reexamine the contents of jobs in the automated sector with special regard to skill requirements. If it is found that existing skills are modified or new skills are demanded, the personnel manager needs to make arrangements for training programs to be conducted either by company personnel or by outside instructors frequently provided by the manufacturers of the new equipment.

Changes in the existing jobs and the establishment of new jobs also necessitate their evaluation or reevaluation. The performance of this personnel function has been aggravated not only by the large number of jobs involved but also by the inapplicability of the existing methods to some jobs created by automation. For example, Cutler-Hammer and the Machinists have recently agreed that the duties of an operator running the Telecontrol, an electronic monitoring device, do not permit the application of the usual job evaluation plan.

What are some of the reasons why it is difficult to evaluate automated jobs by the conventional methods? First, there is a high degree of interdependence among automated jobs, and therefore, it would be insufficient to analyze only the content of an individual job. Second, the rigid description of traditional job evaluation programs would hamper the flexibility in job assignments that is of critical importance under automated systems [13, p. 283].

Then what are the modifications needed to make job evaluation viable in automated situations? Among others, consideration of interrelationship among automated jobs; giving more weight to such factors as the value of equipment and the amount of discretion and initiative required. The unions particularly insist on the fundamental revision of job evaluation systems to take into account increased responsibility and tension as some of the consequences of automation [13, p. 283].

Automation and Industrial Relations

With the expansion of unionism, the industrial relations (IR) function has become an integral part of the personnel manager's job. The traditional personnel functions associated primarily with the administration of the work force have blended with activities involved in negotiating and administering collective agreements. Although in some of the large companies the IR function has become organizationally separate from the personnel function proper, they have remained interrelated. In the majority of the companies the personnel manager is still in charge of both the personnel and the IR functions. It is, therefore, a necessity for personnel managers to get firmly involved with the dramatic developments caused by automation in the area of IR. Three major aspects of this function have been affected by automation: (1) bargaining power relations, (2) issues of bargaining, and (3) approaches to bargaining.

In this chapter only the first aspect will be discussed in detail as it is less known among personnel managers. On the other hand, so many new bargaining issues have been created by automation that even a superficial survey would greatly exceed the space available for this treatise. It is suggested that interested personnel managers look up some definitive works or one of the labor services which systematically list and analyze the bargaining issues [11, pp. 168–196]. As to the new approaches to collective bargaining, the continuous bargaining and the coalition or coordinated bargaining have been subjects to numerous discussions and analyses lately and probably are well known to the readers [16].

Changes in Bargaining Power between Management and Unions

The outcome of negotiations between unions and management is decided largely by the nature of power relations that exists between them at the time of the bargaining. Preliminary observations seem to indicate that shifts in bargaining power caused by automation have resulted in a decline of union power. Several developments have contributed to declining union strength in automated situations. Some of them have affected unionism in general. Changes in the industrial and occupational composition of employment have eroded union strength in the traditional bastions of trade unionism. Industries such as mining, manufacturing, and transportation, with steadily declining shares in total employment, are by far the most highly unionized in our economy. Similarly, those occupational groups such as the blue-collar workers which are heavily organized are losing ground to white-collar workers who have traditionally resisted unionization. Movement of the production facilities from the industrial centers to suburbs and small towns (which was made possible by the labor-saving effects of automation) also hurts the cause of unionism. Instead of organizing in the friendly environment of a large city, unions have to face the indifferent or even hostile attitude of suburbanites and small-town people [11, pp. 122–129].

Besides these general factors there are some particular developments which have exerted adverse impact on the sources of union power primarily at the firm's level. Exclusive jurisdiction over an industry or occupation has been one of the sources of power. Automation, by opening up new industries and occupations, has created a growing number of jurisdictional disputes among two or more unions which intend to organize employees in the new situations. Any jurisdictional rivalry among unions, however, results in a loss of power due to interunion bickerings and reduces the effectiveness of their bargaining power.

The size of the bargaining unit for which a union has the exclusive right to bargain is another source of union power which is affected by automation. First, the absolute size of the bargaining unit is apt to decrease parallel with the decline in the number of production workers. Second, an erosion of union power may occur when the bargaining unit, following the introduction of automation, includes only the lesser part of the nonsupervisory work force and a portion of the workers is no longer represented by the union. Third, the strength of the bargaining unit may also be affected in situations in which, due to automation, the work force is divided into several bargaining units. With the decline of semiskilled production workers, skilled workers, particularly in maintenance, will get out of the unit of the production workers and form their own unit.

Finally, perhaps the most significant adverse development for union bargaining power is the impact of automation on the strike weapon. The possibility of a strike bringing production to a complete halt has long constituted the most important source of union bargaining power. Automation appears to endanger the two necessary preconditions of an effective strike: total control over the nonsupervisory labor supply of a firm, and the ability of a union to bring production to a complete halt.

Few strikes can be effective without the full support of the nonsupervisory work force. If only a portion of the blue-collar group is organized by a union, the operation of a plant can hardly be shut down. Any effect of automation that may loosen the control of a union over the whole work force in the plant may make strikes less effective than before.

But even if a union had full control over the nonsupervisory work force a strike would remain an ineffective threat if such action could not close down the plant. In an increasing number of industries, however, management has been able to maintain the continuity of production despite a strike for two reasons: first, the size of the group of production workers in relation to the total work force has been on the decline in automated firms; second, many of the functions previously performed by production workers have been taken over by automated equipment [11, pp. 162–166].

The degree of failure or success of strikes generally depends on the type of automation that prevails in a particular company. In this respect a marked difference exists between the continuous-flow type and the automatic-transfer type. Although the automobile industry has been equipped with automatic machines of the latter type, the strike conducted by UAW against Ford in fall 1967 proved to be highly successful for the union. But in industries which can take advantage of the continuous-flow type, the degree of automaticity has increased to such an extent that in case of a strike a relatively small crew of production workers can easily be replaced by supervisory personnel, even for an extended period of time.

But unions may derive some benefits of automation. Organizers usually refer to the threat of technological unemployment and insecurity in both automated plants and offices. Unions also use the computers to improve the efficiency of their organizing and bargaining activities. The Industrial Union Department of the AFL-CIO has recently installed a data-processing center so that an organizer or negotiator will be able to get information on contracts covering workers at a target company. It is contended that data on wages and other terms of employment will furnish a broad profile of a particular company's behavior when faced by a union [11, pp. 129–131].

The Status of the Personnel Manager in Automated Companies

How do the previously discussed organizational and functional changes affect the status of personnel management in automated companies? This is a question which is asked by many personnel managers with some anxiety in a rapidly changing business environment. The great majority of experts studying the automation effects on the personnel function view the new role of the personnel manager rather positively. Bueschel contends that the new problems created by automation have resulted in an increasing recognition for the personnel manager [4, p. 5].

A U.S. Department of Labor study *(Management Decisions to Automate)* suggests that the personnel manager is consulted already in the planning phase of automation. Some of the factors which influence the decision of top management to automate are related to the personnel function (high rates of turnover, shortage of skilled workers, dissatisfaction with temporary labor).

Leonard Rico is in minority when concluding that the status of the personnel department was rather low in the automated companies surveyed by him and that situation inhibited the contribution of personnel management to the management of change [14, p. 210].

It is interesting to learn about how personnel managers view their own role in an automated company. A survey was conducted on this subject among personnel managers in Chicago in 1965. The majority of the respondents believed that the status of personnel management is going to be enhanced by the advent of automation for the following reasons:

Automation and modern approaches to management tend to coincide.

Personnel managers will have a greater role in corporate planning.

Personnel selection will become of greater importance in securing high-caliber personnel who will be in great demand and short supply.

With the use of the computer, personnel management will be in a position to collect and process data efficiently and use it to upgrade its function [12, p. 80].

The challenges that confront personnel managers in the era of automation require them to update their training and education. Personnel executives in automated companies will have difficulty in performing their upgraded functions without a graduate degree in personnel, the curriculum of which should include such subjects as organization and manpower planning, organization theory, and some knowledge in the area of computer applications. Advanced training and added responsibility will make the job of the personnel manager more complex than it is today. But he will be rewarded by his increased status in the corporate hierarchy.

REFERENCES

[1] *Automation and the Middle Manager,* American Foundation on Automation, New York, 1966.
[2] Beaumont, Richard A., and Roy B. Helfgott: *Management, Automation and People,* Industrial Relations Counselors, New York, 1964.
[3] Berkwitt, George: "Middle Manager vs. the Computer," *Dun's Review,* vol. 88, November, 1966.
[4] Bueschel, Richard, T.: *EDP and Personnel,* AMA Research Study 86, American Management Association, New York, 1966.
[5] Burlingame, John: "Information Technology and Decentralization," *Harvard Business Review,* vol. 39, November–December, 1961.
[6] Canning, Richard, G., and Roger L. Sisson: *The Management of Data Processing,* John Wiley & Sons, Inc., New York, 1967.
[7] Higginson, Valliant M.: *Managing with EDP,* AMA Research Study 71, American Management Association, New York, 1965.

[8] Myers, Charles A.: "New Frontier for Personnel Management," *Personnel,* vol. 41, May–June, 1964.

[9] National Commission on Technology, Automation, and Economic Progress: *Technology and the American Economy,* Report—Vols. I–VI in Appendix, Washington, D.C., February 1966. The cited work consists of seven volumes. The first volume constitutes the main report of the Commission; the additional six volumes containing various source materials on which the main report is based are marked Appendix Volume I to VI.

[10] Reichenbach, R. R., and C. A. Tasso: *Organizing for Data Processing,* AMA Research Study 92, American Management Association, New York, 1968.

[11] Rezler, Julius: *Automation and Industrial Labor,* Random House, Inc., New York, 1969.

[12] Rezler, Julius: "Automation and the Personnel Manager," *Advanced Management Journal,* vol. 32, January, 1967.

[13] Rezler, Julius: "Effects of Automation on Some Areas of Compensation," *Personnel Journal,* vol. 48, April, 1969.

[14] Rico, Leonard: *The Advance against Paperwork—Computers, Systems, and Personnel,* Bureau of Industrial Relations, University of Michigan, Ann Arbor, Mich., 1967.

[15] Sanders, Donald H.: "Computers, Organizations, and Managers," *Advanced Management Journal,* vol. 34, July, 1969.

[16] Siegel, Abraham J. (ed.): *The Impact of Computers on Collective Bargaining,* The M.I.T. Press, Cambridge, Mass., 1970.

[17] Simon, Herbert A.: *The Shape of Automation for Men and Management,* Harper & Row, Publishers, Incorporated, New York, 1965.

[18] Taylor, J. W., and N. J. Dean: "Managing to Manage the Computer," *Harvard Business Review,* vol. 42, September–October, 1966.

[19] "Technology, Information, and Management Organization," in *Proceedings of the Nineteenth Meeting,* Winter, 1966, Industrial Relations Research Association, 1967, pp. 156–206. The title denotes Part IV of the Proceedings which includes four papers written by four different authors. The notation was made in this way in order to avoid three additional references. The names of the authors and the title of their papers are as follows: Perrow, Charles, "Technology and Organizational Structure" (156–64); Wilensky, H. L., "The Failure of Intelligence" (164–76); Simon, Herbert, "Programs as Factors of Production" (177–88); Myers, Charles A., "Some Implications of Computers for Management" (189–201); Whisler, T. L., "Discussion" (202–06).

[20] U.S. Department of Labor: *Technological Trends in Major American Industries,* BLS Bulletin No. 1474, Washington, D.C., 1966.

chapter 64

Job Dislocations: Retraining and Relocating Employees

LAWRENCE L. STEINMETZ *Professor and Head, Management and Organization Division, Graduate School of Business Administration, University of Colorado, Boulder, Colorado*

One of the most difficult problems facing the manager of personnel is the dislocated employee. Part of the problem is that a great deal of confusion surrounds the definition of a dislocated employee. Therefore, any discussion of job dislocation and how to cope with it must be preceded by a definition of what it is and when it occurs.

THE DISLOCATED EMPLOYEE—WHO HE IS

Broadly speaking, the dislocated employee is any employee whose job has outgrown him or who is incapable (for whatever reason) of satisfactorily performing the requirements of his job. It should, therefore, be obvious that employees seldom become dislocated overnight because job requirements are rarely that flexible and employee skills (barring an accident) are usually a stable commodity. Most employees become dislocated through a slow process: a gradual erosion of one's skills and capabilities, the course or dictates of the job, its production processes, its technology, and possibly changes in the economic situation under which the work is done.

WHEN DISLOCATION OCCURS

The job dislocation which occurs as a result of the erosion of one's skills and capabilities or the changing of job requirements and technology is the most serious form of job dislocation. Any employee who is dislocated because his job has outgrown him must be dealt with the same as the employee who is dislocated because his job has been abolished. But, in final analysis, the slow erosion process causes the most turmoil, the greatest pressure, and the most difficulty for both the manager of personnel and the employee(s) affected.

One of the big problems with the slowly eroding job dislocation is that of defining when the employee truly is dislocated. The only way to determine this is through the process of a very formalized appraisal system. Thus, a company operating an effective management-by-objectives system has a distinct advantage in this area although the fine line is not always clear-cut even with the best evaluations. A good rule of thumb used by many personnel managers is "An employee is dislocated when he is incapable of performing, or unwilling to perform, a significant portion of his work in a satisfactory manner."

HOW EMPLOYEES SLIP INTO JOB DISLOCATION

The most common excuse for an employee becoming dislocated in his job is inability to adjust to change. Many managers, in trying to reconstruct the reason for an employee becoming incapable of performing his job satisfactorily will blame it all on the employee's unwillingness to learn new skills and to keep up with the times.

While it is true that many employees do fail to keep up with the times, the reason is not necessarily "resistance to change." In fact, one IBM training director, reflecting on his company's capabilities at keeping up with the times, is very fond of making the point that employees do not *simply* resist change by raising the rhetorical question: "Have you ever seen an employee resist the change of going from a lower salary to a higher salary?" The obvious answer to this question underscores the fact that people do not resist change; rather they fail to change because of fear of the unknown.

REASONS EMPLOYEES FAIL TO CHANGE WITH THE TIMES

There are fundamentally two reasons that men permit their jobs to outgrow them: attitudinal and physical. Attitudinal causes are far and away the most serious because they not only are the most common cause of job dislocation, but they also are the least tangible to deal with. Yale Laitin years ago enumerated some of the most common fears and worries that people have when they are confronted with changing ways of doing things. They include: the fear of losing one's job, the fear of being made a fool, the fear of losing status in the eyes of co-workers, the fear of losing privileges, and the fear of reduced chance for promotion. It is, of course, ironical that these attitudes which cause employees to resist change are the very things which occur as a result of their resistance to change (i.e., when they resist change they come closest to losing their job, being degraded, losing status or privileges, and becoming ineligible for promotion).

OVERCOMING RESISTANCE TO CHANGE

The textbook solution to helping people overcome those attitudes which lead them to actions which create dislocation are as follows:

Tell the employee why the new method or technique is necessary. "Mary, learning to mark sense cards is essential to proper billing of long distance calls."

Permit the employee to participate in how the change will be implemented. "Fellows, the problem we are facing is that we are breaking off too many radio antennas while the cars are going through the wash line. Do you have any ideas as to how to minimize this loss?"

Avoid surprise. "I want you all to know that we hope by the end of the summer to have eliminated all hand winding of cord and to have all our cordwinders employed as operators on our semi-automatic machines."

Recognize that the employees will have difficulty doing the new job and that they are not expected to be perfect on first trial. "Jack, it's pretty tricky getting all four clips positioned correctly at one time, but we'll work with you until you learn the knack of it."

Provide a standard of performance which has realistic and obtainable goals. "Al, ultimately you will be required to assemble thirty units an hour, but the first month we won't expect you to do more than fifteen per hour."

Utilize the grapevine and especially the informal leaders of the organization. "Bill, I know the group looks to you for leadership and I wanted to particularly spend a little extra time with you so that maybe you could help me in accurately conveying what is going to happen when we move into the new offices."

Commend the employee on his efforts. "Dick, you're coming along on that new technique a lot better than I figured you'd be able to and that sure has helped us a lot over in quality control."

Repeat explanations of all instructions to the employee. "No problem, Harry, but let's go through it one more time just to make sure."

Allow time for the employee to become adjusted to the new way of doing things. "Don't rush it, George, it just takes a while to really get in the swing of things."

HARD-CORE PROBLEMS

While the above serves as a guideline to overcoming the problem of a job outgrowing a man because of resistance to change, it is good advice only in those circumstances where the erosion of skills has not assumed major proportions; that is, it is not as likely to work in hard-core cases when the extent of the dislocation has assumed chronic proportions.

There are numerous reasons for hard-core job dislocations. The most common ones can be enumerated as follows:
1. Physical deterioration of the individual
2. Aging and senility
3. Indifference to work
4. Group pressure

Let us look at each of these factors, how they can cause job dislocation, and why prognosis is bleak in respect to satisfactory results from retraining and relocation efforts with these employees.

1. *Physical Deterioration:*   Although it is uncommon, it is possible that an employee may become unfit for a particular job from a physical standpoint. Sometimes, of course, the job itself is the cause of the physical unfitness, as in the case of miners getting lung disease. In other cases, an accident or chronic illness can cause the person to become incapable of satisfactorily performing a significant portion of the job.

Obviously, when an employee becomes physically unfit to do a job, he is dislocated and corrective action must be undertaken. Normally, if it is a question of physical prowess, retraining is not the answer. Sometimes relocation of the employee to a different job is effective, sometimes it is not. One advantage accruing to the manager of personnel in the instance of physical unfitness for a job, however, is the fact that the employee's mental attitude is quite conducive and receptive toward being reinstated in a different job. The problem is primarily complicated by the fact that he may be physically unfit to do any job satisfactorily, whether or not he is relocated.

2. *Age and Senility:*   A second factor which may cause chronic or hard-core job dislocation is aging and senility.   It is a commonly observed phenomenon that people's motivational drives change as they age.   If anything, it would appear that the effect of aging on one's motivational drive is negative—people find, as the saying goes, "Their get up and go has got up and gone."

While most people look at aging as a physical process, the manager of personnel, in facing the problem of a dislocated employee, must recognize that aging is more of a mental problem than it is physical; that it is as much a problem of the ability of the grey matter of the mind to function effectively as it is a question of kinesthesis.

Figure 1 illustrates the problem of aging and senility.   There it can be seen that when it comes to the question of man's capabilities to perform effectively at work, his mental ability to learn new things rises while he is a youngster, reaches a peak at about age sixteen, and then begins to deteriorate.   This means that it is literally possible, in those cases where a person undergoes premature aging or experiences an early onset of senility, that he may become completely ineffective in his capability to perform mentally by the time he reaches his late thirties or early forties.   Mother nature, of course, has seen fit to anticipate this problem, and for the normal person who is performing his job satisfactorily, the normal deterioration of mental capacity poses no problem.   What the older person lacks in mental agility, he makes up for in experience.

An example of the importance of the factor of experience and how it is additive when it comes to the capacity of an older person to normally perform jobs can best be given as follows: An older person knows not to drop a glass full of water on a concrete floor, for he knows, *based upon experience,* that the glass will break and he will be sprayed with water.   However, the younger person (in this case an infant) does not necessarily *know* that the glass will break until he has experienced the dropping of a glassful of water on a concrete floor.   In just the same manner the example holds true in responsible, adult jobs.   The senior pilot knows he must have faith in his instruments; the novice, to his own demise, may trust his "feel" more than his instruments and fly straight into the ground.

The problem of aging and the onset of senility should be clear at this point.   It is not only that one physically is not as good as he used to be; it is also a problem that mentally he is less alert.   Mental slowing down, however, is not a chronic prob-

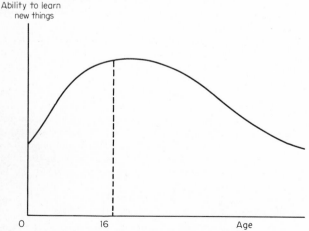

Figure 1.   **Relationship between aging and mental deterioration.**

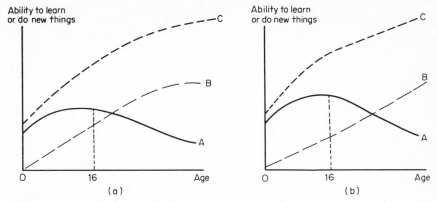

Figure 2.   Ability to function satisfactorily at work (A = ability to learn curve, B = experience factor, C = total of both capabilities). *(a)* Normal person.   *(b)* Person whose mental capabilities have deteriorated but whose experiential capabilities are continuing to increase.

lem until it is compounded by the circumstance wherein the employee has permitted himself to lapse into dull, unimaginative, repetitive, and mentally undemanding work.   The cliché that one person has had one year's experience ten times rather than ten years' experience one time clearly makes this point.   It can graphically be shown in Figure 2 that there is no particular problem with the mental slowing down *as long as one has a wealth of experiences to rely on and utilize in effectively performing at work.*   It becomes a problem when a person lapses into a job dislocation pattern and fails to continually upgrade and update himself via the processes of new experiences.   When that happens, his total ability to function effectively at work is impaired.   If and when this combination of circumstances occurs, the prognosis for retraining the employee is extremely bleak, primarily because he has become much of a dullard who has no experience quotient to implement in learning new tricks.   That situation is, of course, chronic job dislocation; the prospects of being successful in retraining are bleak, and job relocation to a less challenging, less demanding job is about all that will prove successful.

3. *Indifference to work:*   The third chronic job dislocation is the attitudinal problem of indifference.   Basically the problem of indifference is that the employee develops an attitude which is super-negative toward the organization for which he works.   Based on the old adage that behavior is a function of attitudes (not the facts of the situation) and that one can only change behavior by changing attitudes, it is critical that the manager of personnel recognize the magnitude of the problem and the characteristic actions and thought processes of the super-indifferent employee. They include: withdrawal from participation and/or identification with his job, reluctance to compete for any kind of reward, animosity toward his supervisor, contempt for co-workers, and depreciation of the work he performs.   In view of the truistic nature of the statement, "Don't confuse me with the facts, my mind is made up!", the prognosis for the indifferent employee, when job-dislocated, is rather dismal.   Attitudes are extremely difficult to change without extensive psychological counseling, and most personnel departments are not equipped to handle the problem.

4. *Group pressure:*   Another cause of extreme difficulty when an employee is job-dislocated is the factor of group pressure.   It has been well documented that

the pressures of the group on the individual are far more causal of behavior than any other pressure which can be brought to bear upon him. Furthermore, not only may group pressure be significant in determining the behavior of any individual, it must also be recognized that the behavior of any given group can in fact be infectious to any given individual. The power of suggestion is a potent weapon; when the suggestion comes from a group rather than an individual, it is overwhelming. In much the same manner that a group of children in Salem, Massachusetts, became obsessed with notions of witchcraft (with the resultant catastrophic behavior upon the part of a whole population) just so can a union convince an employee whose job has been automated of the impropriety of the employer hiring machines to do the work which was formerly done by the employee. The company can explain until it is blue in the face trying to convince the employee that the change is to his benefit (and it may very well be), but if the group (or union) is opposed, the situation is near hopeless. When a group plants seeds of malcontent and mistrust in the minds of any individual, it is nigh impossible to get him to think along constructive lines, i.e., to use thought processes which would make him amenable to possible retraining or relocating within the employment of the employer.

HELPING THE DISLOCATED EMPLOYEE

The above section of this chapter has outlined the various employee-related causes of job dislocation. Obviously many employees become displaced in their jobs not as a result of their own failings but as a result of technological advancement, changes in production processes, changing economic circumstances, etc. Inasmuch as these causes of job dislocation are outside the control of any individual employee or manager of personnel, there was no need to discuss the myriad of ways in which such exogenous causal agents may bring about job dislocation. However, it was important to discuss individual attitudes which contribute to and make the problem of job dislocation more serious when it does occur. With the above framework now established, it is possible to evaluate what can be done to cope with the dislocated employee.

WHAT THE UNION REQUIRES

Basically, coping with the replaced or dislocated employee can be effectively accomplished in only one of two ways: via the process of retraining or via the process of relocating the employee. In some cases, of course, retraining is the most advisable. In other cases relocating the employee (including discharging him) is the only solution advisable. However, before considering when either of these procedures is most suitable, it may be wise to review procedures which unions attempt to enforce upon employers in coping with job dislocation.

It can be safely stated that the union's concern with job dislocation basically will revolve around giving advance notice of the dislocation to the employee and recompensing the employee who is dislocated. The methods used by the union and the demands which they levy are multifaceted to say the least, and it is therefore impossible to review all the ingenious devices and techniques that they employ in attempting to protect dislocated employees. However, a brief general review is warranted.

THE UNION PHILOSOPHY TOWARD JOB DISLOCATION

Typically, the union will have an attitude toward job dislocation which runs as follows:

1. To learn, as soon as possible, who is and who is not considered dislocated in his job

2. To provide their membership with suitable substitute employment within or outside the employment of the current employer

3. To provide time to cushion the shock of job displacement and relocation if it is to occur

4. To prolong as long as possible the employment of all union members

It should be obvious from the above that it can be generally stated that unions *do not* like job dislocation and will attempt to *immunize* their membership as long as possible from the effects of job dislocation.

HOW JOB DISLOCATIONS ARE COMMUNICATED TO THE EMPLOYEE

One problem which must be considered, and one which the union will have strong emotions about, is the question of when and how the news of job dislocation is communicated to the employee. As a rule of thumb, three months is probably an average, sensible lead time. However, it must be recognized that no average figure is meaningful without consideration of the peculiar problems being faced by the employer. For example, even when job dislocation is caused by technological displacement, the need to be rid of a particular employee on a specified day, week, or month may be unclear. Technology and technical factors themselves may, in fact, limit the speed in which a plant can be automated or mechanized. Furthermore, maintaining a given level of production may dictate only broadly when an employee will no longer be needed. In a situation where a large number of employees are being dislocated, the company's image in the community may affect the timing, propriety, and circumstance under which advance notice is required. Therefore, anyone faced by the prospect of having to lay off or relocate displaced workers has to consider all the factors involved, not only from the employee's standpoint, but also from the standpoint of the employer's needs for production, customer services, etc.

NOTICE OF PENDING JOB DISLOCATIONS

Notice can be given dislocated employees in a variety of ways. Some general rules which can be developed on communicating to the employee that he is being phased out of a job or that a job is being eliminated by the company run as follows:

1. Precautions must be taken to avoid the premature leaking of information to employees via the process of the grapevine.

2. Managerial and supervisory employees should be notified of pending action prior to the time affected employees are told.

3. Union officials should be informed at the same time the managerial and supervisory staff is informed of the pending situation.

4. The announcement should be made to all affected employees at the same time if possible; if not, the largest segment of the employees should be informed first.

5. Oral communications are better received than written notices, especially if it is possible for affected employees to ask questions of the man making the announcement.

6. A written follow-up is desirable. The written communication should contain as much relevant information as possible concerning effective dates or the decision to terminate a job, etc.

It should be recognized that in the union situation the above procedure may not be permissible when there is conflicting policy established in the labor contract.

However, according to the Bureau of Labor Statistics, less than half of the union contracts in the United States contain language governing how or when notice of dislocation is to be communicated to affected employees and most of those that contain provisions are consistent with the above rule of thumb.

RETRAINING—KEY TO AVOIDANCE OF RELOCATION OR SEVERANCE

The obvious solution to dealing with the dislocated employee is to retrain the employee. However, it is a good deal easier to state the practical answer than it is to actually perform the feat satisfactorily. Questions which arise concerning employee retraining run as follows: How are retraining needs determined? What time should a company consider retraining employees and under what circumstances? Is it possible to retrain at all levels of employment? Are the problems in retraining significantly different between the skilled and unskilled employees?

The question is really not so much whether it is desirable to attempt to train or retrain job dislocated employees as *at what point* should training or retraining techniques occur. Therefore, let us consider the above questions of retraining in order that policy decisions can be made effectively in this area.

How Retraining Needs Are Determined

Determining a company's training or retraining needs is largely a question of being able to adequately project what new skills and capabilities will be required on the part of any employee who is apt to be dislocated in his job. There are some guidelines which can be useful in this area:

Surveying retraining needs: One of the first steps in determining retraining needs is that of surveying future needs of the corporation via the process of both formal and informal consultations and discussions with corporate policy makers and decision makers. This is to ascertain the direction of corporate efforts (i.e., what the organization will be producing or providing in the future and how the demand for such products or services will be met, especially in relation to employee requirements).

Evaluating statistical indicators: When a survey is made of projected training needs, a second guideline which can be invoked is the evaluation of statistical indicators which serve as indicators of employees who are at or near the point of being job dislocated. Some of these indicators are: a high accident rate; increase in the incidents of scrappage, spoilage, or waste; a slow rising trend in production costs (especially direct labor cost); increase in the amount of absenteeism and tardiness; increasing incidents of complaints and grievances (especially grievances associated with methods under which work is done); and finally, an increase in disciplinary actions. The use of a statistical analysis of data and records maintained on the above indicators should serve to emphasize areas in which people are becoming less than content and capable at performing their jobs. When there is an increasing incidence in any of these statistical indicators surrounding a certain kind of job or, especially, a particular employee, it is a sure sign of portending problems in the area of job dislocation; and they serve to underscore the fact that immediate training is probably warranted in these areas.

Job and worker analysis: A third indicator of retraining needs is that of making a thorough job and worker analysis. Basically, making a job and worker analysis comprises the following steps:

1. Establishing, via the process of analyzing future job needs, the requirements of the job which is to be performed in the future.

2. Determining the (prospectively dislocated) employee's aptitudes, skills, and capabilities.

3. Comparing the skills, aptitudes, and capabilities of the worker with the description of the future job's needs.

When the future job needs are compared with the skills and aptitudes which the employee has, the void areas are underscored as areas in which training should be conducted for the employee.

If the manager of personnel does an effective survey of future needs, if he keeps attuned to those physical indicators which top off latent dislocation problems, and if he conscientiously sets down and makes a future job and present worker capability analysis, he will be able to adequately predict his retraining needs.

When a Company Should Consider Retraining Employees

From a humanitarian standpoint, the answer to the question of when a company should consider retraining employees is *always.* Unfortunately, such an answer does little for the manager of personnel other than increase his worry quotient. Probably the most functional answer which can be given to the question of when a company should consider retraining an employee is whenever, based upon the determination of future training needs, it is determined that without such training an employee will become job dislocated. When such a decision is warranted, however, it is extremely difficult to quantify. The practice most companies appear to use in making such a decision is that job retraining begins *for those employees determined as trainable* when the company's retraining assessment program shows that these employees are becoming marginal in their performance of 10 percent or more of their jobs and/or when they are incapable of performing *any* critical or significant portion of their jobs. The other guideline used by companies, in those circumstances wherein a totally new method or technique is to be employed and the old method or technique is to be abolished, is to immediately begin training once such a decision is made.

Is It Possible to Retain at All Levels of Employment?

There is no question that it is possible to retrain at all levels and in respect to all skills within an organization. The problem is not so much one of what level in the organization as it is a question of the age and attitude of the trainee. While it must not be contended that older employees are impossible to train, it nevertheless is a truism that as an employee becomes older, the less interested he normally is in undertaking new and different tasks and job duties. Therefore, in dealing with all levels of employment, one basic guideline emerges: Retraining can be conducted at any level and with any employee in an organization assuming *he is mentally and physically up to it.*

Determining whether or not the man is physically up to it merely involves a simple assessment of the physical capability of the individual, perhaps including a talk with the person and if possible, a review of the man's general health with the company physician, close associates, and friends. Determining the man's mental capability, of course, requires a far more careful assessment of the employee's attitudes, mental alertness, and willingness to undertake retraining. Such a determination requires, in most cases, a very careful review of the man's performance appraisals over the past several years (with special attention to the question of sluggishness toward new tasks and duties, outmoded thinking, rigidity toward new ways of doing things). If the employee rates poorly in the assessment of his attitude toward learning new things, there is probably ample argument *not* to waste time and money retraining the individual. It is more advisable to expend such resources in attempting to find suitable alternative employment (possibly with a different employer) for that individual.

The usual problem which will confront the manager of personnel in making the physical and mental assessment of the individual and determining whether to undertake training is the problem that some factors argue for retraining while others argue against it. It is indeed difficult to make the decision in the borderline cases. However, one rule which seems to hold true is that if an error is made, it is in favor of the employee and against the employer in respect to the expenditure of funds. Therefore, the following table is not submitted as a sure-fire way of determining when to train (or not to train) but as a guideline to shape the thinking of the personnel manager faced with the retraining problem. It should be noted that the scoring on the table runs as follows: A man gets a +1 if the particular feature argues for retraining and −1 if it argues against retraining; a 0 is received if the situation has no relevance to the question of retraining or if the factor has both positive and negative arguments in respect to the possible success of a retraining program for the employee. Once the table is completed, the decision is guided (but should not be rigidly enforced) on the basis of whether or not the majority of the evidence argues for retraining the individual or for relocating the individual within or outside the company.

Figure 3. Factors to consider in determining whether an employee should be retrained.

Factor	+1	Weight 0	−1
Mental alertness			
Physical fitness			
Attitude and personality			
Length of service			
Performance record			
Attendance record			
Investment in man			
Personal implications			
a. For man			
b. For company			
c. For boss			
Effect on morale of organization			
Totals			

Score +1 if factor argues for retraining, −1 if against training, 0 if not relevant or if pros and cons rule out the factor.

RELOCATION—THE STRONGER MEDICINE FOR JOB DISLOCATION

If the employee cannot be retrained the only other solution is to relocate him. Relocation means that the employee is transferred, demoted, possibly promoted, dehired, or flatly fired from the organization. Therefore, it should be recognized that relocating an employee means to move him to a different job in the organization *or* to sever his relationship with the company. The strongest technique of relocation is, of course, the severance of the individual. How this is done has been outlined in the book *Managing the Marginal and Unsatisfactory Performer*[1] and will not be dwelt upon at length here. Suffice it to say that the technique runs as follows: When an error is made, it is probably in favor of the employee and against the company, i.e., the employee is more often not fired when he should be rather than fired when he should not be. Therefore, it should be recognized that the main

[1] Lawrence L. Steinmetz, *Managing the Marginal and Unsatisfactory Performer,* Addison-Wesley Publishing Co., Reading, Massachusetts, 1969.

problem the manager of personnel will face in the chronically dislocated employee is a problem of how to relocate him somewhere else within the organization. The remainder of this chapter will address this question.

The Probability of Successful Relocation

At the outset of any discussion on how to relocate employees, it should be recognized that relocation is frequently not successful As a general rule, it can be assumed that any dislocated employee who is relocated elsewhere in the organization *as an individual* will probably *not* be pleased with his circumstance. He may, in fact, be outwardly hostile toward the organization and resentful of the change. While there are well documented cases of people who have been willing to accept transfers to new communities and new jobs, many consultants place the odds of a successful relocation of an individual as low as one in five.

The manager of personnel should not be fooled into thinking that a job relocation is necessarily successful just because a man accepts such an offer whether he moves his family to a new area or he himself goes to work at a different plant but remains in the same community. Normally the disruption of the household, the unspoken resentments, and the frictions generated, both at home and at work, argue against considering such a relocation as being successful. However, if success is defined as the outward acceptance by the man and there are no union problems, the odds of a successful job relocation may run as high as 60 to 70 percent.

Even though the prospects of relocating an employee in a different job are bleak in respect to true success for the *individual* person, the odds are extremely high that the relocation will be successful for a *large group of individuals*. The reason for the success of massive relocations is that group feelings and common misery tend to be less important than individual suffering. Perhaps there is truth to the saying that "misery loves company," but it is easy to observe the relative complacency with one's plight in life for individuals in large groups as compared to the strong feelings held by individuals who have had a singularly difficult circumstance. The group camaraderie often injects a note of humor to lighten what would otherwise appear grim, and the feeling that everyone is in the same boat may lend a spirit of adventure to a frightening situation.

Any employee should be relocated when he is the victim of a job dislocation and when it is considered likely or probable that a relocation is both feasible and likely to be successful. If an employee is to be relocated the timing is critical. Whether it is possible to relocate an employee without cost to him or without lost wages, timing is more a question of what is expedient for the organization than anything else. However, before transferring an employee, the personnel manager must be carefully attuned to such mundane matters as school, vacation, holidays, weather, real estate markets, etc., for all these factors will affect the happiness of the employee. In short, as a policy decision, relocation should occur at *the company's convenience,* with a special effort made to make the company's convenience commensurate with the employee's convenience and needs.

How to Relocate

The actual job of relocating an employee contains many facets. One, of course, is having the man trained to undertake his new duties. This problem was dealt with above, and it is assumed here that any person who is to be relocated has already been trained or will receive the necessary training at his new post. Another problem involves the mechanical procedures of actually relocating the man. This involves what the company should do to ameliorate or minimize the problems which the man and his family will face as a result of the move, both financially and emotionally.

The emotional relocation: When it comes to the question of the emotional problems to be faced by the man and the family who is being relocated, the obligation of the organization is to attempt to familiarize the man and his family with the new situation.   The question of what kind of a community he is going to, living conditions, travel and commuting problems, schools, marketplaces, and city government are all unknown to the relocating employee.   Even though the company may have had a plant or facility in the new location for many years, it cannot be assumed that any individual employee knows all he needs or would like to know about the new community in which he is to live and the new job at which he is to work.   Therefore, it is considered necessary by most organizations who relocate employees to at least send the man on an expense paid familiarization tour of his new work area and situation.   Furthermore, most company's, in the event that the new job requires moving to a new community, take it upon themselves to supply the relocating employee with Chamber of Commerce information and various vital statistics in an effort to minimize the concerns which any person would have when faced with the prospects of moving to a new locale.

Financial problems: Attempting to physically relocate an employee at a new site is expensive.   Not only are moving expenses involved, but the expenses of selling a home, canceling a lease, finding temporary quarters, etc., all linger in the shadows.   Not only do these potential expenses lie heavy on the mind of the relocating employee but many times he feels inadequately prepared or incapable of coping with the financial outlay required.

Policies of companies who relocate employees vary tremendously and depend upon many factors: the practice of the industry, the geographical location of the company, and the level of the relocated employee in the organization.   Normal policy for most companies is to establish a policy for various levels of employees, e.g., top level executives, supervisory and managerial personnel, and rank and filers. It is safe to say that the more generous and liberal allowances, when policies differentiate between lower and upper level employees, are always in favor of the upper level employees.   Many companies, of course, have the same policies for all people—one of picking up virtually all attendant expenses involved in the relocation.   Other companies are very careful to specify which expenses will be borne by the company and which are the employee's responsibility.   As a normal rule, the following expenses are probably most generally absorbed by the company: expenses for the man and his wife to visit the new work site, losses entailed in the sale of the man's residence, the cancellation of his lease or the subletting of leased property, all moving and transportation expenses (one way) to the new site, and temporary living expenses up to a period of one month.   Also, a miscellaneous draw (which seldom exceeds more than a few hundred dollars) is frequently provided to absorb any of the unanticipated out-of-pocket costs.

The list above is a good general guideline to use with supervisory personnel. With rank and file personnel, it is probably more common for a company not to recompense the employee for loss on the sale of his residence, lease cancellation, or subletting expenses.   All other expenses are commonly covered.

Summary

The problem of the dislocated employee is serious and can become acute.   Any policy designed to cope with this problem, no matter what, must call for immediate and forceful action.   Such action, hopefully, will be preventive but may necessarily have to take a more harsh orientation.   Whatever the shape of plan, however, the manager of personnel must recognize that unless it is aggressively implemented with a firm goal orientation (as to the desired outcome of the implemented plan), it will fail and, in end result, will be less than useful toward the alleviation of the omnipresent problem of job dislocation.

BIBLIOGRAPHY

Baldwin, George B., and George P. Shultz: "Automation: A New Dimension to Old Problems," *Proceedings of the Seventh Annual Meeting, Industrial Relations Research Association,* 1954, pp. 114–128.

Bennis, W. G., K. D., Benne, and R. Chin (eds.): *The Planning of Change,* Holt, Rinehart and Winston, Inc., New York, 1961.

Coch, Lester, and John P. French: "Overcoming Resistance to Change," *Human Relations,* August, 1948.

Judson, Arnold S.: *The Manager's Guide to Making Changes,* John Wiley & Sons, Inc., New York, 1966.

Lippitt, Ronald, Jeanne Watson, and Bruce Westley: *The Dynamics of Planned Change,* Harcourt, Brace & World, Inc., New York, 1958.

Schoderbek, Peter P., and William E. Reif: *Job Enlargement: Key to Improved Performance,* Bureau of Industrial Relations, University of Michigan, Ann Arbor, Mich., 1969.

Steinmetz, Lawrence L.: "Do Him a Favor—Fire Him!" *Nations Business,* vol. 55, no. 11, November, 1967, pp. 96–98.

———: *Managing the Marginal and Unsatisfactory Performer,* Addison-Wesley Publishing Company, Inc., Reading, Mass., 1969.

———: "The Unsatisfactory Performer: Salvage or Discharge?" *Personnel,* vol. 45, no. 3, May-June, 1968, pp. 46–54.

Weber, Arnold R., and David P. Taylor: "Procedures for Employee Displacement: Advance Notice of Plant Shutdown," *Journal of Business,* vol. 36, no. 3, July, 1963, pp. 302–315.

chapter 65

Employee Terminations

AURORA PARISI *Personnel Administrator, McGraw-Hill, Inc., New York, New York*

There are a variety of reasons and causes for employee terminations. In general, they fall into three broad categories: resignation, dismissals, and other. The last group covers terminations of such a special nature (mandatory retirement, death, layoff, physical incapacity to perform job, etc.) that they do not properly belong in either of the first two groups.

In all cases of terminations, from the simplest resignation for maternity to dismissal for misconduct, there are certain responsibilities of line management and of the personnel administrator which must be carried out. Of course, the extent of the role to be played by each will vary with the type of termination.

RESIGNATIONS

Resignations are terminations which are initiated by the employee. It is important in the case of resignations to determine whether or not the action could have been prevented. The many reasons why employees quit their jobs can be divided into two broad areas: avoidable and unavoidable. Nothing can be done about the latter, which covers amicable resignations for reasons of marriage, maternity, relocation, and even pursuit of an entirely different career. These reasons usually do not reflect unhappiness or dissatisfaction with the job or the company. On the other hand, resignation that could have been avoided may indicate the need for improvement in some aspect of personnel administration. It is for this reason that line managers should be encouraged to sit down with the employee with the intent of finding out the *real reason* for the resignation. The stress on the words "real reason" stems from the fact that many employees are, at times, understandably reluctant to be completely truthful. In many cases they fear that any criticism or evidence of dissatisfaction on their part might cause them to get poor references as they seek employment elsewhere. Because this is a natural reaction, it is doubly imperative that the manager not only try to create the proper atmosphere, but that he not automatically accept at face value the reason for resignation as first given by the employee. Discussion with the employee should be aimed at probing into the real reason behind the stated reason. Resignations for such well-known phrases as "personal reasons" and "another position" are often the easy way out for the employee; "another position" is frequently found to be nonexistent. Even where there is another position, the question should be asked, "What motivated the employee to seek another job?"

The following excerpt from an exit interview held by a personnel administrator, Mr. Smith, and a departing employee, Miss Jones, whose stated reason for resignation is "dissatisfaction with pay," is a good example of what can be learned when looking for the *real reasons* for resignation:

> Mr. Jones: Do you have another job as yet?
> Miss Smith: Yes, I start next Monday.
> Mr. Jones: Will you be making appreciably more money?
> Miss Smith: (very hesitatingly) Well, not really.
> Mr. Jones: May I ask just how much more?
> Miss Smith: (again after rather long pause) To be perfectly honest, I will be getting exactly what I was making here.
> Mr. Jones: There must be an error on your termination notice. It states here that you are leaving because you are dissatisfied with your pay.
> Miss Smith: (looking Mr. Jones straight in the eye) Mr. Jones, if you had *my* boss, you would want more money too!

What May Be Gained by Discussion

Although, as the above example indicates, a manager may not always be pleased with what he hears, there is much to be gained from having a serious discussion with the employee:

Salvaging a good employee. In trying to determine what led to the employee's decision to resign, the manager may find that the employee feels his opportunities for growth and/or advancement are limited. If the manager is truly interested in keeping the employee, he should take this opportunity to outline future plans which could influence the employee's thinking. If in the immediate or foreseeable future the manager cannot honestly see change, he should encourage and help the employee to explore the possibilities of another more promising job within the company. In either case, the mere evidence of interest in the employee may be enough to be the basis on which the employee will reconsider.

Learning shortcomings of departmental personnel administration. During a serious discussion with an employee, a manager may learn much about his or his subordinate's handling of human relations problems. If an employee indicates dissatisfaction with pay it should alert the manager to review his interpretation and application of the company's salary administration policies and guidelines. If the company has a formal job evaluation program, he should reexamine the job content. He may find that the job over the years has grown, but no attempt was made at having it reevaluated.

If an employee cites dissatisfaction with the manner in which he has been treated regarding such matters as special requests for time off the job, docking for lateness, payment of overtime, reprimands for excessive use of telephones for personal business, and long lunch hours, it would be well for the manager to ascertain how uniformly the applicable company policies or practices are being applied throughout his department.

Realistic appraisal of job requirements and qualifications. Last, in discussing the job with the departing employee, a manager may gain a better insight into the qualifications he should be seeking in replacing the job being vacated. For example, a secretary who is leaving because she takes so little dictation that she is afraid she will lose her skills, should cause the manager to reappraise the real need for stenography in that job. Perhaps he should be looking for a good typist who is willing to use a dictaphone.

Resignation Procedure

Once it is determined that an employee's resignation is unalterable, either because it is an unavoidable one or because the supervisor has been unable to have the employee reconsider, the resignation should be accepted in good grace. It is advisable to request a signed letter of resignation so that the company has prima facie evidence that the termination was voluntary. This information, for example, can be very helpful in cases involving claims for unemployment insurance.

The question of what is considered adequate notice can sometimes be a basis of friction between manager and employee. Although reasonable notice will vary from case to case, two weeks to one month seems to be the customary period of notice depending on the type of job. In any event, when, because of the nature of the job and the probable difficulty in finding a replacement quickly, the manager may deem the amount of notice inappropriate (e.g., two weeks or less, the latter sometimes made necessary by circumstances beyond the employee's control), he must still accept the resignation gracefully. Members of management should *never* make short notice an excuse for changing a resignation into a dismissal.

Where companies have a definite probationary period, less than two weeks notice is generally acceptable. In such cases, the company policy does not require notice although in practice it may be given as well as received.

Under some conditions, it may be desirable to make a resignation effective sooner than the date stipulated by the employee. This may often be the case where a person has decided to resign as a result of having been put on final warning and his continued appearance at work might have an adverse effect on the job or office morale. In this situation, however, the manager must achieve his goal in such a way that the employee does not get the impression that he is being dismissed.

DISMISSALS

Dismissals are terminations initiated by the company. Because dismissal is the most drastic step an employer can take toward an employee, it is imperative that such action be given the most careful deliberation and action. Good personnel administration, therefore, dictates that dismissal must be for *just and sufficient cause* and *only after* all practical steps toward rehabilitation or salvage of the employee have been taken and failed. However, it is equally important that, if the welfare of the company indicates that dismissal is necessary, the decision be arrived at and carried out forthrightly.

Responsibility for Dismissal

Since the decision to dismiss an employee is a grave responsibility, it should not be made solely by one person. The immediate supervisor, who is normally the person responsible for appraising performance, must review with, and get approval from, at least the next higher authority, regardless of the level at which the action occurs. Where there is a personnel administrator or manager, he too should be consulted before any action is taken. It is only in this way that complete objectivity and fairness to the employee can be assured.

Acceptable Reasons for Dismissal

Reasons for dismissal should be clearly defined so as to assure that each manager is applying the same criteria to all employees. Broadly speaking, reasons for dismissal may be categorized under four major headings:

1. Unsatisfactory performance
2. Misconduct
3. Lack of qualifications for the job
4. Changed requirements of the job

Unsatisfactory performance may be defined as persistent failure to perform assigned work duties or to meet prescribed standards on the job. This failure may be due to various causes, any of which normally justifies dismissal as follows:

1. *Absenteeism* is cause for dismissal regardless of the reason for absence. Excessive absenteeism cannot help but eventually affect an employee's effectiveness on the job as well as have a demoralizing influence on other members of the staff. What constitutes excessive absenteeism is often the basis for disagreement among managers as well as between supervisor and employee. For example, in the past, twelve absences a year was considered by many companies sufficient cause for dismissal. There are many "old school" supervisors who still hold to this rule, while other managers are far more permissive. Although there often are extenuating circumstances, some company guidelines should be established to assure equitable treatment of all employees.

Even where the absenteeism is due to health reasons, an employer may have to take action. Here it is important to differentiate between excessive absenteeism due to one- and two-day absences for illness as against absenteeism for long periods of serious illness. In the case of the habitual one or two "sick days," the supervisor should treat the situation as a regular absentee problem, and if, after several warnings, the employee's attendance does not improve, he should be dismissed. The case of the prolonged illness is discussed later on in the chapter under the heading of "physical incapacity to perform job."

2. *Tardiness* should be treated in much the same manner as absenteeism. Very often the excuse is offered that the employee stays late or takes shorter lunch periods. When one's position requires that he work with and through others, his habitually starting work at other than the prescribed company hour can be very irritating and frustrating to fellow employees. As such it has the same detrimental effect on job performance and employee morale as excessive absenteeism, and therefore the "makeup" rationalization should not be condoned.

3. *Lack of application to job* is evidenced by the employee's persistent failure to meet normal job requirements of quantity and quality of work. In such cases, the employee is deemed to be qualified and capable of performing the job assigned to him, but is not giving the job either the attention or the energy required.

4. *Adverse attitude* toward the company, one's supervisor, fellow employees, work assignments, and/or established policies and procedures pertaining to job assignment all constitute cause for dismissal. Care must be exercised here not to confuse a reserved manner or unwillingness to fraternize with a truly uncooperative attitude which seriously affects job performance and *work* relationship with fellow employees.

Misconduct may be defined as deliberate and willful violation of company or departmental rules by an employee. The same is true for insubordination, dishonesty, rowdyism, or other serious breaks of acceptable behavior. An employee guilty of any of these infractions should be dismissed without notice. Because of the extreme action called for here, it is important that a supervisor check with his boss and any available personnel help before the employee is dismissed. In this way, the possibility of a person acting hastily without true cause or substantiation may be avoided.

Lack of qualifications for the job may be defined as an employee's incapability of doing the work assigned to him or of meeting prescribed goals and objectives, even though the employee applies himself diligently and has a commendable attitude.

This situation, when it occurs, is usually related to a newly hired or newly promoted employee. The employee's probable success on the job can only be measured by his education and experience prior to taking on the new job responsibilities. Because it is not absolutely possible to predict success in a hiring or promotion situation and the employee is taking as much risk as the employer, dismissals in such cases are *not* considered the fault of the employee. Therefore, every effort should be made to salvage such an employee.

Changed requirements of the job may be defined as an employee's incapability of doing the work assigned or of meeting prescribed job goals and objectives where the nature and/or scope of the job he has held has changed. In this case, the employee's qualifications have not changed, but the demands of the job have. This, for example, is often the case in sales when a salesman cannot, despite all his efforts, meet the new goals dictated by increasingly competitive business pressures which call for a different or high-powered sales approach. It can also be the result of a change in emphasis in a job such as the added requirement that a promotion manager have an extensive background in research. In either case, the employee is truly applying himself but cannot meet the new requirements of the job. As in the case of lack of qualifications for the job, dismissal here, too, is *not* considered the fault of the employee.

Preventing Dismissals

There are many steps a manager can and should take in the hope of salvaging or rehabilitating an employee. The key factor here is *timing*. All too often a problem situation is allowed to go on until there is almost no alternative but dismissal. It is the manager's responsibility to attack unsatisfactory performance before the problems become insurmountable. If an employee is not meeting job goals, is not adhering to departmental or company rules, or is not showing the proper cooperative attitude, all of which are danger signals pointing toward possible dismissal, the manager may be able to salvage the situation by having frank discussions with the employee "early in the game."

How far the manager will go in giving the employee an opportunity to save his job will, of course, depend on the nature of the problem. In the case of nonadherence to company policy about matters as absenteeism or tardiness, or in the case of a problem attitude, where it is within the employee's ability to show marked improvement quickly, long trial periods after sufficient warnings are not usually required or advisable. On the other hand, where an employee's attitude and willingness are commendable, a manager should make every effort to work with and counsel the employee, and to set reasonable targets of achievement for him. For example, in the case of a salesman, it would be unrealistic to expect him to turn around a poor sales record in a month's time.

It is also recommended that a manager follow up discussions with the employee in writing. Written confirmations should be aimed at clarifying job responsibilities and goals and offering assistance to the employee. In essence, the tone and spirit of these early discussions and written confirmations should be such as to convince the employee of his supervisor's sincerity and thereby to encourage him to put forth his best efforts.

If, in spite of all the foregoing attempts to salvage the employee in his present job, it appears certain that things will not work out, consideration should be given to possible transfer to a more suitable position. Care, however, should be taken to honestly evaluate the employee's worth to the company. It is all too common a practice for a manager to take the easy way out and pass on what should be *his* problem to another unsuspecting manager or department head. If the employee has qualifications that can truly be of value elsewhere in the company and his attitude and willingness are *plus* attributes, then all avenues for transfer should be fully explored. If not, the manager should take the proper steps toward dismissing the employee.

Dismissal Procedure

The importance of establishing and adhering to specific guidelines in all the steps that lead to termination cannot be stressed too strongly. Not only is this dictated by ethical business practice in dealing with human relations problems, but the increasingly greater role being played by governmental agencies at all levels makes it incumbent on the employer. A company must be in a position to defend itself against charges of unfairness or discrimination. Therefore, to the extent possible, company policy and the procedures to be followed by managers in cases of impending dismissal should be clearly set forth and closely administered.

In general, the action to be taken in impending dismissals is as follows:

Warning discussions should precede any final action; an employee *must* be made aware that he is not performing satisfactorily. Ideally, all such discussions should be followed by confirming letters. At this stage, especially if the manager is hopeful of salvaging the employee, copies to those who need to know (the manager's superior and the personnel representative) should be "blind carbons" to prevent unnecessarily demoralizing the employee.

Careful documentation of warning discussions should be kept by the supervisor, if it is deemed inappropriate to follow each such discussion with a confirming letter. Wherever possible detailed records should also be kept, as in the cases of absenteeism, tardiness, and failure to meet production goals. Adequate evidence furnished by the employer can have a direct bearing on possible claims for unemployment insurance. For example, an employee dismissed for excessive absenteeism or tardiness cannot normally claim unemployment insurance, but the State Division of Employment usually requires that such evidence be documented, and it must also be shown that the employee was warned.

Final warning, when all else has failed, should be extremely explicit. The employee *must* be made to realize that his job is in jeopardy. All too often some of the techniques used in the so-called corrective interview can be misinterpreted by the employee. No one wants to believe he really could be *fired*. Therefore, the use of ambiguous phrases which can be misleading should be avoided. The following synopsis of a final warning discussion illustrates this point:

The manager, wishing to set a friendly atmosphere, invites the employee to lunch. They order a drink and discuss their respective golf games of the preceding weekend. Sometime during the meal the manager tells the employee (in this case a salesman) that he is somewhat disappointed in his sales record over the past year and that if his sales don't improve over the next few months, he, the manager, is "going to have to do something about it." Dessert is ordered, they exchange a few more pleasantries and then return to work. The manager thinks to himself, "Well I really laid it on the line to him." The employee says to his wife that night, "You know honey, my boss and I had a real nice talk at lunch today."

The final warning should spell out to the employee exactly (1) where and how his performance is not meeting the standards and goals set for his job, (2) the length of time he has in which to meet these standards and goals, and (3) that termination will result if he is unsuccessful.

Written confirmation of final warning is an absolute *must* as protection to both the employee and the company. As for the employee, the written warning cannot be easily ignored or misunderstood. Even the frankest of discussions can fall short of achieving the purpose because of the very human reaction of screening out what one does not wish to hear or accept. As for the company, it assures that managers have indeed carried out their responsibilities in the critical area of dismissal in accordance with prescribed policy. It also provides documentation of proper handling should the company be called upon to prove same in possible subsequent claims for unemployment insurance or allegations by the employee, directly or through some governmental agency, of unfair or discriminatory treatment.

Adequate notice should be given the employee *in addition* to the final warning. The warning states to the employee that he has to a specified date to meet job requirements and/or standards of performance. At that date, if he was unsuccessful he then should be put on notice of termination.

Minimum notice is usually two weeks for employees with one or more years of service. Employees with less than one year of service usually receive a minumum of one week's notice. Companies that have specified probationary periods for new employees normally do not, by policy, require that advance notice be given. However, practice indicates that probationary employees are usually told up to a maximum of one week before dismissal. On the other hand, temporary employees and those dismissed for misconduct very rarely are given advance notice.

Consideration of notice beyond two weeks should be given depending on the employee's length of service and the circumstances surrounding job failure. For example, it is not uncommon to give an employee with twenty years or more of service up to three months notice.

Pay in lieu of notice should be considered in cases where it is to the advantage of the company to do so. Such cases would include a disgruntled employee who might adversely affect the morale of his fellow workers or an employee whose presence would cause acute embarrassment or who might be expected to "drag his feet" after notice of dismissal.

In those cases where pay in lieu of notice is deemed appropriate, this pay should be given regardless of whether separation allowance is paid.

Careful selection of reason for dismissal is of importance to the company as well as to the employee. The *true* reason for dismissal should be officially indicated on whatever form or document the company uses for this purpose. It should be clearcut and substantiated by adequate evidence. It is equally important that the dismissed employee know the reason for dismissal as officially stated by the company, since it will have a direct bearing on whether he will be eligible for unemployment insurance and, depending on company policy, may determine whether or not he will receive separation allowance. Giving the employee other than the real reason for dismissal is doing him a disservice, and may work to the disadvantage of both the employee and the company. When a former employee applies for unemployment insurance, the reason he gives for dismissal is verified by the State Division of Employment, which, in turn, checks company records. If there is any discrepancy, it may lead to the payment of unemployment insurance in cases where none is justifiably due, and vice versa. Furthermore, the employee must be made aware of his position with regard to any possible reference checks made by prospective employers. Although companies should exercise extreme care in answering reference requests, as well as being as fair as possible, they should be consistent.

OTHER TERMINATIONS

The types of terminations that fall into this category are also initiated by the company, but to include them under dismissals would unjustly place them under the umbrella which carries with it somewhat of a stigma. For in all true cases of dismissal the employee, to varying degrees, had some control over the final outcome. This does not apply to terminations for the following reasons: reduction of force, layoff, physical incapacity to perform job, mandatory retirement, and death.

Reduction of Force

Terminations are classified as reduction of force when an employee's job is eliminated because of combining job functions, changing methods, or by elimination or relocation of certain operations.

Company responsibility for such action over which the employee has no control makes it incumbent on the company management to make every effort to find a suitable transfer for that employee. The transfer sought should be to a position of comparable skills, responsibilities, growth potential, and rate of pay. Failing this, the employee should be given adequate notice and separation allowance in accordance with company policy (see section on separation allowance later on in chapter). If emergency operating problems call for immediate cessation of a unit or department, the employee should be given pay in lieu of notice. This payment should *not* take the place of any separation allowance due the employee.

Employee responsibility for accepting a comparable job and his possible forfeiture of any termination pay is often a very difficult question to resolve. The employee should not be obliged to accept just *any* job. He should have the right to refuse a transfer to a job where skills, responsibilities, growth potential, and rate of pay are not comparable to the position he had held. The same should be true of a transfer, even if comparable, that would require his relocation. Because of the difficulty of determining true comparability to the satisfaction of both the company and the employee, in cases where there is disagreement, it is recommended that leniency be exercised in favor of the employee.

Layoff

A layoff, although it is initiated by the company, differs from other terminations in that it is normally a temporary situation, resulting from lack of work. To be properly classified as a layoff, *all* the following conditions should exist:

1. There is not enough work for the employee.
2. It is anticipated that this will be a short-term, temporary situation.
3. The supervisor intends to recall the employee as soon as the work load permits.

Differentiating between layoff and reduction of force is of importance since it significantly affects the employee's status with the company. In a layoff situation, the aim is to protect a permanent employee's tenure and all related benefits and privileges. To accomplish this, the employee who is laid off because of a temporary lack of work is still regarded as an employee, but one who is not currently working and not receiving any regular pay.

Time limits for layoffs should be spelled out by the company to assure that:

1. All employees are treated equitably in similar situations.
2. The layoff will not be used by managers as a device for avoiding the necessity of "facing up" to what might otherwise be an unpleasant dismissal case.

Setting the time limits will vary from one company to another depending on the nature of the work; especially where such work is cyclical and is readily anticipated. Usually the maximums set for the duration of layoffs are tied in with length of service. For example, a typical time allowance formula is as follows:

1. One month per year of continuous service, not to exceed twelve months.
2. Two days per month of continuous service for employees with less than one year of service, not to exceed one month.

The effect on continuous service should also be defined, since most company benefits and privileges accruing to an employee are usually based on his continuous service date. Therefore, it is necessary to establish: (1) that continuous service is *not* broken by a layoff, and (2) at what point and how the continuous service date should be adjusted if the layoff were to become prolonged. The following guidelines are typical:

1. Continuous service continues to accrue during the first six months.

2. If the layoff were to exceed this six-month period, there would be no further accrual and the employee's continuous service date would be adjusted by the amount of time the layoff went beyond this period when he returned to work.

The effect on employee benefit programs will usually vary with the type of benefit. During a layoff, the insured benefits such as medical, life, and disability coverage can and should be continued to afford the greatest possible protection to the employee. If any or all of these programs are contributory, the employee should be given the opportunity of arranging for his regular premium payments. He should also be given the option at the beginning of the layoff period of making these payments in advance, during layoff, or after recall. If he is not recalled and subsequently terminated, any premium payments due can be withheld from severance pay.

If a company has a retirement and/or a profit-sharing plan, the provisions of the plan should clearly define the status and the extent of the employee's participation during the layoff period.

Vacation rights and holiday pay will depend on the company policy regarding these benefits. Where a company looks upon vacation as "earned," the employee should be given the option of charging all or part of his layoff time to unused earned vacation. If he chooses not to, he then should be given pay in lieu of vacation if the duration of the layoff makes it impossible for him to take his vacation within prescribed time limits.

In the case of holidays, companies normally pay for holidays that fall either at the beginning or end of a layoff period. However, except in the case of some union contracts, it is *not* the usual practice to pay for holidays that fall *within* this period.

Layoffs should become terminations for reduction of force under the following circumstances:

1. When the layoff has continued without recall for the maximum period permitted as specified by the company policy.

2. When the department head determines, with the concurrence of his superior, that the lack of work is not, as first thought, a temporary condition.

3. When the layoff lasts more than a specified time, (usually two weeks) and the employee notifies his supervisor that he wishes to be terminated. In this case, it is the right of the employee to seek and accept what he considers more stable employment without being penalized. The notification to his supervisor should be accepted in good graces, and the termination should be regarded as a reduction of force.

Explaining layoff policy and action to the employee so affected should be the responsibility of the immediate supervisor. The employee should understand all the details of the layoff including probable duration, the effect on and the handling of benefits, the effect on continuous service, maximum duration permissible, and the circumstances under which the layoff may become a reduction of force.

Physical Incapacity to Perform Job

This type of termination, initiated by the company, should be restricted to *only* those cases where an employee is incapable of fulfilling his responsibilities because of illness or injury. Generally speaking, it covers absence due to chronic illness or protracted disabilities of indefinite duration where the outcome is not readily determinable or where rehabilitation is doubtful. It also applies to employees who are at work, but whose performance fails to meet minimum standards due to clearly established health problems. These situations should *not* be confused with cases of acute illness or temporary disability where the terminal date of enforced absence can be predicted with some degree of accuracy. The only exception might be a very short-term or probationary employee.

Responsibility for determining whether an employee is physically incapable of performing his job should not rest solely with line management. When such a serious decision is based on an employee's physical or mental condition, the advice and guidance of the company doctor or whoever the company uses for medical services should be sought.

There are many factors which must be given careful consideration in deciding if and when such an employee is to be terminated:

1. The nature of the disability or illness
2. The prospects for return to work and/or returning to a satisfactory level of performance
3. The employee's length of service
4. The importance of the position and its impact on the effective operation of the unit or department

The importance of fairly weighing all the facts cannot be stressed too strongly. The danger of adverse reaction from the employee involved as well as the possible effect on general employee morale is great. Care must be taken to avoid the impression of "kicking a person when he is down." Consultation with a medical authority and a personnel representative should assure that the employee receive all the consideration and protection the company policy provides. It should also assure that "physical incapacity" will not be used as a guise for dismissing an unsatisfactory employee whose discharge is warranted on other grounds.

How long the employee should be kept on payroll will, because of the various considerations listed above, necessitate a case-by-case determination. However, certain minimum and maximum limitations should be prescribed to be fair to both the employee *and* the company:

1. *Minimum periods* before which termination may *not* be effected are usually based on: (*a*) the employee's length of service and (*b*) the company's salary continuation plan, if any. For example, a typical formula for length of service is one week for each six months of service. This would mean that an employee with five years of service could not be terminated before ten weeks of absence. If the company salary continuation plan would pay for a period beyond ten weeks, the termination could not take place before the "sick pay" was dissipated. If the reverse were true, again the longer period of time would set the earliest date for termination.

2. *Maximum periods* after which termination *must* be effected should also be defined. Retention of a nonproductive employee on the payroll for an indefinite period is contrary to good management. If a position can be unmanned for a protracted period, its essentiality may very well be questioned. On the other hand, if a temporary replacement must be hired to do the job, operating costs are increased. In addition, consideration must be given to the impact on the company's benefit programs. None of the foregoing considerations should be misconstrued as "license" for termination, but it should motivate action when inaction stems from carelessness or inertia.

When replacement of the physically incapacitated employee takes place is still another determination which must be made by line management. The established company guidelines for keeping the disabled employee on payroll should normally set the time period during which the job must be held open for him. However, there are times when circumstances do not permit adhering to this general rule. If it is known in advance that termination is inevitable (e.g., terminal illness), or if the pivotal nature of the position makes it impossible to keep it open for the required period, replacement of the employee may have to be considered. Such a decision, however, must *not* be made *unless absolutely necessary*. In the first case, the medical authority must confirm that a recovery from the disabling condition is improbable before the projected termination date. In the latter instance, the "pivotal" nature of the job and all possible alternatives for interim coverage must be thoroughly investigated and ascertained.

Mandatory Retirement

Many companies have a policy requiring the retirement of employees when they attain a specified age, usually sixty-five. There are many sound reasons for establishing mandatory retirement. Although it is not necessarily true that the effectiveness of all employees diminishes with age, it is unrealistic to deny that there are many who "start running out of gas" as they approach the senior years. Because it is *often* difficult from a management viewpoint, and *almost always* impossible from a human relations viewpoint, to differentiate between the two, the only equitable solution is to make retirement mandatory. In addition, enlightened management recognizes the need for encouraging new talent and bringing new blood to a company. Younger employees with initiative and know-how will seek career opportunities elsewhere, if they see no real advancement to jobs of greater responsibilities within the company.

Factors to be considered with regard to retirement are:
1. How is vacation to be treated in the last year?
2. Are retirees eligible for severance pay?
3. What effect will retirement have on insurance benefits?
4. What employee privileges are retained by retirees?
5. Who has the responsibility for (*a*) explaining company policy on all of the above, (*b*) counselling the employee regarding such matters as Medicare and social security, and (*c*) handling all the details necessary to expedite the payment of pension benefits where applicable.
6. What type of recognition (e.g., party or gift) should the company sponsor and/or encourage.

The answers to these questions will vary depending on company policy and the type of benefit programs in force. Whatever the answers are, it is important that the retiree be informed well in advance about those things he needs to know. It is equally important that notification of the approaching retirement to the necessary departments and people be done early so that the termination of a long career proceeds smoothly.

Throughout the entire termination procedure, the retiring employee should be made to feel that his service with the company is truly appreciated.

Death of an Employee

Termination in the case of the death of an employee is, of course, perfunctory. However, there are certain company responsibilities which call for immediate action, as well as special consideration in the handling of all details which involve the deceased employee's family.

The factors to be considered and acted upon are:
1. *What monies are due the deceased employee?* The period through which regular salary and/or other compensation is to be paid needs to be determined. It is common practice to use the particular pay period cycle under which the deceased employee was normally paid as the basis for all such computations. For example, if the deceased employee was paid semimonthly, salary and other compensation would be paid for the entire semimonthly period regardless of whether death occurred at the beginning, the end, or the middle of this period. Where a

commission arrangement was in effect, compensation would, of course, include the commission on business that the management decides was written by the deceased employee. Any vacation money due should be in accordance with company policy pertaining to terminated employees.

2. *What disposition is to be made of monies due?* It is normal to pay all such monies either to the deceased employee's next of kin or to his estate. Where large sums of money are involved (e.g., over $1,000), it may be advisable to seek legal counsel for instructions on how and to whom remittance should be made. This does not apply, of course, to insurance benefits where a beneficiary is named.

3. *Who should be notified?* News of the death of an employee should be reported promptly to the members of line management directly concerned, to the person responsible for expediting any death benefit payments, and to the payroll department. Where there is a personnel administrator, he would normally be responsible for coordinating these activities.

Depending on the size of the company and how well known the deceased employee was, a departmental or company-wide memorandum might be appropriate. In such cases, information regarding funeral services and the family's wishes concerning flowers, donations, etc. should be included.

4. *Who should contact the family of the deceased?* If the immediate supervisor or another fellow employee is acquainted with the family, it is desirable to have him be the person through whom all communications be made. It would then be his responsibility to obtain documents necessary to expedite any insurance benefits due and to explain any other payments or death benefits which might be due. Needless to say, in such difficult times, a personal contact is usually appreciated by the bereaved family.

SEVERANCE PAY

"Severance pay" or "separation allowance," as it is often referred to, is the terminology used for special payments made by the employer to terminating employees. The conditions under which such payments are made vary from the extremely liberal to the very restricted. On the liberal side can be found those companies (admittedly few in number) which look upon the period of employment as a time during which employees are accruing a vested interest in the company, and which therefore pay separation allowance even to those who resign. On the other hand, there are some companies (also few in number) which pay severance only under the most limited conditions, such as only in the case of reduction of force.

In the majority of companies, however, it has become the generally accepted practice to pay separation allowance to permanent employees when termination is initiated by the company. Normally separation is *not* paid to temporary employees, regardless of the reason for termination.

Within the group of companies that pay severance only to employees terminated by the company, there are generally two schools of thought about eligibility for this payment:

1. *All employees,* with the possible exception of those dismissed for misconduct, terminated by the company are eligible for severance pay.

2. *Only those employees,* terminated by the company, who are considered to have lost their jobs through no fault of their own are eligible for severance pay.

There are rationales for these differing viewpoints on severance pay eligibility. Those who adhere to the philosophy of paying severance to all but those employees who are terminated for outright misconduct, point to the difficulty, if not the impossibility, of determining "fault" on the part of the employee. Even in the more easily evaluated situations of excessive absenteeism or lateness, it is argued that unless the word excessive is *defined* in numbers, and *strictly enforced* by all super-visors, unfair or inequitable treatment can easily result.   In essence, the greatest argument for paying severance to all dismissed employees is that it avoids the pos-sibility of any error in human judgment or of any prejudice.

Good and responsible management, however, should and can overcome these arguments.   If the guidelines on proper warning and written confirmation of such warnings are followed, inequitable treatment of employees and questionable deter-mination of "cause" or "employee fault" can be avoided.   Furthermore, a company has a responsibility to those employees who are putting forth their best efforts and making a real contribution to the company.   Paying separation allowance to un-deserving employees is not only a wasteful expenditure, it is demoralizing to the hardworking, productive employee when poor performance is rewarded.   The payment of separation allowance, on the other hand, to those who are truly losing their jobs through no fault of their own is easily understood and accepted.   In fact, it does much to label the company as *fair* in the eyes of all employees.

In addition to creating confidence in a company's sense of fair play, the payment of separation allowance *only* to deserving employees tends to assure that problem situations that might lead to termination are handled properly.   If managers know they will have to defend their designation of an employee's eligibility for severance pay based on reason for termination, it will be incumbent on them not only to take all the prescribed steps in the termination procedure, but to document such action as well.

Following the more responsible philosophy of paying separation allowance only to those employees who lose their jobs through no fault of their own, the following reasons for termination as described earlier in this chapter would qualify:

1. Lack of qualifications for job
2. Changed requirements of job
3. Reduction of force
4. Physical incapacity to perform job
5. Mandatory retirement if there is no company-sponsored retirement plan
6. Death of an employee only in those cases where there is no insurance death benefit

Amount of severance pay is usually based on length of service.   It is recommended that a specific formula be developed to assure equitable treatment of all employees. A common formula is as follows:

Length of Service	*Separation Allowance*
Less than twelve months.	One day's pay for each full month of service up to a limit of two weeks pay
One year and over.	One week's pay for each half year of service

There are, in many companies, two special situations in which the above formula would not apply or would be altered:

1. In those companies that have specified probationary periods, no severance pay applies if termination takes place during this time.

2. In cases of reduction of force, a minimum of two weeks' severance is paid, regardless of length of service.

Computation of severance pay is usually based on regular salary, commissions and/or contingent compensation.   It does not include special bonus payments or overtime pay.   In those cases where commissions or additional compensation agreements are involved, "weekly pay" may be figured by taking the average of earnings over the twelve months preceding termination.

Setting limits on severance pay is a common practice. Cutoffs may be set on the number of weeks and/or at a maximum dollar amount. Although it might be considered desirable from a human relations standpoint to set no limits, the cost factor to the company cannot easily be ignored. A compromise to the dilemma of being as fair as possible to the employee while recognizing the necessity for keeping costs within reasonable boundaries is to set limits on the number of weeks rather than on the dollar amount. Such limits usually range between twenty-six to fifty-two weeks.

Where dollar maximums are applied, it tends to penalize the longer service employee. For example, if a company, using the formula of one week's pay for each six months of service, terminated an employee with ten years of service, that employee would be eligible for twenty weeks of separation pay. However, if there were a dollar maximum in force, it is very likely that the dollar limit would be reached before the twenty-week limit. This, in effect, invalidates much of the service factor which should be the prevailing consideration. At the same time, a relatively short-term employee usually receives severance pay which is in direct correlation to his years of service. In such a situation, it is not a question of doing too much for the short-term employee but, rather, not doing enough for the long-term employee.

BIBLIOGRAPHY

Gellerman, Saul W.: *When the Job Outgrows the Man,* International Business Machines Corporation, June, 1960.

National Industrial Conference Board, Inc.: "Forms and Records in Personnel Administration," *Studies in Personnel Policy,* no. 175, New York, 1960, pp. 116–121.

———: "Severance Pay Patterns in Nonmanufacturing," *Studies in Personnel Policy,* no. 178, New York, 1964.

———: "Corporate Retirement Policy and Practices," *Studies in Personnel Policy,* no. 190, New York, 1964.

Sheer, Wilbert E.: *Personnel Director's Handbook,* The Dartnell Corporation, Chicago, 1969, pp. 219–234.

chapter 66

The Role of Legal Counsel

ROBERT H. SAND *Labor Counsel, Allied Chemical Corporation, New York, New York*

The ever-increasing number of federal, state, and municipal laws affecting personnel administration makes the extensive use of legal counsel unavoidable. To assure the effective use of counsel the personnel administrator should be able to recognize the need for legal assistance at the earliest moment. Toward this end, the personnel administrator needs a general familiarity with the various laws affecting personnel and labor relations, enabling him to identify those situations where an attorney might be of assistance.

What type of attorney? Normally a personnel administrator should seek a legal specialist, a labor lawyer who is familiar with the particular, often peculiar laws and practices affecting employee relations. Where a specialist is not available, the personnel administrator can nevertheless call upon any attorney's basic skills: the ability to guide a client in light of the attorney's analysis of the law and thereafter to defend his client's position.

With a view then toward the timely and effective use of labor counsel, this chapter provides a brief and necessarily less than exhaustive description of the circumstances in which legal counsel should be consulted, suggesting not only the assistance counsel can provide the personnel administrator but also the assistance the latter must provide his attorney.

I. WAGE AND HOUR LAWS

It is deceptively easy to achieve almost complete compliance with the federal, state, and local minimum wage laws without the assistance of counsel. There are various companies which publish guides to the law, while federal and most state authorities issue generally comprehensible materials summarizing and explaining the law.

However, less than complete compliance can prove very expensive. In addition to minimizing the possibility of overlooking a simple mistake, there are various more complex requirements that can be met more readily with the aid of an attorney. Interpreting and applying exemptions for professional, executive, and administrative employees can be expedited by counsel. There are also the technical aspects of the laws and regulations where resort to counsel is often mandatory: over-the-road drivers; outside salesmen; fixed salaries for a fluctuating work week; and special exemptions, such as those for fishing and agriculture.

Despite the apparent dangers, many employers are lulled into a false sense of security, believing that their employees are too loyal to complain to the U.S. Department of Labor. But all too often the employee who retires, is laid off, is given only a small raise, or has a lawyer in the family walks the well-beaten path to the Wage and Hour Division. It is similarly dangerous to ignore a company's compliance status because, up to the present time, it has not been visited by the Wage and Hour Division.

At the outset, the personnel administrator should review corporate pay practices, unassisted by counsel. He should consider practices for record keeping, minimum wages, and overtime payments as well as the correct classification of exempt personnel. Throughout this review, problem areas should be identified and relevant materials assembled so that any difficulties may be reviewed thereafter with legal counsel.

After a careful and thorough review with counsel, paying particular attention to the exempt payroll, a company should have nothing to fear from a surprise visitor from the Wage and Hour Division. When the investigator arrives, be polite, be cooperative, and generally call for an attorney to intercede if significant violations are indicated. The investigator is normally willing to meet again with the administrator and his attorney at some later date. Given the opportunity to muster the facts and perhaps some citations on the employer's behalf, legal counsel may be able to reach a reasonable settlement, normally involving some back pay, changed procedures or both. He may even convince the investigator that the company is entirely correct and that no remedial action is called for.

II. EQUAL PAY FOR EQUAL WORK

The Wage and Hour Division of the Department of Labor is also charged with assuring women equal pay for equal work since this requirement is part of the Fair Labor Standards Act. The Division will determine whether women do "substantially" the same work as men, and if they do, it will compel payment equal to that of the men if the latter are higher paid. Although the determination seems fairly simple, in practice employers often err in determining whether or not the work is substantially the same.

The government, attuned to the temper of our times, is somewhat more generous to women in making this determination than many companies. Since mistakes can be costly, the personnel administrator should review salary structures and, with respect to any problem area, review with counsel the work performed, the skills, effort, and machinery involved and any other relevant factors.

Bear in mind that a legal question in this area, or any area, will not always receive an immediate answer from an attorney. He should have an opportunity to digest the facts, go back to his office, review the law, and if need be contact the Wage and Hour Division for its opinion. Then he can give his client a proper opinion.

III. MINORITY RIGHTS

The Civil Rights Act of 1964 presents a challenge and an opportunity to personnel administrators and their attorneys, particularly where the employer deals in federal contracts or subcontracts and is thus subject to Executive Order 11246. Essentially both the act and the order prohibit discrimination based on race, color, religion, sex, or national origin. There are also the various comparable municipal and state laws as well as the federal law banning discrimination based on age for individuals from forty through sixty-five. Most state laws, moreover, protect individuals of all ages.

Once again the best advice is to get a head start by reviewing *all* corporate employment practices and then, having obtained and organized data affecting possible problem areas, call in legal counsel to review the company's compliance posture. The areas to be reviewed with counsel include:

1. *Recruiting Practices.*   At the top of an attorney's checklist will be recruiting. How and where does the company recruit?   At black schools as well as white? Women's schools as well as men's?   Help-wanted ads will be scrutinized carefully. Are they directed at all labor markets?   Do they contain any illegal references to sex or age?   Do they indicate the company is an equal opportunity employer?

2. *Applications, Interviews, and Records.*   There is a long and ever-growing list of dos and don'ts concerning employment applications and interviews.   Once a company's procedures and forms have been tentatively developed, they should be reviewed by counsel.   Among the legal tests to be considered are whether the information requested is reasonably related to the job and whether any otherwise innocent question has the effect of barring employment or promotion to any group or individual entitled to statutory protection.

Legal counsel will also indicate the information an employer is required to keep concerning applicants and employees, as well as when to request and record such information.   Counsel will also detail local, state, and federal rules concerning the length of time applications and personnel records must be kept.

3. *Hiring and Promotion Practices.*   Testing procedures used before hiring or promotion must be thoroughly reviewed and, as legally required, validated.   Similarly, education or experience requirements that affect job entry or advancement must be reviewed.   The basic legal requirement is that tests be "job related" and free from any cultural bias.

4. *Government Reports.*   If a company does not file annually the employment profile report known as EEO-1 with the Equal Employment Opportunity Commission, counsel should be consulted to verify the presumed exemption.   In any event, counsel should review the company's contracts and bulletin boards to assure that any legally required compliance provisions appear or are incorporated by reference as necessary.

The success of a company's minority rights program is most easily measured by the census figures appearing in the EEO-1 report, particularly the figures for the more skilled and responsible positions.   Moreover, these figures must be judged in light of the percentage of minority group members in the relevant labor market.

IV. AFFIRMATIVE ACTION PROGRAMS

It is advisable and often necessary that a company's practices and policies with respect to minority rights be formalized, normally in a document known as an affirmative action program.   Federal authorities have announced what such programs should cover and many companies have published theirs so that ample guidelines now exist.

The preparation of an affirmative action program necessarily involves a review of the basic compliance areas suggested above as well as a review of company practices and benefits in general.   Legal counsel will ask such questions as, "Are women given maternity leaves of absence?"   Are they barred from lucrative jobs or overtime because of dubious state laws designed to "protect" women. And many more questions. Although veteran's rights are protected by other statutes, the legal protection offered this group might well be reviewed at the same time.

V. INVESTIGATIONS, CONCILIATION, AND LAWSUITS

Once a formal investigation begins, it is in many ways too late. But much remains that can be done. The notice of the charge normally names the complaining party and states the grievance. Generally there is sufficient time to meet with legal counsel and assemble the facts for the immediate case. Federal and most state investigators will also wish to examine the company's overall compliance picture, and witnesses and documentation toward this end should also be readied.

Following the investigation or as part of it, the various state and federal authorities will institute voluntary compliance negotiations if they believe corrective action called for. An attorney can be of crucial assistance since the government representatives are frequently lawyers themselves and since the end result is a legal and all too often legalistic document.

In the event of an actual lawsuit, make certain that your attorney is fully briefed of the facts, recognizes the full implications of the suit from the company's point of view, and receives the cooperation of all company personnel. Do not try to direct or motivate a lawyer by giving him only some of the facts. This technique is rarely helpful, never welcome and frequently damaging. Just as a doctor needs a true picture of his patient's illness, so does a lawyer.

VI. UNION ORGANIZING CAMPAIGNS

There is an old adage that unions are organized by employers. Thus the employer who takes his workers' loyalty for granted is the employer most apt to sit in his lawyer's office, pass the union's demand for recognition across the desk to his attorney and say, "This comes as a complete surprise. What can I do now?"

Despite the restrictions imposed by the National Labor Relations Act and the National Labor Relations Board, much can still be done. But remember that union supporters and activists are entitled to considerable protection at all times, and once a demand for recognition has been made, a very formidable array of legal restrictions are imposed on the employer who wants to "do something" to prevent unionization. Once the union has started its campaign or actually demanded recognition, it is in many respects too late to do anything. Therefore an employer's initial actions should take place before the union arrives.

As any personnel administrator knows, an employer should continuously review working conditions, pay, benefits and communications, all the while asking himself "Am I doing anything now that tomorrow may assist a union in organizing my employees?" Most of this review is the peculiar province of the personnel and labor relations specialist. However a labor lawyer experienced in the ways of union organizing campaigns can often recognize nonlegal aspects of a company's personnel policies that unions are apt in his experience to use to their advantage at some later date. Moreover, there are a number of legal or legally oriented practices which should be discussed with counsel as part of this review:

1. *Solicitation Rules.* Plant or office rules allowing solicitation during working time and on the work floor should be reviewed with counsel with a view toward the protection and opportunity they may afford union organizers. Such solicitation rules should be clarified with a view toward a future organizing campaign as well as productivity requirements.

2. *Periodic Reviews.*   As already indicated, once a union organizing campaign begins and particularly after the demand for recognition, the law normally prevents an employer at that point from improving salaries or other benefits.   But there is a crucial exception whereby an employer with a clearly established practice of reviewing and upgrading the company's wage and benefits program may continue this practice even during the election period.   Similarly an improvement planned before the union appeared on the scene need not be suspended just because the effective date followed the demand for recognition.   Indeed a company is not merely entitled but required to continue its normal policies and practices during the campaign period.

As a result, the company with such a clearly established program of regularly reviewing benefits and policies can maintain some freedom of action during the union organizing campaign.   The continuation of regular review practices immediately prior to a representation election can result in a union's filing unfair labor practice charges and objections to the election.   It is therefore particularly important that advice of counsel be obtained in establishing, documenting, applying, and communicating such a review program.

3. *Separate Gates.*   Companies using contractors for special construction, shipping, or the like should review with counsel the establishment of separate gates for the exclusive use of such employees.   The advantage of such separate gates, in the event of picketing by plant employees, is that it may be possible to bar such primary pickets from properly established secondary employee gates.   Conversely, picketing directed at the contractor's employees may be barred from the main employee gate, if the gates and the use of the contractor's employees meet the legal tests.

4. *Unit Definition.*   Employers can be hurt if a union petitions for only a segment of the overall bargaining unit, rather than a plant-wide or company-wide unit.   Or an employer may be hurt if a "high-priced" union that normally represents a single skilled trade is able to petition for an entire plant, not just for a smaller unit of drivers or machinists.   This is an area where timely consultation, i.e., before the petition is filed, can prove extremely helpful.

The factors which the NLRB will consider in determining whether a union is requesting an appropriate unit are generally well defined, even though the emphasis given one or another factor has varied over the years.   Since many of these factors are within the control of the employer, he can quite properly control or at least affect the scope of the unit a union may represent at some later date.

Among the factors the board will consider and which the company might wish to adjust are location, functional integration, lines of promotion, interchange, common supervision, uniformity of benefits, training, skills, and other indications of a general community of interest or lack thereof.

Once a union organizing campaign is under way, legal counsel is necessary if an employer is to progress successfully through the legal thicket.   Common sense is no substitute here for actual knowledge of the law.   The commonsense answer to a question concerning what an employer may do during a union organizing campaign is rarely correct.   And mistakes are costly.

Legal advice in the following areas will prove helpful:

1. *Instructions to Supervisors.*   Ill-advised statements by supervisors can lead to a Board's order setting aside the election or, in extreme cases, to a Board order requiring the employer to recognize and bargain with a union, even without an election or even if the union lost the election.

Written instructions to supervisors assist the supervisors, while establishing a record for a possible board proceeding.   The instructions are designed to assure "laboratory conditions" in accordance with board rulings. The instructions should be drafted with legal counsel and must be adapted to the particular campaign, the sophistication of the supervisors, the position of the company in the campaign, the types of employees and union (or unions) involved.

2. *Responding to Demands for Recognition.* Most often unions demand recognition by letter, giving the company ample opportunity to consult with counsel as to the appropriate response. However management should be coached by counsel on how to respond to a face-to-face request for recognition, particularly a demand by a union representative for an employer review of authorization cards.

Depending upon the employer's circumstances and the ever developing Board law in this area, counsel will normally suggest that requests for immediate recognition be answered with a brief statement that the company believes in good faith that, despite the claim of the union, a majority of the employees do not wish to be represented by the union. Moreover, this response should be made without viewing the cards either directly or by a third party.

3. *NLRB Conferences and Hearings.* When the union goes the election route the Board will ask the employer to file certain jurisdictional information, prepare certain lists, have legal counsel file a notice of appearance, and attend an informal conference in an attempt to reach voluntary agreement on the appropriate unit and the time, place, and other details of the election.

Employers are well advised to be represented by counsel throughout these board procedures. Although unions are often represented by a full-time organizer, unassisted by counsel, they have been well trained by their unions and experience to handle such NLRB election proceedings.

4. *Campaign Materials.* Unions will review every aspect of management's campaign in an attempt to find a basis for filing unfair labor practice charges or objections to the election. To avoid mistakes, the company's attorney should review all speeches, letters, posters, and pamphlets with a view toward their legality. At the same time, company counsel should be provided with information concerning union campaign materials to assure that the union is similarly complying with the law.

In the preparation of its campaign materials, companies relatively inexperienced in the ways of organizing campaigns might well allow their attorney, who should be experienced, a more active role in the original drafting of the materials.

5. *Unfair Labor Practice Charges.* The procedural and substantive difficulties surrounding the defense or instigation of Board charges make the immediate use of legal counsel advisable. If the employer is filing a charge, or an objection to an election, legal counsel will know and probably have the necessary NLRB forms. Counsel can prepare the supporting affidavits in accordance with the preferences and practices of local NLRB officials. Where issues of law are concerned, an attorney can cite precedents to the Board and thereby expedite and strengthen the employer's case.

Where the employer is on the receiving end of the charge, the marshalling of company evidence is particularly important. The company's attorney can be particularly helpful in directing the Board's field attorney to the proper cases and witnesses. When the board attorney is taking depositions from members of supervision, it is often most helpful to have the company's attorney present.

If Board investigation gives rise to a formal complaint and hearing, the company will normally be represented by counsel. If the company is the charging party, NLRB attorneys will carry the burden of preparing and presenting the case, but the employer's counsel can and should appear as well.

6. *Collective Bargaining.* Most employers do not make the mistake of underestimating the union representative. Although he may be underpaid and over-

worked, the labor leader knows his business: negotiating labor agreements. The union representative has learned, perhaps the hard way, that negotiations require study, hard work, guile, sensitivity, knowledge of the law, draftsmanship, theatrical flair, and experience. His management counterpart, at the least, should be similarly qualified. Even when the union's representative is inept, management's representative must be all the more capable since control over the union's bargaining committee and ratification from the membership at large will be even harder to come by.

Many companies find that an experienced labor lawyer, one who spends a substantial part of his time in labor negotiations, can best serve as management's spokesman in negotiations. He can be of particular assistance in a first negotiation when the company is less apt to have an experienced negotiator. Moreover, the drafting of the initial contract places a particular premium on legal draftsmanship. Negotiating the termination or transfer of a unionized shop similarly calls for an attorney's skills. An attorney may also be of assistance in drafting more legalistic or complex contract clauses such as those dealing with arbitration, resort to legal action, the right to strike or lock out, subcontracting, contributions to funds, and supplementary unemployment benefits.

It should also be borne in mind that many negotiations involve the legal question of what is negotiable. The limits of the duty to bargain in good faith are still being defined by the Board and by the courts. Even experienced negotiators are well advised to review the legal status of their demands and those of the union. If legal counsel is not a member of management's negotiations team, then it is wise to have copies of company and union proposals reviewed by him at the earliest moment.

The use of an attorney as management spokesman should also be considered for negotiations best characterized as "unpopular." While the personnel administrator or other local management representative need not be loved by the workers, it is also true that their long-term function will not be assisted by serving as spokesman in a negotiation where management finds it necessary to take a particularly hard line. Another "unpopular" negotiation where companies often find the use of an attorney advisable, is where top management decides for one reason or another to sacrifice the desires of local management in the interest of some broader corporate policy. In such negotiations, legal counsel is rarely popular with local management, but he is nevertheless performing a necessary and often thankless task.

VII. ARBITRATION

The preparation for and trial of an arbitration calls into play the skills of an attorney: preliminary advice about the proper position for a client to adopt in light of the immediate facts, the labor agreement and the applicable case law; and thereafter the effective advocacy of that position in an adversary procedure. However effective the attorney is in actually trying the arbitration, it is often true that he would have been more successful had he been consulted at an earlier stage, before the facts and perhaps the arbitrator's award had been preordained by ill-advised action.

Of course most grievances are neither so sensitive nor so difficult as to require legal assistance until a demand for arbitration is filed. The experience, knowledge, and training of each personnel administrator, the complexity of the case and the company's willingness to pay legal fees should determine, on a case-by-case basis, just how soon legal counsel should be consulted.

Once a grievance is to be arbitrated, the company must decide if it is to be tried by an attorney or by a member of the personnel staff who, though not a lawyer, has the necessary skills and the experience. Again it is often a mistake to assume that the company need not use a lawyer just because the union's representative is not an attorney. The union's representative, albeit not a lawyer, normally tries dozens of cases a year. He generally has had extensive training, as well as years of intensive experience. Indeed, he may do nothing but handle grievances and try arbitrations.

Even when a personnel administrator possesses the skills and experience, there are situations where it may nevertheless be advisable to retain counsel. Highly controversial or political cases can compromise the administrator's long-term rapport with the employees or the union. Thus the arbitration of a union official's discharge is often assigned to an attorney; if the case is lost, the attorney, unlike the personnel administrator, may not have to face the reinstated official in the plant or at the bargaining table. In many discipline cases, a firm statement of the company's case and cross examination are not necessarily consistent with the sympathetic posture of a personnel administrator.

Whenever an attorney handles an arbitration he will need the assistance and guidance of the labor relations staff. Aside from briefing counsel on strategic or political considerations, the personnel administrator should provide (1) a copy of the grievance forms showing the positions taken by the company and union at the various stages of the grievance procedure, (2) copies of all relevant or possibly relevant forms from the employee's personnel folder, (3) the labor agreement and any plant rules, (4) summaries of any relevant past practices or disciplinary cases, (5) a list of the supervisors involved in the case, along with advice as to the role of each supervisor, and (6) a brief summary of the facts. Counsel should have direct access to potential witnesses, and finally, he should be told of any weaknesses in the company's case.

VIII. THEFT

It is an unfortunate commentary on our times that employee theft is no longer an occasional nuisance but a constant threat. The direct dollar cost is staggering. As a result, it is all too easy to forget that expensive and embarrassing false arrest or invasion of privacy suits can accompany ill-advised attempts to attack theft or embezzlement.

Legal counsel should be apprised of your problem, be it executive embezzlement or petty theft. Counsel can assist in dealings with the police, the district attorney, or a private detective. He should also review any insurance or bonding implications.

IX. EMPLOYMENT CONTRACTS

With the possible exception of top management and employees covered by union agreements, most employees are not covered by formal employment contracts. However, the executives who do receive employment agreements are normally key personnel, and their contracts deserve the attention of legal counsel. Of particular importance from the company's point of view are covenants not to compete. These provisions must be carefully drawn to meet the changing law in the area, as well as the needs of the company and the employee.

Although they are not full employment contracts, agreements protecting company "secrets" can be equally important and may be necessary even where a broader employment contract is not. Such agreements should be drafted by counsel to protect such matters as customer lists, inventions, research development, company documents, and other trade secrets.

X. WAGE GARNISHMENTS

The Consumer Credit Protection Act provides employees with relatively clear protection against creditors and employers. It limits the amount of earnings subject to garnishment and prevents discharge based upon garnishment for any one indebtedness. However, this federal law does not necessarily replace state laws, and legal counsel should be consulted to assure compliance with any applicable state law.

Moreover, any questions that arise concerning the proper method of calculating the amount that may be withheld pursuant to a garnishment or application of the phrase "garnishment for any one debtedness." Such debts should also be referred to counsel who will have access to the latest rulings.

SUMMARY

The personnel administrator who relies too heavily on his attorney is almost as unwise as the administrator who relies too little, or too late. How often and how soon he calls his attorney will depend upon his familiarity with the legal principles involved, the scope of his labor relations library, and the size of his staff. Labor lawyers recognize that excessive reliance on counsel is not only expensive, but undermines the primary responsibility and functions of the personnel and labor relations staff.

On the other hand, the personnel administrator who is reluctant to expose his company to the abilities and expertise of an attorney is needlessly limiting his own usefulness. Moreover, any client who acts as his own attorney is apt to overestimate his objectivity.

An attorney is a valuable tool to be used by the personnel administrator. To get full value, the administrator must remain alert for those situations where counsel may be helpful so as to obtain legal guidance before the law is broken. Once counsel has been called in, the personnel administrator should assure counsel access to the facts, the individuals concerned, and the company's objectives.

BIBLIOGRAPHY

Bureau of National Affairs: *The New Wage and Hour Law,* Washington, D.C., 1967.

Elkouri, Frank and Elkouri, Edna: *How Arbitration Works,* Bureau of National Affairs, Washington, D.C., 1960.

McGuiness, Kenneth: *How to Take a Case before the National Labor Relations Board,* Bureau of National Affairs, Washington, D.C., 1967.

Monthly Labor Review, U.S. Department of Labor, Bureau of Labor Statistics.

National Association of Manufacturers: *Equal Employment Opportunity: Compliance and Affirmative Action,* 1969.

National Labor Relations Board—Rules and Regulations—Labor Management Relations Act, U.S. Government Printing Office, 1965.

Summary of the National Labor Relations Act, U.S. Government Printing Office, 1970.

chapter 67

Food Services

RICHARD J. BENOIT *Manager, Recruiting and Training, Interstate United, Chicago, Illinois*

The modern personnel department and the modern executive play an integral part in the management and guidance of company-sponsored food service programs. This is especially true when the service of an outside professional food service contractor is required. There is general agreement that the food service improves health, reduces absenteeism, increases productivity, and boosts morale. Because of this impact on employee relations programs, the personnel executive has been required to gain new expertise in many new areas that were previously foreign to his background and training.

The need for providing food service to employee groups was recognized by many progressive companies in the early 1900s. However, the greatest emphasis was felt during World War II. At that time, the more progressive companies recognized the need to play an active role in providing food service facilities for their employees. The earlier trends in the industry were to have companies operate their own cafeterias with full control over menu planning, price and portions, and labor costs. However, as the food service industry became more sophisticated and it became apparent that more professional food service management was required, companies moved to outside contractors.

Thus, with the trend of utilizing outside food service contractors firmly established, top management experts and personnel executives have been required to become informed about the complexities of selecting an outside contractor.

Today, such organizations as insurance firms, banks, colleges, hospitals, and manufacturing firms prefer to contract with outside professional food service companies. As a normal practice, outside contractors operate either on a profit and loss basis, a cost-plus-fee basis, or a subsidized basis with the company absorbing a percentage of the food and labor costs along with providing eating facilities and equipment.

The majority of companies with food service programs operate them at a loss. Since individual circumstances vary within each company, there is no average subsidy for a food service program.   However, the amount of subsidy can be controlled by management policy in setting food prices.   These prices should be set to cover the food costs, salaries, and wages of food service personnel and other fixed expenses.   If the prices do not cover these expense elements, then the company must increase its subsidies.   As indicated, this might take the form of providing space, equipment, maintenance, and utilities.

This chapter will highlight the different types of food services available to companies interested in providing food and automatic vending service to their employees, along with a discussion of the pros and cons of various types of food service management.   In addition, it will cover general rules and regulations connected with the various types of service and special rules regarding eating at work stations. Further, it will present specific guidelines for obtaining the special permits and licenses required to operate food service and automatic vending facilities.   The chapter will conclude with a presentation of a recommended approach in selecting an outside contractor.

TYPES OF FOOD SERVICE

Full-line Cafeterias

This type of service is considered one of the most effective ways to serve large numbers of employees quickly and efficiently.   Further, this service offers a wide variety of freshly prepared hot and cold entrees, salads, and desserts, all attractively served and merchandised.   Preparation, presentation, and menu planning are keys to the success of a full-line cafeteria operation.

Professional food service contractors have the capabilities to create the necessary cycle menus and establish the merchandising and food standards which ensure a quality food program.   Full-line cafeterias are designed with the capability of offering complete services during peak dining hours and partial line service for break times and during low employee shifts.

Automatic Vending Services

Personnel executives are turning increasingly to this system, which offers employees the maximum in round-the-clock convenience with a wide selection of hot and cold foods, beverages, and single items.   Automatic vending service centers offer the versatility of single or multiple satellite locations placed throughout work areas in offices, industrial plants, and institutions for added convenience and efficiency.   It is also highly adaptable for space utilization or when conversion of "odd-lot" spaces is required in the food service installation.

Combination Cafeteria and Vending Services

Installations provide the efficiency and convenience of vending with the personal touch of cafeteria service.   Highly adaptable to business hours and shift schedules, it can function as a full-line cafeteria supplemented by vending during meal periods and as a separate twenty-four-hour vending service center for hot and cold food and beverages during work shifts of lower employment.   The combination can also be used as a short-order grill service in conjunction with vending service during certain hours or shifts.

Executive Dining Rooms

In these facilities, food, service, atmosphere, and decor are combined to present a dining area that allows management to enjoy a relaxing luncheon with colleagues or to entertain business associates in their own restaurant.   This type of service is normally tailored to the management people who use the facility. The typical executive dining room may provide for group dining to facilitate lunchtime discussions, while others are designed to promote more private dining at tables of from two to four.

Mobile Food Service

This type of service is used to provide food and beverage to employee groups who are not able to reach centrally located cafeterias or are unable to leave their work areas. The most common type of equipment used is coffee carts or small or large wagons that carry an assortment of light lunches and sandwiches, along with cold and hot drinks. By the very nature of this type of service, special rules regarding eating at work stations are required. In addition to automatic vending, coffee-cart or lunch-wagon service is the most common means of providing in-between snacks to isolated areas of employee population. This type of service normally supplements a full-line cafeteria and executive dining room.

TYPES OF FOOD SERVICE MANAGEMENT

One of the first considerations that you must make in determining the type of food service management that will be required to administer your food service program is to examine your own capabilities in-house to determine whether or not you can be your own food service operator or whether this special program requires more expertise than you have on your payroll and are willing to commit. Further, by examining the technical and support aspects of operating an effective food service facility that will meet corporate objectives, a written or mental checklist of whether or not these components are available within your organization will be helpful in evaluating the pros and cons of operating your own service.

Additional requirements of a successful food and/or vending operation is a set of well-defined and well-documented operating procedures. These operating procedures should reflect the latest techniques of professional food service management. These procedures must be flexible enough to:

1. Allow your food service manager to display his managerial skill and knowledge
2. Produce a quality product, menu, and merchandising techniques
3. Be enlarged, revised, and augmented when need arises, which in most cases is constant

Depending on the outcome of the above analysis, you should be in a position to select the type of food service management that will meet your corporate objectives.

The majority of companies that operate their own food service cafeterias do so in order to exercise greater control over such elements as:

Cafeteria layout and design
Types of service
Food price structuring
Sanitation standards
Scheduling of cafeteria hours
Developing employee nutrient needs and preferences
Menu planning
Food costs
Employee-to-management handling of complaints and suggestions for improvements
Control over selection and training of management and service personnel
Costs of operations, especially labor costs
However, it has become more difficult for companies over the past few years to

exercise total control over food prices and labor costs. This is due to the fact that it is becoming more and more fashionable in situations where the plant or office force has unionized and where the company operates its own food service to have the plant union raise at negotiation time the issues of prices charged in the company cafeteria as well as other items such as food quality, variety, and portions, as items to be negotiated with the unions.

In many situations, the company which utilizes the service of an outside independent contractor can point to recent court decisions to blunt the union's demand to bargain concerning cafeteria operations as "a condition of employment." The negotiator for the company which runs its own food service will have a much harder time and if he refuses to bargain over these items may, if conditions warrant, find the NLRB directing him to negotiate with the union.

If the manufacturing plant has become subject to an intensive union organizing drive and the plant is operating its own cafeterias, the cafeteria employees are generally swept up into the manufacturing union along with plant employees. The outside contractor, on the other hand, is a separate legal entity, which automatically requires the union directing the organizing drive to conduct a double approach in its effort. Faced with the effort and expenditure in conducting two organizing drives for two separate bargaining units with two different employers to result in two separate labor agreements, many industrial unions usually have second thoughts about organizing the handful of cafeteria employees of the outside contractor.

The Federal Fair Labor Standards Act, as well as many state wage and hour laws, set different and lower standards for wage payments and conditions for food service workers versus manufacturing or clerical employees. The employee in a cafeteria operated by a food service company and employed by that company is clearly under food service rates and regulations. The cafeteria worker on the payroll of a manufacturing plant might be considered by a wage and hour investigator to be covered by a more stringent and higher paying manufacturing statute.

This recent trend has caused some companies operating their own food service to go to outside contractors.

The advantages of contractor-operated facilities are that company management is relieved of details, the contractors are more experienced, and the costs are lower to the operator, primarily due to greater purchasing power and better control of labor cost.

The chief criticisms of company-operated facilities are that they are too expensive to operate and there are too many administrative details. On the other hand, the chief criticism of contractor-operated facilities is normally the lack of control over food quality.

SPECIAL RULES RELATING TO FOOD SERVICE

As indicated earlier, mobile service (coffee carts and lunch wagons) presents certain related problems—specifically, sanitation and housekeeping. The majority of food and beverages served from coffee carts or lunch wagons utilize paper plates and containers along with various forms of plastic spoons, forks, and knives. Therefore, specific guidelines must be set up to ensure that work areas are kept clean and sanitary. This is especially true when you are not in a position to provide special dining rooms for your employees. Where glass bottles or other types of china are used, specific storage areas must be provided to avoid breakage and safety hazards.

In utilizing coffee carts and lunch wagons, it is suggested that special dining rooms be set up to encourage employees to eat away from their work area. The determination of whether you set up separate dining rooms for men and women will best be determined by a survey of the attitudes of your employee group and financial consideration.

In many cases, the problems connected with employees eating at their work stations can best be resolved by providing adequate supervision. Everything should be done to provide facilities away from work areas. Otherwise this could be a cause for additional problems.

SPECIAL PERMITS AND LICENSE REQUIREMENTS

There normally are many different types of licenses and permits required in order to operate food service and automatic vending facilities. Prior to opening a new location, the company must contact state and local officials to ascertain the particular licensing involved. Once the necessary applications are obtained and completed, it is recommended that the legal and/or tax department review for compliance to local requirements. The following are permits and licenses that are usually reviewed annually:

State sales tax permit
Board of Health permit
County, town, or city license
Liquor license
Vending machine license
Cigarette dealer's license
Cigarette tax bonds
Sales tax bonds

In summary, the individuals responsible for setting up the food service should work closely with their respective legal and/or tax departments in order to comply with all licensing and permit requirements of the local jurisdiction involved. In all cases, adequate follow-up must be maintained on a recurring basis to assure constant compliance.

SELECTING OUTSIDE CONTRACTOR

With the absence of professional food service managers on company payrolls, the job of selecting an outside contractor can be difficult. Management must seek to provide food and automatic vending services which will contribute to employee satisfaction along with improving on-the-job productivity while providing the company an opportunity for potential added income. It should be emphasized that potential added income from food service and automatic vending facilities should never be a factor in selecting a contractor. However, the two can be accomplished if each is kept in proper perspective. In order to assure the best-quality food service program, specifically designed for you by the outside contractor, analysis of each and every segment of a contractor's proposal is necessary.

Specific policies and guidelines should be established that will enable the personnel department executive to meet basic management objectives and operate the food and vending services on professional standards. It is suggested that management clearly define what it is they want to accomplish before attempting to classify the criteria for selecting a food service contractor. These policies and operating facilities provide for required steps in choosing an outside contractor, including initial recommendations from designated contractors (a system of bidding by contractors based on standards drawn up by management and joint control over the awarding of contracts, which should involve a corporate official as well as local operating management). There must be full agreement among management with regard to the selection process. Specific consideration must be given to developing a uniform bidding system conforming with company policy and requiring all contractors to adhere to the same format when submitting proposals.

To accomplish the objective of receiving uniform bids, the company must be prepared to provide certain information to the outside contractor. The following information must be provided in order for him to prepare a realistic operational forecast. At the time the information below is given to the contractor, he should also be provided with the deadline when the proposal is due and to whom it should be addressed as well as the number of copies required.

Location of facility
Date service is to start
Type of service (manual, vending, or combination of both)
Employee population—salaried and hourly, by shift and location
Length and scheduling of lunch periods for each facility
Location and layout of equipment provided by client
List of additional equipment and number of vending machines required
Dishes, glassware, and flatware requirements
Sanitation and temperature controls
Details of required service personnel—manning charts, etc.
Utility requirements
Quality of food
Price and portion controls
Menu cycles
Number of machines by type
Products to be vended
Vending prices and portions
Frequency of vending service
Commission rates
Specific events and promotions required
Maintenance and housekeeping requirements
Insurance
Accounting and auditing requirements
Existence of any union contracts
Licenses
Plant rules and regulations that affect food service

The determination of who will absorb the cost of such items as dishes, glassware, maintenance, and housekeeping services should be made prior to submitting the above information to contractors.

With the above requirements spelled out, the contractor will be in a position to develop a proposal that will be within the framework and ground rules laid out by management and will enable management to evaluate all bids on an objective basis. Further, the contractor will now be in a position to develop a realistic operational plan providing adequate profits for their needs and possible additional income for the company. It is important that the contractor have an opportunity to survey the locations in question. (Normally, one or two days is sufficient for a contractor to survey the various shifts.)

In addition to the contractor's sales manager, it is suggested that the company require the presence of the operating personnel who will subsequently be responsible for the day-to-day operation of the unit.

The list below highlights some of the more pertinent information that will be required to analyze each of the contractor's proposals. However, it is not meant to be all-inclusive as there will be certain information required that is unique to the company's particular operation.

1. An operating statement projecting for a one-year period
- Sales
- Cost of sales
- Labor costs
- Administrative expenses
- Other operating expenses
- Breakdown of resulting profit or loss for each manual and vending operation
2. Sample menus and suggested menu cycle
3. Purchasing specifications
4. Staffing chart for manual service, including
- Job titles
- Wage rates
- Hours scheduled
- Type of work to be performed
- Fringe benefit costs
- Payroll recap showing taxes and cost of fringe benefits
5. Staffing chart for vending or mobile service personnel (same information required in No. 4 above)
6. Management qualifications—request résumé of education and work experience of proposed manager
7. Request name and address of other clients served by contractor in same geographical area
8. Management staff available for local support and frequency of visits
9. Copy of contractor's last annual report

The time and effort invested in preparing the uniform bidding system will pay dividends when it comes time to analyze each of the contractor's proposals. Each proposal should be checked against the bidding requirements for completeness, making sure that the contractor has answered each part of your bid request. After that, the next step should be a section-by-section analysis to evaluate the factors affecting the financial statement. Careful consideration must be given to items such as existing labor contracts, staffing plans, and food costs. These factors, if projected erroneously, can greatly affect the efficiency and quality of service that will ultimately be provided to your employees. Inadequate portion sizes and unrealistic prices can significantly influence the overall financial proposal. Further, a hard look at the proposed staffing patterns and salary scales will indicate whether or not the contractor can provide the service you require. If the proposal reflects an understaffing, it will only lead to poor service and products, which will affect employee morale. Also, an appraisal of the ratio of the vending to food service volumes and projected incomes might indicate an invalid assignment of gross sales leading to an inflated picture. Whenever large discrepancies show up between bidders in similar sections of the bid, further examination for accuracy in proposed operating format and results is recommended. In the final analysis, however, the company must ask the questions: Does the proposed food service/vending program fit the company's needs? Does it meet established corporate objectives? Does the contractor have a good organization with modern techniques and practices with the reputation for the quality wanted? Once the areas suggested have been analyzed and the above questions answered, it is usually possible to narrow the field down to the top two or three proposals. After that, the personnel executive and/or selection committee must get down to the task of evaluating each of the contractor's past performance on a local basis, along with analyzing the financial terms of the proposal. The next step should be to invite each of the contractors in to review the proposals before a final decision is reached. If the steps that are outlined in this section are followed, the selection of a contractor can be reduced to a very systematic and objective procedure.

Figure 1 reflects a typical food and vending service survey form that would be used by an outside contractor. This form provides all the information required in order for the company and the contractor to evaluate the economics involved in operating the food and/or vending service.

SUMMARY

Food and vending services are not intended as another source of revenue. The purpose of providing food and vending services must be clearly established. If this purpose is misconstrued as a means of additional income, your service will

INTERSTATE UNITED

SURVEY
VENDING AND FOOD SERVICE

CLIENT NAME				BRANCH/DISTRICT	DIVISION
				DATE PROPOSAL IS REQUIRED	
ADDRESS				INSTALLATION DATE	
CITY	STATE	ZIP CODE	PHONE NUMBER	SALESMAN	
CONTACT			CONTACT'S TITLE		

PRESENT VENDING AND FOOD SERVICE FACILITIES

	NO. OF UNITS	OPERATED BY - (✓) CLIENT	CONTRACTOR	ESTIMATED ANNUAL SALES	IF NOT CLIENT OPERATED - STATE BY WHOM AND FINANCIAL ARRANGEMENTS:
MANUAL CAFETERIA				$	
COMBINED VENDING & MANUAL SER.					
VENDING BANKS					
SNACK BARS OR CARTS					
DINING ROOM(S)					
TOTAL				$	

POPULATION AND SERVICE PERIODS

	WORK HOURS FROM	TO	NO. OF EMPLOYEES WK. DAYS	SAT.	SUN.	BREAKFAST FROM	TO	LUNCH FROM	TO	DINNER FROM	TO	BREAKS FROM	TO	FROM	TO	FREE FLOW (✓)
PLANT - SHIFT #1																
PLANT - SHIFT #2																
PLANT - SHIFT #3																
OFFICE																
TOTAL						POPULATION				% MALE,				% FEMALE		

	THRU VENDING MACHINES	THRU MANUAL FOOD SERVICE
AVERAGE WEEKLY SALES PER CLIENT EMPLOYEE	$	$

CLIENT HOLIDAYS:

CLIENT VACATION POLICY - SHUTDOWN
OTHER - EXPLAIN:

		CLOSED SHOP	OPEN SHOP
NON UNION	☐		
CLIENT UNION(S)		☐	☐
PRESENT FOOD SERVICE EMPLOYEES UNION(S)		☐	☐

PRESENT FOOD SERVICE EMPLOYEES BENEFITS

BENEFIT	TERMS
PENSION PLAN	
VACATION	
INSURANCE	
SICK LEAVE	
HOSPITALIZATION	

CHARGE AND CREDIT DATA:

EXPLAIN ANY NON-CASH SALES AND METHOD OF HANDLING:

EQUIPMENT AND FACILITIES

EQUIPMENT: CHECK (✓) COST	INSTALLATION CLIENT	CON-TRACTOR	REPLACEMENT CLIENT	CONTRACTOR
SMALL KITCHEN EQUIPMENT				
CHINA, GLASSWARE, SILVERWARE				
OFFICE EQUIPMENT				

SERVICES: CHECK (✓) COST	CLIENT	CONTRACTOR
UTILITIES - PREPARATION AREAS		
UTILITIES - DINING ROOM AREAS		
GARBAGE REMOVAL		
DINING ROOM - FLOORS, WALLS, WINDOWS, ETC.		
REPAIRS AND MAINTENANCE OF EQUIPMENT		

DESCRIPTION AND CONDITION OF STORAGE SPACE, EQUIPMENT, AND REFRIGERATION:

ATTACHMENTS: LAYOUT ☐ MENUS ☐ PRICE LISTS ☐
OPERATING STATEMENTS ☐ UNION CONTRACTS ☐

Form 605 12/68

Figure 1. Food and vending service survey form.

suffer.   Management will then subsequently lose in employee morale and production.

The personnel executive must always be cognizant that management and the contractor are in business together.   Thus, a carefully drawn contract is a necessity and will provide management with a control over performance, liability, accounting, commissions or fees, and quality of service.   For the contractor it will provide assurance that his investment and equipment and installation costs will be protected from premature cancellations of the contract without cause.   The food and vending service will function better if the contract is clearly understood by both parties.

By the very nature of the industry, food and vending contractors will incur approximately the same operating and product costs.   There will, however, be some minor regional variations in food and labor costs, based on the contractor's purchasing

VENDING PRO FORMA

SALES AND MERCHANDISE COST

SALES: PRODUCT TYPE	VENDING PRICE	SIZE	PER CAPITA SPENDING WEEKLY	TOTAL WEEKLY SALES	NO MACH.	AVERAGE SALES PER MACHINE PER WEEK	ANNUAL GROSS SALES	MERCHANDISE COST AMOUNT	%	SALES ARE:
COFFEE	$		$	$		$	$	$		☐ ACTUAL
COLD DRINK W/ICE										☐ ESTIMATED
CANNED SODA										IF ACTUAL:
CIGARETTE										PERIOD COVERED
CANDY										
PASTRY										
MILK										SOURCE OF SALES INFO.
ICE CREAM										
HOT CANS										
FOOD MERCHANDISER										
OTHER										
TOTAL ALL PRODUCTS	$		$			$	① $	② $		

LABOR AND COST RELATED

TYPE	NO.	HOURS PER DAY	REGULAR WEEKLY COST	WEEKLY O/T OR PREMIUM COST	ANNUAL COST
SERVICEMAN			$	$	$
HOSTESS					
MECHANIC					
SUPERVISOR					
DELIVERY					
TOTAL			$	$	

COST RELATED TO PAYROLL   % OF TOTAL

TOTAL ANNUAL LABOR AND COST RELATED   ③ $

DIRECT OPERATING EXPENSE

VEHICLE EXPENSE: ($40.00 PER WEEK PER VEHICLE OR FRACTION THEREOF)	
SERVICE	$
MAINTENANCE	
DELIVERY (BRANCH EXPERIENCE)	
INSTALLATION	
FREIGHT (IF EXPENSED)	
RETAIL SALES TAX	
OTHER TAXES & LICENSES RELATED TO THIS JOB & EQUIPMENT	
UNIFORM EXPENSE (BRANCH EXPERIENCE)	
SALESMAN'S COMMISSION	
TOTAL ANNUAL DIRECT EXPENSE	④ $

INDIRECT OPERATING EXPENSE

RENT	$
UTILITIES	
TELEPHONE	
OTHER (SPECIFY)	
TOTAL ANNUAL INDIRECT OPERATING EXPENSE	⑤ $

OTHER INCOME OR EXPENSE

NET EFFECT OF SUBCONTRACT ITEMS (INCOME) OR EXP. - SPECIFY	
	$
OTHER (INCOME) OR EXP.	
TOTAL ANNUAL (INCOME) OR EXP.	⑥ $

COMMENTS:

Figure 1.   Food and vending service survey form.   (continued)

DEPRECIATION EXPENSE

| PRODUCT TYPE | MODULAR | | | NON MODULAR | | | INVESTMENT | ANNUAL DEPRECIATION |
	NO.	UNIT COST	TOTAL COST	NO.	UNIT COST	TOTAL COST		
CANDY		$	$		$	$	$	
CIGARETTE								
SALES TAX								
FRT.								
TOTAL 8 YEAR LIFE			$			$	$	$
INVESTMENT ÷ 8 = DEPRECIATION								
COFFEE		$	$		$	$	$	
SODA								
CANNED SODA								
PASTRY								
MILK								
ICE CREAM								
HOT CAN FOOD								
FD. MERCHANDISER								
OVEN								
CHANGER								
PANEL & DECOR								
OTHER								
SALES TAX								
FRT.								
TOTAL 6 YEAR LIFE			$			$	$	$
INVESTMENT ÷ 6 = DEPRECIATION								
VEHICLE INVESTMENT REQUIRED FOR THIS JOB							$	
OTHER EQUIPMENT INVESTMENT REQUIRED FOR THIS JOB								
OTHER EQUIPMENT INVESTMENT ÷ YEAR LIFE = DEPRECIATION								
TOTAL INVESTMENT							$	
TOTAL ANNUAL DEPRECIATION EXPENSE								

VENDING AND FOOD SERVICE SUMMARY

| KEY | VENDING SUMMARY | ANNUAL PROJECTION | |
		AMOUNT	%
①	ANNUAL SALES	$	100.0
②	LESS: MERCHANDISE COST		
	SALES LESS MERCHANDISE COST = GROSS PROFIT	$	
③	LABOR & COST RELATED	$	
④	DIRECT OPERATING EXPENSE		
⑤	INDIRECT OPERATING EXPENSE		
	MISC. EXPENSE (2% RESIDENT BRANCH 3% ALL OTHER)		
⑥	OTHER (INCOME) OR EXP.		
⑦	ANNUAL DEPRECIATION		
	TOTAL EXPENSES		
	JOB CONTRIBUTION (GROSS PROFIT LESS TOTAL EXPENSES)	$	

TOTAL AVAILABLE FOR BRANCH O/H, COMMISSIONS, FIELD & CORP. O/H & PROFIT	$

* WHEN FOOD SERVICE SALES VOLUME EXCEEDS $100,000, ATTACH MANNING CHARTS AND COSTS WORK PAPERS

NOTE: TRANSFER SALES AND AVAILABLE TO COMBINED SUMMARY.

| FOOD SERVICE SUMMARY | ANNUAL PROJECTION | |
	AMOUNT	%
SALES: *	$	
TOTAL SALES		100.0
TOTAL FOOD COSTS		
PAYROLL REGULAR		
PAYROLL RELATED COSTS %		
TOTAL LABOR COSTS		
LAUNDRY		
REPLACEMENTS		
PAPER & OTHER SUPPLIES		
CLEANING SUPPLIES		
OTHER EXPENSE		
DEPRECIATION		
TOTAL DIRECT EXPENSE		
TOTAL COST & EXPENSE		
UNIT OPERATING GAIN OR LOSS		
COMMISSION RECEIPTS AND OTHER INCOME		
NET INCOME (LOSS) FROM OPERATIONS	$	

Figure 1.   Food and vending service survey form.   (continued)

power and individual labor practice and/or state minimum wage laws. In the final analysis, the reputation and ability of the contractor on a local basis will be of primary importance in determining the selection of an outside contractor.

BIBLIOGRAPHY

Anderson, Harriet: *"Frozen Convenience" Solves Problems of Inplant Manual Feeding Operation*, institutional ed., E. W. Williams Publications, Inc., New York, May, 1969.

Employers' Food Services in Manufacturing Plants: "Marketing Research Report," no. 325, U.S. Department of Agriculture, 1959.

Interstate United Corporation Brochure, Professional Food Service Management, Chicago, 1968.

COMMISSION EXPENSE

PRODUCT TYPE	GROSS SALES	COMM. CODE **	COMMISSIONABLE SALES	COMM. %	COMMISSION AMOUNT		
CANDY	$		$		$	** COMMISSION CODE LEGEND	
CIGARETTE							
COFFEE						FLAT % OF SALES	1
SODA						FLAT AMOUNT PER UNIT SOLD	2
CANNED SODA						NO COMMISSION	9
PASTRY						OTHER (EXPLAIN)	0
MILK							
ICE CREAM							
HOT CAN FOOD							RETRO. SCALE / STEP SCALE
FOOD MERCHANDISER						INDIVIDUAL MACHINES	7 / 8
						TOTAL MACHINES	3 / 5
						AVERAGE MACHINES	4 / 6
TOTAL	$	■	$		$	** SEE VENDING COMMISSION PROCEDURES	

PROPOSED OTHER FINANCIAL TERMS:

RENEWAL AND TERMINATION PROVISIONS:

COMBINED VENDING AND FOOD SERVICE SUMMARY

	VENDING	%	FOOD	%	TOTAL	%
SALES	$	100.0	$	100.0	$	100.0
BRANCH/UNIT AVAILABLE (PER FINAL LINE OF SUMMARY)						
CLIENT PARTICIPATION						
LESS COMMISSIONS						
LESS RENT						
PLUS SUBSIDY (INCLUDING FEE)						
NET AVAILABLE - IUC - FOR FIELD & CORP. O/H & PROFIT	$		$		$	
TOTAL INVESTMENT	$	■	$	■	$	■
RATIO OF SALES TO INVESTMENT	TO		TO		TO	
AVAILABLE TO INVESTMENT	■	%	■	%	■	%

		APPROVALS:	
PREPARATION AND SURVEY BY		DIVISION SALES	DATE
SALES	DATE	DIVISION OPERATIONS	DATE
OPERATIONS	DATE	CORPORATE MARKETING	DATE
		CORPORATE OPERATIONS	DATE

Figure 1.   Food and vending service survey form.   (continued)

Mather, Richard W.: "Selecting a Catering Contractor," *Cornell Quarterly,* vol. 2, no. 1, May, 1970.

McCall Corporation vs. NLRB, CA 4, 1970, 75 LRRM 2223.

National Industrial Conference Board, Inc.: "Company Food Services," *Studies in Personnel Policy,* No. 104, New York, May, 1950.

Reed, Walter W.: "There's Nothing Automatic about Achieving a Good Vending Operation," *Recreation Management,* November, 1967.

Westinghouse Electric Company vs. NLRB, 387 F20 542.

Part 15

Special Employee Groups

chapter 68

Supervisory Employees

W. E. KOGER*   *Vice President, Personnel and Industrial Relations, Ingersoll-Rand Company, New York, New York*

In singling out supervisory employees as a separate group for review and consideration, it would be well to attempt to answer the following questions:

Who is the supervisor?

What does he do?

Which personal qualities and skills are important to his successful performance?

Successful examination of all the above factors will lead to consideration of the relationship of the personnel staff to the supervisory staff and the role the personnel department plays in regard to the special problems the supervisor has with his subordinates.

The supervisor occupies a unique position in the structure of an organization. It is this unique position that shapes many of the problems he faces, that accounts for many of the peculiarities in his relationships with others. It is only through an understanding of his place and role in the total organizational structure that one can deal effectively with these problems and relationships.

WHO IS THE SUPERVISOR?

The supervisor has been called many things by many people. Like others in the organizational hierarchy, he has suffered his share of descriptive adjectives.

Cynics and humorists aside, many have approached the problem in a serious attempt to identify the supervisor. Some have placed him on "the front line of management." Others seek to locate him within the organizational structure by relegating him to "the bottom rung of the management ladder."

While both definitions do help to locate and identify the supervisor, both also tend to do some injustice to the man who has the job and to the important responsibilities he must fulfill. On the one hand, he is depicted as a member of the management shock troops, designated to lead a battle against the workers. On the other, he is located by placing him on the first rung of a ladder that may have little relation to the

* Deceased.

job he has to do. Each definition inclines toward drawing a sharp line between the supervisor and those who work under his leadership. Regretfully, in this age of proliferating knowledge, such sharp lines of difference do exist, though they are far from ideal. (See Figure 1.)

To the Worker the Supervisor Is the Company

The supervisor is *tangible, immediate management.* He is not a thirty-two-page booklet describing company benefits and worker obligations. He is not a notice on the bulletin board. He is neither a layoff nor a recall telegram. He is none of the manifestations of upper-level management, but he represents them all. He is also a living human being. As such he is subject to angers, jealousies, lapses of memory, mistakes, difficulties in interpreting directives sometimes couched in bureaucratic language, and the myriad other frailties that plague us all.

He is tangible, immediately accessible from above and below. If a student needs a vivid example of the word pressure, he might try "supervisor." Few suffer from pressure as he does. And few are so inadequately prepared for that pressure as he is. More on that later.

The supervisor should not be a protagonist in an eternal employee-management confrontation. He need not be a man on the first rung of a ladder that leads directly to the company presidency, though he could be. He is in fact the *first level* of management to those he supervises. As such, he is the first person within the management structure charged with the old and always valid definition of managing—getting things done through others.

At the functional or operational level, he is the one charged with planning, organizing, integrating, and measuring the human, physical, and financial resources into a cohesive unit which produces results. Whether he is called a foreman, group leader, assistant manager, manager, general manager, or any other title, he is charged with promulgating, enforcing, and implementing the company policies, plans, programs, and procedures—concise or rambling, clear or obscure—which are designed to achieve the desired results.

At his best, the supervisor is a leader, teacher, and coach. He has the authority of knowledge and leads through persuasion. He is capable of creating a work climate that motivates people and maximizes their human assets. He can often get extraordinary results from ordinary people by helping them recognize and develop their abilities.

At his worst, the supervisor is a tyrant. He possesses only the authority of command and rules by decree. His chief tool is fear. He destroys morale. He breeds shoddiness of person and work habits, and at times actual sabotage. He stifles initiative, pride, and dignity. At the most, he gets from those under him only those results that they must produce to hold their jobs.

The foregoing "best" and "worst" descriptions may be trite—but they are true. The supervisor is a very important person. He is a vital member of the organization's management structure and can have tremendous impact on the financial profit and loss statements, as well as on the organization's human assets.

WHAT DOES THE SUPERVISOR DO?

As cited above, the supervisor is charged with planning, organizing, integrating, and measuring. These are functions which we have come to believe are common to all managers. First and foremost a supervisor must manage. As such, these functions are applicable to the supervisor in a very specific way. It is he who must deal with the day-to-day realities of machinery breakdown, getting out production,

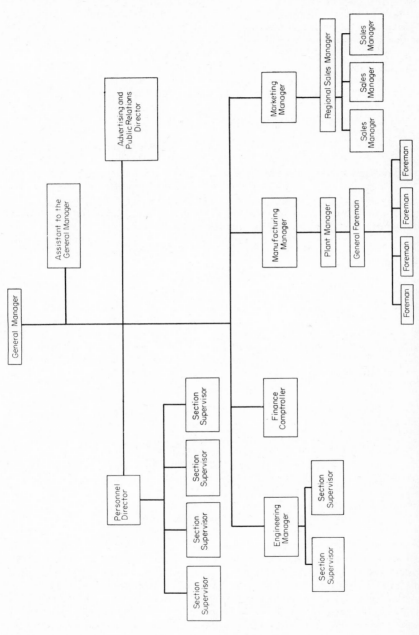

Figure 1. A sample organization chart showing the reporting relationships of the various foremen and supervisors.

maintaining quality, and the hundreds of other diverse problems that go into the makeup of the actual work situation.

"Nonsense," say the dissenters. "In our company, all the supervisor must do is keep an eye on the men and make certain they get out their quotas. Planning, organizing, and integrating are accomplished at *true* management levels. Measuring is the function of the controller's organization."

The company that operates with this attitude is underestimating and underutilizing its supervisors. The company that allows its so-called supervisors to be nothing more than disciplinary watchdogs is robbing itself. Production may go up temporarily, but quality is certain to suffer in the long term. It is only a matter of time until profits suffer also. There are men and women who worked on production lines not many years ago who remember the "pushers" or "expediters," as they came to be euphemistically titled. Also remembered are the lengths to which individual workers went to injure the pushers through sabotaging the product. That this type of job has largely disappeared from our manufacturing society is a blessing.

Broad policies and operating procedures, rendered from above, have their proper place as a general framework and as guidelines for decision making. Because they cannot cover every possible situation or condition, however, they must allow flexibility. No reader who has any knowledge of military history, or who has watched "war movies," is unfamiliar with the number of times junior officers have snatched victory from the jaws of defeat by throwing away the book—or conversely, how many times defeat was inevitable because the junior officer was forbidden to exercise his own judgment in a situation he knew best.

So it is with the supervisor. Production schedules are designed with an average number of machines operating and an average number of workers present as a base. What happens, however, when an abnormal number of machines are down, or half the work force is off ill? The good supervisor goes to work: organizing and integrating the assets he has at hand, planning a feasible work schedule for the day and following up and measuring the results. Innovative action is incompatible with rigidity of command. No company has ever reached its maximum potential by handing its managers a set of "standard operating procedures" and an "or else" directive.

The Supervisor's Tasks Are Definable, His Problems Limitless

While it is possible to delineate the duties of a supervisor, within certain limits, it is also recognized that each area of responsibility has enough and varied aspects that he never seems to have all his problems solved at any one time.

What is meant by planning, organizing, integrating, and measuring as these terms apply to a supervisor? What are the general duties of the supervisor within each category?

Planning. He must look ahead. What is the production schedule? What tools and equipment will be needed? Which machine is not functioning properly and may require unscheduled maintenance? Which worker has a personal problem or a health problem that may interfere with his ability to perform his tasks? He must anticipate so as to be able to create and not simply meet the next situation. Within the framework of the broad company policies, he must establish specific policies for his unit. He must formulate plans and schedules for his group and ascertain that these elements are clearly understood by both his subordinates and his superiors. He must make known and understood the organization's objectives, policies, plans, and standards to those who work under his leadership. He must be able to use the results of his evaluations to alter schedules and training.

Organizing. The supervisor must be able to classify the work to be done into realistic and manageable components when the situation changes from the normal.

Within the structures of the labor contract and job descriptions, he must group tasks in an orderly manner. He must be able to clearly explain the methods and procedures for performing the work to be done. And he must be able to organize his own time and work.

Integrating. The first-line manager must be able to explain the common purpose which integrates all the activities into a common goal for the benefit of the company and the workers. He must be able to listen so as to generate positive communication, and he must demonstrate patience and tolerance for differing views. He should be able to secure voluntary acceptance of work assignments. He must be able to create and maintain a cooperative, friendly, and productive working situation. He must have the ability to encourage the development of his workers.

Measuring. Using the systems and forms provided, he must record and report the performance of his workers. He must also be able to establish his own evaluation criteria, since no form will supply all the answers. He must make known to the workers the standards by which they will be evaluated. He must be able to continually refine the measuring function in light of changing tasks and requirements.

The above are but brief, representative descriptions of the supervisor's generalized responsibilities.

Some of the supervisor's specific responsibilities, that combine all or some of the broad areas listed above, include:

Seeing that the work gets out. While the production requirements may well be established by someone else, he is charged with meeting them.

Maintaining quality control. While others set the parameters of product quality and still others measure and inspect for quality, he is responsible for maintaining it in the first instance.

Interpreting, promulgating, and implementing company policies. The supervisor is management's representative in matters of communication. Failure to convince the supervisor of the importance of his role in the communication process can only have harmful effects. Well-intentioned policies and directives are of little value without competent interpretation and implementation.

Handling disciplinary problems fairly, promptly, and uniformly—without malice or favoritism. The degree of discipline must bear relationship to the severity of the act.

Building team spirit through his roles as teacher, coach, and leader. He must be able and willing to help the workers develop and maximize their skills and not try to hold them back.

Delegating responsibility. Only through the delegation of responsibility can the supervisor relieve himself of the responsibility of "doing it himself. " Only then can he truly begin to manage and get work done through others.

Measuring, with the help of others, individual performance and providing guidance toward improvement. He must be able to develop results-oriented people.

Interpreting and administering, with the aid of the labor relations staff, the labor contract where one exists. He is the first person to whom grievances are brought, and he handles them before they reach the written stage. His initial response to a grievance can often affect the outcome of the arbitration procedure if the matter is carried that far.

The supervisor is at the crossroads, representing management to the workers and vice versa. In his position he can put into motion a process that will administer away in day-to-day affairs that which has been gained at the bargaining table. If he knows his job and the contract, he can cut down on the number of real grievances and the number of grievances that reach arbitration. He must know when and how to say no, and he must know how to explain his position when the company is not in violation of the contract. A lack of such understanding has caused a great many unnecessary problems. This is not to say that the effective foreman is the one who has no grievances charged against him. If one finds such a supervisor, it might be well to suspect that something is amiss. He could by buying the workers' apparent goodwill with the assets of the company.

One could easily cite many other responsibilities of the supervisor which have not been specifically named here. But those listed above should serve to describe the nature of the position and indicate some of the problems that must be faced and solved.

It is obvious to the thoughtful that the job of supervision is becoming more difficult every day. The proliferation of knowledge is taking its toll. Each person in this position of stewardship is required to learn and understand more and more. The changes in the marketplace as well as in the shop and office are occurring at an increasing rate.

It is not enough, then, that the supervisor simply keep up with changing methods and procedures. For he is being barraged with an ever-growing body of knowledge concerning product, quality, new machine technology, incentives, time studies, wage and benefits administration, labor law, and countless other areas.

The nature of the time in which we find ourselves prompts, if not demands, added effort, knowledge, increased competence, and continued education on the part of the supervisor.

It takes a special competence and talent to adequately fill this position in the organizational hierarchy.

PERSONAL QUALITIES

The position obviously makes certain demands upon the supervisor in terms of the work to be done. Additionally, there are *certain desired qualities which ideally he should bring to the job.* To generalize, these are the qualities to be sought in anyone who is going to hold down a position of business or industrial leadership.

He should possess reasonable knowledge of the work to be performed or the function to be managed. While this does not mean he must be able to do the job as well as those he supervises, he should be able to understand the problems they face. While many basic skills are transferable, it would be unreasonable to expect an accountant to do a superior job of running a research laboratory. Of course, some accountants will take exception to this premise.

He should have a past record of success in interpersonal relationships. "But what if he's never been a supervisor before; how can you tell?" His prior record in dealing with others in any type of situation should be determined. What has he accomplished in union, social, community, civic, and church activities? What have been his activities in fraternal and service organizations? There are countless ways in which he could have demonstrated his success in getting along with others. People are seemingly creatures of habit. That which they have done, they are likely to do again. If the dynamics of any set of situations are roughly comparable, we are likely to repeat our successes. Assuming a knowledge of the work to be accomplished, a person who has been able to get things done through others in the past has a reasonable chance at succeeding again.

He should have a degree of mental acuity sufficient to deal with the scope of the department or function to be supervised. Admittedly, this is a relative matter. The problems faced by thirty men putting nuts on widgets differ from those faced by twelve men in a highly sophisticated numerically controlled machining center. In each case, however, the supervisor should be able to grasp the complexity of the product being manufactured and the difficulty of the procedures and processes to be followed.

He should be able to generate enthusiasm and competence.

He must be able to motivate and lead a team.

He should be able to communicate. In addition to understanding the problem, he must be able to describe it to others.

Conversely, he should be able to listen and understand. The supervisor who turns a deaf ear to one of his subordinates is cheating himself, the worker and the company. He should be able to handle both the giving and the receiving of instructions and criticism.

He should be able to delegate responsibility. If a company appoints a man to be a supervisor who is unable to delegate and who tries to do too much himself, the man is unfortunately doomed to failure as a supervisor.

He should possess empathy, that capacity to identify and understand the feelings or ideas of another person. If the supervisor does not have this quality, his personnel problems will be multiplied.

Again, the above are just some of the personal qualities one should bring to a supervisor's job. These are skills that are transferable, skills that would prompt success in many endeavors, qualities which management should look for in an individual if he is to be successful and capable of future success, growth, and development.

SELECTION AND SOURCES

It is a function of the personnel department to provide the tools for the selection process and to guide the manager in his consideration of available candidates. In accomplishing this function, the personnel department assists in the following ways:

Identifies the various factors of the job to be done and writes a job description.

Conducts a manpower inventory in an effort to predict the future need for new supervisory personnel and as an aid in identifying potential candidates within the group to be managed and within other units of the company.

Recruits possible candidates, including college graduates, from outside the company.

Where possible, aids in establishment of a preselection and pretraining program.

Through checking records, interviewing, and testing, identifies the few best candidates for the job.

The First Step Is Defining the Job to Be Done

The idea may appear too basic to put forth, but it is not possible to evaluate a person's chances of success if the tasks that person will be asked to perform are not first clearly defined. This is true of all jobs; if the position exists as a valid job to be done it can be specifically defined. The description will lead to identification of the necessary skills.

"Everybody knows the job. He's going to supervise the gamma department." That's fine. But does the candidate know exactly what the gamma department is supposed to accomplish? Does he know the *scope* of the job he is being asked to consider? Is he aware of all its *functions?* Does he know the *reporting relationships* that will be required? Have his *future responsibilities* been detailed? Is he cognizant of the *standards* of *performance* that will be expected? "He's worked in the department for four years. He ought to know." Perhaps, but does he? For that matter, does anyone? Why did the last person leave or get fired?

Too often a man is assigned to a job and those who make the assignment are not clear themselves on just what is to be done. After a period of time, someone decides the man is not cutting it, and he is "let go." Another man is then placed in the position, again without a clear idea of what is expected. One could get the impression that management is hoping the man in the job will define it through his performance and save everyone a lot of trouble. Then, all that will have to be told the next man in the job is, "Do what Joe did."

It is not enough. A job description must be set forth, a description that:

Gives the scope of the job

Lists the primary functions and necessary skills

Details the responsibilities

Cites the reporting relationships

Sets the standard of performance expected

Once this step has been taken it becomes easier to evaluate whether or not the job is being done properly.

A Manpower Inventory Aids in Forecasting Need and Helps to Identify Possible Candidates for the Job

While these are not the only benefits to be gained from a manpower inventory, they are most important to a discussion of the selection of supervisors.

An assessment of the talent that exists within an organization is a vital first step in determining the means by which any organization will continue to grow. The soundness of such an inventory, however, is predicated upon the assumption that realistic planning has been done in all other areas of the organization. These include:

Establishment of challenging but practical long- and short-range objectives.

Organization of the company in a fashion necessary to accomplish its stated objectives.

Establishment of policies which provide the framework for decision.

Formulation of plans and programs relating to markets, money, production, sales, and other functions.

Given the above, the manpower inventory seeks to forecast vacancies that will be created by promotion, retirement, normal turnover, plant expansion, and other causes. It next aims to identify all possible candidates for promotion and relate them to the predicted vacancies.

The procedure normally requires the managers to appraise the supervisors reporting to them, while the supervisors evaluate their subordinates. This forces all, some for the first time, to make an organized effort to inventory their groups. (The procedure has the additional benefit of pointing out those who are not critical enough in their appraisal of others or have not studied their group with sufficient depth or care. These weaknesses often correlate with mediocre performance in other areas and further point up a need for corrective action.)

The manpower inventory highlights the units with pending replacement problems and prompts the serious consideration of beginning to prepare for the filling of such vacancies. It tends to point up the need for better identification of individuals in other units who might be possible candidates for a given position.

The Most Frequently Used Source of Supervisory Talent Is the Group to Be Managed

While this group is the most available and normally the most practical source, it often presents a special type of problem if all the necessary steps of the selection process are not completed. It is unfortunate, but true, that some managements hold the view that the best salesmen, measured in dollar achievements, make the best sales managers—or the best machinists make the best foremen. Some newspaper editors believe the best reporters make the best editors. It may be only natural for a man to feel he was promoted to his present position because he was "the best" at the step below.

On the one hand we say a man must demonstrate a certain technical competence in the work he is to supervise (as mentioned above in the personal qualities or skills he should bring to the job), while on the other hand promotion on this factor alone can often lead to selection of the wrong man.   Herein lie many problems.

To illustrate.   A managing editor of a medium-sized metropolitan daily newspaper was one of those who believed that the best reporters make the best editors.   (Was he not the living proof of his theory?)   A vacancy occurred when the city editor of the second shift resigned.   The managing editor recommended that the star reporter on the second shift be offered the job, and the paper's editor agreed.   The reporter accepted and, for a time, everything appeared to be working out.

The new editor was able to plan and organize the work of his staff.   He ran a reasonably well-organized "desk."   He spent time training and bringing along the younger reporters.   He came prepared for and contributed to the weekly editorial meetings.   Although his judgment differed from that of his superiors at times, that was chalked off to lack of desk experience.   All things considered, however, he appeared well suited to his job.

But there were other factors that neither he nor his superiors had considered — factors that were to eventually lead to his dissatisfaction with the position.

All his working life, the new editor had been "on the move." Never before had he been tied to a desk.   After several months, a feeling of entrapment came over him.   He differed with his superiors over the relationship of editors with newsmakers.   While he felt editors should be personally acquainted with as many news sources as possible in order to properly evaluate stories concerning them, his superiors felt objectivity could be best served by maintaining a distance.   Worse, he took his job too seriously.   He found himself unable to forget it and relax at any time.   This affected his family life and nearly led to a divorce.

In the end, he requested to return to his old position as a reporter.   His superiors refused, and he left the paper.

A good reporter was lost because neither he nor those above him had looked at all the factors, evaluated all the risks.   Everyone involved proceeded on one basic, unfounded assumption: "The best reporter makes the best editor."   Whose responsibility was it to evaluate the risks?   Both sides, of course.   But management bore the greater responsibility.   More on this below.

Is there anyone in industry who has not seen a company promote its top salesman, often over his protestations, to a manager's job and lose a good salesman and gain a poor manager in doing so?   It happens all too often.

Therefore, a major problem facing the person who is charged with the selection of a supervisor is separating the man's skill at his task from his potential skills as a supervisor.

A professional manpower inventory, conducted under the supervision of the personnel department, can go a long way toward helping to solve this problem.   Properly structured, the program aids the evaluators by delineating the prime areas to be appraised, setting standards and methods, and providing guidance.   The process is an aid to the effective preidentification of potential supervisors.

The manpower inventory may uncover units with more than one person capable of succeeding at the supervisory level, as well as units where no one has shown the capacity to move ahead.   The consequences of such a situation in a plant where management simply picks the "best at the task" from within the group to be managed can easily be seen:

In the first case, a potentially excellent supervisor will be left to languish — normally in frustration — because there was another man in the unit who showed slightly better potential than he.

In the second case, the best of the worst will be promoted — normally to the detriment of the unit.

The results of the inventory should call attention to this potential problem and thus help management in taking steps to correct it.

The Personnel Department Is Responsible for Outside Recruiting Activities

There are times when a firm, particularly a smaller company with a limited number of potential supervisors, may have to go outside its present employees to find a new supervisor. This situation can also arise in a larger company when an unusually large number of new supervisors are needed because of expansion and growth.

The manpower inventory described above is an excellent aid in forecasting if outside help will be needed, and it helps to identify and clarify the sources which should be considered. In seeking applicants from the outside the personnel department can place classified advertisements, contact state and private employment agencies, post notices in appropriate locations, etc. Other sources are the man who walks in "off the street" to submit a job application, and friends and relatives of present employees.

One additional source of supervisory personnel is the college campus. There are many in industry who now advocate placing college graduates in supervisory positions, after first orienting the graduate to the task through some other job—project engineering, production control, industrial engineering, etc. Working as a foreman or first-line supervisor undoubtedly prepares the new graduate for higher-level positions by giving him a feel for production and its problems. The experience can be a very beneficial one for the rest of his working career.

The foreman's job today is much more complicated than it was twenty-five years ago. Then, the job may have required no more than an eighth-grade education. Today it requires at least a high school education, and the trend is to select foremen from among graduates of the two-year colleges and post–high school technical and vocational schools. Who is to say whether, or when, the day is coming that the four-year degree will be a prerequisite for becoming a foreman or first-line supervisor?

Identify Potential Supervisors in Advance of Need

While this type of program is effective in any size company, it is particularly effective for smaller companies that lack formal personnel development procedures. Prior identification is a valuable tool that may avoid a later expedient choice.

Where possible, a man who shows supervisory potential should have to do part of his boss's job upon occasion. "Working up" provides an excellent framework, not only for preidentification but also for pretraining. Opportunities can arise whenever the supervisor must be absent from his job, or the candidate can be required to accomplish certain work—record keeping and training of new employees, for example—while the boss is on the job.

Preidentification allows management to further evaluate the potential candidate. It aids in determining how well the person reacts to instruction and criticism, and in evaluating the reaction of other employees to his leadership; and it provides an excellent measure of his overall attitude.

There are cases where classroom training can be offered as part of the preidentification process. If there is a tuition assistance program in existence, the potential supervisor might be encouraged to attend outside classes. He should also be encouraged to attend any general training sessions held in the plant. But there is a limit to how much you can ask of a man before he is actually told he has the job.

Another benefit of the preidentification process is that it gives the worker who thinks he wants to be a supervisor a better look at himself and the job. He may decide, after short experiences, he does not want the problems and responsibilities of the position.

It is not wise to have so many men involved in the pretraining process that most will never have the opportunity to attain the higher position because of a limited number of openings. The manager has an obligation to identify those whom he believes have the most potential for future success. A company that has progressed far enough to preidentify its potential supervisors should also have the wisdom not to build up its employees' hopes while sending them down dead-end streets.

The step from worker to supervisor is a step from labor to management. For many people, it is filled with dread. It can change the patterns of a lifetime. These changes will affect his family, too. Part of that which he must consider is his chance for success — or even further promotion.

Limiting the number of men receiving preselection training or coaching to the number of real and potential openings lets them know they are competing on the basis of their personal abilities — only! If a man does fail, it is infinitely better to let him do so during this identification period than after he has actually been placed in the supervisor's job. This is a prime purpose of such prior identification and training.

Management stands to gain also. While it may be disappointed in the performance of a certain candidate during this period, the advance program will normally allow time to evaluate others within the company or alert management to the need to look outside.

Selection procedure. The sources for possible supervisory candidates and various techniques for evaluating persons found within those sources have been discussed, but what are the steps of the actual selection process? They include record checking, interviews, and testing. While these subjects have been covered in other chapters of this handbook, let us briefly review the manner in which they affect the selection of a new supervisor.

A Man's Past Record Is Probably the Best Indicator of his Future Performance

Where the dynamics of situations are comparable, the candidate's past record correlates more accurately and affords more reliable predictions as to what he is likely to do in the future.

A review of the candidate's past record can be accomplished with the aid of an interview and by checking records. If the man is proposed for advancement from within the company, his personnel records, his supervisor's evaluation of his work and ability to deal with people, his salary progress, and the observations of others who work with and near him should be readily available. (If they are not, it probably indicates that the company has no set procedures for evaluating and upgrading its personnel, and that all selections are made on the basis of intuition. Where this is the case, little that has been stated here applies.)

Where the candidate is coming from outside the firm, it is vitally important to check his prior references. There are many companies that are reluctant to carry out this step. They fear the man's current employer may learn he is unhappy and seeking to improve or change his situation.

Most candidates for supervisory positions, however, have had more than one prior job. These prior employers can be checked. In seeking a reference, personal contact is best, but a telephone conversation must usually suffice. A letter reference check is generally as useless as no check at all.

Most of us do not want to be guilty of blacklisting a fellow human. Letter reference checks, therefore, usually reveal only the candidate's prior title, length of employment, salary, and some nebulous reason for his departure.

A telephone call to the candidate's prior supervisor, not the personnel department, will usually provide a more accurate description of the candidate's performance and the circumstances surrounding his departure from the other firm. As in the case of the interviewer, the prospective employer also has the advantage of being able to gauge what the former employer does *not* say. At times the unsaid, along with the tone of voice, are more important than the words spoken. Every telephone reference check should be concluded with the question, "Would you rehire him?" Figure 2 shows a typical telephone reference check reporting form.

A necessary adjunct to the records check is a review of the man's performance by his immediate superior. This brings his evaluation up to date. Figure 3 illustrates the type of form that can be used in structuring and recording this evaluation.

The Interview

Where the skills, abilities, experience, and qualities of the individual are matched with the job requirements, the interview, conducted by one skilled and trained in

TELEPHONE INVESTIGATION REPORT

Applicant-First Name ______ Last Name ______

Person Contacted ______

If not applicant's supervisor, state relationship. ______

Company ______ Location ______ Telephone Number ______

1. I wish to verify some of the information given us by Mr.______, who has applied for a position with us. Do you remember him? What were the dates of his employment with your company? From______19____to______19____
2. What was he doing when he started? ______When he left?______
3. What were the main duties and responsibilities on his final job? (If he sold, what type of selling did he do?) ______ Do you understand fully the nature of his job?
4. He says he was earning $______per______Is this right?______
5. How much of this was salary? $______commission $______expenses $______
6. How did he take to training and instructions? ______ Intelligent? Adaptable? Curious?
7. Was he alert and enthusiastic in his approach to his job? ______ Energetic? Didn't Bore Easily?
8. How was he at organizing and planning his work? ______ Self-Disciplined? Flexible?
9. How was he at handling figures? ______ Adept? Accurate? Analytical?
10. Does he like or dislike detail? ______ Methodical? Thorough? or Slip-Shod?
11. What kind of impression did he make on customers and other outsiders? Does he meet people easily? ______ Sincere? Understanding? or Argumentative?
12. Can he express himself well in talking? ______ Poised? Clear-Thinking? Organized?
13. Can he express himself well in writing? ______ Clear-Thinking? Organized?

Figure 2. Employment investigation report.

the process, is the most sound selection device.   As with all selection steps, the interview serves as a guide to the final decision.   Reputable and proficient firms, such as the Psychological Corporation, Dartnell Institute, and others conduct interviewer training and have published reliable guides to interview and evaluation techniques.

Suffice it to say the interviewer should cover work history, education and training, and present health as well as attitude, interests, and abilities so as to match the man and the job.

Immediately after the interview, the interviewer should record his observations on a reporting form.

What are the differences between an interview and a test?   Both solicit answers

14.   How hard did he work?

Conscientious?   Ambitious?

15.   Did he require more or less supervision than average?

Self-Starter?   Diligent?   or Hard to Manage?

16.   How did his results compare with others?   Quality?   Quantity?

Industrious?   Competitive?

17.   Did he supervise anyone?   How did he go about it?

Leader?   or Driver?   or Follower?

18.   How did he react to criticism?

Mature?   or Emotional?

19.   Did he have any domestic or financial difficulties that interferred with work?

Immature?   Involved?

20.   What about gambling?

Immature?   Poorly Adjusted?

21.   What about drinking?

22.   How dependable was he?   Did he miss much time from work?

Conscientious?   Healthy?

23.   Is he ambitious?   What were his aspirations?

Does he have a goal?   Is he realistic?

24.   What was he doing to improve and develop himself while with you?

Night School?   Willing to work to advance?

25.   Why did he leave your company?

Good Reasons?   Do they check?

26.   What are his outstanding strong points?

Potential for Growth

27.   What were his weak points?

Do strengths outweigh weaknesses?

28.   What type of work do you feel he would do best?

Does this fit?

29.   Would you reemploy him.   If not, why?

30.   Is there anything else you feel we should know about him...for help us make the right decision...for him and for us?

NAME OF INTERVIEWER_____DATE_____

Figure 2.   Employment investigation report.   (continued)

```
PERSONNEL APPRAISAL FORM
PART I - PAST EXPERIENCE

(Last Three Job Assignments)
```

JOB TITLE	NATURE OF ASSIGNMENT	MANAGER	DATES (FROM-TO)

```
PART II - PRESENT PERFORMANCE
```

Overall Performance (Circle) A*|B*|C*   Comp. Ratio _____ % (if you
                                           use the Hay System - other-
                                           wise current salary)

Brief Description of Present Position

_____

_____

_____

_____

Knowledge, Skills and Abilities Required in Present Position
(e.g., Ability to Manage Others, Knowledge of Product Design,
Knowledge of Records Keeping, Product Knowledge, Knowledge of   Degree to Which
Methods, etc.)   Mastered at This Time*

1. _____   A   B   C

2. _____   A   B   C

3. _____   A   B   C

4. _____   A   B   C

Action Required to Improve Present Performance	Action to Be Taken by (✔)
	The Manager | The Individual
1. _____	_____ | _____
2. _____	_____ | _____
3. _____	_____ | _____
4. _____	_____ | _____

Date of Last Performance Review _____ Conducted By _____

*   A - Outstanding   B - Above Average   C - Average

Figure 3.   Personnel appraisal form.

to questions.   The skilled interviewer, however, can more adequately observe and measure the various factors of human response and react to the unexpected.   In an unstructured situation, the interviewer can delve deeper.   He can also evaluate what the candidate does *not* say, which is often as important as what he does say.

The Third Aid to Selection Is Testing

In American industry, there are many types of tests that can be used—aptitude, intelligence, physical, personality.   If the employee is being promoted from within the company, if he has been with the company for a sufficient length of time, if he has been placed in enough preselection situations, testing may be deemed unnecessary.   There are many who question the personnel department that administers a

```
                        PART III - FUTURE RESPONSIBILITY
```

Probable Next Position, _____   Approx. Date of Probable
Assignment, or Type   Next Position/Assignment_____
of Assignment   _____

  Requirements/Qualifications of Next Position:

  _____

  _____

  _____

  _____

  Present Qualifications (Exp. and/or Education) for Future Position

  _____

  _____

  _____

  Experience and/or Education Required to Qualify for Future Position

  _____

  _____

  _____

Action(s) to Be Taken to Qualify Individual for Next Position	Action to Be Taken by (✓)	
	The Manager	The Individual
1. _____	_____	_____
2. _____	_____	_____
3. _____	_____	_____
4. _____	_____	_____

  Have these plans been discussed with the individual?   (Circle)   Yes   No

      If "Yes," by whom? _____   When? _____

  Overall Promotability at This Time:

       _____Ready Now   _____Ready in 3-6 Mos.   _____Ready in 6-12 Mos.   _____Ready
                                                                                        in 1-2 Yrs.

                   PLEASE USE OTHER SIDE FOR ADDITIONAL COMMENTS

Figure 3.   Personnel appraisal form.   (continued)

full battery of tests to a man who has been employed by the firm for several years. Has he not been evaluated and tested many times over?

Where the candidate is from outside the firm or work unit which it is proposed he supervise, some forms of testing may be desired as an additional aid to selection. Such results, if tests are given, should be used in combination with records checking and interview results in making the decision rather than as a sole basis for selection.

In spite of their popularity in some quarters, there are still many personnel departments that choose not to rely too heavily on psychological tests of any type. As stated before, it seems more appropriate to rely on the judgment of a skilled interviewer and an evaluation of the candidate's past track record.

One test evaluation states, for example, that "in all probability" the man who scores 60 or above will succeed, while "in all probability" the man who scores below 60 will not. What about the candidate who scores 61? or 59? The candidate who scores 65? or 55? Has the test actually qualified some while ruling out others? Of course not. It has provided a "chances are" answer to a question and is only a guide and can well be mitigated by other factors. No one wants his future decided by one percentage point on a scale of probability.

Total reliance on test scores may well be a sign of a weak personnel department and a weak management. The weaker they are, the more apt they are to rely solely on test results. Tests may serve as a crutch for inability to make objective analyses of the candidate's abilities and liabilities and to relate these analyses to the job to be performed.

The question the person charged with the responsibility for selection decision must ask is, "Does the use of this test truly help and improve our selection batting average?" If it does, there probably is no harm in using the test—so long as it has been professionally developed and administered and evaluated by a trained individual.

It is unfortunate, however, that many managers and some personnel practitioners are unable to accurately state how well the tests they use work. They have not followed through. They have never troubled to determine whether the claimed validity and reliability equate with their history of success and failure. Did the candidates with the best scores become the best supervisors? How many with passing grades failed to succeed on the job? Is the test accurate as a predictor of success within their company as often as the developer of the test claimed it would be? These are some of the questions that must be asked in an effective follow-up program.

There are tests that serve a purpose and which may provide useful selection data. One is a physical examination where physical and health characteristics are an integral part of the ability to perform the tasks required. Others are aptitude and intelligence tests that measure basic abilities and skills. Care must be taken when using the latter, however, to ascertain that the tests are not actually measuring cultural differences.

The interview, record check, and testing provide the guides for selection, but the final selection decision must still be made by correlating the data from all sources.

Generally, the responsibility for decision should rest with the line manager to whom the supervisor will report. It should not be made by the personnel department. If the person responsible for the decision can pass the buck to the personnel department, he can also pass the responsibility for the candidate's failure. It is seldom that he will pass the credit for success. He therefore should make the final selection decision.

The Role of Management in Selection

Management has a continuing responsibility to evaluate its attitude toward the supervisor selection program. It has a particular obligation to help the candidate evaluate all the risks included in his decision to try to move up so as to minimize the likelihood he will not be successful and have to move down again.

To be fair to the candidate, management must accept the theory that most men want to do a good job. If this is done, the chances are the candidate will be given enough information to truly understand the job, to know what is expected of him—in terms of performance and the qualities he will be asked to bring to the job.

Management must continue to realize, as it has come to, that selection is a matching process. It is no longer a matter of placing the individual in a position and expecting him to be able to learn all he has to know without considering the personal attributes he must bring to the job. It must also be realized there is seldom, if ever, a perfect match—one man who has all the abilities and none of the liabilities required of the perfect supervisor. To some extent every candidate represents a compromise.

The candidate should not be laden with a "temporary" title. This is another crutch of indecisive management. It tells the worker the manager has little faith in his own ability to decide. "Temporary" added to a title is an insult. It puts the supervisor on edge, and makes him uneasy and insecure. The best man should be selected and should be given the job, the title, and the money. He should never be paid under rate "until he proves himself." This works to limit his chances for success. Responsibility without appropriate compensation breeds resentment.

A good generalization is that one should select from within where possible. If a man is a competent worker, commands the respect of his fellow workers, and has the other skills and qualities to be a supervisor, promoting him can be a morale builder. Conversely, reaching outside the group when there is a member of the group who should be considered is demoralizing. People lose their incentive when they do not see their own progressing. Many people profess to be uncreative, but it is amazing to witness the number and diversity of ways individual workers can help another man fail if they do not like or respect him. The worker promoted from within, who has the necessary qualifications, probably has a greater chance of success than the outsider—although this does not rule out the possibility that the outsider can also succeed.

While individual workers may applaud one of their own getting promoted, it is not unusual for unions to have contracts that act to keep a man among the union's members. Many contracts cause the man who accepts a supervisor's post to lose his seniority should he have to return to the bargaining unit for some reason. Some contracts actually deprive him of the right to return to the bargaining unit. It is incumbent upon management, therefore, to be as right as possible in assessing a man's chances for success. If he fails as a supervisor and has to return to the lowest level within the union structure, he is not going to be a happy employee. Industry must do a better job in this area, for its own good and for the sake of the potential success of the men it asks to be supervisors.

It is management's obligation to assess all the risks for the proposed supervisor. Too often, the candidate sees only the future benefits. He fails to measure these against the difficulties, the setbacks he will suffer should he fail to succeed, the real problems he will face with his former union should he have to return. Management must assess the risks and make certain the candidate understands them. To fail to do so is criminal.

TRAINING THE SUPERVISOR

Near the beginning of this chapter it was stated that few persons are normally subjected to job pressure with as little opportunity for formal preparation as the new supervisor. In the section immediately above, mention was made of the lack of early identification and pretraining in industry and the tendency to wait until a vacancy occurs and before choosing the most available candidate. Not mentioned before was the propensity of some managements to select the supervisor, by whatever means, and then let him fend for himself.

Not surprisingly, many men succeed when put in this situation. These are the ones who absorb and learn through observation and the ones who are motivated and able to seek educational opportunities for themselves. But a more enlightened approach in this era of shortage of competent supervisors is to use formalized and carefully developed supervisory training programs.

Managers have the responsibility to help develop the company, but management has the obligation to help the supervisor develop himself, to provide him with the challenge, the motivation, and financial assistance. If it is a crime to make a man a victim of a haphazard selection system, it is more so not to provide him with the tools he needs to succeed.

Some managements take the viewpoint that the man in a responsible position should not require more training—that he was promoted because he has sufficient knowledge. They feel the men who do need training are weak. That this attitude is wrong goes without saying. Training is not therapy for the sick; *it is calesthenics for the healthy.* The man has been appointed a supervisor because he shows the best potential. To help him fulfill that potential, management must analyze his educational needs and make provision for offering him the training that will satisfy those needs. It should be recognized that the man who seeks further training is trying to improve himself to the benefit of the company, and he should be suitably assisted in his efforts.

A supervisor's training should begin as soon as he has been selected and placed on the supervisory payroll. The best type of training is on-the-job instruction, giving him a job to do and letting him do it and then supplementing his experience with formal instructions as needed. Giving a man a "how to supervise" course alone will not make him a supervisor. He should be provided with the opportunity to relate new knowledge learned in a classroom with the work to be performed, to see how this newly acquired knowledge will affect his performance. This procedure most often leads to true insight, to true training and development. True training and development occurs as knowledge is put to use. It has been found that when the two types of instruction are combined, they tend to reinforce one another.

Another facet of the new supervisor's training is coaching. Failure the first time he tries something new does not mean he is incapable of accomplishing the assignment. He wants to do a good job, but perhaps he has not grasped a core fact or concept. Through coaching, this can be determined, and his motivation can be maintained. When the new supervisor realizes that his superiors are truly interested in seeing him succeed, his chances of doing so are enhanced.

Among the many subjects that can be covered in the new supervisor's training program are:

Planning
Delegation
Discipline
Human relations
Contract administration
Record keeping
Machine processes
Industrial engineering
Quality control
Time study
Employee benefits and obligations
Company policies and procedures
Communications

It is not necessary that the supervisor become an expert in all of the above subject areas, but he should have a knowledge of his responsibilities in each area. No one, for example, expects the supervisor to be an expert in all the legal ramifications of the labor contract. But he should be aware of the rights held by both management and labor. He should be able to recognize legitimate grievances and handle them before they reach arbitration. He should know where and how to seek help regarding contract provisions when he needs it. When management is in the right, he should be able to clearly explain the matter. As has been noted, the labor contract is just one area where it is vital that he be knowledgeable. He should know as much about all the subject areas that bear on the performance of his work.

Where Is the Supervisor Going to Get this Knowledge?

Much of the information can be supplied by the various sections within the particular organization. The labor relations staff, for example, would be responsible for providing the information on the union contract. Films, lectures, teaching machines, discussion, role playing, and case studies all can be used to aid in this training. Likewise other needed information can be supplied by the controller, purchasing agent, general foreman, etc.

Other, more generalized knowledge, can be acquired from night school or community college courses where they are available. Not only should the supervisor be encouraged to attend such courses, he should be helped. This help is provided in two ways:

The company should provide appropriate financial assistance. If the supervisor successfully completes any course recommended by the company, many companies refund the full tuition.

The supervisor may well be given time off from the job to take the courses. A man cannot be expected to work a full shift five days a week and then attend night classroom instruction for extended periods and fully apply himself—not if he is performing up to expectations on the job.

It is recognized that local educational institutions are often most helpful in developing and offering courses in which the community has an interest. It is always wise to approach the school's administrators and identify the courses that would be helpful to new supervisors. They will normally canvass the business community to see if sufficient interest exists for the suggested subject matter. If the interest is apparent, and the revenue available, many schools will make the courses available.

When a major manufacturing company opened a new plant near Roanoke, Virginia, for example, the community college responded with both classroom and in-plant instruction for new employees. This was later supplemented by additional training for new supervisors. The entire program was tailored for the need that existed, as should be the case with all training.

Any instruction provided by the company personnel should normally be accomplished during the work shift. It is extremely difficult to get a man to come in early or stay late for a lecture or training session even if its contents are of vital importance to him.

Another excellent source of continuing education is the seminars provided by such groups as the American Management Association. These normally require a week or less of the supervisor's time. Many companies, particularly smaller firms, believe they cannot afford the time or the money to send a supervisor to such seminars. Can they afford to keep him on the job if he is poorly prepared? It should be realized that one mistake on the part of a supervisor can cost even the smallest firm many times the small and tax deductible investment required to send him to a good professionally led seminar.

If none of these avenues are open, there are hundreds of excellent publications available for the development and advancement of supervisors. Professional associations such as the AMA will provide reading lists to fit the particular needs of a member.

The new supervisor should be exposed to the required knowledge that will help him understand and perform his job. He must be armed with appropriate knowledge if he is to successfully direct the work of others to achieve the desired results.

THE SUPERVISOR'S RESPONSIBILITIES AND THE PERSONNEL DEPARTMENT

In its relationship to the supervisor, we have already seen how the personnel department aids in his identification, selection, and training. What does the department do, however, once the supervisor is on the job? It helps the supervisor solve his problems and meet his responsibilities in regard to the work to be done and to the people who work for and with him.

The personnel department justifies its existence to the extent that it helps the organization solve its people problems. All the functional specialists in the personnel group should be readily available to the supervisor and should establish reputations as men who are willing to listen and ready and able to help. If the supervisor is rejected or ignored a few times, he is not apt to turn to the personnel department for assistance when he should.

There are many specific ways in which the personnel department can be of assistance to the supervisor:

The competent personnel department can and should be a counselor to the new supervisor. While the supervisor worked within the production unit, for example, he could measure his performance in a tangible way, i.e., how many pieces did he assemble that day. His satisfaction was derived from the actual work done. Now that he has become a supervisor and is charged with getting work done through others, he must learn and internalize a new set of values. He needs to develop the sensitivity and skills of working through other people. He must establish a new set of personal achievement measures, for he no longer does the work with his own hands. In all of this, the personnel department should be of assistance. The personnel people act as counselors to the new supervisor in his adjustment to this new situation. Once he has come to understand the difference, he can usually learn to live with it and thrive on it.

In an ideal situation, the supervisor should have not only the right, but the responsibility, of selecting the new men who will work in his unit. The personnel department should help screen the qualified applicants for the job and let the supervisor make the final selection of men to work in his unit. The personnel department should also make certain the supervisor knows as much as possible about the new man before he joins the group.

In conjunction with the above, the personnel department should develop manpower studies, succession plans and similar devices to allow the supervisor to predict when he will need new workers.

The personnel department should aid in the administration of discipline.

The personnel department should see that salaries are equitable and assist the supervisor in carrying out his salary administration responsibilities. Salary inequity between men of equal ability, equal performance, and equal service creates resentment and unnecessary problems for the supervisor. The personnel department is responsible to see that such unwarranted variations are not permitted to exist.

The personnel department is responsible for seeing that the educational opportunities and programs the supervisor needs to succeed and develop in his job are available.

The personnel department helps the supervisor help his workers to grow and develop through appropriate skills and training programs. It is also the agency that must convince the supervisor he cannot keep the "best group in the shop" together forever. This might be good for the supervisor so long as he is in his position, for he is measured on his workers' success, but holding back the workers from individual development and promotion is damaging to their morale and eventually to their productivity.

The personnel department aids as an avenue of communication from higher management to the supervisor. It assists the supervisor in interpreting and implementing company programs and policies. In doing so, it helps the supervisor develop his own communication skills. In carrying out this communications function, the personnel department should act as a monitor to ascertain that everyone is "talking from the same script."

The personnel department assists the supervisor in maintaining records of all types. These include federal, state, and local government records, social security records, employee benefits records, seniority lists, unemployment compensation records, insurance records, and medical and safety records. The supervisor should be able to obtain all the information he requires from any of these records by a call or visit to the personnel department.

The personnel department helps the supervisor in measuring the *results* of his workers. This is fairly easy to accomplish in manufacturing areas where there are known machining capabilities and known production requirements. In other areas, however, measuring becomes much more subjective. The inexperienced man may not yet have learned to trust his personal subjective evaluations, and the personnel department can aid in attempting to evaluate the more important aspects of the workers' performance.

Finally, if the supervisor is coach and teacher to his men, the personnel department serves the same function to the supervisor. The personnel department helps the supervisor's superior as well as the supervisor himself to identify the supervisor's needs for development and growth. It continually counsels him and sustains his morale. It helps him with personal problems if and when this is necessary.

The relationship between the personnel department and the supervisor is unique indeed. An effective personnel department can do much in the way of aiding a supervisor toward success in his position. In turn, the personnel department can gain the satisfaction of making a constant and recognizable contribution to the enterprise.

CONCLUSION

We have outlined who the supervisor is and what he does, what qualities he should possess, and how he is selected; and we have pointed to the fact that training is required after he is placed in this important spot in the organizational structure. The supervisor truly manages at the first level, and if he is to be successful, he must get results through efforts of others.

As stated in the beginning, to the worker the supervisor is the company. A competent supervisor can greatly assist a company in achieving its profit and growth objectives. A poor one can offset many good intentions, policies, and procedures of an enlightened management. Management, therefore, must select him carefully and see that he is properly trained and equipped to do the job.

The supervisor is truly a manager and should be prepared and treated as such.

BIBLIOGRAPHY

Drucker, Peter: *Managing for Results,* Harper & Row, Publishers, Incorporated, New York, 1964.

Famularo, Joseph J.: *Supervisors in Action,* McGraw-Hill Book Company, New York, 1961.

McGregor, Douglas: *The Human Side of Enterprise,* McGraw-Hill Book Company, New York, 1960.

Merrihue, W. V.: *Managing by Communication,* McGraw-Hill Book Company, New York, 1960.

Proctor, John H., and Thorton, Wm. M.: *Training: A Handbook for Line Managers,* AMA, New York, 1961.

chapter 69

Minorities and
the Disadvantaged

LEE S. GASSLER   *Director of Industrial Relations, Kodak Park Division, Eastman Kodak Company, Rochester, New York*

Jimmie R., a trainee in a large northern corporation, recently told his supervisor that he wanted to quit. He was intent, but gave no immediate reasons for wanting to leave his job. And that might have been the end of it if the supervisor had not had a real concern for Jimmie's future—a future that could have been filled with despair, dead-end jobs, and years of frustration, because Jimmie is a Negro belonging to that ill-defined category of Americans often referred to as "disadvantaged."

On the advice of his supervisor he had several talks with persons in the personnel department. It soon became apparent to them that Jimmie was homesick. He wanted to return to his hometown in Georgia to visit his mother. It also was learned that Jimmie had not understood that because of the length of time he had been employed by the company, he would not have to quit to return home for a short visit. He was encouraged to take several days of his vacation to see his family and then return to his job. However, had there been less concern about him, or an unwillingness on the part of his supervisor to take the little extra time involved to understand his plight and seek a solution, both Jimmie and the company would have suffered.

While Jimmie's case may be unique in some details, the overall situation whereby managers, supervisors, and personnel people are becoming more sensitive to the special needs of the "disadvantaged" in industry—who in most cases bring with them life-styles very different from those of their fellow workers—is becoming more common as industry seeks ways to provide opportunities for those who otherwise might be unemployable. Men and women who in the past were considered for only the most rudimentary, unskilled work or none at all, are now viewed as potentially valuable human resources that can be upgraded through training to take their places in responsible, productive positions.

By examining some of the historical, legal, and managerial aspects of what New York State Senator Thomas Laverne, chairman of the Committee on Labor and Industry, calls the "manpower paradox"—people without jobs, jobs without people—in. the United States, this chapter will attempt to show what can be done to help alleviate this paradox.

DEFINING TERMS

The manpower paradox is not a recent development.   Decades of societal development, short-run economic behavior, and governmental action (or inaction) in the United States have created problems that only positive, concerted action will alleviate.   Throughout the history of this country (see Appendix A), many positive, constructive virtues grew side by side with prejudices, misconceptions, and myths. Even today, despite the strides made in the fields of psychology and sociology, many people are guided in their interpersonal relationships by stereotypes to the point where it is necessary to define even the most basic terms encountered frequently by the personnel manager.

So before proceeding to examine the upgrading of workers distinguished by their economic position in society or because of their "race, religion, color, sex, or national origin," it may be worthwhile to define some commonly misused terms.   Let's begin with one of the most ill-used and overworked of all—*race*.   Probably no pure race exists in the world today, unless it has been completely isolated from contact with other groups, which is hardly likely because of centuries of exploration and population movements everywhere on earth.   A race, in a workable, sociological context, is "a large division of human beings distinguished from others by relatively obvious characteristics presumed to be biologically inherited and remaining relatively constant through numerous generations" [1].   Three broad classifications of human beings by race are commonly used—Caucasoid, Mongoloid, and Negroid.

Minority group person is a term frequently used as a euphemism for "Negro." But racial characteristics *alone* do not in themselves place persons into minority groups.   (The hundreds of millions of Mongoloids in Asia certainly are not a minority, although they constitute a minority of people in the Western world.)   Rather, according to sociologist Louis Wirth, a minority is

> . . . A group of people who, because of their physical or cultural characteristics, are singled out from the others in the society in which they live for differential and unequal treatment, and who therefore regard themselves as objects of collective discrimination.   The existence of a minority in a society implies the existence of a corresponding dominant group with higher status and greater privileges.   Minority status carries with it the exclusion from full participation in the life of the society [2].

Note that the *number* of persons in a minority group as defined above is not the sole determining criterion of what constitutes a minority.   The number of blacks in South Africa, for example, exceeds the whites, and yet they are the minority group under this definition.   (It is generally true that a minority person—despite personal attributes—will be treated as a member of the minority group to which he belongs.) Where several minority groups exist within a society, a *hierarchy* is likely to develop among them, and each group may be treated differently.   Generally, members of minority groups tend to marry within the group and to transmit characteristics of the group by a "rule of descent which is capable of affiliating succeeding generations even in the absence of readily apparent special cultural or physical traits" [3].

Subculture is another sociological term that is used with little regard for its meaning.   Simply stated, a subculture is related to the general culture of the society of which it is a part, but is distinguishable from it in one or several ways.

Occupation, religion, social class, and age are some of the characteristics setting sub-cultures apart from the overriding culture. Negroes in the United States today are probably better classified as a subculture than as a race, and best classified as a minority group rather than a subculture. An *ethnic group*, on the other hand, is one which as a group uses isolation techniques such as geographical or social barriers to maintain its distinctiveness. It tends to remain distinct if the barriers are kept high. But an ethnic group should not be confused with a race, although in some instances characteristics of each *may* overlap.

Other frequently misused terms outside the realm of sociology relate to groups within the economy of a country. *Disadvantaged* is one of them, and while there are many definitions of it, to the personnel manager it denotes a person (or group) who through membership in a minority group or subculture or for other reasons, has been *denied* access to certain privileges of the dominant society such as a "good" educa-tion, fair hiring practices, and so forth. The National Alliance of Businessmen has defined the disadvantaged in an attempt to establish criteria for eligibility of persons into entry-level jobs programs.

These persons are poor and without suitable employment and are characterized by one or more of the following: school dropouts (less than twelve grades of school completed, with the exception of some Southern schools that graduate students after eleven grades); less than twenty-two years of age; forty-five years of age or older; handicapped (physical, mental, or emotional impairment); and those who face "special obstacles to employment" [4].

Perhaps the most overworked phrase in the entire scope of upgrading minority persons is *hard-core unemployed*. According to the federal government, a person is "hard-core" if he does not have suitable employment and is characterized by one or more of the above five criteria.

The Board for Fundamental Education, an organization that trains the hard-core unemployed for industry, notes that hard-core persons labor under a range of handi-caps such as "race," language, functional illiteracy, lack of job skills, poor health, and in many instances, prison records. The hard-core person is neither from one race alone nor from any single minority group.

Underemployed workers are those who are at work below their skill, or potential skill, levels; they are usually in low-paid, dead-end jobs.

MINORITIES IN THE UNITED STATES

Although many minorities exist within the United States—Negroes, Puerto Ricans, Filipinos, Koreans, Japanese, Chinese, American Indians, Polynesians, Indonesians, Hawaiians, Mexican-Americans, Aleuts, and Eskimos—Negroes as a group are the most visible. First, Negroes make up the largest minority group in the country. Their numbers are estimated at more than twenty-one million or about one-tenth the total United States population. Second, information about this group is readily available from the results of many studies over the years. Third, Negroes have migrated to all areas of the country and have settled in urban areas where industry is concentrated. And fourth, while some minorities such as the Puerto Rican may be of special concern to particular regions or urban areas such as the City of New York, the Negro minority is more diffuse and is likely to be encountered almost every-where.

The great majority of members of minority groups wants to be assimilated into the larger society—peacefully. On the other hand, while most minorities are readily assimilated in our society, racially distinguishable groups, by and large, have been excluded. Assimilation is *not* a one-way street. Reciprocity is the key. And whereas the dominant groups in this country have not made it easy for racial minorities to be assimilated, they have nonetheless granted legal protection to minorities in the Thirteenth, Fourteenth, and Fifteenth Amendments to the United States Constitution, and through national, state, and local fair employment practices acts granting equal work rights to minority group persons. For nearly a century the Constitutional amendments did little to protect the rights or guarantee the equality of minorities. But within the last twenty-five to thirty years, laws and a series of executive orders (see Appendix B) have begun to open the door to opportunity and equality. The Civil Rights Act of 1964 is the most significant piece of legislation in the realm of equal employment opportunity.

TITLE VII—THE CIVIL RIGHTS ACT OF 1964

On July 2, 1964, the long-debated Civil Rights Act of 1964 was enacted into law to become effective one year from its passage on July 2, 1965. Of particular importance to employees in the United States is Title VII of the act, headed "Equal Employment Opportunity." It prohibits overt discriminatory employment practices by businesses (whose employment is affected by interstate commerce) because of race, color, creed, sex, or national origin. The title also sets forth provisions for an appointed commission and enforcement of compliance orders in federal courts. The non-discrimination provisions of Title VII apply not only to employers, but also to employment agencies, unions, and apprenticeship committees in the areas of hiring, compensating, promoting, training, discharging, and gaining union membership. The act prohibits segregated working conditions; advertising for employees on the basis of race, color, creed, etc.; and reprisals against persons filing complaints under provisions of the law.

Although employers, employment agencies, and unions falling under provisions of the act must meet the qualifications of being "engaged in an industry affecting commerce . . . or the agent of such a person" [5], the act applies to nearly every employer of any consequence. The commerce clause is included to give the federal government authority to regulate economic affairs under the Constitution. Past decisions by the Supreme Court and federal courts show that the commerce clause does very little to hold back federal agencies from intervening in economic affairs.

Contrary to what many believed, however, the provisions of Title VII did not go into effect immediately in 1965. Only employers of 100 or more persons were affected in that year. A diminishing scale based on numbers of employees was established wherein on July 2, 1968, employers of twenty-five to forty-nine persons would come under the law. A similar scale was applied to labor unions, also. Now, of course, the law is in full effect, and it is noteworthy that it represents the first time that Congress has outlawed discrimination in private industry.

Besides setting forth rules against discriminatory employment practices, Title VII also created a five-member Equal Employment Opportunity Commission (EEOC) to investigate alleged wrongdoings by those covered by the act. A complainant under the law can file a grievance with the EEOC within ninety days after the alleged incident occurred. The commission is—by law—compelled to investigate the charge and, if "reasonable cause" is found for believing it to be true, to use the techniques of conference, conciliation, and persuasion to correct the situation. Unlike many state fair employment practice commissions, however, if voluntary compliance does not come within thirty days (or within an additional thirty days which can be granted by the commission), a public hearing is *not* held. Rather, the EEOC informs the complainant that it has failed to gain compliance. At his option, the aggrieved person may, within thirty days of the commission's notice, institute a court suit. The case is then out of the commission's hands as it has no authority to provide legal assistance. Under Section 706(e), depending upon the financial circumstances of the complainant, the court may provide him with legal counsel to seek remedies provided in the act such as issuance of an injunction to stop the defendant from engaging in unlawful employment practices, ordering affirmative action which may—not *must*—include reinstating an employee, or hiring one, with or without back pay [6].

If the court refuses to act on behalf of the complainant—or even if court action is under way—the complainant may seek out the assistance of the Justice Department. Title VII states that "Upon timely application, the court may, in its discretion, permit the Attorney General to intervene in such civil action if he certifies that the case is of general public importance" [7]. Thus if the Attorney General agrees that the case meets these qualifications, and if the court allows him to intervene, the Justice Department can take over much of the burden of the prosecution of the case.

Under the provisions of Section 707 of Title VII, the Attorney General is allowed to *initiate* court action when he "has reasonable cause to believe that any person or group of persons is engaged in a pattern or practice of resistance to the full enjoyment of any of the rights secured by this title, and that the pattern or practice is of such a nature and is intended to deny the full exercise of the rights herein described" [8]. Thus he may initiate court action independently of the complainant's suit. Unlike the restriction of "general public importance" which must be present for the Attorney General to intervene in an individual's suit, suits brought under Section 707 carry no such limitation. This enables the Attorney General to bring suit *whether or not* the complainant does. Suits may also be brought where no specific complainant even exists. Under this section the Attorney General must sign personally each complaint and, although he can bypass the EEOC, a "pattern or practice" of discrimination must be shown before he intervenes. This qualification requires more than just an isolated instance of discrimination, however [9].

If an employer, employment agency, or union is found by the court to have committed an act that is unlawful under Title VII—and refuses to comply with the court order—the EEOC can ask that the guilty party be held in contempt, which could mean, under civil contempt proceedings, daily fines and/or imprisonment. This procedure is outlined in Subsection (3) of Section 706 [10]. Other sections of the act under Title VII allow the EEOC to work closely with the Attorney General in civil actions.

A member of the EEOC under Section 706(a) can file a written charge "where he has reasonable cause to believe a violation of this title VII has occurred (and such charge sets forth the facts upon which it is based) . . ." [11]. Filing such a charge requires a subsequent investigation by the commission. Hence the EEOC is endowed with "self-starting" powers. But this does not mean that it has the power to dig up the facts required to file a charge *before* a charge is filed. On the other hand, two factors modify this limitation of the commission. First, commission members can gain cooperation from employees or union members who may be victims of discriminatory practices as well as information from respondents during *informal* investigations. Second, Section 709(c) requires employers and labor organizations to make reports and to keep and preserve records of hiring practices after a public hearing. (Filing reports is nothing new to most government contractors, who are required to make such reports anyway.) Employers who do not comply with the reporting aspect of the law can be sued to comply by the EEOC under Section 710(b). Again, the commission must go to court to gain compliance. If this is done, and the employer still fails to report, he could be held to be in contempt of court. Also, under the federal criminal code, an employer can be fined, imprisoned, or both, for falsifying reports to the commission.

The EEOC may be restricted in how it can obtain compliance information, but no such limitations set forth by the act apply to the Attorney General. He can use resources in the Justice Department such as the Federal Bureau of Investigation to gather information for a possible suit brought under Section 707. If the evidence does not warrant prosecution under this section, but it appears that some action should be taken, the Attorney General may give the information he has collected to the commission which could then file a charge.

Despite the broad coverage and detailed provisions of Title VII, it must be borne in mind that the Secretary of Labor has the most responsibility for seeing to it that federal contractors hire, train, and employ persons on a nondiscriminatory basis. With his power to withhold or cancel contracts he has more powerful sanctions at his command than does the EEOC. He can also refer cases beyond his authority to the EEOC for action.

The Congressional sponsors of the Civil Rights Act of 1964, Title VII, were very careful to see that this legislation would not preempt state fair employment practices laws and commissions *unless* those laws were proved to be inconsistent with the national legislation. Section 708 of Title VII states specifically:

> Nothing in this title shall be deemed to exempt or relieve any person from any liability, duty, penalty, or punishment provided by any present or future law of any State or political subdivision of a State, other than any such law which purports to require or permit the doing of any act which would be an unlawful employment practice under this title [12].

Another section of the act, 709(1), allows the EEOC to cooperate with state and municipal fair employment practices commissions, even to the extent of entering into written agreements not to process charges when state or local commissions are handling the cases (unless, of course, such agreements are found not to serve the purposes of Title VII, in which cases the written agreements can be rescinded).

Two reasons for the passage of state laws were (1) that there was no federal fair employment practices commission (before 1964), and (2) that state commissions can operate in areas that the federal government cannot (notably local service industries and the distributive trades). It also is legal for states to pass such laws and create commissions because the Supreme Court of the United States has ruled that neither the due process clause nor the equal protection clause of the Fourteenth Amendment forbade such legislation. Provisions of the state fair employment practices legislation[1] are similar to the national legislation wherein discrimination with regard to race, creed, color, sex, or national origin is prohibited in hiring and firing, in conditions and privileges of work, in job advertisements, and in reprisals against persons complaining under the law. Employment agencies and labor unions also come under provisions of the law. Exceptions to the law are employers with less than four employees, and churches are allowed to hire employees of their own faith.

Grievance procedures under state laws usually follow similar patterns. A person who believes himself to be the victim of a discriminatory act by an employer, union, or employment agency writes a complaint (usually with the assistance of a commission member) which he is required to sign. A field representative will make an investigation and file a report. On the basis of the report the commission decides whether or not any action should be taken, determined by the presence or absence of "probable cause." Should the commissioner decide that probable cause to believe an illegal act had been committed was lacking, the complainant can appeal the de-

---

[1] In 1945, the New York legislature passed the Ives-Quinn bill which was incorporated into Sections 290-301 of New York's Executive Law. The state is cited often as a leader among states enacting fair employment practices legislation. Similar laws in more than thirty other states have been, in general, patterned after the New York example.

cision, and seek court action if he is not satisfied with the appeal decision. (In actuality, this rarely occurs because of the expense involved and the courts' reliance on commissioners' reports.) If probable cause does exist, then the commission will attempt to remedy the situation through conference and conciliation (private negotiations in which the employer promises to comply with the law), and if these approaches to obtaining compliance fail, a public hearing is held.

In a public hearing several commissioners (usually not including the one who originally handled the case) hear charges by the commission and the reply of the employer. The commission and the employer have the power to subpoena witnesses, books, and records. A majority vote by the commissioners decides the guilt or innocence of the respondent. If found guilty, the employer will be issued a cease and desist order, and he may have to pay all back wages to the aggrieved party, or what he would have earned if he had been hired. Cease and desist orders are not self-enforcing. Therefore, if the employer ignores it, the commission has to seek judicial enforcement. (By the same token, an employer may seek to have the order invalidated by court action.) If the court finds the employer is at fault through substantial evidence, and upholds the commission's decision, it can order the employer to comply with the order and if he refuses, find him to be in contempt of court. However, it must be noted that few cases ever reach the stage at which cease and desist orders are issued [13].

Other important functions of state fair employment practices commissions are (1) the information services about FEP laws aimed at probable victims who are members of minority groups and (2) informing employers, employment agencies, and unions of their obligations under the law. Commissions may also produce and distribute printed material, notices, and so forth, to inform the public of its rights and the services available.

Laws similar to those at the state level have been enacted by more than fifty cities across the country. Between 1948 and 1960, more than forty cities passed such laws, in some instances in lieu of state action. Counties, too, may have fair employment practices acts.

JOB OPPORTUNITIES

Until recent years, management had not taken the lead in finding ways to employ more effectively the socially and economically disadvantaged. No longer so. Through the National Alliance of Businessmen, for example, United States business is engaged in a massive effort to help solve this problem. More than 20,000 companies are participating and more than 100,000 people and jobs are already involved.

Managements are on the move to find solutions to the problem of people without jobs and jobs without people. Voluntary action—positive, affirmative programs—are constantly under review to meet the requirements of changing times. In furthering the principle of equal employment opportunity, companies are striving:

1. To develop new ways of recruiting and hiring people whose educational, economic, and social backgrounds otherwise would show them to be unqualified for industrial employment

2. To establish training programs designed to make up for the deprivations so that the disadvantaged can become productive and, it is hoped, promotable individuals

There are at least three reasons why management is acting in accordance with its professed beliefs in equal employment opportunity:

1. The unemployment of the disadvantaged has become a high priority of management. Although short-term profit objectives sometimes seem to conflict, achiev-

ing better results in improving the utilization of minority people is a continuing goal.

2. Many managers who heretofore believed that they did not discriminate are reexamining their positions. In the North, for example, employers who traditionally have stated that they will hire "qualified" Negroes, now are seeking ways and modifying their standards to "screen in" rather than "screen out" persons having the potential to succeed.

3. Management has become more aware that nondiscriminatory policies established by top management are not self-enforcing. Better ways are being found for conveying the message all the way down the line and, through supervision and training, deep-seated and largely unconscious prejudice at lower management levels less frequently distorts the message.

By taking a practical approach to minority hiring—and without sacrificing profits to any social "do-good" programs—management can benefit from upgrading and increasing its work force during a labor shortage, as well as perform a significant contribution to the community. With ever-increasing percentages of young persons remaining outside the work force because they have either dropped out of school or are continuing their educations in college, it is estimated that by 1975, 145 *skilled* workers will be needed for every 100 that will be available. Nearly six million more teenagers entered the work force in the 1960s than during the previous decade, while the unskilled jobs that had absorbed them in the past were diminishing.

And although extensive training programs are operated by the government and in the school systems, most of the training in the United States is carried on in the private sector. A survey made by the Labor Department in 1962 showed that 2.5 million workers were in company-sponsored training programs. (Cooperative programs of training such as those carried on under the Manpower Development and Training Act, and the Job Opportunities in the Business Sector program of the National Alliance of Businessmen, add significantly to the number of persons in the 1962 survey.)

Largely because of automation, the number and type of jobs opened for the unskilled have been reduced. A decrease in railroad employment of 700,000 persons has occurred since 1947; 168,000 fewer jobs exist in the steel industry today than in 1951; and although over a million more automobiles were produced in 1963 than in 1953, there were 20 percent fewer automobile workers. As the economy continues to grow, more workers will be needed. However, it should be noted that the *major industries* within the economy will move at different rates.

Recent estimates by the U.S. Department of Labor set the number of "chronically poor people for whom unemployment could be an escape route from poverty" at 11 million: 4.5 million from the disadvantaged minorities; 4 million under twenty-one years of age; and 3 million who live in urban slums [14]. These are the men and women who now spend their working lives at the periphery of the urban economy, moving in uncertainty, having job after job with low pay and often with long periods of unemployment in between. The challenge to companies, then, is to open a way for these disadvantaged people into more productive, higher-paid employment.

HIRING AND TRAINING THE DISADVANTAGED

The employer who decides to recruit and train the disadvantaged may find to his surprise that applicants are not flocking to his door. He will learn soon that communication with the disadvantaged person is not always easy. To actively recruit minority people it may be necessary to send personnel recruiters into inner-city areas; cooperate with local groups that refer job applicants; solicit workers by advertising job openings over television or radio; or work with state employment services for referrals of minority applicants. Many innovative approaches have been used to reach the disadvantaged. The Flick-Reedy Corporation of Bensenville, Illinois, for example, operates a van that visits job centers, agencies, and churches. It serves as a mobile interviewing and hiring center. Inland Steel sponsors a weekly television show known as "Opportunity Line," which features one of its black personnel executives. Job openings in the area are announced and viewers are invited to call in for interviews. The show stimulates about 2,000 calls from viewers each week.

Perhaps the most crucial point in hiring the minority applicant, therefore, is the job interview. The undereducated worker is often unable to get over even the first hurdle in obtaining a decent job in our technically oriented society. A simple employment application holds terror for someone who can neither read the questions nor write the answers required by the form. Saddled with his inability to comprehend or communicate the written word, he loses another job even before he has begun. Interviewers are often startled by what they consider to be rudeness, a lack of responsibility, and unconventional (to the interviewer) dress and modes of fashion. What the interviewer must realize is that members of minority groups are usually members of subcultures, also, having different value patterns, mores, and what are commonly known as "life-styles." Such characteristics of these persons are not indicative of their intelligence, capability, or on-the-job performance, however. The interviewer must look beyond the outward appearance and overt behavior (which may be "put on" as a defense) of the applicant and weigh other, more pertinent factors.

Similarly, there is the danger of "credentialism" when interviewing prospective minority people. Credentialism refers to an overemphasis on applicants' formal training. Thus while a high school diploma may be desirable for some types of work, for others it may not be essential. Employers who desire to recruit minority workers should strive to be flexible in their requirements for formal education.

Another danger that exists at the interviewing stage is that the interviewer may "overidentify" with the applicant. While some degree of empathy is desirable, one should not go overboard in trying to make him feel at ease. Disrespect for the interviewer (and others in the company) may result if the company representative tries too hard to identify with him in an artificial way. On the other hand, the interview should not be a time for the interviewer to espouse his theories on how to solve the "Negro problem." Most applicants want to be treated just the same as any other person.

Because the applicant may be functionally illiterate, and for other reasons, standard testing procedures are often meaningless. Thus the interviewer must be able to ask questions and evaluate the interviewee by his verbal replies. Expressions of willingness to work, informal experience or previous training, stated goals, and aspirations are some indications of the applicant's chances for success in training or on the job, however "unscientific" these responses may be. Also, if the interviewer must assist the applicant in filling out forms, this is an excellent opportunity to gain rapport with the job seeker. The use of job-related tests, and application forms, however, may be useful in determining whether or not the applicant may be helped by basic education, orientation to work discipline, and assistance with personal affairs. Inability to make out an application, or poor performance on a test, can alert the company to these special needs.

At least six problem areas exist during the job interview. First, a disadvantaged job applicant is likely to become defensive if he is questioned too directly. He may have been the victim of blunt, direct strings of questions by policemen or credit investigators, and may consider such a procedure punishment or rejection. Second, the applicant probably will not see any relationships between personal questions and job performance, so it is best to keep questions about personal life, domestic problems, and marital status, for example, to a minimum. Third, the interviewee may make mistakes in filling out his application, or may purposely omit information because he does not understand its importance. Thus the interviewer should be wary of embarrassing the applicant when making corrections or requesting additional information. Fourth, the interviewer should make it a point to try to keep up with the expressions and speech patterns often encountered when speaking to disadvantaged persons. It even may be helpful to know a little of the Spanish language. Fifth, unless unconventionalities of dress or hairstyle of the applicant could create a health or safety problem on the job, they should be overlooked. Sixth, applicants should not be forced into revealing arrest records.

Two general approaches to training the disadvantaged are open to industry. The first is business-supported programs carried on within the community. In many cases programs are undertaken in cooperation with local high schools. Students, especially vocational students in their last semester of high school, attend classes for a portion of the school day, and receive additional training in the shops of local plants. Their performance is evaluated by company instructors, reported to school officials, and becomes part of the pupils' records. The cooperative approach may also involve training persons in outside community facilities funded by concerned businessmen. In many communities, instruction in clerical skills, for example, is given in classes conducted by local branches of the National Urban League. The league trains workers and serves as a placement service for graduates. Instruction may include also on-the-job experience for a specified period within participating businesses. Such programs are beneficial especially to small companies that need clerical help, but cannot afford formal, internal training.

Innovative variations of this type of training are being undertaken by many large corporations. In Cleveland, business and the school system have teamed up and are using a General Electric Company warehouse in the inner city as a work-study center to train school dropouts for jobs. In Buffalo, New York, the Iroquois Brewery sponsors a summer program for twenty-five potential high school dropouts, giving them instruction in many phases of the company's operation. Chase Manhattan Bank for several years has operated its Business Experience Training Program which gives potential dropouts part-time jobs and training that encourages them to remain in school. Three out of four participants are hired to permanent positions at the bank.

The second general approach is in-company training. Benefits to the company may include more efficient work; fewer accidents; better communication with supervisors; and increased initiative to perform. Training sessions afford good opportunities to ensure that minority employees understand the company, learn proper work attitudes, and learn what is expected of them in the plant and on the job.

Because "attitudes" of the disadvantaged trainees may be unacceptable, the instructor must be sensitive to different behavior patterns. At times trainees may attempt to provoke the instructor to anger as a "test" of the sincerity of his interest in their well-being. Frequently, they will come to the instructor with personal problems. If he is able, the instructor should offer advice or suggest to the trainees that they take their problems to someone else in the company or community who can be of assistance. The instructor must be also alert to problems that may not be expressed overtly, but which manifest themselves in work or training performance. The story is told of the migratory farm worker who in his first industrial job was performing well, but would frequently and sporadically be absent during the summer months. Investigation into this behavior revealed that the worker was not ill or abusing his job. Rather, he was not coming to work on rainy days because he believed factory workers—like migrant farm workers—did not work when it rained. A simple talk with his supervisor remedied this misunderstanding. Had his supervisor been unwilling to get to the bottom of this absenteeism, a good worker might have been dismissed.

In-company training may be carried on in classrooms, workshops, on-the-job, or any combination of the three. One corporation that has used these methods of in-company training is Eastman Kodak Company.

CASE STUDY: EASTMAN KODAK COMPANY

In 1962, Kodak was one of the first companies to volunteer to join the late President Kennedy's Plans for Progress program, and in 1964, the company began an experimental program to upgrade persons who would not normally have been qualified for regular employment. Beginning with a class of fifteen trainees, the program had a specific goal: To bring these men in one year to a level that would enable them to meet the entry requirements for the company's long-established skilled trades apprentice training program. Besides the regular on-the-job training, the initial group received 221 hours of special classroom instruction which included 80 hours of mathematics, a minimum of 14 hours of writing, 15 hours of reading, 56 hours of blueprint reading, and 56 hours of mechanical comprehension.

Today, the employment and training programs have been expanded and structured differently at the various Kodak divisions. At all sites, programs are designed to help people from Rochester's inner city, many of them lacking in education and industrial skills, upgrade themselves. However, the basic ingredient in each case is training in technical or special skills which will enable the individual to meet job requirements. Training in basic communication skills is also offered to new people who need such instruction and to those already employed who feel their progress in the company has been limited because of a lack of education.

At the Kodak Park Division, the company's largest manufacturing facility, trainees are hired for three basic programs—trade trainee, laboratory trainee, and production trainee.

The trade trainee program prepares young men for work in the skilled trades. The duration of this preparatory type training is up to one year, and can lead to qualification in apprenticeships, or to jobs as skilled trades helpers.

The trainees receive instruction in such subjects as shop and safety practices, shop mathematics, and blueprint reading. Most acquire good work habits. The course includes at least twelve weeks of Hands-On Training (HOT). In the HOT program, while doing needed jobs, they cover some ninety-one procedures to become familiar with hand and simple power tools. They learn also the importance of the normal job-holding requirements of attendance, punctuality, and teamwork.

When they complete the program, qualified trainees enter the regular Kodak skilled trades apprenticeship course—a three-year program. The others are either continued in the special training program, reclassified as trade helpers with continued on-the-job training, or transferred to other areas of the company.

The one-year laboratory program prepares trainees to qualify as laboratory assistants. It provides on-the-job training and classroom work in elementary chemistry, laboratory techniques, instrumentation, and safety practices.

Production trainees are hired for entry-level jobs in service or production work. During their training, which also may extend up to one year, depending on individual abilities, the trainees receive on-the-job training with special assistance. At the completion of the training program—or earlier, if the supervisor feels that the minimum qualifications have been met—production trainees may be classified in the job which they are performing.

Another example of Kodak's special training activities is the Industrial Trainee Program at the Kodak Apparatus Division. This affirmative action program is handled on a direct, on-the-job basis in assembly, manufacturing, or optics operations. The trainee may be in the program from six months to a year. In that time, he is given simple duties and responsibilities, and receives instruction about good work habits, industrial environment, and the requirements of a production department. The length of time a trainee is in the program depends on his progress and the availability of regular jobs. Upon completion, the trainee can be placed in a warehouse, stock handling, or production line job within the area he is working. He might also be placed in another area if there is an earlier opening. This encourages early advancement and versatility.

The opportunity to improve basic communication skills is available concurrently to trainees in these programs through the Board for Fundamental Education (BFE), a private, nonprofit organization chartered by Congress in 1954. BFE has been retained by Kodak since 1966, and hundreds of Kodak employees have participated in classes since then. (Employees with many years at Kodak have also benefited from participation in the BFE program.)

BFE operates a flexible, self-help instructional program designed to develop an individual's potential. In this way, BFE keeps abreast of the needs of the students while offering methods of instruction that give the greatest opportunity to develop the students' abilities to learn. The program upgrades skills in reading, writing, and arithmetic. There are two levels of instruction. The first brings the trainee up from the 0.0 grade (or no education level), to the equivalent of a fourth-grade education. The second level brings the trainee to eighth-grade equivalency in the basic communication skills.

The usual course requires a total of 120 hours of classroom work at each level. The normal format is for trainees to attend classes two hours each day for up to twelve weeks. During the classes, the students and the instructor use a seminar approach. Classes are informal, and studies are related to activities that the student sees and hears in his daily life.

Kodak also is involved in other special training programs such as a clerical training program—Advancement through Clerical Training (ACT)—undertaken in cooperation with the Rochester Urban League, Inc. In the ACT program, girls and women learn office skills such as typing, filing, and office procedures, and attain familiarity with office machinery such as Mimeograph and collating equipment. They also devote some time to learning good grooming habits in the program's "charm school." Black history, office mathematics, and English are taught to the students during their training which extends for a period of sixteen weeks—ten in class and six on the job with participating local businesses. (Several girls are now receiving this training at Kodak and, if they perform well, will be employed by the company.) Refresher courses are offered to graduates who may wish to brush up on their clerical skills.

Kodak also participates in a high school program to prevent dropouts. High school seniors, a high percentage of whom are members of minority groups, are employed by various Kodak divisions for half a day while spending the other half day in school. The students employed at Kodak Park, for example, spend the working portion of their day participating in Kodak's Hands-On Training program and are paid wages for the hours they work. Upon graduation from high school, the students who have done well are considered for full-time employment in Kodak's trade, laboratory, or production training jobs. Almost all the students have done well, school officials report, and about 85 percent of those who have participated have been employed by Kodak. Most of the remaining 15 percent have left for military service.

Kodak also assists in other ways to help keep youngsters in school. Through lecture programs, plant visits, audio-visual presentations, and meetings with guidance counselors, the company encourages youngsters to stay in school by informing them, among other things, of what industry is looking for in potential employees.

For many years the company has had a special cooperative program for high school technical and vocational students. These students also go to school half a day, but their work experience is more in the form of on-the-job training. They are good students who have specialized in a trade or skill during their high school training, and they work at Kodak in their last year or two of school.

Rochester Jobs, Inc. (RJI), which administers the NAB and Concentrated Employment programs in Rochester, is a community-wide organization established in 1967 with the active support of virtually all the city's major employers, including Kodak. It was formed as a nonprofit corporation that would coordinate the efforts of all employers and agencies in the city who are seeking to resolve the problems of unemployment and underemployment. RJI has placed an average of 100 persons a month who were categorized previously as hard-core unemployables. This organization has the support of educational institutions, governmental agencies, churches, and many other public and private organizations concerned with helping the chronically unemployed. More than 100 businesses and industries in Rochester are now RJI members. Many of the trainees at Kodak were referred to the company by this agency.

By the beginning of the new decade, RJI had placed more than 3,550 disadvantaged persons into local industry. Eighty-five percent were hired at rates of $2 or more an hour, and more than 90 percent of those hired are members of minority groups. The RJI program works this way: staff members provide lists of job openings to participating agencies which, in turn, refer applicants directly to employers. Employers also are advised to work with participating agencies under RJI sponsorship.

Another important function of RJI is the presentation of "understanding seminars" through its Employer Education Committee. These seminars have been attended by leaders of business, industry, community agencies, and labor, together with more than 2,000 foremen. The program is designed to create understanding and sensitivity towards the problems of the disadvantaged. As a result of these seminars, some RJI employees have been encouraged to conduct in-plant sensitivity seminars.

SUMMARY

During the past decade the combined efforts of business and government in equal employment opportunity have been directed to overcoming the manpower paradox in the United States. Through federal, state, and local legislation; innovative training and education programs developed by industry; and cooperative programs undertaken jointly, inroads are being made into employing minorities and the disadvantaged. But even though these endeavors are beginning to show many positive results, they cannot—nor are they meant to—be the final solutions to employment inequities. Perhaps they can be best described as the impetus, the first step toward finding better long-term programs that will reach the root causes of the problems. We should hope that today's special training programs will lead us to discoveries that will alleviate some of the current employment difficulties and provide us with knowledge useful in the future, but there is the ever-present danger that today's programs will become permanent and institutionalized. If they do, business and government will be admitting that they cannot prevent the manpower paradox, but must continue to design eleventh-hour programs as new and more difficult problems arise. Thus our efforts today should be looked upon as temporary, allowing society to look around to find more fundamental answers while preventing us from losing ground to increasing numbers of people without jobs and jobs without people.

Industry and government should not have to provide basic education for adults. The elementary and secondary school systems should provide sound, basic educations so that adults are employable when they seek jobs, and so that they have the backgrounds necessary for furthering their educations. They should be able to enter into training programs which are often highly technical. The alternative to today's programs is clear: industry in cooperation with the schools will have to make its requirements known, and assist in developing educational programs, so that young men and women can be prepared adequately for entry-level jobs—at many levels. The long-range approach to alleviating the employment problems facing us today lies with our young people who must learn to understand each other, besides learning job skills so that they can be utilized effectively within society.

APPENDIX A. PREINDUSTRIAL AMERICA

During the colonial period of this country's history, we were predominantly an agricultural people struggling to provide the necessary staples to sustain a growing population. In the colonies of America the land was tilled much in the same way as had been done in ancient Egypt with crude wooden plows. And for the most part, European methods of cultivation were applied in the New World. Staples from the "bread colonies" of New York and Pennsylvania supported the other colonies for many years. Because of the farmers' vital role in the early economy—and survival —of colonial settlements, it is no wonder that they became looked upon as the backbone of democracy.

The farmers' natural right to own land gave them status, social position, and economic security, and encouraged the individualism that is characteristically American. As freeholders, they set the stage for the right to own private property— a right that has been extended to other forms of production down to the present day.

The role of agrarians in America made them a potent force in society because of their influence in government, the dependency of others upon them, and the philosophy of independence that they set forth for the entire country. Such great American colonial leaders as Franklin and Jefferson propounded the concept of the freeholder and agrarian nationalism that characterized early American life. From an eighteenth-century almanac the veneration of the farmer is clearly stated in a characteristic poem of the time:

> To render service, and perfection give
> To this great *Art,* by which all others live:
> To twine the laurel round the farmer's brow,
> And learn to *use*—to *venerate* the PLOUGH [15].

But the colonists also were manufacturers of sorts. Necessities were produced in each household, and until the end of the colonial period, this home production persisted on the farms. Soon, however, artisans such as carpenters, coopers, weavers, and tailors appeared in the growing towns. By the mid-eighteenth century, nearly one-third of all Philadelphia residents, for example, lived exclusively on the income derived from craft work.

Slave labor was employed in the agricultural development of the country—which led to many of the problems facing us today. During the period of active slave trading, more than five million blacks were shipped to America from Africa. And although great losses occurred during the rugged ocean voyages, more Negroes than whites reached the East coast before 1800. Slaves were used in great numbers in dike building to prevent salt water of the incoming tides of the Georgia and Carolina coasts from flooding the rice paddies, and were utilized to an even greater advantage on a year-round basis on the growing tobacco plantations of the South.

But even in these early days, slaves were not all farm or plantation workers. The ablest blacks received special training to become skilled laborers on plantations and in towns—blacksmiths, carpenters, bricklayers, and cobblers. Some slaves with special training served their masters, others were contracted out to private or public employers, and still others were allowed to work for themselves provided they remitted a specified portion of their earnings to their masters. (Expanding industries such as mining and manufacturing called for increased manpower, and thus some slaves worked in quarries, coal mines, iron mills, foundries, textile mills, and tobacco factories. Steamboats and railroads also employed slave labor.) By 1865, there were as many as five Negro mechanics for every white mechanic in the South [16].

The mechanization of agriculture began during the Civil War when thousands of farm laborers were drafted into military service. The resulting manpower shortage compelled farm owners to seek—and employ—labor-saving implements. The use of mechanical reapers during the war, for example, increased 2.5 times from 100,000 to 250,000. New devices such as the iron plow, disc harrow, reaper, and grain planter also came into widespread use. But more important during this period in American history was the shift in emphasis of the entire structure of agriculture after the Civil War. The position of the American farmer as an independent, self-reliant yeoman of Franklin's and Jefferson's time was becoming little more than fiction by the 1860s: The ideal was killed by the shift from subsistence to commercial farming, i.e., the farmers' specialization in a cash crop to be sold in the national or international marketplace. This kind of farming benefited the farmer because he could buy goods from outside producers which were of superior quality to the homemade articles.

But commercial farming meant also that the farmer became a part of a more complex—and impersonal—market, and that individually he has little control over economic factors such as interest and freight rates, supply and demand, or even his own production.

The impersonal forces of the market were soon evident to the farmer in the decades of the 1860s and 1870s when high prices for produce during the war years dropped. In relation to the overall population of the country, farm population decreased, although between 1860 and 1910 the number of farm families increased fourfold. The number of mortgaged farms also increased, but the wealth of the farmers' production in comparison with other sectors of the economy dropped from 50 percent in 1860 to 20 percent at the turn of the century. Tenant farming was on the upswing.

Well into the twentieth century the farmers were becoming the depressed portion of the economy. In the 1920s farmers' incomes decreased, while those of other workers increased. Farmers on marginal lands abandoned thirteen million acres between 1919 and 1924. Between 1920 and 1930, the number of tractors in farming rose from 230,000 to 920,000, replacing 7,450,000 horses and opening up farming possibilities on thirty-five million acres. The large-scale farmer was successful, but his small-scale brother suffered, and the farm population dropped by three million persons between 1921 and 1928 [17].

For our purposes in evaluating the manpower scene and its paradox, the dramatic changes in farming of the middle and late nineteenth century mark one of the beginnings of urbanization, industrialization, and the needs for new kinds of labor. It also signaled the beginnings of the problems of utilization of human resources which faces the businessman today, for the shift to commercial farming meant new population patterns and new labor demands.

Rural residents began moving to urban areas as new job possibilities and the prospects of higher income arose in burgeoning industry.

Industrialization

Two revolutions occurred simultaneously in the world of the late eighteenth century: the American Revolution and the Industrial Revolution in England. In the latter, power-driven machinery was replacing hand-operated tools in production. Workers were in demand and were relocated to plant sites where they worked together tending machines near power sources. Factory towns arose and a new class of workers soon became dependent upon the owners of the new productive capacity.

In America, much of the new technology was borrowed from England and adapted to manufacturing cotton thread and cloth. Corporations began to grow in the early 1800s. More labor and capital were needed, with labor being scarcer. During this period, nearly 90 percent of the population was tied to the soil, and the city dwellers were likely to be artisans who worked within their own shops, or persons who ran small commercial businesses. Few unskilled workers existed, and a labor shortage developed as industry expanded. It is not surprising that a new class began to form from among the farmers who left their farms in the East when they could not compete in the market with their western counterparts. The developing economy also attracted workers from Europe and the British Isles.

By 1840, the value of manufactured goods by new American industry stood at just under $500,000,000, and by 1860 this figure had increased to nearly $2 billion— nearly the worth of agricultural production. The number of inventions patented during a similar period is indicative also of industrial growth. In 1830, 544 inventions were patented; in 1850, 993; and in 1860, 4,778 [18].

The succeeding era between 1865 and 1900 witnessed a fantastic increase in productive capacity. The number of workers in industry jumped from less than 1.5 million in the early 1860s to more than 5.5 million in 1900. Invested capital stood at 12 billion dollars and the annual value of production topped 11 billion dollars. This rate of growth was twice as rapid as England's. And it can be attributed to America's utilization of technology, ingenuity, and adaptability; specialization of labor, industrial organization, and mass production; the availability of raw materials; a favorable government giving encouragement to growth; and internal markets protected by high tariffs.

If corporations were the identifying large business structure of large-scale enterprise in the United States during the mid-1860s, then trusts, pools, and holding companies characterized bigness at the turn of the century. The actual number of individual firms decreased between 1865 and 1900, but total production increased fifteenfold. Two percent of the manufacturing establishments accounted for nearly 50 percent of all United States manufactured goods.

But while this may have been a time of great advancement for the leaders ("captains") of industry, it was far from a boon to the workers or the Negroes. After the Civil War, Negroes became day laborers, wage earners, or tenant farmers. Negroes in occupations other than agriculture began to be replaced by whites and with the gains of the labor movement, white workers got—and for the most part retained—control of jobs formerly held by Negroes.   Blacks also were edged out by women entering industrial jobs in the South, restrictive racial legislation, and the depression of the 1890s.

Profits resulted from cheap labor made possible by unrestricted immigration. In fact, many employers actively recruited workers through agents in foreign countries.   Hence immigrants settled in the cities to work in the factories as the labor demand increased.   Southern Negroes moved north in search of work.   Their numbers in nonagricultural production rose from 275,000 in 1900 to nearly a million in 1920, while the number of those employed as domestics or in personal service dropped nearly 20 percent [19].

With the advent of World War I, labor recruiters from the North were sent into Southern rural areas to bring Negroes back to work in industry.   This recruitment was much like what had been done earlier to attract Irish and Italian workers.   As a result of their efforts and the Negro migrations, the black population in the North and West increased by one million persons as European migration slackened and blacks were displaced from Southern agriculture.   The work awaiting them included a variety of unskilled jobs in the steel, automobile, and meat-packing industries, as well as railroad maintenance, food processing, and needle trades. Despite the unglamorous occupations that absorbed most of the Negro labor in the North, the 1920s were relatively prosperous for blacks as well as whites, with unemployment rates holding nearly equal for both groups.   This did not last long—the Great Depression of the 1930s wiped out many gains that Negroes had made in employment and may have actually set them back—something they could ill afford, especially at that point in the development of the nation's economy.   Devastating to the Negro's position in the economy was the failure of the Southern cotton crop; scant opportunities for employment in the Northern urban-industrial regions, and the movement of whites into the manual, unskilled jobs formerly held by Negroes. Their numbers in manufacturing, mechanical trades, and mining dropped from 1,100,000 in 1930 to 738,000 in 1940.   A similar drop occurred in Negro employment in the wholesale and retail trades from 398,000 to 288,000 [20].

World War II

Unlike the period of the First World War and its aftermath, the Second World War was a greater boon to white workers, many of whom were unemployed throughout the Depression.   The employment of Negroes migrating from the South was not as important as in previous years of higher labor demand.   And the opposition of unionized immigrants who remembered the Negroes' earlier strike breaking was a force with which Negroes had to contend [21].

In certain industries, however, Negroes were able to find work.   Besides their traditional jobs in the iron, steel, and meat-packing industries, they entered the expanding consumer and service industries and construction projects related to the war effort such as airports and military bases.

During the war years, Negro employment increased by about one million workers (exclusive of those in the military).   Many of these had backgrounds in agriculture or domestic service and were employed as unskilled labor.   Some gains, however, were made in semiskilled and skilled trades.   Gains also were made in public employment.   Total employment for all workers rose from 46,500,000 to 53,000,-000 in 1940, and included a broad stratum of ages, and millions of women.   The migration of Southern whites and blacks to war plants involved five million persons *within* the Southern states, while more than 1,500,000 moved out of the South entirely.   What happened to the undereducated workers, many from the South, after the war production boom remains a paradox today: Workers were plentiful and so were jobs, but the gap between them widened.   The labor force became better educated. But technological development created new demands for even higher educational attainments among workers, making it difficult for unskilled, poorly educated workers to find employment. As Garth L. Mangum has so succinctly observed of the postwar changes in the supply and demand for a more sophisticated work force, "All of these trends proved irreversible, but their profound consequences were hidden for nearly a full generation by postwar adjustments and internal competition" [22].

Thus, today, industry is faced with a shortage of skilled workers and technicians on the one hand, and a large number of unskilled, undereducated people in the labor market, on the other. There is a need to provide training for the unemployed so that they will be able to compete for jobs. There is a need to help those who are still in school but may drop out. These tasks are faced by government, education, and industry. Of private concerns employing 800 or more employees, for example, three-fourths had ongoing training programs [23]. This figure is not limited to the training of Negroes exclusively, of course, but certainly they as a group represent— in proportion to their percentage of the population—a major challenge to training in industry.

APPENDIX B. THE LAW AND EQUAL EMPLOYMENT OPPORTUNITY

The first significant moves toward equitable employment policies came with a series of Executive Orders issued by Presidents Roosevelt, Truman, Eisenhower, Kennedy, and Johnson.

In July, 1941, President Franklin D. Roosevelt was faced with the threat of a demonstration march on Washington, D.C., that was likely to attract 100,000 blacks led by A. Philip Randolph, president of the Pullman Porter's Union. The Negro union leader was speaking for hundreds of thousands of blacks who were angered at being excluded from work in government and defense industries since the defense program began in 1940. For example, the proportion of blacks in manufacturing had dropped 1.1 percent (from 6.2 percent to 5.1 percent) since 1910. In fact, proportional decreases had occurred in other areas of Negro employment except domestic services. In 1940, the percentages of Negroes in industry were as follows:

> Aircraft and related parts—0.1 percent;
> Electrical machinery—0.5 percent;
> Other machinery—1.0 percent;
> Rubber products—2.1 percent;
> Nonferrous metals—2.4 percent;
> Apparel—2.3 percent;
> Automobile equipment—3.6 percent;
> Iron and steel—5.5 percent; and
> Ships and boat building—6.4 percent [24].

Meetings were held in an attempt to discourage the demonstration but finally Roosevelt issued Executive Order 8802 in June, 1941. This order—which was to become the root of all equal employment opportunity laws in the United States— prohibited discrimination in government agencies and defense industries. It prohibited discrimination in the above areas because of race, color, or national origin. Both employers and unions were asked to treat workers nondiscriminatorily. Provisions for equal employment under the order were to be included in contracts made by government agencies and government training and vocational programs were ordered desegregated.

Administration of Executive Order 8802 was given to the Committee on Fair Employment Practice within the Office of Production Management. A nominal sum of $80,000 was allotted for the committee's first year of operation. The four members and chairman of the committee, appointed by Roosevelt, held a series of public hearings in various regions of the country to get the President's message across, and they issued directives to try to correct discriminatory employment practices when discovered. But the committee was hindered because no sanctions were set forth in the executive order.

In 1942, the committee was transferred to the War Manpower Commission and abolished on May 29, 1943, by Executive Order 9346.

This subsequent order established a new Committee on Fair Employment Practice in the Office for Emergency Management of the Executive Office of the President. The committee had a full-time chairman—and no more than six members could be appointed by the President. It was empowered to seek assistance from other governmental departments, agencies, and volunteers. The members could work also in cooperation with state and local officials. But most significant, Executive Order 9346 required a nondiscrimination clause in *all* government contracts, not merely defense contracts. The budget for the new committee was increased, also. As with the old committee, the new one could not have its directives enforced by legal process. Again, public hearings were held (or closed hearings in cases involving governmental agencies). "Satisfactory adjustments" were sought where grievances were aired and wrong-doings uncovered.

In August, 1944, the committee began follow-ups on cases "settled" by satisfactory adjustments. The inquiries were made by regional staff members, and by the time the committee terminated its activities on June 30, 1946, commendable gains in minority employment had been made. During the lives of the two committees more than fourteen thousand complaints had been received (30 percent of the appeals were brought by Negroes); fifteen public hearings had been held; five thousand cases had been dispatched through satisfactory adjustments, including forty racially inspired strikes. In 1942, only 3 percent of the work force was composed of minority group workers. By 1944, the figure stood at more than 8 percent. With the end of World War II, however, many of the Negroes who lacked seniority because they were hired late in the war industries were discharged as production fell off and veterans returned seeking their former jobs. And yet the war years for Negroes meant gains never achieved at any time following the Civil War.

The next executive order dealing with fair employment—Executive Order 9980 — was issued by President Harry S. Truman on July 26, 1948. It placed responsibilities for carrying out equitable, nondiscriminatory labor practices and policies with the head of each governmental department who in turn was advised to select a Fair Employment Officer. Persons so designated could appeal their findings directly to the department heads whose appeals were then subject to the Fair Employment Board of the Civil Service Commission [25].

With a change of administrations, new governmental policies for fair employment were adopted. In January, 1955, President Dwight D. Eisenhower abolished the Fair Employment Board and established a five-man committee to carry out Executive Order 10479. The five committee members no longer worked under the auspices of the Civil Service Commission, but reported to the President directly. Under the Eisenhower order, discrimination because of race, color, religion, or national origin against any person applying for work, or already employed, in the federal government was prohibited. The committee could make inquiries and advise the President regarding compliance.

Previous to this, the President on August 13, 1953, had done away with the Committee on Government Contract Compliance, establishing the Committee on Government Contracts in its place. Among this new committee's responsibilities was seeking compliance of contractors and subcontractors in nondiscriminatory hiring and employment practices where government work was being performed.

Between 1957 and 1960, nearly two thousand compliance reviews were completed.

Shortly after his inauguration, President John F. Kennedy issued Executive Order 10925 which created the Committee on Equal Employment Opportunity. This heralded a new approach to fighting discrimination because now the committee was responsible for overseeing the policies of the federal government, government contractors, and labor unions.

Soon after the order was issued, nine large corporations with defense contracts met and promised to comply voluntarily with the President's order. Thus evolved the well-known Plans for Progress program which would eventually gain pledges of nondiscrimination from hundreds of major defense contractors in the United States. Lockheed was the first to sign up for the program and by 1963, 104 additional firms had followed suit.

In other executive orders of 1963, the President gave his Committee on Equal Employment Opportunity the authority to withdraw federal funds from state, local, and private projects that had employment practices contrary to Executive Order 10925. Another order forbade discrimination in hiring minorities for federal projects, especially federal construction projects. A task force soon after, under the direction of the Secretary of Labor, began reviews of employment policies on construction projects involving federal funds. Noncompliance could mean cancellation of contracts.

Another major executive order came from President Lyndon B. Johnson on October 24, 1965, and superseded Kennedy's Executive Order 10925. The Johnson order—11246—did not alter drastically the provisions of the Kennedy order, but it did dismantle the Committee on Equal Employment Opportunity while shifting responsibility for compliance by government contractors to the Labor Department.

Provisions of 11246 prohibit government contractors from discriminatory policies as set forth by previous orders, and require contractors also to take *affirmative action* to employ minority applicants, and treat minority employees without regard to race, religion, color, or national origin. (A subsequent order, Executive Order 11375, expanded the realm of nondiscrimination to include sex.) As part of the program, contractors are required to post their obligations of equal employment opportunity on their premises and signify that they are Equal Employment Opportunity employers in solicitations and advertisements for employees. Compliance with the order is mandatory and contractors must submit to compliance investigations; follow additional rules set forth by the Secretary of Labor in the Office of Federal Contract Compliance, and file reports with the Joint Reporting Committee (for the Equal Employment Opportunity Commission, OFCC, and National Alliance of Businessmen) containing relevant information that is requested. Government contractors also must include nondiscriminatory provisions in subcontracts and follow the orders of the OFCC via the contracting governmental agency to enforce those provisions.

Effective since January 30, 1970, is Order No. 4, signed by Secretary of Labor George P. Shultz, and John L. Wilks, director of the Office of Federal Contract Compliance. This new order sets forth rules for federal contractors and subcontractors (not in the construction trade who employ fifty or more workers on government contracts of at least $50,000), who must develop written affirmative action compliance programs within 120 days from the start of their contracts. An analysis of major job categories must be made at each company facility where government contract work is conducted. Underutilization of minority group members must be explained in each analysis, based on such considerations as minority population in the area around each facility; minority unemployment within that area; proportion of minority people in the total work force of the area; availability of minority group people with skills in the area whom the contractor can recruit; availability of minority employees who could be promoted within the company; anticipated changes in the size and composition of the work force; existence of institutions capable of training minority group people in requisite skills; and the degree of training that the employer is reasonably able to undertake for making all job classes available to minorities. "Identifiable deficiencies" call for the contractor to set goals, and make timetables and affirmative action commitments to correct them. These must become part of the employer's written affirmative action program, and include supporting data and analyses. Support data for the affirmative action program which show the statuses of minority group members must be kept, also. Six categories—officials and managers, professionals, technicians, sales workers, office and clerical, and skilled craftsmen—are identified in Order No. 4 to receive special attention when analyses are made and goals are set by the contractor.

If the government finds the contractor's affirmative action program to be unacceptable, the contractor will be notified that he has thirty days to "show cause why enforcement proceedings under Executive Order 11246 should not be instituted." If the contractor cannot show good cause for the deficiency, or fails to correct it with an acceptable affirmative action program within thirty days, "the compliance agency, with the approval of the OFCC director, may issue a notice of proposed cancellation of existing contracts or subcontracts and debarment from future contracts or subcontracts" [26]. Contractors, however, have ten days within which to request a hearing. If such a request is not made, the contractor will be "ineligible for future contracts and present contracts will be terminated for default. During the 'show cause' period, the federal compliance agency will make every effort to resolve through conciliation, mediation, and persuasion the deficiencies that led to the noncompliance determination" [27].

REFERENCES

[1] Walter, Paul A. F.: *Race and Culture Relations*, McGraw-Hill Book Company, New York, 1952, p. 5.
[2] Wirth, Louis: in George E. Simpson and J. Milton Yinger, eds., *Racial and Cultural Minorities*, Harper & Row Publishers, Inc., New York, 1965, p. 16.
[3] Wagley, Charles, and Marvin Harris, in *ibid.*, p. 17.
[4] National Alliance of Businessmen, *JOBS '70*, Washington, D.C., 1969, pp. 87–88.
[5] Sovern, Michael I.: *Legal Restraints and Racial Discrimination in Employment*, Twentieth Century Fund, New York, 1966, p. 64.
[6] *Ibid.*, p. 75.
[7] *Ibid.*, p. 76.
[8] *Ibid.*, p. 77.
[9] *Ibid.*, pp. 77–78.
[10] *Ibid.*, p. 79.
[11] *Ibid.*, p. 84.
[12] *Ibid.*, p. 93.
[13] *Ibid.*, p. 26.
[14] National Industrial Conference Board: "Managing Programs to Employ the Disadvantaged," *Studies in Personnel Policy*, No. 219, New York, 1970, p. 6.
[15] Eisinger, Chester E.: "The Farmer in the Eighteenth Century Almanac," in Abraham S. Eisenstadt, ed., *American History*, vol. 2, Thomas Y. Crowell Co., New York, 1962, p. 44.
[16] Ross, Arthur M., and Herbert Hill: *Employment, Race, and Poverty*, Harcourt, Brace & Jovanovich, Inc., New York, 1967, pp. 8–9.
[17] Current, Richard N., T. Harry Williams, Frank Freidel, *American History: A Survey*, Alfred A. Knopf, New York, 1961, p. 695.

[18] *Ibid.,* p. 288.
[19] Ross and Hill, *op. cit.,* p. 12.
[20] *Ibid.,* p. 15
[21] *Ibid.,* p. 16.
[22] Mangum, Garth L.: "The Why, How, and Whence of Manpower Programs," in *Annals of the American Academy of Politics and Social Science,* Philadelphia, pp. 51–52, September, 1969.
[23] Somers, Gerald G.: "Training the Unemployed," in Joseph M. Becker, ed., *In Aid of the Unemployed,* Johns Hopkins, Baltimore, Md., 1965, p. 242.
[24] Simpson and Yinger, *op. cit.,* p. 267.
[25] *Ibid.,* p. 299.
[26] News release, U.S. Department of Labor, Jan. 30, 1970.
[27] *Ibid.*

chapter 70

Women, the Handicapped, and Older Workers

JAMES M. KELLY *Dean, College of Business, Idaho State University, Pocatello, Idaho*

In a free enterprise system, such as our own, administrators make employment decisions based primarily upon the expected productivity of workers. Successful placement of women, the handicapped, and older persons, therefore, requires that they be handled in a manner whereby they "fit" the existing work environment and can compete effectively with other workers.

GENERAL SELECTION PROCEDURES

A careful examination of any business organization reveals that it consists of a group of departments rationally determined to accomplish these three objectives: First, the function of the departments is determined. Then as a logical result, the number and the types of jobs to be included in each department are decided upon. This determination is built upon a setting forth of the requirements of each job, or its "job factor." And finally, from the job factors, the employer is able to establish a "job description" (literally a description of the duties and responsibilities inherent in the job); and more important to the selection process, the job specification. The specification is virtually synonymous with the term "man specification" as it depicts the qualities of the desired occupant of the position. In short, the job description sets forth the duties of the job, while the job specification establishes the personal qualifications or the sum of the individual's skills, talents, education, and experience needed to perform the job in an effective manner.

Experience and research suggest that the factors which should be considered in the employment selection process are those of: (1) level of skill needed, which often includes education, experience, initiative, and ingenuity; (2) responsibility undertaken for manipulating material and human resources; (3) physical, mental, and emotional effort required; and (4) working conditions experienced, especially those conditions which are especially disagreeable or hazardous. Unfortunately, many employers neglect consideration of these factors in making selection choices from groups of job seekers, or if they do consider them, they often relegate them to a subordinate position.

EMPLOYMENT OF WOMEN

Female workers represent a substantial segment of the United States human resource population. Recent statistics reveal that women make up approximately one-third of the United States' labor force. Further, the largest segment of these are employed in clerical positions; few enter managerial, professional, and blue collar fields.

Historically, women have received less pay than men for similar jobs. The Equal Pay Act of 1963 amends the Fair Labor Standards Act in an attempt to prohibit discrimination in wage levels on the basis of sexual status. The Equal Pay Act provisions apply to those employees who are subject to minimum wage provisions of the Fair Labor Standards Act. These equal pay provisions apply to those employees whose jobs require equal skill, effort, and responsibility under similar working conditions. Those jobs offering lower rates of remuneration to one sex than to the other are justifiable if that differential is based upon a valid seniority system, a merit system, a system measuring earnings by quantity or quality of production, or on any factor other than sex.

Almost half of the states have laws that prevent discrimination in pay rates between men and women for the same amount and type of work performed. Paradoxically, however, almost half of the states also prohibit or limit night work for women, and proscribe them from working in hazardous occupations. This in some respects may protect women on the job; but simultaneously, it places such potentially burdensome demands on employers that employment opportunities for women are substantially lessened.

John B. Miner observes that:

> The sexes do not appear to differ very much, if at all, in terms of the most important type of mental ability in our society, verbal ability.

Further, he relates that there are in fact important differences in some other characteristics.

> In the area of manipulative abilities, for example, there is evidence that women are clearly superior, both in the speed of their movements and in their accuracy. However, the ability to pay attention visually to some specific object without being disturbed by the surrounding context, an occupational skill of some importance in these days of dial watching and automated equipment, is much more pronounced among males. In fact, men generally do somewhat better than women in tasks related to the spatial and mechanical abilities, apparently because of the differences in what society expects of members of the two sexes. As indicated previously, men tend to be rather markedly superior in activities involving the use of numbers and arithmetic or mathematical reasoning [25, pp. 42–43].

Miner indicates that female employees may develop highly negative attitudes toward change because they fear that the change would upset social relationships in the work environment; and he further relates that women may be oriented toward attempting to gain high scores

> . . . on a specially constructed test when their superior performance might lead to social, rather than intellectual, acceptability. Men, on the other hand, are much more strongly oriented toward achievement and advancement in an intellectual sense.

This pattern, with social orientation paramount among women and achievement orientation more pronounced among men, receives further substantiation from research that has been done with a variety of psychological measures [25, p. 44].

Following another line of thought, Miner states that:

> Another important difference that probably has both biological and cultural origins is the greater aggressiveness of the male sex. . . . Finally, a very important difference between the sexes occurs in the area of emotional adjustment. There is good reason to believe that many more women than men experience considerable emotional distress and that symptoms of an emotional nature are more prevalent among women [25, pp. 44–45].

In contrast, Edwin Flippo postulates that:

> There are many difficulties derived from the employment of women, particularly when women are given jobs normally allocated to men. Some managers feel that the female will be more emotional and sensitive, and, as a result, less objective. There is always the possibility that she will replace some man, thus depriving him of an income necessary to support a family. Her absenteeism and turnover rates are higher than for her male counterpart. Most of these conclusions are, however, based on stereotypes; the only fear which is based on facts is that of absenteeism and turnover; various studies have shown these rates to be higher on the average than those of men [23, pp. 509–510].

Flippo's comments, cogent as they are, should be tempered. Miner clarifies the issue:

> It appears, then, that there are certain types of work for which women are much less likely to be qualified than men, and other types where the reverse is true. This fact may well serve to limit the alternatives open to a personnel manager as he attempts to solve the problems facing him. Thus, if a company employing primarily semiskilled female workers engaged in individual manual assembly tasks, wishes to move to an automated production process requiring primarily spatial and mechanical skills of the operators, the existing work force could constitute a major problem. There is every reason to believe that the abilities required for the change would not be available in sufficient quantity among the present employee group. To prevent this constraint, it would be necessary to either go outside the company, presumably so as to keep recruiting costs at a minimum among the male populations, to find the skills now required or perhaps something could be done to overcome the barrier imposed by the existing characteristics of the present employee group. Perhaps the abilities of the women could be changed [25, p. 45].

The entrance of women into the labor force, especially in professional occupations, will be facilitated by factors such as increased acceptance by society, the opportunity and willingness to take work of increased responsibility, the desire for requisite education and training, commensurate pay as a return for career investment, and adequate facilities for child day care. Experience in some countries suggests that all these are possible in this country [10, p. 12].

EMPLOYMENT OF THE PHYSICALLY HANDICAPPED

Another group of individuals who often suffer discriminatory treatment at the workplace is the physically handicapped. Again, stereotyped thinking, mythology, folklore, and outmoded rules of thumb on the part of employers frequently produce marginal occupational status for those in this category. Experience and research demonstrate that the physically handicapped employee, when properly placed, is equal or better to the normal employee in terms of productivity.

> The major avenue through which physical disorders contribute to ineffective performances is absence from the job, although quantity and quality of output may be affected. And there may even be an increase in uncooperative, conflict-producing behavior, which

occurs with certain kinds of brain disorder.   Handicapped employees have generally proved as competent as other workers, if their handicaps do not bar working at all, but in some instances certain disabilities may contribute to failure on specific jobs.   There are things that the deaf, the blind, those with heart conditions, epileptics, and other handicapped people just cannot do effectively.

A number of physical symptoms, such as headaches, fainting, ulcers, high blood pressure, hay fever, backache and skin disorders are caused, at least in part by emotional factors.   When this is the case, the symptoms and the work disruption are to be expected to be substantially identical to that which would exist if no emotional element were present; only the causation is different.   Yet, to select an appropriate corrective action, disorders of this kind must be differentiated from those due partially or entirely to physical illness or handicap.

Abnormal physical characteristics are those features of bodily proportion and aesthetics that, although not significant in all occupations, may be of strategic importance in certain jobs.   A large man may have difficulty working in a cramped space, as may a small man in a truck cab with the seat far removed from the controls, or an unattractive woman in a fashion modeling position.   Many physical characteristics are less important today than in the past, as a result of strides in human engineering, and the consequent emphasis on designing equipment to fit the human operator, but these factors can become crucial at times [25, pp. 423–424].

EMPLOYMENT OF THE MENTALLY RETARDED

Closely related to the physically handicapped, as regards employer job discrimination, as well as the sources of discriminatory attitudes, are the mentally retarded. This disprivileged group is a potentially valuable and largely untapped labor source. It is estimated that there are approximately 5.6 million retarded persons in the United States.   Of this total retarded population, approximately 4 percent are confined to institutions, and the other 96 percent live in private homes.[1]   Presently about 125,000 mentally retarded are detected each year.   Estimates are that by 1970, approximately 139,000 persons with some degree of mental retardation will be discovered annually.   Further projections suggest that, of the total 6.3 million mentally retarded in 1970, almost 3.7 million will be of working age (sixteen to sixty-four).   Thus, by 1970, 1.7 percent of an estimated United States population of 208 million, and almost 5 percent of an estimated labor force of 75 million, will be of working age, yet be disadvantaged because of their mentally retarded condition.[2]

Today, approximately 3.3 million of the almost 6 million individuals in the United States thought to be mentally retarded are of working age.   These have a higher rate of unemployment, and participate in gainful employment far less than workers of average intelligence.[3]   Many of the retardates residing in institutions and private homes can be competently trained and successfully employed, for although mental retardation implies limited learning ability, this is not always a severe handicap.   One reason is that the employable mentally retarded often realize that their capabilities are limited and, therefore, strive harder to perform their duties very diligently.   They may not aspire to more highly skilled positions, but often perform lower-level jobs—the dull ones—considerably better than workers of average intelligence.

Federal officials estimate that between 60 and 75 percent of the nation's 5.6 million mentally retarded persons can be taught minimum skills needed to hold

---

[1] *The Mentally Retarded: Their Special Training Needs* (U.S. Department of Labor, Office of Manpower, Automation and Training, Bulletin No. 6, October, 1964), pp. 1–6.

[2] Ibid.

[3] Ibid.

jobs as messengers, warehousemen, stock clerks, gardeners, and restaurant workers. The federal government began hiring retardates in 1964 and now employs some 1,700, mainly as laborers, clerks, and mail handlers.[4]

While it is true that mental retardates vary considerably in mental capacity, most can be trained for unskilled, semiskilled, and service jobs. Approximately 2.9 million of the 3.3 million retarded persons of working age (over 85 percent) in 1963 had intelligence quotients between 50 and 70 and were capable of being trained for some of the jobs requiring minimal levels of skill.[5] This means that 110,000 mental retardates of "educable" intelligence quotient are now being born each year, and that by 1970, the birth rate of these "educable" retardates will reach over 118,000 per year. This raises the question of the provision of training for employable retardates. Although there are additional costs for training, substantial reductions of social costs, i.e., institutionalization, follow training periods.[6] If the training program is successful, the cost of institutionalization is reduced. An increase in income tax contributions also may occur.[7]

There are many managers, however, who are dubious about employing these people and who, although they agree with the principle, continue to ask very pragmatic and difficult questions, such as: Are they actually as productive as others? Is extra training needed? How does speed of performance compare? What degree of supervision is needed? What about physical endurance? How do their safety records compare with those of the average worker?

The drift of the research and case analysis findings point to the following conclusions:

When properly placed, the majority of mentally retarded employees perform tasks assigned to them as effectively and as rapidly as do their normal counterparts. In fact, they perform routine and/or repetitive tasks better than do their nonhandicapped co-workers, and tire less quickly.

The use of retarded individuals in repetitive jobs reduces labor costs caused by tardiness, absenteeism, and high turnover.

Since mentally retarded workers enjoy a high degree of job satisfaction on routine jobs, generally do not actively seek promotions, and usually are more strongly motivated than their counterparts, turnover rates are lower. As a corollary, costs of training, retraining, and effecting personnel procedures of the employment process are reduced.

Clearly, there are many jobs for which the retardate cannot be recommended. For example, one would definitely not utilize such an individual to perform a task — even a "dull" one — that might tend to endanger the safety of himself, co-workers, or the public at large, as might be the case should he be placed in charge of a large truck, crane, or pile driver.

On the other hand, the findings set forth above uphold the view that, just as with the nonhandicapped employee, the major factors to be considered in hiring mental retardates are attitude, ability, and the degree of skill required for the specific positions at hand. The primary advantage that they offer to the hirer is that they can be expected to perform effectively and diligently in the dull, routine tasks that

[4] "More Companies Hire the Mentally Retarded to Offset Labor Pinch," *The Wall Street Journal* (Pacific Coast Edition, September 20, 1966), p. 1.

[5] *Mental Retardation: A National Plan for a National Problem* (The President's Panel on Mental Retardation, August, 1963), p. 8.

[6] Theodore Schultz, "Investment in Human Beings," *The Journal of Political Economy,* 70:1, October, 1962.

[7] *The Rehabilitated Mentally Retarded* (U.S. Department of Health, Education and Welfare, Vocational Rehabilitation Administration, April, 1964), p. 2.

offer no job satisfaction to most normal persons. Further, it is possible that the degree of job satisfaction that they encounter when properly placed, and the consequent low turnover, tardiness, and absenteeism rate, may, in all probability, exert a positive effect on the morale of other employees.

A number of states have encouraged employment of handicapped workers by passing a statute that is commonly termed the "second injury clause." This legislation specifies that the workmen's compensation authority will assess the employer only for those injuries that the worker actually incurred within his employ, as contrasted to those experienced prior to the current job. As a case in point—an individual who is partially disabled prior to coming to work for the immediate enterprise and who receives further disablement on the job, will not cause the employer's liability to be commensurate with the total disability suffered to date, but only that portion which was acquired on the immediate job. Only the specific and proximate injury is to be charged to him, and in most states, the disabled worker is paid out of a special state fund, not dependent on the employer's contributions.

If the physically and mentally handicapped are to achieve a satisfactory level of productive and meaningful employment in our complex society, understanding of the problems of the handicapped, especially their abilities and disabilities is necessary. The need arises both in the institutions and agencies responsible for job placement of the handicapped and in the business firms and other organizations who hire these persons for competitive work situations.

EMPLOYMENT OF THE ELDERLY

The Age Discrimination in Employment Act of 1968 bans discrimination based on the age of the applicant, in positions offered by employers of twenty-five persons or more, in those industries identified as belonging in "interstate commerce" by the Fair Labor Standards Act.

The popular myths that "You can't teach an old dog new tricks" and "Older people can't keep up the pace" have a very damaging effect upon the careers of the men belonging to these age groups. Presumably, many are, in fact, unaware of this discriminatory influence and often deny its existence. The effect of this attitude on the individual's self-image and consequently on his performance is usually quite negative. This may have effects, in turn, not so much on what could be done but on what is likely to be done, the way the worker now perceives what he is capable of doing. Further, this usually produces a significant lowering and narrowing of their level of aspiration, often in conflict with long-established desires to fulfill the dictates of responsibilities and position in society. The worker, even though he does not actually possess a disability, may feel that he does, and may attempt to compensate for it, or, on the other hand, to overcompensate for the disabilities that he does have. This, in turn, may accentuate the negative effects on performance of some real disability that might not have arisen had it never been mentioned. If this leads to further self-examination and introspection, the adverse effects may be to bring into consciousness many buried habits, activities, and peculiarities which, if left undisturbed, would have remained in the subconscious, but which now when under scrutiny, break up the normally quiet and efficient work pattern [9, p. 118]. In sum, the influence of the cycle may be to magnify actual disabilities, and/or felt disabilities, many times over.

In many enterprises, young persons enjoy preferential hiring status. In general, employers appear to prefer younger to older employees because they feel that younger workers complete larger volumes of work, are more adaptable to change, and are in better health than their older colleagues. Research shows that advancing age does produce a "slowing down" of bodily actions. In an early study, the main cause of this in older people was focused in the physical movements, rather than in the central thought activities of comprehending relevant data and selecting a proper response [9, pp. 114–119]. This should not be construed to mean that the cause of decline lies more in the motor mechanism than in the central brain processes. It may be explained more in terms of a "conservation of effort."

On the other hand, recent studies indicate that slowing with increased age is a result of declines in the functioning of perceptual and translatory mechanisms controlling movement. In other words, it is reaction time and not movement time that becomes slower with age. The slacking pace with age is due, not to longer time required to execute movements as such, but to time needed for the central thought processes to initiate, guide, and monitor performance. If there is a choice available to the individual between accuracy and speed, older persons tend to shift toward accuracy. Management should consider this in training older people for sensory-motor-type skills, especially if accuracy is of great importance to them. If, however, the time available for completing a task is limited, older people are at a disadvantage [18; 27, pp. 70–108].

It is very difficult to determine whether younger persons (late teens and early twenties) or older (mid-forties to early eighties) do better at specific tasks. If the total quantity of work completed, aside from other performance criteria, is of concern, younger people are, on the average, somewhat better. Older subjects achieve their results with less wasted effort on errors, and might be termed to be more "efficient" for this reason.

There is a tendency for most individuals to increase the amount of planning engaged in, as age advances. Coupled with this is, of course, the popularly held idea that younger people are more likely to act "on the spur of the moment," that is, without serious aforethought. Management should consider this advance thought process of older persons where they are involved in selecting workers for jobs where planning is essential for successful performance. If accuracy is of concern, as where errors are costly to the enterprise, older subjects should be considered as being potentially superior, on the average. Some writers trace the planning phenomenon to an increased carefulness on the part of older behavers [27, pp. 65–69].

One of the central activities in job performance is learning or retention of ideas, habits, and skills. Learning is a process which results from an individual's effort to satisfy a need. Repetition, habit, or drill are not necessary or sufficient prerequisites to learning. On the contrary, only if a need is satisfied will learning occur. Further, the need which the individual perceives may change from one moment to another. Combs reports that a child may seem to be learning to give the appearance of practicing as a means of satisfying another need. Consequently, management, during a retraining situation, must be aware that training and/or retraining satisfies a need for the behaver. The probability of learning in a given case will depend on the importance of the need to learn [22, pp. 193–194; 15].

Learning is, in essence, a product of differentiating one object, idea, or symbol from others; whether it occurs through trial and error, conditioning, or observation, it does not usually take place "all at once," in a flash of understanding, as it sometimes appears to the casual observer. Instead, it is the result of a sequence of previous related differentiations. Management may, therefore, be well rewarded should they choose to investigate thoroughly the lengths of time required for different individuals to learn various skills. They should keep in mind that retained differentiations that are based upon previous perceptions may assist in faster retraining [22, p. 193; 15, p. 264]. The training process may, thus, be enhanced by treating it as a sequential chain—a building-block approach—rather than as one or more isolated events. Studies indicate that rates of learning are greater if the behaver's need is strong than if it is weak. Opportunities for differentiations must not be too limited, of course, or the need, alone and unsupported, will not increase the rate of learning. The need may become so strong, however, that the behaver perceives it to be sufficiently powerful, and other perceptions disappear: the need overpowers him. The implication is that management may attempt to overemphasize the need for retraining and in doing so, lead the trainee to try so hard that he fails [1, p. 4; 22, pp. 194–195].

The peak age for high performance at learning tasks occurs in the late teens or early twenties (depending on the nature of the task) and declines from that time on. However, as set forth earlier, many older people can be trained to achieve satisfactorily for jobs in which younger persons might fail. This suggests that management must utilize careful selection procedures and policies, in order to avoid mistakes in filling positions. Rigid age bars may not be justifiable for many training courses, because, although training may take longer, lower labor turnover of the older workers selected might well offset the cost of extended training [4; 7; 13, p. 392; 24, pp. 516–526].

The method of instruction sometimes has a significant influence on the results of training. In one study, older (above thirty) subjects had fewer errors than younger subjects when the instructions were written, but produced more errors when the method of tackling the problem was demonstrated through physical example. If a trainee is slow to comprehend, he is in a position to refer to written instructions several times. Similarly, if he forgets a detail he can refer back to the written material. This, of course, is impossible when the demonstration method is used, and although the trainee could ask to have the demonstration repeated, it may become embarrassing to do this frequently. On the other hand, it cannot be assumed that written instructions always solve the problem. This is especially the case if the instructions are complex or are difficult for the trainee to understand. In general, if the educational level of the worker is adequate, written instructions should be considered [27, pp. 270–271].

Of further interest is that older subjects learn better by "doing" than by conscious memorization of instructions. In an investigation of this process it was revealed that performance learned through the "activity" (demonstration) method was more rapid than through a written instruction method. Surprisingly, this quicker performance achieved by the "activity method" was not acquired at the expense of accuracy. Accuracy, especially that of the oldest group tested, tended to be higher when based upon subjects trained by the activity method. In some cases, subjects were unable to do the task at all when instructed through a memorization method, but performed reasonably well following training by "doing." Perhaps present retraining programs which emphasize classroom activities should be reviewed to consider possible changes to activity learning [27, pp. 271–275].

Numerous investigations have revealed that shorter training periods produce significantly better training results. This may be attributable to frustration, lack of interest, and apprehension under strange conditions, among other things. Where this is economically feasible and operational, management should attempt to incorporate sessions of limited duration in training programs. However, older workers may not perform as well under these conditions[8] [4].

The results of aging differ widely between one task and another, depending upon the extent to which various capacities are required for performance. Experience factors and organic capabilities must be considered in the case of numerous positions. This does not imply that experience should be granted overriding importance as a selection criterion in these jobs. Frequently, all that is required of the worker

---

[8] Floyd L. Ruch, "The Differentiative Effect of Age upon Human Learning," *Journal of General Psychology*, vol. XI, p. 264, 1935.

is certain specialized knowledge or understanding or skill, and if the individual possesses this, he may be expected to fulfill management's expectations, unless limited by organic disabilities and/or off-the-job "personal" problems.   Any performance improvement resulting from long experience would probably be most useful in the event of rare occurrences—those that confront the worker very infrequently, if at all.   Thus, it appears that management should consider people of all ages for those tasks that are limited in organic or experience requirements [27, pp. 8–15].

The extent of the complexity inherent in job duties has a bearing on utilizing older workers.   Complicating a given task (adding one complication to another in a task) may result in a disproportionate lowering of performance for older people. On the other hand, removal of a source of complexity may, in some instances, result in a disproportionate improvement of performance.   Certainly, the area of job design for older workers has been neglected.   This is unfortunate, especially in some industries where it is the only way of keeping at the job older workers who are still productive, a goal that is especially desirable under conditions of labor shortage [12, p. 47].   Management may be able to save considerable time and effort in retraining older workers if the jobs for which they are retrained, and the job training process itself, are reduced in complexity, thereby bringing many formerly impossible tasks within the capabilities of older workers.   As a by-product, management may discover that a number of nonproductive duties and responsibilities have been eliminated [27, pp. 129–152].

In situations where several data variables must be related together there is a decline of performance with age.   Further, and perhaps even more perplexing, the decline becomes greater with a more complex problem.   This does not mean that older people do not have the insight necessary to relate two variables.   Rather, the limitations lie in the process of gathering and holding firmly in mind that data upon which the insights depend.   In short, insight does not decline, but this necessary precondition for its occurrence does.   In retraining older persons for somewhat complex jobs, time and expense of training can be reduced and job performance enhanced by minimizing short-term memory requirements through the use of "notes" or more efficient coding methods and procedures [27, pp. 192–223].

The performance of individuals of different ages varies in the case of paced or, on the other hand, unpaced tasks, as paced tasks result in lesser performance at an earlier age than do unpaced tasks, where the level of difficulty of tasks remains as equal as possible.   In selecting individuals for retraining, management should consider this phenomenon.   When older workers apply, or on the other hand are being considered for discharge because they cannot keep up with assembly line production, it should be kept in mind that the early fifties is the age at which difficulties with paced industrial tasks becomes important.   On the other hand, the age for encountering difficulties with unpaced activities seems to be about sixty [27, pp. 109–113].

Some fragmentary evidence exists that suggests that lack of education may be a serious handicap for older workers in retraining.   It indicates that workers with substantially identical levels of education differed little in performance, regardless of age.   This finding is tempered since older workers had a lower average level of education and lacked recent school experience.   If educational opportunities are made more readily available for older workers in the future, this serious problem may be mitigated and, it is to be hoped, erased [19].

Employers, especially those in the industrial and construction setting, are highly concerned about accident prevention.   Edwin Flippo indicates that older workers are less prone to experience accidents than are their younger colleagues.   Accidents, of course, are a source of labor turnover.   Another source of turnover is the attitude of the employee. Older workers, in many cases, are less likely to produce substantial labor turnover, inasmuch as they are aware of the discriminatory attitudes held concerning older workers, and as they are more likely to remain on the job than to seek other positions or to change employment for reasons that are significant to younger workers [23, pp. 507–508]. Necessarily, the type of injury potential in a given industry is an important determinant of selection practices. The greatest causes of agricultural accidents, for instance, as age increases, are falls or being hit by a falling or moving object. If possible, older workers should be assigned to jobs and/or work areas where this type of hazard is less prevalent [27, pp. 117–123].

In a study of coal miners, there was a significant positive correlation between accident proneness in the audiovisual and auditory acuity—the accident prone were more likely to possess this attribute in abundance. There was little relation between acuity and accidents in any one particular age group, however. Management should consider a wide range of personal attributes, such as these, in establishing safety programs. The tremendous costs of industrial accidents might be reduced if this information were investigated and made to become more widespread. Contrary to the implications of research at present, many employers probably assign workers with better visual and auditory acuity to hazardous jobs [27, pp. 117–120].

Heavy jobs, especially those that demand a continued effort without intermission, seem to cause considerable difficulty to most older people. Older people are capable of performing jobs in which occasional or discontinuous heavy muscular effort is required, however, provided that they are relatively healthy. Retraining programs and job assignments should take this into consideration, rather than operating on the assumption that older persons cannot perform the duties required [27, pp. 112–128].

SUMMARY

Experience suggests that some segments of the labor force do not participate fully in the employment process, due, at least in part, to mistaken impressions on the part of managers regarding the potential productivity of these individuals. Some of these impressions border on folklore.

Numerous business enterprises have found that women, the physically handicapped, the mentally handicapped, and the elderly are effective workers in a wide range of occupations. When the selection, training, placement, job design, and supervision tasks are properly implemented, persons in these categories often outproduce others. Employers who draw from these sources of personnel frequently find that they have enhanced the quality of the work force, and in addition, they sometimes experience a sense of fulfillment of social responsibilities.

BIBLIOGRAPHY

PERIODICALS
[1] Abel, Lorraine B.: "The Effects of Shift in Motivation upon the Learning of a Sensory-Motor Task," *Archives of Psychology*, no. 205, pp. 1–6, June, 1936.
[2] Auman, Fred A.: "Retraining—How Much of an Answer to Technological Unemployment?" *Personnel Journal*, vol. 41, pp. 505–507, November, 1962.
[3] Fichter, The Rev. Joseph H.: "Career Expectations of Negro Women Graduates," *Monthly Labor Review*, vol. 90, no. 11, November, 1967.
[4] Hoy, George A.: "Maintenance Training," *Factory*, vol. 118, pp. 89–100, February, 1960.
[5] Landay, Donald M.: "Private Pension Plan Coverage of Older Workers," *Monthly Labor Review*, vol. 90, no. 8, August, 1967.
[6] Lundquist, Clarence T.: "The Age Discrimination in Employment Act," *Monthly Labor Review*, vol. 90, no. 5, May, 1968.

[7] McNamara, Walter J.: "Retraining of Industrial Personnel," *Personnel Psychology,* vol. 16, no. 3, pp. 233–247, Autumn, 1963.

[8] McNulty, Donald J.: "Differences in Pay between Men and Women Workers," *Monthly Labor Review,* vol. 90, no. 12, December, 1967.

[9] Miles, Walter R.: "Age and Human Ability," *The Psychological Review,* vol. 40, no. 2, pp. 99–123, March, 1933.

[10] Perrella, Vera C.: "Women and the Labor Force," *Monthly Labor Review,* vol. 31, no. 2, February, 1968.

[11] Rosenfeld, Carl, and Vera C. Perrella: "Why Women Start and Stop Working: A Study in Mobility," *Monthly Labor Review,* vol. 88, no. 9, September, 1965.

[12] Rothberg, Herman J.: "Job Redesign for Older Workers: Case Studies," *Monthly Labor Review,* vol. 90, no. 1, January, 1967.

[13] Ruch, Floyd L.: "Adult Learning," *Psychological Bulletin,* vol. 30, pp. 387–414, 1933.

[14] "The Differentiative Effects of Age upon Human Learning," *Journal of General Psychology,* vol. 11, pp. 261–285, 1935.

[15] Schneirla, T. C.: "Motivation and Efficiency in Ant Learning," *Journal of Comparative Psychology,* vol. 15, pp. 243–266, Baltimore, Md., 1933.

[16] Somers, Gerald G.: *"Evaluation of Work Experience and Training of Older Workers,"* a report prepared for the National Council on the Aging, Chap. 3, III, pp. 24–42, 1967.

[17] Wells, Jean A.: "Women College Graduates 7 Years Later," *Monthly Labor Review,* vol. 90, no. 7, July, 1967.

[18] "Hard Realities of Retraining," *Fortune,* vol. 64, pp. 505–507, July, 1961.

GOVERNMENT PUBLICATIONS

[19] *Industrial Training Programs for Technological Change,* U.S. Department of Labor, Bureau of Labor Statistics, Bulletin No. 1368, June, 1963.

[20] *Manpower Development and Training Act — A Report and Evaluation of Research, Trainees, Training Programs, and Training Activities,* U.S. Department of Labor, Office of Manpower, Automation, and Training, February, 1963.

BOOKS

[21] Chruden, Herbert J., and Arthur W. J. Sherman: "Manpower Requirements and Resources," in *Personnel Management,* South-Western Publishing Company, Incorporated, Cincinnati, 1959.

[22] Combs, Arthur W., and Donald Snygg: *Individual Behavior,* Harper & Brothers, New York, 1959.

[23] Flippo, Edwin B.: *Management: A Behavioral Approach,* Allyn and Bacon, Inc., Boston, 1970.

[24] McGeoch, John A.: *The Psychology of Human Learning,* Longmans, Green and Co., London, 1952.

[25] Miner, John B.: *Personnel and Industrial Relations: A Managerial Approach,* The Macmillan Company, New York, 1969.

[26] Strauss, George, and Leonard R. Sayles: *Personnel: The Human Problems of Management,* Prentice-Hall, Inc., Englewood Cliffs, N.J., 1967.

[27] Welford, A. T.: *Aging and Human Skill,* Oxford University Press, London, 1958.

chapter 71

Long-service and Retiring Employees

CHESTER T. O'CONNELL *Vice President, Industrial Relations, KLEIN-SCHMIDT, Division of SCM Corporation, Deerfield, Illinois*

The employee about whom we are talking in this chapter can be either a man or a woman. Everything in this chapter refers to either sex in the same degree. A long-service employee is identified as one who at the age of fifty-five has been with the company approximately fifteen years or more, so that by the time normal retirement age of sixty-five is reached that employee has accumulated more than twenty years of active employment in the company. A retiring employee is anyone close to age sixty regardless of the number of years of active service.

DIFFERENCE IN TREATMENT

Frequently these employees are treated differently in the same company. The long-service employee is usually rewarded with a longer vacation because of his years of service. Most companies honor long service with service awards of one form or another—pins, watches, or some sort of remembrance. The employee about to retire is not favored with these awards because of his short length of service.

RECOGNIZE THE CONDITION

Either of these employees, the long-service employee or the employee about to retire, can be a problem, but he need not be. Companies are becoming aware that unless some recognition is given to an employee beginning with his last ten years of employment or after age fifty-five, these years could be the least productive of all of his employment. When a company keeps an employee strictly from a moral obligation point of view, it has a depressing effect on him. Poor work and/or less efficiency is the result.

Except the newer companies, who usually do not have long-service employees, most companies are doing something for this older group either consciously or unconsciously. Some companies' programs on a hit-and-miss basis are productive to some degree, but companies which have a definite plan for taking care of the older employee are finding that he can be productive to the extent of his ability right up to the week of his retirement.

WHAT MAKES THE OLDER EMPLOYEE DIFFERENT?

It is the fear of what is ahead which causes the employee to lose interest in his work. It is the approaching retirement for which he is totally unprepared that causes him to resent the company's policy of "retirement at sixty-five." When he attains the age of fifty, he becomes aware of his declining work years and fear develops. When he becomes fearful of retirement, realizing that it is the company that is compelling him to retire, his resentment is expressed towards the company, its supervision, its product, or its good image. In short he becomes a problem.

HIS RESENTMENTS AND FRUSTRATIONS

Thinking that the company will not terminate him before sixty-five, he may barely comply with the rules of employment feeling that he is in some way getting back at the policy that is pushing him out. He resents younger people moving up into positions for which he will no longer be considered. He resents the younger employees' ability to learn newer approaches to modern products and frequently becomes a morale problem, by dragging his feet.

His incentive to advance is gone. Frustrations are setting in. Younger employees are taking his place in the inner circle, and they are learning much more rapidly than he is now able. He knows that he is being tolerated. He is also aware that his health must be guarded and this causes him to be more conservative. His last years at work are spent in not wanting to "rock the boat." He lives in the past with ideas that are definitely out of date. He gets to a point where he is hanging on and becomes an innovator of nothing. Even his boss bypasses him in favor of the younger employee either to do the physical work which he can no longer do or to learn something which he is no longer able to learn. His flexibility is gone, he has no tolerance for new and modern ideas or modern conduct, and all in all he gets the feeling of not being needed or wanted. But nevertheless he hangs on. He hangs on maybe because he would lose so much or maybe because if he did leave the nest he might not be able to get a job as good as the one he has because of his being "over forty."

HE MAY BE WORKING FOR YOU

This is the employee that we must recognize as being in our company. The older the company, the more of these employees there are likely to be. It is important for each company to ask itself how many such people it can tolerate. These older employees cannot be thrown out because the younger people seeing this treatment would have no incentive to stay around themselves. Something has to be done for the older employee so that the work he performs until his day of retirement represents his best efforts. Any programs which will bring out the best in these employees are well worth while.

TOP-LEVEL POLICY

Any company worth its salt will acknowledge that it does have a responsibility to formulate policies which will help all levels of supervision to understand the position of the older employees. Its policies will be in the direction of acknowledging and reciprocating for the employees long years of good service. The long-range goal will be to help him acquire and maintain happiness as long as he is on the payroll and for years afterwards.

ATTITUDE OF SUPERVISION

Line management also must recognize its responsibility to the men who have been good employees for a number of years. They must assign work which will maintain dignity, they must tolerate some unintentional inefficiencies, and they must be made well aware of the fears that are in the minds of the employees who are approaching retirement age.

ACTION BY THE PERSONNEL RELATIONS STAFF

Once the management of the company accepts its responsibilities, the personnel relations staff should implement the policies regarding older employees. They must develop tolerance and understanding of the problems in the minds of immediate supervision or line management. They must work directly with the employee to instill a feeling of being wanted and needed. They must maintain recognition of the employee. They must eliminate fear of retirement, by preretirement counseling. They must maintain postretirement contact. In other words they must be a friend in need as the employee approaches retirement and after he is in retirement. They must eliminate the resentment of compulsory retirement by developing positive attitudes toward retirement. They must develop in the employee the thought that he is not retiring from work but that he is retiring into a life that is full of time to do what he has always wanted to do. A personnel relations staff should have on it a mature and interested person who is capable of developing good mental health in the last years of the employee's work life and the rest of the years of his retirement life.

VARIETY OF APPROACHES

Some companies, both large and small, that are not equipped with a trained counselor are doing something for their employees to prepare them for retirement. More and more in recent years these companies are subscribing to retirement planning magazines which are sent directly to the employee's home. The thought here is that the employee and his wife, through reading, will prepare themselves for retirement. While these magazines, periodicals, and other forms of literature are quite helpful, they nevertheless lack the personal attention that can only be given through group counseling and therapy. Many companies subscribe to these magazines, but they are sent directly to the employee's home under the company's name. Subscriptions start at somewhere between five and ten years prior to retirement. Subscriptions to magazines are better than nothing but they do not approach individual attention. Some companies enroll their senior employees in retirement associations. The employee then receives benefits of the retirement associations plus a subscription to its magazines, and they are able to participate in the association meetings that are held throughout the country. This is an improvement over subscriptions to magazines alone.

PRERETIREMENT PLANNING COURSES

The ultimate in preparing older employees for retirement is a combination of all these efforts. Namely: subscriptions to magazines, membership in retirement associations, and group counseling or group therapy with individual counseling where it would seem beneficial. Progressive companies that have on their personnel relations staff a person capable of conducting group counseling sessions feel that this is the road to go.

Each company varies its group counseling efforts to fit its own plan. Some conduct these meetings at work on company time, others do it in the evening hours on the employee's time. The group can consist of employees alone, or it can be a combination of employees and spouses. Some companies permit the employee to bring his spouse and friends as well. It is generally thought that the ideal size of the group is somewhere between twelve and twenty-two people. The group is kept this size to encourage discussions from the floor.

ONE COMPANY'S PROGRAM

One of the more successful companies in the field of group counseling conducts its sessions in the evenings, one night a week for six consecutive weeks. It is done in March and April when the weather is becoming more pleasant and people feel "spring in the air." An announcement of the group counseling course is sent to the home of each employee who is fifty-five years of age and older. The approach in the announcement is very casual and is the first step toward a positive approach to retirement planning. Spouses and friends are encouraged to attend as well. (See Figure 1.)

COST IS NEGLIGIBLE

At the very first session each person attending is given a blank notebook for taking whatever notes he chooses to make. A slight additional cost is cake and coffee at each session. Beyond these two items there is practically no cost to the course. As the counselor is a staff member, there is no additional cost for his services, and the people attending the course do so on their own time. There are no textbooks and only a minute cost of using the conference room could be charged to the course.

First Meeting: Preretirement Planning

Developing the correct attitude for happy retirement. At the very first meeting, the counselor concentrates on developing a positive line of thinking. He encourages the participants to think in terms of retiring to a beautiful life in which they will have time to do the things that they always wanted to do. He discourages them from thinking of retiring from work but rather he encourages them to think in terms of retiring to a fuller life. To do this he tells them what is ahead for the retirees. He advises them of the many changes that have taken place in our society in recent years which benefit the older or retired person. To name just a few of the changes in society: (1) In many communities the theater permits the retiree to attend performances during nonbusy times at half rate. (2) Golf courses permit retirees to play a round of golf when the golf course is empty at a reduced rate. (3) More and more cities have public transportation available to retirees during the nonrush hours at lower fares. (4) Housing projects are going up all over the country; not only is the government financing and controlling such projects, but also many church organizations are building retirement communities. These homes or apartments run anywhere from taking care of the retiree who has a minimum income in retirement

KLEINSCHMIDT
DIVISION OF SCM CORPORATION
DEERFIELD, ILLINOIS 60015

TELEPHONE
945-1000
AREA CODE 312

WANT TO LOOK FORWARD TO A HAPPY LIFE IN RETIREMENT?

WE CAN'T GUARANTEE ONE, BUT WE CAN HELP!

Beginning Monday, March 23, and ending April 27, those of us who are fifty-five years of age and up are going to be kicking around the idea of retirement.

How about joining us each Monday for six weeks?

There will be

NO textbooks,

NO homework,

NO speeches (unless you want to make one),

just a guided search for what must be considered to better prepare us for a beautiful retirement. Some of the subject matter covered is listed on the attached sheet.

Your spouse is more than welcome to come along and join in. It will be an enjoyable and productive evening for him or her also.

Sessions will meet in the Company Cafeteria. They will begin at 7 pm and be through about 8:30.

Needless to say there is no cost - just a smile and a desire to plan for a better life. It is not too soon to start planning.

So that we may begin to prepare for these meetings, please let us know if you will be with us by Friday, March 13.

If you want any further information, stop in to Personnel and let's talk about it.

Chet. O'Connell

Figure 1.   Invitation to retirement planning course.

to the one who has no financial problems at all. (5) Many states offer fishing licenses to older people for as little as 50 cents or $1 as opposed to $5 and $6 for the average citizen. (6) The city automobile tax in many communities instead of being the customary $10, $20, and $30 can be purchased by any retiree for $1. (7) Even in filing an income tax return, a person who has attained age sixty-five and/or his spouse of sixty-five gets credit for a double exemption. And so the counselor could go on almost indefinitely and show how the senior citizen of today is by far not a forgotten citizen. Efforts to improve their conditions are constantly being made by the lawmakers so as to win the favor of the senior votes. After the counselor has painted the true picture for the senior citizen of the future, he goes a step further to help him acquire the proper attitude.

Helps to acquiring a proper mental attitude.   The counselor will encourage the retiree to develop a proper mental attitude by using as many of his senses as he can. The participants are encouraged to read things that are positive in nature rather than only those "headline stories." The participants are encouraged to develop a healthy outlook on life by seeing things which are humorous, good, and wholesome. They are further encouraged to listen to those things which are encouraging, particularly those speeches or reports which are not only factual but inspirational as well. The counselor will then advise the participants to refrain, not 100 percent but to a great degree, from those magazines or pages of the newspaper which are depressing in tone. Somewhat flippantly but nevertheless realistically he might suggest that if the participants are going to look for news, "Concentrate on the birth notices and wedding announcements rather than the death notices."

Keeping mentally active. The participants are told of the churches of almost all denominations which have fifty plus clubs. Almost every community has golden age organizations. The YMCA has educational courses that are particularly slanted toward older persons. Every community that has a high school has night classes which can prove very interesting to older people. These courses are usually inexpensive and cover such subjects as needlework, real estate, handwriting analysis, investments, dressmaking, cake decorating, and many other subjects that will help to enrich a retiree's life.

Developing and keeping a happy frame of mind. It is generally recognized that once an older person understands and follows the suggestions below he will have acquired the proper mental health necessary for a happy retirement.

1. *Face the facts.* He should accept the fact that he is growing older and that in spite of his gray hair, false teeth, and hearing aid he is just as desirable in the company of his friends as he was in his earlier years provided his outlook on life is a positive one. People in retirement must acknowledge their inability to play touch football, basketball, and those other sports in which they engaged in their youth. However, they can find proper substitutes. Regardless of age they can play golf, swim, walk, and do a number of things that require a moderate amount of physical effort.

2. *Use the mind.* A constant effort should be developed to improve ourselves mentally. This is done by reading, not only books but magazines as well. Enrolling in night school courses, attending meetings, going to exhibitions such as the auto, sport, and flower shows. Speakers, whether they be at church, civic, or social activities, help us to improve our minds. Travel courses and travel itself are very educational and help us to fit in with the crowd much more easily. Retired people should especially expose themselves to things which are different from their normal routine. One should make a point of subscribing to a different type of magazine at least every year.

3. *Have a goal.* Care should be taken lest the retiree become as a ship without a rudder. If he has direction he will know where he is going at all times. To accomplish this he should have a goal. He should have a goal not only for tomorrow and for next month but even for next year. With the fulfillment or the attainment of each goal the good feeling of success will help him over some of the rough spots.

4. *Be available to help others.* With additional time on his hands, an effort should be made by the retiree to be useful not only to another person but also to society itself. When there is a need for his help, he should strive to be ever available. However, this desire to be helpful to others should never give him a license to meddle in other people's affairs.

5. *Keep up to date.* At this period in history many changes are taking place. Transportation systems and religions are changing. Housing, work habits, leisure time, even sport games have changed. If the retiree insists upon living in or constantly talking about the good old days he will be taking a shortcut to the good old people's home. By becoming part of the changes that are going on he will stay alive and attractive to others rather than become rocking chair material.

6. *Don't pass the buck.* If the retiree does the best he can with the knowledge he has at the time and accepts the results, he is in a position to take full responsibility for himself. By not blaming others, or the times, or the government, etc., he will avoid being labeled an "old man."

7. *Be forever thankful.* If he does not have it now, he should develop the ability to be thankful. Once he can count his blessings, the next step is to be able to declare them aloud. The person who is able to say to his spouse "I am thankful that I have a wife who loves me" will make himself and his wife happy. The person who is able to say, "I am thankful that I truly have the desire to be tolerant," spreads another ray of sunshine and everyone likes the sun. An audible expression of thanks should be one of his habits.

By following the above seven suggestions, one cannot help but acquire the proper mental attitude that will carry him until his retirement and after retirement into a state of happiness. With these suggestions anyone can enter a new stage of life with confidence.

Second Meeting: Leisure Time Converted to Happiness

At the second meeting of preparation for retirement the subject matter might be leisure time. The experienced counselor will point out that leisure time plans are an individual matter. Ability to enjoy plans will change from time to time, and therefore one must be willing and able to change plans which are not working well at the moment. As an example: A retiree might think that his retirement will be one golf game after another, day after day. However if it should rain seven days in a row, it would behoove him to have something else to occupy his time. A person who thinks that retirement is going to be one journey after another may do well to prepare himself for the time when he may no longer be able to drive a car. A grandmother who thinks her retirement will be spent in unlimited hours with her grandchildren must prepare herself to realize that these grandchildren someday are going to grow up and that other interests than their grandmother may prevail. The more one does to prepare himself with many interests after retirement, the fuller his retirement will be.

What he should do. For a key to what might be the best way for the prospective retiree to occupy himself in his leisure time, he might ask the following questions: What have I always wanted to do and never had time for? What do I really enjoy doing at the present time? If I have a talent for something, is it feasible in my retirement that I pursue these talents? What is it that other people think I do well which in my retirement I will still have enough money to continue doing? Which of the interests of my friends do I wish I could develop for myself? Finally, but certainly not the least of all, which things do my spouse and I both enjoy doing together?

The answer to the above questions will give one some idea of where he should start in developing interests to occupy his leisure time. The retiree should pursue as many of these as he can. He should attain as much variety as possible. His final list should permit him to get some physical exercise, to enjoy some relaxation, to expose himself to the friendship of others, to be a spectator, to stimulate himself mentally, and to be useful in some manner. If his final list will enable him to accomplish these things and if he is still within his financial budget, he will have found his niche in life. He need never fear boredom.

Third Meeting: Is Working in Retirement for Me?

At the third meeting of preretirement planning the experienced counselor will point out the relationship between work and play. To people taking the course who are currently employed, work can have many different meanings. While it is generally thought that people work for money this is not true in all cases.

Why people work.   Many of the leaders of our country are men of wealth, and yet they work as hard as or harder than people who have to work to live.   Examples of people who do not or have not worked for money are Howard Hughes, the men in the Rockefeller family, the men in the Kennedy family, and ex-President Johnson while President.   These men worked hard but not for the money.   Some people work because they feel either that they want to contribute something to society or that they do not want to be stagnant.   They feel that people will look up to them if they are employed, and therefore they are able to maintain a high degree of self-respect.

Dedicated people.   People whose lives are dedicated to the service of others seldom are engaged in such activities for the pay involved.   This group of people is getting out of work the satisfaction of being helpful to others rather than money.   Examples of such people are ministers, priests, rabbis, teachers, social workers, nurses, etc.   To them work means dedication.

Some people work for the enjoyment they get from what they are doing.   The pay is secondary, as evidenced by the fact that many who are engaged in working for enjoyment are people of wealth.   There are many people who play in orchestras for the sheer enjoyment of music.   The same is true of people in the other performing arts, racing car drivers, and even famous lawyers who take on cases which permit them to become completely involved in an issue, even though there may be no pay at all.

Some people work because it is the best way they know to be with others.   Most often these people derive a great deal of satisfaction and pleasure from being with others most of the day.

There is even a group of people who work because they have nothing else to do.   And rather than sit around the house, even if they are well able to do so financially, they prefer to keep occupied and they do it by working.

Work if you choose.   The skilled counselor will point out to the retirement planning class that there is nothing wrong with working after retirement.   It does not indicate that the retiree was not frugal in his earlier years.   It does not mean that he was not prepared for retirement.   It is not a disgrace to be gainfully occupied.   If people want to work in retirement it is entirely up to them.   The retiree, if he is going to work, should decide inwardly his reason for working.   If, on the other hand, the retiree does not choose to work, it behooves him to determine what it was that he did get out of work, so that in his retirement he can find a real substitute for what work meant to him.

Substitutes for work.   If he worked exclusively for money it will be hard for him to find a substitute in his retirement to compensate for his loss of pay.   However, if in his employment he enjoyed the respect of others, he can still enjoy this position by being a leader; by being fair with all those with whom he will be coming in contact; by being honest, diplomatic, and tolerant of others.   If he is all of these things, respect of others will continue to come his way.   If in employment he truly enjoyed what he was doing, then in retirement there is now an even better chance to do the things that he really enjoys doing.   There will be more time available and the selection will be unlimited.

If employment during his work life permitted him to be of service to others, then in retirement he should have no trouble getting a substitute for that dedication. A substitute can come in many forms, including doing something for the blind, taking a boy fishing, showing a girl how to sew, babysitting for someone who needs our help—the list goes on forever.   If besides earning a living in earlier years, he found that working kept him from being bored and considered it an ideal way of passing away the time, he should conscientiously try to keep from being a burden to himself. With additional free time it will be required that he plan a daily routine.   He should lay out a program for regularly occupying himself on say Monday, Wednesday, and Friday. He should awake and retire at regular times and eat at regular intervals. By setting routines for himself, he only has to fill in the gaps. This can be done by regularly corresponding with friends, choosing hobbies to be performed at certain times, etc.

If in addition to the pay of his work life he enjoyed the social life that comes with working with others, then in his retirement he may consider joining various organizations, thereby gaining exposure to the company of others as much as possible. By doing this, he will not miss that element of satisfaction that work gave him.

Is it play or work?   Play, unlike work, is never a burden because play is something we do of our own free will. The retiree should determine what work means to him and substitute the correct remedy in the form of play. The skilled counselor will point out that the income of a retired person can be increased by either full-time or part-time work. If income can be derived from working at a hobby or an intense interest, then the work will be more like play. For example, a personnel director who enjoyed playing golf and in his retirement secured a part-time job as a starter at a golf course found himself in seventh heaven. Then there was the truck driver who enjoyed umpiring and refereeing at baseball, football, and basketball games; in his retirement he secured a part-time job driving a school bus, including driving the athletic teams to the various games. While he did not officiate at the games, he did enjoy watching them, and besides he got some pay for it. There is also the story, and it is a true one, of the highly skilled cabinet maker who was also a bachelor. During his work life he spent his vacations fishing in the far north, and in his retirement he spent three months of every year in that same area as a guide. All these people got part-time jobs in their retirement and were extremely happy at them. What they were doing was more like play.

Fourth Meeting: Money Matters

Income can also be derived during retirement from selling items produced as a hobby. The list of things that can be made in the basement or workshop and sold through gift shops is unlimited. And if the retiree has any skill at all at his hobby he will be able to convert it into income without really working.

The retirement planning class should be told that while income during retirement under age seventy-two has a limit before social security is affected, most people feel that at some time this limit will be discontinued. If this ceiling is erased, then those people who will be retiring a few years from now should plan now about whether or not they are going to want to work. If work is important to them, it may be best for them to work at something that they really like to do in their retirement. The job possibilities for the elderly are practically unlimited now, and the list of opportunities seems to be growing all the time.

Income from social security.   At this fourth meeting of the retirement planning course, it is fitting that other money matters be discussed if time permits. Some companies and counselors invite a representative of the social security administration to the course to give an explanation of the social security benefits which the retiree is going to enjoy. However, even though the presentation may be a very good one, the information given today may be all wrong the day the employee retires. For this reason and this reason alone, having a representative from the social security office is not recommended. It does an employee no good to learn what benefits are now when he is going to retire five years from now. Most anyone in the personnel relations department of a company is well enough equipped to give an estimate of benefits and to spell out the percentage difference when a person retires early. Since social security benefits are of individual concern, the participants should be encouraged to contact the social security office directly and individually for a determination of their own benefits. They should also be advised about when applications should be made for these benefits.

Company pension plan. It is at this meeting that the company pension plan is explained in a general way. It is suggested that each participant consult individually with the personnel staff for an estimate of his own retirement pension.

How to lessen the shock of a greatly reduced income. Income during retirement is usually less than during work life. If the retiree estimates that his income during retirement is going to be as much as $2,500 less than his present income, the following is a way to minimize the shock of his reduced income.

From his fifty-ninth birthday to his sixtieth birthday, the employee should keep track of all his expenses. This record should be in detail and should account for every dollar spent, although the cents may be rounded off to the nearest dollar. A record should be kept of all money spent for the house, car, clothes, pleasure, food, contributions, recreation, medical bills, etc. On his sixtieth birthday, therefore, the employee will know with reasonable accuracy what it costs him to live at the present time. He is now in a position to see clearly what adjustments he is going to have to make. If he is serious about making this adjustment gradually he will set up a budget for the period from his sixtieth birthday to his sixty-first birthday, cutting his present budget by $500.00 over what it actually cost him to live in his fifty-ninth year. He can then set up his budget for the period from his sixty-first to his sixty-second birthday, reducing it $1,000 below his budget for his fifty-ninth year. Between his sixty-second and his sixty-third birthdays he should reduce that same budget by $1,500.00. Between his sixty-third and sixty-fourth birthdays, the cut should be $2,000.00. And between his sixty-fourth and sixty-fifth birthdays, his budget should be cut by $2,500.

This program will accomplish two things. First of all it will show him that he can live on less than he is making and will get him accustomed to doing so. It will better prepare him for living on less money. Second, if he saves all the reductions that he made, he will have an extra $7,500 in cash. This will go a long way toward cleaning up any outstanding debts, and if there are no debts, it will permit him to buy, without installment payments, those things which he is going to need during his retirement.

Fifth Meeting: Relocating in Retirement

Whenever the subject of retirement is discussed, some people automatically think that retirement is moving to another climate. There is no doubt that there are some advantages to moving from a present location, but there are also some disadvantages. Very few people in their retirement move from a warmer climate to a colder one. Most people, if they move, are relocating to the South, the West Coast, or the Southwest area of the country.

Advantages of moving. What are the advantages of moving? (1) A warmer climate is likely to mean a longer life. (2) More time can be spent out of doors. (3) Living in a warmer climate is an easier, more relaxed type of living. (4) Depending upon where one locates, it usually means lower living costs. However, the congested metropolitan areas do not offer this advantage. (5) It is easier to make new friends and engage in activities when one is not confined indoors because of inclement weather. (6) In a more relaxed atmosphere, the retiree is much freer to do what he wants to do, as it is not necessary to comply with someone else's ideas of what a grandparent should do. (7) Moving away from his present location permits him to get away from overly protective children. (8) Because of modern expressway systems throughout the United States, the trip "back home" is not too difficult. (9) If he relocates he can select the area that will give him the climate he wants. (10) He can select the community that has the recreational activities that he desires.

(11) He can move to a town of his own choice, whether he prefers a large one, a small one, a college town, or a small country community. (12) He can select new, bright living quarters for himself. (13) Finally, he can select the religious or cultural environment that he desires. It can be seen therefore, that moving does have some advantages; however, before any move is made it is strongly suggested that the retiree spend at least one full year in the location he selects before investing his money in a permanent home.

Advantages of not moving. Not all people find that there is an advantage to moving. Some feel that staying where they are gives them most for their retirement. What are the advantages of staying put? (1) The retiree knows what he has. If he is not a particularly adventuresome person, the unknown may be frightening. It may be better for him to stay where he is with the ashes of a burnt mortgage. (2) Most likely his family and many of his old friends are still close by. Not everybody relocates. His family ties may be close and if he has a circle of friends adequate for himself, he may not want to try the unknown. (3) Even though the living cost may be higher in his present community it may in the long run be more economical. The cost of moving some distance away could be a very appreciable amount, which he would not have to spend if he stayed where he is. (4) If he is going to have to work to increase his income during retirement it may be very advisable for him to stay in his present location. Undoubtedly he knows his way around better, and he has friends and relatives who may be able to help him find work. Having to find employment during retirement in a strange area can be a very harrowing experience.

Counselor must keep up to date. The experienced counselor will point out to those in his retirement planning course that there is no one answer to the question: Should I move or should I stay where I am? It is a very personal, individual decision. What is good for one may not be good for the other. But if the retiree does consider all the advantages and disadvantages of relocating, he will be able to make a wise decision for himself. The counselor will have learned either by reading or by actually visiting various locations those things which are attractive to retiring people. He will caution them about buying land sight unseen, for five dollars down and five dollars a month. He will be able to tell them what happens at these land sale dinners and how pressure is put on particularly the older people to "sign now." He will also be able to tell them about the many legitimate retirement communities in which there are many people living very happily. In this category, just to mention a few, are the Sun City locations in Arizona and Florida; Dreamland Villa in Arizona; Leisure World in California; Whispering Oaks in McHenry County, Illinois; Willow Estates in Elgin, Illinois; and the many communities sponsored by churches. The Baptists, Presbyterians, Catholics, etc., all over the country sponsor retirement communities. The counselor, to do the best job for his older employees, will have this knowledge, and relaying it on to the employees will help to allay their fears about what lies ahead in their retirement.

Move in with the children? While on the subject of where to live in retirement, the counselor will also include some thoughts on living with the children. He will note that except under unusual circumstances, the retired couple is far better off living alone if they are able to. And he will caution retirees against giving their money to their children in return for "perpetual care." In this arrangement, if by any chance the retired couple lives longer than the children think has been paid for, they may find themselves eventually placed in old peoples' home.

The knowledge that he will not be a burden to his children in his later years can be one of the most appreciated gifts to his children. If children are permitted to raise their own families with their own money, they will have satisfaction in having accomplished successfully their own obligations and without interference from the old folks. At the time of retirement it is proper that the apron strings be cut if they have not been already. The counselor will advise the employees to tell their children as far ahead as possible that, upon retirement, the retirees will be on their own and plan to live independently of their children so that both generations can live the way each of them wants to.

Sixth Meeting: All Other Subjects Relating to Retirement

The sixth meeting of the retirement planning course can be devoted to all the various miscellaneous subjects which have not been covered in the first five meetings. Among these subjects the counselor should include the adoption of hobbies, life insurance policies and how they may be converted to improve retirement living, and the various frauds that are continuously being perpetrated on older retired people. Some time should be spent on how to maintain proper health during later years of life.

Medicare. It is almost certain that at this meeting the subject of Medicare will be brought up. A general explanation of what it covers and what it does not cover should be given; however, the experienced counselor will avoid too much detail because by the time the employees are ready for retirement the detailed provisions of Medicare as well as social security will have changed.

Publications. The employees will be told about various publications that are circulated primarily for increasing the happiness of retired people. Copies of *Harvest Years, Modern Maturity,* etc., will be available at this meeting.

Marital relations. The experienced counselor will also cover the subject of marital relations during advanced years. What one can expect and not expect in a present marriage, or one entered into in later years, should be adequately discussed.

Wills. Another miscellaneous subject which should always be discussed is whether or not to make out a will. The local bar association usually has brochures on this subject, which are quite informative and helpful.

It is at this last and sixth meeting of the retirement planning course that any subject which is interesting to any participant is discussed. Anything not covered in previous meetings is covered. It is at this meeting that frequently the counselor himself broadens his own knowledge.

What we have seen in this chapter is a way to make the older employee, to the extent of his ability, a productive employee rather than one whose morale and efficiency are declining. It is believed that in addition to monetary rewards, courtesies, and benefits which come with long service, the employee will become a minimum problem if the fears of the future can be eliminated. A good retirement planning course could be more helpful in maintaining employee morale than many of the dubious benefits that are showered upon him by some companies. Any single company who has upwards of ten people retiring each year would do well to develop a program of preretirement planning. Small neighboring companies may find it advisable to sponsor a joint program for their older employees. Personnel associations might consider sponsoring a course particularly for their smaller members. If a retirement planning counselor has to be engaged annually from the outside, experienced people are available at nominal costs.

In conclusion we should treat the older employees the way we ourselves would wish to be treated. We would want to be taken care of properly at the present time, and if we are prepared for the future we need have no fear for the present or the future. This is nothing more than the obligation of a good company, even though the dividends are great and the cost is small.

SINCERE PHILOSOPHY—A REQUISITE

No matter what gimmicks, policies, or benefits are used to motivate the older employee they will all be for naught unless he is convinced that the true underlying philosophy of the company is one that protects his job security.

The foreman of one company refused to attend the annual service banquet because he could not find it within himself to fuss over his employees one night and crack the whip with threat of job security the next 364 days. The company philosophy must go deeper than the surface at executive level.

YOU HAVE "SALESMEN"; USE THEM

Companies that have the ability to communicate their concern for the older employee are the ones that need not be concerned with motivation. Retired employees who contribute some of their happiness to the company for which they worked can be a big morale booster if they are not only permitted but encouraged to visit the plant, to "Come back to see us," so to speak. Their visits do not greatly disrupt production, and really only those who have a good feeling for the company actually come back "to see the boys or the girls."

People still at work appreciate the opportunity to learn firsthand how the retiree is doing, to ask a few questions about what is unknown to them, to be able to set their own minds at ease. After all, the company cannot be such a bad place to work if retirees still have the desire to remain attached to it after they leave.

Far-sighted companies have policies which make it possible for retired employees to come back. A happily retired employee can do more in one visit to keep a working employee motivated to do his best for the company than a good personnel man can do in weeks.

AN INCENTIVE + A REWARD = A COMPANY GAIN

One company has before its executive board a proposal designed to improve and keep alive the morale and motivation of its exempt salaried employees who receive no overtime pay for hours worked beyond a normal day. If approved and put into effect it will accomplish more than just aid in "firing up" the employee.

The policy, simply stated, grants vacation in addition to that which the employees are normally entitled. These extra vacations are as follows:

At age sixty, he will receive three extra weeks of vacation.

At age sixty-one, he will receive four extra weeks of vacation.

At ages sixty-two, sixty-three, and sixty-four, he will receive five extra weeks vacation.

At age sixty-five he will be retired.

All the extra vacation must be taken either immediately before or immediately after the employee's regular vacation. This is the only restriction and is necessary to accomplish the end for which this policy is proposed. It is felt that the extra vacation being over and above what is now considered appropriate will cause no ill feeling if it is placed at normal vacation time.

The company figures to accomplish the following results from the extra vacation policy:

1. Being an added something in recognition of age and service, it should be a morale booster and a motivator.

2. Being associated with age, it comes at a time in life when health can stand an additional "get away for a while."

3. A rested man will be able to do almost as much work in ten months as he could in eleven months of fight with health and job.

4. It compels the employee to train a substitute, to designate and prepare his successor.

5. At the employee's retirement, there is no gap in knowledge, experience, or authority when the position changes hands.

Needless to say, the extra vacation must be taken as time off away from the company. No one will be permitted to work through it and receive extra pay.

This policy after it is approved will be watched carefully with the expectation that the results will be very favorable, and then consideration will be given to extending it to other classifications of employees.

VOLUNTARY PHYSICAL EXAMS

Another policy that indicates concern for the older employee and pays dividends in the form of attitude, effort, and motivation is the simple offer of a complete physical exam to all, beginning at age sixty. This is not compulsory but is made available free of charge, with the results made known only to the employee. To further assure the employee that the company is only concerned with his well-being, the employee selects his own doctor. Usually a liberal maximum fee is specified, and seldom is this abused.

The reaction to this policy is always favorable, and if it is adopted as outlined above, the employee will inevitably advise the company if the results of the exam are unfavorable. Where an employee at age sixty or above knows his health is good, he is not afraid to work at his fullest capacity and to be a real living part of the good company he works for. On the other hand, if a danger signal is evident from the examination the company will certainly want to take whatever precautions are necessary.

A physical exam by a company doctor, whether compulsory or not, accomplishes nothing to motivate the employee. His suspicions far outweigh the sought results. Having the physical exam must be at the option of the employee, and he must be able to choose his own doctor.

PROMOTION AND DEMOTION

A general pattern is evident among companies with regard to promotion and demotion. Beginning at age fifty-five employees are considered less and less for promotion. Occasionally an exception is found, but by and large companies look for their promotable material in the thirty- to forty-year bracket. If an employee has not "made it" by fifty-five he may as well forget it.

Companies will try to keep him as a productive and efficient contributor to the operation and will form policies that are designed as rewards or incentives to maintain an employee's level of contribution, but seldom is the average man of fifty-five or over considered for greater responsibility leading to even more responsibility. He is not the one selected for grooming for the future.

An employee with both years of age and years of service is demoted only at times of economic necessity. A policy to the contrary when a company is enjoying normal business conditions would be disastrous for morale, motivation, productivity, and efficiency. If a company has to demote an employee, the reason should be so serious that termination is really called for. Unless an older employee is let go, he should be helped to attain retirement and be a company booster all the way.

PENSION PLANS

Pension plans invariably permit early retirement. This feature was meant to be at the option and discretion of the employee. It never was meant to be an easy way for expelling an unsatisfactory employee. Rather than use it as a way of termination the company would do well to concentrate on improving instead of removing the employee.

It does not necessarily follow that because there are some benefits that come to an early pensioner they are adequate for him. His retirement is usually geared to working until full retirement at age sixty-five. Forcing early retirement on an unprepared employee will have the same effect as a mild explosion among the employee's friends who are still expected to look to their company for fair treatment and to give their all. They will not do either.

WAGES AND SALARIES

There is nothing in the "book of fair treatment" that says that the paycheck has to increase with regularity. Older employees realize this although the younger work force may not. To stop a salary or wage increase because of age or because the employee cannot go anywhere else is wrong. To continue increases which are not deserved is equally wrong. The more paid, the more is expected. If the decision to increase or to freeze is a just one for the individual, he may be agreeable to accepting the decision, knowing that he no longer has the carrot out in front of him which could cause his collapse in trying to get it or justify it. It must be realized that people are mature at age fifty-five and that most of them want fairness above anything else. While it is nice for him to be paid more than he is worth, he will accept his true value to the company if it is explained to him.

When a man reaches the top of his salary bracket he should not only be so advised but complimented as well. Everyone likes to reach the top of any goal, and the older employee is no exception. The top of the bracket is his goal and reaching it creates a sense of accomplishment and fulfillment. With fair treatment in other respects the older employee at the top of the bracket is no problem. Instead he can be the best morale booster the company has. The author knows of no company that exceeds the top of the bracket because of age or length of service.

Part 16

Communicating to Employees

chapter 72

Corporate Policy, Programs, and Communications Media

THOMAS A. KINDRE *Senior Vice President, Hill and Knowlton, Inc., New York, New York*

THE FUNCTION OF EMPLOYEE COMMUNICATIONS

Communication is considered a function of modern management. Communicating with employees is a most important aspect of that function. Employee performance, vital to the success of any enterprise, is importantly affected by how well employees can identify their own goals with those of the company. Helping them to do so is the central objective of employee communications programs.

To be fully effective, a communications program must (1) be properly organized and integrated into the structure of the corporate enterprise, (2) have the support of top management to operate in a climate favorable to free and open exchanges of views and attitudes, and (3) have continuity.

Management's credibility is established when a regular schedule of communications is maintained, helping employees to understand the significance of bad news as well as good. If communications are confined to crises, employees will become skeptical of management's motives and its interest in them.

Studies of employee attitudes show that the individual in a corporate enterprise has a need to identify with the organization and to be assured that his particular role is essential to the success of the group effort. A steady program of well-planned communications helps to fulfill both needs.

PROFIT-ORIENTED PROGRAMS

Communications programs should not be regarded merely as corporate window dressing, nor should they be based simply on the nebulous concept of "building workers' morale." The editor of a company newspaper or the manager of employee communications who takes that approach to his job may find he is expendable when the organization is caught in a cost-price-profit squeeze.

The principal purpose of internal communications is to help management operate the business more successfully. Placed in this perspective, communications programs can be created and implemented with a mixture of factual and persuasive articles, with presentations aimed at bolstering or changing employee attitudes toward the company and helping to solve problems confronting it.

There is ample evidence that programs planned to attain specific goals and fully backed by management can be instruments for making money rather than gimmicks for spending it.

For example, many firms are plagued by a high rate of employee turnover. The cost of recruiting, training, and carrying new workers during the early period of low productivity adds up to a formidable sum annually in a large organization. Research should be able to disclose the reasons why employees quit. A number of the reasons usually can be eliminated by a properly constructed communications program. Such a program can counter suspicion and uncertainty with facts. At the same time, it can foster recognition of employee achievement and help workers identify worthwhile personal goals with those of the company. If communications can reduce turnover rate by only a few percentage points, they contribute to profitability.

TANGIBLE RESULTS A MUST

Every facet of a business enterprise must show tangible results to justify its existence. Initiative and imagination are required to sell a company's products or services to the consuming public. The identical elements are equally essential in selling the company to its most important "public"—its employees.

Motivation experts agree that people tend to be cooperative when there is an acceptable reason for their cooperation. Sound information programs can convince workers that their future security and advancement are directly related to the company's prosperity and growth. When that task is handled skillfully, the department of employee communications becomes an indispensable component of a successful business.

DEVELOPING COMMUNICATIONS OBJECTIVES

The first, most crucial step in setting up a communications program is to establish objectives. Objectives, practically speaking, take many forms. Some are specific, some general. The most useful combine both long- and short-term goals. Most important is that they be thoroughly thought out, realistic, and understandable, and that they have the approval of top management.

The following steps will provide a useful guide to the process of developing practical and meaningful objectives:

Through consultation with top management, determine their views of corporate objectives.

Through interviews with various members of management, gain as much information as possible on present and expected problem areas.

Consider how employees will need to be motivated in order to achieve corporate objectives and help solve corporate problems.

Formulate objectives in terms of employee motivation.

Submit draft objectives to management for approval.

Circulate approved objectives to all management and supervisory levels.

Further refine objectives by developing lists of themes or categories of communications content aimed at achieving them.

EXAMPLES OF CORPORATE OBJECTIVES

Broad Objectives for a Large Company

A giant corporation, a leader in developing new chemical products, has four major objectives in its master plan of employee communications:

To build the individual's pride in, and identification with, the organization.

To foster understanding of the organization's nature, problems, and needs.

To increase understanding of the individual's role and function within the organization.

To encourage participation in efficiency measures.

Company with Many Branches

An airline with more than 100 offices and facilities throughout the United States charts these communications objectives:

To promote a feeling of "family" unity among 40,000 employees in scattered locations.

To keep employees and their dependents informed about company policies, programs, and future plans.

To report on industry-wide developments which affect the company.

To build pride in the company and understanding of management problems and decisions.

Labor-oriented Management Objectives

Companies in basic industries with a strong tradition of unionism often are troubled by sharp conflicts in attitudes between management and blue-collar workers. A mining company, after studying areas of misunderstanding among employees, decided it wanted to get across the following seminal ideas:

General business conditions affect company operations.

Automation creates, not eliminates, jobs by cutting costs which, in turn, stimulates consumption.

Responsible unionism is a stablizing economic force.

Steady work and steady pay are linked to the company's profits and progress.

Profits are the source of social and economic advances.

Productivity is the source of profits.

Community-oriented Objectives

A large, diversified organization that acquired a new company in a small town found the previous management's policies had aroused a good deal of hostility among residents of the community. To establish favorable acceptance of the company and promote rapport in the community, special objectives were built into the communications program:

Participation in civic events.

Donations of equipment for vocational and commercial courses in high school.

Recruiting programs and part-time jobs for students.

Executives and supervisors to serve on nonpolitical committees, on company time.

Open house meetings, lectures by visiting authorities on social and economic issues.

Periodic surveys underscoring the company's importance to the economy of the community by showing:

1. The proportion of its payroll to the town's total income.

2. The importance of employees' expenditures to local merchants.

3. Business given to small suppliers in the area, extending the benign influence of the company beyond its plant.

Other Generalized Objectives

To stress the interdependence of employee, organization, and community.

To gain support for specific projects.

To recognize individual achievement as an incentive for others.

To promote employee understanding of benefits and of personal aspects of his work.

PRACTICAL COMMUNICATIONS: SOME EXAMPLES

The best piece of advice that can be given to the director of a communications program is: Think like a member of top management. The end purpose of every department is to contribute to the corporation's success. Creative, imaginative ideas can be as valuable to a company as brilliant production and sales programs.

Costly Losses Cut

A 50 percent decrease in eye accidents in a plant manufacturing heavy equipment promptly followed an article in the company paper reporting the hazards that could be averted by using a new type of safety glasses.

A food-processing company's insurance costs were being pushed through the roof by a soaring rate of accidents among its car fleet salesmen. The editor concentrated on driving safety themes and ran tips from the AAA and National Safety Council for correcting common mistakes on the open highway. The accident rate was reduced 80 percent, although mileage increased 52 percent. And the company saved substantially on insurance charges.

Labor Trouble Averted

Exorbitant demands by an independent union for wage increases threatened a company with a damaging strike. The director of employee relations prepared a series of brochures explaining in simple terms how the competitive system works, and indicating where the company stood among its competitors. He also prepared a chart, which was enlarged and posted prominently throughout the plant, showing that employee salaries accounted for more than 60 percent of the operating costs, with stockholders receiving less than 5 percent on their investments. The company president credited the campaign with persuading the union to settle for much lower, more realistic increases.

Labor Force Held Intact

An electronics company moving its base of operations from Los Angeles to a smaller city was worried that many skilled workers would be reluctant to pull up stakes and disrupt their families. Since the company was not in a position to offer such inducements as salary increases or full moving expenses, management feared that fully 30 percent of its personnel would not make the change. (This was during a period of high employment in the industry.)

The editor of the company newspaper initiated a campaign to persuade employees to move. He ran a series of articles describing the schools, shopping facilities, climate, and recreational and cultural advantages of the new location. He ran interviews with some people in the advance party who had shifted to the new location and were commuting temporarily to Los Angeles. As a result, employee departures were held to 14 percent; only two key supervisors did not follow the company.

Sales Up, Costs Down

A chemical company developed a new product that marked a sharp improvement in controlling the growth of weeds along highways. The editor of the company's technical magazine wrote a feature article describing the principle of the product and reporting on tests conducted before it was put on the market.   The article was read by the highway director of a state which never had done business with the company.   Its first order was for a carload of the product.

Another company making precision instruments was plagued by high returns of products that did not function properly.   After a series of features in the company newspaper on individuals in the quality control department and the importance of their work, customer returns and complaints dropped 80 percent.

THREE-WAY COMMUNICATIONS

A viable system of employee communications does not operate on a one-way switch from the president's office.   Three interlocking circuits should be built into it to transmit information and opinions up, down, and laterally.

In a large corporation, management insulated on executive row from problems, gripes, and frustrations, from ambitions and personality clashes among employees, can easily lose touch with the psychological climate.   To learn what employees think about their work and the organization, the communications program must be conceived as an intelligence network for feedback and danger signals of potential trouble.

The key factor in enlisting the support of employees is attentive listening to their comments and opinions—then acting on them when they are valid and useful.   Contrary to the suspicions of some choleric critics of labor, employees are not determined to revamp high-level policy.   All they want is to have their views and complaints taken seriously by top managers.

Formal statements of company policy and major management decisions are best explained in internal newspapers and letters.   If they include only management views, however, employees often feel the chief officers are talking down to them instead of soliciting their opinions.   In addition, the intimacy of face-to-face meetings with executives, at least occasionally, provides an opportunity for venting views.

Supervisors' Roles in Communications

Unfortunately, supervisors who are closest to the rank and file generally are weak links in the upward chain of communications.   They are not necessarily chosen for their skills as communicators; in too many instances they suppress expressions of honest opinion as implied criticism of their own ability.

Management must demonstrate that an employee in no way endangers his or her job by speaking out.   A good deal of patience may be necessary to lend an attentive ear to tales of woe and harebrained ideas, but it is the only way to convince employees that management values their opinions.   One organization considers this so important that it offers middle-management personnel free sixteen-hour courses in oral communications skills.

Upward Communications

Two methods effective in stimulating an upward flow of communications at departmental and company-wide meetings are:

Provide paper and pencil so employees can jot down questions which occur to them during an executive's speech.   At the conclusion he answers them off the cuff.   The questions are anonymous, of course.

Encourage employees to submit in advance questions which a panel of executives answers at open meetings.

The advantage of the first method is that spontaneous answers seem more convincing and candid than a carefully worded response.   The second means helps control the inevitable loudmouths who are enchanted by the sound of their voices and try to monopolize the floor.   Also, there is time to frame answers to tricky, difficult questions.

One of the best methods for probing employees' attitudes, however, is for top managers to walk about the plant and offices and speak to workers.   There is no adequate substitute for face-to-face discussions.

Lateral Communications

The failure in many large organizations to maintain open channels of communication linking all departments on the same wavelength adds up to staggering losses of time and money.

A corporation is built on the great interdependence of its various functions, yet there is a common, persistent tendency to neglect the integration of pertinent information.   The inevitable result is confusion, misunderstanding, internal rivalries, and a lack of coordination among units doing related work.

It should be a rigid rule that all essential information concerning every phase of a company's operations be distributed to all department heads and their supervisors.   Verbal reports are not good enough; they usually are garbled and distorted in transmission.

Formal written directives should be issued as soon as orders are received or management reaches important decisions.   Overall operations should be described in summaries that are distributed weekly to promote company-wide coordination.

PUBLICATIONS AND THEIR CONTENTS

The most significant change in employee communications in recent years has been in the editorial content of company publications.   The social chitchat once spoon-fed to employees has been largely scrapped in favor of more solid fare.

Surveys consistently show that employees want substantive information that directly affects their job security, wage scales, and chances for advancement.   They want to know the company's plans for future growth, new products, projections of sales and profits, news on what competitors are doing, the effect of news events and legislation on operations.

Content Related to Objectives

Following is an example of objectives translated into story themes:

To build the individual's pride in, and identification with, the organization.   Plant products provide a valuable contribution to the public.   The research program is outstanding.   The company provides training to upgrade employees.   Management respects personal dignity.   Employees enjoy liberal benefits, good working conditions, and a high degree of job security.   The plant is a good force in the community.

To foster understanding of the organization's problems and needs.   Its size is determined by its function.   Large and small business are interdependent.   Huge investments in research and production facilities make possible huge contributions to the nation, benefiting everyone.   Improved technology is the key to plenty.   Profits provide jobs and security.   Oppressive taxation can kill incentive and limit growth.

To increase understanding of the individual's role and function within the organization.   It has no existence apart from people.   Its performance is the sum of all individual efforts.   The modern employee possesses a high degree of skill and special knowledge.   The worker is responsible for the successful operation of complex equipment and processes unheard of only a few years ago.   Membership in an organization makes possible feats impossible to attain by the individual working alone.

To encourage participation in efficiency measures.   Cost reduction keeps product prices down, markets expanding.   Conservation of materials is the first step in meeting competition.   Quality workmanship is the foundation of job security.   Suggestions for improving efficiency keep a plant up to date and progressive.

Bad News and Good News

Employees should not be told only of good news.   Awareness of a company's problem may gain their sympathetic understanding and cooperation in correcting an adverse condition.   Employees always should be informed of all news, good and bad, before outsiders hear it.   Unchecked rumors of a company crisis can do more damage than disclosure of the truth.

Management sometimes may be reluctant to communicate as fully as it should in certain situations, such as an impending merger, a cutback in the work force, a shift to a new location or legal action brought by a regulatory agency.   Employees, however, have a valid stake in such developments.   The communicator should counsel management on the value of bringing such information to their attention.

Controversy

Until a few years ago there were rigid taboos against using company publications and other communications media as vehicles for stating management's position in labor-management disputes.   Among a growing number of companies, the taboo is rapidly disappearing.

The National Labor Relations Board repeatedly has affirmed management's right to challenge union allegations by presenting its side of a dispute to employees.   The company's story should be told, vigorously and forthrightly, where it does the most good—in its own shop.

The Audience for Communications

The audience is difficult to determine in a large organization that includes professionals, blue-collar workers, and office staffs.   An editorial mix aimed at all groups may be diluted so thinly it contains substance for none.   Most companies produce separate publications for management.   Where there is considerable disparity among employee groups, some firms publish several different editions.   If this is not practical, a mixture of articles appealing to different groups can also make for successful communication, though in less concentration.

COSTS OF COMPANY PUBLICATIONS

So many variables—staff salaries, circulation, use of color, distribution charges—govern the cost per issue of internal newspapers and magazines that only an approximation can be given.   The following representative costs in each category are for tabloid-size newspapers handed out to employees biweekly and for monthly magazines (8½ x 11 inches) sent through the mail (as of 1970):

NEWSPAPERS

Pages	Circulation	Cost per Copy
4	1,400	18¢
4	9,000	9¢
4	31,000	8¢
6	1,000	20¢
6	35,000	5¢
8	30,000	6¢

MAGAZINES

16	15,000	32¢
24	8,900	50¢
24	55,000	20¢
32	12,000	60¢
32	27,000	33¢
32	60,000	25¢
52	10,000	70¢

MEETINGS

The written word is the basic tool of communications, but meetings providing face-to-face verbal exchanges with employees are highly effective—if planned carefully. Such group sessions, involving the interactions of people, can give a sensitive manager a better barometer of employee attitudes than any other facet of a program.

Meetings should be conducted regularly, optimally once a month for the entire labor force and biweekly for departments. The sessions, lasting no more than one hour, should be held during working hours to ensure full attendance and to forestall complaints of intrusions on leisure time. The benefits a company can derive from such sessions will more than compensate for any production loss.

Planning Meetings

Experience has proved the best results are obtained by following certain procedures. The purpose of the meeting should be stated in advance in the company paper or in notices posted on bulletin boards. If management has nothing to say, skip it. Although the last fifteen or twenty minutes should be reserved for questions from the audience, there may be occasions when management prefers not to answer them. In that case, the departure from the usual practice should be announced in advance.

There is one "must" that never should be neglected: Any change in company policy or procedure that affects employees should be announced at a meeting. Also, when employees are agitated by alarming rumors, the truth should be told at a meeting—even though it may confirm their worst suspicions.

General meetings should be conducted by an articulate executive, preferably one with a sense of humor. If none is on the staff, it is a good investment to have a few men take courses in leading discussions.

Types of Meetings

Supervisor and workers. Should be open discussions of problems relating to their jobs and explanations of the economics of the business. If the supervisor cannot answer a question, he should promise to find the answer, if at all possible, before the next meeting.

Departmental. Often organized on a series basis, with each one addressed by a company officer or a specialist in some phase of the operation.

Company-wide. Useful for promoting a unity among the entire labor force by commenting on problems and prospects. It is important for the company's chief officer to appear fairly regularly at mass meetings. Even if he is a retiring type and an ineffectual speaker, he should say a few words at least to show his interest in the employees, to whom he may be a shadowy, aloof figure. After a brief statement, he then can turn the discussion over to a competent leader, who should be a top executive.

Follow-up

Résumés of meetings should be posted on bulletin boards or carried in the company newspaper to help interpret the purposes of them for employees. If suggestions from the floor helped to influence a management decision, employees will be gratified to know the part they played.

An excellent way to evaluate the impact of meetings is to distribute cards to employees and ask them to rate a session as good, indifferent, or dull. More important, leave a space for comments. Stress that the cards should *not* be signed. Analysis of the cards can give management valuable insights into employee attitudes and the psychological climate in the company.

OTHER MEDIA AND METHODS

A wide variety of new techniques have been added to time-tested materials available to communicators. Some are designed to transmit news quickly, others to provide background information, while still others are useful for a variety of communications jobs.

There are so many items in the communications kit that it is impossible to describe them fully. The following summary reviews several broad categories of tools. Detailed information on each method can be obtained from the National Industrial Conference Board and a number of other organizations that publish reports on business practices and procedures.

Electronic and Visual Aids

Films and television have been adapted to business use with excellent results. The universal appeal of motion pictures can be capitalized on by showing films prepared by nonprofit organizations on such topics as safety, plant security, and health protection. Films also are extremely effective in training salesmen and technicians.

Many major industries have produced films on broad social issues—pollution control, how automation creates new jobs, the importance of active participation in the democratic process, advances in research and technology sponsored by private enterprise and the nation's economic structure.

Few small companies can afford to produce their own films, of course, but filmstrips can make a comparable impact. A firm can assemble at low cost a series of still photographs showing its history, the activities of its divisions, and demonstrations of new products, which will be useful for induction programs and other specific campaigns. If the synchronized commentary is spoken, it will be more effective; however, it can be recorded on tape.

Closed-circuit TV, a relatively new development, is the most effective addition to employee communications. It is very useful to a company with branches throughout the country for telecasting from one central point explanations of new technical processes or product lines.

A novel use of closed-circuit TV has been made in training salesmen. A tape is made of a trainee's approach to a prospect, then played back immediately. It points up graphically flaws in his speech, personality, and presentation that should be corrected.

There are innumerable visual aids on the market useful for training technicians, displaying products, and explaining charts, blueprints, sales areas, merchandising problems, and the organization of a large company.

Institutional Announcements

The oldest device for disseminating company news—the bulletin board—still is the one in widest use. More than 85 percent of the firms surveyed recently resort to bulletin boards for announcements. Newsletters and statements sent to stockholders—financial reports, explanations of policy—are often also distributed to employees. Ads in local newspapers beamed mainly to employees usually are more convincing than statements in company publications.

In-house Publications

Booklets explaining the benefits offered to employees are distributed by virtually every large company. Procedure and organization manuals stress company objectives. A dictionary of industrial terms is a useful feature. Humorous cartoon books can effectively convey company messages to production and clerical staffs.

Surveys

Attitude surveys are invaluable for exploring employees' attitudes and possible misconceptions about a company. They should be conducted by outside consultants who have the professional knowledge and objectivity to plan the survey and weigh the answers. Anonymity must be promised—and observed scrupulously—to elicit complete candor from respondents. Merit rating interviews are another extension of surveys.

Recreational and Social Activities

The scope of such programs depends entirely on the money a company wishes to spend. Goodwill is intangible but valuable. It can be cultivated by open houses, family nights, civic celebrations, and clubs for long-time or retired employees.

Contests

Friendly rivalry for modest prizes stimulates participation in company activities. It also can be a source of ideas in sales, slogan, safety, art, and photographic contests. That venerable institution, the suggestion box, has returned savings in untold millions for American industry. It should be given strong boosts periodically.

Giveaways

Slogans and inspirational messages can be circulated inexpensively by giving away such useful items as matchbooks, auto stickers, calendars, blotters, diaries, almanacs, eyeglass wipers, and vacation kits.

EVALUATING PUBLICATIONS

The communicator who does not review and evaluate his performance periodically is groping in the dark without direction or purpose. Management wants results for its money. The communicator must be able to furnish tangible evidence that he is interpreting company policy effectively.

There are four methods for appraising the effectiveness of employee communications, which the communicator should, over a period of time, utilize in varying degree.

Two approaches are more scientific and reliable than the others, though all are helpful. The communicator needs as many yardsticks as possible for measuring the value of his program.

1. *Top of the Head.* Intuition, casual observation and informal interviews are helpful in measuring effectiveness, but since they involve subjective impressions, conclusions must be drawn carefully. Spot checks will tell whether the paper is discarded quickly or taken home for careful reading. Employees can be asked for their honest opinion of certain stories—which the editor rarely will get. He can compile figures on the response to contests or free offers. Phone calls about controversial articles also may be revealing.

2. *Content Analysis.* Content analysis involves measuring the amount of space devoted to various categories of information in each issue of a publication, then figuring the cumulative totals for the year or a fairly extended period. The chief

value of such a box score is that it tells a communicator what his editorial "mix" is and shows him how it compares with the ideal proportions he originally set for himself.

The contents of company publications may include many types of material: general news and features, personals, club and organization activities, sports, technical and economic stories, company policy, safety, products, employee benefits, civic and charity, classified ads, public affairs, and government.

The communicator should decide, when his objectives are approved, what categories of material the publication should contain and in what ideal proportion. He will not be able to obtain that proportion in each issue of a publication, but content analysis will show him how well he is doing over a period of time.

3. *Readership Surveys.* Questionnaires investigating readers' reactions to a publication, the attention certain stories command, and preferences in content are a standard technique. Whenever feasible, it is advisable to have an outside consultant prepare and process the questionnaire.

Although the forms are returned unsigned, care must be exercised in choosing and wording questions so respondents do not give the answers they think management wants to hear.

If polling all employees is too expensive, scientific sampling techniques must be applied to make sure participants are selected on a completely random basis and reflect a statistically accurate and representative cross section of the labor force.

Finally, raw figures are misleading if they are not carefully interpreted. It should be remembered that the purpose of communications is to instill or strengthen certain attitudes in employees and to bring certain types of information to them. The communicator must, in effect, construct a grid between what employees want and what management needs, then strike a balance in each communications medium.

Standard questions in a publication survey cover:
- Frequency and degree of thoroughness of readership
- Circulation among other members of the family
- Credibility of contents
- Individuals' preferences for various types of stories
- Respondents' major sources of information about the company
- Suggestions for improving the publication.

All employees should be informed of the findings, after they have been analyzed, by personal letters or a news story in the publication. If they are not told, they will suspect management's motives and may refuse to cooperate in future surveys.

4. *In-depth Surveys.* This is the costliest method, but the most valuable because "proven" and "claimed" readers are clearly identified. Each participant is interviewed and asked to recall from memory the specific ideas or information contained in a given article or articles.

The employee may be shown the front page or cover of a publication and its table of contents. He then is asked to give an account of any article in that issue. He is not counted as a "proven reader" unless he can give a fairly accurate description of an item, photograph, or idea in that issue.

The same technique is used to test readership of selected articles. This second stage provides a fairly accurate gauge of a publication's impact and the clarity of writing in it. Some readers often are left with exactly the opposite interpretation or conclusion the editor meant to convey.

In-depth surveys are not foolproof. Some readers can scan an article and give a satisfactory playback to an interviewer without really absorbing the content and the point of it. Improvements in the method, however, hold the promise of making it the best device for measuring the value of communication programs.

BIBLIOGRAPHY

I. Graphics and Mechanics

BOOKS

Arnold, E. C.: *Modern Newspaper Design,* Harper & Row Publishers, Inc., New York, 1969.

Baird, Russell N., and Arthur T. Turnbull: *The Graphics of Communication,* 2nd ed., Holt, Rinehart and Winston, Inc., New York, 1968.

Bruce, Helen F.: *Your Guide to Basic Photography,* Barnes & Noble, Inc., New York, 1965.

Croy, P.: *Graphic Design and Reproduction Techniques,* Hastings House Publishers, Inc., New York, 1968.

Dair, C.: *Design with Type,* University of Toronto Press, Toronto, 1967.

Rothstein, A.: *Photojournalism,* 2d ed., Chilton Company, Trade Book Division, Philadelphia, 1965.

PERIODICAL

Better Editing, American Business Press, Inc., 205 East Forty-second Street, New York, N.Y., 10017.

ARTICLES

Campbell, Bruce: "Are Corporate Graphics Clarifying or Confusing?" *Public Relations Journal,* vol. 23, no. 2, pp. 16–17, February, 1967.

Haskins, Jack B.: "Increasing Visual Efficiency of Headlines," *Editor and Publisher,* vol. 102, no. 10, p. 14, March 8, 1969.

Roth, Joel A.: "Publishing's Multi-media Future," *Book Production Industry,* vol. 44, no. 12, pp. 35–39, December, 1968.

Snyder, Mel: "How to Get the Best Pictures," *Public Relations Journal,* vol. 25, no. 3, pp. 18–21, March, 1969.

II. Contents, Writing, and Editing

BOOKS

DeMare, G.: *Communicating for Leadership,* The Ronald Press Company, New York, 1968.

Gunther, M.: *Writing the Modern Magazine Article.* The Writers, Inc., Boston, 1968.

Root, R.: *Modern Magazine Editing,* Wm. C. Brown Company Publishers, Dubuque, Iowa, 1966.

Shidle, N. G.: *The Art of Successful Communication,* McGraw-Hill Book Company, New York, 1965.

PERIODICALS

Reporting, 407 South Dearborn Street, Chicago, Ill. 60605.

Score, 3200 North Lake Shore Drive, Chicago, Ill. 60657.

ARTICLES

Brown, Lenore: "Something's Missing from Employee Papers," *Editor and Publisher,* vol. 101, no. 11, pp. 44–45, March 16, 1968.

Charlton, R. G.: "A Bigger Job for House Organs," *Public Relations Journal,* vol. 25, pp. 16–17, January, 1969.

Kuran, Charles L., and Graham B. Bell: "Reading Ease as a Factor in Improved Communication Effectiveness," *Journal of Psychology,* vol. 68, no. 1, pp. 49–53, January, 1968.

Lipper, J. J.: "Who Says a House Organ Has to Be Dull?" *Public Relations Journal,* vol. 25, no. 9, pp. 30–31, September, 1969.

Tingey, S.: "Six Requirements for a Successful Company Publication," *Personal Journal,* vol. 45, pp. 638–642, November, 1967.

Werth, P. M.: "How to Produce Effective Employee Publications," *Public Relations Journal,* vol. 23, no. 12, pp. 21–23, December, 1967.

PAMPHLET

Anderson, Walter G.: *The Industrial Communications Handbook,* American Association of Industrial Editors, 802 Kenmore Avenue, Buffalo, N.Y. 14216.

MANUAL

Dover, C. J.: *Effective Communication in Company Publications,* 2d printing, BNA Inc., Washington, D.C., 1961.

III. Audience, Publics, Social Reaction

PERIODICALS

Public Relations Journal, 845 Third Avenue, New York, N.Y. 10022.
Public Relations Quarterly, 305 East Forty-fifth Street, New York, N.Y. 10017.

ARTICLES

Anderson, J.: "Giving and Receiving Feedback," *Personnel Administration,* vol. 31, pp. 21–27, March, 1968.
Baxter, John D.: "Who Has the Right to Communicate with the Employees?" *Public Relations Journal,* vol. 21, no. 5, pp. 8–10, May, 1965.
"Getting the Message to Employees," *Administrative Management,* vol. 28, p. 42, September, 1967.
Hurley, Gerald D.: "The Making of an Industrial Editor: The Editor and Creative Photography," *Public Relations Journal,* vol. 22, no. 9, p. 10, September, 1966.
Kaufmann, C. B.: "The Making of an Industrial Editor: The Editor as an Advocate," *Public Relations Journal,* vol. 22, no. 9, p. 11, September, 1966.

IV. Government, Law, History, Research, and Theory

BOOKS

Nafziger, R. O., and M. M. Wilkerson (eds.): *An Introduction to Journalism Research,* Greenwood Press, New York, 1968.
Thayer, L. O.: *Communication and Communication Systems,* Richard D. Irwin, Inc., Homewood, Ill., 1968.

V. Audio-Visual

BOOKS

Gould-Marks, L.: *Management Communications through Audio Visual Aid,* Leonard Hill Books Ltd., London, 1966.
Kemp, J. E., and others: *Planning and Producing Audio-visual Materials,* 2d ed., Chandler Publishing Company, San Francisco, 1968.
Stevenson, G. A.: *Graphic Arts Encyclopedia,* McGraw-Hill Book Company, New York, 1968.
Wittich, W. A., and C. F. Schuller: *Audio-Visual Materials; their Nature and Use,* 4th ed., Harper & Row Publishers, Inc., New York, 1967.

PERIODICAL

Audio-Visual Communication Review, Department of Audio-Visual Instruction, 1201 Sixteenth Street, Washington, D.C. 20036.

ARTICLES

Gelman, M. J.: "Closed Circuit TV; Its Applications Are Infinite but Only Surface Has Been Scratched So Far," *Television,* vol. 22, pp. 40–43, July, 1965.
McGehee, W.: "Audio-Visual Aids; Where They Fit into Training," *Textile World,* vol. 116, pp. 98–100, May, 1966.
"Motion Pictures for Effective Communication," *Audio-Visual Communications,* vol. 2, no. 4, pp. 22–26, August, 1968.

chapter 73

Company Newspapers
and Magazines

N. L. RUNGER, JR. *Editorial Director, New Jersey Bell Telephone Company, Newark, New Jersey*

Why should your organization have a company newspaper or magazine?

There are at least three good answers to this question. First, a well-informed employee will probably be a better employee: more productive, more cooperative, better motivated. Your employees will probably never identify themselves quite as closely with the company's interests as you would like them to do. Nevertheless, an employee who knows the objectives and problems of the company is more likely to work toward the objectives and view the problems sympathetically than is an employee who does not even know what they are.

Second, perhaps of broadest impact—is the "employee ambassador" concept. Every time one of your employees discusses his job or his company with one of his friends or a member of his family, he is automatically doing public relations work for you. Whether it is good or bad public relations work depends on how effectively he identifies his own interests with the broad company position. And he cannot do that unless you have taken the time to let him know something about the company's situation.

One major firm once discovered through a customer survey that customers who knew its employees and discussed the company with them had poorer attitudes toward the company than customers who did not know any company employees! Employees will be ambassadors—you cannot stop them. What you *can* do is try to make them good ambassadors.

A third reason for having company publications is the increasing desire on the part of people to become really involved in what they do. In a work situation, this means that they feel they have a right to know more about the company than previous generations of employees generally cared to learn. This rising desire for involvement means, in effect, that in order to turn them on you have to fill them in. The companies that do this have employees who care; the ones that do not have employees who pick up paychecks.

As a communications medium, print has some special characteristics. An awareness of them can be helpful to those responsible for publications.

Print delivers a standard message to all readers, as opposed to the distortion that often accompanies word-of-mouth communication.

Print provides a high level of content control; you need not print your material until you are sure it is just the way you want it.

Print costs can be quite moderate, as compared with such relatively exotic media as closed-circuit television.

Print can be used anywhere and at the reader's convenience; it does not rely on a schedule or special equipment.

Not all the qualities of print are positive:

It requires more work—reading—on the part of the receiver than such communications media as film and television.

It generally lacks the personality and direct impact of live, filmed, or televised presentations.

By itself, it does not allow feedback or discussion, such as question-and-answer sessions. It should be realized, though, that these features can be built into a program that includes print.

WHO IS IT FOR?

Whether you call your publication a *company* magazine or an *employee* magazine may indicate quite a bit about how you look at its job (and yours!). Are you producing your publication for the company or for the employee?

On the one hand, the company pays for it, so considering it a company publication is easily justified. And this in turn leads to its use as a carrier of information that higher management wants employees to have; it is a vehicle of corporate propaganda.

On the other hand, if its content and style are so heavily oriented around the brass in the executive suite, many potential readers may very likely reject it. It just will not appeal to their interests and tastes.

Therefore, to be effective, it must be constantly viewed as both a company and an employee publication. Its job is to explain company matters to employees. Its readers must be approached with contents and style that will appeal to them. This means including some material with high reader interest even though it might not be directly related to the business. It also means writing about business matters with a style that will appeal to the broad range of employees—most of whom are *not* officers of the corporation.

A related danger—and even more damaging to the effectiveness of a publication —is underrating the interests and tastes of employees. Contemporary research indicates that most employees are not interested in wedding reports, birth announcements, and pictures of all the fish Pat caught on vacation last month. One of the nation's largest manufacturers recently polled its employees about what they wanted to see in the company magazine. The subjects that rated highest were about the company's history and future prospects, the outlook for more and better jobs, employee fringe benefits, and the company's competitive position.

THE ORGANIZATION CHART

Who should be responsible for the company publications? The first (and only solid) rule is that sound writing and creative talent is essential. Wherever that talent is in your organization is where responsibility for producing the publications should be also. This responsibility includes the establishment of objectives for the publications.

A recent survey documented the public relations department as the one responsible for most company publications, with personnel second. Again—the name of the department is not important; the availability of talent is.

NUTS AND BOLTS

Words are the logical subject with which to start any discussion of the mechanics involved in producing a publication. Most articles and features begin with words. Assuming that you have a qualified writer who has done his research and his writing with competent craftsmanship, the next step is getting his copy—what he has written—approved for publication in the magazine or newspaper.

Approvals are an important and often worrisome aspect of industrial publication. They fall into three basic areas:

Content and policy approvals should be obtained from the highest man in the department responsible for the publication. When you want to do a story on cost control, and your main thrust will be to show that each employee benefits personally when costs are kept down, the top man is the one to say yes or no. It is his job to interpret and administer company policy. He is most likely to know of any situations or plans not yet announced which could have a bearing on the timing and appropriateness of any particular article. Story ideas and approaches should be cleared at his level.

Accuracy approvals have to be obtained from whatever people in the company have the knowledge to verify the material. The accuracy of a story on a manufacturing process can possibly be best judged by a shop foreman. An article about internal corporate debt structure may have to be approved—for accuracy—by the comptroller. There are no hard and fast rules about accuracy approvals.

Editorial approvals are the responsibility of the editor's supervisor, provided he is competent to judge the editorial suitability of the material. It is his job to make sure the story has been told in the most effective way. He should know what objective and approach were cleared at the content and policy stage and make sure the finished story is consistent with them. Where he feels the nature of the material warrants further review, he can of course go higher—or lower—in the organization for additional opinions.

These different types of approval should steer most stories safely from concept to printed page. Most approval troubles occur when the distinctions among them become blurred. If, for example, you are asking an engineer to approve the accuracy of a story about stress in metal fabricating, make sure (tactfully) in advance that he understands what you want. Unless you want his comments about your style, ask him specifically for an accuracy judgment only. The writer, the editor, and the engineer will work better together if the lines of distinction are kept clear.

PUTTING THE PIECES TOGETHER

Once the words are established, and the pictures to illustrate the article are in hand, the next job is arranging the elements for printing. This is the layout or design stage of production, and it can be effectively done only by a competent, trained commercial artist or designer. His job is to arrange the various elements on the printed page in a way that will attract the eye of the reader, and at the same time make the story as easy as possible to read. Plain columns of clean type are easy to read, but many potential readers are not attracted to pages made up only of type. On the other hand, graphic elements such as photographs and draw ings can make the page eye-appealing, but may also interfere with smooth reading to the point where the reader just quits. Finding the proper balance is what produces good layouts, and they are the work of professional designers.

If you have such a person in your company, you are ahead of the game. If you do not, consult some of the people listed under Artists in your telephone directory's classified section, or make inquiries at a nearby art school. Layout services can be hired from an art studio, and this is often a better arrangement than an "in-house" artist, particularly where the amount of this kind of work in the company is quite small.

If your budget restrictions are so rigid that the person who writes your material must also lay it out, be sure he gets some sound training in graphic arrangement. The industrial editors association in your area generally will know where such training can be obtained. Another source for this information (and perhaps for the training itself!) is the journalism department of a nearby college or university.

One helpful technique that can save time and money during layout is the use of what is often called space paper. This is 8½- by 11-inch paper with a wide right margin and numbered lines set for double-space typing (see Figure 1). Typing each article on space paper lets the designer know immediately how many column inches of set type the manuscript copy will produce. He then knows how much space in the allotted pages is left for other elements such as photographs, artwork, and white space (page area left completely blank to help avoid an impression of closely packed type).

HOW ABOUT SOME COLOR?

One important decision generally made during layout is whether or not to use color; that is, color in addition to the basic printing color, which is usually (though not always) black. About the only two generalities that can safely be made about the use of extra color are that it can be quite attractive and it is usually quite expensive.

Spot pieces of color can add a lot of attractiveness to a layout. These are small elements of solid color that do not require expensive processing. They can be in shapes that relate somehow to the article; they can also be used for printing the headline or title of the article. Their function is to brighten up the page, and they may be the deciding factor in whether your reader quickly flips the pages past a feature or pauses long enough to be drawn into reading. Such uses of color can be moderate in cost.

But do not think you can use full-color photographs like the ones you admire in commercial magazines, unless you are prepared to pay the price. This kind of color reproduction—involving color separations and color correction—can be achieved only by highly skilled and highly paid craftsmen. When you need the kind of drama that this kind of treatment makes possible, there is nothing more effective. But go into it only with your eyes wide open (and an estimate from your printer!)

SOME PRESSING DETAILS

A detailed knowledge of printing production methods and processes is not necessary for those responsible for most industrial publications. Printing is an industrial science that is becoming increasingly complex and innovative. However, a general familiarity with fundamentals can help the manager communicate better with printers and other publications technicians.

Most company publications are now being printed on *sheet-fed offset* presses.

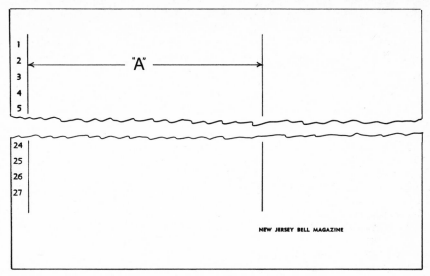

Figure 1. Space paper tells the designer how much set type the manuscript will produce. Type face, point size, and publication column width are used to determine the space paper column width. For example, 10-point Times Roman type, set 18 picas wide, will produce 48 characters to the line; 48 characters on a pica typewriter will require 4-7/8 inch—the column marked "A."

This term means that: (1) the paper is fed into the press in sheets, rather than from the giant rolls used to produce major newspapers, and (2) the printed image is applied to the paper from a rubber-surfaced blanket rather than directly from metal type.

Several newspapers and magazines are being produced on web presses. These use the large rolls of paper and print at much higher speeds than sheet-fed presses. There is some loss of image quality in web printing compared with sheet-fed printing. But this difference is steadily decreasing as new technology is incorporated into press manufacture. Even today, the difference may or may not be apparent to the reader, depending upon his ability to detect subtle quality distinctions.

The two primary ways of setting type are of some interest in industrial publication, especially where copy changes in late production stages may be a factor.

Cold type is set by typewriter-like machines that produce typed copy with justified margins (both left and right margins flush, like this book). This typed copy is subsequently converted photographically into printing plates for use in the presses.

Hot type is molten lead cast into word forms, usually on a Linotype machine, a line at a time. These lines, called *slugs,* are then assembled into complete stories and in offset printing are used to produce reproduction proofs for conversion into printing plates.

The significance of hot type's being set a line at a time is the relative ease with which one or two words may be changed, often without affecting more than one line. If your copy, once approved, is not subject to further review and possible change, this feature is of little value. In this case, the generally slightly lower cost of cold type might be the deciding factor in determining which method to use.

It should be stressed, however, that type methods as well as other technical details like stock (the paper on which you print your publication), ink, and binding methods are matters that should be settled in consultation with your printer. Once you have selected a printer with whom you can work in mutual confidence, he is your best adviser on production matters.

TIME: THE TWO-EDGED SWORD

One of the most critical elements in publication production is time. The time required to turn a story idea into a printed feature will have an important bearing on how current your publication is. This is one of the forks in the road where newspapers and magazines part company.

If your newspaper is to function as a genuine news medium, it must feature fresh material, so that your readers will come to think of it as the place to get authoritative reports about recent company matters. (If it is made up of "news" reports of events more than a week or two old, do not even bother to think of it as a newspaper.) Some of the ways you can keep your material and your newspaper timely are:

Establish a late deadline. This will give your editor some harried moments when late-breaking stories upset his page makeup, but it will also make sure your readers get fresh news.

Streamline your approval routine. When your material has been approved, let your editor work out its position in the paper. If you think he is doing it ineffectively, review each issue with him after publication, or get a new editor; don't hamper him with arbitrary "suggestions" in late production stages.

Work ahead where possible. Late stories cannot, of course, be done ahead of time, but there are lots of features that can and should be done early. Some of these are: organization changes, editorials, safety features, classified ads, and personnel features like retirements and service anniversaries. Take care of them early in your production cycle, so that you will be free late in the game to handle the late-breaking flashes.

Time is an important element in the production of magazines, too, but in a different way. The primary concern of the magazine is generally not speed, but quality: this is your company's showcase publication, and you want it to reflect quality and purpose in its appearance and content.

You will be carefully examining proofs and other materials at each stage of preparation to detect and eliminate errors and mechanical imperfections. All of this takes time, and this time must be built into your production schedule in advance. Again, give your printer a chance to participate in the preparation of your schedule; if he has had a hand in determining the schedule, he will be more likely to feel committed to keeping his part of it.

The lead time required in magazine printing may mean, for example, that if your magazine is to be available on June 1, you cannot submit any new material later than April 15. You may need as much as six weeks to go through all the steps necessary to produce the quality product your company magazine should be. Naturally, this means you will not have May's events in your June magazine. Never mind: that's what your newspaper is for.

If your decision is to have only a magazine, you must compromise in one or more areas. If it is to include fresh events, its production must be more hasty and less polished. If it is to retain top quality, it cannot at the same time include late-breaking material. There are hard choices to be made here, because each hour contains only sixty minutes and there are no real shortcuts to genuine quality.

Since you will be keeping track of perhaps a dozen or more features for each issue—and may be working on more than one issue at a time—a status record of some sort is almost essential for administrative control. Such a record will tell you the status of each story at any time and will help you spot—in time to take corrective action—stories that may be lagging and could cause delays. (See Figure 2 for one form of status record.)

Since printing involves a considerable amount of transferring materials back and forth between you and your printer, the distance between the two is of some importance. The best arrangement is to have your printer in the same city, and as close as possible. This allows frequent face-to-face contact and can prevent delay-causing and expensive misunderstandings.

If conditions force you to use a printer located some distance away, your copy, photographs, artwork, and other materials may have to be transported by mail. This can be slow and risky, with the hazard of possible loss of original material.

One way of expediting some things in this situation is the use of devices currently available for sending printed matter over telephone lines. Several manufacturers now market these products. All the material you can get on an 8½- by 11-inch sheet of paper can be sent from your office to your printer (provided he also has one of the devices) in about six minutes. Even photograph quality is fairly good (though not good enough for reproduction purposes) so you can get a good idea of the composition of photographs and artwork.

The difference between the time elements in newspaper and magazine production deserves repetition. Since the newspaper should be fresh, your deadline must be late in order that you can include late stories. Since the magazine should be of

APEX POINTER July, 1971	Copy Aprvd.		Layout Aprvd.		Galleys Corrected		Final Proof	
	*S	*A	S	A	S	A	S	A
Benefits are Money	5/10	5/6	5/14	5/13	5/24	5/20	6/4	6/2
How Safe Can You Get?	5/10	4/28	5/14	4/30	5/24	5/6	6/4	6/2
She's a Tough Boss	5/10	5/3	5/14	5/6	5/24	5/4	6/4	6/2
A Penny Saved	5/10	5/7	5/14	5/11	5/24	5/14	6/4	6/2
From the Drawing Board	5/10	4/30	5/14	5/5	5/24	5/12	6/4	6/2
Our New 4-Ton Baby	5/10	4/29	5/14	5/4	5/24	5/7	6/4	6/2
High Cost of Giving	5/10	5/10	5/14	5/14	5/24	5/24	6/4	6/7
APEX: Where It's At!	5/10	5/7	5/14	5/12	5/24	5/7	6/4	6/2

Advance Copies: 6/15 S / A 6/5
Run Complete: 6/18 6/18

*S = Scheduled
*A = Actual

Figure 2. Status record gives the editor and his supervisor quick-glance control over material in various states of production. Checking it frequently can help identify potential difficulties (like the story in the figure called "High Cost of Giving") and prevent serious delays.

top quality, your deadline must be early in order that you will have time to exercise the necessary care. If these distinctions are maintained, each of your publications will be effective—in its own way—when you are ready to distribute it.

DISTRIBUTION OPTIONS

Distributing your publication opens up a wide variety of possibilities. In the case of a single factory company, distribution may be quite simple. (But do not assume it is!) On the other hand, if your employees are in 200 different locations around the world, distribution complexities may make your production problems look simple by contrast.

Publication distribution boils down to a series of choices.

The first choice is whether to distribute on the job or at home. Distribution on the job is relatively inexpensive, fast, and makes it easy for employees to pick up extra copies. On the other hand, it is unlikely that all copies will be taken home for other members of the employees' families to read (and this could result in the loss of a very important secondary audience), and some work time may be consumed by reading (though if your publication is doing its job, this should not bother you or the operating managers).

Distribution to the home costs more, is a little slower (though it need not be too much so), and does not provide easy access to extra copies. But it does get your publication to the families of your employees (and if you are trying to promote things like the importance of fringe benefits, the employee's wife may be an even more influential reader than the employee himself). Home distribution also means that your publication may be read on the employee's time instead of on the company's.

You are the only one who can decide which of these factors is most important in your situation. If you feel family involvement and understanding are essential to the building of a motivated employee group, the additional cost and slight delay of home distribution will be worthwhile. If minimum cost is desired above all other factors, having workers pick up their copies in the cafeteria may be the best choice.

One other distribution matter deserves mention. Assuming you rule in favor of home distribution, the next choice is between first-class and third-class mail. First-class mail is relatively expensive, fast, and can be delivered to the post office in random order. It enhances the importance and timeliness of your publication and provides for undelivered copies to be forwarded or returned to the sender.

Third-class mail is less expensive, considerably slower, and must usually be sorted by zip code. It does not enhance the timeliness of your publication or allow undelivered copies to be returned or forwarded.

Since your newspaper is the timely and usually smaller of your two publications, a reasonable program might be first-class mailing for the newspaper and third-class mailing for the magazine. Again—it is a matter you must decide to fit your own situation and your own employee communications priorities.

SOME MISCELLANEOUS MECHANICS

There are a number of factors that will influence the effectiveness of your employee publication program—factors that do not relate to any specific stage of production or distribution.

Overall cost is one of these. Cost will be determined by many factors—the size of the printing run, the section of the country in which you print, how much extra color you use, the grade of stock on which you print, the number of changes you make in type already set (these are called "author's alterations"), and how much use you make of such special devices as gatefold covers, unusual die cuts, the binding inclusion of lightweight vinyl phonograph records, etc. A magazine will generally cost more than a newspaper, but there are probably instances where even that seemingly safe generalization is not true.

Perhaps the best advice in the area of cost is to consult with your printer. He should be willing and able to give you a fairly accurate estimate of printing and typography costs—in advance. What *you* must remember, however, is that such additional items as photographs, artwork, graphics services, postage, mail handling, and overtime will all be additional costs.

Cost control is a difficult area in the publication business. Expenses can easily skyrocket as you move from one attractive element and design device to another. Printers are not in business to perform your cost control function for you. If you find a printer who will voluntarily communicate with you about the costs of projected treatments, treasure him.

One way of getting some extra mileage out of your publications (and thereby in a sense reducing their cost) is the use of reprints. A four-page feature on new products currently in the development stage might make an effective handout for your company's salesmen. If so, the marketing department will very likely pay for the small cost of reprinting the feature from existing printing plates. When reprints are made, be sure your publication gets credit for them: a short line—"Reprinted from the *Apex Pointer*"—will do it neatly.

Should you have a contract with a printer or print each issue on separate bids? There are things to be said for either alternative. A two- or three-year contract assures you of some stability in printing costs for a predictable time. On the other hand, one of the world's largest insurance companies finds that obtaining bids for each issue of its magazine enables it to take advantage of slack times in various printing shops. Experience and the presence or absence of a choice of printers will be your best guides here.

Another choice you must make is between the use of independent, free-lance photographers and the hiring of staff photographers. A staff photographer can, of course, only be in one place at a time. The chances are that if the company is big enough to afford a staff photographer, it is big enough to have more than one event occurring at one time and will have to cover one of them with an outside photographer anyway.

Then, too, the editor and designer will quickly determine that certain features call for the talents of certain photographers. Using free-lance professionals leaves them with a free choice each time. Good free-lance photography is expensive, but not as expensive in the long run as bad pictures.

Should you use "local reporters" to help gather the news from various areas? This question may be answered by the nature of the company's organization. If it is a one-factory operation of moderate size, you may not need anyone beside the editor of the paper. If the company is international in scope, you almost certainly will need some news-gathering help. At any rate, local reporters can help keep tabs on what is happening in various parts of the company.

You can increase the true usefulness of local reporters if you make sure they are selected carefully: they should be people who will be likely to know what is going on and willing to pass it on to you. You will have to train them (the editor can help you do that) and motivate them. A periodic newsletter is one way of doing this, and recognizing a particularly good reporting job in your paper is another.

HOW ARE YOU DOING?

Assuming you have done all the right things—made all the right decisions and chosen all the right production and distribution methods—how do you know what your readers think about your publications? Answering this question brings us up against the matter of readership surveys.

The first thing to be said about readership surveys is that there is no substitute for the judgment of a good editor. He should know how his publication is being received. Voluntary feedback (excepting the "Hey, I found a typo!" variety) is rare, so measuring his audience means footwork for the editor. When he is out on a story, attending a meeting, or at a company party—these are all occasions when he should be asking what his readers think about the publication.

If you decide that, in addition to your editor's judgment, you want to survey your readers formally, you must consider the various types of surveys.

A Letters to the Editor column in your paper or magazine is one form of survey —one that can backfire with explosive suddenness. The primary hazard is the potential for critical letters, the kind that ask why general salary increases are not given at more frequent intervals and why foremen do not treat production workers more like human beings. Unless you're prepared to publish and comment on some of these letters along with the neutral and laudatory ones, running a Letters to the Editor column may only create a credibility gap for your publications. Your readers will assume that *some* critical letters must have been submitted; when they do not see *any* of them in print, they will soon begin to doubt the fairness and objectivity of the newspaper or magazine.

The random mail survey is a safer kind of readership test. It is relatively easy to conduct and inexpensive, but it may yield only a low response. A large insurance company sends readership questionnaires to 100 randomly selected readers following each issue of its magazine, asking which stories were particularly interesting and which less interesting. This company generally receives about 50 percent of the questionnaires back. When a major Northeastern utility tried the same thing, its returns were only about 10 percent. Even a small return *may* be helpful, but it can also be misleading.

The most elaborate survey method (also the most expensive and most time-consuming) is the "in-depth" survey which usually includes individual and/or group interviews as well as detailed questionnaires. If your organization's statistical group is willing to take on the job of conducting such a survey, you can save the considerable fee that will normally be charged by an independent research organization.

In any of these and other types of surveys, the least certain aspect is likely to be interpreting the data. Even if the sample size and composition satisfy the statistician's standard of validity, there are still value judgments to be made about the meaning of the summarized results.

For example, one in-depth survey showed that readers of a newspaper wanted more information about what was happening in their town or district and less about what was happening in other sections of the company's territory. This puts the editor in a dilemma: *any* town is "other" territory to a majority of readers in any but the smallest, most compact companies.

One solution to this problem would be to organize the local news into clearly marked sections of the publication so that each reader could find his town or district easily. Another solution would be to prepare regional editions, which would emphasize as well as localize the nature of the news, but would also add to the cost and complexity of the publications job, particularly in the area of distribution.

Another situation requiring caution occurs when responses are about equally split between favorable and unfavorable reactions. If a particular story was interesting to 47 percent of respondents, of little interest to 49 percent, and aroused no reaction from the remaining 4 percent, what do you do? On the basis of those results alone, it would be difficult to substantiate a decision either to run a similar feature or to avoid the subject. If a large majority of respondents lines up on one side of the "like-dislike" fence, you are much safer in accepting the result and basing future plans on it. But if your readers are that unanimous about something, you may very well have known it without the survey!

Surveys can give you valuable support and substantiation. They can indicate areas where some further feature possibilities should be considered. And they give your readers a feeling of participation in the company publication. But they are not a substitute for editorial judgment. Your editor should frequently review his publication for balance of many kinds—characteristics of his audience such as age, sex, geography, and operating departments and divisions. He should know his readers and take advantage of every opportunity to find out what kind of job they think he is doing.

IN CONCLUSION

There are a couple of points that should be kept in mind about the special business of supervising creative people—the kind of people who are involved in writing, editing, and designing publications. These kinds of people are different from most corporation employees—different enough to warrant awareness of their special needs.

Creative people have large egos; they are sensitive and rather easily hurt, though on the surface they may appear blasé and callous. They are motivated largely by internal satisfaction—the fulfillment that comes to creative people when *they* feel they have exercised their craft skillfully. Praise is a powerful element in encouraging them, as long as it is sincere praise. Material rewards such as money and office surroundings—beyond what is necessary—will not buy as much performance from a creative person as they will from a production manager or salesman.

Just as praise motivates creative people, overbearing supervision is withering and flip criticism is nearly fatal. A heavy-handed supervisor can increase his own feeling of importance while he is smothering the motivation of the people who are supposed to make him look good. On the other hand, a skillful leader of creative people can—by supervising only when and as necessary—keep his group at a high level of morale and production while appearing to let his shop run itself.

Unless you are an editor, learn to resist the urge to edit. It is a natural desire: everyone feels he can write better than the next fellow, even when the next fellow is a professional writing craftsman.

If you are an editor, try to use restraint and avoid overediting. If something is wrong or misleading, by all means change it (or better yet ask the writer to change it). But do not substitute words or phrases just because you happen to prefer one expression or idiom over another.

Properly motivated creative people will knock themselves out to excel—that is what makes them feel good. Oversupervised or otherwise abused, they may be worse than harmless. They have been trained to be articulate; privately they can be just as articulate about what a poor company they work for. Use their intense desire for inner satisfaction and make it work *for* you.

Similarly, the relationship between editors and artists is one of the most important elements in a publication program. Working harmoniously, they make an inventive team that can perform wonders. Out of balance, or working at cross purposes, they can seriously undermine the effectiveness of your publication effort.

Maintaining proper balance between their different disciplines is a delicate but essential job. Your magazine can win top honors in art directors and printing competitions, and yet be using page layouts that make your message hard to read. And you can be printing truly fine, straightforward prose, yet lose your readers because unimaginative layouts just do not attract them.

One workable arrangement seems to be that of giving the editor the responsibility and authority to review and approve graphic work. If you have a good editor, he will use this authority gently. After all, his own interests are best served by keeping the designer highly motivated and proud of the publication they produce together, just as he wants his own boss to keep *him* that way.

The road to successful employee publications has many turns, many hills, and more than enough hazards to make it interesting. There will be mistakes and embarrassment; that is why it is often said that while doctors bury their mistakes, editors publish theirs. There will be well-intentioned articles that do not quite come off as planned. But if you are working hard at it, there will also be cases of direct, effective information that helps shape attitudes and channel behavior in desirable directions. And is that not a large part of what employee communications is all about?

BIBLIOGRAPHY

Arnold, Edmund G.: *Modern Newspaper Design,* Harper & Row, Publishers, Incorporated, New York, 1969.

Breth, Robert D.: *Dynamic Management Communications,* Addison-Wesley Publishing Company, Inc., Reading, Mass., 1969.

Burack, A. S., (editor): *The Writer's Handbook,* The Writer, Inc., Boston, 1968.

Merrihue, Willard V.: *Managing By Communication,* McGraw-Hill Book Company, New York, 1960.

Wolseley, Roland E.: *Understanding Magazines,* Iowa State University Press, Ames, 1966.

Pocket Pal, International Paper Company, New York, 1966.

chapter 74

Employee Handbooks

RICHARD M. MACHOL *Electrical World, McGraw-Hill, Inc., New York, New York*

EDGAR M. BUTTENHEIM *President, Buttenheim Publishing Corporation, Pittsfield, Massachusetts*

Why a Handbook?

Well-thought-out personnel policies are a sure road to building employee morale — and any improvement in employee morale and job satisfaction is bound to result in increased employee efficiency and lower levels of employee unrest. But the finest possible personnel policies will have little or no impact unless they are clearly explained to, and clearly understood by, your employees. One of the best ways to achieve this vital understanding of your policies is through an employee handbook.

Advantages of Having a Handbook

Handbooks are an advantage to employees and supervisors alike. We all tend to forget what our benefits and privileges are. What better way than a handbook to avoid the answering of repetitive questions: "Do we get Election Day off?" "How many years do I have to have with the company before I get three weeks' vacation?" "When do my pension plan rights begin?" All these, and many more, can be covered fully in the handbook.

The handbook can have peripheral benefits, too. With all the facts about the company at hand, for instance, employees can be more articulate about the company as they mix in the community. This can lead to a feeling that the company is "a good place to work." Result: Higher-quality applicants will apply for job vacancies.

The very process of setting all company personnel policies down in one place may well lead to discovery of gaping holes in the policies, or of inconsistencies. Thus, the act of compiling a handbook of your personal policies may result in improvement of those policies.

What Should Be Included

Many factors combine to determine what information should be included in an employee handbook. Among them: How big is your company? Are all employees at one central location, or do you operate at many scattered sites? What type of business are you in: light or heavy manufacturing, retail or wholesale trade, service industry, etc.? Are your employees primarily white-collar desk workers, or are they mostly blue-collar assembly-line men? Are you unionized or not? Thus, any company's employee handbook must be custom-tailored to fit that company. For guidance, however, Figure 1 lists the tables of contents of several representative employee handbooks.

Everybody Is Involved

Compiling an employee handbook is *not* a one-man job; nor should it be done entirely within the personnel department. To start with, top-management support and cooperation are essential. But even that is not enough; all major sections of your company's organizational structure should be involved, too. With that in mind, here is one way to go about it:

1. Prepare an outline, or even a rough draft, of what *you* think should be included in your handbook.

2. Set up a meeting with all the managers and supervisors who head up the different parts of your organization structure. (If you cannot get them all together at one time, a series of meetings may be needed.) If you have the firm support of one of the members of top management for your project, get him to call the meeting; his summons will carry more weight.

3. At this meeting, describe the project and the reasons for it. Present in detail

---

Figure 1.   Contents of typical employee handbooks

Company A
Who we are—What we do
History of our company
Hours of work
Salary review
Promotions
Holidays and vacations
Illness and accidents; hospital and
    medical bills; group insurance
Termination of employment
Use of the telephone
Our pension plan
Company B
Company history
Pictures of plants and products
You and your job
Employee benefits and services
Company policies and rules
An insert of the union contract
Company C
A letter explaining the handbook
Company history
Organization charts
Your earnings and your hours
Your working conditions
Your security and your future

the advantages that will accrue to the company, the employees, and the supervisors from having a handbook. In other words, "sell" the idea of the handbook to the people in the organization whose support is essential if the project is to be successful.

4. After you have them convinced, distribute copies of your outline or draft to everyone present, and ask each one to study it, and to submit to you a memorandum listing suggested changes, additions, and deletions. Depending on your company's size and organization structure, it might be wise to suggest that they, in turn, have meetings with their subordinates, to invite comment and contributions. Assign a definite (but realistic) deadline date for getting all memorandums back to your office. (This is the stage at which omissions or inconsistencies in your company personnel policies will become apparent.)

5. Once you have received all the memorandums, it is time to put your handbook together. Write out a full working draft of the handbook as you think it should be, taking into consideration all the suggestions embodied in the memorandums. (Obviously, you will not be able to accept all the suggestions; many of them, in fact, may be diametrically opposed. But somebody has to choose among them, and that is *your* job.) Rather than do the actual writing of the text yourself, it may be better to get someone else to do it; more on that below.

6. Submit copies of this draft for further comment and suggestions. At this point in the project, it is usually too unwieldy to include everyone who attended your original meeting; just send the draft to the key executives and managers.

7. As soon as you get this round of comments back, write the final draft, check it once more with your key top-management supporter, print it, and distribute it.

Why all this "democracy"? Because, as every good personnel man knows, no one in an organization likes to be handed a fait accompli, in the preparation of which he has had no part, and to be told to use it. He will not; instead of cooperation, you will get criticism, backbiting, possibly even sabotage of your project.

After consultation as suggested above, however, even though all the ideas have not been accepted, the company's executives and managers will have the psychological satisfaction of having been in on the project from the beginning. They will consider the completed handbook as partly theirs, and they will cooperate accordingly in pushing its distribution and its use.

An Editor's Work Is Never Done

Personnel policies and employee benefits are always changing. As they change, the employee handbook must change too. If you have issued the handbook in loose-leaf form, change is easy; just print revised pages. If you have issued it as a bound booklet, however, a complete new edition must be compiled from time to time. (The time between editions in most companies ranges from 18 months to 3 years.)

Even loose-leaf handbooks should be completely reissued occasionally—employees lose them, or forget to insert revisions as they are issued, and a thoroughly out-of-date handbook is worse than no handbook at all.

For a complete revision, you may want to consider going through the whole consultation process over again. It will be shorter this time. You have your existing handbook as your "first draft"; your managers and supervisors already know what is expected of them; and they and their employees have had experience using the existing handbook, so its lacks and drawbacks, if any, will be apparent to them.

Appearance Counts

Even the best-planned handbook will be a failure if your employees do not read it, or if, having read it, they do not understand it. So you have to make it attractive enough so they will want to read it, and you have to write it so they will understand what they read.

Figure 2. Subjects covered in an employee handbook. Company size: 10,000 employees

The company and your job
  How we earn our living
  How the company originated and grew
  Employees with initiative
  Your contribution to future success
Your employee status
  Your employee classification
    Nonexempt employees
    Exempt employees
    Probationary employees
    Permanent employees
    Temporary employees
    Full-time employees
    Part-time employees
    On-call employees
    Domestic employees
    International employees
    Foreign employees
  Your continuous-service date
  Your adjusted anniversary date
  Your responsibility to keep company informed
Your hours and pay
  Working hours
  Paycheck and deductions
  Paydays
  Overtime pay
  Supper allowance
  Evaluation of your job
  Review of your pay
  Separation allowance
Time off your job
  Vacations
  Military service—active duty
  Military reserve training
  When you are sick
  Jury duty
  Death in family
  Widespread emergencies
  Maternity
  Personal business
  Coffee break
  Tardiness
How you and the company communicate
  Oral communication
  Written communication
  Keep company up to date on you
More training or education—for yourself or others
  Company training courses
  Tuition refund
  Gift matching
  Merit scholarships
Employee services and activities
  Discounts on books and magazines
  Credit union
  Classified advertisements
  Savings-bond purchasing
  Libraries
  Restaurant and cafeterias

Figure 2.   Subjects covered in an employee handbook.   (continued)

Award for recruiting
Monthly investment plan
Medical services
If company moves you
Twenty-five-year club
Social, artistic, and athletic activities
Charitable activities
Membership drives and solicitations
Gifts to other employees
Security benefits—introduction
Eleven benefit plans
Automatic plans
If you are ill or injured
Emergencies
Protection of your earnings during brief disabilities
Salary—continuation plan
When injured on the job—workmen's compensation
Off-the-job disabilities
State required disability benefits
Protection of your earnings during prolonged or permanent disabilities
Workmen's compensation
Travel accident insurance
Social security
Group life insurance
Long-term disability insurance
An example of payments for total and permanent disability
Payment of your hospital and surgical medical bills
Workmen's compensation
Medical expense insurance plan—its two components
Expenses covered by hospital and comprehensive medical
Claim filing procedures
Effects of employment interruptions on hospital and comprehensive
    medical
Blood bank
Regional benefit offices
General matters concerning absence due to disability
Your responsibilities
Effect on benefit plans
Your retirement program
Company's retirement policy and two plans
Pension plan
Supplemental retirement income plan
Social security
Medicare
Continuation of benefits at retirement
Conversion of benefit plans at retirement to individual
    direct-payment policies
Miscellaneous retirement privileges
Vacation due you at retirement
In case of death
Pay due employee at death
Workmen's compensation
Group travel—accident insurance
Social security
Group life insurance
Pension plan
Supplemental retirement income plan (SRIP)
If you die while on leave of absence or on military leave

How attractive you can make the handbook depends in part on your budget. Obviously, a book printed in two colors, or even with four-color picture reproductions, is more attractive than photo-offset or mimeographed sheets stapled together. But even if the latter is all your budget allows, there are still some steps you can take. Do not use type that is too small for easy reading. Do not put your lines of type too close together—and do not make them too long. If you are using 8½ by 11-in. paper, it is better to use two columns of text to a page rather than run your lines all the way across. Even if you have a very small budget, you should still consider small illustrations or line drawings to make your pages more alive.

Communicate

Most of this chapter so far has been devoted to *what* to say in your handbook. Equally important, however, is *how* you say it. The essence of good communications is to make your material both understandable and interesting to those who are expected to read it. It is amazing how many companies that practice this religiously in their advertising completely forget about it when it comes to communicating with employees.

Far too often, messages intended for employees are written at a level too difficult for the typical employee to comprehend. Also, they are all too frequently dull and uninteresting. Davis and Hopkins, in a study of employee handbooks,[1] found that 91 percent of the handbooks they surveyed were too difficult for their intended readers. Be sure you do not fall into that trap; if you do, your handbook will not be worth the paper it is written on.

Rudolph Flesch and others have developed methods by which you can measure, objectively, the degree of interest and understandability of your writing. But all these methods come down, more or less, to a few simple rules.[2]

1. Use simple words instead of complex ones. Never use a word of several syllables when a word of one or two syllables will do just as well. In general (and there are many exceptions, of course), a word of Germanic origin will be easier to understand than the corresponding word of Latin origin.

2. Use personal words. The generous use of personal pronouns (you, we, etc.) will make your material more interesting to the reader. Thus, "We want you to . . ." will get far better readership than "The company wants its employees to. . . ."

3. Use short sentences and simple sentence structure. Avoid sentences full of dependent clauses and qualifying phrases. Remember *The New York Times'* basic recommendation to its reporters and writers: "One idea, one sentence."

4. Use the active rather than the passive voice. Do not say, "Your vacation must be completed during the official vacation year"; say "You must complete your vacation within the official vacation year"; or, even better, "You must take all your vacation before the end of the official vacation year."

5. Eliminate unnecessary words. This applies particularly to adjectives. Go back over a page or a section after you have written it; you will be surprised how many words you can cut out without changing the meaning at all.

6. Keep your paragraphs short. Any paragraph of more than eight or ten lines can almost always be broken up into two or more paragraphs. Use subheadings often, to add interest to the page.

7. Be sure that the emphasis in any sentence or paragraph falls on the important

[1] Keith Davis and James Hopkins, "Readability of Employee Handbooks," *Personnel Psychology,* vol. 3, no. 3, Autumn, 1950, pp. 317–326.
[2] Rudolph Flesch, "How to Test Readability," Harper & Bros., New York, 1951, pp. 25–27.

point that you want to make. Often this can be done by proper use of punctuation; the use of the colon is particularly helpful here. But often you will find on rereading that you have to rearrange your sentence to drive home the important point.

Writing simple, clear, interesting, understandable prose is not easy for everyone. It requires some basic talent for the job, plus a lot of practice. So before you start on the handbook, perhaps you had better ask yourself whether this is really a job you should do yourself. Or is there anyone in your department who is better qualified to handle it? If not, perhaps there is someone else in the company you could borrow—someone from the public relations department, perhaps, or from the company house organ, if you have one. If there is no one in your company who is really qualified to do the job properly, the extra expense of hiring someone from outside can more than pay for itself in increased readability, and therefore effectiveness, of your handbook.

Putting It Together

If your budget allows only for in-house mimeographing, your job is about over. But if your budget allowance is greater, now is the time to look into methods, and costs, of printing. There are two basic methods of printing today—letterpress and photo-offset—and each has its advantages. In general, it is best to get bids on both types from several printers. Most printers, incidentally, have artists or layout men working for them who can help to make your handbook better looking if you have no company artist of your own to turn to.

But before you get bids, you have to decide how many copies you want. As a general rule of thumb, consider ordering three to four times as many handbooks as your number of employees. In addition to distributing a copy to every present employee, you will want to use the handbook extensively with prospective employees and, of course, to give one to each new employee. Also, copies should be in your reception room—you will be amazed at how many are taken away, which is good community relations for your company.

Remember, all the basic costs of a printing job—layout, typesetting, proof-reading, press make-ready, and so forth—are included in the price of the first 100 copies. The incremental cost of each copy after that is based only on press running time, paper, and binding. So if there is any question in your mind as to how many, choose the higher figure; the extra cost is not very significant.

Bound or Loose-leaf?

A major question in producing a handbook is whether to issue it as a bound booklet or in a loose-leaf binder with replaceable sheets for revisions. There is no definite answer; each method has its advantages and disadvantages, and only you can decide which is better for your company. Here is a list of the advantages and disadvantages of the loose-leaf binder, as determined from a nationwide survey of both large and small companies:

Advantages

1. It is more impressive in appearance.
2. It is easy to issue revisions promptly and inexpensively.
3. It is more adaptable to companies with mixed benefit packages—sections can be added or omitted for certain locations or groups.
4. It is less apt to be misplaced by the employee, because of its important appearance.
5. It is less costly in the long run.

Disadvantages

1. It costs more initially.
2. Employees may not bother to insert revisions in the binder when they are issued.
3. All copies in storage have to be corrected every time a revision is issued.
4. Binders are thick and bulky.

Although all these points are important, the comments that accompanied the responses to the survey make it apparent that the handling of revisions, particularly whether employees will bother to insert new sheets in loose-leaf binders, is the key question. The companies that responded were sharply divided on this point. Some typical comments:

> We feel that issuing [loose-leaf] supplements each time we make a benefit improvement provides an added opportunity for communication of the improvement, and at the same time reinforces the value of the program as a whole.
>
> Personally, I doubt that employees take the trouble to make insertions, and my guess is that they [improvements in benefits] have more impact when given to employees in new booklets containing the latest changes.
>
> What little evidence we have indicates that they [loose-leaf binders] usually are not kept up to date.
>
> We tried [loose-leaf binders] about four years ago. It was a disaster because employees simply did not keep the books up to date. We found it cheaper and easier to use brochures, which we up-date about every 18 months or so.
>
> In theory, the loose-leaf binder seems to have everything on its side. In practice, however, it usually does not work out that way.

So it is up to you to decide which is best for your company. *Hint:* White-collar workers, who are used to paperwork, are a lot more likely to keep loose-leaf binders up to date than are blue-collar assembly-line workers.

One company's solution to the bound versus loose-leaf question: Issue the handbook in the form of several small brochures, each covering a specific area, so that any one can be revised without the expense of reprinting the entire handbook.

Distribution

There are many methods of distributing your finished handbook to employees. But whichever one you choose, make sure it is done with fanfare; the more important you can make the occasion seem to your employees, the better the chance that they will read the handbook, and hold onto it for future reference.

You may simply hand out the books on a specified day. Or the managers and supervisors who had a part in the handbook's preparation may want to distribute copies to their sections personally. In either case, make sure your managers arrange that copies are given later to employees who were absent on the distribution day. You may prefer to mail the handbooks to the employees' homes, so that members of the family will see it too. (This costs extra, of course.)

Regardless of the method of distribution, an accompanying letter from the company president is a must. Be sure that it, too, is written to be interesting and understandable.

BIBLIOGRAPHY

Management Information Center: *How to Prepare an Employee Handbook,* Chicago, 1966.
Ross, H. John: *How to Make a Procedure Manual,* 4th ed., Office Research Institute, South Miami, 1956.
Scheer, Wilbert E.: *Dartnell's Personnel Director's Handbook,* Dartnell Corporation, Chicago, 1969.
SESCO: *How to Develop a Company Personnel Policy Manual,* Dartnell Corporation, Chicago, 1967.

chapter 75

Personnel Policy Manuals

HOWARD T. MAIER *Director of Personnel Administration, McGraw-Hill, Inc., New York, New York*

WHAT IS A PERSONNEL POLICY MANUAL?

The personnel policy manual is a companion volume to the employee handbook. It presents personnel policies in detail for a specialized group who have particular responsibilities for communicating them and carrying them out. The employee handbook is for everybody. The personnel policy manual is written for the guidance of managers primarily.

Personnel policies can look deceptively simple. Applying them to everyday situations is something else. An uncomplicated leave-of-absence policy, for example, permits an employee to request unpaid time off for personal needs. Fine. But now look at the questions that can arise. Who authorizes the leave? Can the request be turned down if it is inconvenient for the company? Can a new employee ask for one? How long may a leave be? Does it make any difference why he wants it? Can it be used to extend a vacation? To have a baby? How about trying out a new job? Does he get sick pay if he goes into the hospital while on leave? Holiday pay? Will his insurance coverage continue? At whose expense? Does the time off affect vacation credits for next year? What happens if the employee does not return at the end of a stated leave?

Faced with a multiplicity of subsidiary questions, a borderline case, a problem that does not quite match a policy statement, or a request for an exception, what does a supervisor do? Ask his superior? Call the personnel director? Follow his instincts? Or just take a healthy guess? Left on his own, the most conscientious supervisor can inadvertently create inequities and even rewrite a personnel policy through his actions. If the most effective supervisor is one who assumes intelligent responsibility for the personnel administration of his department, he must be encouraged to make his own decisions, but decisions that are consistent with company aims. For precisely this reason, many companies have concluded that their managers should be supported with a well-organized personnel policy manual that helps them understand the objectives of specific policies, interprets key aspects of the policies, defines terms, and outlines approved procedures.

A personnel policy manual then, serves two main purposes. First, it provides a written expression of policies to ensure consistent application throughout an organization. Second, it enables a manager to administer his own personnel relations at the most desirable level—first-line supervision. How a typical manual is developed, what should be included, how it is distributed and updated, who gets a copy, and how it is used as a communications device will be covered in this chapter.

HOW IS A PERSONNEL POLICY MANUAL DEVELOPED?

What steps are needed to develop a personnel policy manual depend on the material already available. If comprehensive personnel policies have already been written (see Chapter 7), the task consists of gathering the policies together, organizing them into logical units, and writing them according to some acceptable format. Properly done, the process is highly analytical. Each policy should be dissected so that the manager using it can determine what its basic objective is, to whom it applies, who has the responsibility for carrying it out, and how it is implemented—to mention just some of the questions a good manual answers.

The person responsible for developing the manual usually discovers serious deficiencies in the body of policies he is trying to codify. The job then grows to the extent that new policies must be written or old ones revised. Even if the policy appears to be carefully and completely developed before it is incorporated in the manual, the spotlight now put upon it will often encourage reconsideration. Many companies will, therefore, treat the development of a manual for existing policies in the same way they would if the policies were being newly developed. Thus the development of the manual becomes an audit of personnel policies with final approval reserved to top management.

The manual developed for the line manager has special requirements. The targets are the practical problems of the operating man. For example, does he have to clear with the shop steward before he cracks down on a tardiness problem? He is not interested in personnel theories couched in pretentious jargon. That wastes his time. He wants to know how to use action forms he, not someone else, is responsible for. The form sent to the insurance company by the personnel department has no interest for him. Keep it out of his manual. The final authority on how successfully the supervisor's needs have been met is the supervisor himself. If the manual remains in mint condition at the bottom of a desk drawer, somebody wasted a lot of time.

HOW IS THE FIRST DRAFT HANDLED?

It is not necessary to wait until the book is published to find out if it is a best-seller. It can be tried out as the work of writing the manual proceeds, by sending a draft of each section to a review list that is representative of the eventual users. Do they understand it? Does it answer their everyday questions? Are the procedures practical? Can they live with it? From their point of view, what changes would make it more effective? Because good reviewers are critical, companies that use such an approach spend more time developing a manual than it would take if the project were kept in the hands of the personnel expert until the job is done. The reviewers may surprise (and frustrate) the specialist by negative reactions to some of his pet ideas. To gain acceptance, basic concepts may have to be revised or compromised, procedures reworked. But if the result is less than a personnel textbook, it will still be a solid and accepted tool for the managers who have to use it.   The manager will not think of it as simply the personnel department's rule book.

The assignment of responsibility for writing the first draft of a personnel manual will depend on the size and organization of the company, and the nature of the subject matter covered.   If the company is large enough to have a personnel department, the job is typically assigned to that staff.   The smaller the department, the greater the probability that the personnel manager or his assistant will work on it. The larger personnel department has greater resources that can be tapped—the employment manager, the salary administrator, the benefits manager, etc.   The functional specialist is usually best qualified to write the first draft on policy concerned with his subject.   Some personnel departments set up a research or policy section with responsibility for maintaining current information on trends and needs in the personnel area, and then drafting policy proposals in response.   Regional personnel managers in multilocation companies may also have responsibility for offering first drafts of policy if local conditions seem to require a statement.

HOW IS APPROVAL OBTAINED?

However dispersed the responsibility is for originating a proposal for a policy, it must go through some coordinating procedure and then on to approval channels. The head of the personnel department will of course review drafts of functional subordinates.   Review by other personnel staff members and discussion with them can serve to check on overlap problems and to obtain additional insights from different points of view about the probable impact of the policy.   The personnel director can profit from this kind of internal departmental consultation on drafts that he has written as well as on those originated by his subordinates.

In most companies, the personnel department does not have final approval authority for personnel policy.   Drafts for personnel manuals in these organizations must be submitted to other staff members whose functions relate to the subject matter and to operating management personnel.   The reviewers may function simply as critics who are expected to comment on possible effects and offer suggestions for revisions.   Others, such as the company legal officer, may have veto power.   There is an added dimension if the material is covered by a collective bargaining agreement.   The text must be checked against the contract and arbitration decisions.   The company labor relations or legal staff must participate.

Ultimate approval may reside in top management—an executive committee, the chief operating executives of major organizational units, or even the board of directors.

Approval levels may vary according to subject matter and the extent of the policy. A completely new job evaluation program, for example, might require board approval, but new parking lot regulations would go no further than the plant manager. Some flexibility is needed if the manual ranges widely in its coverage.

HOW IS THE MANUAL DISTRIBUTED?

The personnel policy manual is an official management document.   Distribution should be carefully controlled.   Most companies maintain authorized user lists. Copies can be numbered and recorded by name of user.   If an organization chart or some other such device is not available or adequate for identifying the proper recipients, individual requests to the personnel department from some authorized echelon of management may be required.

In general, access to the manual should be based on the need to know.   How far down the supervisory line this need exists depends on the purpose of the manual and the extent of delegation of responsibility for making the decisions that the policies are designed to control. If it is a supervisor's manual, a copy should be available to every first-line supervisor as well as the managerial echelons above him.

Of course, access to the manual does not necessarily mean possession. Distribution may be limited to a middle management level but made available to lower-level supervisors when required. For that matter, even nonsupervisory personnel are permitted to refer to a policy manual in some companies that have copies available for reference on particular questions. There should be little need for the general employee to refer to the manual, however, especially if he has a good employee handbook designed especially for his use.

If it is a supervisor's manual, it is preferable that every supervisor have his own copy unless cost and security reasons dictate more limited distribution. The new supervisor should receive a copy from his superior as part of his introduction to his responsibilities. Just finding it in his desk is not enough. The supervisor will use it seriously if his manager emphasizes its importance to his success in dealing with personnel problems. It should be a symbol of his office.

Users are ordinarily informed that manuals are company property that must be returned when terminating employment or transferring to a position where responsibilities do not require reference to the volume. It is helpful if a procedure has been established for handling the manual of a manager who is transferred to another managerial office. Does he take it with him, or leave it for his successor, and then obtain the manual kept in his new office? A well-used manual is often annotated by the supervisor and supplemented with pertinent memos and other materials he finds helpful. Personalized in this way, a supervisor prefers to keep the manual with him as he moves about in his company career.

HOW IS THE MANUAL KEPT UP TO DATE?

The conditions that call for particular personnel policies are seldom static. A policy manual is useful only if policies are changed to meet new requirements. A policy changed but not recorded in the manual is an invitation to disaster. Responsibility for keeping the manual up to date should be assigned to one person. As in developing the manual initially, that responsibility can be further delegated to specialists each of whom is accountable for the departmental unit covering his province. The benefits manager recommends changes of procedure for filing accident insurance claims, the salary administrator asks for revisions in job evaluation standards. When they obtain approval for modifications of their programs, they are the ones who initiate a request for manual changes. The manual coordinator, most often the personnel administrator or his assistant, carries the changes through to completion, usually following the same review and approval procedures as used for the new manual. He can also serve as the editor who watches for inconsistencies between sections, and the originator of recommendations for changes in more general subject matter not otherwise covered by the specialists.

The manual itself can be used as a vehicle for making changes instead of just recording changes after they have been instituted. The more comprehensive the manual is, the more useful it can be in effecting revisions of policies. Members of management who have authority to approve changes can review them best if they understand what the new objective is, who will implement it, and how it will be carried out—points a good manual will cover. With the present and proposed versions in the same format, comparisons and the decision to approve or disapprove can be made with greater confidence.

Because it is so important that a personnel manual be kept responsive to current needs, revision should be practically continuous. It is generally accepted that in addition to making changes when obviously needed, some kind of periodic audit of the entire manual should be conducted. A good rule is to examine every chapter no later than one year after its issue or last revision. The manual coordinator should do this himself and also request that the specialist on individual chapter subject matter make the same review.

If the manual is kept in a loose-leaf binder (the overwhelming preference of personnel men), changes can and should be made as frequently as the policies change, section by section. A good personnel manual is generally too big a project to revise in its entirety or to replace when just some parts are changed.

Getting new or changed pages into a manual should follow the same routine as the initial distribution. A master list of users is important of course. A covering note summarizing the essential change will help the user decide whether he should study it immediately or file for reference when needed. The recipient should be told to clean out the old pages. If pages are dated (a common practice), it is recommended that both the original issue date and date of revision appear on new pages. The need to change tables of contents and indexes corresponding to changes in text should not be neglected.

HOW CAN THE MANUAL BE USED AS A COMMUNICATIONS DEVICE?

A personnel policy manual can be used in two very effective ways to communicate with users. It can become a two-way communication tool in the development stage, and an authorized announcement method after a policy has been approved.

A supervisor's opinion should be weighed before making policy or changes in policy that directly affect his relationships with his employees. One way of doing this is to prepare a proposed version of the policy for the manual and send it to all or a selected sampling of supervisors for their comments. Meetings can be called to discuss the draft with personnel department staff to explore its effect and the problems of implementation. Letting supervisors know what is being planned, thus, not only prepares them for the job of eventually putting it into effect, but brings their practical experience into its development.

When the manual is used to make the official announcement of new policy, it provides the detail that answers questions before they are asked. Immediate execution becomes possible. There may be a disadvantage to the busy supervisor in a long statement, perhaps discouraging him from reading it. This is easily overcome, however, by attaching it to a brief memorandum that summarizes the policy.

HOW CAN THE MANUAL BE USED AS A TRAINING DEVICE?

A good personnel policy manual may be the best personnel textbook a supervisor will ever see. Here are the nuts and bolts of today's personnel theory as applied by his company. It can be the cornerstone of a supervisory training program in human relations. A training program that helps him supervise more effectively can be designed in units corresponding to chapters in the manual. Reading assignments, lectures, and films can expand the background aspects. Case studies, role playing, and other problem-solving techniques can be designed around the policy manual.

One company held seminars on its manual, several chapters at a time as it finished writing them. After the manual was completed, refresher sessions were held to emphasize proper treatment of especially difficult subjects. Tapes were made of problem cases that actually occurred in that company as a result of poor application of policy. Top executives recorded the material on the tapes to emphasize management concern with human relations problems and their desire that guidelines in the manual be followed. The same material was then reworked into an introductory program for new supervisors who had just been given their copies. As a by-product of training sessions based on a policy manual, a company gains insights into the effectiveness of its policies. Discussions among supervisors in the context of the company's policy manual generates comment and criticism that are invaluable feedback for consideration of further revisions. The education process becomes two-way.

HOW SHOULD THE MANUAL BE ORGANIZED?

The easiest way to organize the material in a manual is by date of issue of policies. As new policies are written, they are inserted in the back or front of the manual. If there are not too many policies, this can be quite satisfactory. But as the manual grows, it becomes increasingly difficult to locate a given subject, and some system should be devised to avoid unnecessary searching by the user. Most commonly, this takes the form of a table of contents, a simple listing of the topic heading of each policy in the same order that it was bound in the manual.

A more refined method of organization is needed for the truly comprehensive policy manual covering a multiplicity of topics. The best arrangement is by subject matter, preceded by a table of contents and followed by a detailed index. Subject groupings can follow the main areas of concern of the personnel department such as employment, compensation, training, benefits, and recreation. Such groupings may be designated as chapters and related matter within each chapter further grouped into subsections. Chapters can follow various orders—by subject matter in alphabetical sequence (the first chapter is on absenteeism and the last chapter on workmen's compensation), or by career sequence (the first chapter covers recruitment and the last one discusses terminations).

A sufficiently detailed table of contents that shows both chapter and section headings may obviate the necessity for an index. An alternate approach to the table of contents shows chapter headings at the front of the book, and section headings in a table of contents at the beginning of each section.

A subject index, if used, is usually placed at the back of the manual. It serves the purpose of drawing attention to every page where reference is made to the subject of interest. If, for example, a supervisor is contemplating a disciplinary discharge, reference to the index under Termination may send him to different chapters or sections of the manual for guidance and policy on warning procedures, separation pay, conversion of insurance for terminated employees, unemployment insurance, etc. Of course, if every aspect of each subject were thoroughly covered in each of the several places it appeared in the manual, the index might be superfluous. Writing a manual on this basis, however, would result in an impractical size. An index is more efficient. Also helpful are cross references, or parenthetical notes listing other places where the subject is treated.

A separate section may be used to collect items that would clutter text material unnecessarily. Action forms, for example, may be shown more conveniently in an appendix rather than adjacent to the pages that discuss them. Salary conversion tables, benefit plans, and union contracts, and other similar material also appear in some manuals this way.

Numbering of pages offers several alternatives. The most important thing to remember here is that the best manuals keep changing. Additions, deletions, and substitutions will play havoc with a rigid sequential system. One way is to avoid numbering pages at all. Instead, paragraphs can be numbered with a decimal system or a letter-number combination so that the first part of the code is constant for a given subject and the second part advances with each paragraph or subsection. For example, a chapter on recruitment would find paragraphs numbered like this:

Recruitment Sources 1.10, 1.11, 1.12, 1.13
Job Specifications   1.20, 1.21
Interviewing Procedure   1.30, 1.31, 1.32

Another numbering method starts from page 1 in each chapter, or even each section of each chapter. Thus the subject of compensation would appear as, perhaps, Chapter F. Section I in that chapter would cover general policies, Section II job evaluation, Section III merit and promotion increase standards, etc. Each section would start with page 1. But whatever approach is used, and these are not the only methods, the idea is to allow room for revisions without the necessity of reissuing large numbers of pages that actually have no text changes.

In view of the foregoing, it should be almost unnecessary to urge a loose-leaf binder as the container for the manual. Unless the manual is highly specialized and covers a limited subject field, loose-leaf format is about the only one used in business today. The most common page size is the standard 8½ by 11 inches. Furthermore, since manuals of this type are referred to frequently, a little extra initial expense to obtain a durable cover will turn into a long-range saving.

WHAT SHOULD BE INCLUDED IN A POLICY MANUAL?

Define the objectives of a personnel policy manual, and a good start will have been made in deciding what should be included. The table of contents illustrated in Figure 1 shows by its chapter headings comprehensive coverage of personnel subject matter in a manual used by a managerial staff. Figure 2 shows the further breakdown of topics for one chapter of the same manual. The company's intent is apparently to cover the entire range of their managers' personnel administration responsibilities, and to provide them with guidance in considerable detail.

Limits on the coverage of a manual may be based on a variety of conditions. The types of employees to whom the policies apply is a common basis for individual manuals. Policies applicable to employees under a collective bargaining agreement

Figure 1.   Manual table of contents.

PERSONNEL POLICIES AND PROCEDURES

TABLE OF CONTENTS

Chapter	Subject
A.	Recruitment, Selection, and Placement
B.	Termination of Employment
D	Job Fundamentals
F.	Compensation
H	Privileges and Responsibilities
J	Transfer and Promotions
L.	Security Benefits
M	Miscellaneous Benefits
N	Employee Health and Safety
P.	Social and Recreational Activities
R.	Internal Communications
T.	Time Off the Job
Z.	Other Personnel Policies and Procedures
Index. .	

Figure 2.   Chapter table of contents.

CHAPTER T
TIME OFF THE JOB

TABLE OF CONTENTS

Subject	*Section*
Vacations	I
Holidays	II
Leave of Absence	III
Personal Business	IV
Death in the Family	V
Military Service	VI
Jury Duty	VII
Illness or Injury	VIII
Official Closing	IX
Individual Absence Due to Emergency	X
Religious Observance	XI
Tardiness	XII
Effect of Time Off on Overtime Pay	XIII

may be treated in a separate manual, sometimes with the complete text of the union contract included. Whether unionized or not, policies for plant personnel are often sufficiently different from those affecting office employees to suggest separate manuals. A comparable distinction is sometimes made between exempt and non-exempt employees or salaried versus hourly personnel.

Multilocation companies might have a manual for each plant if policies vary sufficiently. Corporate headquarters and subsidiary companies may also have their own manuals. Overseas operations will obviously require different policies in many categories and so justify a distinct manual.

The decision to break out a body of policy for a separate manual is usually determined by the extent of the differences applicable to the distinct unit. Large-scale differences suggest a separate manual. Otherwise the same manual can be used more broadly with notations where variations apply or even with separate chapters if needed.

The existence of other procedure manuals in a company will also influence the contents of the personnel manual. An office procedure manual, for example, may provide full treatment of the use of standard company forms. An accounting manual may cover such items as payroll procedures and expense account policies. The industrial relations department may provide its own manual analyzing the union contracts and providing detailed guidance on administration at the supervisory level. There may be an insurance manual covering certain employee benefit plans. To the extent that the supervisor has access to these sources, the personnel manual may be restricted instead of duplicating material unnecessarily.

Indiscriminate inclusion in the personnel manual of the details of every personnel program in an effort to make it complete can result in such a ponderous tome that the average supervisor will be repelled by the idea of trying to find anything in it. Before something new is added to the manual, two basic questions should be asked about the material:

1. Does the user absolutely need it to do his job effectively?
2. Is it available elsewhere in more convenient form?

A few examples will illustrate considerations that might keep even important material out of a manual. A union contract is often separately printed for union members and supervisors. A convenient-size edition that the supervisor keeps readily available on his desk or in his shirt pocket may be all he needs. Pension plans and group insurance programs are administered by company specialists. The supervisor should know the main features but does not need the fine detail of such plans. If the eligibility rules and filing procedures are printed fully on suggestion plan application blanks, inclusion of this same material in the supervisor's personnel manual may also be superfluous.

Where all facets of a company's operations are detailed in writing, the personnel policy manual may be just one of a bookshelf of volumes used by a manager. Such material may be organized in separate manuals or grouped between the covers of only one volume. Although the personnel department may have responsibility then for its section alone, some attention is usually given to avoiding repetition of material available in other sections by use of cross references. It will keep the volume as a whole down to a reasonable, usable size.

HOW MUCH DETAIL IS NEEDED IN A MANUAL?

In deciding how much detail to put into a manual, the company's objectives must be weighed. How much help does the supervisor need? How much discretion does the company want him to exercise? To what extent has the company developed a body of viable policy, and how much does it want to share with lower echelons of management?

Obviously, there will be quite a range of answers to these questions from company to company and, therefore, a corresponding variety of treatment of manuals. At one end of the spectrum is a simple listing of plant rules. Then there are the collections of occasionally published bulletins on personnel subjects, organized in no special manner. Moving toward the more complete approach are the manuals that assemble more detailed standard practices on certain subjects, not necessarily covering the entire personnel area.

The most comprehensive manuals carry sections on all major human relations subjects. For each subject, policies and procedures are segregated, interpretations discussed, forms exhibited, and an attempt made to anticipate all questions facing supervisors in practical work situations.

To do a thorough job, a manual for supervisors must be complete and detailed. The result is usually a volume of impressive size. The criticism that few busy managers have time to read something so formidable is valid only if they are expected to read it literally from cover to cover. Generally speaking, that is not why a manual is given to a supervisor. It should be treated primarily as a reference work. When a personnel problem faces him, the supervisor must have all the policy guidelines that apply and answers to all the questions that the company wants treated consistently. There are some obvious specifications for a manual of this kind. Not only must it be complete, but it must be logically organized.

The best organization of policy pins down five things:
1. The objective or purpose of the policy
2. The principal features of the policy
3. The assignment of responsibility for carrying the policy out
4. Definitions of terms
5. The procedures to be followed.

A SAMPLE POLICY STATEMENT

One company's policy on the subject of dismissal of employees will be used to illustrate.

The section begins with a question calling for a definition of basic policy. The company sets forth its overall objective, its philosophy on dismissal. A statement of this kind should be made in fairly general terms. It is very fundamental, and seldom changes even though procedures for implementation often do.

DISMISSAL

What Is the Basic Policy?
To resort to dismissal for just and sufficient cause only, and only after all practical steps toward rehabilitation or salvage of the employee have been taken and failed. However, if the welfare of the company indicates that dismissal is necessary, then that decision should be arrived at and carried out forthrightly.

Then a series of statements are made covering the principal features of the policy, more detailed than the opening statement.

Must An Employee Be Given A Final Warning Before Dismissal?
Yes, except in cases of misconduct.
What Form Must A Final Warning Take?
Any permanent employee, full time and part time, including probationary employees, should be told in what way he fails to meet required standards of performance, and that failure to attain these standards within a reasonable period of time and subsequently maintain them will result in notice of dismissal.
Must A Final Warning Be Put In Writing?
Yes. A memo to the employee confirming the essentials of the discussion in which the warning was given will avoid misunderstanding on the part of the employee. Such written warning must have prior approval of the manager who would be required to approve the dismissal, and a copy is to be forwarded to the appropriate Personnel Administrator for the employee's file.

Assignment of responsibility is established with the following question and answer:

Who May Dismiss An Employee?
The decision to dismiss an employee cannot be made solely by his immediate supervisor. It must be approved by the next higher authority, no matter at what level the action occurs. Moreover, the appropriate Personnel Administrator must be consulted before any definite action is taken.

Now key terms are introduced and defined:

What Are Acceptable Reasons For Dismissal?
An employee may be dismissed for any of the following reasons:
1. Unsatisfactory performance
2. Misconduct
3. Lack of qualifications for job
What Constitutes "Unsatisfactory Performance"?
Persistent failure to perform assigned work duties or to meet prescribed standards on the job constitutes unsatisfactory performance. This failure may in turn be due to various causes, any one of which justifies dismissal, as follows:
1. Absenteeism. This is cause for dismissal regardless of the reason for absence, and if, after several warnings, the employee's attendance continues to be such that it affects his performance or has a bad influence on other members of the staff, he should be dismissed.
2. Tardiness. Likewise, repeated or habitual tardiness is cause for dismissal.
3. Lack of Application to Job. An employee may be qualified and capable of performing the job assigned to him, but if he persistently fails (despite warnings) to apply himself to meeting normal requirements of quantity and quality, he should be dismissed.
4. Attitude. If the employee's attitude affects seriously his performance or his relationship with his fellow employees, he should be dismissed, but only after adequate warning.

By attitude is meant the sum total of all his feelings towards the company, his supervisor, his fellow employees, his work assignments, and the established policies and procedures pertaining to his work.

The definitions continue with two questions covering "misconduct" and "lack of qualification for the job." Additional policies follow covering the details of special payments for dismissed employees. (Notice cross references made to other chapters of the manual. An alternative to cross references is repetition of needed material to save the user from turning pages excessively. Too much duplication results in a bulky manual, however.)

When Does Separation Allowance for Dismissal Apply?
A separation allowance is paid to any permanent employee, either full-time or part-time, who has completed his probationary period and who is dismissed because of lack of qualifications for the job, or for some other reason that is not considered the fault of the employee.

When Does Separation Allowance for Dismissal NOT Apply?
Separation allowance is not paid when dismissal occurs under any of the following circumstances:
1. Unsatisfactory performance
2. Misconduct
3. Some other reason that is considered the fault of the employee
4. Before the completion of the probationary period
5. During temporary employment.

How Much Separation Allowance Is Paid?
The amount of separation allowance depends upon the employee's length of service and his earnings at the time of dismissal. In each case, the exact amount will be computed and included in the final check by the Payroll Department.

A similar question is then asked to cover how much vacation is paid for, and then several questions follow on notice of dismissal:

When Should Notice of Dismissal Be Given? . . .
When Should A Dismissed Employee Receive Pay In Lieu of Notice? . . .
How Much Payment Is Given In Lieu Of Notice? . . .

The section concludes with several paragraphs under the heading Procedure on Dismissal. The manager is told what action steps he must take to carry out a dismissal according to the stated policies. It is a brief how-to dissertation.

Consider Dismissal Action Carefully.
No employee should be dismissed without a careful study of all the factors involved. Before reaching a decision to dismiss an employee, the supervisor should be satisfied in his own mind that all practical steps have been taken to salvage the employee. In cases of employees who lack qualifications for the job, it is possible that their deficiencies might be overcome by further on-the-job training or by the employee taking outside courses. Frank discussions between the employee and the supervisor should be held to assure a thorough understanding of the problem and what corrective steps should be taken.

The supervisor should consult with his Personnel Administrator before any definite action is taken to remove the employee from the payroll. The Personnel Administrator will work with the Recruitment Section to explore transfer possibilities, if it is believed that the employee could be useful elsewhere in the company.

If all other steps taken do not have the desired effect, the employee should be warned that his failure to meet required standards of performance within a reasonable period of time and subsequently maintain them will result in dismissal.

Confirm the warning with a written memo to the employee. Clear the memo with your manager before giving it to the employee and send a copy to your Personnel Administrator for the employee's file. Consult your Personnel Administrator if you need help in writing this memo.

Select Reason Carefully.

The true reason for dismissal should be officially indicated in each dismissal case. It should be clearcut, and substantiated by adequate evidence. It must be kept in mind that the reason given for an employee's dismissal will have an important bearing on whether the dismissed employee will be eligible for separation allowance and for unemployment insurance. For example, an employee dismissed for excessive absenteeism or tardiness cannot normally claim unemployment insurance, but the State Division of Employment usually requires that the evidence of excessive absenteeism or tardiness be documented, and it must also be shown that the employee was warned. If an employee begins to follow a pattern of absence or lateness, the supervisor should keep his own record of dates and times, and copies of written warnings, for future reference.

Another paragraph in this manner is headed "Discuss The Matter With The Employee," and the section ends with instructions for filing the notice of termination according to regular company procedure.

With this material, a supervisor has solid guidance on a very sensitive subject. He knows what his company's general intentions are, how to carry them out, and where to go for help if he needs it. His manual is a practical management tool.

Two more examples of well-thought-out policy statements appear in Figures 3 and 4.

CONCLUSION

There are many fine personnel policy manuals in use in the business world today. The successful ones follow the general principles outlined in this chapter. But an examination of a sampling of them will also show considerable diversity, and this illustrates a final point that contributes to their success. The unique conditions of each company must be considered when its manual is designed. Borrowing another company's manual will not work. Each step of development must be consistent with the particular company's objectives, resources, managerial organization and employee characteristics. It is a tailor-made project. And it calls for imagination as well as sound judgment.

Furthermore, the job is never finished, as conditions inevitably and continuously change. What does not change if the manual is on a sound basis are the two fundamental purposes of striving for consistent application of personnel policies, and putting the administration of those policies in the hands of the most effective level of line supervision.

Figure 3.   Leave of absence policy.

SUBJECT: *Leaves of absence*   EFFECTIVE DATE: *May 2, 1969*

1. *Policy*

1.1 It is the policy of the corporation to keep intact the continuity of service of permanent full-time and part-time employees who have been granted time off from work without pay.

2. *Length of Leaves of Absence*

2.1 Requests for approved absences without pay of two weeks or less are not considered "leaves of absence" and are approved by supervisors by time card entry.

2.2 The maximum length of a leave of absence is six months.

3. *Failure to Return from Leave of Absence*

Figure 3. Leave of absence policy. (continued)

3.1 Failure to return to work at the expiration of a leave of absence shall be construed as a resignation unless an extension has been requested and approved before the expiration of the leave.

4. *Guides for Approving Leaves of Absence*

4.1 The employee must be a permanent employee, either full-time or part-time.

4.2 The employee must have at least one year of service.

4.3 The effect of the absence upon the operation of the department must be considered and will not be approved if the position cannot be held open until the employee returns, or if the department cannot meet its work requirements while the employee is on leave.

4.4 The employee must have a serious purpose for requesting the leave such as:

4.4.1 Serious illness in the family

4.4.2 Health reasons not covered by corporation disability benefits plan

4.4.3 Special scholarship

4.4.4 Election to public office

4.4.5 Urgent personal business such as settling an estate

4.4.6 Extended travel for purposes of personal growth and improvement as an employee.

4.5 Leave of absence cannot be approved for the purpose of seeking another position.

5. *Maternity Leaves of Absence*

5.1 If a pregnant woman's job can be held open or filled on a temporary basis, her request for a leave of absence must be granted. Forcing her to resign would be a violation of the Civil Rights Act. Limitations under the leave of absence policy as outlined in this subject section apply equally to maternity leaves as well as other leaves. This includes the requirements of one-year service and permanent status, and the maximum permissible period of leave of six months.

6. *Effect of a Leave of Absence on Benefit Plans*

6.1 Holidays—The employee will be paid for an official corporation holiday that falls the day before the start of or the day after the end of an unpaid leave of absence, but he will not be paid for any holidays that fall within the leave of absence period.

6.2 Vacations—Vacation credits are reduced proportionate to the amount of leave if the time off exceeds two months.

6.3 Retirement Plan—Contributions to the Retirement Plan are based upon monthly earnings and therefore may not be continued during a leave of absence.

6.4 Group Life Insurance and Medical Expense Insurance—To continue in effect the group life insurance and medical expense insurance coverage, the employee must indicate on the application form for the leave of absence his authorization for advance payment of premiums that normally fall during the period of the leave. If the employee does not give authorization for advance payments, membership in these plans will be suspended.

6.4.1 Deductions in effect prior to the employee's leave of absence will be reinstated automatically when the employee returns to work, regardless of whether or not advance deductions were authorized by the employee for the period of the leave.

7. *Procedure for Requesting Leave of Absence*

7.1 When an employee requests a leave of absence, have him complete the form "Application for Non-Military Leave of Absence." Forms are available in the Personnel Department.

7.2 The department head must endorse the application if all aspects of the application conform to guides listed in paragraph 4 above, and forward the form to the Personnel Department for review.

7.2.1 Maternity leave requests must be forwarded to the Personnel Department for review even if the department head feels he cannot endorse it because of operational problems.

7.3 If the leave is approved, a "Non-Military Leave of Absence" notice is prepared in quadruplicate by the Personnel Department and distributed to the employee, department head, Payroll Department, and personnel files.

7.4 If the leave is not approved, the department head will be advised of the reason and he should tell the employee why it was turned down.

Figure 4. Tuition refund policy.

INDUSTRIAL RELATIONS POLICY

Title   *Tuition refunds*

COVERAGE: All Domestic Operations—Plant and Office Personnel

AUTHORIZED BY: Employee Services Manager

DATE OF LATEST ISSUE: January 3, 1970

PURPOSE: To encourage permanent, full-time employees to improve their technical and intellectual competence as employees by pursuing and successfully completing appropriate courses of study, in addition to carrying out their regular full-time duties.

I. Eligible Courses

A. The course must be a serious technical, intellectual, or cultural undertaking, successful completion of which will improve the competence of the student as an employee. Courses taken for a recreational purpose, whether intellectual or physical, are not eligible.

B. The course must be offered by a well-established institution. Courses given by an individual tutor operating independently will not qualify for a tuition refund.

II. Ineligible Employees

A. Temporary employees

B. Part-time employees

C. Probationary employees

III. Employee Responsibility

An application for refund must be submitted to the personnel department no later than one month after the course begins. If the employee wishes to know before paying for courses whether the tuition refund will be granted, the application should be submitted prior to registering for courses. Applications will not be approved if received after the one-month filing period, unless an adequate explanation for the delay is furnished.

IV. Manager Responsibility

The manager must complete the tuition refund application form by answering the question concerning the applicability of the course to the employee's present job. This helps determine taxability of the refund under government regulations. The manager must then forward the application, regardless of the answer to the tax question, to the personnel department.

V. Personnel Department Responsibility

The employee services manager of the personnel department approves or disapproves requests. If the request is approved, he also decides whether the refund is subject to withholding taxes.

VI. Amount of Refund

A. Refunds are 50 percent of the cost of tuition including registration fees, but not including books or laboratory fees.

B. By law, refunds will be subject to income tax withholding unless courses taken are immediately applicable to the improvement of skills or add to knowledge now required in the employee's present job.

C. Courses covered by the plan and subsidized under the GI Bill or by other public or private funds are eligible for a refund of 50 percent of the employee's nonsubsidized tuition cost.

VII. Limitations

A. A course will not be approved under the plan if it covers the same subject matter as a course that is sponsored by the company and given at no expense to the employee, and which the employee is either actually scheduled to take or will be able to take in the foreseeable future.

B. Refund payments will be limited to tuition for not more than six credit hours a week. Where credit hours are not given, six actual class hours will be the limit. The company does not encourage a more strenuous schedule because of the possible effect on the employee's health and work performance.

C. The amount of refund for courses not directly related to the employee's present job will be limited as follows:

1) Not more than $175 per term

2) Not more than $350 per any twelve-month period

Figure 4.   Tuition refund policy.   (continued)

VIII. Verification and Completion

    A. Refund payments are made to employees after they have submitted tuition receipts and records of satisfactory completion of the course.

    B. Employees must complete courses while still employed except that those terminated due to a reduction in force are eligible for refund for all approved courses started before termination.

    C. Required documents must be submitted within sixty days of completion of the course.

IX. Procedure

    A. The employee obtains an application for participation in the Tuition Refund Plan from the Personnel Department, Employee Services Section.

    B. The employee fills in the form and gives it to his manager for completion.

    C. The manager sends the completed form to the employee services manager.

    D. The applicant is notified by the employee services manager whether the request was approved or disapproved, and whether or not the refund will be subject to withholding taxes. He is also given instructions on what records must be produced upon completing the course in order to obtain the refund.

    E. After the course ends, the employee whose application was approved sends the required records showing successful completion of the course and cost to the employee services manager who then sends a request for check to payroll or accounting (depending on whether taxes must be withheld or not). The check is sent via interoffice mail to the student by the employee services manager.

BIBLIOGRAPHY

Cooper, Joseph D.: *How to Communicate Policies and Instructions,* Bureau of National Affairs, Washington, D.C., 1960.

Kellogg, M. Graham: *Preparing the Office Manual,* Research Study No. 36, American Management Association, New York, 1959.

McLaughlin, T. J.: *Communication,* Charles E. Merrill Books, Inc., Columbus, Ohio, 1964.

Management Information Center, Inc.: *How to Write a Personnel Policy Manual,* Deerfield, Ill., 1968.

National Industrial Conference Board, Inc.: *Personnel Procedure Manuals,* Studies in Personnel Policy No. 180, New York, 1961.

Neuschel, Richard F.: *Management by System,* 2d ed., McGraw-Hill Book Company, New York, 1960.

Redfield, Charles E.: *Communication in Management,* The University of Chicago Press, Chicago, 1958.

Ross, H. John: *How to Make a Procedure Manual,* Office Research Institute, Miami, Fla., 1958.

chapter 76

Other Written Materials and Devices

DANIEL D. CANTOR   *Deputy Director, American Peace Corps, New Delhi, India*
Formerly Vice President, Employee Relations, Itek Corporation, Lexington, Massachusetts

The preceding chapters have covered the four most frequently utilized methods of employee communications.   However, a mistake is often made in regarding these major areas—newspapers, magazines, handbooks, manuals—as the primary or even the only way of getting the word to the people.   No one in the personnel field should turn his back on the many other avenues of communication that are readily available.   This chapter will examine as many of these approaches as possible, but new ones can be and are being developed and used almost all the time.   Keep in mind that there are no "right" or "only" ways to communicate; there are some that are to be preferred for certain purposes, but even these are limited only by the innovativeness and judgment of the personnel people utilizing them.

For clarification, the methods to be discussed here will be more specialized, and directed toward more specific purposes, than those previously described.   They are "on-the-spot" ideas that can be easily tailor-made to fit specific situations.   They tend, as a group, to be less expensive than the more conventional methods, with exceptions as noted.   But the main thing to keep in mind about them is that you can use them—or any others they bring to mind—as specifically designed and, it can be hoped, very effective communications tools.

For each method described, these key factors will be considered:

What purpose can it best serve?

When is it not useful?

Advantages and disadvantages

Hints to consider

Dangers to avoid

I. BULLETIN BOARDS

Bulletin boards are like aspirin—cheap, easily available, very useful, and quite often badly used. Traditionally, they have sometimes become the object of employee scorn or they have been misused as a depository for inappropriate graffiti. Do not discard the good with the bad; good bulletin boards are good communications. With a modern, current approach, bulletin boards can be a very effective device. Build up good readership and some respect, and your company's bulletin boards will earn their keep.

Purposes best served

1. Certain postings that are legally required—minimum wage notices, equal employment compliances, workmen's compensation coverage
2. Timely notices of interest to all employees—vacation shutdowns, holiday notices, schedule changes, cafeteria information
3. Timely notices of employee activities—recreation association, theatre parties, athletic contests or results
4. Employee personal services—lost and found, car pools, housing

When Is It Not Useful?

1. Information that is of limited interest, such as material with a high and narrow technical content
2. Material needing a "personal" touch
3. Material that requires a long reading time

Advantages

1. Bulletin boards are readily available and highly visible, and can secure broad readership.
2. They are inexpensive, and get away from all the reproduction and distribution problems associated with most written communications.
3. The information can be quickly changed and updated.

Disadvantages

1. Bulletin boards are easily subject to abuse, and require some active control of posting procedures.
2. They must be physically placed in a location with good traffic flow.
3. They need an approval procedure, sometimes bulky to administer, that will ensure posting of only authorized material.

Hints to Consider and Things to Avoid

1. The interest level of your employees must be maintained:
- By the information posted and what it says and how well it says it
- By the appearance and attractiveness of the board itself, so that people want to see what is posted.
2. The material should be brief and readable.
3. The board should be uncluttered, and material should be sorted out by area of interest or subject matter or audience. Your readers should not have to search for the subjects they want to read about.
4. The board and material *must* be current. There is nothing more destructive to a bulletin board's effectiveness than out-of-date material. If you think you might tire of reading today's newspaper for ten more consecutive days, then imagine how your people feel about seeing the same dead, outdated notices up on the board. And once your people have decided that there is "nothing new," you will have a difficult time recapturing their interest.
5. The board should be placed in a heavy traffic area; people generally will not go out of their way to find the board.

In summary, bulletin boards can be revitalized to serve as an effective method of reaching your people. But like any medium, this one must be responsive and reactive to the needs of your changing population. The bulletin board of old may have been "required reading," and the employer did not have to worry whether his people read the requirement about sweeping out the store or not chewing tobacco. Today, people have to be—and can be—attracted to read what you want to tell them. Effectively set-up and maintained bulletin boards can carry messages effectively.

II. EMPLOYEE LETTERS AND MEMOS

As in the case of the bulletin board, personnel people sometimes tend to downgrade or even ignore this area, perhaps again because it can be deceptively simple and relatively inexpensive. However, letters and memos have their place—and a very real place—in any overall plan of communications. For ease of understanding, let us divide these letters and memos into two basic types; first, the normal, periodic ones, and second, the letters and memos used for special occasions. This done, we can examine a number of examples of each type to see and analyze their use and their purpose.

1. *Periodic.* Included here would be such examples as management or employee newsletters, quarterly or monthly or other periodic business summaries, and regular reports on union relations (when called for or permitted by contract).

2. *Special.* Examples of this type would include announcements of new appointments or organization changes, current and immediate information on any state-of-the-business matter, updating on current union negotiations, holiday or vacation send-offs (including safety messages if appropriate). See Figure 1 for a sample special memo. *Note:* The use of memos or any other communications in situations involving unions or organizing efforts can be treated as a subject all its own. Much of what will be covered here—timing, advantages of mail-homes, flexibility on who sends it out, etc.—applies to union situations as well, but the entire labor law problem must be given primary attention. That is left for a separate chapter, and communications methods discussed here must not be considered as automatically applicable or legal in a situation involving a labor union.

Purposes best served

1. *Periodic*
   a. Good when personal communications with large numbers of people are desired.
   b. The established practice of regular letters or memos makes them acceptable in the "special" cases, such as a need to communicate with people about a potentially sensitive subject such as union organizing efforts or adverse business conditions.
   c. Helpful if it is desired to have considerable degree of "privacy."
   d. Useful if it is important to involve the employee's family.
2. *Special*
   a. Excellent for situations requiring rapid communications.
   b. Good when added emphasis is needed on any subject.
   c. Can be as flexible as you want them; witness just a small sampling of the subject matter covered by a recent sampling.

   ■ Answering a newspaper editorial that showed the company in a poor light
   ■ Telling people about actions taken in a bomb scare incident
   ■ Explaining to people just what the stock price movement means to them
   ■ Congratulating the people on a commendation received from a major customer

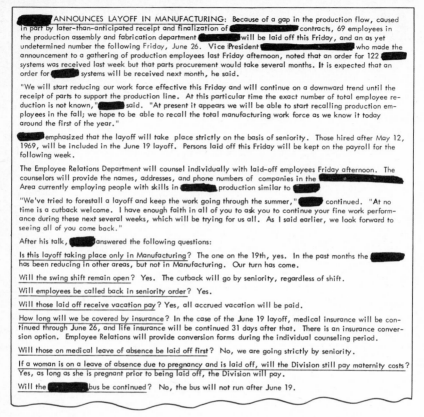

Figure 1.   Special release to employees.

When it is not a useful method

1. *Periodic*

a. Obviously, when the timing is the paramount objective. There is nothing sadder and less effective than the bimonthly management newsletter that contains the "hot" news of a new acquisition or a new appointment that happened seven weeks ago. This type of dead-news reporting will not only severely restrict the effectiveness of the periodic publication, but it will effectively, if inadvertently, serve as a growth stimulus for the grapevine and rumor mill.

b. When it is clearly outside the subject scope of the periodic publication. Do not try to squeeze fire safety rules or other specific pieces of information into a publication with known limits of audience.

2. *Special*

a. If used correctly, and because the "special" implies a tailor-made response to any need, there should be virtually no purpose for which such approaches are inappropriate. The major problem is in picking the *best* one for each problem as it arises. Consider the essentials—the specific readership, the timing, the anticipated reactions—then get on with it.

b. Recognize only the intrinsic *time* limitations of interoffice mail and of the regular postal system. There is often the tendency to assume that putting 500 envelopes in the post office Tuesday night means that the people will all get them Wednesday morning. Make sure you *know* how your local postal office system works, and allow for its foibles in your schedule. (Also, do not overlook a simple, obvious fact—if the people are to receive that mail-home Wednesday morning, most of them will be at work when the mail arrives.)

Hints to consider

Improvise.
Break the habit.
Invent.
Develop.

In this whole area of notes or letters or memos to employees, we tend to fall back far too often on the "doing-it-again-because-it-worked" syndrome. If the company president has traditionally written a mail-home letter to each employee every Christmas season, *do not* assume it should be done again this year. What is the mood of your people? What is the state of your business? Are there special problems or situations that, for *your* people at *this* time, indicate that a different letter, no letter, a card, a phonograph record, or some other approach would do the job more effectively?

Answer the need, not the habit.

And try to avoid these dangers

1. *Lack of Timeliness.* Again, if the news is cold, you might be well advised to avoid sending out anything at all.

2. *Lack of Real Interest in the Subject Matter.* Do not try to artificially stimulate employee interest in something you know is of no interest to them.

3. *Lack of Appropriate Appearance of the Letter.* I.e., if you are telling it straight about a tough business situation that will require belt tightening, do not print it in four colors on expensive stock.

III. AUDIO-VISUAL METHODS

A new, rapidly developing type of media, audio-visuals have become virtually an art form in some quarters. Unlike the bulletin board or the letter or the notice, audio-visuals are a relatively new method of getting messages across to audiences. And because of this, they have several characteristics that are typical of almost any new communications approach, including:

- They are relatively expensive.
- They are highly specialized.
- They are done best by technically trained people.
- They rely on developing and evolving techniques of a mechanically oriented methodology.

Because of these specific characteristics, audio-visual methods have strengths and weaknesses that vary considerably from those found in our other approaches to employee communications.

What purposes are best served? Here we are looking at an educational effort that has opened up whole new teaching approaches. Personnel people and communicators in general must learn to adapt this new methodology to their needs so that they can make most effective use of it. Audio-visuals can serve a host of purposes very effectively—but also probably quite expensively.

Example: An audio-visual house, in its internal communications program for its own people, has replaced the traditional bulletin board with a self-contained slide viewer and changer. Every thirty seconds the next "bulletin board item" flashes on the screen, and watchers can use a "Hold" button to keep a more lengthy item on the viewer longer. Costs aside, the company reports a dramatically improved readership—in terms of numbers of readers and retention of the information presented—with the new system.

Probably the areas best served by an audio-visual approach include:
- Employee orientation
- Employee training
- Explanations of benefit programs
- Dramatization of any specific subject matter to be communicated in a teaching-type approach.

There seems to be no doubt about the validity of studies reflecting the efficiency of audio-visuals as a teaching tool. Interest, comprehension, and retention all show significant and measurable increases when *good* audio-visual techniques are utilized in a teaching process. Therefore, if you want your employees to understand their benefits program, a well-done movie or slide presentation will do an effective job for you. Here, so long as the cost factor can be understood and justified, audio-visuals are right for the job.

Purposes not well served. We have purposely leaned heavily on two aspects of audio-visuals; they are costly and they must be done well. Therefore, the portion of the communications spectrum it can cover tends to be limited. It should not be used when the supply of available time or money (or both) is limited. Resist the temptation to do a polished job of presenting a status report on union negotiations, or an analysis of the new organization chart—these things change so relatively quickly that any costly effort to "sell" them are not justified by the need. (Ridiculous as it sounds, there were strong suspicions in one case that a company preserved an organization arrangement beyond its useful time limits because they had just completed a very fine series of color slides illustrating and demonstrating, clearly and dearly, how the organization chart worked.)

Advantages and disadvantages, then, come out looking like this:

Audio-visuals are fine as a teaching tool, when necessity for thorough comprehension of a major subject matter justifies the cost of a professionally prepared and presented format.

Audio-visuals balance out badly if the communications need calls for speed, low cost, flexibility or individualization.

Hints and dangers

1. If you are going to do it, do it right. The penny-wise, pound-foolish complex is no place more obvious than in an almost-effective safety program that does not quite reach the people. The additional cost may be burdensome, but get someone to do it who knows how, give him the time and money needed, and *do not cut that corner!*

2. Take advantage of the many new and innovative methods and techniques that are continually being developed in this growing field. Rapid sequencing, music integration, multimedia concepts, and a host of other approaches make for attractive learning devices—but again, leave it to the experts. Tinkering with a Model A is fun and even productive, but it does not qualify one to be Mario Andretti's chief mechanic.

In summary, then, audio-visuals are a relatively costly and truly effective teaching device; used wisely, sparingly, and well, they make a very worthwhile addition to the supply of communications media.

IV. BOOKLETS

Described in an earlier chapter were employee handbooks, newspapers, magazines, and policy manuals. This section deals with other types of bound booklets, primarily:

- Recruitment brochures
- Wage and salary handbooks
- Benefits booklets
- Policy handbooks
- Union contracts
- Job information handbooks

It is quickly obvious that many of these booklets or handbooks are based on material derived from other programs; i.e., a benefits booklet arises out of the benefits program developed by the company and contained in a legal document or contract. However, the booklet so derived becomes a very important communicating tool, because it will be the concise, summarized, attractive booklet (and not the legal contract or the bulky policy) that your employees will tend to read and remember.

These handbooks and booklets can be treated together as a broad group, because the advantages and disadvantages, the areas of usefulness, and the guidelines generally apply to all of them. Therefore, let us first examine briefly each type of booklet, and then we can look broadly at how best they can be used.

1. *Recruitment Brochures.* Here is an excellent example of how we can use the spillover benefit of something, developed for one purpose, as a valid communicating device. And, because it is incidental to its primary use, we too often tend to overlook this avenue. One company, for example, began making general distribution of its recruitment material, and then questioned a number of its current employees about their reactions. The results tended to bear out the fact that a significant number of the employees were not aware of much of the information that was being given to nonemployees. Some of the things the employees apparently learned from the recruiting brochures were:

- What kind of businesses (other than their own plants) their company was in
- The geographical locations of company plants (other than their own)
- Products and customers of the company
- The types of people being considered for employment
- Company benefits programs (and this, despite a sincere company effort to communicate in this area)

2. *Wage and Salary Handbooks.* An easy-to-read rewrite of its policy on compensation gave another company an excellent tool for telling employees about their wages (see Figure 2). In straightforward, readable fashion the company presented its program for establishing, maintaining, and administering competitive and equitable wage rates. It outlined the establishment of jobs, the preparation of descriptions, the process of job evaluation, methods of structure construction, wage surveys, and the process of updating the program. Supervisors, at first fearful that this information in the hands of their people would lead to many (and potentially embarrassing) questions or challenges, were surprised to see how a better-informed employee group actually helped in program administration.

3. *Benefits Booklets.* This represents probably the most single vital form of communication in this category. Traditionally, no one understands a benefits program until he or she has to use it. This, in face of ballooning costs of these programs, has been of real concern to many companies and to virtually all personnel people. Booklets that, because of:

- The way in which they are presented

The policy of the laboratory sets forth three basic steps in the program to establish your rate of pay--

Your Rate of Pay

1. JOB EVALUATION

2. AREA SURVEYS

3. INDIVIDUAL APPRAISAL

Figure 2.   From a booklet describing the company's job evaluation plan.

- The continuing emphasis on them
- Their readability
- Their accessibility

really call out to be read and referred to, can be the best tool management has to use in securing an understanding and an appreciation of a benefits program (see Figure 3).

4. *Policy Handbooks.*   If the assumption is made (and it appears safe to do so) that hardly anyone reads or recalls clearly the detailed manual write-up of a company policy or practice, there remains a real need for readable digests of key policies. The definition of "key" will vary from company to company, and even from time to time, but the list probably should include policy statement summaries on such major areas of employee concern as:

- Equal employment and advancement opportunities
- Salary and wage practices
- Internal promotional opportunities
- Length of service and job security concepts
- Development and training
- Education assistance

IN BRIEF
HERE IS WHAT YOUR GROUP INSURANCE PLAN PROVIDES —

FOR YOU AND YOUR FAMILY

MEDICAL CARE BENEFITS

See Page

Protection from most hospital-surgical and out-of-hospital diagnostic X-ray bills and, after a deductible amount, from a major part of almost all other charges for reasonable and necessary medical care. — 10

PART 1—BASIC PLAN

Hospital Expense Insurance
Includes room and board up to $40 a day for 70 days, and up to $300 of Hospital Special Services. — 11

Physicians' Attendance Insurance (While in the Hospital)
Up to $5 times the number of days for which hospital daily benefits are paid, up to a maximum of $350. — 13

Surgical Operation Insurance
Benefits to help pay the surgeon's fee up to $570, depending upon the type of operation performed. — 14

Diagnostic X-ray and Laboratory Examinations
Up to $50 for all X-ray and laboratory examinations during any consecutive 12-month period. — 16

Additional Accident Insurance
Up to $300 for medical expenses incurred because of an accident. — 18

PART 2—MAJOR MEDICAL INSURANCE
(Picks up Where Your Basic Plan Leaves Off)
Up to $25,000 for you and $25,000 each for your eligible dependents for covered medical expenses in or out of the hospital. You pay a $100 deductible and then the Plan pays 80% of remaining covered expenses up to the maximum. Plan features a $200 family deductible. (See pages 25-26 for additional details.) — 22

2

FOR YOU

See Page

Disability Income
Benefits when you are disabled and unable to work.
(See special insert in back pocket of this booklet) — 6

Accidental Dismemberment Benefits
Cash amounts provided for loss of limb or eyesight.

Travel Insurance
In addition to your regular Disability Income benefits or Accidental Dismemberment Insurance, cash benefits are provided for total disability or bodily dismemberment or loss of eyesight caused by accident while traveling on Company business. — 8

FOR YOUR FAMILY

Life Insurance
A basic $5,000 life insurance amount will be provided at no cost to you. Optional plans can be purchased in amounts totalling either two (2) or three (3) times base annual salary (including the first $5,000 free coverage). — 6

Accidental Death Benefit
In addition to your Life Insurance, 1½ times your annual salary.

Travel Insurance
In addition to Life Insurance and Accidental Death & Dismemberment benefits, your beneficiary can receive death benefits should you die by accident while traveling on Company business. Also, certain dismemberment benefits are payable in cases of injuries incurred while traveling on Company business. — 8

FOR FEMALE EMPLOYEES AND DEPENDENTS

Maternity Benefits
HOSPITAL EXPENSE INSURANCE
Up to $200 for room and board and special services combined (normal delivery). — 21

SURGICAL OPERATION INSURANCE
Up to $150 for normal delivery. — 21

MAJOR MEDICAL INSURANCE
For severe complications of pregnancy. — 24

3

Figure 3. A page out of an employee handbook.

- Benefits programs
- Health and safety
- Employee communications
- Conflict of interest and proprietary information
- Security
- Civil disorders

These subjects can be covered in booklets that combine them appropriately, or treat them individually. The important thing is that they say, succinctly, what is to be said in a manner that will be read and understood and, it is hoped, retained.

5. *Union Contracts.* This category represents a substitute for some or many of the areas covered under policy handbooks. The problem is that managements seem to feel that, once the union contract is written and until and unless contract interpretation difficulties arise, the contract is the union's sole property and responsibility. These contracts govern much of the working life of the employee in the bargaining unit, and have a very real effect on all other employees, too. It therefore seems clear that management should be at least as interested as—and probably more interested than—the union in making sure its people receive, read, and understand the provisions which guide their working relationship.

With this in mind, personnel people have another very valid reason for fighting for contract language that the employee can understand. The legal requirements are not to be ignored, but efforts must continue toward language that will make the contract a useful communications device.

6. *Job Information Handbooks.* Although primarily training tools, these publications can also serve as good ways to communicate. Handbooks for secretaries, for salesmen, for purchasing people, for researchers, for clerical people—they all focus on the "how-to" aspects of job performance. But integrally a part of the description of ways in which the job can best be done is a whole area of information about the company, its people, products, customers, and procedures. Again, with some minor modifications of wording, we have here a very valuable tool for employee communications that we cannot afford to overlook.

With these descriptions in mind, let us next examine the general dos and don'ts about this general communications area.

The purposes best served. These booklets are instructional in nature. They are teaching-communicating devices by which we can help the employee to learn more about all facets of his job with his company. The booklets are most useful when presented in conjunction with some type of learning program that will motivate the employee to read, learn, and retain. They are fundamental to many other types of communications, and as such, they deserve the time and attention necessary to get their message across.

These booklets *are least useful* in instances requiring quick communication. They do not serve on-the-spot needs, are not helpful in getting out instant messages to your employees. They can be considered as a sort of textbook of communications, and therefore need to be supplemented by all the other methods that have been and will be covered.

The *advantages* of all these employee booklets include:

Cost. Because these booklets are often the offspring of some other write-up, they can be relatively inexpensive.

Availability. The employee is given the booklet and, if he can be persuaded to hold on to it and remember where it is, he has a ready reference in which he can find answers to his questions.

Flexibility. The booklets can be arranged in just about any fashion or style to fit the need. Subjects can be combined, illustrations used, texts written imaginatively; the only limits are money, legal or contractual controls, and the innovativeness of the writer.

There are, of course, several *disadvantages* as well, including:

Obsolescence.   Probably the major difficulty lies in keeping these booklets up to date.   Plans, programs, methods all change, and the effectiveness of the booklet is destroyed when it no longer is accurate.   Many solutions have been tried, including loose-leaf booklets with dated replacement pages, but none of them have been very effective without being clumsy and expensive.

Disinterest.   Despite our best efforts, people often are not really interested in what the booklet has to say.   Given this indifference, the booklet is not very good at getting employees to open it up and read it.

Hints and dangers

1. Watch the language.   It must be accurate, but do not sacrifice clarity and readability for accuracy.

2. Keep your reading audience in mind.   The material can be tailored to meet the reading needs of your people, so take advantage of this.   Do not write down to the employee, write to him.   You may even want two or more versions of a booklet on the same subject.

3. Remember the breadth of your potential readers.   This can and often does include the employee's family, so write for them, too.

4. Do not be stodgy, in either language or format.   Crisp, easy-reading, attractive booklets need not cost any more than dull ones.   Let the booklet do a little reader-enticing for you.

5. Keep an eye on the problem of booklet updating.   As noted above, there is no easy answer to this problem, but it is something you must continue to work on.

V. ANNUAL AND PERIODIC REPORTS

Here is another instance in which a reporting device, traditionally designed for and aimed toward another audience, can be made into an excellent and very effective mode of employee communications.

In other sections of this chapter we talk about this possible use of a communications device for a purpose other than that initially intended.   This is a very key factor in the employee communications area generally, and this may well be an appropriate place to look briefly at this dual purpose approach.   A brief example illustrates what is meant.   A company had an adequate audio-visual program for new employee orientation; with minimum editing, it was used most effectively in summing up the company to groups of executives in a newly acquired firm.

The same dual approach is directly appropriate in reviewing annual and other company reports for possible use in communicating to employees.   Historically, annual reports have grown into a broad-based communications tool, and every company should now be making good use of its reports for a variety of reasons.

These financial-type reports, since that is what they are basically, can serve well the purpose of explaining the company, outlining company programs or philosophies, summarizing company business, and examining company goals.   Reports are a teaching and updating device, and can work well in conjunction with employee meetings called to review these areas.

They are not useful if time is a factor, nor can they be very well tailored to include any information on anything outside their "normal" scope.   (However, as will be outlined below, the definition of scope can be changed in such a way that report utilization can be broadly improved.)

Advantages of report-type communications:

1. They can be inexpensive. With just a little or even no change in editing, the only real direct cost is running extra copies.

2. Reports are distributed to stockholders regularly; as such, a growing number of employees of publicly held firms get them anyway, and ones sent specifically to employees can have a more positive impact.

3. A company's business is a changing thing, and the report is a good reminder of the need to update employees on a regular basis.

There are *disadvantages,* of course, and they include:

1. The time table is relatively inflexible, so this is a communications medium that will not help serve some other time need. Also, reports are subject to extensive legal, financial, and management editing, and there can be interminable delays encountered in their production.

2. It is not easy, in reports whose primary purpose is to describe the financial and business conditions of the company, to develop a style, approach, and language that appeal to broad groups of employees. Outstanding progress has been made over the past few years, however, and readable reports are now a target within reach for any company. Even so, the report may well have limited reader appeal among your employees.

There are a number of *hints* to consider and *dangers* to avoid:

1. We talked earlier about being innovative in employee communications; innovation continues to be very important here. There are legal and financial requirements for company reports, but there is no law that says the report must be dull, unimaginative, or unreadable.

2. In trying to design a report to be used for many and sometimes diverse audiences, your writers or editors can work themselves into a language corner. It may be better to decide that, first, the primary audience remains the financial and investing public; second, however, that the words and pictures and charts used can be presented attractively and simply and understandably without detracting from their accuracy or value.

Note: One company took the bull by the horns and split its annual report into two parts. The first included the material conventionally found in reports of this type — financial tables, president's letter, auditor's statement, etc. The second and larger part of the report was the narrative section, describing the company's divisions and operations clearly and interestingly.

3. Just because annual reports make an appealing approach to communicating with some of your people, do not assume everyone will react the same way. And, as part of the same problem, the fact that your report is an artistic success does not mean it will be a really good employee communicator.

VI. MISCELLANEOUS METHOD

After reviewing the various types of written material and devices noted in the preceding parts of this chapter, we are left with a significant — if not easily identified — collection of communications methods that deserve emphasis. In fact, in this day of categorization and specialization, we sometimes may tend to ignore things we cannot label, so that many of these useful devices can be forgotten or ignored.

Instead, we should continue to concentrate on *what* we want to communicate, and then should improvise, innovate, and invent any valid method that fits our need. Here, indeed, the end can often justify the means. The method chosen can be costly or very inexpensive; it can be reflective of the company's image, or can be the "quick and dirty" type; the approach can gain its strength from a well-conceived, carefully implemented and integrated editorial approach, or it can simply and quite literally be the "back-of-an-envelope" method.

The important thing to do is to devise and produce that piece of communication material that:

- Carries the message
- Does it in a timely fashion
- Reaches the right audience
- Is read by that audience
- Is understood by that audience

Let us look at some examples of this so-called "miscellaneous" grouping of communication media.

A. Notes on the Doors

Here is one of the "quick-and-dirty" school of communications tactics that can be most effective. One company has adopted a very simple, straightforward philosophy of employee information; they want their people to learn things *about* the company *from* the company, before they learn about it from any other source. Good news or bad, they feel they can tell it more effectively and have it better understood if the firm's people learn about it "from the horse's mouth" rather than from a regular newspaper, or a labor union, or a neighbor. Even good news loses value when the employee's first awareness of it comes from an outside source, and bad news can be distorted in the worst possible way if it is learned from unreliable sources. To be the first to get to their employees with news, this firm has used a very simple method. "Spot" news in the form of a press release is taped onto all regular employee entrances, so that it is quickly and easily available to every person leaving or coming into the building (see Figure 4).

What is best communicated this way?   Anything that you want people to know about quickly, before they read it in the morning paper. Examples include:

- News on gaining or losing major contracts or customers
- Current status of merger or acquisition talks
- Factual stories about bomb scares or other emergencies affecting the employees
- Recent major appointments
- Explanation of stock price movements

This "notice-on-the-door" method does not serve well in areas involving company images, in-depth information or explanation, or the "selling" of any program. It is the antithesis of the audio-visual approach described earlier, and will not serve those programs well which lend themselves to the formality of audio-visuals. "Door postings" are, in effect, portable bulletin boards with only one subject at a time (or most often no subject at all) posted, and then only in cases of real need.

Advantages are timeliness, low cost, flexibility, and an appearance of hot-off-the-press priority that almost demands full readership.

Disadvantages include:

- If you say it quickly, you may say it wrong. Speed sometimes makes people forget the necessity of careful checking.
- Notices are easily defaced.
- Notices age quickly, and tend to be left up too long.

Hints and dangers

1. Use discretion. Do not "door-post" items of questionable immediate interest; maintain the reader reaction that, based on past experience, if there is a notice up it is of too much interest to be passed unread.

2. Let one person have the responsibility for final review; these notices are news

PRESS INFORMATION

ITEK CORPORATION, LEXINGTON, MASSACHUSETTS 02173 / (617) 276-2645 / HOWARD J. HALL, MANAGER OF PUBLIC RELATIONS.

TO ALL EMPLOYEES: The following announcement was released to the press
today for immediate publication.

ITEK AWARDED NEW CONTRACTS FOR ELECTRONIC COUNTERMEASURES

For Immediate Release - (October 4, 1968) - Lexington, Mass. - Itek Corporation
announced recent government contract awards amounting to more than $26 million
for production and installation of airborne electronic countermeasures equipment
(ECM).

The work will be performed for the Air Force and the Navy by Itek's
Applied Technology Division at facilities in Sunnyvale, Calif. and Lincoln,
Neb.

The largest of the new orders is a $14 million Air Force contract for
producing electronic countermeasures equipment and installing it on F-4 "Phantom"
jet fighter-bombers. Two other Air Force contracts totalling more than $5 million
are for the manufacture of advanced ECM equipment. An additional $1.5 million
was awarded for spare parts.

The Air Force also awarded Itek a $6 million contract to produce ECM
equipment and spare parts for use on Navy aircraft.

#   #   #

Figure 4.   A press release.

about the company and must stand the same analysis as does anything else your
company releases.

3. Let another person bear full responsibility for posting and taking them down;
twenty-four or thirty-six hours should be the total useful life of any notice.

4. Pick your posting places carefully; then, stay with them.

5. Watch your outlying locations, if any, and give them a crack at the same timeliness through prenotification.

B. Pay Envelope Stuffers

This is an effective tool that has tended to become "typecast" too much.   Again,
keep the basic guidelines in mind: first, decide what your communication goal is,
then use whatever device is appropriate.   Just because the pay envelope may have

only been used in the past for community chest appeals is no reason at all not to use it for something radically different.

Purposes best served include areas than can, first, wait until payday. (This sounds too obvious to even mention, but it is a very real limitation.) Next, probably the material covered should have some tie-in with wages (but you can certainly have exceptions to this). Finally, the stuffer itself should be easily handled, in terms of size and bulk.

Payroll stuffers are not useful if:

- The subject matter actually interferes with simple fact that it accompanies the employee's paycheck.
- You have many different types of payrolls that are paid on different time schedules or under different arrangements.
- Your payroll handout is done by an outside agency, and "stuffing" becomes complicated.
- There are any problems of timing or confidentiality.

Hints and dangers

1. Keep the stuffers brief, readable, pertinent. The employee is interested in his paycheck, and will not spend a lot of time worrying about an insert unless it grabs his interest and is important to him at that time.

2. Watch the subject matter. Although, as pointed out above, you can get away occasionally from material that has no bearing on the pay itself, this can be a tricky approach. Telling people, for example, about an unfavorable change in working conditions through a payroll stuffer could have a doubly negative effect.

3. Do not overdo it. Continually stuffing pay envelopes can result in people destroying anything else except the pay itself without even looking at the insert.

C. Special-occasion Handouts

This is a fertile field for exploration. There are many occasions that render employees very amenable to being communicated with; take advantage of them. These cover many types of occasions, including:

- Company anniversaries
- New product introductions
- Facility openings
- Reorganizations
- Employee achievements on or off the job
- Company awards or recognition
- Public policy statements

All of these instances, and many more, can result in a natural and anticipated employee communication. All you have to do is tailor a communications handout to fit the occasion.

The primary advantage of this approach is that it contains a built-in audience expectation that guarantees, in advance, a high level of readership.

The disadvantage, obviously, is that this method is very limited in application; your company will have only one ten-year anniversary.

There are many different actual methods that can work effectively in this area, and rather than analyze them all perhaps the best approach would be to look at some typical occasions and review communications methods that have worked.

1. *Company Anniversary.* Many firms have put out an anniversary issue of the company house organ. It can feature a review of the development of the organization, review high spots of past histories, describe major milestones, and probably take a look ahead at the future. Done well, these issues are read avidly by employees—the older ones to relive what once was, the newer ones to catch up. The

copies become an excellent orientation device to be used with people just joining the company; in addition, they can be very handy recruiting tools. The papers also are useful with community agencies, schools, and local papers, because of the way in which they give outsiders a thumbnail sketch of the company.

2. *Employee Achievements.* Here again a multifaceted use can be made of another good "excuse" for communicating. The employee involved receives considerable recognition. Local papers get a newsworthy item about a local resident, and the releases contain valid information about the company, too. Fellow employees read and follow the recognition enthusiastically. The employee's family becomes involved, too, and recognition at home can strengthen the business recognition.

3. *Public Policy Statement.* One company mailed home a clear-cut statement on the company's equal employment philosophy. Here again the results were manifold and worthwhile, in spite of a not unanticipated negative reaction by a few. The mailed-home brochure not only reached all current employees, but was also included in the recruiting brochure. The statement formed the basis of an interview with a nationwide business magazine, and became an integral part of the company's submission to a government regulatory agency involved in this area.

In summary, these special occasion communications are limited, because you need the basic occasion to begin with, but are advantageous from two major points of view; first, they have a strong built-in tendency toward favorable responses, and second, they generally capture a broad spectrum of interested audiences.

D. Reading Racks

This tool is indeed an old one, and even the name may conjure up visions of the factory making buggy whips. However, we must continue to avoid being misled; used appropriately, this employee communications approach can be as effective as any other.

Reading racks, in their traditional form, represented a sort of changing library of commercially purchased pamphlets designed to encourage people to do their job better or safer or faster. As they evolved, they became a source of general (sometimes petty) information to people on health, hobbies, finance, or home repairs. If it is to be used, today's modern reading rack must reflect today's approach to personnel administration; in this framework, it can be an effective communications tool.

Reading racks can be *best used* as a reference library for information that employees want and need about their jobs, or job-related education, safety, training, or extracurricular activities.

The rack is *not a useful tool* for day-to-day communications. It should not be considered if the timeliness of the information is critical, if the distribution of the material should be limited, or if the information is of a proprietary nature.

Advantages lie in the fact that people always know that information they want in certain areas is readily available. Material is easily put into very readable form, and is theirs for the taking.

Disadvantages center first about the residual feeling that many people have about the "do-good" nature of some of their past experiences with reading racks. Second, there is the human failing that we often do not actively seek out information without some sort of urging or prodding.

There are several *hints to consider* if we wish to increase the effectiveness of reading racks.

1. Set up and maintain one well-known, accessible, centrally located spot for the rack. Let people know, on a regular periodic basis, where it is and what it contains.

Remember, the reading rack will not seek out the readers; they should be constantly reminded about it.

2. Keep the material current and changing. Supply information which will be of interest to at least one major or representative segment of your employee population. Be flexible in your choice of material, and be prepared to stock enough material about a sufficient number of subjects so that, in total, you will achieve a good readership coverage.

3. Watch the way in which your material is written, so that your people's interest is maintained by the literature itself. See that the level of writing matches the level of understanding of its readers.

4. Keep the reading rack orderly. Consider it a library, with a logical arrangement that can be followed easily by the people using it.

5. Utilize some simple ways of testing readership. Libraries today are gearing their books to their reader's desires; this technique, using opinion survey forms tucked into the literature itself or set up separately in the reading rack area, can be your best guide to what form and direction your material should take.

In a parallel manner, there are *dangers* in these various situations that can reduce or even destroy the effectiveness of your reading rack.

1. An out-of-date rack is as bad as a tired bulletin board. How many of us have seen the same old pamphlets on having a safe vacation or avoiding hazards at home, so old-fashioned that we do not even bother to open them up. Safety is an old subject, but its presentation can be kept fresh and immediate. Paperback books have enjoyed a phenomenal reader interest, and this is in large measure due to their packaging; follow this concept in your reading rack material.

2. Do not spoon-feed people. If you feel it is advantageous for them to read about company products or progress, do not apologize for it or try to give it to them in pablumlike form.

3. Do not assume one writing approach is appropriate for all your employees, nor for all the material. The comic-book approach is indeed a truly effective way to treat certain material, but it is equally inappropriate—and even insulting—to approach all your literature in this fashion. Do not tailor your pamphlets or booklets to some outsider's view of your reading public; rather, put it together in a way that you know will be read and understood by *your* users.

4. Do not let the supply of material in the rack become disproportionate to the demand. An overabundance of one booklet almost tells the "shopper" that it cannot be a very interesting one, but, at the same time, the employee may not return often to pick up the pamphlet that is out of stock.

In closing, these are a few illustrative types of material effectively used in today's reading racks:

- Education offerings at nearby schools and colleges
- Employee association announcements, charters, by-laws, activities
- Descriptions of company-sponsored seminars, health programs, employee programs
- Civic and community activities, programs, and agencies
- Explanations of social, political, or economic facts about the community or the country
- Training and development hints and guides
- Safety facts, on the job, at home, on the highways
- Employee handbooks, union contracts, benefits programs booklets
- Company annual reports or other periodically issued financial or business reports

E. Appointment Circulars and Organizational Announcements

Here is a ready-made source of employee communications that may easily be over-looked.   Too many of us make the assumption that such releases should go only to people directly concerned with the appointment or change, and thereby we lose out on an effective communications channel.   For example, the realignment of a purchasing department could be of direct interest to only a few people in or dealing directly with purchasing, but it is of at least ancillary interest to many more.   Or the promotion or employment of a new manager may affect reporting relationships of relatively few, but news of this nature will be sure to receive wide circulation.

> *Keep in mind an easy guide: If the news is going to end up on the "grapevine hit parade," why not* tell *people what they will hear anyway?   If you do, you can tell it the way you want and, at the same time, make many more employees feel part of the team.*

Obviously, there may be much information in this area that will have to be re-stricted in distribution and, for that reason, this communications tool has built-in limits.   However, the advantages are clear:

- News comes out in a form you want.
- People do feel more involved.
- The person or organization about whom the news revolves gets the added psy-chic income of good publicity.

Disadvantages are focused mainly in the fact that not all such announcements can be broadcast widely.   Here you run into a doubly adverse affect because you have communicated other announcements freely; this negative must be taken into con-sideration if you are deciding on whether or not to use this communications medium.

Here are some *hints* to consider:

1. Timeliness is essential.   Most organizations are different from the charts describing them almost from the day the chart is used.   Any significant delay in the announcement itself will make it even more obsolete.   The positive aspects of announcements about people are similarly lost, because the person promoted or employed needs the publicity when the event occurs.   Finally, under any circum-stances, if you are to beat the grapevine, you must react quickly.

2. Watch your wording.   Be specific as possible, to avoid misinterpretation.   A vague, potentially misleading organization chart or description of a new person's responsibilities can fuel the fire of the rumor mill rather than cool it.

There are also some *dangers* to avoid:

1. Do not forget to clear any people announcements with the person involved. You may have a standard approach that ends up with a sentence on the man's family situation, but if there happens to be a personal problem involved, such an approach could do serious harm.

2. Broadly distributed organizational announcements should be checked more carefully.   These can be customer impact, competitive company problems, legal involvements, union implications, or financial community situations that can be-come important.

Note: However, once again it should be the personnel responsibility to hit the correct balance.   So many functions claim they must have prior approval authority that, unless controlled, your communications ability can be throttled.

F. Computer Printouts

This represents probably the newest field for employee communications, one that is attractive and yet complex, and one that can be harnessed and used effectively. Because it is still so new, the printout as a communications method (like the audio-visual approach described earlier) must rely heavily on the guidance of the technical experts. To the personnel man, nothing can be more frustrating than to be told something cannot be done "because the computer won't take it." Nevertheless, machine requirements and limitations are real and have to be dealt with. While information is cranking out of computers at a fantastic rate, most personnel people have made little or no use of the machines for communications purposes. Therefore, it bears emphasis here that we are not talking about personnel records or salary information or turnover reports; we are discussing the direct utilization of specially designed machine printouts as a communications medium.

An example may be the easiest way of clarification. Probably the best one now available is that of a personalized printout of an employee's fringe benefits package (see Figure 5). This is in use by several companies as a precise and impressive way to get across to the people, on a periodic basis, the benefits and protection they enjoy as part of their job picture, and how much it costs to support the program.

Obviously, the major advantage of computer printouts is the completeness and accuracy of the detail they can present and the speed and efficiency (after initial programming) with which they can be prepared.

The disadvantages may be a little less obvious, but must not be ignored.

1. There is a tendency to overutilize the computer's capability. The fact that much information can be stored and recalled easily tempts people to use redundant or inappropriate details, thereby blunting the focus of the communication itself.

2. In a similar vein, there is a tendency to spend a disproportionate amount of time—and money—to secure just a little more detail.

3. The first time is always the worst time because of the programming effort. This can represent a real problem in getting a program off the ground; both time and cost factors cannot be ignored.

There are a number of *hints and dangers* that have already been discovered by companies using this approach, and some of these can be summarized briefly here. However, keep in mind that the entire approach is too new for any of us to be very definitive; you will have to add to this list based on your own experiences.

▪ Because of its newness (and potential profitability), the field has attracted a number of consultants who, for a price, will do this job for you. Weigh your facts carefully; get some valid cost comparisons; keep in mind that you will have to supply all basic information no matter who does the program; do not get sold what one union man once described as "a tuxedo for an amoeba."

▪ Make sure your distribution method matches your product. A well-conceived, well-presented printout can be severely downgraded if it is mishandled. Consider individual mailouts, even though they add to the cost.

▪ Remember the need for timeliness. Lots of detailed facts become pretty unimpressive if they are six months old.

▪ Arrange the printout for employee readability. Here again the machine can be a powerful opponent, but the form and the way and order in which the material is presented should first focus on the needs of the people reading it.

▪ Remember that your audience, you hope, will include your employee's spouse, and even family; include them as appropriate in coverage descriptions.

▪ Do not forget the legally required (as well as the discretionary) benefits you make available to your people.

▪ Finally, keep in mind the law of diminishing returns. If certain pieces of information require extensive background work, you may be able to estimate a benefit or a cost (and tell your people it is an estimate) to the point where you will have a meaningful figure without a lot of work.

MEDICAL CARE BENEFITS	**HOSPITAL ROOM AND BOARD:** up to $ per day for days or $ **ATTENDING PHYSICIAN:** up to $ per day for doctor's hospital visits to total of $ **ADDITIONAL ACCIDENT EXPENSES:** up to $ for bills from each accident which exceed or are not covered by basic benefits. **DIAGNOSTIC EXAMINATIONS:** X-Ray and Laboratory fees according to schedule to maximum of $ per accident and $ for combined illnesses during any 12 consecutive months. **HOSPITAL SPECIAL SERVICES:** up to $ for anesthesia, drugs, blood, operating room, etc. **SURGEONS FEES:** benefits for surgery, according to schedule, up to $ **MATERNITY EXPENSES:** up to $ for hospital and $ for physician for normal delivery. **MAJOR MEDICAL EXPENSES:** % of covered expenses to $ for yourself and each covered dependent after basic plan payments and annual deductible of $ per person or $ per family.
DEATH AND SURVIVOR BENEFITS	**ITEK LIFE INSURANCE BENEFIT:** $ **SOCIAL SECURITY DEATH BENEFIT:** Total normal death benefit $ **ITEK ACCIDENTAL DEATH BENEFIT:** in addition to normal coverage $ **ITEK TRAVEL ACCIDENT DEATH BENEFIT:** for employees on company business $ **SOCIAL SECURITY ESTIMATED MONTHLY SURVIVOR INCOME** for wife from age or from any age if there is a dependent child $ **AND SOCIAL SECURITY ESTIMATED MONTHLY SURVIVOR INCOME** for each dependent child. $

ITEK SICK PAY: up to   days per year at full pay

DISABILITY INCOME BENEFITS

For longer term disabilities Itek Insurance and Social Security Benefits supplement sick pay as follows:
(For convenience, all amounts are expressed weekly)

Your Itek benefits begin on the day of accident or day of illness and pay the amounts below:		Your Estimated Social Security Benefit	Your Estimated Total Benefit	Plus Social Security for wife age or from any age if there is a dependent child.	Plus Social Security for each dependent child.
1st	weeks of benefits	$	$	$	$	$
after	weeks of benefits	$	$	$	$	$

Itek Disability Income Plan Benefits extend for   for an accident or   for an illness.

RETIREMENT INCOME BENEFITS

ITEK RETIREMENT PLAN MONTHLY BENEFIT assuming you continued employment at Itek to age 65 (at your present salary): $

SOCIAL SECURITY ESTIMATED MONTHLY BENEFIT from age 65 assuming maximum quarters of coverage: $

SOCIAL SECURITY ESTIMATED MONTHLY BENEFIT FOR WIFE from her age 65 $
Total Estimated Monthly Retirement $

Your total contribution to the Itek Retirement Plan including interest as of $

If you terminate employment before retirement and elect to leave your present contribution in the plan, your monthly retirement benefit at age 65 would be: $

ANNUAL COST

ESTIMATED ANNUAL COST to you based on your current salary and contribution rates:

MEDICAL AND LIFE	DISABILITY INCOME	RETIREMENT INCOME	SOCIAL SECURITY	HOLIDAYS	SICK PAY	VACATIONS
$	$	$	$	$	$	$

Your Estimated Total Cost: $ Itek's Estimated Total Cost: $

Itek provides other special benefits for its people that are not included in the costs above such as: educational assistance, workmen's compensation insurance; jury duty differential pay; and military reserve differential pay.

NAME _____

ADDRESS _____

EMPL. NO. _____

FAC. DEPT. NO. _____

BIRTH DATE _____

Figure 5. A personalized employee benefit report.

In summary, personnel people have available to them a large assortment of devices, tools, and methods which they can use to enhance company communications with employees. Presented briefly in this chapter is a collection of many of them that can work for you. It is hoped that, if you have identified your needs, this chapter will make available some proven guidelines in the selection and use of the appropriate communications method.

BIBLIOGRAPHY

Davis, Keith: *Human Relations at Work,* McGraw-Hill Book Company, New York, 1967.

Dooher, M. J., and V. Marquis: *Effective Communications on the Job,* American Management Association, New York, 1956.

Roethlisberger, F. J.: *Management and Morale,* Harvard University Press, Cambridge, Mass., 1962.

Saltonstall, Robert: *Human Relations in Administration,* McGraw-Hill Book Company, New York, 1959.

Yoder, D.: *Personnel Principles and Policies,* Prentice-Hall, Inc., Englewood Cliffs, N.J., 1959.

Breslow, H. S.: "Employee Communications: A Personnel Man's View Point," *Personnel Journal,* December, 1969.

McElreath, M. P.: *Employee Publications: The Medium and the Message "Reporting,"* International Council of Industrial Editors, Akron, Ohio, December, 1969.

Seybold, G. (ed.): *Employee Communication: Policy and Tools,* Studies in Personnel Policy, No. 22 National Industrial Conference Board, New York, No. 220, 1966.

Zeyher, L. R.: "Improving Your Three-dimensional Communications," *Personnel Journal,* May, 1970.

Part 17

Records, Reports, and Statistics

chapter 77

Essential Personnel Records and Reports

FRANK JAY WOLLING *Manager, Reference and Library Service, The Rockefeller Foundation, New York, N.Y.*

JOHN S. BERCEN *Director, Industrial Relations, Coro Inc., Providence, Rhode Island*

As businesses continue to grow and the administration of personnel becomes more professional and sophisticated, the volume of paper records increases in proportion, with the new technologies creating new and vastly different kinds of records.

Sound records management administration can provide an organization with the necessary "checks and balances" in paper work. What are the component functions of a records management program?

1. Records creation
2. Records maintenance
3. Records disposition

Records creation involves the basic capture of data in man or machine readable form; records maintenance provides the means of controlling, analyzing, classifying, arranging, and retrieving active recorded information; and records disposition provides for:

1. The systematic removal of semiactive records from expensive space
2. The orderly disposal of nonactive records
3. The protection of vital records
4. The preservation of legal and historical documents

In this chapter our attention is directed to the essential records and reports necessary to effectively carry out the personnel administration of an organization.

FORMS

It is inconceivable that any personnel department can operate efficiently for even one day without the use of forms. Webster defines a form as "a printed or typed document with blank spaces for insertion of required or requested specific information." Good forms are created to save work and time. They permit a company to retain necessary information in a uniform way. Many organizations have a separate department which is solely responsible for forms creation and control.

Be sure all personnel forms are systematically reviewed and analyzed to be certain they call for the information needed. Continuity of information is important. Does the information requested follow a logical pattern? Check the forms for layout. Is the form intelligible to the person who will be completing it? Make sure the information is consolidated. Unless it is absolutely necessary, do not ask for the same repetitious information on several forms, if it will serve its purpose on only one. Be sure the forms designer designates each copy of a multipart form with its purpose, as file copy, personnel copy, payroll copy. This will aid in orderly distribution and filing, and permit the establishment of a "copy of record" for official retention purposes. Update and revise forms when necessary. Be sure the date of a revision appears on the form. Number each form for easy reference and control. If possible, try to have management limit the preparation of forms to one department. Personnel forms should be created within the forms design unit in cooperation with the personnel department or, in the absence of a forms design unit, by the personnel department. This will aid the control of repetitious, unnecessary, and nonofficial forms.

By now it should be obvious that a good personnel forms control program plays a vital role in implementing good records management.

Forms Used in Personnel Administration

Personnel records represent the accumulation of personnel forms. Among others, they include the forms completed to secure, interview, employ, appraise, evaluate, and terminate and/or retire employees. The various forms used will be discussed in this chapter and several examples included.

The forms described and illustrated in this section are arranged in chronological sequence, i.e., from the initial request for an employee, to the employment application, wage and salary authorization, benefit plans, etc., ending with employment termination.

Employment requisition. Requisitions for new or replacement employees can be initiated in a number of ways. Some companies use a simple memorandum to the personnel department, stating the title of the position to be filled and a brief description of the position, the qualifications needed, and the salary range. Others use printed forms.

The department should be identified on the form, as well as the position title and a brief description of the job duties. If there is a formal salary or wage evaluation program, the proper grade and salary level should also be shown. Some forms contain background requirements, such as education, experience, and unusual skills, and the date the job needs to be filled. If the requisition has been generated to replace an employee currently on the payroll, the form may provide for information on the reasons for termination of the employee. If the requisition is for a new position, some justification for the addition should be given. Figures 1 and 2 are samples of employee requisitions.

Interviewing. *Preliminary application.* The stage in employee recruitment termed interviewing may involve the completion of several forms. For example, there may be a preliminary application used by employers who receive many ap-

REQUISITION FOR PERSONNEL

Date _____   Requisition No. _____

A. DEPARTMENT   DEPT.   INC. PLAN
NAME _____   NO. _____   CODE NO. _____

B. JOB TITLE   Contact Salary Administration if this job title is not listed on the Departmental Job Rating sheet.

SALARY
CLASS _____

REQUIRES: ☐ Male   ☐ Female   ☐ Either   WORKING HOURS _____   DATE NEEDED _____

C. EMPLOYMENT STATUS (CHECK ONE)

☐ REGULAR OR PROVISIONAL   ☐ PART-TIME EMPLOYEE   ☐ TEMPORARY EMPLOYEE   ☐ OTHER _____
☐ RESERVE EMPLOYEE   ☐ UNDER 20 HRS./WK.   ☐ CO-OPERATIVE STUDENT
☐ SUMMER EMPLOYEE   ☐ 20 HRS. OR MORE/WK.   ☐ VOCATIONAL TRAINEE

D. TYPE OF REQUEST AND PROVISIONS FOR FINANCING

☐ ADDITION TO DEPARTMENT: (Report submitted by requestor and/or Industrial Engineering.)

☐ In Profit Plan as _____ in Department _____
(Job Title)

☐ In Profit Plan by cancellation of open Requisition No. _____ in Department _____

☐ In Profit Plan by non-replacement of _____ in Department _____
☐ In Profit Plan due to production work-volume support in areas not requiring specific budget provision.
☐ Not in Profit Plan

☐ NO ADDITION TO DEPARTMENT:
☐ Promotion from within—no replacement needed.
☐ Replacement for (name) _____ because of (☐ promotion); (☐ resignation);
other—
(☐ transfer to Dept. _____); (☐ retirement); (☐ specify _____) on _____ (date).

☐ Cancellation of open Requisition No. _____ in same department.

☐ Other—specify _____ .

E. STATEMENT OF NEED:

F. SUPPORTIVE REQUIREMENTS:
Facilities:
Estimated expenditures for revised or additional space and equipment resulting from approval of this requisition.
☐ None   ☐ Under $5,000   ☐ $5,000 and Over (If over $5,000 contact Industrial Engineering for assistance.)
Personnel:
Estimated supportive personnel resulting from approval of this requisition. (Number and Job Titles)

G. APPROVALS AND ROUTING

Date	Submitted		Date	Reviewed	
	Submitted	Department Head		Reviewed	Industrial Engineering
	Approved	Division Director		Reviewed	Financial Planning & Budgeting
	Approved (Required for additions to a department)	Vice-Pres. or Exec. Director		Approved	Salary Classification Committee
	Job Control	Salary Administration		Approved	Budget Committee

H. FOR PERSONNEL USE
NAME _____   Personnel
DATE FILLED _____ DATE ON JOB. _____   ☐ NEW EMPLOYEE   TRANSFERRED FROM DEPT. _____

09 DN 9000 PRINTED IN U. S. A. DECEMBER 65   Copy No. 1
Personal History File

Figure 1.   Sample requisition for new employee.

plicants.   The preliminary application calls for sufficient information to assist the personnel department in determining if the applicant warrants further consideration.   Figure 3 provides an example of the type of preliminary application used by McGraw-Hill, Inc.   Figure 4 is an example of a short form.   This form is completed by the applicant at the reception desk and is then referred to the personnel department.

Employment application.   Next in the recruitment process is the completion of the employment application.   This is essential to the screening and interviewing process and provides basic data about an employee which remains unchanged and serves as a permanent file on an individual's background.

In most cases the initial exposure a person has with a company is in the employ-

McGraw-Hill, Inc.
Personnel Requisition

10151

Job Title_____ Grade Level_____ Date Needed_____
Div/Co_____ Pub/Dept._____
☐ Other than McGraw-Hill (Explain in
☐ Work Location   Comments)
Section_____ Work Location_____
City   State

Pay Agency Fee: ☐ Yes ☐ No   Pay New Employee Relocation Expenses, If Necessary: ☐ Yes ☐ No

Refer Questions and Applicants To: _____ Location _____ Fl._____ Ext._____
In His Absence To:_____ Location _____ Fl._____ Ext._____

JOB REQUIREMENTS

I. Brief Description of Duties_____

II. Special Experience or Qualifications Required_____

III. Education Required_____

SALARY AND WORK STATUS

I. Hiring Range: From $_____ To $_____ Per Year_____ Month_____ Week_____ Hour_____
II. Charge Salary   G/L_____ S/L_____ Dept._____ %_____   G/L_____ S/L_____ Dept._____ %_____
Expense To: G/L_____ S/L_____ Dept._____ %_____   G/L_____ S/L_____ Dept._____ %_____
III. ☐ Permanent Full Time ☐ Temporary Full Time   If Temporary, For How Long_____
☐ Permanent Part Time ☐ Temporary Part Time   If Part Time, What Hours & Days_____
☐ Day Shift ☐ Night Shift   If Night Shift, What Hours_____ What Rate Differential_____

JUSTIFICATION AND HISTORY

I. Is This an   ☐ Yes - Give Reasons In "Comments"
Increase to Staff?   ☐ No - Replacement For: Name_____ Title_____
Grade Level_____ Salary_____ Per_____ Date Off Job_____ Reason (Check One Below)
☐ Promoted ☐ Transferred ☐ Terminated ☐ Military Service ☐ Other (Explain)_____

II. Is This Position Budgeted? ☐ Yes ☐ No   If No, Explain in "Comments"

IMPORTANT: SEND CONFIRMATION 5090 TO

Name

Address (or Location)

IF ADDRESS HAS INTEROFFICE
MAIL SERVICE—CHECK HERE ☐

COMMENTS

SEE INSTRUCTIONS ON OTHER SIDE

APPROVALS

First_____ Date_____
Second_____ Date_____
Third_____ Date_____
Agency Fee_____ Date_____
Relocation Expenses_____ Date_____

PERSONNEL DEPT. ONLY
Job Class_____ Grade Level_____
Salary Structure_____
FLSA_____
Signature_____ Date_____
Signature_____ Date_____

FORM 51-50850 (REV. 1-71)

Figure 2.   Sample requisition for personnel.

ment process; therefore, the employment application should be neat in appearance and readable with sufficient space provided so that the applicant has ample room to answer questions which necessitate lengthy explanations. The information requested should be arranged in a logical sequence, as shown in Figure 5.

Most forms are 8½ by 11 inches in size and utilize four pages. Some companies use color in the form layout to give it eye appeal. The form should be designed so that the applicant can complete it in a relatively short time. Lengthy applications may tend to make the applicant ill at ease, which will then be reflected in the employment interview.

Note the reference on the form shown in Figure 6 to the company's position on equal employment opportunity. Some employment applications may include a statement alerting the candidate to the fact that a preemployment physical examina-

MCGRAW-HILL POLICY AND FEDERAL LAW FORBID DISCRIMINATION BECAUSE OF RACE, COLOR, RELIGION, AGE, SEX OR NATIONAL ORIGIN.

PERSONNEL RELATIONS

McGRAW-HILL, INC.

PRELIMINARY
EMPLOYMENT APPLICATION

Date _____

Personal Data

Applying For Position As _____ Salary Desired _____ Date Available _____

Name: _____
        (Last)   (First)   (Middle)

Address _____
        (Street)   (City)   (State)   (Zip Code)

Telephone No. _____ Social Security No. _____   Are you a U. S. Citizen or an
             (Area Code)   Alien Immigrant? ☐ Yes ☐ No

Are you (check appropriate box) over 16 ☐, over ☐ 18, and/or under ☐ 65?

How were you referred to McGraw-Hill, Inc.?   ☐ Agency ☐ School ☐ Advertisement ☐ Direct Contact ☐ McGraw-Hill Employee ☐ Other

Name of referral source above: _____

Educational Data

SCHOOLS	NAME OF INSTITUTION	ADDRESS	MAJOR	COURSES TAKEN	No. Yrs. Attended	Yr. Grad.	Degree
GRADE			XXXXX	XXXXX			XX
PREPARATORY OR HIGH			XXXXX				XX
COLLEGE							
OTHERS							
PRESENT							XX

Employment Data   Begin with more recent employer.

FORMER EMPLOYERS and ADDRESS	YOUR POSITION and DUTIES	DATES	SALARY RECEIVED	SUPERVISOR'S NAME	REASON FOR LEAVING
		From	Start $		
NATURE OF BUSINESS		To	Finish $	TITLE	
		From	Start $		
NATURE OF BUSINESS		To	Finish $	TITLE	

Skills

Typing Speed _____ words per minute   ☐ Electric ☐ Manual   Steno Speed _____ words per minute Method _____

Business Machines _____

Figure 3.   Sample preliminary employment application.

```
              Preliminary Application     Date_____
Name_____
          Last              First           Middle
Address_____ Tel. No._____
Position Desired_____
Date of Birth_____ Referred by_____
Check or Fill in Items Below Which Apply to You:
Shorthand speed_____ Length of Business or Profes-
Typing speed_____ sional Experience_____
High School Graduate ⌐⌐⌐ Name of Present Employer
College Graduate     ⌐⌐⌐
Business Training     ⌐⌐⌐
Postgraduate Degree_____   Unemployed ⌐⌐⌐
Per.15
```

Figure 4.   Sample preliminary employment application.

GENERAL ELECTRIC

AN EQUAL OPPORTUNITY EMPLOYER

APPLICATION FOR EMPLOYMENT

THE NEW YORK LAW AGAINST DISCRIMINATION PROHIBITS DISCRIMINATION BECAUSE OF AGE

It is the policy of the General Electric Company to provide employment, training, compensation, promotion and other conditions of employment without regard to race, color, religion, national origin, sex or age, except where age or sex are bona fide occupational requirements.

INTERVIEWER'S SUMMARY

BEST QUALIFIED JOB CODE NO.

PERSONAL

PRINT NAME ____ LAST / FIRST / MIDDLE / (MAIDEN)

SOC. SEC. NO.

TEMPORARY ADDRESS ____

PERMANENT ADDRESS ____ NO. & STREET / CITY / STATE / ZIP CODE / TELEPHONE

CHECK ALL THAT APPLY

☐ SINGLE ☐ MARRIED ☐ DIVORCED ☐ SEPARATED ☐ WIDOWED ☐ REMARRIED

CITIZEN OF U.S.A.? ☐ YES ☐ NO*

☐ MAN ☐ WOMAN

NAME, RELATIONSHIP & AGE OF HUSBAND OR WIFE, AND DEPENDENT CHILDREN — NAME / RELATION & AGE / NAME / RELATION & AGE

IF SINGLE, GIVE PARENTS' NAMES

HEIGHT ____ WEIGHT ____

BIRTH DATE ____ MONTH / DAY / YEAR

* If you are not a U.S. citizen have you a legal right to remain permanently in the U.S.? Yes ☐ No ☐

NOTIFY IN EMERGENCY ____ NAME / ADDRESS / TELEPHONE

HAVE YOU ANY DEFECTS OR LIMITATIONS? (Physical, Mental, other.) ☐ YES ☐ NO IF YES, EXPLAIN FULLY

HAVE YOU EVER BEEN CONVICTED OF A MISDEMEANOR OR A FELONY? ☐ YES ☐ NO IF YES, EXPLAIN FULLY

JOB INTEREST

POSITION DESIRED

WAGES OR SALARY EXPECTED $ PER {HR. / WK. / MO.

OTHER POSITIONS FOR WHICH YOU ARE QUALIFIED

DATE AVAILABLE

WHAT INTERESTED YOU IN G.E.?

LIST NAMES AND COMPANY LOCATIONS OF RELATIVES EMPLOYED BY G.E.

WERE YOU EVER EMPLOYED BY G.E.? IF YES, WHERE & WHEN?

HAVE YOU EVER APPLIED FOR WORK AT G.E.? IF YES, WHERE & WHEN?

TRAINING

CIRCLE HIGHEST GRADE *COMPLETED* IN *EACH* SCHOOL CATEGORY	GRADE SCHOOL	HIGH SCHOOL	COLLEGE	GRAD. SCHOOL
	1 2 3 4 5 6 7 8	9 10 11 12	1 2 3 4	1 2 3 4

	NAME	LOCATION	COURSE—DEGREE	YEAR GRADUATED	CLASS STANDING
GRADE SCHOOL					
HIGH SCHOOL					
COLLEGE					
GRADUATE SCHOOL					

APPRENTICE, BUSINESS OR VOCATIONAL SCHOOL

OTHER TRAINING OR SKILLS (Factory or Office Machines Operated, Special Courses, etc.)

HOBBIES

MILITARY

BRANCH OF U.S. SERVICE	DATE ENTERED	DATE DISCHARGED	FINAL RANK	SERVICE NO.

SERVICE SCHOOLS OR SPECIAL EXPERIENCE

TYPE DISCHARGE

SELECTIVE SERVICE NO. CLASSIFICATION & DATE

LOCAL BOARD NO. AND ADDRESS

RESERVE OR NATIONAL GUARD STATUS

NAME & ADDRESS OF COMMANDING OFFICER

FF-75-B (5-70) Rev.

PLEASE COMPLETE OTHER SIDE

Figure 5. Sample employment application.

tion is necessary. Others may include provision for a candidate to authorize the company to check credit references before employment, with the understanding that any derogatory remarks will be made known to the individual. It is mandatory that the employment application be reviewed and revised as often as necessary so that it adheres to the constantly changing governmental requirements concerning employment practices. A personnel manager of a large retailing corporation stated that his company's employment application was revised as many as six times within a year. Many companies will go beyond subscribing to the "letter of the law" and also set up their practices and forms to take into account the "spirit of the law" as well. Management has a responsibility to protect the interests of the company and the individual, and this is possible only if it is alert to new developments. Additional samples are shown in Figures 7 and 8.

EMPLOYMENT HISTORY

PLEASE LIST ALL EMPLOYMENT STARTING WITH PRESENT OR MOST RECENT EMPLOYER.

ACCOUNT FOR ALL PERIODS, INCLUDING UNEMPLOYMENT & SERVICE WITH U.S. ARMED FORCES. USE ADDITIONAL SHEET IF NECESSARY.

DATES	NAME & ADDRESS—EMPLOYER	1 JOB TITLE / 2 DEPARTMENT / 3 NAME OF SUPERVISOR	DESCRIBE MAJOR DUTIES	WAGES	REASON FOR LEAVING
FROM MONTH / YEAR TO MONTH / YEAR		1 / 2 / 3		STARTING $ per / FINAL $ per	
FROM MONTH / YEAR TO MONTH / YEAR		1 / 2 / 3		STARTING $ per / FINAL $ per	
FROM MONTH / YEAR TO MONTH / YEAR		1 / 2 / 3		STARTING $ per / FINAL $ per	
FROM MONTH / YEAR TO MONTH / YEAR		1 / 2 / 3		STARTING $ per / FINAL $ per	
FROM MONTH / YEAR TO MONTH / YEAR		1 / 2 / 3		STARTING $ per / FINAL $ per	
FROM MONTH / YEAR TO MONTH / YEAR		1 / 2 / 3		STARTING $ per / FINAL $ per	

PRE-EMPLOYMENT STATEMENT

I voluntarily give the General Electric Company the right to make a thorough investigation of my past employment and activities, agree to cooperate in such investigation, and release from all liability or responsibility all persons, companies or corporations supplying such information.

I consent to taking the pre-employment physical examination and such future physical examinations as may be required by the Company. I agree to wear or use protective clothing or devices as required by the Company and to comply with the safety rules.

I agree that the entire contents of this application form, as well as the report of any such examination, may be used by the Company in whatever manner it may wish.

If employed by the Company, I understand that such employment is subject to the security policies of the Company. I further understand that if the position for which I am hired requires access to classified information and I am not able to obtain a security clearance, I will not be allowed to work in this position. My employment with the Company in a position not requiring security clearance depends upon the existence of such a position for which I am qualified.

I further understand that any false answers or statements made by me on this application or any supplement thereto, or in connection with the above mentioned investigation, will be sufficient grounds for immediate discharge.

APPLICANT'S SIGNATURE _____ DATE _____

INTERVIEWER'S COMMENTS

INTERVIEWED BY _____ DATE _____

Interview Guides.   Bingham and Moore, in their classic book *How to Interview,* state that "interviews need to be planned."[1]   Once the prospective employee completes the application form, the interviewing process begins.   Some companies use guide sheets which are completed by the interviewer after the interview takes place. Figures 9 and 10 provide examples of interview guides which utilize a check-off procedure.   Note that provision is made for additional comments.

Reference checks.   Reference checks are made by most organizations.   Note the authorization concerning reference checks on the sample form in Figure 7.   Some companies rely on oral reference checks.   Figure 11 is a form to be completed by

[1] Walter V. Bingham and Bruce V. Moore, *How to Interview,* Harper & Brothers, New York, 1931, p. 17.

PERSONNEL RELATIONS

McGRAW-HILL, INC.

EMPLOYMENT
APPLICATION

Date_____

Personal Data

Applying For Position As_____ Salary required_____ Date available_____

☐ Male
☐ Female

Name:_____
     (Last)   (First)   (Middle)

Figure 6. Sample employment application.

Application and Personal History Record

PERSONAL INFORMATION

DATE_____

NAME
   LAST   FIRST   MIDDLE

SOCIAL SECURITY
ACCOUNT NUMBER

PRESENT ADDRESS
   STREET   CITY   ZONE   STATE

PERMANENT ADDRESS
FILL IN IF OTHER THAN PRESENT ADDRESS

RESIDENCE TELEPHONE

BUSINESS TELEPHONE

REFERRED BY

DATE OF BIRTH   AGE   ARE YOU A CITIZEN OF THE U. S. A.   YES ☐   NO ☐

FOR WOMEN APPLICANTS ONLY: IF MARRIED, STATE MAIDEN NAME AND HUSBAND'S FIRST NAME FOR REFERENCE PURPOSES

MAIDEN NAME   HUSBAND'S FIRST NAME

MARRIED ☐ SINGLE ☐ DIVORCED ☐	NO. OF DEPENDENTS	HUSBAND ☐ WIFE ☐	NO. OF CHILDREN	TOTAL	AGE OF EACH				NO. OF OTHER DEPENDENTS

IF HUSBAND OR WIFE IS EMPLOYED GIVE EMPLOYER   POSITION

RELATED TO ANYONE IN OUR EMPLOY — IF SO STATE NAME, RELATIONSHIP & LOCATION

MILITARY OR NAVAL SERVICE IN U. S. FORCES   PRESENT MEMBERSHIP AND RANK, IN ANY U. S. MILITARY ORGANIZATION

BRANCH   DATES   RANK

EDUCATION   SHOW COMPLETE RECORD COMMENCING WITH GRAMMAR SCHOOL, INCLUDING MAJOR COURSE, NOTING IF DAY OR EVENING

KIND OF SCHOOL	NAME OF SCHOOL	LOCATION	DATE STARTED	DATE LEFT	DATE GRADUATED	COURSES TAKEN AND DEGREES
ELEMENTARY						
HIGH SCHOOL						
COLLEGE						
GRADUATE						
OTHER						

FORM 488

Figure 7. Sample employment application.

the person making a telephone reference check. Many personnel departments prefer this method to written reference checks. Often a more frank opinion is obtained through a telephone check. If possible, an applicant's reference should be checked before the employment confirmation is finalized. If this is impractical, employment should be contingent upon receiving satisfactory references. Some companies prefer not using personal references since they feel that these tend to be less objective than business references.

Health records.   Health records are important to an organization because they provide crucial information about the physical condition of a company's most valuable asset—the employee. Preemployment physical examinations are required by most companies. Note the checklist, in Figure 12, provided for medical personnel to evaluate the candidate's health status in terms of employment. During the past

2.

FOREIGN LANGUAGES (INDICATE WHETHER SLIGHT—FAIR—FLUENT)				LIST ANY SCHOLASTIC HONORS OR EXTRACURRICULAR ACTIVITIES
LANGUAGE	SPEAK	READ	WRITE	

BUSINESS SKILLS

SHORTHAND SPEED		SYSTEM USED		TYPING SPEED		TOUCH SYSTEM?	

LIST BUSINESS MACHINES USED ON PREVIOUS POSITIONS

BUSINESS RECORD AND REFERENCES

IMPORTANT   LIST EVERY EMPLOYMENT WHETHER OR NOT IT SEEMS RELEVANT TO POSITION APPLIED FOR. IF LAPSES OCCURRED BETWEEN PERIODS OF EMPLOYMENT GIVE DATES OF, AND REASON FOR UNEMPLOYMENT.

PRESENT OR LAST EMPLOYER

NAME OF EMPLOYER			TELEPHONE NO., IF KNOWN
ADDRESS—STREET	CITY	ZONE STATE	NATURE OF BUSINESS
EMPLOYMENT DATES (MO. AND YR.)	TITLE OF POSITION	NO. OF PEOPLE SUPERVISED	NAME AND TITLE OF IMMEDIATE SUPERVISOR
FROM: TO:			
REASON FOR DESIRING CHANGE OR LEAVING			STARTING SALARY FINAL SALARY

MAY WE CONTACT?

DESCRIPTION OF DUTIES

NEXT PREVIOUS EMPLOYER

NAME OF EMPLOYER			TELEPHONE NO., IF KNOWN
ADDRESS—STREET	CITY	ZONE STATE	NATURE OF BUSINESS
EMPLOYMENT DATES (MO. AND YR.)	TITLE OF POSITION	NO. OF PEOPLE SUPERVISED	NAME AND TITLE OF IMMEDIATE SUPERVISOR
FROM: TO:			
REASON FOR LEAVING			STARTING SALARY FINAL SALARY

DESCRIPTION OF DUTIES

3.

NEXT PREVIOUS EMPLOYER

NAME OF EMPLOYER				NATURE OF BUSINESS

ADDRESS—STREET   CITY   ZONE   STATE   NAME AND TITLE OF IMMEDIATE SUPERVISOR

EMPLOYMENT DATES (MO. AND YR.)	TITLE OF POSITION	NO. OF PEOPLE SUPERVISED	STARTING SALARY	FINAL SALARY
FROM: TO:				

REASON FOR LEAVING

DESCRIPTION OF DUTIES

NEXT PREVIOUS EMPLOYER

NAME OF EMPLOYER				NATURE OF BUSINESS

ADDRESS—STREET   CITY   ZONE   STATE   NAME AND TITLE OF IMMEDIATE SUPERVISOR

EMPLOYMENT DATES (MO. AND YR.)	TITLE OF POSITION	NO. OF PEOPLE SUPERVISED	STARTING SALARY	FINAL SALARY
FROM: TO:				

REASON FOR LEAVING

DESCRIPTION OF DUTIES

ADDITIONAL DETAILS

PLEASE LIST ANY ADDITIONAL EMPLOYMENT NOT SHOWN ABOVE. ALSO INCLUDE ANY FOREIGN TRAVEL OR ANY INFORMATION YOU BELIEVE WOULD BE HELPFUL TO US.

THE NEW YORK LAW AGAINST DISCRIMINATION PROHIBITS DISCRIMINATION ON ACCOUNT OF AGE OR SEX.

PLEASE NOTE

PERMANENT EMPLOYMENT IS CONDITIONAL ON PASSING A PHYSICAL EXAMINATION AND UPON THE FOUNDATION'S RECEIVING SATISFACTORY REPLIES TO REFERENCE INQUIRIES.

DATE   APPLICANT'S SIGNATURE

two decades, preemployment physical examinations have taken on a new significance in the organization because of group insurance and major medical programs. These plans have brought about the practice of a periodic physical examination by company doctors. The physician's medical report is usually kept in a confidential file in his office and may be released to the individual's personal physician upon request. A simple form can be completed by the physician and used as a vehicle to advise the personnel department about the status of the individual's health.

Wages and salary. Once the candidate has successfully completed all interview procedures and is made a part of the staff, notification must be sent to the payroll department. In many companies the payroll function is maintained separately from personnel, and consequently forms are prepared in duplicate.

```
                                    4.
                              FOR OFFICE USE ONLY
   INTERVIEWED BY
   _____
   NAME                                              DATE
   _____  _____

   _____  _____

   _____  _____

   _____  _____

   EMPLOYED_____  DATE_____
                        TITLE
   REPLACING_____  _____
                                                      DEPARTMENT OR PROGRAM
   NEW POSITION_____  _____
                                                      DEPARTMENT OR PROGRAM
```

The form shown in Figure 13 is used to inform the payroll department of an addition to the staff.

The salary recommendation form in Figure 14 is an all-purpose salary administration form used to initiate personnel action on new hires, reinstatements, promotions, and transfers.

The forms shown in Figures 15 and 16 are used as companion forms in a nonprofit organization. The form in Figure 15 is completed by the supervisor at the time of salary review. Provision is made in the lower portion of the form for comments by the personnel department. Note the provision on the form for information about absenteeism and lateness. These factors are taken into account in the salary review and are made available to the supervisor at the time the individual is considered for review. The completed form is then returned to personnel and the pertinent information transferred to the form in Figure 16, which is the official payroll change form. The supervisor's signature is provided for in the space marked "Recommended," and final approvals are registered by the personnel director and the administrative vice-president in the two spaces indicated as "Approved." The section in the upper left corner is used for routing purposes, thereby avoiding the necessity of a multipart form. The form is prepared only in duplicate, with a copy held in

```
   IN ACCORDANCE WITH ALL APPLICABLE FEDERAL AND STATE LAWS, ALL APPLICANTS WILL RECEIVE EQUAL CONSIDERA-
   TION WITHOUT DISCRIMINATION ON THE BASES OF RACE, RELIGION, SEX, NATIONAL ORIGIN OR AGE.
```

Figure 8. Sample employment application.

the individual's personnel file. The original is routed to the payroll department and is included in that file and serves as the authorization to change the payroll status of the individual.

In most companies only nonexempt employees are reimbursed for overtime. Figure 17 represents a form which can be used for the recording of overtime. It is

INTERVIEW EVALUATION GUIDE   PERSONNEL RECRUITMENT and SELECTION

Applicant _____ Date _____

Position _____

Please complete and return this form to Personnel Relations within 24 hours of interview.
In all District Offices, please attach this form to the application and keep on file.

CHARACTERISTICS	EXCEPTIONAL	ABOVE AVERAGE	AVERAGE	BELOW AVERAGE
Appearance				
Education				
Experience				
Expression				
Maturity–Attitude				
Ambition–Drive				
Judgment				
Job Interest–Enthusiasm				
Growth Potential				
Sales Ability (Where Applicable)				

Willingness to Travel _____ To Relocate _____

Additional Comments_____

_____

Major Shortcomings_____

_____

The Interviewer's Recommendation is: ☐ Employ

☐ Consider

☐ Refer to Another Department
_____

☐ Advise Applicant We Have No
Interest at This Time

Interviewer_____ Department _____

Figure 9.   Sample interview evaluation guide.

```
                          INTERVIEW REPORT


    Applicant_____        Replacement for_____

    Title_____        New Position_____
                                                   Date Authorized_____

    Applicant should be:    _____ offered position )   please
                                                              )   check
                            _____ rejected          )   one

    If applicant is to be accepted please indicate:

           Suggested starting date_____

           Pax number_____

    If applicant is to be rejected please indicate reason or reasons:

           _____Lack of educational background or training

           _____Lack of appropriate experience

           _____Lack of proficiency in needed skills

                _____Typing                _____Shorthand

                _____Accounting             _____Purchasing

                _____Record keeping         _____Other (please specify)

           _____Personal (Appearance, Personality, Attitude, etc.)

    Comments: _____

    _____

    _____

    _____



    Date: _____    Signature: _____

    PLEASE RETURN TO THE PERSONNEL DEPARTMENT WITHIN 24 HOURS AFTER INTERVIEW.

    Per. 28
```

Figure 10.   Sample interview evaluation form.

PERSONNEL RECRUITMENT
AND SELECTION

TELEPHONE REFERENCE CHECK

Applicant's Name_____

Firm Contacted_____

Person Contacted_____ Position_____

Confirm Dates of Employment: Started _____Left _____

Job Title and Brief Description of Duties:_____

_____

_____

Overall Job Performance: ☐ Outstanding ☐ Average ☐ Poor

Did the Applicant Work Well with Others? ☐ Yes ☐ No

Strong Points:_____

_____

Weak Points:_____

_____

Reason for Leaving:_____

Rate of Pay: _____ Absenteeism: _____

Would You Recommend for Our Position? ☐ Yes ☐ No

Would You Rehire? ☐ Yes ☐ No   If Not, Why?_____

_____

Additional Specific Questions: _____

_____

_____

_____

Reference Done By:_____ Date: _____

STRICTLY CONFIDENTIAL
Upon Completion Forward To Personnel Relations Department

Figure 11.   Sample telephone reference check.

PERSONNEL INTERVIEWER: PLEASE COMPLETE UPPER-HALF OF FORM AND SEND TO THE DOCTOR WITH A PRE-EMPLOYMENT MEDICAL EXAMINATION FORM.

DOCTOR: PLEASE RETURN WHITE AND PINK COPIES TO PERSONNEL INTERVIEWER. ATTACH GREEN COPY TO COMPLETED PRE-EMPLOYMENT MEDICAL EXAMINATION FORM AND SEND WITH YOUR BILL TO MEDICAL DIRECTOR, McGRAW-HILL, INC., NEW YORK, N.Y. 10036.

☐ CORPORATE
☐ PUBLICATIONS
☐ BOOK
☐ SYSTEMS CO.
☐ REAL ESTATE

PRE-EMPLOYMENT MEDICAL EVALUATION FORM

McGRAW-HILL, INC.
330 WEST 42nd STREET
NEW YORK, N.Y. 10036

☐ REGULAR
☐ TEMPORARY
☐ REHIRE
☐ TRANSFER

______ MEDICAL APPOINTMENT—DAY, DATE, AND TIME ______ EXPECTED DATE OF EMPLOYMENT

______ (APPLICANT) IS BEING CONSIDERED FOR ______ (POSITION OR TYPE OF WORK)

IN ______ (DEPARTMENT) REPORTING TO ______ (REQUISITIONER OR SUPERVISOR) ______ (TEL. NO.)

SPECIAL PHYSICAL REQUIREMENTS (IF OTHER THAN OFFICE WORK) ______ E.G. DRIVING, TRAVELING, HEAVY LIFTING, PROLONGED STANDING, ETC.

______ PERSONNEL INTERVIEWER ______ TEL. NO.

IF APPLICANT HAS HAD ANY UNUSUAL OR SERIOUS ILLNESS, A SUMMARY FROM HIS DOCTOR WILL BE HELPFUL TO THE EXAMINING PHYSICIAN.

MEDICAL EVALUATION

☐ A Approved for employment without restrictions.

☐ B1 In the opinion of the medical examiner performance may be adversely affected by health problems. The requisitioner should weigh this with other factors in deciding whether or not to employ.

☐ B2 Approved for TEMPORARY work only not to exceed 5 months. Not eligible for company benefits. Medical department will review evaluation within 5 months.

☐ C Approved for this particular job only. Because of existing physical conditions, no transfer should be made to another job without prior consultation with the medical director.

☐ D Not approved for employment.

______ EXAMINING PHYSICIAN'S SIGNATURE—TEL. NO.

ALTHOUGH CONFIDENTIAL MEDICAL DETAILS CANNOT BE DISCLOSED, THE EXAMINING PHYSICIAN WILL BE GLAD TO DISCUSS ANY RATING.

FORM 01-27000 6/69 5M

PERSONNEL INTERVIEWER'S COPY

Figure 12. Sample pre-employment medical evaluation form.

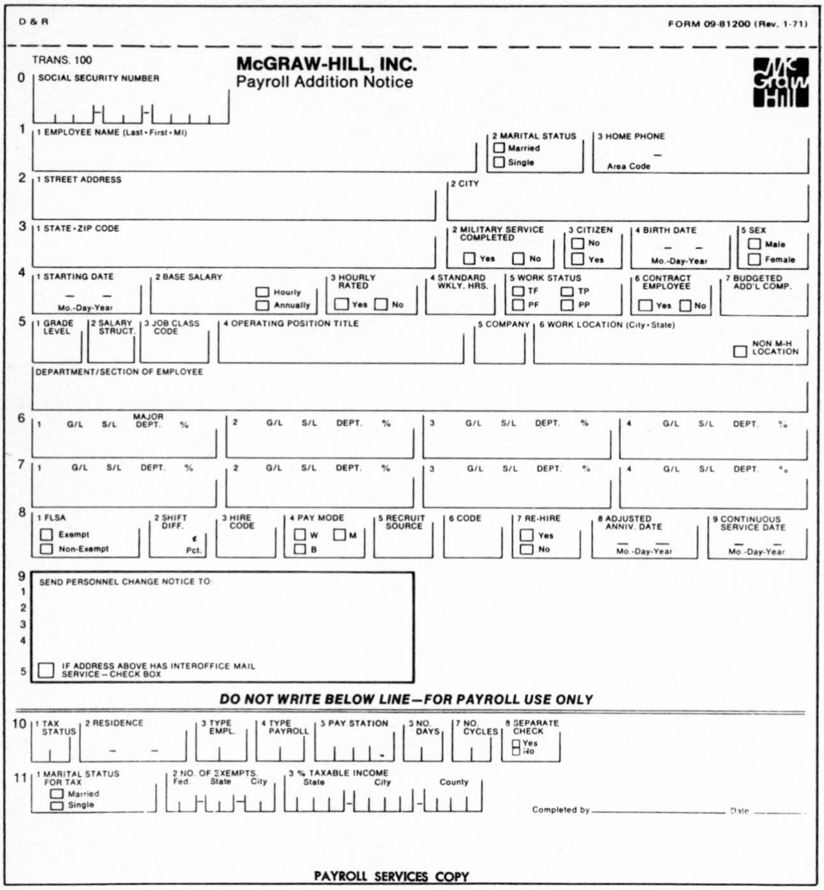

D & R

FORM 09-81200 (Rev. 1-71)

TRANS. 100

McGRAW-HILL, INC.
Payroll Addition Notice

0 SOCIAL SECURITY NUMBER

1 — 1 EMPLOYEE NAME (Last • First • MI) | 2 MARITAL STATUS ☐ Married ☐ Single | 3 HOME PHONE Area Code

2 — 1 STREET ADDRESS | 2 CITY

3 — 1 STATE • ZIP CODE | 2 MILITARY SERVICE COMPLETED ☐ Yes ☐ No | 3 CITIZEN ☐ No ☐ Yes | 4 BIRTH DATE Mo.-Day-Year | 5 SEX ☐ Male ☐ Female

4 — 1 STARTING DATE Mo.-Day-Year | 2 BASE SALARY ☐ Hourly ☐ Annually | 3 HOURLY RATED ☐ Yes ☐ No | 4 STANDARD WKLY. HRS. | 5 WORK STATUS ☐ TF ☐ TP ☐ PF ☐ PP | 6 CONTRACT EMPLOYEE ☐ Yes ☐ No | 7 BUDGETED ADD'L COMP.

5 — 1 GRADE LEVEL | 2 SALARY STRUCT. | 3 JOB CLASS CODE | 4 OPERATING POSITION TITLE | 5 COMPANY | 6 WORK LOCATION (City • State) ☐ NON M-H LOCATION

DEPARTMENT/SECTION OF EMPLOYEE

6 — 1 G/L S/L MAJOR DEPT. % | 2 G/L S/L DEPT. % | 3 G/L S/L DEPT. % | 4 G/L S/L DEPT. %

7 — 1 G/L S/L DEPT. % | 2 G/L S/L DEPT. % | 3 G/L S/L DEPT. % | 4 G/L S/L DEPT. %

8 — 1 FLSA ☐ Exempt ☐ Non-Exempt | 2 SHIFT DIFF. ¢ Pct. | 3 HIRE CODE | 4 PAY MODE ☐ W ☐ M ☐ B | 5 RECRUIT SOURCE | 6 CODE | 7 RE-HIRE ☐ Yes ☐ No | 8 ADJUSTED ANNIV. DATE Mo.-Day-Year | 9 CONTINUOUS SERVICE DATE Mo.-Day-Year

9 SEND PERSONNEL CHANGE NOTICE TO:
1
2
3
4
5 ☐ IF ADDRESS ABOVE HAS INTEROFFICE MAIL SERVICE — CHECK BOX

DO NOT WRITE BELOW LINE—FOR PAYROLL USE ONLY

10 — 1 TAX STATUS | 2 RESIDENCE | 3 TYPE EMPL. | 4 TYPE PAYROLL | 5 PAY STATION | 6 NO. DAYS | 7 NO. CYCLES | 8 SEPARATE CHECK ☐ Yes ☐ No

11 — 1 MARITAL STATUS FOR TAX ☐ Married ☐ Single | 2 NO. OF EXEMPTS. Fed. State City | 3 % TAXABLE INCOME State City County

Completed by ____________ Date ______

PAYROLL SERVICES COPY

Figure 13. Sample payroll addition notice.

FORM 1001   REV. 8

SALARY RECOMMENDATION

LOCATION

Date   Department

Name   Date of Birth

Home Address   Social Security No.

Married ☐   Permanent No.

Single ☐   Employment Date   Telephone No.

New Position — Grade — No. and Title   DATE STARTED

                                                                        Overtime Class

Present Position — Grade — No. and Title   DATE STARTED

                                                                        Overtime Class

TYPE ADJUSTMENT		SALARY		

TYPE ADJUSTMENT

Initial Employment ☐
Re-employment ☐
Return from Leave ☐
Service ☐
Merit ☐
Promotion ☐
General ☐
Shift Change ☐
Transfer ☐

Mo. Base Salary

Per Cent Increase
Proposed Salary
Present Salary
Amt. Last Increase
Date Last Increase

Salary Rate Range for Position $

Effective Date of this Adjustment

SHIFT PREMIUM
Per Cent   Amount

TOTAL SALARY
Month   Annual

EXPLANATION OF RECOMMENDATION:

PLANT OR CORPORATION DEPARTMENT APPROVALS

Signatures   Titles

Salary Committee Action: Approved ☐   Disapproved ☐

Authorized Salary $_____   Effective Date _____
                                                SALARY COMMITTEE

SALARY FIGURES: Monthly and Annual Basis.   By _____
                                                         Secretary

Figure 14.   Sample salary recommendation form.

Employee _____   Date of Employment _____

Job Title _____

Change of position since last increase: Yes ____   No ____

If answer is yes give a brief description of new duties: _____

_____

_____

Record of attendance and lateness for the past year:

Number of days late _____   Number of days of personal absences _____
                                            (a) sick _____
Number of hours late _____   (b) death in family _____
                                            (c) personal _____
                                            (d) leave without pay _____
                                         Number of days of official absences _____

Present Salary _____   Date of last increase _____

Present Grade _____   Amount of last increase _____

Present Salary Range _____   Standard for Grade _____

Supervisor's Comments: _____

_____

_____

Recommendation for pay increase:

Effective date of recommendation _____   Amount of increase _____

Today's Date _____   Signature _____
                                                              Supervisor

Personnel Department's Comments: _____

_____

_____

Per.27

Figure 15.   Sample salary review form.

PAYROLL CHANGE REPORT

FROM: DATE:

TO:

LINE NO.	EXPLANATION	PRESENT	PROPOSED
1	Employee's Name		
2	Title		
3	Department or Division		
4	Nature of Change		
5	Rate of Pay	$.............. per	$.............. per ....
6	Salary to be charged to:		
7	Effective Date		

Recommended..   Approved..

Approved..

Form 464

Figure 16.   Sample payroll change report.

```
              MEMORANDUM OF OVERTIME

Overtime must be approved in advance and verified by
an officer or department head.

                            Date _____

TO:  _____

     AT  ___

     HH  ___

     MHF ___

        This is to certify that I have worked overtime

as follows:

   Date          From - To       No. Hours   Approved
_____      _____      _____    _____
_____      _____      _____    _____
_____      _____      _____    _____
_____      _____      _____    _____
_____      _____      _____    _____
_____      _____      _____    _____

              Total            _____

              (Signed)        _____

              (Approved)      _____

Please submit this form to the Personnel Office at the
end of each week in which you have worked overtime.



   Per.4
```

Figure 17. Sample overtime memo.

prepared by the employee, approved by the supervisor, and routed to personnel and payroll. Note the statement at the top of the form concerning advance approval.

Job description. A basic component of a wage and salary program is the determination of basic rates of pay. Some companies use job analysis or evaluation to determine the content of the job, the experience required, and the degree of supervision necessary, etc. This analysis is usually made by an independent company team and involves a visual observation of the job incumbent at work together with an interview with the incumbent. In other companies a job description is required, and this is usually completed by the incumbent and used as a basis for salary rating. This is not meant to imply that other techniques are not in use; the two methods mentioned are the ones most widely used. Both of them involve the completion of forms. Figure 18 is a sample of the type used in analysis, and Figure 19 is a three-page form which serves as a job description questionnaire.

A variety of forms may be used by an organization, depending upon the level of the position to be evaluated. For example, there may be separate forms for clerical positions, technical personnel, supervisory personnel, etc. It is not always possible to design an all-purpose form to serve job analysis or description purposes. Whenever possible, however, the number of forms should be limited.

Performance appraisal. Traditionally, most companies periodically conduct a performance appraisal of each employee. The appraisals are usually made by an immediate supervisor and are used at the time a salary is to be reviewed, promotion is available, or service is to be terminated. Ratings of this type are most effectively

```
┌─────────────────────────────────────────────────────────────────────────┐
│                    JOB ANALYSIS QUESTIONNAIRE                              │
│ ═══════════════════════════════════════════════════════════════════════  │
│                                                                           │
│ Suggested Position Title _____  Department _____   │
│                                                                           │
│ Supervisor _____    Title _____    │
│ ═══════════════════════════════════════════════════════════════════════  │
│                                                                           │
│ Primary Function of Position:                                             │
│                                                                           │
│                                                                           │
│                                                                           │
│ Principal Duties:                                                         │
│                                                                           │
│                                                                           │
│                                                                           │
│                                                                           │
│ Experience Required:                                                      │
│                                                                           │
│                                                                           │
│                                                                           │
│ Educational Requirements:                                                 │
│                                                                           │
│ Type of Supervision (i.e. close, general, works independently, etc.):     │
│                                                                           │
│ Number of Employees and Job Areas Supervised:                             │
│                                                                           │
│ Decisions and Judgment Required:                                          │
│                                                                           │
│                                                                           │
│ ═══════════════════════════════════════════════════════════════════════  │
│                                                                           │
│ Submitted by: _____  _____  _____           │
│                    Name               Title             Date             │
│    ER-7                                                                   │
│ Revised 4-1-71                                                            │
└─────────────────────────────────────────────────────────────────────────┘
```

Figure 18.   Sample job analysis questionnaire.

used if they are followed up by a constructive counseling interview. As with job analysis, a number of forms may be necessary, depending upon the level and type of position. The form shown in Figure 20 is used to appraise nonexempt personnel.

Personnel status change.   Some employees will inevitably change their address, telephone number, or marital status during their employment, and such changes must be noted in several departments. A multipurpose form such as the one shown in Figure 21 is designed to serve many of these changes. It is a five-part form for distribution to personnel records, payroll, employment benefits, and medical departments and the supervisor.

Attendance records.   Attendance records are used to (1) compute wages for hourly employees, (2) determine the number of sick days when benefits are to be paid, and (3) aid the supervisor and management in evaluating an individual's status at the time of salary review.

Date _____
Issue No. _____
Job No. _____
Soc. Sec. No.

POSITION DESCRIPTION

Emp. Name _____ Loc. & Div. _____

Occ. Title _____ Occ. Code No. _____

Org. No. _____ Org. Title _____

Reports to: _____
            Name   Rank   Title

List All Positions in This Department (Identify Incumbent with Asterisk):

Number   Title   Level or Grade

Principal Purpose of Position (A Capsule Statement Explaining Reason for Job's Existence):

2.

Major Job Functions Performed to Fulfill Principal Purpose (Concise Statements Listing Main
Job Responsibilities): _____
_____

3.

Specific Knowledge and Experience Required:

Most Difficult Kinds of Problems:

Accountability (How Does Position Affect Operations of Company):

Approvals:

_____   _____
            Incumbent   Date

_____   _____
         Assistant Manager   Date

Figure 19.   Sample position description form.

C
O
M
M
E
N
T
S

ADAPTABILITY: Consider the ability of the employee to learn, to grasp new ideas and work, remember instructions and adjust to job changes._____

RELIABILITY: Consider the extent to which you can depend upon the employee to complete assignments._____

ADDITIONAL OBSERVATIONS: _____

Provide additional information below only if Employee is in Trainee capacity:

Newly Hired____; newly hired, but experienced___; new to the job through promotion___; transferred from similar job in Company or System___; rehired to old job___; other (specify)_____

Did you rate this employee at the last performance review?_____

If yes, compare previous with current performance appraisal :

Was this appraisal discussed with employee ?_____ Date: _____
What was the employee's reaction ?

O
F

C
O
U
R
S
E

A
C
T
I
O
N

Based on your rating, what do you recommend?

Action:
  Merit Increase ( ) Have you initiated "Personnel Action" form?_____
  Promotion   ( ) To what position?_____
  Training   ( ) What type?_____

  Transfer   ( ) To what type of work?_____
  Separation   ( ) Does employee know of unsatisfactory performance ?_____

_____   _____   _____
TITLE OF IMMEDIATE SUPERVISOR   SIGNATURE   DATE

_____   _____   _____
TITLE OF DEPARTMENT HEAD   SIGNATURE   DATE APPROVED

IR-4
MAY, 1968

Figure 20. Sample performance appraisal form.

Educational benefits. Tuition refund plans are common in business and industry today. The percentage of reimbursement may depend on the type of course in which an employee is enrolled. Some companies will reimburse toward work-related courses, others toward a degree program of study. This information is usually spelled out in employee handbooks. The form shown in Figure 22 is completed in duplicate prior to course registration. Note that approvals must be obtained prior to registration. The form shown serves not only as a request vehicle but also as an authorization and eventually for receipt purposes.

Suggestion systems. The objective of a suggestion system is to stimulate employees to contribute ideas for improving either their department or company operations. Most suggestion systems provide for cash awards and company recognition for accepted ideas.

	NON – EXEMPT PERFORMANCE APPRAISAL					

NAME:

( ) Semi-Annual Review
( ) Annual Review

DEPARTMENT & SECTION:

JOB TITLE:

DATE OF APPRAISAL:

Please rate and comment on the employee's performance in his present classification

	OVERALL PERFORMANCE:	OUTSTANDING:	ABOVE STANDARD:	STANDARD:	FAIR:	UNSATISFACTORY:
R A T I N G	Refers to the manner in which the employee carries out assigned responsibilities and duties:	Results are consistently in excess of job requirements.	Excellent, made some improvements on objectives of job. While some areas of performance are excellent, there is not enough consistency to warrant an outstanding rating.	Good performance, somewhat more than adequate. Meets job requirements.	Inadequate performance. Meets minimum job requirements infrequently. Must improve.	Performance unacceptable; Performance is such that consideration should be given to demotion or release.
		☐	☐	☐	☐	☐

C O M M E N T S

JOB KNOWLEDGE: Refer to the degree that the employee understands and can perform the assignments within the scope of the job duties (consideration should be given to the amount and type of supervision required)._____
_____
_____
_____

QUALITY OF WORK: Refer to the accuracy, thoroughness, and neatness of work produced. Indicate relationship with quantity required._____
_____
_____

QUANTITY OF WORK: Consider such factors as meeting schedules and amount of acceptable work accomplished. Indicate relationship with quality required._____
_____
_____

INITIATIVE: Consider the ability of the employee to take action without being told or continually supervised and to suggest and try new ideas, methods._____
_____
_____

Some companies will entertain suggestions submitted in memorandum form. Most companies which have suggestion systems, however, use printed forms. While the primary purpose of the form is to provide a means for submitting a suggestion, it can also be used as a promotional piece, and often cartoons and multicolored printing are used.

As a rule, the forms are 8½ by 11 inches. The suggestion form used by Western Electric is shown in Figure 23. Note the preprinted number on the reverse side of the form. This number provides a means of identification and ensures a degree of impartiality. Instructions for completion are included on the reverse side, together with a partial list of areas in which suggestions are welcome. After completion, the form is enclosed and sealed in a preaddressed envelope and forwarded to the secretary of the suggestion committee.

Termination of employment. Many companies conduct exit interviews when an employee is leaving the organization. This interview often discloses departmental or job-related problems. In most instances a form is used by the interviewer to record the substance of the interview. Some forms are designed so that the reasons for leaving and other attendant reasons can be checked off; others which are depth designed permit extensive interviewer comments.

In addition to the exit interview, personnel must also advise various departments of an individual's termination in order to compute final salary payments, adjust benefits plans, retrieve charged-out equipment, etc. The form shown in Figure 24 serves most of these purposes. Instructions are printed on the reverse side. Note that coding is used to simplify completion.

Personnel Reports

Personnel departments are invariably required to compile statistics on company employment, turnover, absenteeism, lateness, salaries, training, employee benefits, etc. Some reports can be completed with a "yes" or "no" answer, and consequently a checklist form is appropriate; others require a narrative-type form which

STRUCTIONS: TYPE or PRINT WITH BALL POINT PEN ONLY.
DETACH LAST COPY AND GIVE TO YOUR SUPERVISOR.
SEND ALL REMAINING COPIES TO THE PERSONNEL RELATIONS DEPT.

51•54700 (Rev. 5/71)

McGraw-Hill, Inc.
Personal Status Change Notice

TRANS. 140

I hereby authorize McGRAW-HILL, INC. to make the following revisions to my personnel and payroll records effective: Date________

0 SOCIAL SECURITY NUMBER | NAME: Last Name (Currently on Company Records) First Name Initial

DIVISION | PUB./DEPT. and SECTION | WORK LOCATION: City State

☐ NAME change to: 1 | 1 Last Name | First Name | Initial

☐ MARITAL STATUS change to: 2 | 1 Change to | Date of Marital Status Change

☐ ADDRESS change to: 3 | 1 Street Address | 2 City

4 | 1 State | Zip | 2 Residence Code (Payroll Use Only)

☐ HOME TELEPHONE change to: 5 | 1 Telephone (Area-Number)

PLEASE NOTE: If you are changing your marital status and now wish to enroll or exclude dependent(s) for coverage under EMPLOYEE BENEFIT PLANS, you must complete a new benefits enrollment card, and forward it to your appropriate REGIONAL BENEFITS OFFICE within 30 days of change of status. Mark the card "REVISED." A benefits enrollment form may be obtained from your local office manager or your Regional Benefits Office.

To change your withholding exemptions for tax purposes, obtain a withholding tax form from your local office manager or Personnel Relations Department and forward it to the Payroll Department, Hightstown, New Jersey.

Signature________ Date________

COPY 1: PERSONNEL RECORDS & BENEFITS

Figure 21. Sample personal status change notice.

Tuition Reimbursement Application

Name_____ Request Date_____

Department_____ Position_____

Name of School_____ Purpose of Study_____

Degree Program: Yes___ No___ Degree Expected_____ Date Expected_____

COURSES TO BE TAKEN

Course Title & Description	Credit Hours	Course Duration	Class Time & Schedules	Cost of Course

Employee Signature_____ TOTAL $_____

APPROVALS

Supervisor_____ Dept. Head_____

Employee Relations Dept._____

Amount Eligible for Reimbursement		
by $_____	Check Request Initiated	Date
	Check Received	Date

NOTE: Complete this form in duplicate prior to course registration. Obtain
signatures of Supervisor and Department Head and forward the two copies to
Employee Relations. One copy will be returned to the employee indicating
department approval. Upon completion of the course/s, submit this approved
copy to Employee Relations, together with a tuition receipt and course
transcript, for reimbursement.

Revised 4-15-71
ER-1T

Figure 22. Sample tuition reimbursement application.

usually provides for justification for certain trends which are observable from the statistics.

The frequency of reports is determined by the nature of the information and the level of management to be advised. For example, absenteeism and lateness reports are usually compiled weekly or monthly, whereas turnover statistics may be reported quarterly. Charts, graphs, and tables are often used to aid visual comprehension. Many of the personnel reports are computer generated; this is discussed under Electronic Data Processing.

RECORDS MAINTENANCE

There are a number of books and periodicals included in the bibliography which will serve as excellent reference tools in a search for information about filing meth-

ods and systems. Therefore, this section will merely mention a few suggested guidelines.

The basic methods of arranging records are alphabetically, chronologically, and
numerically. For example, individual personnel file folders are most conveniently
arranged alphabetically, while papers within file folders are customarily arranged
chronologically. General personnel correspondence, to be most useful, can be filed
according to subject, which in turn may be numerically coded for ease of filing and
retrieval.

A brief sample outline of personnel subjects, coded numerically, is shown below:

PERSONNEL	PER
PER 1	General policy
PER 2	Employment
PER 2-1	Recruitment
PER 2-2	Discrimination
PER 2-3	Examinations and tests
PER 3	Positions
PER 3-1	Job evaluation
PER 4	Salaries and wages
PER 4-1	Policy and procedure manuals
PER 4-2	Fringe benefits
PER 5	Attendance and absenteeism
PER 5-1	Vacations
PER 5-2	Overtime
PER 5-3	Holidays
PER 6	Health and safety
PER 6-1	Accident prevention
PER 6-2	Blood bank
PER 6-3	Disability

Remember every filing system should be tailor made to the needs of the organization.

Records Retention

Records pass through three stages in their life cycle:
1. Active use
2. Occasional reference
3. Inactive use

In order to determine the stage personnel records are in, it is first necessary to
conduct a records inventory or audit. This will indicate what records are available,
where they are and the quantity. See Figure 25 for a sample inventory form.

Once the records which are in the second and third cycles have been determined,
investigate the availability of low-cost storage space. Office space which is used
for the storage of infrequently used records is an unjustifiable use of space. It is
also costly. Take advantage of the greatest amount of filing space per square foot
of floor space for the storage of inactive records. Many companies set up their own
inactive records center in a low-cost secondary location. Others use commercially
operated centers which will receive, retrieve, and service records and handle disposal, for a fee.

If a company-operated center is created, make sure there are adequate controls
built into the system to assure quick retrieval and systematic follow-up on borrowed
records.

Review the inventory and analyze each record for retention. Consult with the
record user about his administrative need of the record. How long does he require

S-246 (1-69)

What's Your Idea?

EMPLOYEES' *Suggestion*

SYSTEM

Ⓐ **Western Electric**

HEADQUARTERS COMMITTEE

(SEE BACK OF THIS FORM FOR INSTRUCTIONS)

FOLD HERE

I SUGGEST_____

DETAILED EXPLANATION AND WHAT THIS SUGGESTION WILL ACCOMPLISH:_____

IF YOU ARE ELIGIBLE AND YOUR SUGGESTION IS ADOPTED FOR USE, YOU WILL BE GRANTED AN AWARD AND YOUR RIGHTS IN THE SUGGESTION THEREUPON BECOME THE PROPERTY OF THE COMPANY

IF FURTHER SPACE IS REQUIRED USE PLAIN PAPER OR USE SPACE ON BACK OF THIS FORM IF NOT NEEDED FOR SKETCH

IF OTHER SHEETS ARE ATTACHED SHOW NUMBER HERE ☐   IF YOU HAVE A MODEL TO SUBMIT CHECK HERE ☐

DO NOT FILL IN FROM THIS LINE TO PERFORATION   THIS SPACE FOR OFFICE USE ONLY

DATE RECEIVED   SERIAL NUMBER

FOLD HERE

DO NOT DETACH THIS COUPON BEARING YOUR NAME

TO ASSURE IMPARTIAL CONSIDERATION OF YOUR SUGGESTION, THE SECRETARY WILL DETACH THIS COUPON AND HOLD IT IN CONFIDENTIAL FILE. YOUR SUGGESTION, THEREAFTER, WILL BE IDENTIFIED BY THE SERIAL NUMBER ASSIGNED TO IT. YOU WILL RECEIVE PROMPT ACKNOWLEDGMENT OF THIS SUGGESTION SHOWING THE NUMBER ASSIGNED AND WILL BE ADVISED OF THE COMMITTEE'S ACTION.

SIGN YOUR NAME HERE_____   DEPT._____   DATE_____

TELEPHONE EXTENSION_____   LOCATION_____

NAME   DO NOT WRITE IN THIS SPACE   FOR OFFICE USE ONLY

PRINT YOUR NAME IN SPACE BELOW CLOSE TO DOUBLE RULE   DATE RECEIVED   SERIAL NUMBER

(WOMEN SHOW MISS OR MRS.)   LAST   INITIALS

Figure 23.   Sample suggestion system form.

the record to ensure efficient operation in his department? If usage statistics have been compiled, use them as a basis for establishing a retention. Check the company legal counsel to see what the law requires in terms of retention. If there is a company historian or archivist, consult him about historical documentation. Negotiate a reasonable retention for every record on the inventory. Be sure that the records retention schedule has the approval of top management. Build a periodic review into the system so that forms, records, and reports no longer used are deleted and new ones added. Include all types of records: paper, punch cards, tapes, disks, microfilm, etc.

For excellent coverage on records retention, see *Records Retention* by William E. Mitchell, or *Records Control and Storage Handbook*.

VITAL RECORDS PROTECTION

In the early 1950s, American businessmen threatened by possible nuclear attack began to consider what measures should be taken to ensure the company's ability

SKETCH

YOUR SKETCH DOES NOT HAVE TO BE DRAWN TO SCALE—BUT IT SHOULD SHOW SUFFICIENT DETAIL TO ILLUSTRATE YOUR IDEA CLEARLY.

INSTRUCTIONS

IF SUGGESTION CONTAINS CLASSIFIED INFORMATION, SUBMIT TO THE LOCAL SECURITY SUPERVISOR.

EXPRESS YOUR IDEAS AS CLEARLY AND IN AS FEW WORDS AS POSSIBLE ON FRONT OF THIS FORM. USING SPACE IMMEDIATELY ABOVE FOR SKETCH OR DIAGRAM OR, IF NEEDED, FOR FURTHER EXPLANATION OF YOUR SUGGESTION.

YOUR SUPERVISOR WILL BE GLAD TO HELP YOU IN PREPARING THIS SUGGESTION AND ALSO WILL ARRANGE TO HAVE THIS FORM TYPED IF YOU WISH.

REVIEW WHAT YOU HAVE WRITTEN TO BE SURE THAT YOU HAVE SAID WHAT YOU WANTED TO SAY.

FOLD THIS FORM AT INDICATED FOLD LINES, SEAL IT IN A PRE-ADDRESSED ENVELOPE WHICH IS PROVIDED IN THE SUGGESTION FORM HOLDER AND FORWARD IT TO THE SECRETARY OF THE SUGGESTION COMMITTEE THROUGH INTERDEPARTMENTAL MAIL. OR IF YOU WISH, YOU MAY MAKE PERSONAL DELIVERY.

IF YOU HAVE OTHER SUGGESTIONS YOU WISH TO SUBMIT MAKE OUT SEPARATE FORMS FOR EACH ONE. THERE IS NO LIMIT TO THE NUMBER YOU MAY SUBMIT.

N⁰ 0466

SUGGESTIONS ARE PARTICULARLY WELCOME ON THE FOLLOWING SUBJECTS:

1. IMPROVEMENT IN QUALITY OF PRODUCT.
2. IMPROVEMENT IN SERVICE TO OUR CUSTOMERS.
3. BETTER STORAGE, PACKING OR SHIPPING.
4. IMPROVEMENT IN WORKING CONDITIONS AND REDUCTION OF FATIGUE.
5. SAFETY PRECAUTIONS TO ELIMINATE HAZARDS IN WORK OR TO PROPERTY.
6. IMPROVEMENT IN OPERATING METHODS.
7. METHODS FOR INCREASING PRODUCTION.
8. SAVINGS OF LABOR, MATERIALS OR SUPPLIES.
9. PREVENTION OF WASTE OF EVERY KIND.
10. REDUCTION OF DEFECTIVE WORK.
11. IMPROVEMENT OF TOOLS OR MACHINERY.
12. IMPROVEMENT IN HANDLING METHODS.
13. ELIMINATION OF UNNECESSARY RECORDS, DATA, MATERIALS OR EQUIPMENT.
14. IMPROVED METHODS OF MAINTAINING COMPANY PROPERTY.

THIS LIST IS NOT NECESSARILY COMPLETE, SO SEND IN ANY IDEAS WHICH YOU THINK HAVE VALUE.

N⁰ 0466

to function following a catastrophe. Thus was born the "vital records security" concept.

Nuclear threats have lessened in the decades since then, but other hazards such as fire, theft, civil insurrection, and employee sabotage now loom before management as threats to the safety of the memory of the organization: its records. Vital records protection can be likened to a casualty insurance policy. You may pay for it for years and never have to use it, but it affords protection to the family if and when an accident occurs.

Personnel records and reports have a place in any vital records protection program. Earlier in the chapter, reference was made to a company's most valuable asset: the individual. Management has a responsibility and obligation to protect the interests of its employees.

Consult with the person or department responsible for record keeping in the organization, and develop a list of the records vital to personnel needs. In a study undertaken by the Association of Records Executives and Administrators in 1966, the following personnel records were included as vital in the programs of the companies surveyed:

Employee savings plans
Federal income tax computations and returns
Forms (copy of important)
Insurance policies and schedules
Labor contracts
Officers, list of
Payroll registers
Personnel records
Retirement plans

Detach last copy.   Forward remaining 5 copies intact to Personnel Relations Department:
Division Personnel Administrator or your Regional Personnel Representative.

FORM 51 50910

McGraw-Hill, Inc.
Termination of Employment

EMPLOYEE
NAME
CO /DIV
DEPT /SECTION
LOCATION

NOTE: The Latest Personnel Change Notice (5090) for the above employee must be
attached to this Termination Notice.

DEPARTMENT HEAD

1 EFFECTIVE 'CLOSE OF BUSINESS' DATE	2 REASON CODE			Termination Reason
		☐ Resignation ☐ Dismissal ☐ Other		

Would you re-employ, without reservations, in a final position? ☐ Yes ☐ No (Explain in Comments) Is employee on an Expense Account? ☐Yes☐No Final Payment will not be made, until expense account is cleared.
Would you recommend for a transfer or re-employment elsewhere? ☐ Yes ☐ No

If no exit interview by Personnel send final pay check to: NAME   DEPARTMENT   LOCATION

If Retirement, last scheduled day of work ▶   Number of Vacation days taken since June 1: ▶   NUMBER OF DAYS

If Dismissal ▶ Final warning memo sent to employee on ▶   DATE   Employee was or will be advised of dismissal on ▶   DATE   No. of weeks Salary to be paid in lieu of notice ▶

COMMENTS: _____

APPROVALS— Present Department		OTHER APPROVALS— As Required		PERSONNEL REVIEW	
Signature	Date	Signature	Date	Signature	Date

PAYROLL DEPARTMENT

PAYMENTS TAXABLE:

REGULAR SALARY: From ____ to ____	$ ____
LESS: ____ (days-hours) overpaid for period ____	$ ____
OVERTIME PAY: ____ hours, for period ending ____ 19____	$ ____
OVERTIME PAY: ____ hours, for period ending ____ 19____	$ ____
UNUSED EARNED VACATION PAY: ____ days	$ ____
ACCRUED VACATION PAY ____ twelfths of ____ weeks	$ ____
SEPARATION ALLOWANCE: ____ weeks	$ ____
PAY IN LIEU OF NOTICE: ____ weeks	$ ____
MILITARY INDUCTION BONUS: ____ weeks	$ ____
OTHER: ____	$ ____

LESS: OVERPAYMENTS: REGULAR PAY: ____   ____
                       OTHER: ____   ____

TOTAL GROSS TAXABLE PAYMENT $ ════

REFUNDS: Add to payment   OTHER DEDUCTIONS: Subtracted from payment

BOND BALANCE ____ $ ____   EXPENSE ACCOUNT $ ____
                                     DINING ROOM BILLS $ ____
OTHER ____ $ ____   CREDIT UNION $ ____
                                     OTHER ____ $ ____

BENEFIT PLANS:

☐ YOU WERE AUTOMATICALLY ENROLLED IN: YOU HAD ELECTED THE FOLLOWING OPTIONAL PLANS:

Life Insurance   ☐ Long Term Disability Insurance
Travel Accident Insurance   ☐ Comprehensive Medical Plan ☐ Self ☐ Dependents
Hospitalization   ☐ Life Insurance
Weekly Accident   ☐ Employee Retirement Plan
    and Sickness Plan   ☐ Supplemental Retirement Income Plan

PAYROLL SERVICES COPY

COMPLETED BY PAYROLL ____

**INFORMATION CONCERNING FUTURE COVERAGES OR AUTOMATIC DISCONTINUANCE
OF VARIOUS BENEFIT PLANS ARE EXPLAINED ON THE ATTACHED FORM**

Figure 24.   Sample termination of employment form.

Stock purchase plans (in-house)
Succession of management lists
Wage rates
Workmen's compensation
This list can serve as a guide—it is not meant to be all inclusive.

Once the list is developed, decide upon the methods of protection.   Some companies which have multilocations send copies of vital documents to outlying company locations.   Others consider records routinely distributed outside the company to banks, insurance companies, governmental agencies, etc., as protected by dispersal.

TERMINATION NOTICE INSTRUCTIONS

This is a combined form used to seek approval, process terminations and provide the statement of final pay.

It is important that the Termination Notice be completed and processed as soon as it is known that an employee will terminate. Prompt processing of the Termination Notice will enable the Payroll Department to clear the employee's account prior to the termination date and issue the correct final pay check by the employee's last day of work.

INSTRUCTIONS:

1. Fill out the Termination Notice immediately upon reaching a decision to terminate an employee. Refer to section B of the Personnel Policies and Procedures Manual for guidance.

   Note: If termination is a Dismissal, a copy of the Final Warning Letter to employee must be on file in Personnel Relations.

2. Obtain proper approvals, detach the Department Head's file copy, attach the current computer produced Personnel Change Notice, form 5090.

3. Send the completed, approved Termination Notice with the attached 5090 to the Personnel Relations Department: division Personnel Administrator or the regional Personnel representative for your location.

TERMINATION REASONS AND CODES

Select the appropriate termination reason and corresponding code below and enter it in the space provided on the Termination Notice. If more than one reason applies, enter the primary reason and code in the space provided and note other reasons in comments.

CODE	RESIGNATION	CODE	DISMISSAL
01	Dissatisfied with pay	61	Absenteeism
01	Offered higher pay	62	Tardiness
02	Dissatisfied with present duties	*63	Attitude
02	Change in career interest	*64	Lack of application to job
03	Personal relations on job	*65	Misconduct
04	Physical working conditions	*66	Other — Employee's fault
05	Dissatisfied with promotion opportunities	70	Lack of qualifications for job
05	Offered better opportunity		(Eligible for Separation Allowance)
		70	Changed requirements of position
10	Moving out of area		(Eligible for Separation Allowance)
11	Marriage	*71	Other — Not employee's fault
12	Maternity		(Eligible for Separation Allowance)
13	To remain at home		
14	To return to school (permanent employee)	CODE	OTHER
15	Commuting problem	90	Military service (Copy of orders or draft notice
16	Hours not suitable		must be attached for induction bonus)
		91	Reduction of force
20	Unknown (Left without notice)		(Eligible for Separation Allowance)
		92	Temporary work completed
		*93	Physical incapacity to perform job — Needs
40	Voluntary retirement		concurrence of Medical Director
*50	Health reasons but not physically		(Eligible for Separation Allowance)
	incapacitated	95	Mandatory retirement (Eligible for Separation
*55	Other		Allowance if not eligible for pension)
		99	Deceased

*Explain in Comments

Many corporations send duplicate records to off-site record centers or to one of the many underground security centers.

It is important to remember that the purpose of a vital records program is to protect the essential information which is contained in the record, not necessarily the hard copy itself. Therefore, duplication may be one of many processes, i.e., microform, magnetic tape, photocopy, carbon copy, etc. The more sophisticated means of recording information are discussed elsewhere in this chapter.

If duplication is carried out through one of the newer technologies, make sure the vital records protection plan assures the capability of producing a readable

RECORDS INVENTORY WORK SHEET						
YEARS	RANGE	AREA	LOCATION	EQUIPMENT	CU. FT.	ACTION

DESCRIPTION:	OFF.	C.F.
	STOR.	C.F.
	VAULT	C.F.
RECORDS TITLE:	DEPARTMENT:	

Figure 25.   Sample records inventory work sheet.

printed copy when it is needed. Every vital records program should be systematically reviewed and obsolete records deleted and new ones added. Make sure the plan provides for scheduled times when current data are to be substituted for out-of-date information.

Some informative articles on vital records are included in the bibliography at the end of the chapter.

NONCONVENTIONAL FILING SYSTEMS

No chapter on modern record keeping would be complete without a reference to the use of microfilm and electronic data processing (EDP).

Microfilm

A microfilm systems application may be the solution for improving filing and retrieving. Companies which have experienced problems in maintaining file integrity and control have turned to one of the microforms available. Others which have multiplant locations and find it necessary to keep complete files on all employees at headquarters with duplicate files of local personnel in divisional or plant locations, film their personnel records and send back to the field either the hard copy or microfilm copies. If space is a factor, a microform file may be considered. However, microfilming may not be an economical substitute for storage. Record center storage space rental is usually considerably less than the cost of microfilm. Consider the following before deciding on microfilm as a space saver.

Compute storage space and equipment costs on an annual basis for the period of time the records must be kept. Compute the cost to microfilm the identical amount of records. For example, assume that 6 cubic feet of records can be stored at $0.80 per cubic foot per year, whereas the cost of microfilming the same amount is $12 per cubic foot. Plot this information on a graph as shown in Figure 26 to determine the "break-even" point.

The most practical microform for personnel record keeping is the micro-thin jacket. This form permits additions to the file as needed and can conveniently be indexed on the jacket header by typing the individual's name, social security number, or any other indexing factor. The availability of a reader printer permits quick retrieval and fast copy capability.

Most microfilm manufacturers have a variety of literature available, and their systems personnel can be of assistance to a company in surveying any records problem. In-house filming equipment is not always necessary; many fine service companies can do the filming, processing, and inspecting, etc., at a reasonable cost.

Electronic Data Processing

Is there a place for electronic data processing (EDP) in personnel record keeping? This question can be resolved only after a careful study and analysis of present manual methods versus the advantages and disadvantages of an EDP system.

Some personnel departments which issue long reports informing management of such facts as the number of employees on the payroll, tardiness and absenteeism records, turnover rates, and participation in company benefit programs may find an EDP system better equipped to manipulate and interpret such data. Skill inventories of personnel are often computer programmed. When a promotion is to be made or a new position created, the inventory data bank is queried and asked to print out the employees, for example, within the ages of 25 to 35, with a B.A. in economics, with five years experience, and who are fluent in Spanish.

Computer systems are used to prepare payrolls, paychecks, tax computation, and employee earning records.

Do not overlook the possibilities which are available through microfilm, EDP, and computer output microfilm (COM). Keep abreast of these technologies so that when management is ready to move into these areas, you are prepared to make a meaningful contribution.

Archives

Personnel records should not be overlooked as a source of information for a company archives. Interest in organizational memorabilia is generated when someone decides to write a company history. No history is complete without a record of the accomplishments of personnel, and very often an individual's personnel file is the only source of such information. In the past few decades, oral histories have been prepared by retired executives and key personnel of an organization, and personnel files are often consulted for background information before the researcher begins the project with the individual.

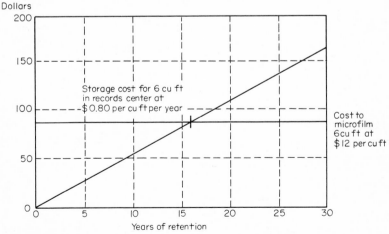

Figure 26. Chart to compute costs of storage space for records retention.

In addition to individual's personnel files, personnel policy files also contain a rich source of information not only for historical purposes but also for making current decisions in the light of past experience.

BIBLIOGRAPHY

Books

Forms and Records in Personnel Administration, Studies in Personnel Policy, No. 175, National Industrial Conference Board, New York, 1960.

Kish, Joseph L., Jr., and James Morris: *Microfilm in Business,* The Ronald Press Company, New York, 1966.

Leahy, Emmett J., and Christopher A. Cameron: *Modern Records Management,* McGraw-Hill Book Company, New York, 1965.

Mitchell, William E., *Records Retention,* Ellsworth Publishing Company, Evansville, Indiana, 1966.

Place, Irene, and Estelle L. Popham: *Filing and Records Management,* Prentice-Hall, Inc., Englewood Cliffs, N.J., 1966.

Periodicals and Pamphlets

Bibliography for Records Managers, Superintendent of Documents, U.S. Government Printing Office, Washington, D.C. 20402.

Company Continuity in Case of Disaster, The Conference Board Business Record, November, 1961, pp. 7–16.

Data Processing in Personnel Work, The Conference Board Management Record, September, 1962, pp. 32–34.

Information and Records Management, 250 Fulton Avenue, Hempstead, N.Y. 11550.

Protection of Vital Records, report by Association of Records Executives and Administrators, July, 1966.

Records Control and Storage Handbook, Bankers Box, 2607 North 25 Avenue, Franklin Park, Illinois 10131.

Records Management Journal, published quarterly by the Association of Records Executives and Administrators, P.O. Box 4259, Grand Central Station, New York, N.Y. 10017.

Records Management Quarterly, published by American Records Management Association, 24 North Wabash Avenue, Chicago, Illinois 60602.

Subject Filing, Superintendent of Documents, U.S. Government Printing Office, Washington, D.C. 20402.

The Company Looks Backward, The Conference Board Business Record, February, 1959, pp. 95–99.

chapter 78

Personnel Statistics

WALLACE W. GARDNER   *Professor of Management, The University of Utah, Salt Lake City, Utah*

INTRODUCTION

The personnel administrator cannot avoid dealing with masses of quantitative information as he goes about the business of tracking the personnel organization. Over a long time period a variety of methods, principles, and concepts have been devised for dealing with such information. As usually stated, these methods may be classified as (1) techniques for meaningful summary description of mass phenomena, (2) concepts and methods useful in the drawing of inferences under conditions characterized by uncertainty.

Though such classifications are useful, the reader should be warned against adopting a mechanical view of this subject matter. The aim should be, of course, to gain a sufficient understanding of statistical method so that it may be employed with imagination and precision to further an analytic process of broader scope. In application, the critical questions involve such matters as: What needs to be accomplished, and why? Basic deficiencies in reasoning or in data cannot be removed or ameliorated by arithmetic manipulation of those data.

The following presentation is subject to the serious constraint of space limitations. The reader is seriously urged to seek further statistical advice as the need arises. Such help is ordinarily readily available within the organization.

Measurement

Statistical methods imply a quantification of the phenomena which are subject to analysis. Further, each statistical technique available *assumes* a given *level* of measurement. In addition, the analytic process must be carried out within the framework of the "knowledge" held by the analyst.

In this respect it is useful to remind ourselves that knowledge consists, first of all, of an organized body of "theoretical concepts," which are defined in terms of more basic constructs that are assumed to be understood. Examples are "racial discrimination" and "worker skill." When it is possible to add to a theoretical concept a definition of means and methods for *measurement,* it becomes an "operational concept."

In the social sciences, this is often a very big step. An understanding of the manner in which this step was taken is fundamental to an assessment of the quality of measurement information being applied to any specific analysis. Often, for example, the measurement is not upon the subject construct but upon some reflection of it. There is no great harm in this, of course, if such is the best that can be done. But the rather uncertain correspondence between the measure and the real-world phenomena must be made clear and maintained as a part of the reporting structure. The danger lies in the tendency for such information to somehow gain in quality as one becomes familiar with its quantitative form.

Level of measurement.   Another essential aspect of the "quality" afforded by a measurement lies in the level of differentiation it represents. Four such levels of differentiation are possible: the *nominal, ordinal, interval,* and *ratio* scales.

Nominal Scale: The sorting of individual events into classes on the basis of a name attached to each event when that name implies nothing about relative desirability between events having different names. Example: A classification of employees by skill—plumbers, machinists, and metalworkers.

Ordinal Scale: A classification which adds a desirability vector to the information conveyed by a nominal scale, thus allowing an ordering of individual events. For two individual events placed in different classes it becomes possible to make statements such as: "A is greater than (or better than) B" but no inference may be drawn about how much better. Example: Employees categorized into groups such as high skill, average skill, and low skill.

Interval Scale: Classifies individual events not only by their possession of a characteristic but also by specifying the extent to which they possess the characteristic. This extends the information from the ordinal scale to allow a definition of differences between events found in different classes. Example: Classification of employees by scores on a placement test.

Ratio Scale: An interval scale which has a meaningful zero value. This additional element is necessary before it is possible to compare individuals by use of a ratio between the values of the class to which they are assigned. For example, an individual who receives a score of 120 on a placement test cannot be said to "know" twice as much as one who receives a score of 60, and thus the scale is not a ratio scale. An employee who produces 140 units of output per hour can be said to be 70 percent as productive as one who produces 200 units per hour; on this scale the zero value is meaningful.

DESCRIPTIVE STATISTICS

As information in the mass is difficult to interpret, it is necessary to carry out summarizing procedures in order to define the essential qualities of such information. The basic tool serving this purpose is the frequency distribution.

Frequency Distribution

Essentially a visual concept, the frequency distribution is useful as a means for communicating the central qualities held by a mass of information. The procedure is that of classifying each of the events in the group into one of a number of defined categories upon a measurement scale and showing the result as a graph (Figure 1). When the individual events are categorized upon an ordinal or nominal scale, interpretation will consist only of noting the relative importance in the group of each defined category.

When the level of measurement is at the level of an interval scale, a somewhat more meaningful interpretation is available. Now the frequency distribution has three important concepts associated with it: (1) central tendency, descriptive of

Figure 1. Frequency distribution —nominal scale.

the way in which the events tend to be alike; (2) dispersion, descriptive of the way in which the events tend to be different; and (3) shape of the distribution, which adds a further dimension to the description of differences among events.

For example, suppose a mass of raw data of interest consists of 200 individual test scores which range from values of 23 to 86. As the essence of "summarization" is the "reduction of detail," we change our measurement scale from units to frequency classes containing ten units per class and categorize the individual events to produce the following:

Test score	Frequency
20–29	7
30–39	16
40–49	48
50–59	74
60–69	39
70–79	12
80–89	4
	Total 200

To present a clearer visual impression, we chart the frequency table (Figure 2). The typical value is seen to be the class 50–59. The bulk of the test scores were found within the values 40–69. The dispersion around the typical scores exhibits a considerable degree of symmetry.

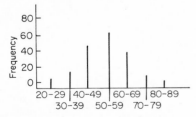

Figure 2. Frequency distribution —interval scale.

A few words need to be said about the choices made in converting the raw data into the frequency distribution above. Seven classes were used. If the data should have been rounded into two classes, too much detail would have been lost. If twelve or fifteen classes were used, so much detail would still have been present that the underlying qualities of central tendency and dispersion would have been submerged. This decision is made largely on the basis of a choice which produces convenient class limits and results in a visual impression which conveys the above qualities. A rough guide often used is that the number of classes should be in the neighborhood of $1 + 3\ 1/3$ (logarithm of the number of observations).

Measures of central tendency.   These measures are defined, and ordinarily calculated, from the raw data rather than from the frequency distribution. The most common in use are the mode, the median and the arithmetic mean.

The *mode* is the observation which appears with the greatest frequency.

The *median* is that scale value which separates the larger half from the smaller half of the observations.

The *arithmetic mean* is defined as that value about which the squared differences between it and the observations is a minimum value. For a variable measured in one dimension this quality is assured by calculating in the familiar manner: summing the observations and dividing by the number of observations.

Measures of dispersion.   These are also defined, and ordinarily calculated, from the raw data. Those most commonly employed are the range and the standard deviation.

The *range* is a very simple measure merely defining the difference between the largest and smallest value observed.

The *standard deviation* is more complex but best understood as a measure of the average distance between the observed measurements and their arithmetic mean. It is calculated as $\sigma = \sqrt{\Sigma x^2/N}$ where σ = standard deviation, Σ implies summation, $x = X - \bar{X}$, X = observed value, $\bar{X}$ = arithmetic mean, and N = number of observations.

Identification of Relationship

Multiple measurements upon the individual employee exist and may be drawn from the employee record or obtained by special survey. These may provide a fruitful source of insight into means for improved managerial and administrative practices. To accomplish this requires a means for organizing the information so that meaningful relationships are exposed if they do, in fact, exist.

The means available for this purpose depend upon the level of measurement presented in the observation. For illustration we shall limit ourselves to those cases where two measures upon each individual constitute the factors of interest. Three different situations are ordinarily found.

Both factors measured at the nominal or ordinal level.   In this case, the analytic mechanism is the frequency table. As an example, suppose we wish to investigate the possibility that the degree to which a policy is accepted within an employee group depends upon the job classification of the employee. Information bearing upon this question would be organized as follows:

ATTITUDE TOWARD POLICY

Job	Accept	Neutral	Hostile	Sum
Clerk	15	45	8	68
Electrician	200	240	170	610
Machinist	20	15	22	57
Sum	235	300	200	735

We face two analytic questions: (1) Are the differences observed among the classifications significant? (2) If they are, what is the nature of the pattern of relationship? It does appear that differences exist, e.g., among the 68 clerks, 22 percent indicated acceptance of the policy while among the 57 machinists, 35 percent indicate acceptance.

The answer to the analytic questions lies in the chi-square model. Though the statistical foundations of chi-square lie outside the scope of this chapter, its application is relatively straightforward.

First we use the chi-square transformation to answer the question: If many random samples with the same row and column totals as in our table above were obtained from a population in which job and attitude were independent (no relationship), what fraction of these random samples would indicate an apparent relationship of as much as, or more than, that indicated in our table? If this fraction is not small, we conclude that the apparent relationship here observed is not to be taken as real.

For each cell of our table we calculate chi-square equals (frequency observed-frequency expected)^2 divided by frequency expected and sum over all cells. The frequency expected for any cell equals (row total associated with the given cell divided by total events in the table) multiplied by column total associated with the given cell. Thus for the cell clerk-accept policy:

Frequency expected $= (68 \div 735)\ 235 = 21.7$
Chi-square $= (15 - 2.17)^2 \div 2.17 = 2.07$

For use later in our analysis, we take note of the fact that the difference between frequency observed and frequency expected was negative in sign.

Over all cells, the value of chi-square so calculated adds to 25.5. From a table of chi-square probability values, it may be found that such a value, or one more extreme, is extremely unlikely as a matter of chance under the given hypothesis. A relationship may thus be said to exist.

What is the nature of the relationship which exists between job and attitude? Though it may not be defined in any specific way, the cell values for chi-square are quite helpful in drawing a "picture" which is reasonably informative. Create a new table similar to the original with the chi-square values (with sign attached) replacing the observed frequencies. Now change the order in which rows and/or columns are shown until a pattern emerges. In this example, the following will result:

ATTITUDE TOWARD POLICY

Job	Neutral	Accept	Hostile
Clerk	+10.8	+2.1	−6.0
Electrician	− 0.3	+0.1	+0.1
Machinist	− 3.0	+0.2	+2.8

Statements such as these are now possible: Given the attitudes of all employees, a considerably greater proportion than expected of the clerks were neutral while a smaller than expected proportion of machinists exhibit a neutral attitude. Machinists exhibit more hostility than might be expected while clerks exhibit less. In each dimension, the scale runs from clerks to machinists at the extremes with electricians in the central position.

One theoretical consideration: The chi-square model requires that no cell contain fewer than something like five frequencies. If this problem presents itself, either "pool" (or combine) two or more rows and/or columns or seek expert assistance.

Relationship test when a factor measured upon an interval scale may be dependent upon a factor measured upon a nominal or ordinal scale: Analysis of this type of situation calls for an analysis of variance, a statistical technique of sufficient complexity to be ruled out of the scope of this chapter. When presented with a problem of this nature, it is not only suggested that statistical advice be sought, but also that it be sought early in the investigation.

For an example of this type of problem, suppose there exist three different ways of approaching the training task in the case of new employees. Further, it has been decided that a reasonable "measure of merit" for training is the number of hours required for an employee to attain a "standard output" proficiency. You design an experiment which seeks to discover whether a relationship exists between "method" and "time" in this context. The following data were obtained:

TIME TO ACHIEVE PROFICIENCY

	Method A	Method B	Method C
	7.5	9.5	4.3
	9.2	6.5	9.1
	10.1	10.8	6.0
	7.4	8.5	8.0
	5.5	8.8	7.5
	8.1	6.5	3.5
	11.4	5.2	9.0
	5.0	10.5	7.0
	4.5	8.5	4.5
	7.8	11.0	6.1
Arithmetic mean	7.64	8.58	6.50

The preceding evidence is the result of a random assignment of thirty new employees to one of the three "method" treatments. On the basis of this evidence, it might be tempting to conclude that a relationship does in fact exist which ranks the methods as C being best, A next best, and B poorest. But the thought occurs that, even though the methods applied were equal in training efficiency, it might be highly probable that apparent differences equal to, or greater than, those found here might occur simply as a matter of chance. How may this question be resolved? The statistician follows this logical path.

All factors other than teaching method which might influence the time to gain proficiency have been randomly assigned, and thus this source of variation (as well as purely random influences) contributes to the variability (dispersion) *within* each set of ten measurements. This dispersion defines the influence of chance, is measured by the squared standard deviation (variance) for each set of measurements, and is assumed equal (except for chance differences) in the measurements resulting from each method.

Any difference in the measured observations due to method employed results from an effect which has equal influence upon each individual subject to that method and thus may be considered equivalent to an effect which adds a constant to each observation. Therefore, if a method effect actually exists, it is excluded as a contribution to variance in the estimation of the influence of chance. *Note:* Any large constant value could be added to the values shown for a given method and it would not change the variance among those values.

If there exists no relationship, the variability among the method means is the result of the same chance cause system as that producing dispersion among the events within columns. Calculating the variance between the means and converting it to the variance among items should produce the same estimate of the influence of chance estimated from within columns. If the variance estimated from between the means differs (larger) by more than can be attributed to chance, the hypothesis of statistical homogeneity among method means may be rejected and one may conclude that a relationship does exist.

Relationship when both variables are measured upon an interval scale. The means for analysis of relationship in this case is known as regression. As was observed previously, the key to analysis both in the case of the frequency table and analysis of variance lies in a test of a hypothesis. A similar test of hypothesis is available in the case of regression, and is important when the number of observations is *small*. When, however, the number of observations is reasonably large, regression tends to be used in the purely descriptive sense. To be more specific: In most applications a relationship is known, or assumed, to exist and regression techniques are used as a means for *definition* of that relationship. The information to be conveyed pertains to the qualities of a bidimensional frequency distribution.

For example, suppose a set of observations are in hand showing for each employee a measure of job success paired with a measure of performance on a test given at time of employment. Plotting these data might provide a graph like that shown in Figure 3.

$$Y_c = 20 + 5X$$
$$s_{y.x} = 8$$

Figure 3. Scatter diagram: Job success related to test score.

Each employee (of a Y and an X pair) contributes one point to the plot. The arithmetic mean for the bivariate sample, the line of regression, is defined as $Y_c = 20 + 5X$. This was obtained by an arithmetic routine which assures that the sum of the squared differences between each Y value and the point on the regression line with the same value for X is a minimum value. For any test score, there exists a point on the regression line; this point is interpreted as the arithmetic mean or expected value of job success measures associated with this test score. The "average difference" expected between the mean success value and the actual success value is measured by the "standard error of estimate" (standard deviation of Y values, given a specific X value), here shown to have a value of $s_{y.x} = 8$.

The nature of the relationship is defined by the "regression coefficient," the slope of the line of regression, here indicated to have a value of five units. For each unit of increase in test score, the average value of the measure of job success is expected to increase by five units.

The Correlation Coefficient: When the problem concerns the measurement of the degree of association between two independent variables rather than a definition of the predictive relationship between a dependent (Y) and an independent (X) variable, the applicable statistical model is correlation. The arithmetic procedures result in a single value, symbolized by r, measuring the strength of association along a scale from 0 to 1.

The correlation coefficient is a rather complex measure which does not readily lend itself to interpretation. When the problem is truly one of assessing the extent of association, no alternative to its use exists. Unfortunately, it is possible to calculate the correlation coefficient from data which should have been analyzed by regression. (The phrase "should have been" is used in order to imply that regression would be more informative.) When presented with this situation, the "statistical consumer" is badly in need of a means for assessing the correlation coefficient in terms of the strength of the predictive relationship which it implies. A very useful means for accomplishing this lies in the index of predictive efficiency.

The Index of Predictive Efficiency: What is really meant by the phrase "predictive quality of a relationship"? The most direct answer to this question is: The extent to which the predictor X decreases the error of estimate below that value which would exist should the predictive relation not be available.

Given the evidence from a sample of Y values, the best estimate of another value not in this set is the arithmetic mean of these values; the error in this estimate is measured by the standard deviation of the Y values. If a regression relationship exists upon another variable, X, the bivariate mean (line of regression) is the best estimator, with the error of estimate now measured by the dispersion around the line of regression. This is shown graphically in Figure 4. Without X, the error of

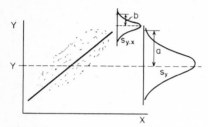

Figure 4.   Reduction in error of estimate achieved through regression.

estimate is a; using X as predictor, the error of estimate is b. A convenient way of measuring the relative advantage gained is by the ratio $s_{y.x} \div s_y$. Or, to reverse the direction of the scale, the form $1 - (s_y \div s_{y.x})$ may be preferable. We shall call this the index of predictive efficiency.

This index has an invariant relation to the correlation coefficient: index of predictive efficiency $= 1 - \sqrt{1 - r^2}$

A graph of this relation between index of predictive efficiency and r provides a picture which should be kept in mind whenever the need exists for interpreting the predictive quality implied by a reported correlation coefficient (Figure 5).

Thus, suppose a reported value of the correlation coefficient was $r = .5$. This implies an index of predictive efficiency of .135. Use of X as a predictor has reduced the error of estimate by 13.5 percent ($s_{y.x}$ is still 87.5 percent of s_y).

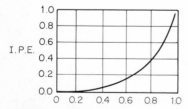

Figure 5.   Relation between the index of predictive efficiency and the correlation coefficient.

THE ROLE OF STATISTICAL MODELS

A central role in all statistical applications is played by the statistical models drawn from the discipline of mathematics. Each "model" specifies the results of a long-run random sampling process carried out upon a defined universe. Such results are expressed as a "probability distribution," a frequency distribution in which the frequencies total unity. For our purpose here, we define "probability" as relative frequency.

As an example, suppose we had available a very large set of events (universe) in which each event was measurable upon a two-valued ordinal or nominal scale. Let us call the relative frequency with which one of these two values exist in the universe π, and the relative frequency of the other value $1 - \pi$. Let us also distinguish the two values as "success" and "failure," respectively. We draw a sample of five events at random from this set ($n = 5$).

Each sample of five items may be described by counting the number of "successes" (r) found within it. The "model" describes the relative frequency with which the six different results would be observed over a very large number of repeated trials of this experiment. Rather than carry out such an experiment, we simply use the formula below to evaluate the probabilities:

$$P_r = C_r^n \pi^r (1 - \pi)^{n-r}$$

This is the binomial model, one of the simplest and most basic in the theoretical structure.

In this brief treatment, it will be impossible to present a catalog of the specific models available, even though any one of them may, at some time, be very useful to the personnel administrator. We emphasize the concept of the model as a frequency distribution which *could be* derived through a long-run sampling experiment under specified conditions. These conditions define the *assumptions* of the model. *These assumptions are a part of the information conveyed whenever a statistical model is employed.* If not understood by the "consumer," he must ask that they be explicitly stated by the reporter-analyst.

In application, there are three fundamental ways in which statistical models are used. First, they provide a means for attaching a measure of precision to an uncertain estimate. Second, they provide a means for testing hypotheses. Third, they provide a means for identifying elements of stability in real-world systems.

Estimation

Suppose it has been decided that it would be useful to estimate the proportion of newly hired employees who are now using or have used drugs. In the entrance examinations, every tenth inductee is subjected to special scrutiny in the medical-psychological phase of the procedure. Out of 200 such cases, 12 percent were identified as "users." How good is this estimate?

One aspect of "quality" lies outside the province of statistics (though it is encompassed within the statistical investigator's sphere of responsibility). This is the question of *accuracy*, i.e., does the measuring instrument correctly assess what it purports to measure? Is the quality "user-nonuser" correctly defined for each subject observed?

The statistical aspect of "quality" lies in the concept of *precision*. If this measuring instrument were applied to a very large universe of these subjects, how much difference might exist between the universe proportion (π) and the sample proportion reported ($p = .12$)?

We assume the existence of a (perhaps theoretical) universe, of very large size, and that our sample of 100 subjects was randomly drawn from this universe. Thus we have one sample out of an infinite number of such samples which might have been obtained, as a matter of chance, from the universe. This large number of possible samples may be described by use of the binomial model. (Actually, with $n = 200$ and π not small, we shall use a reasonably good approximation to the binomial, the normal curve. The arithmetic is much simpler, and tabulated probability values are easily available.) The model, with arithmetic mean and standard deviation as shown, would appear as in Figure 6.

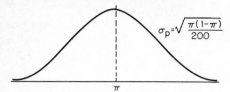

Figure 6. Binomial model for
n = 200.

We may reason in this manner. If the sample proportion of .12 is one of the 90 percent most likely sample proportions which could be obtained as a matter of chance from this universe, then the following statement is true:

$$.12 - 1.65\sigma_p < \pi < .12 + 1.65\sigma_p$$

The value 90 percent was chosen arbitrarily and indicates the level of faith, or confidence, in the statement. It can be said that, for many such statements resulting from different sample evidence when statements like the above are made, 90 percent of those statements will be true.

The statement made is normally given in the following form:

$$\pi = .12 \pm 1.65\sigma_p = .12 \begin{array}{l} +.042 \\ -.032 \end{array}$$

The best estimate of π is the value $p = .12$. The *reliability* of this estimate (for a 90 percent confidence statement) is $\begin{array}{l} +.042 \\ -.032 \end{array}$. This reliability statement measures the statistical precision of the instrument used to produce the estimate of π. It is exactly the same type of statement as that used by the engineer when he says that a micrometer will produce measurements with a precision of $\pm.0001$.

Testing Hypotheses

A test of a statistical hypothesis arises whenever we have some basis, flowing from the environment in which the inferential problem is found, for an expression of what the value of an unknown universe quality should be along with sample evidence which differs from that expressed value.

To continue our example above, suppose a similar investigation in another division of our company produced a sample of 300 in which 15 percent of the subjects were identified as drug "users." Can we say that the previous work force (division A) constitutes less of a problem in this regard than the work force in this area (division B)?

We hypothesize that both samples came from a universe with equal "user" proportions, i.e., $\pi_a = \pi_b$, and that the difference between $p_a = .12$ and $p_b = .15$ is due to chance.

The relevant model is now the "distribution of differences between two sample proportions." This model is well approximated by a normal distribution with

$$\text{Mean} = \pi_a - \pi_b = 0$$

$$\text{Standard   deviation} = \sigma_{p_a} - p_b = \sqrt{\pi(1 - \pi)\frac{1}{200} + \frac{1}{300}}$$

The common value of π must be estimated from the samples as

$$\pi = \frac{200(.12) + 300(.15)}{500} = .138$$

Thus $\sigma_{p_a} - \sigma_{p_b} = .031$

The decision which follows from a test of an hypothesis is made on the basis of an assessment of the degree of doubt cast upon the hypothesis. Let the graph in Figure 7 be a picture of the distribution of all possible sample results under a given hypothesis.

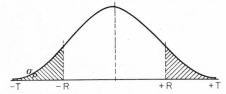

Figure 7. Distribution of sample results given that hypothesis is true.

If the sample evidence were located within the distribution at point R, little doubt is cast upon the hypothesis. The measure of the degree of doubt lies in the relative frequency with which sample results equal to, or more extreme than the sample evidence occur (the crosshatched area above). Should the sample evidence be located at point T, great doubt would be cast upon the hypothesis.

A similar picture for our example is shown in Figure 8. If our hypothesis is true, $p_a - p_b = .03$ is seen not to be a highly unusual event; a sample event equal to, or more extreme than this could occur as a matter of chance in 17 percent of the trials. It is difficult to reject the hypothesis.

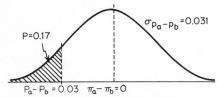

Figure 8. Location of the sample result within the distribution.

Notice that we cannot say that we *know* that the hypothesis is true. The evidence from the sample may be shown not to be inconsistent with alternative hypotheses so long as such alternatives specify small negative values for $\pi_a = \pi_b$. By accepting the hypothesis, we must bear a risk; that of accepting a hypothesis which is not true.

Identification of Stability

If it can be shown that real-world events follow a pattern of variability which agrees closely with a given probability model, then it is possible to attribute to those events the properties (or "laws" of behavior) assumed in the construction of the model.

The application of this approach in analytic effort often provides enormous insight into an environment.   Among the many examples of this form of an attack upon the development of "information," one of the most interesting to the personnel administrator may well lie in the statistical analysis of "life" properties.

For an example, suppose there exists a department in which the rate of turnover among employees is a cause for concern.   One way to analyze turnover defines the "life" of an individual as the time between hiring and separation, and examines the properties of this phenomenon by use of actuarial concepts.

It might be found convenient to begin with the historical record which starts at a date 80 months prior to the present time.   For each employee hired over this period, record the "life" of employment (months between hiring and separation). After choosing a convenient "life" interval, this information is summarized in tabular form below:

DISTRIBUTION OF EMPLOYMENT LIFE

Life, Months	Separations in Interval: No. of Employees	Employees Surviving at Beginning of Life Interval
0 to less than 5	170	1000
5 to less than 10	155	830
10 to less than 15	130	675
15 to less than 20	95	545
20 to less than 25	90	450
25 to less than 30	50	360
30 to less than 35	35	310
35 to less than 40	35	275
40 to less than 45	15	240
45 to less than 50	5	225
50 to less than 55	30	220
55 to less than 60	25	190
60 to less than 65	15	165
65 to less than 70	15	150
70 to less than 75	10	135
75 to less than 80	10	125
80 and larger	115	115
Total	1,000	

A convenient means for analysis of data such as this is to choose a "law" which might define the pattern of "disappearance," seek a scale transformation upon which the data would plot as a straight line if it does indeed follow that law, plot the data upon this scale, and make a judgment.

Let us first try a "law" which requires that a constant fraction of employees surviving a given employment life will be separated in the next life interval.   The mathematical description of the expected "employee survival" pattern under this law would be $Y = 1000\ e^{-\lambda t}$; where Y = employees surviving at time t, λ = probability of separation of an individual during time interval t to $t + 1$, and t = any conveniently small time measure, say one month.   If this "law" is operative, the "employees surviving" data should appear as essentially a straight line upon a semilogarithmic chart (Figure 9).

In this case, the law specified does indeed appear consistent with the data.   However, a very interesting feature of this data appears.   The discontinuity at about 30 months indicates that the constant probability of an individual quitting employment suddenly changes to a much lower level at this time.   Though estimation of

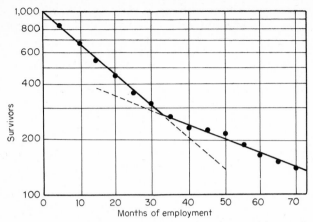

Figure 9.   Employers surviving a given employment time period—semilogarithmic scale.

this value is beyond the scope of this material, the value of λ is about 4 percent during months 0 to 30, and about 2 percent for the later period.

As is usually the case, information of this kind generates many new questions. Its enormous value lies in the fact that a new level of understanding has been achieved.   A complex phenomenon now appears somewhat less so.

BIBLIOGRAPHY

Chou, Y. L.: *Statistical Analysis with Business and Economic Applications,* Holt, Rinehart, and Winston, Inc., New York, 1969.

Croxton, F. E., and D. J. Cowden: *Applied General Statistics,* Prentice-Hall, Inc., New York, 1955.

Hamburg, Morris: *Statistical Analysis for Decision Making,* Harcourt, Brace & World, Inc., New York, 1970.

Neter, J., and W. Wasserman: *Fundamental Statistics for Business and Economics,* Allyn and Bacon, Inc., Boston, 1961.

Spurr, W. A., and C. P. Bonini: *Statistical Analysis for Business Decisions,* Richard D. Irwin, Inc., Homewood, Ill., 1967.

chapter 79

The Computer in Personnel Administration

DAVID R. WEBB *Management Information Systems Manager, Ritter Company, Rochester, New York*

PERSONNEL DATA SYSTEMS

Throughout the last decade personnel departments have made increasing utilization of computers as a management tool in fulfilling their objectives. This expanding utilization of computer systems in the personnel function has basically come about for the same reasons that data systems are being utilized more and more in other functional areas. Personnel management has recognized the need for more data obtained more rapidly and in a more accurate form, in order to make sound business decisions. In the past, the need for such data may have been recognized but because the data was scattered throughout the organization, inaccurately maintained, or in some cases not available at all, decisions had to be made in the absence of meaningful information. Therefore, today many organizations have recognized this need for timely and accurate information on employees and have developed and implemented personnel data systems.

In industry today the term "personnel data systems" normally refers to a mechanized method for the creation and maintenance of personnel data, the reporting of such data, and the subsequent destruction of such data. A personnel data system may encompass all the functional area within the personnel department, or it may be limited to only one or two areas such as records and administration and wage and salary data. Personnel data systems vary from company to company, reflecting the specific needs of the company's personnel department which in turn will reflect such variables as: city, county, and state laws; company personnel practice; and union contract agreements. Therefore, there is no one concise definition for the term personnel data system. However, for purposes of this chapter the term shall be used to apply to computerized personnel information systems in general as depicted below:

PERSONNEL DATA SYSTEM

Types of Input Data	*Master Files*	*Output Reports*
Salary	Employee status	Wage and salary
Resume		Employee history
Performance appraisal	Pension	Pension
Open requisitions	Skills inventory	Benefits
Applications	Job	Skills inventory
Payroll and benefits	Safety	Selection and placement
Safety	Benefits and pension	Safety statistics
Attendance	Suggestions	Dispensary statistics
Pension	Grievance	Lost-time reports
Skills inventory		Manpower utilization
		Manpower planning
Suggestions		Grievance status and analysis reports
Dispensary		Personnel statistics
Grievance		

ADVANTAGES OF PERSONNEL DATA SYSTEMS

The growth in the number of personnel data systems in industry today has come about due to the advantages that such systems can provide to the personnel function. One advantage is that such systems make it possible to store and retrieve the vast amounts of information about employees which are so vitally needed to properly exercise the responsibilities of the personnel department. Normally, such systems are capable not only of providing large quantities of information but also of relating various pieces of information which would be virtually impossible via manual means. For instance, in many systems it is possible to relate employee absenteeism to salary grades, work departments, seasonal fluctuation, etc. Another advantage is that such data can be made available at a very nominal incremental cost where heretofore it would only be possible to provide the information by a laborious manual means. Still another advantage of a personnel data system is that it provides for a degree of accuracy that otherwise might not be obtained. For example, the recording of employee data in personnel jackets, etc., is normally carried out by a personnel clerk and is reviewed or audited only at such time that the data is needed. However, in a properly designed personnel data system error checks are built into the system which would reject and call to the attention of responsible individuals missing or erroneous data. Also, since such data are normally provided to management in various summary reports, there is a tendency to place a greater emphasis upon the accuracy of data throughout the personnel function. The elimination of duplicate records and the function of maintaining the duplicate records is another distinct advantage of the implementation of a personnel data system. In organizations today that do not have some form of a mechanized personnel data system, one will find various functional areas maintaining separate files on personnel data. For example, there will be files in the medical department, safety department, wage and salary administration, employee benefits, and pension department. Although some of the files pertain to the department's function specifically, in many cases there are files or portions of files that are duplicated in each one of these areas. Also, there probably are multiple files in each area in order to have information more rapidly available concerning employee matters. An example of this would be the situation of filing employee grievances where one copy of the grievance is filed by employee, another copy by subject, and yet another by disposition. Finally an advantage which is often sighted is a savings in clerical costs. However, such savings normally are not realistic. Although there may be a savings in the pure clerical function of maintaining employee data, such savings dissolve when one considers the cost of mechanically creating and maintaining the data and the cost of analyzing such data. In other words, the number of people and the cost involved in the personnel department probably will not be reduced through the implementation of a personnel data system. The real savings is not realized in the creation and maintenance of data but rather in the improved management decisions which are possible through the availability of such data.

USES OF PERSONNEL DATA SYSTEMS

Today many progressive personnel departments of large organizations are realizing considerable operating benefits through the availability of more data on a more timely and accurate basis. The utilization of computers within these personnel departments has usually taken place in four broad areas; records and administration, wage and salary, skills inventory, and employment.

Personnel records and administration is an area where the most tangible clerical savings can be realized. Therefore, it is not surprising that this is the area in which most computer applications have begun. In general the main advantages of applications in this area are the savings in clerical time, increased accuracy, imposed standardization, and time necessary to prepare routine and special reports. This area includes such items as keeping track of the status and progress of employees, and basic employee data.

Wage and salary applications have been cited to have four principle advantages. One advantage is that they provide a rapid means of simulating the effects of wage and salary changes, which can be especially useful during union contract negotiations. Another advantage is that it is possible to derive comparisons of wages by job class, by department, etc., on a rapid and efficient basis so that internal wage and salary surveys may be conducted. Still another advantage is that wage and salary applications can be utilized to control and analyze salary administration. Finally such applications can facilitate the preparation of data for outside salary surveys.

One of the most recent areas to be encompassed by personnel data systems is the area of skills inventory programs. Companies are recognizing that they must keep track of a multitude of employee skills in order to properly fulfill their replacement responsibilities. Skills inventory systems can provide an objective means of selection and placement of employees, thereby utilizing in-house talent to a maximum.

Another recent area to be considered for computer application is the area of employment. This area has come under study primarily due to the high cost of recruiting technical personnel. Such systems are credited with speeding the hiring decision, coordinating the internal routing of information and files concerning prospective employees, reducing the time required to determine the disposition of applications, and reducing clerical costs.

The above presentation of the four categories of personnel data systems is not intended to be all-encompassing. Today and in the future there will be a growth in the utilization of computer services in more areas of the personnel function. Data systems will be utilized to simulate the effects of wage and salary changes, benefit changes, manpower levels, etc. They will be used to increase and intensify the control of personnel costs in all areas of operation such as pension, medical insurance, and recruiting. The level of control in absenteeism, job evaluation, the selection of job candidates, and other areas where the absence of data on a timely and accurate basis has limited the level of control will be increased. Still other applications will deal with training, safety, and suggestion programs; preemployment testing; manpower planning; and employee appraisals. Two very recent developments in this area have been the development of systems for the evaluation of various compensation plans available to company executives. Through such systems it is possible for an executive to select, from options such as current pay, deferred pay, and stock options, that combination which most precisely meets his personal objectives. Another development has been the preparation of annual employee benefits reports. Companies utilizing such programs believe that employee morale is improved by providing employees with a report illustrating the worth of the various company fringe benefits.

WHAT DATA SHOULD BE STORED

In order for a personnel data system to be able to provide information such as outlined in the previous section, it is necessary to provide for the creation, storage, and maintenance of a vast amount of data in a form which will provide for the rapid and efficient availability of such data for reporting purposes. As was mentioned earlier, personnel data systems will vary greatly between companies reflecting the needs of the particular personnel function. In turn, the need for keeping specific pieces of information will also vary between organizations. Therefore, the following presentation of data fields should only be interpreted as a general example and not as a recommendation for all personnel data systems.

Appraisal rating (current)	The employee's appraisal rating in his current job in comparison with performance standards.
Appraisal rating (rotation)	If the employee has been promoted this will be his appraisal rating on his previous job.
Birth date	Month, day and year.
Birth date verification	A code to indicate whether the employee's birth date has been verified by the inspection of a birth certificate, etc.
Career accrued earnings.	The total earnings of the employee while working for the company.
Continuous service date	The month, day, and year in which the employee's credited service with the company began.
Current salary rates	The employee's current salary in terms of hourly, weekly, or annual rate depending upon the employee's classification.
Salary rate date	The month, day, and year in which the employee first received his current rate.
Current salary step or range	The location of the employee's current salary rate in relation to the salary ranges or steps within his job.
Date of hire	The month, day, and year that the employee was last hired.
Educational level	The number of years of formal education completed (i.e., 12 equals completed high school, 16 equals completed college, etc.).
Employee classification.	The employee's classification code (i.e., supervisor, unit head, specialist, technician, hourly, etc.).

Employee status . . . . The employee's status (i.e., regular, part-time, etc.)

Exit type. Defines the type of exit and reason (i.e., quit to return to school, quit for new job, quit for health reasons, layoff, etc.).

Exit date. The month, day, and year that the employee terminated.

Employee name. . . . . The employee's first name, middle initial, last name.

Department number . . . . The employee's current department number.

Department number date . . . . The month, day, and year that the employee became a member of the department.

General wage increase code . . . . A code to indicate whether the employee is eligible for the next general wage increase or not.

Graduate degree . . . . A numeric code to define the college, graduate degree, and year of graduation. (Note: There should be room in the master file for several sets of such data.)

Group life insurance plan . . . . A code to indicate whether the employee is eligible for group life insurance plan and to what extent he is eligible.

Job entrance date . . . . The month, day, and year that the employee entered his current job.

Job classification . . . . The month, day, and year from which the employee's seniority on his current job is computed.

Job classification date code . . . . If several employees have the same job classification code, this code is assigned by union relations to indicate which employee will be considered the senior.

Job number. . . . . A unique number assigned to each company job title.

Job points . . . . The number of job points which have been assigned to the various jobs within the company to reflect the level of the duties and responsibilities.

Job salary range or steps . . . . The number of salary steps in the job.

Job standard or maximum rate of pay. . . . . The midpoint or high point of the salary grade.

Current salary rate code. . . . . A code to indicate hourly, weekly, or annually paid employee.

Job title . . . . The title of the employee's current job.

Job wage grade . . . . The grade of the employee's job within the broad job categories (i.e., salaried office job, supervisor, specialist, etc.).

Last year's total earnings . . . . The employee's gross earnings for the previous year.

Marital status . . . . Whether the employee is single, married, separated, or divorced.

Next salary review date . . . .   The date of the employee's next merit salary review.

Occupational group . . . .   A code to indicate which series of jobs is assigned a single promotional sequence for purposes of determining seniority of unionized employees.

Extra compensation amount . . . .   The amount paid to management as extra compensation, such as bonuses.

Pension eligibility . . . .   The number of full years of continuous service that an employee will have served upon normal retirement.

Pension fund interest class . . . .   The code to indicate the interest class of the employee based upon his continuous service date.

Pension number . . . .   A unique number to identify the employee within the pension system.

Resident address . . . .   The employee's home mailing address.

Rotation of assignment . . . .   A code indicating whether the employee is on rotation of assignment and if so, the reason (i.e., training, special assignment, task force, etc.).

Sex . . . .   Male or female.

Social security number . . . .   The employee's social security number.

Undergraduate degree . . . .   The college degree, year, and rank in the class. (*Note:* There should be room for multiple sets of dates if necessary.)

Race . . . .   A code to indicate the employee's race.

Number of dependents . . . .   The number of dependents for personnel department use which may be different than the number of dependents claimed for federal tax deduction purposes.

Date of last increase . . . .   The month, day, and year of the employee's last salary increase.

Reason for increase . . . .   A code to indicate the reason for the increase (i.e., merit increase, cost of living increase, etc.).

Citizen of what country . . . .   A code to indicate the employee's citizenship.

Year-to-date hours of pension service added . . . .   The number of hours, on a year-to-date basis, to be credited for pension purposes.

Hospital insurance code . . . .   A code to indicate the type of hospital insurance coverage.

Overseas code . . . .   A code to indicate whether the employee has had overseas assignments or not, and if so, in what countries.

Hospital contract number . . . .   The employee's hospital contract number.

Shareholder code . . . .   A code to indicate whether the employee is a shareholder or not.

Year-to-date paid hours . . . .   The number of hours the employee has been paid for on a year-to-date basis.

Year-to-date weeks worked . . . .   The number of weeks that the employee has worked during the current year to date.

Accidental death class of coverage . .	A code to indicate the type and extent of accidental death coverage.
Security clearance code	A code to indicate the security clearance for the employee.
Year-to-date vacation hours taken . . .	The number of hours that the employee has taken in vacation time during the vacation period.
Vacation eligibility.	The number of hours of vacation time that an employee is eligible for.
Division or branch code	A code to indicate which division or branch the employee works at.
Location code	A code to indicate which of several physical locations within a branch the employee works in.
Home telephone number	The employee's home telephone number.
Office telephone number	The employee's office telephone number.
Military service information	Information such as the employee's service classification, reserve obligation in terms of obligation, and the length of the obligation, the branch of the military, and his rank.
Achievement.	A coding structure for the employee's achievement such as patents, disclosures, books, articles, etc.
Employment and advancement tests and scores	A coding structure to indicate the specific tests and scores that the employee has taken.
Leave of absence.	A coding structure to indicate a leave of absence, reason code, date granted, and number of days. (*Note:* There might be several groups of such information.)
Disciplinary actions	A coding structure to indicate date and type of disciplinary action taken. (*Note:* There should be room for several such codings.)
Workmen's compensation code	A code to indicate the particular class of workmen's compensation that the employee falls within.

The various data fields listed above apply in general to personnel data systems within many organizations. In organizations where the payroll function falls within the personnel department, of course, there would be many more data fields required in the system. The fields would deal with gross and net pay; withholding information at the federal, state, and municipal levels; various deductions amounts such as credit union, charity, insurance, union dues, safety equipment, etc.; bonus eligibility hours; bonus paid dollars; and other data fields involved in the payroll function.

PERSONAL SKILLS INVENTORY DATA

Very often in order to do an effective job of manpower planning, complete, accurate, and readily accessible information concerning the employee's skill is necessary. Consequently, many large organizations have implemented a "skills inventory data system" either as a stand-alone system or as a subsystem of their personnel data system. Data concerning employees' skills is collected mechanically for evaluation, classification, and reporting.   Through such systems it is possible to readily screen hundreds of employees in order to react to a personnel requisition or to develop manpower development programs.   Generally in skills inventory systems each particular skill is coded and also there is a field to represent the relative degree of achievement. For instance, concerning an employee's ability in the area of a foreign language, one would want to know what language or languages the employee is familiar with and what degree of skill he possesses (i.e., whether he can read them, speak them, or speak them fluently).   In addition, many skills often can be evaluated based upon the number of years of experience or exposure.   Therefore, there may be three specific fields for each skill (i.e., the skill code, the skill level, and the years of experience).   The data that are collected and stored for a skills inventory system should include only information that the company really needs.   It would be of little value to list specific data fields for inclusion in a skills inventory system.   There are a few comments in general, however, that should be followed when designing and implementing such a system.

1. Each element of data should have a specific purpose and should serve to answer a management question.

2. Extreme care should be exercised in the definition of each data element so that there will be no confusion about what the various codes or degrees of skill mean.

3. Before a particular element is included in this system, it should be determined whether auditing such information would be possible.

DEVELOPMENT AND IMPLEMENTATION

The development and implementation of a personnel data system is a large and expensive undertaking which must be thoroughly planned, organized, and controlled if it is to be successful.   The first step should be a comprehensive economic feasibility study.   The study should be conducted under the direction of a task force composed of representatives from the various functions involved and chaired by the representative from the personnel department.   The study should encompass the following elements:

1. A definition of the objectives of the projects including time and cost estimates.

2. A definition of the problem and its parameters in writing for mutual understanding and communication.

3. An evaluation of various alternative methods and recommendations of an optimum solution including possible degrees of automation and associated equipment required.

4. A definition of the potential benefits to the personnel department and the line organization from the point of view of information retrieval and utilization.

5. A description of the degree of standardization of various personnel plans and programs and their adaptability for conversion.

6. The identification of the short- and long-term impact on the organization structures of the elements involved.

7. The identification of the impact on manpower, training, and retraining during and after conversion.

8. A timetable for conversion and phase out of the present system.

9. An estimate of labor and other costs for the development and annual operation of the system.

10. An estimate of the payback period and cost breakeven point.

The second step should be the presentation and selling of the recommended solution to top management.   This is particularly important in that the acceptance and effectiveness of the new system will hinge largely on the understanding and endorsement of top management.

The third step involves planning the details of the conversion. Here, the thinking and planning done in the first step should be refined. In addition, the system should be defined in terms of a conceptual model with associated system flowcharts and diagrams. This, of course, should be reviewed and approved by top management before the actual conversion is undertaken.

As part of the planning, the kinds of personnel information needed to satisfy the various requirements of the organization should be reviewed:

1. First-line supervision
2. Department, division, and corporate level
3. Government
4. Employees
5. Personnel department
   a. Employment
   b. Labor relations
   c. Control
   d. Salary administration
   e. Training, development, safety
   f. Medical
   g. Census
   h. Benefits
   i. Manpower capability
   j. Research, organization planning

A technique that can be utilized for this review is to conduct an audit of every report generated by the personnel department and then to survey the organization about the reports, asking:

1. Do you need this information?
2. Is it in the best form?
3. Do the data cover the best time period?
4. Is the frequency of distribution proper?
5. Is the report timely?
6. What other information do you need?
7. Do you circulate it further, discard it, or file it?

The results of this survey would help in determining what information is presently needed. Also, as a result of this type of survey it might be possible to eliminate a large number of reports, consolidate many others, and revise many to make them more effective.

MANUAL VERSUS MECHANIZED SYSTEM CONSIDERATIONS

During the design of a personnel data system, it should be recognized that not all data should be computerized and also that even with a computerized system there must be a certain amount of manual record keeping to support the system. The question of what data should be mechanized can only be answered by examining each piece of data in order to identify what alternatives are available for the creation and maintenance of such data and what are the advantages, disadvantages, and cost of each alternative. During this investigation certain questions must be answered, such as: How often are the data referred to? How long must they be kept? How useful are they? In general, it can be said that mechanized systems should deal with current information whereas manual systems should deal with historical information. Also, in a mechanized system, data are used to identify, classify, and report status rather than to report voluminous historical and descriptive information. For example, concerning the topic of employee grievances, in a mechanized system one may want to capture grievance number, date, disposition, date of disposition, type of grievance, and a basic subject code of grievance. The actual description of the grievance and how it was settled should be captured within a manual filing system. This approach provides, via the mechanized systems, a means of summarizing, reporting, indexing, and identifying grievances in a rapid and inexpensive manner, while at the same time the manual system provides historical and detailed descriptive information concerning the grievance. If one were to attempt to capture in a mechanized system all the details concerning each grievance, the cost would be prohibitive and in reality would not provide more meaningful and useful results than the combination of manual and mechanized systems.

Another question to be considered in manual versus computerized record keeping deals with how definitely management's needs have been defined. For instance, if a company were to be initiating a skills inventory system, they should probably not attempt to mechanize the system initially if there were many questions concerning what data should be kept, how often the data are needed, and how useful they are. In other words, if it is not possible to precisely define the systems specification, then it is more appropriate to approach the system on a manual basis for a year or two. Once the manual system has been in operation and management needs have been defined, then the system can be mechanized.

Still another question in this topic of mechanized versus manual is a recognition that there must be a manual record-keeping system to support a mechanized system. The manual system, in such an environment, plays a supportive role to the mechanized system for the filing of imput transactions to the system, and in filing and retrieving reports prepared by the system. It also would provide the extensive history files of various transactions concerning each employee. For instance, in an "integrated payroll and industrial relations system," it is a requirement in some states that the original employee time cards with the foreman's authorizing signature must be filed for seven years. These documents, within that environment, should be processed through the mechanized system to capture paying information and then should be filed and maintained in a manual system in order to meet the state requirements.

A final consideration in whether or not to mechanize certain pieces of data concerns the question of how many different functional areas have need for this information. If the information is required by many areas rather than a single functional area, it probably would be far more efficient and effective to capture such data mechanically and prepare the reports for distribution to the various functional areas. An example of this would be the difference between employee office phone numbers versus employee home phone numbers. It would be practical to capture in a mechanized system employee office phone numbers so that such information could be used to prepare employee phone directories for distribution throughout the company. On the other hand, the employee's home phone number may only be used by the personnel department for reference and therefore should be filed and maintained through manual means rather than a mechanized system.

INFORMATION CODING

A very critical area during the design and implementation phase of a personal data system is that of assigning numbers to various data elements. The design of a numbering structure, although it may appear to be a very simple task, is a task that can have a major impact upon the results and success of the system. *Numbers should be used to identify, not to classify information.* Often numbers are used both to identify and to classify information, with the results that the whole numbering structure must be revised over and over again to reflect revisions in operating conditions. There is a tendency for people to want to look at a number and be able to tell something about the number rather than just to use the number to identify. For instance, often employee numbers not only identify the employee but also indicate the employee's department. As a result every time an employee changes departments not only must his number be changed, but also all the historical data concerning him must receive his new number. On the other hand if the employee number were used only to identify the employee and another field on the master employee record was used to identify his department, then all that would have to be changed would be his department number since all the other records with his employee number would still be correct. Violation of this principle of identification versus classification should only be allowed if there has been a very thorough analysis of all alternatives. Another advantage of using a numbering system only to identify and not to classify is that it prevents the problems associated with assigning numbers. For instance, it is easier to assign a new employee the next available employee number in the company on a random basis rather than to be concerned with which numbers are open in a particular department. In summary, identification numbers should be used to identify data elements such as employee number, insurance policy number, department number, etc., and not to classify the element. There should be separate data fields for the purpose of classification. This approach provides for greater flexibility in the system, fewer errors, and a minimum amount of maintenance expense.

TYPICAL PROBLEMS TO BE AVOIDED

With any large computer system development, installation, and maintenance, there are many potential problems that can arise. Through proper planning, however, the potential problems can readily be avoided, and hence the usefulness and value of the system will be ensured.

One of the most typical and most serious problems can occur during the development of the personnel data system and can result in the system being totally useless. The problem specifically is a lack of communication and coordination between the personnel and data-processing functions. What can occur is that representatives from each of these functions fail to learn and understand the role and objectives of each others' functions. Each functional area has certain functional responsibilities to the overall organization. Also each functional area has its own set of terms and operating procedures that are unique to the area. Therefore, if there is to be a successful effort in the development and installation of a personnel data system, there must be good communication and coordination between the functional areas. However, very often the representatives from the respective departments fail to fully understand each other, and therefore, even though there are many meetings conducted on the objectives of the installation of the personnel data system and many memos exchanged, in reality the proper communication between the two elements is never achieved. Representatives from each element believe they understand and comprehend, but after the system is developed and installed, it is discovered that the system is not capable of performing at the desired level. This situation can be serious enough to require the whole system being designed, developed, and implemented all over again, which is a very costly and time-consuming process.

Another potential problem which can occur is one arising from the electronic data-processing department's overzealous enthusiasm to serve the organization. This can result in the establishment of target dates and cost estimates that are too optimistic and practically unachievable. Another result can be that the implementation of proper controls, the documentation of procedures, and the training of personnel are neglected in an attempt to reduce costs and meet unrealistic target dates. In order to prevent these very serious problems, the overall project should be approached in phases which can be audited at the completion of each phase. Of course, there also should be a comprehensive reporting system established on the project itself. In this manner, the progress and cost can be evaluated during the project and corrective actions can be taken if necessary.

Still another potential problem can result from the lack of training, motivation, and documented procedures within the personnel department for the maintenance of the personnel data system. As a result, after the system is installed and operating, the accuracy of the reports generated by the system deteriorates rapidly. Further, if the proper controls have not been established, this deterioration can go unnoticed for a long period of time which in turn can result in poor management decisions being made based upon inaccurate data. There is a very serious tendency in industry today to accept reports as accurate and unchallengeable just because they were printed on a computer. Management fails to recognize that the data were supplied to the computer by the same individuals as under a manual system and hence are subject to the same level of human errors as always. Also, because the data are processed by computer programs written by humans, there is the possibility that the programs do not function properly under all conditions and situations. Still another factor that can lead to the inaccuracy of reporting is that, through the installation of a mechanized system, the people supporting the system lose the visibility and understanding of the data. Whatever the causes of this phenomenon may be, the results can mean that people fail to recognize gross errors that would have been caught in a manual system. Apparently, once a mechanized system is installed, the people begin to function just as mechanically as the system, and hence the data flowing across their desk become meaningless as individual pieces of information such as names, social security numbers, and employee numbers. In order to prevent the very consequential results of the deterioration of the data files, stringent controls and procedures should be established and audited periodically. There should be controls established to check the validity of the data being entered into the system. There should be checks not only for the presence or absence of data, but also for the reasonableness of the data. Also there should be controls for the presence and reasonableness of related pieces of data. For instance, when a new employee is being added to the file, there should be a check not only to ensure that he has been given a salary rate, but also to determine whether the salary rate is reasonable, i.e., not less than $60 a week or more than $1,000 a week, and also that there is a positive correlation between the man's salary and the salary grade of his job.

Finally, another potential problem is the situation where the personnel data system was not designed to be flexible enough to meet changes in the business environment, and/or management fails to be aware of certain limitations in operating policies and practices imposed by the mechanized system. This situation can arise from improper communications during the design and development of the system, lack of understanding of how the system operates, or lack of recognition that once the system is designed and implemented it may be very difficult and costly to change. For example, in a hypothetical situation, a whole personnel data system can be designed and implemented to operate in a one-plant company. Subsequently, the company could expand into a multiplant operation and as a result have the need to know personnel data not only on an overall company basis but also on a plant-by-plant basis. A change such as that may require thousands of dollars worth of expense and many months to implement under a mechanized system which did not provide for a plant number as a basic piece of information for each employee. It should be noted that this same change under a manual system would require probably even more effort and more expense; however, since the costs are more readily identified under a mechanized system, such a change can be very upsetting to management in terms of time and expense and can lead to dissatisfaction with the mechanized system. Another fairly frequent situation in this area is the failure on management's part to recognize that the mechanized system was designed and implemented to be operated under certain specific ground rules, and further, the failure to recognize that changing the ground rules may require some very drastic and expensive overall system changes. For instance, under a manual systems environment to change employee number from three digits to four digits may not be very costly, especially if the old employee numbers are to be expanded to four digits by just adding a zero before the number. However, in a mechanized system such a change can mean changing twenty or thirty programs that deal with employee numbers. The programs would specify employee numbers as being three digits, and therefore to change to four digits could be a very expensive and time-consuming task.

BIBLIOGRAPHY

Bueschel, Richard T.: *EDP and Personnel,* American Management Association, Management Bulletin 86, New York, 1966.

Danner, Jack: "Management Information Systems: A Tool for Personnel Planning," *Personnel Journal,* Stamford, Conn., July, 1971.

MacGuffie, John V.: "Computer Programs for People," *Personnel Journal,* Stamford, Conn., April, 1969.

Morrison, Edward J.: *Developing Computer-Based Employee Information Systems,* American Management Association, Research Study 99, New York, 1969.

Part 18

Personnel Research

chapter 80

Sources of
Personnel Information

ROBERT I. DAWSON   *Director, Research and Consulting, Personnel Department, The Equitable Life Assurance Society of the United States, New York, New York*

The decade of the 1960s was regarded as a period of rapidly expanding knowledge in all scientific fields. This expansion was particularly evident in the social sciences, a field which got a relatively late growth start, and yet is the focal point of many of society's major breakdowns. It is this new knowledge in the social sciences reported in the literature, the new theories developed in the universities, the new research experiences obtained in organizations, that provide basic information for personnel research.

If the sixties are noted as a period of knowledge expansion, the seventies may well be looked back upon as the decade in which we became concerned about the utilization of knowledge, the degree to which we can take research findings out of the laboratory and build them into the fabric of organization life. Gaining support and allegiance to a new theory of motivation is far more difficult than introducing a new polio vaccine, as troublesome as the latter may be. Moving behavioral science knowledge over into the practices of personnel management is a difficult and torturous conversion process. In view of this knowledge-utilization problem, the approach in this chapter will be directed both at increasing familiarity with data sources and at implementing these data effectively in the business organization.

But first, what are the parameters of this topic? The breadth of scientific fields which serve as input sources for personnel research may be judged from the following list:

Anthropology.   The functions of a culture and the development of social customs, norms, and values.

Educational Psychology. Understanding individual differences, the growth process, learning theory, and the measurement of change.

General Psychology. The way in which habits, intelligence, attitudes, motivation, and emotions influence the adjustment and behavior of the individual.

Industrial and Organizational Psychology. The analysis of human behavior in industry in order to provide for the maximum utilization of human resources.

Political Science. The analysis of socioeconomic systems, the use of power and authority, governing systems, and resolution of conflict.

Psychiatry. An understanding of individual personality dynamics, deviations, and retraining and readjustment procedures.

Social Psychology. A study of interpersonal relations, leadership, group behavior, and communication processes.

Sociology. An analysis of social systems, group norms, and social institutions.

There are bits and pieces of knowledge being generated in each of the above fields that are relevant and useful to the professional in industrial relations and personnel. From anthropology comes the concept of group norms and their meaning for resistance to change; from educational psychology comes much of the new knowledge about programmed instruction; from general psychology and psychiatry comes an interest in individual ability measurement, career planning, and counseling; from industrial and organizational psychology comes an interest in controlled experimentation and the impact of new motivation systems; and from social psychology and sociology comes an awareness of the influence carried by the group and the complexity of the leadership process. However, rather than attempt to follow this subject outline as a basis for reviewing new knowledge in personnel research, let this structure be considered as illustrative of the scope of the topic.

To be most useful to the personnel specialist or the operating line manager, three broad functional areas of personnel research will be identified along with a sampling of questions helping to define each of the areas; we can then proceed to specify relevant sources for information and help. The three functional areas of personnel research to be used here are:

1. Establishment and interpretation of personnel statistics
2. Personnel program evaluation and development
3. Consultation on organizational problems

There are elements of increasing complexity in each of these three functions. Refining personnel statistics is an essential beginning step in any personnel research program. Working by means of consultation and action research on organizational problems is difficult and risky for both the researcher and the organization. But successful efforts in the consultation area hold out great rewards for both parties. Although not all personnel research programs progress sequentially through all three functional areas, many do follow this maturation pattern.

ESTABLISHMENT AND INTERPRETATION OF PERSONNEL STATISTICS

The application of the scientific method to human behavior in organizations requires the quantification of variables to be analyzed. While organizations are small and information can be assessed intuitively, there is less concern with the accurate assessment of personnel variables. As organizations grow in size, these intuitive assessments become more difficult to make; the increasing psychological distance between individuals and between parts of the organization make such informal readings less accurate.

The following are examples of questions likely to be raised in this functional area:

1. What is our termination rate month by month? How does the rate in plant X compare with the rate in plant Y?

2. Of those employees terminating, what proportion represent a significant loss to the company?

3. How long does an employee have to produce on a job before he has "paid back" his initial hiring and training investment?

4. How does the absence rate in this plant compare with that of other plants in this area having the same type of labor force? Or with the industry as a whole?

5. How does the productivity (the error rate, absence, safety, or grievance rate) of one type of employee (say, part-time employees) compare with that of other types of employees?

6. Are more employees terminating for salary reasons this quarter of the year than during the same quarter last year?

To establish and interpret personnel statistics requires both the use of sources within the company and within the local labor market or the industry. The more refined the internal statistics become, as described in Chapter 78, the more critical the comparability of external measures becomes. It becomes important not only to have uniform definitions with a group of similar companies with whom turnover information is exchanged; it is vital to be sensitive to other closely associated organizational variables such as age and service patterns, male-female ratios, salary distributions, etc. Marked differences on these organizational variables will produce significant variations in performance statistics. An organization in which 50 percent of the staff have more than twenty-five years of service will have a much lower rate of turnover than another company in the same business and same area in which only 20 percent of the staff have more than twenty-five years of service.

There are few local personnel associations that do not make periodic surveys among their members to compile area rates on turnover, absence, salary, safety, or other personnel statistics. Similar surveys are conducted by groups in the local business association, such as the Chamber of Commerce or the Commerce and Industry Association. Both federal and state departments of labor, as well as city administrations, release periodic studies dealing with local employment conditions and practices. A number of trade and business associations, as well as numerous scientific and technical associations, are listed and described in the *Encyclopedia of Associations* [6] and the *National Trade and Professional Associations of the United States* [16]. Each month the activities and conferences of selected personnel associations are reported in the *Personnel Journal* (see Periodical Listing in the Appendix).

The most fruitful, though also the most time-consuming, approach to comparative statistics is the selection of a limited number of similar companies operating in the same labor market who agree to share among themselves certain specified personnel statistics. With these data, each company can construct its own external standard and regularly measure its performance against this external standard. As some historical record is compiled, it becomes possible for the company to establish realistic objectives on the personnel statistics for the entire organization or for a specific segment of the company. Used as performance targets, these measures are more likely to become considered "changeable" and open to influence by the managers themselves.

PERSONNEL PROGRAM EVALUATION AND DEVELOPMENT

Either jointly with the administrative group responsible for the program or singly by itself, the personnel research group is asked to evaluate an ongoing personnel activity or program. Such an examination is most likely to be productive when clear and well-defined objectives have previously been established for the activity or program. If the effectiveness of a college recruiting and training program is under study, the research is most meaningful if the program objectives specified the number of trainees to be recruited and trained to take a specific job. Of course, the company is concerned with the ultimate objectives of operating efficiency and with the satisfaction and personal growth of employees, but additional, short-run objectives are essential to effectively examine a particular program.

Questions about program are numerous and easily framed; the following are samples:

1. Following a change from the traditional organization structure in a field sales unit to a decentralized structure, what is the impact of this change on sales volume or on service?

2. A special program to recruit and train hard-core unemployed has been in operation for two years; how effective has it been in terms of the time and effort invested by the company?

3. An appraisal program covering all management employees has been operating for a number of years; how well is it achieving its twin objectives of identifying promotable talent and facilitating individual growth?

4. Modifications were introduced into the grievance procedure several years ago; did these changes result in an increase in the effectiveness of the company's upward communications?

5. Should the proportion of incentive compensation for sales representatives be increased and the proportion of basic salary decreased? What should the ratio be between these two factors?

6. Is it more economical and efficient to recruit and train your own analysts (or typists, draftsmen, machine operators, or whatever), or is it more economical to hire experienced personnel?

Again, there are two major sources of help: sources within the company and sources external to the company. Too frequently the internal sources are not utilized and program assessments become overly dependent on outside "experts." If an appraisal program is to be studied, some means of collecting information from the superiors (the appraisers) and from the participants (the appraisees) should be devised. A reading from the superiors should indicate the adequacy and competence of the promotable talent; a reading from the participants should indicate their expectations regarding their own growth and the extent to which they feel the appraisals are facilitating this growth. Illustrative of this approach was the technically sound and organizationally meaningful study conducted by Dr. Herbert H. Meyer and his associates at General Electric [15].

Intimately involved in assessing operating policies such as an appraisal program should be the line managers who are expected to apply the policy and make the appraisals. If these managers can have a real voice, not just a superficial gesture at participation, the policy is more likely to be adhered to and made to function. These are the same managers who will apply the policy constructively on the job or will undercut it and eventually eliminate it.

At the same time, much breadth of perspective can be obtained from the judicious use of sources of help outside the company. These sources would include: (1) the technical literature published in book form and in journals, (2) staff members in academic departments and research groups at the universities, (3) staff members in nonprofit, independent research groups, and (4) the consulting organizations.

As indicated earlier, relevant articles or books may be published in any of the eight scientific fields enumerated at the beginning of the chapter. A number of the standard references are shown in the References; some of the relevant periodicals are listed separately. Up-to-date bibliographies covering the field can also be found in Dr. Gordon L. Lippitt's *Organizational Renewal* and in Harold Rush's National Industrial Conference Board Personnel Policy No. 216, *Behavioral Science: Con-*

cepts and Management Applications. Of course, standard personnel administration texts such as Dalton E. McFarland's *Personnel Management: Theory and Practice* and Stanley Sokolik's *The Personnel Process* contain extensive bibliographies.

Maintaining a grasp of the current research literature is always difficult, especially for individuals working full time in business where they may not have a ready access to library facilities. Yet, some scanning of the journals is essential to maintain the standing of the professional. Abstracts and reviews are helpful devices in working with the literature, particularly *Psychological Abstracts, Personnel Management Abstracts,* and the *Annual Review of Psychology.*

The university research groups not only have their university ties, they are very interested in maintaining their connections with the "real world" of business and industry. For this reason, they are very approachable. Many university staff members also operate as independent consultants. A sampling of university research groups is shown below:

Boston University,
Human Relations Center
Boston, Mass.

University of California
Institute of Human Development
Berkeley, Calif.

University of California
Institute of Industrial Relations
Berkeley and Los Angeles, Calif.

University of Chicago
Industrial Relations Center
Chicago, Ill.

Cornell University
Social Science Research Center
Ithaca, N.Y.

Harvard University
Laboratory of Social Relations
Cambridge, Mass.

University of Illinois
Laboratory of Personality Assessment and
Group Behavior
Urbana, Ill.

Massachusetts Institute of Technology
Industrial Relations Section
Cambridge, Mass.

University of Minnesota
Industrial Relations Center
Minneapolis, Minn.

New York University
Research Center for Human Relations
Research Center for Industrial Behavior
New York, N.Y.

University of Michigan
Institute for Social Research
Survey Research Center
Research Center for Group Dynamics
Bureau of Industrial Relations
Ann Arbor, Mich.

Princeton University
Industrial Relations Section
Princeton, N.J.

Purdue University
Occupational Research Center
West Lafayette, Ind.

Stevens Institute of Technology
Laboratory of Psychological Studies
Hoboken, N.J.

University of Wisconsin
Industrial Relations Research Center
Madison, Wisc.

Yale University
Labor and Management Center
New Haven, Conn.

Nonprofit research groups such as the National Industrial Conference Board and the American Management Association can be helpful sources of information, particularly when comparative information is desired with regard to a particular policy or practice. Both of these New York City–based organizations maintain extensive library facilities of their own and are very ready to handle inquiries from the company researcher.

The consultants, as out-of-company professionals, can bring years of experience to a question or company problem; their answers can be provided with objectivity, status, and believability. The services of outside consultants are expensive, yet these services may be inexpensive in terms of extending the regular staff for short intervals while major problems are being resolved.

A starting point when considering management consultants might be their professional association called the Association of Consulting Management Engineers (ACME) with offices located in New York City. This group published a directory of its membership with a brief description of each of its member firms and a list of guideline requirements for the effective use of management consultants. These requirements cover the following points:

1. Careful definition of the problem
2. Careful selection of the consultant
3. Agreement with the consultant on mutual obligations
4. Proper supervision and support of the consultant's work
5. Implementation of the final recommendations
6. Measurement of the consultant's and the company's results

CONSULTATION ON ORGANIZATIONAL PROBLEMS

Unlike the activities described above in which the research starts with a policy or a program, consultation research uses as a starting point the diagnosis and analysis of organizational problems. An effort is made to get behind the superficial evidence of the problem to the causes which underlie the difficulty, to generate constructive alternatives from among the employees in the work group, and to introduce changes which will solve the immediate problem and increase the long-run effectiveness of the group.

There is growing movement toward experimental action research which relies heavily on the organization's own internal staff resources, is directed at carefully designed interventions, and devises measurements that gauge the impact of any change. Generally this means a heavy reliance on what Schein refers to as "process consultation." A detailed review of the history and procedures involved in "process consultation" are presented in his latest book, *Process Consultation: Its Role in Organization Development* [18]. A brief outline of the steps and techniques involved in this type of action research are shown in Figure 1.

The above pattern of consultation and action research will continue to be developed and refined; however, there are a growing number of consultants, particularly those with backgrounds in the National Training Laboratories, who are skilled in and devoted to this approach.

This last approach employed by personnel research faces squarely the difficult problem of knowledge utilization and organizational change. This research process permits the type of involvement of the employees concerned which will result in knowledge utilization. Only to the extent that we learn to use knowledge to solve organizational problems will we be able to bring about an increase in organizational effectiveness.

REFERENCES

[1] *Annual Review of Psychology,* vol. 20, Annual Reviews, Palo Alto, Calif., 1970.
[2] Argyris, C.: *Interpersonal Competence and Organizational Effectiveness,* The Dorsey Press and Richard D. Irwin, Inc., Homewood, Ill., 1962.
[3] Bennis, W. G.: *Changing Organizations,* McGraw-Hill Book Company, New York, 1966.
[4] Byham, W. C.: *The Uses of Personnel Research,* American Management Association, New York, 1968.
[5] *Directory of Membership and Services 1970–1971,* Association of Consulting Management Engineers, New York, 1970.

FIGURE 1.   Participative Steps and Techniques Involved in Action Research

Participative steps	Techniques
1. Gaining recognition of the problem and the need for change. Members of the group need to feel some discomfort and some dissatisfaction. Members need to feel there is the possibility of "constructive change."	Boss directs attention to problem or sets new standard. Examination of our performance data. Introduction of new cognitive input, such as work simplification or motivation theory.
2. Defining the problem precisely. Obtaining agreement within the group about the problem. Clarifying the cause.	Use survey techniques. Follow up with group discussion.
3. Generating proposals for change. Enumerating a variety of alternatives. Selecting the most promising "starting point."	"Green lighting" for new ideas with no evaluation. Giving priority to "green-light" items.
4. Setting up experimental tryout. Obtaining agreement on objectives. Providing for measurement and a feedback system.	Don't need a control group. Do need historical records of performance.
5. Evaluating the tryout and making the necessary modifications.	Evaluation made by the line organization.

[6] *Encyclopedia of Associations, National Organizations of the United States,* vol. 1, Gale Research Company, Detroit, 1970.

[7] Gellerman, S. W.: *Management by Motivation,* American Management Association, New York, 1968.

[8] Herzbert, F.: *Work and the Nature of Man,* The World Publishing Company, Cleveland, 1966.

[9] Likert, R.: *The Human Organization,* McGraw-Hill Book Company, New York, 1967.

[10] Lippitt, G. L.: *Organizational Renewal,* Meredith Press, New York, 1969.

[11] Litwin, G. H., and R. A. Stringer: *Motivation and Organizational Climate,* Harvard Business School, Division of Research, Boston, 1968.

[12] Marrow, A. J., D. Bowers, and S. E. Seashore: *Management by Participation,* Harper & Row, Publishers, Incorporated, New York, 1967.

[13] McFarland, D. E.: *Personnel Management: Theory and Practice,* The Macmillan Co. of Canada, Limited, Toronto, 1969.

[14] McGregor, D.: *The Professional Manager,* McGraw-Hill Book Company, New York, 1967.

[15] Meyer, Herbert H., E. Kay, and R. O. P. French: "Split Roles in Performance Appraisal," *Harvard Business Review,* January–February, 1965.

[16] *National Trade and Professional Associations of the United States,* C. Colgate, Jr. (ed.), Columbia Books, Washington, D.C., 1970.

[17] Rush, H. M. F.: *Behavioral Science: Concepts and Management Application,* National Industrial Conference Board, New York, 1969.

[18] Schein, E. H.: *Process Consultation: Its Role in Organization Development,* Addison-Wesley Publishing Company, Inc., Reading, Mass., 1969.

[19] Sokolik, S. L.: *The Personnel Process: Line and Staff Dimensions in Managing People at Work,* International Textbook Company, Scranton, Pa., 1970.

APPENDIX: PERIODICAL LISTING

Advanced Management Journal
Society for the Advancement of
Management
16 West 40th Street
New York, N.Y. 10018

Business Week
McGraw-Hill
330 West 42nd Street
New York, N.Y. 10036

California Management Review
Periodical Department
University of California Press
Berkeley, Calif. 94720

Canadian Personnel and Industrial Relations Journal
William Dawson Subscription Service
6 Thorncliffe Park Drive
Toronto 354, Ontario, Canada

The Conference Board Record
National Industrial Conference Board, Inc.
845 Third Avenue
New York, N.Y. 10022

Employment Service Review
Superintendent of Documents
Government Printing Office
Washington, D.C. 20402

Harvard Business Review
Soldiers Field
Boston, Mass. 02163

Industrial and Labor Relations Review
New York State School of ILR
Cornell University
Ithaca, N.Y. 14850

Industrial Management Review
Massachusetts Institute of Technology
Cambridge, Mass. 02139

Journal of Applied Behavioral Science
NTL Institute for Applied Behavioral Science
1201 16th Street, N.W.
Washington, D.C. 20036

Journal of Applied Psychology
American Psychological Association
1200 17th Street, N.W.
Washington, D.C. 20036

Management of Personnel Quarterly
Bureau of Industrial Relations
Graduate School of Business Administration
University of Michigan
Ann Arbor, Mich. 38104

Management Review
American Management Association
135 West 50th Street
New York, N.Y. 10020

Monthly Labor Review
Superintendent of Documents
Government Printing Office
Washington, D.C. 20402

Personnel
American Management Association
135 West 50th Street
New York, N.Y. 10020

Personnel Administration
484 National Press Building
529 14th Street, N.W.
Washington, D.C. 20004

Personnel Journal
100 Park Avenue
Swarthmore, Pa. 19081

Personnel Management Abstracts
Bureau of Industrial Relations
University of Michigan
Ann Arbor, Mich. 38104

Personnel Psychology
Box 6965, College Station
Durham, N.C. 27708

Psychological Abstracts
American Psychological Association
1200 17th Street, N.W.
Washington, D.C. 20036

Training and Development Journal
American Society of Training and Development, Inc.
313 Price Place
Box 5307
Madison, Wisc. 53705

chapter 81

Constructing Personnel
Research Programs

ROBERT J. PAUL *Associate Professor of Management, University of Missouri, Columbia, Missouri*

INTRODUCTION

The goal of research is to enlarge the perimeter and scope of knowledge. The behavioral sciences, like the natural sciences, progress toward new understandings through refinement and through closer study of more minute aspects of their specialties. By subdividing and by concentrating on smaller aspects, scientists can describe phenomena and processes with greater exactness, and therefore can observe things which had previously gone unnoticed.

However, the mere gathering of facts does not constitute research. The task of research is the selection of facts pertinent to a specific problem and the search for a pattern in these selected facts that will aid in the solution of the problem under investigation. From selected facts and the uncovering of a pattern in those facts a premise can be formulated. Thus, in summary, gathering facts is only one part of research activity; the determination of relevancy of these facts is the second stage, and reflection upon and analysis of the facts is the starting point of meaningful research.

The Nature of Scientific Findings

It is quite likely that the arguments over definitions will continue for a long time; there is, however, general agreement on at least two basic characteristics that differentiate scientific inquiry. These characteristics are the scientist's skeptical attitude and his methodology.

The scientific attitude is best characterized as an attitude of doubt. The scientist must appraise findings and accept explanations with caution, tentativeness and a realistic appreciation of probable error. Because of this attitude of doubt, scientific investigation is engaged in with skepticism, and scientific convention dictates the use of methodologies which demonstrate validity and generality of findings.

Rigorous standards of methodology in scientific investigation have been in use since the early seventeenth century. Scientific convention demands that a hypothesis, to be considered meaningful, must be capable of support by public demonstration. The essential characteristics are prediction and verification.

EVALUATING EMPIRICAL PERSONNEL RESEARCH

As stated above, to be consistent with scientific convention, empirical research findings must be appraised and accepted cautiously, tentatively, and with a realistic appreciation for probable error. This convention of skepticism encourages a careful examination of findings and induces both the researcher and the ultimate user to search for methods of verifying hypotheses. It follows, therefore, that all reports of scientific research must include adequate information and description to permit an understanding of the methodology sufficient for replication and public demonstration.

The objective of public demonstration is to ensure a corrective method to compensate for intended error by preventing the construction of general laws and the formulation of theories which are based on inadequately tested hypotheses. The requirement of public demonstration is satisfied when the research design includes: (1) a priori hypotheses, (2) a priori criteria that can be used to measure the acceptability of those hypotheses, (3) isolation and control of the variables under consideration, (4) methods of measuring and verifying the variables under consideration.

Stating a Priori Hypotheses and Criteria

In an effort to reduce the amount of judgment required in accepting or rejecting hypotheses on the basis of empirical findings, the hypotheses and criteria for evaluating the hypotheses should be stated in advance. Demonstration of a predicted outcome is one of the surest ways of increasing confidence that the outcome can be repeated. The use of a predictive hypothesis and a criterion for measurement provides both the researcher and the witness with a standard for evaluation which is not influenced by subjective evaluation. In such instances assumptions are expressed explicitly in advance, and acceptance or rejection of the hypotheses is determined by a comparison of findings with the priori criteria. The comparison process can be quite objective if both hypothesis and criterion are stated clearly in advance and it is unnecessary to make findings comparable with the criterion by the use of judgment. The statement of a priori hypotheses and criteria thus limits the use of subjective evaluation to the predictive portions of the research rather than to the evaluation of the validity of the findings.

Isolating and Controlling Variables

There are a great number of methodologies that can be employed to isolate and control relevant variables. In the area of personnel research the method of correlation analysis and the method of difference are among those most widely used. Correlation analysis shows the degree to which variables are related. Correlation between numbers is expressed by a single number which gives an immediate picture of how closely two variables move together. In correlation analysis there is no concern with or proof of cause and effect. Correlation between X and Y can be estimated regardless of whether X affects Y or vice versa, whether both affect each other, or whether neither affects the other but they move together because some third variable influences both. The value of correlation analysis in personnel research is that if the change in one set of values is known, it is possible to predict the change in another set of values. For example it is logical to expect that increased training would be related to increased productivity and that by studying the relationship it would be possible to predict a certain increase in productivity when there has been a given increase in training.

The method of difference, which is expressed in basic experimental design, involves physical manipulation and control of variables. The basic logic of experimentation is straightforward. Two groups are matched by similarity of known characteristics or by random assignment of subjects. Variables are measured in both groups under study. One of the groups is then subjected to some type of change such as work environment, leadership style, or role definition, and the affect of the experimental variable is then measured by studying the variables in both groups. The difference in the two groups before and after the experiment is attributed to the change introduced in the manipulated group. Cause and effect relationships are simulated experimentally by this method as nearly as possible.

The use of control groups in personnel research is particularly appropriate because it ensures that change in one of the groups is the result of the manipulation and not due to the passage of time or some other uncontrolled change. The basic experimental design applies to individual or group analysis and may be used in the real world as well as the research laboratory.

Measuring and Verifying Variables

A clear expression of empirical findings is required to meet the requirement of measurement. If research findings are to be evaluated in terms of degree as well as type, it is necessary to develop numerical indices and classifications based on precisely stated assumptions. It then becomes possible to state findings precisely and to compare different studies.

Prediction and observation are the basic requisites of scientific verification. Research design provides a valid basis for generalization when it is directed by a priori hypotheses developed from theory and the variables can be isolated and studied by rigorous scientific methodology.

LEVELS OF RIGOR IN PERSONNEL RESEARCH

The methodologies most commonly employed in personnel research constitute three levels of scientific rigor which can be judged by criteria employed in research design.

First Level of Rigor

The lowest level of rigor consists of qualitative and narrative analysis of variables with a minimum of classification or enumeration of data. Studies conducted at this low level of rigor can do little more than indicate relevant variables and hypotheses to be examined by tests at higher levels of rigor. The methods included at the first level of rigor are: collective opinions, single-case study, and historical analysis.

Collective opinions includes descriptive writings of actual observations of experienced practitioners or persons who have direct contact with the phenomena they try to describe. Much of the existing body of personnel management literature, especially the earlier writings, has been based on a retrospective analysis of the individual's career and therefore fall into this category. The collective opinions approach suffers from the fact that the observations are not experimentally controlled and are subject to personal selection and interpretation. The opinions are based on random samples which are sometimes small in size and recorded a considerable length of time after occurrence. The extensive time lag presents difficult problems of recall, and of course the objectivity of reporting is subject to personal bias in spite of efforts to the contrary.

The single-case study is an investigation of an individual or a group in which the variables which are measured and analyzed are unique to the individual or group and not of some subunit. The basic shortcomings of single-case analysis include (1) an inability to compare cases meaningfully since the environment is not controlled, (2) an inability to repeat case studies since facts are gathered without attempting to control or classify data, (3) an inability to interpret the findings objectively since the data are usually not collected to test on a priori hypotheses, (4) an inability to present findings briefly in narrative form and to make these findings broad enough in scope to apply to more than a particular set of circumstances whose recurrence is highly uncertain, (5) an inability to generalize broadly from case studies.

Narrative history is a look back and an analysis of past events. The objective of retrospective study is to find causes for certain events, cause and effect relationships, and the probable outcome under varying circumstances. It is intended that a study of narrative history will provide prospective concerning current events in view of similar past experiences. Historical study also provides a basis for generalization concerning large-scale developments or major movements. The basic limitation of historical study results from the time lag that exists between occurrence of an event and its analysis. Because of this time lag the researchers must estimate both the validity of the data and its classification. Tests of validity are conducted by comparison with data gathered for other purposes and are limited to major events. Conclusions must always be somewhat tentative, and dependence on conditional statements and assumptions necessarily makes the historical analysis lengthy.

Second Level of Rigor

Research at the second level of rigor includes survey research, time study analysis, and uncontrolled experimentation.

Survey research consists of polls and analytical surveys. Polls focus on current practices or events and are focused upon the distribution of events concerning one item. Analytical surveys are the second phase of polls as they consist of statistical analysis of data gathered by the poll. The objective of polls is to collect data concerning the degree of existence of certain practices or elements at a given time. Information gathered by polls permits the identification of trends and a comparison with contemporary and predecessor trends.

The basic advantage of polling surveys is the ease with which they can be replicated at different times and places thus permitting comparison with other studies. Their basic disadvantage is that they are limited to descriptions of current events, which do not indicate whether existing situations are desirable or undesirable. Evaluation of findings requires an analytical survey which can test the relationship between factors and research findings. However it must be kept in mind that the establishment of statistically significant relationships does not show how the variables are related. Significant too is the fact that analytical surveys indicate relationships for the given situation under analysis and that findings cannot be applied to other conditions and other times.

Time series analysis involves records of environmental change over time. The data gathered are usually classified and observations should be controlled if hypotheses are to be tested. With control over observations and isolation of variables, findings from time series analysis can be compared with other studies and subjected to public demonstration. However it is infrequent that the variables will be within the control of the researcher and this constitutes the basic limitation of time series analysis. Even a knowledge of extraneous variables may not permit their measurement, and of course cause and effect relationships cannot be established.

Uncontrolled experimentation consists of collecting data at a point in time and then comparing these data with subsequently collected data. The findings from the first collection become the standard of comparison for data gathered at later points in time. In the interval between the two measurements some experimental variable, whose influence is to be studied, is inserted. It is assumed that variation in observations is due to the introduction of the experimental variable. A cause and effect relationship can be assumed to exist between the experimental variable and measured data when there is no change in all other variables that could account for change. As can be noted above, the requirements of the method of uncontrolled experimentation are quite confining, therefore its application is very limited.

Third Level of Rigor

Methodology employed at this highest level of research rigor should permit both manipulation of variables to verify cause and effect relationships and also isolation of critical variables and relationships. These methodologies include laboratory experimentation and controlled field experimentation. Methodologies at this level of research rigor are especially apt when the research situation involves cause and effect relationships rather than descriptive phenomena or when the objective of the research is to develop or verify a theory.

Laboratory experimentation is conducted in an environment which permits the analyst to control the conditions under which observations are made. The environmental conditions are varied so that effects of the change and the prior conditions can be contrasted. The objective is to isolate theoretically significant variables and to measure the results when either the dependent or the intervening variables are altered. Laboratory experimentation is an attempt to simulate "real-world" conditions; hence it is especially useful in situations where natural conditions cannot be repeated or observed readily. In most instances the number of variables manipulated is kept small and limited to variables assumed to be relevant to the phenomena being studied.

Laboratory experimentation must be based on the assumption that there is relevance between laboratory findings and "real-world" events if valid conclusions are to be drawn. Both laboratory and "real-world" events must be relevant to the same propositions if they are to be related to each other. The same basic features must be present in both situations and laboratory replication of real situations must be possible if the methodology is to be valid.

Controlled field experimentation is the same as laboratory experimentation except that the study is conducted in the natural environment. Both methods attempt to control all variables except an experimental variable and note changes by use of a before-and-after technique. Controlled field experimentation is based on the assumption that only the experimental variable effects either group alone and that other variables will affect both groups in the same manner and to the same extent. These assumptions can be tested by repeating the experiments with the control group and experimental group interchanged. If the results are unchanged the experimental findings are reliable. Field experimentation can also be controlled by statistical comparison of data classified within the experimental sample.

CONTROLLED EXPERIMENTATION IN PERSONNEL RESEARCH

It is frequently argued that the nature of personnel research, with its complex interrelationship of a great number of variables, is such that controlled experimentation methods are not relevant or reliable. A summary of the thinking with regard to this question is in order. The proponents of controlled experimentation argue that it is superior to either intuitive opinion or case-study methodologies as a basis for theory formulation or decision making. They present two points in support of their argument. First, the researcher using controlled experimentation can maintain control over the variables which he considers relevant to the problem. Control over variables permits an analysis and interpretation of the findings. Second, the researcher is compelled to design the study so that he will have exact knowledge of the environment from which his data was gathered. This grasp of the environment makes possible generalizations based on specific findings as conditions of study are known and cause and effect relationships are understood.

In addition to their contention concerning the superiority of experimental methodology the proponents further contend that it is applicable to situations where other methodologies cannot be used. The supporters of this research methodology recognize, however, that simulation of relevant variables from the "real world" in the laboratory presents the greatest challenge of this approach. The experimental situation will be relevant to the natural environment to the degree to which it retains properties of the setting, task, and participation associated with reality. The user of the findings of controlled experimentation must be satisfied that the real and experimental environments were similar. Finally it must be recognized that the methodology of controlled experimentation is subject to the limitations of time, practicality, and the ethics concerned with using human subjects.

LEVELS OF RIGOR AND QUALITY IN PERSONNEL RESEARCH

The limitations of the lower levels of rigor in personnel research may lead to a tendency to discount these techniques. It must not be forgotten that quantitative and intuitive understanding of the variables being analyzed can be of vital importance in formulating hypotheses and in pinpointing areas for study. Experience and familiarity with other studies permits logical treatment of the unexpected. However a study based on descriptive methodology such as the first two levels of rigor must still stand the test of controlled experimentation.

It is significant to note that levels of rigor are not necessarily directly correlated with research quality. Research can be conducted at the highest level of rigor and still yield low-quality results. Research quality depends on the nature of the data, the care exercised in collecting and analyzing data, the degree to which a priori criteria guided the study, how logical the criteria are, and how precise the hypothesis is.

THE NEED FOR PERSONNEL RESEARCH

It has become "old hat" to point out that understanding of human behavior has lagged behind man's understanding of his physical environment by a considerable margin. There may be several reasons for this lag. Among the major reasons is the complex nature of the subject. Man is probably more difficult to research than the physical or material world. Perhaps it is significant too that everyone, as a result of his own experience, assumes that he possesses a degree of expertise in the field of human relations. Such an attitude is not very conducive to scientific investigation. Personnel research provides a means of taking an objective look at problems and developing policies and procedures that are based on facts gained through scientific investigation instead of opinions based on limited personal experiences.

Basic topics of discussion for investigation into the need for personnel research include:

1. The inadequate status of present knowledge
2. The need for adapting to changing conditions
3. The need for research to encourage improvement

The Inadequate Status of Present Knowledge

As mentioned previously, much of our existing knowledge and methodology of personnel management are based on common sense and personal experience that have been passed along from manager to trainee through the ages. Frequently these rules of thumb and methodologies are essentially "art" and involve very little scientific or logical foundation. The present-day personnel manager quickly realizes that he operates in an increasingly complex environment and that he simply does not have the answers to his problems. He must make quick decisions and hope for the best. His situation is further complicated by the fact that he is part of and subject to the influence of the environment he is attempting to control.

Just as all learning requires an admission that a lack of knowledge exists, the inadequacy of the present status of existing knowledge in personnel management provides a starting point and an incentive to personnel research. By pushing back the frontiers of knowledge and applying the scientific method to his own work the personnel manager can enlarge the base from which he and others can make more effective personnel management decisions.

The Need for Adapting to Changing Conditions

So much has been written about the rapid change in business environment that it hardly needs reiteration here. This rapid change initiates new problems that must be solved even before the old problems are solved completely. The new problem areas require adjustment in personnel policy as well as procedures. Since business research tends to concentrate on day-to-day problems it is the research of the social scientist that will probably provide most of the information utilized by business, industry, and government in coping with future problems. Thus the empirical findings of the researcher eventually become available to the personnel manager who seeks them. Unfortunately, as stated earlier, there is a time lag in the application of these research findings to "real-world" problems. This time lag has the effect of reducing the benefit of the research findings, as the social environment at the time the research was conducted may have changed appreciably by the time of application.

The Need for Research to Encourage Improvement

The constant need for improvement can easily be overlooked by the busy personnel manager in his endeavor to cope with his daily problems. However, alert managers, aware of the value of research, must constantly emphasize the importance of a continuous search for improved methods and procedures by all employees. This attitude of receptiveness to improvement must permeate the entire organization. Personnel managers should tap the experimental information gained from specialized sources and even add to this body of information by conducting studies of their own.

ORGANIZING PERSONNEL RESEARCH

Research work requires a comparatively stable organization and one that requires time to develop. Researchers cannot be hired today, laid off tomorrow, and re-hired the next day. There must be commitment to a continuing program.

The firm's personnel research organization, in a sense, represents technical capital. Frequently it is both cause and effect of the firm's success, as personnel research contributes to and benefits from the firm's success. Capability in personnel research is a matter of having behavioral scientists who are outstanding in the area. It is necessary to decide upon what is involved in the area of personnel research and then to build the technical organization and the physical facilities to provide the capability necessary to carry on the desired research. Unlike product or process research, personnel research offers little opportunity for developing areas that have "fallout" value in line with commercial operations. A possible exception to the policy of making profit on research contracts and also acquiring frontier knowledge that can be used in commercial operations is the personnel management consulting firm which sells its research findings to other firms in the form of recommended programs.

Personnel management research occurs in many settings which dictate to some degree the organization that should be designed. Three of these settings constitute the bulk of the research done. These include:

1. Company personnel research groups
2. Outside association
3. Universities

Company Personnel Research Groups

Intracompany personnel research effort varies widely from none at all to highly advanced behavioral research teams working out of staff research offices. Most company research programs are organized under two basic schemes. (See Figure 1.) Research sections within the employee relations department under the supervision of a department director are the most common. The behavioral research

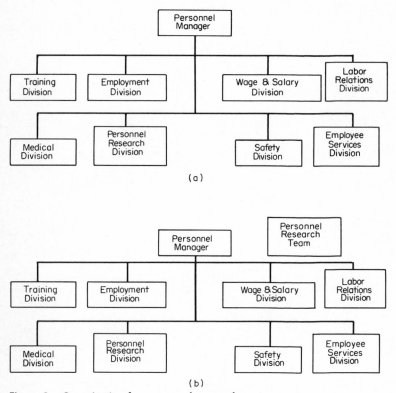

(a)

(b)

Figure 1.   Organization for personnel research.

team constitutes another, though less common, structure of organization. Behavioral research teams are usually independent of the employee relations section and report to a staff officer or to the company's chief executive.

Employee Relations Research Sections

The task of the employee relations research section is usually pragmatic in nature, concentrating on administrative and problem-solving requirements, although theoretical concepts may also be researched. The staff encompasses professional research personnel of various backgrounds although it may not be competent to deal with all personnel problems. Some research work may be contracted out except in the case of very large firms which may employ specialists for personnel research work.

Some of the research conducted by employee relations research sections is initiated by other personnel sections or operating sections although the research section also pursues its own research. Some of the projects undertaken are repetitive in nature as when the research group conducts measurement and evaluation of entrance examinations for the employee relations department on a continuous basis. Employee relations and other operating groups may do their own research depending upon the company size and the degree of autonomy of the groups. A balanced program of effective research services within the restrictions of its budget and company policies and needs, presents the research unit with its greatest challenge. It is essential that the research unit gain the respect of other personnel and operating units if it is to expect their cooperation and support as well as requests for assistance.

Continuity and consistency in the collection of the data are the basic advantages of internal employee relations sections. Thus it becomes possible to conduct longitudinal analysis (comparison over several time periods). Internal research groups are also more flexible and adaptable to the changing needs of a dynamic environment, an advantage which is particularly significant in short-range survey work and for evaluating the firm's employee relations programs.

On the debit side, company research sections are usually somewhat limited to short-range research of a small-scale variety. Usually, because of their limited and uncertain budget, they must concentrate on immediate organizational problems and limit theoretical pursuits and preventive studies. These limitations frequently mean that the company research section will be occupied with temporary solutions and continuous repetitive performance. The nature of these activities is not conducive to the development of meaningful liaison with outside research groups, and thus the findings of these outside groups may not be available for incorporation into the firm's policies and programs.

Behavorial Research Teams

Behavorial research teams are usually composed of university faculty members with advanced degrees and good standing in their respective disciplines. Their work objectives are twofold: to assist the company in the solution of its operating problems and to contribute to the body of knowledge in their respective disciplines. Some of the research team activities are on a "call-in" basis in which specific company problems are researched, but occasionally the team may define its own problem and conduct theoretical research which is not directly related to current company problems. Thus at times the firm's operating departments serve as "real-world" laboratories for behavorial research.

Since the behavorial research team is not directly involved in day-to-day operating problems, it can undertake long-range problems of great complexity. The team members tend to be better versed in the literature of their field and thus more aware of related findings of other researchers. The validity of the findings is enhanced by the fact that the researchers are independent of the firm's operating groups. Since they have to be brought in from outside the organization by conscious decision they usually have strong top-level interest and budgetary support. Their close association with diverse groups provides them with a broad scope of knowledge and exposes them to the most modern concepts and techniques in their discipline.

The behaviorial research team has its disadvanatages. The long-range nature of their work involves greater cost and more remote payoff applications. The higher degree of specialization of the researchers makes cooperation with operating people more difficult and application of findings more involved. It is somewhat more difficult to evaluate the work of behaviorial research teams since operating executives are usually untrained in the terminology and methodology of research. Behaviorial research teams may be limited to large-firm research.

A review of the last few paragraphs reveals that there are advantages and disadvantages to both departmental research sections and behavioral research teams. The specific approach to be used must be determined in view of the demands and resources available in a given situation. Some large firms may employ both approaches, thus gaining flexibility and providing a method of comparison of results with outside sources.

An Appraisal and a Look Ahead

Personnel research programs have not fared very well in the eyes of the critics. It is argued that these research programs have not contributed any really new ideas and therefore have added very little to the body of scientific knowledge in employee relations. A survey of personnel research programs may cast light on the validity of these claims. In summary, personnel research seems to be largely the domain of the large firm. Most of the research budget is devoted to applied research concerning day-to-day problems, and this budget is usually a very small percentage of gross sales. Most of the research is done by the firm's own staff, and the studies employ several research methodologies but are usually conducted at low levels of scientific rigor.

In spite of the tendency to pay lip service to personnel research, while restricting research budgets, the number of research projects conducted is increasing. The firms tend to engage the services of a research specialist and to use advanced techniques of research and analysis. Unfortunately most of the research findings are not disseminated beyond the confines of the firm or organization.

PERSONNEL RESEARCH—OUTSIDE ASSOCIATIONS

Outside agencies which conduct personnel research include universities, which will be discussed separately, trade and business associations, professional societies, labor unions, and government bureaus. The methods and objectives of these agencies vary widely, and the scope of their research frequently extends far beyond personnel problems. Of course these outside associations are independent of company control and have access to association funds. Their semipublic nature permits greater ease in obtaining data for historical and comparative study, and their greater permanence is conducive to more successful longitudinal study. Their ability to offer more stable employment encourages employment of highly competent, full-time specialists. These agencies tend to publish their findings and suffer only from difficulty in garnering cooperation from companies in doing their research.

Trade and Business Associations

Trade and business associations contribute to personnel research in several ways. Primarily their efforts consist of direct research conducted by their own organizations or of sponsoring research conducted by other agencies either private or public.

Most of their research is industry-wide in scope and is concerned essentially with the specific problems; their broad scope encourages publication and dissemination of research findings. Unfortunately the data are not readily available to nonassociation members.

Labor Union Research

Most national and international unions are seriously involved in research. They have competent research staffs and are well aware of the need for data and for education of their members. Hence they spend significant amounts of money on research, publication, and political activity. Much of their research effort is applied research.

Unlike trade and business associations which restrict research publications to their own members, unions attempt to make their findings available to other unions, to management, to their members, and to the general public. Although much of their research concerns day-to-day problems there is a trend toward more study of broad social, political, and economic problems. The research interests of unions are quite similar to those of the trade and business associations, but differences in their aims and emphasis may lead to vastly different conclusions. However, both provide valuable sources of research data, although the task of verifying and interpreting the results may become formidable.

As with company personal research, most of the programs exist in large units. The national or international headquarters staffs perform most of the research. The findings are then analyzed and attractively written up for use by the local unions. This specialization and concentration provides a consistent unified policy for guiding the local officials in the conduct of their daily operations.

There are, of course, limitations to labor union research. Funds are often limited as the rank and file member and the local union leadership may question expenditures for research, especially broad-based studies. The local may resent the lack of autonomy implied in the policy directives which suggest problem-solving approaches. Changing membership composition requires constant review to keep research objectives consistent with member goals. Finally research interpretation is subject to bias, so that union research as well as trade association research must be used carefully.

Professional Societies

Professional societies include a great variety of member-oriented service organizations. These societies usually consider research and member education among their primary objectives. Since the composition of the professional society includes academicians as well as professional people the goals and methodologies employed vary. The societies do little research themselves but they finance and encourage both pure and applied research at various levels of scientific rigor. The journals of these associations, their channels of communication between researchers, and the platforms for exchange of thought provided by their professional meetings facilitate dissemination of research findings.

BUSINESS RESEARCH ORGANIZATIONS

Business research organizations may be classified as profit-making organizations or nonprofit organizations.

Nonprofit Organizations

This classification of business research organization can be subclassified into groups which conduct their own research and those which engage the services of full-time researchers from outside agencies. The primary focus is large-scale in-depth studies of very important social, economic, and political problems. Some of these nonprofit organizations maintain publications and sponsor educational programs to make their findings available to outside interests. Generally these organizations enjoy the respect and cooperation of other research organizations and sometimes issue joint research designs and evaluations.

Commercial Services

Some research organizations rely on various types of subscriptions to finance their study and disseminate their findings. These reports are usually periodic and regular although special reports are sometimes issued. Since considerable cost is involved commercial subscriptions must be selected and placed carefully. A desirable approach seems to be to strive for wide distribution of summary write-ups with detailed information available upon request. The data gathered usually concern day-to-day problems and frequently cannot be obtained in any other manner. Since the data are collected on a periodic continuous basis, they are timely and usable.

Research by Government Bureaus

Federal and state government bureaus are an excellent source of low-cost personnel research data. The government bureaus are full-time collectors of data, and hence they can tap high-quality specialists whose work is reliable and dependable. Government research is done as a public service and is therefore accurate and impartial. The data are readily available as each of many bureaus publishes its findings as well as keeping very complete up-to-date files of relevant data. Governments also make financial grants to outside research agencies for specific types of research, and publish the findings.

UNIVERSITY RESEARCH

Although universities are best known as preservers and dispensers of knowledge they are also great centers of research. There is considerable variation in the excellence of university research, both intrauniversity and interuniversity. The better-financed universities are of course more capable of maintaining high-level research programs. Some university research is interdisciplinary in nature, but most of the personnel research is conducted by departments of social science (psychology, sociology, anthropology, etc.) or business administration, and by research centers and special institutes.

Schools of Business Administration

Primary contributors to personnel research in schools of business administration are the departments of management, bureaus of business research, and departments of economics. Most of this work is accomplished by individual researchers working alone or with assistance from graduate students and research assistants. These research projects provide funding for graduate students and supply opportunities for study and experience. The methodologies used by the university professors varies widely, but commonly used techniques include statistical surveys, questionnaires, interviews, library research, and case-study approaches.

Bureaus of business and economic research serve chiefly as publishers of faculty research findings, although they frequently do some research also. Most of these bureaus publish their findings through the publication of journals, books, and papers.

Like most other research organizations, business schools find their research efforts hampered by a lack of funds. Staffing also presents a problem, as good researchers are in short supply and the demand for their services is great. Research education is a long and difficult course of study, and experience must be gained if the research scholar is to be productive. Present-day research is highly specialized and advanced, requiring up-to-date techniques and large-scale operations. Finally the university researcher has many other duties and cannot devote his full time to research.

Research Institutes

The development of centers for the analysis and publication of labor and industrial relations research findings is a relatively recent development in American universities. These research centers are usually attached to one of the university divisions (see Figure 2). The basic objective of these research centers is to provide an interdisciplinary approach to the study of employee relations. Frequently they also engage in continuing education programs for labor and management. The teaching and research aspects of the research institute's activities supplement each other and serve the dual purpose of discovering and dispensing knowledge. Since a substantial portion of the center's budget is allocated to research, it is possible to undertake broad-gauge problems which require experimentation and team study involving several disciplines.

Research institutes publish and distribute their findings widely. Since successful operation of the institute requires combined support of labor and management groups, top leaders from these areas frequently participate in their operations. This broad foundation in labor, management, and public programs permits these institutes to tap several sources of operating funds. Education, consultation, and sale of published material are also fund-raising activities.

University research has been subject to criticism for failing to live up to expectations as a science. It is said to suffer from lack of attention to scientific methodology. Specifically, it supposedly lacks a sharp theoretical focus since it does not encompass the whole organization in its complex, multiple environment. The critics also point out that there appears to be a tendency for each researcher to interpret the problem and devise solutions on the basis of his own background and experience rather than fitting the analysis to the problem. It is further emphasized that much university research in personnel management is not conducted at a level of rigor which permits meaningful utilization. Often the research is done at low organization levels, thus limiting the usefulness of the findings for higher-position analysis. Finally, it is argued that human relations research is not intellectually adequate

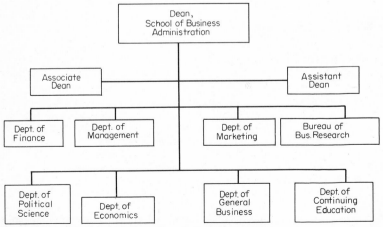

Figure 2. Organization of a university research center.

because it is not socially relevant and sufficiently influential to meet public demands; because it has not contributed to related, organized disciplines; and because it has been unable to attract top-flight scholars.

The criticisms mentioned above no doubt have some validity. However, these criticisms should serve as instruments of self-correction and as constant reminders that efforts toward improvement must continue unabated. The opportunities for meaningful research in human relations are vast. As research skills are upgraded and new techniques are developed and employed, the quality and usefulness of findings will improve. The future promise is nearly unlimited and the outlook is optimistic.

SUBJECT AREAS FOR PERSONNEL RESEARCH

The introduction to the subject of personnel research suggests that the basic objective of research in this area is to introduce the scientific method as the basis for decisions involving human behavior or the utilization of human resources. It is appropriate to consider the various types of decisions which are concerned with various aspects of personnel management. Areas of decision and the corresponding personnel research activities implied by each of them are summarized below.

Decisions Structured by Organizational Requirements

This decision area assumes that certain variables in the organizational or industrial environment remain unchanged. The problem involves the selection of personnel whose behavior on the job is consistent with the requirements of the organization.

Personnel Selection

The personnel selection process is based upon determining the job requirements, establishing manpower needs, and recruiting personnel. The objective is to select from among the persons recruited the individuals most likely to succeed on the job. Scientific methodology requires that these inferences be tested empirically by demonstrating that the testing methods utilized in measuring human qualifications are actually related to success on the job. Most firms have a multitude of jobs to be filled and must assess the characteristics of applicants so that they may be assigned to the jobs in a manner which contributes most to the firm's overall efficiency. The decisions made concerning these assignments are the ones involved in any program of personnel selection.

Personnel Training and Development

Another step toward improved job performance is to teach or train employees in the skills and knowledge required by the job. The personnel researcher's role in training concerns determining what skills and knowledge need to be gained, establishing procedures for instructing employees, and designing and conducting experiments to determine whether or not training programs are achieving their stated objectives. The areas of personnel selection and personnel training are inseparable. The selection process must secure persons who are capable of being trained, and the design of the training program must be geared to the quality of the persons to be trained. In some circumstances the personnel researcher will have to develop several training programs to encompass the varying levels of skill, experience, ability, and current knowledge of prospective trainees.

Personnel Counseling

The most intimate learning situation offered by industry is the personnel counseling experience. The requirements and objectives of the organization sometimes conflict with the capabilities and objectives of the individual. Such instances may result in dissonance and if severe could result in the need for psychological guidance. Counseling may concentrate on discrepancies between the individual's qualities and the requirements of the job. In such cases either a learning program to help the individual learn new skills or modes of behavior or placement on a job more in line with the individual's talents is usually recommended. In other situations there may be problems which involve the individual's total life experience. There are serious moral questions involved in determining the extent to which the firm should involve itself in the personal and emotional problems of its employees. There is a great need for further research in the area of personnel counseling in industry.

Decisions Structured by Individual Characteristics

It is implied here that the organizational requirements may have to be modified by the characteristics, capabilities, and limitations of people. It should not be assumed, however, that individual differences among people are unimportant. To take such a stand would seriously limit the effectiveness of human relations research in industry. Of course the consideration of individual differences complicates personnel research greatly, but any assumption of a "block vote" or "mass" would be an unrealistic and erroneously simplified model. The basic question then becomes how many ways must industry be modified to consider the varying capabilities of a collection of individuals, not how must the industry be modified to consider the capabilities of man.

Engineering Psychology

Only in the last thirty years has industry witnessed the coordinated effort between engineers and psychologists made necessary by the always existing need to design machines in the light of operator capacities and limitations. This need was brought to attention by wartime experiences and by studies of accident reports especially in the aircraft industry. Basically engineering psychology is the study of the characteristics of the human operator with a view to designing equipment and man-machine systems for most efficient operation. The objective is to design the mechanical components of an industrial system for most efficient and effective use of the capabilities of the human elements of the system.

Human Motivation

Perhaps few decision areas are more important than the area of human motivation. The research and effort devoted to recruiting, training, and placement as well as the careful design of jobs and system will be essentially wasted if the employee cannot be induced to contribute his efforts with a high degree of willingness. There is a great multitude of theories concerning human motivation in industry, but unfortunately there is little empirical evidence to support them. The personnel researcher is commissioned with the task of determining conditions within the employment situation which contribute to high employee motivation. Of course individual differences must be considered as different persons have different wants and needs and will therefore be differently motivated in varying situations. The researcher must search for the essentials of human motivation and use these essentials as a basis for structuring an incentive program that will enhance employee motivation.

Organizational Psychology

The last fifteen years has seen the focus of widespread attention on the effects of organizational structure upon human efficiency. There are conspicuous industrial examples in which organizational structure was altered resulting in beneficial changes in span of control, hierarchal levels, and decentralization of authority and decision making. These structural changes in organization were based upon the findings of behavioral research which suggest an appeal to individual sense of importance and belongingness through participation and supportive behavior. It is not certain that research is adequate to support these theories for long periods or in diverse environments, but the impact of these changes merits attention. Organizational psychology is a far-reaching and complex area of psychology applied to industry. The objective of the organizational psychologist is to develop a better understanding of the human interactions which make up organizations. Organizational psychology merges differential, experimental, and social psychology. By employing this interdisciplinary team approach it becomes perhaps the most comprehensive approach to an understanding of human behavior in industry undertaken to date.

Decisions Concerning Group Perceptions and Group Influences

Frequently group perceptions and group influences precipitate group conflict which much be resolved. A basic human characteristic appears to be the desire to belong. Persons of similar needs and interests form groups to facilitate achievement, and the formation of these groups in turn defines and intensifies their needs and wants. Industrial employees are members of many groups ranging from their own work group to their unions or professional societies and to religious, political, and community groups outside the work environment. Decisions in industry can be made more intelligently when information concerning all these groups is considered. The personnel research scientist can help to gain this information.

Industrial Communications and Union-Management Relations

Any industrial activity must involve communication between people or groups of people. A significant barrier to interpersonal or intergroup behavior is that individuals hold different perceptions. A given request or directive might be viewed quite differently by various recipients depending on their personalities. An accurate communication must represent an authentic transmission of the mechanical components of the message but also an authentic transmission of the sender's intent and purpose. Intelligent personnel decision-making in industry requires a faultless process of gathering relevant information. The implementation of decisions requires accurate transmission of information to individuals and groups in the organization. Personnel research in industry is aimed at identifying and removing barriers to accurate communication so that relevant information for decision making can be transmitted rapidly and faithfully and so that misunderstanding can be reduced to a minimum. The different perceptions of the goals of labor and management constitute one of the major areas of misunderstanding and conflict in industry. Both groups would, no doubt, agree that their primary goal is to maximize output in an efficient, effective, and humane manner. Their disagreement would arise over their different definitions of efficient, effective, and humane. Quite probably they differ in their definition of the work environment necessary to achieve maximum output. Specific union-management areas of conflict might include the degree to which loyalty to the union may interfere with the employees' company loyalty, the circumstances which contribute to union-management cooperation or conflict, the factors which enhance employee satisfaction or dissatisfaction with the union or the company, and the characteristics of successful and unsuccessful bargaining sessions between the company and the union. Personnel management researchers have, to date, conducted only a limited amount of research in the labor-management relations area. The field represents a vast and potentially profitable area for personnel research.

For practical purposes it is frequently useful to summarize a personnel research unit's activities by functional area. A detailed summary might appear as follows:

1. To keep current with new developments and trends in personnel research both within the company and within the industry.
2. To design experiments, and to collect and analyze data in such areas as:
    a. Wage and incentive plans
    b. Personnel utilization and productivity
    c. Performance evaluation
    d. Innovations and developments in personnel administration
    e. Computer applications in personnel research
    f. Spinoffs from space technology and research
3. To conduct applications in personnel research:
    a. Social, legal, and ethical viewpoints
    b. Public image
    c. Campus views of company practices
    d. Ecological consequences of company practices
4. To design and supervise pilot programs for company divisions:
    a. Local divisions
    b. International divisions
    c. Cultural and environmental studies
5. To store, maintain, and update research data files relevant to company activities:
    a. Computer possibilities
    b. Reciprocal agreements with other researchers
    c. Publishing findings
    d. Systematic search of literature at selected intervals
6. To assemble, analyze, and advise on current trends concerning personnel relations:
    a. Real versus dollar wages
    b. Wage and salary increase ratios
    c. Cost of living
    d. Current economic outlook
    e. Strike trends, losses and costs on a company, industry and national basis

The job description in Figure 3 of a typical personnel research director position outlines in greater detail the duties involved in personnel research.

GAINING SUPPORT FOR PERSONNEL RESEARCH

Efforts toward gaining support for personnel research should probably be divided into two categories: First, efforts applicable to situations where a research department already exists and where research has been done and is currently being done. Second, efforts in situations where no research unit exists and the firm is trying to determine whether or not it should engage in personnel research. Although the problems of gaining support for and justifying continued existence of personnel research unit are troublesome, the existence of the research unit provides some advantages. In these instances much of the preliminary management education will have been done already as it can probably be assumed that management recognizes the role and contribution of research if there has been prior exposure to it. The fact that there is a research unit is indicative of management support. This of course does not mean that the research unit will not be subject to continued review and questioned concerning its costs and contribution.

If there is no personnel research unit presently but the firm is considering the development of such a unit some initial groundwork must be done. The need for personnel research must be demonstrated. There are several aspects of need demonstration. First it should not be difficult to provide a great deal of data which

Figure 3.   Job description for the position of director of personnel research.

DIRECTOR OF PERSONNEL RESEARCH

TITLE: Director of personnel research
ALTERNATE TITLES: Planning and research director, director of research and development.
  PROMOTION TO: Industrial relations director.
  PROMOTION FROM: Personnel statistician, personnel director.
  DUTIES: The person holding this position is responsible for research engaged in by the department of industrial relations. He plans and assigns research projects and directs and supervises his assistants in their work; coordinates the research activities of this department with those of similar departments in other firms and agencies; exercises control over standards; prepares a periodic progress audit; performs advisory and service functions to the other departments; assists with the development of job analyses and the preparation of job specifications, and the development and standardization of selection tests. He supervises and directs research on: wages, job evaluation, collective bargaining, labor supply, labor turnover, absenteeism, accident proneness, employee attitudes, morale, qualifications for jobs, incentive plans, statistical reports, special reports, merit rating plans, employee induction procedures, and rehabilitation of returning veterans.
  He engages in analyses and writes reports on new developments and progress in methods, standards, and administrative trends in other companies; studies questionnaires and functional charts and arranges desk audits for classification problems; keeps departmental officials informed of tentative conclusions from surveys; acts as a consultant on special problems concerning manpower; continually evaluates policies in order to determine better methods of accomplishing the divisions' objectives; prepares all final survey reports and compiles statistics and reports on various personnel activities for management, Department of Labor, and other agencies.
  RESPONSIBILITY FOR POLICY: Makes policy recommendations to the industrial relations director based on evaluations of data obtained through research.
  INITIATIVE REQUIRED: A high degree of self-motivation is required in originating and carrying out research ideas.
  RESPONSIBILITY FOR WORK OF OTHERS: Supervises the statisticians, business machine operators, and clerks involved in research work.
  TRAINING: Some on-the-job training is necessary, but general professional training and experience are of primary importance.
  QUALIFICATIONS FOR EMPLOYMENT:
    Sex: Either.
    Education: A minimum of four years of college training, and a Ph.D. degree in economics, psychology, and statistics are desirable. Important college courses are: labor economics, psychometric and advanced statistical methods, research techniques, personnel management, industrial, personnel and experimental psychology, industrial methods, safety engineering, labor problems and labor legislation, time and motion study, production standards, IBM machine operation, and accounting.
    Experience: Several years of experience in research work and in assigning and directing the work of others are desirable.
    Personal qualities: Ability to handle factual data with accuracy; thoroughness; intellectual integrity; ability to assign and direct work of others.
    Special knowledge: Familiarity with a great variety of statistical techniques together with a knowledge of the most effective ways of reporting results of research work.

have been gathered through personnel research and to show how these data have been or can be used in management decision making. Even without economic analysis it will usually be quite clear that better decisions have been made as a result of the information provided by research. Second, economic tests can be applied. If research has made a contribution it should be evident in the form of reduced turnover, increased productivity, shorter training times required, faster promotion rates, and a series of other events which can be measured in dollars of reduced cost or increased profit contribution.   A third contribution of personnel research, that will assist in gaining support for a research program, is the recognition and respect that can be garnered from publication of research findings.   Although this benefit is intangible it can do much to enhance the firm's reputation and public image.   As a fifth point it must be recognized that management education may be required. It might be necessary to make management personnel as well as union members aware of the assistance available to them.   They should be made familiar with types of problems that can be solved by the research unit, and the great amount of data and theory which is at their command.

Last and perhaps most important is the contribution of an atmosphere of science, based upon the use of the scientific method, which exists in research environments. It is to be hoped that this atmosphere will permeate the entire organization and encourage submission of all decision making to tests of scientific logic, for intuition and experience must be supplemented with research if the perimeter and scope of knowledge are to be enlarged.

SUGGESTED READING

Conant, James B.: *Modern Science and Modern Man,* Columbia University Press, New York, 1952.
——— : *Science and Common Sense,* Yale University Press, New Haven, Conn., 1951.
Goode, Cecil E.: *Personnel Research Frontiers,* Public Personnel Association, Chicago, 1958.
Hertz, David B.: *The Theory and Practice of Industrial Research,* McGraw-Hill Book Company, New York, 1950.
Komarovsky, M. (ed.): *Common Frontiers of the Social Sciences.*   The Free Press of Glencoe, Inc., New York, 1957.
Luck, Thomas J.: *Personnel Audit and Appraisal,* McGraw-Hill Book Company, New York, 1955.
Seybold, Geneva: *Personnel Audits and Reports to Top Management,* Studies in Personnel Policy, No. 191, National Industrial Conference Board, New York, 1964.
Shuchman, Abe: *Scientific Decision Making in Business,* Holt, Rinehart and Winston, Inc., New York, 1963.
Strother, George G. (ed.): *Social Science Approaches to Business Behavior,* The Dorsey Press and Richard D. Irwin, Inc., Homewood, Ill., 1962.
Whyte, William F., and E. Hamilton: *Action Research for Management,* Richard D. Irwin, Inc., Homewood, Ill., 1965.

BIBLIOGRAPHY

Arensberg, Conrad M., et al.: *Research in Industrial Human Relations,* Harper & Brothers, New York, 1957.
Aronson, Robert L.: "Research and Writing in Industrial Relations—Are They Intellectually Respectable?" Reprint Series No. 124, New York State School of Industrial and Labor Relations, Ithaca, N.Y., 1961.
Bales, Robert F.: "Small Group Theory and Research," in Robert K. Merton et al., eds., *Sociology Today: Problems and Prospects,* Basic Books, Inc., Publishers, New York, 1959.
Berelson, Bernard: *Content Analysis in Communications Research,* The Free Press, Glencoe, Ill., 1952.
Blake, Robert R., and Jane S. Mouton: "The Experimental Investigation of Interpersonal Influence," in Albert D. Biderman and Herbert Zimmer, eds., *The Manipulation of Human Behavior,* John Wiley & Sons, Inc., New York, 1961.
Cartwright, Dorwin, and Alvin Zander, eds.: *Group Dynamics: Research and Theory,* 2d ed., Harper & Row, Publishers, Incorporated, New York, 1960.
Chamberlain, Neil W., Frank C. Pierson, and Theresa Wolfson (eds.): *A Decade of Industrial Relations Research, 1946–1956,* Harper & Brothers, New York, 1958.

Child, Irvin L.: "Socialization," in Gardner Lindzey, ed., *Handbook of Social Psychology,* vol. 2, Addison-Wesley Publishing Company, Inc., Reading, Mass., 1954.

Cochran, W. G., and Gertrude M. Cox: *Experimental Designs,* 2d ed., John Wiley & Sons, Inc., New York, 1950.

Cohen, B. D., H. I. Kalish, J. R. Thurston, and E. Cohen: "Experimental Manipulation of Verbal Behavior," *Journal of Experimental Psychology,* vol. 47, 1954.

Coman, Edwin T., Jr.: *Sources of Business Information,* rev. ed., University of California Press, Berkeley, 1964.

Cooley, William W., and Paul R. Lohnes: *Multivariate Procedures for the Behavioral Sciences,* John Wiley & Sons, Inc., New York, 1962.

Cronbach, Lee J., *Essentials of Psychological Testing,* 2d ed., Harper & Row, Publishers, Incorporated, New York, 1960.

Dahl, Robert A., Mason Haire, and Paul F. Lazarsfeld: *Social Science Research on Business: Product and Potential,* Columbia University Press, New York, 1959.

Derber, Milton, "Research in Union-Management Relations: Past and Future," *Proceedings of the Annual Meetings, 1965,* Industrial Relations Research Association, Madison, Wisc., 1956.

Edwards, A. L., *Experimental Design in Psychological Research,* rev. ed., Holt, Rinehart and Winston, Inc., New York, 1960.

Festinger, Leon, and Daniel Katz, eds.: *Research Methods in the Behavioral Sciences,* Holt, Rinehart and Winston, Inc., New York, 1953.

Fisher, R. A.: *The Design of Experiments,* 4th ed., Oliver & Boyd Ltd., Edinburgh, 1947.

Goode, Cecil E.: *Personnel Research Frontiers,* Public Personnel Association, Chicago, 1958.

Goode, William J., and Paul Hatt: *Methods in Social Research,* McGraw-Hill Book Company, New York, 1952.

Guide to the Use of the General Aptitude Test, U.S. Government Printing Office, 1958.

Hyman, Herbert H.: *Survey Design and Analysis,* The Free Press of Glencoe, Ill., Chicago, 1955.

Industrial Relations Counselors: *Behavioral Science Research in Industrial Relations,* Industrial Relations Monograph No. 21, New York, 1962.

Institute of Industrial Relations: "Research Developments in Personnel Management," *Proceedings of First Conference on Industrial Relations,* University of California, Los Angeles, 1957.

Lazarsfeld, Paul F., and Morris Rosenberg, eds.: *The Language of Social Research: A Reader in the Methodology of Social Research,* The Free Press of Glencoe, Ill., Chicago, 1955.

Lindzey, Gardner, ed.: "Part 3. Research Methods," in *Handbook of Social Psychology, Vol. I: Theory and Method,* Addison-Wesley Publishing Company, Inc., Reading, Mass., 1954.

Meehl, Paul: *Clinical vs. Statistical Prediction: A Theoretical Analysis and Review of the Evidence,* The University of Minnesota Press, Minneapolis, 1954.

National Industrial Conference Board, Round Table Discussion: "Behavioral Science—What Is In It for Management?" *Business Management Record,* June, 1963.

National Referral Center for Science and Technology: *A Directory of Information Resources in the United States, Social Sciences,* Washington, D.C., 1965.

Osgood, Charles E.: *Method and Theory in Experimental Psychology,* Oxford University Press, Fair Lawn, N.J., 1953.

Rogers, Carl R.: "An Overview of the Research and Some Questions for the Future," in Carl R. Rogers and Rosalind F. Dymond, eds., *Psychotherapy and Personality Change,* The University of Chicago Press, 1954.

Sayles, Leonard R.: "The New Look in Industrial Relations Research: Organization Behavior," in *Research Frontiers in Industrial Relations Theory,* McGill University, Industrial Relations Center, Montreal, 1962.

Selltiz, Claire, et al.: *Research Methods in Social Relations,* rev. ed., Holt, Rinehart and Winston, Inc., New York, 1959.

Skinner, B. F.: *Science and Human Behavior,* The Macmillan Company, New York, 1953.

Webbink, Paul: "Methods and Objectives of Industrial Relations Research," *Proceedings of the Industrial Relations Research Association,* 1954.

Wechsler, David: *The Measurement and Appraisal of Adult Intelligence,* 4th ed., The Williams & Wilkins Company, Baltimore, 1958.

Whyte, William F., "Needs and Opportunities for Industrial Relations Research," Reprint Series No. 125, New York State School of Industrial and Labor Relations, Ithaca, N.Y., 1960.

Index

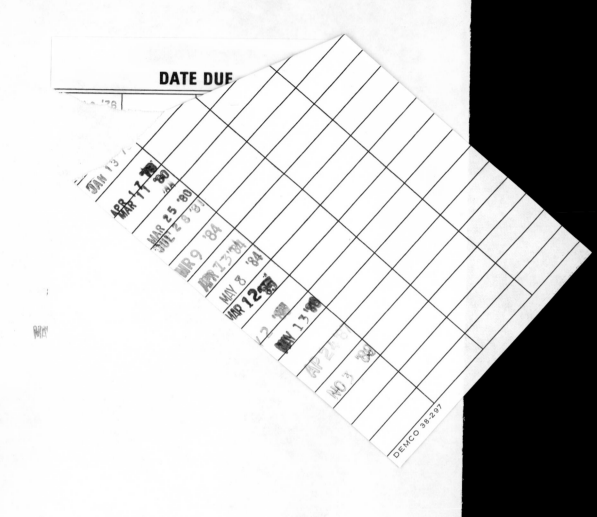

DATE DUE